# Basic Geometry

## TEACHER'S EDITION

Ray C. Jurgensen
Richard G. Brown

Editorial Adviser:
Albert E. Meder, Jr.

Teacher Consultant:
Robert J. McMurray

Houghton Mifflin Company, Boston
Atlanta Dallas Geneva, Illinois
Lawrenceville, New Jersey Palo Alto Toronto

## The Authors

**Ray C. Jurgensen,** Chairman of the Mathematics Department and holder of the Eppley Chair of Mathematics at the Culver Academies, Culver, Indiana. Mr. Jurgensen has been a lecturer at the National Science Foundation institutes for mathematics teachers and meetings of the National Council of Teachers of Mathematics.

**Richard G. Brown,** Mathematics teacher at the Phillips Exeter Academy, Exeter, New Hampshire. Mr. Brown has taught a wide range of mathematics courses for both students and teachers at several schools and universities, including Newton, Massachusetts, High School and the University of New Hampshire.

## Editorial Adviser

**Albert E. Meder, Jr.,** Dean and Vice Provost and Professor of Mathematics, Emeritus, Rutgers, The State University of New Jersey.

## Teacher Consultant

**Robert J. McMurray,** Mathematics teacher in the Albuquerque, New Mexico, Public School System. Mr. McMurray has many years of experience teaching geometry in secondary schools.

1986 Impression



Printed in U.S.A.
ISBN: 0-395-34052-7

# Contents



# Introduction

This textbook has been designed for those students who would normally have difficulty with a standard course in geometry. It provides a simple, yet thorough, introduction to the fundamentals of Euclidean geometry. The lessons are short and easy to read, with many interesting activities for group and individual work. The plentiful exercises are graded according to difficulty and serve a dual purpose: to help students develop basic geometric skills; and to teach the many applications of geometric principles. A clear, colorful design and many special features help make the text interesting and effective.

We invite you to browse through the next few pages of this Teacher's Edition, which illustrate many of the features of BASIC GEOMETRY with reduced sample pages from the text.

# Organization of the Text

# Chapter 2

# Introducing Proof

## 1 • Areas of Rectangles

Which of the rectangles shown at the right covers more surface? Count the squares to see.

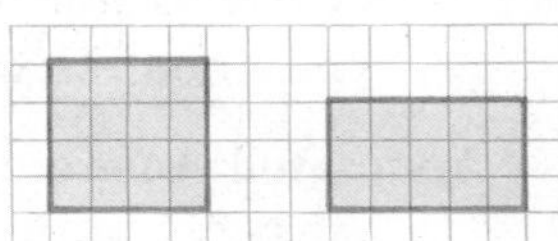

The $4 \times 4$ rectangle is made up of 16 squares. The $5 \times 3$ rectangle is made up of 15 squares. We say that the $4 \times 4$ rectangle has the greater *area.* The amount of surface in a region is its **area.**

A square with sides one unit long has an area of *one square unit*. A common unit of area is the square centimeter.

1 cm | 1 cm | 1 square centimeter

Rectangle *ABCD* has a *base* 5 cm long. Its *height* is 2 cm. Since the rectangle is made up of 10 square centimeters, its area is 10 square centimeters (written 10 cm²). Notice that the area is the product of the lengths of the sides:

$$10 = 5 \times 2.$$

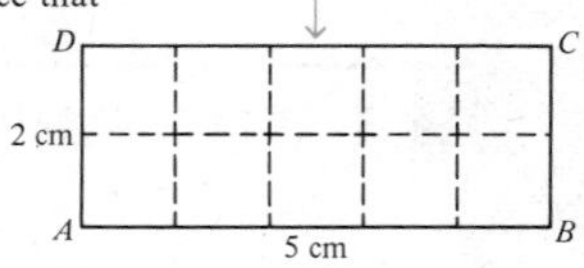


This example suggests the following postulate.

**POSTULATE 12**

The area of a rectangle is given by the formula:

Area = base × height

EXAMPLE 1 Find the area of a rectangle with base length 12 and height 6.

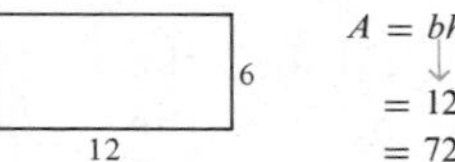


$A = bh$

$= 12 \times 6$

$= 72$

*Answer:* 72 square units

216

The text is organized into six units, each comprising two chapters. The chapters consist of short lessons, employing many worked-out examples and illustrations. The lessons include a generous number of classroom and written exercises.

## SELF-TEST

**Find the area of each triangle.**

1. 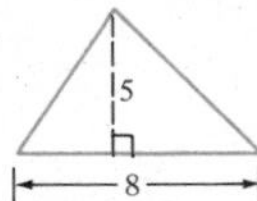


2. 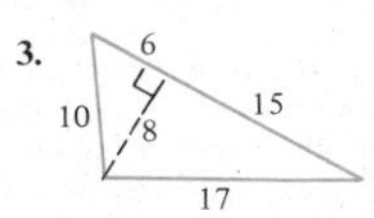


3. 


## Reviewing the Chapter

### Chapter Summary

1. The following formulas for area can be used.

**Rectangle**
$A = bh$

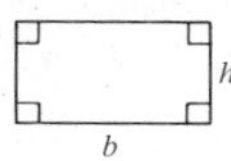


**Square**
$A = s^2$

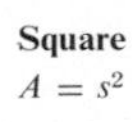


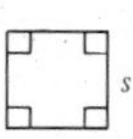

**Parallelogram**
$A = bh$

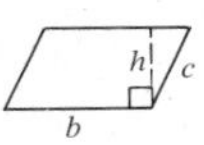


Unless a parallelogram is also a rectangle, $h \neq c$.

**Triangle**
$A = \frac{1}{2}bh$

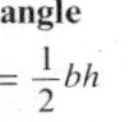
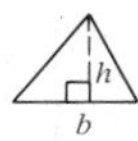


**Trapezoid**
$A = \frac{1}{2}h(b_1 + b_2)$

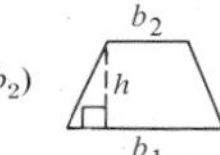


### Chapter Review Test

**Copy and complete the table about rectangles.** *(See pp. 216–220.)*

| | 1. | 2. | 3. | 4. |
|---|---|---|---|---|
| base $b$ | 5 | 30 | 7 | 7.2 |
| height $h$ | 2 | 20 | ? | 4 |

## Reviewing Arithmetic Skills

| | a | b | c | | d | e | f | g | | | h | i | j | k | | l | m | n | |
|---|---|---|---|---|---|---|---|---|---|---|---|---|---|---|---|---|---|---|---|
| | o | | | | p | | | | | | q | | | | | r | | | |
| s | | | | | t | | | | | | u | | | | | v | | | w |
| x | | | | | y | | | z | | | | | aa | | | | bb | | |
| | | | cc | | | | | | | | | | dd | | | | | | |

**Copy the pattern above on squared paper. Then work the exercises and fill in the blanks just as you would in a crossword puzzle.**

*Across*

**a.** 905 − 219 **d.** 5 × 847 **h.** 6421 − 3804 **l.** 2826 ÷ 9
**o.** $(19)^2$ **p.** 96 × 74 **q.** 709 + 517 **r.** 1172 ÷ 4

## Cumulative Review / Unit B

**Complete.**

1. In $\triangle PAT$ at the right, $\angle 4 = \angle$ ? $+ \angle$ ? .
2. A triangle with no equal sides is called ? .
3. A triangle with two equal sides is called ? .
4. If a triangle has two 40° angles, the third angle equals ? °.

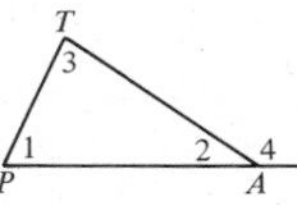


Self-Tests occur after a cluster of related lessons, providing frequent opportunity for review. Answers to the Self-Tests are included at the back of the student text.

Each chapter is followed by a *Reviewing the Chapter* 2-page spread. This feature includes a *Chapter Summary,* which lists the main ideas of the chapter, and a *Chapter Review Test*. The Teacher's Edition provides alternative chapter tests in a permission-to-reproduce format. In addition, there is a set of review exercises for each chapter, starting on page 466.

In each chapter, a full-page *Reviewing Arithmetic Skills* or *Reviewing Algebraic Skills* section helps students to maintain the skills they will need in geometry. Each unit ends with a *Cumulative Review* of its content.

# Teaching Features

Each lesson is short and easy to read, with the amount of text minimized. Postulates, Theorems, Constructions, and other important concepts are displayed in colorful panels. Illustrative examples are included frequently. Numerous lessons include *Explorations* activities which lead students to discover geometric principles for themselves. Color is used effectively in the text and diagrams to clarify and emphasize important concepts.

## 6 • Proving Figures Are Parallelograms

How can you show that quadrilateral $ABCD$ is a parallelogram? Of course, one way is to show that its opposite sides are parallel. But there are other ways of showing that $ABCD$ is a parallelogram. See if you can decide what these are by trying the explorations below.

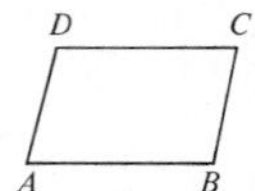


### Explorations

1. Use lined paper to draw two segments, $\overline{AB}$ and $\overline{DC}$, which are both parallel and equal.

2. Draw $\overline{AD}$ and $\overline{BC}$.
   Do $\overline{AD}$ and $\overline{BC}$ appear to be parallel?

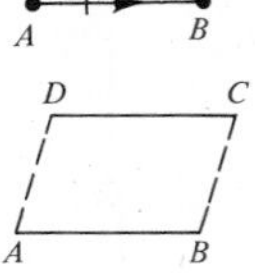


3. What kind of quadrilateral is $ABCD$?

Repeat steps 1–3 using other segments which are both parallel and equal.

**THEOREM 10**

If a quadrilateral has one pair of opposite sides that are both parallel and equal, then the quadrilateral is a parallelogram.

*Given:* $\overline{AB} \parallel \overline{DC}$
$AB = DC$

*Prove:* $ABCD$ is a $\square$.

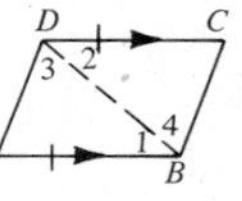


Here are the key steps:

1. Draw $\overline{DB}$. Then $\angle 1 = \angle 2$. (Why?)
2. $\triangle ABD \cong \triangle CDB$ (Why?)

Summaries of important methods and strategies are displayed in panels for easy reference.

We now have four ways to show that a quadrilateral is a parallelogram.

1. Show that both pairs of opposite sides are parallel. (Definition of $\square$)

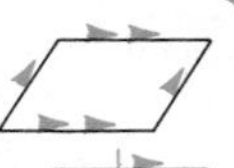

2. Show that one pair of opposite sides are parallel and equal.

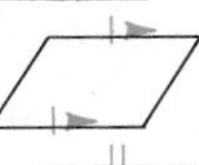

3. Show that both pairs of opposite sides are equal.

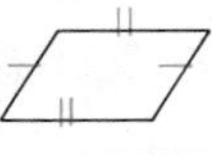

4. Show that the diagonals bisect each other.

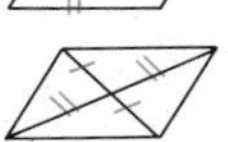

### Classroom Practice

**State the definition or theorem that allows you to conclude that *CDEF* is a parallelogram.**

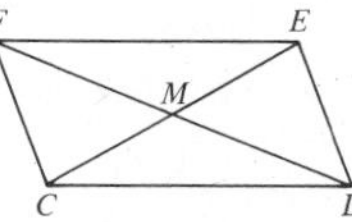


1. $CD = EF$; $DE = CF$
2. $\overline{CD} \parallel \overline{EF}$; $\overline{DE} \parallel \overline{CF}$
3. $CM = ME$; $DM = MF$
4. $CF = DE$; $\overline{CF} \parallel \overline{DE}$
5. $M$ is the midpoint of $\overline{CE}$ and $\overline{DF}$.
6. $CD = EF$; $\angle CDE = 70°$; $\angle DEF = 110°$

### Written Exercises

**In Exercises 1–4, write the definition or theorem which supports the statement "*ABCD* is a ▱."**

A 1.

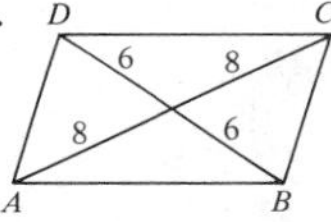


2. D 11 C, 7, 7, A 11 B

There is an abundance of classroom and written exercises. Written exercises are graded A, B, and C in order of increasing difficulty. Many exercise sets include sample exercises with complete solutions.

### Experiments

EXPERIMENT 1

1. Take a large sheet of paper and fold it down the middle. Cut from the corner to any point on the fold as shown. Unfold.
2. What kind of triangle did you form?
3. Explain why the fold is both an altitude and a median.
4. Complete: The median and the altitude to the base of an __?__ triangle are the same segment.

fold cut

EXPERIMENT 2

1. Plot points $A(0, 0)$, $B(6, 12)$, and $C(12, 0)$ on graph paper. Draw $\triangle ABC$.
2. Draw dots at the midpoints of the sides of $\triangle ABC$. Draw the three medians. Use $P$ to label the point where the medians meet. Use $M$ to label the midpoint of $\overline{BC}$.
3. $M$ is point (__?__, __?__) and $P$ is point (__?__, __?__).
4. Measure $AP$ and $AM$ with your ruler. If you worked carefully, $AP = \frac{2}{3}(AM)$.

The Written Exercises often are supplemented by an *Experiments* section. These experiments serve to reinforce concepts already taught and to introduce new ideas for enrichment.

BASIC GEOMETRY contains several additional reference aids for students. A Table of Special Symbols appears on page xi. A List of Postulates, Theorems, Constructions starts on page 477, followed by an illustrated Glossary and a comprehensive Index.

# Special Features

Each chapter includes an *Applications* or *Extra for Experts* feature. The Applications illustrate the many ways in which geometric principles are used in art, science, and everyday life. Several *Calculator Corner* features enable students to explore computational topics in geometry.

## applications

### *Surface Area and Volume*

Geometry tells us that, in general, a small object has more surface area *per unit of volume* than a large object has. Let us compare a baseball with radius 3.5 cm and a basketball with radius 12.4 cm.

Baseball: $\frac{\text{Surface area}}{\text{Volume}} \doteq \frac{153.9}{179.5} \doteq 0.86$

Basketball: $\frac{\text{Surface area}}{\text{Volume}} \doteq \frac{1931.2}{7982.4} \doteq 0.24$

Now let us see how this principle affects a relatively small animal, a mouse, and a larger animal, a human being. Having more skin area per unit of volume, a mouse loses body heat faster than a person does. Just to keep warm, a mouse must eat and burn more food relative to its size. A mouse needs to eat about one half of its weight in food each day. How much food would you have to consume if you ate at that rate?

## CALCULATOR CORNER

Can you see that any two equilateral triangles are similar polygons?

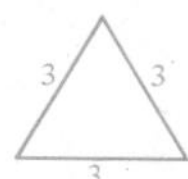


The area of an equilateral triangle is given by the formula

$$A = \frac{s^2\sqrt{3}}{4} \quad \text{where } s \text{ is the length of a side.}$$

Use your calculator to compute the perimeter and area of each triangle described. ($\sqrt{3} \doteq 1.732$) Round each area to the nearest tenth.

| $s$ | 1 | 2 | 3 | 4 | 5 | 6 | 7 |
|---|---|---|---|---|---|---|---|
| perimeter | 3 | ? | ? | ? | ? | ? | ? |
| area | 0.4 | ? | ? | ? | ? | ? | ? |

Now copy and complete each graph.

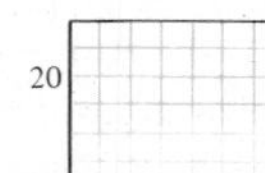


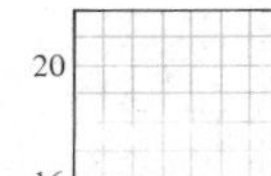

*Career Notes* illustrate jobs that utilize a background in mathematics. Practical tips for students are presented in *Consumer Corner* sections.

## CAREER NOTES

### Helicopter Pilot

Helicopter pilots work in many different situations. For example, they deliver mail, herd cattle, transport building materials and fully assembled towers, rescue people from mountains and jungles, drop food and medical aid to flood and disaster victims, and broadcast traffic reports. Helicopters perform important tasks in farming. For example, helicopters are used to seed and to fertilize large areas of land.

## CONSUMER CORNER

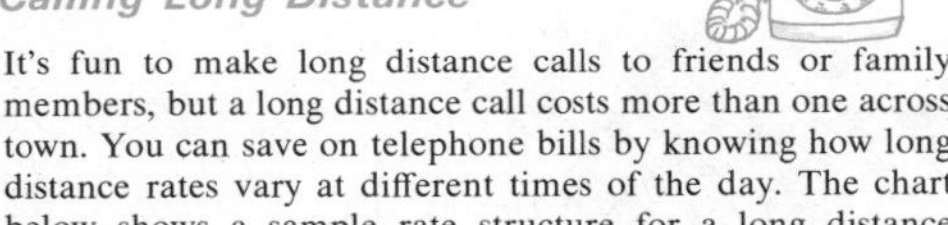

### Calling Long Distance

It's fun to make long distance calls to friends or family members, but a long distance call costs more than one across town. You can save on telephone bills by knowing how long distance rates vary at different times of the day. The chart below shows a sample rate structure for a long distance direct-dial call.

*Puzzles & Things* sections provide entertaining challenges and cartoons provide a light touch, helping to make BASIC GEOMETRY an enjoyable text.

## Puzzles & Things

Sid and Gregory were hiking in the woods when they came to the Red Hawk River. Sid challenged Gregory to guess the width of the river. This is what Gregory did:

He stood at $B$ and looked out across the river. He then adjusted his cap until the tip of his visor was in line with his eye and point $X$.

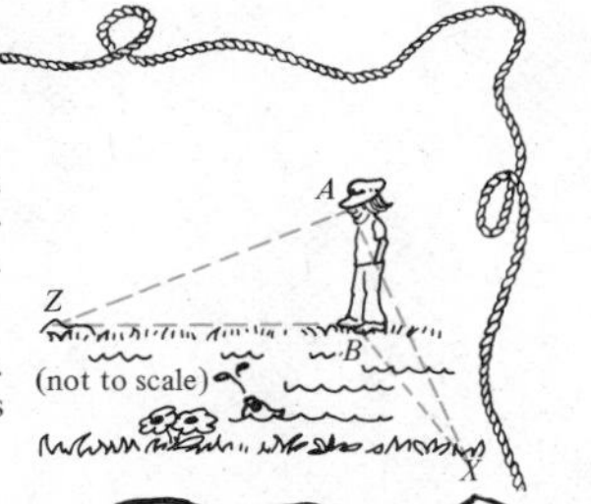

# Supplementary Materials

This Teacher's Edition contains lesson-by-lesson commentary on the student text, with teaching suggestions, chalkboard examples, and extensions. Chapter tests and answers, an individualized assignment guide, and a table of related references are also provided. Answers to classroom and written exercises appear on full-sized facsimiles of the student pages.

Progress Tests are a convenient way to keep track of each student's performance. Each test is keyed to the student text. Answers to all tests appear in the Teacher's Annotated Edition of the Progress Tests.

The Solution Key provides step-by-step solutions for every written exercise and puzzle.

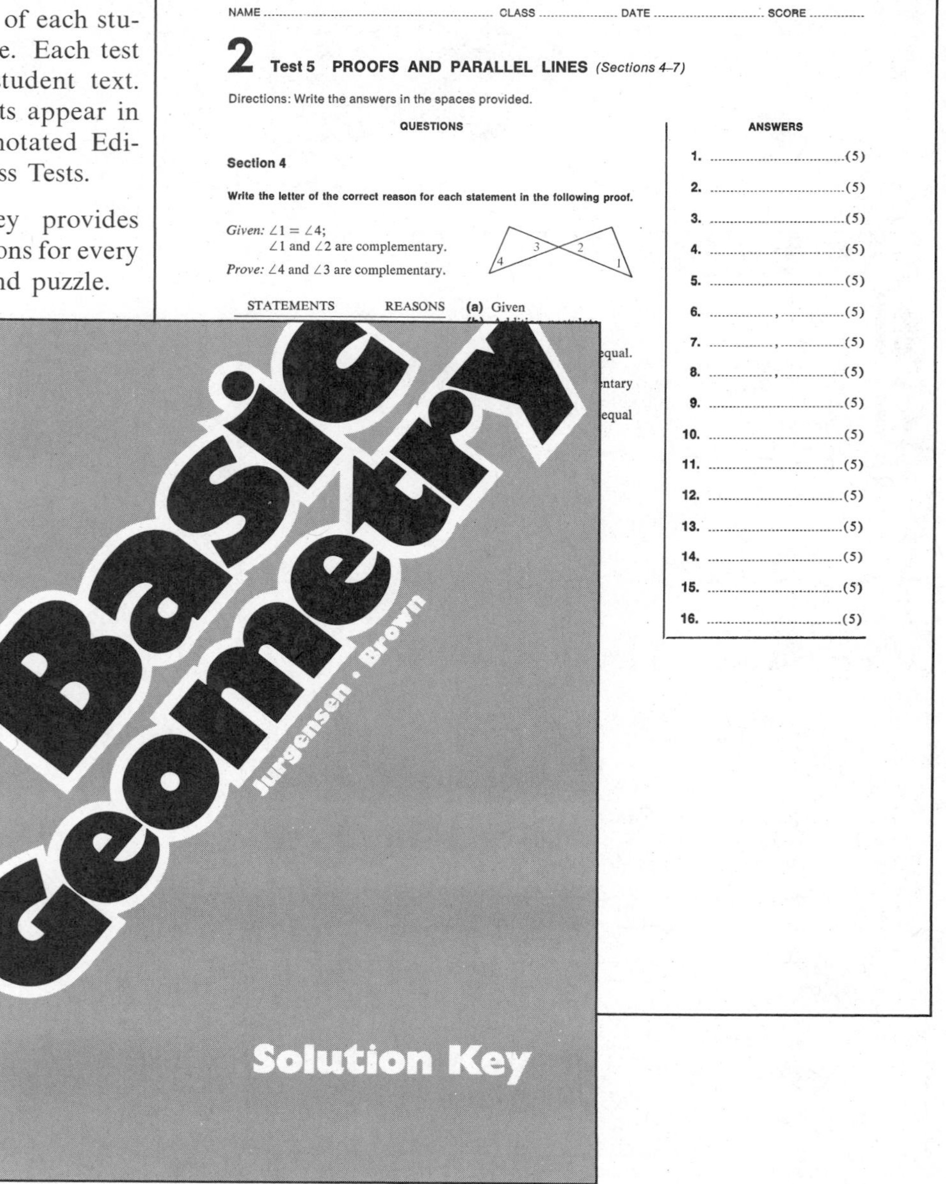

NAME ............ CLASS ............ DATE ............ SCORE ............

**2** **Test 5 PROOFS AND PARALLEL LINES** *(Sections 4–7)*

Directions: Write the answers in the spaces provided.

**QUESTIONS**

**Section 4**

**Write the letter of the correct reason for each statement in the following proof.**

*Given:* $\angle 1 = \angle 4$;
$\angle 1$ and $\angle 2$ are complementary.
*Prove:* $\angle 4$ and $\angle 3$ are complementary.

| STATEMENTS | REASONS |
|---|---|

**(a)** Given

...equal.

...ntary

...equal

**ANSWERS**

1. ............(5)
2. ............(5)
3. ............(5)
4. ............(5)
5. ............(5)
6. ......, ......(5)
7. ......, ......(5)
8. ......, ......(5)
9. ............(5)
10. ............(5)
11. ............(5)
12. ............(5)
13. ............(5)
14. ............(5)
15. ............(5)
16. ............(5)

# Chapter Tests

## Chapter 1

**Complete.**

1. Another name for $\overleftrightarrow{QR}$ is __?__.
2. Another name for $\overrightarrow{SQ}$ is __?__.
3. $PQ =$ __?__ and $QS =$ __?__.
4. If $R$ is the midpoint of $\overline{QS}$, then the coordinate of $R$ is __?__.

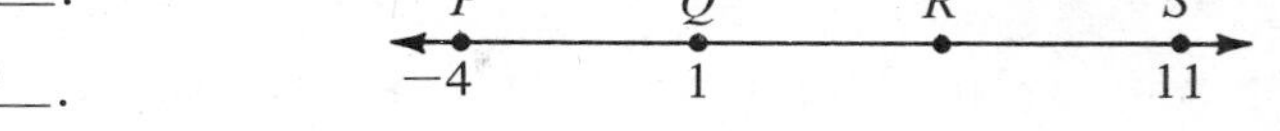


5. Another name for $\angle GTA$ is __?__.
6. $\angle 8 + \angle 9 = \angle$ __?__ (use 3 letters)
7. $\angle 4 + \angle 5 =$ __?__ °
8. $\angle 3$ and $\angle$ __?__ are vertical angles.
9. If $\overrightarrow{AN}$ bisects $\angle TAG$ and $\angle 8 = 35°$, then $\angle TAG =$ __?__ °.

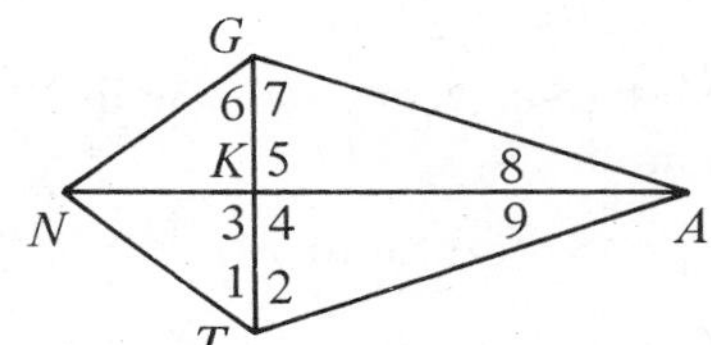


**In the diagram above, $\overline{TG} \perp \overline{NA}$. Classify each angle as acute, right, obtuse, or straight.**

10. $\angle NTA$ 11. $\angle NKA$ 12. $\angle NKG$ 13. $\angle ANG$

14. Construct a right angle.
15. Construct a 45° angle. (Use your answer to Exercise 14 if you wish.)

**Which postulate can be used to justify each statement?**

16. If $3x + 7 = 31$, then $3x = 24$.
17. If $3x = 24$, then $x = 8$.
18. If $\angle 1 = \angle 2$ and $\angle 1 + \angle 5 = 50°$, then $\angle 2 + \angle 5 = 50°$.
19. If $\angle 1 = \angle 2$ and $\angle 3 = \angle 4$, then $\angle ABC = \angle ACB$. (See diagram.)

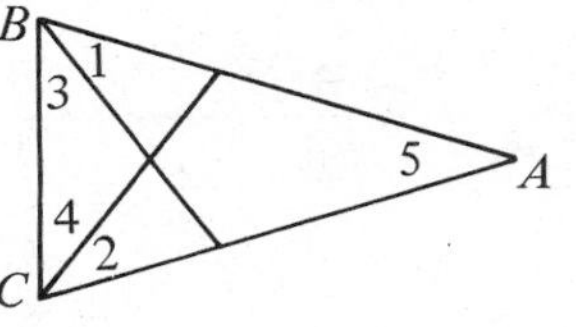


**Refer to the rectangular solid shown. Complete.**

20. Plane $SBTN \parallel$ plane __?__.
21. $J$, $N$, $L$, and __?__ are coplanar points.
22. $\overleftrightarrow{AJ}$ is formed by the intersection of plane __?__ and plane __?__.

## Chapter 2

*Given:* $\overline{DC} \perp \overline{FC}$

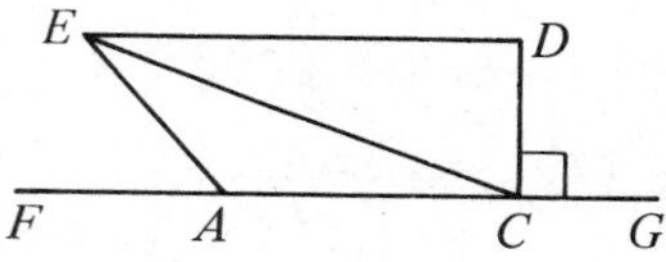


1. Name a complement of $\angle ACE$.
2. Name *two* pairs of supplementary angles.
3. If $\overline{DE} \parallel \overline{AC}$, then $\angle DEC = \angle$ _?_.
4. If $\overline{DE} \parallel \overline{AC}$, then $\angle FAE = \angle$ _?_.

**Use the statement "two coplanar lines each perpendicular to a third line are parallel."**

5. Write the statement in "if . . . then" form.
6. State the converse of the given statement.

**Find the values of $x$ and $y$ in each diagram.**

7. 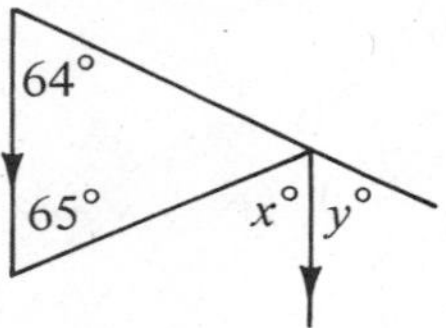


8. 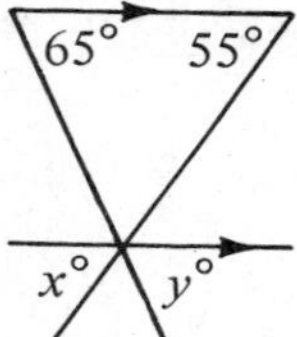


9. 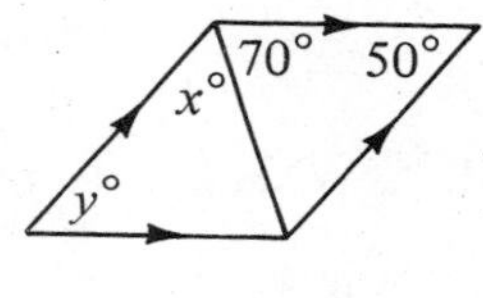


**Supply the reasons to complete the proof.**

10. *Given:* $\angle 1 = \angle 2$; $\angle 3 = \angle 4$
*Prove:* $\overline{AN} \parallel \overline{LB}$

| Statements | Reasons |
|---|---|
| 1. $\angle 1 = \angle 2$; $\angle 3 = \angle 4$ | 1. _?_ |
| 2. $\angle 2 = \angle 3$ | 2. _?_ |
| 3. $\angle 1 = \angle 4$ | 3. _?_ |
| 4. $\overline{AN} \parallel \overline{LB}$ | 4. _?_ |

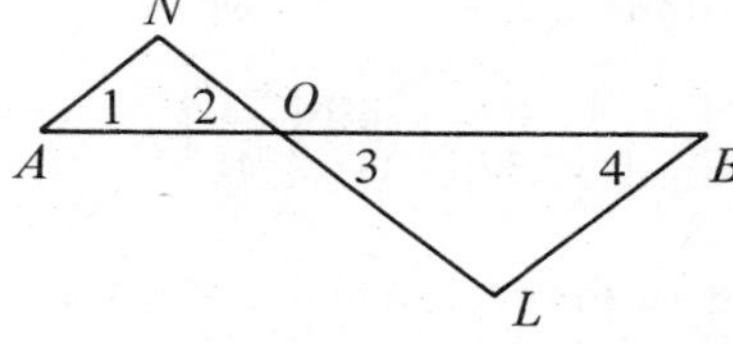


11. Use the figure for Exercise 10.
*Given:* $\angle 1 = \angle 2$; $\overline{AN} \parallel \overline{LB}$
*Prove:* $\angle 4 = \angle 3$

12. Draw a triangle $ABC$. Construct a line through $A$ parallel to $\overline{BC}$.

## Chapter 3

**Find the value of $x$.**

**1.** 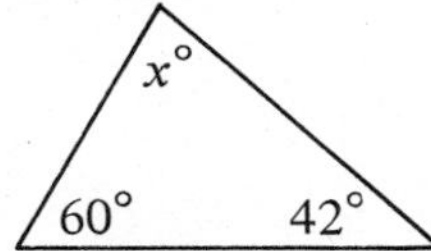


**2.** 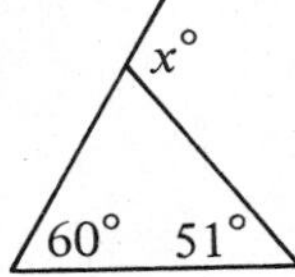


**3.** 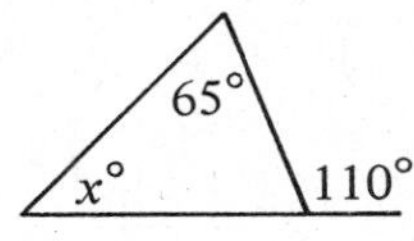


**4.** Two angles of a triangle have measures 46° and 44°. Is the triangle *acute, right,* or *obtuse?*

**5.** A triangle has three unequal sides. Is the triangle *isosceles, equilateral,* or *neither* of these?

**Complete: If $\triangle TOW \cong \triangle RAN$, then . . .**

**6.** $\angle W = \angle$ _?_ **7.** $TW =$ _?_

**8.** Which *two* of the following indicate correct ways of proving triangles congruent?

SS HL SSS AAA

**9.** Complete the statement correctly:

$\triangle XYZ \cong \triangle$ _?_ _?_ _?_

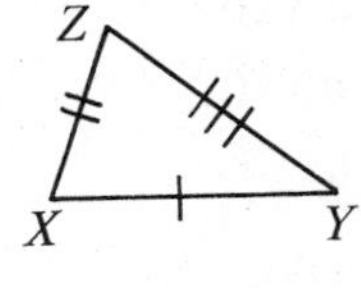


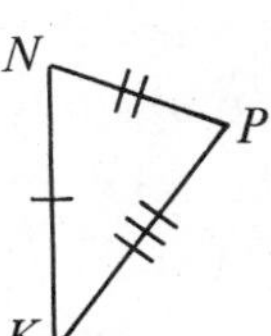


**10.** Supply the reasons to complete the proof.

*Given:* $\overrightarrow{AB}$ bisects $\angle XAY$

$AX = AY$

*Prove:* $\triangle BAX \cong \triangle BAY$

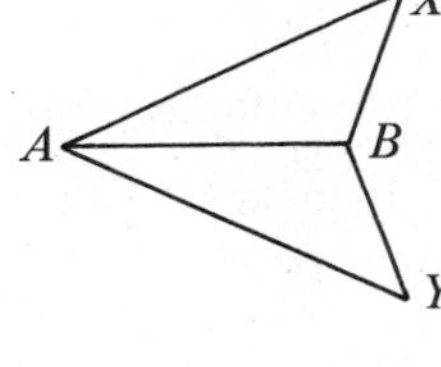


| Statements | Reasons |
|---|---|
| 1. $AB = AB$ | 1. _?_ |
| 2. $\angle BAX = \angle BAY$ | 2. _?_ |
| 3. $AX = AY$ | 3. _?_ |
| 4. $\triangle BAX \cong \triangle BAY$ | 4. _?_ |

**11.** Write a complete proof in two-column form.

*Given:* $VT = SR$

$\overline{VT} \parallel \overline{SR}$

*Prove:* $\triangle RST \cong \triangle TVR$

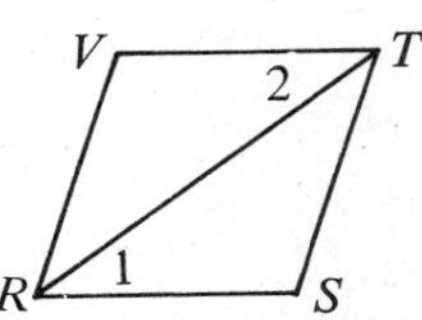

## Chapter 4

**1.** Suppose $\angle SAT$ has been bisected, by construction. Then $\overline{XP}$ and $\overline{YP}$ have been drawn. Supply reasons to complete the proof that $\angle SAT$ really has been bisected.

| Statements | Reasons |
|---|---|
| 1. $AX = AY$ | 1. By construction |
| 2. $XP = YP$ | 2. ? |
| 3. $AP = AP$ | 3. ? |
| 4. $\triangle XAP \cong \triangle YAP$ | 4. ? |
| 5. $\angle XAP = \angle YAP$ | 5. ? |

**2.** $M$ is the midpoint of $\overline{JK}$.

**a.** Name three bisectors of $\overline{JK}$.

**b.** $\overleftrightarrow{DE}$ is a perpendicular bisector of $\overline{JK}$ if $\angle DMK =$ ___?___.

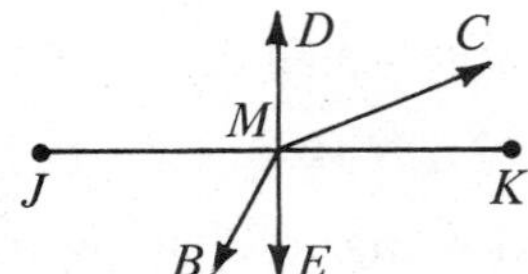


**3.** Draw a triangle like the one shown, but much larger.

**a.** Construct the altitude from $T$.

**b.** Construct the median from $T$.

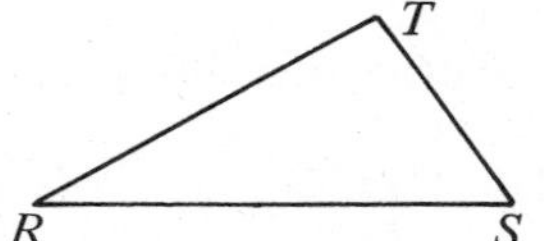


**4.** Draw a $\triangle ABC$. Circumscribe a circle about $\triangle ABC$.

**5.** In $\triangle GUM$, $GU = MU$ and $\angle U = 40°$. $\angle G =$ ___?___ °

**Write a proof in two-column form.**

**6.** *Given:* $\overrightarrow{WX}$ bisects $\angle YWZ$; $WY = WZ$

*Prove:* $XY = XZ$

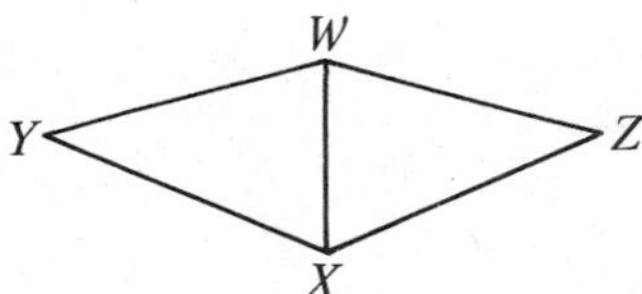


**7.** *Given:* $\angle 3 = \angle 4$

*Prove:* $AT = AV$

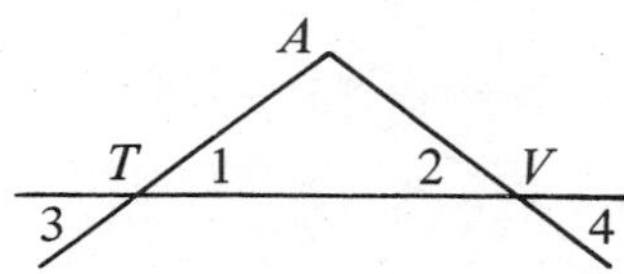

## Chapter 5

1. The perimeter of a regular pentagon is 450 cm. How long is a side?

2. Find the interior angle sum of a polygon with 12 sides.

3. Find the exterior angle sum of an octagon.

4. Find the measure of each interior angle of a regular hexagon.

***Given:* ▱*STAL* and ▱*BANK*.**
**Find each length and angle measure.**

5. *NK* 6. *LS* 7. *LN*

8. ∠*T* 9. ∠*A* 10. ∠*K*

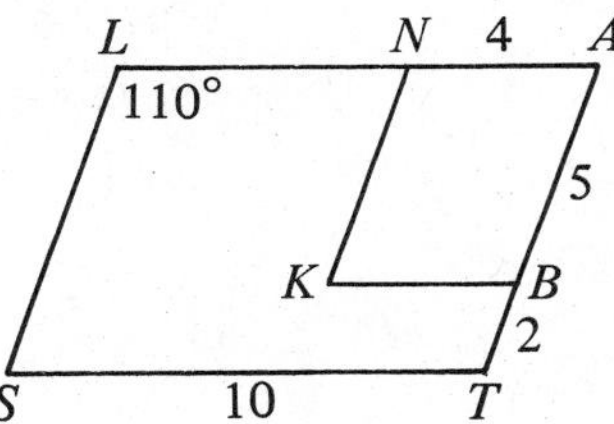


***Given:* Rectangle *ABEF* and rhombus *BCDE*.**
**Find each length and angle measure.**

11. *AE* 12. *BF* 13. *OF*

14. *BC* 15. ∠*BAE* 16. ∠*BEC*

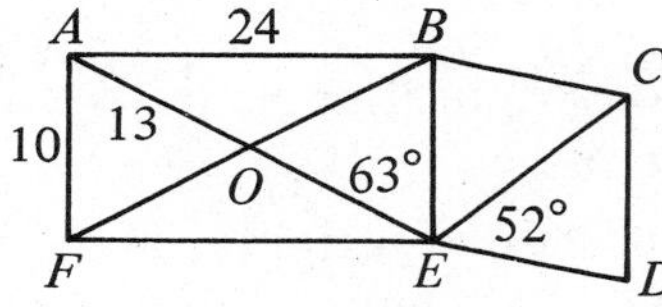


***PRIM* is an isosceles trapezoid with bases $\overline{PR}$ and $\overline{MI}$.**
***PR* = 30, *MI* = 16, and *RI* = 12.**

17. Find the length of the median of the trapezoid.

18. If ∠*P* = 54°, find the measures of ∠*R*, ∠*I*, and ∠*M*.

***D*, *E*, and *F* are midpoints of the sides of △*PQR*.**

19. *DE* = _?_ 20. *RQ* = _?_ 21. *PE* = _?_

22. If ∠*Q* = 90°, what kind of quadilateral is *FEQD*?

23. State the definition of a parallelogram.

24. State a theorem which can be used to prove that a quadrilateral is a parallelogram.

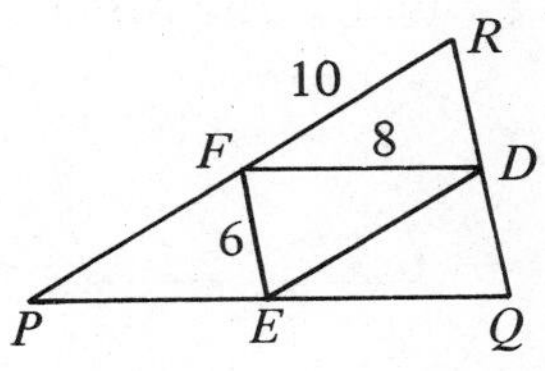

## Chapter 6

**Match the expressions or statements in the column at the right with the phrases in the column at the left. *If* the area of a parallelogram were $2\pi r$, for instance, you would write 1j.**

| | |
|---|---|
| **1.** Area of a parallelogram | **a.** $\pi r^2$ |
| **2.** Area of a square | **b.** $s^2$ |
| **3.** Circumference of a circle | **c.** $bh$ |
| **4.** Area of a trapezoid | **d.** $c^2 > a^2 + b^2$ |
| **5.** Area of a circle | **e.** $\frac{1}{2}(bh)$ |
| **6.** Area of a triangle | **f.** $4s$ |
| **7.** Perimeter of a square | **g.** $\frac{1}{2}h(b_1 + b_2)$ |
| **8.** Obtuse triangle | **h.** $c^2 < a^2 + b^2$ |
| **9.** Acute triangle | **i.** $2b + 2h$ |
| **10.** Perimeter of a rectangle | **j.** $2\pi r$ |

**11.** The legs of a right triangle have lengths 6 and 8. Find the length of the hypotenuse.

**12.** The hypotenuse of a right triangle is 13 m long and one leg is 12 m long. Find the length of the other leg.

**13.** The sides of a rectangle are of length 4 and 13.
**a.** perimeter = __?__ **b.** area = __?__ **c.** length of a diagonal = __?__

**14.** The radius of a circle is 6. Find the area (in terms of $\pi$).

**15.** The radius of a circle is 8. Using 3.14 for $\pi$, find the area (correct to the nearest integer).

**16.** The area of a circle is $100\pi$. Find the circumference (in terms of $\pi$).

**Find the area of each figure.**

**17.** Parallelogram

6 5
8

**18.** Triangle

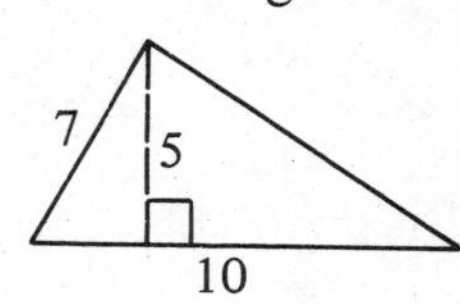


**19.** Trapezoid

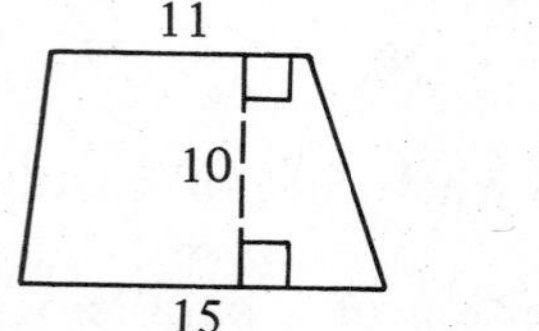


**20.** Trapezoid

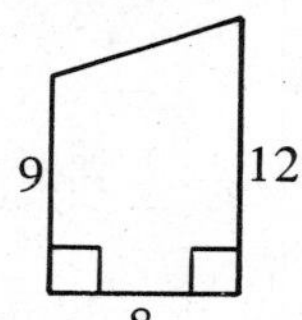


**21.** The area of a certain rectangle is 84 cm². Each of the longer sides is 14 cm. How long is each of the shorter sides?

**22.** The perimeter of a certain square is 28 cm. Find the area.

## Chapter 7

**Express each ratio in simplest form.**

**1.** $\frac{12}{16}$ **2.** $\frac{18}{21}$ **3.** $\frac{15x}{35x}$

**4.** 30:45 **5.** $xy:yz$ **6.** 48:36:60

**7.** 8 cm:2 m **8.** 400 m:4 km **9.** 15 min to 5 h

***Given:* $\square ABCD$. Find each ratio in simplest form.**

**10.** $\frac{DE}{DC}$ **11.** $\frac{AF}{FB}$

**12.** $\frac{AG}{AC}$ **13.** $\frac{BC}{AD}$

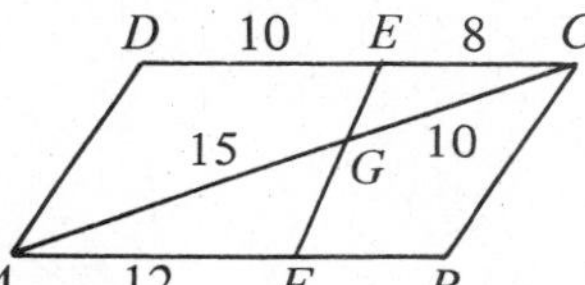


**Complete each statement. All variables represent nonzero numbers.**

**14.** If $\frac{a}{b} = \frac{5}{7}$, then $\frac{a+b}{b} = \underline{\quad ? \quad}$.

**15.** If $\frac{k}{8} = \frac{7}{9}$, then $\frac{k}{7} = \underline{\quad ? \quad}$.

**Find the value of $x$.**

**16.** $\frac{x}{6} = \frac{3}{2}$ **17.** $\frac{27}{18} = \frac{x}{6}$ **18.** $\frac{x-5}{4} = \frac{6}{12}$

**19.** It takes 5 cans of paint to paint a floor 5 m wide and 8 m long. How many cans will it take to paint a floor 4 m wide and 6 m long?

**Use the diagram at right.**

**20.** Measure the map distance between Stow and Lee to the nearest centimeter. Then give the scale of the map.

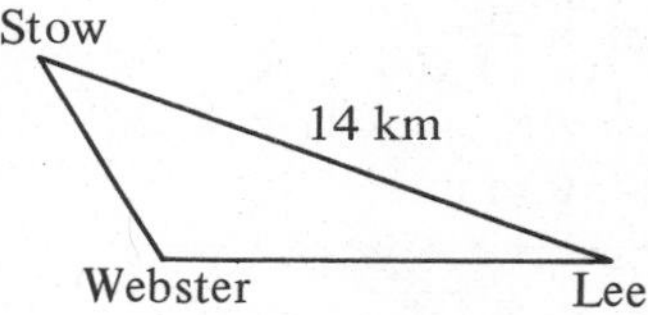


**21.** Find the actual distance between Stow and Webster.

**22.** Find the actual distance between Lee and Webster.

**23.** Make an accurate scale drawing of a rectangular plot of land 180 m long and 120 m wide. Give the scale of your drawing.

## Chapter 8

**The two trapezoids are similar. Complete each statement.**

1. $RAFT \sim$ __?__
2. The scale factor is __?__ : __?__
3. $\frac{12}{8} = \frac{x}{?}$
4. $y =$ __?__

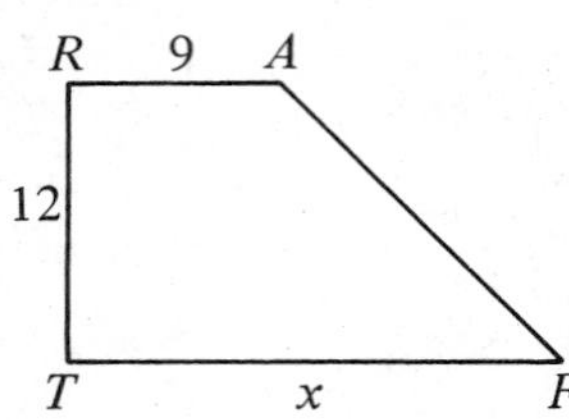


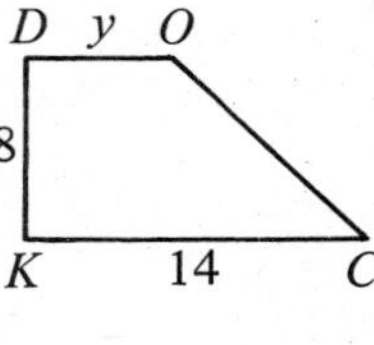


5. The ratio of the perimeters of the figures is __?__ : __?__.
6. The ratio of the areas is __?__ : __?__

**Find the values of $x$ and $y$.**

**7.**

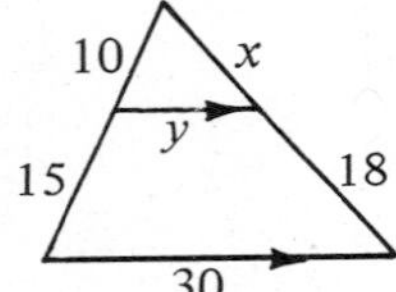


**8.**

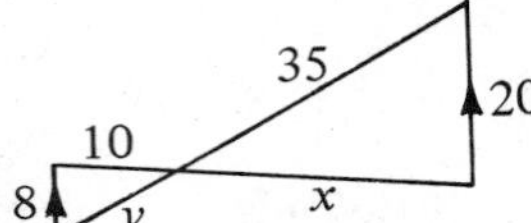


**9.**

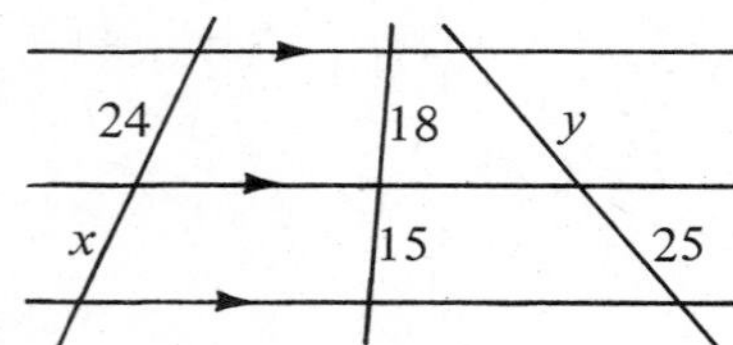


**10.**

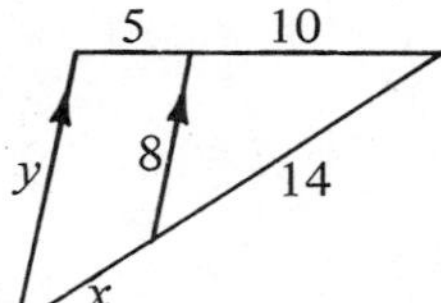


**11.** Supply the reasons to complete the proof.

*Given:* ▱$PQRS$

*Prove:* $\frac{NO}{QO} = \frac{RO}{PO}$

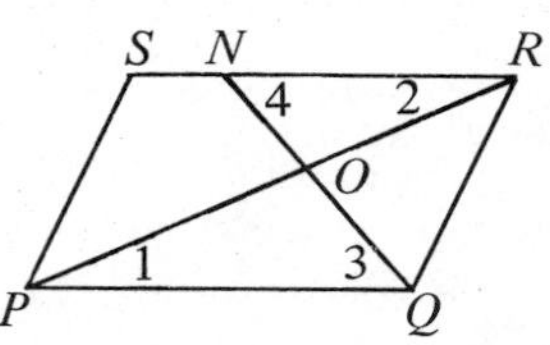


| Statements | Reasons |
| --- | --- |
| 1. $PQRS$ is a ▱ | 1. __?__ |
| 2. $\overline{NR} \parallel \overline{PQ}$ | 2. __?__ |
| 3. $\angle 1 = \angle 2$; $\angle 3 = \angle 4$ | 3. __?__ |
| 4. $\triangle NOR \sim \triangle QOP$ | 4. __?__ |
| 5. $\frac{NO}{QO} = \frac{RO}{PO}$ | 5. __?__ |

## Chapter 9

**Refer to the figure and use letters to name the following:**

**1.** A tangent **2.** A radius

**3.** A chord **4.** A secant

**Refer to the diagram and complete the statements.**

**5.** The number of common external tangents that can be drawn to $\odot P$ and $\odot R$ is _?_.

**6.** The number of common internal tangents that can be drawn to $\odot P$ and $\odot R$ is _?_.

**7.** $\odot P$ and $\odot Q$ are _____?_____ (internally/externally) tangent.

**8.** Suppose a line is drawn perpendicular to $\overline{QX}$ at $X$. That line will be _?_ to $\odot Q$.

**Write numerical values to complete the statements.**

**9.** If $\widehat{BC} = 40°$, $\widehat{AC} =$ _?_ °. **10.** If $\widehat{AC} = 150°$, $\widehat{ABC} =$ _?_ °.

**11.** If $\angle 1 = 36°$, $\widehat{BC} =$ _?_ °. **12.** If $\widehat{AC} = 142°$, $\angle 1 =$ _?_ °.

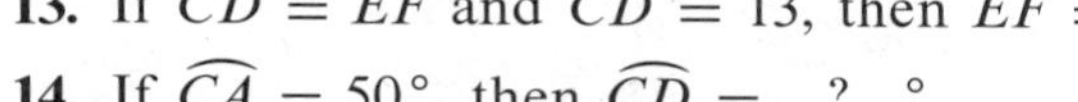

**13.** If $\widehat{CD} = \widehat{EF}$ and $CD = 13$, then $EF =$ _?_.

**14.** If $\widehat{CA} = 50°$, then $\widehat{CD} =$ _?_ °.

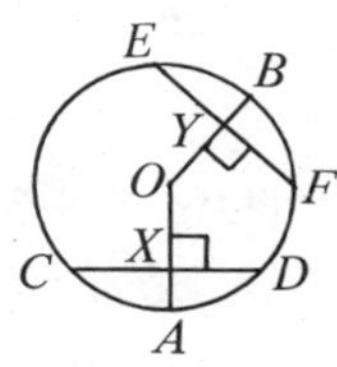


**15.** If $OY = OX$ and $EF = 18$, then $CX =$ _?_.

**16.** If $CD = 16$ and $OX = 6$, then $OC =$ _?_.

**State the numerical value of $x$.**

**17.**

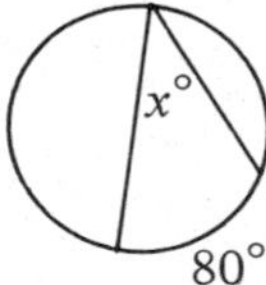


**18.**

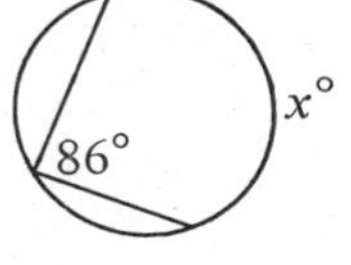


**19.**

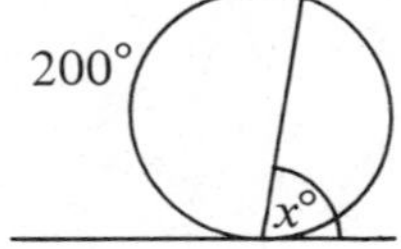


**20.**

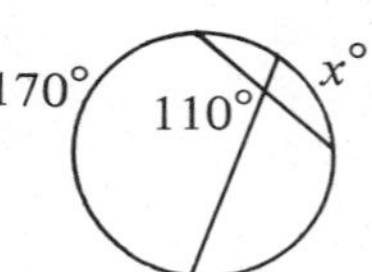


**21.**

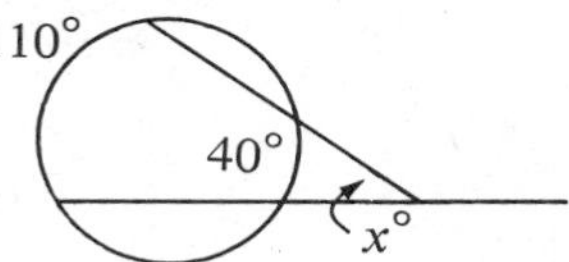


**22.**

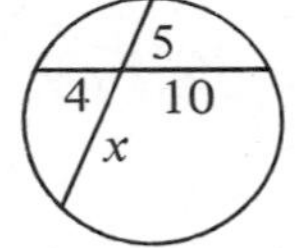


**23.** Construct a circle and choose a point $P$ on the circle. Construct a line tangent to the circle at point $P$.

## Chapter 10

**Tell whether the statements are true or false.**

1. Two parallel lines must be coplanar.
2. If two lines are skew, there is one plane that contains both lines.
3. If a line does not lie in a plane, the line must intersect the plane.
4. If $\overleftrightarrow{XY}$ is perpendicular to plane $P$, then every plane that contains $\overleftrightarrow{XY}$ must be perpendicular to $P$.

**Refer to the right prism shown.**

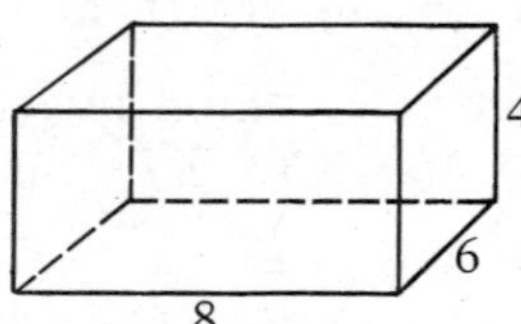


5. $B =$ _?_ 6. L.A. = _?_
7. T.A. = _?_ 8. $V =$ _?_

**Refer to the cylinder shown. Answer in terms of $\pi$.**

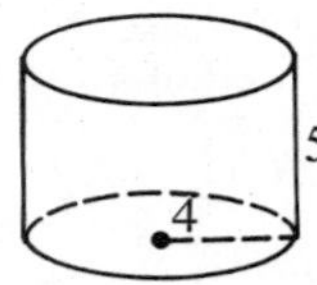


9. $C =$ _?_ 10. L.A. = _?_
11. T.A. = _?_ 12. $V =$ _?_

**Refer to the regular square pyramid shown.**

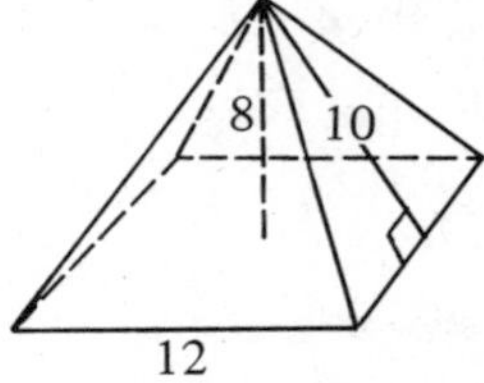


13. $B =$ _?_ 14. L.A. = _?_
15. T.A. = _?_ 16. $V =$ _?_

**Refer to the cone shown. Answer in terms of $\pi$.**

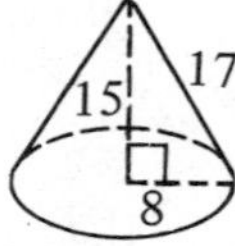


17. $C =$ _?_ 18. L.A. = _?_
19. T.A. = _?_ 20. $V =$ _?_

21. Find, in terms of $\pi$, the area of a sphere in which $r = 8$.
22. The area of a sphere is $36\pi$. Find the volume, correct to the nearest integer.

## Chapter 11

**Find the exact values of $x$ and $y$.**

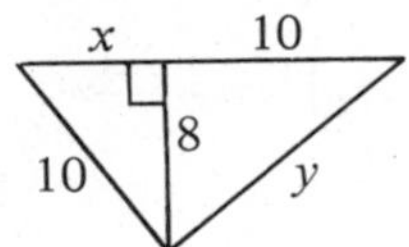


2.

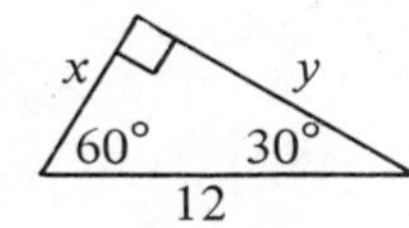


x
45°
30°
6
y

**Find the area of each figure.**

4.

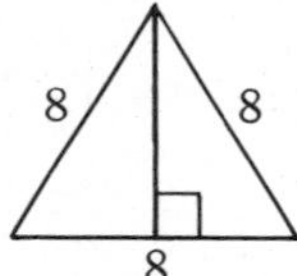


5.

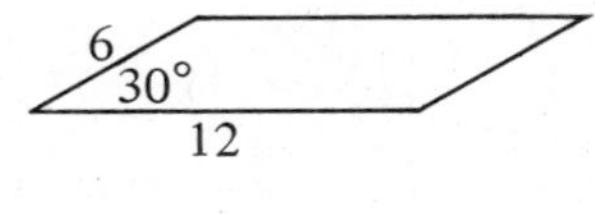


6.

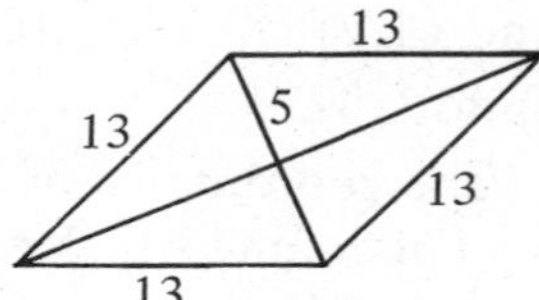


7. The length of a diagonal of a square is $8\sqrt{2}$. What is the area of the square?
8. The dimensions of a rectangular solid are 6 cm, 3 cm, and 2 cm. How long is its diagonal?

**Chord $AB$ is 16 cm long and is 6 cm from the center of the circle.**

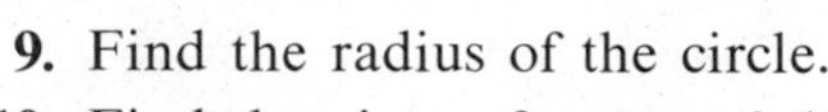

9. Find the radius of the circle.
10. Find the circumference of the circle.

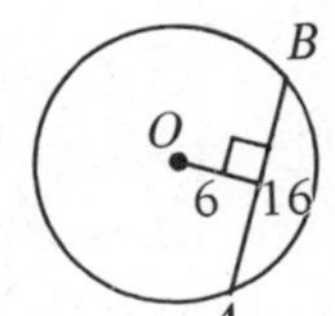
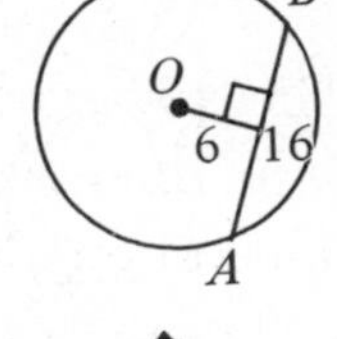


11. Find the lateral area of the regular square pyramid.
12. Find the height.
13. Find the volume.
14. Draw a cone with height 9 and slant height 15.
15. Find the radius of the cone.
16. Find the volume of the cone (in terms of $\pi$).

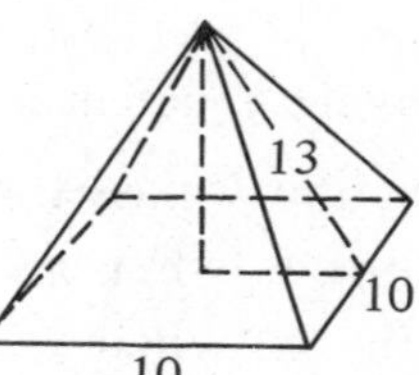


**Find the value of $x$ to the nearest tenth. Use the table on page 418.**

17.

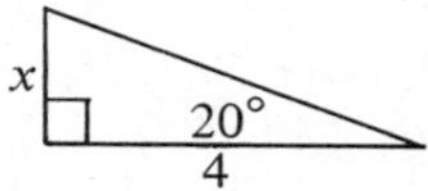


18.

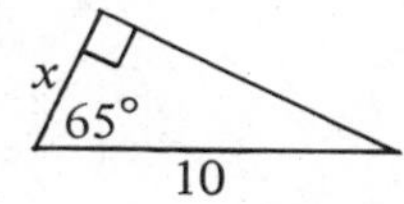


19.

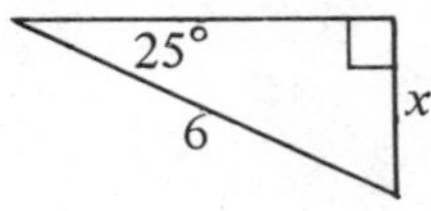

## Chapter 12

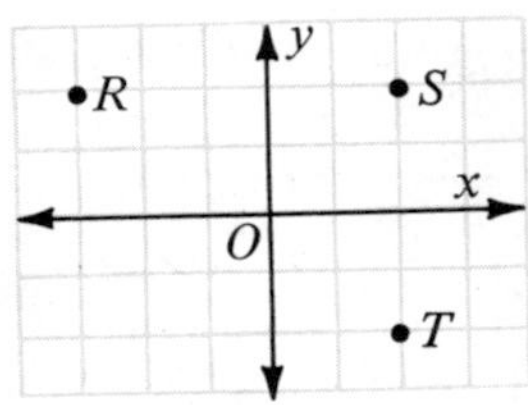


1. Point $R$ lies in Quadrant __?__.
2. The $x$-coordinate of point $R$ is __?__.
3. The $y$-coordinate of point $S$ is __?__.
4. If point $U$ is chosen so that quadrilateral $RSTU$ is a rectangle, then $U$ has coordinates (__?__, __?__).

**Find the distance between the points named. Use graph paper if you wish.**

5. (4, 1) and (4, 7)
6. (0, −3) and (−2, −3)
7. (0, 0) and (3, 4)
8. (−4, 1) and (2, −7)

9–12. Find the coordinates of the midpoint of the segment that joins the points named in Exercises 5–8.

**State the slope of the line. If the slope is not defined for a particular line, write *not defined.***

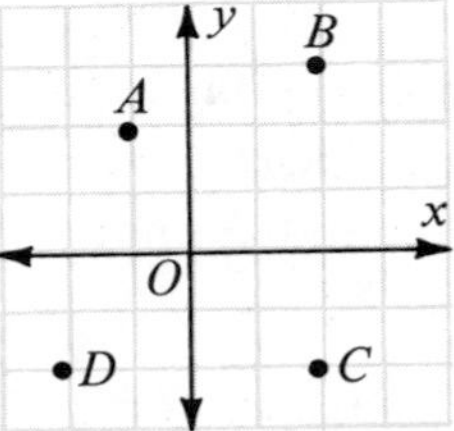


13. $\overleftrightarrow{OA}$
14. $\overleftrightarrow{AB}$
15. $\overleftrightarrow{BC}$
16. $\overleftrightarrow{DC}$

**Line *t* has slope $\frac{5}{2}$.**

17. Does line $t$ *rise,* or does it *fall,* to the right?
18. The slope of any line parallel to $t$ equals __?__.
19. The slope of any line perpendicular to $t$ equals __?__.

**Line *k* has the equation $3x - 2y = 12$.**

20. Does line $k$ pass through point (5, 1)?
21. On line $k$, when $x = 0$, $y =$ __?__.
22. On line $k$, when $y = 6$, $x =$ __?__.

**Points *E*, *F*, *G*, and *H* have the coordinates shown.**

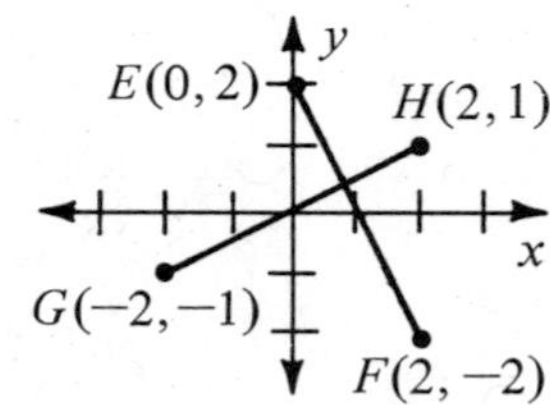


23. *Prove:* $\overline{EF} \perp \overline{GH}$
24. *Prove:* $EF = GH$

# Answers to Chapter Tests

**Chapter 1**

**1.** $\overleftrightarrow{PQ}$, $\overleftrightarrow{QS}$, $\overleftrightarrow{PS}$, and so on. **2.** $\overrightarrow{SR}$ or $\overrightarrow{SP}$ **3.** 5; 10 **4.** 6 **5.** $\angle 2$, $\angle KTA$, $\angle ATG$, or $\angle ATK$ **6.** *GAT* or *TAG* **7.** 180 **8.** 5 **9.** 70 **10.** obtuse **11.** straight **12.** right **13.** acute **14.** **15.**

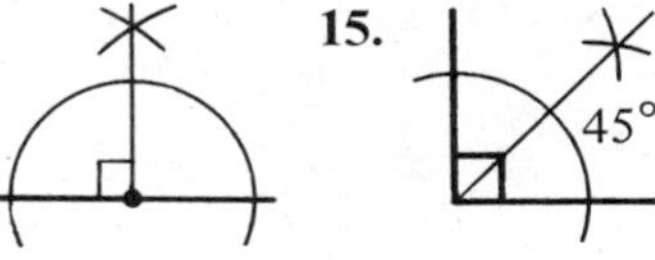


**16.** Subtraction **17.** Division **18.** Substitution **19.** Addition **20.** *ARLJ* **21.** *T* **22.** *ARLJ*; *AJNS*

**Chapter 2**

**1.** $\angle ECD$ **2.** $\angle EAF$ and $\angle EAC$; $\angle DCA$ and $\angle DCG$; $\angle ECA$ and $\angle ECG$ **3.** *ECA* **4.** *AED* **5.** If two lines are coplanar and each is perpendicular to a third line, then the two lines are parallel. **6.** If two lines are parallel, then they are coplanar and each is perpendicular to a third line. **7.** $x = 65$; $y = 64$ **8.** $x = 55$; $y = 65$ **9.** $x = 60$; $y = 50$

**10.** 1. Given 2. Vertical angles are equal 3. Substitution (twice)
4. If two lines and a transversal form equal alternate interior angles, then the lines are parallel.

**11.** 1. $\angle 1 = \angle 2$ (Given) 2. $\angle 2 = \angle 3$ (Vertical angles are equal.)
3. $\angle 1 = \angle 3$ (Substitution) 4. $\overline{AN} \parallel \overline{LB}$ (Given)
5. $\angle 1 = \angle 4$ (If two parallel lines are cut by a transversal, then alternate interior angles are equal.)
6. $\angle 4 = \angle 3$ (Substitution)

**12.**

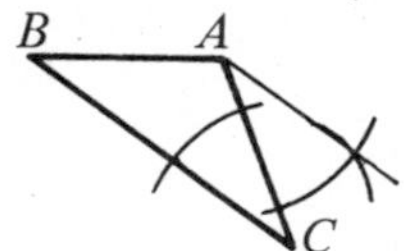


**Chapter 3**

**1.** 78 **2.** 111 **3.** 45 **4.** right **5.** neither (scalene) **6.** *N* **7.** *RN* **8.** HL; SSS **9.** *NKP*

**10.** 1. From algebra 2. Given: $\overrightarrow{AB}$ bisects $\angle XAY$ 3. Given 4. SAS Postulate

**11.** 1. $VT = SR$; $\overline{VT} \parallel \overline{SR}$ (Given)
2. $\angle 1 = \angle 2$ (If two parallel lines are cut by a transversal, then alternate interior angles are equal.)
3. $TR = RT$ (From algebra) 4. $\triangle RST \cong \triangle TVR$ (SAS Postulate)

## Chapter 4

**1.** 2. By construction 3. From algebra 4. SSS Postulate 5. Corresponding parts of congruent triangles are equal

**2. a.** $\overleftrightarrow{CM}$; $\overleftrightarrow{MB}$; $\overleftrightarrow{DE}$ **b.** 90° **3.**

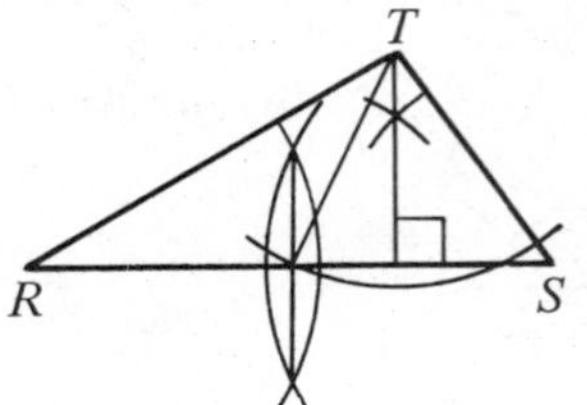


**4.**

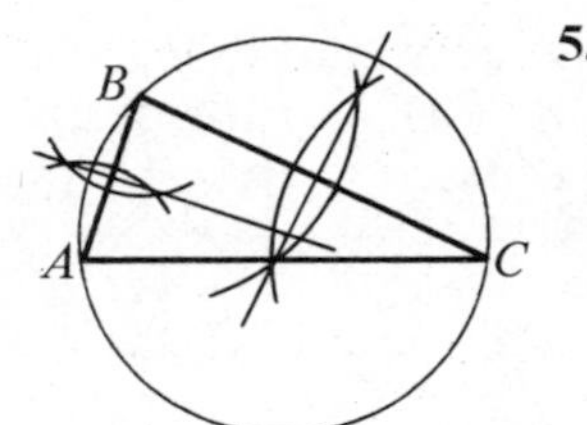


**5.** 70

**6.** 1. $WY = WZ$ (Given) 2. $\angle YWX = \angle ZWX$ (Given: $\overrightarrow{WX}$ bisects $\angle YWZ$) 3. $WX = WX$ (From algebra) 4. $\triangle YWX \cong \triangle ZWX$ (SAS Postulate) 5. $XY = XZ$ (Corresponding parts of congruent triangles are equal.)

**7.** 1. $\angle 3 = \angle 1$; $\angle 4 = \angle 2$ (Vertical angles are equal.) 2. $\angle 3 = \angle 4$ (Given) 3. $\angle 1 = \angle 2$ (Substitution – twice) 4. $AT = AV$ (If two angles of a triangle are equal, then the sides opposite those angles are equal.)

## Chapter 5

**1.** 90 cm **2.** 1800° **3.** 360° **4.** 120° **5.** 5 **6.** 7 **7.** 6 **8.** 110° **9.** 70° **10.** 70° **11.** 26 **12.** 26 **13.** 13 **14.** 10 **15.** 27° **16.** 52° **17.** 23 **18.** $R = 54°$; $\angle I = \angle M = 126°$ **19.** 10 **20.** 12 **21.** 8 **22.** rectangle **23.** A parallelogram is a quadrilateral with both pairs of opposite sides parallel. **24.** Theorems 10–12, pages 195–196

## Chapter 6

**1.** c. **2.** b. **3.** j. **4.** g. **5.** a. **6.** e. **7.** f. **8.** d. **9.** h. **10.** i. **11.** 10 **12.** 5 **13.** a. 34 b. 52 c. $\sqrt{185} \doteq 13.6$ **14.** $36\pi$ **15.** 201 **16.** $20\pi$ **17.** 40 **18.** 25 **19.** 130 **20.** 84 **21.** 6 cm **22.** 49 cm²

## Chapter 7

**1.** $\frac{3}{4}$ **2.** $\frac{6}{7}$ **3.** $\frac{3}{7}$ **4.** 2:3 **5.** $x:z$ **6.** 4:3:5 **7.** 1:25 **8.** 1:10 **9.** 1:20 **10.** $\frac{5}{9}$ **11.** $\frac{2}{1}$ **12.** $\frac{3}{5}$ **13.** $\frac{1}{1}$ **14.** $\frac{12}{7}$ **15.** $\frac{8}{9}$ **16.** 9 **17.** 9 **18.** 7 **19.** 3 cans **20.** 4 cm; 1 cm:3.5 km **21.** 5.6 km **22.** 10.5 km **23.** (The length:width ratio of the drawing should be 3:2.)

## Chapter 8

**1.** *DOCK* **2.** 3:2 **3.** 14 **4.** 6 **5.** 3:2 **6.** 9:4 **7.** $x = 12$; $y = 12$ **8.** $x = 25$; $y = 14$ **9.** $x = 20$; $y = 30$ **10.** $x = 7$; $y = 12$

**11.** 1. Given 2. Opposite sides of a parallelogram are parallel. 3. If two parallel lines are cut by a transversal, then alternate interior angles are equal. 4. AA Postulate 5. Corresponding sides of similar triangles are in proportion.

## Chapter 9

**1.** $\overleftrightarrow{VZ}$ **2.** $\overline{OX}$ **3.** $\overline{YZ}$ **4.** $\overleftrightarrow{YZ}$ or $\overleftrightarrow{OX}$ **5.** 2 **6.** 2 **7.** internally **8.** tangent **9.** 140 **10.** 210 **11.** 36 **12.** 38 **13.** 13 **14.** 100 **15.** 9 **16.** 10 **17.** 40 **18.** 172 **19.** 80 **20.** 50 **21.** 35 **22.** 8 **23.**

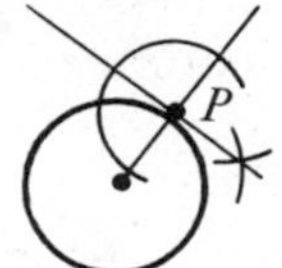


## Chapter 10

**1.** true **2.** false **3.** false **4.** true **5.** 48 **6.** 112 **7.** 208 **8.** 192 **9.** $8\pi$ **10.** $40\pi$ **11.** $72\pi$ **12.** $80\pi$ **13.** 144 **14.** 240 **15.** 384 **16.** 384 **17.** $16\pi$ **18.** $136\pi$ **19.** $200\pi$ **20.** $320\pi$ **21.** $256\pi$ **22.** 113

## Chapter 11

**1.** $x = 6$; $y = \sqrt{164} = 2\sqrt{41}$ **2.** $x = 6$; $y = 6\sqrt{3}$ **3.** $x = 6\sqrt{2}$; $y = 6\sqrt{3}$ **4.** $16\sqrt{3}$ **5.** 36 **6.** 120 **7.** 64 **8.** 7 cm **9.** 10 cm **10.** $20\pi$ cm **11.** 260 **12.** 12 **13.** 400 **14.** (Drawing omitted) **15.** 12 **16.** $432\pi$ **17.** 1.5 **18.** 4.2 **19.** 2.5

## Chapter 12

**1.** II **2.** −3 **3.** 2 **4.** (−3, −2) **5.** 6 **6.** 2 **7.** 5 **8.** 10 **9.** (4, 4) **10.** (−1, −3) **11.** (1.5, 2) **12.** (−1, −3) **13.** −2 **14.** $\frac{1}{3}$ **15.** not defined **16.** 0 **17.** rise **18.** $\frac{5}{2}$ **19.** $-\frac{2}{5}$ **20.** no **21.** −6 **22.** 8

**23.** 1. Slope of $\overline{EF} = \dfrac{2-(-2)}{0-2} = -2$; Slope of $\overline{GH} = \dfrac{1-(-1)}{2-(-2)} = \dfrac{1}{2}$ (Definition of slope)

2. $\overline{EF} \perp \overline{GH}$ $(-2(\frac{1}{2}) = -1$; If the product of the slopes of two lines is −1, then the lines are perpendicular.)

**24.** 1. $(EF)^2 = 2^2 + 4^2 = 20$; $EF = \sqrt{20}$; $(GH)^2 = 4^2 + 2^2 = 20$; $GH = \sqrt{20}$ (Pythagorean Theorem and algebra)

2. $EF = GH$ (Substitution)

# Guide to Individualized Assignments

The following Guide to Individualized Assignments provides suggested assignments for an average course and a comprehensive course. The average course includes all topics that are considered essential and any concepts which are prerequisites for the lessons to follow. The comprehensive course includes all of the topics presented in the text. You will find that the assignments for the comprehensive course provide somewhat less drill than do the assignments for the average course.

**Summary Time Schedule for the Assignments**

| Chapter | 1 | 2 | 3 | 4 | 5 | 6 | 7 | 8 | 9 | 10 | 11 | 12 | Total |
|---|---|---|---|---|---|---|---|---|---|---|---|---|---|
| Average Course | 16 | 13 | 15 | 15 | 15 | 17 | 8 | 11 | 15 | 14 | 10 | 11 | 160 |
| Comprehensive Course | 15 | 15 | 13 | 14 | 14 | 17 | 8 | 10 | 13 | 13 | 14 | 14 | 160 |

| Lesson | AVERAGE COURSE Pages | AVERAGE COURSE Assignment | COMPREHENSIVE COURSE Pages | COMPREHENSIVE COURSE Assignment |
|---|---|---|---|---|
| | **Chapter 1** | | **Chapter 1** | |
| 1 | 3 | all | 3 | all |
| 2 | 6,7 | 1–20 | 6,7 | 1–20 |
| 3 | 7 | 21–29 | 7 | 21–30 |
| 4 | 11 | 1–12 | 11<br>12 | 1–22<br>Self-Test |
| 5 | 11<br>12 | 13–22<br>Self-Test | 14,15 | 1–20 |
| 6 | 14,15 | 1–16 | 17 | 1–17 |
| 7 | 17 | 1–16 | 19 | 1–13 |
| 8 | 19 | 1–13 | 20 | Experiments, all; Self-Test |
| 9 | 20 | Experiments, all; Self-Test | 23,24 | 1–15 |
| 10 | 23,24 | 1–15 | 24 | 16–24 |
| 11 | 27,28 | 1–14 | 27,28 | 1–17 |
| 12 | 32,33 | 1–17 | 32,33 | 1–22 |
| 13 | 33<br>34 | 18–22<br>Self-Test | 33<br>34 | 23<br>Self-Test |

| Lesson | AVERAGE COURSE Pages | Assignment | COMPREHENSIVE COURSE Pages | Assignment |
|---|---|---|---|---|
| 14 | 35<br>36,37 | Reviewing Arithmetic Skills<br>Applications (optional) | 36,37<br>38,39 | Applications<br>Reviewing the Chapter |
| 15 | 38,39 | Reviewing the Chapter | T11 | Chapter 1 Test |
| 16 | T11 | Chapter 1 Test | **Chapter 2**<br>44,45 | 1–22 |
| 17 | **Chapter 2**<br>44,45 | 1–18 | 48,49 | 1–24 |
| 18 | 48,49 | 1–20 | 49 | 25–28; Self-Test |
| 19 | 49 | 21–24; Self-Test | 52,53 | 1–11 |
| 20 | 56–58 | 1–6 | 56–59 | 1–6; 7–11 odd |
| 21 | 58,59 | 7–12 | 59 | 13–16 |
| 22 | 63,64 | 1–25 odd | 63,64 | 1–25 |
| 23 | 68,69 | 1–21 odd | 64,65 | 26–32 |
| 24 | 73 | 1–10 | 68–70 | 1–22 |
| 25 | 74<br>75 | Self-Test<br>Reviewing Algebraic Skills | 70 | 23–27 |
| 26 | 76,77 | Applications | 73 | 1–10 |
| 27 | 78,79 | Reviewing the Chapter | 74 | 11–14; Self-Test |
| 28 | T12 | Chapter 2 Test | 76,77<br>78,79 | Applications<br>Reviewing the Chapter |
| 29 | 80 | Cumulative Review | T12 | Chapter 2 Test |
| 30 | **Chapter 3**<br>86,88 | 1–27 odd | 80 | Cumulative Review |
| 31 | 91 | 1–14 | **Chapter 3**<br>86–88 | 1–29 odd; 30 |
| 32 | 92 | 15–19; Self-Test | 91 | 1–14 |
| 33 | 96,97 | 1–12 | 92 | 15–20; Self-Test |
| 34 | 101,102 | 1–10 | 96,97 | 1–21 odd |
| 35 | 102,103<br>104 | 11–14<br>Self-Test | 101–103 | 1–17 |

| Lesson | AVERAGE COURSE Pages | AVERAGE COURSE Assignment | COMPREHENSIVE COURSE Pages | COMPREHENSIVE COURSE Assignment |
|---|---|---|---|---|
| 36 | 107,108 | 1–13 | 103<br>104 | 18–20<br>Self-Test |
| 37 | 108,109 | 14–17 | 107,108 | 1–15 |
| 38 | 112–114 | 1–9 | 109 | 16–20 |
| 39 | 114<br>115 | 10–11<br>Self-Test | 112–114 | 1–9 |
| 40 | 118–120 | 1–19 odd | 114–115 | 10–15; Self-Test |
| 41 | 122<br>123 | Self-Test<br>Reviewing Algebraic Skills | 118–122 | 1–26 |
| 42 | 124–125 | Applications | 122<br>124–125<br>126,127 | Self-Test<br>Applications<br>Reviewing the Chapter |
| 43 | 126,127 | Reviewing the Chapter | T13 | Chapter 3 Test |
| | | | **Chapter 4** | |
| 44 | T13 | Chapter 3 Test | 132–134 | 1–6; 8–22 even |
| | **Chapter 4** | | | |
| 45 | 132,133 | 1–14 | 136–138 | 1–11 |
| 46 | 136 | 1–6 | 138<br>139 | 12–16<br>Self-Test |
| 47 | 137–138<br>139 | 7–11<br>Self-Test | 142 | 1–11 |
| 48 | 142 | 1–11 | 143 | 12–17 |
| 49 | 143 | 12–15 | 146,147 | 1–15 |
| 50 | 146 | 1–10 | 147<br>148 | 16–18<br>Experiments |
| 51 | 148 | Experiments | 151,152 | 1–15; Self-Test |
| 52 | 151,152 | 1–10; Self-Test | 155–157 | 1–19 odd; 20–22 |
| 53 | 155,156 | 1–20 even | 160–162 | 1–17 |
| 54 | 160–162 | 1–14 | 162<br>163 | 18–23<br>Experiments; Self-Test |

| Lesson | AVERAGE COURSE Pages | AVERAGE COURSE Assignment | COMPREHENSIVE COURSE Pages | COMPREHENSIVE COURSE Assignment |
|---|---|---|---|---|
| 55 | 163 | Experiments; Self-Test | 165<br>166,167 | Applications<br>Reviewing the Chapter |
| 56 | 164<br>165 | Reviewing Arithmetic Skills<br>Applications (optional) | T14 | Chapter 4 Test |
| 57 | 166,167 | Reviewing the Chapter | 168 | Cumulative Review |
| | | | **Chapter 5** | |
| 58 | T14 | Chapter 4 Test | 174,175 | 1–31 odd |
| 59 | 168 | Cumulative Review | 178,179 | 1–22; Self-Test |
| | **Chapter 5** | | | |
| 60 | 174,175 | 1–19 | 182–184 | 1–23 odd |
| 61 | 178 | 1–11 | 187,188 | 1–25 odd; 27–32 |
| 62 | 178<br>179 | 12–18<br>Self-Test | 188,189 | 33–36; Self-Test |
| 63 | 182,183 | 1–15 | 192,193 | 1–10; 11–23 odd |
| 64 | 187 | 1–29 odd | 194 | 25–28 |
| 65 | 188<br>189 | 30–32<br>Self-Test | 197–199 | 1–12 |
| 66 | 192,193 | 1–10; 12–24 even | 200 | 13, 15, 17; Self-Test |
| 67 | 197,198 | 1–6 | 204,205 | 1–21 odd; 22–26 |
| 68 | 199<br>200 | 8–12 even<br>Self-Test | 207,208 | 1–18 |
| 69 | 204 | 1–15 | 208,209 | 19–25; Self-Test |
| 70 | 207,208 | 1–13 odd | 211<br>212,213 | Applications<br>Reviewing the Chapter |
| 71 | 208<br>209 | 15–21 odd<br>Self-Test | T15 | Chapter 5 Test |
| | | | **Chapter 6** | |
| 72 | 210<br>211 | Alg. Skills: 1–31 odd<br>Applications (optional) | 219,220 | 1–31 odd |
| 73 | 212,213 | Reviewing the Chapter | 220 | 32–35 |
| 74 | T15 | Chapter 5 Test | 223 | 1–13 |

| Lesson | AVERAGE COURSE Pages | AVERAGE COURSE Assignment | COMPREHENSIVE COURSE Pages | COMPREHENSIVE COURSE Assignment |
|---|---|---|---|---|
| | **Chapter 6** | | | |
| 75 | 219 | 2–24 even | 223<br>224 | 14–15<br>Self-Test |
| 76 | 219,220 | 25–31 | 227 | 1–15 |
| 77 | 223 | 1–9 | 228 | Calculator Corner |
| 78 | 223<br>224 | 10–13<br>Self-Test | 231,232 | 1–7; 8–24 even |
| 79 | 227 | 1–14 | 232,233 | 25–27; Self-Test |
| 80 | 231,232 | 1–16 | 236,237 | 2–28 even |
| 81 | 232<br>233 | 17–24<br>Self-Test | 240<br>241 | 2–24 even<br>Self-Test |
| 82 | 236 | 1–12 | 245 | 1–35 odd |
| 83 | 240<br>241 | 1–19 odd<br>Self-Test | 246 | 36–40 |
| 84 | 245 | 1–23 odd | 248,249 | 1–27 |
| 85 | 245,246 | 24–36 even | 249,250 | 28–33; Self-Test |
| 86 | 248,249 | 1–21 odd | 252,253<br>254,255 | Extra for Experts<br>Reviewing the Chapter |
| 87 | 249<br>250 | 22–26 even<br>Self-Test | T16 | Chapter 6 Test |
| 88 | 251<br>252,253 | Alg. Skills: 1–17 odd<br>Extra for Experts (optional) | 256 | Cumulative Review |
| | | | **Chapter 7** | |
| 89 | 254,255 | Reviewing the Chapter | 261,262 | 2–40 even |
| 90 | T16 | Chapter 6 Test | 265,266 | 2–38 even |
| 91 | 256 | Cumulative Review | 268–269 | 1–11; Self-Test |
| | **Chapter 7** | | | |
| 92 | 261,262 | 1–31 odd | 272 | 1–17 |
| 93 | 265,266 | 2–28 even | 273–274 | 1–9 odd |
| 94 | 268<br>269 | 1–8<br>Self-Test | 274<br>275,277 | 11<br>Self-Test; Applications |

| Lesson | AVERAGE COURSE Pages | AVERAGE COURSE Assignment | COMPREHENSIVE COURSE Pages | COMPREHENSIVE COURSE Assignment |
|---|---|---|---|---|
| 95 | 272 | 1–12 | 278,279 | Reviewing the Chapter |
| 96 | 273,274<br>275 | 1–7 odd<br>Self-Test | T17 | Chapter 7 Test |
| | | | **Chapter 8** | |
| 97 | 276<br>277 | Alg. Skills: 1–27 odd<br>Applications (optional) | 284–285 | 1–16 |
| 98 | 278–279 | Reviewing the Chapter | 285–286 | 17–26 |
| 99 | T17 | Chapter 7 Test | 289–291<br>292 | 2–24 even<br>Self-Test |
| | **Chapter 8** | | | |
| 100 | 284–285 | 1–16 | 293,294 | 1–12 |
| 101 | 289,290 | 1–15 odd | 299 | Experiments |
| 102 | 291<br>292 | 16–21<br>Self-Test | 302,303 | 1–21 odd; Self-Test |
| 103 | 293,294 | 1–9 | 304 | Calculator Corner |
| 104 | 297 | 1–14 | 306,307<br>308,309 | Applications<br>Reviewing the Chapter |
| 105 | 302 | 1–13 | T18 | Chapter 8 Test |
| 106 | 302,303 | 14–20 even; Self-Test | 310 | Cumulative Review |
| | | | **Chapter 9** | |
| 107 | 305<br>306,307 | Alg. Skills: 1–29 odd<br>Applications (optional) | 316 | 1–26 |
| 108 | 308,309 | Reviewing the Chapter | 317 | 27–32; Experiments |
| 109 | T18 | Chapter 8 Test | 321,322 | 1–25 odd |
| 110 | 310 | Cumulative Review | 325,326<br>327 | 2–26 even<br>Self-Test |
| | **Chapter 9** | | | |
| 111 | 316 | 1–18 | 331,332 | 2–30 even |
| 112 | 316<br>317 | 19–26<br>Experiments | 335,336 | 1–29 odd |
| 113 | 321 | 1–4 | 336,337 | 30–33; Self-Test |

## AVERAGE COURSE

| Lesson | Pages | Assignment |
|---|---|---|
| 114 | 325,326<br>327 | 2–16 even<br>Self-Test |
| 115 | 331 | 1–16 |
| 116 | 332 | 17–23 |
| 117 | 335 | 1–14 |
| 118 | 336 | 15–20 |
| 119 | 340,341 | 1–12 |
| 120 | 341 | 13–20 |
| 121 | 344 | 1–12 |
| 122 | 346 | Self-Test; Puzzles & Things |
| 123 | 347 | Alg. Skills: 1–35 odd |
| 124 | 350,351 | Reviewing the Chapter |
| 125 | T19 | Chapter 9 Test |

### Chapter 10

| Lesson | Pages | Assignment |
|---|---|---|
| 126 | 356,357 | 1–24 |
| 127 | 357<br>358 | 25–29<br>Experiments |
| 128 | 362 | 1–14 |
| 129 | 363 | 15–23 |
| 130 | 366,367 | 1–12 |
| 131 | 367,368 | 17–20; Self-Test |
| 132 | 371 | 1–14 |
| 133 | 371 | 15–22 |
| 134 | 374,375 | 1–12 |

## COMPREHENSIVE COURSE

| Lesson | Pages | Assignment |
|---|---|---|
| 114 | 340,341 | 2–24 even |
| 115 | 344 | 2–12 even; 13–16 |
| 116 | 345,346 | 17–20; Self-Test |
| 117 | 346<br>348,349 | Puzzles & Things<br>Extra for Experts |
| 118 | 350,351 | Reviewing the Chapter |
| 119 | T19 | Chapter 9 Test |

### Chapter 10

| Lesson | Pages | Assignment |
|---|---|---|
| 120 | 356,357<br>358 | 1–35 odd<br>Experiments |
| 121 | 362,363 | 1–18 |
| 122 | 363,364 | 19–27 |
| 123 | 366,367 | 1–16 |
| 124 | 367,368 | 17–21; Self-Test |
| 125 | 371,372<br>372 | 1–20; 21–25 odd<br>Class Experiment |
| 126 | 374,375 | 1–17 |
| 127 | 375<br>377 | 18–20<br>Calculator Corner |
| 128 | 379<br>380 | 1–15 odd; 17, 18<br>Self-Test; Calculator Corner |
| 129 | 382,383 | 1–17 odd |
| 130 | 385<br>386,387 | Applications<br>Reviewing the Chapter |
| 131 | T20 | Chapter 10 Test |
| 132 | 388 | Cumulative Review |

### Chapter 11

| Lesson | Pages | Assignment |
|---|---|---|
| 133 | 393,394 | 2–18 even; 19–28 |
| 134 | 394 | 29–36 |

| Lesson | AVERAGE COURSE Pages | AVERAGE COURSE Assignment | COMPREHENSIVE COURSE Pages | COMPREHENSIVE COURSE Assignment |
|---|---|---|---|---|
| 135 | 379 380 | 1–8 Self-Test | 397,398 | 1–13 odd; 14–25 |
| 136 | 384<br>385 | Alg. Skills: 1–33 odd<br>Applications (optional) | 398,399 | 26–36 |
| 137 | 386,387 | Reviewing the Chapter | 400,401 | 1–9 odd; 10–25 |
| 138 | T20 | Chapter 10 Test | 401,402 | 26–38; Self-Test |
| 139 | 388 | Cumulative Review | 405 | 1–13 |
| | **Chapter 11** | | | |
| 140 | 393,394 | 2–18 even | 408 | 1–15 |
| 141 | 397,398 | 1–25 odd | 408,409 | 16–23; Self-Test |
| 142 | 400,401 | 1–13 | 412,413 | 1–21 odd; 22–24 |
| 143 | 401,402 | 14–19; Self-Test | 416,417 | 1–39 odd |
| 144 | 405 | 1–6 | 418<br>420,421 | Self-Test<br>Extra for Experts |
| 145 | 408 | 1–12 | 422,423 | Reviewing the Chapter |
| 146 | 408 409 | 13–15 Self-Test | T21 | Chapter 11 Test |
| | | | **Chapter 12** | |
| 147 | 419 | Alg. Skills: 1–29 odd | 427,428 | 1–22 |
| 148 | 422,423 | Reviewing the Chapter<br>Exercises 1–19 only | 429 | 23–32 |
| 149 | T21 | Chapter 11 Test<br>Exercises 1–16 only | 431,432 | 2–24 even |
| | **Chapter 12** | | | |
| 150 | 427,428 | 1–22 | 436,437 | 2–26 even; Self-Test |
| 151 | 431 | 1–12 | 441,442 | 1–21 odd; 22–23 |
| 152 | 436 | 1–12 | 445,446 | 1–17 odd |
| 153 | 436,437 | 13–18; Self-Test | 446,447 | 19–22; Self-Test |
| 154 | 441,442 | 1–13 | 451 | 1–16 |
| 155 | 445 | 1–12 | 451,452 | 17–27 |
| 156 | 447<br>459 | Self-Test<br>Applications | 454,455 | 1–6 |

| Lesson | Average Course: Pages | Average Course: Assignment | Comprehensive Course: Pages | Comprehensive Course: Assignment |
|---|---|---|---|---|
| 157 | 457 | Alg. Skills: 1–27 odd | 456 | 7–8; Self-Test |
| 158 | 460,461 | Reviewing the Chapter<br>Exercises 1–23 only | 458,459<br>460,461 | Applications<br>Reviewing the Chapter |
| 159 | T22 | Chapter 12 Test<br>Exercises 1–19 only | T22 | Chapter 12 Test |
| 160 | 462 | Cumulative Review | 462 | Cumulative Review |

## Table of Related References

| Chapter | Progress Tests | Sections |
|---|---|---|
| Chapter 1 | Test 1<br>Test 2<br>Test 3 | 1–3<br>4–6<br>7–9 |
| Chapter 2 | Test 4<br>Test 5 | 1,2<br>4–7 |
| Chapter 3 | Test 6<br>Test 7<br>Test 8<br>Test 9 | 1,2<br>3,4<br>5,6<br>7 |
| Cumulative Review/Test | Test 10 | |
| Chapter 4 | Test 11<br>Test 12<br>Test 13 | 1,2<br>3–5<br>6,7 |
| Chapter 5 | Test 14<br>Test 15<br>Test 16<br>Test 17 | 1,2<br>3,4<br>5,6<br>7,8 |
| Chapter 6 | Test 18<br>Test 19<br>Test 20<br>Test 21 | 1,2<br>3,4<br>5,6<br>7,8 |
| Cumulative Review/Test | Test 22 | |

| Chapter | Progress Tests | Sections |
|---|---|---|
| Chapter 7 | Test 23<br>Test 24 | 1–3<br>4,5 |
| Chapter 8 | Test 25<br>Test 26 | 1,2<br>3–5 |
| Chapter 9 | Test 27<br>Test 28<br>Test 29 | 1–3<br>4,5<br>6,7 |
| Cumulative Review/Test | Test 30 | |
| Chapter 10 | Test 31<br>Test 32 | 1–3<br>4–6 |
| Chapter 11 | Test 33<br>Test 34<br>Test 35 | 1–3<br>4,5<br>6,7 |
| Chapter 12 | Test 36<br>Test 37<br>Test 38 | 1–3<br>4,5<br>6,7 |
| Cumulative Test/Review | Test 39 | |

# Lesson Commentary

## *Chapter 1. Points, Lines, and Angles*

Many students beginning geometry look to the course as a fresh change from algebra. The classroom experiments and constructions in Chapter 1 and throughout the book will help to create a new outlook on mathematics. This does not mean, however, that students may forget algebra during their course in geometry. Algebraic skills are needed to solve many of the exercises in this text. We hope that teachers will frequently assign such exercises.

You will probably want to move students quickly through the first four or five sections of this chapter. The first three sections in particular should not be allowed to drag. The ideas involved are already familiar to many students. Even students who have no previous experience with the ideas or the notation usually do not find them difficult.

### Objectives for Pages 2–11

1. To become acquainted with the types of questions involved in the study of geometry.
2. To name points, lines, rays, and segments.
3. To name angles and use a protractor to measure angles.

### 1•BEGINNING YOUR STUDY OF GEOMETRY (pp. 2–3)

### Teaching These Pages

We hope that the optical illusions which open this text will provide an entertaining "curtain-raiser" for students. They also illustrate the point that one can't always depend on appearances. Sometimes, measurements must be made. Other illusions are presented in Exercise 1 on page 2 and in Chalkboard Examples 1 and 2 below.

In Experiment 1, many students may not know the term *rhombus,* or may call the figure a "diamond." Try not to let vocabulary problems be a stumbling block. The important thing is that students see that the sides of the figure inside the rectangle all have the same length. Let students test their conjectures by measuring the sides and angles of the inner figures. Then point out two things: (1) no measurement is completely accurate; (2) it would be impossible to test every rectangle since there are an unlimited number of them. With this in mind, students should appreciate the fact that, later in the course, they will be able to prove without measuring that the figure formed by joining the midpoints of any rectangle is a rhombus. (See Suggested Extension 2 on page T78.)

Although the results of Experiment 1 may not be surprising, Experiment 2 is completely astounding to many people. Exercise 3 on page 3 suggests the fact that the space between the hoop and the object will be the same no matter what size object is used. You might do this exercise in class and have students repeat it with different-sized containers as homework. A proof of this surprising result is developed in Written Exercise 40 on page 246. The proof depends on the formula $C = 2\pi r$.

Chalkboard Example 3 below gives students an opportunity to piece together clues to arrive at a "theorem" of a nongeometric nature.

Be sure to remind students that they will need a protractor (for Section 3) and a straightedge and compass (for Section 7).

### Chalkboard Examples

1. Are the line segments straight? Test your answer with a ruler. yes

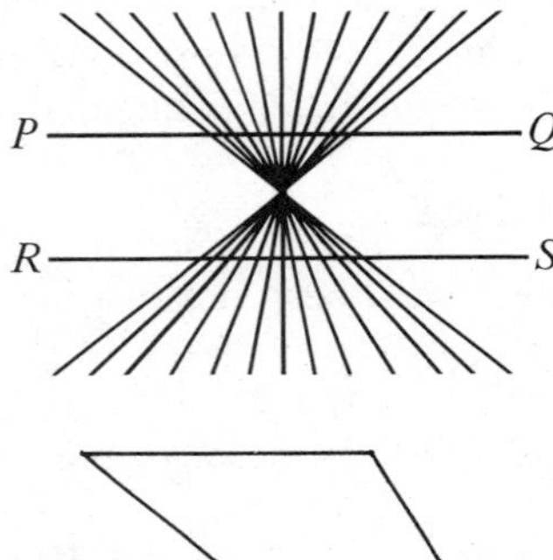


2. Are the segments parts of the same line? yes

3. In a certain corporation, the positions of sales manager, vice-president, and treasurer are held by Arnold, Carnathan, and Brown, although not necessarily in that order. The sales manager, who was an only child, earns the least. Carnathan, who plays bridge with Arnold's sister, earns more than the treasurer. What position does each person occupy? Carnathan is vice-president; Arnold is treasurer; Brown is sales manager.

## 2 • POINTS AND LINES (pp. 4–7)

### Teaching These Pages

Some students will have been exposed to the basic ideas of this section in previous mathematics courses. You might ask whether anyone in the class can suggest ways of symbolizing line $AB$, ray $AB$, segment $AB$, and distance $AB$. The Classroom Practice Exercises will help to acquaint students with the notation $\overleftrightarrow{AB}$, $\overrightarrow{AB}$, $\overline{AB}$, and $AB$.

The introduction of the *midpoint* concept enables students to practice numerical skills while developing geometric intuition. The idea of a number line should be familiar to all students. However, practice with negative coordinates is still advisable. Classroom Practice Exercises 11–15 will help, as will Chalkboard Examples 8–13 below.

## Chalkboard Examples

**Give the symbol for each:**

**1.** Line $PQ$ $\overleftrightarrow{PQ}$ **2.** Segment $ST$ $\overline{ST}$ **3.** Ray $ST$ $\overrightarrow{ST}$ **4.** Ray $TS$ $\overrightarrow{TS}$

**5.** Are points $P$, $S$, and $T$ collinear? no

**6.** Name three points which are collinear. $P$, $S$, and $Q$; $R$, $S$, and $T$

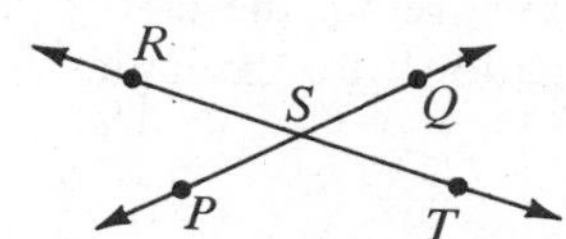


**7.** If $PS = SQ$, then $S$ is called the _?_ of $\overline{PQ}$. midpoint

**Use the number line below to find the following:**

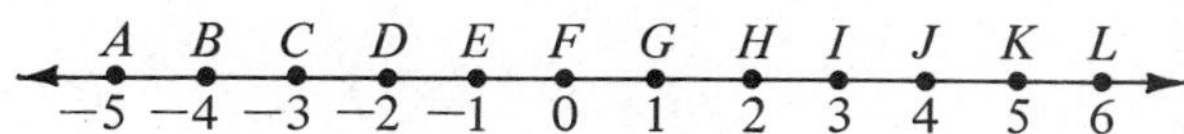


**8.** $GL$ 5 **9.** $EJ$ 5 **10.** $AD$ 3 **11.** $BL$ 10

**12.** The midpoint of $\overline{AK}$ F **13.** The midpoint of $\overline{BH}$ E

## Suggested Extension

**Find the approximate position on the number line of points having these coordinates:**

**1.** $2\frac{1}{2}$ **2.** $-\frac{3}{4}$ **3.** 3.9 **4.** −3.99 **5.** $\sqrt{2}$

## 3 • ANGLES (pp. 8–11)

### Teaching These Pages

Familiarize students with the notation used for angles. You might begin by asking them to suggest a notation for the first angle shown on the next page. Probably, students will suggest "$\angle ABC$" or "$\angle B$." Some may also suggest "$\angle CBA$."

To illustrate that "$\angle ABC$" is sometimes preferable to "$\angle B$," draw the diagram at right, below. Here, the symbol "$\angle B$" is ambiguous. It could refer to $\angle ABC$, but also to $\angle ABD$ or $\angle DBC$.

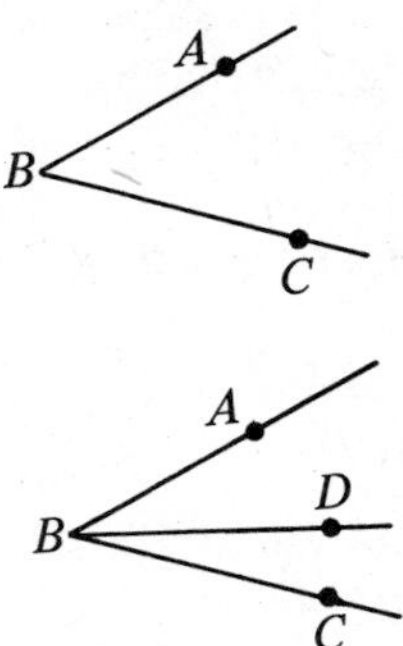


You might illustrate the use of the protractor by drawing angles and having students measure them with a protractor. This can be done on the chalkboard with a large protractor or on an overhead projector with a small transparent protractor. The footnote on page 8 describes our use of the notation "$\angle 1 + \angle 2 = \angle AOC$" instead of "$m\angle 1 + m\angle 2 = m\angle AOC$." We retain the use of the term "measure" in some situations: for example, "Find the measure of $\angle 3$."

## Chalkboard Examples

Students' answers may vary.

1. Give other names for each angle.
   a. $\angle RSQ$ $\angle 3$  b. $\angle QTR$ $\angle 8$
   c. $\angle SUR$ $\angle RUS$  d. $\angle 7$ $\angle TQU$
   e. $\angle 5$ $\angle QRT$  f. $\angle 6$ $\angle RQS$

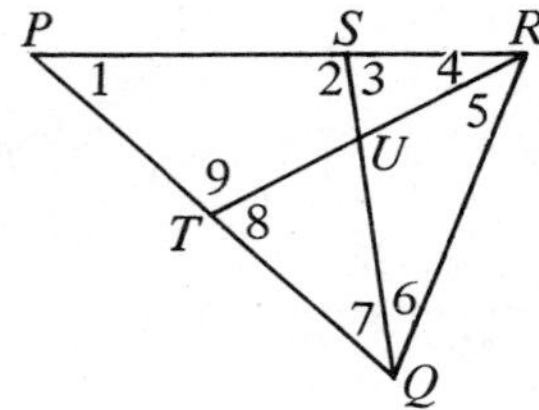


2. $\angle 4 + \angle 5 = \angle$ _?_ $SRQ$
3. $\angle 6 + \angle 7 = \angle$ _?_ $RQT$
4. $\angle 2 + \angle 3 =$ _?_ ° 180

## Objectives for Pages 13–20

1. To classify angles as *acute, right, obtuse,* or *straight*.
2. To name and calculate the measures of vertical angles.
3. To use angle bisectors in calculating the measures of angles.

## 4•CLASSIFYING ANGLES (pp. 13–15)

### Teaching These Pages

You may want to introduce the terms *right angle* and *perpendicular* first, since they are more familiar than *acute* and *obtuse*. One method of introduction is to ask students to estimate the measures of the angles formed by intersecting horizontal and vertical lines. In addition, be sure to give examples of right angles whose sides are not horizontal and vertical. Then present the special names given for angles smaller than right angles and angles larger than right angles.

To describe 180° angles, we have decided to use the term *straight angle.* Note that we use the notation $\angle B = \angle C$ ("angle *B* equals angle *C*") to state that angles have equal measures. "Equal angles have equal measures" is an idea students find easy, so you need not belabor it.

### Chalkboard Examples

Draw several angles on the board and have students classify them as *acute, right, obtuse,* or *straight* angles. You might also have them estimate the measure of each angle.

## 5 • VERTICAL ANGLES (pp. 16–17)

### Teaching These Pages

The figure at the top of page 16 illustrates the idea of vertical angles. To develop the relationship between vertical angles, let $\angle 1 = 30°$ and have students find the measures of $\angle 2$, $\angle 3$, and $\angle 4$. You may want to repeat this exercise, letting $\angle 1 = 20°$, $\angle 2 = 40°$, and so on, recording your answers in a table like that shown on page 16. Have students make a conjecture about vertical angles (vertical angles are equal). You might challenge students to prove their conjecture, letting the class decide which arguments should be accepted as "proofs." Students may enjoy naming the result after the discoverer and prover. It appears as Theorem 3 in Chapter 2 (page 43).

### Chalkboard Examples

**Suppose $\overline{QT} \perp \overline{UR}$ and $\angle POQ = 35°$. Find the measure of each angle.**

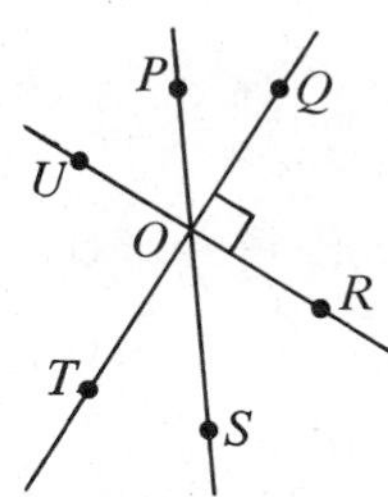


**1.** $\angle SOT$ 35° **2.** $\angle POU$ 55° **3.** $\angle ROS$ 55°

**4.** $\angle POR$ 125° **5.** $\angle SOU$ 125° **6.** $\angle TOU$ 90°

**7–12.** Repeat Examples 1–6 using $\angle POQ = 27°$.
**7.** 27° **8.** 63° **9.** 63° **10.** 117° **11.** 117° **12.** 90°

## 6 • ANGLE BISECTORS (pp. 18–20)

### Teaching These Pages

You might begin this lesson by holding up a piece of string and having a student "bisect" it with a pair of scissors. This will demonstrate dramatically the "cutting in half" concept. Then ask a student to draw a ray which will bisect an angle you've drawn on the board. When students have grasped the basic concept, move on to the numerical exercises.

Experiment 2 offers students a chance to propose a theorem concerning paper folding, and then to argue the correctness of the theorem. The Suggested Extension for this lesson uses paper folding to introduce the concept of a circle inscribed in a triangle. In Classroom Practice Exercise 5, students show that the line bisecting an angle is unique. Since many students are confused by detailed considerations of uniqueness and existence issues, the text omits such a discussion. Some of your more advanced students might be interested in using Postulate 6 on page 31 to justify the uniqueness of the angle bisector.

### Chalkboard Examples

**Draw $\angle ABC$ with the given measure. Using a protractor, draw $\overrightarrow{BD}$ which bisects the angle. Name the measures of $\angle ABD$ and $\angle DBC$.**

**1.** $\angle ABC = 70°$ 35°, 35°  **2.** $\angle ABC = 90°$ 45°, 45°

**3.** $\angle ABC = 150°$ 75°, 75°  **4.** $\angle ABC = 180°$ 90°, 90°

### Suggested Extension

**1.** Draw a large triangle on a sheet of paper and cut the triangle out.

**2.** Can you discover a way of folding the paper so that the fold will bisect $\angle A$?

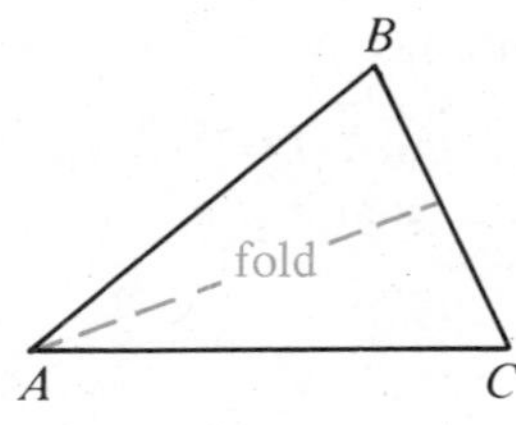


**3.** Now unfold the paper and refold it to bisect $\angle B$.

**4.** Finally, bisect $\angle C$ with a fold.

**5.** If you have worked accurately, your three folds meet in a point. Do they?

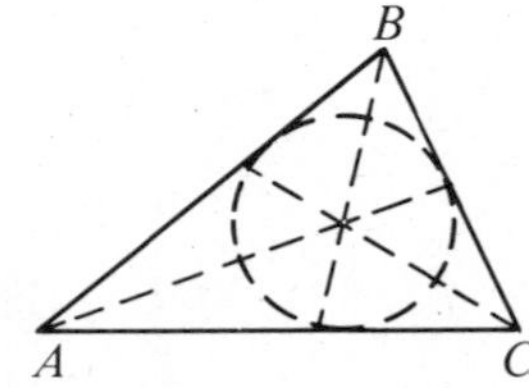


**6.** Put the point of a compass where the three folds meet. Can you use the compass to draw a circle that will just touch the three sides of the triangle?

## Objectives for Pages 21–33

1. To construct bisectors of angles and perpendiculars to segments.
2. To use postulates of equality to draw conclusions about geometric figures.
3. To use postulates of geometry.

## 7 • THREE CONSTRUCTIONS (pp. 21–24)

### Teaching These Pages

Demonstrate these constructions one at a time, allowing students to practice each before you show the next one. After students have learned all three constructions, you might try the Classroom Practice Exercises and then the Chalkboard Examples below, which use the three constructions in a different order. Proofs that these constructions are valid are developed in the text and exercises of Section 2 of Chapter 4 (pages 135–138).

### Chalkboard Examples

**Draw a figure similar to, but larger than, the one shown.**

1. Construct a line through $A$ perpendicular to $\overline{BC}$.
2. Bisect $\angle C$. Call the bisector $\overrightarrow{CX}$.
3. Bisect $\angle BCX$.

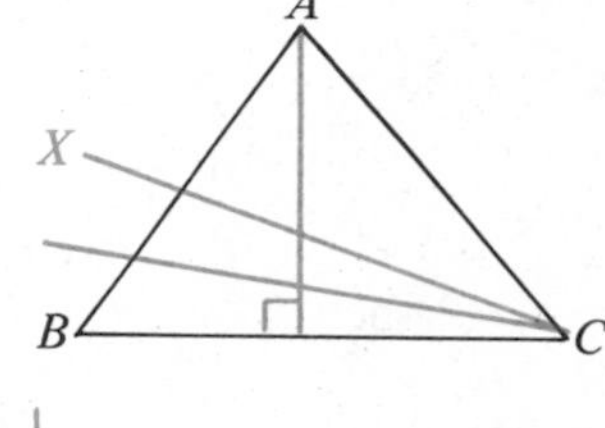


4. Construct a line perpendicular to $\overleftrightarrow{PQ}$ at $P$. (Note: $\overline{PQ}$ must be extended to the left.)

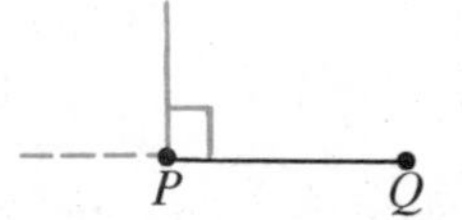


### Suggested Extension

The designs below were made using a compass only. Have students experiment and make designs of their own.

## 8 • POSTULATES OF EQUALITY (pp. 25–28)

### Teaching These Pages

Your students may not be able to quote the postulates of equality, but they have used these postulates in their study of algebra. You may wish to illustrate the postulates with the algebraic examples below before taking up the geometric examples in the text.

Addition Postulate

$$\begin{array}{r} \text{If } x - 5 = 7 \\ \text{and } \quad 5 = 5 \\ \hline \text{then } (x - 5) + 5 = 7 + 5. \end{array}$$

Simplify: $x = 12$.

Subtraction Postulate

$$\begin{array}{r} \text{If } x + 9 = 25 \\ \text{and } \quad 9 = 9 \\ \hline \text{then } (x + 9) - 9 = 25 - 9. \end{array}$$

Simplify: $x = 16$.

Multiplication Postulate

If $\frac{1}{3}x = 21$,

then $3\left(\frac{1}{3}x\right) = 3(21)$.

Simplify: $x = 63$.

Division Postulate

If $13x = 52$,

then $\frac{13x}{13} = \frac{52}{13}$.

Simplify: $x = 4$.

Substitution Postulate

If $y = 2x + 7$ and $x + y = 10$,

then $x + (2x + 7) = 10$.

Written Exercises 13–17 offer students a chance to draw their own conclusions. You probably won't want to insist on a written formal proof to support these conclusions: a student's oral argument to the class is sufficient. You may wish to partially formalize the argument by writing the steps on the chalkboard. Having students make a list of steps may help to prepare them for the transition to writing formal proofs in Chapter 2.

### Chalkboard Examples

**Name the postulate of equality used in each step.**

**1.** $3x - 7 = 8$ Given
$3x = 15$ _?_ Addition
$x = 5$ _?_ Division

**2.** $2x + 18 = 5x$ Given
$18 = 3x$ _?_ Subtraction
$6 = x$ _?_ Division

3. $\frac{x+5}{4} = 9$ Given

$x + 5 = 36$ _?_ Multiplication

$x = 31$ _?_ Subtraction

4. $y = 3x - 5$ and $x = 10$ Given

$y = 3(10) - 5$ _?_ Substitution

$y = 25$ _?_ Substitution

5. Suppose $AB = CD$. Which postulate allows you to conclude that $\frac{1}{2}AB = \frac{1}{2}CD$?

Multiplication

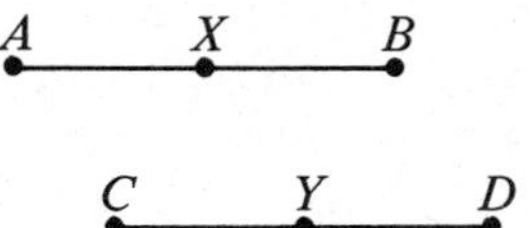


Suppose you also know that $AX = \frac{1}{2}AB$ and that $CY = \frac{1}{2}CD$. Which postulate allows you to conclude that $AX = CY$?

Substitution

## 9•POSTULATES OF GEOMETRY (pp. 29–33)

### Teaching These Pages

Use your classroom to illustrate some of the terminology and postulates of this section:

*plane*—desk top; floor; walls
*collinear points*—points along one edge of a desk
*coplanar points*—points on one wall
*non-coplanar points*—two points in the middle of the floor, one in the middle of the ceiling, and one in a side wall
*parallel planes*—floor and ceiling; opposite walls

It is probably unwise to prolong the presentation of the postulates in this section. Deal with them matter-of-factly, and move on to the exercises, which reinforce the learning of the postulates.

Some students may note that the Ruler Postulate is true only after a coordinate system has been selected for the line. Most students, however, feel satisfied with the postulate as it is stated in the text. Similarly, some students may note that there are two numbering schemes for rays, corresponding to the two scales on a standard protractor.

## Chalkboard Examples

1. Mark two points on the chalkboard and have a student indicate a third point "in space." Have another student indicate the plane determined by these points (Postulate 2).
2. Mark three collinear points on the chalkboard. Have a student indicate several planes which contain these points.
3. Describe the intersection of:
   - **a.** a side wall of the classroom and the floor line
   - **b.** a side wall and the front wall line
   - **c.** the plane containing a desk top and the floor no intersection

## Suggested Extension

A carpenter sometimes checks the flatness of a board by laying a straightedge across the board. Suppose there is a part of the board where the endpoints of the straightedge lie on the board but the middle of the straightedge does not. The carpenter then concludes that the board is not flat. State the postulate to which this conclusion is related.
Postulate 3: If two points lie in a plane, then the line joining them lies in that plane

## Chapter 2. Introduction to Proof

This chapter begins with proofs of three simple theorems. The informal, step-by-step presentation of these proofs paves the way to the usual two-column format. In their first exposure to two-column proof, students supply "Reasons" to complete proofs. Then they construct their own proofs concerning parallel lines. The chapter closes with a construction of parallel lines using straightedge and compass.

### Objectives for Pages 42–49

1. To use theorems about complementary, supplementary, and vertical angles.
2. To write "if . . . then" statements and their converses.

### 1•THREE THEOREMS (pp. 42–45)

### Teaching These Pages

You might begin the introduction of proof by supplying students with the *Given* information from the Example on page 42. Ask them to draw their own conclusion. Then have a student present an oral argument to justify the conclusion. Summarize the argument in writing, then compare with the five steps given on page 42.

The same strategy could be used for Theorems 2 and 3. For Theorem 3, a proof could be based on Theorem 2 (as on page 43) or could follow the steps suggested in Chapter 1 on page 16.

The proofs of the three theorems in this section are written in a style which is intended to provide a transition between oral proof and the more formal two-column proof to be introduced in Section 4.

### Chalkboard Examples

**Find the complement and supplement of $\angle A$ if:**

1. $\angle A = 10°$ 80°, 170°
2. $\angle A = 80°$ 10°, 100°
3. $\angle A = 45°$ 45°, 135°
4. $\angle A = 16°$ 74°, 164°
5. *Given:* $\overline{AB} \perp \overline{CD}$.

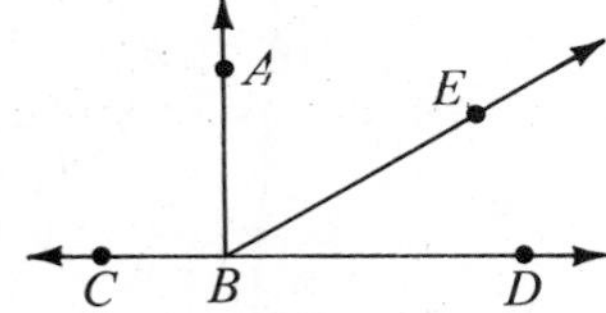


a. Name the complement of $\angle DBE$. $\angle ABE$
b. Name the supplement of $\angle DBE$. $\angle CBE$

6. **a.** Name two supplements of $\angle 2$. $\angle 1$, $\angle 7$
**b.** Name two supplements of $\angle 4$. $\angle 3$, $\angle 5$
**c.** If $\angle 2 = \angle 4$, tell why $\angle 1 = \angle 3$.
If two angles are supplements of equal angles, then they are equal. (Theorem 2)
**d.** Why does $\angle 3 = \angle 5$? Vertical angles are equal.

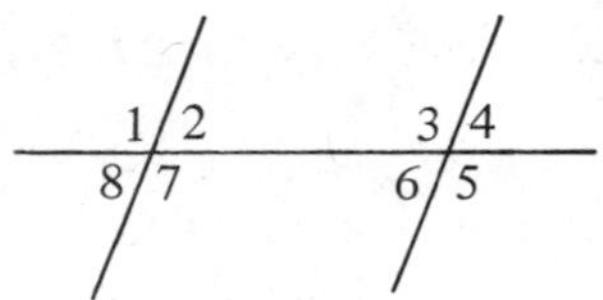


## Suggested Extension

1. **a.** If $\angle A = x°$, what is the measure of a complement of $\angle A$?
$(90 - x)°$
**b.** What is the measure of a supplement of $\angle A$? $(180 - x)°$
**c.** Write an equation, in terms of $x$, which says that a supplement of $\angle A$ is four times as large as a complement of $\angle A$.
$180 - x = 4(90 - x)$
**d.** Solve your equation for $x$. $x = 60$

2. A supplement of $\angle B$ is six times as large as a complement of $\angle B$. Find the measure of $\angle B$. 72°

## 2•"IF . . . THEN" STATEMENTS (pp. 46–49)

### Teaching These Pages

You might like to supply examples of "if . . . then" statements from a current newspaper or magazine. Your students can supply other examples from their daily lives. Examples 1 and 2 on page 46 illustrate the key ideas of the section: (1) An "if . . . then" idea is often expressed without the words "if" and "then;" (2) The converse of a true statement may be false.

### Chalkboard Examples

**State the hypothesis and the conclusion of each statement.**

1. If he remembers, then we're sunk. Hyp: he remembers Conc: we're sunk
2. She should stay home if she is sick. Hyp: she is sick Conc: she should stay home

**State the converse of each statement.**

3. If $n$ is an integer, then $n + 1$ is an integer. If $n + 1$ is an integer, then $n$ is an integer.
4. All cats are animals. All animals are cats.
5. Decide if the statements in 3 and 4 above are true. **3.** True **4.** True
Then decide if their converses are true. **3.** True **4.** False

## 3 • USING "IF . . . THEN" STATEMENTS (OPTIONAL) (pp. 50–53)

### Teaching These Pages

Type 1 reasoning is the kind most commonly used in geometry. Most students view this kind of reasoning as common sense. Unfortunately, students too often employ Type 3 and Type 4 reasoning in their geometry proofs. The fallacy committed in Type 3 reasoning is called "arguing from the converse." The fallacy committed in Type 4 reasoning is called "arguing from the inverse." Type 2 reasoning ("arguing from the contrapositive") is valid. It is the logical basis of indirect proof. (See Extra for Experts, pages 348–349.)

If time is a problem, consider omitting all of the text, but including the Classroom Practice Exercises. As the class discusses the exercises, you can illustrate the correct and incorrect types of reasoning.

### Chalkboard Examples

***Given:* "If Dan is in Duluth, then Valerie is in Seattle."**
**From each statement below, draw a conclusion or state "no conclusion possible."**

**1.** Valerie is in Seattle.
**2.** Dan is in Duluth.
**3.** Valerie is not in Seattle.
**4.** Dan is not in Duluth.

1. no conclusion
2. Valerie is in Seattle.
3. Dan is not in Duluth
4. no conclusion

**Decide whether the reasoning is correct.**

**5.** (1) All persons 18 and over are qualified to vote.
(2) Gregory is 18.
*Conclusion:* Gregory is qualified to vote. Correct

**6.** (1) Those who brush their teeth with Dentashine have no cavities.
(2) Louise has no cavities.
(3) *Conclusion:* Louise brushes her teeth with Dentashine. Not correct

### Objectives for Pages 54–74

1. To understand and write basic geometry proofs.
2. To use the properties of parallel lines cut by a transversal.
3. To use facts about transversals to prove lines parallel.
4. To construct an angle equal to a given angle.
5. To construct parallel lines.

## 4·WRITING PROOFS (pp. 54–59)

### Teaching These Pages

Teaching students to write proofs is one of the toughest jobs of a geometry teacher. Most students find it easier to write a proof after understanding the broad outline of the reasoning. One way to help students to develop this kind of understanding is by having them present oral arguments, and allowing them to make heavy use of a figure.

Once the outline of a proof is given orally, help students refine it into a written proof. You may wish to use this procedure with the Classroom Practice Exercises and the Chalkboard Examples below.

The order of the steps, even the basic strategy, may vary from one student's proof to another's. This is as it should be. One of the beauties of geometry is that there is so much room for individuality in constructing proofs.

We suggest that, at this early stage, you not risk destroying students' interest in proof by being overly fussy about details. With more experience, many students will come to appreciate the finer points of logical argument.

### Chalkboard Examples

**Write a proof in two-column form.**

**1.** *Given:* $\angle 1 = \angle 4$
*Prove:* $\angle 2 = \angle 3$

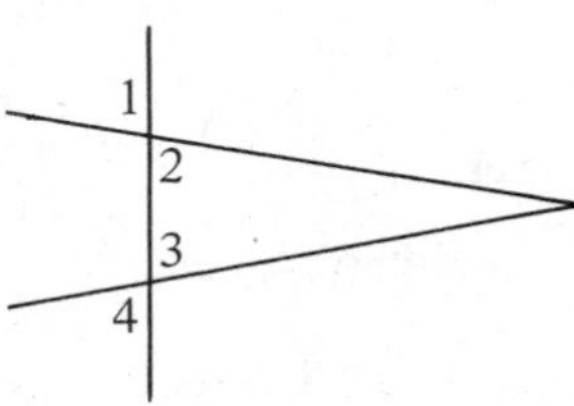


1. $\angle 1 = \angle 2$ (Vert. angles)
2. $\angle 1 = \angle 4$ (Given)
3. $\angle 2 = \angle 4$ (Substitution)
4. $\angle 3 = \angle 4$ (Vert. angles)
5. $\angle 2 = \angle 3$ (Substitution)

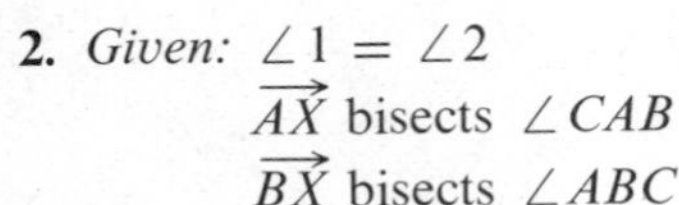

**2.** *Given:* $\angle 1 = \angle 2$
$\overrightarrow{AX}$ bisects $\angle CAB$
$\overrightarrow{BX}$ bisects $\angle ABC$
*Prove:* $\angle 5 = \angle 6$

**3.** *Given:* $\angle 3 = \angle 4$
$\overrightarrow{AX}$ bisects $\angle CAB$
$\overrightarrow{BX}$ bisects $\angle ABC$
*Prove:* $\angle 5 = \angle 6$

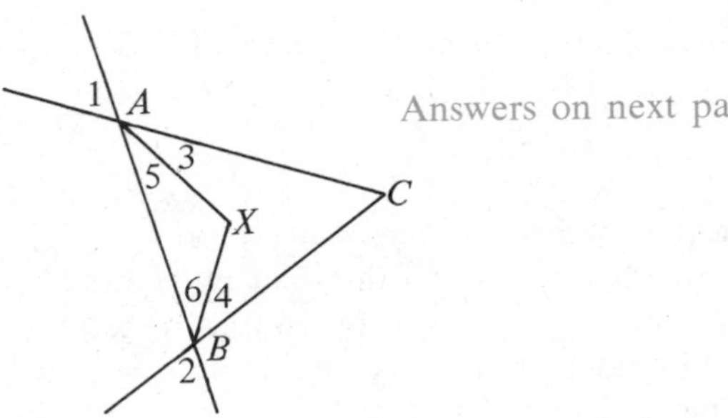


Answers on next page.

Ex. 2
1. $\angle 1 = \angle CAB$; $\angle 2 = \angle CBA$ (Vertical angles)
2. $\angle 1 = \angle 2$ (Given)
3. $\frac{1}{2}\angle 1 = \frac{1}{2}\angle 2$ (Mult. Post.)
4. $\frac{1}{2}\angle CAB = \frac{1}{2}\angle CBA$ (Subst.)
5. $\angle 5 = \frac{1}{2}\angle CAB$; $\angle 6 = \frac{1}{2}\angle CBA$ (Given: angle bisectors)
6. $\angle 5 = \angle 6$ (Subst.)

Ex. 3
1. $\angle 3 = \frac{1}{2}\angle CAB$; $\angle 4 = \frac{1}{2}\angle CBA$; $\angle 5 = \frac{1}{2}\angle CAB$; $\angle 6 = \frac{1}{2}\angle CBA$ (Given: angle bisectors)
2. $\angle 3 = \angle 5$; $\angle 4 = \angle 6$ (Subst.)
3. $\angle 3 = \angle 4$ (Given)
4. $\angle 5 = \angle 4$ (Subst.)
5. $\angle 5 = \angle 6$ (Subst.)

## 5•PARALLEL LINES (pp. 60–65)

### Teaching These Pages

You can illustrate skew and parallel lines using your classroom. The intersection lines of ceiling, walls, and floor provide good examples of both concepts.

The word *transversal* may have more meaning for students if compared with *reversal*:

reversal—a turning back        transversal—a turning across

Point out that the prefix *trans* means "across," as in *transfer* and *transport*. You may wish to teach students exterior-angle terminology. A suggested sequence follows.

interior angles: $\angle 1$, $\angle 2$, $\angle 3$, and $\angle 4$
exterior angles: $\angle 5$, $\angle 6$, $\angle 7$, and $\angle 8$
alternate interior angles: $\angle 1$ and $\angle 3$; $\angle 2$ and $\angle 4$
same-side interior angles: $\angle 2$ and $\angle 3$; $\angle 1$ and $\angle 4$
alternate exterior angles: $\angle 5$ and $\angle 7$; $\angle 6$ and $\angle 8$
same-side exterior angles: $\angle 6$ and $\angle 7$; $\angle 5$ and $\angle 8$

5 6
1 2
4 3
8 7

Note that Postulate 7 and Theorem 4 are sometimes worded this way:

Postulate 7: Corresponding angles of parallel lines are equal.

Theorem 4: Alternate interior angles of parallel lines are equal.

In this text, we have often chosen an "if . . . then" phrasing of a theorem or postulate instead of another, shorter phrasing. We have found that learning "if . . . then" forms enables students to understand better the relationships among statements and their converses.

Postulate 7 is roughly equivalent to Euclid's "Parallel Postulate." Some texts use the following instead of Postulate 7: "Through any point outside a line, there is exactly one line parallel to the given line."

## Chalkboard Examples

**Classify each pair of angles as (1) *alternate interior,* (2) *same-side interior,* (3) *corresponding,* or (4) *none of these.***
**(You may wish to add: (5) alternate exterior angles and (6) same-side exterior angles.)**

**1.** ∠2 and ∠6 (1) **2.** ∠3 and ∠1 (3)
**3.** ∠1 and ∠5 (4) or (5) **4.** ∠2 and ∠4 (3)
**5.** ∠7 and ∠6 (2) **6.** ∠5 and ∠8 (4) or (6)
**7.** ∠8 and ∠6 (3) **8.** ∠2 and ∠5 (4)

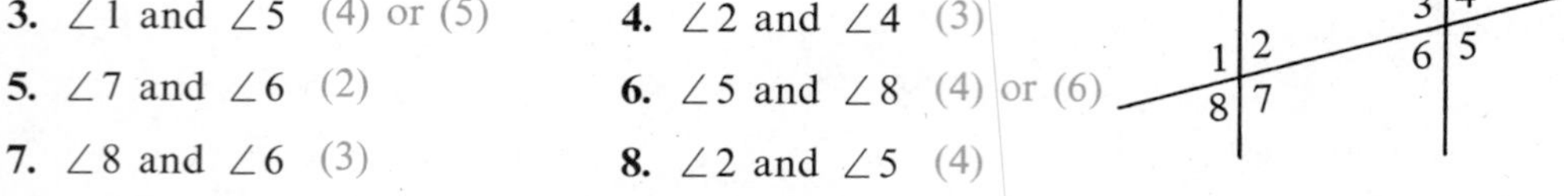


**Find the values of $x$ and $y$ in each diagram.**

**9.**

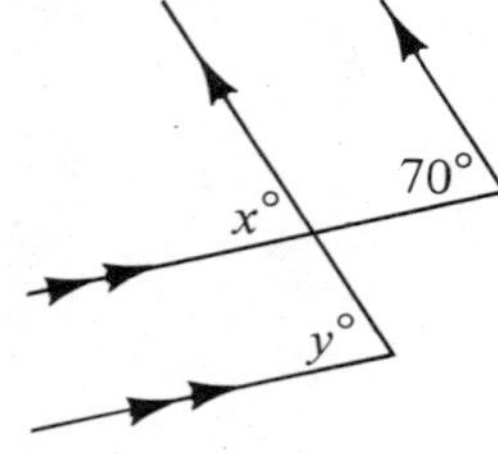


$x = 70°$; $y = 70°$

**10.**

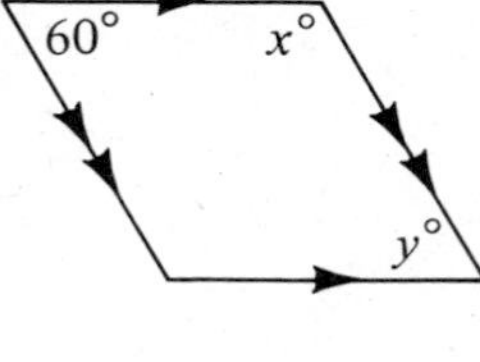


$x = 120°$; $y = 60°$

**11.**

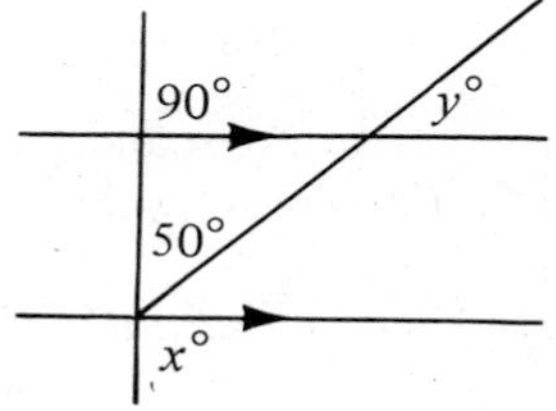


$x = 90°$; $y = 40°$

## Suggested Extension

If you decide to teach exterior-angle terminology, have students discover two additional theorems:

*Theorem:* If two parallel lines are cut by a transversal, then alternate exterior angles are equal.

*Theorem:* If two parallel lines are cut by a transversal, then same-side exterior angles are supplementary.

You may wish to have some students confirm the converses of these theorems as an extension of their work in Section 6.

## 6 • PROVING LINES PARALLEL (pp. 66–70)

### Teaching These Pages

Postulates 7 and 8 are converse statements, as are Theorems 4 and 6 and Theorems 5 and 7. It is important that students realize that Theorems 6 and 7 are not automatically true just because their converses have been proved. Theorems 6 and 7 do not follow from Theorems 4 and 5, but from Postulate 8.

You may wish to use the following example to remind students that the converse of a true statement is not necessarily true.

TRUE: If two lines are parallel, then they do not intersect.

FALSE: If two lines do not intersect, then they are parallel.

The converse is true in a plane, but in three dimensions, lines may be skew.

## Chalkboard Examples

**In each figure, tell which lines are parallel. Give reasons for your answers.**

**1.**

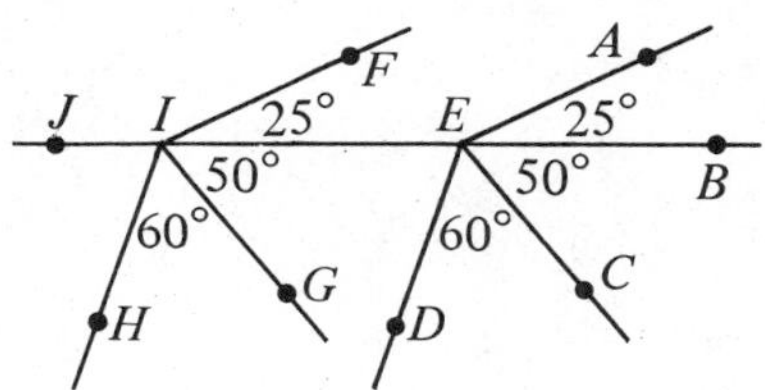


$\overleftrightarrow{IF}$ and $\overleftrightarrow{EA}$ (corr. angles)
$\overleftrightarrow{IG}$ and $\overleftrightarrow{EC}$ (corr. angles)
$\overleftrightarrow{HI}$ and $\overleftrightarrow{DE}$ (corr. angles)

**2.**

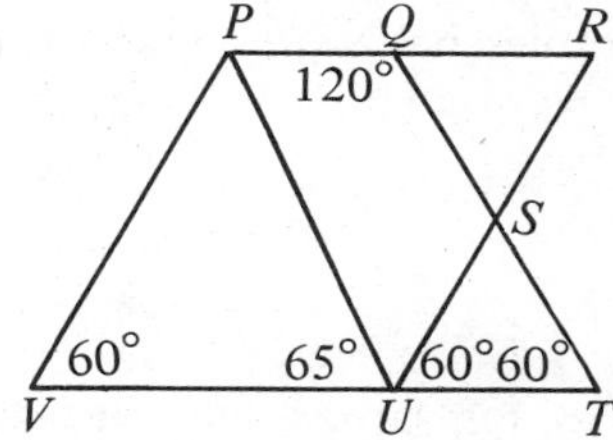


$\overleftrightarrow{PV}$ and $\overleftrightarrow{RU}$ (corr. angles)
$\overleftrightarrow{PQ}$ and $\overleftrightarrow{TU}$ (same-side int. angles)

**Find the value of $x$ which makes lines $s$ and $t$ parallel.**

**3.**

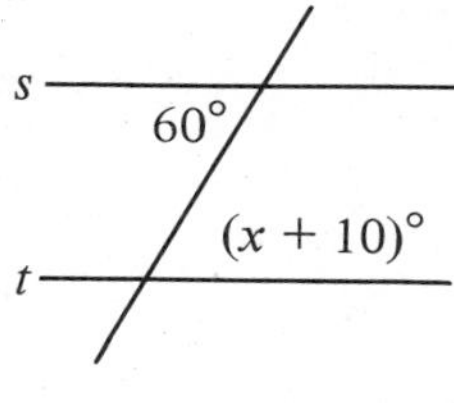


$x = 50$

**4.**

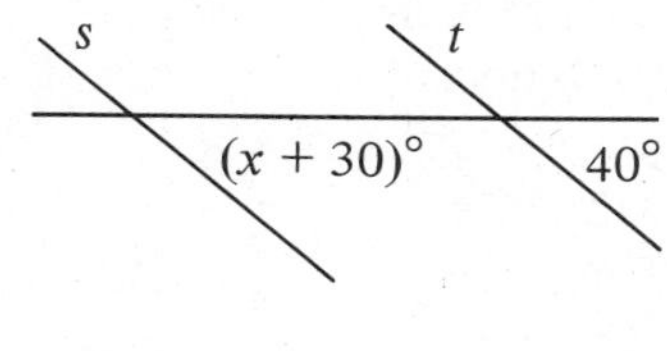


$x = 10$

**5.**

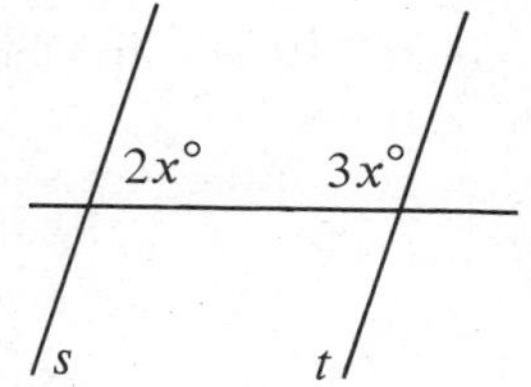


$x = 36$

## Suggested Extension

If $l \parallel m$ and $l \perp n$, what are the possible relationships between $m$ and $n$? Draw a diagram to illustrate each possibility.

If $l$, $m$, and $n$ are coplanar, then $m \perp n$.
Otherwise, $m$ and $n$ are skew.

## 7 • CONSTRUCTING PARALLEL LINES (pp. 71–74)

### Teaching These Pages

You may wish to challenge students to copy an angle using straightedge and compass only (no protractor). After explaining Construction 4, let students practice copying angles of various sizes. Then see if any student can describe a strategy for Construction 5. The method given in the text is based on Postulate 8. Methods based on Theorems 6, 7, or 8, or on exterior angles are equally possible. (See Written Exercises 7 and 10.) Students will use the SSS Postulate to prove the validity of Construction 4 in Written Exercise 9 on page 137.

The proof that the lines constructed in Written Exercise 9 on page 73 are perpendicular depends on a fact that some students may not yet know: The angle sum of a triangle is 180°.

The Chalkboard Examples below preview the Midpoints Theorem. (See Chapter 5, Section 8.)

### Chalkboard Examples

**Draw a triangle similar to, but larger than, the one shown.**

1. Draw a line through $A$ parallel to $\overleftrightarrow{BC}$.
2. Draw a line through $B$ parallel to $\overleftrightarrow{AC}$.
3. Draw a line through $C$ parallel to $\overleftrightarrow{AB}$.
4. Measure $\overline{AB}$, $\overline{BC}$, $\overline{AC}$, and the sides of the new triangle just constructed. What relationships do you find?
   The sides of the new triangle are twice as long as the sides of the original triangle.

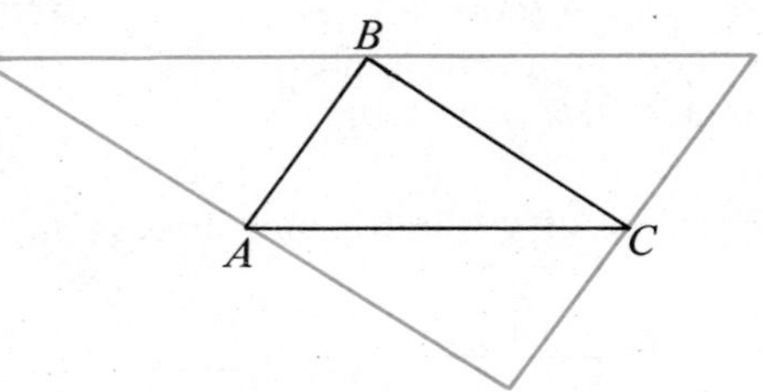


### Suggested Extension

Written Exercises 7 and 10 offer other methods of constructing a line parallel to a given line. Those methods are based on Theorems 6 and 8. Challenge your students to find a method based on Theorem 7.

Some of your students may be interested in finding out the methods that commercial artists use to draw parallel lines (drafting board with T-squares and triangles, folding parallel rules, rolling rules).

## *Chapter 3. Triangles*

This chapter opens with a proof of a property that many students already know: The angle sum of a triangle is 180°. Terminology is presented which enables students to classify triangles according to their sides and their angles. After the meaning of congruent triangles is developed, the SSS, SAS, and ASA Postulates are considered in separate sections. The final section is devoted to the AAS and HL Theorems.

### Objectives for Pages 84–92

1. To use the angle sum theorem to find angle measures.
2. To use the exterior angle corollary to find angle measures.
3. To classify triangles by sides.
4. To classify triangles by angles.

## 1•THE ANGLE SUM OF A TRIANGLE (pp. 84–88)

### Teaching These Pages

Encourage students to draw large diagrams for the investigation of the angle sum of a triangle. The impact will be greater and the memory stronger. Some students may suggest measuring angles with a protractor. They shouldn't expect to get an angle sum of exactly 180° on each trial, but they shouldn't miss by much if they work carefully and use large triangles. A proof of the corollary to Theorem 1 is outlined in Written Exercise 25 on page 88. Exercises 26 and 27 anticipate the theorem concerning the angle sum of a convex polygon (Theorem 1, page 176).

### Chalkboard Examples

**Given:** $l \parallel \overline{AC}$

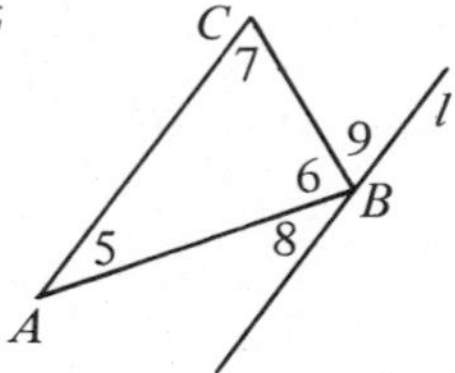


1. What angle of $\triangle ABC$ equals $\angle 8$? $\angle 5$
2. What angle of $\triangle ABC$ equals $\angle 9$? $\angle 7$
3. $\angle 8 + \angle 6 + \angle 9 =$ ____° 180
4. $\angle 5 + \angle 6 + \angle 7 =$ ____° 180

**Complete the table, referring to the diagram below.**

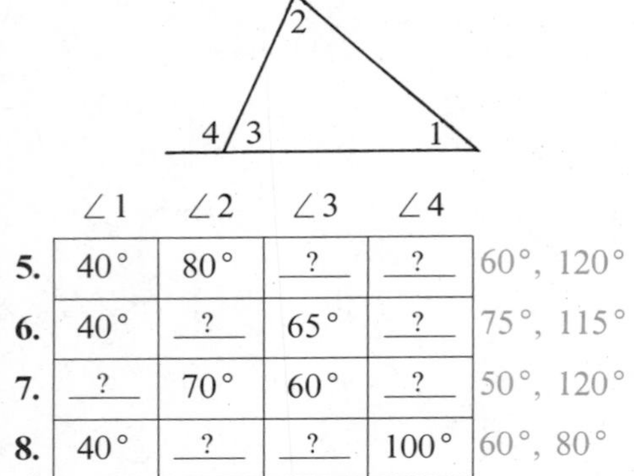


| | ∠1 | ∠2 | ∠3 | ∠4 | |
|---|---|---|---|---|---|
| **5.** | 40° | 80° | ? | ? | 60°, 120° |
| **6.** | 40° | ? | 65° | ? | 75°, 115° |
| **7.** | ? | 70° | 60° | ? | 50°, 120° |
| **8.** | 40° | ? | ? | 100° | 60°, 80° |

## Suggested Extension

**Is it possible for two angles of a triangle to have the measures listed?**

**1.** 90° and 80° yes

**2.** 90° and 90° no

**3.** 90° and 100° no

**4.** 81° and 93° yes

**5.** Can there be a triangle with:

- **a.** Two obtuse angles? no
- **b.** Two right angles? no
- **c.** One right angle and one obtuse angle? no
- **d.** Two acute angles and one non-acute angle? yes

## 2 • CLASSIFYING TRIANGLES (pp. 89–92)

### Teaching These Pages

Group activity as well as individual study may make mastery of new vocabulary more pleasant. You might like to conduct an oral drill in which students classify different triangles as you draw them on the chalkboard.

Students should realize that more than one term may apply to a figure. If, in $\triangle ABC$, $AB = 10$ and $AC = 10$, then one can conclude that $\triangle ABC$ is isosceles. It is possible that additional information, acquired later, will permit a further conclusion: for instance, it may develop that $\triangle ABC$ is acute, obtuse, or even equilateral. Be sure students understand that it remains true that $\triangle ABC$ is isosceles, because $AB = AC$.

## Chalkboard Examples

**Draw a triangle that fits the description. If the condition cannot be met, write *not possible.***

1. An acute triangle that is isosceles (drawings are omitted)
2. A right triangle that is isosceles
3. An obtuse triangle that is isosceles
4. A scalene triangle that is isosceles not possible
5. A right triangle that is equilateral not possible
6. An isosceles triangle that is equilateral
7. A right triangle in which the hypotenuse equals a leg not possible

## Objectives for Pages 93–103

1. To name congruent triangles and their corresponding parts.
2. To use the SSS Postulate to prove that two triangles are congruent.

## 3•DEFINING CONGRUENT TRIANGLES (pp. 93–97)

### Teaching These Pages

In some situations, it is convenient to make informal statements such as "The triangles are congruent" or "Triangle I is congruent to Triangle II." But students must realize that in a statement of the form $\triangle \_\_\_ \cong \triangle \_\_\_$, the order in which the letters appear is crucial. An advantage of the more formal statement is that we can identify corresponding parts of congruent triangles without needing to consult a diagram.

Written Exercises 5–8 involve graphing skills. You may wish to assign Reviewing Algebraic Skills, page 75, to students who need extra practice using the coordinate plane.

### Chalkboard Examples

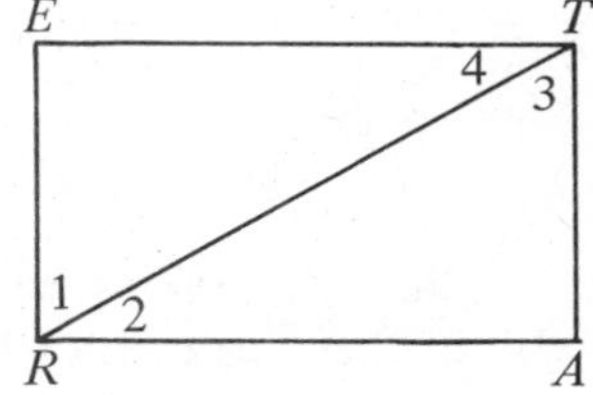


1. Name the six parts of $\triangle RAT$. $\overline{RA}$, $\overline{AT}$, $\overline{TR}$, $\angle 2$, $\angle A$, $\angle 3$
2. Name the six parts of $\triangle ERT$. $\overline{ER}$, $\overline{RT}$, $\overline{TE}$, $\angle E$, $\angle 1$, $\angle 4$

**In the diagram above, $\angle 1 = 60°$, $\angle 2 = 30°$, $\angle 3 = 60°$, and $\angle 4 = 30°$. Tell whether the following statements are correct or incorrect.**

3. $\triangle RAT \cong \triangle RTE$ incorrect
4. $\triangle RAT \cong \triangle TER$ correct
5. $\triangle TAR \cong \triangle RET$ correct
6. $\triangle ERT \cong \triangle ART$ incorrect

## Suggested Extension

Have students check to see that these two statements are both correct:

$$\triangle ABC \cong \triangle RST \qquad \triangle ABC \cong \triangle XYZ$$

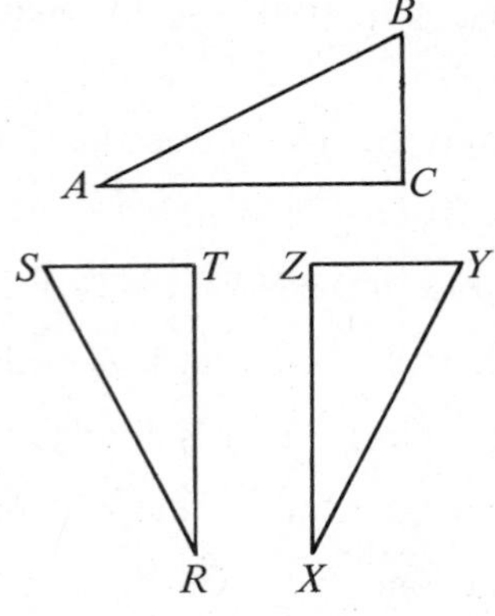


The first statement seems easier, however, because we can slide $\triangle ABC$—mentally—and get a fit with $\triangle RST$. To fit $\triangle ABC$ over $\triangle XYZ$ we must both *flip* and slide.

Point out that congruence in solid geometry is more complicated. The two solids shown are *oppositely congruent*. One cannot be made to fit over the other, no matter how much flipping and sliding is done.

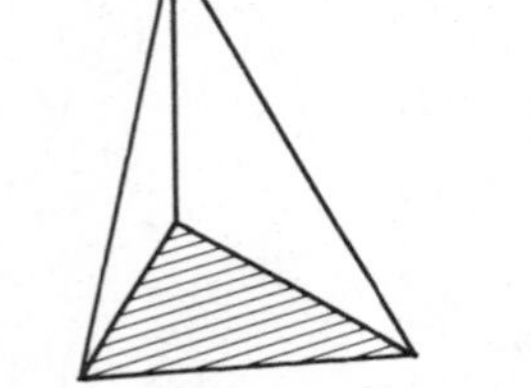

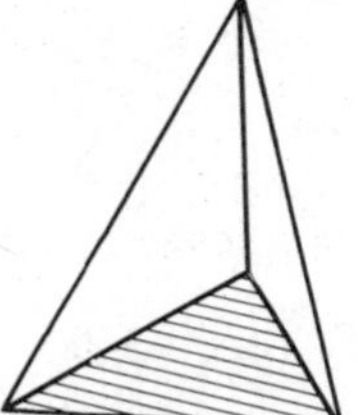

You might ask students to name pairs of oppositely congruent objects which we meet in everyday life. gloves, shoes

## 4•THE SSS POSTULATE (pp. 99–103)

### Teaching These Pages

Some students will be convinced of the validity of the SSS Postulate by the diagram on page 99. Other students may need to handle some sticks like those in the diagram. Students who like woodworking may enjoy preparing several sets of three sticks 20 cm, 30 cm, and 40 cm long.

### Chalkboard Examples

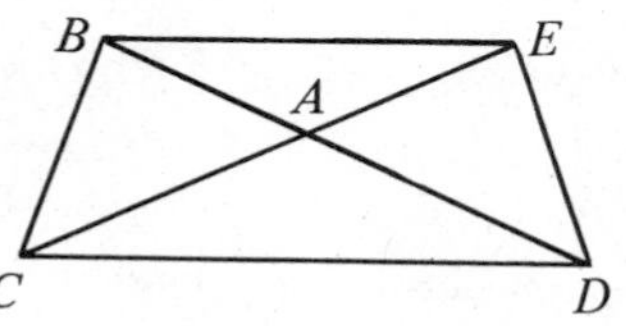


1. Suppose you want to prove $\triangle BAC \cong \triangle EAD$ by using the SSS postulate. List the three pairs of sides of these triangles which you must prove equal.
   $\overline{BA}$ and $\overline{EA}$; $\overline{AC}$ and $\overline{AD}$; $\overline{CB}$ and $\overline{DE}$

2. Repeat Exercise 1, but work with $\triangle BCD$ and $\triangle EDC$.
   $\overline{BC}$ and $\overline{ED}$; $\overline{CD}$ and $\overline{DC}$; $\overline{DB}$ and $\overline{CE}$

3. *Given:* $GX = JX$
E is the midpoint of $\overline{GJ}$
*Prove:* $\triangle XEG \cong \triangle XEJ$

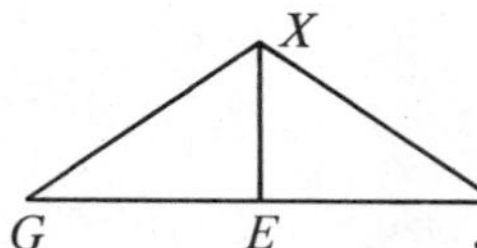


1. $GX = JX$ (Given)
2. $GE = JE$ (Given: $E$ is midpt.)
3. $XE = XE$ (From algebra)
4. $\triangle XEG \cong \triangle XEJ$ (SSS Post.)

4. Suppose you want to prove that $\triangle ABC \cong \triangle DEF$. You find that $BC = 17$ and $EF = 18$. Should you continue your proof? no

5. Suppose you want to prove that $\triangle RST \cong \triangle XYZ$. You find that $RS = 102$ and $YZ = 103$. Should you continue your proof? yes

## Suggested Extension

The Applications feature, Rigidity of Triangles, on pages 124–125 discusses a very important practical use of the SSS Postulate. The exercises in this feature encourage students to experiment with one of the fundamental concepts of architecture.

## Objectives for Pages 105–115

1. To use the SAS Postulate to prove that two triangles are congruent.
2. To use the ASA Postulate to prove that two triangles are congruent.

# 5•THE SAS POSTULATE (pp. 105–110)

## Teaching These Pages

If some students prepared sticks for use with Section 4, the sticks can be adapted for use here. An angle indicator like the one pictured at right should be made for each set of sticks.

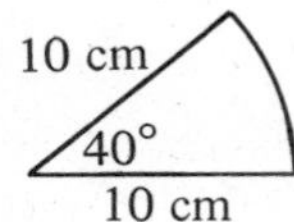


## Chalkboard Examples

**State whether the SSS Postulate or the SAS Postulate could be used to prove $\triangle RUG \cong \triangle TUG$.**

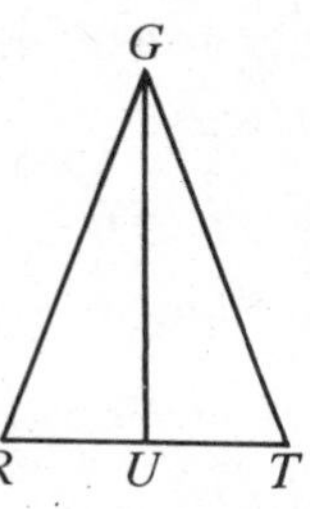


1. *Given:* $\angle RGU = \angle TGU$; $RG = TG$ SAS
2. *Given:* $\angle RUG$ and $\angle TUG$ are right angles; $RU = TU$ SAS
3. *Given:* $RG = TG$; $RU = TU$ SSS
4. *Given:* $\angle RGU = 25°$; $\angle TGU = 25°$; $RG = TG$ SAS
5. *Given:* $U$ is the midpoint of $\overline{RT}$; $RG = TG$ SSS
6. *Given:* $RU = TU$; $\overline{GU} \perp \overline{RT}$ SAS

## Suggested Extension

**Supply reasons to complete the proof.**

*Given:* $XY = XZ$
*Prove:* $\triangle XYZ \cong \triangle XZY$

| Statements | Reasons |
|---|---|
| 1. $XY = XZ$ | 1. ? Given |
| 2. $\angle X = \angle X$ | 2. ? From algebra |
| 3. $XZ = XY$ | 3. ? Given |
| 4. $\triangle XYZ \cong \triangle XZY$ | 4. ? SAS Post. |

This strategy can be used in an alternate proof of Theorem 3 on page 153.

## 6 • THE ASA POSTULATE (pp. 111–115)

### Teaching These Pages

You may wish to have students make stick models similar to the one pictured on page 111 to demonstrate the ASA Postulate. Two angle indicators should be made for each set of sticks. Such models help students to understand the activity described on page 111.

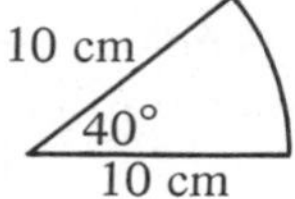


The constructions in Written Exercises 7–9 on page 114 also serve to convince students of the validity of the ASA Postulate.

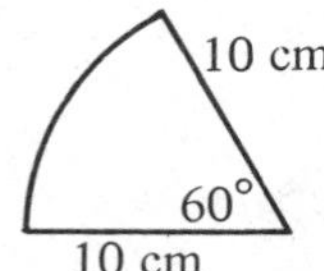


### Chalkboard Examples

**State whether the SAS Postulate or the ASA Postulate could be used to prove $\triangle RED \cong \triangle REN$.**

**1.** *Given:* $RD = RN$; $\overrightarrow{RE}$ bisects $\angle DRN$ SAS

**2.** *Given:* $\angle DRE = \angle NRE$; $RD = RN$ SAS

**3.** *Given:* $\overline{RE} \perp \overline{DN}$; $\angle D = \angle N$; $DE = NE$ ASA

**4.** *Given:* $\overrightarrow{RE}$ bisects $\angle DRN$; $\overline{RE} \perp \overline{DN}$ ASA

**5.** *Given:* $DE = NE$; $\angle RED = \angle REN$ SAS

**6.** *Given:* $\angle RDE = 65°$; $\angle RNE = 65°$; $DR = NR$; $\overrightarrow{RE}$ bisects $\angle DRN$ ASA

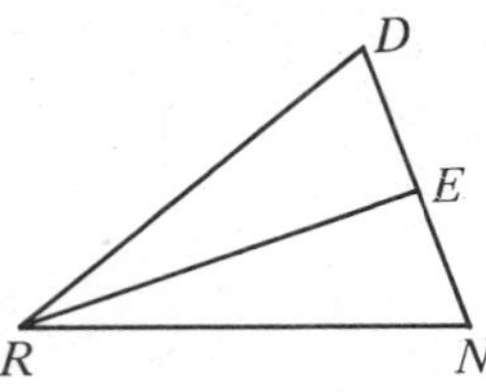

**7.** *Given:* $\angle F = \angle G$
$\angle 1 = \angle 2$
$\overline{DE} \perp \overline{FG}$
$E$ is the midpoint of $\overline{FG}$.
*Prove:* $\triangle FEH \cong \triangle GEK$

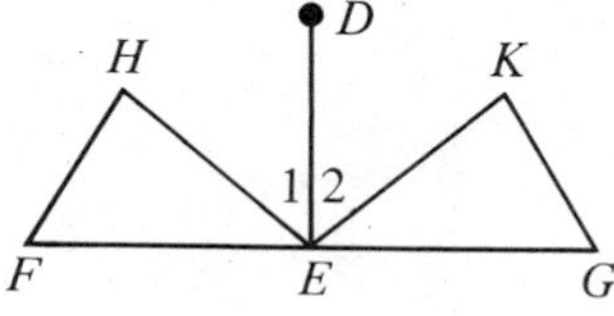


1. $\angle DEF = \angle DEG$ (Given: $\overline{DE} \perp \overline{FG}$)
2. $\angle 1 = \angle 2$ (Given)
3. $\angle HEF = \angle KEG$ (Subtr. Post.)
4. $FE = GE$ (Given: $E$ is midpt.)
5. $\angle F = \angle G$ (Given)
6. $\triangle FEH \cong \triangle GEK$ (ASA Post.)

## Suggested Extension

**Supply reasons to complete the proof.**

*Given:* $\angle A = \angle B$
*Prove:* $\triangle ACB \cong \triangle BCA$

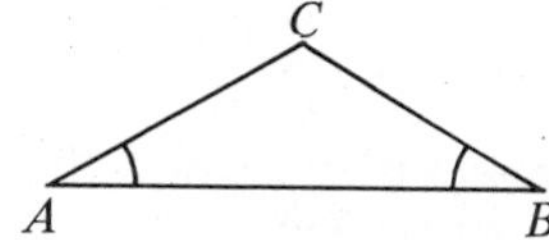


| Statements | Reasons |
|---|---|
| 1. $\angle A = \angle B$ | 1. ? Given |
| 2. $AB = BA$ | 2. ? From algebra |
| 3. $\angle B = \angle A$ | 3. ? Given |
| 4. $\triangle ACB \cong \triangle BCA$ | 4. ? ASA Post. |

This strategy can be used in an alternate proof of Theorem 4 on page 158.

## Objectives for Pages 116–122

**1.** To use the AAS Theorem to prove that two triangles are congruent.
**2.** To use the HL Theorem to prove that two triangles are congruent.

## 7•THE AAS AND HL THEOREMS (pp. 116–122)

### Teaching These Pages

Point out that these two congruence statements are theorems, not postulates. In introducing Theorem 2, the text uses one numerical case to suggest a strategy for a general proof.

The proof of Theorem 3 is long and hard, and has been omitted from the text. The Class Experiment on page 122 is convincing at an informal level.

## Chalkboard Examples

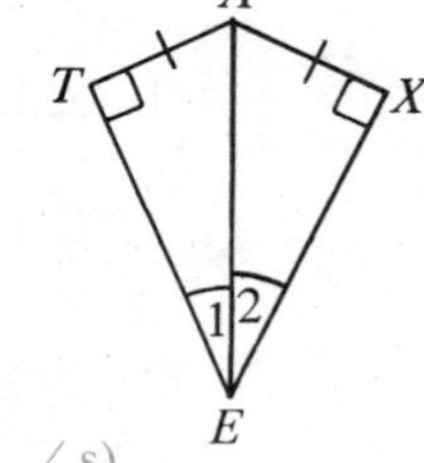


***Given:*** **$\angle T$ and $\angle X$ are right angles**
**$AT = AX$; $\angle 1 = \angle 2$**

1. Use the AAS theorem to prove $\triangle ATE \cong \triangle AXE$.
2. Use the HL theorem to prove $\triangle ATE \cong \triangle AXE$.

Ex. 1
1. $\angle T = \angle X$ (Given: $\angle T$, $\angle X$ are rt. $\angle$s)
2. $\angle 1 = \angle 2$; $AT = AX$ (Given)
3. $\triangle ATE \cong \triangle AXE$ (AAS Thm.)

Ex. 2
1. $\triangle ATE$, $\triangle AXE$ are rt. $\triangle$s (Given: $\angle T$, $\angle X$ are rt. $\angle$s)
2. $AT = AX$ (Given)
3. $AE = AE$ (From algebra)
4. $\triangle ATE \cong \triangle AXE$ (HL Thm.)

3. Use the HL Theorem to prove that a diagonal of a rectangle divides it into two congruent triangles.

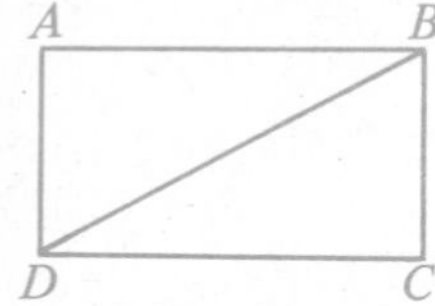


1. $\angle A$, $\angle C$ are rt. $\angle s$ (Def. of rectangle)
2. $\triangle ABD$, $\triangle CDB$ are rt. $\triangle$s (Def. of rt. $\triangle$)
3. $AD = CB$ (Opp. sides of a rect. are =)
4. $DB = DB$ (From algebra)
5. $\triangle ABD \cong \triangle CDB$ (HL Thm.)

## Suggested Extension

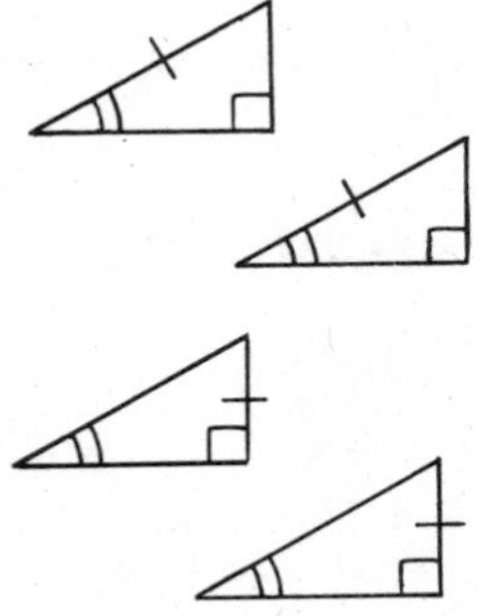

1. Some books prove an HA theorem (hypotenuse and acute angle theorem) that could be used for the triangles shown at right. What method have you studied that you could use to prove the triangles congruent? AAS Theorem

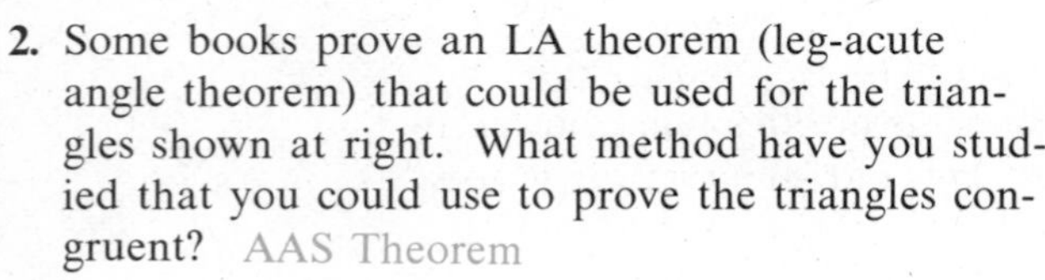

2. Some books prove an LA theorem (leg-acute angle theorem) that could be used for the triangles shown at right. What method have you studied that you could use to prove the triangles congruent? AAS Theorem

## Chapter 4. Using Congruent Triangles

This chapter opens by calling attention to six things that must be true when two triangles are congruent. After a section which introduces the use of the reason *Corresponding parts of congruent triangles are equal,* there is a section dealing with proofs that Constructions 1–4 are logically sound. Three new constructions are presented and justified. Altitudes and medians of triangles are defined and constructed. Important theorems concerning isosceles and equilateral triangles are used in proofs, in computational work, and in justifying the construction of a 60° angle.

### Objectives for Pages 130–138

1. To prove segments and angles equal by using the reason: Corresponding parts of congruent triangles are equal.
2. To show that the following constructions are logically sound:
   - **a.** Bisecting an angle
   - **b.** Constructing a perpendicular at a point on a line
   - **c.** Constructing a perpendicular to a line from an outside point (Exercise 7, page 137)
   - **d.** Constructing an angle equal to a given angle (Exercise 9, page 137)

### 1 • PROVING CORRESPONDING PARTS EQUAL (pp. 130–134)

### Teaching These Pages

Encourage students to use the time-honored wording *Corresponding parts of congruent triangles are equal.* Quoting the definition of congruent triangles doesn't appeal to most students, and many find writing "Definition of congruent triangles" unconvincing. The strategy which appears in the panel on page 130 is a very useful tool for the geometry student. Urge students to learn these steps.

### Chalkboard Examples

**Supply reasons to complete the following proofs:**

**1.** *Given:* $\overline{AO}$ bisects $\overline{EU}$; $\overline{EU}$ bisects $\overline{AO}$
*Prove:* $\angle 3 = \angle 4$

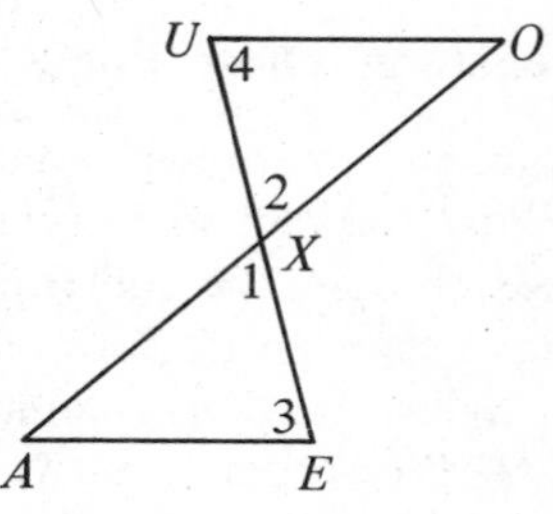


| Statements | Reasons |
|---|---|
| 1. $XE = XU$ | 1. ? Given: $\overline{AO}$ bisects $\overline{EU}$ |
| 2. $XA = XO$ | 2. ? Given: $\overline{EU}$ bisects $\overline{AO}$ |
| 3. $\angle 1 = \angle 2$ | 3. ? Vertical angles are equal. |
| 4. $\triangle AXE \cong \triangle OXU$ | 4. ? SAS Postulate. |
| 5. $\angle 3 = \angle 4$ | 5. ? Corresponding parts |

**2.** *Given:* $AB = AC$; $BD = CE$
*Prove:* $BE = CD$

| Statements | Reasons |
|---|---|
| 1. $BD = CE$ | 1. ? Given |
| 2. $AB = AC$ | 2. ? Given |
| 3. $AD = AE$ | 3. ? Addition Postulate |
| 4. $\angle A = \angle A$ | 4. ? From algebra |
| 5. $\triangle ABE \cong \triangle ACD$ | 5. ? SAS Postulate |
| 6. $BE = CD$ | 6. ? Corresponding Parts |

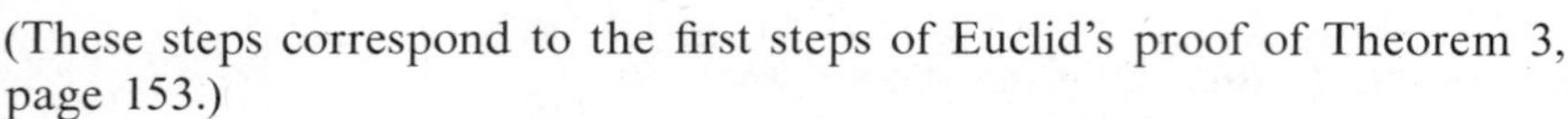

(These steps correspond to the first steps of Euclid's proof of Theorem 3, page 153.)

### Suggested Extension

**Have students prove the *transitive* property of congruence: If two triangles are congruent to the same triangle, they are congruent to each other.**

*Given:* $\triangle ABC \cong \triangle XYZ$;
$\triangle DEF \cong \triangle XYZ$
*Prove:* $\triangle ABC \cong \triangle DEF$

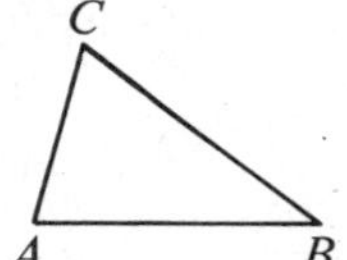

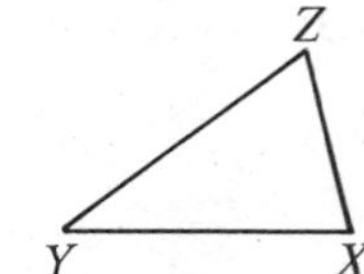

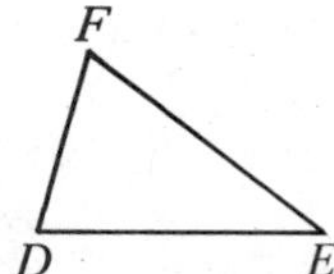


1. $\triangle ABC \cong \triangle XYZ$; $\triangle DEF \cong \triangle XYZ$ (Given)
2. $AB = XY$; $DE = XY$; $BC = YZ$; $EF = YZ$; $AC = XZ$; $DF = XZ$ (Corr. parts)
3. $AB = DE$; $BC = EF$; $AC = DF$ (Subst. Post.)
4. $\triangle ABC \cong \triangle DEF$ (SSS Post.)

## 2•CONGRUENT TRIANGLES AND CONSTRUCTIONS (pp. 135–138)

### Teaching These Pages

Point out to students that in showing Constructions 1 and 2 to be correct, we use the fact that corresponding parts of congruent triangles are equal. In each case, the construction involves locating the vertices of congruent triangles, even if the procedure does not, itself, require drawing complete triangles. In Construction 1, for instance, we must complete $\triangle OXP$ and $\triangle OYP$ in order to prove that the construction is correct. The justifications of Constructions 3 and 4 are left as Written Exercises 7 and 9, respectively, on page 137.

## Chalkboard Examples

1. Draw an $\angle AOB$ and bisect the angle in this particular way: After you draw an arc with point $O$ as center, use the *same* compass setting to draw the arcs that intersect at $P$.

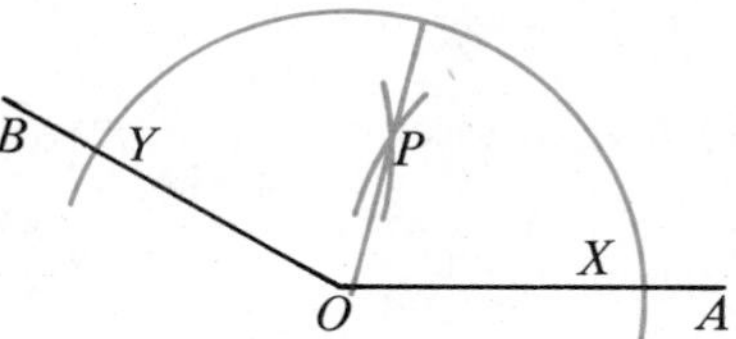


2. Are the five steps of the proof of Construction 1 on page 135 true for your figure? yes
3. What special kind of triangle is $\triangle OXP$? isosceles

## Suggested Extension

Prove that:

(1) Any point on the bisector of an angle is equidistant from the sides of the angle.

(2) Any point that is equidistant from the sides of an angle is on the bisector of the angle.

Note the similarity between these two facts and Theorems 1 and 2 on page 141.

## Objectives for Pages 140–152

1. To construct the perpendicular bisector of a segment.
2. To construct the altitudes of a triangle.
3. To construct the medians of a triangle.
4. To inscribe a circle in a triangle and circumscribe a circle about a triangle.

## 3•SEGMENT BISECTORS (pp. 140–143)

### Teaching These Pages

To most students, it is quite clear that we can always construct a line which is a perpendicular bisector of a segment, and that there is only one such line. As in the case of angle bisectors (Chapter 1, Section 6), the text omits a discussion of existence and uniqueness issues. Students may refer either to *the* perpendicular bisector or to *a* perpendicular bisector of a segment.

You may want to help students who appreciate these issues use Theorems 1 and 2 to show that, in a plane, every segment has one, and only one, perpendicular bisector. Some students may be interested in showing that, in space, the perpendicular bisector of a segment is the *plane* of points equidistant from the endpoints of the segment.

Written Exercise 17 outlines a justification for Construction 6, page 140.

## Chalkboard Examples

**Begin each example by drawing a segment $AB$.**

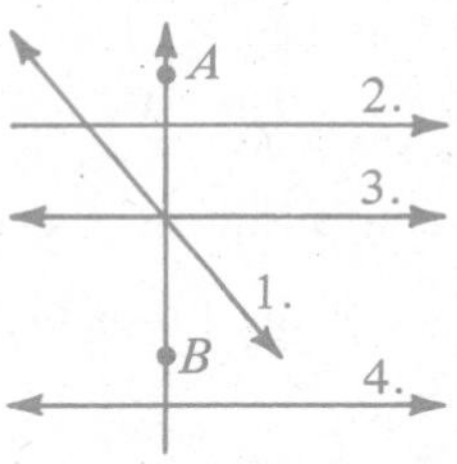


1. Draw a line that bisects $\overline{AB}$ but is not perpendicular to $\overline{AB}$.
2. Draw a line that is perpendicular to $\overline{AB}$ but does not bisect $\overline{AB}$.
3. Draw a line that is the perpendicular bisector of $\overline{AB}$.
4. Draw a line that is perpendicular to $\overleftrightarrow{AB}$ but does not intersect $\overline{AB}$.

## Suggested Extension

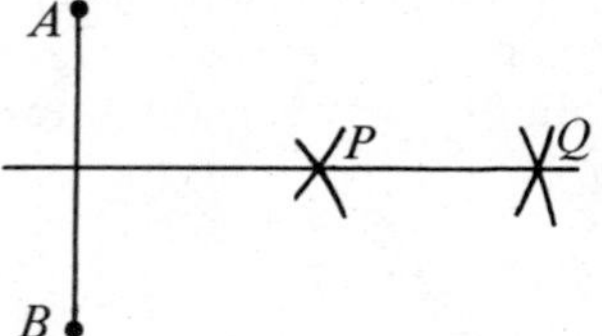


1. Draw a segment $AB$. Construct the perpendicular bisector of $\overline{AB}$ using the procedure suggested by the diagram at right.
2. Draw the appropriate segments in your construction and prove that $\angle PAQ = \angle PBQ$.
   1. $PA = PB$; $QA = QB$ (Construction)
   2. $PQ = PQ$ (From algebra)
   3. $\triangle APQ \cong \triangle BPQ$ (SSS Post.)
   4. $\angle PAQ = \angle PBQ$ (Corr. parts)

# 4 • ALTITUDES AND MEDIANS OF A TRIANGLE (pp. 144–148)

## Teaching These Pages

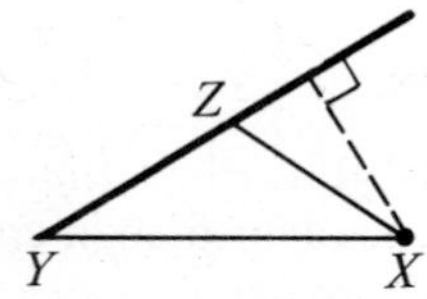


Some students find it a formidable challenge to draw the altitude from $X$ in $\triangle XYZ$ pictured at right. You might suggest that they draw line $YZ$ and point $X$ very prominently. In this way, they can focus their attention, properly, on a line and a point.

Experiment 1 on page 148 and the Suggested Extension below provide two demonstrations that the altitude and median to the base of an isosceles triangle are the same segment.

## Chalkboard Examples

1. In each triangle on the next page, decide which altitude is the shortest, the one from $X$, $Y$, or $Z$.

**a.** 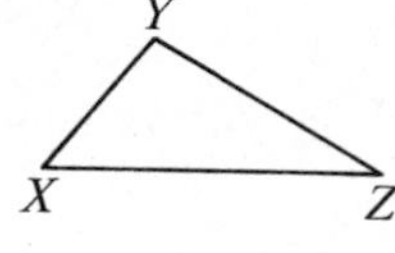


altitude from $Y$

**b.** 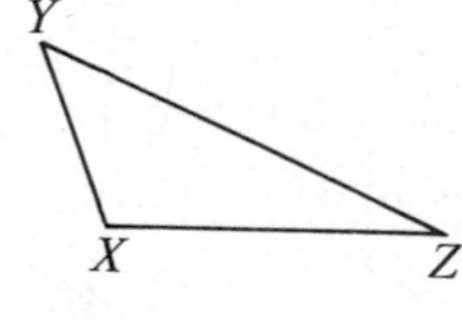


altitude from $X$

**c.** 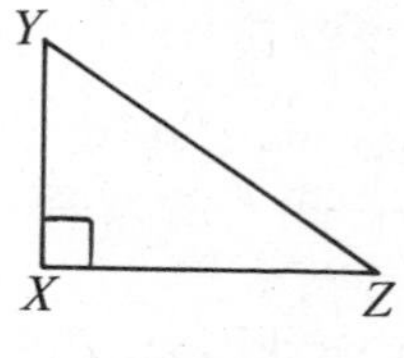


altitude from $X$

2. In each triangle above, decide which median is the shortest, the one from $X$, $Y$, or $Z$. **a.** median from $Y$ **b.** median from $X$ **c.** median from $X$

3. $\triangle RST$ is an isosceles triangle, with $RS = RT$. Which two altitudes of $\triangle RST$ are equal? altitudes from $S$ and $T$

4. Why must the medians of a triangle meet *inside* the triangle? The medians themselves are entirely inside the triangle.

## Suggested Extension

1. Draw a $\triangle ABC$ in which the median from $A$ is longer than the altitude from $A$. Can $\triangle ABC$ be an isosceles triangle, with $AB = AC$? no

1. 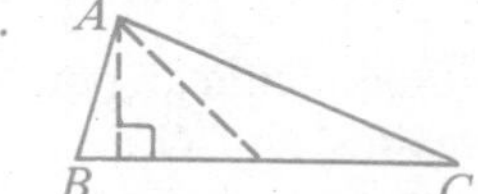


2. Draw a $\triangle ABC$ in which the median from $A$ is the same segment as the altitude from $A$. (isosceles, with vertex A)

2. 

3. Can you draw a $\triangle ABC$ in which the median from $A$ is shorter than the altitude from $A$? no

4. In Exercise 2 above, note that the altitude from $A$ is the perpendicular bisector of $\overline{BC}$. From Theorem 1 on page 141, you can conclude that $\underline{\ ?\ } = \underline{\ ?\ }$.
   $AB$ $AC$

## 5•INSCRIBED AND CIRCUMSCRIBED CIRCLES (pp. 149–152)

### Teaching These Pages

Students should realize that all three perpendicular bisectors of the sides of a triangle intersect at one point. (See Classroom Practice Exercise 5.) Students may select any pair of sides to bisect in order to locate that point, the *circumcenter*. You may want students to construct all the perpendicular bisectors as a check on their mechanical accuracy.

## Chalkboard Examples

1. Draw an acute $\triangle ABC$ with the shortest side at least 10 cm long. Inscribe a circle in $\triangle ABC$.

2. Use your work from Example 1. Label as $R$, $S$, and $T$ the points where the circle touches $\overline{AB}$, $\overline{BC}$, and $\overline{AC}$. Draw $\triangle RST$ and inscribe a circle in $\triangle RST$.

3. Do the circles in Examples 1 and 2 have the same center? no

4. Which of the circles in Examples 1 and 2 can be called a circumscribed circle? the circle through points $R$, $S$, and $T$

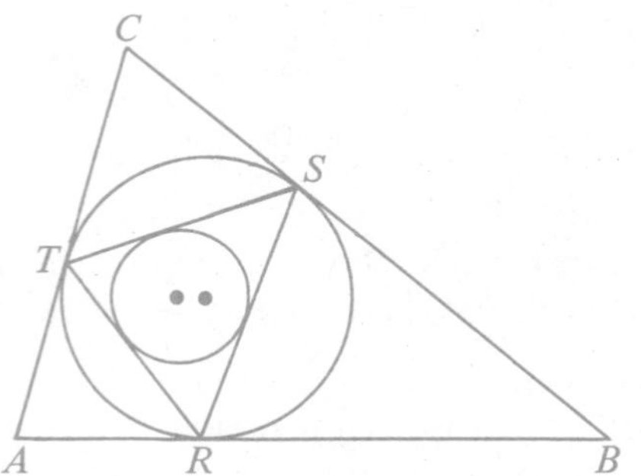


## Suggested Extension

The steps below are an attempt to adapt Construction 7 on page 149 to construct a circle that passes through three collinear points.

1. Draw three collinear points $A$, $B$, and $C$ so that $B$ is between $A$ and $C$.

2. Construct the perpendicular bisectors of $\overline{AB}$ and $\overline{BC}$.

3. What can you say about the intersection of the perpendicular bisectors? They do not intersect (Theorem 8, page 66).

4. Is there any circle that contains points $A$, $B$, and $C$? no

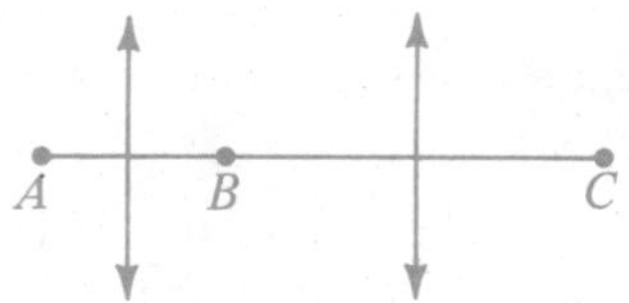


## Objectives for Pages 153–163

1. To use the theorem: If two sides of a triangle are equal, then the angles opposite those sides are equal.
2. To use the theorem: If two angles of a triangle are equal, then the sides opposite those angles are equal.
3. To construct a $60°$ angle.

## 6 • TRIANGLES WITH TWO EQUAL SIDES (pp. 153–157)

### Teaching These Pages

We have chosen a somewhat lengthy phrasing for Theorem 3 on page 153.

Some teachers prefer to have students use a simpler statement of this theorem: Base angles of an isosceles triangle are equal. A disadvantage of the latter phrasing, however, is that many students find it difficult to formulate the converse (Theorem 4, page 158).

The corollary on page 153, along with Theorem 1 on page 84, provides the logical basis for the construction of a 60° angle (Construction 9, page 159).

### Chalkboard Examples

***Given:* $\triangle RST$ with $RT = ST$. Classify each statement as *true, false,* or *cannot be determined.***

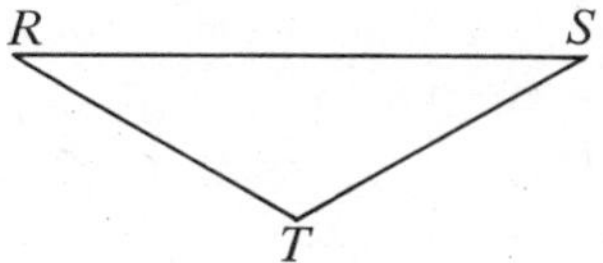


1. $\triangle RST$ is isosceles. true
2. $\triangle RST$ is equilateral. can't be det.
3. $\triangle RST$ is equiangular. can't be det.
4. $RT > RS$ can't be det.
5. $\angle R = \angle S$ true
6. $\angle S = \angle T$ can't be det.

**Find the value of $x$.**

7. 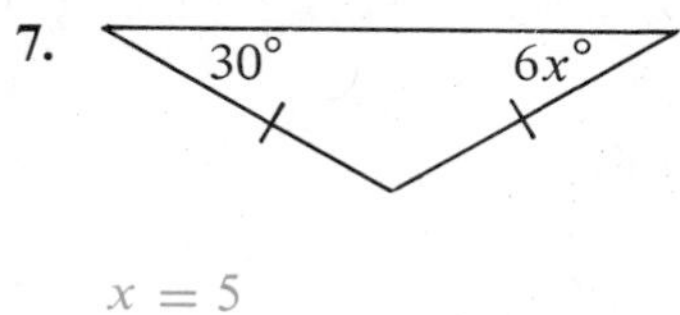


$x = 5$

8. 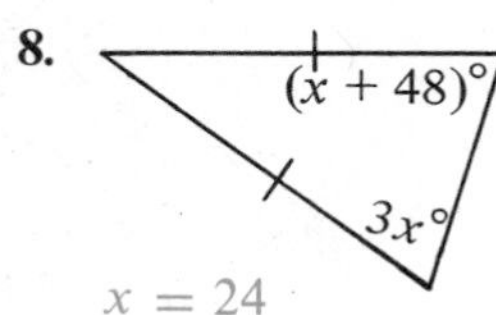


$x = 24$

9. 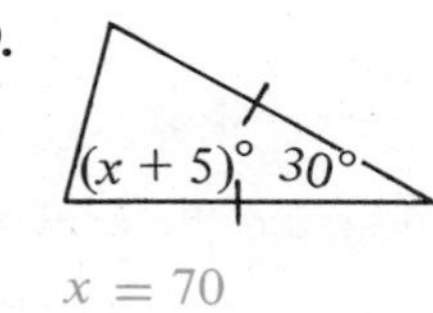


$x = 70$

### Suggested Extension

In the diagram $OA = OB$, and $\angle O = 20°$. Triangles $ABC$, $BCD$, and $CDE$ are isosceles. What is the measure of $\angle ODE$? 20°

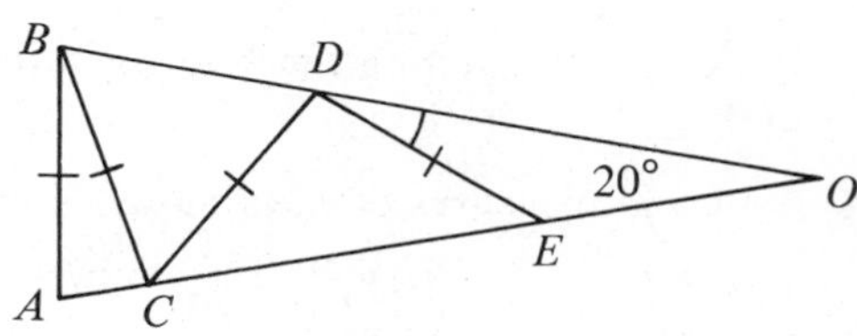


## 7 • TRIANGLES WITH TWO EQUAL ANGLES (pp. 158–163)

### Teaching These Pages

Point out that we construct a 60° angle as part of an equilateral (and therefore equiangular) triangle. The outline of a proof justifying Construction 9 appears on page 159 following the construction.

## Chalkboard Examples

**Equal angles are marked. Name the sides that must be equal. Then find the value of $x$.**

**1.**

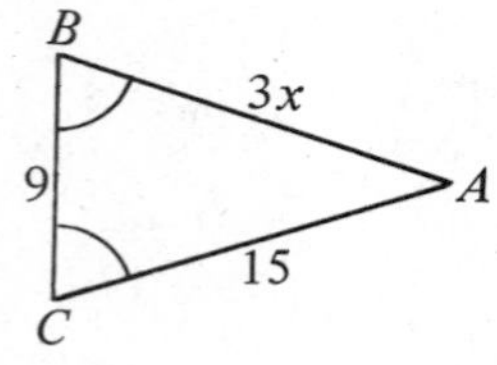


$AB = AC$; $x = 5$

**2.**

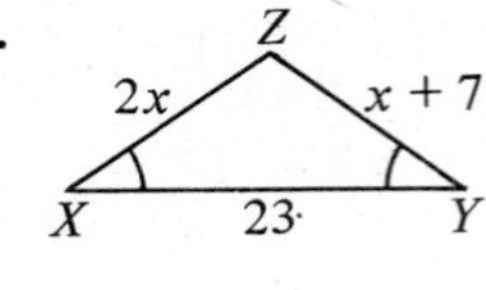


$XZ = YZ$; $x = 7$

**3.**

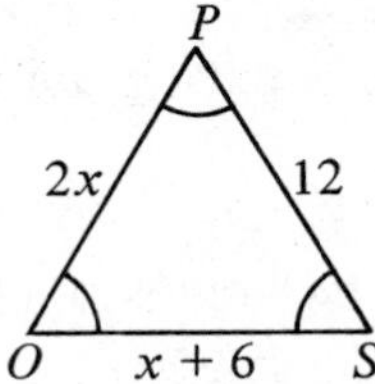


$PO = OS = PS$; $x = 6$

**4.**

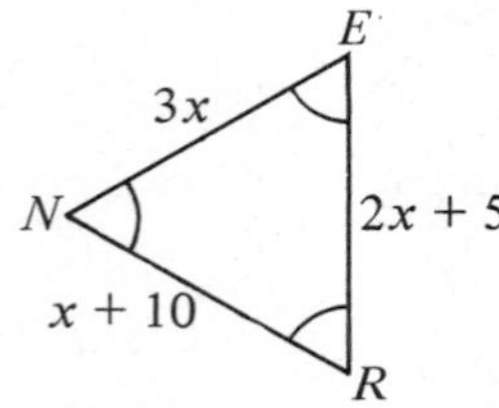


$NE = ER = NR$; $x = 5$

**5.**

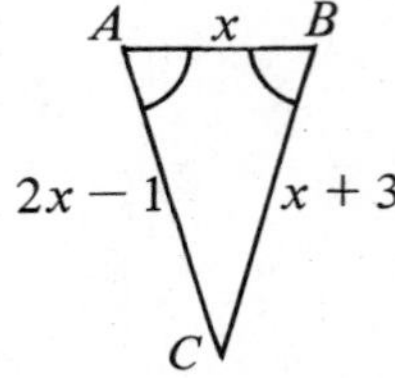


$AC = BC$; $x = 4$

**6.**

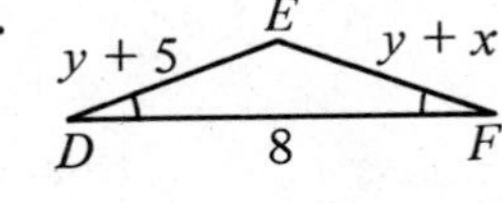


$DE = FE$; $x = 5$

## Suggested Extension

**Steps 1–3 describe the construction of a 75° angle.**

1. Construct an equilateral $\triangle ABC$.
2. Bisect $\angle ABC$, letting the bisector intersect $\overline{AC}$ in $X$.
3. Bisect $\angle ABX$, letting the bisector intersect $\overline{AX}$ in $Y$.
4. State the measures of the following angles:

| $\angle ABC$; | $\angle ABY$; | $\angle YBC$; | $\angle BYC$ |
|---|---|---|---|
| 60° | 15° | 45° | 75° |

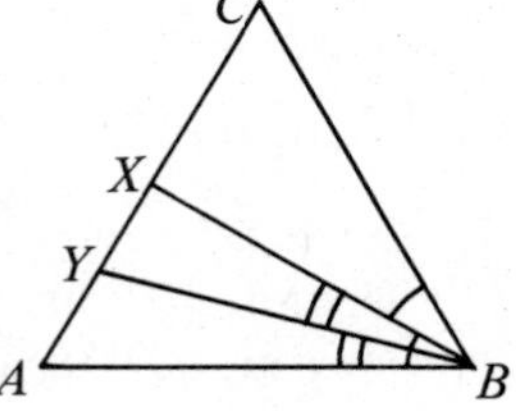

# Chapter 5. Polygons

In the first two sections of this chapter, polygons and their angle sums are discussed. In the remaining sections, the properties of special quadrilaterals are investigated. Included in the latter sections of the chapter are several Explorations. You might have students try these Explorations in class or as homework, encouraging them to hypothesize the properties of special quadrilaterals.

Allowing students to be a part of the discovery process is especially important in the study of geometry. Proving one's own conjectures is much more rewarding and motivating for a student than proving a theorem listed in a book or stated by a teacher.

## Objectives for Pages 172–179

**1.** To classify polygons by the number of sides, and by the terms *equilateral, equiangular, regular,* and *convex.*
**2.** To find the interior and exterior angle sums of a convex polygon.
**3.** To find the measures of the interior and exterior angles of a regular polygon.

## 1•INTRODUCING POLYGONS (pp. 172–175)

### Teaching These Pages

The easiest way to teach the polygon concept is to give examples. A formal definition of *polygon* can be complicated and not very helpful to beginning geometry students.

> A polygon is a figure formed by three or more coplanar segments such that:
>
> 1. No two segments with a common endpoint are collinear.
> 2. Each segment intersects exactly two other segments, but only in endpoints.

You may wish to present this only as an illustration of how difficult a formal definition can be. Some students might have fun trying to make their own precise definitions of "polygon" or "convex polygon."

> A convex polygon is a polygon with the property that every segment which joins two points of the polygon's interior lies wholly in the interior.

*Example:* The figure at right is not a convex polygon because segment *PQ* does not lie wholly in the interior of the figure.

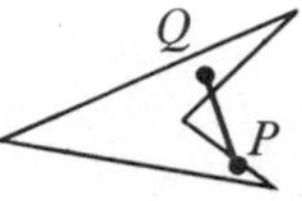

In the study of triangles, the terms *equilateral, equiangular,* and *regular* all denote the same figure. You might use a nonsquare rhombus, a rectangle, and a square to demonstrate that the terms are not equivalent in general. You can provide further reinforcement with the three hexagons pictured below.

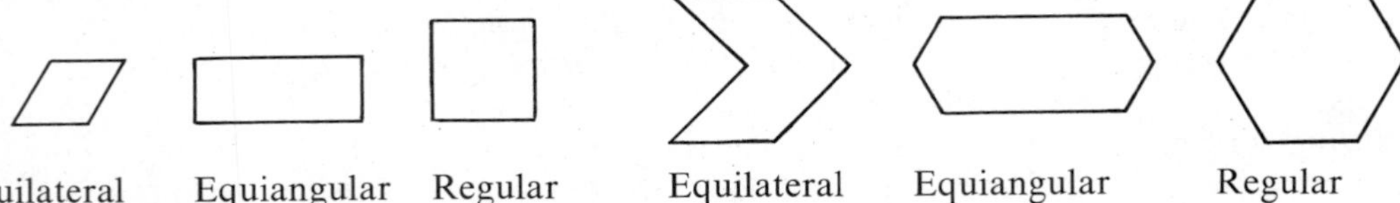


### Chalkboard Examples

**Draw each of the following figures.** (drawings are omitted)

**1.** A pentagon

**2.** An octagon

**3.** A nonconvex quadrilateral

**4.** An equilateral triangle

**5.** An equiangular triangle

**6.** A regular quadrilateral

**7.** Is it possible to draw an equiangular triangle that is not equilateral? no

**8.** What is a regular quadrilateral usually called? square

### Suggested Extension

Challenge students to find a pattern in the table given for Written Exercises 28–32 on page 175. They can use this pattern to predict the number of diagonals if the number of sides is 9, 10, 11, and so on. Some students may like to find a formula that gives the number of diagonals, $d$, in terms of the number of sides, $s$.

$$d = \frac{s(s-3)}{2}$$

From each of the $s$ vertices, $s - 3$ diagonals can be drawn, for a total of $s(s - 3)$. But each diagonal has been counted twice in this scheme. Divide by 2 to get the correct count.

## 2 • ANGLE SUMS OF POLYGONS (pp. 176–179)

### Teaching These Pages

Remind students that one case has already been settled: all triangles have an angle sum of 180°. You may wish to begin further investigation with the "simplest" quadrilaterals: squares and rectangles. Students will quickly see that the interior angle sum is always $4 \times 90° = 360°$. Then try another quadrilateral (perhaps one with just 2 right angles): will its angle sum also be 360°? Suggest to students that they "break" the quadrilateral into triangles and use what they already know about a triangle's angle sum.

You might get more than one proof of the 360° angle sum for the quadrilateral. Here are two possibilities, both of which suggest the general formula, $S = (n - 2) \times 180°$.

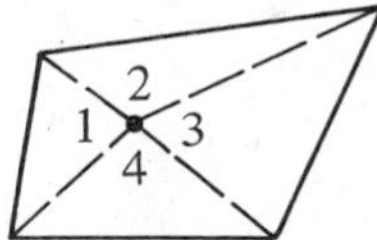


Sum $= 2 \times 180°$

Sum $= 4 \times 180° - (\angle 1 + \angle 2 + \angle 3 + \angle 4)$
$= 720° - 360° = 360°$

Generalize:
Sum $= (n - 2) \times 180°$

Sum $= n \times 180° - 360°$
$= n \times 180° - 2 \times 180°$
$= (n - 2) \times 180°$

The measure of each angle of a regular polygon is given by the formula $A = \frac{(n - 2) \times 180°}{n}$, as illustrated in the Example on page 177. Students, however, usually prefer the formula $A = 180° - \frac{360°}{n}$, which follows from the fact that each interior angle is the supplement of an exterior angle whose measure is $\frac{360°}{n}$.

## Chalkboard Examples

**Complete the table for convex polygons.**

| | 1. | 2. | 3. | |
|---|---|---|---|---|
| Number of sides | 5 | 7 | 102 | |
| Interior angle sum | ? | ? | ? | 540°, 900°, 18,000° |
| Exterior angle sum | ? | ? | ? | 360°, 360°, 360° |

**Complete the table for regular polygons.**

| | 4. | 5. | 6. | |
|---|---|---|---|---|
| Number of sides | 6 | 10 | 20 | |
| Each exterior angle | ? | ? | ? | 60°, 36°, 18° |
| Each interior angle | ? | ? | ? | 120°, 144°, 162° |

## Suggested Extension

Some students may be interested in the art of M. C. Escher. Many of his works involve filling the plane with interesting and bizarre repeated figures. An excellent reference is: Sheila Haak, "Transformation Geometry and the Artwork of M. C. Escher," *The Mathematics Teacher,* 69:647–652 (December, 1976).

## Objectives for Pages 180–189

1. To classify quadrilaterals as parallelograms, rectangles, rhombuses, squares, and trapezoids.
2. To use the properties of parallelograms.

## 3•SPECIAL QUADRILATERALS (pp. 180–184)

### Teaching These Pages

We suggest that you present examples of the five special quadrilaterals one at a time, in the order implied by the chart on page 180: trapezoid, parallelogram, rectangle, rhombus, and square. You may wish to have students suggest definitions for the figures. Listed below are some possible definitions.

Rectangle: A parallelogram with 4 right angles
A parallelogram with 1 right angle
Rhombus: An equilateral parallelogram
A parallelogram with two adjacent sides equal
Square: A rhombus which is a rectangle
A rectangle which is a rhombus
A regular quadrilateral

Note that the text defines a trapezoid as having *exactly* one pair of parallel sides. Hence, a parallelogram is not a special case of a trapezoid. More advanced students might like to contrast this situation with that for isosceles and equilateral triangles.

### Chalkboard Examples

1. Draw a parallelogram and one of its diagonals. What appears to be true about the two triangles formed? congruent

2. *PQRS* is a rhombus. $\angle 1 =$ __?__; $\angle 2 =$ __?__
70°; 70°

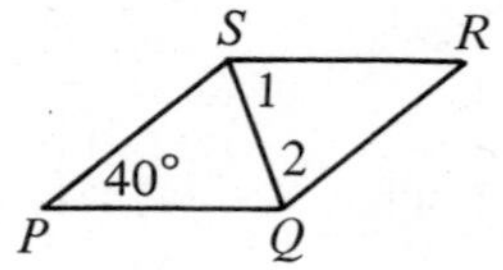

3. $ABCD$ is a rectangle. $\angle 1 =$ _?_; $\angle 2 =$ _?_
65°; 25°

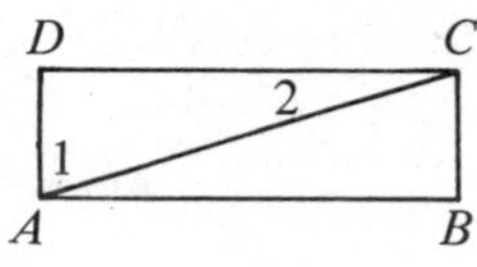


4. $PQRS$ is a square. $\angle 1 =$ _?_; $\angle 2 =$ _?_
45°; 45°

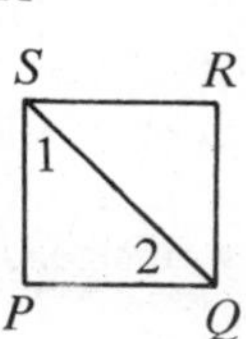


## 4•PROPERTIES OF PARALLELOGRAMS (pp. 185–189)

### Teaching These Pages

We suggest that you teach this section by following the steps of the Explorations in the text. Allow plenty of time for students to form and test their conclusions. Students should be able to express the theorems on page 186 in "if . . . then" form. For example: "Theorem 3: If a polygon is a parallelogram, then opposite sides of the polygon are equal." The converses of the theorems will be considered in Section 6.

### Chalkboard Examples

***ABCD* is a parallelogram. Find:**

1. $CO$ 50 2. $BD$ 60

3. $CD$ 70 4. $AD$ 44

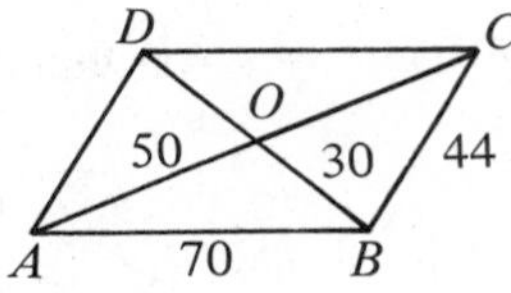


***LOAB* is a parallelogram. *SAOT* is a rhombus.**
**Find each length and angle measure.**

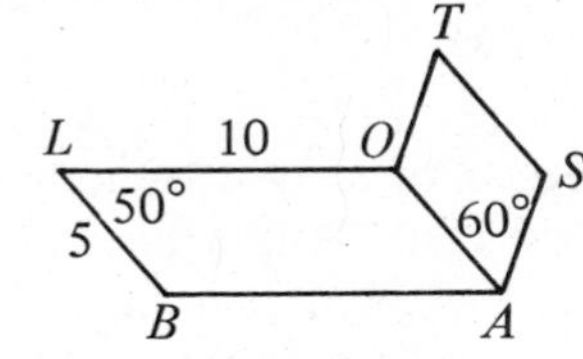


5. $AO$ 5 6. $OT$ 5 7. $AB$ 10

8. $\angle LBA$ 130° 9. $\angle BAS$ 110° 10. $\angle TSA$ 120°

### Objectives for Pages 190–200

1. To use the properties of rectangles, rhombuses, and squares.
2. To prove that quadrilaterals with particular properties are parallelograms.

## 5•PROPERTIES OF SPECIAL PARALLELOGRAMS (pp. 190–194)

### Teaching These Pages

We suggest that you teach this section by following the steps of the Explorations in the text. Theorem 9, a corollary of Theorems 6 and 7, appears unexpectedly, providing information about right triangles. The Suggested Extension below shows how this result sheds light on the construction of circumscribed circles.

### Chalkboard Examples

***TRAK*** **is a rectangle.** ***BARS*** **is a square. Find the measure of each angle.**

**1.** $\angle KAT$ 39° **2.** $\angle TRO$ 39°

**3.** $\angle RXS$ 90° **4.** $\angle XRS$ 45°

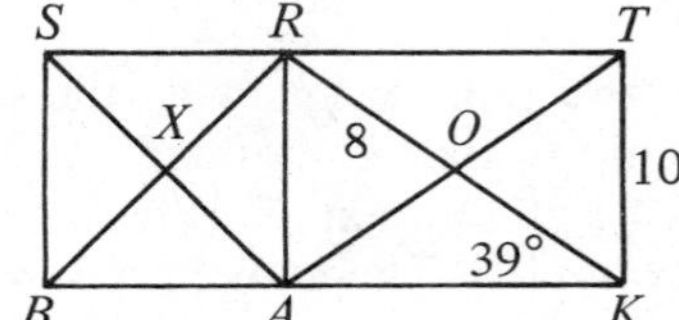


**Find each length.**

**5.** KO 8 **6.** $OT$ 8 **7.** $AT$ 16 **8.** $AB$ 10

***BLUR*** **is a rhombus. Find the measure of each angle.**

**9.** $\angle LRU$ 67° **10.** $\angle BOR$ 90°

**11.** $\angle RBO$ 23° **12.** $\angle LBO$ 23°

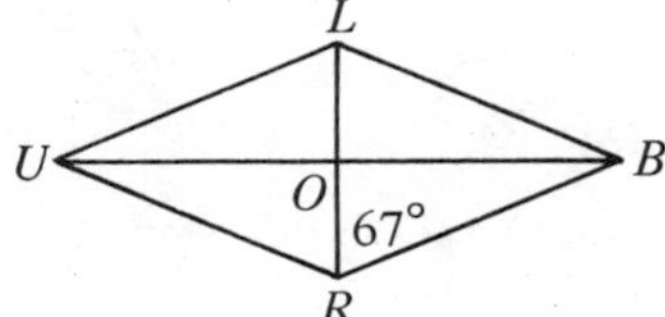


### Suggested Extension

Theorem 9 implies that the midpoint of the hypotenuse of a right triangle is also the center of the circumscribed circle. Some students might like to verify these related facts: if a triangle is acute, the center of the circumscribed circle is inside the triangle; if a triangle is obtuse, the circumcenter is outside the triangle.

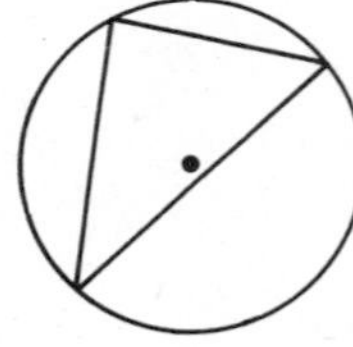
Acute triangle

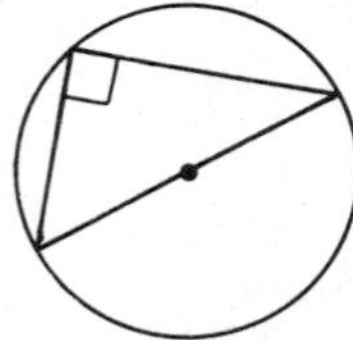
Right triangle

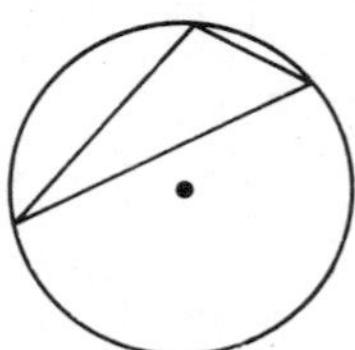
Obtuse triangle

## 6•PROVING FIGURES ARE PARALLELOGRAMS (pp. 195–200)

### Teaching These Pages

As a sequel (or an alternative) to the Explorations in the text, you might have students review the properties of a parallelogram (Theorems 3–6, page 186). Then ask whether or not they think the converse of each theorem is true. (They all are!)

The converse of Theorem 4 is not listed on page 197 as a method for proving a figure is a parallelogram, because this method is not used very often (but see Suggested Extension 4 for this lesson). Students can prove the validity of this method in Written Exercise 15 on page 200.

In Written Exercises 16 and 17 on page 200, students use conditions on diagonals to prove that figures are special parallelograms. Point out to students that if *both* conditions are met, then it follows that the figure must be a square.

We have not included in this text the theorem that *if two lines are parallel to a third line, then they are parallel to each other.* This useful principle is mentioned and used in Written Exercise 8 on page 199 and in Chalkboard Example 3 below.

### Chalkboard Examples

**1.** *Given:* $PQRS$ is a parallelogram
$TR = UQ$
*Prove:* (a) $RTUQ$ is a parallelogram
(b) $STUP$ is a parallelogram

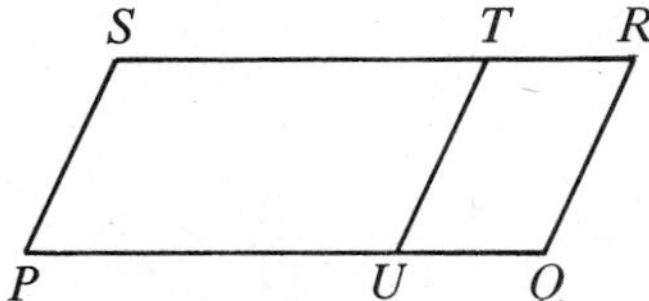


1. $TR = UQ$ (Given)
2. $\overline{TR} \parallel \overline{UQ}$ (Opp. sides of a ▱ are parallel)
3. $RTUQ$ is a ▱ (Thm. 10)
4. $SR = PQ$ (Opp. sides of a ▱ are =)
5. $ST = PU$ (Subtraction Post.)
6. $\overline{ST} \parallel \overline{PU}$ (See step **2.**)
7. $STUP$ is a ▱ (Thm. 10)

**2.** *Given:* $LANK$ is a parallelogram
$\overrightarrow{KX}$ bisects $\angle LKN$
$\overrightarrow{AY}$ bisects $\angle NAL$
*Prove:* $\triangle XLK \cong \triangle YNA$

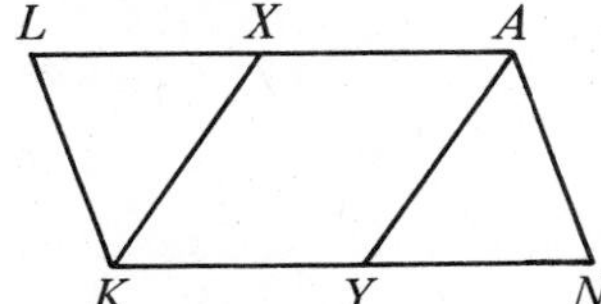


1. $\angle LKN = \angle NAL$; $\angle L = \angle N$ (Opp. $\angle$s of a ▱ are =)
2. $\angle LKX = \frac{1}{2}\angle LKN$; $\angle NAY = \frac{1}{2}\angle NAL$ (Given: angle bisectors)
3. $\angle LKX = \angle NAY$ (Mult. and Subst. Postulates)
4. $LK = NA$ (Opp. sides of a ▱ are =)
5. $\triangle XLK \cong \triangle YNA$ (ASA Post.)

**Supply the reasons to complete the proof. Use the fact that *if two lines are parallel to the same line, then they are parallel to each other.***

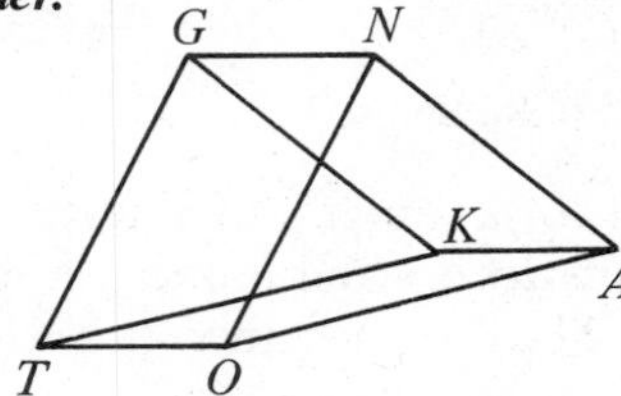


**3.** *Given:* *TONG* is a parallelogram
*KANG* is a parallelogram
*Prove:* *TOAK* is a parallelogram

| | | |
|---|---|---|
| 1. $TO = GN$; $GN = KA$ | 1. ? | Opp. sides of a ▱ are equal |
| 2. $TO = KA$ | 2. ? | Substitution Postulate |
| 3. $\overline{TO} \parallel \overline{GN}$; $\overline{GN} \parallel \overline{KA}$ | 3. ? | Definition of parallelogram |
| 4. $\overline{TO} \parallel \overline{KA}$ | 4. ? | If two lines are $\parallel$ to the same line, then they are $\parallel$ to each other. |
| 5. *TOAK* is a parallelogram. | 5. ? | If a quad. has one pair of opp. sides both = and $\parallel$, then it is a ▱. |

(Note: Written Exercise 8 on page 199 extends the strategy used in Example 3.)

## Suggested Extension

**1.** Construct a rhombus whose diagonals have lengths 4 cm and 7 cm.

**2.** Construct a rhombus which has a 60° angle and sides with length 5 cm.

**3.** Construct a rectangle having one side with length 6 cm and a diagonal with length 8 cm.

**4.** Use the converse of Theorem 4 in a proof of the following theorem.
*Given:* *PQRST* is a regular pentagon.
*Prove:* *STOR* is a rhombus.

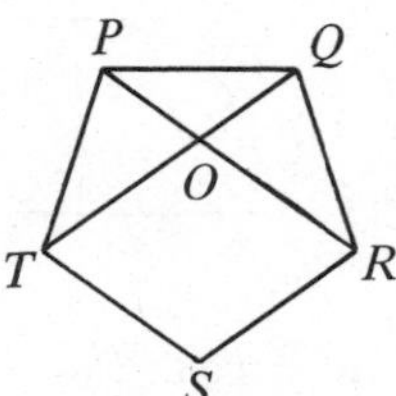


*Strategy:* (1) Regular pentagon: $\angle TPQ = \angle PQR = \angle S = 108°$.
(2) In isos. $\triangle$s *TPQ* and *QPR*, show $\angle PTQ = \angle QRP = 36°$.
(3) Show $\angle OTS = \angle ORS = 72°$.
(4) Use angle sum of quad. to show $\angle TOR = 108°$.
(5) Opp. angles in *STOR* are =. Hence it is a ▱.
(6) Since $TS = SR$, ▱*STOR* is a rhombus.

## Objectives for Pages 201–209

**1.** To use the properties of trapezoids.
**2.** To apply the Midpoints Theorem.

## 7•PROPERTIES OF TRAPEZOIDS (pp. 201–205)

### Teaching These Pages

You may wish to introduce the isosceles trapezoid by slicing off the vertex of an isosceles triangle with a cut parallel to the base. If you adopt this approach, students should be able to reason that the base angles of an isosceles trapezoid are equal (Theorem 13, page 202). An outline of a formal proof appears on page 202 after the statement of the theorem.

Students should note that, unlike a median of a triangle, the median of a trapezoid does not contain a vertex of the polygon. The properties of the median developed in Exploration B are listed in Theorem 14. A formal proof of this theorem is postponed until Chapter 12 (see page 453), but Classroom Practice Exercises 8 and 9 make the result seem very reasonable. (Better students may note that Theorem 5 on page 62 is needed to prove that the two trapezoids "fit together" to form a parallelogram.)

### Chalkboard Examples

**For each trapezoid, find the length of its median $\overline{XY}$ and the measures of its angles.**

**1.** M 7 P; X Y; 70° 40°; S 12 T

$XY = 9.5$; $\angle N = 110°$; $\angle P = 140°$

**2.**

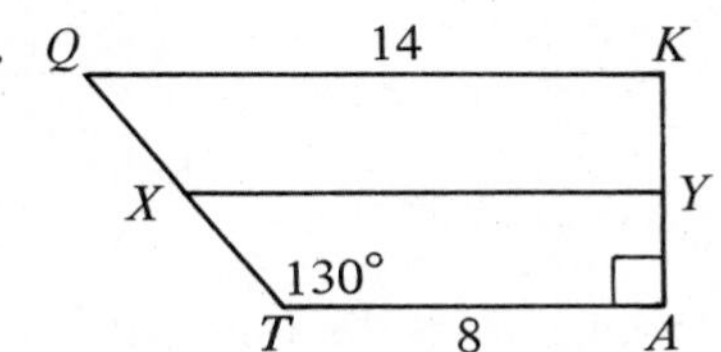


$XY = 11$; $\angle Q = 50°$; $\angle K = 90°$

**3.**

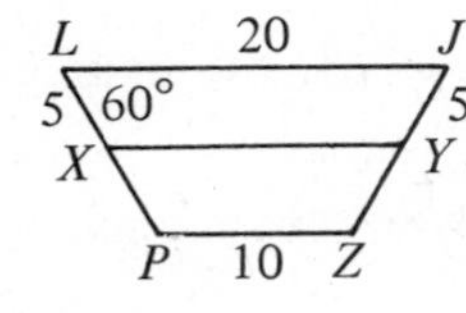


$XY = 15$; $\angle P = \angle Z = 120°$; $\angle J = 60°$

### Suggested Extension

The Puzzles & Things feature on page 205 reviews several skills which students have learned in this course: the angle sum of a triangle (Chapter 3), the measure of a straight angle (Chapter 1), vertical angles (Chapter 1), and inscribed circles (Chapter 4).

## 8•THE MIDPOINTS THEOREM (pp. 206–209)

### Teaching These Pages

You might begin this lesson by drawing figures (a), (b), and (c) of page 206 on the chalkboard. Ask students what they know about the median $\overline{MN}$. $\overline{MN} \parallel \overline{AB}$ and $MN = \frac{1}{2}(AB + DC)$ Then draw figure (d) and ask for their conjectures about $\overline{MN}$. (Remind students that in a triangle, $\overline{MN}$ is *not* called a median.)

The strategy of considering a triangle to be a quadrilateral with one side of zero length often yields theorems about triangles from theorems about quadrilaterals. (See the Suggested Extension for this lesson.) Here, Theorem 15 becomes a special case of Theorem 14. The formal proof of Theorem 15 has been postponed until Chapter 12. (See Classroom Practice, page 454.)

## Chalkboard Examples

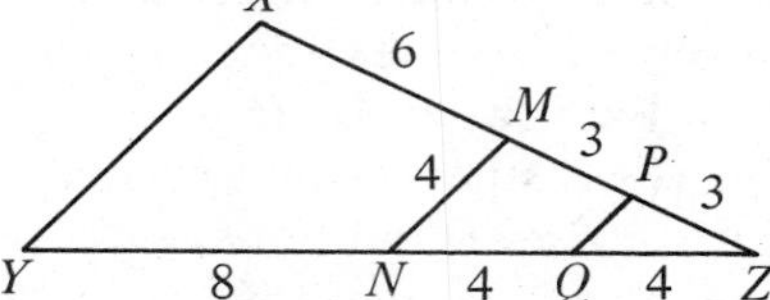


1. $PQ =$ __?__ 2
2. $XY =$ __?__ 8
3. Why is $\overline{MN} \parallel \overline{XY}$? Midpoints Thm.
4. Why is $\overline{PQ} \parallel \overline{MN}$? Midpoints Thm.
5. Draw equilateral $\triangle ABC$ and $\overline{DE}$, the segment joining the midpoints of sides $\overline{AB}$ and $\overline{AC}$. What kind of triangle is $\triangle ADE$? Why? equilateral; $AD = \frac{1}{2}AB$ and $AE = \frac{1}{2}AC$ by construction; $DE = \frac{1}{2}BC$ by Midpoints Thm.; $AB = AC = BC$ by hypothesis, so $\frac{1}{2}AB = \frac{1}{2}AC = \frac{1}{2}BC$ by Mult. Post. of Equality; $AD = AE = DE$ by substitution.

## Suggested Extension

1. Derive a theorem about triangles from the following theorem about trapezoids. To do this, let one base of the trapezoid shrink to zero length, turning the figure into a triangle.

   *Theorem:* The area of a trapezoid with base lengths $a$ and $b$ and height $h$ is $A = \frac{1}{2}h(a + b)$.

   Let $a = 0$ in the formula $A = \frac{1}{2}h(a + b)$: $A = \frac{1}{2}h(0 + b) = \frac{1}{2}h(b) = \frac{1}{2}bh.$

   Hence, the area of a triangle is given by the formula $A = \frac{1}{2}bh.$

2. Prove that the polygon formed by joining the midpoints of a rectangle is a rhombus. (At long last, we can prove the result of the Exploration on page 2!)

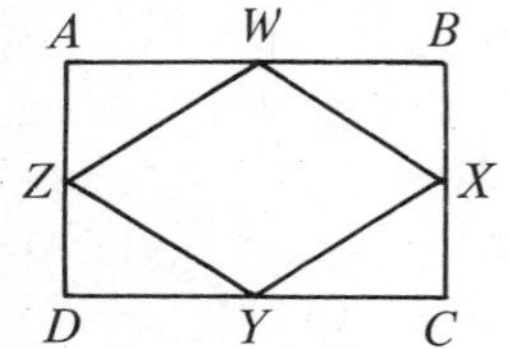


*Strategy:* (1) Show $AW = BW = CY = DY$.
(2) Show $AZ = DZ = BX = CX$.
(3) In rectangle $ABCD$, $\angle A = \angle B = \angle C = \angle D$.
(4) SAS Postulate: $\triangle AZW \cong \triangle BXW \cong \triangle CXY \cong \triangle DZY$.
(5) Corr. parts: $ZW = XW = XY = ZY$.
(6) By definition, $WXYZ$ is a rhombus.

## *Chapter 6. Areas*

The formula for the area of a rectangle is postulated and used. In succeeding sections, area formulas for parallelograms, triangles, and trapezoids are derived and used. The Pythagorean Theorem is developed by reasoning with areas. The last two sections of the chapter deal with circumferences and areas of circles. Every section provides opportunities for students to sharpen their computational skills, a change of pace from the deductive work of the three preceding chapters.

### Objectives for Pages 216–223

1. To find the perimeter and area of a rectangle and a square.
2. To find the perimeter and area of a parallelogram.

### 1 • AREAS OF RECTANGLES (pp. 216–220)

### Teaching These Pages

Make sure students see that whenever a rectangle has sides with integral lengths, segments can be drawn to divide the rectangle into unit squares. Students will soon learn that after they count the squares in the first row, they automatically know the number of squares in each of the other rows. Hence, the total number of unit squares can be found by multiplying. For rectangles whose sides have lengths involving irrational numbers, the counting method breaks down. For this reason, we postulate the formula for the area of a rectangle: $A = bh$.

Note: In Postulate 12 on page 216, the term *base* is used to mean *base length*. This abbreviation is convenient and widely accepted. We occasionally shall use *base* to denote *base length* and *side* to denote *side length* when no confusion is likely.

### Chalkboard Examples

1. Find the area of each of the five non-overlapping rectangles. (see figure)
2. The sum of the areas of the five rectangles is ___?___. 35
3. In the complete rectangle, $b =$ ___?___ 7 and $h =$ ___?___. 5

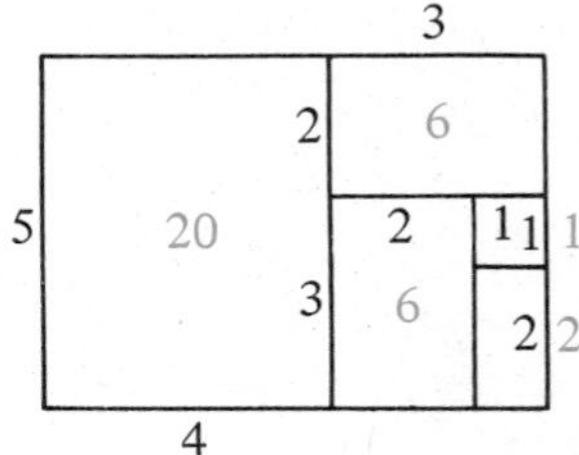


4. Find the area of the large rectangle by using the values of $b$ and $h$ found in Example 3. 35 Compare with your answer to Example 2. they are equal
5. Find the area of a square with sides 3 cm long. 9 cm$^2$

## Suggested Extension

**Each side of a square is 4 m long.**

1. The number of meters in the perimeter is __?__. 16
2. The number of square meters in the area is __?__. 16
3. The number of centimeters in the perimeter is __?__. 1600
4. The number of square centimeters in the area is __?__. 160,000
5. Is it proper to say: "The perimeter of this square is numerically equal to its area"? no, since the numbers depend on the unit of measure used

# 2 • AREAS OF PARALLELOGRAMS (pp. 221–223)

## Teaching These Pages

Plan to reinforce repeatedly the statement on page 221: the area of a parallelogram is not equal to the product of two consecutive sides (unless the parallelogram is a rectangle). Sometimes you will merely want to give a verbal reminder. As a stronger reminder, you might suggest that students study the three parallelograms above Classroom Practice Exercise 5 on page 222. They should see that these parallelograms cannot all have areas of (15 × 8) square units.

Some students may benefit from handling an actual stick model like that described on page 221.

## Chalkboard Examples

**For each parallelogram find a. the area, and b. the perimeter. When the area or the perimeter cannot be computed, write *cannot be found.***

**1.**

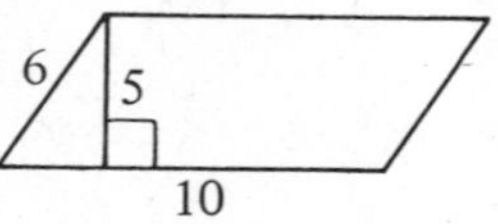


a. 50
b. 32

**2.**

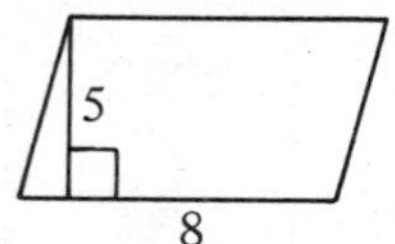


a. 40
b. can't be found

**3.**

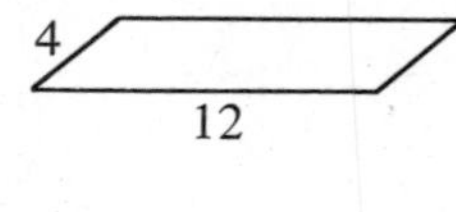


a. can't be found
b. 32

## Suggested Extension

1. Find the areas of the three parallelograms.
   I. 200 II. 200 III. 200

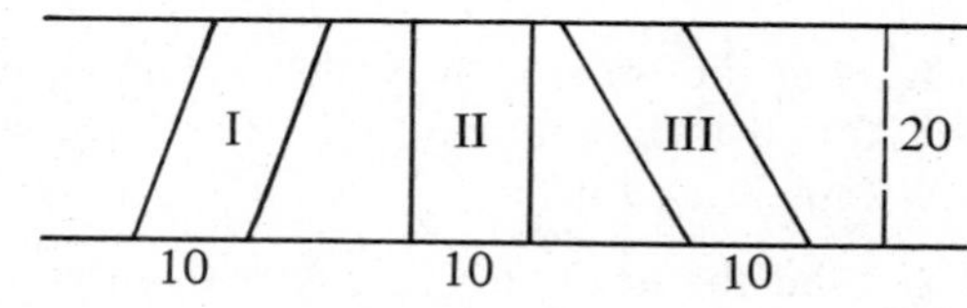

2. Can a parallelogram be drawn with $b = 12$ cm, $A = 24$ cm$^2$, and $p = 50$ cm? yes

3. Can a parallelogram be drawn with $b = 12$ cm, $A = 24$ cm$^2$, and $p = 25$ cm? no

## Objectives for Pages 225–233

1. To find the area of a triangle.
2. To find the area of a trapezoid.

## 3•AREAS OF TRIANGLES (pp. 225–227)

### Teaching These Pages

To develop the idea that the area of a triangle is half the area of a parallelogram, you might begin by having a student draw any triangle on the chalkboard. Complete a parallelogram and point out that the triangles are congruent, so that the original triangle has half the area of the parallelogram. Draw an altitude and emphasize that the triangle and the parallelogram have the same base length and height. The area formula follows easily from this point.

### Chalkboard Examples

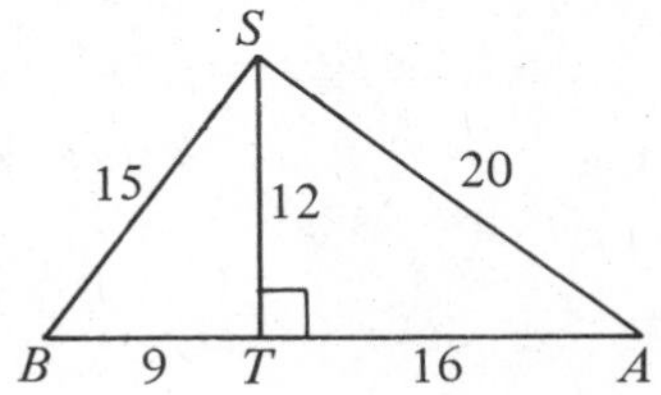


1. Area of $\triangle ATS =$ _?_ 96
2. Area of $\triangle BTS =$ _?_ 54
3. Add the areas found in Examples 1 and 2. Area of $\triangle ABS =$ _?_ 150
4. Using $AB$ as $b$ and $ST$ as $h$, Area of $\triangle ABS =$ _?_. $\frac{1}{2}(25)(12) = 150$
5. $\angle ASB$ is a right angle. Using $SB$ as $b$ and $SA$ as $h$, Area of $\triangle ABS =$ _?_. $\frac{1}{2}(20)(15) = 150$

**Find the area of the shaded triangle.**

6. 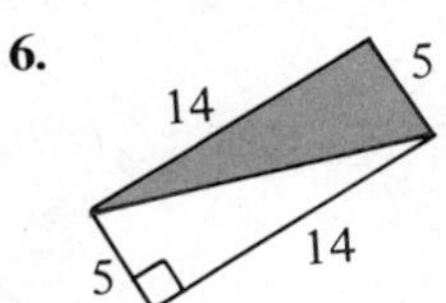

35

7. 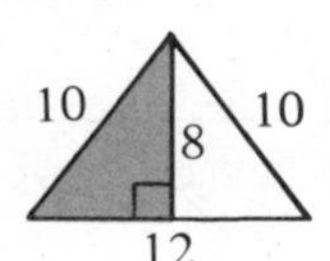

24

8. 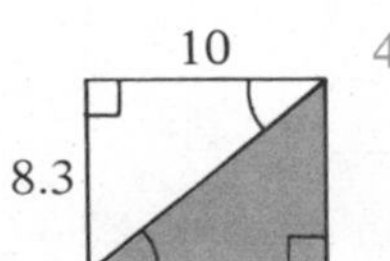

41.5

## Suggested Extension

The exercises below illustrate the idea of indirect proof. See Extra for Experts, pages 348–349.

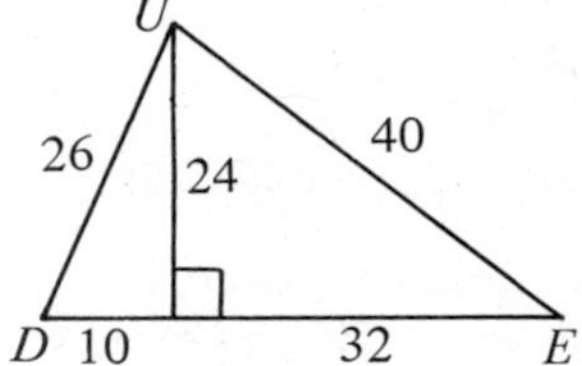


1. Using $DE$ as $b$, find the area of $\triangle DUE$. 504
2. Assume that $\angle DUE$ is a right angle. Using $UE$ as $b$ and $DU$ as $h$, find the area of $\triangle DUE$. 520
3. Compare the results of the first two exercises. Can $\angle DUE$ be a right angle? no

## 4 • AREAS OF TRAPEZOIDS (pp. 229–233)

### Teaching These Pages

You may wish to split the class into groups, each doing one of the Explorations on page 229. Then the class as a whole can focus on just one method, explained at the chalkboard.

### Chalkboard Examples

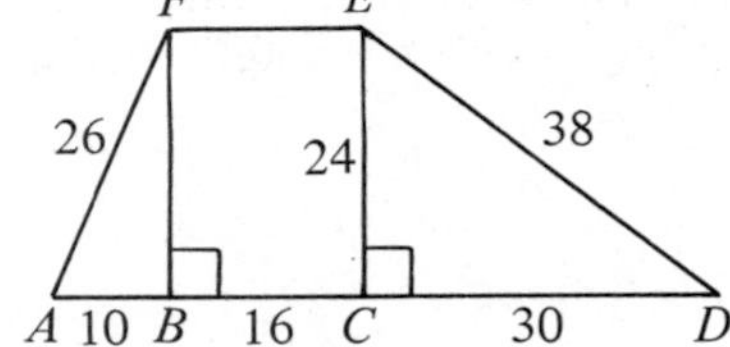


1. Area of $\triangle ABF$ = _?_ 120
2. Area of rectangle $BCEF$ = _?_ 384
3. Area of $\triangle DCE$ = _?_ 360
4. Add the areas found in Examples 1–3. Area of trapezoid $ADEF$ = _?_ 864
5. In trapezoid $ADEF$: $b_1$ = _?_; $b_2$ = _?_; $h$ = _?_ 56; 16; 24
6. Using the formula $A = \frac{1}{2}h(b_1 + b_2)$, find the area of trapezoid $ADEF$. 864

### Suggested Extension

**In trapezoid $QRST$, $\overline{QX}$ has been drawn parallel to $\overline{TS}$.**

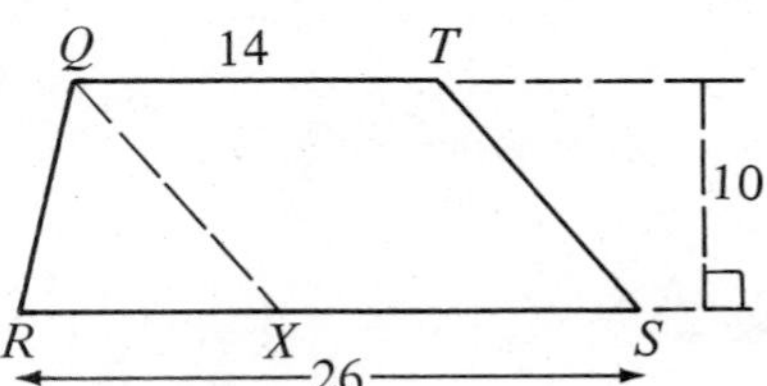


1. $XS$ = _?_ 14
2. $RX$ = _?_ 12
3. Area of $\triangle RXQ$ = _?_ 60
4. Area of $\square XSTQ$ = _?_ 140
5. Add the areas found in Exercises 3–4. Area of trapezoid $QRST$ = _?_ 200

6. Using the formula $\frac{1}{2}h(b_1 + b_2)$, find the area of trapezoid $QRST$. 200

## Objectives for Pages 234–240

1. To find the hypotenuse of a right triangle, given the legs.
2. To find a leg of a right triangle, given the hypotenuse and the other leg.
3. To determine, given the three sides of a triangle, whether the triangle is acute, right, or obtuse.

## 5•THE PYTHAGOREAN THEOREM (pp. 234–237)

### Teaching These Pages

You might begin by having a student draw any right triangle on the chalkboard. Then you can build the rest of the figure shown at the bottom of page 234 step-by-step. Use ruler and protractor to draw the diagram so that students aren't distracted by straightedge and compass constructions.

The text uses the symbol "≐" to mean "is approximately equal to" in situations involving irrational square roots. Another symbol with the same meaning is "≈".

The Puzzles & Things feature on page 241 provides another area-based demonstration of the Pythagorean Theorem.

### Chalkboard Examples

**Find the indicated values. When necessary, use the square root table on page 465 and round to the nearest tenth.**

1. $OB$ 5
2. $OC$ 13
3. $OD$ 10.2
4. $PR$ 1.4
5. $PS$ 1.7
6. $PT$ 2

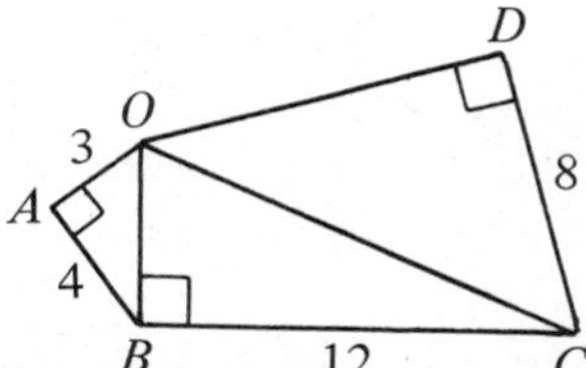


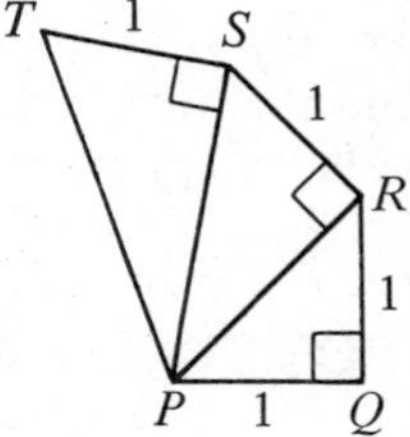


### Suggested Extension

Have students use the Pythagorean Theorem to prove the validity of the HL Theorem (page 116).

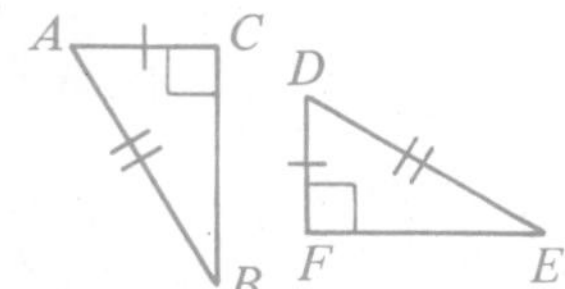


*Strategy:* (1) *Given:* $AB = DE$ and $BC = EF$
(2) $(AC)^2 = (AB)^2 - (BC)^2$; $(DF)^2 = (DE)^2 - (EF)^2$
(3) Subst. Postulate: $(AC)^2 = (DF)^2$, so $AC = DF$
(4) SSS Postulate: $\triangle ABC \cong \triangle DEF$

## 6•CONVERSE OF THE PYTHAGOREAN THEOREM (pp. 238–240)

### Teaching These Pages

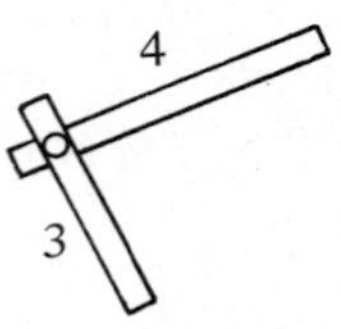


The text does not prove the theorem which underlies the strategy on page 239. You might use a 4-unit stick and a 3-unit stick fastened together to offer the class some visual evidence in support of the theorem. By holding one stick stationary and rotating the other, you can show how the distance between the free ends determines the angle which the sticks make. Only when the free ends are 5 units apart do we have a right angle.

Many students will see that the angle between the sticks determines the distance between the free ends (SAS Postulate). Hence, the converse strategy can be used to determine whether $c^2 < a^2 + b^2$, $c^2 = a^2 + b^2$, or $c^2 > a^2 + b^2$.

### Chalkboard Examples

**The lengths of the three sides of a triangle are given. Is the triangle a *right* triangle, an *acute* triangle, or an *obtuse* triangle?**

**1.** 9, 12, 16 obtuse

**2.** 5, 12, 13 right

**3.** 4, 4, 6 obtuse

**4.** 11, 60, 61 right

**5.** 10, 10, 14 acute

**6.** 15, 112, 113 right

### Objectives for Pages 242–250

**1.** To find the circumference, radius, or diameter of a circle.
**2.** To find the area, radius, or diameter of a circle.
**3.** To state an approximation for $\pi$, correct to the nearest hundredth.

## 7•CIRCUMFERENCES OF CIRCLES (pp. 242–246)

### Teaching These Pages

You might like to have some student volunteers measure the diameter and circumference of circular objects. When different students report that their measurements of a basketball hoop, a tractor tire, a pie tin, a coffee can, and so on, all support the statement $\frac{C}{d} \doteq 3.1$, all students should be convinced that $\frac{C}{d}$ really does have just one value—whatever circles are used.

### Chalkboard Examples

**Complete the table about circles. When necessary, express answers in terms of $\pi$.**

| | 1. | 2. | 3. | 4. | 5. | 6. | |
|---|---|---|---|---|---|---|---|
| $r$ | 5 | ? | ? | 12 | ? | ? | 6, 9, 4.5, 5.5 |
| $d$ | ? | 12 | ? | ? | 9 | ? | 10, 18, 24, 11 |
| $C$ | ? | ? | $18\pi$ | ? | ? | $11\pi$ | $10\pi$, $12\pi$, $24\pi$, $9\pi$ |

**Complete. Use 3.14 for $\pi$.**

7. When $r = 7.21$, $C =$ __?__ (correct to tenths). 45.3
8. When $C = 10$, $r =$ __?__ (correct to tenths). 1.6

## 8 • AREAS OF CIRCLES (pp. 247–250)

### Teaching These Pages

Some students enjoy subjecting the formula $A = \pi r^2$ to a test. Have them draw circles of various radii on graph paper. They can estimate the areas of the circles by counting the unit squares that lie entirely inside the circle or appear to have at least half their area inside the circle. Then they can compare the counts to the values obtained for $A$ using the formula $A = \pi r^2$.

### Chalkboard Examples

**Copy and complete the table about circles. When necessary, express answers in terms of $\pi$.**

| | 1. | 2. | 3. | 4. | 5. | 6. | |
|---|---|---|---|---|---|---|---|
| $r$ | 3 | ? | ? | $\frac{3}{4}$ | ? | ? | 7, 4, 2.5, $\frac{4}{7}$ |
| $d$ | ? | 14 | ? | ? | 5 | ? | 6, 8, $1\frac{1}{2}$, $1\frac{1}{7}$ |
| $A$ | ? | ? | $16\pi$ | ? | ? | $\frac{16\pi}{49}$ | $9\pi$, $49\pi$, $\frac{9\pi}{16}$, $6.25\pi$ |

7. Find the area of a circle whose circumference is $10\pi$. $25\pi$
8. Using 3.14 for $\pi$, find the area—correct to the nearest integer—of a circle whose radius is 7. 154

## Chapter 7. Ratios and Proportions

In this chapter, we have two broad goals. First, we seek to teach soundly the fundamental ideas of ratio and proportion which are crucial to the study of similarity in Chapter 8. Second, we seek to show applications of ratio and proportion which are not part of the traditional study of similarity. These applications include the reading and making of maps, scale drawings, and mechanical drawings. Students should enjoy these ideas and find them helpful in their lives.

### Objectives for Pages 260–269

1. To find the ratios of numbers and the ratios of lengths of segments.
2. To write and solve proportions.
3. To solve problems using proportions.

### 1•RATIOS (pp. 260–262)

#### Teaching These Pages

Even if your students are good at algebra, it would be wise to review the concept of ratio and to run through both methods of Example 2 on page 260. Classroom Practice Exercises 13–15 and Written Exercises 17–28 are particularly important preparation for work with similar figures. The Consumer Corner on page 275 discusses an important ratio in most everyone's life:

$$\text{Consumer Price Index} = \frac{\text{current total price of selection of typical consumer purchases}}{\text{total price during "base year"}}$$

#### Chalkboard Examples

**Express each ratio in simplest form.**

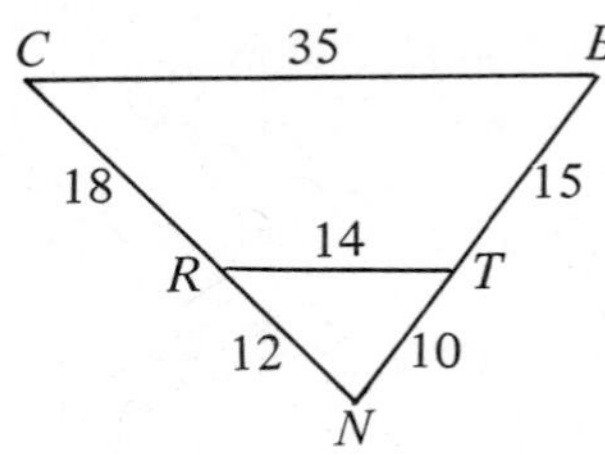


1. $\frac{RT}{CB}$ $\frac{2}{5}$
2. $\frac{BT}{TN}$ $\frac{3}{2}$
3. $\frac{BT}{BN}$ $\frac{3}{5}$
4. $\frac{RN}{CR}$ $\frac{2}{3}$
5. $\frac{RN}{CN}$ $\frac{2}{5}$
6. $\frac{TN}{RN}$ $\frac{5}{6}$
7. $\frac{\text{Perimeter of } \triangle RTN}{\text{Perimeter of } \triangle CBN}$ $\frac{2}{5}$

**Express in simplest form:**
**a. the ratio of the area of the shaded part to the area of the unshaded part**
**b. the ratio of the area of the shaded part to the total area.**

**8.** 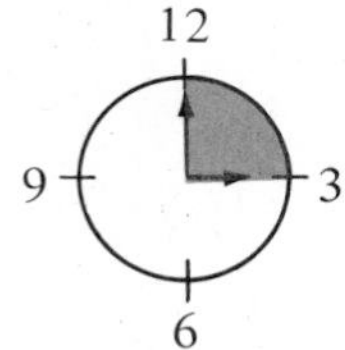


a. $\frac{1}{3}$ b. $\frac{1}{4}$

**9.** 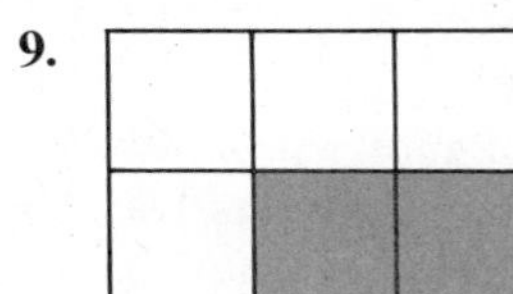

a. $\frac{1}{2}$ b. $\frac{1}{3}$

## 2 • PROPORTIONS (pp. 263–266)

### Teaching These Pages

After explaining that a proportion is an equation that states two ratios are equal, try Classroom Practice Exercises 1–4. Then discuss the four properties of proportions. (These properties are given names for reference purposes, but it is not necessary that students learn these names.) Classroom Practice Exercises 5–18 and the Chalkboard Examples below drill these four properties.

### Chalkboard Examples

**Complete each statement.**

**1.** If $\frac{4}{12} = \frac{1}{3}$, then $\frac{4}{1} = \frac{?}{?}$ and $\frac{3}{12} = \frac{?}{?}$. $\frac{12}{3}$; $\frac{1}{4}$

**2.** If $\frac{x}{y} = \frac{3}{5}$, then $\frac{x+y}{y} = \frac{?}{?}$. $\frac{8}{5}$

**3.** If $\frac{2}{12} = \frac{3}{18}$, then $2 \times 18 =$ _?_ $\times$ _?_. 12; 3

**4.** If $\frac{a}{b} = \frac{4}{5}$, then $\frac{b}{a} = \frac{?}{?}$ and $5a =$ _?_. $\frac{5}{4}$; $4b$

**5.** If $\frac{13}{2} = \frac{x}{y}$, then $\frac{x+y}{y} = \frac{?}{?}$ and $\frac{x-y}{y} = \frac{?}{?}$. $\frac{15}{2}$; $\frac{11}{2}$

**6.** If $\frac{3}{a} = \frac{4}{b}$, then $\frac{3}{4} = \frac{?}{?}$ and $\frac{b}{a} = \frac{?}{?}$. $\frac{a}{b}$; $\frac{4}{3}$

**7.** If $\frac{2}{x} = \frac{5}{15}$, then $5x =$ _?_ and $x =$ _?_. 30; 6

## 3•USING PROPORTIONS (pp. 267–269)

### Teaching These Pages

This section applies proportions to the algebraic solution of word problems. Several exercises reinforce students' work with area in Chapter 6. The Suggested Extension for this lesson presents two very *non*standard proportion problems. Students should find them both entertaining and valuable in showing the use of proportions in estimation.

### Chalkboard Examples

1. Mr. Garcia used 30 liters of gasoline for driving to and from work last month. Estimate how many liters he uses in a year of driving to and from work. 360 liters
2. In a certain school with 1000 students, 10 students chosen at random are asked for whom they are going to vote for student council president. Seven of these students say "Smith." Estimate the number of votes that Smith will receive in the election. 700 votes

### Suggested Extension

1. Guide students through the following procedure, which estimates the number of ping-pong balls needed to fill your classroom.
   - **a.** Fill a small box with ping-pong balls. Count the balls.
   - **b.** Find the volume of the box and of your classroom by determining the length, width, and height and using the formula $V = lwh$.
   - **c.** Solve the proportion

$$\frac{\text{number of balls in box}}{x} = \frac{\text{volume of box}}{\text{volume of classroom}}$$

2. Have students discuss a procedure for estimating the number of hot dogs eaten in the entire nation in one day.

### Objectives for Pages 270–274

1. To use maps and scale drawings.
2. To make maps and scale drawings.

## 4•MAPS AND SCALE DRAWINGS (pp. 270–272)

### Teaching These Pages

The map of Lakeville and the floor plan of the Briggs home (pages 270–271) are appropriate classroom examples for this topic. Note that both the

Classroom Practice Exercises and the Written Exercises refer to the map and floor plan on pages 270 and 271. Emphasize to students that different scales are used to interpret the same diagrams. Hence, for instance, the kitchen has different "real" dimensions in the Written Exercises than it has in the Classroom Practice Exercises.

### Chalkboard Example

Have students name 3 or 4 fictitious cities and place them as dots at random on the chalkboard. Then arbitrarily set the distance in kilometers (or miles) between any two of the cities. The diagram at right shows one possible situation.

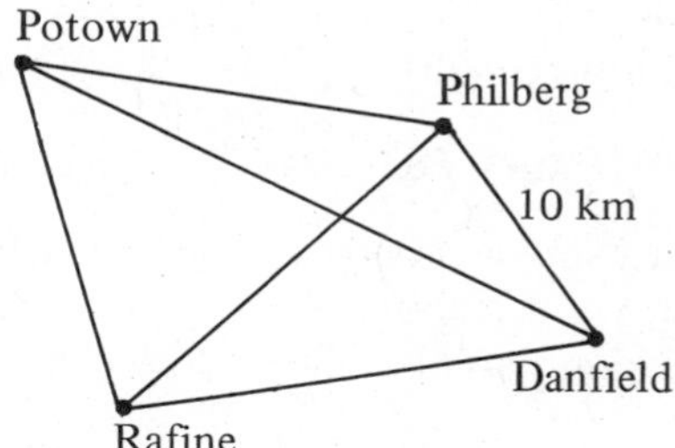


Then have students:

1. Measure the distances between the pairs of dots on the chalkboard.
2. Calculate the scale factor.
3. Determine the "real" distances between all pairs of cities.

## 5•MAKING MAPS AND SCALE DRAWINGS (pp. 273–274)

### Teaching These Pages

An excellent project for teaching the ideas of scale drawings is to have small groups of students work together to make scale drawings of your classroom. If there are not enough tape measures or measuring sticks available, students can measure dimensions in paces or shoe lengths. For example, your classroom might be "30 shoe lengths by 20 shoe lengths." You may wish to point out that no matter what unit of measurement is used, the dimensions of the classroom will be in the same ratio.

The Applications feature on page 277 illustrates how the concepts presented in this section can be applied to mechanical drawing.

### Chalkboard Example

Make a map using the following information.

**a.** Johnston is 40 km north of Sayville.
**b.** El Placido is 20 km east of Sayville.
**c.** Everton is 32 km northeast of Johnstown.
**d.** Sherborn is 32 km west of Everton.

(At the chalkboard, use the scale 2 cm : 1 km. Students may use the scale 0.25 cm : 1 km to produce maps which fit on standard size notebook paper.)

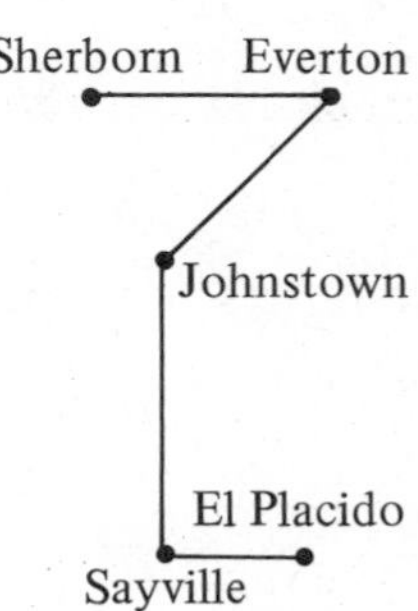

## *Chapter 8. Similar Polygons*

Students have already been introduced to similar figures in their study of scale drawings and maps (Chapter 7, Sections 4 and 5). In this chapter, students first learn how to decide whether two figures are similar. Then they use proportions to calculate lengths in similar figures. Students learn the important case of a line parallel to one side of a triangle cutting off a similar triangle. Finally, they use the relationships involving the perimeters and areas of similar figures.

### Objectives for Pages 282–291

1. To recognize similar polygons and use their properties.
2. To use the AA Postulate.
3. To find missing parts of similar triangles.

### 1 • DEFINING SIMILAR POLYGONS (pp. 282–286)

#### Teaching These Pages

You might begin this lesson by drawing the pairs of figures shown in the Chalkboard Examples below, and asking which pairs are similar. Then ask the same question for the pairs of figures in Classroom Practice Exercises 1–3. Students usually can recognize similar figures even if they can't formulate a definition.

Such a lesson might lead to students making up a definition of similar figures. The examples they have discussed should make clear to them why *both* of the following conditions are necessary:

(1) Corresponding angles are equal
(2) Corresponding sides are in proportion

This definition applies to polygons, but not to figures like circles. You might ask students which of several circles are similar. If you remind them that "similar figures have the same shape," they should conclude successfully that *all* circles are similar.

#### Chalkboard Examples

**State why the polygons are, or are not, similar.**

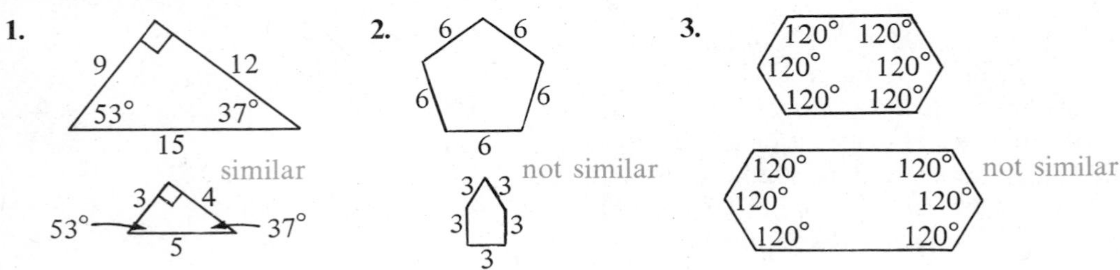

**In each example, the two polygons are similar. Find the values of $x$ and $y$.**

**4.** 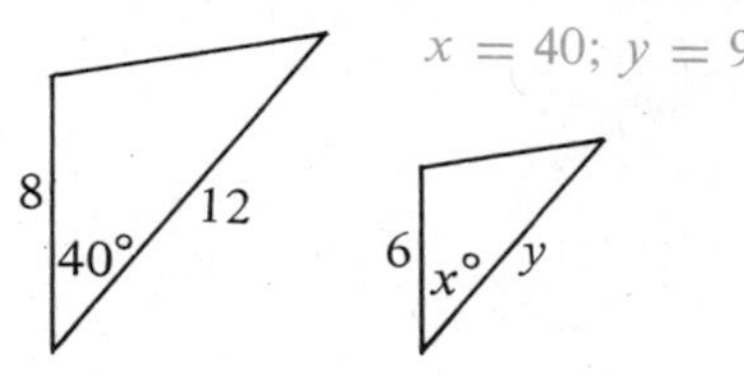

$x = 40$; $y = 9$

**5.** 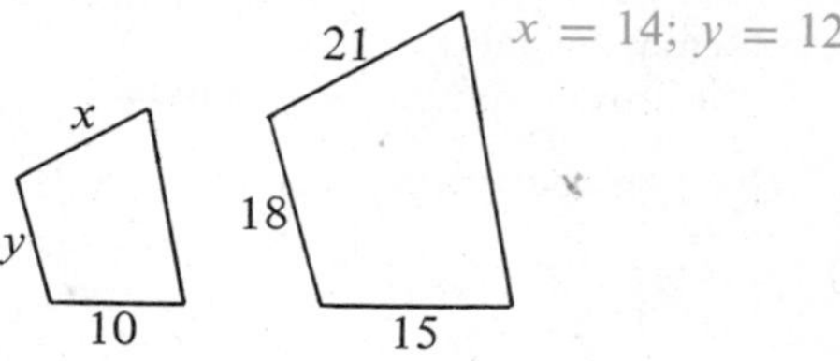

$x = 14$; $y = 12$

**6.** What is the scale factor of two congruent polygons? 1

**7.** If the symbol $\sim$ is used for similar polygons, why is the symbol $\cong$ used for congruent polygons? Congruent figures are both similar and of equal size.

**8.** The sides of a quadrilateral are 6 cm, 9 cm, 12 cm, and 15 cm long. The longest side of a similar quadrilateral is 20 cm long. How long are its other sides? 8 cm, 12 cm, 16 cm

### Suggested Extension

Students may find the game Encounter (page 286) challenging and entertaining. To "solve" the game, a student must realize that player B traces a figure which is similar (with scale factor 2:1) to that of player A. You might vary the rules of the game as follows:

1. Player B draws a segment three times as long as player A's segment.
2. Player B draws a segment in the *opposite* direction and twice as long as player A's segment.

(*Warning:* In the second variation, the "meeting point" is the point $X$ on $\overline{AB}$ such that $BX = 2AX$. If this point $X$ does not have integral coordinates, it will be impossible to force player B to move to the same point as player A.)

## 2•THE AA POSTULATE (pp. 287–291)

### Teaching These Pages

We suggest that you begin this lesson with the remarks and the Explorations on page 287. These Explorations should make the AA Postulate seem reasonable to students. The AA method of showing triangles to be similar can be proved as a theorem instead of being postulated. However, the proof is so involved that it seems wise to postulate the result and have students learn it by *using* it.

Note that Written Exercise 16 proves the special case of similar triangles treated in the next section. Written Exercise 24 proves a result which will help students understand the area ratio of similar triangles. (See Section 5.)

## Chalkboard Examples

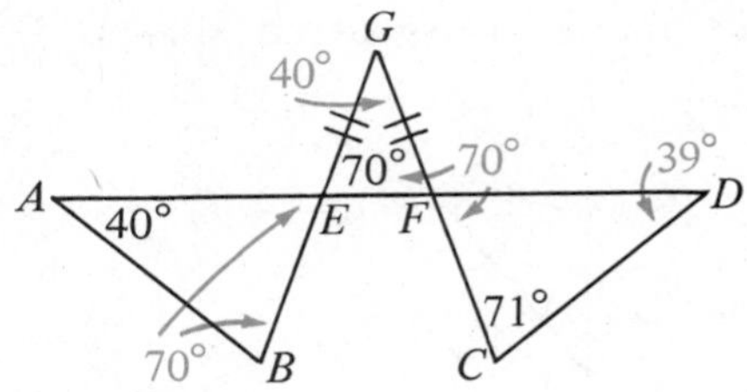


**1.** Find the measures of all angles in the three triangles. (see figure)

**2.** Which of the triangles are similar?
$\triangle ABE \sim \triangle GEF$

**Supply the reasons to complete the proof.**

**3.** *Given:* $\overline{PQ} \parallel \overline{ST}$

*Prove:* $\frac{PR}{TR} = \frac{QR}{SR}$

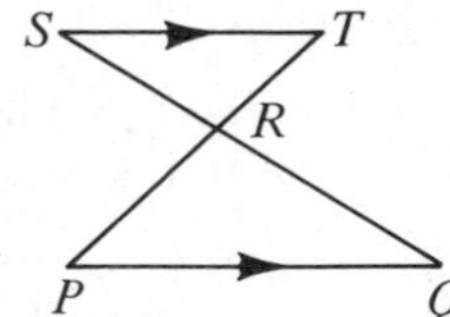


| | |
|---|---|
| 1. $\overline{PQ} \parallel \overline{ST}$ | 1. __?__ Given |
| 2. $\angle P = \angle T$; $\angle Q = \angle S$ | 2. __?__ Alt. int. angles |
| 3. $\triangle PQR \sim \triangle TSR$ | 3. __?__ AA Postulate |
| 4. $\frac{PR}{TR} = \frac{QR}{SR}$ | 4. __?__ Def. of similar triangles |

## Suggested Extension

To prove that two polygons are similar, one must, in general, show two things:

(1) Corresponding angles are equal
(2) Corresponding sides are proportional

The AA postulate asserts that (1) alone suffices to prove that two *triangles* are similar. The activity outlined below should convince students that (2) alone also suffices to prove similarity in the case of triangles.

1. Draw any triangle *ABC*. (drawings are omitted)
2. Draw or construct $\triangle DEF$ with sides twice as long.
3. Draw or construct $\triangle GHI$ with sides three times as long.
4. Draw or construct $\triangle JKL$ with sides 3.5 times as long.
5. Use a protractor to measure the angles of all the triangles. Are corresponding angles equal? yes Are the triangles similar? yes

## Objectives for Pages 293–303

**1.** To use similar triangles involving parallel segments.
**2.** To use the Triangle Proportionality Theorem.
**3.** To find the perimeters and areas of similar polygons.

## 3•A SPECIAL CASE OF SIMILAR TRIANGLES (pp. 293–294)

### Teaching These Pages

Of all the circumstances in which similar triangles appear, the most common is the one discussed in this section. Make a point to assign or discuss Written Exercise 16 of the previous section, since this exercise proves the key result needed in this section:

> If a line through two sides of a triangle is parallel to the third side, then it cuts off a triangle similar to the original triangle.

When using this result, students commonly make the error of using segments which are not sides of triangles, but only parts of sides.

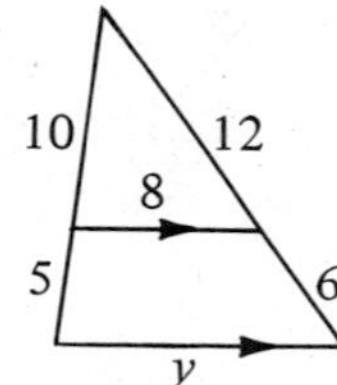


Common Student Error:

$$\frac{10}{5} = \frac{8}{y}, \text{ so } y = 4$$

The Triangle Proportionality Theorem (Section 4) will enable us to draw conclusions about parts of sides of triangles. For now, it is best to emphasize to students that we can make proportions only with the lengths of *complete* sides of similar triangles. Some students may need to make additional diagrams in order to identify correctly the corresponding sides.

### Chalkboard Examples

**Complete each statement. Then find the values of $x$ and $y$.**

**1.**

$$\frac{x}{12} = \frac{18}{?} = \frac{y}{?}$$

30 20

$x = 7.2;\ y = 12$

**2.**

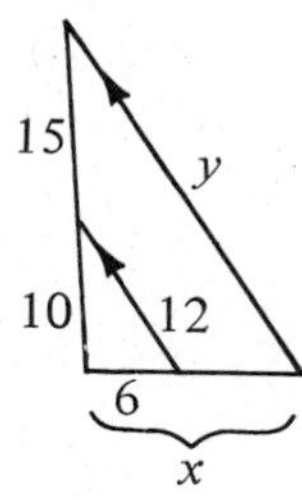


$$\frac{x}{6} = \frac{?}{10} = \frac{y}{?}$$

25 12

$x = 15;\ y = 30$

**3.**

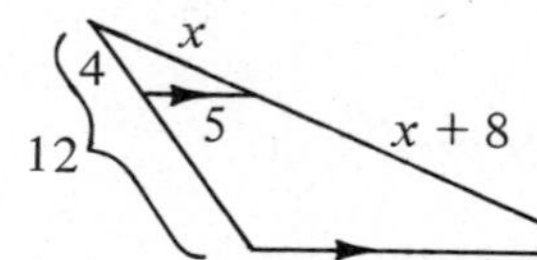


$$\frac{x}{2x + 8} = \frac{?}{12} = \frac{5}{?}$$

4 y

$x = 8;\ y = 15$

## 4 • THE TRIANGLE PROPORTIONALITY THEOREM (pp. 295–299)

### Teaching These Pages

In the previous sections, students have worked only with complete sides of similar polygons. Theorem 1 in this section deals with *parts* of two different sides of a triangle. You might summarize the situation with the diagram and discussion below.

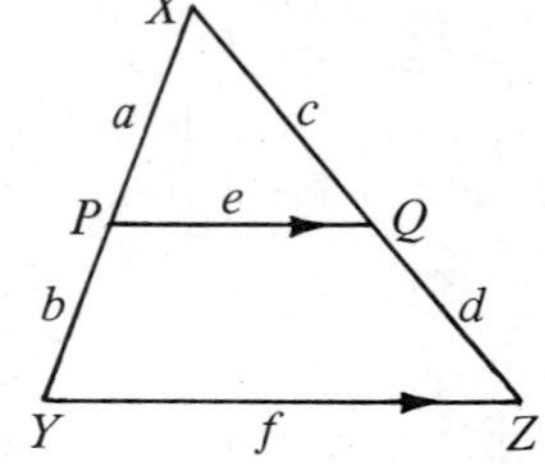


A. When dealing with $\overline{XY}$ and $\overline{XZ}$, the two sides intersected by the parallel $\overline{PQ}$, we may form proportions using whole sides or parts of sides.

1. The top-to-whole ratios are equal:

$$\frac{a}{a+b} = \frac{c}{c+d}$$

2. The top-to-bottom ratios are equal:

$$\frac{a}{b} = \frac{c}{d}$$

B. When dealing with the parallel sides, we must not form proportions with parts of sides. We must form ratios of complete sides of similar triangles.

$$\frac{e}{f} = \frac{a}{a+b} = \frac{c}{c+d}$$

### Chalkboard Examples

**Find the values of $x$ and $y$.**

**1.** 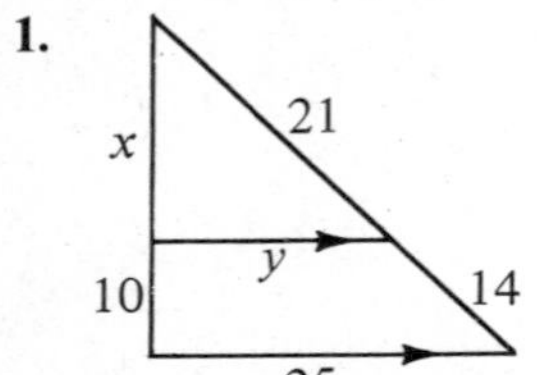


$x = 15$; $y = 15$

**2.** 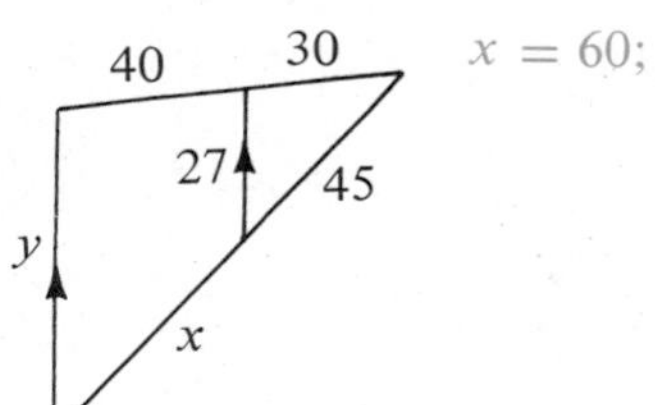


$x = 60$; $y = 63$

**3.** 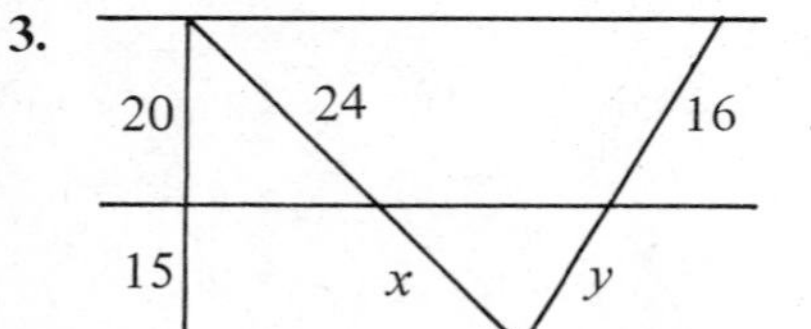


$x = 18$; $y = 12$

**4.** 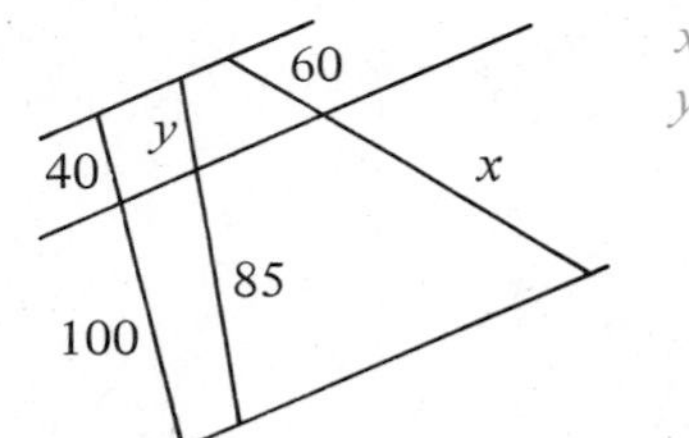


$x = 150$; $y = 34$

## Suggested Extension

1. An extension of the corollary on page 296 asserts:

   If three or more parallel lines cut off equal segments on one transversal, then they cut off equal segments on any transversal.

   A page of lined notebook paper has a set of lines meeting this description. Challenge students to use notebook paper to divide a segment 10 cm long into 3, 4, or 5 equal segments.

2. Have students supply reasons to complete the following proof of the converse of the Triangle Proportionality Theorem.

   *Given:* $\frac{b}{a} = \frac{d}{c}$

   *Prove:* $\overline{PQ} \parallel \overline{YZ}$

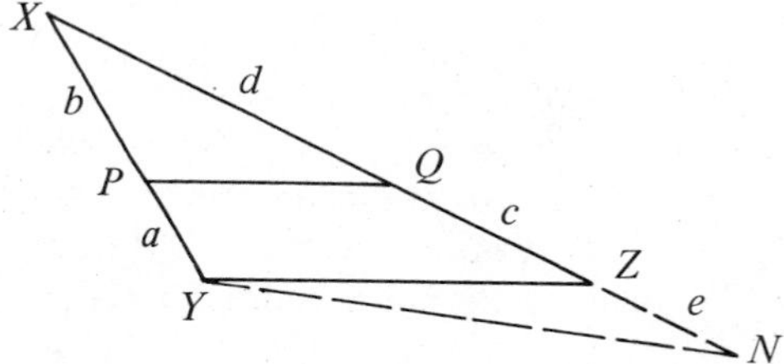


| Statements | Reasons |
|---|---|
| 1. Draw $\overline{YN} \parallel \overline{PQ}$, as shown. (We wish to show that point $N$ is the same as point $Z$ so that "$\overline{YN} \parallel \overline{PQ}$" becomes "$\overline{YZ} \parallel \overline{PQ}$.") | 1. _?_ Construction 5, page 72 |
| 2. $\frac{b}{a} = \frac{d+e}{c}$ | 2. _?_ Triangle Proportionality Thm. |
| 3. $\frac{b}{a} = \frac{d}{c}$ | 3. _?_ Given |
| 4. $e = 0$ | 4. _?_ Subst., Subtr., Mult. Post. |
| 5. $N$ coincides with $Z$ and $\overline{YZ} \parallel \overline{PQ}$ | 5. _?_ Ruler Postulate |

Point out that the Midpoints Theorem (page 206) is a special case of this theorem. In the Midpoints Theorem, $a = b$ and $c = d$.

## 5 • PERIMETERS AND AREAS (pp. 300–303)

### Teaching These Pages

You may wish to let students discover for themselves the relationships described in this section. To start simply, draw the following pairs of rectangles and have students calculate **a.** the ratio of the perimeters and **b.** the ratio of the areas.

$$\frac{\text{perimeter of I}}{\text{perimeter of II}} = \frac{8}{16} = \frac{1}{2}$$

$$\frac{\text{area of I}}{\text{area of II}} = \frac{3}{12} = \frac{1}{4}$$

$$\frac{\text{perimeter of III}}{\text{perimeter of IV}} = \frac{2(a + ka)}{2(b + kb)} = \frac{(2k + 2)a}{(2k + 2)b} = \frac{a}{b}$$

$$\frac{\text{area of III}}{\text{area of IV}} = \frac{a(ka)}{b(kb)} = \frac{ka^2}{kb^2} = \frac{a^2}{b^2}$$

The work with the second pair of rectangles proves Theorem 2 for the special case of rectangles.

Students may continue their investigation by guessing (or calculating) the perimeter and area ratios of two similar rectangles with scale factor 1:3, or 1:4, or 2:3. Try different scale factors until students get the idea. The billboard illustrated on page 300 provides yet another example of similar rectangles.

You might want to have students investigate other polygons, or simply tell them that the principles they've discovered are true for all pairs of similar polygons. The Calculator Corner on page 304 provides practice with perimeters and areas of equilateral triangles, any two of which are similar. Optional Section 7 of Chapter 10 extends the consideration of similar figures to solids.

## Chalkboard Examples

**In each example, there is a pair of similar figures. Find a. the ratio of the perimeters and b. the ratio of the areas.**

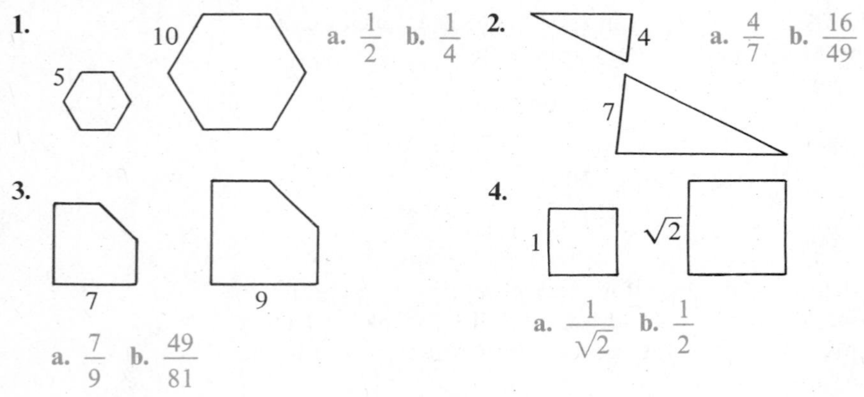

**1.** a. $\frac{1}{2}$ b. $\frac{1}{4}$

**2.** a. $\frac{4}{7}$ b. $\frac{16}{49}$

**3.** a. $\frac{7}{9}$ b. $\frac{49}{81}$

**4.** a. $\frac{1}{\sqrt{2}}$ b. $\frac{1}{2}$

5. *Given:* $\triangle PST \sim \triangle PQR$. Find **a.** the ratio of the perimeters of $\triangle PST$ and $\triangle PQR$ and **b.** the ratio of the areas.

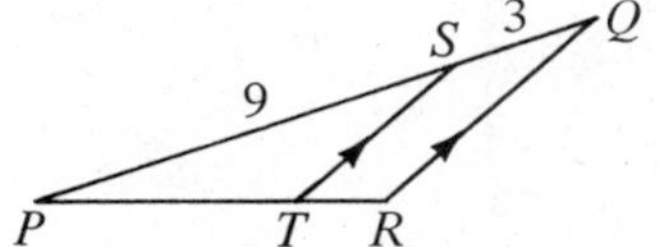


**a.** $\frac{3}{4}$

**b.** $\frac{9}{16}$

## Suggested Extension

Point out to students that if we calculated the volumes of the trash cans on the billboard on page 300, the ratio would be 1:8. In general, we can add a clause to Theorem 1:

> If two similar solids have a scale factor $a:b$, then the ratio of their volumes is $a^3:b^3$.

Some students might like to verify this fact using pairs of similar rectangular solids and the formula $V = lwh$.

## Chapter 9. Circles

Circumferences and areas of circles were treated in Chapter 6. In this chapter, other aspects of circles are studied. The measures of angles are calculated using the measures of intercepted arcs. Relationships among radii, chords, and tangents are developed. Because the theorem about the products of the lengths of the segments of two intersecting chords seems rather unlikely (it runs contrary to the intuition of most people), the theorem is treated in detail.

### Objectives for Pages 314–326

1. To use terms related to circles.
2. To construct a tangent to a circle at a given point on the circle.
3. To apply theorems relating tangents and radii.
4. To find measures of minor arcs, major arcs, and central angles.

### 1•BASIC TERMS (pp. 314–317)

#### Teaching These Pages

Brief, fast-moving drills on vocabulary will ease the learning process for students and promote retention. You might draw a circle and then add a radius, a chord, and so on, one at a time. Remind students that we use the term radius in two senses, to denote a certain segment and to denote a length. Both senses are equally correct.

#### Chalkboard Examples

**State whether the figure named (though not necessarily drawn in the diagram) is a chord of circle *O*. If the figure has another name, give that name.**

1. $\overline{OA}$ no; radius
2. $\overleftrightarrow{AB}$ no; secant
3. $\overline{AC}$ yes; diameter
4. $\overleftrightarrow{OA}$ no; secant
5. $\overrightarrow{AB}$ no
6. $\overline{BC}$ yes

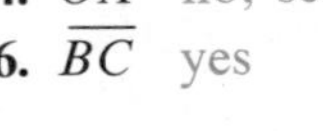

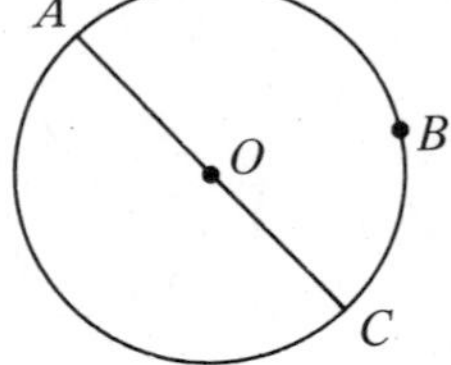


#### Suggested Extension

**Point *X* lies on a sphere.**

1. How many chords of the sphere contain point *X*? an indefinite number

2. How many diameters of the sphere contain point *X*? one

## 2•TANGENTS (pp. 318–322)

### Teaching These Pages

The displayed statements on page 318 are referred to as theorems, since they can be proved. We recommend that you not use class time for proofs. Most students accept these statements as being quite reasonable without needing a formal argument. Caution students to distinguish carefully between a common internal tangent and the common tangent of internally tangent circles. As the figures on page 319 illustrate, these phrases apply to quite different situations.

### Chalkboard Examples

**$\overleftrightarrow{AB}$ is externally tangent to $\odot X$ and $\odot Y$.**

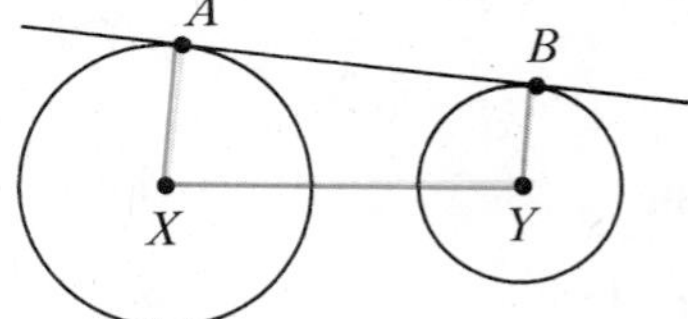


1. Copy the diagram. Draw $\overline{XA}$ and $\overline{XB}$.
2. $\overline{XA}$ _?_ $\overline{AB}$; $\overline{YB}$ _?_ $AB$ $\perp$; $\perp$
3. $\overline{XA}$ _?_ $\overline{YB}$ $\parallel$
4. Draw $\overline{XY}$. What kind of quadrilateral is $AXYB$? trapezoid
5. Suppose $\odot X$ and $\odot Y$ were intersecting circles. Would your answers to Examples 3–5 be different? no

### Suggested Extension

Construct a circle $O$ and draw a diameter $CD$. Construct a diameter $UV$ that is perpendicular to $\overline{CD}$. Construct lines tangent to the circle at points $C$, $U$, $D$, and $V$. What kind of quadrilateral is formed? square

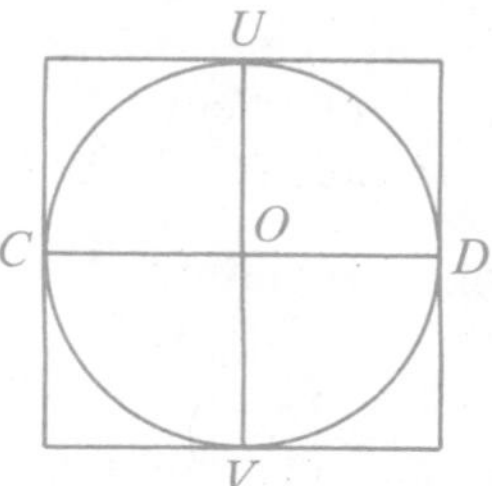


## 3•ARCS AND CENTRAL ANGLES (pp. 323–326)

### Teaching These Pages

You might want to show students that the use of a protractor is based on the idea that a minor arc and its central angle have the same degree measure. Explain that when we use a protractor to draw a 40° angle, we are really drawing a central angle which cuts off an arc with measure 40° in a certain circle.

## Chalkboard Examples

**$\overline{AC}$ is a diameter of $\odot O$. Find the measure of:**

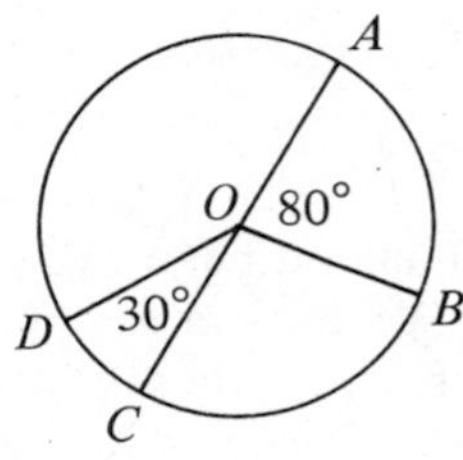


**1.** $\overset{\frown}{BC}$ 100°

**2.** $\overset{\frown}{DA}$ 150°

**3.** $\overset{\frown}{BD}$ 130°

**4.** $\overset{\frown}{BAD}$ 230°

**5.** $\angle AOD$ 150°

**6.** $\angle BOC$ 100°

## Objectives for Pages 328–337

1. To apply theorems about chords and arcs.
2. To find the measure of an inscribed angle, given the measure of its intercepted arc.
3. To find the measure of an angle formed by a chord and a tangent, given the measure of its intercepted arc.

# 4•CHORDS (pp. 328–332)

## Teaching These Pages

We suggest that you have students discover the properties described in Theorems 5, 6, and 7 by having them do the Explorations on page 328. You might challenge more advanced students to devise proofs of these theorems. Written Exercise 30 outlines a proof of Theorem 7.

The construction in the Puzzles & Things feature on page 346 can be justified using the converse of Theorem 7:

> The perpendicular bisector of a chord passes through the center of the circle.

## Chalkboard Examples

**In $\odot O$, $JY = KY$. Copy the figure, then draw $\overline{OJ}$, $\overline{OY}$, and $\overline{OK}$.**

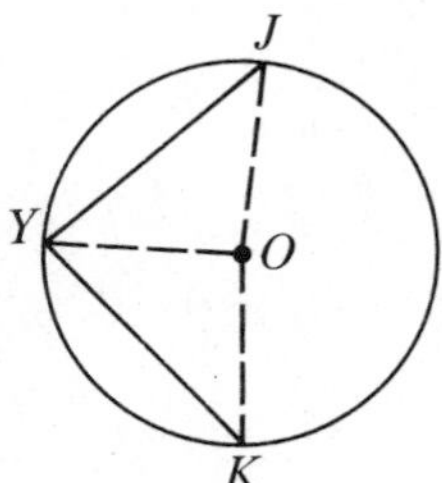


**1.** Why is $\triangle JOY \cong \triangle KOY$? SSS Post.

**2.** Why is $\angle JOY = \angle KOY$? Corr. parts

**3.** Why is $\overset{\frown}{JY} = \overset{\frown}{KY}$? Thm. 3 *or* Thm. 5

## Suggested Extension

Suppose you wish to circumscribe a circle about a square. How would you find the center of the circumscribed circle? How would you find the center of the inscribed circle? What can you say about these two circles? The circles have the same center. The larger circle has twice the area of the smaller circle.

## 5 • INSCRIBED ANGLES (pp. 333–337)

### Teaching These Pages

You may want to review what it means for a triangle to be inscribed in a circle. Students should realize that when $\triangle ABC$ is inscribed in a circle, each of the angles $A$, $B$, and $C$ is inscribed in the circle. For example, if side $BC$ is erased—except for endpoints $B$ and $C$—then inscribed $\angle A$ remains.

Note that the omission of the term "measure" simplifies the statements of Theorems 8 and 9 in this section and Theorems 10 and 11 in Section 6.

### Chalkboard Examples

**Given: $\overleftrightarrow{YZ}$ is tangent to $\odot O$; $\widehat{XB} = 80°$; $\angle AXZ = 70°$**

1. $\angle YXB =$ __?__ ° 40
2. $\widehat{XA} =$ __?__ ° 140
3. $\widehat{AB} =$ __?__ ° 140
4. $\angle AXB =$ __?__ ° 70
5. $\widehat{XA} + \widehat{AB} + \widehat{BX} =$ __?__ ° 360
6. $\angle AXZ + \angle AXB + \angle YXB =$ __?__ ° 180

### Suggested Extension

**In the diagram below, $\angle TEY$ intercepts $\widehat{TY}$. We say that $\angle TEY$ is inscribed in $\widehat{TEY}$. What can you say about the measure of:**

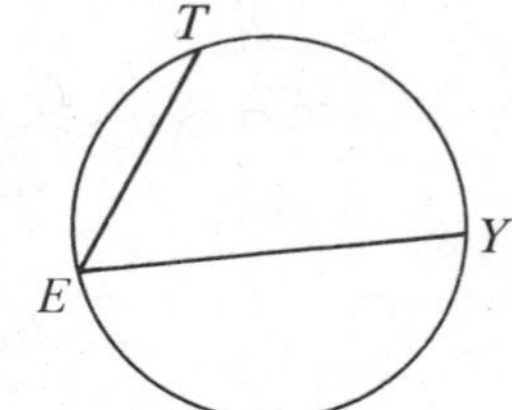


1. An angle inscribed in a semicircle? right angle
2. An angle inscribed in a major arc? obtuse angle
3. An angle inscribed in a minor arc? acute angle

### Objectives for Pages 338–345

1. To find the measure of an angle formed by two chords.
2. To find the measure of an angle formed by two secants.
3. To apply the theorem about the lengths of the segments of two intersecting chords.

## 6 • OTHER ANGLES (pp. 338–341)

### Teaching These Pages

We suggest that you have students discover the properties described in Theorems 10 and 11 by having them do the Explorations on page 338. You might like to lead students through the following verification of a special case of Theorem 10: the two chords are diameters.

Suppose $\angle 1 = 30°$.

Since $\angle 1$ is a central angle, $\widehat{AC} = 30°$.

Since $\angle 1$ and $\angle 2$ are vertical angles, $\angle 2 = 30°$.

Since $\angle 2$ is a central angle, $\widehat{BD} = 30°$.

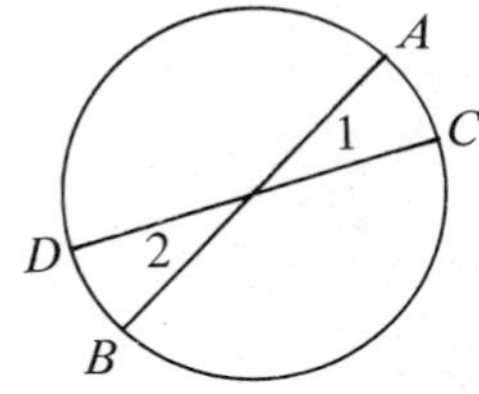


Now test: $\angle 1 \stackrel{?}{=} \frac{1}{2}(\widehat{AC} + \widehat{BD})$

$$30° \stackrel{?}{=} \frac{1}{2}(30° + 30°)$$

$$30° \stackrel{?}{=} \frac{1}{2}(60°) \quad \checkmark$$

Thus the definition of central angle and Theorem 10 both lead to the same result.

### Chalkboard Examples

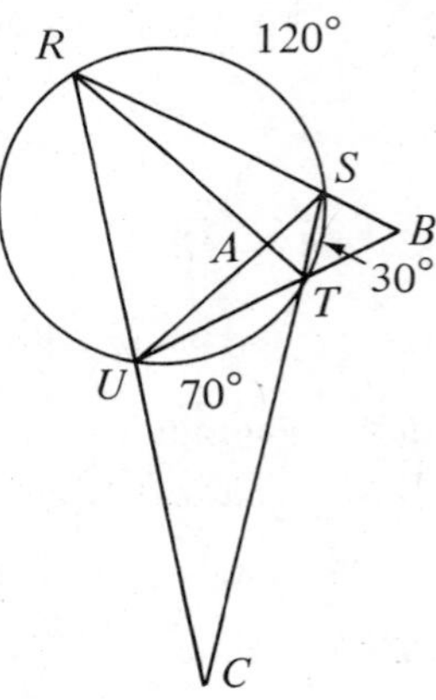


**Draw a circle. Place points *R*, *S*, *T*, and *U*, in that order, on the circle so that $\widehat{RS} = 120°$, $\widehat{ST} = 30°$, and $\widehat{TU} = 70°$.**

1. $\widehat{UR} =$ __?__° 140

2. Let the intersection of $\overleftrightarrow{RT}$ and $\overleftrightarrow{SU}$ be $A$. $\angle SAT =$ __?__° 85

3. Let the intersection of $\overleftrightarrow{RS}$ and $\overleftrightarrow{UT}$ be $B$. $\angle RBU =$ __?__° 55

4. Let the intersection of $\overleftrightarrow{RU}$ and $\overleftrightarrow{ST}$ be $C$. $\angle RCS =$ __?__° 25

### Suggested Extension

**In $\odot O$, $\widehat{AB} = 100°$. Point *X* lies on the same side of $\overleftrightarrow{AB}$ as *O* does. Does *X* lie inside, outside, or on the circle:**

1. If $\angle AXB = 50°$? on the circle
2. If $\angle AXB = 40°$? outside
3. If $\angle AXB = 52°$? inside

## 7 • SEGMENTS OF CHORDS (pp. 342–345)

### Teaching These Pages

Point out to students that almost all the theorems they have encountered in geometry "look true." But in Theorem 12, we have a theorem which "looks false" to many people.

### Chalkboard Examples

**Draw a diagram for each exercise. Chords $\overline{RS}$ and $\overline{TV}$ intersect at *P*, inside a circle. Find *PV*.**

**1.** $RP = 3$, $PS = 4$, and $TP = 6$ $PV = 2$

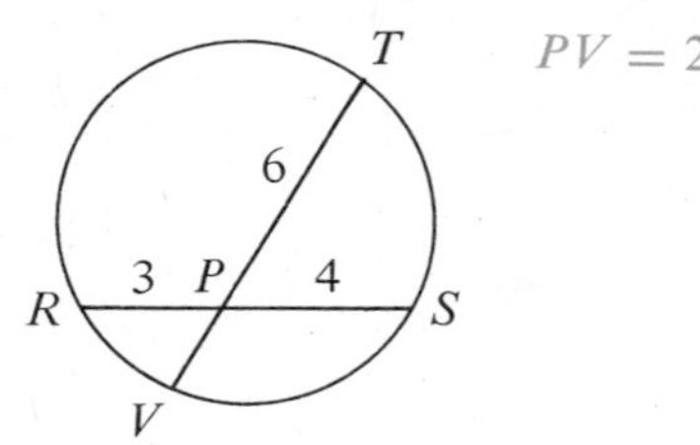


**2.** $RP = 6$, $PS = 10$, and $TP = 5$ $PV = 12$

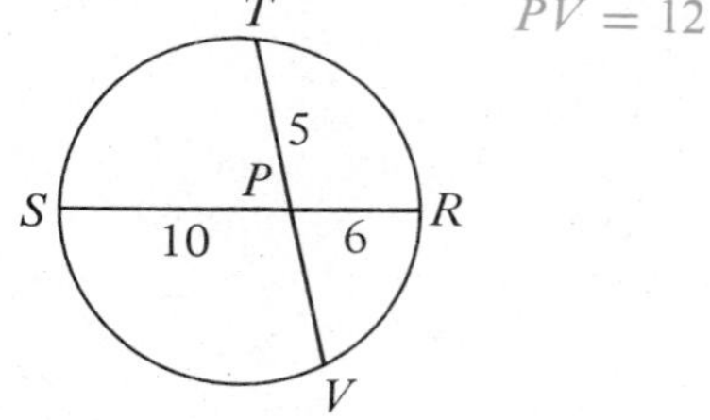


**3.** $RP = 12$, $PS = 12$, and $TP = 16$ $PV = 9$

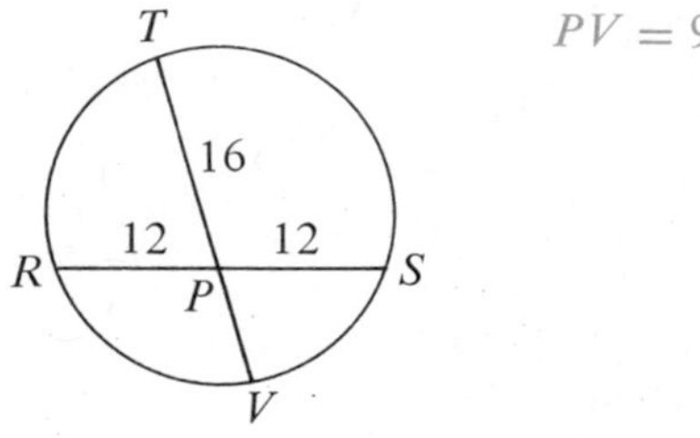


### Suggested Extension

In the Chalkboard Examples above, it is difficult to draw accurate diagrams. Here is a method for drawing an accurate figure for Chalkboard Example 1.

1. Draw a segment *RS* that is 7 cm long.
2. Take *P* on $\overline{RS}$ so that $RP = 3$ cm and $PS = 4$ cm.
3. Take a point *T*, not on $\overline{RS}$, so that $TP = 6$ cm.
4. Draw $\triangle RTS$ and circumscribe a circle about $\triangle RTS$.
5. Extend $\overline{TP}$ to the point where it intersects the circle and call that point *V*.

The resulting figure should be quite accurate. If another point *T* had been chosen 6 cm away from *P*, would the circumscribed circle be the same? no

## Chapter 10. Areas and Volumes of Solids

This chapter opens with a section that develops students' awareness of geometric relationships in three dimensions. The possible relative positions of two lines, two planes, and a line and a plane are explored. The rest of the chapter deals with the most common solids. The material on prisms emphasizes rectangular solids. The cylinders and cones studied are the types that students see most often, right circular cylinders and cones. The pyramids studied are regular pyramids. After a section on spheres, there is an optional section on similar solids. The chapter as a whole helps students to develop the ability to picture three-dimensional figures while reinforcing their arithmetic and algebraic skills.

### Objectives for Pages 354-367

1. To draw and to interpret drawings of solid figures.
2. To find the lateral area, total area, and volume of a right prism.
3. To find the lateral area, total area, and volume of a right circular cylinder.

### 1 • LINES AND PLANES IN SPACE (pp. 354-358)

#### Teaching These Pages

The classroom itself provides examples of lines and planes in space: for instance, the floor, ceiling, and walls, and the lines in which they intersect. You might use a chalkboard pointer and a desk top to illustrate possible relative positions of a line and a plane.

Encourage students to make drawings and to use handy objects (desk top, pencils, notebooks, and so on) in making judgments about three-dimensional relationships. Remind students that lines and planes extend indefinitely: The plane suggested by the ceiling, for instance, doesn't end at the walls of the classroom.

#### Chalkboard Examples

**Classify as true or false.**

1. If two lines are parallel, there must be a plane that contains both lines. true
2. If two lines are skew, there must be a plane that contains both lines. false
3. Any line in the ceiling must be parallel to the floor. true
4. There are many lines in the floor that intersect the front wall. true

5. There are many lines in the floor that are parallel to the front wall. true

6. If a pencil is held parallel to a desk top, then any plane that contains the pencil must be parallel to the desk top. false

7. A line and a plane may be skew. false

### Suggested Extension

The exercises below make use of a cylinder and a cone. Some students may not be familiar with these figures.

1. Draw a plane. Show two points, $A$ and $B$, in the plane. Does $\overleftrightarrow{AB}$ have to lie in the plane? yes (Postulate 3)
2. Draw a cylinder. Show two points, $A$ and $B$, such that $\overline{AB}$ lies in the cylindrical (the curved) surface. Also show two points, $X$ and $Y$, both in the cylindrical surface but such that $\overline{XY}$ does not lie in the cylindrical surface.

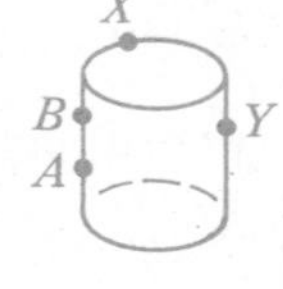


3. Repeat Exercise 2, using a cone and its conical surface.

A X B Y

## 2•RIGHT PRISMS (pp. 359–364)

### Teaching These Pages

Use the classroom or a cardboard packing box to illustrate a rectangular solid. If you don't have a set of models, you can find objects around the classroom to illustrate other prisms. A pencil can be cut twice to form a right prism with a hexagonal base. It could be cut at a slant to form a prism that is not a right prism. (Round pencils can be used to illustrate cylinders, which the class will be studying next.) An open textbook, standing upright, suggests a right prism with a triangular base.

### Chalkboard Examples

**A rectangular solid has edges that are 10, 8, and 3 units long.**

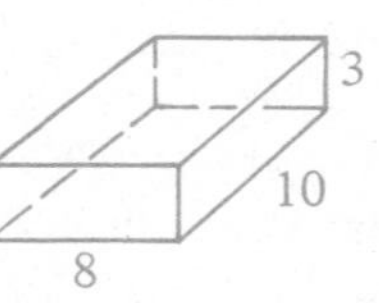


1. Draw the solid, showing the $10 \times 8$ face as the base. Find:
   **a.** the lateral area 108 **b.** the total area 268 **c.** the volume 240

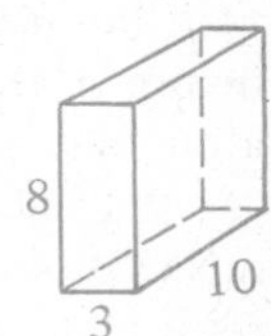


2. Repeat Exercise 1, but show the $10 \times 3$ face as the base.
   **a.** 208 **b.** 268 **c.** 240

For each right prism, find: a. the lateral area b. the total area c. the volume.

3. 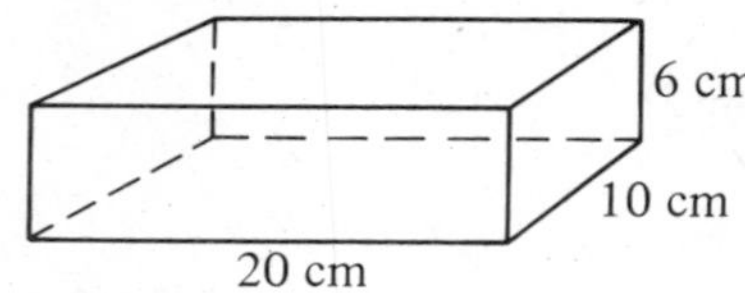


a. 360 cm² b. 760 cm²
c. 1200 cm³

4. 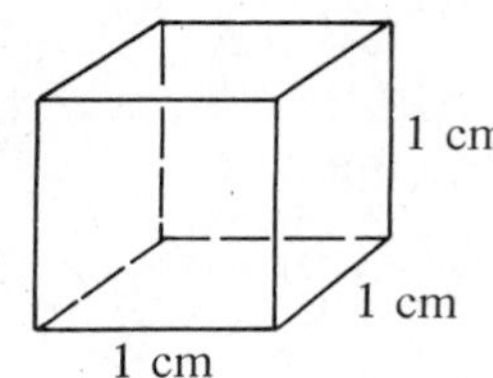


a. 4 cm² b. 6 cm²
c. 1 cm³

5. 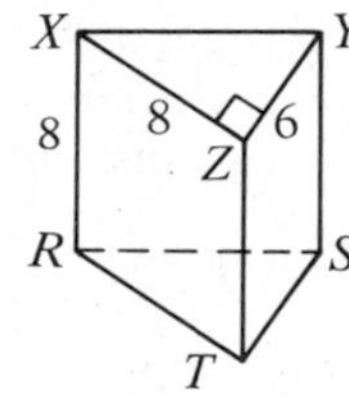


a. 192 b. 240
c. 192

## Suggested Extension

**Think of a cube whose edges are 6 cm long.**

1. The volume of the cube is __?__ $cm^3$. 216
2. The total area of the cube is __?__ $cm^2$. 216

**Now use the fact that the edges of the cube are 60 mm long.**

3. The volume of the cube is __?__ $mm^3$. 216,000
4. The total area of the cube is __?__ $mm^2$. 21,600
5. Look at your results in Exercises 1 and 2; then at your results in Exercises 3 and 4. Is it proper to say that the volume of the cube is numerically equal to the total area? no, since the numbers depend on the unit of measure used

## 3•RIGHT CIRCULAR CYLINDERS (pp. 365–367)

### Teaching These Pages

Use a few minutes to show the class that not all cylinders are circular. You might place a large oval paper cutout on the classroom floor, and then trace its boundary with a chalkboard pointer held upright. A round pencil with both ends cut off at an angle provides another example. You could demonstrate that a circular cylinder need not be a right cylinder by tracing a circular cutout with a chalkboard pointer kept at an angle to the floor.

After such demonstrations, point out that right circular cylinders are the most common ones; for simplicity, the class may use the term *cylinder* for *right circular cylinder.*

## Chalkboard Examples

**Express answers in terms of $\pi$.**

1. The radius of a cylinder is 10; the height is 2. Find:
   **a.** circumference of base $20\pi$
   **b.** area of base $100\pi$
   **c.** L.A. $40\pi$
   **d.** T.A. $240\pi$
   **e.** $V$ $200\pi$

2. Repeat Exercise 1, using a cylinder in which $r = 2$ and $h = 10$.
   **a.** $4\pi$ **b.** $4\pi$ **c.** $40\pi$ **d.** $48\pi$ **e.** $40\pi$

**Use 3.14 for $\pi$.**

3. A 20 cm by 30 cm sheet of paper is rolled, without overlap, to form the lateral surface of a cylinder with height 30 cm. Find the volume to the nearest tenth of a cubic centimeter. 955.4 $cm^3$

4. Repeat Example 3, but roll the paper so that the height of the cylinder is 20 cm. 1433.1 $cm^3$

## Suggested Extension

1. Describe a cylinder with height 10 cm whose lateral area (in $cm^2$) is many times as great as its volume (in $cm^3$). radius much smaller than 10 cm

2. Describe a cylinder with height 10 cm whose volume (in $cm^3$) is many times as great as its lateral area (in $cm^2$). radius much larger than 10 cm

## Objectives for Pages 369–379

1. To find the lateral area, the total area, and the volume of a pyramid.
2. To find the lateral area, the total area, and the volume of a cone.
3. To find the area and the volume of a sphere.

## 4•REGULAR PYRAMIDS (pp. 369–372)

### Teaching These Pages

It is helpful to have a model pyramid on which you can show students the parts of a pyramid. Some students might enjoy making cardboard models based on the pattern at right.

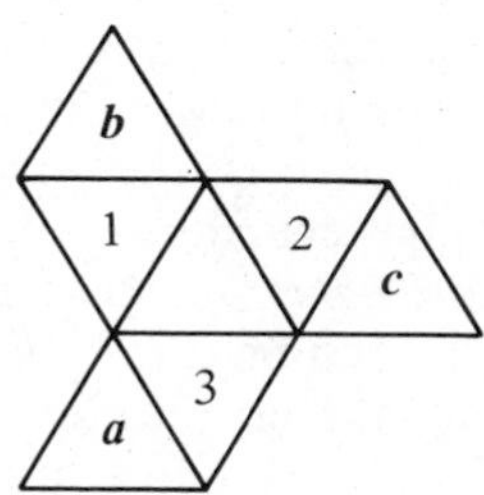

## Chalkboard Examples

1. Draw a pyramid so that the base is a $10 \times 10$ square and the height is 12. The slant height of this pyramid is 13.

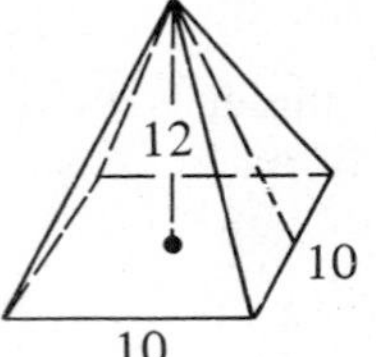

2. Find: **a.** the area of the base 100
   **b.** the area of one lateral face 65
   **c.** the total area 360
   **d.** the volume 400

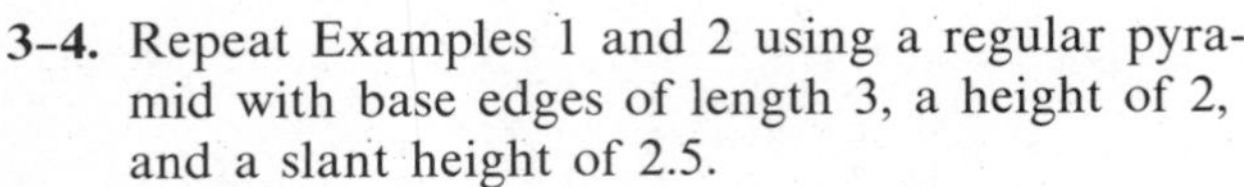

3–4. Repeat Examples 1 and 2 using a regular pyramid with base edges of length 3, a height of 2, and a slant height of 2.5.
   4. **a.** 9 **b.** 3.75 **c.** 24 **d.** 6

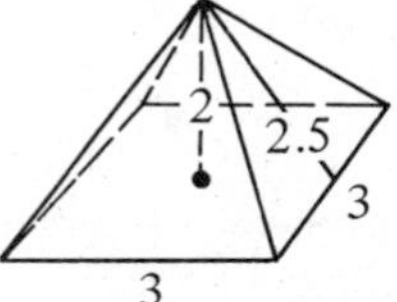


## Suggested Extension

**The four diagonals of a cube meet at a point *V*. Consider the six congruent pyramids *VABCD*, *VBCTS*, and so on, that have vertex *V*.**

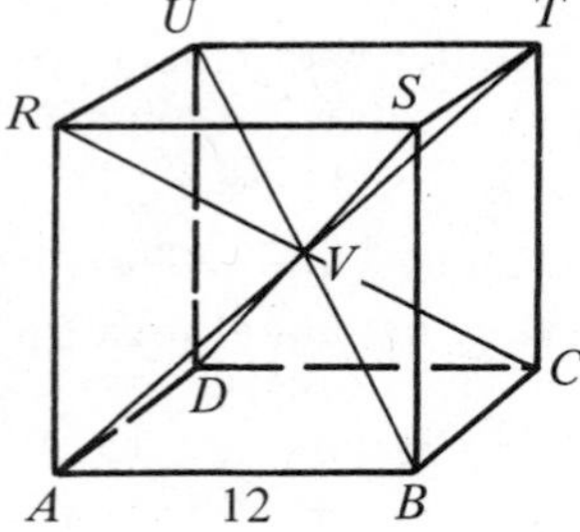


1. Use the formula $V = \frac{1}{3}Bh$ to find the volume of one of these pyramids. 288
2. Does your answer in Exercise 1 indicate that each of the congruent pyramids "fills" one-sixth of the cube? yes, $288 = \frac{1}{6}(12 \times 12 \times 12)$

## 5 • RIGHT CIRCULAR CONES (pp. 373–376)

### Teaching These Pages

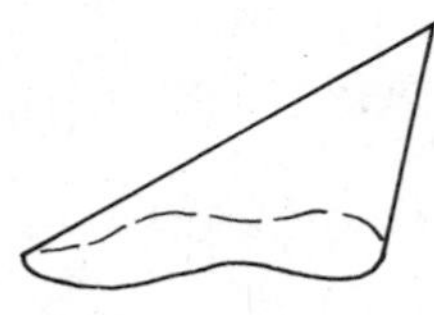

Explain that just as not all cylinders are right circular cylinders, not all cones are right circular cones. You might draw a figure like the one shown at right as an example of a cone in the broad sense of the word. Recalling the agreement concerning cylinder terminology, tell students that *cone* will mean *right circular cone* in this course.

The activity described in Classroom Practice Exercises 2–10 justifies the formula $A = \pi rl$ for the lateral area of a cone by showing that this area is two-thirds the area of a certain circle.

### Chalkboard Examples

**Express answers in terms of $\pi$.**

1. In a certain cone: $r = 9$; $h = 12$; $l = 15$. Find:
   **a.** L.A. $135\pi$ **b.** T.A. $216\pi$ **c.** $V$ $324\pi$
2. Repeat Exercise 1, using: $r = 12$; $h = 9$; $l = 15$.
   a. $180\pi$ b. $324\pi$ c. $432\pi$
3. A cone and a cylinder both have a radius of 5 and a height of 2. Find the ratio of their volumes. 1:3

## 6 • SPHERES (pp. 378–379)

### Teaching These Pages

The formulas for the area and volume of a sphere are very difficult to prove. Most students are quite willing to accept these formulas without proof. You may want to point out that the area formula involves "$r^2$" and the volume formula involves "$r^3$," corresponding to the fact that area is measured in square units and volume is measured in cubic units.

### Chalkboard Examples

**Find, in terms of $\pi$, the area of a sphere whose radius is:**

**1.** 3 cm $36\pi$ cm$^2$ **2.** 4 cm $64\pi$ cm$^2$ **3.** 5 cm $100\pi$ cm$^2$

**4.** Does the area of the largest of the three spheres equal the sum of the areas of the other two? yes

**5–8.** Repeat Examples 1–4, calculating volumes instead of areas.
5. $36\pi$ cm$^3$ 6. $85\frac{1}{3}\pi$ cm$^3$ 7. $166\frac{2}{3}\pi$ cm$^3$ 8. no

### Suggested Extension

Show that the volume of the cylinder is three times that of the cone, and that the volume of the sphere is twice that of the cone.

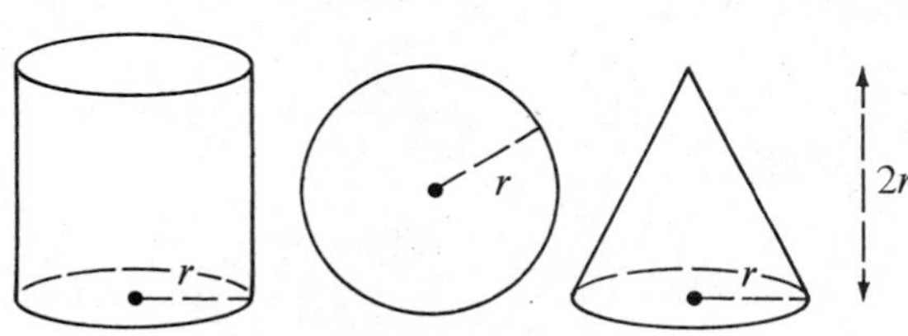


$$V_{CY} = \pi r^2(2r) = 2\pi r^3;\ V_{SP} = \frac{4}{3}\pi r^3;$$

$$V_{CO} = \frac{1}{3}\pi r^2(2r) = \frac{2}{3}\pi r^3$$

$$V_{CY} = 2\pi r^3 = 3\left(\frac{2}{3}\pi r^3\right) = 3(V_{CO})$$

$$V_{SP} = \frac{4}{3}\pi r^3 = 2\left(\frac{2}{3}\pi r^3\right) = 2(V_{CO})$$

## 7 • SIMILAR SOLIDS (OPTIONAL) (pp. 381–383)

### Teaching These Pages

This section extends the treatment of measurements of similar figures begun in Section 5 of Chapter 8. We suggest that you have students do the Explorations on page 381. Explain that Theorem 1 on page 381 is an extension of Theorem 2 on page 301. Students may find Theorem 1 easier to remember if they note that the exponent (1, 2, or 3) in the ratio of measurements corresponds to the unit of measure involved (for example: m, $m^2$, or $m^3$).

### Chalkboard Examples

1. A photograph is enlarged to form a new one that is twice as long and twice as wide as the original.
   **a.** Are angle measures changed in the enlarging process? no
   **b.** Suppose the picture shows a bridge. What is the ratio of the length of the bridge in the enlargement to the length in the original photograph? 2:1
   **c.** What is the ratio of the area of the enlarged photograph to the area of the original? 4:1

2. One ball bearing has one-third the diameter of another. There are 10 g of steel in the smaller one. How many grams of steel are there in the larger one? 270 g

3. Two birthday cakes are the same shape, but one is twice as wide as the other.
   **a.** How many times as much icing will the larger cake need? 4 times
   **b.** How many times as many people will the larger cake feed? 8 times

4. Two soup cans are similar solids. The ratio of their diameters is 3:5.
   **a.** The smaller can has a label with area 450 $cm^2$. What is the area of the larger can's label? 1250 $cm^2$
   **b.** The larger can has a capacity of 2500 $cm^3$. What is the capacity of the smaller can? 540 $cm^3$

## Chapter 11. Right Triangles

This chapter offers both a review and an extension of important ideas presented in the course. The Pythagorean Theorem is applied to derive special relationships in 45°-45°-90° and 30°-60°-90° triangles. These relationships are used in exercises which also review a wide variety of topics: properties of circles, triangles, and special quadrilaterals; area and volume formulas; properties of similar figures; inscribed figures. The Pythagorean Theorem is further applied to find the diagonals of rectangular solids and to extend the study of pyramids and cones.

The chapter ends with an introduction to trigonometry. In keeping with the simplified treatment, an abbreviated table of sines, cosines, and tangents is presented on page 418: only degree measures which are multiples of 5° are included, and the values of the trigonometric ratios are given to only three decimal places.

### Objectives for Pages 392–402

1. To solve problems involving some common right triangle lengths.
2. To use the relationships among the sides of 45°-45°-90° triangles and 30°-60°-90° triangles.
3. To apply theorems about 45°-45°-90° triangles and 30°-60°-90° triangles to other figures.

### 1 • REVIEWING RIGHT TRIANGLES (pp. 392–394)

### Teaching These Pages

You might begin by reviewing the Pythagorean Theorem with students, having them recall the common right triangles with integral side lengths. The exercises in the text review many of the situations in geometry in which right triangles occur.

You may wish to move right to Section 2, assigning problems from both of the first two sections for two or three days. You might try the same tactic with Sections 3 and 4, discussing and assigning problems from both sections concurrently.

### Chalkboard Examples

**Find the value of each variable.**

**1.** 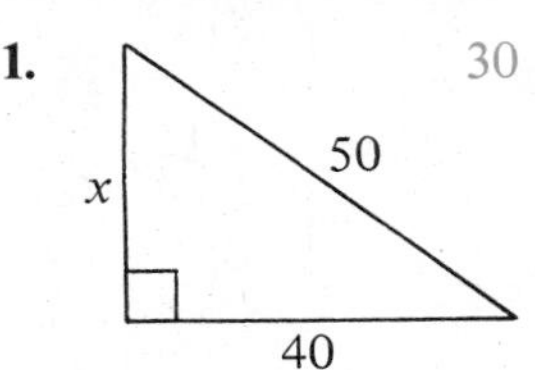

30

**2.** 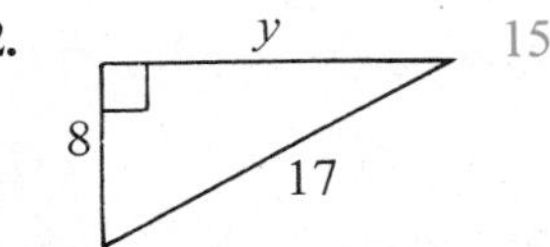

15

**3.** 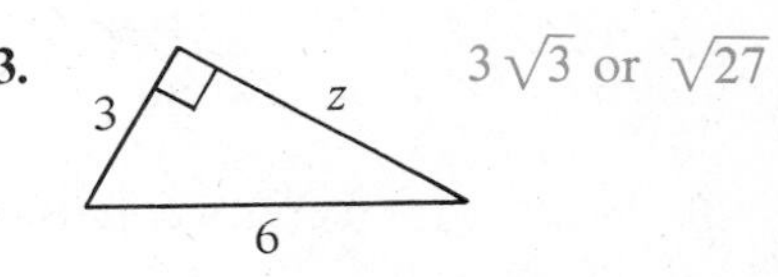

$3\sqrt{3}$ or $\sqrt{27}$

**4.**

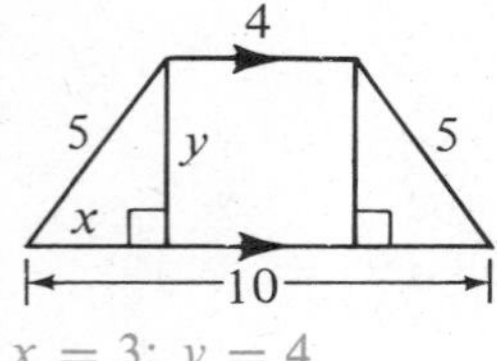


$x = 3;\ y = 4$

**5.**

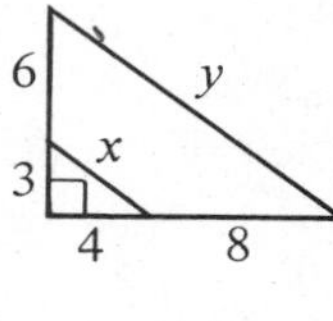


$x = 5;\ y = 15$

**6.**

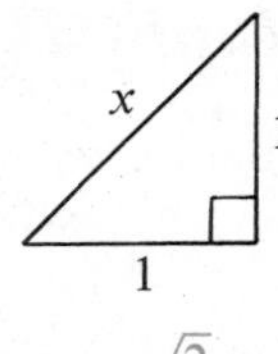


$x = \sqrt{2}$

## Suggested Extension

Some students may be interested in using whole-number values of $r$ and $s$ in the formulas below to generate "Pythagorean triples," sets of whole numbers which are the lengths of sides of right triangles.

For any values of $r$ and $s$:

$$\text{If } a = r^2 - s^2 \qquad \text{then } a^2 + b^2 = c^2$$
$$b = 2rs$$
$$c = r^2 + s^2$$

You might challenge more advanced students to prove the validity of this method. $a^2 + b^2 = (r^2 - s^2)^2 + (2rs)^2 = r^4 - 2r^2s^2 + s^4 + 4r^2s^2 = r^4 + 2r^2s^2 + s^4 = (r^2 + s^2)^2 = c^2$

## 2 • SPECIAL RIGHT TRIANGLES (pp. 395–399)

### Teaching These Pages

To motivate Theorem 1 on page 395, you might use the Pythagorean Theorem to find the hypotenuse of each of the following isosceles right triangles.

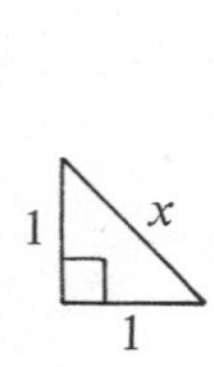


$x^2 = 1^2 + 1^2$
$x^2 = 2$
$x = \sqrt{2}$

$x^2 = 3^2 + 3^2$
$x^2 = 3^2 \cdot 2$
$x = 3\sqrt{2}$

$x^2 = 14^2 + 14^2$
$x^2 = 14^2 \cdot 2$
$x = 14\sqrt{2}$

Note that the above method eliminates the need to reduce the radicals $\sqrt{18}$ and $\sqrt{392}$.

By this time, several students should be ready to state a conjecture (Theorem 1) about 45°-45°-90° triangles. The proof of this theorem in the text uses the algebraic equivalent of the method shown above.

To motivate Theorem 2 on page 396, have students find the altitude of an equilateral triangle with side length 2. Point out that the altitude forms two 30°-60°-90° triangles.

$$x = 1$$
$$y^2 = 2^2 - 1^2 = 3$$
$$y = \sqrt{3}$$

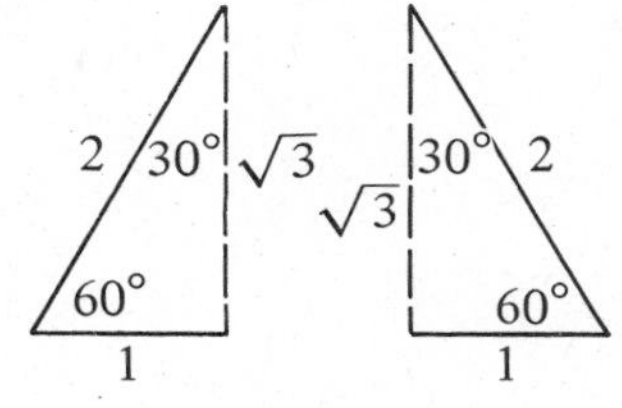


Have students form other 30°-60°-90° triangles in the same way. After working several such examples, students should be ready to suggest Theorem 2 on their own.

### Chalkboard Examples

**In $\triangle ABC$, $\angle A = 90°$, $\angle B = 60°$, and $\angle C = 30°$.**

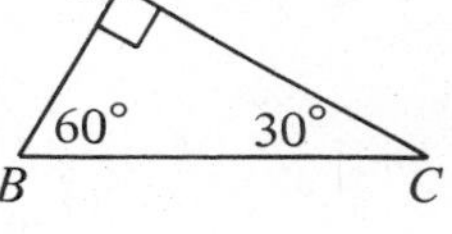


1. If $AB = 6$, $BC =$ _?_. 12
2. If $AB = 10$, $BC =$ _?_. 20
3. If $AC = 4\sqrt{3}$, $BC =$ _?_. 8
4. If $BC = 2$, $AC =$ _?_. $\sqrt{3}$

**In $\triangle PQR$, $\angle P = 30°$, $\angle Q = 90°$, and $\angle R = 60°$.**

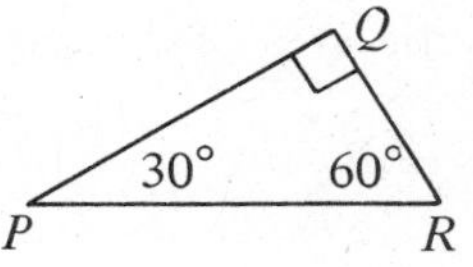


5. If $PR = 8$, $QR =$ _?_ and $PQ =$ _?_. 4; $4\sqrt{3}$
6. If $PR = 12$, $QR =$ _?_ and $PQ =$ _?_. 6; $6\sqrt{3}$
7. If $QR = 5$, $PR =$ _?_ and $PQ =$ _?_. 10; $5\sqrt{3}$
8. If $PQ = 7\sqrt{3}$, $QR =$ _?_ and $PR =$ _?_. 7; 14

## 3 • USING SPECIAL RIGHT TRIANGLES (pp. 400–402)

### Teaching These Pages

Explain to students that the special right triangles they have just studied occur often in geometry problems. The theorems concerning these triangles frequently provide the key to solving such problems.

Work the Example on page 400 with students, pointing out how a knowledge of 30°-60°-90° triangles enables us to find the altitude of the parallelogram and, hence, the area. You may want to work the problem a second time, letting $\angle A = 45°$, and a third time, letting $\angle A = 30°$.

## Chalkboard Examples

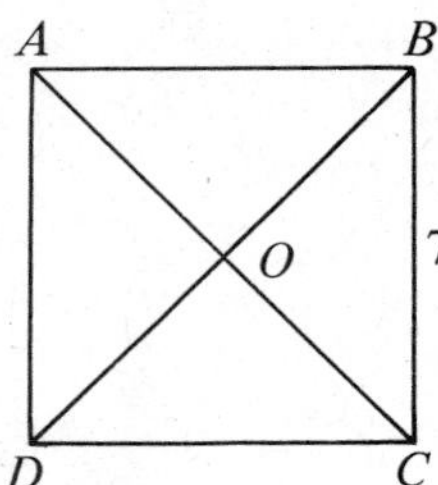


**1.** Figure $ABCD$ is a square with $BC = 7$.
**a.** Find $BD$. $7\sqrt{2}$
**b.** Find $CO$. $\frac{7\sqrt{2}}{2}$

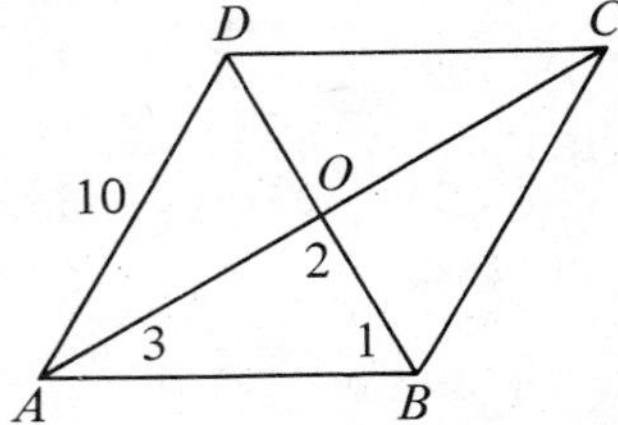


**2.** Figure $ABCD$ is a rhombus with $\angle DAC = 30°$.
**a.** Find the measures of $\angle 1$, $\angle 2$, and $\angle 3$.
$\angle 1 = 60°$; $\angle 2 = 90°$; $\angle 3 = 30°$
**b.** Find $BO$ and $AO$.
$BO = 5$; $AO = 5\sqrt{3}$

**3. a.** Find $PR$. 3
**b.** Find $QR$. 3
**c.** Find $PQ$. $3\sqrt{2}$

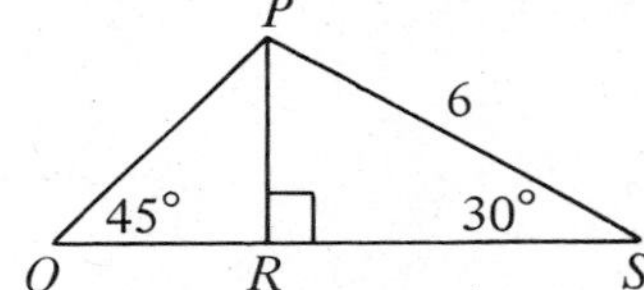


**4.** The altitude of an equilateral triangle is $6\sqrt{3}$.
**a.** What is the perimeter of the triangle? 36
**b.** What is the area of the triangle? $36\sqrt{3}$

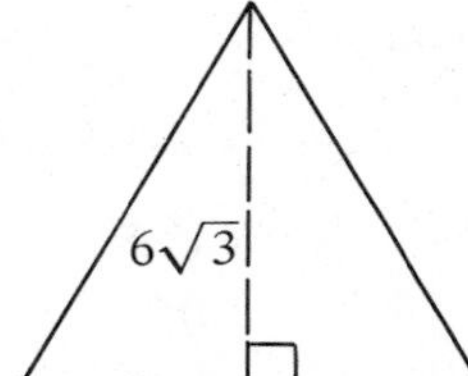


## Objectives for Pages 403–409

1. To find the length of the diagonal of a rectangular solid.
2. To use right triangles to solve problems involving pyramids and cones.

## 4•DIAGONALS OF RECTANGULAR SOLIDS (pp. 403–405)

### Teaching These Pages

Try *leading* your students to the formula $d = \sqrt{a^2 + b^2 + c^2}$ rather than presenting it without justification. This can be done by analyzing several rectangular solids using the three steps illustrated on page 403. These same three steps are used in Classroom Practice Exercises 1–3 and 5–7 and in the Chalkboard Examples below. A few such examples should prepare students for the derivation of the formula.

## Chalkboard Examples

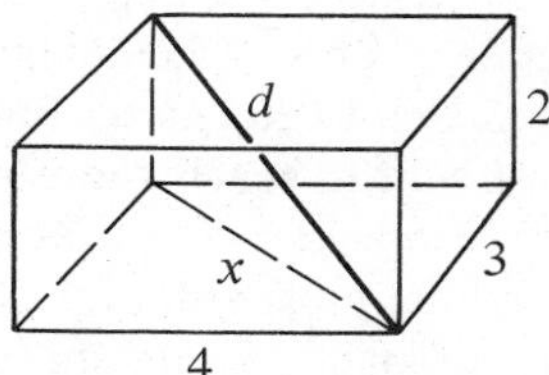


1. $x^2 = (\underline{\ ?\ })^2 + (\underline{\ ?\ })^2$ 3; 4

2. $d^2 = x^2 + (\underline{\ ?\ })^2$ 2

3. Combining the results of Examples 1 and 2:
   $d^2 = (\underset{3}{\underline{\ ?\ }})^2 + (\underset{4}{\underline{\ ?\ }})^2 + (\underset{2}{\underline{\ ?\ }})^2 = \underset{29}{\underline{\ ?\ }}$
   $d = \sqrt{\underline{\ ?\ }}$ 29

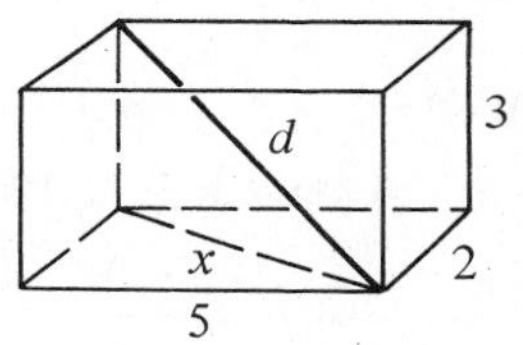


4. $x^2 = (\underline{\ ?\ })^2 + (\underline{\ ?\ })^2$ 2; 5

5. $d^2 = x^2 + (\underline{\ ?\ })^2$ 3

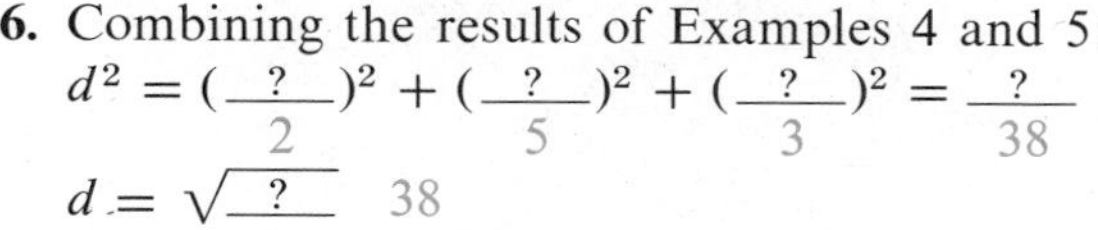

6. Combining the results of Examples 4 and 5:
   $d^2 = (\underset{2}{\underline{\ ?\ }})^2 + (\underset{5}{\underline{\ ?\ }})^2 + (\underset{3}{\underline{\ ?\ }})^2 = \underset{38}{\underline{\ ?\ }}$
   $d = \sqrt{\underline{\ ?\ }}$ 38

## Suggested Extension

Many of your students will enjoy the problem about the ant and the sugar in the Puzzles & Things on page 409. The hint will help students see that the ant crawls a distance of $\sqrt{8^2 + 6^2} = 10$. But what if the box is unfolded differently, suggesting another path for the ant? The work below shows that another path is of length $\sqrt{130}$, which is larger than 10.

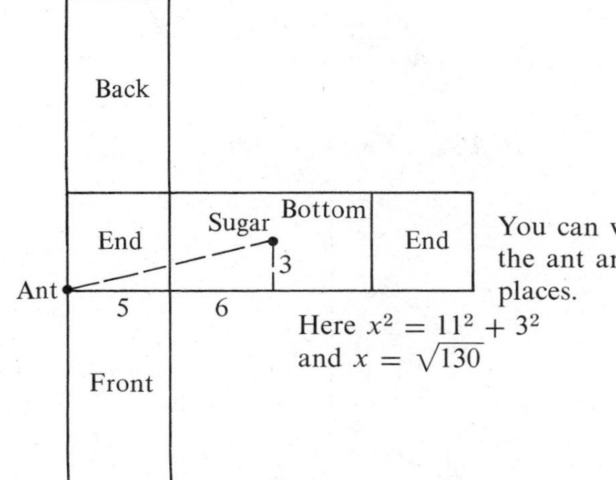


You can vary the problem by placing the ant and the sugar at different places.

Here $x^2 = 11^2 + 3^2$ and $x = \sqrt{130}$

## 5 • RIGHT TRIANGLES IN PYRAMIDS AND CONES (pp. 406–409)

### Teaching These Pages

The work in this section is an extension of the area and volume work in Chapter 10. In that chapter, students were *given* the slant height or the height of a pyramid in order to calculate its area or volume. Now students must use right triangles to *calculate* the slant height or height.

Perhaps the best way to teach these pages is to pose to the class the problems given in Examples 1 and 2 on pages 406–407. After their work with rectangular solids, most students should have little difficulty visualizing right triangles in space. Some students, however, may need to work with models of pyramids and cones.

### Chalkboard Examples

**A cone has radius 6 and slant height 10.**

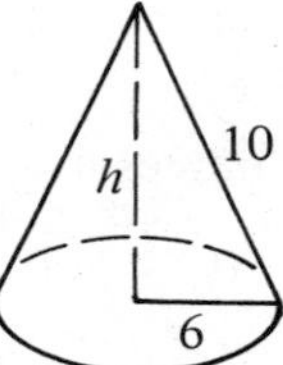


1. What is its height? 8
2. What is its volume? $96\pi$
3. What is its lateral area? $60\pi$

**A square pyramid has base edges of length 6 and a height of 4.**

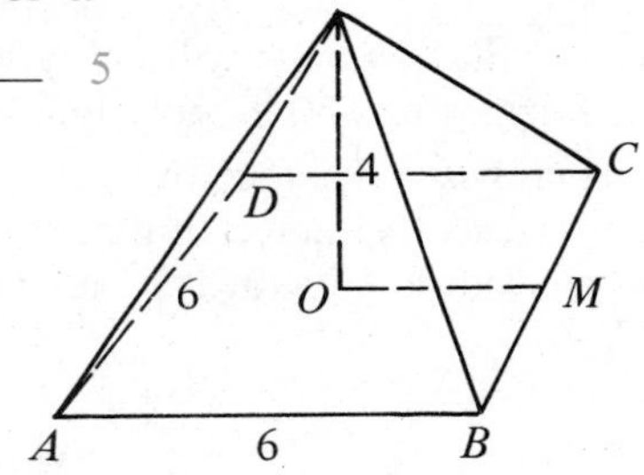


4. $MB =$ _?_ 3
5. $OM =$ _?_ 3
6. $VM =$ _?_ 5
7. Area of $\triangle VBC =$ _?_ 15
8. Lateral area of pyramid = _?_ 60
9. Total area of pyramid = _?_ 96

### Suggested Extension

**A plane slices a sphere, passing 4 cm from the center *O*. It forms a circle with radius 3.**

1. What is the radius of the sphere? 5
2. What is the area of the sphere? $100\pi$
3. What is the volume of the sphere?

   $166\frac{2}{3}\pi$

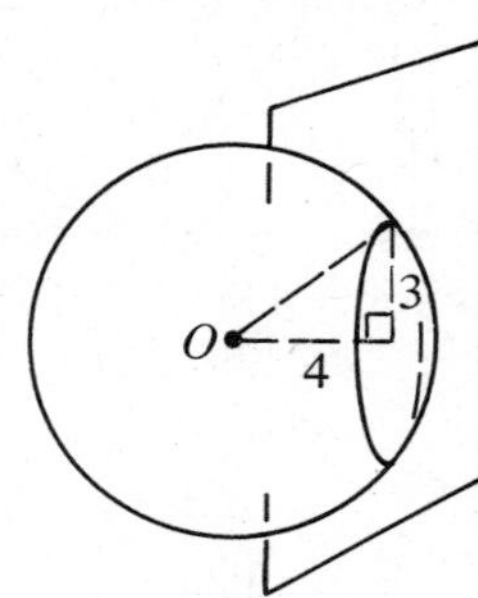

## Objective for Pages 410–417

**1.** To use the tangent, sine, and cosine ratios to find the missing parts of right triangles.

## 6•THE TANGENT RATIO (pp. 410–413)

### Teaching These Pages

If you have a limited time in which to teach trigonometry, you may wish to combine Sections 6 and 7. Explain the terminology "opposite leg" and "adjacent leg," and then define the sine, cosine, and tangent ratios. Then move immediately to the Classroom Practice Exercises for Section 7.

Of course, it is more desirable to do Section 6 by itself before proceeding to Section 7. After you define the tangent ratio, you might work through Example 1 in the text and Chalkboard Examples 1–3 below. To do Example 2 in the text and Chalkboard Examples 4–6 below, students must be introduced to the Table of Trigonometric Ratios on page 418.

Point out to students that in Chalkboard Example 5, we may write either

$$\tan 35° = \frac{x}{2} \quad \text{so that} \quad x = 2\,(\tan 35°)$$

$$\text{or } \tan 55° = \frac{2}{x} \quad \text{so that} \quad x = \frac{2}{\tan 55°}.$$

For those having a calculator, both expressions for $x$ are equally easy to evaluate. For those without a calculator, $2(\tan 35°)$ is easier to evaluate than $\dfrac{2}{\tan 55°}$.

### Chalkboard Examples

**Find tan *A* and tan *B* for each right triangle.**

**1.**

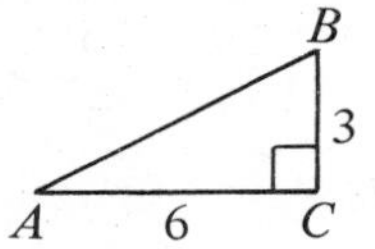


$\tan A = \frac{1}{2}$; $\tan B = 2$

**2.**

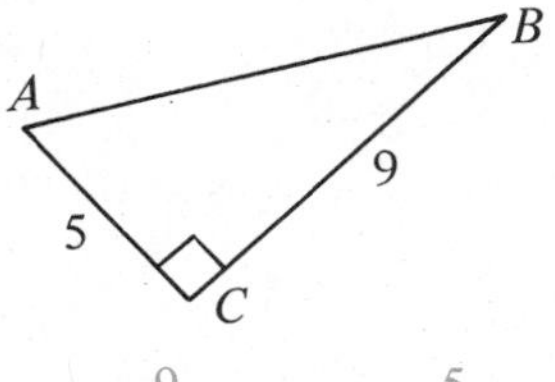


$\tan A = \frac{9}{5}$; $\tan B = \frac{5}{9}$

**3.**

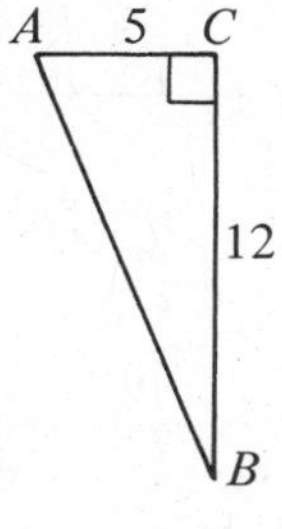


$\tan A = \frac{12}{5}$; $\tan B = \frac{5}{12}$

Find the value of $x$ to the nearest tenth. Use the table on page 418.

4. 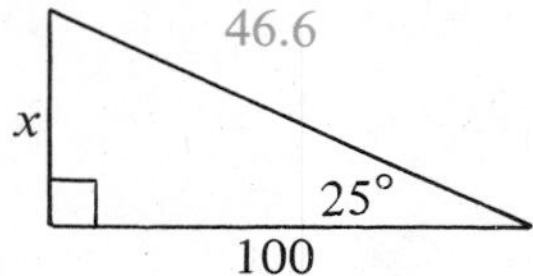


5. 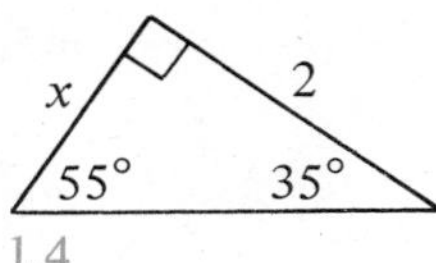


6. a. Express $\tan A$ as a fraction. $\frac{1}{2}$
   b. Express $\tan A$ as a decimal. 0.5
   c. Use the table on page 418 to find the measure of $\angle A$ to the nearest 5°. 25°

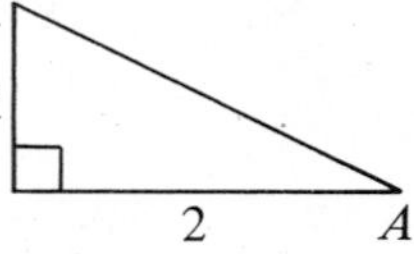


## 7•THE SINE AND COSINE RATIOS (pp. 414–417)

### Teaching These Pages

After you define the sine and cosine ratios, work through Examples 1, 2, and 3 on pages 414–415. Be sure that students understand these ratios thoroughly before you assign the Written Exercises.

### Chalkboard Examples

**Express the sine, cosine, and tangent of $\angle A$ and $\angle B$ as decimals.**

1. 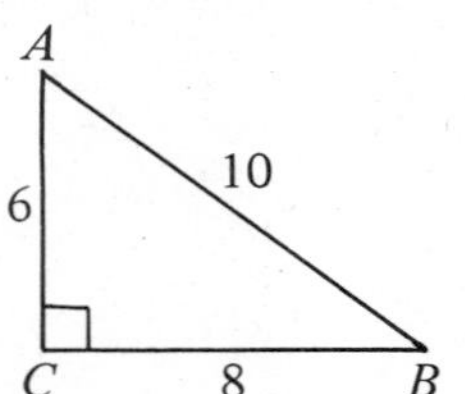


$\sin A = 0.8$; $\sin B = 0.6$
$\cos A = 0.6$; $\cos B = 0.8$
$\tan A = 1.333$; $\tan B = 0.750$

2. 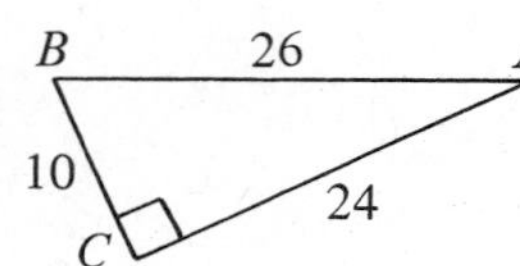


$\sin A = 0.385$; $\sin B = 0.923$
$\cos A = 0.923$; $\cos B = 0.385$
$\tan A = 0.417$; $\tan B = 2.400$

3. 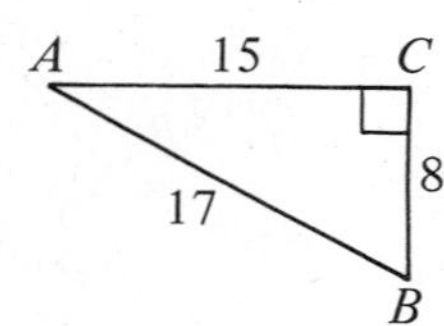


$\sin A = 0.471$; $\sin B = 0.882$
$\cos A = 0.882$; $\cos B = 0.471$
$\tan A = 0.533$; $\tan B = 1.875$

## Suggested Extension

The Extra for Experts feature on pages 420–421 provides a nice introduction to the use of trigonometric ratios in oblique triangles. Advanced students might like to tackle the problems below.

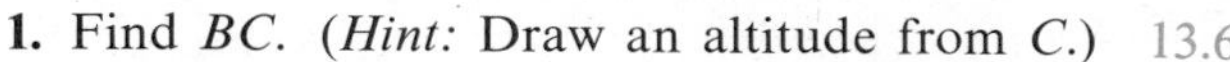

1. Find $BC$. (*Hint:* Draw an altitude from $C$.) 13.6

2. Find $AB$. $8.19 + 12.32 \doteq 20.5$

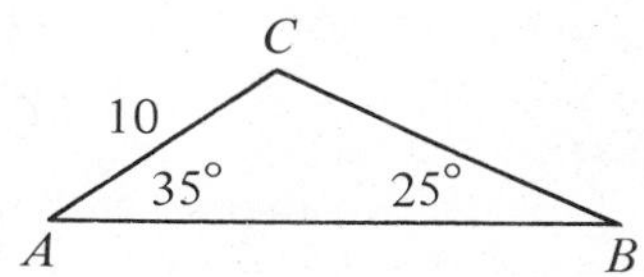


3. Find the area. 58.8
4. Find the length of the altitude from $B$. 11.8
5. Show that $\dfrac{\sin A}{\cos A} = \tan A$.

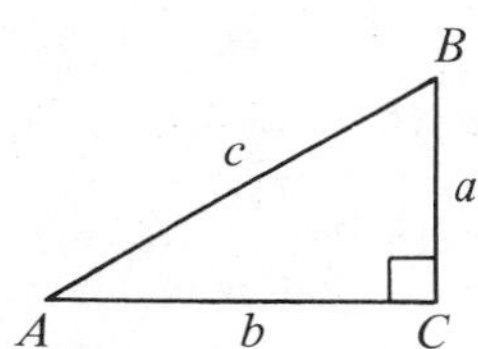


$$\frac{\sin A}{\cos A} = \frac{\frac{a}{c}}{\frac{b}{c}} = \frac{a}{b} = \tan A$$

6. Show that $a \sin B = b \sin A$. (*Hint:* Calculate the length of altitude $CD$ in two ways.)

$$\sin A = \frac{CD}{b};\ \sin B = \frac{CD}{a};\ a \sin B = CD = b \sin A$$

7. Show that $c = b \cos A + a \cos B$. (*Hint:* Find $AD$ and $BD$.)

$$\cos A = \frac{AD}{b}, \text{ so } AD = b \cos A$$

$$\cos B = \frac{BD}{a}, \text{ so } BD = a \cos B$$

$$c = AD + BD = b \cos A + a \cos B$$

## Chapter 12. Coordinate Geometry

This final chapter begins with drill on basic vocabulary and plotting points. After students have had experience finding the distance between two points on horizontal or vertical lines, they move on to finding distances by applying the Pythagorean Theorem. The midpoint formula grows out of an averaging approach. The idea of slope is developed and applied to parallel and perpendicular lines. Linear equations are graphed. In the final section of the book two theorems that lend themselves to coordinate treatment are proved. Students first saw these theorems in Chapter 5, but the proofs were postponed until the introduction of coordinates.

### Objectives for Pages 426–437

1. To specify points by their coordinates in the coordinate plane.
2. To work with simple figures in the coordinate plane.
3. To find the distance between two points in the coordinate plane.
4. To apply the midpoint formula.

### 1 • POINTS AND COORDINATES (pp. 426–429)

#### Teaching These Pages

Drill vocabulary according to needs of the class; what is review to some students may be new material to others. Even experienced students should do most of the exercises, for the ability to make judgments about simple figures is developed along with proficiency in plotting points.

#### Chalkboard Examples

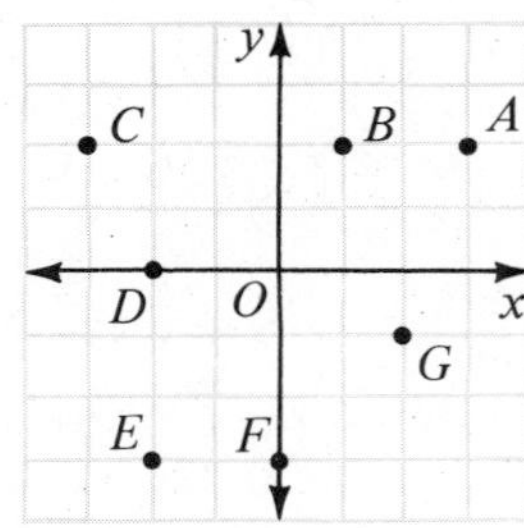


1. State the coordinates of each of the labeled points.
   $A(3, 2)$; $B(1, 2)$; $C(-3, 2)$
2. Find the distance between points:
   a. $A$ and $B$ 2  b. $B$ and $C$ 4
   c. $D$ and $E$ 3  d. $E$ and $F$ 2

#### Suggested Extension

1. Points $(-1, -1)$ and $(3, 3)$ are two of the vertices of a square. Find three pairs of points that could be the other two vertices.
   $(7, -1)$ and $(3, -5)$; $(-1, 7)$ and $(-5, 3)$; $(3, -1)$ and $(-1, 3)$
2. Repeat Exercise 1, using points $(0, 2)$ and $(4, 8)$.
   $(6, -2)$ and $(10, 4)$; $(-6, 6)$ and $(-2, 12)$; $(5, 3)$ and $(-1, 7)$

## 2 • DISTANCE BETWEEN TWO POINTS (pp. 430–432)

### Teaching These Pages

Encourage students to recognize the fact that they don't need a special formula to find the distance between two given points. When a segment is horizontal or vertical its length can be determined by subtraction or by counting squares. For any other segment, students may draw horizontal and vertical segments to form a right triangle, then apply the Pythagorean Theorem.

### Chalkboard Examples

**Plot points and draw segments as necessary. Then find the distance between the two points.** (drawings omitted)

**1.** $(-3, 0)$ and $(-5, 0)$ 2

**2.** $(2, -4)$ and $(2, 1)$ 5

**3.** $(1, 2)$ and $(5, 5)$ 5

**4.** $(-3, 0)$ and $(5, 6)$ 10

**5.** $(0, 2)$ and $(5, 14)$ 13

**6.** $(1, -1)$ and $(-11, -10)$ 15

### Suggested Extension

Plot point $A(2, 1)$. What points lie above the $x$-axis and are exactly 5 units from $A$? One coordinate of several such points is given. Find the other coordinate.

**1.** (7, __?__) 1

**2.** (6, __?__) 4

**3.** (5, __?__) 5

**4.** (2, __?__) 6

**5.** (−1, __?__) 5

**6.** (−2, __?__) 4

**7.** There is one other point that lies above the $x$-axis, has integer coordinates, and is 5 units from $A$. Find the coordinates of that point. $(-3, 1)$

**8.** There are five points that lie below the $x$-axis, have integer coordinates, and are 5 units from $A$. Find the coordinates of the five points. $(-2, -2)$; $(-1, -3)$; $(2, -4)$; $(5, -3)$; $(6, -2)$

## 3 • MIDPOINT OF A SEGMENT (pp. 433–437)

### Teaching These Pages

We suggest that you have students carry out Part A of the Explorations individually. Then do Part B—step by step—as a group, using a large figure like that on page 434. In Steps 4 and 5, be sure students see that we find a midpoint coordinate by averaging the endpoint coordinates.

Some students may need a careful explanation of the use of subscripts in the midpoint formula.

## Chalkboard Examples

**$M$ is the midpoint of $\overline{RS}$. State the coordinates of $M$, using:**

**1.** $R(0, 0)$ and $S(8, -6)$ $(4, -3)$

**2.** $R(5, 0)$ and $S(11, 2)$ $(8, 1)$

**3.** $R(-3, 2)$ and $S(5, -10)$ $(1, -4)$

**4.** $R(0, 7)$ and $S(8, 0)$ $(4, 3.5)$

## Suggested Extension

Have students plot points $A(0, 0)$, $B(8, 0)$, $C(10, 6)$, and $D(2, 6)$. Then have them complete the parallelogram and find the midpoint of each diagonal. $(5, 3)$ The fact that the same point is the midpoint of both diagonals confirms Theorem 6 of Chapter 5 (page 186): *Diagonals of a parallelogram bisect each other.*

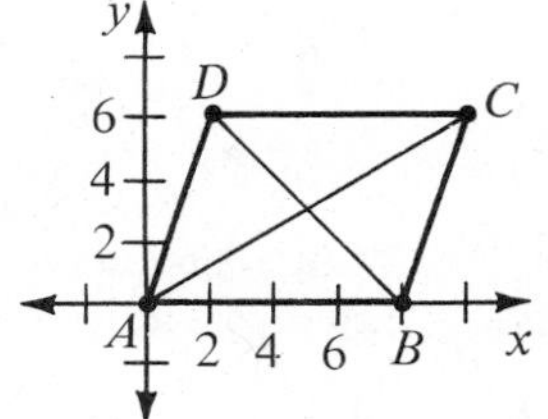


## Objectives for Pages 438–447

1. To find the slope of a line.
2. To apply the fact that parallel lines have equal slopes.
3. To apply the fact that the product of the slopes of two (nonvertical) perpendicular lines equals $-1$.

# 4•SLOPE OF A LINE (pp. 438–442)

## Teaching These Pages

Encourage students to go from left to right when they compute slopes. Then all lines that rise have positive slopes and all that fall have negative slopes. Use language carefully when you talk about vertical lines, but don't be too critical of students who think correctly but express themselves ambiguously. Note how easy it is to go from "That part of the road doesn't slope" to "That part of the road has no slope" to "A horizontal line doesn't have a slope." However, students must learn that a horizontal line does have a slope; the slope is the number zero. Use the phrasing, "If a line is vertical, slope is not defined for the line." Some students may form confusing mental images if you say "A vertical line has no slope."

## Chalkboard Examples

**Use points $A(1, 2)$, $B(5, 4)$, $C(4, 2)$, and $D(4, 0)$. State the slope of the line named. Write *not defined* if the line named is vertical.**

**1.** $\overleftrightarrow{AB}$ $\frac{1}{2}$ **2.** $\overleftrightarrow{AC}$ $0$ **3.** $\overleftrightarrow{AD}$ $-\frac{2}{3}$

**4.** $\overleftrightarrow{BC}$ $2$ **5.** $\overleftrightarrow{BD}$ $4$ **6.** $\overleftrightarrow{CD}$ not defined

## Suggested Extension

In the diagram, $\overline{AR}$ and $\overline{CS}$ are horizontal segments; $\overline{RB}$ and $\overline{SD}$ are vertical segments. Note that $\overleftrightarrow{AR}$ and $\overleftrightarrow{CS}$ are parallel lines cut by transversal $k$. Tell why:

1. $\angle BAR = \angle DCS$ Postulate 7 (p. 61)

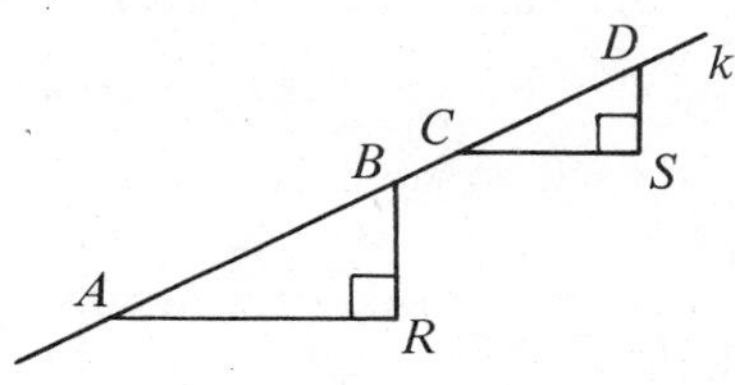


2. $\angle R = \angle S$ Hor. and vert. lines make rt. $\angle$s.
3. $\triangle BAR \sim \triangle DCS$ AA Postulate
4. $\frac{BR}{DS} = \frac{AR}{CS}$ Corr. parts of sim. triangles are in proportion
5. $\frac{BR}{AR} = \frac{DS}{CS}$ Switching Property

Note that $\frac{BR}{AR}$ and $\frac{DS}{CS}$ both represent the slope of line $k$.

## 5•PARALLEL AND PERPENDICULAR LINES (pp. 443–447)

### Teaching These Pages

You should use, without fanfare, the idea that vertical lines are parallel and horizontal lines are parallel. The coordinate grid itself implies this. It is better to say to beginning students, "If two lines are parallel, they have equal slopes" than "If two nonvertical lines are parallel, they have equal slopes." The precision you would achieve by using the second form would come at the expense of simplicity and clarity.

### Chalkboard Examples

**Use points $R(2, 2)$, $S(5, 4)$, and $T(5, 6)$. Find:**

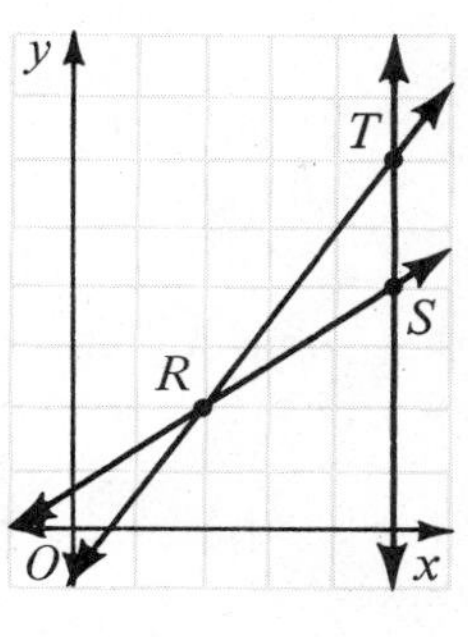


1. The slope of $\overleftrightarrow{RS}$; of $\overleftrightarrow{RT}$ $\frac{2}{3}$; $\frac{4}{3}$

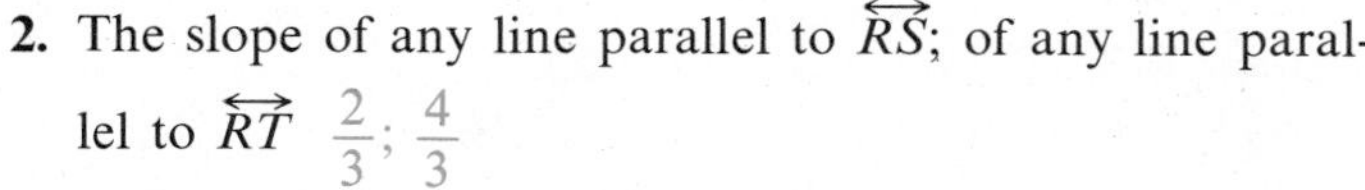

2. The slope of any line parallel to $\overleftrightarrow{RS}$; of any line parallel to $\overleftrightarrow{RT}$ $\frac{2}{3}$; $\frac{4}{3}$

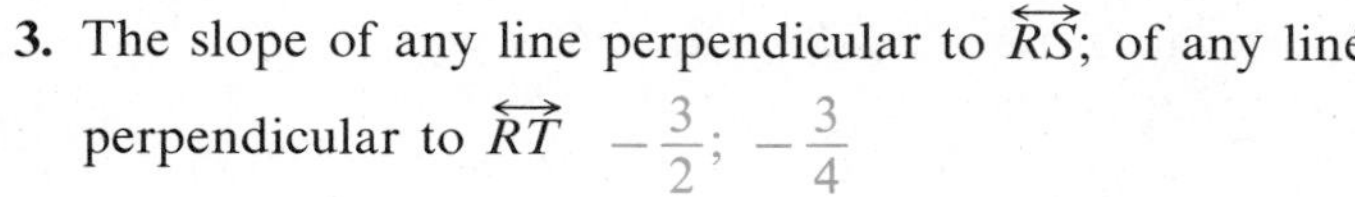

3. The slope of any line perpendicular to $\overleftrightarrow{RS}$; of any line perpendicular to $\overleftrightarrow{RT}$ $-\frac{3}{2}$; $-\frac{3}{4}$

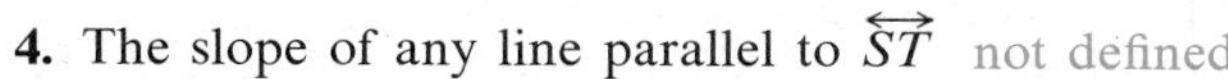

4. The slope of any line parallel to $\overleftrightarrow{ST}$ not defined
5. The slope of any line perpendicular to $\overleftrightarrow{ST}$ 0

## Suggested Extension

**Plot points $A(-2, 0)$, $B(2, 3)$, $C(2, -2)$, and $D(-2, -5)$. Complete.**

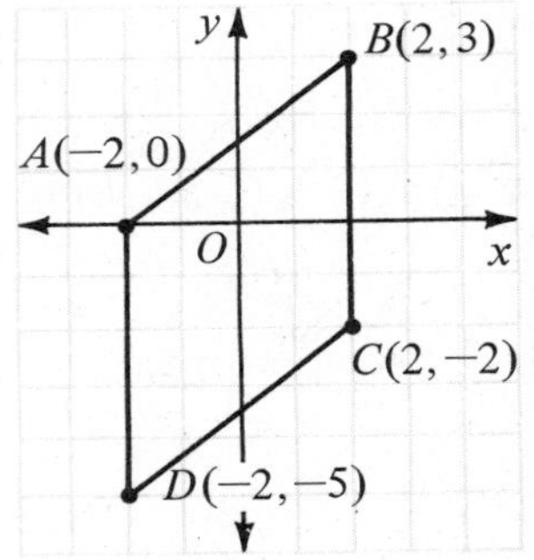


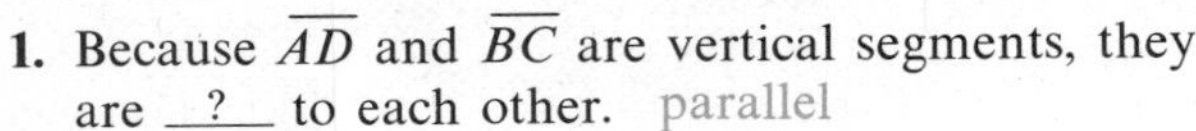

1. Because $\overline{AD}$ and $\overline{BC}$ are vertical segments, they are __?__ to each other. parallel
2. $\overline{AB}$ and $\overline{CD}$ are parallel segments because the slope of each equals __?__. $\frac{3}{4}$
3. Because opposite sides are parallel, quadrilateral $ABCD$ is a __?__. parallelogram
4. The slope of $\overline{AC}$ equals __?__, and the slope of $\overline{BD}$ equals __?__. $-\frac{1}{2}$; 2
5. $\overline{AC}$ and $\overline{BD}$ are __?__ to each other. perpendicular
6. From Exercises 3 and 5 you see that quadrilateral $ABCD$ must be a __?__. rhombus
7. Confirm your conclusion in Exercise 6 by finding the length of each side of quadrilateral $ABCD$. all sides are of length 5

## Objectives for Pages 448–456

1. To make a table of values for a linear equation.
2. To graph the line specified by a given equation.
3. To prove theorems using coordinate geometry.

## 6 • EQUATIONS AND LINES (pp. 448–452)

### Teaching These Pages

Remember that some students have difficulty graphing equations like $x = 3$. When you drill equations of the type $x = a$, all goes speedily. But later on, when students encounter $x = 3$ in the midst of equations like $x + y = 5$, confusion arises. There is no magic remedy. Patience on your part, and willingness to spread the graphing of lines over a period of several days will help. Encourage students to use simple numbers, especially 0, when they make tables of values, and to show fortitude when they need to plot such points as $\left(0, 2\frac{1}{3}\right)$.

## Chalkboard Examples

**Prepare tables of values for the equations.**

**1.** $x + y = 6$

| $x$ | $y$ |
|---|---|
| 0 | 6 |
| 2 | 4 |
| 4 | 2 |
| 6 | 0 |

**2.** $2x - y = 6$

| $x$ | $y$ |
|---|---|
| 0 | −6 |
| 1 | −4 |
| 2 | −2 |
| 3 | 0 |

**3.** $2x + 3y = 12$

| $x$ | $y$ |
|---|---|
| 0 | 4 |
| 3 | 2 |
| 6 | 0 |

**4–6.** Draw graphs of the equations in Examples 1–3.

**4.**

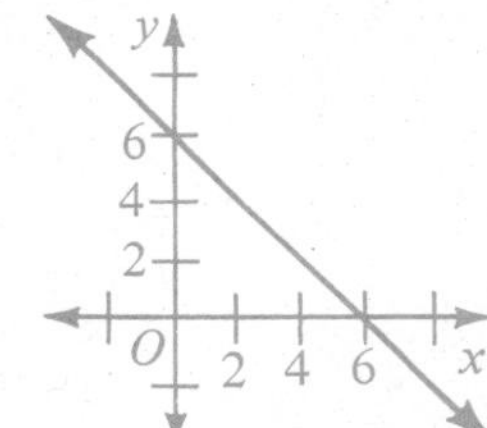


**5.**

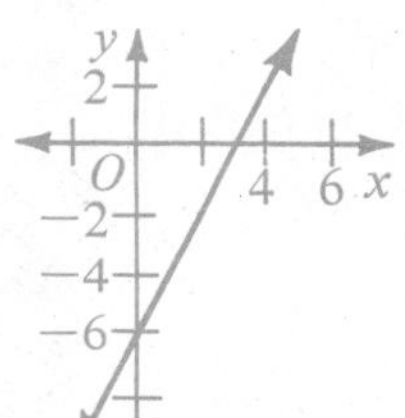


**6.**

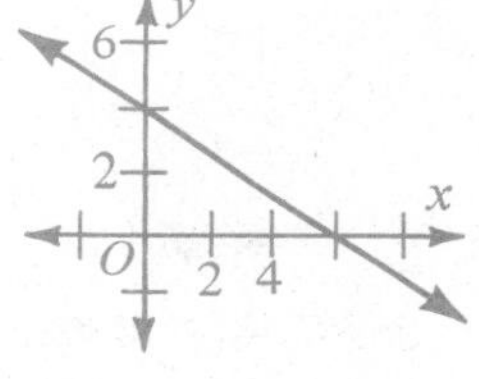


## Suggested Extension

Graph the equations

$$2x - 3y = -4$$
$$7x - 4y = 12$$
$$3x + 2y = -6$$

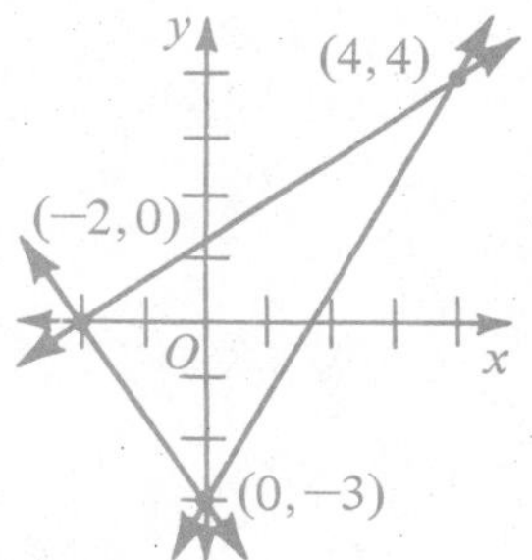


What kind of triangle is formed by the lines? Support your answer using two different arguments. right triangle; Prove this by (1) using the converse to the Pythagorean Theorem, or (2) showing that the line with equation $2x - 3y = 4$ is perpendicular to the line with equation $3x + 2y = -6$.

## 7 • COORDINATE GEOMETRY PROOFS (pp. 453–456)

### Teaching These Pages

Allow students plenty of time to study page 453. You may want to develop the theorem as a class project. Begin with a large figure drawn on the chalkboard. Assign coordinates to the vertices, explaining that we use the coefficient "2" in the coordinates to simplify the calculations. Then find the coordinates of $M$ and $N$. Have students state the slope of $\overline{MN}$, then of $\overline{AB}$ and $\overline{DC}$, leading to the deduction that $\overline{MN} \parallel \overline{AB} \parallel \overline{DC}$. Finally, have students find the lengths of $\overline{MN}$, $\overline{AB}$, and $\overline{DC}$, showing that $MN = \frac{1}{2}(AB + DC)$.

## Chalkboard Examples

**Coordinates have been assigned to three vertices of an isosceles trapezoid.**

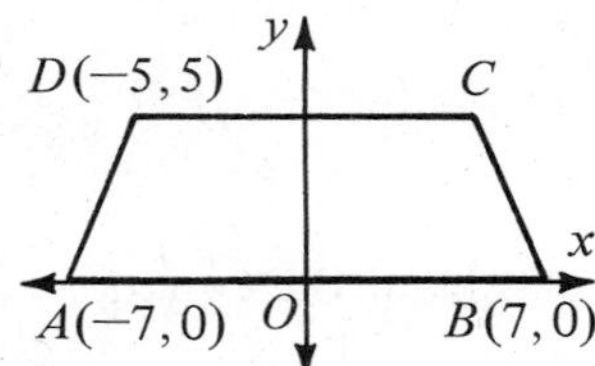


1. Find the coordinates of vertex $C$. (5, 5)
2. Check your work by showing that $AD = BC$.
   $AD = \sqrt{2^2 + 5^2} = \sqrt{29} = BC$
3. Prove that the diagonals of this isosceles trapezoid are equal.
   $BD = \sqrt{12^2 + 5^2} = 13$
   $AC = \sqrt{12^2 + 5^2} = 13$

## Suggested Extension

**Given points $P(a, b)$ and $Q(c, d)$:**

1. Prove that point $J\left(\frac{2a + c}{3}, \frac{2b + d}{3}\right)$ is one of the trisection points of $\overline{PQ}$ by proving that $PJ = \frac{1}{3}PQ$ and $JQ = \frac{2}{3}PQ$.

$$(PJ)^2 = \left(\frac{2a + c}{3} - a\right)^2 + \left(\frac{2b + d}{3} - b\right)^2 = \left(\frac{c - a}{3}\right)^2 + \left(\frac{d - b}{3}\right)^2$$
$$= \frac{1}{9}[(c - a)^2 + (d - b)^2] = \frac{1}{9}(PQ)^2$$

Hence $PJ = \frac{1}{3}PQ$.

$$(JQ)^2 = \left(\frac{2a + c}{3} - c\right)^2 + \left(\frac{2b + d}{3} - d\right)^2 = \left[\frac{2}{3}(a - c)\right]^2 + \left[\frac{2}{3}(b - d)\right]^2$$
$$= \frac{4}{9}[(a - c)^2 + (b - d)^2] = \frac{4}{9}(PQ)^2$$

Hence $JQ = \frac{2}{3}PQ$.

2. Use the triangle at right to prove that the medians of a triangle meet at a point $\frac{2}{3}$ of the way along each median.

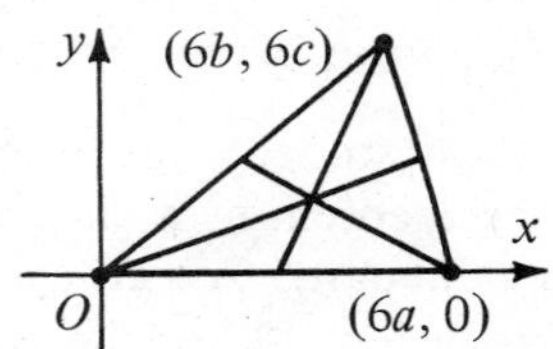


*Strategy:*
1. Find the coordinates of the midpoints of the sides.
2. Use the formula from the exercise above to show that $(2a + 2b, 2c)$ is a trisection point of all three medians.

# ANNOTATED ANSWERS

(Answers too long to be included on the student pages.)

**Written Exercises, page 7**

**29.** Geo-indicates the earth; geometry means to measure land; geography is the study of the earth and its features; geology is the study of the origin, history, and structure of the earth.

**Classroom Practice, page 47**

**7.** If the tent falls, then the rope breaks.
**8.** If you are a genius, then I am smart.
**9.** If $x = 10$, then $3x - 7 = 23$
**10.** If I go, then you will. **11.** If we succeed, then we shall try.
**12.** If you practice, then you want to play in Yankee Stadium.

**Written Exercises, page 48**

**7.** If two angles are complementary, their sum is $90°$.
**8.** If it pours, it rains.
**9.** If $x = 4$, then $5x + 7 = 27$
**10.** If I am there at noon, I'll have taken the bus.
**11.** If we play tennis on Tuesday, then it will be a nice day.
**12.** If a number is greater than 3, then it is greater than 4.

**Written Exercises, page 155**

**1.** $\angle 2 = 65°$; $\angle 3 = \angle 4 = 115°$; $\angle 5 = 50°$ **2.** $\angle 1 = \angle 2 = 60°$; $\angle 4 = 120°$; $\angle 5 = 60°$
**3.** $\angle 1 = \angle 2 = 64°$; $\angle 3 = 116°$; $\angle 5 = 52°$ **4.** $\angle 1 = 70°$; $\angle 3 = \angle 4 = 110°$; $\angle 5 = 40°$
**5.** $\angle 2 = 68°$; $\angle 3 = \angle 4 = 112°$; $\angle 5 = 44°$ **6.** $\angle 1 = \angle 2 = 68°$; $\angle 4 = 112°$; $\angle 5 = 44°$
**7.** $\angle 1 = \angle 2 = 69°$; $\angle 3 = \angle 4 = 111°$ **8.** $\angle 1 = \angle 2 = 65°$; $\angle 3 = \angle 4 = 115°$
**9.** $\angle 2 = j°$; $\angle 3 = \angle 4 = (180 - j)°$; $\angle 5 = (180 - 2j)°$
**10.** $\angle 2 = k°$; $\angle 3 = \angle 4 = (180 - k)°$; $\angle 5 = (180 - 2k)°$

**Classroom Practice, page 248**

**1.** $d = 10$; $C = 10\pi$; $A = 25\pi$ **2.** $d = 18$; $C = 18\pi$; $A = 81\pi$
**3.** $r = 4$; $C = 8\pi$; $A = 16\pi$ **4.** $r = 8$; $C = 16\pi$; $A = 64\pi$
**5.** $r = 14$; $d = 28$; $A = 196\pi$ **6.** $r = 6$; $d = 12$; $A = 36\pi$
**7.** $r = 2$; $d = 4$; $C = 4\pi$ **8.** $r = 1$; $d = 2$; $C = 2\pi$

**Classroom Practice, page 355**

**7. a.** a pencil on a desk **b.** the line of intersection of 2 walls and the floor **c.** a non-vertical chair leg and the floor **d.** the line of intersection of 2 walls and a third wall
**8. a.** the bottoms of 4 chair legs **b.** 3 noncollinear points on a desk and a point on a wall
**10. a.** the lines of intersection of the floor and ceiling with a wall compared with the intersection of that wall and an adjacent wall **b.** the 3 lines of intersection in a corner of the room

**Written Exercises, page 375**

**10.** $C = 6\pi$; $B = 9\pi$; L.A. $= 15\pi$; T.A. $= 24\pi$; $V = 12\pi$
**11.** $C = 24\pi$; $B = 144\pi$; L.A. $= 180\pi$; T.A. $= 324\pi$; $V = 432\pi$
**12.** $C = 16\pi$; $B = 64\pi$; L.A. $= 136\pi$; T.A. $= 200\pi$; $V = 320\pi$
**13.** $r = 6$; $B = 36\pi$; L.A. $= 60\pi$; T.A. $= 96\pi$; $V = 96\pi$
**14.** $r = 4$; $C = 8\pi$; L.A. $= 20\pi$; T.A. $= 36\pi$; $V = 16\pi$
**15.** $C = 10\pi$; $B = 25\pi$; $h = 12$; $l = 13$; L.A. $= 65\pi$; T.A. $= 90\pi$

**Written Exercises, page 379**

**9.** $d = \frac{1}{4}$; $A = \frac{1}{16}\pi$; $V = \frac{1}{384}\pi$

**10.** $r = \frac{3}{8}$; $A = \frac{9}{16}\pi$; $V = \frac{9}{128}\pi$

**11.** $r = 5$; $d = 10$; $V = \frac{500}{3}\pi$

**12.** $r = 6$; $d = 12$; $A = 144\pi$

**13.** $d = 3$; $A = 9\pi$; $V = \frac{9}{2}\pi$

**14.** $r = 6$; $d = 12$; $V = 288\pi$

**15.** $r = 7$; $d = 14$; $A = 196\pi$

**16.** $r = \sqrt{3}$; $A = 12\pi$; $V = 4\sqrt{3}\pi$

**Written Exercises, page 399**

**31.** $BC = 6$; $AC = 6\sqrt{3}$; $CD = 3\sqrt{3}$; $AD = 9$; $DB = 3$
**32.** $AB = 20$; $AC = 10\sqrt{3}$; $CD = 5\sqrt{3}$; $AD = 15$; $DB = 5$
**33.** $AB = 8$; $BC = 4$; $CD = 2\sqrt{3}$; $AD = 6$; $DB = 2$
**34.** $AB = 12$; $BC = 6$; $AC = 6\sqrt{3}$; $CD = 3\sqrt{3}$; $AD = 9$
**35.** $AB = 28$; $BC = 14$; $AC = 14\sqrt{3}$; $AD = 21$; $DB = 7$
**36.** $AB = 12$; $BC = 6$; $AC = 6\sqrt{3}$; $CD = 3\sqrt{3}$; $DB = 3$

# Basic Geometry

# Basic Geometry

Ray C. Jurgensen
Richard G. Brown

Editorial Adviser:
Albert E. Meder, Jr.

Teacher Consultant:
Robert J. McMurray

Houghton Mifflin Company, Boston
Atlanta Dallas Geneva, Illinois
Lawrenceville, New Jersey Palo Alto Toronto

## The Authors

**Ray C. Jurgensen,** Chairman of the Mathematics Department and holder of the Eppley Chair of Mathematics at the Culver Academies, Culver, Indiana. Mr. Jurgensen has been a lecturer at the National Science Foundation institutes for mathematics teachers and meetings of the National Council of Teachers of Mathematics.

**Richard G. Brown,** Mathematics teacher at the Phillips Exeter Academy, Exeter, New Hampshire. Mr. Brown has taught a wide range of mathematics courses for both students and teachers at several schools and universities, including Newton, Massachusetts, High School and the University of New Hampshire.

## Editorial Adviser

**Albert E. Meder, Jr.,** Dean and Vice Provost and Professor of Mathematics, Emeritus, Rutgers, The State University of New Jersey.

## Teacher Consultant

**Robert J. McMurray,** Mathematics teacher in the Albuquerque, New Mexico, Public School System. Mr. McMurray has many years of experience teaching geometry in secondary schools.

1986 Impression



Printed in U.S.A.
ISBN: 0-395-34051-9

# Contents

## UNIT A

## UNIT B

## UNIT C

## UNIT D

## UNIT E

## UNIT F

# Symbols

| Symbol | Meaning | Page |
|---|---|---|
| $\angle$, $\angle$s | angle, angles | 8 |
| $\angle ABC$ | angle $ABC$, measure of $\angle ABC$ | 8 |
| $\overset{\frown}{CD}$ | arc with end-points $C$ and $D$, measure of $\overset{\frown}{CD}$ | 323 |
| $A$ | area | 216 |
| $B$ | area of base | 360 |
| $\odot P$ | circle with center $P$ | 242 |
| $C$ | circumference | 242 |
| $\cong$ | congruent, is congruent to | 93 |
| cos | cosine | 414 |
| $^\circ$ | degrees | 8 |
| $d$ | diameter, | 242 |
| | length of diagonal, | 403 |
| | distance | 430 |
| $=$ | equals, is equal to | 5 |
| $\doteq$ | is approximately equal to | 243 |
| $\neq$ | is not equal to | 52 |
| $>$ | is greater than | 31 |
| $<$ | is less than | 49 |
| L.A. | lateral area | 360 |
| $h$ | length of altitude, height | 216 |
| $b$ | length of base | 216 |
| $s$ | length of a side of a square | 217 |
| $l$ | length of slant height | 369 |
| $XY$ | length of $\overline{XY}$ | 5 |
| $\overleftrightarrow{CD}$ | line through points $C$ and $D$ | 4 |
| $(x, y)$ | point with coordinates $x$ and $y$ | 75 |
| $\parallel$ | parallel, is parallel to | 30 |
| ▱ | parallelogram | 180 |
| $p$ | perimeter | 218 |
| $\perp$ | perpendicular, is perpendicular to | 13 |
| $\pi$ | pi | 243 |
| $r$ | radius | 243 |
| $\frac{a}{b}$, $a:b$ | ratio of $a$ to $b$ | 260 |
| $\overrightarrow{AB}$ | ray with endpoint $A$ | 4 |
| $\overline{AB}$ | segment with endpoints $A$ and $B$ | 4 |
| $\sim$ | similar, is similar to | 282 |
| sin | sine | 414 |
| $\sqrt{x}$ | positive square root of $x$ | 235 |
| tan | tangent | 410 |
| T.A. | total area | 360 |
| $\triangle$, $\triangle$s | triangle, triangles | 13 |
| $V$ | volume | 360 |

### Metric system symbols

| Symbol | Meaning |
|---|---|
| mm | millimeter |
| cm | centimeter |
| m | meter |
| km | kilometer |
| $cm^2$ | square centimeter |
| $m^2$ | square meter |
| $km^2$ | square kilometer |
| $cm^3$ | cubic centimeter |
| $m^3$ | cubic meter |
| L | liter |
| g | gram |
| $g/cm^3$ | grams per cubic centimeter |
| min | minute |
| h | hour |

# Why Study Geometry?

As you begin your study of geometry, you may wonder why geometry is important. Here are a few reasons to consider.

Many careers use geometry. Your studies can help prepare you for work in carpentry, design, mechanics, or architecture.

Geometry will help you organize facts and think logically. These skills will be valuable no matter what career you choose.

The world is full of geometric shapes. The musical instruments below contain many examples of rectangles, triangles, circles, cylinders, and spheres. Geometry will teach you the special properties of these figures.

# UNIT A

### *Here's what you'll learn in this chapter:*

1. To name points, lines, rays, segments, angles, and planes.
2. To measure and classify angles.
3. To do basic constructions with a compass and a straightedge.
4. To use postulates of equality and postulates of geometry to justify statements.

# Chapter 1

# Points, Lines, and Angles

# 1 • Beginning Your Study of Geometry

For each diagram below, tell which line looks longer—the solid green one or the solid black one.

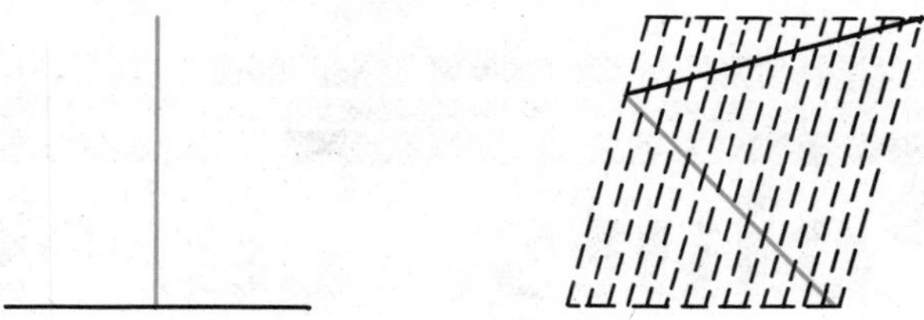

Check your answers by measuring.

Were you fooled by these optical illusions? They show that you cannot always depend on appearances. Sometimes you need to measure. In this course you will need three tools for measuring: a ruler, a protractor, and a compass.

Not all geometry problems can be solved by measuring. Many are solved by reasoning logically, starting with known geometric facts. This is the kind of reasoning you will study in this course. The following experiments preview some of the things that you will learn. Try them.

**1**

1. Draw a rectangle. Join the midpoints of the sides. What kind of figure is formed?
2. Now join the midpoints of the "inside" figure to form a third four-sided figure. What kind of figure is formed? How do its dimensions compare with the dimensions of the original rectangle?
3. Try this experiment again, beginning with a different-looking rectangle.

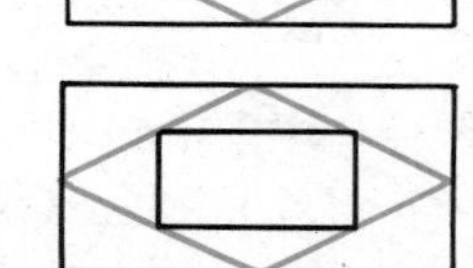

**2**

Imagine that the earth is a perfectly round ball. A giant hoop fits exactly around the earth's equator. The hoop is then stretched so that it is 2 m longer. (Two meters is about the height of a tall person.)

The hoop now floats evenly around the earth. Is there enough room between the earth and the hoop for a flea to crawl under? a fly? a mouse? a cat?

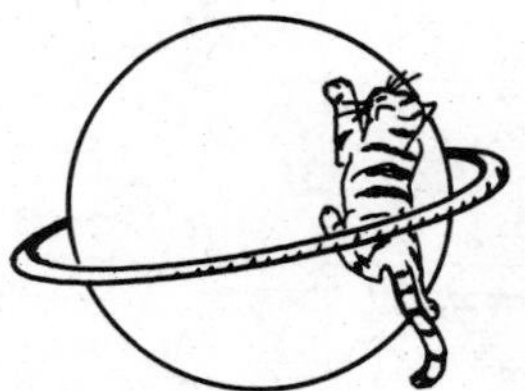

The answers are at the top of the next page.

*Experiment 1:* When you join the midpoints of a rectangle, you form a parallelogram with all sides equal. This figure is called a *rhombus.*

When you join the midpoints of this rhombus, you form a rectangle. The length and width of this rectangle are half those of the original rectangle.

*Experiment 2:* All of them could crawl under the hoop. Later in the course you will be able to prove that there are about 32 cm between the earth and the hoop. See Exercise 40 on page 246.

The experiments should suggest that some geometric problems have surprising results. To get these results, we begin our study with some very *un*surprising ones. We will piece these together to prove more substantial results, called *theorems.* In a way, this process is like detective work. We will fit together geometric clues to arrive at conclusions. The exercises will give you a chance to do some detective work.

## Exercises

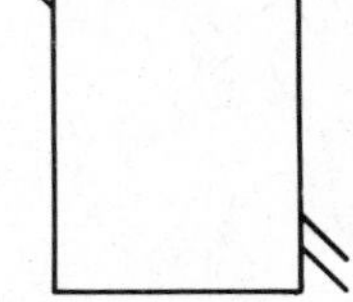

1. Which line at the right of the rectangle is the continuation of the line at the left? the bottom line

2. Draw several four-sided figures. For each, join the midpoints of the sides. In each case, what kind of figure is formed? parallelogram

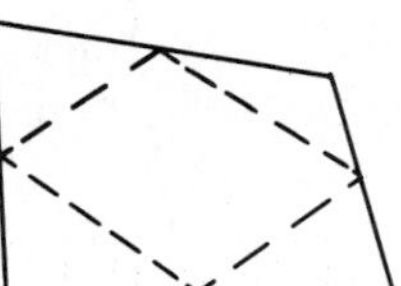
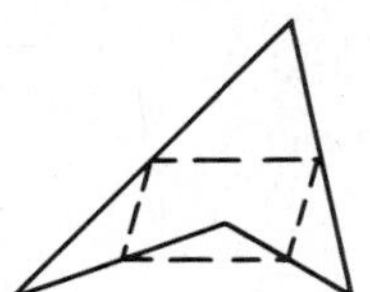
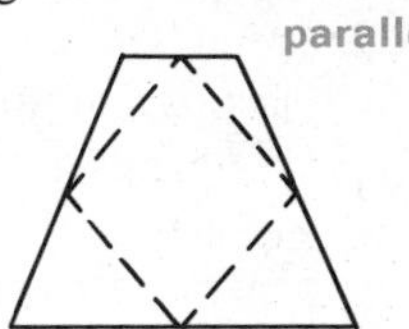

3. Wrap a piece of string tightly around a large wastebasket. Wrap another piece around a small tin can. Then add two meters of string to each piece. Finally, spread the lengthened strings evenly around the wastebasket and the can as shown.

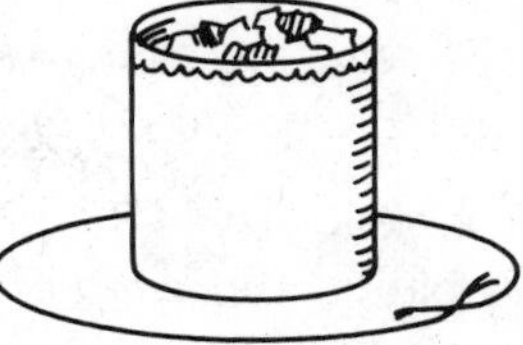

Compare the space between the string and the wastebasket with the space between the string and the can. What do you notice?
The spaces are the same. For any diameter, the distance will be $\frac{2}{\pi}$ meters.

# 2 • Points and Lines

Do you know that a color television picture is composed of thousands of dots? You don't notice the spaces between the dots because the dots are so close to each other.

The idea of tightly-packed dots is sometimes used in mathematics. For example, the picture below suggests that a **line** contains very many **points.**

Each dot represents a point of the line.

Actually, a line contains an unlimited number of points. We usually picture a line by drawing along the edge of a ruler, like this.

The arrowheads in the drawing suggest that a line extends indefinitely far in both directions.

The drawings below explain how we name points and lines.

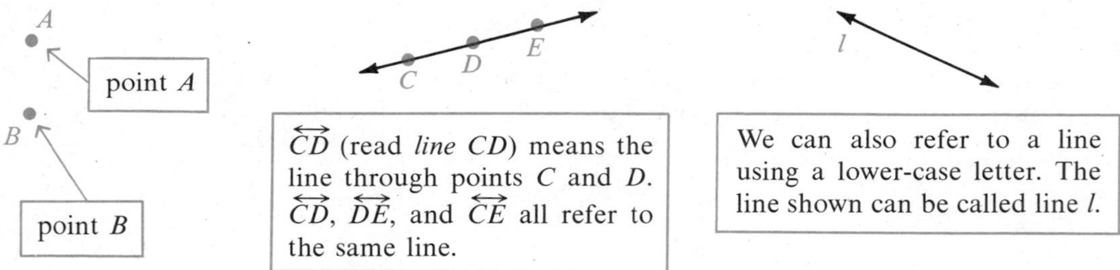


point *A*

point *B*

$\overleftrightarrow{CD}$ (read *line CD*) means the line through points *C* and *D*. $\overleftrightarrow{CD}$, $\overleftrightarrow{DE}$, and $\overleftrightarrow{CE}$ all refer to the same line.

We can also refer to a line using a lower-case letter. The line shown can be called line *l*.

The points *C*, *D*, and *E* in the middle diagram above are called **collinear points.** This means that they are all on one line. On the other hand, the points *X*, *Y*, and *Z* pictured at the right are not collinear points. They do not lie on one line.

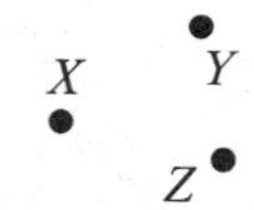


A *segment* and a *ray* are parts of a line as shown below.

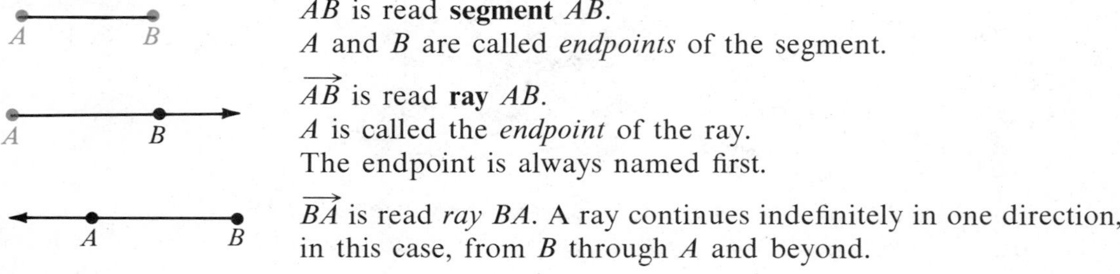


$\overline{AB}$ is read **segment** *AB*.
*A* and *B* are called *endpoints* of the segment.

$\overrightarrow{AB}$ is read **ray** *AB*.
*A* is called the *endpoint* of the ray.
The endpoint is always named first.

$\overrightarrow{BA}$ is read *ray BA*. A ray continues indefinitely in one direction, in this case, from *B* through *A* and beyond.

Notice that $\overrightarrow{BA}$ and $\overrightarrow{AB}$ refer to different rays. On the other hand, $\overline{BA}$ and $\overline{AB}$ refer to the same segment.

Each point of a line can be paired with a real number. Similarly, each real number can be paired with a point.

See The Ruler Postulate, page 31.

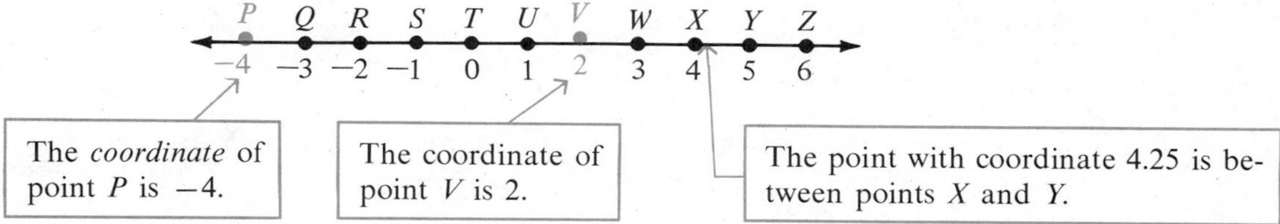


The symbol $XY$ stands for the length of $\overline{XY}$. This length is just the distance between $X$ and $Y$. It can be found by counting the number of units from $X$ to $Y$. It can also be found by subtracting the smaller coordinate (the one on the left) from the larger coordinate (the one on the right). Using the figure above, we find:

$$XY = 5 - 4 = 1$$

$$SU = 1 - (-1) = 1 + 1 = 2$$

$$PS = -1 - (-4) = -1 + 4 = 3$$

In the diagram above, the *midpoint* of $\overline{SU}$ is the point $T$. It is exactly halfway between $S$ and $U$. In general, the **midpoint** of a segment is defined in this way:

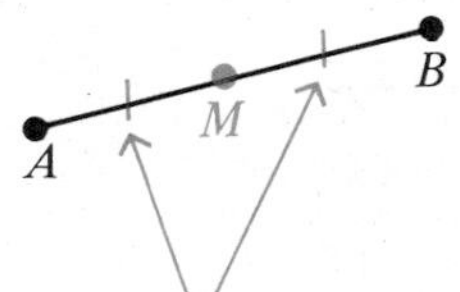


$M$ is the midpoint of $\overline{AB}$ means that

(1) $M$ is on $\overline{AB}$ and

(2) $AM = MB$.

The little marks show that $AM = MB$.

From the definition of midpoint it is clear that $AM = \frac{1}{2}AB$ and $MB = \frac{1}{2}AB$.

In the diagram, $Q$ is the midpoint of $\overline{PS}$, $RS = 2$, and $QR = 3$. Find $PS$.

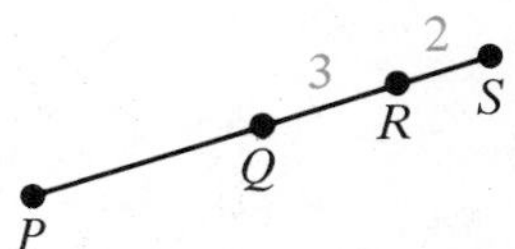


$QS = QR + RS = 3 + 2 = 5$
Since $QS = 5$, $PQ$ also equals 5.
Then $PS = PQ + QS = 10$.

## Classroom Practice

**Two lines meet at $O$ as shown.**
**Tell whether each statement is true or false.**

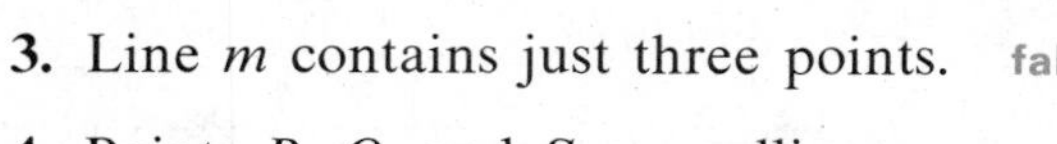


1. $\overleftrightarrow{OS}$ is the same as $\overleftrightarrow{OR}$. true
2. $\overline{OS}$ is the same as $\overline{OR}$. false
3. Line $m$ contains just three points. false
4. Points $R$, $O$, and $S$ are collinear. true
5. Points $N$, $O$, and $S$ are collinear. false

**Exercises 6–10 refer to the diagram at right.**

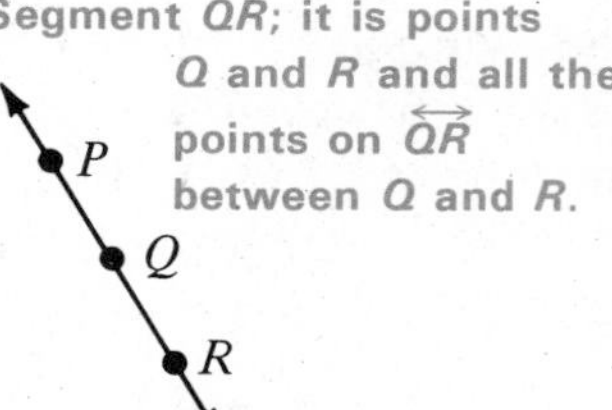


6. Read the symbol $\overline{QR}$ and explain what it means. Segment $QR$; it is points $Q$ and $R$ and all the points on $\overleftrightarrow{QR}$ between $Q$ and $R$.
7. Name the endpoints of **a.** $\overline{PQ}$; **b.** $\overline{QP}$. a. $P$ and $Q$ b. $P$ and $Q$
8. Read the symbol $\overrightarrow{QP}$ and explain what it means. (see below)
9. Name the endpoint of **a.** $\overrightarrow{PQ}$; **b.** $\overrightarrow{QP}$. a. $P$ b. $Q$
10. Which points are in both $\overrightarrow{QR}$ and $\overrightarrow{PQ}$? $\overrightarrow{QR}$

**Exercises 11–15 refer to the diagram.**

B E L G I U M
−3 −2 −1 0 1 2 3

11. Name the coordinate of $B$. −3
12. Name the point with coordinate 3. $M$
13. Name the midpoint of $\overline{IM}$. $U$
14. Find each distance: **a.** $IM$; **b.** $LU$; **c.** $BL$. a. 2 b. 3 c. 2
15. How many real numbers are there between 1 and 2—a limited number or an unlimited number? How many points are there between $I$ and $U$? unlimited number; unlimited number

8. Ray $QP$; it is $Q$ and all points on $\overleftrightarrow{QR}$ on the same side of $Q$ as $P$.

## Written Exercises

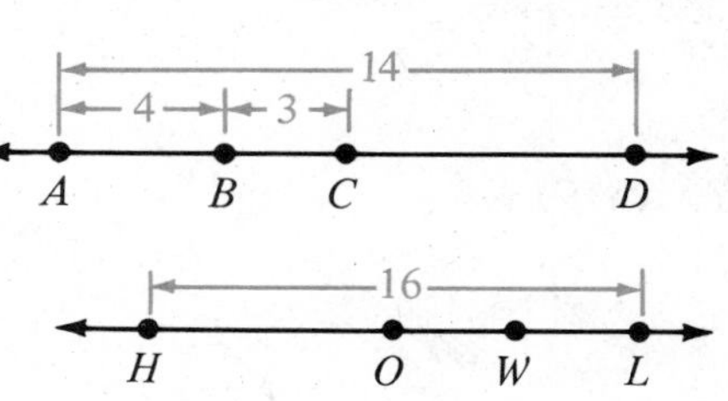


A

1. Suppose $AB = 4$, $BC = 3$, and $AD = 14$.
   **a.** Then $CD =$ _?_. 7
   **b.** Is $C$ the midpoint of $\overline{AD}$? yes
2. Suppose $O$ is the midpoint of $\overline{HL}$.
   **a.** If $HL = 16$, then $OL =$ _?_. 8
   **b.** Suppose you also know that $W$ is the midpoint of $\overline{OL}$. Then $OW =$ _?_. 4

**Exercises 3–10 refer to the figure.**

B L U E F I S H

−5 −3 1 3 7

Exercises 3–10

3. The coordinate of point $L$ is __?__. −3

4. If $I$ is the midpoint of $\overline{FS}$, then the coordinate of $I$ is __?__. 5

5. If $L$ is the midpoint of $\overline{BU}$, then the coordinate of $U$ is __?__. −1

6. If $SH = 2$, then the coordinate of $H$ is __?__. 9

**Find each distance.**

7. $FS$ 4
8. $FL$ 6
9. $BL$ 2
10. $SB$ 12

**The coordinates of $Z$ and $A$ are −10 and 20, as shown. $B$ is the midpoint of $\overline{ZA}$, $ZE = 6$, and $ZR = 23$. Find each of the following.**

11. The coordinate of $B$ 5
12. The coordinate of $E$ −4
13. The coordinate of $R$ 13
14. $ZB$ 15
15. $ER$ 17
16. $EA$ 24

Z E B R A

−10 20

Exercises 11–20

**Using the diagram for Exercises 11–16, tell whether each statement is true or false.**

17. There are an unlimited number of points between $E$ and $B$. true

18. $\overline{ER}$ and $\overline{RE}$ refer to the same segment. true

19. $\overrightarrow{ER}$ and $\overrightarrow{RE}$ refer to the same ray. false

20. $\overleftrightarrow{ER}$ and $\overleftrightarrow{AB}$ refer to the same line. true

**Suppose $S$ is the midpoint of $\overline{RT}$. Complete the table.**

R S T

B

| | 21. | 22. | 23. | 24. | 25. | 26. | 27. | 28. |
|---|---|---|---|---|---|---|---|---|
| coordinate of $R$ | 8 | −4 | −18 | 5 | 17 | −18 | $a$ | $b - 10$ |
| coordinate of $T$ | 12 | 12 | −2 | ? 13 | ? 41 | ? −2 | $a + 6$ | 6 |
| length of $\overline{RT}$ | ? 4 | 16 | ? 16 | ? 8 | ? 24 | ? 16 | ? 6 | ? (see below) |
| coordinate of $S$ | 10 | ? 4 | ? −10 | 9 | 29 | −10 | ? $a + 3$ | ? |

29. Look up the meaning of the prefix "geo-." Relate this meaning to the words "geometry," "geography," and "geology." Answer on page T127

C 30. Points $X$, $Y$, and $Z$ have coordinates 2.001, $\frac{21}{8}$, and $\sqrt{5}$. Which of these points are between points $C$ and $D$? All three

A B C D

0 1 2 3

28. $RT = 16 - b$; the coordinate of $S$ is $\frac{b}{2} - 2$.

# 3 • Angles

As you may know, an **angle** is a figure formed by two rays or segments with a common endpoint. The rays or segments are called the **sides** of the angle and the endpoint is called the **vertex** of the angle. The diagrams below show how angles are named.

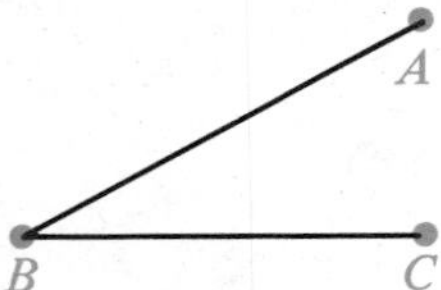

$\angle ABC$ means angle $ABC$.
$\angle CBA$ is another name for $\angle ABC$.
$\overline{BA}$ and $\overline{BC}$ are the sides.
$B$ is the vertex.

$\angle DEF$ means angle $DEF$.
$\angle DEF$ is the same as $\angle DEG$.
$\overrightarrow{ED}$ and $\overrightarrow{EF}$ are the sides.
$E$ is the vertex.

Notice that the vertex is always named in the middle.

Sometimes we use just one letter or one number to name an angle.

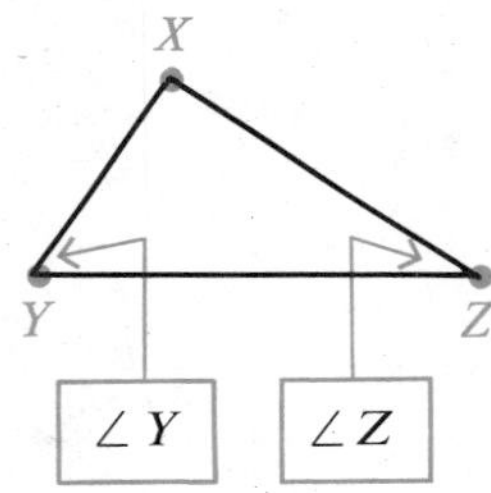


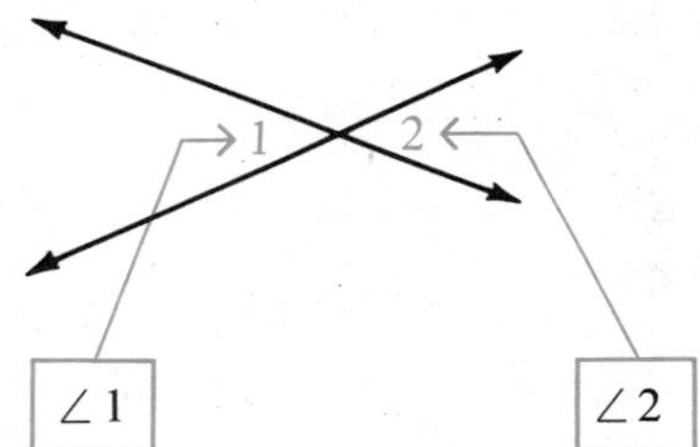


To find the *measure in degrees* of an angle, we use an instrument called a *protractor*. The diagram below shows how to do this. Can you see that the measure of $\angle AOB$ is 40°? This fact is written: $\angle AOB = 40°$.*

See The Protractor Postulate, page 31.

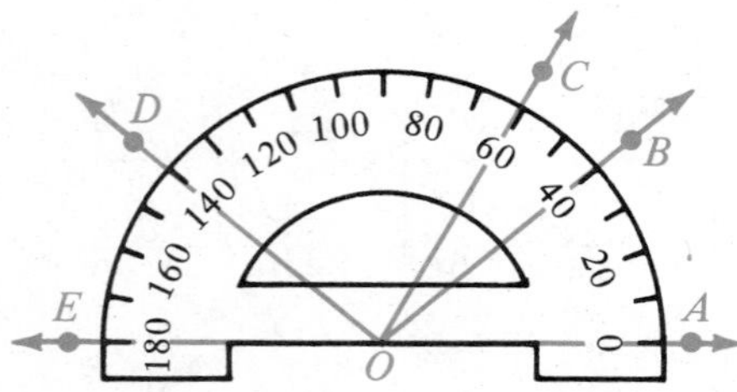


Notice that:

$\angle AOB = 40°$
$\angle AOE = 180°$
$\angle BOC = 60° - 40° = 20°$
$\angle DOB = 140° - 40° = 100°$
$\angle EOC = 180° - 60° = 120°$

* Note: Some books use the notation "$m\angle AOB = 40°$" and say, "the measure of $\angle AOB$ is 40°." In this book, we shall use the simpler notation "$\angle AOB = 40°$" and say, "$\angle AOB$ equals 40°."

Many protractors have two scales, one reading from left to right, and the other reading from right to left. To use this kind of protractor, follow these steps:

1. Estimate: Is the angle measure less than or greater than 90°?
2. Carefully line up your protractor as shown below. If the sides of the angle do not reach the scale, extend them.

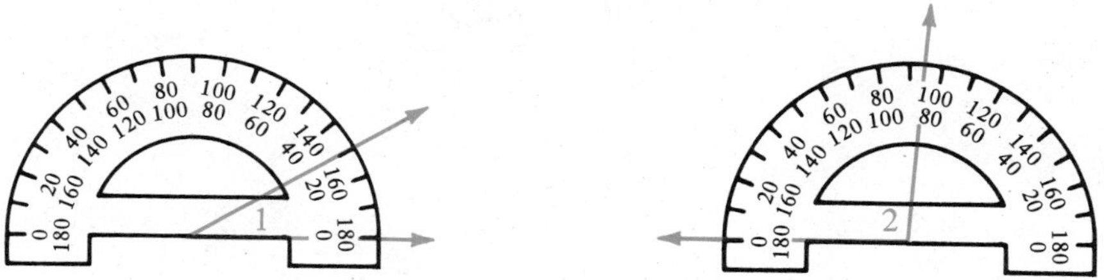


3. Choose the scale that has 0° at one side of the angle.
   Read the measure of the angle.
   Does the measure agree with your estimate?

**EXAMPLE** What is the measure of ∠3?

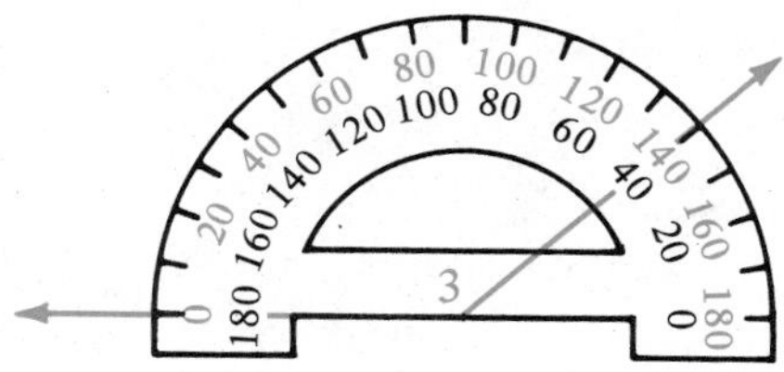


∠3 is greater than 90°.

Choose the scale on top.

∠3 = 140°

The diagram at the bottom of page 8 suggests that we can add and subtract angle measures. Here are some other examples.

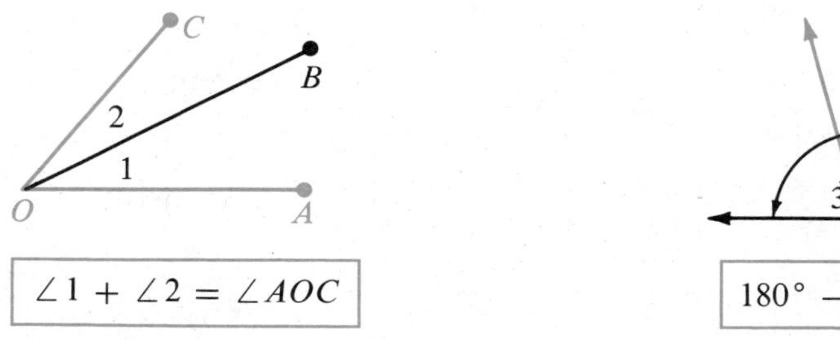


180°

3 4

180° − ∠3 = ∠4

## Classroom Practice

**Exercises 1–7 refer to the diagram.**

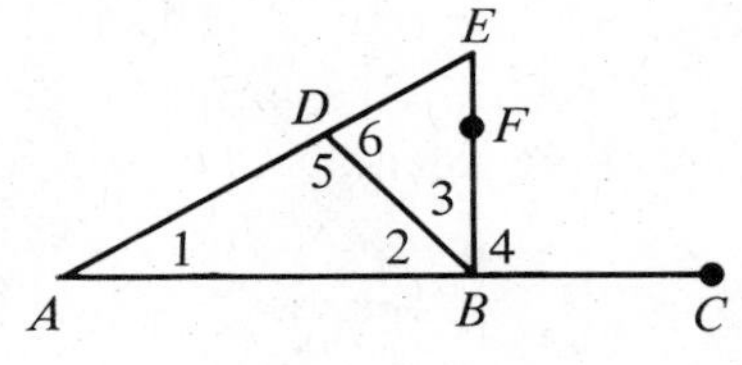


1. Name the vertex of $\angle 4$. B
2. Name the sides of $\angle 2$. $\overline{BD}$ and $\overline{BA}$
3. $\angle BAE$ and $\angle 1$ are names for the same angle. Give another name for each of the following angles:

   $\angle ABD$, $\angle AEB$, $\angle BDE$, $\angle 3$, $\angle 5$, $\angle 4$.

4. $\angle 5 + \angle 6 = \underline{\ ?\ }°$ 180°
5. $\angle ABE - \angle 3 = \angle \underline{\ ?\ }$ 2 or $ABD$
6. Explain why you should not refer to $\angle B$. Because it would not be clear whether you meant $\angle 2$, $\angle 3$, or $\angle 4$.
7. Is it correct to refer to $\angle A$? yes

3. $\angle 2$; $\angle E$, $\angle DEB$, $\angle AEF$, or $\angle DEF$; $\angle 6$; $\angle DBE$ or $\angle DBF$; $\angle ADB$; $\angle EBC$ or $\angle FBC$

**In Exercises 8–10, use the diagram shown.**

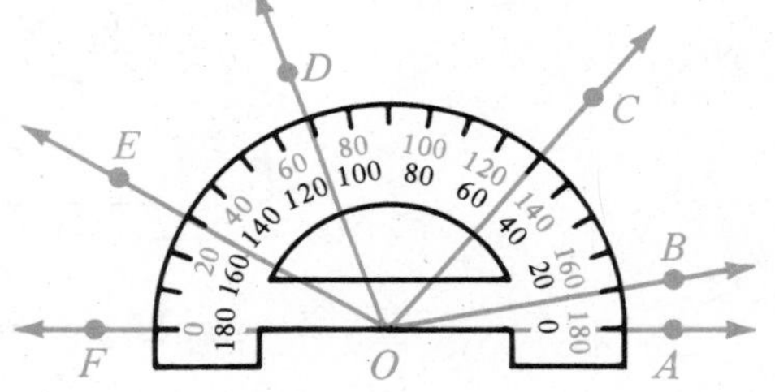


8. Using three letters for each angle, name five angles that have $\overrightarrow{OA}$ as one side. $\angle AOB$, $\angle AOC$, $\angle AOD$, $\angle AOE$, $\angle AOF$
9. Using three letters for each angle, name five angles that have $\overrightarrow{OC}$ as a side. $\angle AOC$, $\angle BOC$, $\angle DOC$, $\angle EOC$, $\angle FOC$
10. State the measure of each of the following:
    $\angle AOB$, 10°, $\angle AOC$, 50°, $\angle AOD$, 110°, $\angle AOE$, 150°, $\angle AOF$. 180°
11. Estimate the measure of each angle shown.

12. Without measuring, sketch each angle. Make your sketches large enough so that you can use a protractor to check the accuracy of your work.

    **a.** 90° angle **b.** 60° angle **c.** 10° angle **d.** 170° angle

## Written Exercises

**Complete each statement.**

A 1. The sides of $\angle AIH$ are ___?___ and ___?___. $\overrightarrow{IA}$ $\overrightarrow{IH}$

2. The vertex of $\angle AIH$ is ___?___. *I*

3. Another name for $\angle OIH$ is $\angle$ ___?___. *HIO*

4. $\angle DIA + \angle AIH = \angle$ ___?___ *DIH*

5. $\angle DIH + \angle HIO = \angle$ ___?___ = ___?___ ° *DIO* 180

6. $180° - \angle DIA = \angle$ ___?___ *OIA*

**Find the measure of each angle named.**

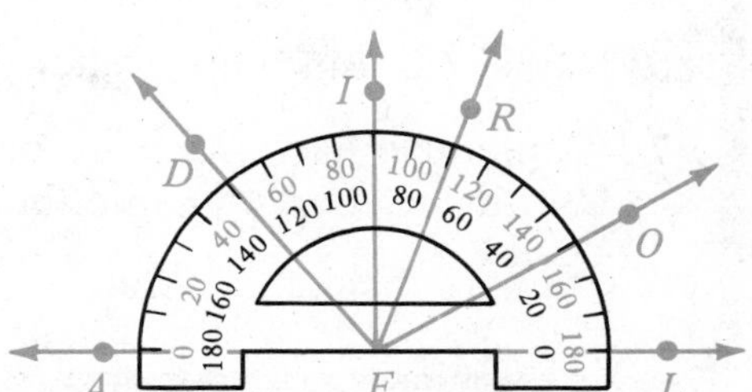


7. $\angle LFO$ 30°

8. $\angle RFA$ 110°

9. $\angle DFO$ 100°

10. $\angle AFL$ 180°

11. $\angle DFR$ 60°

12. $\angle IFL$ 90°

**Use your protractor to draw an angle with the given measure.**

**13.** 20° **14.** 65° **15.** 90° **16.** 140°

**17.** Estimate the measure of each angle shown.

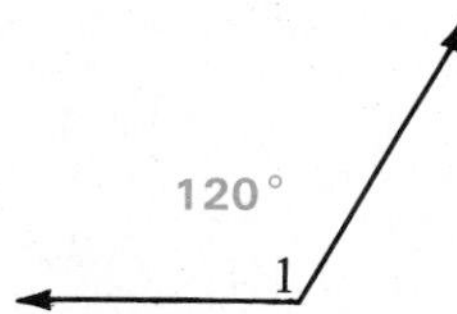


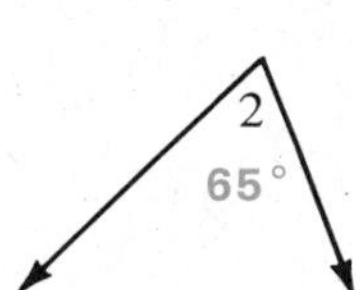


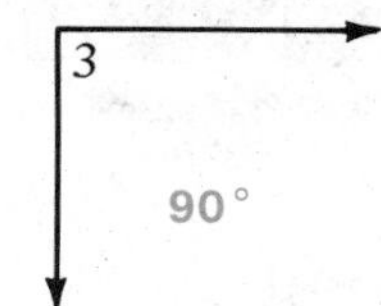


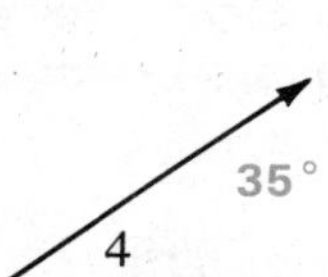


**18.** Without measuring, sketch each angle. Then use a protractor to check the accuracy of your work.

**a.** 45° angle **b.** 15° angle **c.** 85° angle **d.** 160° angle

**Complete each statement.**

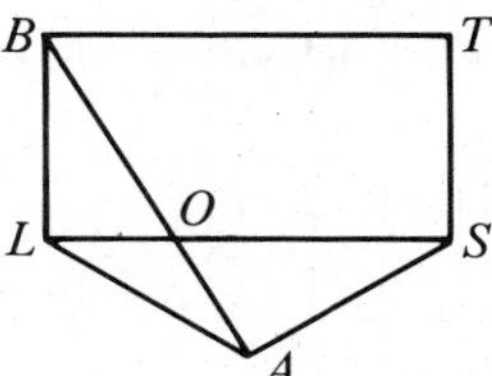


Sample $\angle BLO + \angle OLA =$ ___?___

$\angle BLO + \angle OLA = \angle BLA$

B **19.** $\angle BAS + \angle BAL = \angle$ ___?___ *LAS*

**20.** $\angle TSO + \angle OSA = \angle$ ___?___ *TSA*

**21.** $\angle LAS - \angle LAB = \angle$ ___?___ *BAS*

**22.** $180° - \angle BOS = \angle$ ___?___ $= \angle$ ___?___ *SOA* *BOL*

## SELF-TEST

**True or False?**

**1.** $\overleftrightarrow{AB}$ is the same as $\overleftrightarrow{BC}$. true

**2.** $\overrightarrow{AB}$ is the same as $\overrightarrow{BA}$. false

**3.** $C$ is the midpoint of $\overline{BD}$. true

**4.** $AB = 6$ true

A B C D
−2 4 9 14

**5.** What is the vertex of $\angle PRQ$? $R$

**6.** Name $\angle 2$ using three letters. $\angle PQS$

**7.** What angle has a measure of about 90°? Use three letters to name the angle. $\angle PQR$

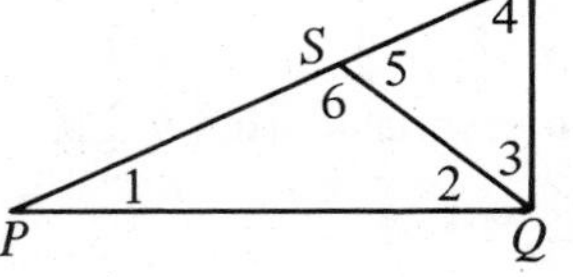


**8.** $\angle 5 + \angle 6 = \underline{\ \ ?\ \ }°$ 180

## CONSUMER CORNER

### *Time is Money*

People use the money they earn in their jobs to buy things they want and need: food, clothing, housing, books, and recreation. How much time must a person work to make these common purchases?

**Exercise**

Suppose a worker takes home $4.50 per hour. How much time will it take the worker to earn the money to pay for the following items?

| | | | |
|---|---|---|---|
| $3\frac{1}{3}$ hr | a $15 toaster | a monthly rent of $279 | 62 hr |
| $43\frac{1}{3}$ hr | a $195 television set | a $20 grocery bill | $4\frac{4}{9}$ hr |
| $\frac{1}{3}$ hr | a $1.50 paperback book | a 5¢ piece of gum | $\frac{1}{90}$ hr |

# 4 • Classifying Angles

Angles are often classified by their measures.

An **acute angle** has a measure between 0° and 90°.

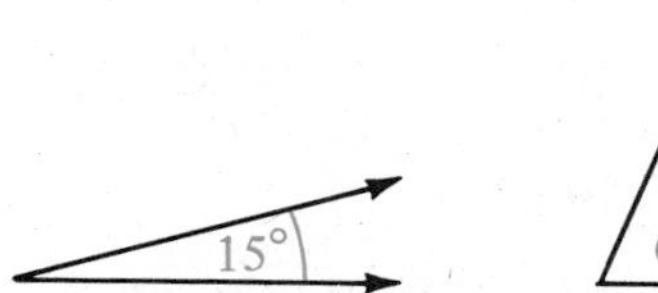


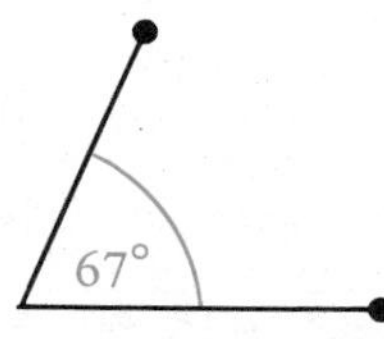


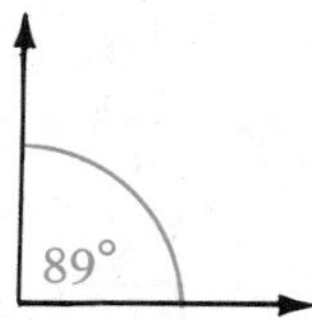


A **right angle** has measure 90°. We indicate a right angle by drawing a small square inside the angle like this. ⟶

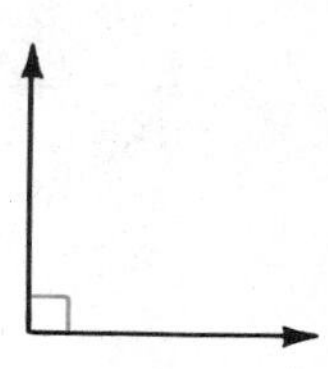

If an angle formed by two lines is a right angle, then the lines are **perpendicular.** Also, if two lines are perpendicular, they form right angles. In the diagram, line *AB* is perpendicular to line *CD*. This is written:

$$\overleftrightarrow{AB} \perp \overleftrightarrow{CD}.$$

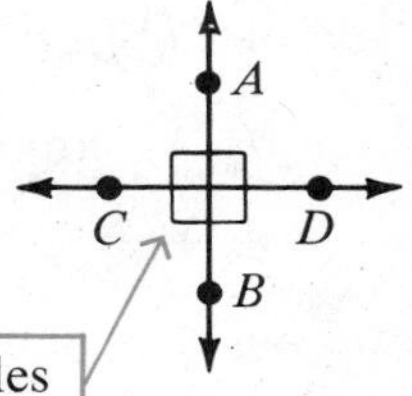


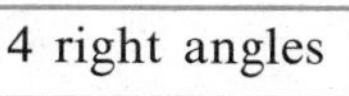


An **obtuse angle** has a measure between 90° and 180°.

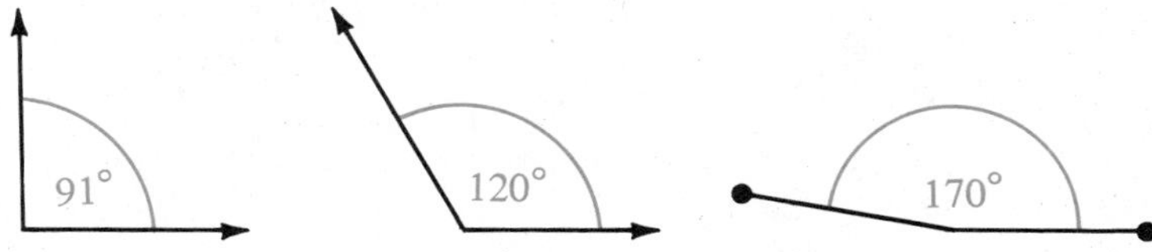


A **straight angle** has measure 180°.

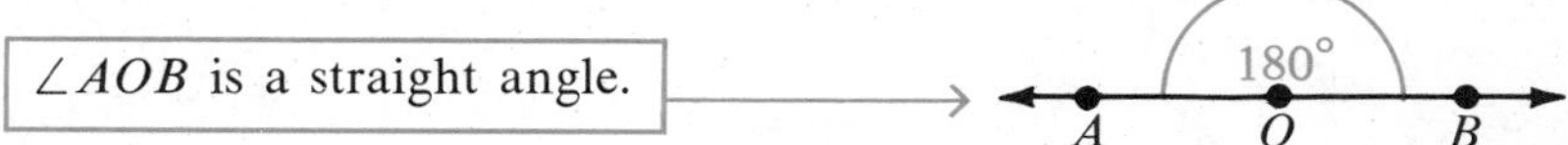


The diagram at the right shows a **triangle** with **vertices** *A*, *B*, and *C*. *Vertices* (sometimes called *vertexes*) is the plural of *vertex*. The triangle pictured is called *triangle ABC* and is represented by the symbol $\triangle ABC$. Since $\angle B$ and $\angle C$ have equal measures, we say that the angles are equal and write

$$\angle B = \angle C.$$

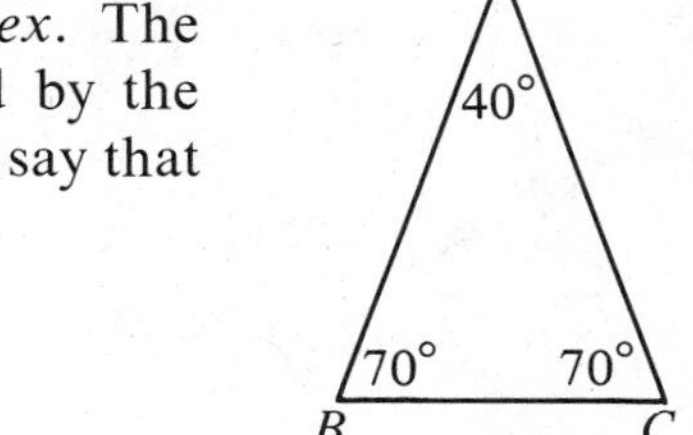


Also, since the measures of $\angle A$, $\angle B$, and $\angle C$ total 180°, we write

$$\angle A + \angle B + \angle C = 180°.$$

**EXAMPLE** In the diagram, $\overline{AC} \perp \overline{EB}$ and $\angle EAD = 40°$.
Find the measure of **a.** $\angle DAC$ and **b.** $\angle DAB$.

**a.** $\angle DAC = \angle EAC - \angle EAD$
$= 90° - 40°$
$= 50°$

**b.** $\angle DAB = \angle EAB - \angle EAD$
$= 180° - 40°$
$= 140°$

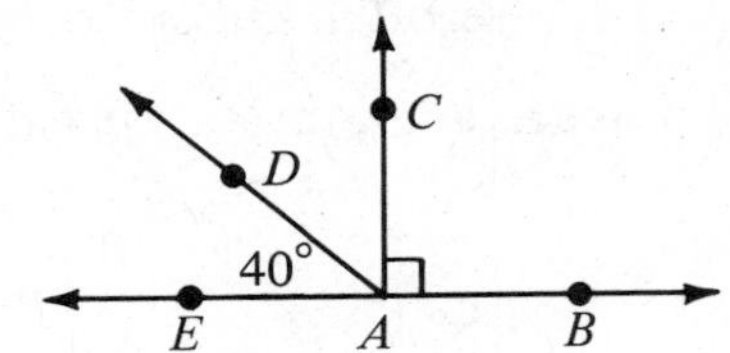


## Classroom Practice

**Classify each angle as acute, right, obtuse, or straight.**

**1.** $\angle 1$ acute **2.** $\angle 2$ right **3.** $\angle DAB$ obtuse

**4.** $\angle ACB$ right **5.** $\angle CAB$ acute **6.** $\angle DCB$ straight

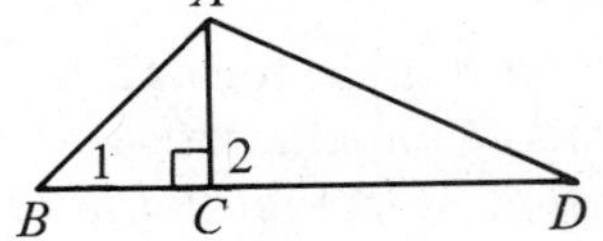


**7.** An angle that is equal to $\angle 2$ is $\angle$ _?_. ACB

**8.** You know that $\overline{AC} \perp \overline{BD}$ because $\angle 2$ is _?_. a right angle

**9.** The three triangles pictured are $\triangle$ _?_ ACB, $\triangle$ _?_ ACD, and $\triangle$ _?_ ABD.

**10.** Name the three vertices of $\triangle ZOS$. Z, O, S

**11.** Name the three angles of $\triangle XOZ$. $\angle XOZ$, $\angle OZX$, $\angle ZXO$

**12.** How many angles are shown in the diagram? (Do not count straight angles.) 15

**13.** How many triangles are shown in the diagram? 8

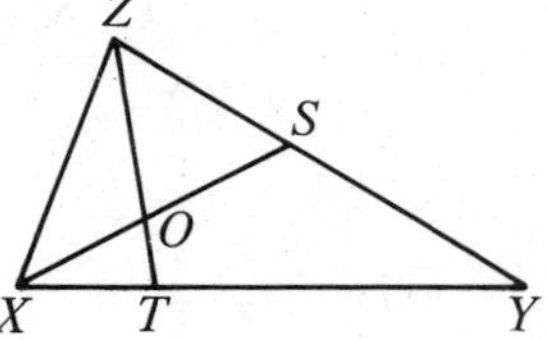


## Written Exercises

**The measures of several angles are given below.**
**Classify each angle as acute, right, obtuse, or straight.**

A **1.** 18° acute **2.** 157° obtuse **3.** 128° obtuse **4.** 90° right **5.** 180° straight **6.** 89° acute

**7.** Name four obtuse angles. $\angle 3$, $\angle 5$, $\angle 7$, $\angle 10$

**8.** Name six acute angles. $\angle 1$, $\angle 2$, $\angle 4$, $\angle 6$, $\angle 8$, $\angle 9$

**9.** Name four pairs of angles whose sum is a straight angle. $\angle 2$, $\angle 3$; $\angle 5$, $\angle 6$; $\angle 6$, $\angle 7$; $\angle 8$, $\angle 10$

**10.** Name four triangles. $\triangle DOG$, $\triangle COA$, $\triangle DAT$, $\triangle GCT$

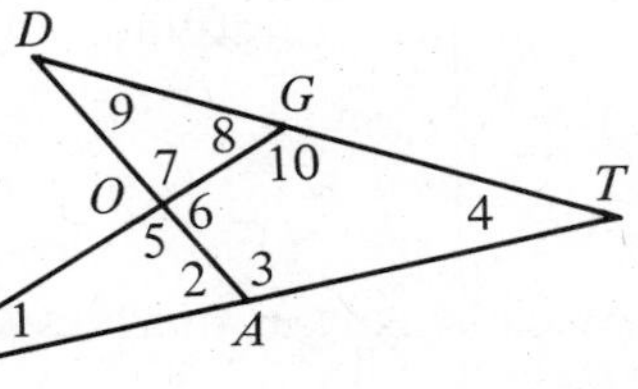


Exercises 7–10

In the figure, $\overline{AB} \perp \overline{CD}$ and $\angle SRD = 30°$.

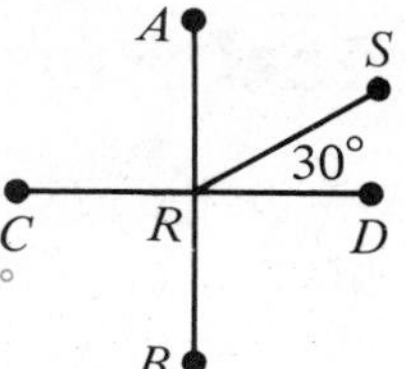


11. Name four right angles. $\angle CRA$, $\angle DRA$, $\angle DRB$, $\angle CRB$

12. Find the measure of each angle named.
   a. $\angle ARS$ 60° b. $\angle CRS$ 150° c. $\angle BRS$ 120°

In the figure, $\overline{TQ} \perp \overline{VR}$ and $\overline{UQ} \perp \overline{QS}$.

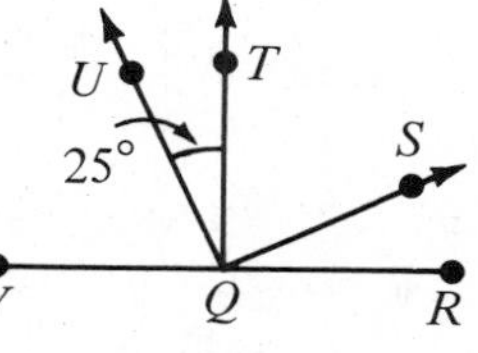


13. Name three right angles. $\angle VQT$, $\angle TQR$, $\angle UQS$

14. Name two obtuse angles. $\angle UQR$, $\angle VQS$

15. Find the measure of each angle named.
   a. $\angle VQU$ 65° b. $\angle TQS$ 65° c. $\angle SQR$ 25°

B 16. a. Draw a triangle with three acute angles.
   b. Draw a triangle with just two acute angles.
   c. Can you draw a triangle with just one acute angle? no

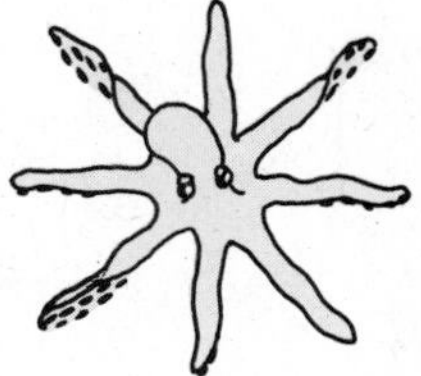

17. If the angles between the legs of an octopus are all equal, find the measure of each angle. 45°

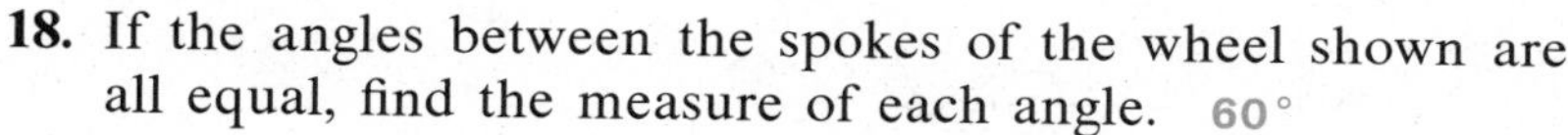

18. If the angles between the spokes of the wheel shown are all equal, find the measure of each angle. 60°

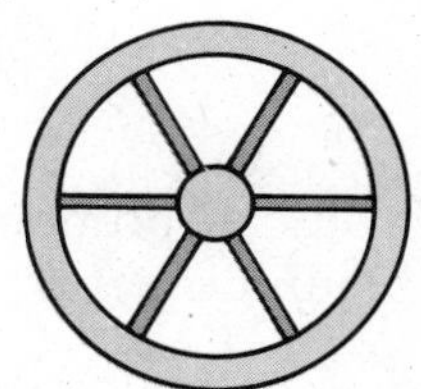

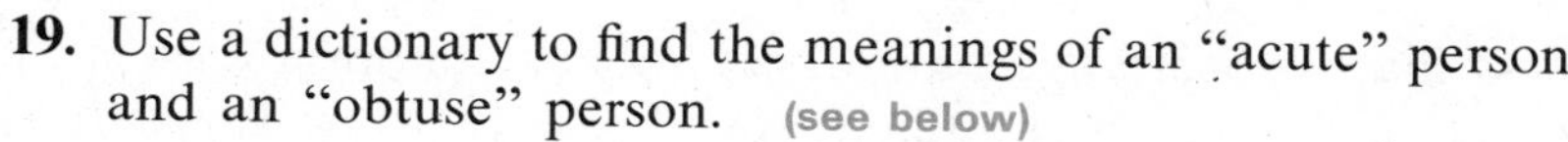

19. Use a dictionary to find the meanings of an "acute" person and an "obtuse" person. (see below)

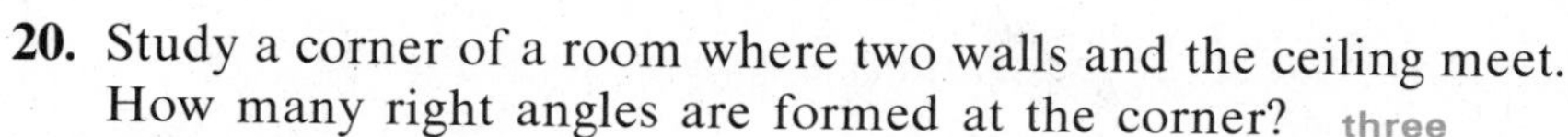

20. Study a corner of a room where two walls and the ceiling meet. How many right angles are formed at the corner? three

19. An acute person is one who is keenly perceptive or discerning; an obtuse person is one who is slow to perceive.

Ron, Jo, and Bobbie each won a contest during class day at their high school. One student won the photography exhibit, another, the math contest, and the third, the track race.

(1) The photographer, who is an only child, does not know how to play tennis.
(2) Bobbie is a friend of the math whiz.
(3) Jo often plays tennis with Bobbie's sister.

Which student won each event? Jo won the math contest, Ron won the photography exhibit, Bobbie won the track race

# 5 • Vertical Angles

When two lines meet, they form four angles. Two angles that are opposite each other, such as $\angle 1$ and $\angle 3$ in the diagram, are called **vertical angles.** $\angle 2$ and $\angle 4$ are also vertical angles.

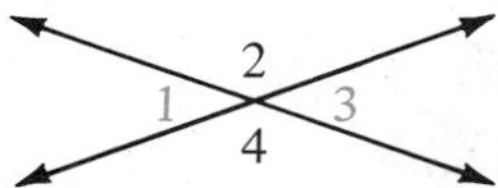


Suppose $\angle 1 = 30°$. Do you see that $\angle 2 = 150°$? (Remember that $\angle 1 + \angle 2 = 180°$.) Now do you see that $\angle 3 = 30°$? How large is $\angle 4$? This information is given in the first row of the table below. Copy and complete rows 2 and 3.

| $\angle 1$ | $\angle 2$ | $\angle 3$ | $\angle 4$ |
|---|---|---|---|
| 30° | 150° | 30° | 150° |
| 20° | ? 160° | ? 20° | ? 160° |
| 25° | ? 155° | ? 25° | ? 155° |

You can probably guess that vertical angles are always equal. Before reading further, see if you can explain why this is so.

The following steps show that *vertical angles are always equal.* Refer to the diagram above.

*Step 1* $\angle 1 = 180° - \angle 2$ because $\angle 1 + \angle 2 = 180°$.
*Step 2* $\angle 3 = 180° - \angle 2$ because $\angle 2 + \angle 3 = 180°$.
*Step 3* $\angle 1 = \angle 3$ because both angles equal $180° - \angle 2$.

See Theorem 3, page 43

In the same way, you can show that $\angle 2 = \angle 4$.

**EXAMPLE** Study the diagram and find the measure of

**a.** $\angle DOE$ **b.** $\angle BOC$ **c.** $\angle COD$.

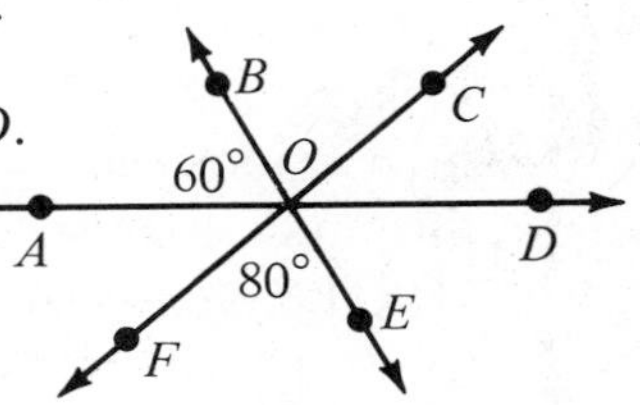


**a.** $\angle DOE$ and $\angle AOB$ are vertical angles. Therefore, both equal 60°.

**b.** $\angle BOC$ and $\angle FOE$ are vertical angles. Therefore, both equal 80°.

**c.**
$$\begin{aligned} \angle AOB + \angle BOC + \angle COD &= 180° \\ 60° + 80° + \angle COD &= 180° \\ 140° + \angle COD &= 180° \\ \angle COD &= 40° \end{aligned}$$

## Classroom Practice

**Find the measure of each angle.**

1. $\angle POU = \underline{\ ?\ }^\circ$ 20  2. $\angle QOR = \underline{\ ?\ }^\circ$ 85

3. $\angle POQ = \underline{\ ?\ }^\circ$ 75  4. $\angle SOT = \underline{\ ?\ }^\circ$ 75

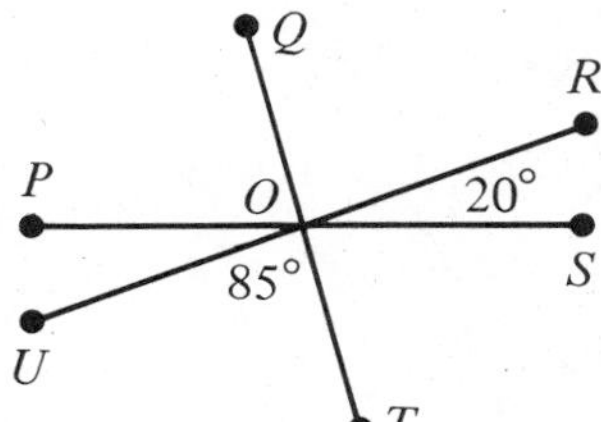


5. There are six pairs of vertical angles in the diagram. Can you find all six pairs?

5. $\angle RAP$, $\angle TAS$; $\angle NAT$, $\angle PAG$; $\angle RAN$, $\angle GAS$; $\angle RAT$, $\angle SAP$; $\angle RAG$, $\angle NAS$; $\angle NAP$, $\angle TAG$

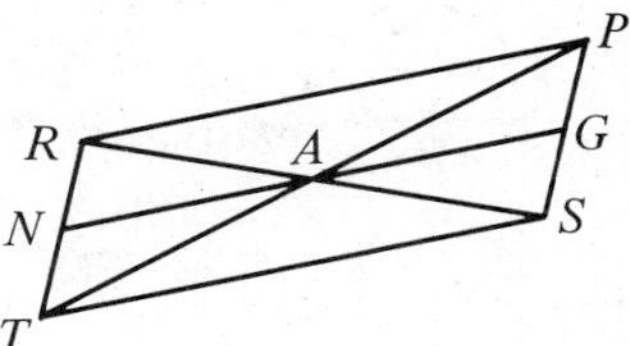


## Written Exercises

**Name an angle equal to the given angle.**

A 1. $\angle BOA$ $\angle DOE$  2. $\angle BOC$ $\angle FOE$  3. $\angle AOC$ $\angle FOD$  4. $\angle DOC$ $\angle AOF$

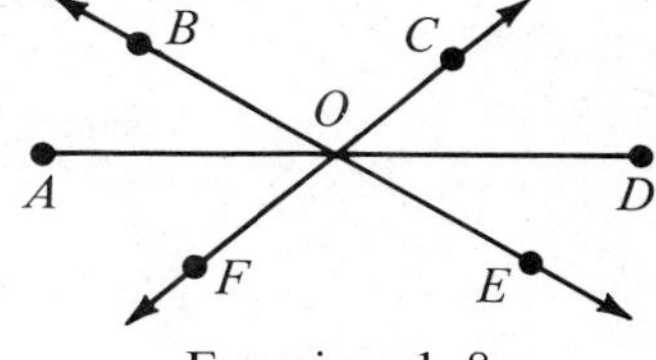

Exercises 1–8

**Suppose $\angle BOA = 30^\circ$ and $\angle DOF = 140^\circ$.**
**Find the measure of each angle.**

5. $\angle COD$ 40°  6. $\angle BOC$ 110°  7. $\angle COE$ 70°  8. $\angle BOF$ 70°

**In the diagram, $\overline{AE} \perp \overline{GC}$, $\angle GOH = 25^\circ$, and $\angle AOB = 35^\circ$.**
**Find the measure of each angle.**

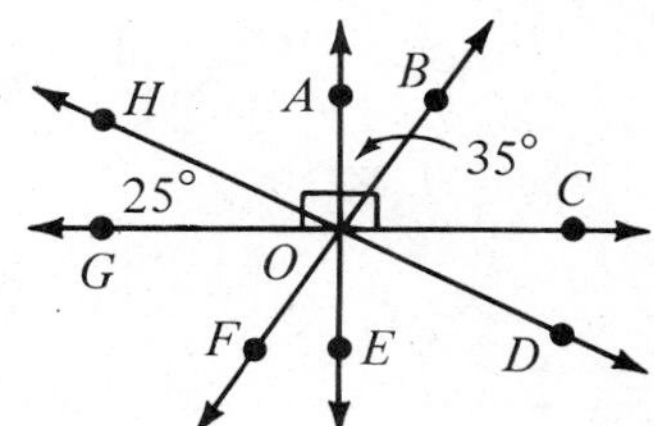


9. $\angle AOH$ 65°  10. $\angle BOC$ 55°  11. $\angle COD$ 25°

12. $\angle DOE$ 65°  13. $\angle EOF$ 35°  14. $\angle FOG$ 55°

**Find the values of $x$ and $y$.**

B 15. $x = 20$
$y = 9$

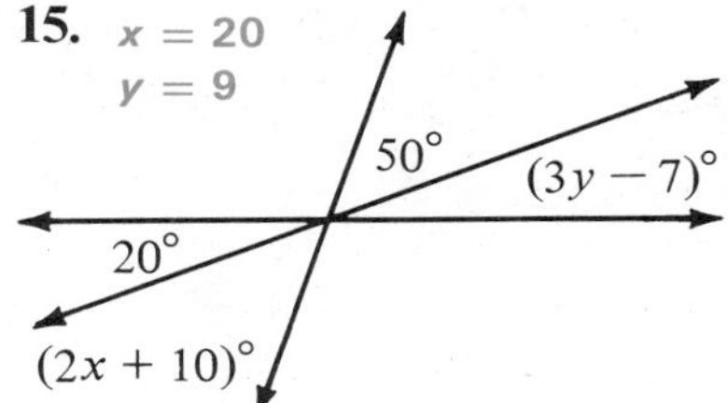


16. $x = 14$
$y = 8$

80° 60°
$(7y + 4)^\circ$ $(6x - 4)^\circ$

C 17. Draw a diagram showing $\overleftrightarrow{AB}$ and $\overleftrightarrow{CD}$ intersecting at point $O$ so that $\angle AOD = \angle BOD$. Explain why $\overleftrightarrow{AB}$ must be perpendicular to $\overleftrightarrow{CD}$. Since $\angle AOD + \angle BOD = 180^\circ$ and $\angle AOD = \angle BOD$, each is 90°. Thus $\overleftrightarrow{AB}$ is perpendicular to $\overleftrightarrow{CD}$.

## 6 • Angle Bisectors

A **bisector of an angle** is a ray or line which divides the angle into two equal angles. In the diagram below, $\overrightarrow{OX}$ *bisects* $\angle AOB$.

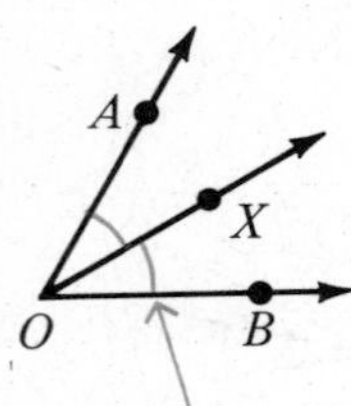


When $\overrightarrow{OX}$ bisects $\angle AOB$, $\angle AOX = \angle BOX$.

Thus $\angle AOX = \frac{1}{2}\angle AOB$

and $\angle BOX = \frac{1}{2}\angle AOB$.

The green marks show that $\angle AOX = \angle BOX$.

**EXAMPLE** $\overrightarrow{OB}$ bisects $\angle AOC$. Find the measure of $\angle AOB$. Then find the number on the protractor that corresponds to $\overrightarrow{OB}$.

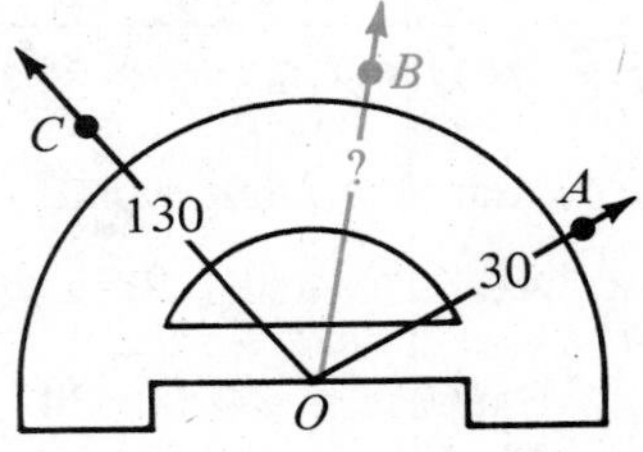


$$\angle AOB = \frac{1}{2}\angle AOC$$

$$= \frac{1}{2}(130° - 30°)$$

$$= \frac{1}{2}(100°) = 50°$$

$\overrightarrow{OB}$ corresponds to $30° + 50°$, or $80°$.

### *Classroom Practice*

**In each diagram, $\overrightarrow{SZ}$ bisects $\angle RST$.**

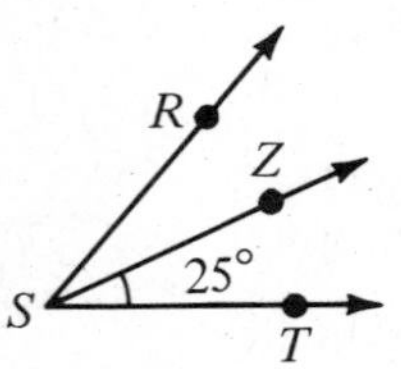


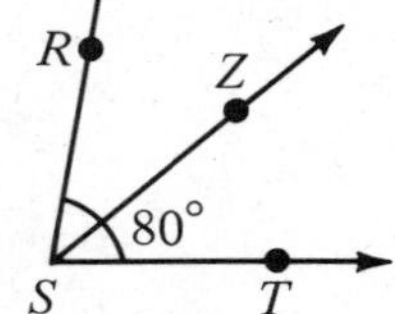


1. $\angle RSZ =$ _?_ ° 25
2. $\angle RST =$ _?_ ° 50
3. $\angle RSZ =$ _?_ ° 40
4. $\angle ZST =$ _?_ ° 40
5. How many lines can bisect a given angle? one

## Written Exercises

A **1.** Draw an acute angle. Label it $\angle JOG$.
Draw a bisector of $\angle JOG$ and call it $\overrightarrow{OP}$.
Now draw $\overrightarrow{ON}$ bisecting $\angle JOP$.
Suppose $\angle JOG = 40°$.
Then $\angle JOP =$ _?_ ° and $\angle JON =$ _?_ °. 20 10

**In each exercise, $\overrightarrow{OB}$ bisects $\angle AOC$.**
**Find a. the measure of $\angle AOB$ and**
**b. the number on the protractor that corresponds to $\overrightarrow{OB}$.**

**2.**

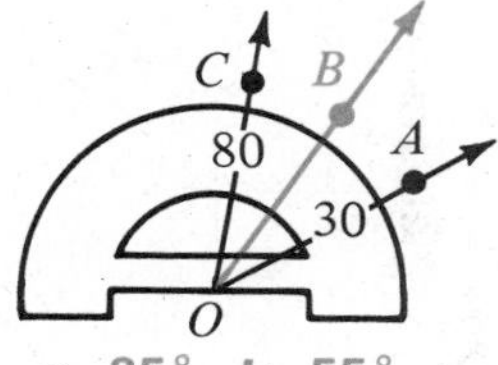


a. 25° b. 55°

**3.**

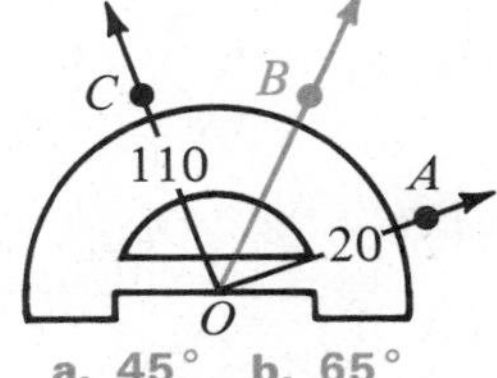


a. 45° b. 65°

**4.**

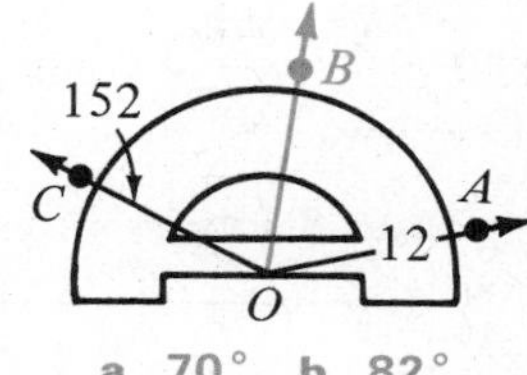


a. 70° b. 82°

***FLEA* is a four-sided figure and $\overline{FE} \perp \overline{LA}$.**

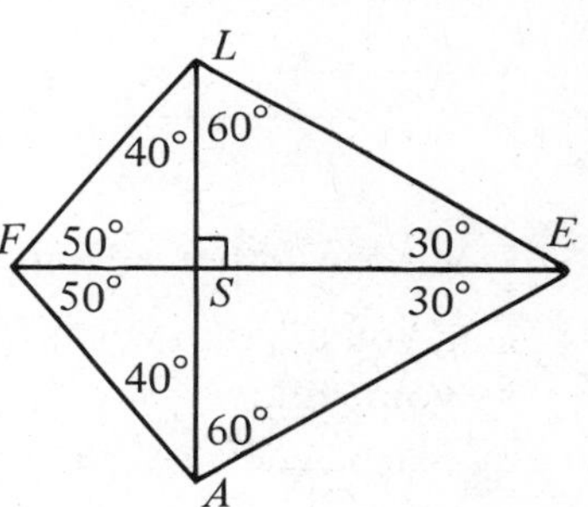


**5.** How many right angles are shown? 4

**6.** How many obtuse angles are shown? 3

**7.** How many acute angles are shown? 9

**8.** Name two pairs of vertical angles. $\angle FSL$, $\angle ESA$; $\angle FSA$, $\angle LSE$

**9.** Name the bisector of $\angle LFA$. $\overline{FE}$

**10.** Name the bisector of $\angle LEA$. $\overline{FE}$

B **11.** Make a paper airplane. Then unfold it and mark on the paper the measure of the angles between the folds. Answers may vary; the angles will be bisected.

**12.** Fold a rectangular sheet of paper to form a square.

**13. a.** Draw any angle and its bisector like this.

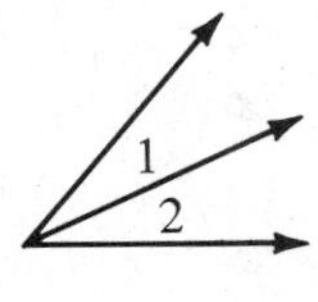


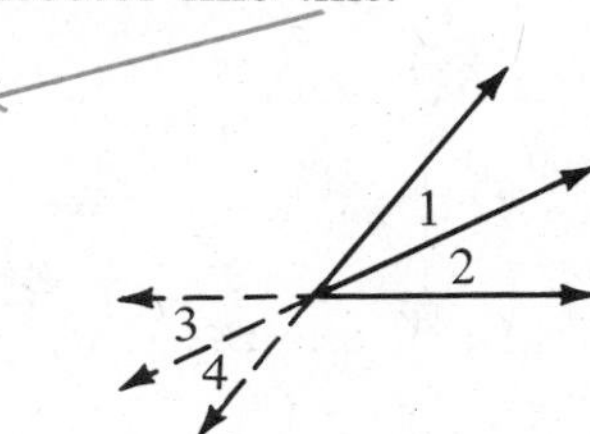


**b.** Now extend each ray in the opposite direction.
**c.** What can you conclude about $\angle 3$ and $\angle 4$? $\angle 3 = \angle 4$
**d.** Explain why you think your conclusion is correct.
$\angle 2 = \angle 3$, and $\angle 1 = \angle 4$; since $\angle 1 = \angle 2$, $\angle 3 = \angle 4$

## *Experiments*

### EXPERIMENT 1

1. Fold a rectangular sheet of paper to form a 45° angle.
2. Can you discover how to form a $22\frac{1}{2}^\circ$ angle? **Bring the two sides of the 45° angle together.**
3. Could an $11\frac{1}{4}^\circ$ angle be formed by the folding process? **Yes; bring the two sides of the $22\frac{1}{2}^\circ$ angle together.**

### EXPERIMENT 2

1. Fold over a corner of a rectangular sheet of paper as in Figure 1 below.
2. Now fold the next corner so the edges touch as in Figure 2.

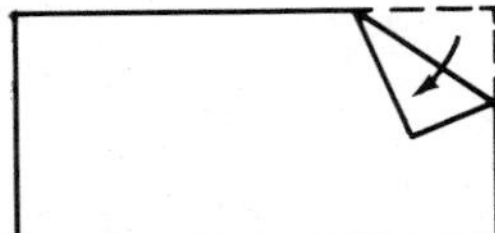

Figure 1

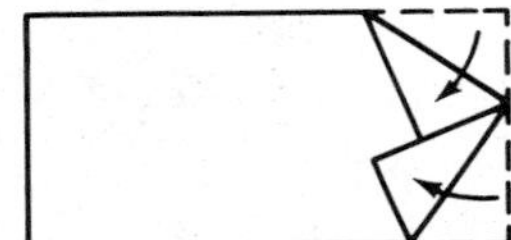

Figure 2

3. Open the paper and measure the angle between the creases. **The angle will be 90°.**
4. Can you explain why your classmates' angles have the same measure as your angle?

   **By folding, we bisect 2 angles whose sum is 180°. Hence the angle between the creases will be $\frac{1}{2} \cdot 180°$ or 90°.**

## SELF-TEST

**In the diagram, $\overline{AD} \perp \overline{BC}$. Classify each angle as acute, right, obtuse, or straight.**

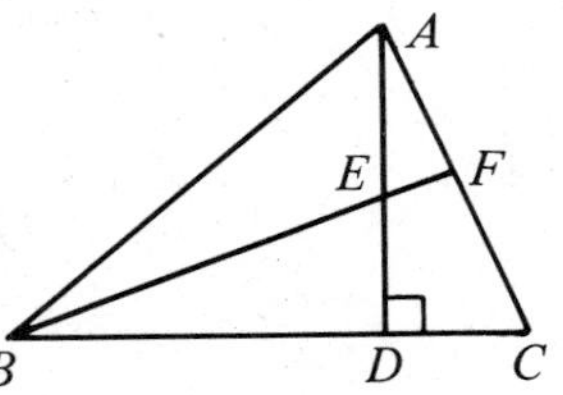


**1.** $\angle ADC$ **right** **2.** $\angle ABC$ **acute**

**3.** $\angle BEA$ **obtuse** **4.** $\angle AFC$ **straight**

**5.** Name two pairs of vertical angles.
**$\angle BED$, $\angle AEF$; $\angle BEA$, $\angle DEF$**

**6.** If $\overrightarrow{BF}$ bisects $\angle ABC$, what two angles must be equal? **$\angle ABF$, $\angle FBC$**

# 7 • Three Constructions

Making a construction is a mathematical game in which figures are drawn using only a *straightedge* and *compass*. The use of a ruler or protractor for measuring purposes is not allowed.

This construction is justified on page 135.

CONSTRUCTION 1 *Given:* An angle
*Construct:* A bisector of the angle

**1.**

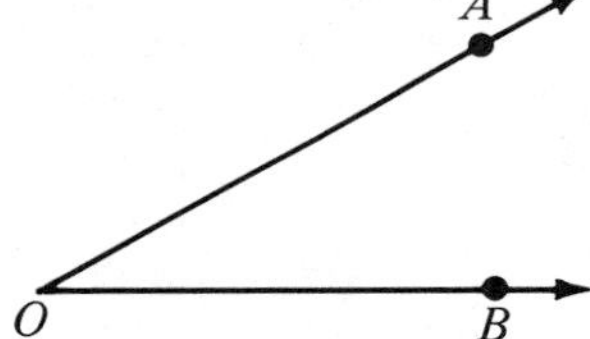


You are given $\angle AOB$.

**2.**

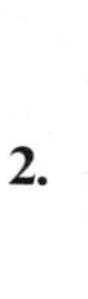

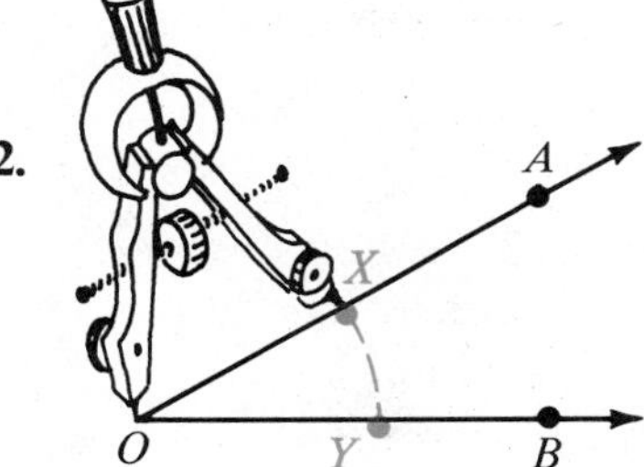


Put the point of your compass at $O$ and swing an arc which cuts the sides of $\angle AOB$ at $X$ and $Y$.

**3.**

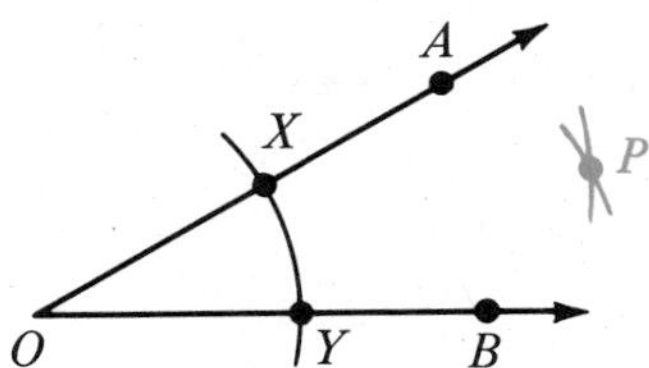


Now draw two arcs, one with the compass point at $X$ and the other with the point at $Y$. Use the same setting of your compass for both arcs. The arcs meet at $P$.

**4.**

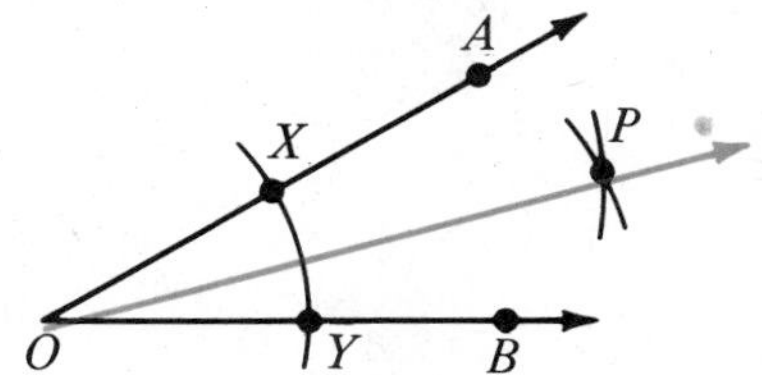


Join points $P$ and $O$. $\overrightarrow{OP}$ is a bisector of $\angle AOB$.

Suppose that $\angle AOB$ given in Construction 1 is a straight angle. When you bisect this straight angle with measure 180°, you form two angles with measure 90°. In other words, bisecting a straight angle produces perpendicular lines. This idea is used in the next construction.

This construction is justified on page 135.

**CONSTRUCTION 2** *Given:* A line and a point on the line

*Construct:* A perpendicular to the line through the point

Turn back to Construction 1. You will notice that the steps in Construction 2 are almost the same as those of Construction 1.

**1,2.**

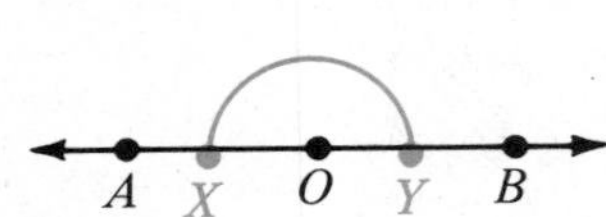


**3.**

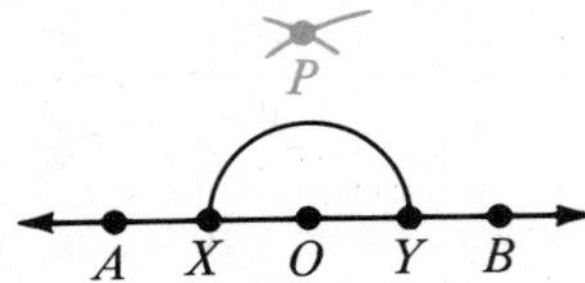


**4.**

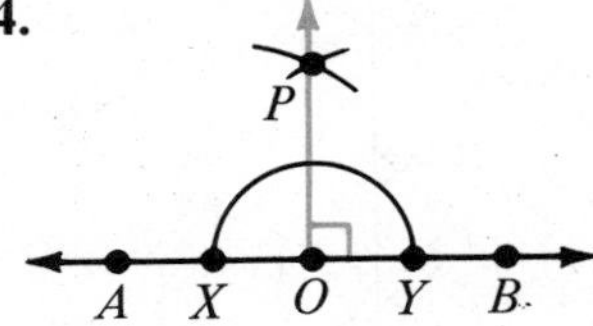


In Construction 2, the perpendicular passes through a point on the given line. In the next construction, the perpendicular passes through a point outside the given line.

This construction is justified in Wr. Ex. 7 on page 137.

**CONSTRUCTION 3** *Given:* A line and a point *not* on the line

*Construct:* A perpendicular to the line through the point

Compare the steps in this construction with those of Constructions 1 and 2.

**1.**

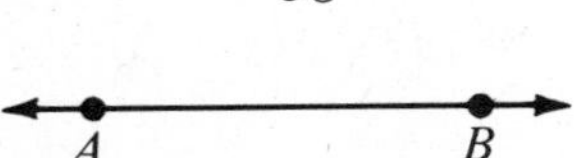


**2.**

**3.**

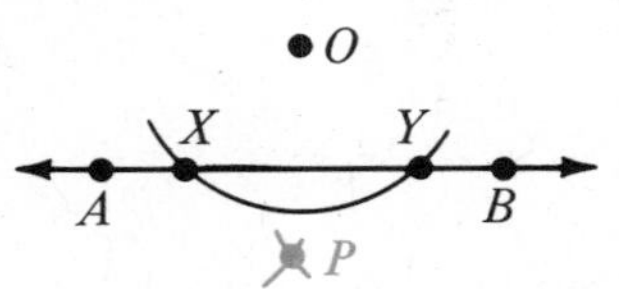


**4.**

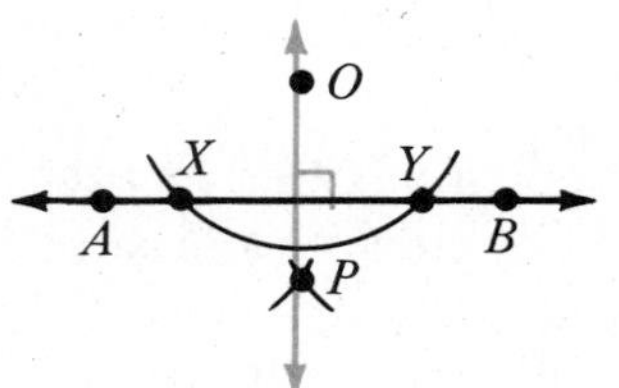

## Classroom Practice

1. Draw an obtuse angle.
   Then bisect it, using a straightedge and compass.
2. Use Construction 2 to construct a 90° angle.
   Then construct a 45° angle by bisecting the 90° angle.
3. Draw a line $l$ and choose a point $O$ not on $l$.
   Use Construction 3 to construct a line, through $O$, which is perpendicular to line $l$.

## Written Exercises

**Draw an angle similar to, but larger than, the one shown. Then bisect it.**

A **1.**

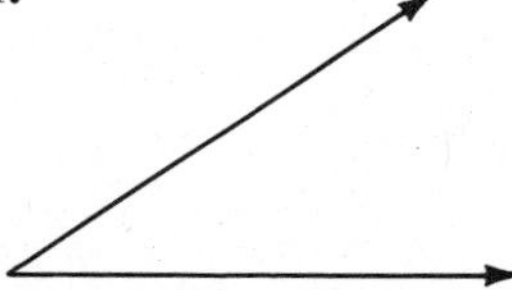

**2.**

**3.**

**Draw a figure similar to, but larger than, the one shown.**
**Then construct a perpendicular to $\overleftrightarrow{AB}$ through point $O$.**

**4.**

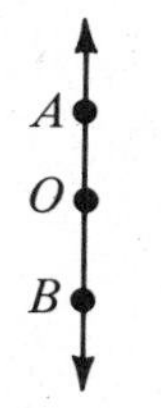


**5.**

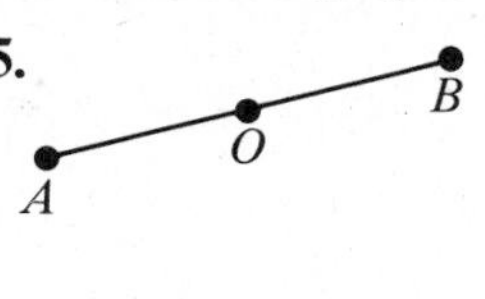


**6.**

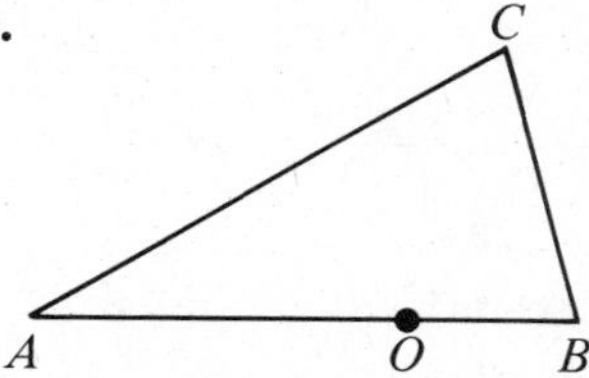


**7.**

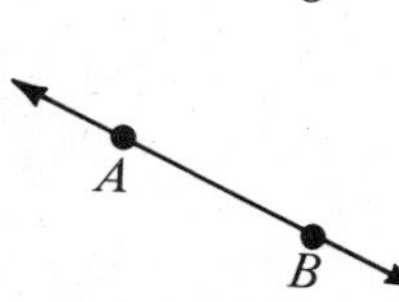


**8.**

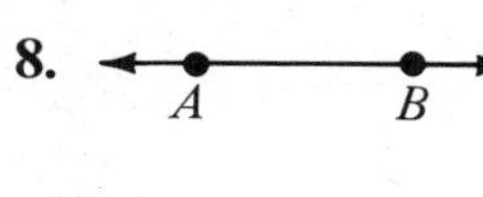


**9.**

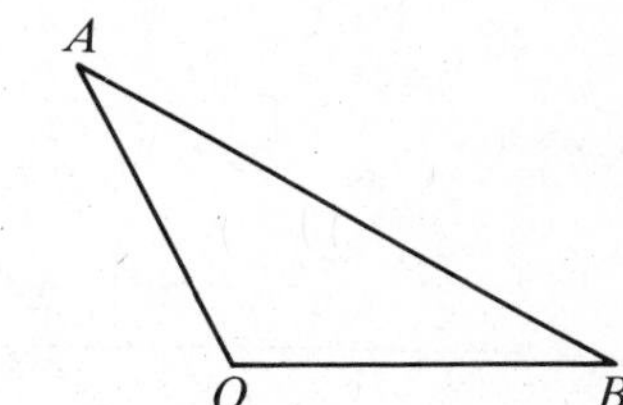


**10.** Draw an acute angle. Construct the bisector of the angle.

**11.** Draw an obtuse angle. Construct the bisector of the angle.

**12. a.** Draw a large triangle.
**b.** Construct the bisectors of the three angles.
The bisectors should meet in a point. Do they?

13. a. Draw a line $m$ and choose a point $K$ on the line.
    b. Construct four right angles, each of which has $K$ as vertex.

14. Use your construction from Exercise 13. Construct a $45°$ angle.

15. Use your construction from Exercises 13 and 14. Construct a $22\frac{1}{2}°$ angle.

**Draw a figure similar to, but larger than, the one shown. Then construct perpendiculars to $\overleftrightarrow{AB}$ from $C$ and $D$.**

B **16.**

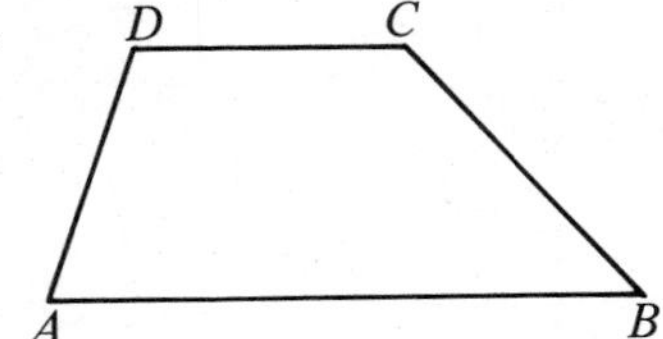


**17.**

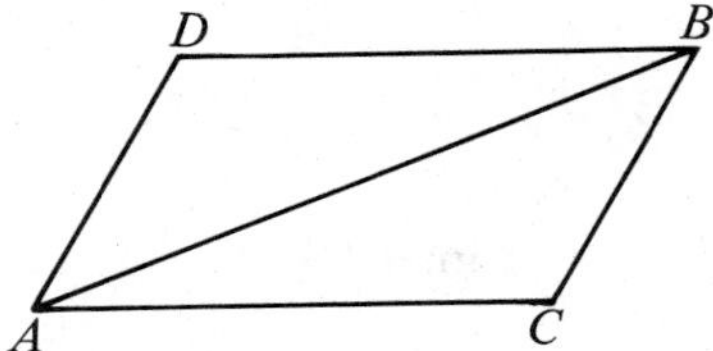


**Draw a figure similar to, but larger than, the one shown. Then construct a perpendicular to $\overleftrightarrow{RS}$ at $S$ and a perpendicular to $\overleftrightarrow{RT}$ at $T$.**

**18.**

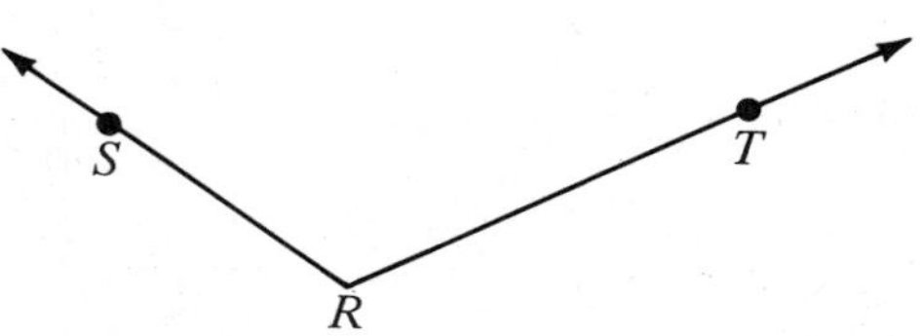


**19.**

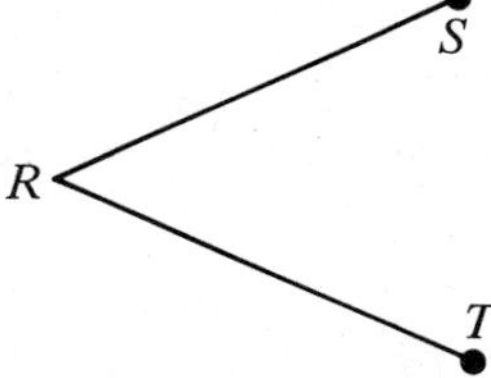


**Draw a figure similar to, but larger than, the one shown. Then construct a bisector of $\angle UVW$ and a bisector of $\angle WVZ$.**

**20.**

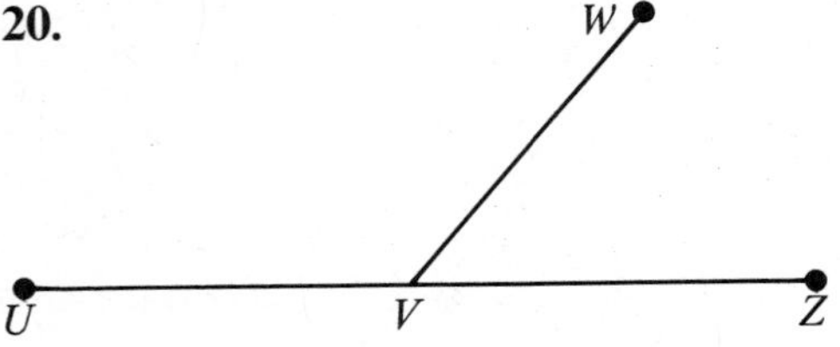


**21.**

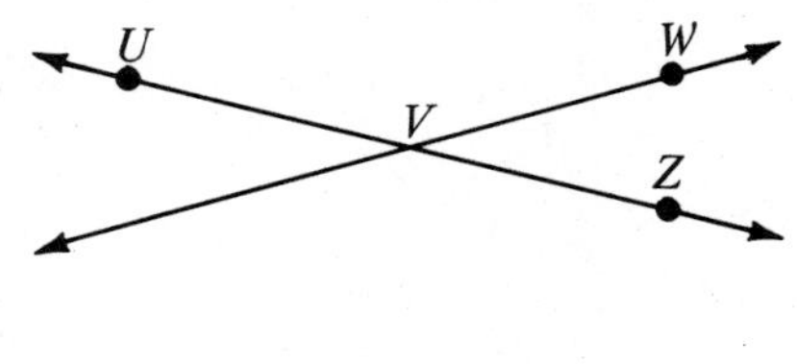


22. In Exercises 20 and 21, how do the two angle bisectors you constructed seem to be related? They are perpendicular.

C 23. Construct a $135°$ angle. (*Hint:* $135° = 180° - 45°$)

24. Construct a square. Remember: You may not use your ruler to measure distances; you may use it only as a straightedge.

## 8 • Postulates of Equality

The following facts about real numbers are called **postulates.** These are statements which are accepted without proof. Postulates are used to prove other statements called *theorems.*

**THE ADDITION POSTULATE**

If $a = b$ and $c = d$, then $a + c = b + d$.

**EXAMPLE 1** In the diagram, $AB = CD$.

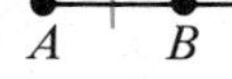


But we know that $BC = BC$.

*Conclusion:* $AB + BC = CD + BC$.

In other words, $AC = BD$.

**THE SUBTRACTION POSTULATE**

If $a = b$ and $c = d$, then $a - c = b - d$.

**EXAMPLE 2** In the diagram, $\angle ABC = \angle ACB$

and also $\angle 1 = \angle 2$.

*Conclusion:* $\angle ABC - \angle 1 = \angle ACB - \angle 2$.

In other words, $\angle 3 = \angle 4$.

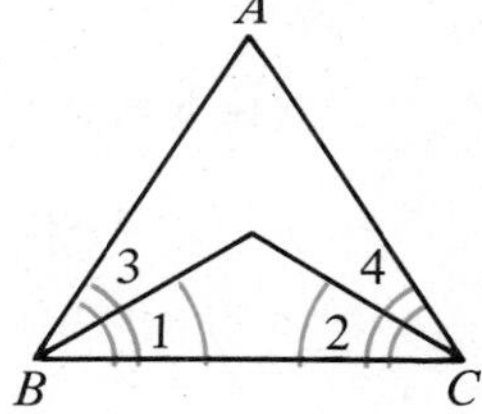

**THE MULTIPLICATION POSTULATE**

If $a = b$, then $ac = bc$.

**EXAMPLE 3** In the diagram, $M$ and $N$ are midpoints of $\overline{AB}$ and $\overline{CD}$, and also $AM = CN$.

*Conclusion:* $2 \times AM = 2 \times CN$.

In other words, $AB = CD$.

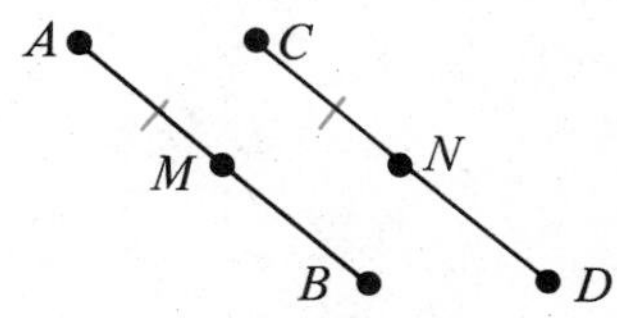

**THE DIVISION POSTULATE**

If $a = b$ and $c \neq 0$, then $\frac{a}{c} = \frac{b}{c}$.

**THE SUBSTITUTION POSTULATE**

If $a = b$, then $a$ can be substituted for $b$ in any equation or inequality.

**EXAMPLE 4** In the diagram, $BC = BD$.
Since $AB + BC = AC$,
we can substitute ↓
and get $AB + BD = AC$.

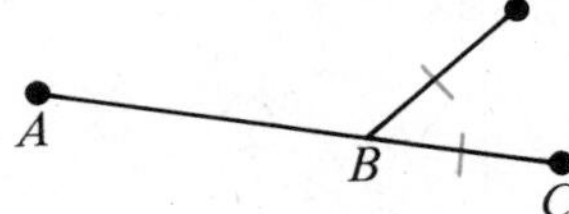


**EXAMPLE 5** In the diagram, $\angle 1 = \angle 2$
and $\angle 3 = \angle 4$.
Since $\angle 2 = \angle 3$, (Why?) Vertical angles are equal.
we can substitute ↓ ↓
and get $\angle 1 = \angle 4$.

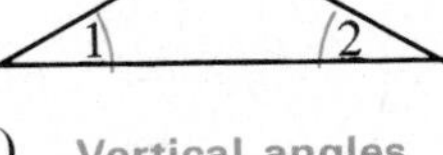

## Classroom Practice

**Name the postulate that can be used to justify each statement below.**

1. If $x - 5 = 21$, then $x = 26$. addition
2. If $\frac{1}{2}x = 5$, then $x = 10$. multiplication
3. If $3x + 4 = 19$, then $3x = 15$. subtraction
4. If $3x = 15$, then $x = 5$. division
5. If $x + y = z$ and $z = 24$, then $x + y = 24$. substitution
6. If $CL = AM$, then $CA = LM$. addition
7. If $CA = LM$, then $CL = AM$. subtraction

8. If $\angle 1 = \angle 3$ and $\angle 2 = \angle 4$, then $\angle ABC = \angle XYZ$. addition
9. If $\angle XYZ = \angle ABC$ and $\angle 1 = \angle 3$, then $\angle 2 = \angle 4$. subtraction

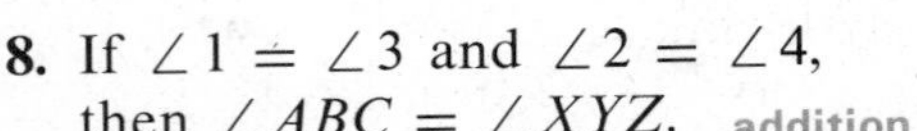

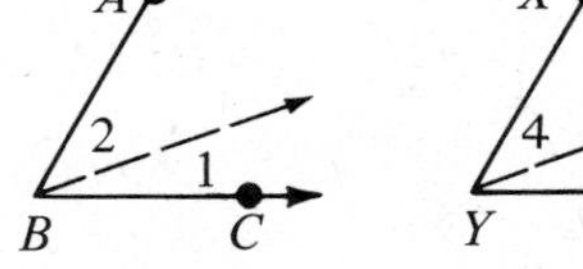

## Written Exercises

**Which postulate can you use to justify each statement below?**

A **1.** If $3x = 18$, then $x = 6$. division

**2.** If $x + 9 = 2$, then $x = -7$. subtraction

**3.** If $\frac{x}{3} = 9$, then $x = 27$. multiplication

**4.** **a.** If $2x - 20 = 22$, then $2x = 42$. addition
**b.** If $2x = 42$, then $x = 21$. division

**5.** If $x + y = 8$ and $x - y = 4$, then $2x = 12$. addition

**6.** **a.** If $x + y = 180$ and $y = 2x$, then $3x = 180$. substitution
**b.** If $3x = 180$, then $x = 60$. division

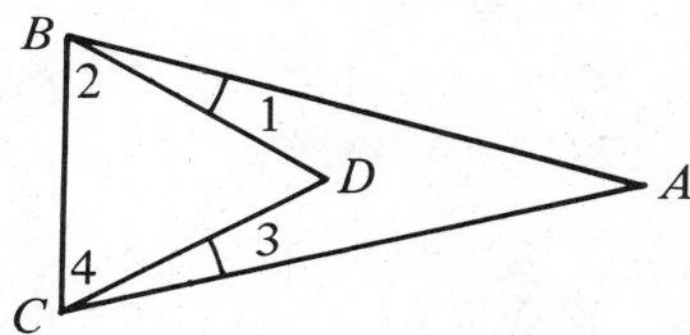


**7.** If $\angle 2 = \angle 4$ and $\angle 1 = \angle 3$, then $\angle ABC = \angle ACB$. addition

**8.** If $\angle ABC = \angle ACB$ and $\angle 1 = \angle 3$, then $\angle 2 = \angle 4$. subtraction

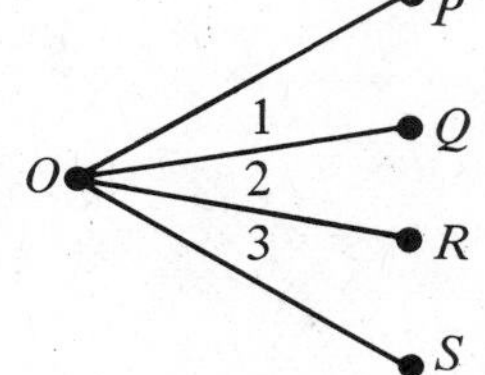


**9.** If $\angle 1 = \angle 3$, then $\angle POR = \angle QOS$. addition

**10.** If $\angle 1 = \angle 2$ and $\angle 2 = \angle 3$, then $\angle 1 = \angle 3$. substitution

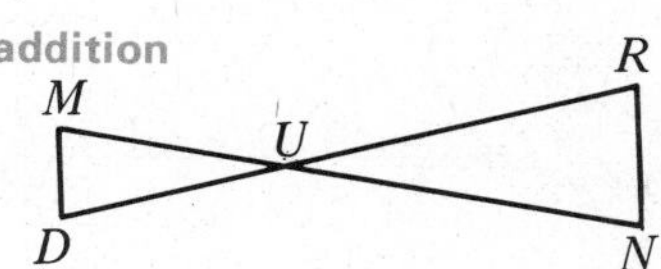


**11.** If $MU = DU$ and $UN = UR$, then $MN = DR$. addition

**12.** If $MN = DR$ and $MU = DU$, then $UN = UR$. subtraction

**Study the given information. Then complete the conclusion. Be sure that you understand how the postulates justify your conclusion.**

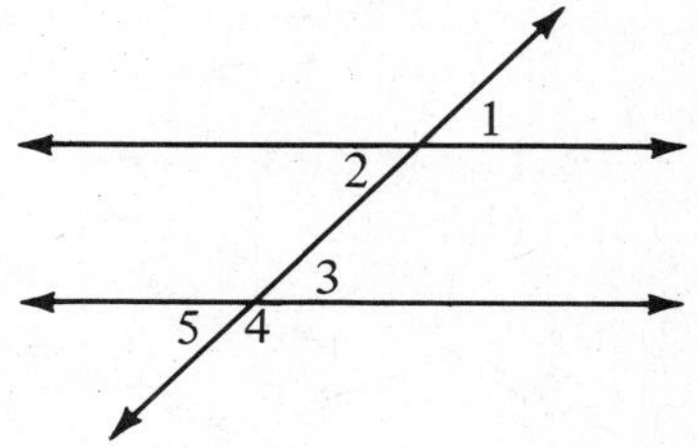


**13.** *Given information:* $\angle 2 = \angle 3$

*Conclusion:* $\angle 1 = \angle \underline{\ ?\ } = \angle \underline{\ ?\ } = \angle \underline{\ ?\ }$ 2, 3, 5

**Study the given information. Then complete each conclusion.**

**14.** *Given information:* $\overline{AB} \perp \overline{BC}$
$\overline{PQ} \perp \overline{QR}$
$\angle 1 = \angle 3$

*Conclusion:* ___?___ $\angle 2$ = ___?___ $\angle 4$

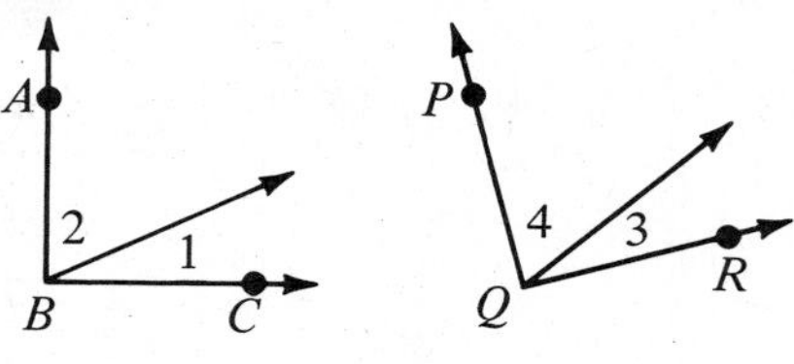


B **15.** *Given information:* $\overrightarrow{AK}$ bisects $\angle CAR$.
$\overline{AK} \perp \overline{TN}$

*Conclusions:* ___?___ $\angle 1$ = ___?___ $\angle 2$
___?___ $\angle 3$ = ___?___ $\angle 4$

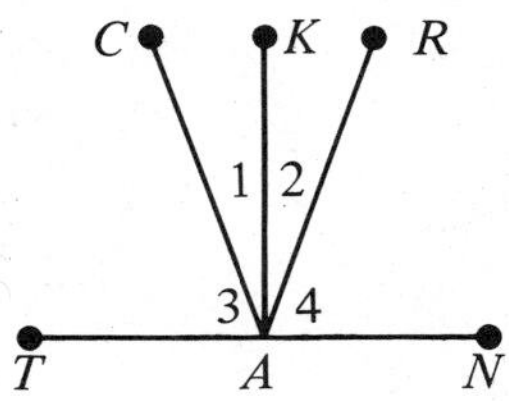


**16.** *Given information:* $\angle 2 = \angle 3$
$\angle 5 = \angle 6$

*Conclusions:* $\angle 2 = \angle 3 =$ ___?___ $\angle 5$ = ___?___ $\angle 6$
$\angle 1 =$ ___?___ $\angle 4$ = ___?___ $\angle 8$ = ___?___ $\angle 7$

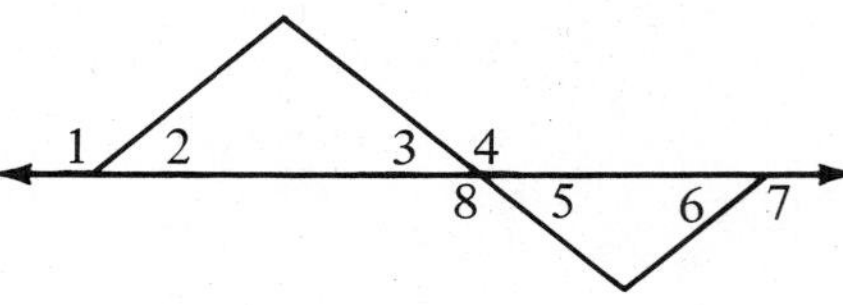


**17.** *Given information:* $M$ is the midpoint of $\overline{AB}$.
$N$ is the midpoint of $\overline{PQ}$.

What additional information would permit you to conclude that $AM = PN$? AB = PQ or BM = QN

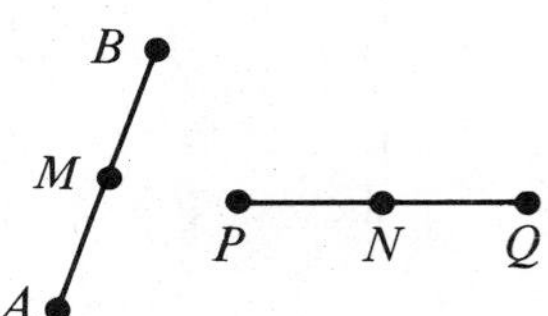


## Puzzles & Things

*Given information:*

(1) Three horses named Steady, Speedy, and Slowpoke ran in a race.
(2) Tic, Tac, and Toe each owned one of the horses.
(3) Tac's horse nearly won.
(4) This was Speedy's fifth race.
(5) The black horse was owned by Toe.
(6) The horse owned by Tic had not previously raced.
(7) Steady broke an ankle after the start of the race.
(8) The horse that won was brown.

The winning horse was ___?___. Slowpoke
The winning horse was owned by ___?___. Tic

# 9 • Postulates of Geometry

A **plane** is a flat surface that extends indefinitely in all directions. A floor suggests part of a plane. So does a wall.

Usually a plane is represented by a four-sided figure. The plane can be named by the four vertices of the figure or by a single capital letter.

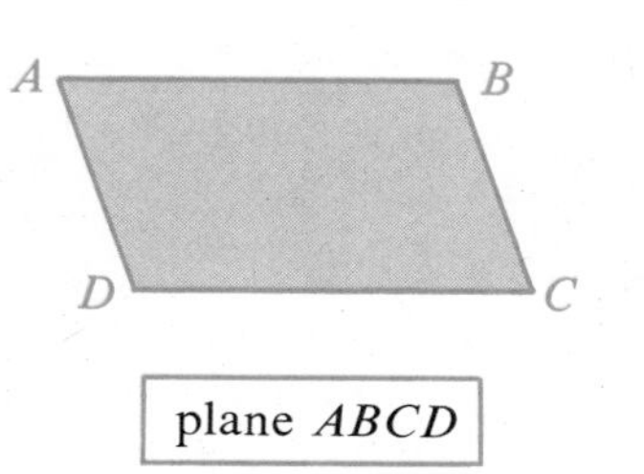


plane *ABCD*

plane *X*

You should realize that drawings like those above only *suggest* planes. There is no good way of showing in a drawing that a plane extends indefinitely. An actual plane does *not* have sides or vertices.

Remember that points all on one line are called *collinear* points. Similarly, points all on one plane are called **coplanar** points.

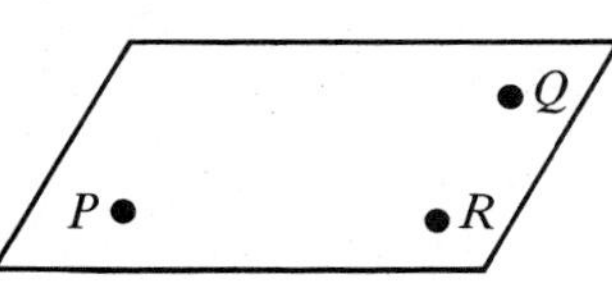


*P*, *Q*, and *R* are *not* collinear. But they are coplanar.

This drawing suggests that there is exactly one plane containing three noncollinear points.

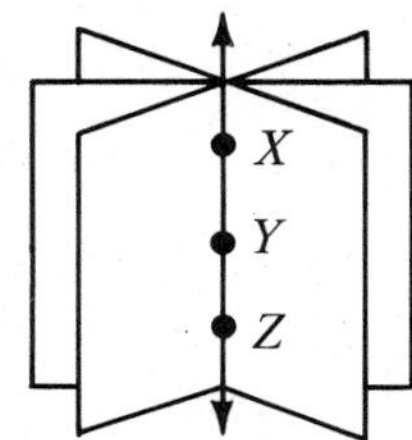


*X*, *Y*, and *Z* are collinear. They are also coplanar.

This drawing suggests that there are an unlimited number of planes containing three collinear points.

A summary of the relationships between points, lines, and planes is given by the postulates on the next page. Remember that postulates are statements which we assume to be true without proof.

**POSTULATE 1**

Through any two points there is exactly one line.

**POSTULATE 2**

Through any three noncollinear points there is exactly one plane.

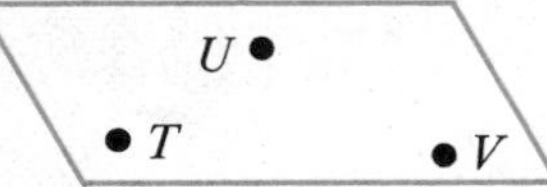


**POSTULATE 3**

If two points lie in a plane, then the line joining them lies in that plane.

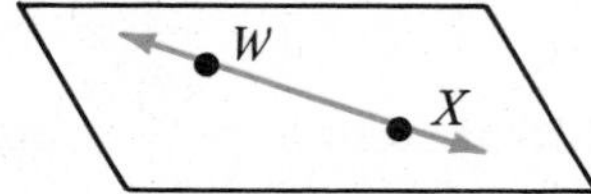


**POSTULATE 4**

If two planes intersect, then their intersection is a line.

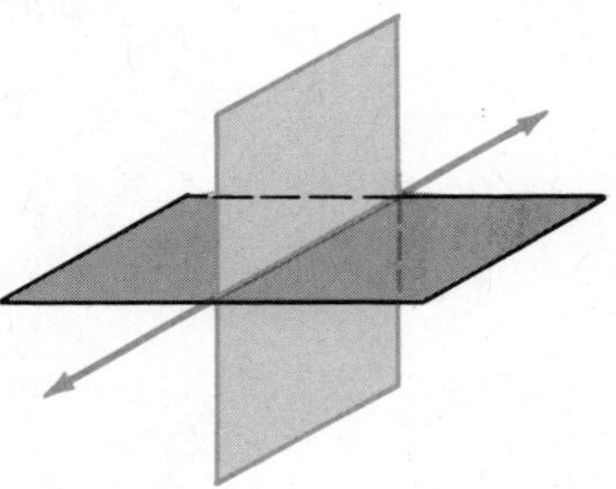

If two planes do not intersect, we say that they are parallel. Planes $M$ and $N$, shown at the right, are parallel planes. We indicate this by writing

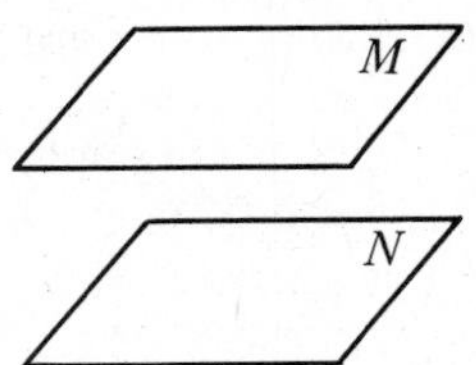


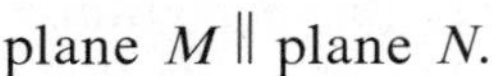

$$\text{plane } M \parallel \text{plane } N.$$

Postulates 1–4 deal with the geometric ideas of *points, lines,* and *planes*. Postulates 5 and 6 connect geometric and algebraic ideas. You do not need to memorize the statements of these two postulates. Just be sure that you understand them.

**POSTULATE 5 (The Ruler Postulate)**

Each point on a line can be paired with exactly one real number called its coordinate. The distance between two points is the positive difference of their coordinates.

If $a > b$, then $AB = a - b$.

**POSTULATE 6 (The Protractor Postulate)**

Suppose $O$ is a point of $\overleftrightarrow{XY}$. Consider all rays with endpoint $O$ which lie on one side of $\overleftrightarrow{XY}$. Each ray can be paired with exactly one real number between 0 and 180, as shown.

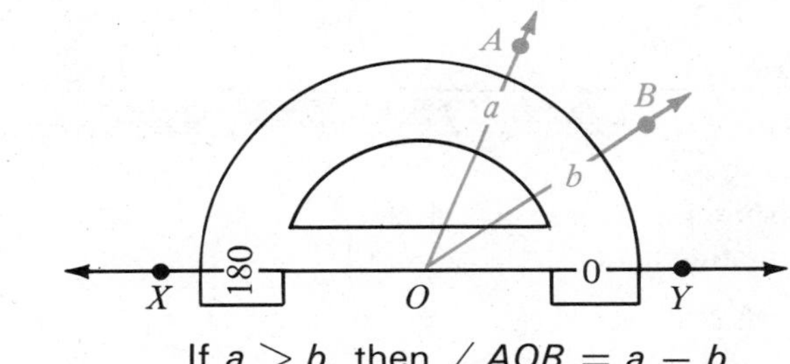


If $a > b$, then $\angle AOB = a - b$.

Do the ideas of the Ruler and Protractor Postulates seem familiar? When we found lengths of segments and measures of angles in Section 1, we were informally using the ideas expressed in these postulates.

## Classroom Practice

**Find each length.**

**1.** $CF$ 3 **2.** $EG$ 2 **3.** $EA$ 4 **4.** $BG$ 5

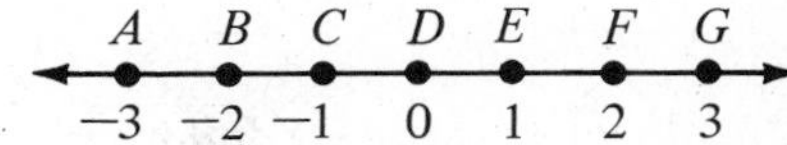


**Find the measure of each angle.**

**5.** $\angle INL$ 100° **6.** $\angle KNJ$ 40°

**7.** $\angle HNM$ 180° **8.** $\angle JNM$ 120°

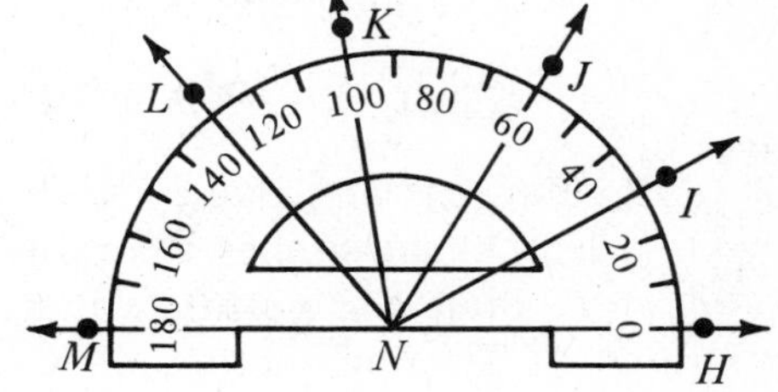

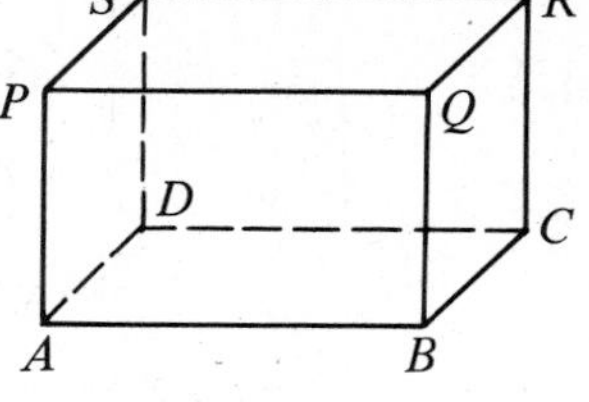

Exercises 9–18

**The diagram shows a figure called a *rectangular solid.* Think of it as a box with six faces (sides). Decide if the given points are coplanar.**

9. $P$, $Q$, $R$, and $S$ coplanar
10. $P$, $Q$, $B$, and $A$ coplanar
11. $B$, $C$, $R$, and $S$ not coplanar
12. $B$, $Q$, $S$, and $D$ coplanar

**Name another point which is coplanar with the three given points.**

13. $A$, $B$, and $D$ C
14. $A$, $D$, and $S$ P
15. $A$, $B$, and $R$ S
16. $A$, $P$, and $R$ C

**Complete each statement.**

17. plane $ABCD \parallel$ plane _?_ PQRS
18. plane $ABQP \parallel$ plane _?_ DCRS

## *Written Exercises*

**The diagram shows a rectangular solid. Complete each statement.**

A

1. Plane $ABCD \parallel$ plane _?_ EFGH
2. Plane $ADHE \parallel$ plane _?_ BCGF
3. Plane $ABFE \parallel$ plane _?_ DCGH
4. Plane $EFGH$ intersects plane $BCGF$ in the line _?_. FG
5. Plane $ABFE$ intersects plane $BCGF$ in the line _?_. BF

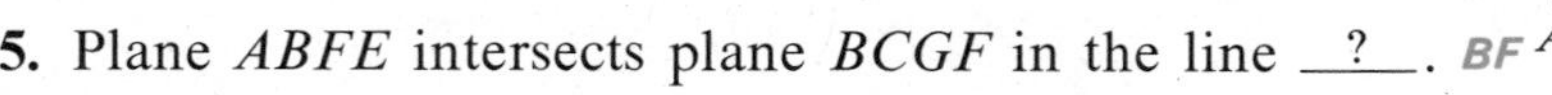

6. Points $E$, $A$, $D$, and _?_ H are coplanar.

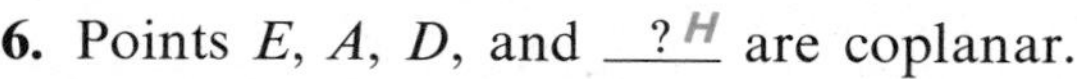

7. Points $B$, $F$, $H$, and _?_ D are coplanar.
8. Points $C$, $G$, $H$, and _?_ D are coplanar.

**Draw each of the following.**

9. Two parallel planes
10. Two intersecting planes
11. A corner of a room where two walls and the floor meet
12. Plane $M$ and plane $N$ both contain point $P$.
    a. Do the planes have any other points in common? yes
    b. State the postulate that answers this question. Postulate 4

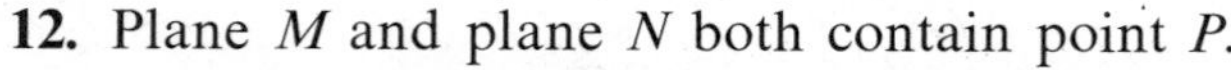

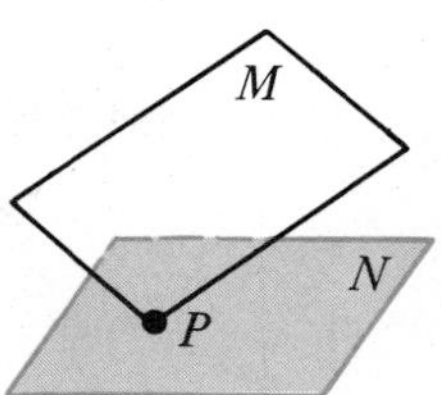

13. The diagram suggests what would happen if two different "lines" both contained points $A$ and $B$. State the postulate that says this cannot happen. Postulate 1

14. A point is given. Is the point contained in just one line or in more than one line? more than one line

15. A line is given. Is the line contained in just one plane or in more than one plane? more than one plane

16. A line and a point not on the line are given. Are the line and the point both contained in just one plane or in more than one plane? one plane

17. A rectangle is given. Is the rectangle contained in just one plane or in more than one plane? one plane

**Tell whether each statement is true or false.**

B 18. If points $P$, $Q$, and $R$ are on plane $M$ and also on plane $N$, then the planes must be the same. false

19. A triangle is contained in exactly one plane. true

20. Any four points are contained in exactly one plane. false

21. If points $A$ and $B$ are on plane $X$, then every point of $\overline{AB}$ must be on $X$. true

22. If points $A$ and $B$ are on a soup can, then every point of $\overline{AB}$ must be on the can. false

C 23. Suppose the rectangular solid represents a tall building. When a three-dimensional figure is represented on a flat surface, it is usually drawn in perspective. That is, for example, angles are drawn larger or smaller than they actually are. In the diagram, $\angle FBC$ is an acute angle but it represents a right angle in the actual building. Using this as an example, complete the table.

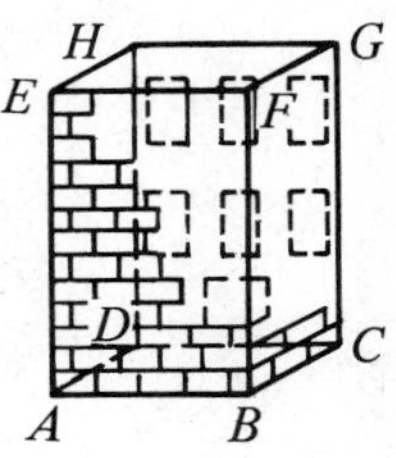


| | $\angle FBC$ | $\angle BFG$ | $\angle HEF$ | $\angle EAB$ |
|---|---|---|---|---|
| In the diagram | acute | ? | ? | ? |
| In the actual building | right | ? | ? | ? |

In the diagram, $\angle BFG$ is obtuse, $\angle HEF$ is acute, and $\angle EAB$ is right.
In the building, $\angle BFG$ is right, $\angle HEF$ is right, and $\angle EAB$ is right.

## SELF-TEST

1. Draw an acute angle. Then bisect it using straightedge and compass.

**Which postulate can be used to justify each statement?**

2. If $x - 7 = 3$, then $x = 10$. addition

3. If $\angle 1 + \angle 2 = 180°$ and $\angle 2 = \angle 3$, then $\angle 1 + \angle 3 = 180°$. substitution

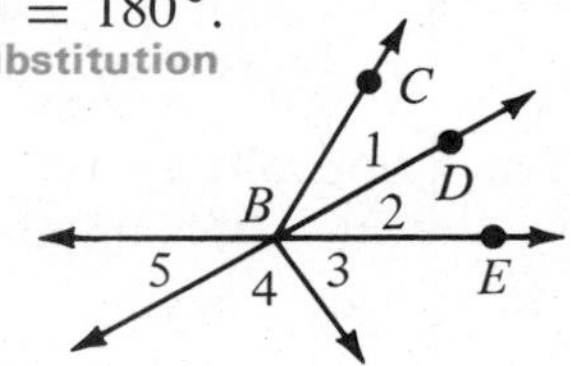


4. Use the diagram at the right.
*Given information:* $\overrightarrow{BD}$ bisects $\angle CBE$.
*Conclusion:* $\angle 1 = \angle$ _?_ 2 $= \angle$ _?_ 5

**The diagram shows a rectangular solid. Complete each statement.**

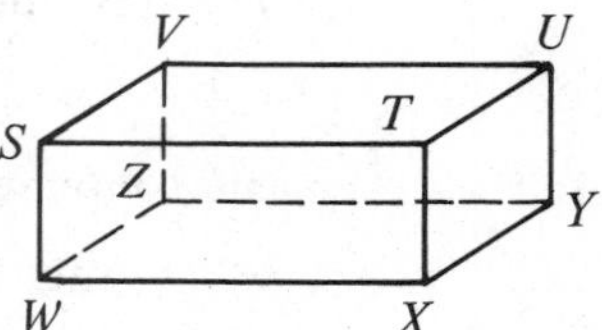


5. $S$, $V$, $Z$, and _?_ W are coplanar points.

6. Plane $STUV \parallel$ plane _?_ WXYZ

7. Plane $STXW$ intersects plane $WXYZ$ in the line _?_. WX

# CAREER NOTES

## Astronomer

Did you ever watch the stars and planets on a clear night? Did you wonder how and where the planets move?

Astronomers who specialize in celestial mechanics deal with the locations and motions of objects in the solar system. These astronomers compute the positions of planets and chart the orbits of comets, meteors, asteroids, and artificial satellites. They use optical devices attached to telescopes to make measurements. To process the data, they use computers and other electronic equipment.

## Reviewing Arithmetic Skills

| | a 6 | b 8 | c 6 | | d 4 | e 2 | f 3 | g 5 | | | h 2 | i 6 | j 1 | k 7 | | l 3 | m 1 | n 4 | |
|---|---|---|---|---|---|---|---|---|---|---|---|---|---|---|---|---|---|---|---|
| | o 3 | 6 | 1 | | p 7 | 1 | 0 | 4 | | | q 1 | 2 | 2 | 6 | | r 2 | 9 | 3 | |
| s 2 | 1 | 2 | 5 | | t 8 | 9 | 1 | 3 | | | u 6 | 5 | 9 | 0 | | v 6 | 3 | 2 | w 1 |
| x | 4 | 9 | | | y 1 | 6 | | z 2 | 0 | 0 | 4 | | aa | 1 | | | bb | 8 | 1 |
| | | | cc | 3 | 5 | 0 | | | | | | | dd | 4 | 0 | 0 | | | |

Box x is 7; box aa is 3; box bb is 6; box cc is 4; box dd is 9.

**Copy the pattern above on squared paper. Then work the exercises and fill in the blanks just as you would in a crossword puzzle.**

*Across*

**a.** 905 − 219
**o.** $(19)^2$
**s.** 25 × 85
**x.** 5992 ÷ 8
**bb.** 3 × 227
**d.** 5 × 847
**p.** 96 × 74
**t.** 995 + 7918
**y.** $2^4$
**cc.** 1833 + 2517
**h.** 6421 − 3804
**q.** 709 + 517
**u.** 7309 − 719
**z.** 2823 − 819
**dd.** 200 × 47
**l.** 2826 ÷ 9
**r.** 1172 ÷ 4
**v.** 21 × 301
**aa.** 2139 ÷ 69

*Down*

**a.** 5406 + 908
**e.** 72 × 305
**i.** 2500 ÷ 4
**m.** $(44)^2$
**b.** 9303 − 674
**f.** 3913 ÷ 13
**j.** 5347 + 7592
**n.** 8001 − 3673
**c.** 15 × 41
**g.** 8 × 679
**k.** 618 × 123
**s.** $3^3$
**d.** 53,913 − 6098
**h.** 968 + 1196
**l.** 49,552 ÷ 152
**w.** 528 ÷ 48

**Simplify.**

**1.** $\frac{7}{8} + \frac{5}{8}$ $1\frac{1}{2}$
**2.** $\frac{9}{16} - \frac{5}{16}$ $\frac{1}{4}$
**3.** $12 - \frac{5}{6}$ $11\frac{1}{6}$
**4.** $\frac{7}{16} + \frac{1}{2}$ $\frac{15}{16}$

**5.** $\frac{11}{12} - \frac{3}{4}$ $\frac{1}{6}$
**6.** $8\frac{5}{9} - 2\frac{1}{3}$ $6\frac{2}{9}$
**7.** $3\frac{2}{5} + 4\frac{3}{10}$ $7\frac{7}{10}$
**8.** $4\frac{3}{8} - 2\frac{1}{2}$ $1\frac{7}{8}$

**9.** $\frac{5}{6} \times \frac{2}{3}$ $\frac{5}{9}$
**10.** $8 \div \frac{2}{7}$ 28
**11.** $\frac{3}{4} \div \frac{9}{10}$ $\frac{5}{6}$
**12.** $\frac{1}{3} \times \frac{4}{5} \times \frac{3}{8}$ $\frac{1}{10}$

**13.** $10\frac{2}{3} \div \frac{1}{3}$ 32
**14.** $4 \times 2\frac{5}{16}$ $9\frac{1}{4}$
**15.** $24 \div 1\frac{1}{5}$ 20
**16.** $3\frac{3}{4} \times \frac{1}{10} \times \frac{2}{9}$ $\frac{1}{12}$

**17.** $6\frac{1}{4} - \frac{7}{8}$ $5\frac{3}{8}$
**18.** $\frac{9}{16} \div 1\frac{1}{2}$ $\frac{3}{8}$
**19.** $3\frac{1}{7} \times 56$ 176
**20.** $8\frac{1}{2} + \frac{9}{10}$ $9\frac{2}{5}$

**21.** $\frac{5}{12} \div \frac{5}{8}$ $\frac{2}{3}$
**22.** $\frac{19}{20} + \frac{4}{5}$ $1\frac{3}{4}$
**23.** $9\frac{5}{6} - 1\frac{2}{3}$ $8\frac{1}{6}$
**24.** $\frac{1}{6} \times 1\frac{3}{5} \times \frac{3}{16}$ $\frac{1}{20}$

# applications

## *Using a Compass*

A magnetic compass is a basic navigational tool for finding direction of travel with respect to magnetic north. A magnetic compass measures direction in degrees, like the protractors you have used to measure angles. Although many protractors only indicate measures from 0° to 180°, a compass includes measures from 0° to 360°, that is, a compass is a complete circle.

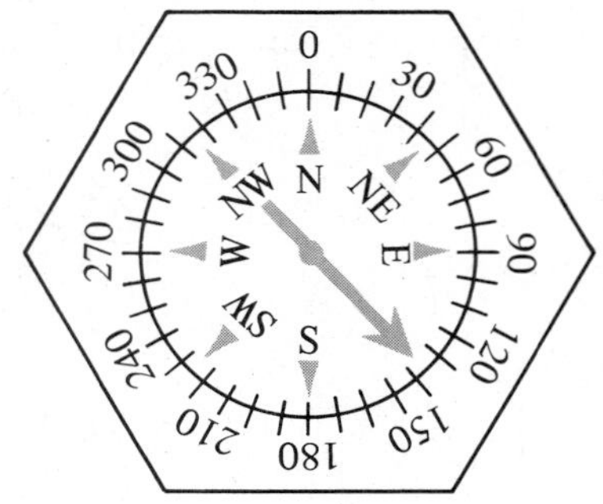


Look at the compass shown here. Notice that 0° indicates a northerly reading while 180° indicates a southerly direction. If you head toward 135°, your direction of travel is southeast. See if you can determine the reading for a southwesterly direction of travel.

Because magnetic north is not located at the north pole, navigators make corrections to accommodate for the difference between the actual direction of travel they wish to take and the magnetic compass bearing they will use. The difference between magnetic north and actual north in any particular area of the earth is called *magnetic variation*. As this variation is not the same everywhere, it is important to know the magnetic variation for your particular location before you use a compass to find your direction.

Because a magnetic compass is such a basic navigational tool, navigational charts are printed with one compass showing actual or true north, and another showing magnetic north. The example shown here is taken from a navigational chart. It shows a magnetic variation of 10° east. This means that the magnetic compass needle will point 10° east of true north. In this location, a magnetic compass reading due west or 270° indicates a true direction of 280°. Suppose you want to head in the true direction of 45°. Find the compass heading by subtracting the magnetic variation, 10°, from the true direction. The magnetic compass heading you should use is 45° − 10° = 35°.

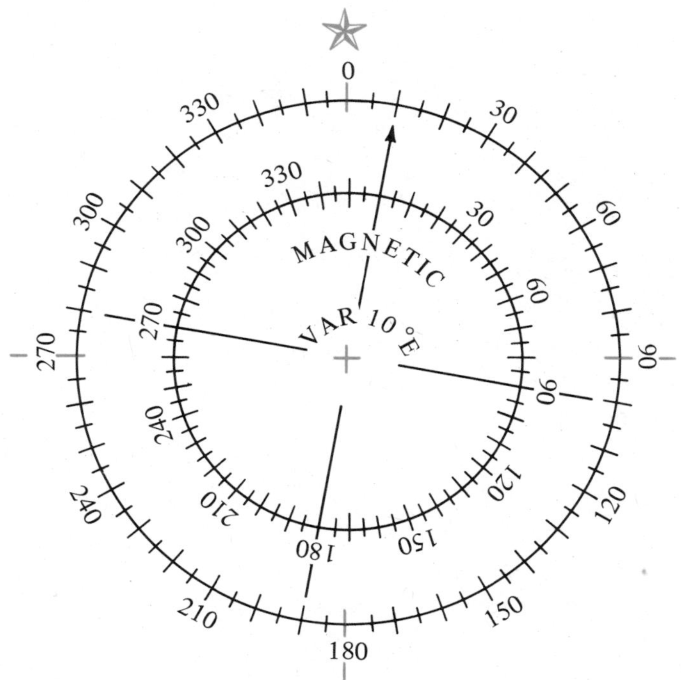


**Exercises**

**If there is no magnetic variation, find the compass heading for:**

**1.** An easterly course 90°

**2.** A northwesterly course 315°

**Find the proper magnetic compass heading for the following:**

**3.** A southwesterly course; magnetic variation 10°E 215°

**4.** A westerly course; magnetic variation 7°W 263°

## Reviewing the Chapter

### Chapter Summary

1. The basic figures studied in this chapter are lines, rays, segments, and angles. Each of these is a set of points.
   Line $AB$ is written $\overleftrightarrow{AB}$.
   Ray $AB$ is written $\overrightarrow{AB}$. $A$ is the endpoint.
   Segment $AB$ is written $\overline{AB}$. $A$ and $B$ are endpoints.
   Angle $AOB$ is written $\angle AOB$. $O$ is the vertex.
2. Angles are classified as acute, right, obtuse, and straight according to their measures. Perpendicular lines form right angles.
3. Vertical angles are equal.

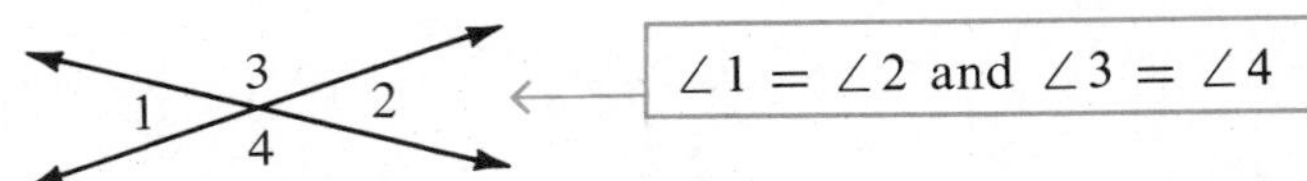


4. If $M$ is the midpoint of $\overline{AB}$, then $AM = MB = \frac{1}{2}AB$.

   If $\overrightarrow{OM}$ bisects $\angle AOB$, then $\angle AOM = \angle MOB = \frac{1}{2}\angle AOB$.
5. In constructing a geometric figure, the only instruments which may be used are a compass and a straightedge. Three basic constructions are shown on pages 21–22:
   (1) a bisector of an angle;
   (2) a line perpendicular to a given line at a point on the line;
   (3) a line perpendicular to a given line through a point not on the line.
6. Postulates are statements which are accepted without proof. They are used to prove other statements and theorems. You should review the postulates of equality on pages 25–26 and the geometric postulates on pages 30–31.

### Chapter Review Test

A permission-to-reproduce chapter test can be found on page T11.

**Complete.** *(See pp. 4–7.)*



**1.** Another name for $\overleftrightarrow{AB}$ is __?__. $\overleftrightarrow{AC}$, for example

**2.** Another name for $\overrightarrow{BD}$ is __?__. $\overrightarrow{BC}$ or $\overrightarrow{BE}$

**3.** $BC =$ __?__ 4

**4.** If $D$ is the midpoint of $\overline{CE}$, then the coordinate of $E$ is __?__. 11

**5.** If $AB = 5$, then the coordinate of $A$ is __?__. −6

**Complete.** (*See pp. 8–11.*)

6. The vertex of $\angle 1$ is __?__. Q
7. The sides of $\angle 7$ are __?__ $\overline{BN}$ and __?__. $\overline{BQ}$ or $\overline{BK}$
8. $\angle 7 + \angle 8 =$ __?__ ° 180
9. Another name for $\angle 5$ is __?__. $\angle KQR$
   (Use three letters.)
10. $\angle SQB - \angle NQB = \angle$ __?__ 3 or $\angle SQN$

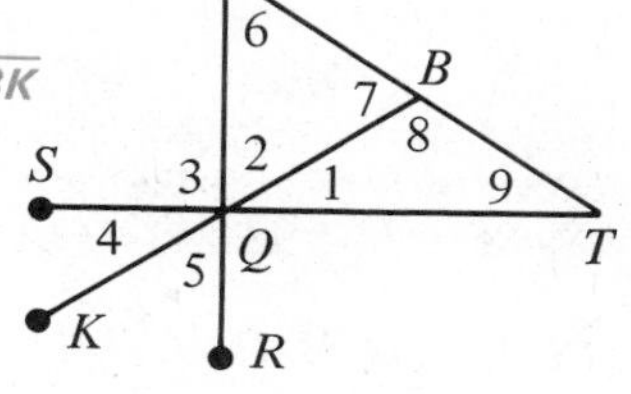

Exercises 6–16

**In the diagram above, $\overline{NQ} \perp \overline{ST}$. Classify each angle as acute, right, obtuse, or straight.** (*See pp. 13–15.*)

11. $\angle RQT$ right
12. $\angle QBN$ acute
13. $\angle QBT$ obtuse
14. $\angle KQB$ straight

**Complete. Use the diagram above.** (*See pp. 16–17.*)

15. $\angle 2$ and $\angle$ __?__ 5 are vertical angles.
16. If $\angle KQN = 122°$, then $\angle$ __?__ RQB $= 122°$.

**Solve.** (*See pp. 18–19.*)

17. When you bisect a right angle, you divide the angle into two smaller angles. What is the measure of each? 45°

**For each exercise, draw a large triangle roughly like $\triangle RST$. Then construct the required figure.** (*See pp. 21–24.*)

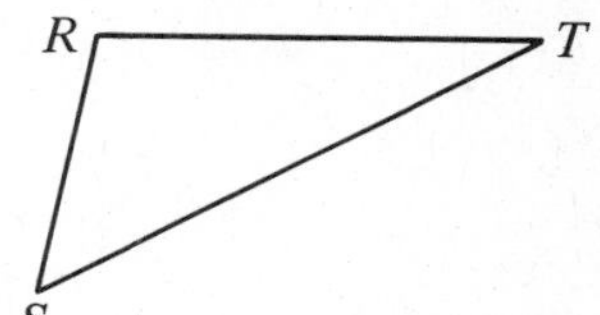


18. Construct a bisector of $\angle T$.
19. Construct a line perpendicular to $\overline{ST}$ through $R$.

**Which postulate can be used to justify each statement?** (*See pp. 25–28.*)

20. If $5x = 35$, then $x = 7$. division
21. If $\angle 1 = \angle 2$ and $\angle 4 = \angle 5$, then $\angle 1 + \angle 4 = \angle 2 + \angle 5$. addition
22. If $\angle 1 + \angle 2 = 180°$ and $\angle 2 = \angle 4$, then $\angle 1 + \angle 4 = 180°$. substitution

**Refer to the rectangular solid shown. Complete.** (*See pp. 29–33.*)

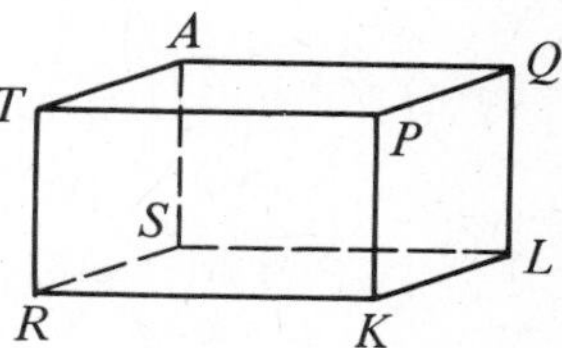


23. $T$, $P$, $Q$, and __?__ A are coplanar points.
24. $A$, $T$, $R$, and __?__ S are coplanar points.
25. Plane $RKPT \parallel$ plane __?__. SLQA
26. Plane $PKLQ$ intersects plane $RKLS$ in the line __?__. KL
27. How many planes contain three noncollinear points? exactly one

## *Here's what you'll learn in this chapter:*

1. To use theorems about complementary, supplementary, and vertical angles.
2. To write "If . . . then" statements and their converses.
3. To understand and write basic geometric proofs.
4. To use the properties of parallel lines cut by a transversal.
5. To prove lines parallel.
6. To construct parallel lines.

# Chapter 2

# Introducing Proof

## 1 • Three Theorems

Logical reasoning is an important part of geometry. You are given certain facts about a geometric figure and you use these facts to reach conclusions. So far, your conclusions have been based on definitions of figures and on the postulates of equality. Here is an example of logical reasoning.

**EXAMPLE** *Given information:* $\overline{AB} \perp \overline{BC}$

$\overline{PQ} \perp \overline{QR}$

$\angle 1 = \angle 2$

*Conclusion:* $\angle 3 = \angle 4$

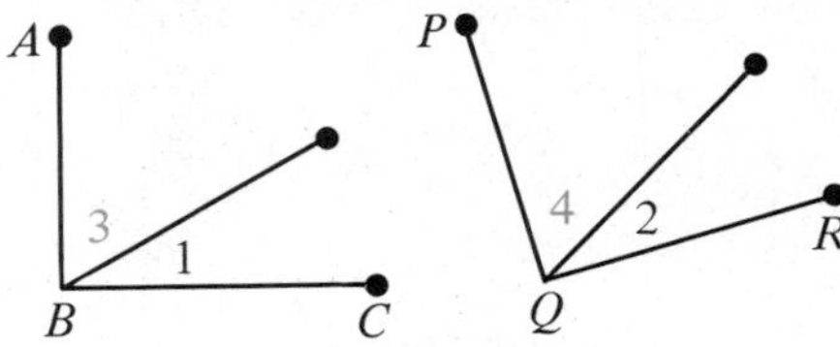


These are the steps used in reaching the conclusion:

*Step 1* $\angle ABC = 90°$ because $\overline{AB} \perp \overline{BC}$, and (by definition) perpendicular lines form 90° angles.

*Step 2* $\angle PQR = 90°$ because $\overline{PQ} \perp \overline{QR}$.

*Step 3* $\angle 1 + \angle 3 = \angle 2 + \angle 4$ because both sums are equal to 90°.

*Step 4* $\angle 1 = \angle 2$ because this is given information.

*Step 5* $\angle 3 = \angle 4$ by using the Subtraction Postulate.

In the example above, $\angle 1$ and $\angle 3$ are called *complementary angles* or just *complements*. **Complementary angles** are two angles whose measures total 90°. In the diagram above, $\angle 2$ and $\angle 4$ are also complementary angles. So are $\angle A$ and $\angle B$ in the diagram at the right.

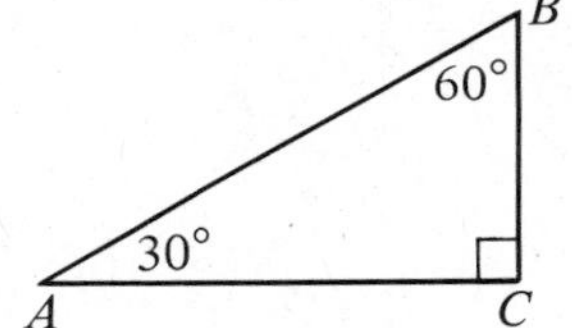


The conclusion reached in the example is really a statement about complementary angles: If two angles are equal (such as $\angle 1 = \angle 2$), then their complements are equal ($\angle 3 = \angle 4$).

Let us list this statement as Theorem 1. Remember that a **theorem** is nothing more than a statement which has been proved. Of course, we won't list every proved statement as a theorem. We'll list only the ones which will be most helpful to us in our later work.

**THEOREM 1**

If two angles are complements of equal angles (or of the same angle), then the two angles are equal.

The next theorem refers to **supplementary angles** (sometimes called **supplements).** These are two angles whose measures total 180°.

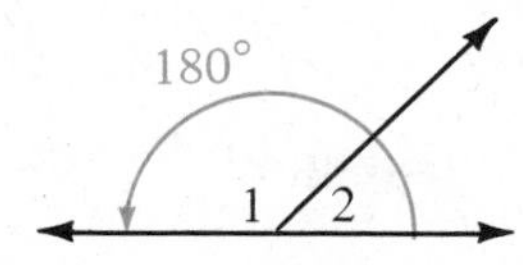


$\angle 1$ and $\angle 2$ are supplementary angles.

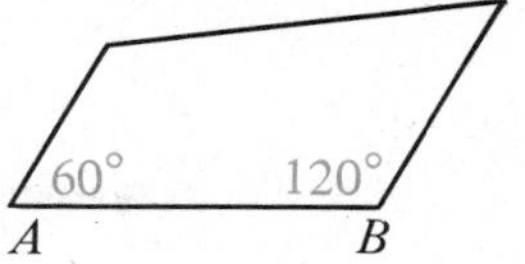


$\angle A$ and $\angle B$ are supplements.

**THEOREM 2**

If two angles are supplements of equal angles (or of the same angle), then the two angles are equal.

Here is a diagram and proof of Theorem 2.

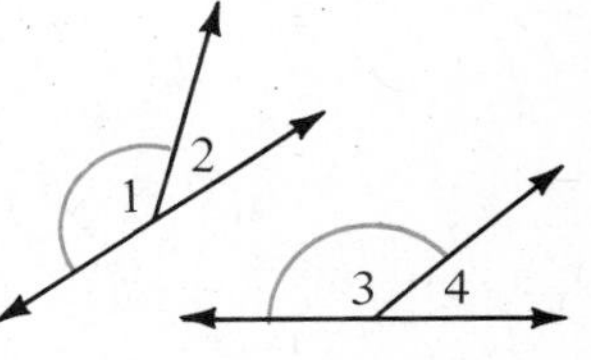


*Given information:* $\angle 1$ and $\angle 2$ are supplements.
$\angle 3$ and $\angle 4$ are supplements.
$\angle 1 = \angle 3$

*Conclusion:* $\angle 2 = \angle 4$

*Step 1* $\angle 1 + \angle 2 = 180°$ because $\angle 1$ and $\angle 2$ are supplements, and (by definition) supplements total 180°.

*Step 2* $\angle 3 + \angle 4 = 180°$ because $\angle 3$ and $\angle 4$ are supplements.

*Step 3* $\angle 1 + \angle 2 = \angle 3 + \angle 4$ because both sums are 180°.

*Step 4* $\angle 1 = \angle 3$ because this is given information.

*Step 5* $\angle 2 = \angle 4$ by using the Subtraction Postulate.

Our next theorem is the familiar statement that vertical angles are equal. Of course, we introduced this result on page 16.

**THEOREM 3**

Vertical angles are equal.

*Step 1* $\angle 1$ and $\angle 2$ are supplements.

*Step 2* $\angle 2$ and $\angle 3$ are supplements.

*Step 3* $\angle 1 = \angle 3$ because supplements of the same angle are equal.

## Classroom Practice

1. If $\angle A = 70°$, what is the measure of a complement of $\angle A$? a supplement of $\angle A$? 20° 110°

2. If $\angle B = 89°$, what is the measure of a complement of $\angle B$? a supplement of $\angle B$? 1° 91°

3. If $\angle C = x°$, what is the measure of a complement of $\angle C$? a supplement of $\angle C$? $90° - x°$ $180° - x°$

4. Name two pairs of complementary angles. $\angle OIA$, $\angle EIA$; $\angle OIA$, $\angle OAI$

5. Name a supplement of $\angle OAE$. $\angle IEA$

6. Name another pair of supplementary angles. $\angle EIO$, $\angle IOA$

7. Name three pairs of supplementary angles. $\angle DHE$, $\angle EHG$; $\angle DHF$, $\angle FHG$; $\angle EFH$, $\angle HFG$

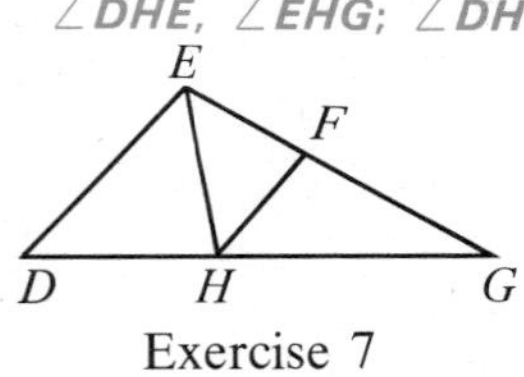

Exercise 7

Exercise 8

8. Suppose that $\angle 1 = \angle 2$. State the theorem that allows you to conclude that $\angle 3 = \angle 4$. Theorem 2

**Suppose $\overline{RY} \perp \overline{SY}$ and $\overline{UY} \perp \overline{TY}$.**

9. Name a complement of $\angle 1$. $\angle 2$

10. Name a complement of $\angle 3$. $\angle 2$

11. State the theorem that allows you to conclude that $\angle 1 = \angle 3$. Theorem 1

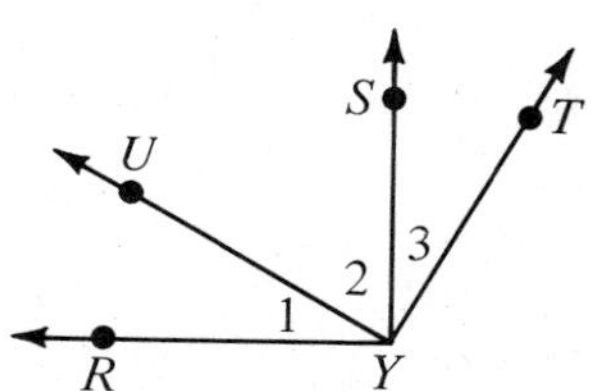


## Written Exercises

**Copy and complete the table.**

A

| | 1. | 2. | 3. | 4. | 5. | 6. | 7. |
|---|---|---|---|---|---|---|---|
| $\angle A$ | 50° | 62° | 18° | ? 20° | ? 42° | ? 80° | ? 45° |
| Complement of $\angle A$ | ? 40° | ? 28° | ? 72° | 70° | 48° | ? 10° | ? 45° |
| Supplement of $\angle A$ | ? 130° | ? 118° | ? 162° | ? 160° | ? 138° | 100° | 135° |

**In the diagram, $\overline{AB} \perp \overline{BC}$ and $\overline{DC} \perp \overline{BC}$.**

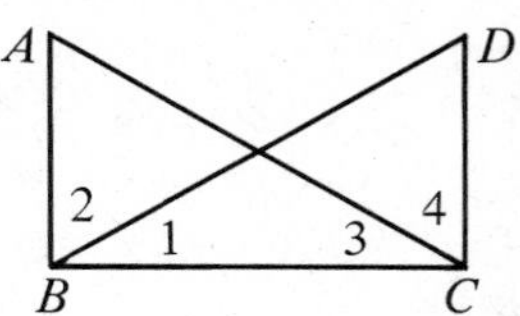


**8.** Name a complement of $\angle 1$. $\angle 2$

**9.** Name a complement of $\angle 3$. $\angle 4$

**10.** If $\angle 1 = \angle 3$, state the theorem that allows you to conclude that $\angle 2 = \angle 4$. Theorem 1

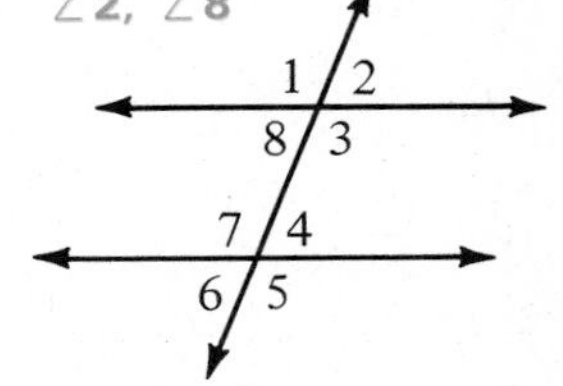


**11.** In the diagram, name two different supplements of $\angle 3$. $\angle 2$, $\angle 8$

**12.** If $\angle 3$ and $\angle 4$ are supplements, state the theorem that allows you to conclude that $\angle 2 = \angle 4$. Theorem 2

**13.** From Exercise 12, you know that $\angle 2 = \angle 4$. State the theorem that allows you to conclude that $\angle 1 = \angle 7$. Theorem 2

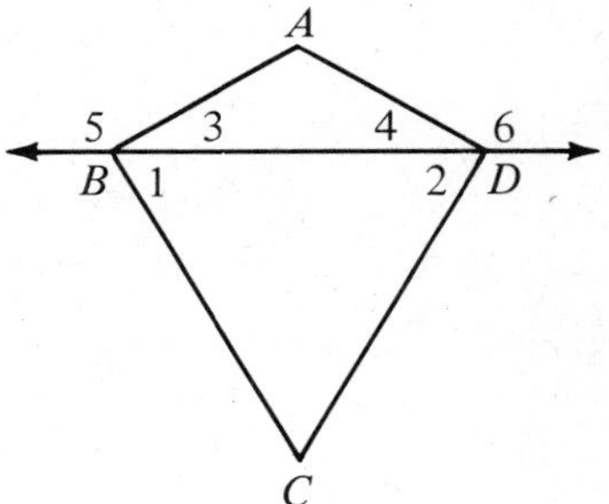


**14.** *Given information:* $\angle ABC = 90°$
$\angle ADC = 90°$
$\angle 1 = \angle 2$

**a.** What theorem allows you to conclude that $\angle 3 = \angle 4$? Theorem 1

**b.** What theorem allows you to conclude that $\angle 5 = \angle 6$? Theorem 2

**15.** Draw an acute angle, $\angle ABC$. Then use Construction 2, page 22, to construct the complement of $\angle ABC$.

**Name the postulate of equality that justifies each statement.**

**16.** If $\frac{5x + 3}{4} = 7$, then $5x + 3 = 28$. multiplication

**17.** If $5x + 3 = 28$, then $5x = 25$. subtraction

**18.** If $5x = 25$, then $x = 5$. division

B **19.** If $3x - 4y = 5$ and $2x + 4y = 10$, then $5x = 15$. addition

**20.** If $\frac{2x}{3} = \frac{7}{5}$, then $10x = 21$. multiplication

**21.** Two angles are complementary and equal. What is the measure of each? 45°

**22.** Two angles are supplementary and equal. What is the measure of each? 90°

## 2 • "If . . . then" Statements

"If . . . then" statements are common in everyday speech and in mathematics. Here are some examples.

1. **If** Jill is 16, **then** she can apply for a driver's license.
2. **If** we win, **then** we'll be in first place.
3. **If** two angles are equal, **then** their supplements are equal.

These "if . . . then" statements all have this form:

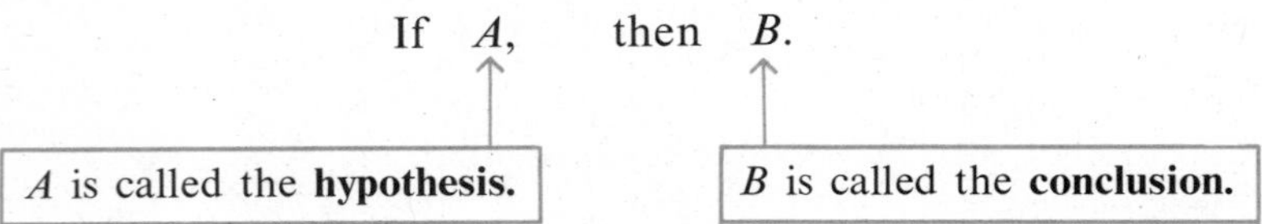


Sometimes you can express an "if . . . then" idea without even using the words *if* and *then.*

**EXAMPLE 1** All sparrows are birds.
*Restatement:* If X is a sparrow, then X is a bird.

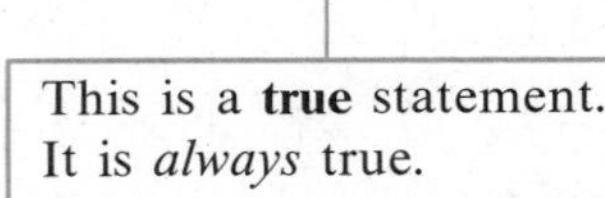

**EXAMPLE 2** All birds are sparrows.
*Restatement:* If X is a bird, then X is a sparrow.

This is a **false** statement.
It is *not always* true.

The statements in Examples 1 and 2 are *converses,* and they say very different things. The **converse** of a statement is formed by exchanging the hypothesis and the conclusion of the statement.

Statement: If *A*, then *B*.

Converse: If *B*, then *A*.

Switch

Some true statements have converses that are true. Other true statements have converses that are false.

1. True statement:
If two lines are $\perp$,
then they form $90°$ angles.

True converse:
If two lines meet at a $90°$ angle,
then they are $\perp$.

2. True statement:
If Kai lives in Texas,
then he lives in North America.

False converse:
If Kai lives in North America,
then he lives in Texas.

True

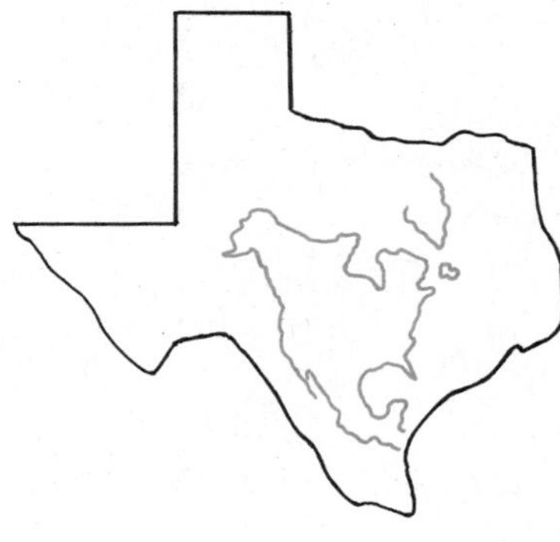

False!

## Classroom Practice

**State the hypothesis and the conclusion of each statement.**

| | |
|---|---|
| ——— | denotes hypothesis |
| - - - - | denotes conclusion |

1. If the rope breaks, then the tent falls.
2. If I am smart, then you are a genius.
3. If $3x - 7 = 23$, then $x = 10$.
4. I will go if you will. (*Warning:* This exercise shows that the hypothesis is not always mentioned first.) Hyp: You go Conc: I will go
5. We shall succeed if we try.
6. If you want to play in Yankee Stadium, then you must practice.

**7–12.** State the converse of each statement in Exercises 1–6. Answers on page T127.

**Express each statement in "If . . . then" form.**

**13.** The integer $n$ is even when $n + 1$ is odd. If $n + 1$ is odd, then $n$ is even.

**14.** All students like vacations. (*Hint:* Begin with "If a person is. . . .") If a person is a student, then he or she likes vacations.

**Express each statement in "If . . . then" form.**

15. All rock collectors are interested in geology. If a person is a rock collector, then he or she is interested in geology.

16. Too many cooks spoil the stew. If there are too many cooks, then the stew is spoiled.

17. $y = 14$ when $y - 8 = 6$. If $y - 8 = 6$, then $y = 14$.

18. Every positive number less than 100 has a square root which is less than 10. If a number is positive and less than 100, then it has a square root which is less than 10.

**In Exercises 19–22:**
**a. decide if the statement is true;**
**b. state the converse;**
**c. decide if the converse is true.**

19. If $t + 4 = 8$, then $8 = t + 4$. a. true b. If $8 = t + 4$, then $t + 4 = 8$. c. true

20. If $a = 2$ and $b = 3$, then $ab = 6$. a. true b. If $ab = 6$, then $a = 2$ and $b = 3$. c. false

21. If $x$ is an even integer, then $2x$ is an even integer. a. true b. If $2x$ is an even integer, then $x$ is an even integer. c. false

22. All right angles have the same measure.
a. true
b. If angles have the same measure, then they are right angles c. false

## Written Exercises

**Write the hypothesis and the conclusion of each statement.**

A 1. If the sum of two angles is 90°, then the angles are complementary.

2. If it rains, it pours.

3. If $5x + 7 = 27$, then $x = 4$.

4. I'll be there at noon if I take the bus.

5. We can play tennis on Tuesday, provided it's a nice day.

6. If a number is greater than 4, it is greater than 3.

———— denotes hypothesis
- - - - denotes conclusion

7–12. Write the converse of each statement in Exercises 1–6. Answers on page T127.

**Write each statement in "If . . . then" form.**

13. All hounds are dogs. (*Hint:* Begin with "If X is. . . .") If $X$ is a hound, then $X$ is a dog.

14. All alligators are dangerous. If $X$ is an alligator, then $X$ is dangerous.

15. Vertical angles are equal. (*Hint:* Begin with "If two angles. . . .") If two angles are vertical angles, then they are equal.

16. $x^2 = 4$ when $x = 2$ or $x = -2$. If $x = 2$ or $x = -2$, then $x^2 = 4$.

17. People who live in glass houses should not throw stones. If a person lives in a glass house, then he or she should not throw stones.

18. Every baseball fan knows about Babe Ruth. If a person is a baseball fan, then he or she knows about Babe Ruth.

19. Every clam is a shellfish. If $X$ is a clam, then $X$ is a shellfish.

20. An obtuse angle has a measure that is greater than $90°$. If an angle is obtuse, then it has a measure greater than $90°$.

**In Exercises 21–28:**
**a. decide if the statement is true;**
**b. write the converse;**
**c. decide if the converse is true.**

B 21. If two angles are equal, then they are vertical angles. a. false b. If two angles are vertical angles, then they are equal. c. true

22. If $x = -3$, then $x^2 = 9$. a. true b. If $x^2 = 9$, then $x = -3$. c. false

23. If a figure is a square, then all its sides have the same length. (see below)

24. If $AM = MB$, then $M$ is the midpoint of $\overline{AB}$. a. false b. If $M$ is the midpoint of $AB$, then $AM = MB$. c. true

C 25. Every rectangle is a square. a. false b. Every square is a rectangle. c. true

26. If $a < 0$, then $a^2 > 0$. a. true b. If $a^2 > 0$, then $a < 0$. c. false

27. Every number divisible by five is also divisible by ten.

28. Whenever each of two numbers is negative, the sum of the numbers is negative.

27. a. false b. Every number divisible by 10 is also divisible by 5. c. true
28. a. true b. If the sum of two numbers is positive, then each is negative. c. false

## SELF-TEST

1. If $\angle A = 20°$, what is the measure of a complement of $\angle A$? 70°

2. If $\angle B = 38°$, what is the measure of a supplement of $\angle B$? 142°

**In the diagram, $\overline{LA} \perp \overline{RK}$.**

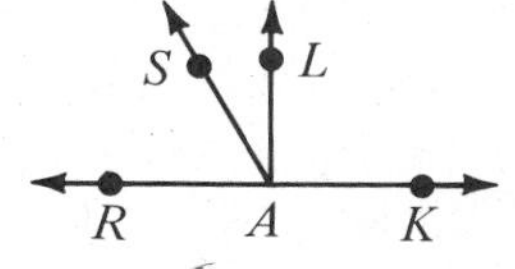


3. Name a complement of $\angle RAS$. $\angle SAL$

4. Name a supplement of $\angle RAS$. $\angle SAK$

**Consider the statement "If you read the newspaper every day, then you are well informed."** Hyp. Conc.

5. Write the hypothesis and the conclusion of the statement.

6. Write the converse of the statement. If you are well informed, then you read the newspaper every day.

23. a. true b. If the sides of a figure are all the same length, then it is a square. c. false

## 3 • "If . . . then" Statements (Optional)

When we try to prove something to others, we often use "If . . . then" statements. In this section, we shall use these statements to reach conclusions. Four kinds of simple reasoning are shown below. The first two are correct, and the last two are incorrect.

### CORRECT REASONING

**Type 1**

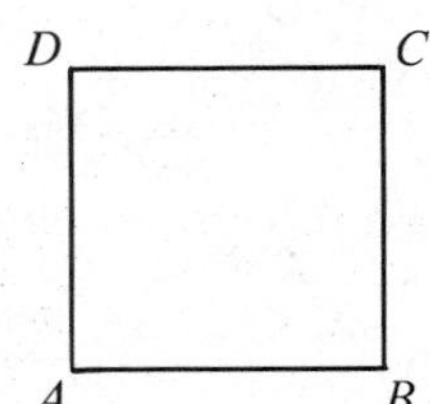


*Given information:* (1) If a figure is a square, then it has four right angles.
(2) *ABCD* is a square.

CORRECT CONCLUSION: *ABCD* has four right angles.

**Type 2**

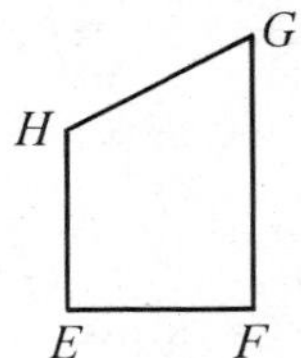


*Given information:* (1) If a figure is a square, then it has four right angles.
(2) *EFGH* does not have four right angles.

CORRECT CONCLUSION: *EFGH* is not a square.

### INCORRECT REASONING

**Type 3**

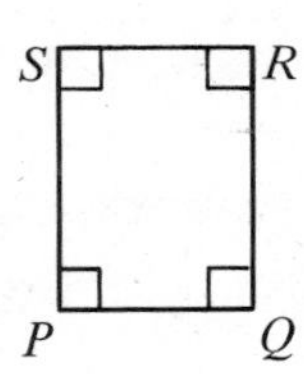


*Given information:* (1) If a figure is a square, then it has four right angles.
(2) *PQRS* has four right angles.

INCORRECT CONCLUSION: *PQRS* is a square.

**Type 4**

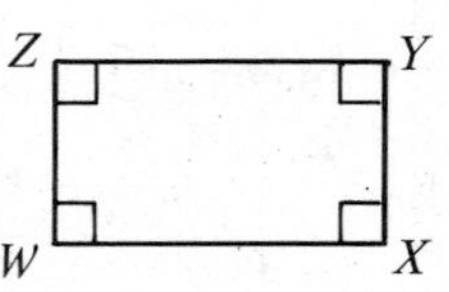


*Given information:* (1) If a figure is a square, then it has four right angles.
(2) *WXYZ* is not a square.

INCORRECT CONCLUSION: *WXYZ* does not have four right angles.

The basic form of each type of reasoning follows, along with a diagram. The diagram at the right illustrates the statement "If *A*, then *B*." When *A* is true, we place a point inside circle *A*. When *A* is not true, we place a point outside circle *A*.

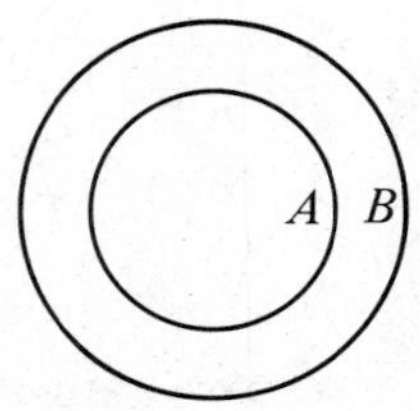

**Type 1**

(1) If $A$, then $B$.
(2) $A$ is true.
CORRECT CONCLUSION: $B$ is true.

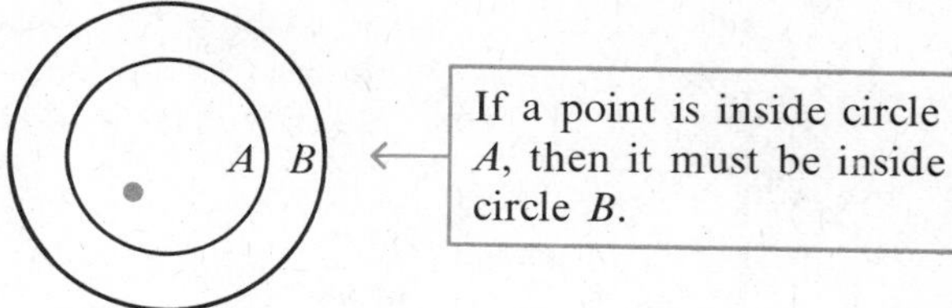


**Type 2**

(1) If $A$, then $B$.
(2) $B$ is not true.
CORRECT CONCLUSION: $A$ is not true.

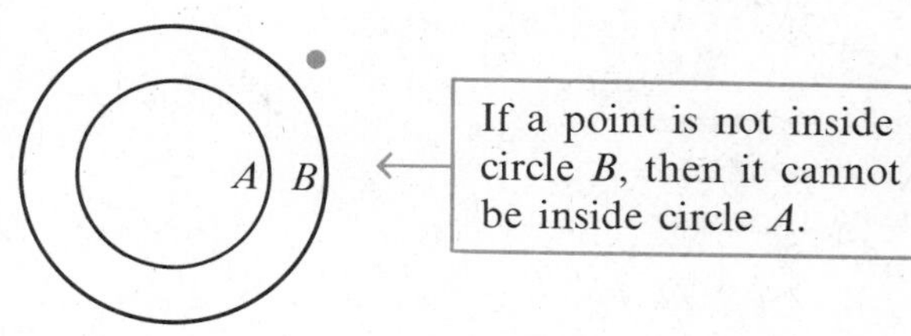


**Type 3**

(1) If $A$, then $B$.
(2) $B$ is true.
No conclusion possible.

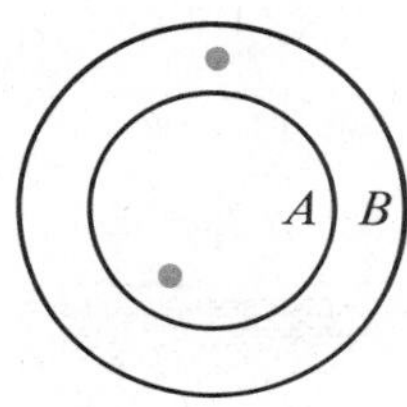


If a point is inside circle $B$, then it may or may not be inside circle $A$.

**Type 4**

(1) If $A$, then $B$.
(2) $A$ is not true.
No conclusion possible.

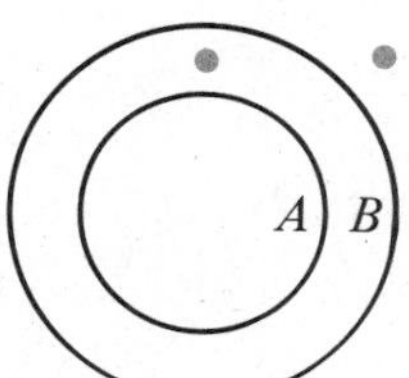


If a point is not inside circle $A$, then it may or may not be inside circle $B$.

## *Classroom Practice*

**Accept this statement as true: "All hedgehogs are hairy."**

1. Reword this statement in "If . . . then" form.
   If an animal is a hedgehog, then it is hairy.
2. Make a circle diagram of this statement.
   (Type 1 diagram)
3. For each statement below, tell what you can conclude. If no conclusion is possible, say so.
   **a.** Horace is a hedgehog. Horace is hairy.
   **b.** Heloise is not a hedgehog. no conclusion
   **c.** Hortense is hairy. no conclusion
   **d.** Bosco is bald. Bosco is not a hedgehog.

**In Exercises 4–5: a. decide whether the reasoning is Type 1, 2, 3, or 4;**
**b. decide whether the reasoning is correct.**
**(*Hint:* Rewrite statement (1) in "If . . . then" form.)**

**4.** (1) All dogs love ice cream.
(2) Shep loves ice cream.
*Conclusion:* Shep is a dog. a. Type 3 b. not correct

**5.** (1) When the product of two numbers is zero, one of the numbers must be zero.
(2) $(x - 2) \cdot (x - 3) = 0$
*Conclusion:* $x - 2 = 0$ or $x - 3 = 0$. a. Type 1 b. correct

**6.** *Given information:* (1) $\angle 1 = \angle 2$
(2) $\angle 3 = \angle 4$
What, if anything, can you conclude about $\angle 1$ and $\angle 3$? Nothing can be concluded.

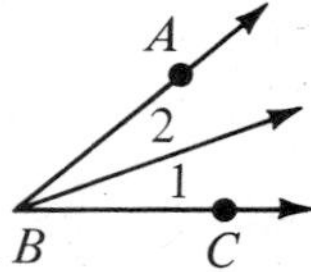


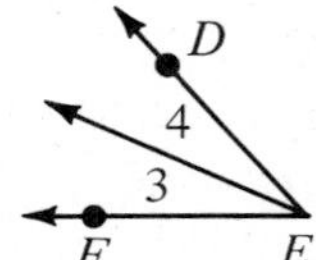


## Written Exercises

**Accept this statement as true: "All sharks have nice teeth."**

**1.** Express the statement in "If . . . then" form. If $X$ is a shark, then $X$ has nice teeth.

**2.** Make a circle diagram of this statement.

**3.** For each statement, tell what you can conclude.
**a.** Salty is a shark. Salty has nice teeth.
**b.** Smiley has nice teeth. no conclusion
**c.** Flipper is not a shark. no conclusion
**d.** Sylvester does not have nice teeth. Sylvester is not a shark.

**4.** Accept this statement as true: "If a figure is a rectangle, then the opposite sides have the same length."
For each statement, tell what, if anything, you can conclude.
**a.** The opposite sides of figure $ABCD$ have the same length.
**b.** The opposite sides of figure $PQRS$ do not have the same length.
**c.** Figure $WXYZ$ is a rectangle.

a. no conclusion
b. $ABCD$ is not a rectangle.
c. The opposite sides in figure $WXYZ$ have the same length.

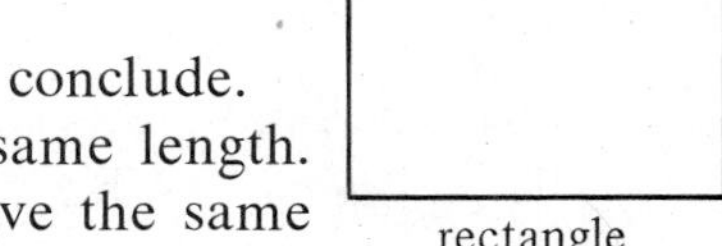
rectangle

**Accept the numbered steps as true. For each exercise:**
**a. decide whether the reasoning is Type 1, 2, 3, or 4;**
**b. decide whether the reasoning is correct.**

**5.** (1) If $x = 5$, then $y = 0$.
(2) $x = 5$
*Conclusion:* $y = 0$ a. Type 1 b. correct

**6.** (1) If $x = 5$, then $y = 0$.
(2) $y = 0$
*Conclusion:* $x = 5$ a. Type 3 b. not correct

7. (1) Vertical angles are equal.
   (2) $\angle 1$ and $\angle 2$ are not vertical angles.
   *Conclusion:* $\angle 1 \neq \angle 2$
   a. Type 4  b. not correct

8. (1) Vertical angles are equal.
   (2) $\angle 3 \neq \angle 4$
   *Conclusion:* $\angle 3$ and $\angle 4$ are not vertical angles.  a. Type 2  b. correct

9. (1) If $\angle D$ is larger than $\angle E$, then $\overline{EF}$ is longer than $\overline{DF}$.
   (2) $\overline{EF}$ is shorter than $\overline{DF}$.
   *Conclusion:* $\angle D$ is not larger than $\angle E$.
   a. Type 2  b. correct

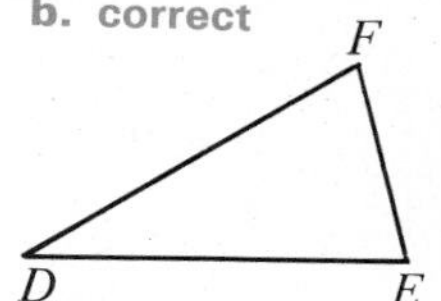


**In Exercises 10–11, try to draw a conclusion from the given information. If none is possible, say so.**

B 10. Given information: (1) $\overrightarrow{EN}$ bisects $\angle AEG$.
(2) $\overrightarrow{EG}$ bisects $\angle NEL$.

What, if anything, can you conclude about $\angle 1$ and $\angle 3$?
$\angle 1 = \angle 3$ since $\angle 1 = \angle 2$ and $\angle 2 = \angle 3$

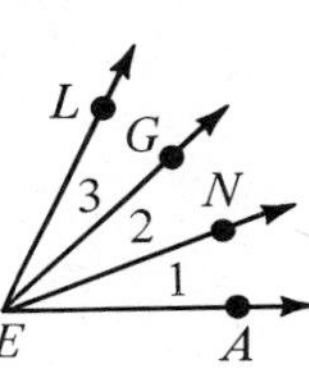


11. Given information: (1) $HE = EN = NS$
(2) $GO = OA = AT$

What, if anything, can you conclude about $HE$ and $GO$?
Nothing can be concluded.

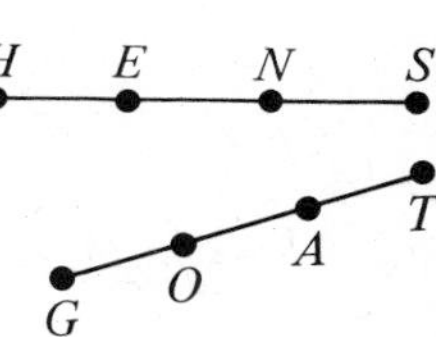


## Puzzles & Things

The sides of a cube are marked with these six symbols:

Here are three views of the cube:

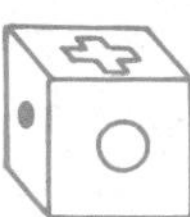  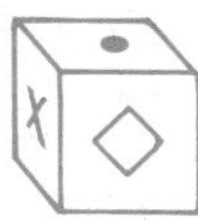

Which symbols are on opposite sides of the cube?
□ is opposite ●; ✕ is opposite ○; ◇ is opposite ✚.

# 4 • Writing Proofs

A geometric proof consists of steps that show how a conclusion follows logically from other statements. As your proofs become longer than just a few steps, it helps to organize them in two columns as shown below.

*Given:* $\angle 1$ and $\angle 4$ are supplements.

*Prove:* $\angle 2 = \angle 3$

Here is the proof:

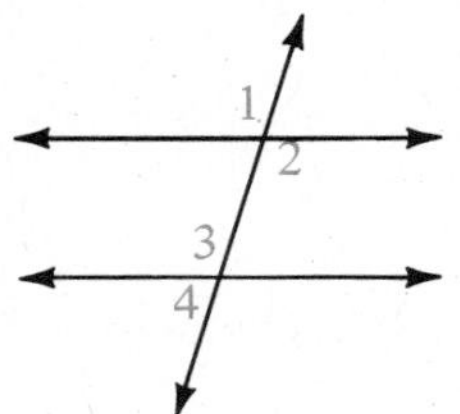


| STATEMENTS | REASONS |
|---|---|
| 1. $\angle 1$ and $\angle 4$ are supplements. | 1. Given |
| 2. $\angle 3$ and $\angle 4$ are supplements. | 2. If the measures of two angles total 180°, the angles are supplements. (A definition) |
| 3. $\angle 1 = \angle 3$ | 3. Supplements of the same angle are equal. (A theorem) |
| 4. $\angle 1 = \angle 2$ | 4. Vertical angles are equal. (A theorem) |
| 5. $\angle 2 = \angle 3$ | 5. Substitution Postulate, using Steps 3 and 4 |

The comments in parentheses are not really necessary. They are included to show you that there are four kinds of reasons which can be used to justify a step in a proof.

**Reasons Used in a Proof**

1. Given information
2. Definitions
3. Postulates (These are statements accepted without proof.)
4. Theorems (These are statements which have been proved.)

These four kinds of reasons are used in the following proof. Notice that Steps 5 and 6 use both the given information and the definition of angle bisector.

*Given:* $\angle 1 = \angle 2$
$\overrightarrow{BX}$ bisects $\angle ABC$.
$\overrightarrow{CX}$ bisects $\angle ACB$.

*Prove:* $\angle 3 = \angle 4$

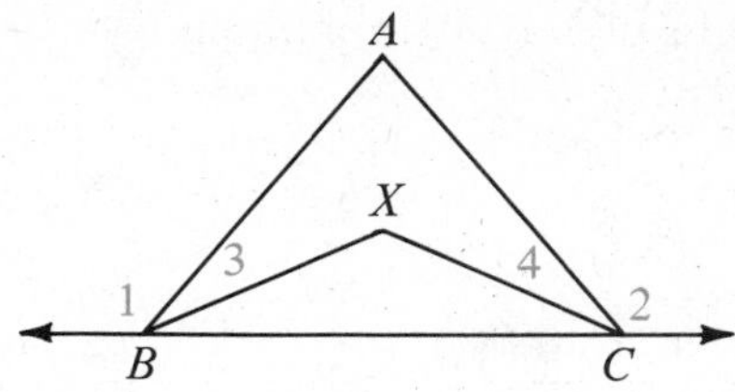


| STATEMENTS | REASONS |
|---|---|
| 1. $\angle 1$ and $\angle ABC$ are supplements. $\angle 2$ and $\angle ACB$ are supplements. | 1. Definition of supplementary angles |
| 2. $\angle 1 = \angle 2$ | 2. Given |
| 3. $\angle ABC = \angle ACB$ | 3. Supplements of equal angles are equal. |
| 4. $\frac{1}{2}\angle ABC = \frac{1}{2}\angle ACB$ | 4. Multiplication Postulate |
| 5. $\frac{1}{2}\angle ABC = \angle 3$ | 5. *Given:* $\overrightarrow{BX}$ bisects $\angle ABC$. |
| 6. $\frac{1}{2}\angle ACB = \angle 4$ | 6. *Given:* $\overrightarrow{CX}$ bisects $\angle ACB$. |
| 7. $\angle 3 = \angle 4$ | 7. Substitution Postulate |

## *Classroom Practice*

**Supply the missing reasons in the proofs.**

**1.** *Given:* $\angle 1 = \angle 2$

*Prove:* $\overleftrightarrow{LI} \perp \overleftrightarrow{NE}$

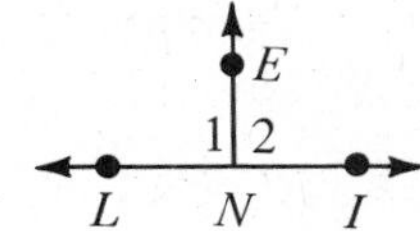


| STATEMENTS | REASONS |
|---|---|
| 1. $\angle 1 + \angle 2 = 180°$ | 1. Their sum is a __?__ angle. straight |
| 2. $\angle 1 = \angle 2$ | 2. __?__ Given |
| 3. $\angle 1 + \angle 1 = 180°$, or $2 \cdot \angle 1 = 180°$ | 3. __?__ Substitution Postulate |
| 4. $\angle 1 = 90°$ | 4. __?__ Division Postulate |
| 5. $\overleftrightarrow{LI} \perp \overleftrightarrow{NE}$ | 5. __?__ Perpendicular lines form right angles. |

**2.** *Given:* $\angle 1$ and $\angle 3$ are supplementary.

*Prove:* $\angle 2 = \angle 4$

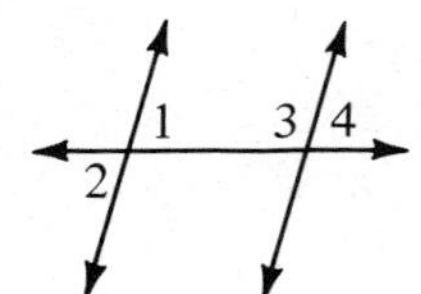


| STATEMENTS | REASONS |
|---|---|
| 1. $\angle 1$ and $\angle 3$ are supplementary. | 1. ? Given |
| 2. $\angle 4$ and $\angle 3$ are supplementary. | 2. ? Their sum is a straight angle. |
| 3. $\angle 1 = \angle 4$ | 3. ? Supplements of the same angle are =. |
| 4. $\angle 1 = \angle 2$ | 4. ? Vertical angles are equal. |
| 5. $\angle 2 = \angle 4$ | 5. ? Substitution Postulate |

## Written Exercises

**Supply the missing statements and reasons in the proofs.**

A **1.** *Given:* $\angle 1 = \angle 2$
$\angle 3 = \angle 4$

*Prove:* $\angle 1 = \angle 4$

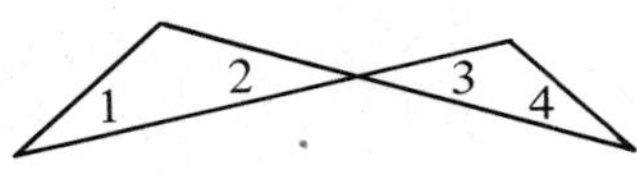


| STATEMENTS | REASONS |
|---|---|
| 1. $\angle 1 = \angle 2$<br>$\angle 3 = \angle 4$ | 1. ? Given |
| 2. $\angle 2 = \angle 3$ | 2. ? Vertical angles are equal. |
| 3. $\angle 1 = \angle 4$ | 3. ? Substitution Postulate |

**2.** *Given:* $\angle 1$ and $\angle 2$ are complements.
$\angle 3$ and $\angle 4$ are complements.

*Prove:* $\angle 1 = \angle 4$

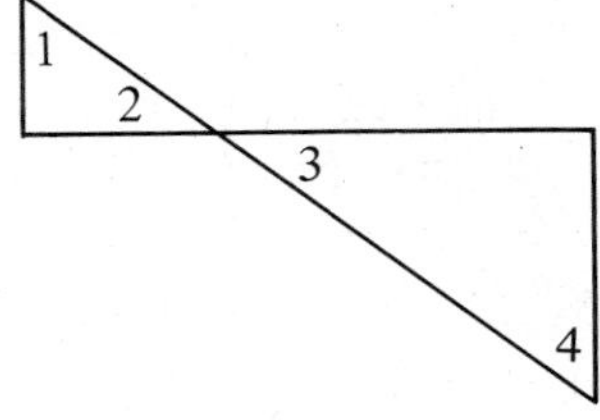


| STATEMENTS | REASONS |
|---|---|
| 1. $\angle 1$ and $\angle 2$ are complements.<br>$\angle 3$ and $\angle 4$ are complements. | 1. ? Given |
| 2. $\angle 2 = \angle 3$ | 2. ? Vertical angles are equal. |
| 3. $\angle 1 = \angle 4$ | 3. ? Complements of = angles are =. |

**3.** *Given:* $\angle 1 = \angle 4$

*Prove:* $\angle 3$ and $\angle 2$ are supplementary.

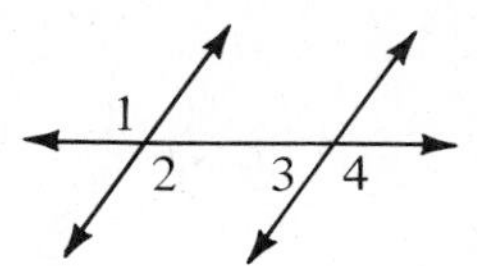


| STATEMENTS | REASONS |
|---|---|
| 1. $\angle 1 = \angle 4$ | 1. ___?___ Given |
| 2. $\angle 2 = \angle 1$ | 2. ___?___ Vertical angles are equal. |
| 3. $\angle 2 = \angle 4$ | 3. ___?___ Substitution Postulate |
| 4. $\angle 3 + \angle 4 = 180°$ | 4. Their sum is a ___?___ angle. straight |
| 5. $\angle 3 + \angle 2 = 180°$ | 5. ___?___ Substitution Postulate |
| 6. ___?___ $\angle 3$ and $\angle 2$ are supplementary. | 6. Def. of supplementary angles |

**4.** *Given:* $\overline{AB} \perp \overline{BD}$

$\overrightarrow{BD}$ bisects $\angle EBC$.

*Prove:* $\angle 1$ and $\angle 3$ are complements.

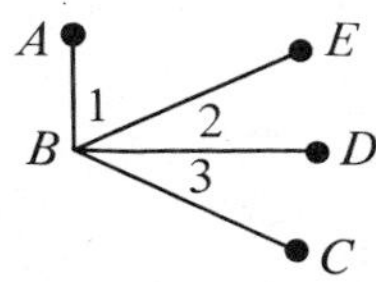


| STATEMENTS | REASONS |
|---|---|
| 1. $\overline{AB} \perp \overline{BD}$ | 1. ___?___ Given |
| 2. $\angle ABD = 90°$ | 2. ___?___ $\perp$ lines form right angles. |
| 3. $\angle 1 + \angle$ ___?___ $= 90°$ 2 | 3. Substitution Postulate: $\angle ABD = \angle 1 + \angle 2$ |
| 4. $\angle 2 = \angle$ ___?___ 3 | 4. *Given:* $\overrightarrow{BD}$ bisects $\angle EBC$. |
| 5. $\angle 1 + \angle 3 = 90°$ | 5. ___?___ Substitution Postulate. |
| 6. $\angle 1$ and $\angle 3$ are complements. | 6. ___?___ Def. of complementary angles |

**5.** *Given:* $\overleftrightarrow{XY}$ bisects $\angle AOC$.

*Prove:* $\overleftrightarrow{XY}$ bisects $\angle DOB$.

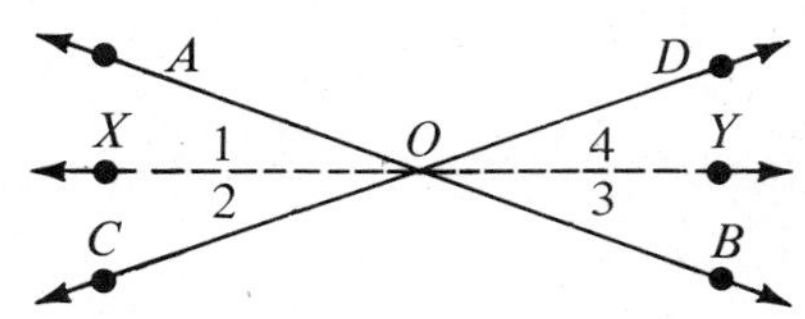


| STATEMENTS | REASONS |
|---|---|
| 1. $\angle 1 = \angle 2$ | 1. *Given:* ___?___ Def. of angle bisector |
| 2. $\angle 1 = \angle 3$ | 2. ___?___ Vertical angles are equal. |
| 3. $\angle 2 = \angle$ ___?___ | 3. ___?___ Vertical angles are equal. |
| 4. $\angle 3 = \angle 4$ | 4. ___?___ Substitution Postulate |
| 5. ___?___ $\overleftrightarrow{XY}$ bisects $\angle DOB$. | 5. Definition of angle bisector |

**6.** *Given:* $AC = BD$
$O$ is the midpoint of $\overline{AC}$.
$O$ is the midpoint of $\overline{BD}$.

*Prove:* $AO = DO$

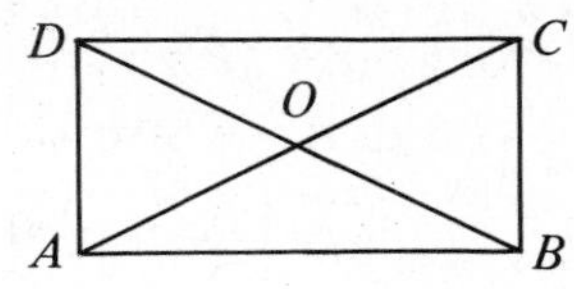


| STATEMENTS | REASONS |
|---|---|
| 1. $AC = BD$ | 1. ___?___ Given |
| 2. $\frac{1}{2}AC = \frac{1}{2}BD$ | 2. ___?___ Multiplication Postulate |
| 3. $AO = \frac{1}{2}AC$ | 3. *Given:* ___?___ $O$ is the midpoint of $\overline{AC}$. |
| 4. $DO = \frac{1}{2}BD$ | 4. ___?___ Given: $O$ is the midpoint of $\overline{BD}$. |
| 5. ___?___ AO = ___?___ DO | 5. Substitution Postulate (Steps 2, 3, 4) |

B **7.** *Given:* $\overrightarrow{RO}$ bisects $\angle YRS$.
$\overrightarrow{SO}$ bisects $\angle YSR$.
$\angle 1 = \angle 2$

*Prove:* $\angle 5 = \angle 6$

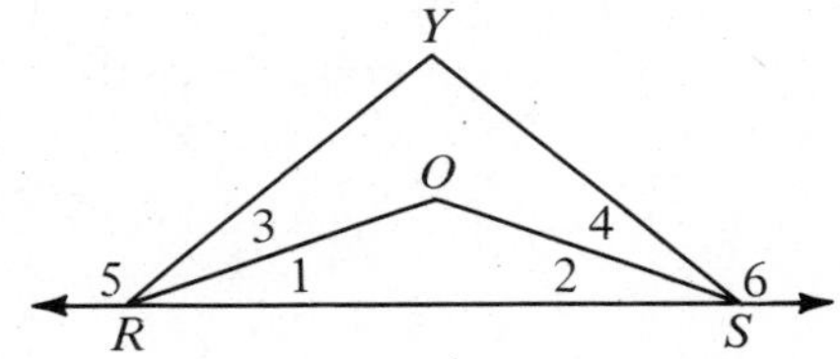


| STATEMENTS | REASONS |
|---|---|
| 1. $\angle 1 = \angle 3$ | 1. ___?___ Given: $\overrightarrow{RO}$ bisects $\angle YRS$. |
| 2. $\angle 2 = \angle 4$ | 2. ___?___ Given: $\overrightarrow{SO}$ bisects $\angle YSR$. |
| 3. $\angle 1 = \angle 2$ | 3. ___?___ Given |
| 4. $\angle 3 = \angle 4$ | 4. ___?___ (Steps 1, 2, and 3) Substitution Post. |
| 5. $\angle 1 + \angle 3 = \angle 2 + \angle 4$, or $\angle YRS = \angle YSR$ | 5. ___?___ Addition Postulate |
| 6. $\angle YRS$ and $\angle 5$ are supplements. $\angle YSR$ and $\angle 6$ are supplements. | 6. ___?___ Def. of supplementary angles |
| 7. $\angle 5 = \angle 6$ | 7. ___?___ Supplements of = angles are =. |

**8.** *Given:* $\angle ABC = 90°$
$\angle ADC = 90°$
$\angle 1 = \angle 4$

*Prove:* $\angle 2 = \angle 5$

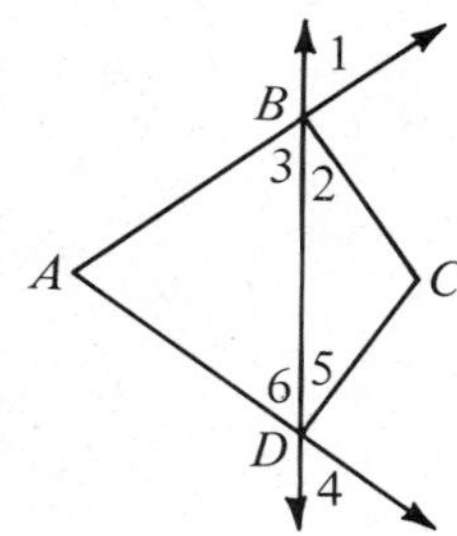

| STATEMENTS | REASONS |
|---|---|
| 1. $\angle 1 = \angle 3$ | 1. ? Vertical angles are equal. |
| 2. $\angle 4 = \angle 6$ | 2. ? Vertical angles are equal. |
| 3. $\angle 1 = \angle 4$ | 3. ? Given |
| 4. $\angle 3 = \angle 6$ | 4. ? Substitution Postulate |
| 5. $\angle 2$ and $\angle$ ? 3 are complements. | 5. *Given:* $\angle ABC = 90°$ |
| 6. $\angle 5$ and $\angle$ ? 6 are complements. | 6. ? Given: $\angle ADC = 90°$ |
| 7. $\angle 2 = \angle 5$ | 7. ? |

Complements of = angles are =.

**For each exercise, copy what is given and what is to be proved. Write a proof in two-column form.**

**9.** *Given:* $\angle 3 = \angle 5$

*Prove:* $\angle 4 = \angle 6$

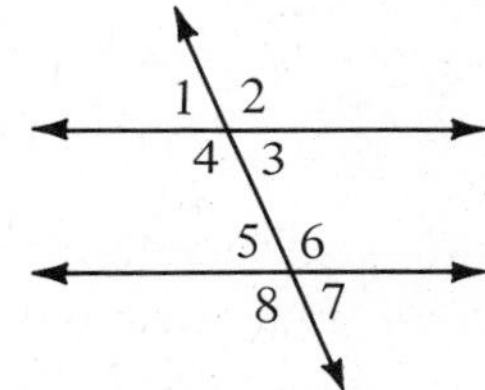

Exercises 9–12

**10.** *Given:* $\angle 2 = \angle 8$

*Prove:* $\angle 4 = \angle 6$

**11.** *Given:* $\angle 3$ and $\angle 6$ are supplements.

*Prove:* $\angle 2 = \angle 6$

**12.** *Given:* $\angle 1 = \angle 5$

*Prove:* $\angle 4$ and $\angle 5$ are supplements.

C **13.** *Given:* $\angle 2 = \angle 3$
$\angle 3 = \angle 5$

*Prove:* $\angle 1 = \angle 6$

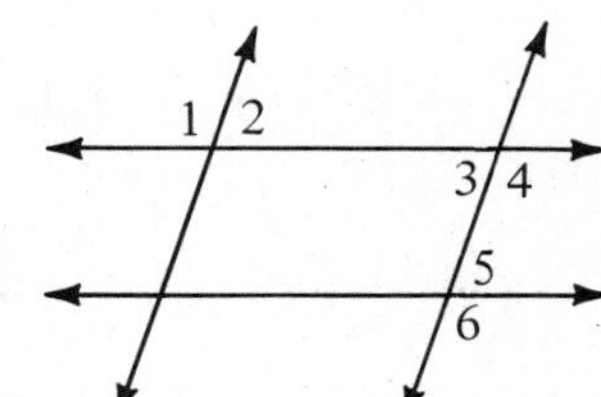

Exercises 13, 14

**14.** *Given:* $\angle 4$ and $\angle 5$ are supplements.
$\angle 2 = \angle 3$

*Prove:* $\angle 2 = \angle 5$

**15.** *Given:* $\angle 1 = \angle 2$
$\angle 3$ and $\angle 5$ are complements.
$\angle 4$ and $\angle 6$ are complements.

*Prove:* $\angle 5 = \angle 6$

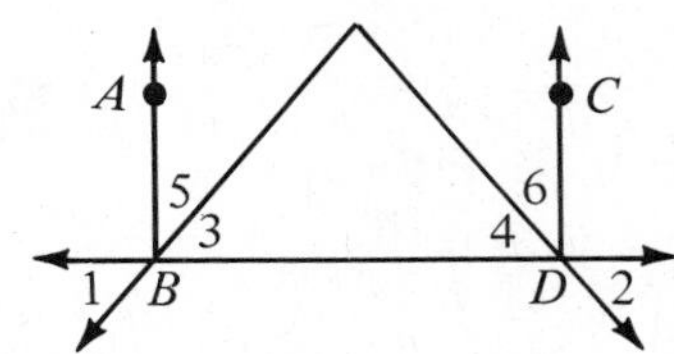

Exercises 15, 16

**16.** *Given:* $\overline{AB} \perp \overline{BD}$
$\overline{CD} \perp \overline{BD}$
$\angle 5 = \angle 6$

*Prove:* $\angle 1 = \angle 2$

# 5 • Parallel Lines

If two lines do not intersect, they are either *parallel* or *skew*.

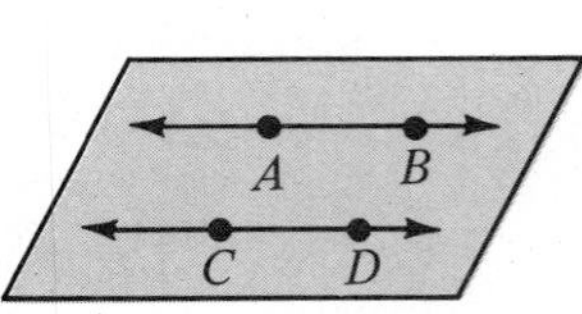


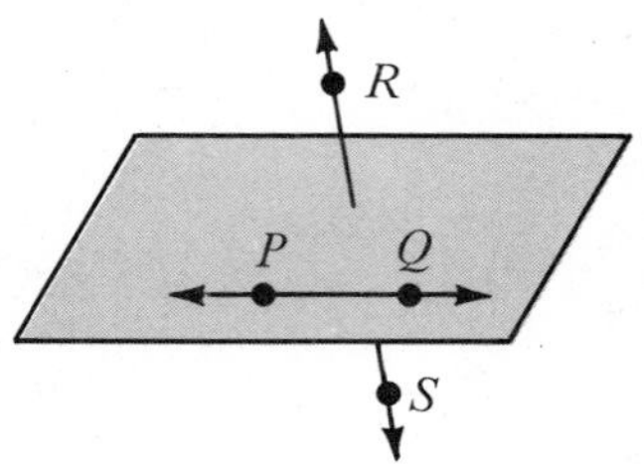


$\overleftrightarrow{AB}$ and $\overleftrightarrow{CD}$ are **parallel lines.**
(1) They are coplanar lines.
(2) They do not intersect.

$\overleftrightarrow{PQ}$ and $\overleftrightarrow{RS}$ are **skew lines.**
(1) They are *not* coplanar lines.
(2) They do not intersect.

We abbreviate the statement "$\overleftrightarrow{AB}$ is parallel to $\overleftrightarrow{CD}$" by writing $\overleftrightarrow{AB} \parallel \overleftrightarrow{CD}$. We shall also say that $\overline{AB} \parallel \overline{CD}$ because the segments are contained in parallel lines. In a drawing, we indicate parallel lines and segments by arrowheads and, if necessary, double arrowheads.

The single arrowheads show that $\overline{AD} \parallel \overline{BC}$.

The double arrowheads show that $\overline{AB} \parallel \overline{CD}$.

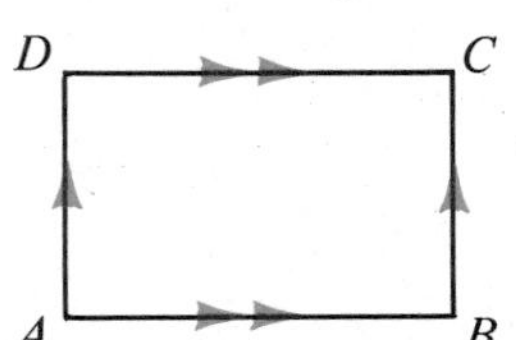


The diagram at the right shows two parallel lines cut by a third line. This cutting line is called a **transversal.** Angles 1, 2, 3, and 4 formed on the inside of the parallel lines are called **interior angles.** Angles formed by parallel lines are given special names as follows:

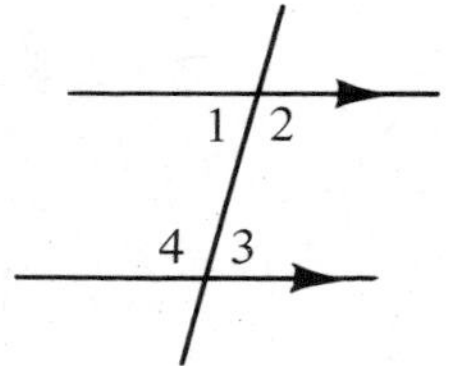


**Alternate interior angles** are interior angles on alternate sides of the transversal. (Examples above: $\angle 1$ and $\angle 3$; also $\angle 2$ and $\angle 4$) To spot alternate interior angles, look for a "Z-shaped" figure in various positions.

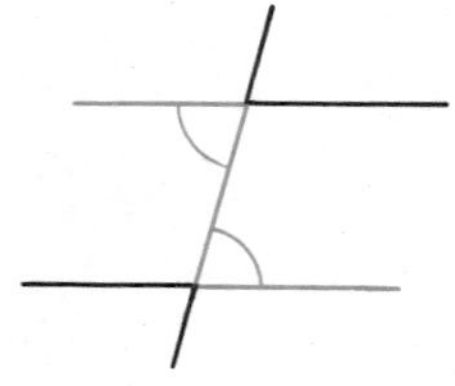

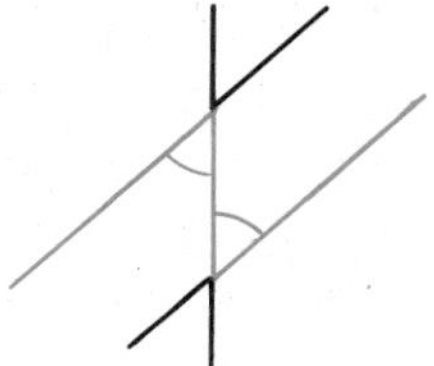

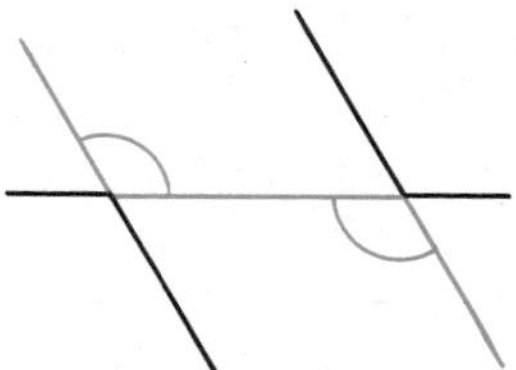

**Same-side interior angles** are interior angles on the same side of the transversal. (Examples above: ∠1 and ∠4; also ∠2 and ∠3) To spot same-side interior angles, look for a "U-shaped" figure in various positions.

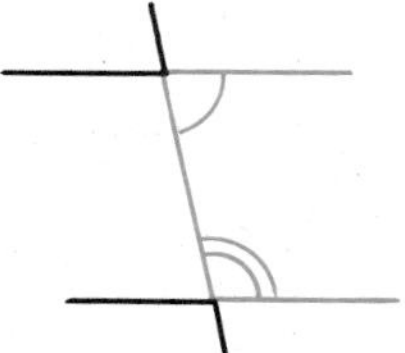

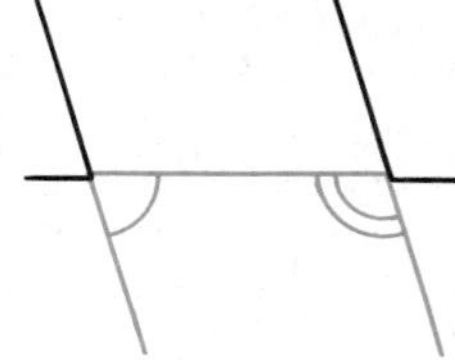

**Corresponding angles** are so named because they appear to be in corresponding positions in relation to the two lines. To spot corresponding angles, look for an "F-shaped" figure in various positions.

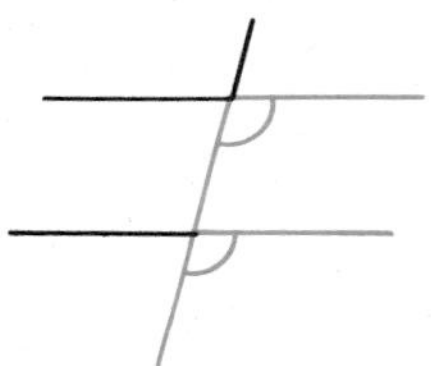

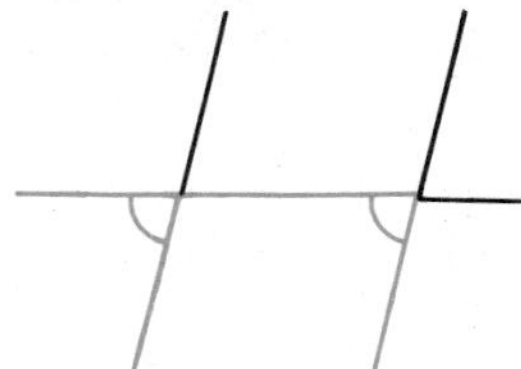

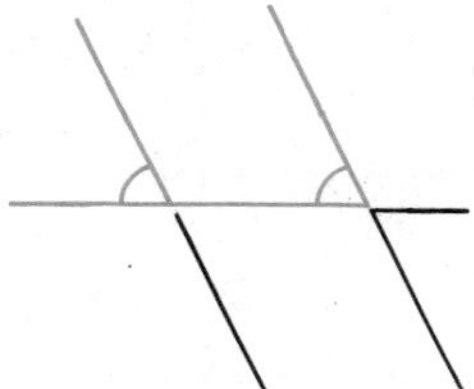

Even when lines cut by a transversal are not parallel, we still use the same vocabulary. For example:

∠4 and ∠8 are corresponding angles;

∠4 and ∠6 are alternate interior angles;

∠4 and ∠5 are same-side interior angles.

Exterior angles: see Lesson Commentary, page T49.

The diagram at the right suggests that when two parallel lines are cut by a transversal, corresponding angles are equal. You can convince yourself of this by drawing and measuring many pairs of corresponding angles formed by different transversals. You may suspect that we can prove this property. However, there is just not enough information in our previous postulates and theorems to deduce this result as a theorem. Let us therefore accept it without proof as a postulate. This is a version of the "Parallel Postulate."

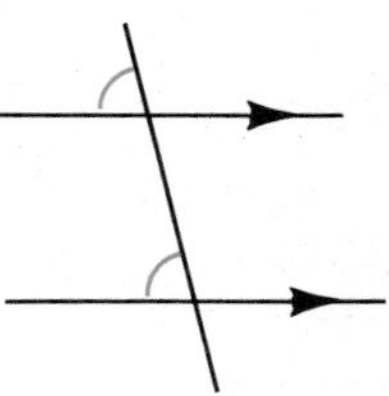

**POSTULATE 7**

If two parallel lines are cut by a transversal, then corresponding angles are equal.

Once we have this postulate, we can immediately deduce the following theorems. The proofs are left as Exercises 31 and 32 on page 65.

**THEOREM 4**

If two parallel lines are cut by a transversal, then alternate interior angles are equal.

**THEOREM 5**

If two parallel lines are cut by a transversal, then same-side interior angles are supplementary.

## *Classroom Practice*

**In the diagram, $l \parallel m$.**

1. Name two pairs of alternate interior angles. $\angle 4, \angle 6;\ \angle 3, \angle 5$
2. Name two pairs of same-side interior angles. $\angle 3, \angle 6;\ \angle 4, \angle 5$
3. Name four pairs of corresponding angles. $\angle 1, \angle 5;\ \angle 4, \angle 8;\ \angle 2, \angle 6;\ \angle 3, \angle 7$
4. What is the special name given to line $t$? transversal
5. Suppose $\angle 4 = 60°$.
   Find the measures of the other seven angles. $\angle 1 = 120°$, $\angle 2 = 60°$, $\angle 3 = 120°$, $\angle 5 = 120°$, $\angle 6 = 60°$, $\angle 7 = 120°$, $\angle 8 = 60°$
6. Suppose $\angle 4 = x°$.
   Find the measures of $\angle 5$ and $\angle 6$. $\angle 5 = 180° - x°$, $\angle 6 = x°$
7. Although we have not discussed *alternate exterior angles,* you may be able to guess what they are. Name two pairs of them. $\angle 1, \angle 7;\ \angle 2, \angle 8$

**State the special name for each pair of angles.**

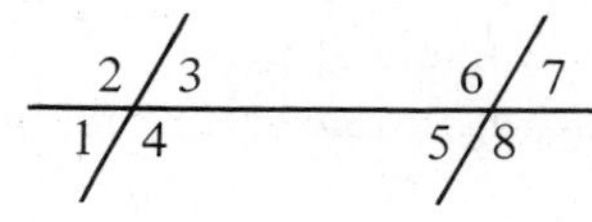


8. $\angle 3$ and $\angle 5$ alternate interior angles
9. $\angle 2$ and $\angle 6$ corresponding angles
10. $\angle 3$ and $\angle 6$ same-side interior angles
11. $\angle 1$ and $\angle 5$ corresponding angles

**Find the values of $x$ and $y$ in each diagram.**

12. $x = 120$, $y = 60$

13. $x = 50$, $y = 85$

14.

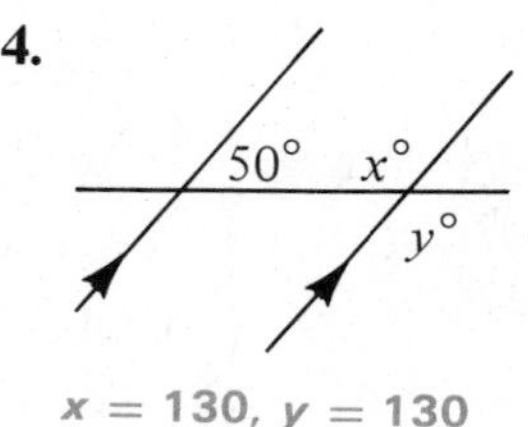


$x = 130$, $y = 130$

## Written Exercises

**Classify each pair of angles as (1) alternate interior angles, (2) same-side interior angles, (3) corresponding angles, or (4) none of these.**

A

**1.** $\angle 1$ and $\angle 5$ (3) **2.** $\angle 3$ and $\angle 8$ (2)

**3.** $\angle 2$ and $\angle 8$ (1) **4.** $\angle 4$ and $\angle 8$ (3)

**5.** $\angle 2$ and $\angle 7$ (4) **6.** $\angle 3$ and $\angle 5$ (1)

**7.** $\angle 2$ and $\angle 5$ (2) **8.** $\angle 3$ and $\angle 7$ (3)

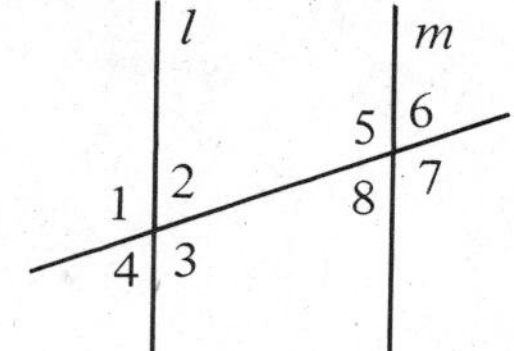


**In the diagram above, suppose $l \parallel m$.**

**9.** If $\angle 1 = 110°$, find the measures of the other seven angles. $\angle 2 = 70°$, $\angle 3 = 110°$, $\angle 4 = 70°$, $\angle 5 = 110°$, $\angle 6 = 70°$, $\angle 7 = 110°$, $\angle 8 = 70°$

**10.** If $\angle 2 = x°$, find the measures of $\angle 5$ and $\angle 8$. $\angle 5 = 180° - x°$, $\angle 8 = x°$

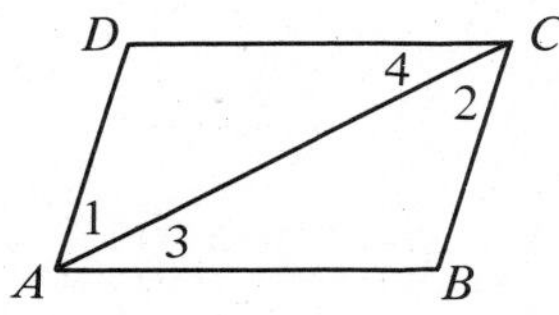


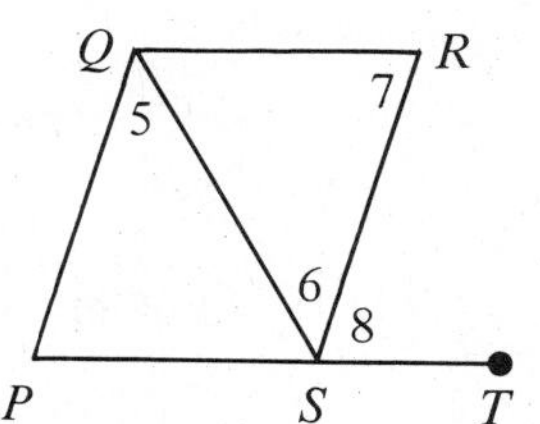


**Complete each statement.**

**11.** $\angle 1$ and $\angle 2$ are formed by lines _?_ *AD* and _?_ *BC* and the transversal _?_ *AC*.

$\angle 3$ and $\angle 4$ are formed by lines _?_ *AB* and _?_ *CD* and the transversal _?_ *AC*.

**12.** $\angle 5$ and $\angle 6$ are formed by lines _?_ *PQ* and _?_ *RS* and the transversal _?_ *QS*.

$\angle 7$ and $\angle 8$ are formed by lines _?_ *QR* and _?_ *PT* and the transversal _?_ *RS*.

**In the diagram, $a \parallel b$ and $c \parallel d$. State the special name for each pair of angles. Then tell if the angles are equal or supplementary.**

**13.** $\angle 6$ and $\angle 10$ corresponding; equal

**14.** $\angle 7$ and $\angle 9$ same-side interior; supplementary

**15.** $\angle 3$ and $\angle 14$ alternate interior; equal

**16.** $\angle 2$ and $\angle 14$ corresponding; equal

**17.** $\angle 9$ and $\angle 16$ alternate interior; equal

**18.** $\angle 8$ and $\angle 10$ (see below)

**19.** $\angle 9$ and $\angle 13$ corresponding; equal

**20.** $\angle 8$ and $\angle 12$ corresponding; equal

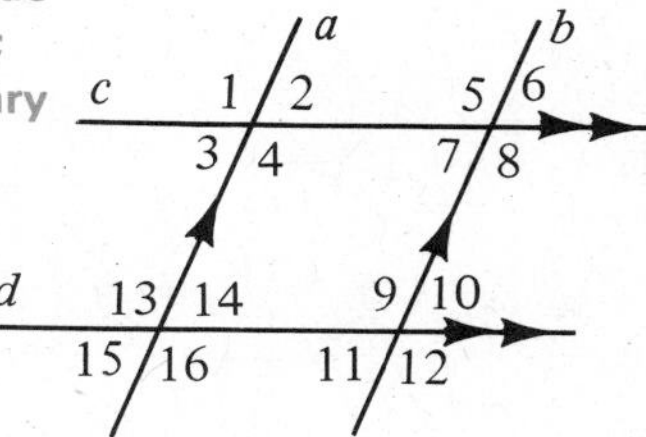


**21.** Refer to the diagram above. Name seven angles equal to $\angle 4$. $\angle 1$, $\angle 5$, $\angle 8$, $\angle 9$, $\angle 12$, $\angle 13$, $\angle 16$

**22.** Name eight angles supplementary to $\angle 4$. $\angle 2$, $\angle 3$, $\angle 6$, $\angle 7$, $\angle 10$, $\angle 11$, $\angle 14$, $\angle 15$

18. same side interior; supplementary

**Find the values of $x$ and $y$ in each diagram.**

**23.**

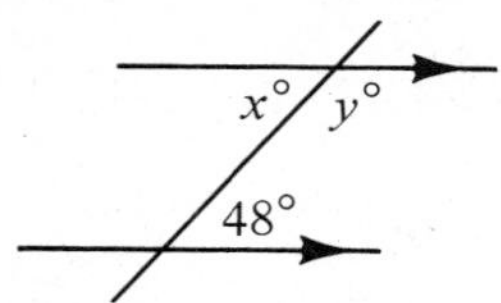


$x = 48,\ y = 132$

**24.**

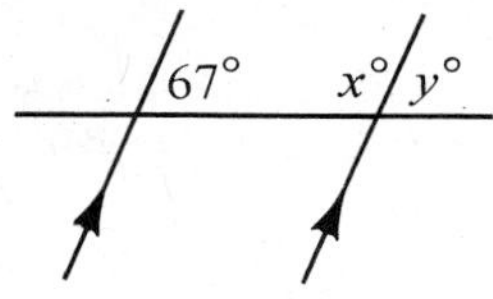


$x = 113,\ y = 67$

**25.**

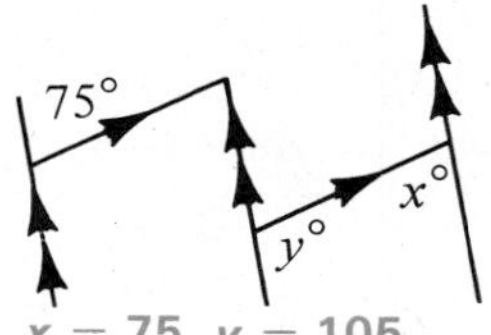


$x = 75,\ y = 105$

B **26.**

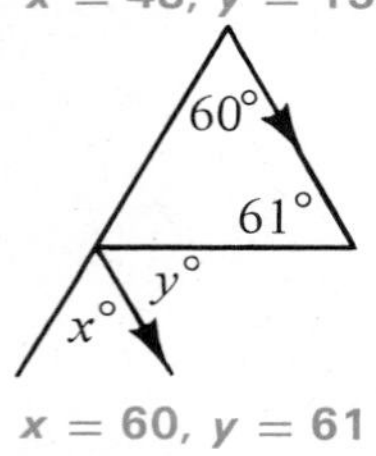


$x = 60,\ y = 61$

**27.**

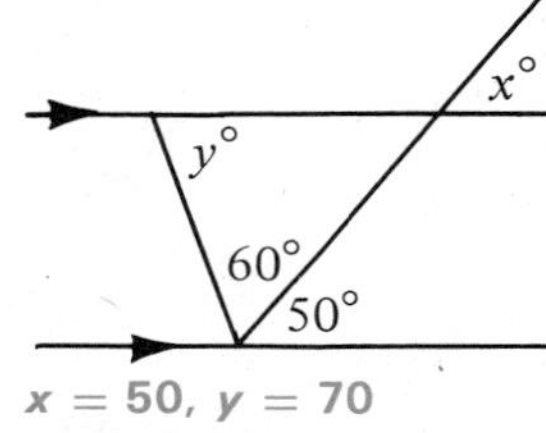


$x = 50,\ y = 70$

**28.**

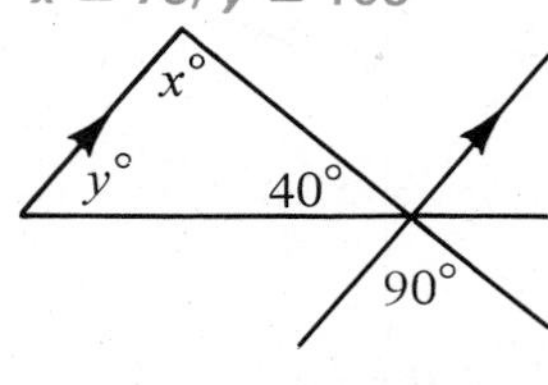


$x = 90,\ y = 50$

**Supply the missing statements and reasons in each proof.**

**29.** *Given:* $\overline{RU} \parallel \overline{ST}$
$\overline{RS} \parallel \overline{UT}$

*Prove:* $\angle R = \angle T$

| STATEMENTS | REASONS |
|---|---|
| 1. $\overline{RU} \parallel \overline{ST}$ | 1. _?_ Given |
| 2. $\angle R$ and $\angle S$ are supplements. | 2. If 2 ∥ lines are cut by a trans., then _?_. same side interior angles are supplementary |
| 3. $\overline{RS} \parallel \overline{UT}$ | 3. _?_ Given |
| 4. $\angle S$ and $\angle T$ are supplements. | 4. _?_ If 2 ∥ lines are cut by a trans., same-side interior angles are supplementary. |
| 5. $\angle R = \angle T$ | 5. _?_ |

5. Supplements of the same angle are equal.

**30.** *Given:* $\angle B = \angle C$
$\overline{AD} \parallel \overline{BC}$

*Prove:* $\angle 1 = \angle 2$

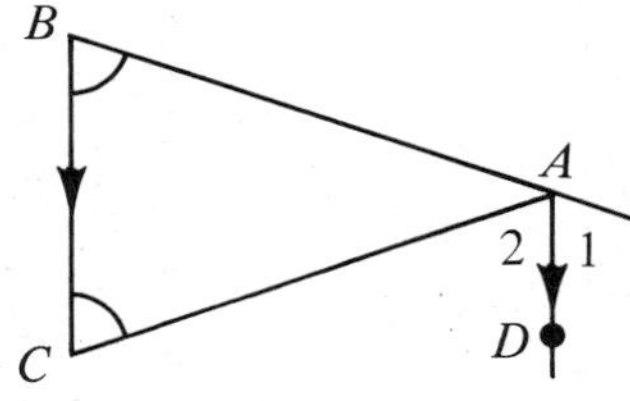


| STATEMENTS | REASONS |
|---|---|
| 1. $\overline{AD} \parallel \overline{BC}$ | 1. _?_ Given |
| 2. $\angle 1 = \angle B$ | 2. If 2 ∥ lines are cut by a trans., then _?_. corresponding angles are equal |
| 3. $\angle 2 = \angle C$ | 3. _?_ (see below) |
| 4. $\angle B = \angle C$ | 4. _?_ Given |
| 5. $\angle 1 = \angle$ _?_ 2 | 5. Subst. Post. (Steps 2, 3, 4) |

3. If 2 ∥ lines are cut by a trans., then alternate interior angles are equal.

C **31.** Prove Theorem 4: If two parallel lines are cut by a transversal, then alternate interior angles are equal.

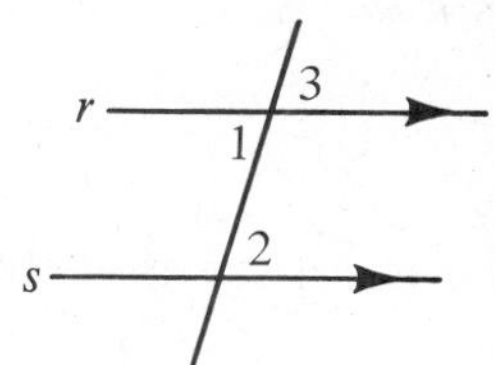


*Given:* $r \parallel s$

*Prove:* $\angle 1 = \angle 2$

(*Hint:* Use $\angle 3$.)

**32.** Prove Theorem 5: If two parallel lines are cut by a transversal, then same-side interior angles are supplementary.

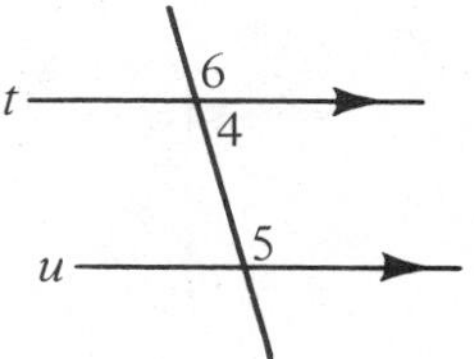


*Given:* $t \parallel u$

*Prove:* $\angle 4$ and $\angle 5$ are supplementary.

(*Hint:* Use $\angle 6$.)

# CAREER NOTES

## Realtor

Did you ever read the newspaper advertisements for houses?

MARSTON, 8 rm. older home in excel. cond., 2 full baths, porch, walking distance to shopping and bus, $52,500. Call 937-1234.

Chances are that this ad was placed by a realtor.

All realtors must obtain licenses by passing written tests. Then they may represent people who wish to sell or rent property.

Realtors examine the property to help determine the value of the real estate. They collect information about tax rates, insurance, and financing. If the property is residential, they find the locations of schools, public transportation facilities, and shopping areas nearby. Then they use advertisements to locate buyers and renters.

# 6 • Proving Lines Parallel

In this section, we shall study ways of proving lines parallel. The first way is given in Postulate 8. Postulate 7 is listed with Postulate 8 so that you can see that these two postulates are converses.

**POSTULATE 7**

If two parallel lines are cut by a transversal, then corresponding angles are equal.

**POSTULATE 8**

If two lines and a transversal form equal corresponding angles, then the lines are parallel.

Postulates 7 and 8 can be written in convenient picture statements as follows:

Postulate 7 If , then .

Postulate 8 If , then .

From Postulate 8, we can easily determine other ways to prove lines parallel. These are given in Theorems 6, 7, and 8 below.

**THEOREM 6**

If two lines and a transversal form equal alternate interior angles, then the lines are parallel.

**THEOREM 7**

If two lines and a transversal form supplementary same-side interior angles, then the lines are parallel.

**THEOREM 8**

In a plane, if two lines are each perpendicular to a third line, then the two lines are parallel.

### Ways to Prove Two Lines Parallel

1. Show that corresponding angles are equal.
2. Show that alternate interior angles are equal.
3. Show that same-side interior angles are supplementary.
4. Show that the lines are both perpendicular to a third line.

**EXAMPLE** Which lines are parallel?

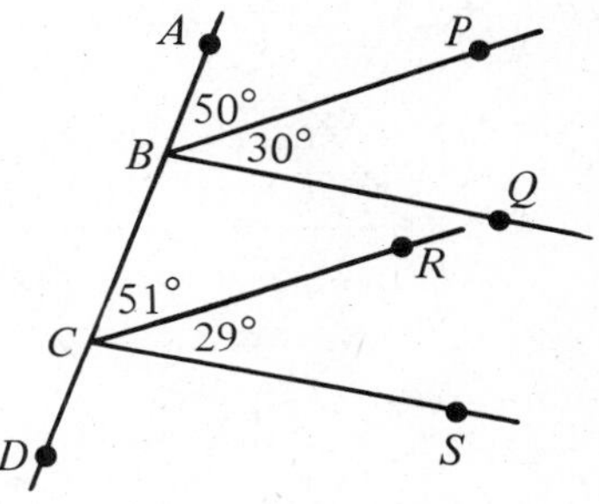


$\overleftrightarrow{BP}$ and $\overleftrightarrow{CR}$ are not parallel because two corresponding angles are not equal ($50 \neq 51$).

$\overleftrightarrow{BQ}$ and $\overleftrightarrow{CS}$ are parallel because two corresponding angles are equal ($50 + 30 = 80$ and $51 + 29 = 80$).

Jules Stauber

## Classroom Practice

**For each figure, tell whether you can correctly conclude that $l \parallel m$.**

**1.** yes

**2.** no

**3.** yes

**In each figure, tell which lines are parallel.**

**4.** $\overleftrightarrow{AB}$ and $\overleftrightarrow{DC}$

**5.** $\overleftrightarrow{WO}$ and $\overleftrightarrow{IS}$

**6.** Suppose $\angle 1 = \angle 2$. Tell which lines are parallel in each figure.

**a.** $\overleftrightarrow{NL}$ and $\overleftrightarrow{MK}$

**b.** $\overleftrightarrow{PS}$ and $\overleftrightarrow{QR}$

**7.** Draw picture statements for Theorems 6, 7, and 8.

**8.** Suppose $\angle 1 = \angle 2$.

**a.** Tell why $\overline{AB} \parallel \overline{CD}$. Theorem 6

**b.** Tell why $\angle 3 = \angle 4$. Postulate 7

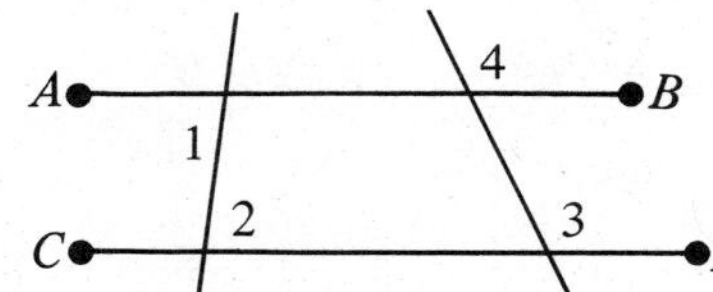


## Written Exercises

**For each figure, tell if you can correctly conclude that $u \parallel v$.**

A **1.** yes

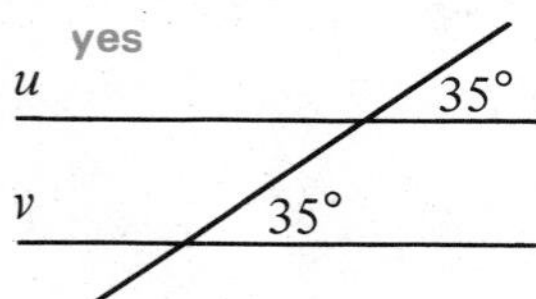


**2.** no

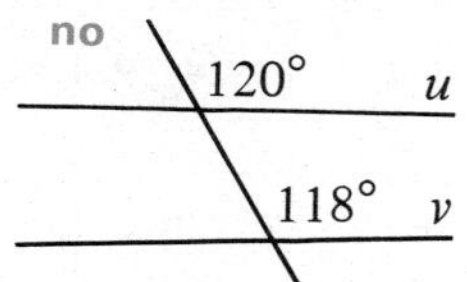


**3.** yes

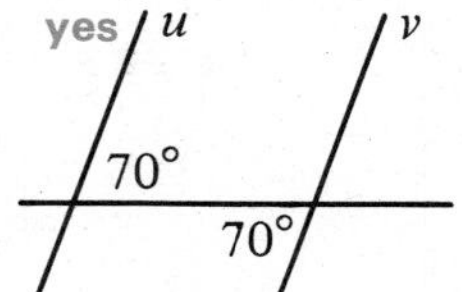


**4.** yes

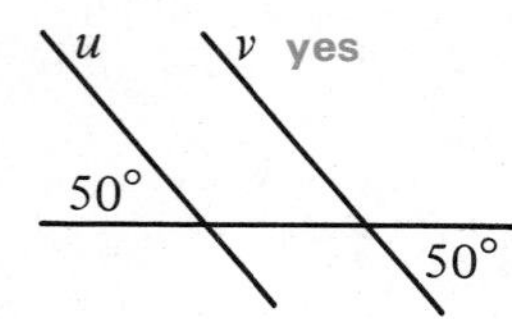


**5.** no

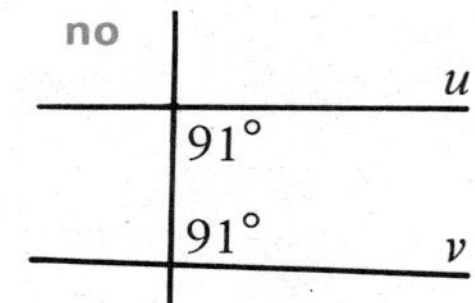


**6.** yes

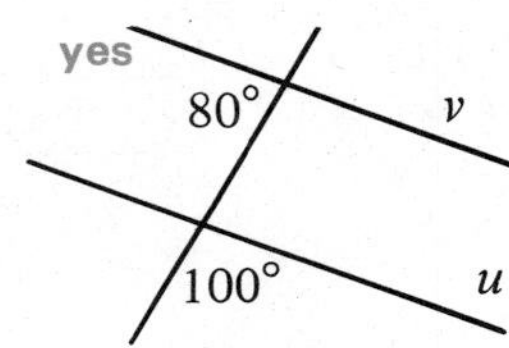

**For each figure, name two pairs of parallel lines.**

**7.**

$\overleftrightarrow{PW}$ and $\overleftrightarrow{RY}$, $\overleftrightarrow{WX}$ and $\overleftrightarrow{YZ}$

**8.**

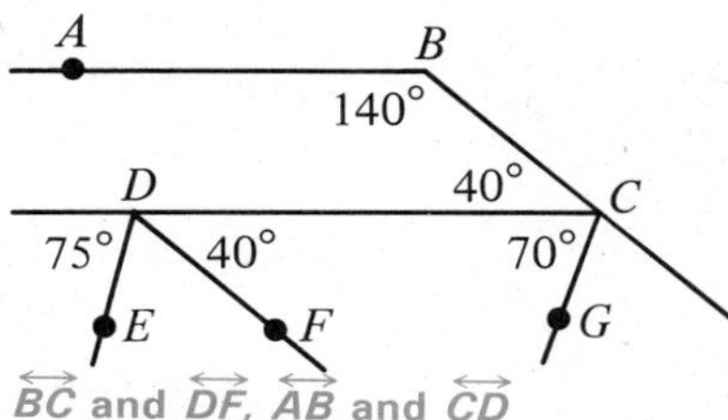


$\overleftrightarrow{BC}$ and $\overleftrightarrow{DF}$, $\overleftrightarrow{AB}$ and $\overleftrightarrow{CD}$

**Find the value of *x* which will make lines *a* and *b* parallel.**

**9.** 35

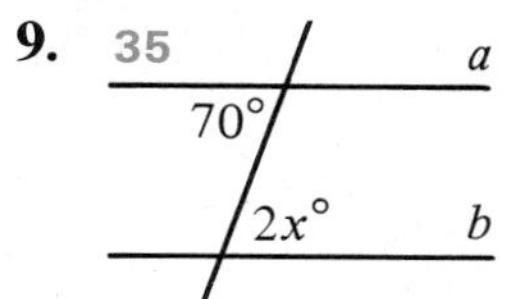


**10.** 120

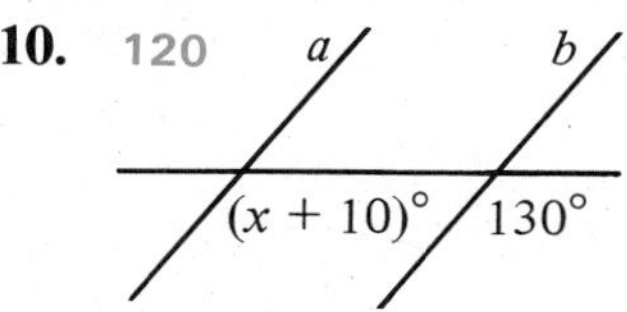


**11.** 40

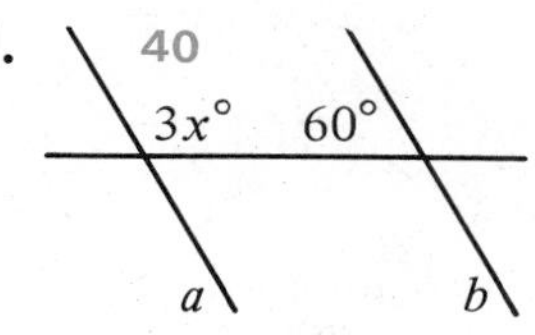


**Use the given information to tell which lines, if any, must be parallel.**

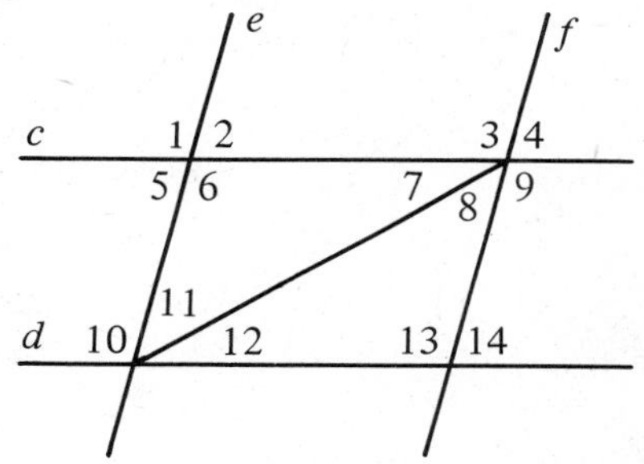


**Sample** $\angle 1 = \angle 3$

Since $\angle 1$ and $\angle 3$ are equal corresponding angles, $e \parallel f$.

**12.** $\angle 2 = \angle 4$ e, f

**13.** $\angle 4 = \angle 14$ c, d

**14.** $\angle 8 = \angle 11$ e, f

**15.** $\angle 7 = \angle 13$ none

**16.** $\angle 5 + \angle 10 = 180°$ c, d

**17.** $\angle 2 + \angle 3 = 180°$ e, f

**18.** $\angle 1 = \angle 10$ c, d

**19.** $\angle 1 = \angle 9$ e, f

**20.** $\angle 9 + \angle 14 = 180°$ c, d

**21.** Complete the following proof of Theorem 6.

*Given:* $\angle 1 = \angle 2$

*Prove:* $r \parallel s$

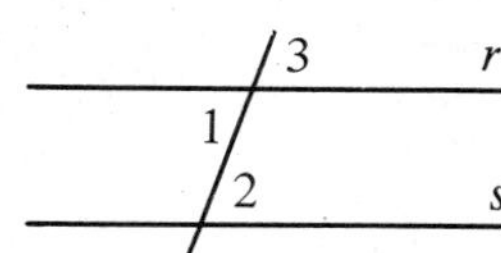


| STATEMENTS | REASONS |
|---|---|
| 1. $\angle 1 = \angle 2$ | 1. ___?___ Given |
| 2. $\angle 1 = \angle 3$ | 2. ___?___ Vertical angles are equal. |
| 3. $\angle 2 = \angle 3$ | 3. ___?___ Substitution Principle |
| 4. ___?___ $r \parallel s$ | 4. If 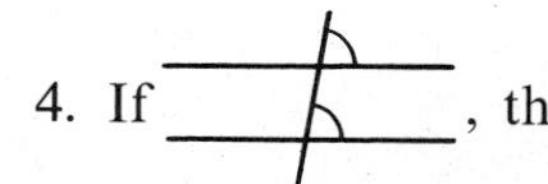, then ___?___. the lines are $\parallel$ |

**22.** Complete the following proof of Theorem 7.

*Given:* $\angle 1$ and $\angle 2$ are supplements.

*Prove:* $l \parallel m$

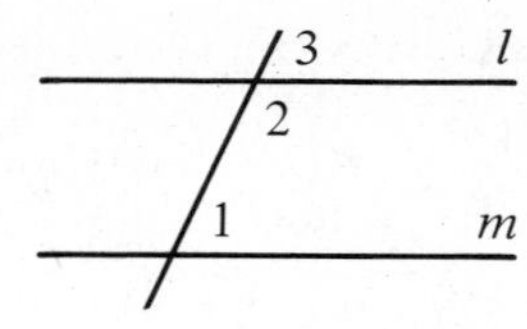


| STATEMENTS | REASONS |
|---|---|
| 1. $\angle 1$ and $\angle 2$ are supplements. | 1. __?__ Given |
| 2. $\angle 3$ and $\angle 2$ are supplements. | 2. Definition of __?__ supplementary angles |
| 3. $\angle 1 = \angle 3$ | 3. Supplements of __?__. the same angle are = |
| 4. $l \parallel m$ | 4. __?__ |

4. If 2 lines and a trans. form = corresponding angles, then the lines are $\parallel$.

**B** **23.** A technical artist sets a plastic triangle in position $ABC$ and draws $\overline{AB}$. Then the artist slides the triangle along the T-square to position $XYZ$ and draws $\overline{XY}$.
Why is $\overline{AB} \parallel \overline{XY}$? Postulate 8; $\angle ABC = \angle XYZ$

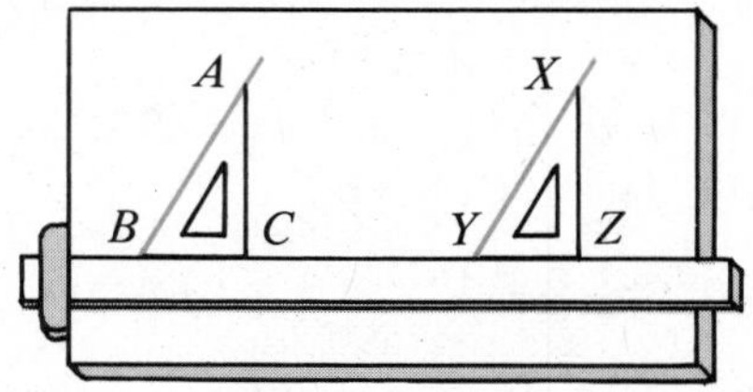


**24.** Explain why the phrase *In a plane* is needed in Theorem 8.
Draw a diagram to illustrate your answer. It is possible for skew lines, or even perpendicular lines, to each be perpendicular to a given line.

**25.** *Given:* $\angle 1 = \angle 2$

*Prove:* $\angle 3 = \angle 4$

(*Hint:* This proof requires just three steps.)

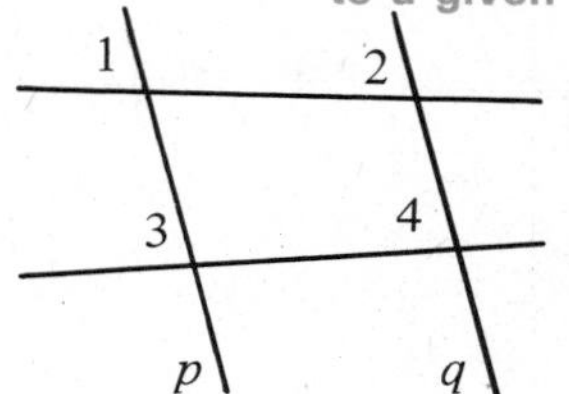


**C** **26.** *Given:* $\angle 5 = \angle 6$
$\angle 7 = \angle 8$

*Prove:* $\overline{AB} \parallel \overline{CD}$

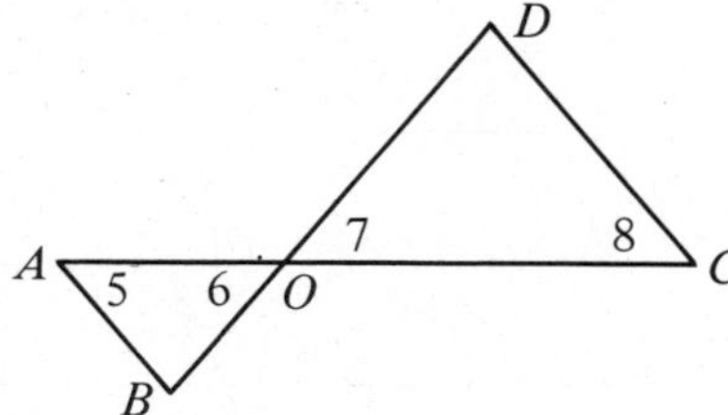


**27.** Prove Theorem 8.

*Given:* $a \perp b$; $a \perp c$

*Prove:* $b \parallel c$

(*Hint:* Use Postulate 8.)

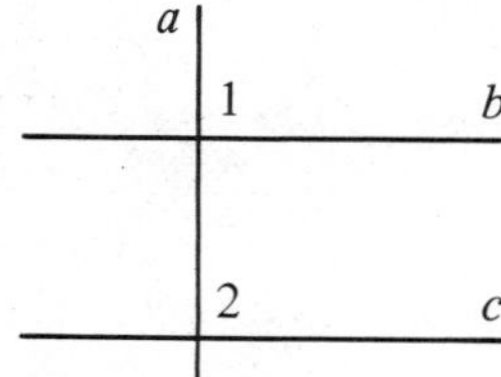

# 7 • Constructing Parallel Lines

Our goal in this section is to construct a line that passes through a given point $P$ and is parallel to a given line $l$. To do this, we must first be able to copy an angle with a compass and straightedge.

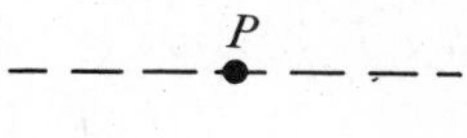


Students are asked to justify this construction in Wr. Ex. 9 on page 137.

CONSTRUCTION 4 *Given:* An angle

*Construct:* An angle equal to the given angle

1. Draw a ray with endpoint $O$.

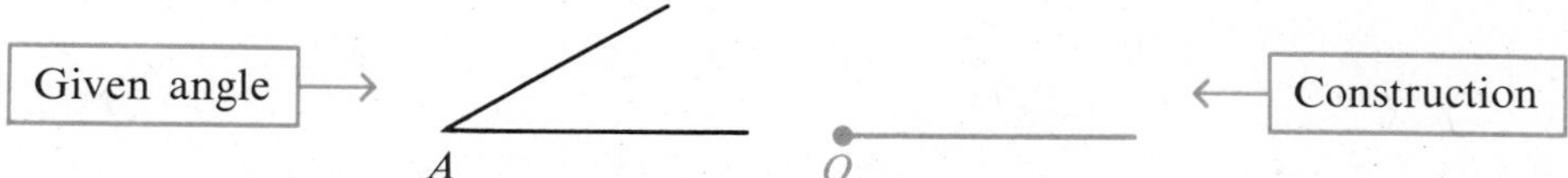


2. Construct an arc with center at $A$.

3. Without changing your compass, construct an arc with center at $O$.

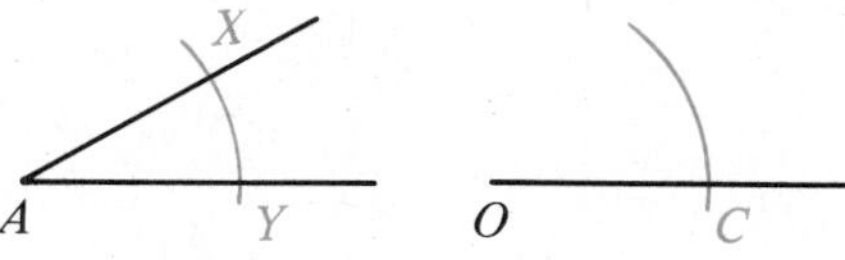


4. Put the compass point at $Y$. Then adjust your compass so that you can draw an arc passing through $X$.

5. Without changing your compass, construct an arc with center at $C$.

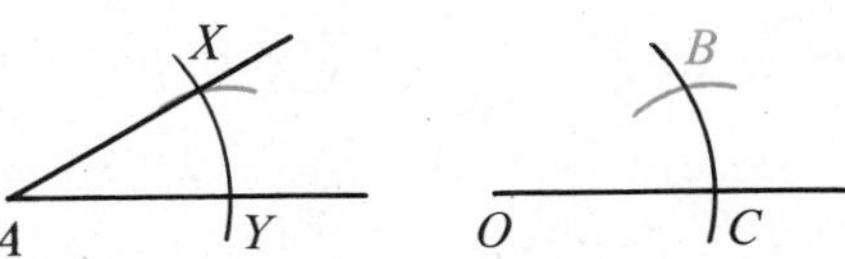


6. Draw $\overrightarrow{OB}$. $\angle BOC = \angle A$.

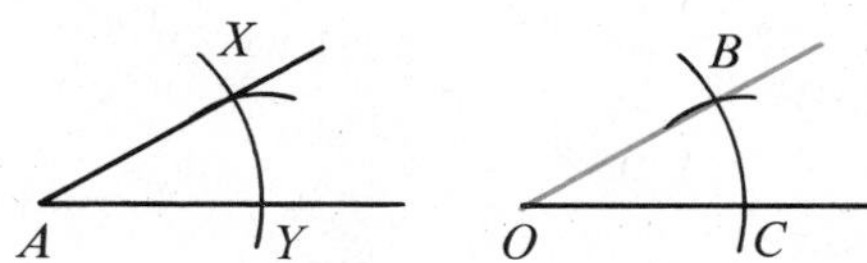

CONSTRUCTION 5 *Given:* A line and a point not on the line

*Construct:* A line that passes through the point and is parallel to the given line

Follow these steps:

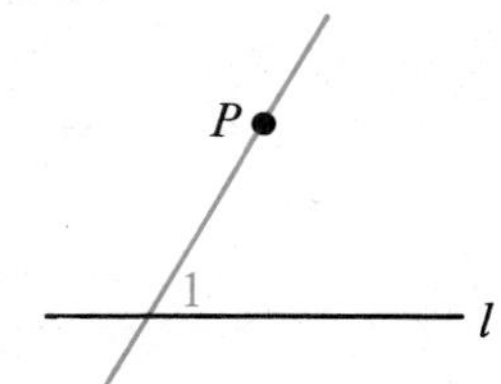


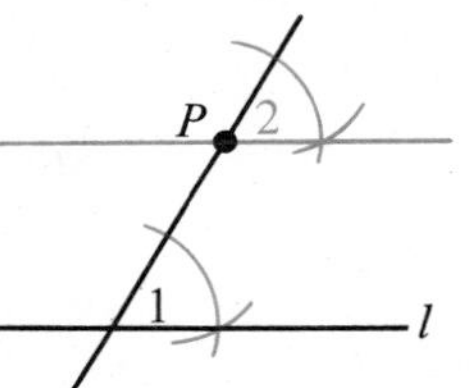


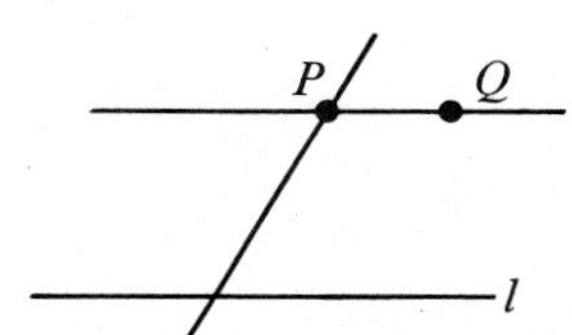


**1.** You are given $l$ and $P$.

**2.** Draw any transversal through $P$. Label $\angle 1$.

**3.** At $P$, construct $\angle 2$, a corresponding angle equal to $\angle 1$.

**4.** $\overleftrightarrow{PQ} \parallel l$. Do you know why?

## *Classroom Practice*

**1.** Draw an acute angle.
Then copy the angle using compass and straightedge.

**2.** Draw an obtuse angle.
Then copy the angle using compass and straightedge.

**3.** Draw a line $l$ and choose a point $P$ not on $l$.
Construct a line through $P$ and parallel to $l$.

**4.** Draw a triangle similar to, but larger than, the one shown.
Then construct a line through $O$ parallel to $\overleftrightarrow{JY}$.

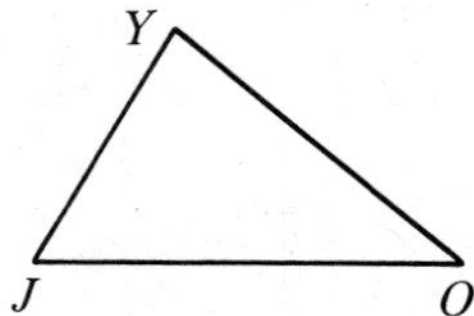

## Written Exercises

**Draw an angle similar to, but larger than, the one shown. Then copy the angle using compass and straightedge.**

A **1.**

**2.**

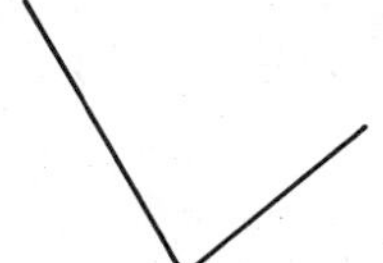

**3.**

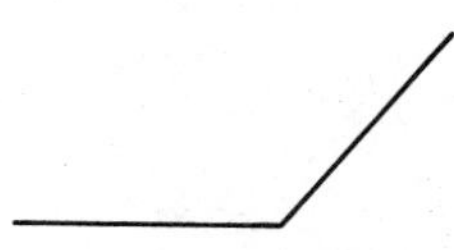

**Draw a figure similar to, but larger than, the one shown. Then construct a parallel to $\overleftrightarrow{RS}$ through point *P*.**

**4.**

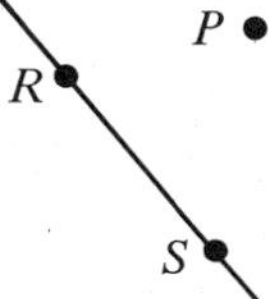


**5.**

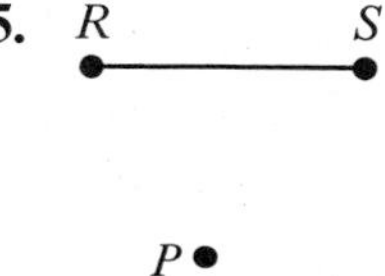


**6.**

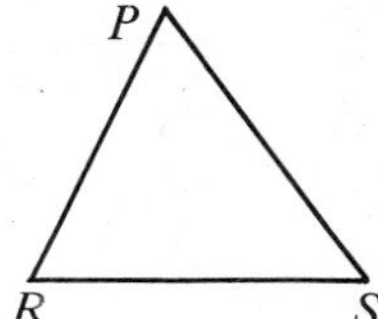


**7.** Draw a line *l* and a point *P* not on *l*. Construct a line which passes through *P* and is parallel to *l* by constructing equal alternate interior angles.

**8. a.** Using lined paper, draw two parallel lines and a transversal as shown. Then construct the bisectors of two alternate interior angles.

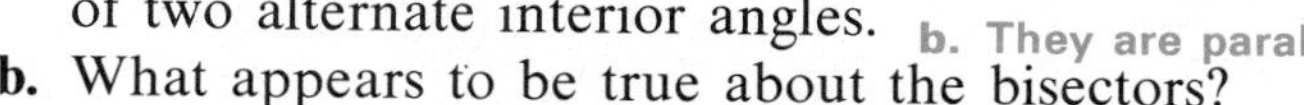

b. They are parallel.

**b.** What appears to be true about the bisectors?

**c.** Explain why your answer in part (b) is true. (see below)

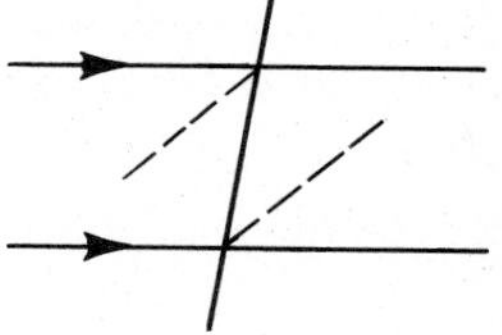

**9. a.** Using lined paper, draw two parallel lines and a transversal. Then construct the bisectors of two same-side interior angles.

**b.** Measure an angle formed by the bisectors. 90°

**c.** Repeat the experiment, using a different transversal. 90°

**d.** What appears to be true about the angles formed by the bisectors? They are right angles.

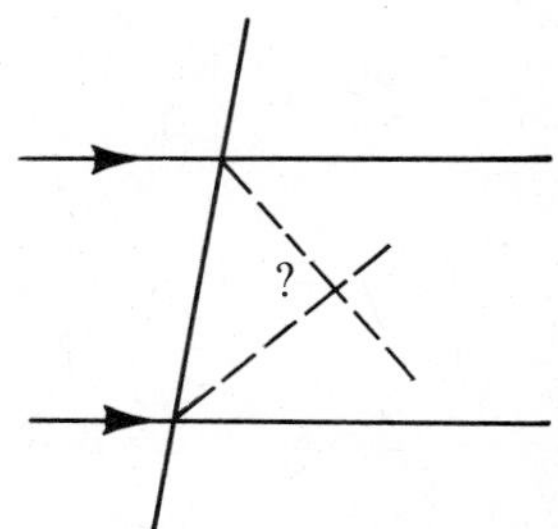


**10. a.** Construct a line through *P* and parallel to *l* by these steps:

(1) Use Construction 3 on page 22 to construct *m*, a line perpendicular to *l* through *P*.

(2) Use Construction 2 on page 22 to construct *n*, a line perpendicular to *m* through *P*.

**b.** Tell why $l \parallel n$. Theorem 8

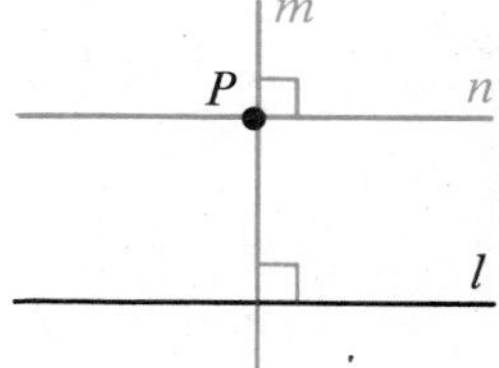


8. c. Since $\angle 1$ and $\angle 2$ are each half the measure of equal angles, they are equal. Thus the bisectors are parallel by Theorem 6.

B **11.** Draw an acute angle. Call it $\angle B$.
Draw a line $t$ and choose a point $Q$ on $t$.
At $Q$, construct an angle that is supplementary to $\angle B$.

**12.** Repeat Exercise 11, using an obtuse $\angle B$.

**Sample** Given $\angle A$ and $\angle B$, construct $\angle A + \angle B$.

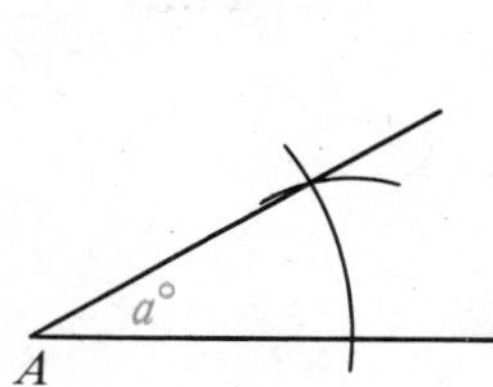


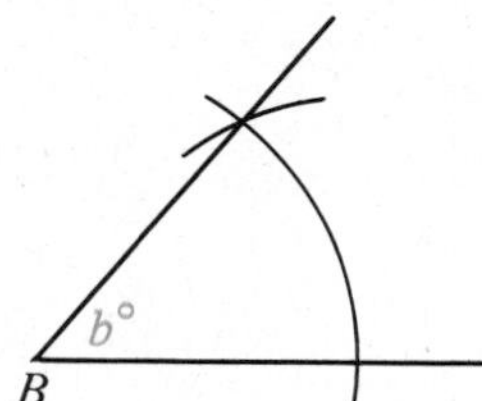


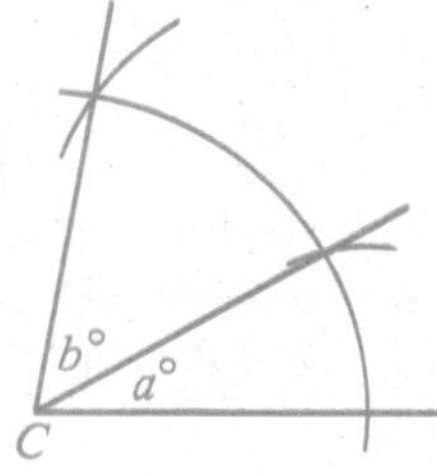


**13.** Draw two acute angles, $\angle X$ and $\angle Y$. Construct $\angle X + \angle Y$.

**14.** Draw an acute angle, $\angle Z$. Construct an angle with measure $2 \cdot \angle Z$.

## SELF-TEST

**1.** What is the difference between a postulate and a theorem? **A postulate is accepted without proof; a theorem is proved.**

**2.** Name two pairs of alternate interior angles. $\angle 2, \angle 7; \angle 3, \angle 6$

**3.** Name two pairs of same-side interior angles. $\angle 2, \angle 3; \angle 6, \angle 7$

**4.** Suppose $\angle 6 = 130°$. Find the measures of the other numbered angles. $\angle 1 = 130°$, $\angle 2 = 50°$, $\angle 3 = 130°$, $\angle 4 = 50°$, $\angle 4 = 50°$ $\angle 7 = 50°$, $\angle 8 = 130°$

1 2 3 4
5 6 7 8

**5.** Find the values of $x$ and $y$ in the diagram. $x = 70°$; $y = 50°$

70°
50°
x°
y°

Exercise 5

**6.** List four ways to prove that two lines are parallel. See page 67.

**7.** *Given:* $l \parallel m$
$\angle 1 = \angle 2$
*Prove:* $\angle 1 = \angle 3$

l 1 2
m 3

**8.** Draw a line $m$. Choose a point $A$ that is several centimeters from $m$. Construct a line through $A$ parallel to $m$.

## Reviewing Algebraic Skills

Give the coordinates of each point.

Sample Point $A$, $(-3, 3)$

1. $B$ (6, 2) 2. $C$ (1, 0) 3. $D$ (−3, −2)
4. $E$ (−5, 5) 5. $F$ (5, −6) 6. $G$ (3, 3)
7. $H$ (−6, 0) 8. $J$ (−7, −4) 9. $K$ (−1, 5)

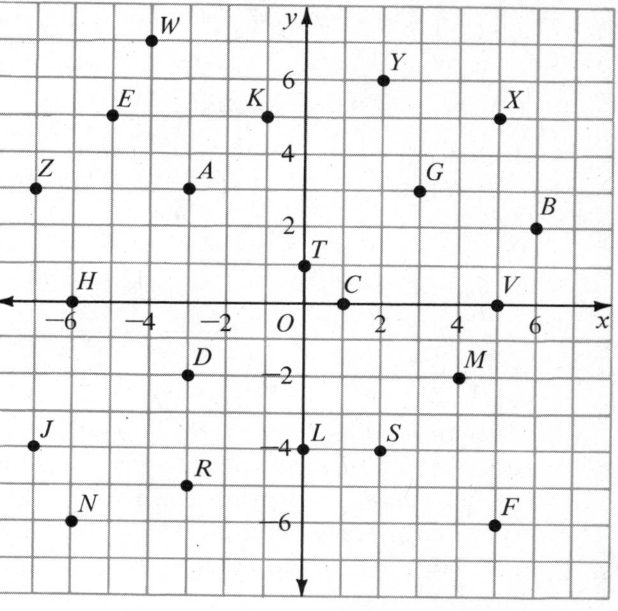


Name the point by its letter.

10. (−6, −6) N
11. (0, −4) L
12. (−4, 7) W
13. (5, 0) V
14. (−3, −5) R
15. (4, −2) M
16. (2, 6) Y
17. (−7, 3) Z
18. (0, 1) T
19. (2, −4) S

Plot the points in Exercises 20–31. Then draw line segments to connect the points in order. You should now have the outline of half a fir tree. (see Solution Key)

20. (0, 6) 21. (−2, 4) 22. (−1, 4) 23. (−3, 2)
24. (−2, 2) 25. (−5, −1) 26. (−3, −1) 27. (−6, −4)
28. (−1, −4) 29. (−1, −6) 30. (−2, −7) 31. (0, −7)

Complete the ordered pairs in Exercises 32–43 to tell how to draw the other half of the fir tree. Start at the top again.

32. (0, __?__) 6
33. (2, __?__) 4
34. (__?__, 4) 1
35. (3, __?__) 2
36. (__?__, 2) 2
37. (__?__, −1) 5
38. (__?__, −1) 3
39. (6, __?__) −4
40. (__?__, −4) 1
41. (__?__, __?__) 1, −6
42. (__?__, −7) 2
43. (__?__, __?__) 0, −7

44. Plot the points (2, −1) and (2, −5). Draw a line segment to connect them. Name the vertices of the two squares that can be drawn with this segment as a side. (2, −1), (2, −5), (−2, −1), (−2, −5); (2, −1), (2, −5), (6, −1), (6, −5)

# applications

## *Mirrors and Billiards*

When a ray of light strikes a mirror, it is reflected at the same angle at which it arrives. For example, in the diagram, $\angle 1 = \angle 2$.

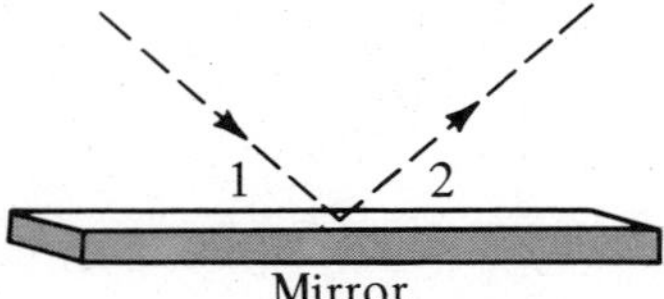


This principle of reflection is applied in the operation of a simple periscope. In the cross section of a periscope shown here, light is reflected twice so that light rays entering the periscope are parallel to light rays leaving the periscope.

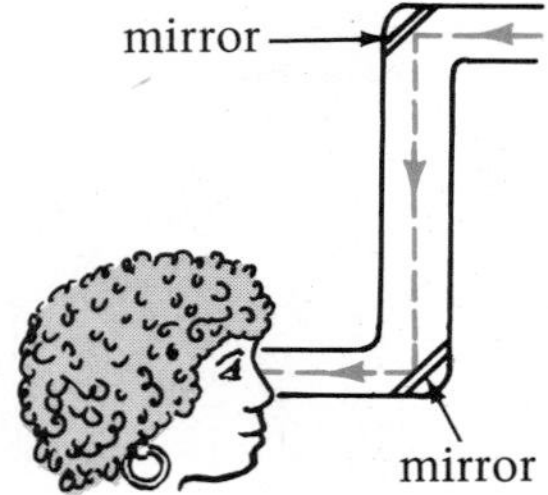


The same principle of reflection also applies to a ball bouncing off the sides of a pocket-billiard table or a miniature-golf course. The ball bounces back at the same angle at which it arrives. A good player uses this principle to sink a shot or to make a hole-in-one.

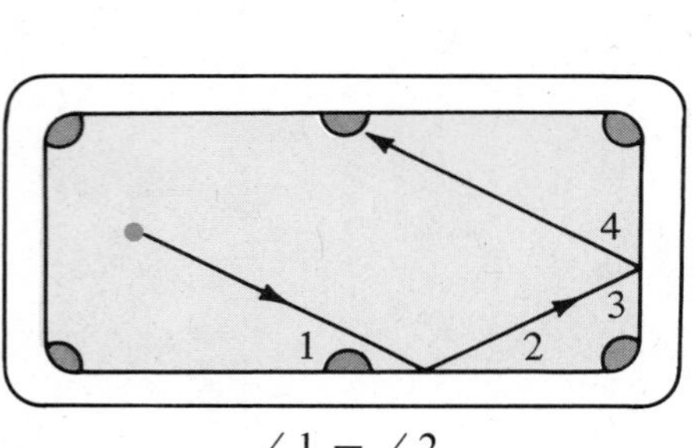


$\angle 1 = \angle 2$
$\angle 3 = \angle 4$

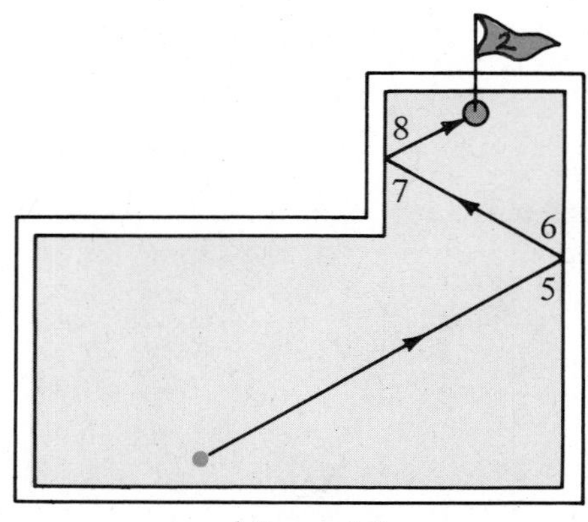


$\angle 5 = \angle 6$
$\angle 7 = \angle 8$

**Exercises**

Two mirrors form a 90° angle as shown.

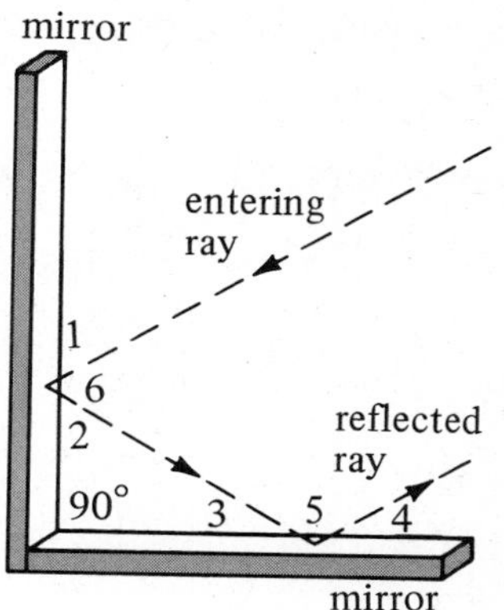


1. If $\angle 1 = 60°$ and $\angle 2$ is complementary to $\angle 3$, find the measure of each numbered angle. $\angle 1 = 60°$, $\angle 2 = 60°$, $\angle 3 = 30°$, $\angle 4 = 30°$, $\angle 5 = 120°$, $\angle 6 = 60°$
2. Complete: $\angle 5 + \angle 6 = \underline{\ ?\ }°$. 180
3. Explain why the entering ray is parallel to the reflected ray. Theorem 7: If 2 lines and a trans. form supplementary same-side interior angles, then the lines are parallel.

In the diagram above, suppose $\angle 1 = 50°$ and $\angle 2$ and $\angle 3$ are complementary angles.

4. Find the measure of each numbered angle. $\angle 1 = 50°$, $\angle 2 = 50°$, $\angle 3 = 40°$, $\angle 4 = 40°$, $\angle 5 = 100°$, $\angle 6 = 80°$
5. Is the entering ray still parallel to the reflected ray? yes

A ball on a billiard table rolls along the path shown. $\angle 1 = 70°$.

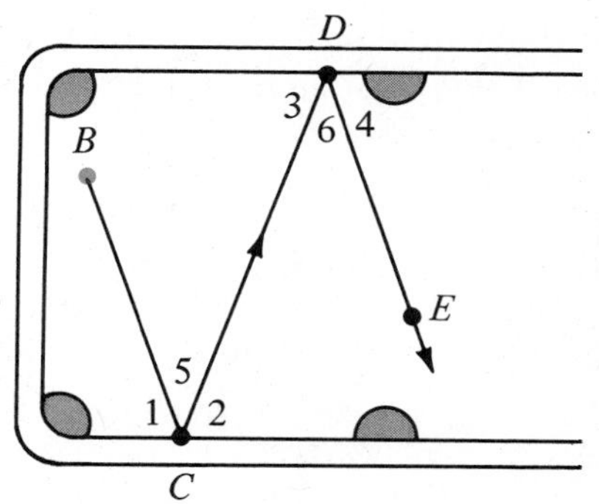


6. Find the measure of $\angle 2$. 70°
7. Explain why $\angle 3 = 70°$.
8. Find the measures of $\angle 5$ and $\angle 6$. $\angle 5 = \angle 6 = 40°$
9. Explain why $\overrightarrow{DE} \parallel \overrightarrow{BC}$. Theorem 6: If 2 lines and a trans. form equal alternate interior angles, then the lines are parallel.

7. Opposite sides of the table are parallel, so alternate interior angles are equal.

10. A billiard ball rolls from point $X$ to point $Y$ as shown. If the ball is hit hard enough, will it go into a pocket? no

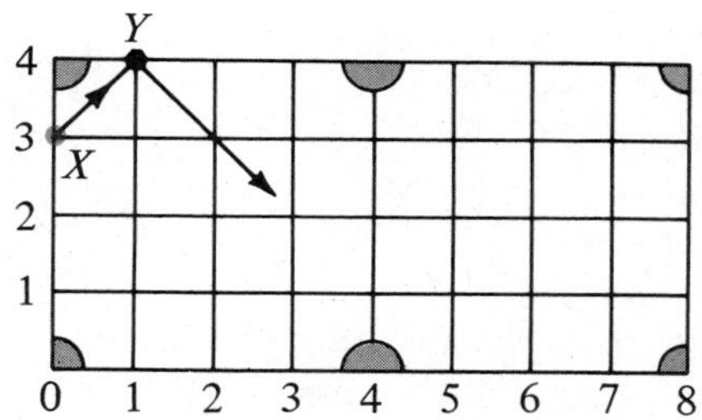

## Reviewing the Chapter

### Chapter Summary

1. Complementary angles are two angles whose measures total 90°. Supplementary angles are two angles whose measures total 180°.

2. "If . . . then" statements are important in logical reasoning.

   Statement: If $A$, then $B$.

   Converse statement: If $B$, then $A$.

3. There are four kinds of reasons used in a geometric proof.
   Given information  Definition  Postulate  Theorem

4. Parallel lines are coplanar lines which do not intersect. Skew lines are not coplanar lines, and they do not intersect.

5. When two parallel lines are cut by a transversal:
   a. corresponding angles are equal;
   b. alternate interior angles are equal;
   c. same-side interior angles are supplementary.

6. Strategies for proving that two lines cut by a transversal are parallel:
   a. show that corresponding angles are equal;
   b. show that alternate interior angles are equal;
   c. show that same-side interior angles are supplementary;
   d. show that both lines are perpendicular to the transversal.

7. It is possible to construct an angle equal to a given angle (Construction 4, page 71). Given a line and a point not on the line, you can construct a line that passes through the point and is parallel to the given line (Construction 5, page 72).

### Chapter Review Test

**In the diagram shown, $\overline{TR} \perp \overline{RO}$ and $\overline{SO} \perp \overline{RO}$.** (See pp. 42–45.)

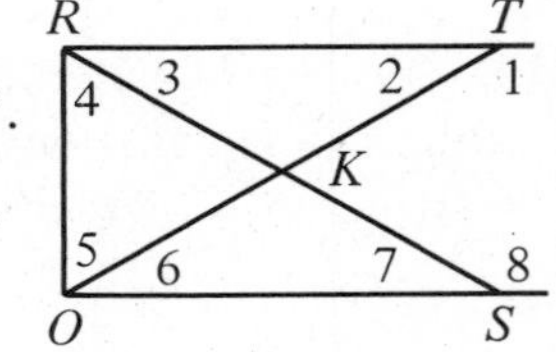


**1.** If $\angle 2 = 30°$, then a complement of $\angle 2$ has measure __?__°. 60

**2.** If $\angle 2 = 30°$, then a supplement of $\angle 2$ has measure __?__°. 150

**3.** Name a complement of $\angle 3$. $\angle 4$

**4.** If $\angle 3 = \angle 6$, state the theorem that allows you to conclude that $\angle 4 = \angle 5$. Complements of equal angles are equal.

**5.** If $\angle 2 = \angle 7$, state the theorem that allows you to conclude that $\angle 1 = \angle 8$. Supplements of equal angles are equal.

Use the statement, "Every acute angle has a measure less than 90°." (See pp. 46–49.)

6. Write the statement in "if . . . then" form. (see below)
7. State the hypothesis and the conclusion. (see below)
8. State the converse of the given statement.
   If an angle has a measure less than 90°, then it is acute.

Supply the reasons to complete the proof. (See pp. 54–59.)

9. *Given:* $\angle 1 = \angle 4$

   *Prove:* $\angle 2 = \angle 5$

| STATEMENTS | REASONS |
|---|---|
| 1. $\angle 1$ and $\angle 2$ are supplements. $\angle 4$ and $\angle 3$ are supplements. | 1. ? Def. of supplementary angles |
| 2. $\angle 1 = \angle 4$ | 2. ? Given |
| 3. $\angle 2 = \angle 3$ | 3. ? Supplements of = angles are =. |
| 4. $\angle 3 = \angle 5$ | 4. ? Vertical angles are equal. |
| 5. $\angle 2 = \angle 5$ | 5. ? Substitution Postulate |

Classify each pair of angles as alternate interior angles, same-side interior angles, or corresponding angles. (See pp. 60–65.)

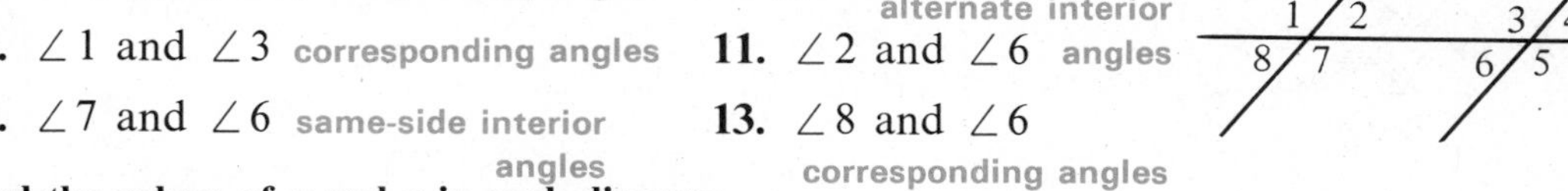

10. $\angle 1$ and $\angle 3$ corresponding angles
11. $\angle 2$ and $\angle 6$ alternate interior angles
12. $\angle 7$ and $\angle 6$ same-side interior angles
13. $\angle 8$ and $\angle 6$ corresponding angles

Find the values of $x$ and $y$ in each diagram.

14.

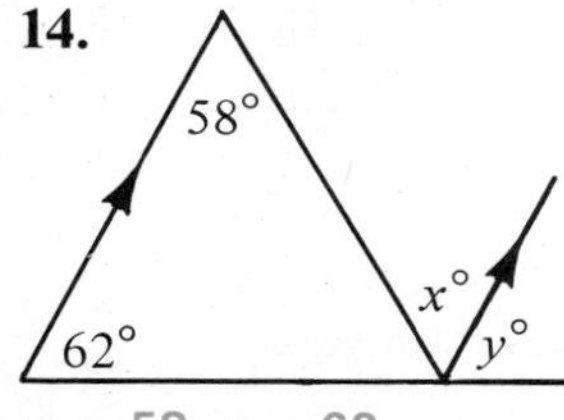


$x = 58$, $y = 62$

15.

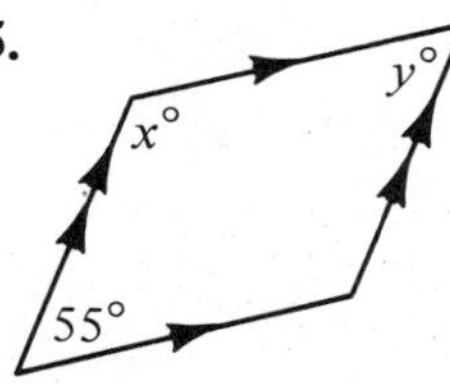


$x = 125$, $y = 55$

16.

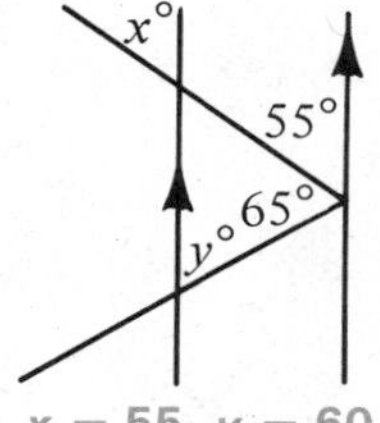


$x = 55$, $y = 60$

Use the given information to tell which lines must be parallel. (See pp. 66–70.)

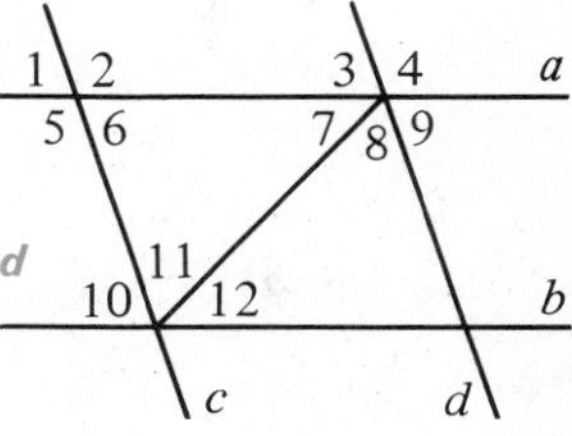


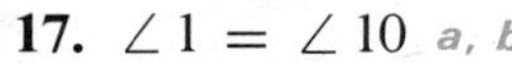

17. $\angle 1 = \angle 10$ a, b
18. $\angle 7 = \angle 12$ a, b
19. $\angle 8 = \angle 11$ c, d
20. $\angle 2 + \angle 3 = 180°$ c, d

Construct the required figure. (See pp. 71–74.)

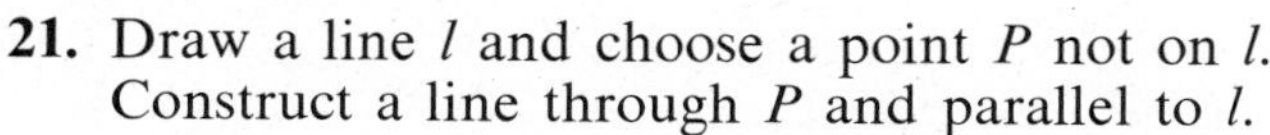

21. Draw a line $l$ and choose a point $P$ not on $l$. Construct a line through $P$ and parallel to $l$.

6. If an angle is acute, then it has a measure less than 90°.
7. hypothesis: an angle is acute; conclusion: it has a measure less than 90°.

# Cumulative Review / Unit A

**Find the following:**

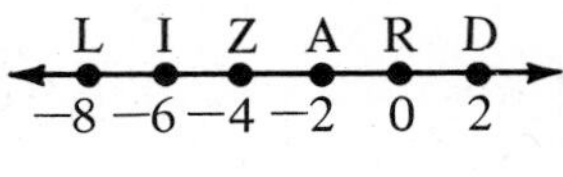


**1.** $AD$ 4 **2.** $LR$ 8 **3.** $ZR$ 4

**4.** The coordinate of $Z$ −4 **5.** The midpoint of $\overline{IA}$ Z

**Tell whether each statement is true or false.**

**6.** $\angle HOJ + \angle JOP = \angle HOP$ true

**7.** $\angle MOY$ is an obtuse angle. false

**8.** $\angle HOM = 45°$ true

**9.** $\overrightarrow{OM}$ bisects $\angle HOY$. true

**10.** $\angle HOY$ is an acute angle. false

**11.** It is possible to draw two different lines containing both points $P$ and $T$. false

**12.** Exactly one plane contains points $P$, $O$, and $Y$. true

**13.** $\angle TOP$ and $\angle HOM$ are complementary angles. true

**14.** Complete.

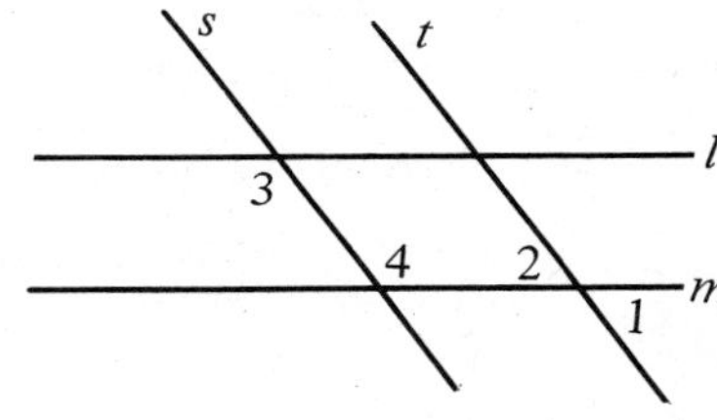


*Given:* $\angle 1$ and $\angle 3$ are supplements.
$s \parallel t$

*Prove:* $l \parallel m$

| STATEMENTS | REASONS |
|---|---|
| 1. $\angle 1$ and $\angle 3$ are supplements. | 1. ? Given |
| 2. $\angle 2$ and $\angle 4$ are supplements. | 2. ? Theorem 5 |
| 3. $\angle 1 = \angle 2$ | 3. ? Vertical angles are equal. |
| 4. $\angle 3 = \angle 4$ | 4. ? |
| 5. ? $l \parallel m$ | 5. ? Theorem 6 |

4. Supplements of equal angles are equal.

**15.** Write the converse of the statement: "If two angles are vertical angles, then they are equal." Is the converse true? If 2 angles are =, then they are vertical angles; not true.

**16.** Draw a line $l$ and points $P$ and $Q$ not on $l$.
**a.** Construct a perpendicular to $l$ through $P$.
**b.** Construct a line through $Q$ parallel to $l$.

# UNIT B

## *Here's what you'll learn in this chapter:*

1. To use the properties of the angles of a triangle.
2. To classify triangles according to their sides or angles.
3. To name congruent triangles and their corresponding parts.
4. To use postulates and theorems to prove that triangles are congruent.

# Chapter 3

# Triangles

## 1 • The Angle Sum of a Triangle

Draw a large triangle on a sheet of paper and cut the triangle out. Then tear off the three corners of the triangle and arrange them as shown. What appears to be true about the angles of the triangle? Try this experiment with a few other triangles and see if your results are the same.

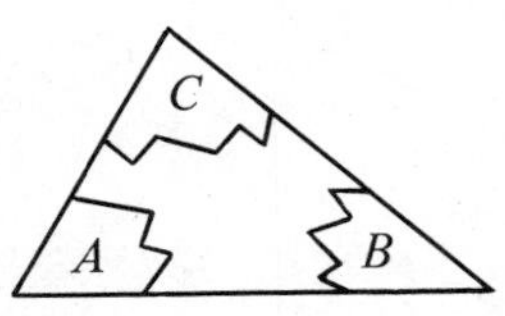


The property illustrated by this experiment is one of the best known and most important theorems in geometry.

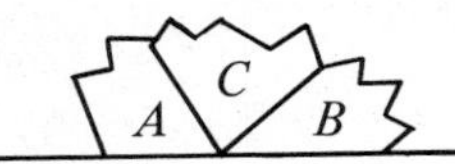

**THEOREM 1**

The angle sum of a triangle is 180°.

*Given:* $\triangle ABC$

*Prove:* $\angle 1 + \angle 2 + \angle 3 = 180°$

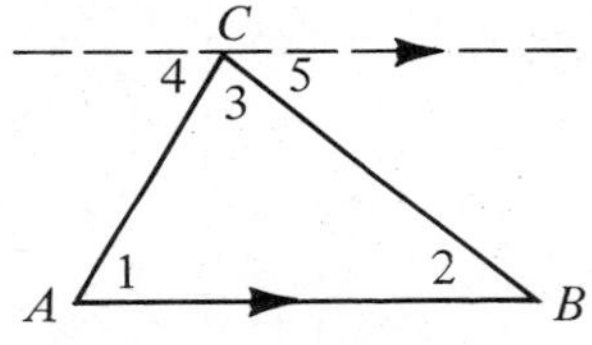


| STATEMENTS | REASONS |
|---|---|
| 1. Through $C$, draw a line parallel to $\overline{AB}$. | 1. Through any point not on a line, a parallel can be drawn to the line. (Recall Construction 5, page 72.) |
| 2. $\angle 4 = \angle 1$ and $\angle 5 = \angle 2$ | 2. If 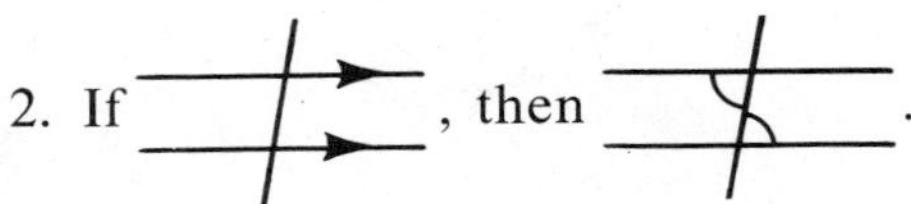, then . |
| 3. $\angle 4 + \angle 5 + \angle 3 = 180°$ | 3. Their sum is a straight angle. |
| 4. $\angle 1 + \angle 2 + \angle 3 = 180°$ | 4. Substitution Postulate |

**EXAMPLE** Find the measures of $\angle 1$ and $\angle 2$.

$$\angle 1 + \underbrace{60° + 70°} = 180°$$

$$\angle 1 + 130° = 180°$$

$$\angle 1 = 50°$$

Since $\angle 1$ and $\angle 2$ are supplements,

$$\angle 2 = 180° - 50° = 130°.$$

In the preceding example, $\angle 2$ is called an **exterior angle** of $\triangle XYZ$. Notice that

$$\angle 2 = 130° = \angle X + \angle Z.$$

Likewise, in the diagram at the right, $\angle QRS$ is an exterior angle of $\triangle PQR$. Do you see that

$$\angle QRS = 100° = \angle P + \angle Q?$$

These observations lead to an important *corollary* of Theorem 1. (A **corollary** of a theorem is a result which follows from the theorem with very little extra work.) The proof of the corollary is left as an exercise.

**COROLLARY**

An exterior angle of a triangle is equal to the sum of the two opposite angles of the triangle.

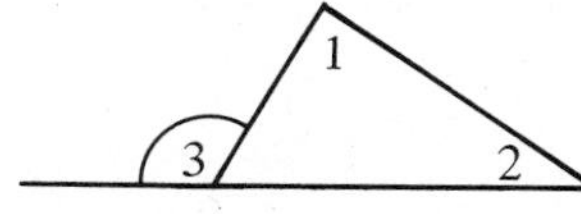


$\angle 3 = \angle 1 + \angle 2$

## Classroom Practice

**Find the measure of each numbered angle.**

**1.**

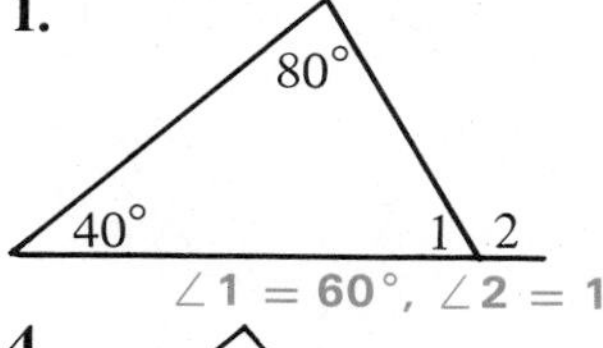


$\angle 1 = 60°$, $\angle 2 = 120°$

**2.**

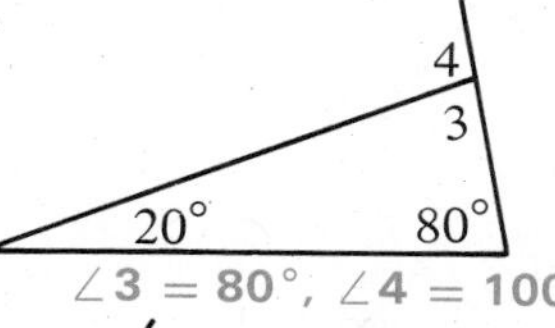


$\angle 3 = 80°$, $\angle 4 = 100°$

**3.**

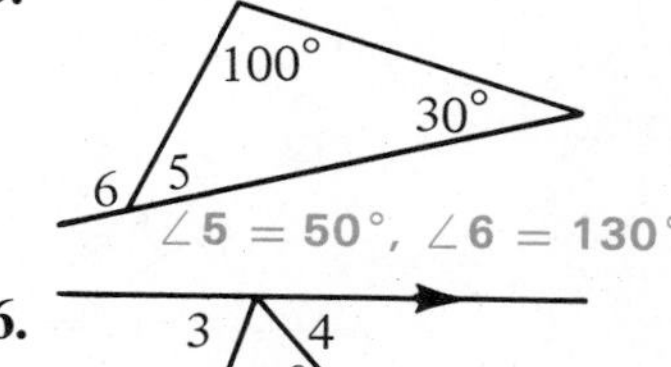


$\angle 5 = 50°$, $\angle 6 = 130°$

**4.**

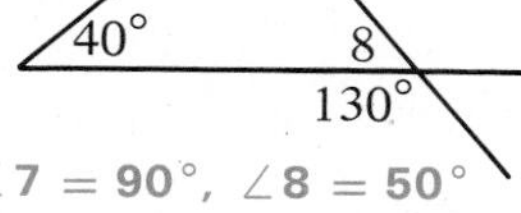


$\angle 7 = 90°$, $\angle 8 = 50°$

**5.**

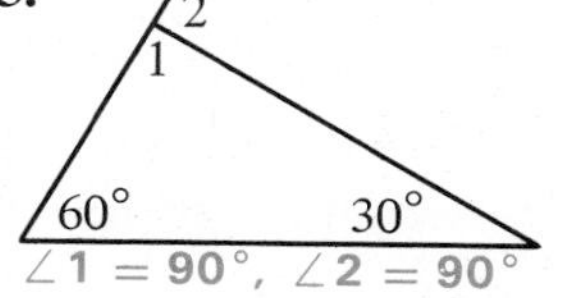


$\angle 1 = 90°$, $\angle 2 = 90°$

**6.**

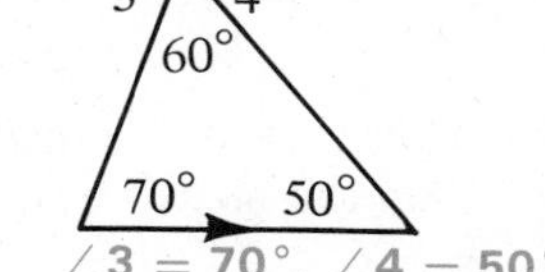


$\angle 3 = 70°$, $\angle 4 = 50°$

**In $\triangle ABC$, $\angle C = 90°$.**

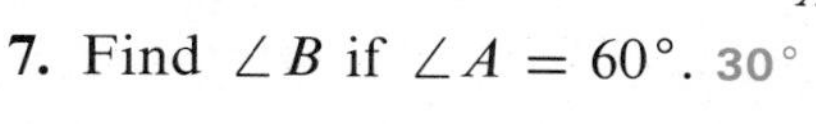

**7.** Find $\angle B$ if $\angle A = 60°$. 30°

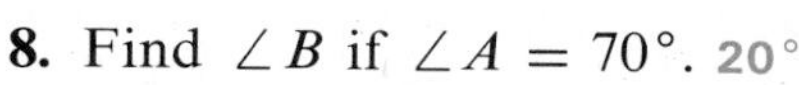

**8.** Find $\angle B$ if $\angle A = 70°$. 20°

**9.** Find $\angle B$ if $\angle A = 65°$. 25°

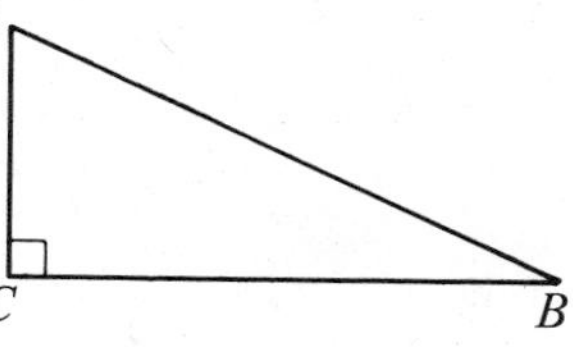

10. From Exercises 7–9, we see that if a triangle has a right angle, then the acute angles are ___?___. complementary

11. In the diagram, $\angle 1 + \angle 2 =$ ___?___°; 90
$\angle 1 + \angle 3 =$ ___?___°. 90

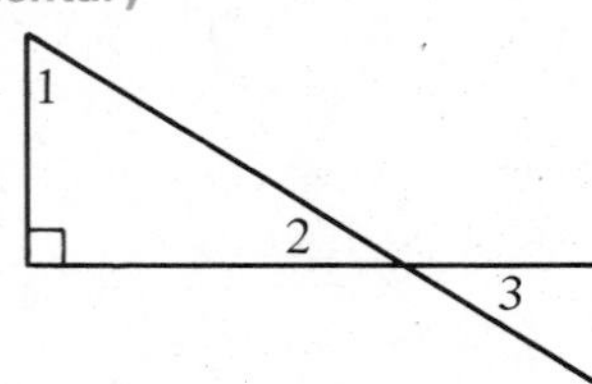


**Find the value of $x$ in each diagram.**

12. 45°

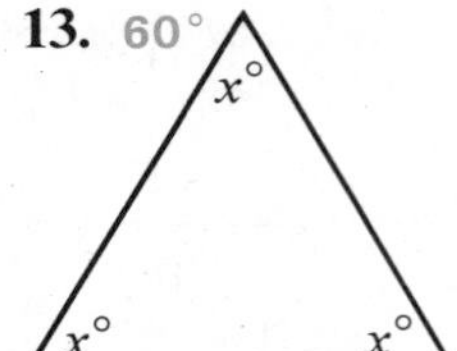


13. 60°

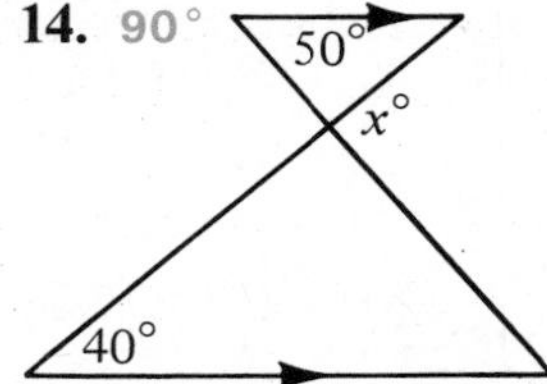


14. 90°



15. How many right angles can a triangle have? Explain your answer. (see below)

16. How many obtuse angles can a triangle have? Explain your answer. One; when the measure of one angle is greater than 90°, the sum of the two remaining angles is less than 90°, so neither is obtuse.

15. One; if it had two, the sum would be 180° and the third angle would have to be 0°.

## Written Exercises

**Find the measure of each numbered angle.**

A

1.

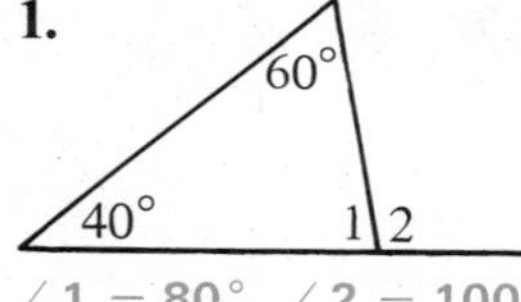


$\angle 1 = 80°$, $\angle 2 = 100°$

2.

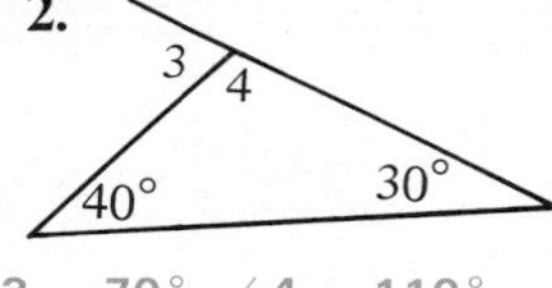


$\angle 3 = 70°$, $\angle 4 = 110°$

3. $\angle 5 = 50°$, $\angle 6 = 130°$

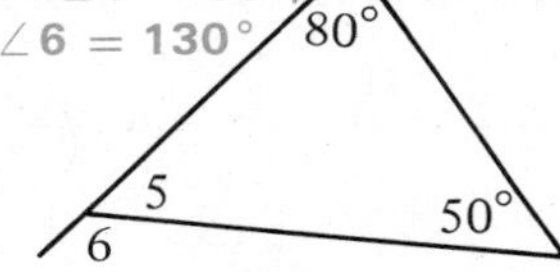


4.

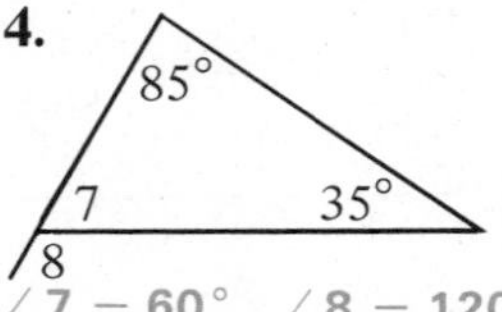


$\angle 7 = 60°$, $\angle 8 = 120°$

5.

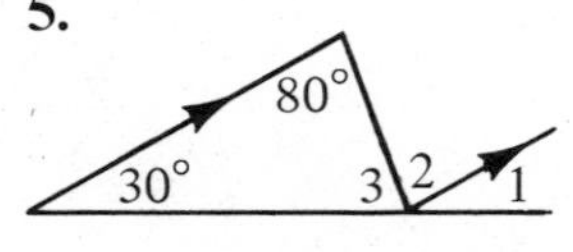


$\angle 1 = 30°$, $\angle 2 = 80°$, $\angle 3 = 70°$

6.

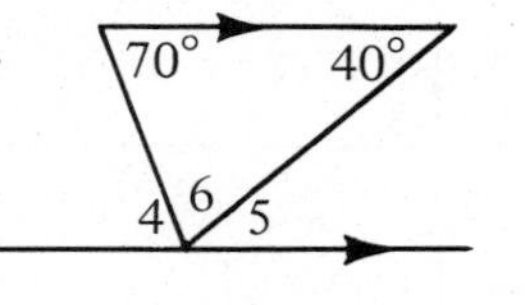


$\angle 4 = 70°$, $\angle 5 = 40°$, $\angle 6 = 70°$

**In Exercises 7–10, the measures of two angles are given. Find the measure of the third angle by using the Corollary of Theorem 1.**

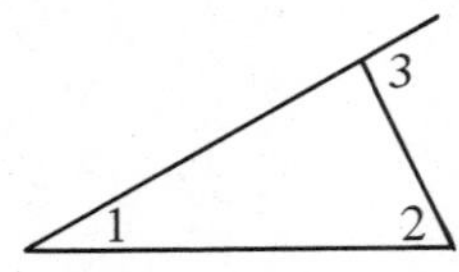


| | 7. | 8. | 9. | 10. |
|---|---|---|---|---|
| $\angle 1$ | 25° | 40° | 30° | ___?___ 50° |
| $\angle 2$ | 65° | ___?___ 70° | 70° | 65° |
| $\angle 3$ | ___?___ 90° | 110° | ___?___ 100° | 115° |

**Find the measures of $\angle 1$ and $\angle 2$.**

11. $\angle 1 = 30°$, $\angle 2 = 50°$

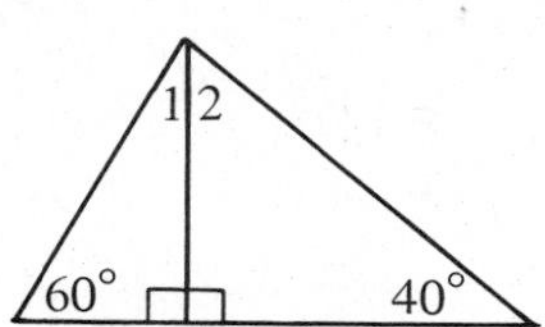


12. $\angle 1 = 60°$, $\angle 2 = 50°$

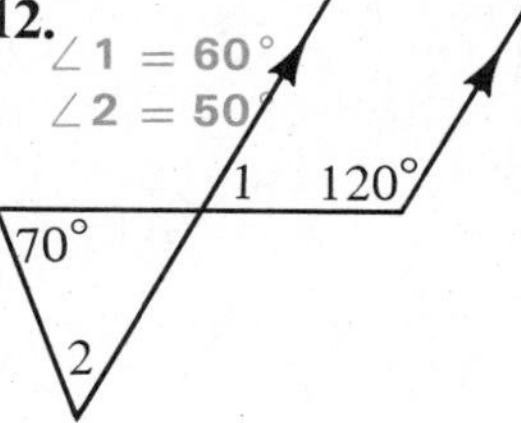


13. $\angle 1 = 45°$, $\angle 2 = 85°$

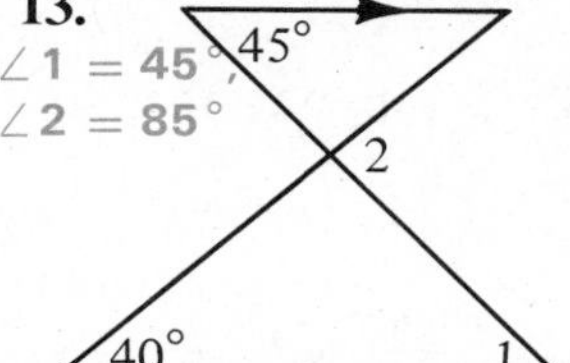


14. The three angles of a certain triangle are all equal. Find the measure of each angle. 60°

15. Find the numerical measure of each angle of $\triangle RST$.
$\angle TRS = 50°$, $\angle RST = 60°$, $\angle STR = 70°$

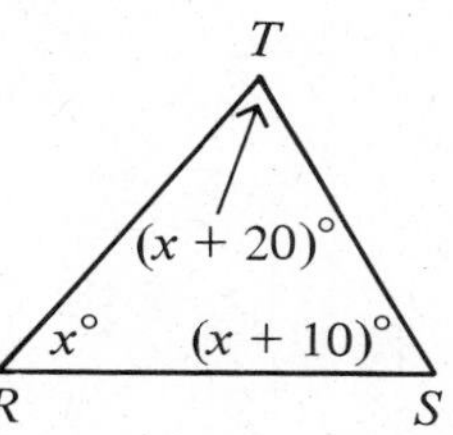


**Find the value of $x$ in each diagram.**

16. 20

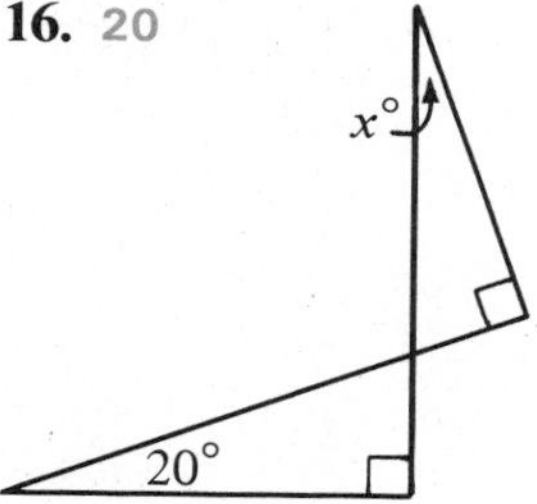


17. 30

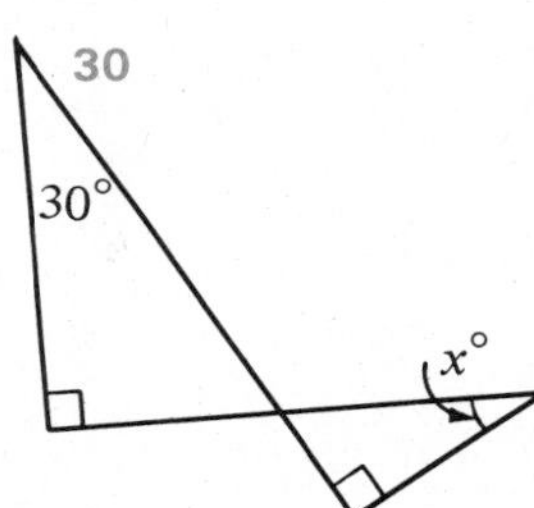


18. 41

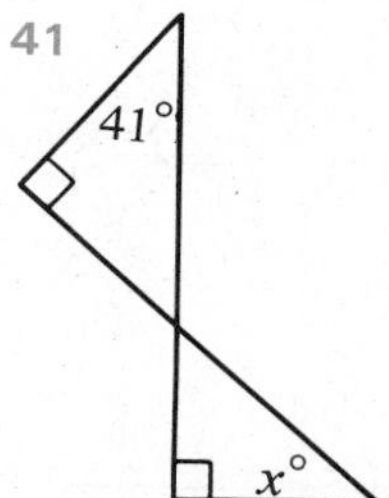


B 19. If two angles of one triangle are equal to two angles of another triangle, what can you say about the third angles of the triangles? Explain your answer. They must also be equal, since each is 180° − (the equal sum of two angles).

**In each diagram, $\overrightarrow{RT}$ and $\overrightarrow{ST}$ are angle bisectors. Find the value of $x$.**

20. 130

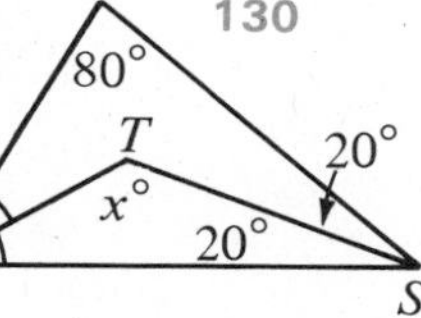


21. 130

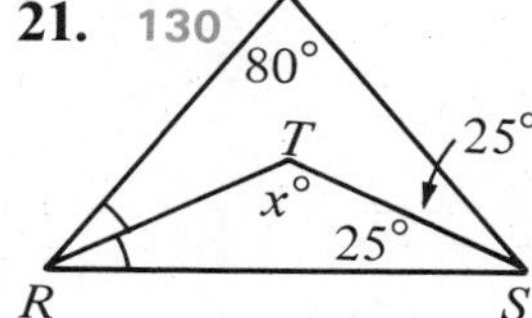


22. 130

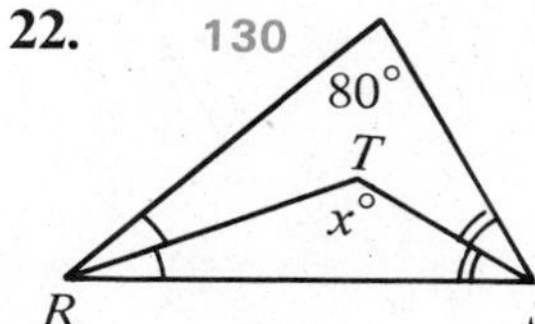


23. In $\triangle DEF$, $\angle E$ is 15° larger than $\angle D$.
Also, $\angle F$ is 45° larger than $\angle D$.
Find the measure of each angle.
(*Hint:* Let $\angle D = x°$. Then $\angle E =$ __?__° and $\angle F =$ __?__°.) 40, 55, 85

**24.** In $\triangle ABC$, $\angle B$ is twice as large as $\angle A$. Also, $\angle B = \angle C$. Find the measure of each angle. $\angle A = 36°$, $\angle B = 72°$, $\angle C = 72°$

**25.** Complete this proof of the Corollary of Theorem 1.

*Given:* $\triangle ABC$

*Prove:* $\angle 3 = \angle 1 + \angle 2$

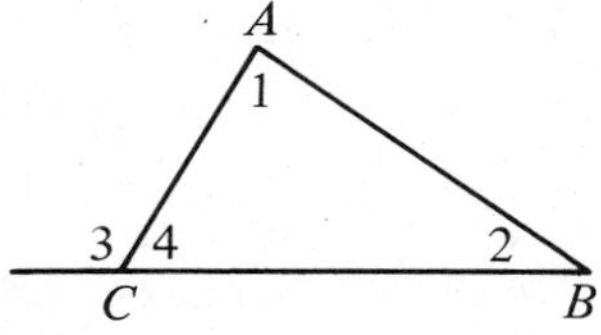


| STATEMENTS | REASONS |
|---|---|
| 1. $\angle 1 + \angle 2 + \angle 4 = 180°$ | 1. __?__ The angle sum of a $\triangle$ is 180°. |
| 2. $\angle 1 + \angle 2 = 180° - \angle 4$ | 2. __?__ Subtraction Postulate |
| 3. $\angle 4 + \angle 3 = 180°$ | 3. Their sum is a __?__ angle. straight |
| 4. $\angle 3 = 180° - \angle 4$ | 4. __?__ Subtraction Postulate |
| 5. $\angle 3 = \angle 1 + \angle 2$ | 5. __?__ Substitution Postulate |

**In each exercise, find the indicated sum.**

**26.**

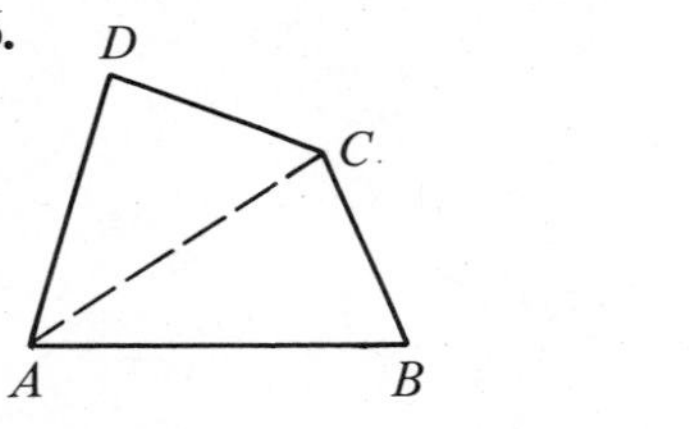


$\angle A + \angle B + \angle C + \angle D =$ __?__ ° 360

**27.**

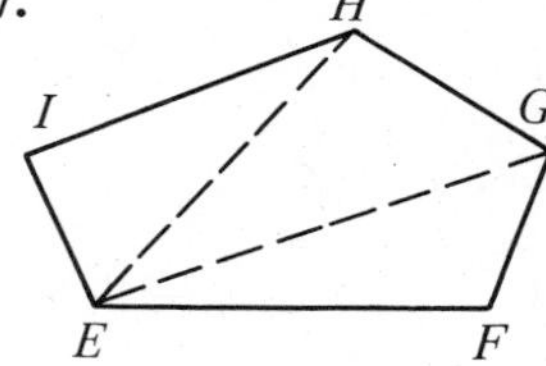


$\angle E + \angle F + \angle G + \angle H + \angle I =$ __?__ ° 540

**In each exercise, find the value of $x$.**

C **28.** 120

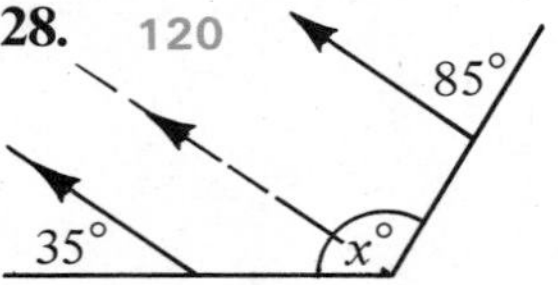


**29.** 90

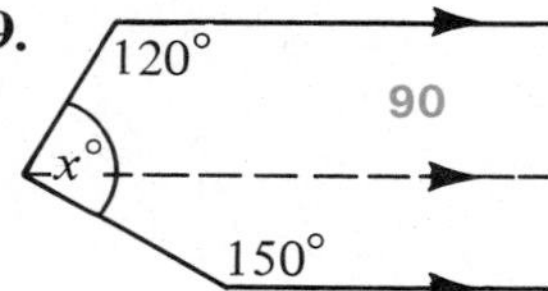


**30.** *Given:* $\angle B = \angle C$

$\overrightarrow{AE}$ bisects $\angle DAC$.

*Prove:* $\overline{AE} \parallel \overline{BC}$

D
A 1 E
2
B C

## 2 • Classifying Triangles

$\triangle ABC$ is shown at the right. The segments $\overline{AB}$, $\overline{BC}$, and $\overline{AC}$ are called the **sides** of the triangle. Notice that two of these sides have equal lengths. We say that the two sides are equal. (This is like saying that two angles are equal if they have equal measures.)

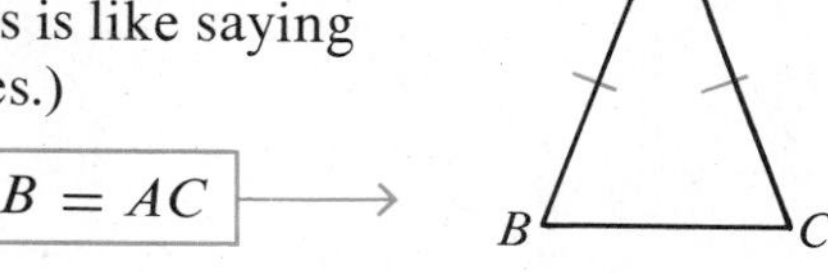


**Classification of Triangles by Sides**

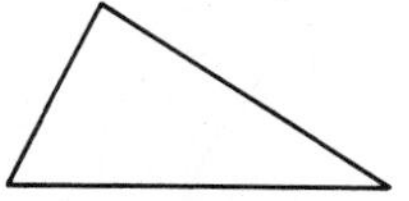

Scalene triangle

No sides are equal.

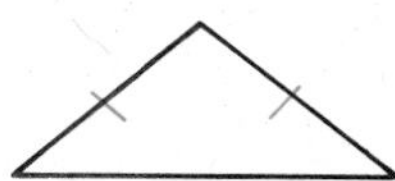

Isosceles triangle

At least two sides are equal.

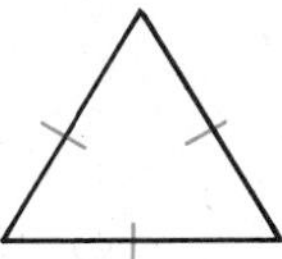

Equilateral triangle

All three sides are equal.

Notice that an equilateral triangle is also isosceles.

**Classification of Triangles by Angles**

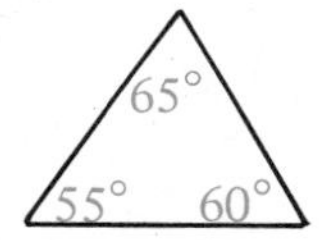


Acute triangle

All angles are acute.

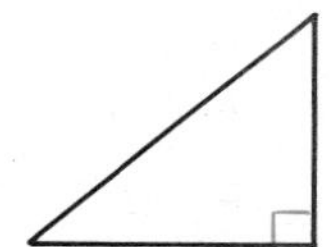

Right triangle

One angle is right.

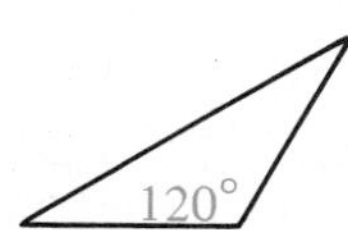


Obtuse triangle

One angle is obtuse.

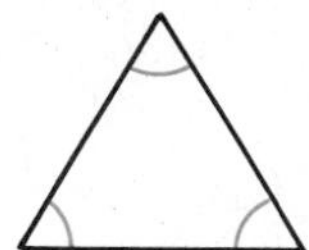

Equiangular triangle

All angles are equal.

**Special Names for Sides**

The two equal sides of an isosceles triangle are called **legs.** The third side is the **base.**

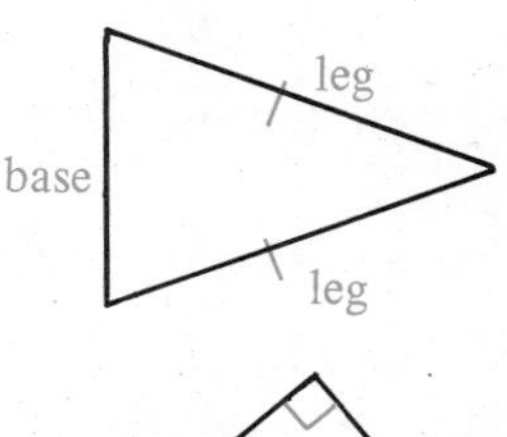


The side opposite the right angle of a right triangle is called the **hypotenuse.** The other sides are called **legs.**

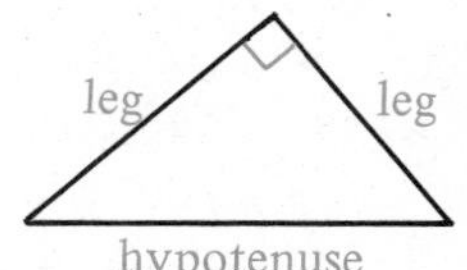

## Classroom Practice

**Classify each triangle shown as scalene, isosceles, or equilateral.**

**1.**

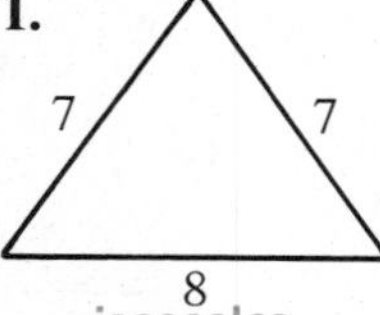


**2.**

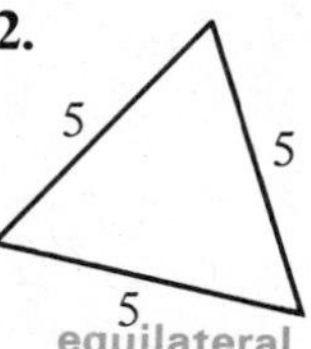


**3.**

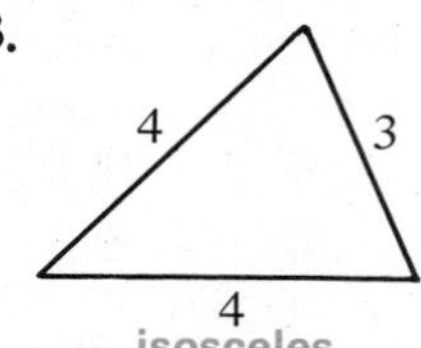


**4.**

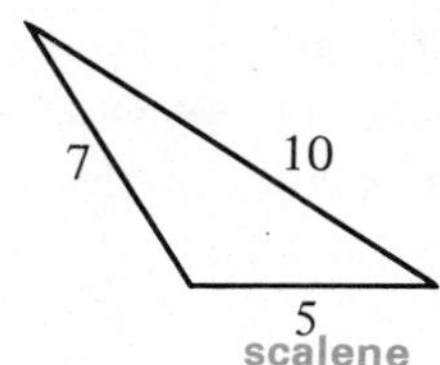


**Classify each triangle shown as acute, right, obtuse, or equiangular.**

**5.**

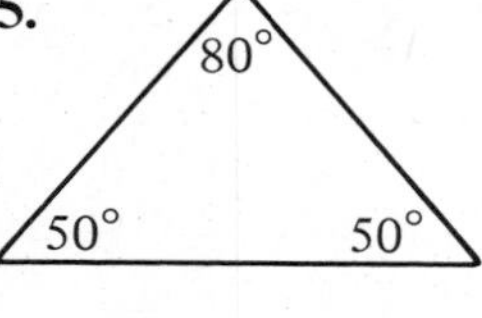


**6.**

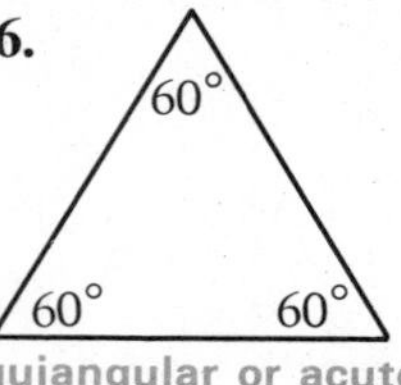


**7.**

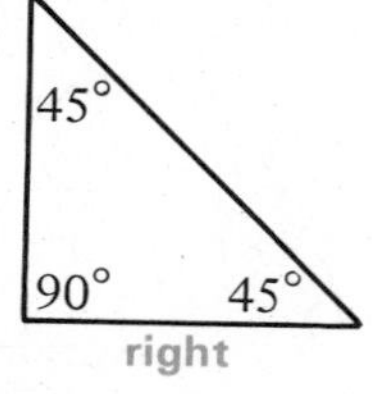


**8.**

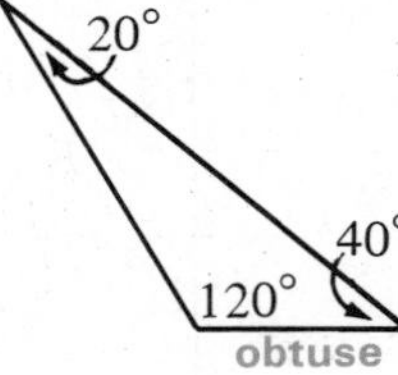


**9.** $\triangle ABC$ is a right triangle.
Sides $\overline{AC}$ and $\overline{BC}$ are called _?_. legs
Side $\overline{AB}$ is called the _?_. hypotenuse

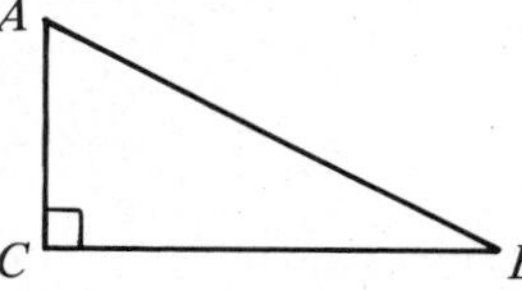


**10.** $\triangle PQR$ is an isosceles triangle.
Sides $\overline{PQ}$ and $\overline{PR}$ are called _?_. legs
Side $\overline{QR}$ is called the _?_. base

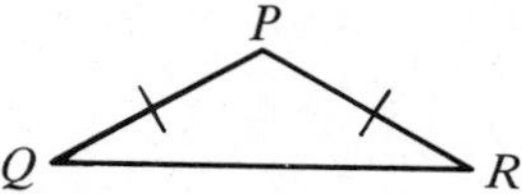


*Given:* $\overline{BE} \perp \overline{AC}$.

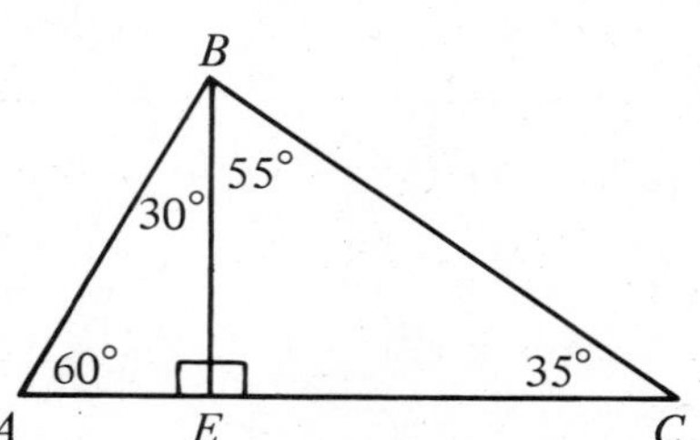


**11.** Name two right triangles. $\triangle ABE$, $\triangle BEC$

**12.** Name an acute triangle. $\triangle ABC$

**13.** Name an exterior angle of $\triangle BEC$. $\angle BEA$

**14.** Name a side common to $\triangle ABE$ and $\triangle BEC$. $\overline{BE}$

**15.** Name a vertex common to $\triangle ABE$ and $\triangle BEC$. E

**16.** Name an angle common to $\triangle ABE$ and $\triangle ABC$. $\angle A$

**17.** If a triangle is equilateral, is it also isosceles? yes

**18.** If a triangle is isosceles, is it also equilateral? no

**19.** The *perimeter* of a triangle is the sum of the lengths of its sides. If the perimeter of an equilateral triangle is 30 cm, find the length of each side. 10 cm

## Written Exercises

**Classify each triangle shown as scalene, isosceles, or equilateral.**

A **1.**

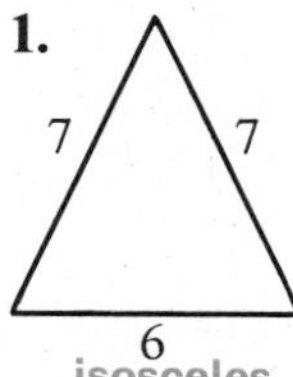


isosceles

**2.**

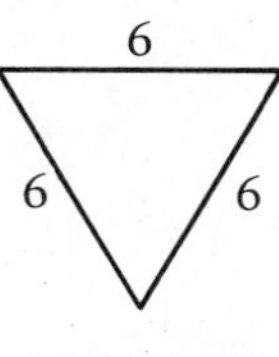


equilateral

**3.**

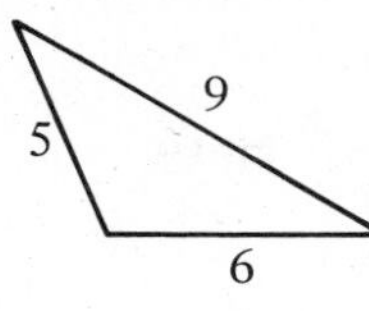


scalene

**4.**

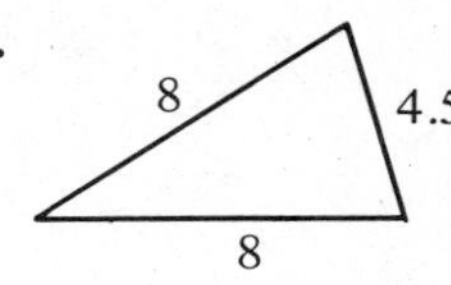


isosceles

**Classify each triangle shown as acute, right, obtuse, or equiangular.**

**5.**

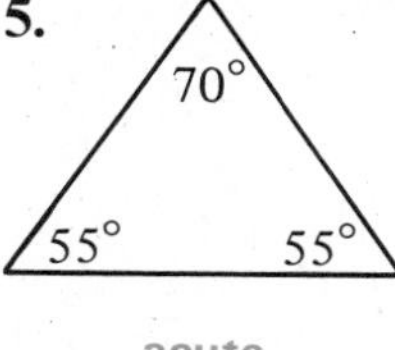


acute

**6.**

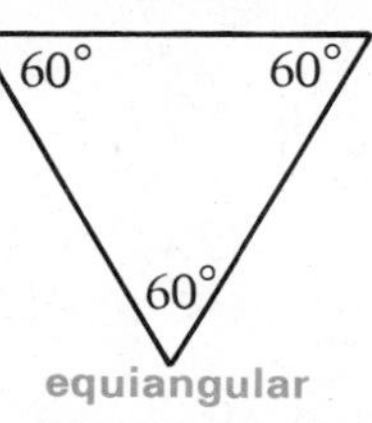


equiangular

**7.**

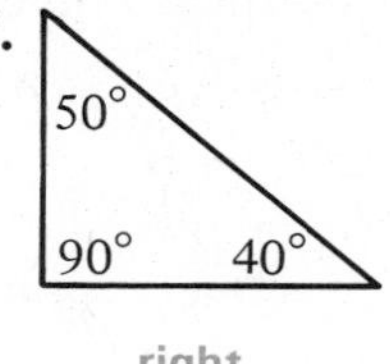


right

**8.**

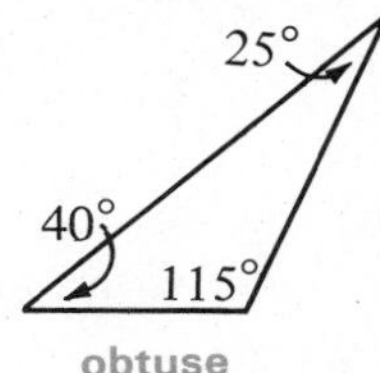


obtuse

**9. a.** Draw an acute scalene triangle. **b.** Draw an acute isosceles triangle.

**10. a.** Draw an obtuse scalene triangle. **b.** Draw an obtuse isosceles triangle.

**11. a.** Draw a right scalene triangle. **b.** Draw a right isosceles triangle.

**12. a.** Fold a sheet of paper in half.
**b.** Use scissors to cut from any point on the fold to a corner point.

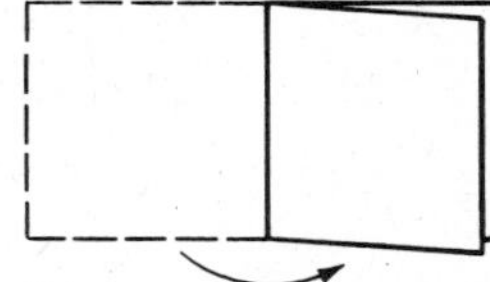

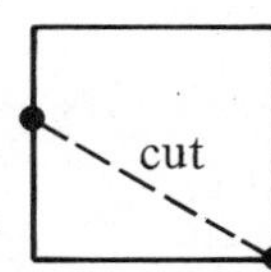


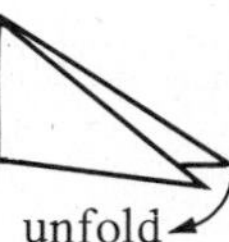


**c.** What kind of triangle is formed when you unfold the paper? isosceles

**13.** *Given:* $\triangle ABC$ is equiangular.
$\overrightarrow{AX}$ bisects $\angle BAC$.

Then: $\angle C = \underline{\ ?\ }°$ 60
$\angle CAX = \underline{\ ?\ }°$ 30
$\angle AXC = \underline{\ ?\ }°$ 90

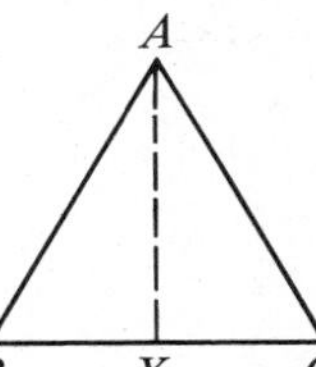


**14.** Figure $ABCD$ has four right angles. (In other words, it is a rectangle.)

**a.** Name two right triangles with hypotenuse $\overline{AC}$.

**b.** Name two right triangles with hypotenuse $\overline{BD}$.

a. $\triangle ABC$, $\triangle ACD$ b. $\triangle ABD$, $\triangle BDC$

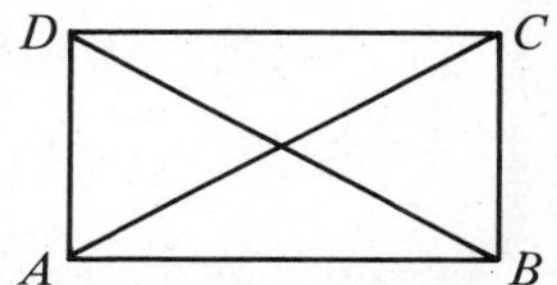

**In Exercises 15–17, find the lengths of the sides of the triangle.**

B **15.**

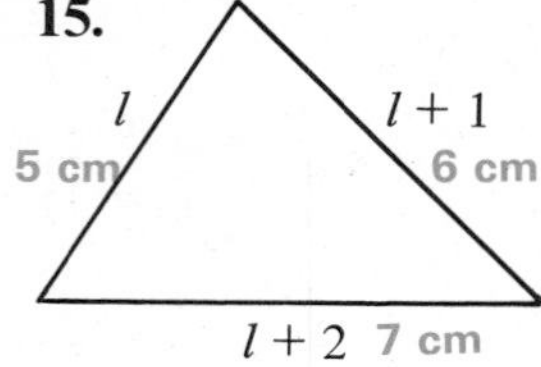


The perimeter is 18 cm.

**16.**

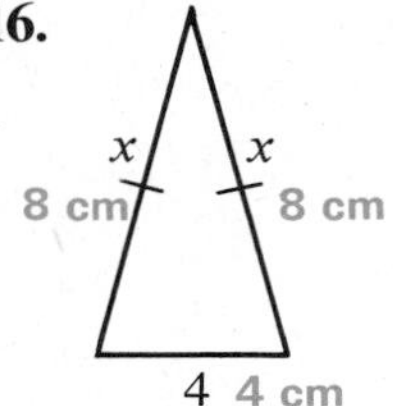


The perimeter is 20 cm.

**17.**

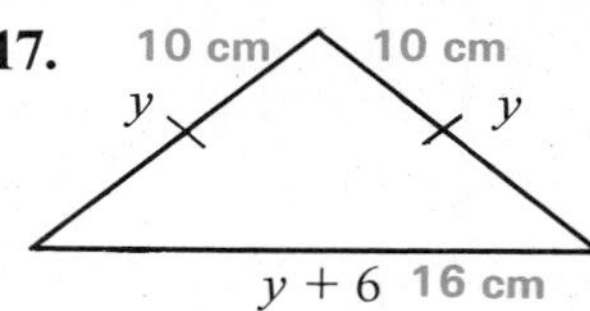


The perimeter is 36 cm.

**Exercises 18–20 suggest some important properties of triangles. Proofs of these properties will be postponed until Chapter 4.**

**18. a.** Construct a triangle with two equal sides. Using a protractor, carefully measure its three angles.
**b.** Repeat this process for other triangles with two equal sides.
**c.** What do you discover about the angles of such triangles? The angles opposite the equal sides are equal.

**19. a.** Construct a triangle with two equal angles. Using a ruler, carefully measure its three sides.
**b.** Repeat this process for other triangles with two equal angles.
**c.** What do you discover about the sides of such triangles? The sides opposite the equal angles are equal.

C **20. a.** Express your discoveries of Exercises 18 and 19 in "If . . . then" form. (see below)
**b.** As a pair, the statements can be called ___?___. converses

a. If 2 sides of a triangle are equal, then the angles opposite these are equal. If 2 angles in a triangle are equal, then the sides opposite these angles are equal.

## SELF-TEST

**Find $x$.**

**1.** 40

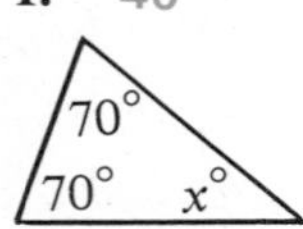


**2.** 120

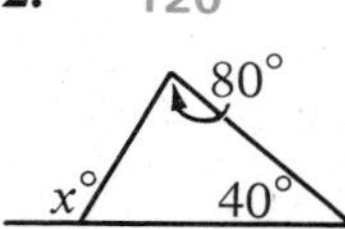


**3.** 70

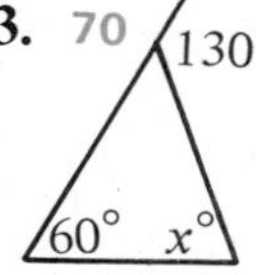


**4.** 74

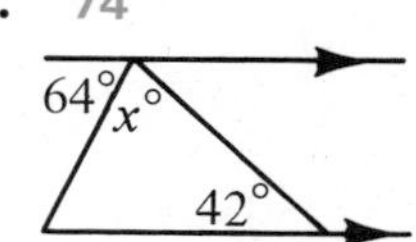


**In Exercises 5–8, write a, b, c, or d to identify a triangle of the type named.**

**a.**

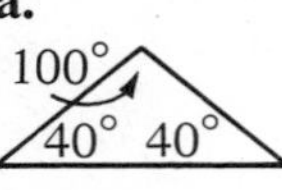


**b.**

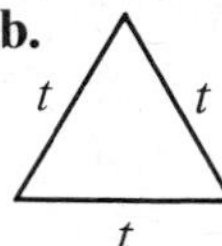


**c.**

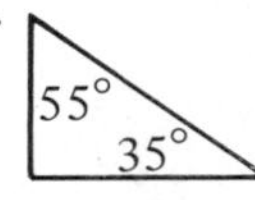


**d.**

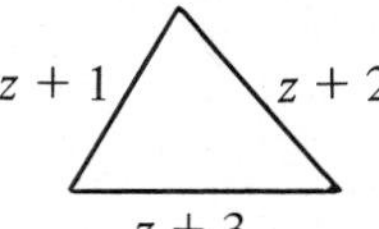


**5.** Scalene triangle d

**6.** Obtuse triangle a

**7.** Right triangle c

**8.** Equilateral triangle b

# 3 • Defining Congruent Triangles

When you buy a package of notebook paper, you get sheets that are all alike. Any two sheets have the same size and the same shape. One sheet will fit directly over another sheet. In the language of geometry, one sheet is *congruent* to another sheet.

Likewise $\triangle CAT$ and $\triangle RUN$ are congruent. They have the same size and shape.

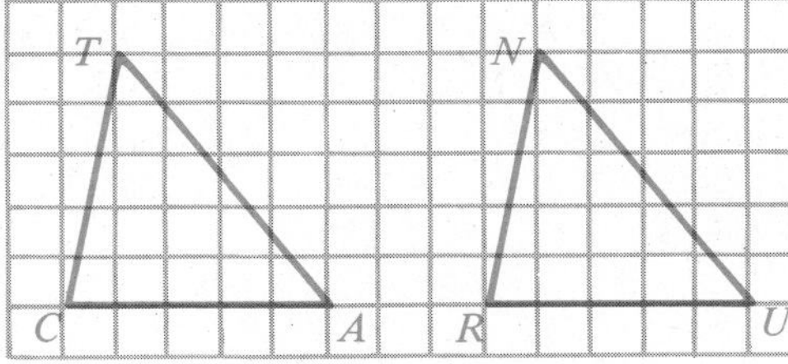


For a discussion of *oppositely* congruent figures, see the Lesson Commentary, page T56.

Imagine sliding one triangle over to fit on the other triangle. You put
point $C$ on point $R$; point $A$ on point $U$; point $T$ on point $N$.

When the vertices are matched in this way:

$\angle C$ and $\angle R$ are called **corresponding angles;**
$\overline{CT}$ and $\overline{RN}$ are called **corresponding sides.**

We often refer to corresponding angles and corresponding sides as corresponding **parts** of the triangles. In congruent triangles, *corresponding parts are always equal.*

When $\triangle CAT$ **is congruent to** $\triangle RUN$ we write

$$\triangle CAT \cong \triangle RUN.$$

$\triangle CAT \cong \triangle RUN$ means that all of the following are true:

$$\angle C = \angle R \qquad \angle A = \angle U \qquad \angle T = \angle N$$
$$CA = RU \qquad AT = UN \qquad CT = RN$$

Suppose that instead of writing $\triangle CAT \cong \triangle RUN$ you started to write:

$$\triangle ACT \cong$$

Having started with $A$ to name one triangle, you must start with the corresponding letter, $U$, to name the other triangle. Corresponding parts are named in the same order. When you begin with $\triangle ACT$, the complete correct statement is:

$$\triangle ACT \cong \triangle URN$$

**EXAMPLE** The two triangles shown are congruent.

**a.** Name the corresponding angles.

**b.** Name the corresponding sides.

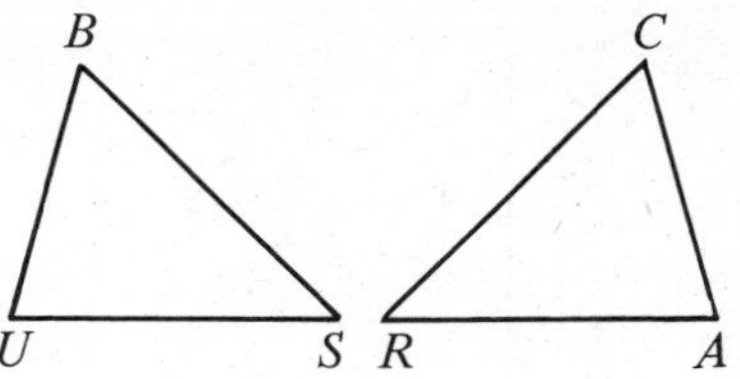


**a.** *Corresponding angles:* $\angle B$ and $\angle C$, $\angle U$ and $\angle A$, $\angle S$ and $\angle R$

**b.** *Corresponding sides:* $\overline{BU}$ and $\overline{CA}$, $\overline{US}$ and $\overline{AR}$, $\overline{SB}$ and $\overline{RC}$

## Classroom Practice

**1.** Name the six parts of $\triangle XYZ$.
$\angle ZXY$, $\angle ZYX$, $\angle Z$, $\overline{XZ}$, $\overline{ZY}$, $\overline{XY}$

**2.** Name the six parts of $\triangle XYW$.
$\angle WXY$, $\angle WYX$, $\angle W$, $\overline{WX}$, $\overline{WY}$, $\overline{XY}$

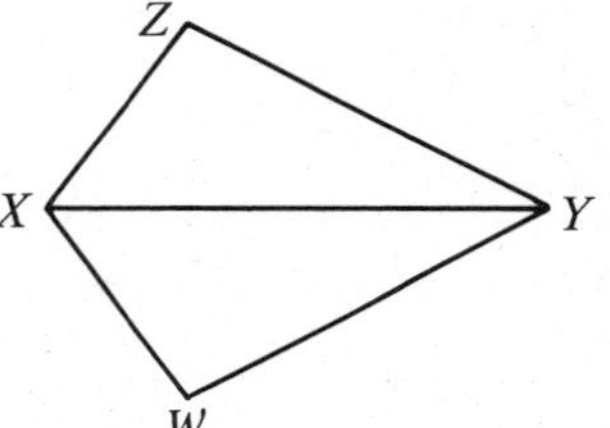


**3.** Kim drew a triangle that is congruent to $\triangle ABC$. Is Kim's triangle acute, right, or obtuse? acute

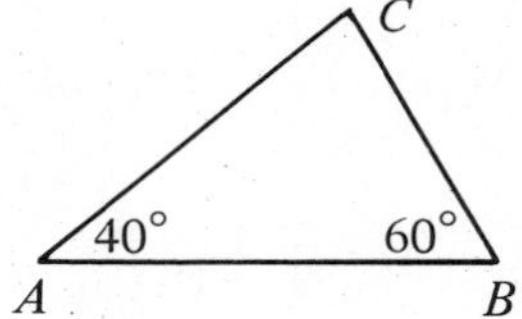


**4.** Aaron drew a triangle that is congruent to $\triangle DEF$. Is Aaron's triangle acute, right, or obtuse? right

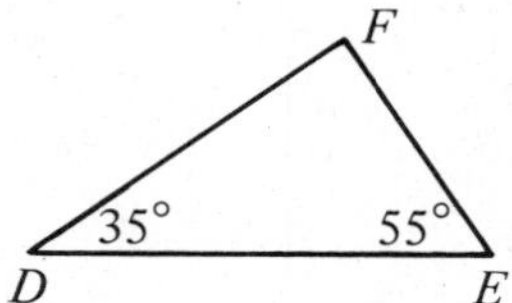


**5.** Do the triangles appear to be congruent? If you can't decide, trace $\triangle ABC$ and slide the tracing over $\triangle XYZ$. Does one triangle fit exactly over the other? yes; yes

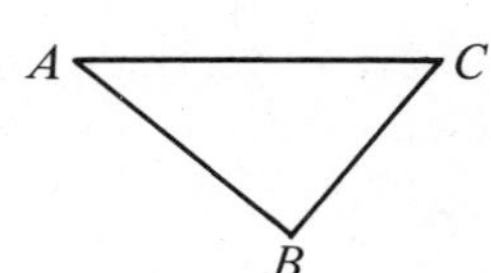


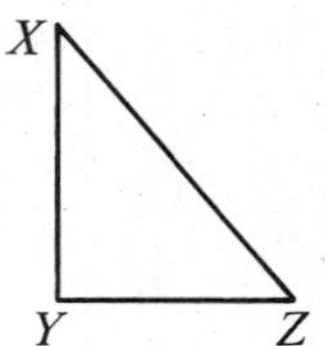

6. Do the triangles appear to be congruent? yes
If you can't decide, trace $\triangle DEF$ and see if your tracing will fit exactly over $\triangle RST$.

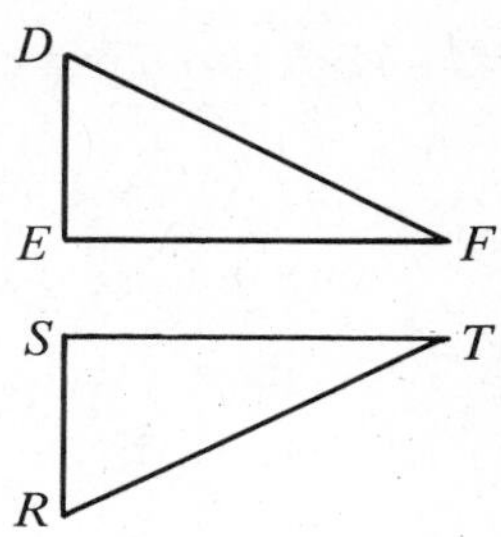


7. *Given:* $\triangle ABC \cong \triangle RST$.

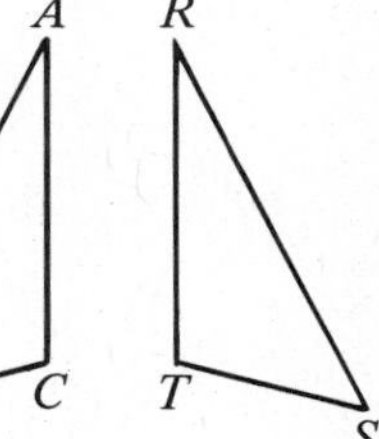


State the part of $\triangle ABC$ that corresponds to the given part of $\triangle RST$.

$\angle R = \underline{\ ?\ }$ $\angle A$ $\quad \angle T = \underline{\ ?\ }$ $\angle C$ $\quad \angle S = \underline{\ ?\ }$ $\angle B$

$RS = \underline{\ ?\ }$ $AB$ $\quad RT = \underline{\ ?\ }$ $AC$ $\quad TS = \underline{\ ?\ }$ $CB$

8. *Given:* $\triangle DEF \cong \triangle VWZ$.

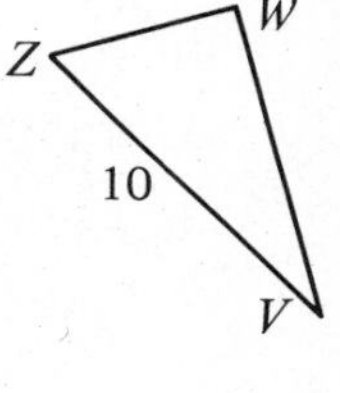


State the angle measures and the segment lengths.

F, 5, 30°, D, $5\sqrt{3}$, E

$\angle W = \underline{\ ?\ }$ 90° $\quad \angle V = \underline{\ ?\ }$ 30° $\quad \angle Z = \underline{\ ?\ }$ 60°

$DF = \underline{\ ?\ }$ 10 $\quad ZW = \underline{\ ?\ }$ 5 $\quad WV = \underline{\ ?\ }$ $5\sqrt{3}$

9. *Given:* $\triangle ABC \cong \triangle RST$.

Complete each statement.

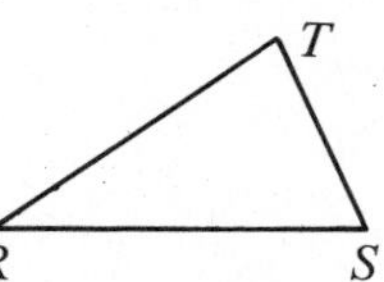


a. $\triangle ACB \cong \triangle \underline{\ ?\ }$ RTS $\quad$ b. $\triangle RST \cong \triangle \underline{\ ?\ }$ ABC

c. $\triangle BAC \cong \triangle \underline{\ ?\ }$ SRT $\quad$ d. $\triangle RTS \cong \triangle \underline{\ ?\ }$ ACB

e. $\triangle CAB \cong \triangle \underline{\ ?\ }$ TRS $\quad$ f. $\triangle TSR \cong \triangle \underline{\ ?\ }$ CBA

g. $\triangle CBA \cong \triangle \underline{\ ?\ }$ TSR $\quad$ h. $\triangle STR \cong \triangle \underline{\ ?\ }$ BCA

T, R, S

10. Mandy said: "Take any three points $X$, $Y$, and $Z$. Draw $\overline{XY}$, $\overline{YZ}$, and $\overline{XZ}$ and you form a triangle."
Was Mandy correct? no

11. Carlos said: "I know a way to pick out three points so you don't get a triangle. Take one point in the middle of the front wall, another point in the ceiling, and a third point on a side wall."
Was Carlos correct? no

## Written Exercises

**In Exercises 1 and 2, copy and complete each statement.**

A **1.** Suppose you know that $\triangle JEM \cong \triangle PIT$.

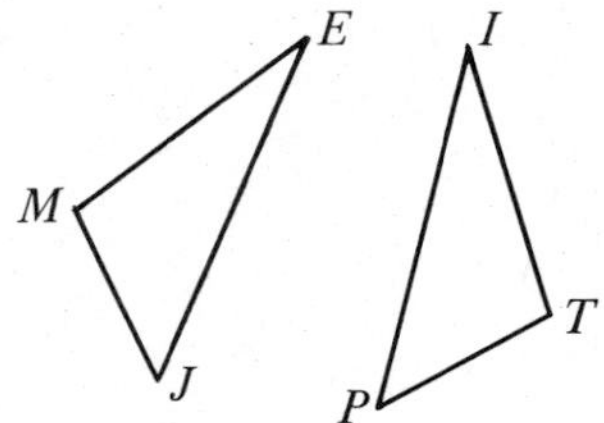


**a.** $\angle J = \underline{\ ?\ }$ ∠P **b.** $\angle M = \underline{\ ?\ }$ ∠T

**c.** $\angle E = \underline{\ ?\ }$ ∠I **d.** $JE = \underline{\ ?\ }$ PI

**e.** $\underline{\ ?\ }$ EJ $= IP$ **f.** $\underline{\ ?\ }$ JM $= PT$

**2.** The statement $\triangle ABC \cong \triangle DEF$ can be a true statement only if:

**a.** $\angle A = \underline{\ ?\ }$ ∠D **b.** $\underline{\ ?\ }$ ∠B $= \angle E$

**c.** $\underline{\ ?\ }$ ∠C $= \angle F$ **d.** $\underline{\ ?\ }$ AB $= DE$

**e.** $\underline{\ ?\ }$ AC $= DF$ **f.** $BC = \underline{\ ?\ }$ EF

**3.** *Given:* $\triangle RST \cong \triangle XYZ$. Write six statements, about equal parts, that follow from the definition of congruent triangles. ∠R = ∠X, ∠S = ∠Y, ∠T = ∠Z, RS = XY, RT = XZ, ST = YZ

**4.** List the six requirements that must be met for the statement $\triangle JKM \cong \triangle PUG$ to be true. ∠J = ∠P, ∠K = ∠U, ∠M = ∠G, JK = PU, JM = PG, KM = UG

**In Exercises 5–8, do the following:**

**a. Plot points *A*, *B*, and *C* on graph paper. Draw $\triangle ABC$.**

**b. Plot points *R*, *E*, and *W*. Draw $\triangle REW$.** (see Solution Key for diagrams)

**c. If possible, complete the statement $\triangle ABC \cong \triangle \underline{\ ?\ }$. Otherwise, write *not congruent*.**

**Sample** $A(-3, -1)$ $B(2, -1)$ $C(2, 1)$
$R(4, 2)$ $E(6, 2)$ $W(6, 7)$

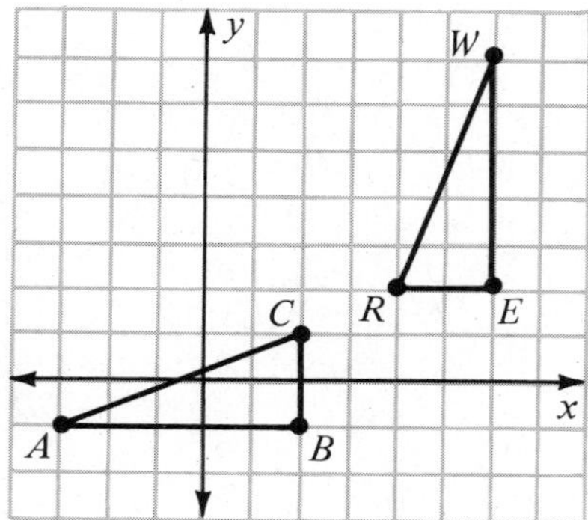


*Answer:* $\triangle ABC \cong \triangle WER$

| | *A* | *B* | *C* | *R* | *E* | *W* |
|---|---|---|---|---|---|---|
| **5.** | $(-3,1)$ | $(2,1)$ | $(0,3)$ | $(4,2)$ | $(9,2)$ | $(7,4)$ |
| **6.** | $(-1,2)$ | $(4,2)$ | $(2,4)$ | $(5,-1)$ | $(7,1)$ | $(10,-1)$ |
| **7.** | $(-6,-3)$ | $(-2,-3)$ | $(-4,0)$ | $(0,1)$ | $(4,1)$ | $(2,2)$ |
| **8.** | $(1,1)$ | $(8,1)$ | $(4,3)$ | $(3,-7)$ | $(5,-3)$ | $(3,0)$ |

5. $\triangle ABC \cong \triangle REW$ 6. $\triangle ABC \cong \triangle WRE$ 7. not congruent 8. $\triangle ABC \cong \triangle WRE$

**Basing your decision on the appearance of the figure, judge whether the statement is correctly written.**

**9.** $\triangle ABC \cong \triangle OND$ no

**10.** $\triangle ABC \cong \triangle DON$ yes

**11.** $\triangle BAC \cong \triangle NOD$ no

**12.** $\triangle CAB \cong \triangle NDO$ yes

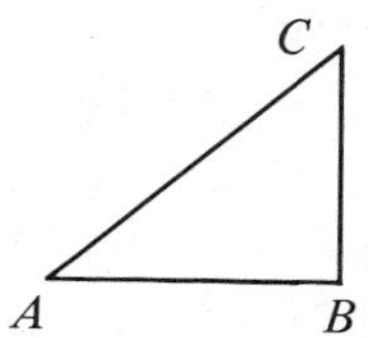

**B** **13.** $\triangle RSJ \cong \triangle CNE$ yes

**14.** $\triangle JRS \cong \triangle ECN$ yes

**15.** $\triangle RJS \cong \triangle NEC$ no

**16.** $\triangle SRJ \cong \triangle ENC$ no

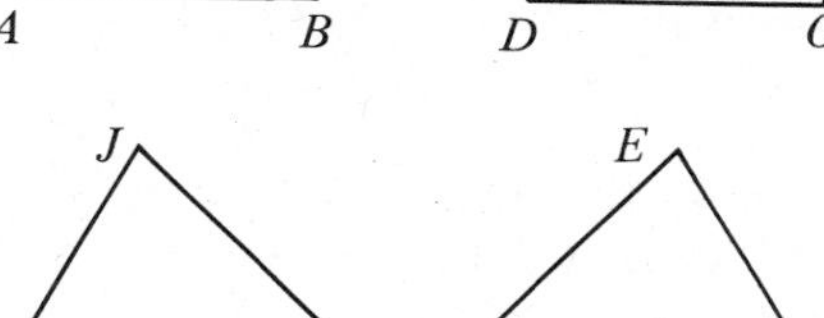

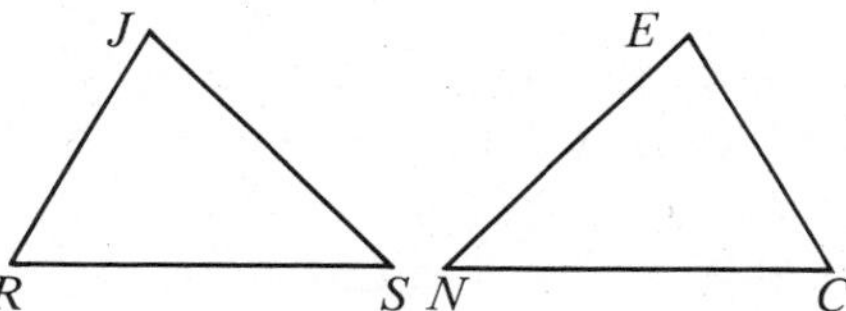

**In each exercise it is given that two triangles are congruent. Judge, from the appearance of the figure, which triangles are congruent. List, in pairs, the corresponding parts.**

**17.** $\triangle MNP \cong \triangle MNQ$

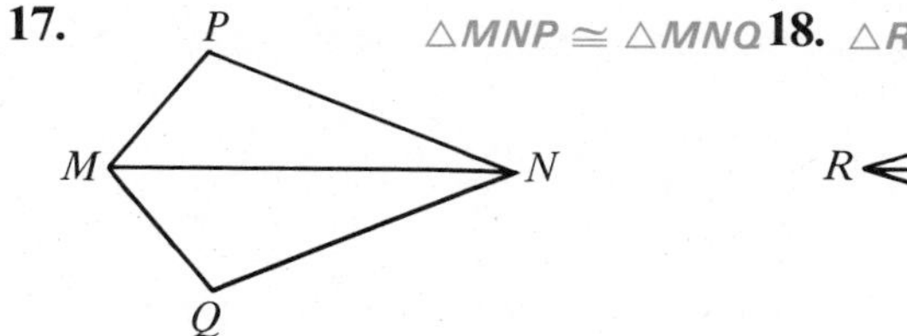

**18.** $\triangle RST \cong \triangle RSQ$

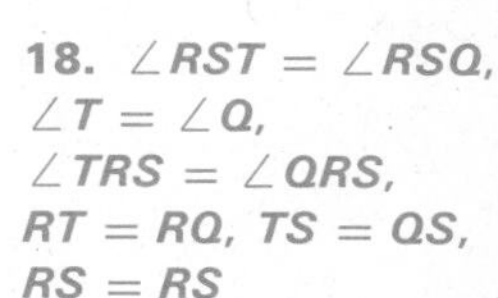

17. $\angle PMN = \angle QMN$, $\angle P = \angle Q$, $\angle PNM = \angle QNM$, $MP = MQ$, $PN = QN$, $MN = MN$

18. $\angle RST = \angle RSQ$, $\angle T = \angle Q$, $\angle TRS = \angle QRS$, $RT = RQ$, $TS = QS$, $RS = RS$

**19.**

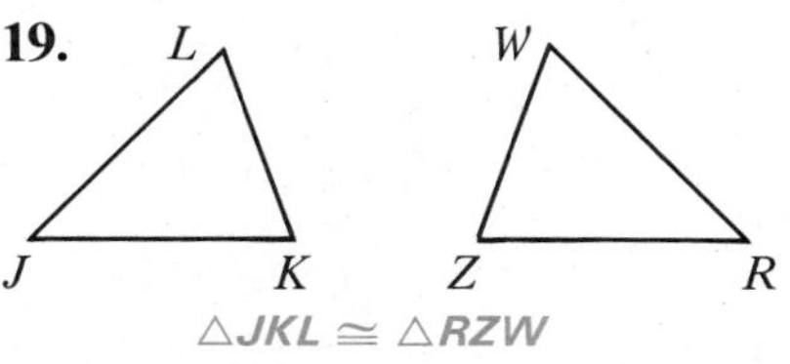

$\triangle JKL \cong \triangle RZW$

**20.**

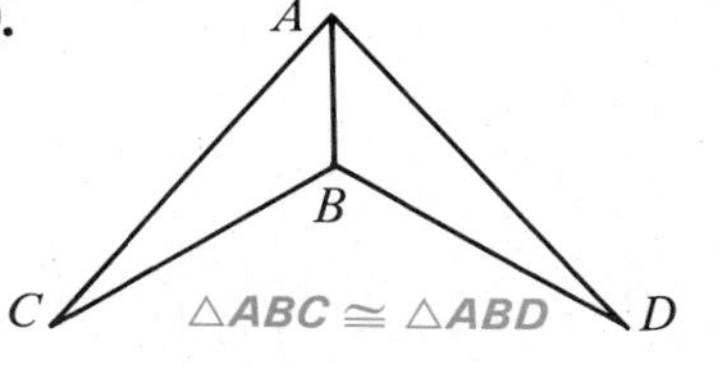

$\triangle ABC \cong \triangle ABD$

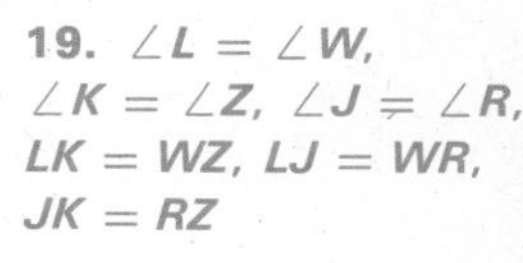

19. $\angle L = \angle W$, $\angle K = \angle Z$, $\angle J = \angle R$, $LK = WZ$, $LJ = WR$, $JK = RZ$

**21.** $\triangle AJX \cong \triangle BKX$

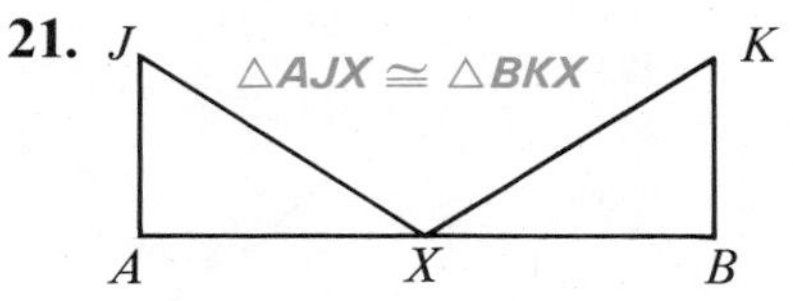

**22.**

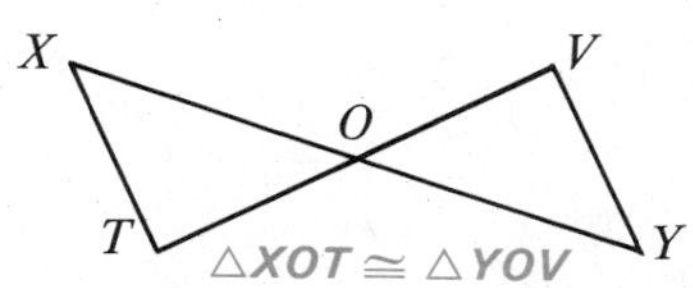

$\triangle XOT \cong \triangle YOV$

20. $\angle C = \angle D$, $\angle CAB = \angle DAB$, $\angle CBA = \angle DBA$, $CB = DB$, $CA = DA$, $AB = AB$

21. $\angle A = \angle B$, $\angle AXJ = \angle BXK$, $\angle J = \angle K$ $AJ = BK$, $AX = BX$, $JX = KX$

22. $\angle X = \angle Y$, $\angle T = \angle V$, $\angle XOT = \angle YOV$; $XT = YV$, $TO = VO$, $YO = XO$

# CAREER NOTES

## *Physical Therapist*

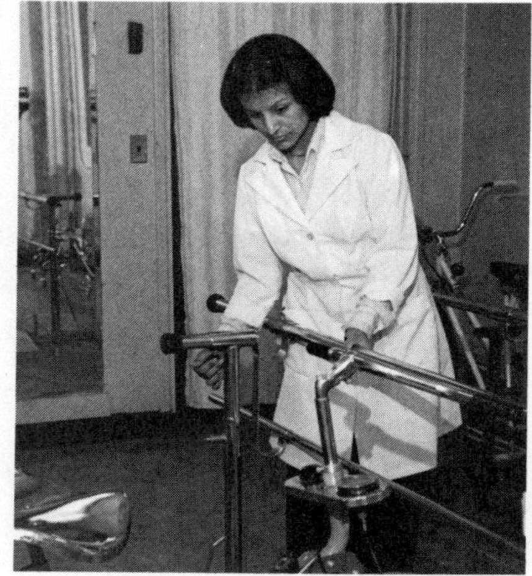

Did you ever squeeze a tennis ball, blow up a balloon, or assemble a jigsaw puzzle? There are millions of disabled people of all ages who find these simple tasks next to impossible. Physical therapists assist people who have nerve, joint, bone, and muscle diseases or injuries.

Physical therapy involves a great deal of knowledge and responsibility. Applicants must earn a degree or certificate from a school of physical therapy and pass an examination to obtain a license to practice.

A significant part of the physical therapist's job is to develop and teach programs for treatment. Therapists use a wide range of tests to chart their patients' conditions. They test for muscular strength, muscular development, respiration, and circulation. They develop exercise programs for their patients. For example, a therapist may prescribe a series of breathing exercises for someone with asthma. Often, when a patient's legs are immobile, a therapist will encourage projects that require hand coordination, such as assembling a jigsaw puzzle.

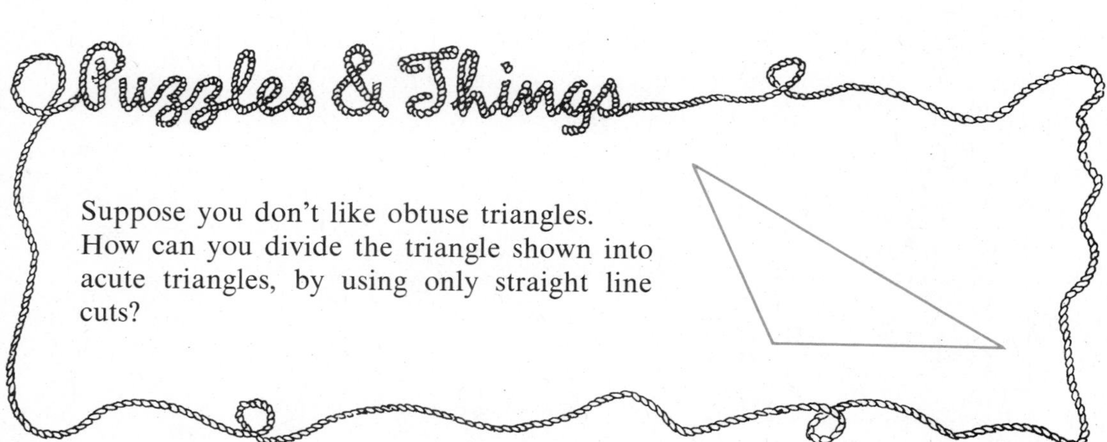


Suppose you don't like obtuse triangles. How can you divide the triangle shown into acute triangles, by using only straight line cuts?

## 4 • The SSS Postulate

Suppose that you are handed the three sticks shown. You fasten the sticks together at the ends to form a triangle.

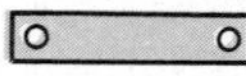

Now suppose someone has a duplicate set of sticks and tries to form a different-looking triangle by joining the sticks at their ends. It is impossible to do this. Only one kind of triangle can be formed from three particular sticks.

The idea suggested by the sticks is a postulate of geometry.

**POSTULATE 9 (SSS Postulate)**

If three sides of one triangle are equal to the corresponding parts of another triangle, the triangles are congruent.

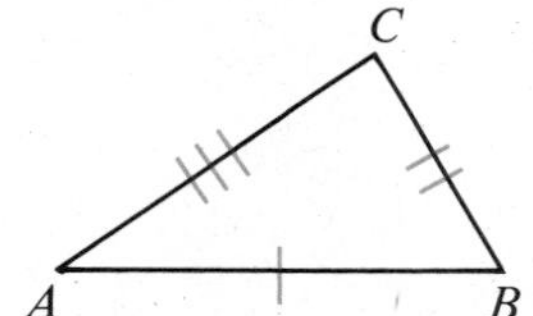


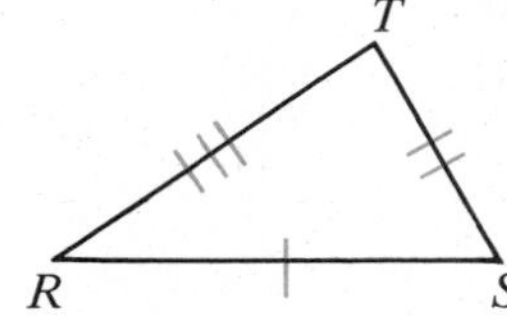


Postulate 9 tells us that $\triangle ABC \cong \triangle RST$.

It follows from the definition of congruent triangles that all six parts of $\triangle ABC$ must be equal to the corresponding parts of $\triangle RST$. Besides the three given pairs of equal sides, we have three pairs of equal angles:

$$\angle A = \angle R \qquad \angle B = \angle S \qquad \angle C = \angle T.$$

Notice in the diagram above that equal sides of the triangles are indicated with marks. $\overline{AB}$ and $\overline{RS}$ each have one mark, $\overline{BC}$ and $\overline{ST}$ each have two, and so on. It is often convenient when writing a proof to mark corresponding sides and angles of congruent triangles.

Suppose someone cannot see that the triangles below are congruent. You can point out:

$AC = RT$ (each length is 10);
$AB = RS$ (each length is 12);
$BC = ST$ (each length is 15).

Then $\triangle ABC \cong \triangle RST$ by the SSS Postulate.

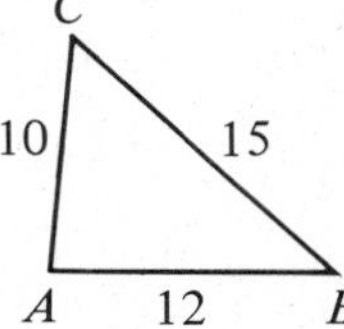


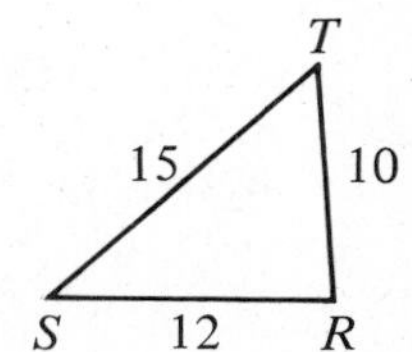

Can you prove that $\triangle XAZ \cong \triangle XBZ$? You can do so if you notice that $\overline{XZ}$ is a side of each of the triangles. Recall, from algebra, that $XZ = XZ$. The length of any segment is equal to itself. We use this idea in the following proof.

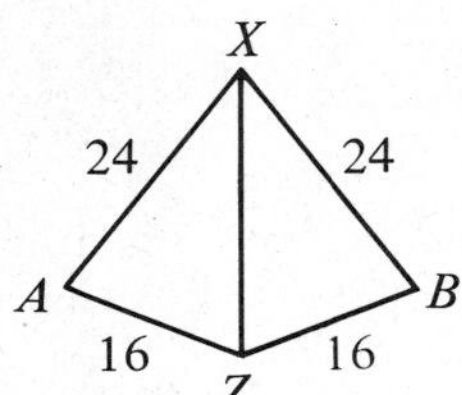


*Given:* $AX = 24$; $BX = 24$
$AZ = 16$; $BZ = 16$

*Prove:* $\triangle XAZ \cong \triangle XBZ$

| STATEMENTS | REASONS |
|---|---|
| 1. $AX = BX$ | 1. *Given:* each length is 24. |
| 2. $AZ = BZ$ | 2. *Given:* each length is 16. |
| 3. $XZ = XZ$ | 3. From algebra |
| 4. $\triangle XAZ \cong \triangle XBZ$ | 4. SSS Postulate |

## Classroom Practice

**1.** To use the SSS Postulate to prove $\triangle JKV \cong \triangle RNC$, you must first show that:

$JK =$ ___?___ RN; $KV =$ ___?___ NC; $JV =$ ___?___ RC.

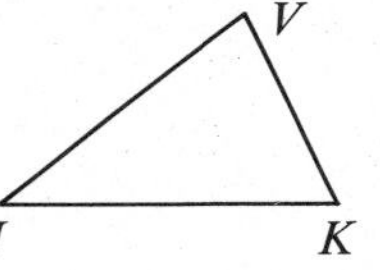


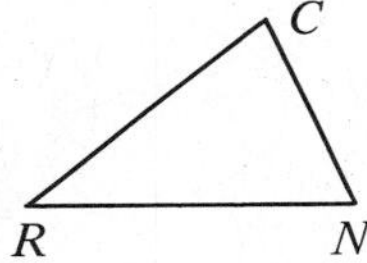


**2.** To use the SSS Postulate to prove $\triangle ABC \cong \triangle VTS$, you must first show that:

$AC =$ ___?___ VS; $AB =$ ___?___ VT; $BC =$ ___?___ TS.

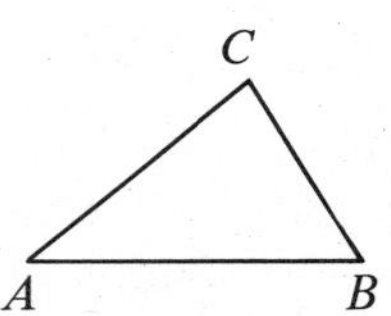


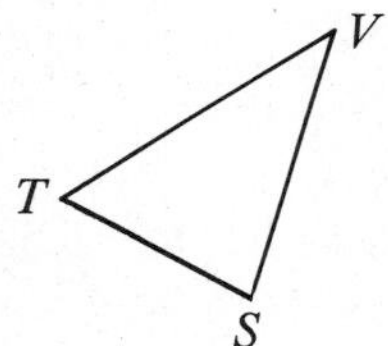


**In Exercises 3–8, the goal is to prove that the two triangles are congruent.**

**3.** Vertex $R$ should be matched with vertex ___?___ H.

**4.** Vertex $T$ should be matched with vertex ___?___ X.

**5.** $\overline{TS}$ and ___?___ $\overline{XK}$ are corresponding sides.

**6.** ___?___ $\overline{TR}$ and $\overline{XH}$ are corresponding sides.

**7.** Is $\triangle RST \cong \triangle KHX$? no

**8.** Is $\triangle RTS \cong \triangle HXK$? yes

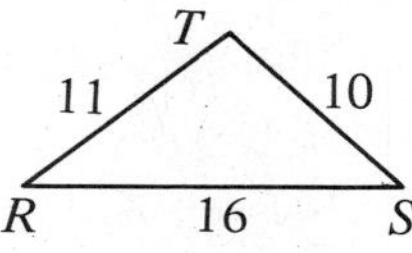


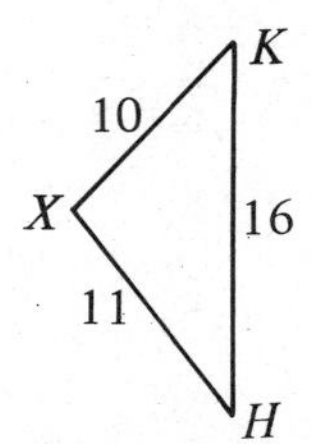

## Written Exercises

**Copy what is shown. Complete the proofs by supplying the reasons.**

A **1.** *Given:* $X$ is the midpoint of $\overline{AB}$ and $\overline{CD}$.
$AC = BD$

*Prove:* $\triangle AXC \cong \triangle BXD$

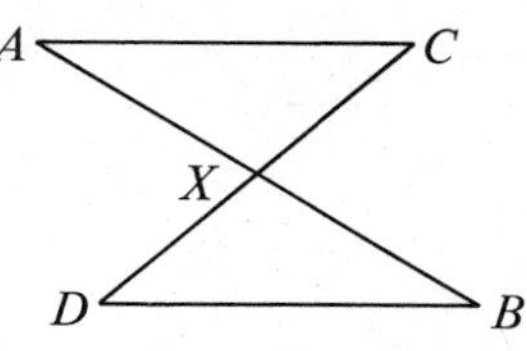


| STATEMENTS | REASONS |
|---|---|
| 1. $CX = DX$ | 1. *Given:* $X$ is the midpoint of ___?___ $\overline{CD}$. |
| 2. $AX = BX$ | 2. ___?___ Given: $X$ is the midpoint of $\overline{AB}$. |
| 3. $AC = BD$ | 3. ___?___ Given |
| 4. $\triangle AXC \cong \triangle BXD$ | 4. ___?___ SSS Postulate |

**2.** *Given:* $S$ is the midpoint of $\overline{TV}$.
$TR = VR$

*Prove:* $\triangle TSR \cong \triangle VSR$

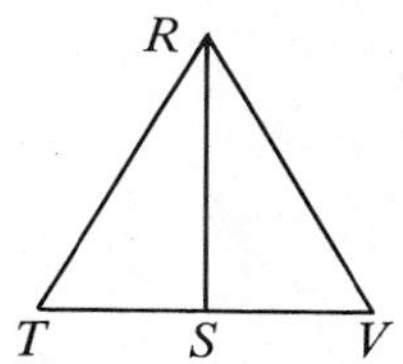


| STATEMENTS | REASONS |
|---|---|
| 1. $TS = VS$ | 1. ___?___ Given: $S$ is the midpoint of $\overline{TV}$. |
| 2. $RS = RS$ | 2. ___?___ From algebra |
| 3. $TR = VR$ | 3. ___?___ Given |
| 4. $\triangle TSR \cong \triangle VSR$ | 4. ___?___ SSS Postulate |

**3.** *Given:* $ZY = WX$
$ZW = YX$

*Prove:* $\triangle WZY \cong \triangle YXW$

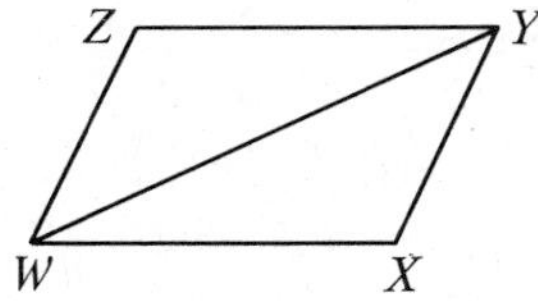


| STATEMENTS | REASONS |
|---|---|
| 1. $ZY = WX$; $ZW = YX$ | 1. ___?___ Given |
| 2. $WY = WY$ | 2. ___?___ From algebra |
| 3. $\triangle WZY \cong \triangle YXW$ | 3. ___?___ SSS Postulate |

**Suppose you wish to use the SSS Postulate to prove that $\triangle DEF \cong \triangle JKM$. What value must $x$ have?**

**4.**

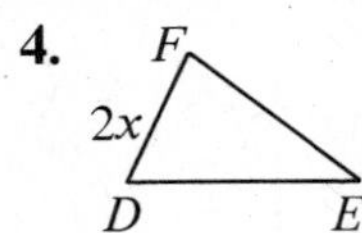


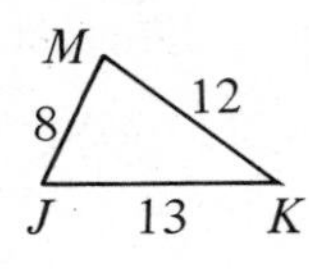


$x = 4$

**5.**

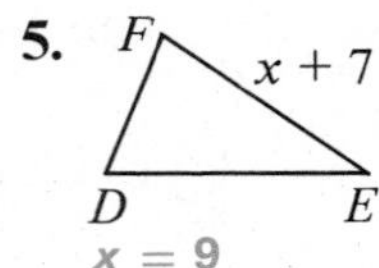


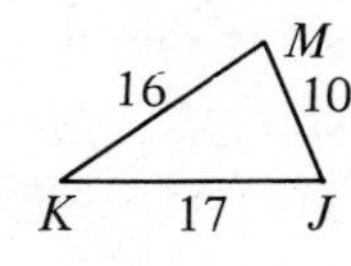


$x = 9$

**6.**

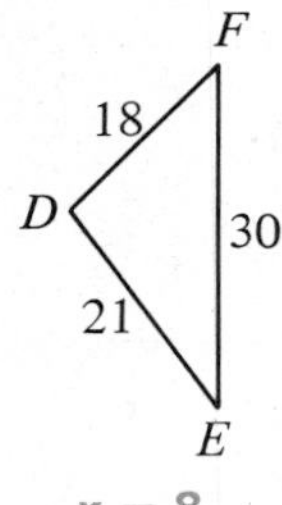


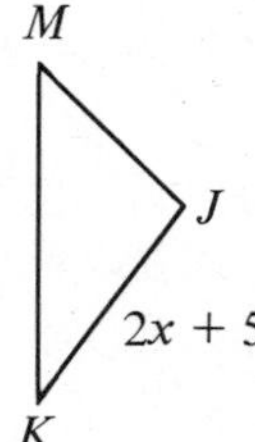


$x = 8$

**7.**

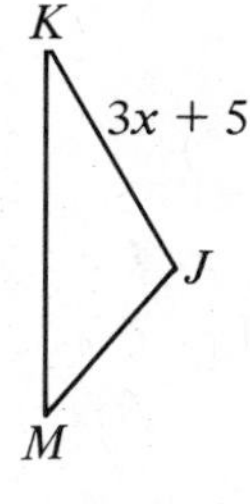


K

3x + 5

J

M

$x = 5\frac{2}{3}$

***Given:*** **$\triangle ABC$ and $\triangle RST$, with $AB = RS$, $BC = ST$, and $AC = RT$. Copy and complete each row of angle measures.**

| | $\angle A$ | $\angle B$ | $\angle C$ | $\angle R$ | $\angle S$ | $\angle T$ |
|---|---|---|---|---|---|---|
| **8.** | 70° | 80° | ? 30° | ? 70° | ? 80° | ? 30° |
| **9.** | 100° | ? 60° | 20° | ? | ? 60° | ? 20° |
| **10.** | ? 65° | 52° | ? 63° | ? 65° | ? 52° | 63° |
| B **11.** | ? $y$° | ? | $x$° | $y$° | ? | ? $x$° |

$\angle R = 100°$

$\angle B = 180° - (x + y)°$, $\angle S = 180° - (x + y)°$

**Draw, on your paper, three segments roughly like those shown.**

A ●————————● B   C ●——————————————● D

E ●————————————————● F

**12.** Construct a segment $\overline{XY}$ so that $XY = AB$.
With $X$ as center, draw an arc with radius $= CD$.
With $Y$ as center, draw an arc with radius $= EF$.
Use $Z$ to label the point where the arcs intersect.
Draw $\overline{XZ}$ and $\overline{YZ}$.

**13.** Construct a segment $\overline{RU}$ so that $RU = AB$.
With $R$ as center, draw an arc with radius $= EF$.
With $U$ as center, draw an arc with radius $= CD$.
Use $N$ to label the point where the arcs intersect.
Draw $\overline{RN}$ and $\overline{UN}$.

14. **a.** Refer to Exercises 12 and 13 to complete the statement:

$$\triangle XYZ \cong \triangle \underline{\ ?\ }.$$ URN

**b.** What postulate supports your answer to part **a**? SSS Postulate

15. **a.** Plot points $A(-7, 1)$, $B(-3, 1)$, and $C(-6, 3)$ on a graph. Draw $\triangle ABC$.

**b.** Plot points $R(2, 0)$ and $S(6, 0)$ on the same graph. Draw $\overline{RS}$.

**c.** On your graph, locate a point $T$ so that the statement $\triangle ABC \cong \triangle RST$ will be true. (*Note:* There is more than one correct point. How many can you find?) There are 2 possible points: (3, 2), (3, −2)

16. **a.** Plot points $D(2, 0)$, $E(2, 7)$, and $F(5, 7)$ on a graph. Draw $\triangle DEF$.

**b.** Plot points $V(-6, 0)$ and $W(-6, 7)$ on the same graph. Draw $\overline{VW}$.

**c.** Locate a point $K$ so that the statement $\triangle DEF \cong \triangle VWK$ will be true. (*Note:* There is more than one correct point.) 2 points: (−3, 7), (−9, 7)

**d.** Locate a point $L$ so that the statement $\triangle DEF \cong \triangle WVL$ will be true. (*Note:* There is more than one correct point.) 2 points: (−3, 0), (−9, 0)

17. To strengthen a triangular frame, Mona fastened three additional sticks as shown. How many triangles were formed? 16 triangles

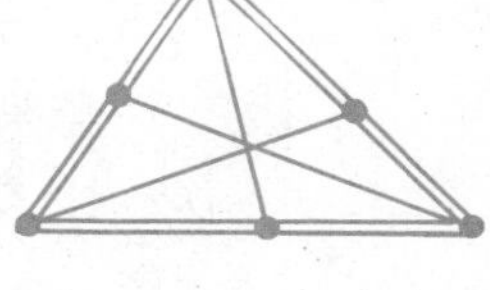

**For each exercise, copy what is shown. Then write a complete proof in two-column form.**

C 18. *Given:* $N$ is the midpoint of $\overline{AB}$.
$AX = BY$
$NX = NY$

*Prove:* $\triangle AXN \cong \triangle BYN$

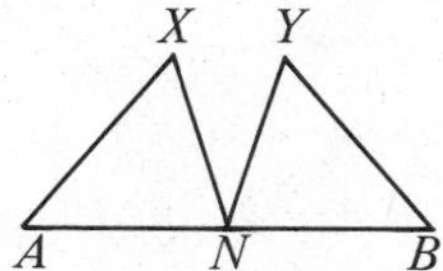


19. *Given:* $RT = RV$
$TS = VS$

*Prove:* $\triangle RST \cong \triangle RSV$

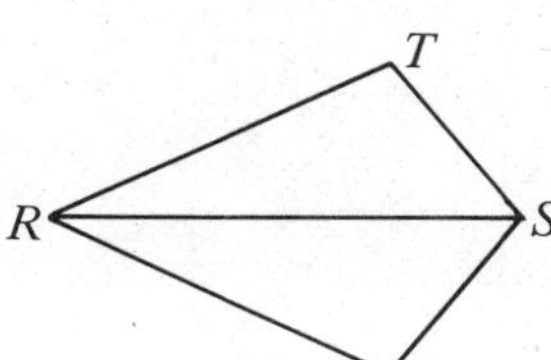


20. *Given:* $JK = MN$
$NJ = 9$
$KM = 9$

*Prove:* $\triangle NJK \cong \triangle KMN$

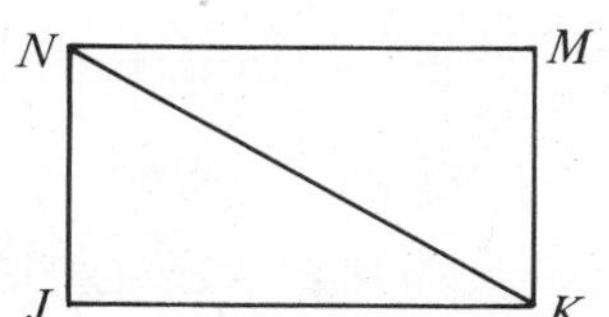

## SELF-TEST

**You are given: $\triangle PEN \cong \triangle JOB$. Complete the statements.**

**1.** $\triangle NEP \cong \triangle$ ___?___ BOJ  **2.** $\angle E =$ ___?___ $\angle O$  **3.** $OJ =$ ___?___ EN

**4.** Supply reasons to complete the proof.

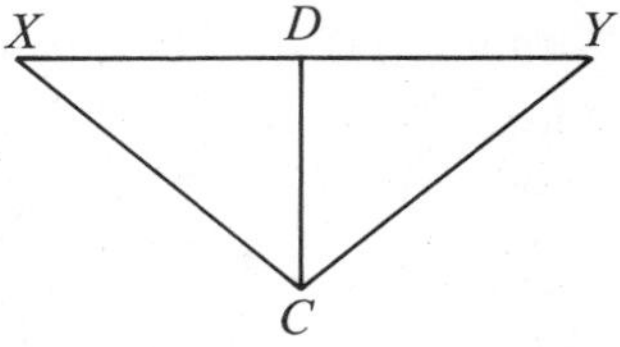


*Given:* $CX = CY$

$D$ is the midpoint of $\overline{XY}$.

*Prove:* $\triangle CDX \cong \triangle CDY$

| STATEMENTS | REASONS |
|---|---|
| 1. $CX = CY$ | 1. ___?___ Given |
| 2. $CD = CD$ | 2. ___?___ From algebra |
| 3. $DX = DY$ | 3. ___?___ Given: $D$ is the midpoint of $\overline{XY}$. |
| 4. $\triangle CDX \cong \triangle CDY$ | 4. ___?___ SSS Postulate |

"DOES ANYONE REMEMBER WHAT WE SET OUT TO PROVE?"

## 5 • The SAS Postulate

Suppose you have two sticks. You fasten them together at a 40° angle.

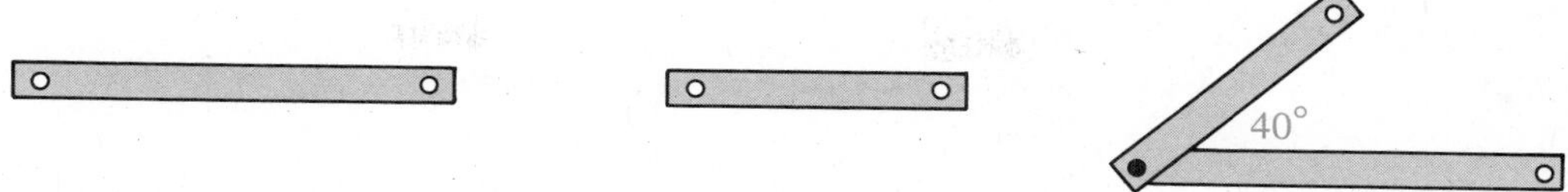


There is only one way to finish forming a triangle. A third stick must be of just the right length.

Think again of the two sticks. What would happen if the sticks were fastened like this?

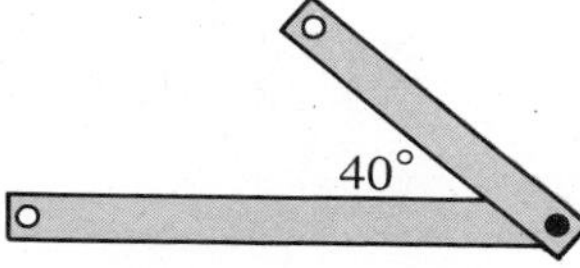


Would the triangle you could form be a different-looking triangle? To decide, you can perform an experiment in your mind.

Flip

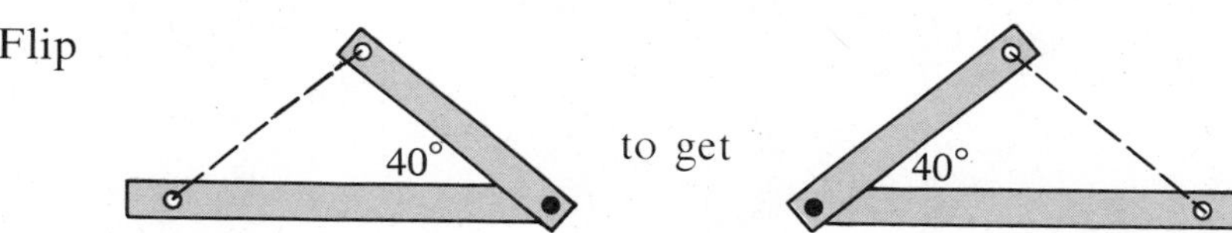


The models are identical.

When two sticks are joined at a certain angle, a third stick must be of just the right length to form a triangle. The triangle can have only one size and shape.

The 40° angle is included between the sides formed by the two sticks. Look at $\triangle DEF$.

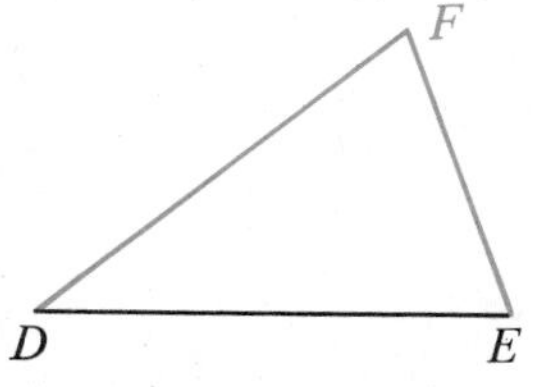


$\angle F$ is *included between* sides $\overline{FD}$ and $\overline{FE}$. $\angle F$ is *opposite* side $\overline{DE}$.

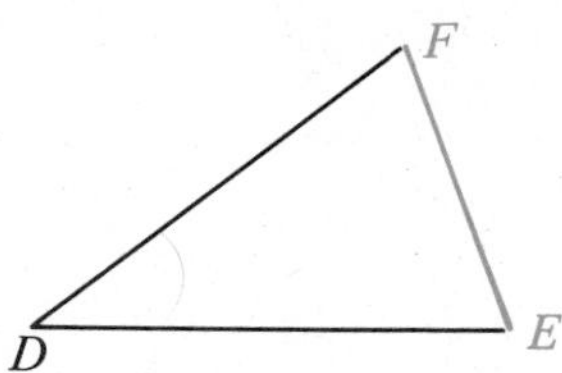


Side $\overline{EF}$ is *included between* $\angle E$ and $\angle F$. $\overline{EF}$ is *opposite* $\angle D$.

**POSTULATE 10 (SAS Postulate)**

If two sides and the included angle of one triangle are equal to the corresponding parts of another triangle, the triangles are congruent.

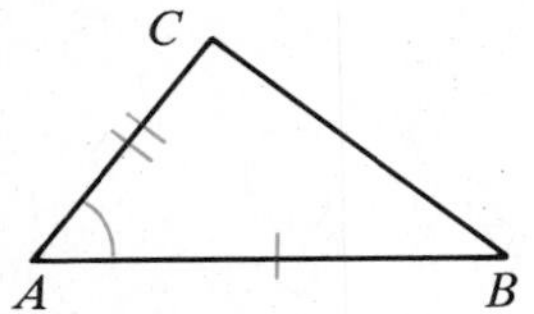


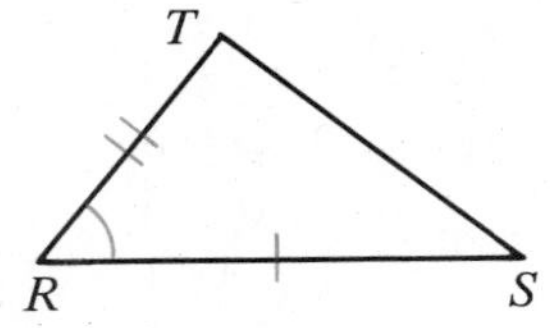


Postulate 10 tells us that $\triangle ABC \cong \triangle RST$.

## *Classroom Practice*

**Complete each statement.**

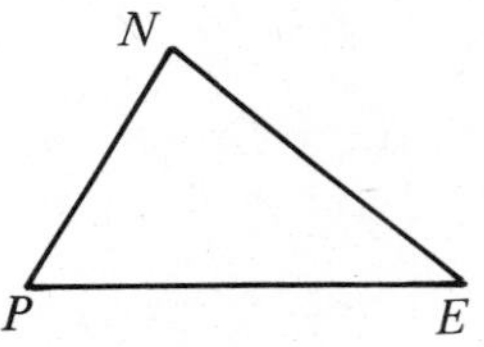


1. $\angle E$ lies opposite side ___?___ $\overline{PN}$.
2. $\angle E$ is included between sides ___?___ $\overline{PE}$ and $\overline{NE}$ ___?___.
3. $\angle$ ___?___ $N$ lies opposite side $\overline{PE}$.
4. $\angle$ ___?___ $P$ is included between sides $\overline{PN}$ and $\overline{PE}$.
5. Side $\overline{NE}$ is included between $\angle$ ___?___ $N$ and $\angle$ ___?___ $E$.
6. Side ___?___ $\overline{PN}$ is included between $\angle P$ and $\angle N$.

**In Exercises 7–12, two triangles are to be proved congruent.**

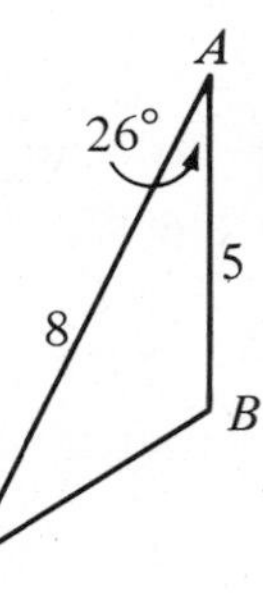


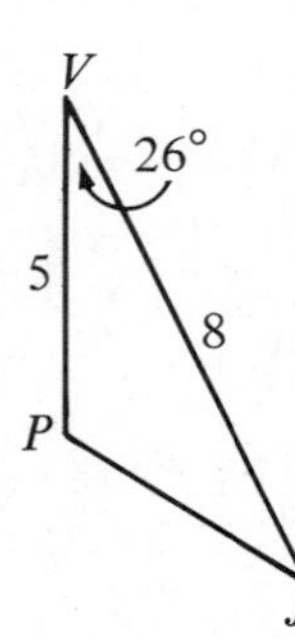


7. Vertex $A$ should be paired with vertex ___?___ $V$.
8. Vertex ___?___ $C$ should be paired with vertex $J$.
9. $\overline{AB}$ and ___?___ $\overline{VP}$ are corresponding sides.
10. ___?___ $\overline{AC}$ and $\overline{VJ}$ are corresponding sides.

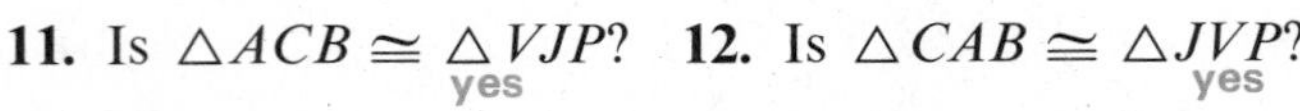

11. Is $\triangle ACB \cong \triangle VJP$? yes
12. Is $\triangle CAB \cong \triangle JVP$? yes

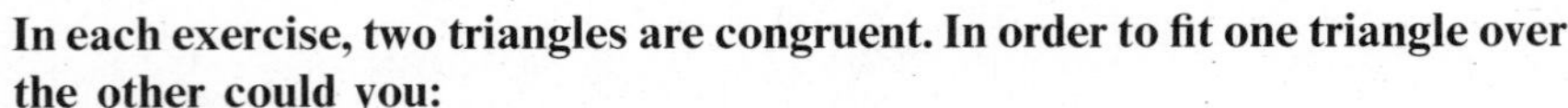

**In each exercise, two triangles are congruent. In order to fit one triangle over the other could you:**
**a. slide the first triangle over the second?**
**b. flip the first triangle and then slide it over the second?**

**13.** b

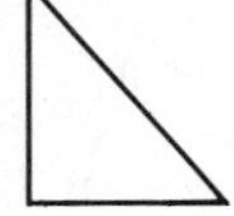
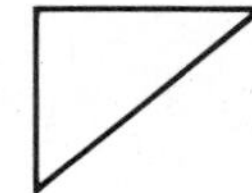

**14.** b

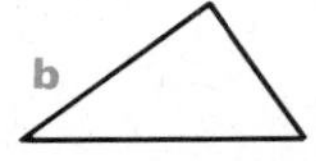

**15.** b

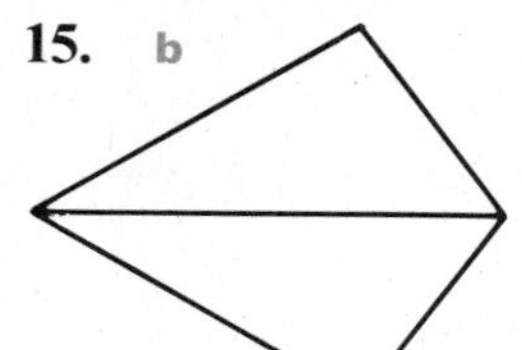

**16.** b

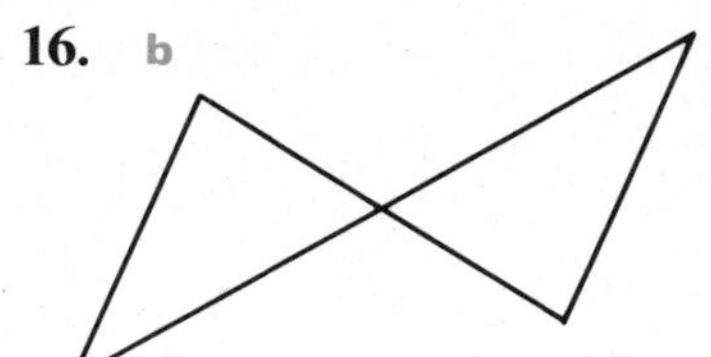

**17.** b

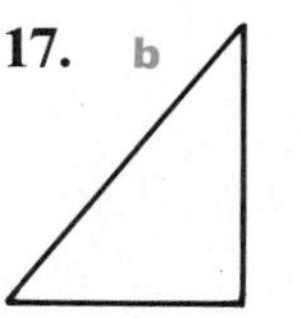

**18.** a

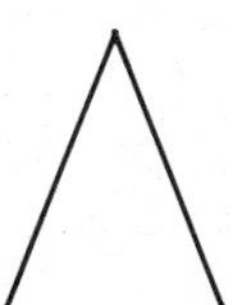

## Written Exercises

**In Exercises 1–4, we will prove that $\triangle ABC \cong \triangle JKN$.**

A **1.** Is $AB = JK$? Is $BC = KN$? Why? Yes; yes; the lengths of each pair of sides are equal.

**2.** Is $\angle B = \angle K$? Why? Yes; each is $90°$.

**3.** Do you know that two sides and the included angle of $\triangle ABC$ are equal to the corresponding parts of $\triangle JKN$? yes

**4.** State the postulate that supports the statement $\triangle ABC \cong \triangle JKN$. SAS Postulate

**In Exercises 5–8, we will prove that $\triangle PXQ \cong \triangle RXS$.**

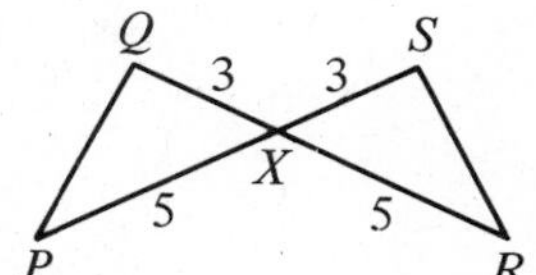


**5.** In $\triangle PXQ$, what angle is included between sides $\overline{XQ}$ and $\overline{XP}$? In $\triangle RXS$, what angle is included between sides $\overline{XS}$ and $\overline{XR}$? $\angle QXP$, $\angle SXR$

**6.** Is $\angle PXQ = \angle RXS$? Why? Yes; vertical angles are =.

**7.** Is $QX = SX$? Is $PX = RX$? yes; yes

**8.** To support the statement $\triangle PXQ \cong \triangle RXS$, would you use the SSS Postulate or the SAS Postulate? SAS Postulate

**State whether the SSS Postulate or the SAS Postulate could be used to prove the triangles congruent.**

**9.**

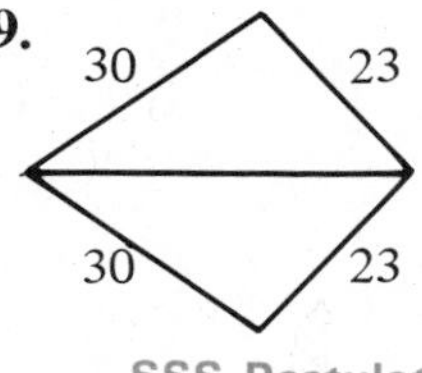


SSS Postulate

**10.**

SAS Postulate

**11.**

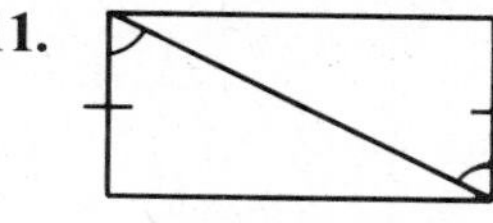

SAS Postulate

**Complete the proofs by supplying the reasons.**

**12.** *Given:* $\angle A = 40°$
$\angle R = 40°$
$AB = RS$
$AC = RT$

*Prove:* $\triangle ABC \cong \triangle RST$

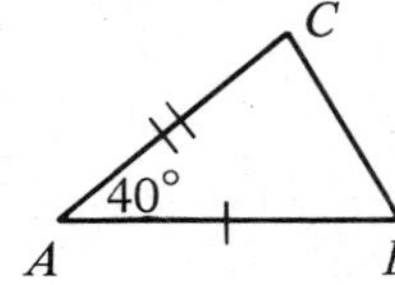


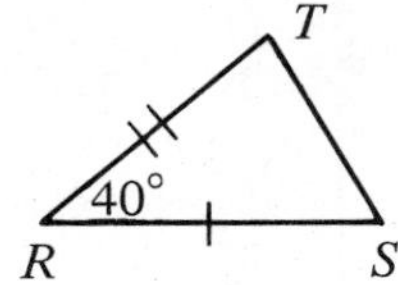


| STATEMENTS | REASONS |
|---|---|
| 1. $\angle A = \angle R$ | 1. *Given:* each angle has measure ?. 40° |
| 2. $AB = RS$; $AC = RT$ | 2. ? Given |
| 3. $\triangle ABC \cong \triangle RST$ | 3. ? SAS Postulate |

**13.** *Given:* $\overrightarrow{ZW}$ bisects $\angle XZY$.
$XZ = YZ$

*Prove:* $\triangle XWZ \cong \triangle YWZ$

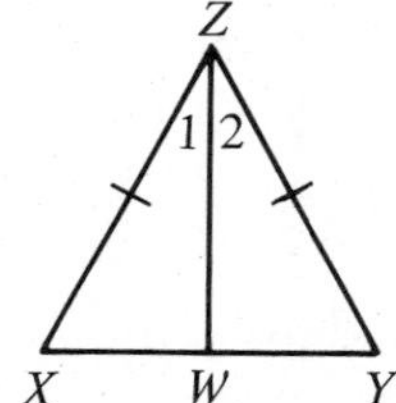


| STATEMENTS | REASONS |
|---|---|
| 1. $\angle 1 = \angle 2$ | 1. ? Given: $\overrightarrow{ZW}$ bisects $\angle XZY$. |
| 2. $ZW = ZW$ | 2. ? From algebra |
| 3. $XZ = YZ$ | 3. ? Given |
| 4. $\triangle XWZ \cong \triangle YWZ$ | 4. ? SAS Postulate |

**Draw, on your paper, an angle and two segments roughly like those shown.**

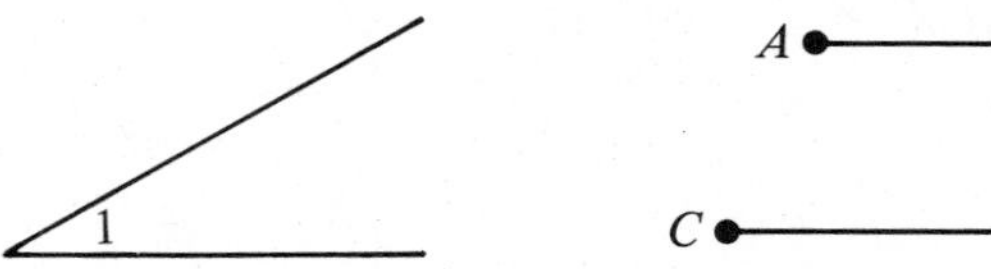


B **14.** Construct an angle equal to $\angle 1$. Call it $\angle R$.
On one side of $\angle R$, construct $\overline{RS}$ so that $RS = AB$.
On the other side of $\angle R$, construct $\overline{RT}$ so that $RT = CD$.
Draw $\overline{ST}$.

**15.** Repeat Exercise 14, using $X$, $Y$, and $Z$ instead of $R$, $S$, and $T$.
What postulate supports the statement: $\triangle RST \cong \triangle XYZ$? SAS Postulate

**16.** Complete the proof by supplying the reasons.

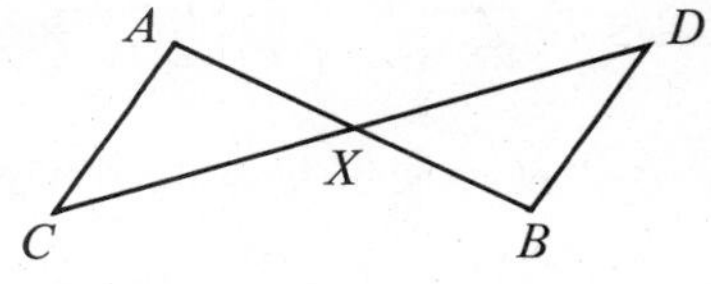


*Given:* $X$ is the midpoint of $\overline{AB}$ and $\overline{CD}$.

*Prove:* $\triangle AXC \cong \triangle BXD$

| STATEMENTS | REASONS |
|---|---|
| 1. $CX = DX$ | 1. *Given:* $X$ is __?__. the midpoint of $\overline{CD}$ |
| 2. $AX = BX$ | 2. __?__ Given: $X$ is the midpoint of $\overline{AB}$. |
| 3. $\angle AXC = \angle BXD$ | 3. __?__ Vertical angles are equal. |
| 4. $\triangle AXC \cong \triangle BXD$ | 4. __?__ SAS Postulate |

**17.** *Given:* $RS = VT$
$\overline{RS} \parallel \overline{VT}$

*Prove:* $\triangle VRS \cong \triangle STV$

Copy what is shown.
Then write a proof in two-column form.

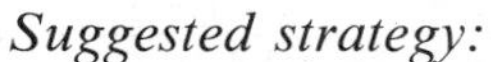

*Suggested strategy:*

A. Use the parallel lines to prove two angles equal.
B. Use the fact that $\overline{SV}$ is a side of each triangle.
C. List enough equal parts so that you can use the SSS Postulate or the SAS Postulate.

**Copy what is shown. Then write a proof in two-column form.**

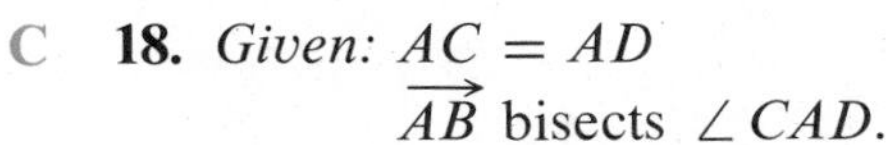

C **18.** *Given:* $AC = AD$
$\overrightarrow{AB}$ bisects $\angle CAD$.

*Prove:* $\triangle ABC \cong \triangle ABD$

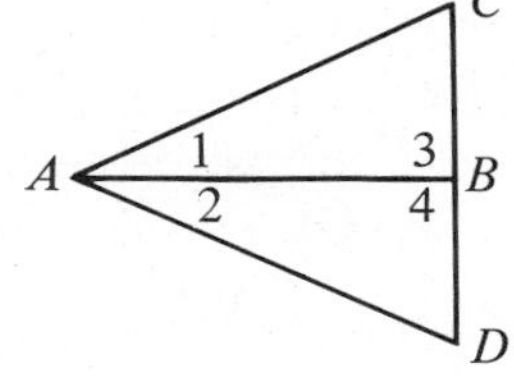


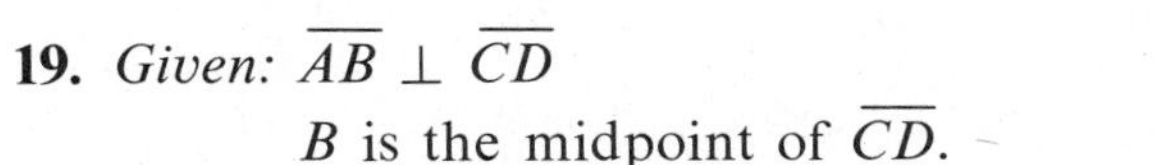

**19.** *Given:* $\overline{AB} \perp \overline{CD}$
$B$ is the midpoint of $\overline{CD}$.

*Prove:* $\triangle ABC \cong \triangle ABD$

**20.** Refer to the figure shown. We wish to prove the following: If the two legs of one right triangle are equal to the two legs of another right triangle, then the triangles are congruent.

**a.** List what is given and what is to be proved, in terms of the diagram. Given: $\triangle ABC$ and $\triangle RST$ are right triangles; $AB = RS$; $BC = ST$. Prove: $\triangle ABC \cong \triangle RST$

**b.** Write a proof in two-column form.

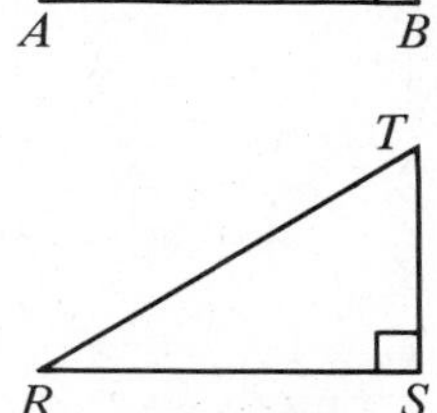

## Class Experiment

**Each student will need paper, scissors, a pencil, a ruler, and a protractor.**

1. Draw a segment 20 cm long.
2. Choosing either endpoint of the segment, draw a ray so that a 35° angle is formed.
3. From the endpoint of that ray, mark off a segment 15 cm long.
4. Connect the two free endpoints to form a triangle.
5. Shade the triangular region and cut out the triangle.

Now students should compare their models until they agree on answers to the following questions.

**a.** Are there some pairs of triangles that fit exactly, one over the other, each with the shaded side up?

**b.** Are there some pairs that fit exactly when the shaded side of one triangle faces up and that of the other triangle faces down?

**c.** Are there any two models that don't fit at all? Should there be?

All the triangles should fit exactly with the shaded side up. (SAS Postulate)

## CONSUMER CORNER

### The Cost of Driving

Buying a car is a major investment. It takes money to operate a car, too. The owner must pay for gas, oil, repairs, parking fees, tolls, taxes, and insurance. A car also loses some of its resale value every day due to normal wear and tear. This loss is called *depreciation.*

Taking all of these factors into account, we can estimate the average cost of 1 km of driving:

| | |
|---|---|
| standard-size car | 18¢ |
| compact car | 14¢ |
| sub-compact car | 13¢ |

For many trips, a car is the most convenient and the least expensive method of transportation. This is particularly true if several people are traveling together. For some short trips, however, public transportation might cost less money. Don't forget that walking is free!

## 6 • The ASA Postulate

The diagram shows three sticks. The fasteners at $A$ and $B$ allow sticks $l$ and $m$ to turn.

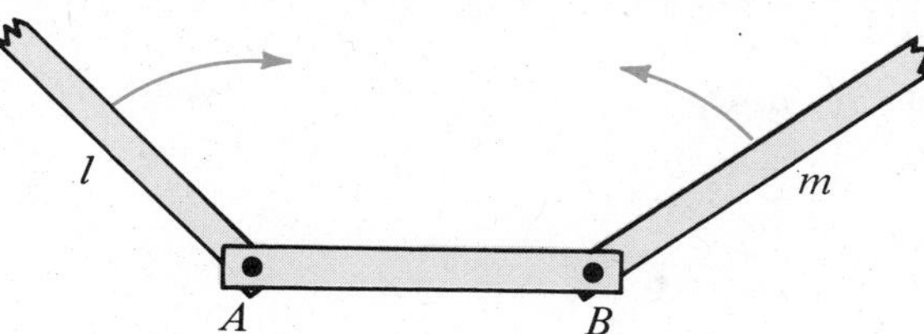


Stick $l$ is rotated until $\angle A = 40°$. Stick $m$ is rotated until $\angle B = 60°$.

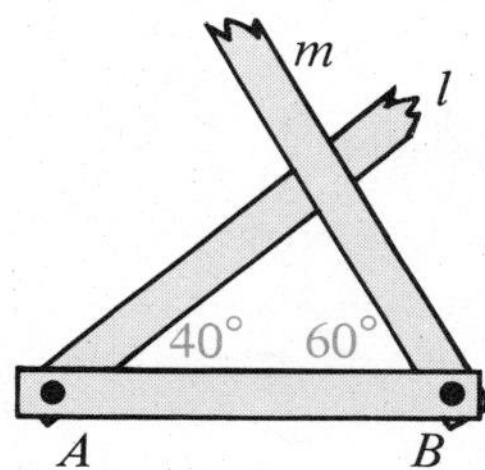


The extra wood is sawed off and a fastener is attached at $C$.

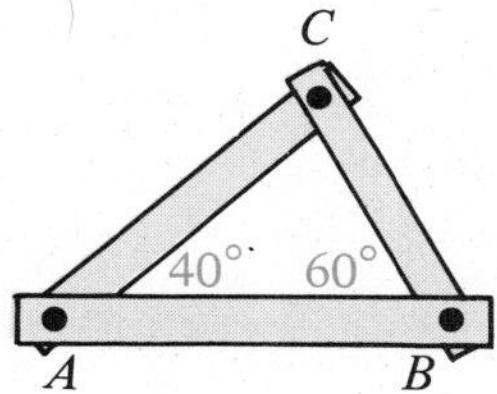


Do you see that for a particular length $AB$, a 40° angle at $A$, and a 60° angle at $B$, only one kind of triangle is possible?

**POSTULATE 11 (ASA Postulate)**

If two angles and the included side of one triangle are equal to the corresponding parts of another triangle, the triangles are congruent.

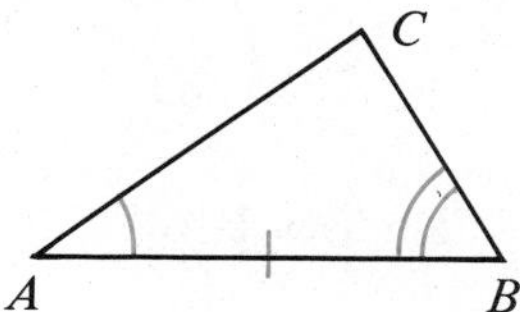


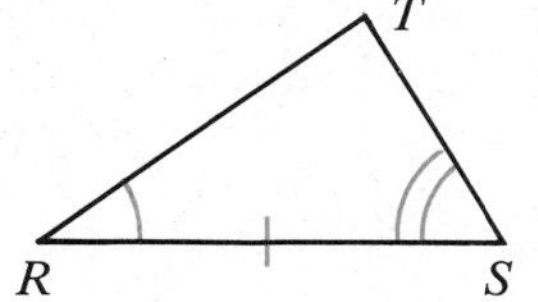


Postulate 11 tells us that $\triangle ABC \cong \triangle RST$.

## Classroom Practice

**Name the side included between the two angles.**

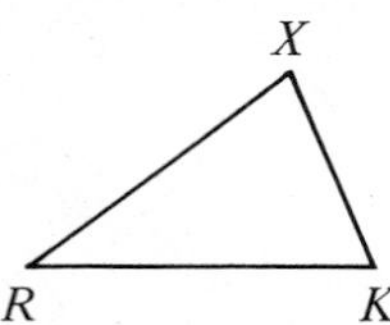


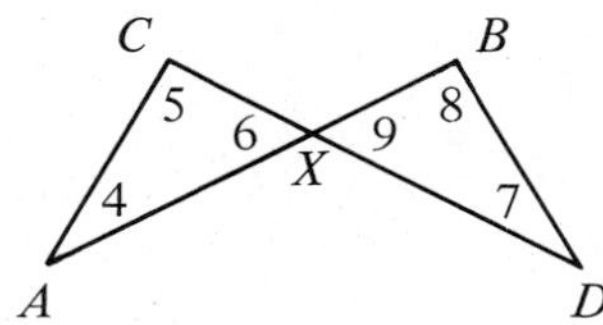


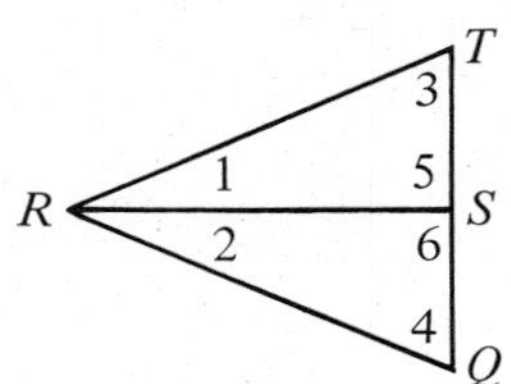


1. $\angle R$ and $\angle K$ $\overline{RK}$
2. $\angle X$ and $\angle R$ $\overline{XR}$
3. $\angle 5$ and $\angle 6$ $\overline{CX}$
4. $\angle 7$ and $\angle 8$ $\overline{BD}$
5. $\angle 1$ and $\angle 5$ $\overline{RS}$
6. $\angle 6$ and $\angle 4$ $\overline{SQ}$

**Suppose you know that $\angle K = \angle X$ and $KL = XO$.**

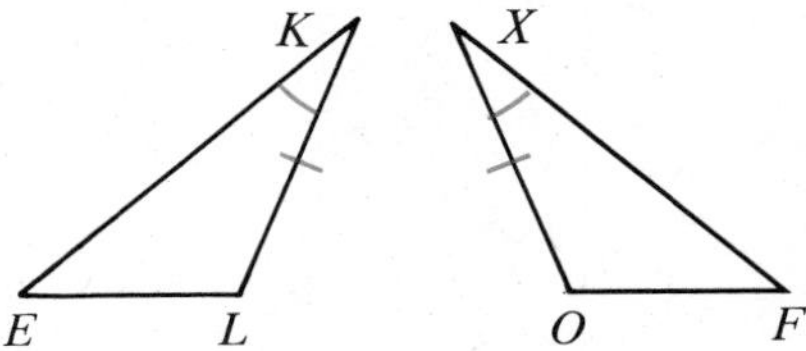


7. To use the ASA Postulate to prove that $\triangle ELK \cong \triangle FOX$, you must also show that __?__. $\angle L = \angle O$

8. To use the SAS Postulate to prove that $\triangle ELK \cong \triangle FOX$, you must also show that __?__. $KE = XF$

9. *Given:* $\overrightarrow{RS}$ bisects $\angle XRY$.
   $S$ is the midpoint of $\overline{XY}$.
   $\overline{RS} \perp \overline{XY}$

   Could you prove that $\triangle RSX \cong \triangle RSY$
   
   **a.** by using the SSS Postulate? no
   
   **b.** by using the SAS Postulate? yes
   
   **c.** by using the ASA Postulate? yes

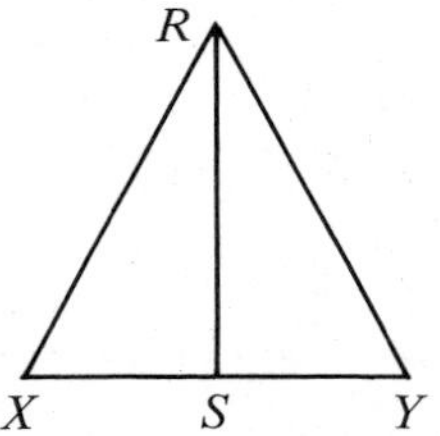


## Written Exercises

A

1. If $\angle A = \angle J$, $\angle B = \angle X$, and $AB = JX$, then you can use the ASA Postulate to conclude $\triangle ABC \cong \triangle$ __?__. $JXP$

2. You intend to use the ASA Postulate to prove $\triangle ABC \cong \triangle JXP$. You have stated that $\angle C = \angle P$ and $\angle B = \angle X$. You also need the statement __?__ = __?__. $CB$ $PX$

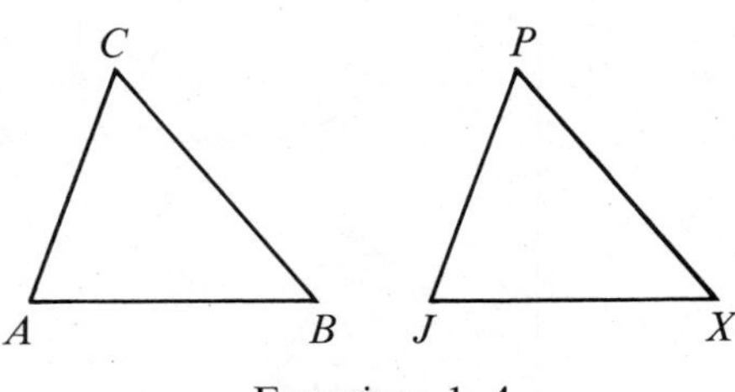


Exercises 1–4

3. You intend to use the SAS Postulate to prove $\triangle ABC \cong \triangle JXP$. You have stated that $\angle A = \angle J$ and $AB = JX$. You also need the statement $\underline{\ ?\ }$ = $\underline{\ ?\ }$.
CA PJ

4. You intend to use the ASA Postulate to prove $\triangle ABC \cong \triangle JXP$. You have stated that $AC = JP$ and $\angle C = \angle P$. You also need the statement $\underline{\ ?\ }$ = $\underline{\ ?\ }$.
$\angle A$ $\angle J$

**In Exercises 5 and 6, state the reasons that are needed to complete the proofs.**

5. *Given:* $\angle D = \angle R$; $\angle F = \angle T$
$DF = 8$; $RT = 8$

*Prove:* $\triangle DEF \cong \triangle RST$

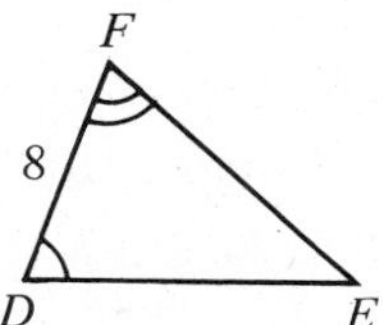


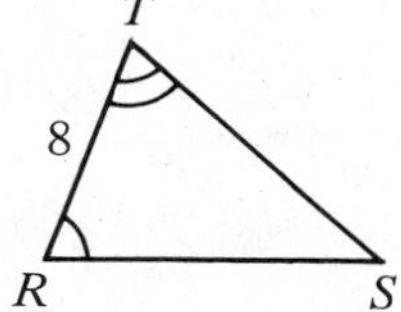


| STATEMENTS | REASONS |
|---|---|
| 1. $\angle D = \angle R$; $\angle F = \angle T$ | 1. ? Given |
| 2. $DF = RT$ | 2. *Given:* each length ? . equals 8 |
| 3. $\triangle DEF \cong \triangle RST$ | 3. ? ASA Postulate |

6. *Given:* $M$ is the midpoint of $\overline{YZ}$.
$\overrightarrow{MY}$ bisects $\angle OMV$.
$\angle Y = \angle Z$

*Prove:* $\triangle YOM \cong \triangle ZUM$

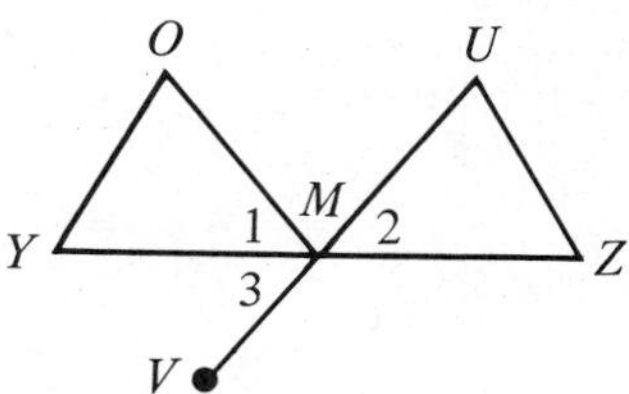


| STATEMENTS | REASONS |
|---|---|
| 1. $\angle 1 = \angle 3$ | 1. ? Given: $\overrightarrow{MY}$ bisects $\angle OMV$. |
| 2. $\angle 2 = \angle 3$ | 2. ? Vertical angles are equal. |
| 3. $\angle 1 = \angle 2$ | 3. ? Substitution Postulate |
| 4. $YM = ZM$ | 4. ? Given: $M$ is the midpoint of $\overline{YZ}$. |
| 5. $\angle Y = \angle Z$ | 5. ? Given |
| 6. $\triangle YOM \cong \triangle ZUM$ | 6. ? ASA Postulate |

**Draw, on your paper, two angles and a segment roughly like those shown.**

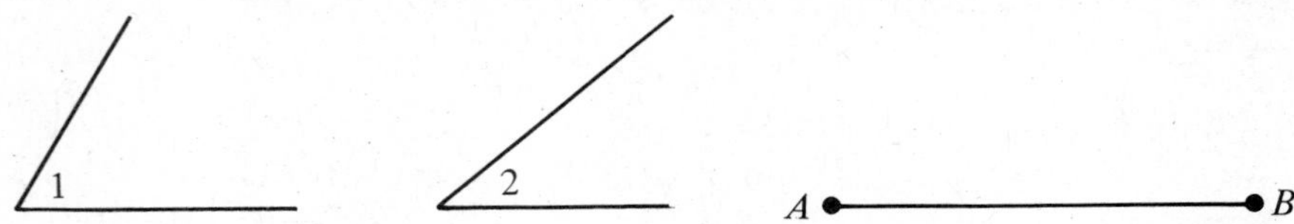


B **7.** Construct a segment $\overline{RS}$ so that $RS = AB$.
Using $\overline{RS}$ as one side, construct $\angle R = \angle 1$.
Using $\overline{SR}$ as one side, construct $\angle S = \angle 2$.
Use $T$ to label the point where two rays intersect.

**8.** Construct a segment $\overline{EZ}$ so that $EZ = AB$.
Using $\overline{EZ}$ as one side, construct $\angle E = \angle 2$.
Using $\overline{ZE}$ as one side, construct $\angle Z = \angle 1$.
Use $N$ to label the point where two rays intersect.

**9. a.** Refer to Exercises 7 and 8 to complete the statement:

$$\triangle RTS \cong \triangle \underline{\quad ? \quad}.$$ ZNE

**b.** What postulate supports your answer to part **a**? ASA Postulate

**Copy what is shown. Write complete proofs in two-column form.**

**10.** *Given:* $AC = AD$
$BC = BD$

*Prove:* $\triangle ACB \cong \triangle ADB$

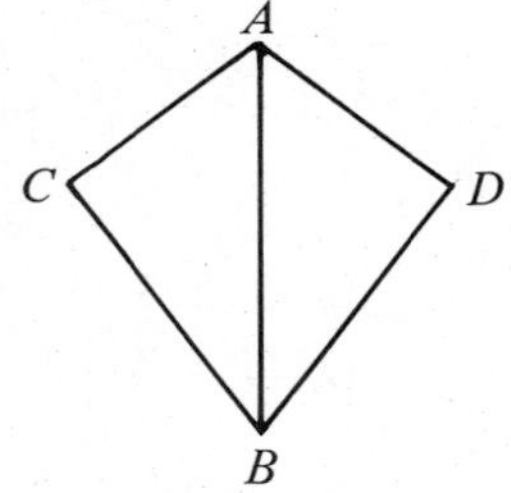


Exercises 10–13

**11.** *Given:* $CB = DB$
$\angle ABC = \angle ABD$

*Prove:* $\triangle ACB \cong \triangle ADB$

C **12.** *Given:* $\overleftrightarrow{AB}$ bisects $\angle CAD$.
$\overleftrightarrow{AB}$ bisects $\angle CBD$.

*Prove:* $\triangle ACB \cong \triangle ADB$

**13.** *Given:* $AC = AD$
$\overrightarrow{AB}$ bisects $\angle CAD$.

*Prove:* $\triangle ACB \cong \triangle ADB$

**14.** *Given:* $\overline{RT} \parallel \overline{VS}$
$RT = VS$

*Prove:* $\triangle RMT \cong \triangle SMV$

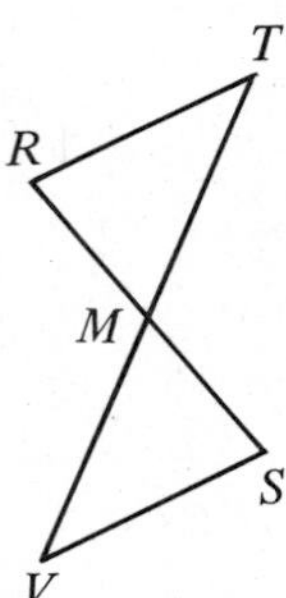


Exercise 14

15. **a.** Draw a large right triangle, $\triangle ABC$, with $\angle B = 90°$.
 **b.** Use Construction 2, page 22, to construct a $90°$ angle. Label it $\angle K$.
 **c.** Construct $KL = BC$.
 **d.** Construct $\angle L = \angle C$. Label the third vertex as $J$.
 **e.** Explain why $\triangle ABC \cong \triangle JKL$. **ASA Postulate**

## SELF-TEST

**Write proofs in two-column form.**

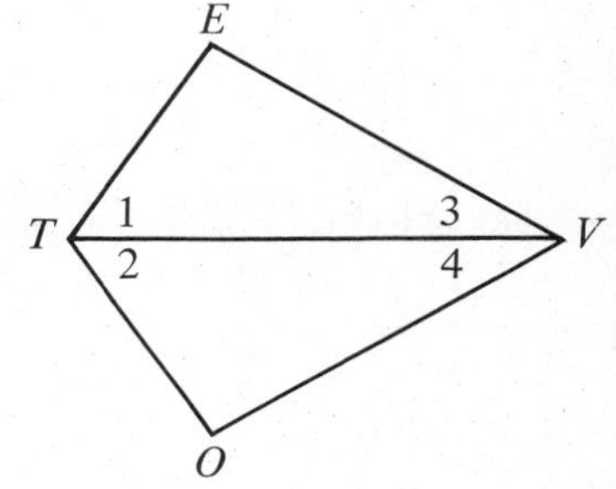


1. *Given:* $\overrightarrow{TV}$ bisects $\angle ETO$.
 $TE = TO$
 *Prove:* $\triangle TEV \cong \triangle TOV$

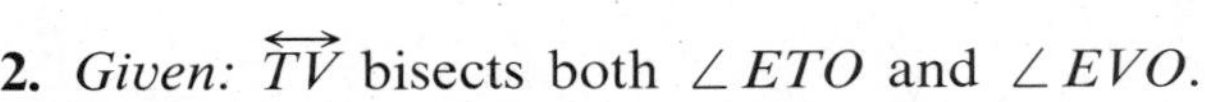

2. *Given:* $\overleftrightarrow{TV}$ bisects both $\angle ETO$ and $\angle EVO$.
 *Prove:* $\triangle TEV \cong \triangle TOV$

## Puzzles & Things

1. Arrange twelve toothpicks as in Figure 1. Now can you rearrange three toothpicks to form three squares of the same size?

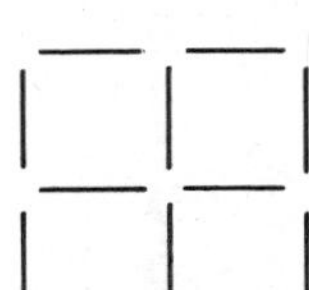
Figure 1

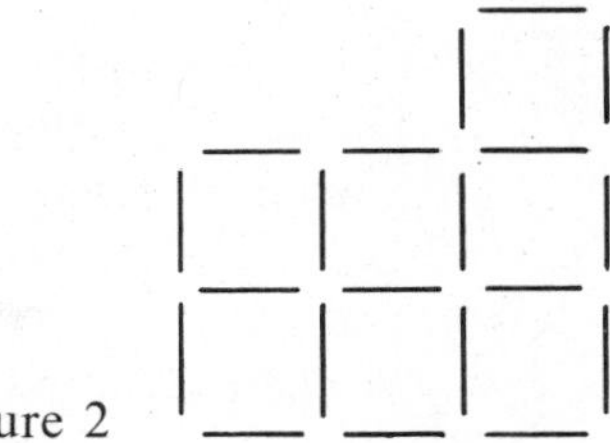
Figure 2

2. In Figure 2, rearrange three toothpicks to form five squares of the same size.
3. Form four equilateral triangles with six toothpicks. (This puzzle is solved in a way completely different from the last two puzzles. Can you see how?) **This puzzle is solved in 3 dimensions rather than on a plane.**

## 7 • The AAS and HL Theorems

In the diagram below, two angles and a *non*-included side of $\triangle RST$ are equal to the corresponding parts of $\triangle XYZ$. Can we prove that the triangles are congruent?

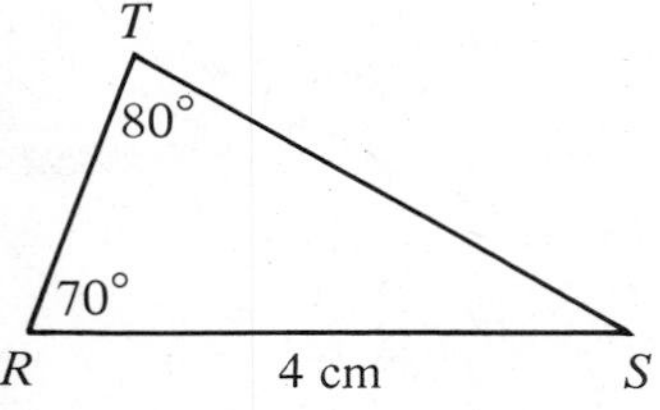


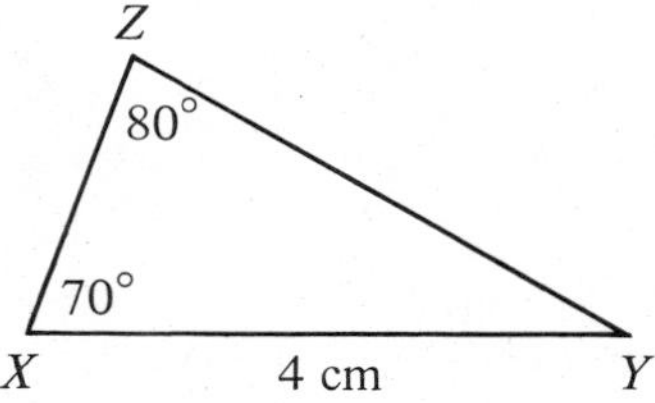


If we use the fact that $\angle R + \angle S + \angle T = 180°$, we can show that $\angle S = 30°$. We can likewise show that $\angle Y = 30°$. Then $\angle S = \angle Y$, and $\triangle RST \cong \triangle XYZ$ by the ASA Postulate.

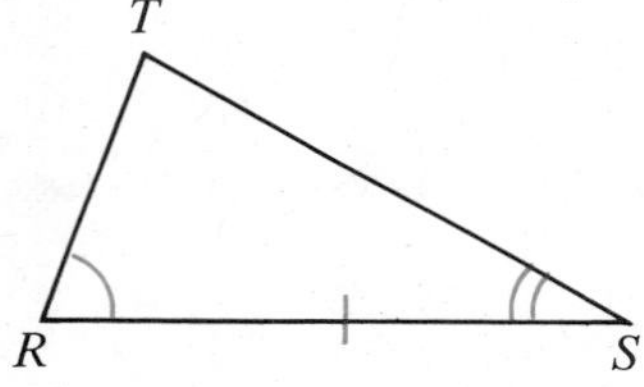


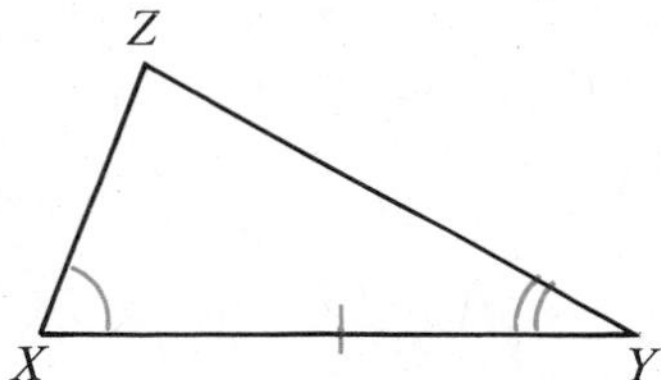


The discussion above suggests our next theorem. Exercise 30, page 122, deals with a proof.

**THEOREM 2 (AAS Theorem)**

If two angles and a non-included side of one triangle are equal to the corresponding parts of another triangle, the triangles are congruent.

A theorem about right triangles is stated here without proof.

**THEOREM 3 (HL Theorem)**

If the hypotenuse and a leg of one right triangle are equal to the corresponding parts of another right triangle, the triangles are congruent.

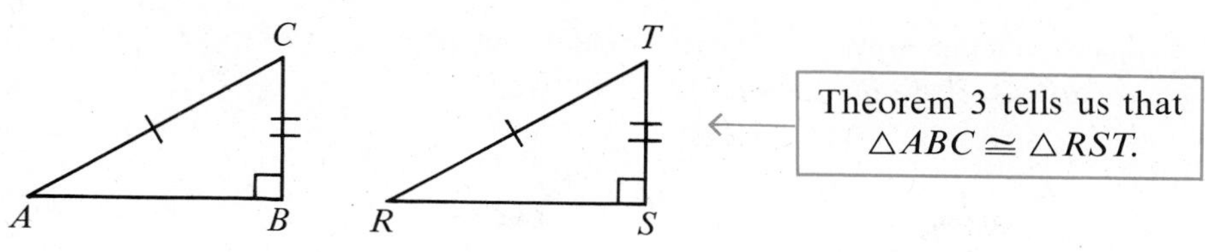


**Ways to Prove Triangles Congruent**

SSS SAS ASA AAS HL

## Classroom Practice

**What is the measure of the angle marked in color?**

Sample

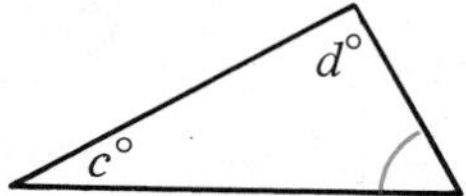


*Answer:* $180° - c° - d°$
*Also correct:* $180° - (c° + d°)$

**1.** $58°$ (32°)

**2.** $180° - 3j°$

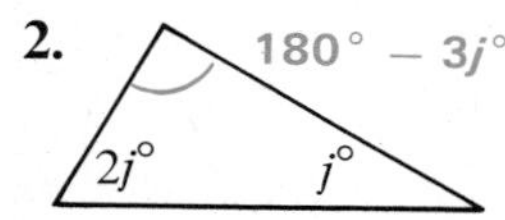


**3.** $90° - n°$ (n°)

**In Exercises 4–7, identify all right triangles shown in each figure. Name the hypotenuse of each right triangle.**

**4.** $\triangle CBA$ with hyp. $\overline{AC}$; $\triangle ABD$ with hyp. $\overline{AD}$

**5.** $\triangle XMW$ with hyp. $\overline{XW}$; $\triangle ZMY$ with hyp. $\overline{ZY}$

**6.** $\triangle RSU$ with hyp. $\overline{RU}$; $\triangle QST$ with hyp. $\overline{QT}$

**7.** $\triangle MJK$ with hyp. $\overline{MK}$; $\triangle JKL$ with hyp. $\overline{JL}$; $\triangle KLM$ with hyp. $\overline{MK}$; $\triangle LMJ$ with hyp. $\overline{JL}$

In Exercises 8–17, state which postulate or theorem you would use to prove the two triangles congruent. If no method applies, say so.

**8.**

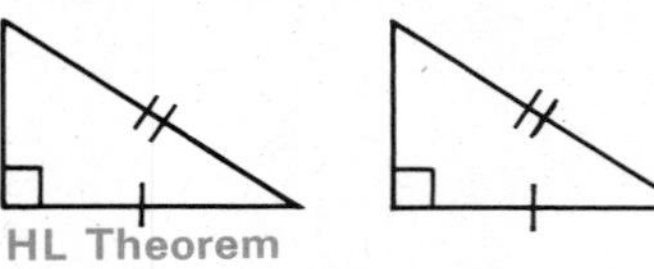

HL Theorem

**9.**

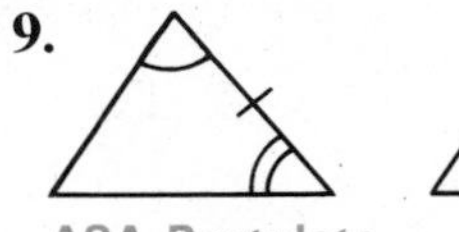

ASA Postulate

**10.**

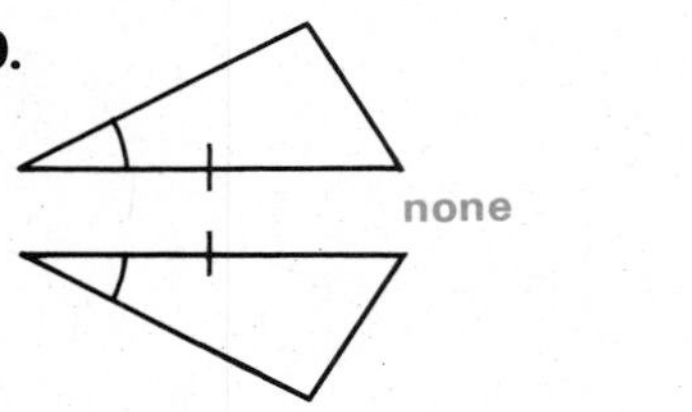

none

**11.**

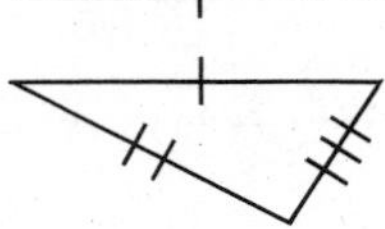

SSS Postulate

**12.**

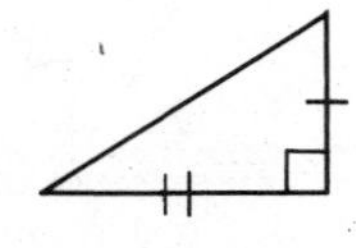

SAS Postulate

**13.**

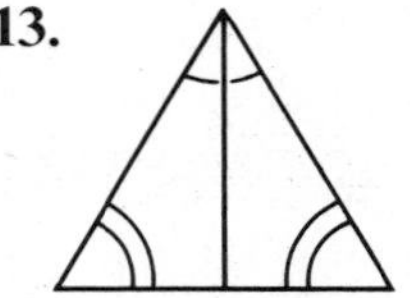

AAS Theorem

**14.**

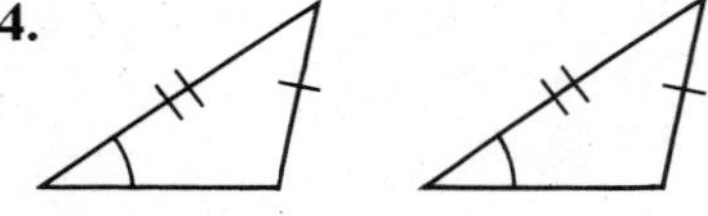

none

**15.**

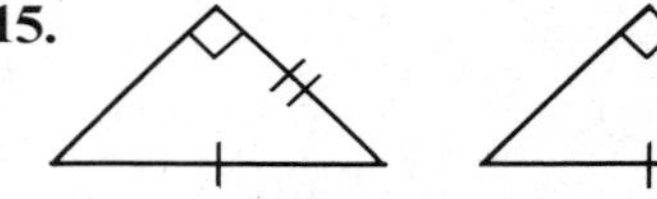

HL Theorem

**16.**

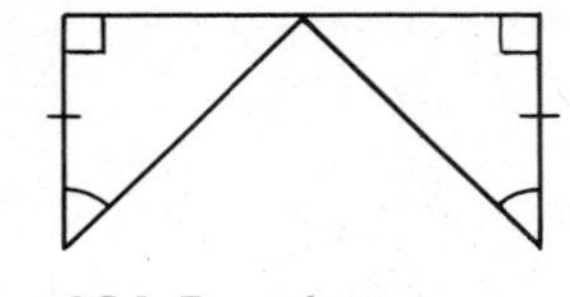

ASA Postulate

**17.**

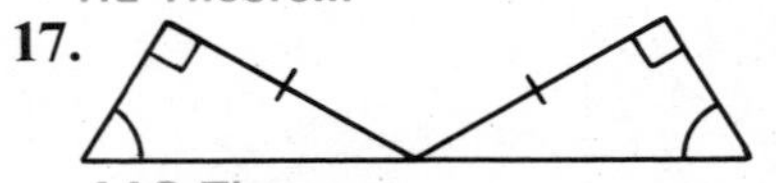

AAS Theorem

## *Written Exercises*

Write SSS, SAS, ASA, AAS, or HL to indicate the method you would use to prove the two triangles congruent. If no method applies, write *none.*

A **1.** HL

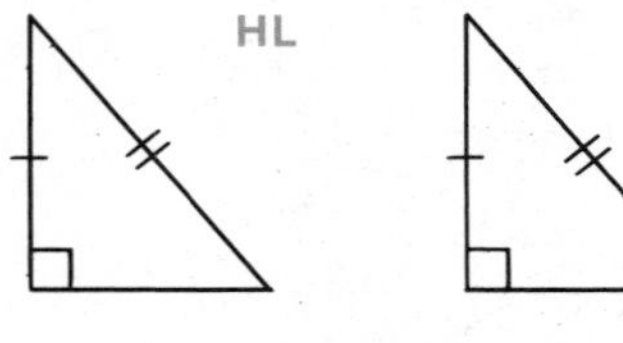

**2.** none

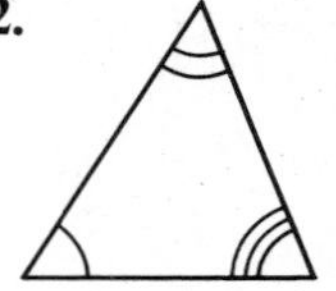

**3.** ASA

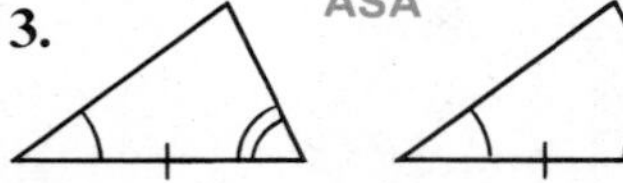

**4.** AAS

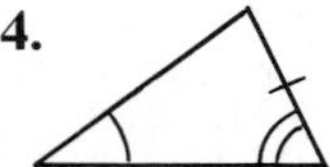

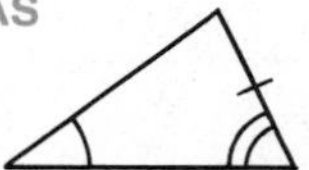

5. HL (or AAS)

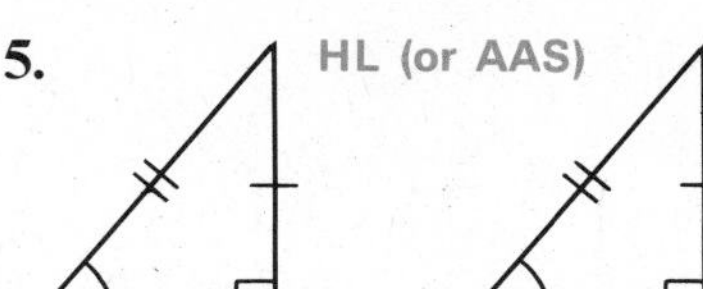

6. SAS

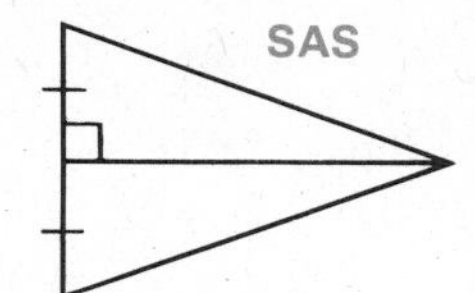

7. AAS

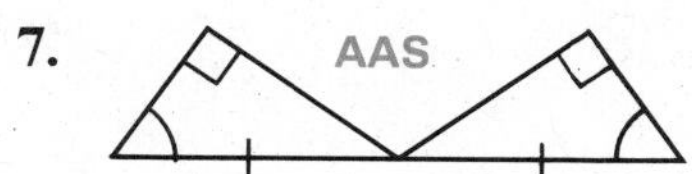

8. HL

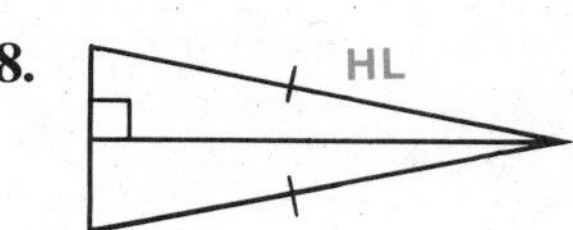

9. SSS

10. ASA

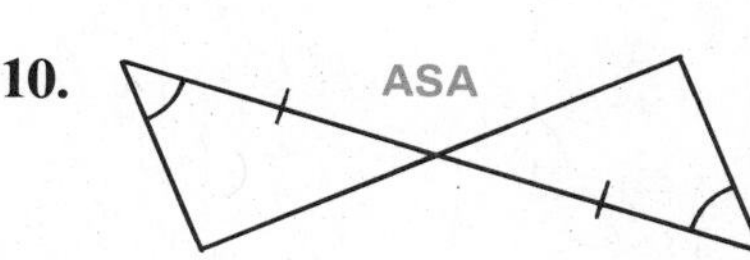

11. none

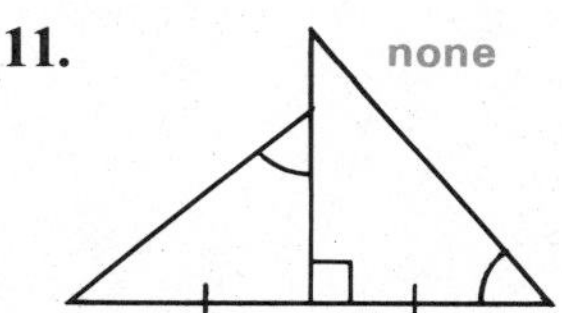

12. AAS

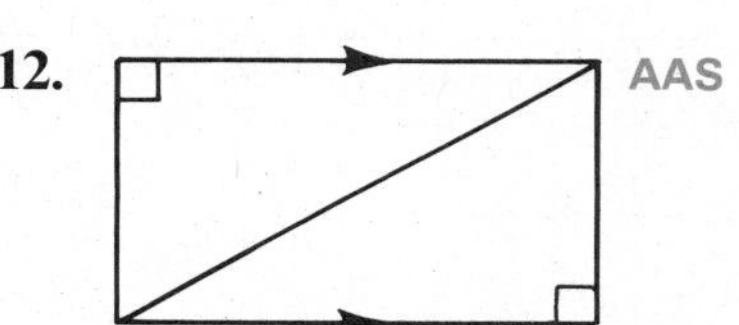

**In Exercises 13 and 14, list *all* possible methods that could be used to prove the two triangles congruent.**

13.

SAS, ASA, AAS

14.

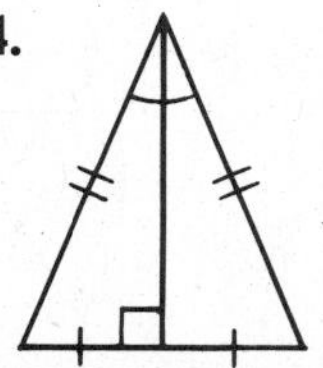

SSS, SAS, ASA, AAS, HL

**In Exercises 15–17, supply the reasons to complete the proofs.**

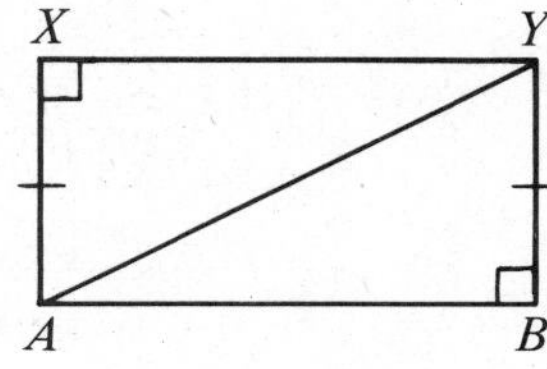


**15.** *Given:* $\angle B$ and $\angle X$ are right angles.
$BY = AX$

*Prove:* $\triangle ABY \cong \triangle YXA$

| STATEMENTS | REASONS |
| --- | --- |
| 1. $\angle B$ and $\angle X$ are right angles. | 1. ___?___ Given |
| 2. $AY = AY$ | 2. ___?___ From algebra |
| 3. $BY = AX$ | 3. ___?___ Given |
| 4. $\triangle ABY \cong \triangle YXA$ | 4. ___?___ HL |

**16.** *Given:* $\overrightarrow{BD}$ bisects $\angle ABC$.
$\angle A = \angle C$

*Prove:* $\triangle ABD \cong \triangle CBD$

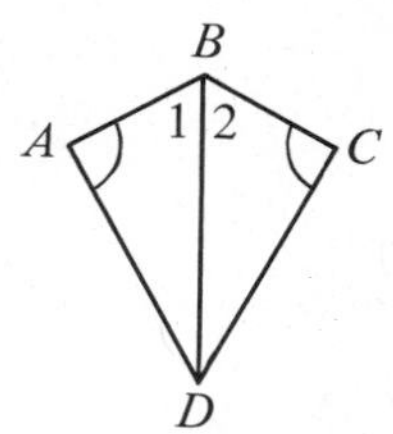


| STATEMENTS | REASONS |
|---|---|
| 1. $\angle 1 = \angle 2$ | 1. ? Given: $\overrightarrow{BD}$ bisects $\angle ABC$. |
| 2. $\angle A = \angle C$ | 2. ? Given |
| 3. $BD = BD$ | 3. ? From algebra |
| 4. $\triangle ABD \cong \triangle CBD$ | 4. ? AAS Theorem |

**17.** *Given:* $\angle 1 = \angle 2$
$\angle 5 = \angle 6$

*Prove:* $\triangle WXY \cong \triangle WXZ$

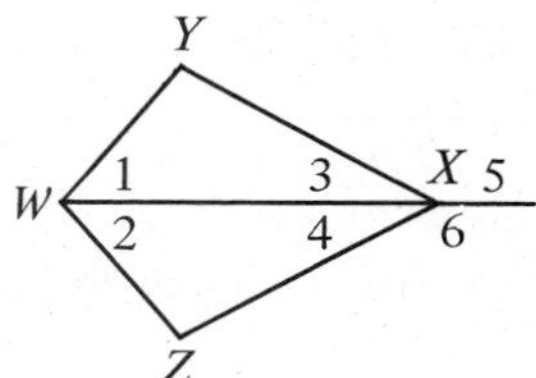


| STATEMENTS | REASONS |
|---|---|
| 1. $\angle 3$ and $\angle 5$ are supplements. $\angle 4$ and $\angle 6$ are supplements. | 1. ? Def. of supplementary angles |
| 2. $\angle 5 = \angle 6$ | 2. ? Given |
| 3. $\angle 3 = \angle 4$ | 3. ? Supplements of = angles are =. |
| 4. $\angle 1 = \angle 2$ | 4. ? Given |
| 5. $WX = WX$ | 5. ? From algebra |
| 6. $\triangle WXY \cong \triangle WXZ$ | 6. ? ASA Postulate |

**Each diagram shows two congruent triangles.**
**Find numerical values for *x*, *y*, and *z*.**

**18.**

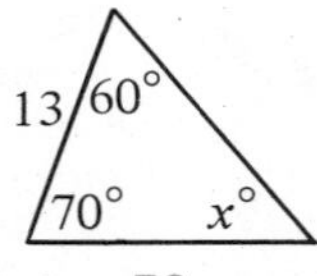


$x = 50$, $y = 60$, $z = 13$

**19.**

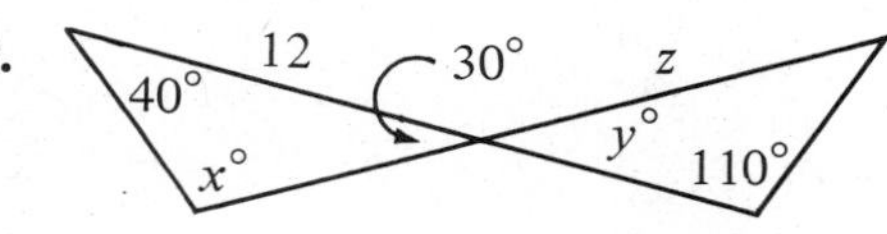


$x = 110$, $y = 30$, $z = 12$

B **20.**

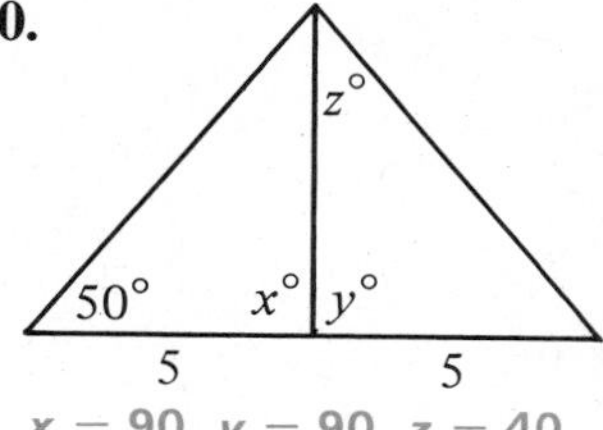


$x = 90,\ y = 90,\ z = 40$

**21.**

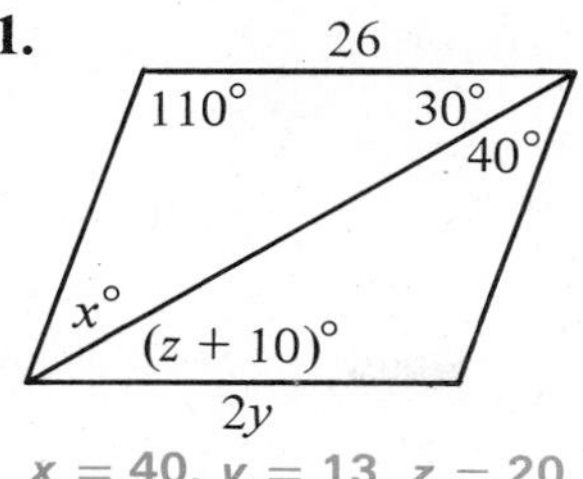


$x = 40,\ y = 13,\ z = 20$

**A geometry class is asked to write this proof:**

*Given:* $\overline{AB} \parallel \overline{XY}$

$M$ is the midpoint of $\overline{AY}$.

*Prove:* $\triangle AMB \cong \triangle YMX$

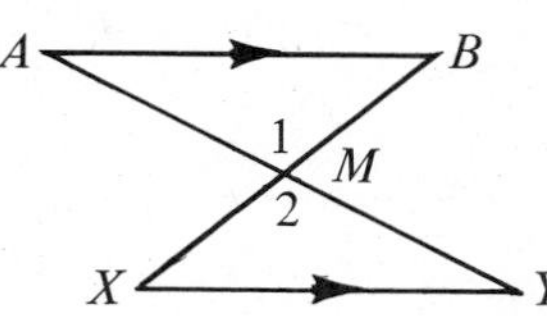


**22.** Ed uses the ASA Postulate. Name the three parts of $\triangle AMB$ that he uses in his proof. $\angle A,\ \angle 1,\ \overline{MA}$

**23.** Rebecca writes $\angle 1 = \angle 2$, and then decides to use the AAS Theorem. List the two parts of $\triangle YMX$, in addition to $\angle 2$, that she uses in her proof. $\angle X,\ \overline{YM}$

**24.** Mike uses the AAS Theorem, but doesn't use $\angle 1$. List the three parts of $\triangle AMB$ that he uses. $\angle A,\ \angle B,\ \overline{MA}$

**25.** Mary remarks: "If I knew that $M$ was the midpoint of $\overline{BX}$, then I could use something other than the ASA Postulate or the AAS Theorem." What theorem or postulate could she use?

SAS Postulate

**26.** *Given:* $M$ is the midpoint of $\overline{YZ}$.

$M$ is the midpoint of $\overline{AB}$.

$\angle Y$ and $\angle Z$ are right angles.

**a.** List four methods you could use to prove $\triangle AYM \cong \triangle BZM$.

**b.** Choose one method and write a complete proof.

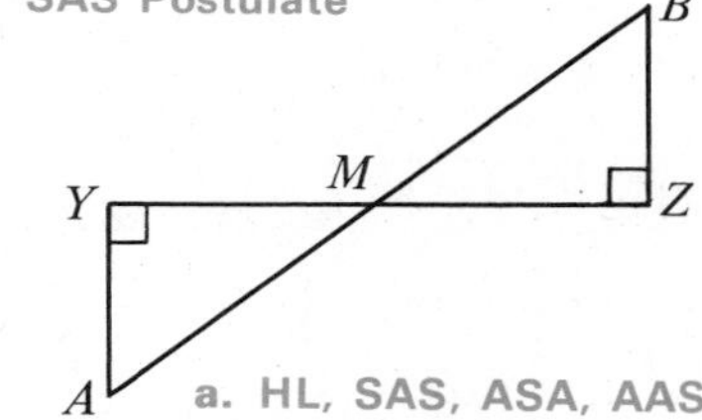


a. HL, SAS, ASA, AAS

Answers may vary.

**In each exercise, equal parts are indicated. Can the two triangles be proved congruent? If so, what postulate or theorem would be simplest to use?**

**27.**

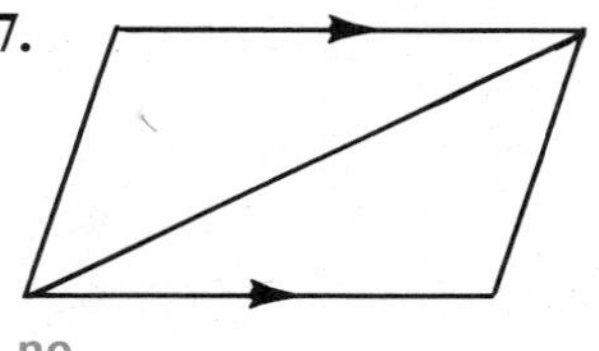

no

**28.**

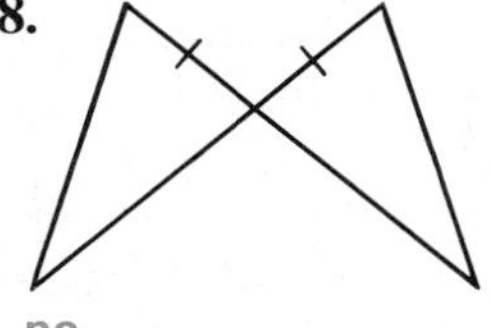

no

**29.**

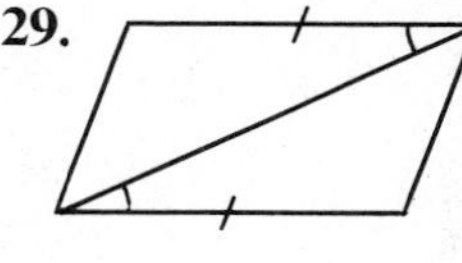

yes; SAS Postulate

C **30.** Prove the AAS Theorem.

*Given:* $\angle R = \angle X$; $\angle T = \angle Z$

$RS = XY$

*Prove:* $\triangle RST \cong \triangle XYZ$

(*Hint:* Let $\angle R = j°$ and $\angle T = k°$. Show that $\angle S = \angle Y$.)

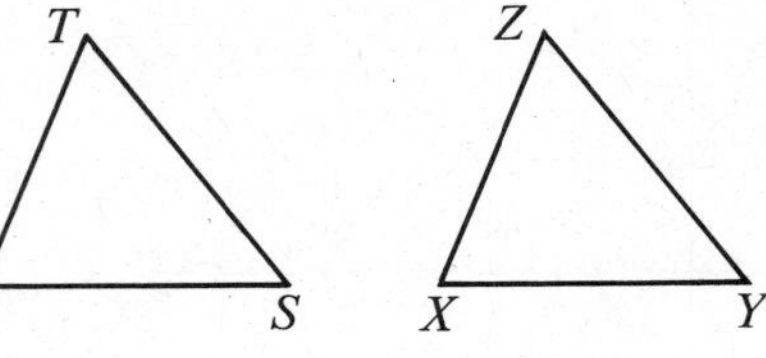


## Class Experiment

**Each student will need paper, scissors, a pencil, a ruler, and a compass.**

1. Draw a segment 8 cm long.
2. Choosing either endpoint of the segment, construct a ray so that a 90° angle is formed.
3. Set your compass for a radius of 12 cm.
   Using the free endpoint of the original segment as center, draw an arc that intersects the ray.
4. Connect the two points to form a triangle.
5. Cut out your triangle and compare it with triangles that other students have made. If each student worked carefully, all the triangles should be congruent.

## SELF-TEST

**1.** *Given:* $\overline{AC} \parallel \overline{DB}$; $AX = BX$; $CX = DX$

Indicate, by abbreviation, three different postulates or theorems you could use to prove

$\triangle AXC \cong \triangle BXD$. ASA, SAS, AAS

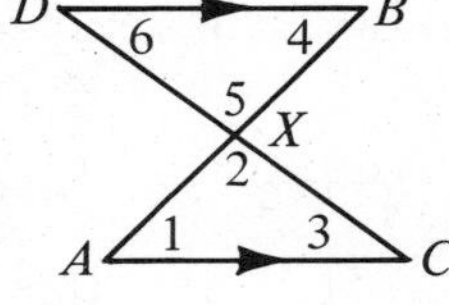


**2.** Write a proof in two-column form.

*Given:* $\overline{RT} \perp \overline{SV}$

$RS = TV$

$RM = TM$

*Prove:* $\triangle RMS \cong \triangle TMV$

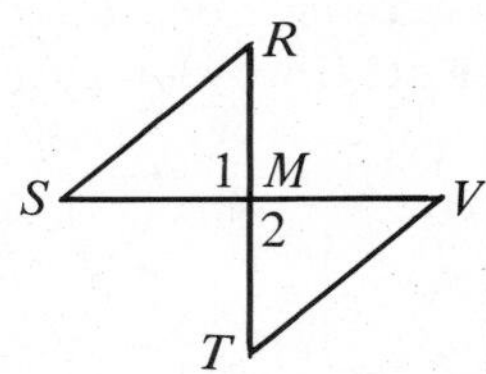

## Reviewing Algebraic Skills

**Add. The samples will help you remember.**

Samples

$7 + 4 = 11$ $\quad -7 + 4 = -3$

$7 + (-4) = 3$ $\quad -7 + (-4) = -11$

**1.** $-3 + 12$ 9 **2.** $0 + (-5)$ $-5$ **3.** $-4 + (-8)$ $-12$ **4.** $9 + (-2)$ 7

**5.** $-15 + (-6)$ $-21$ **6.** $-11 + 19$ 8 **7.** $3 + (-14)$ $-11$ **8.** $-23 + 23$ 0

**Subtract.**

Samples

$4 - 7 = 4 + (-7) = -3$ $\quad -4 - 7 = -4 + (-7) = -11$

$4 - (-7) = 4 + (7) = 11$ $\quad -4 - (-7) = -4 + (7) = 3$

**9.** $13 - 17$ $-4$ **10.** $-2 - 8$ $-10$ **11.** $9 - (-2)$ 11 **12.** $10 - (-10)$ 20

**13.** $-7 - 7$ $-14$ **14.** $20 - 34$ $-14$ **15.** $-16 - (-9)$ $-7$ **16.** $-14 - 30$ $-44$

**Multiply.**

Samples

$3(8) = 24$ $\quad 3(-8) = -24$

$-3(-8) = 24$ $\quad -3(8) = -24$

**17.** $5(12)$ 60 **18.** $-4(20)$ $-80$ **19.** $13(-7)$ $-91$ **20.** $-8(-9)$ 72

**21.** $-29(0)$ 0 **22.** $-3(-50)$ 150 **23.** $8(-11)$ $-88$ **24.** $-6(25)$ $-150$

**Divide.**

Samples

$40 \div 8 = 5$ $\quad -40 \div 8 = -5$

$-40 \div (-8) = 5$ $\quad 40 \div (-8) = -5$

**25.** $-63 \div 9$ $-7$ **26.** $42 \div -6$ $-7$ **27.** $-52 \div -4$ 13 **28.** $-17 \div 17$ $-1$

**29.** $-44 \div -11$ 4 **30.** $-72 \div 8$ $-9$ **31.** $39 \div -13$ $-3$ **32.** $-125 \div 25$ $-5$

**Compare the numbers. Write $<$, $=$, or $>$.**

**33.** $17 + (-10)$ __?__ $5$ $>$ **34.** $(-5)^2$ __?__ $10$ $>$ **35.** $-2(-9)$ __?__ $0 + 18$ $=$

**36.** $-(-3)^2$ __?__ $9$ $<$ **37.** $-13 - (-4)$ __?__ $-7$ $=$ **38.** $0(-10)$ __?__ $5 - 8$ $>$

# applications

## *Rigidity of Triangles*

The SSS Postulate states that if three sides of one triangle are equal to the corresponding sides of another triangle, the triangles are congruent. We have seen that to change the shape of a triangle we must change the length of at least one of its sides. Thus, we say that a triangle is a *rigid* figure.

Architects and builders use the fact that triangles are rigid when they want to build a structure that is strong enough to hold its shape when acted upon by external and internal forces.

Many roofs have a triangular cross-section. In a properly designed triangular roof, all the force is exerted down. None of the force pushes out. As a result, the walls do not need to be reinforced to hold their shape.

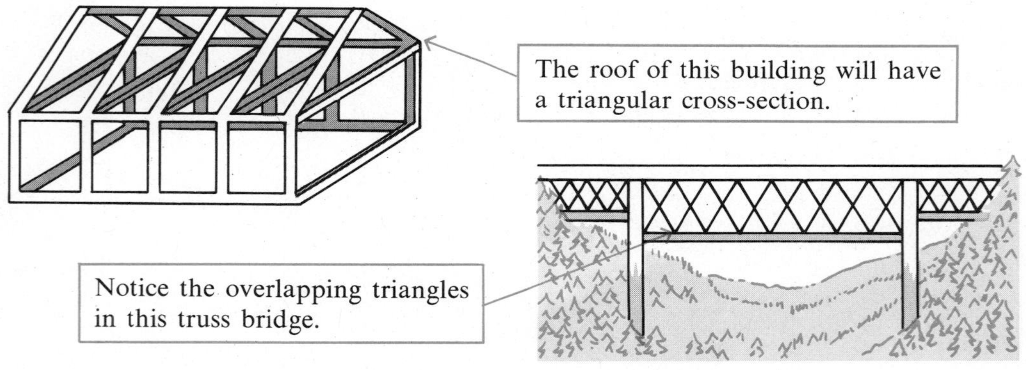


Another example of the use of triangles in construction is the truss bridge. Builders often combine several triangles to make a strong bridge with a wide span. Many covered bridges built in the late 18th century and early 19th century are of simple truss-type construction.

R. Buckminster Fuller used the rigidity of triangles in designing his famous geodesic dome. His design combines many triangular surfaces to form a dome that is strong, but lightweight. Large geodesic domes form pavilions for fairs, sporting events, and horticultural exhibits. Smaller domes make interesting houses.

Geodesic dome in Montreal, Canada

**Exercises**

Cut some cardboard into 1 cm strips of various lengths. Punch holes in the strips 1 cm from each end. Use metal fasteners to attach the ends and form models like those pictured here. Which of the models are rigid figures? Models 3 and 6 are rigid figures.

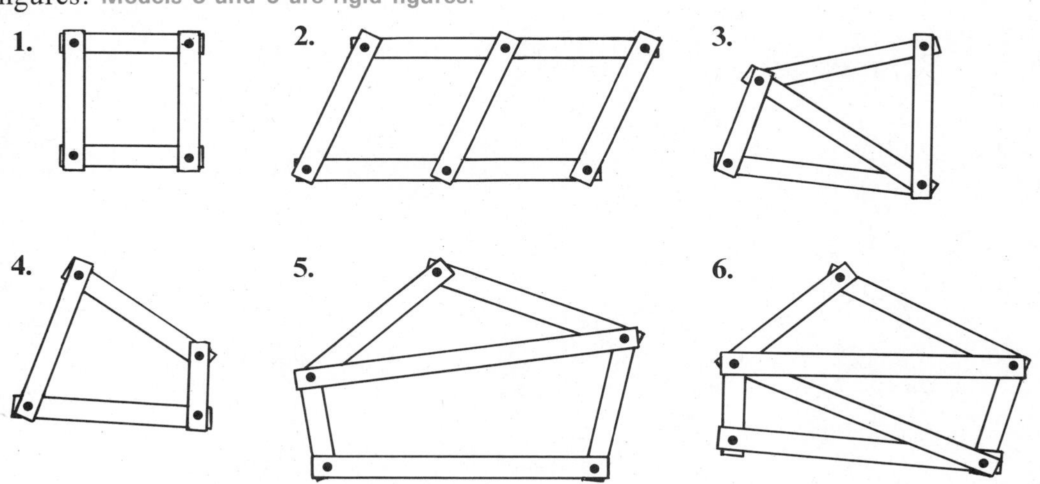


See if you can combine your strips into other models that form rigid figures.

# Reviewing the Chapter

## Chapter Summary

1. In any triangle,
   a. the sum of the angles is 180°.
   b. an exterior angle is equal to the sum of the two opposite angles.
2. Corollaries, like theorems, are proved. A corollary follows directly from a theorem.
3. Triangles can be classified as scalene, isosceles, or equilateral according to their sides.
4. Triangles can be classified as acute, right, obtuse, or equiangular according to their angles.
5. $\triangle ABC \cong \triangle DEF$ means that each part of $\triangle ABC$ is equal to the corresponding part of $\triangle DEF$. Corresponding parts are named in the same order. That is, $\angle A = \angle D$, $\angle B = \angle E$, $\angle C = \angle F$, $AB = DE$, $BC = EF$, and $AC = DF$.
6. Postulates and theorems used to prove triangles congruent are abbreviated by:

   SSS SAS ASA AAS HL

## Chapter Review Test

**Find the value of $x$ in each diagram.** *(See pp. 84–88.)*

**1.** 80

**2.** 70

**3.** 35

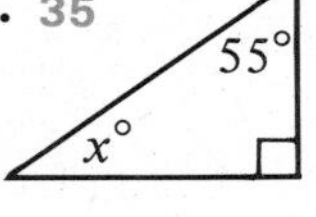


**4.** 132

**5.** 15

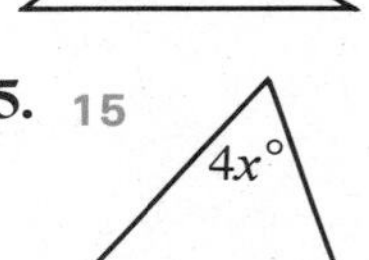


**6.** 40

**Complete.** *(See pp. 89–92.)*

**7.** If the perimeter of an equilateral triangle is 42 cm, the length of each side is __?__ cm. 14

**8.** The base of an isosceles triangle is 8 cm long, and a leg is 7 cm long. The perimeter of the triangle is __?__ cm. 22

9. An isosceles triangle cannot be $\underline{\quad ? \quad}$ scalene
scalene/equilateral.

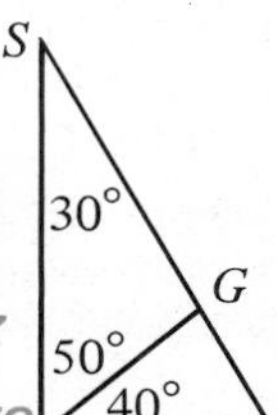


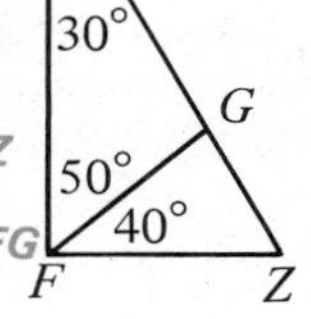

10. A right triangle found in the diagram is $\underline{\ ?\ }$. △SFZ

11. An acute triangle found in the diagram is $\underline{\ ?\ }$. △GFZ

12. An obtuse triangle found in the diagram is $\underline{\ ?\ }$. △SFG

**Complete.** (*See pp. 93–97.*)

If $\triangle CAP \cong \triangle DIR$, then:

**13.** $\angle P = \angle \underline{\ ?\ }$ R **14.** $PC = \underline{\ ?\ }$ RD **15.** $\triangle PCA \cong \triangle \underline{\ ?\ }$ RDI

**Write SSS, SAS, ASA, AAS, or HL to indicate the method you would use to prove the two triangles congruent. Do not write the proof.** (*See pp. 99–122.*)

**16.** *Given:* $AY = BY$ and $AX = BX$
*Prove:* $\triangle AXY \cong \triangle BXY$ SSS

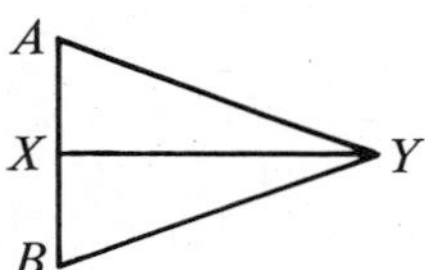


**17.** *Given:* $\angle C = \angle X$ and $CO = XO$
*Prove:* $\triangle BOC \cong \triangle YOX$ ASA

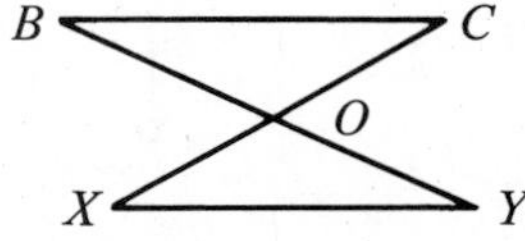


**18.** *Given:* $\overline{AB} \perp \overline{CD}$ and $AC = AD$
*Prove:* $\triangle ABC \cong \triangle ABD$ HL

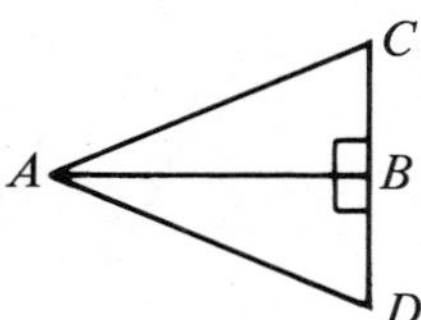


**19.** *Given:* $\angle S$ and $\angle V$ are rt. ∠s;
$M$ is the midpoint of $\overline{SV}$;
and $RS = TV$
*Prove:* $\triangle RSM \cong \triangle TVM$ SAS

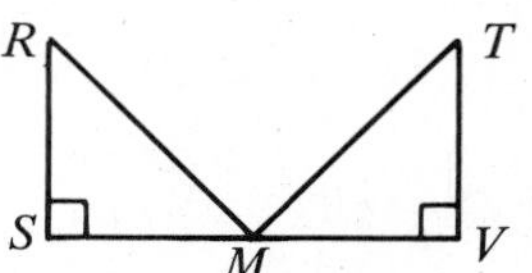


**20.** Write a complete proof in two-column form.
*Given:* $\angle R = \angle S$ and $\overrightarrow{GH}$ bisects $\angle RGS$.
*Prove:* $\triangle RHG \cong \triangle SHG$

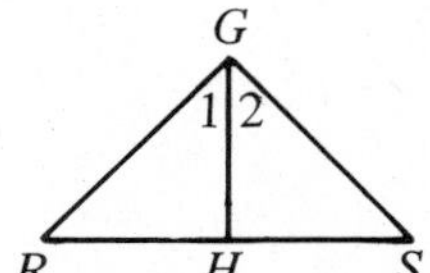

## *Here's what you'll learn in this chapter:*

1. To use congruent triangles to prove that two segments or two angles are equal.
2. To use congruent triangles to justify constructions.
3. To name the altitudes and the medians of a triangle.
4. To inscribe a circle in a triangle and circumscribe a circle about a triangle.
5. To use the properties of isosceles triangles.

# Chapter 4

# Using Congruent Triangles

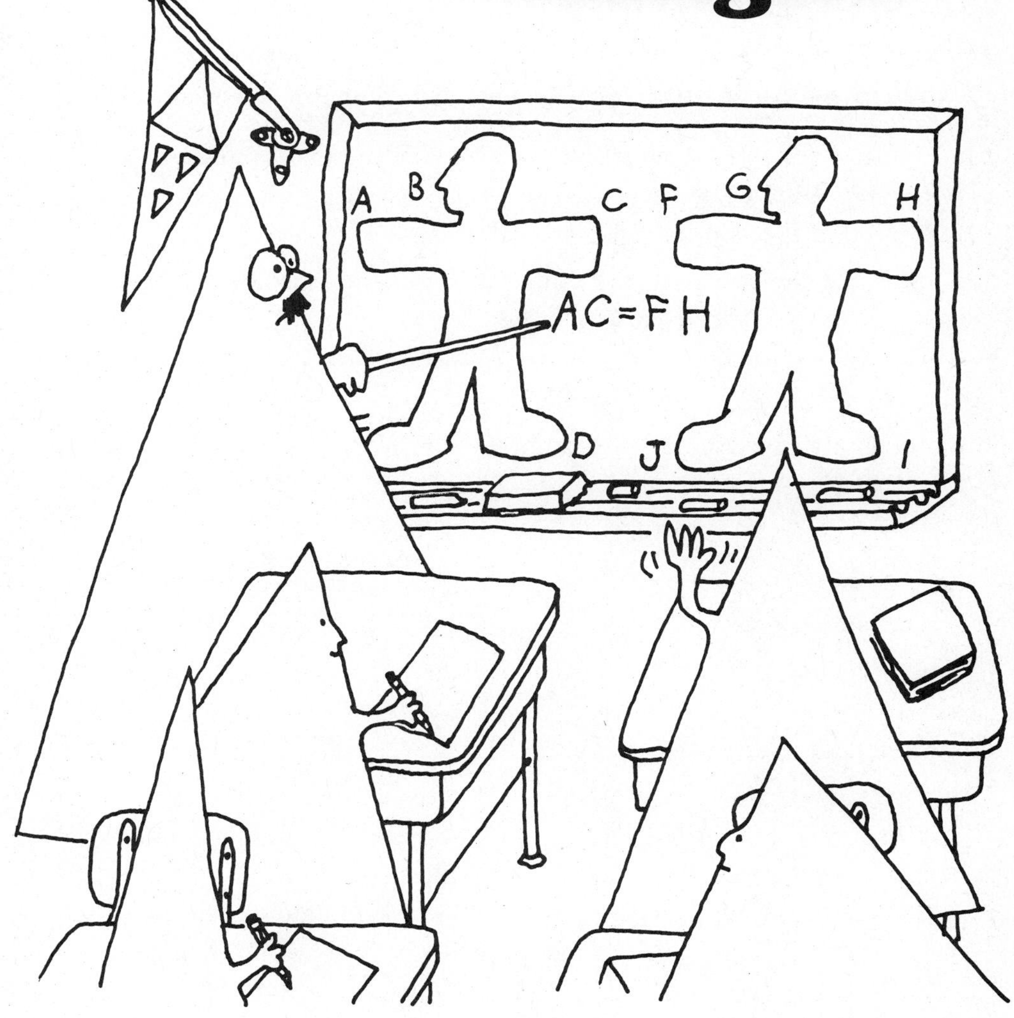

## 1 • Proving Corresponding Parts Equal

Suppose you are told that $\triangle ABC \cong \triangle RST$. Then you know that six things must be true. You should be able to complete the statements below:

$\angle A = \angle R$ $\quad AB = RS$

$\angle B = \underline{\ ?\ }$ $\angle S$ $\quad BC = \underline{\ ?\ }$ $ST$

$\angle C = \underline{\ ?\ }$ $\angle T$ $\quad AC = \underline{\ ?\ }$ $RT$

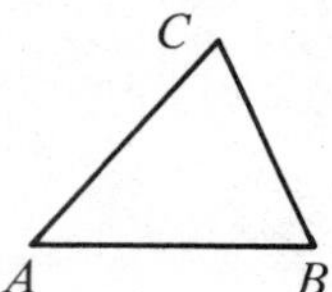


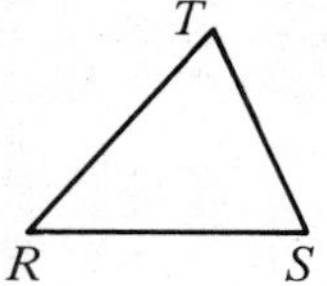


The six statements are true because of the definition of congruent triangles. *Corresponding parts of congruent triangles are equal.*

**A strategy for proving that two segments or two angles are equal:**

1. Find two triangles in which the two sides or the two angles are corresponding parts.
2. Prove that the two triangles are congruent.
3. State that the two parts are equal, using as the reason, "Corr. parts of $\cong$ $\triangle$s are $=$."

This strategy will be used in the examples that follow.

### EXAMPLE 1

*Given:* $JP = JQ$
$PK = QK$

*Prove:* $\angle P = \angle Q$

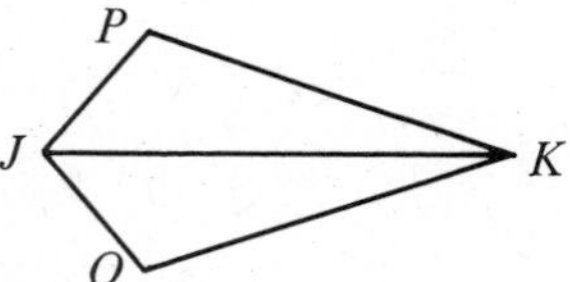


| STATEMENTS | REASONS |
|---|---|
| 1. $JP = JQ$ | 1. Given |
| 2. $PK = QK$ | 2. Given |
| 3. $JK = JK$ | 3. From algebra |
| 4. $\triangle PJK \cong \triangle QJK$ | 4. SSS Postulate |
| 5. $\angle P = \angle Q$ | 5. Corr. parts of $\cong$ $\triangle$s are $=$. |

## EXAMPLE 2

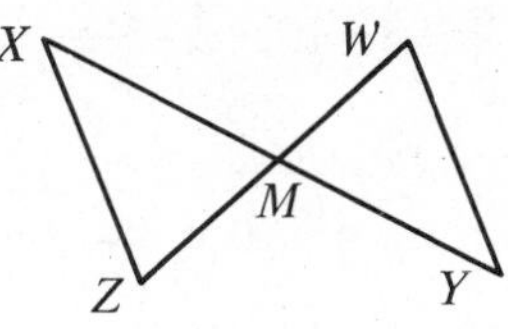


*Given:* $M$ is the midpoint of $\overline{XY}$.
$M$ is the midpoint of $\overline{ZW}$.

*Prove:* $XZ = YW$

| STATEMENTS | REASONS |
|---|---|
| 1. $XM = YM$ | 1. Given: $M$ is the midpoint of $\overline{XY}$. |
| 2. $ZM = WM$ | 2. Given: $M$ is the midpoint of $\overline{ZW}$. |
| 3. $\angle XMZ = \angle YMW$ | 3. __?__ Vertical angles are =. |
| 4. $\triangle XMZ \cong \triangle YMW$ | 4. SAS Postulate |
| 5. $XZ = YW$ | 5. Corr. parts of $\cong$ ⚠ are =. |

## *Classroom Practice*

**In Exercises 1–8, it is known that $\triangle ABC \cong \triangle JTN$.**

**1.** $\angle A =$ __?__ $\angle J$ **2.** $\angle B =$ __?__ $\angle T$ **3.** $\angle C =$ __?__ $\angle N$

**4.** What reason supports each of statements 1, 2, and 3 above? Corr. parts of $\cong$ ⚠ are =.

**5.** $AB =$ __?__ $JT$ **6.** $BC =$ __?__ $TN$ **7.** $AC =$ __?__ $JN$

**8.** What reason supports each of statements 5, 6, and 7 above? Corr. parts of $\cong$ ⚠ are =.

**Suppose, in Exercises 9–14, that you want to prove that $\angle 1 = \angle 2$. Does the figure suggest that congruent triangles might be used?**

**9.** 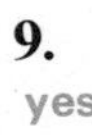 yes

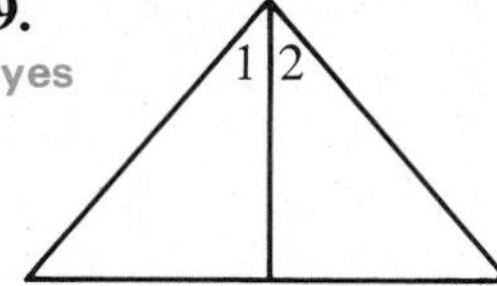


**10.** 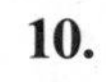 yes

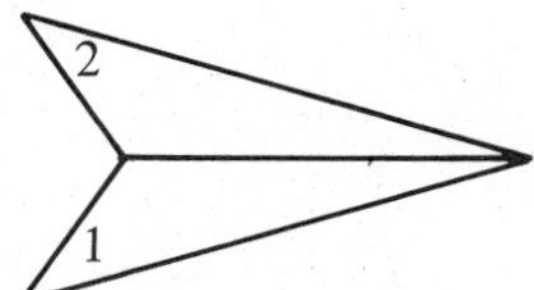


**11.** yes

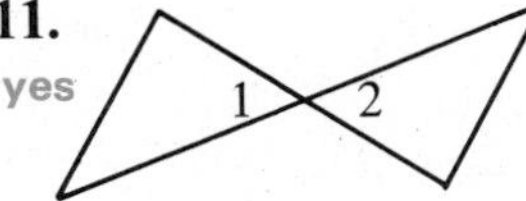


**12.** yes

**13.** yes

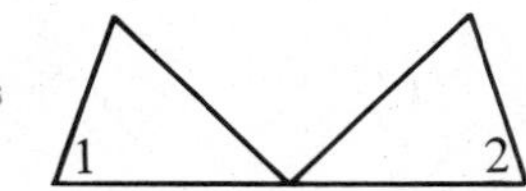


**14.** no

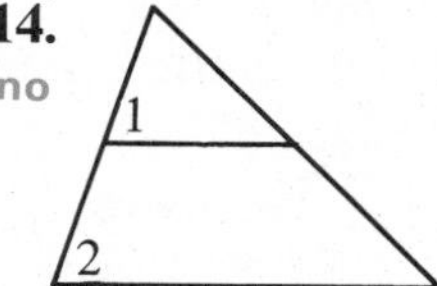

## Written Exercises

A **1–6.** *Given:* $\triangle GAR \cong \triangle DEN$.

Write the six statements that can be supported by the reason:

Corr. parts of $\cong$ $\triangle$s are $=$.

$\angle G = \angle D$
$\angle A = \angle E$
$\angle R = \angle N$
$GA = DE$
$AR = EN$
$GR = DN$

**Name the triangles you might try to prove congruent in order to prove each of the following.**

**7.** $NM = NO$ — $\triangle MEN \cong \triangle OLN$

**8.** $EO = LM$ — $\triangle OEL \cong \triangle MLE$

**9.** $\angle 1 = \angle 2$ — $\triangle OEL \cong \triangle MLE$

**10.** $EN = LN$ — $\triangle ENM \cong \triangle LNO$

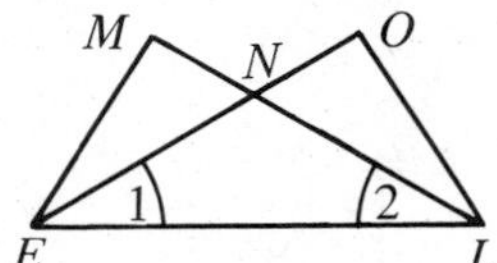


**In Exercises 11–14, supply the reasons needed to complete the proofs.**

**11.** *Given:* $AC = BC$
$\overrightarrow{CD}$ bisects $\angle ACB$.

*Prove:* $AD = BD$

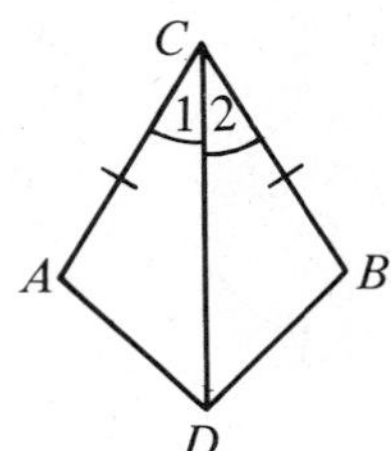


| STATEMENTS | REASONS |
|---|---|
| 1. $AC = BC$ | 1. ? Given |
| 2. $\angle 1 = \angle 2$ | 2. ? Given: $\overrightarrow{CD}$ bisects $\angle ACB$ |
| 3. $CD = CD$ | 3. ? From algebra |
| 4. $\triangle ACD \cong \triangle BCD$ | 4. ? SAS Postulate |
| 5. $AD = BD$ | 5. ? Corr. parts of $\cong$ $\triangle$s are $=$. |

**12.** *Given:* $\angle O$ and $\angle E$ are right angles.
$RO = ES$

*Prove:* $\overline{RO} \parallel \overline{ES}$

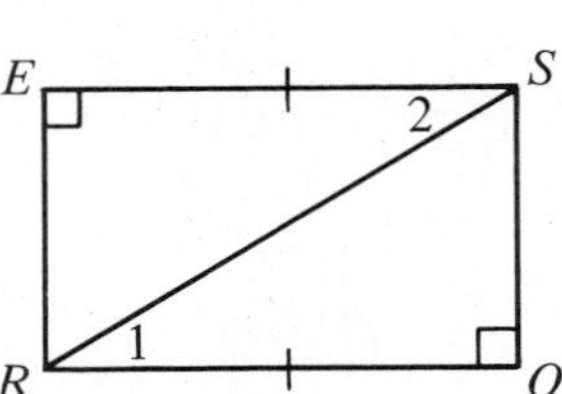


*Strategy for proof:*

A. Prove that two triangles are congruent.

B. Think of a transversal. Use corresponding parts to show that angles are equal.

C. Use the equal angles to prove that two lines are parallel.

| STATEMENTS | REASONS |
|---|---|
| 1. $\angle O$ and $\angle E$ are right angles. | 1. ___?___ Given |
| 2. $RO = ES$ | 2. ___?___ Given |
| 3. $RS = RS$ | 3. ___?___ From algebra |
| 4. $\triangle ROS \cong \triangle SER$ | 4. ___?___ HL Theorem |
| 5. $\angle 1 = \angle 2$ | 5. ___?___ Corr. parts of $\cong$ $\triangle$s are $=$. |
| 6. $\overline{RO} \parallel \overline{ES}$ | 6. ___?___ Thm. 6, p. 66 |

B **13.** *Given:* $\angle A = \angle B$
$\angle 1 = \angle 2$

*Prove:* $AX = BY$

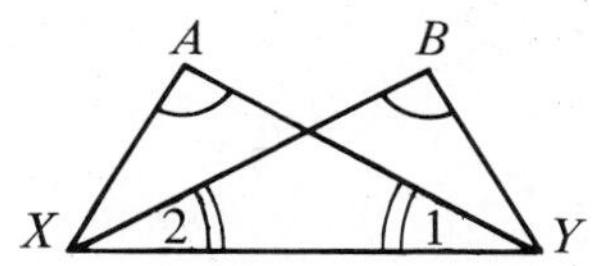


| STATEMENTS | REASONS |
|---|---|
| 1. $\angle A = \angle B$; $\angle 1 = \angle 2$ | 1. ___?___ Given |
| 2. $XY = XY$ | 2. ___?___ From algebra |
| 3. $\triangle AXY \cong \triangle BYX$ | 3. ___?___ AAS Theorem |
| 4. $AX = BY$ | 4. ___?___ Corr. parts of $\cong$ $\triangle$s are $=$. |

**14.** *Given:* $\overline{EB} \perp \overline{AC}$
$\angle E = \angle C$
$EB = BC$

*Prove:* $AB = BD$

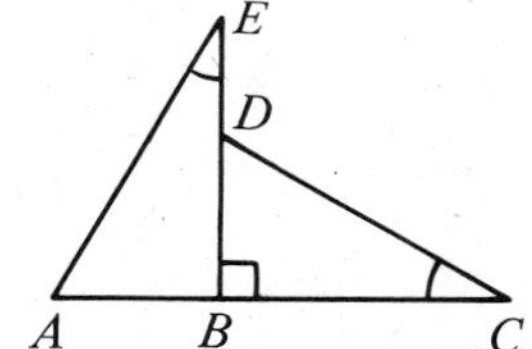


| STATEMENTS | REASONS |
|---|---|
| 1. $\angle EBA$ and $\angle DBC$ are right angles. | 1. ___?___ *Given:* $\overline{EB} \perp \overline{AC}$ |
| 2. $\angle EBA = \angle DBC$ | 2. ___?___ Substitution Post. |
| 3. $\angle E = \angle C$; $EB = BC$ | 3. ___?___ Given |
| 4. $\triangle EBA \cong \triangle CBD$ | 4. ___?___ ASA Postulate |
| 5. $AB = BD$ | 5. ___?___ Corr. parts of $\cong$ $\triangle$s are $=$. |

**Copy what is shown. Then write a proof in two-column form.**

**15.** *Given:* $AX = BX$; $\angle A = \angle B$

*Prove:* $CX = DX$

**16.** *Given:* $AX = BX$; $\angle C = \angle D$

*Prove:* $AC = BD$

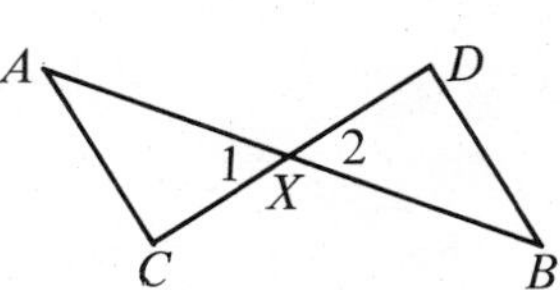

**Copy what is shown. Then write a proof in two-column form.**

17. *Given:* $RT = RQ$; $ST = SQ$
    *Prove:* $\angle T = \angle Q$

18. *Given:* $\angle 1 = \angle 2$; $RT = RQ$
    *Prove:* $ST = SQ$

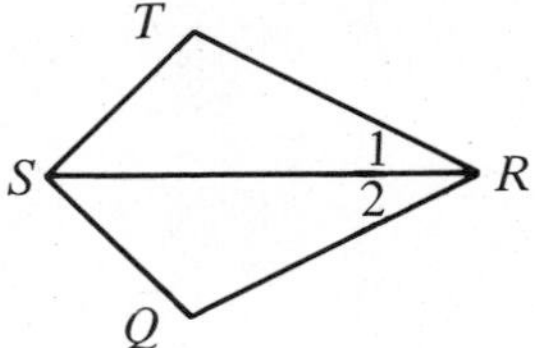


C 19. *Given:* $\overline{JK} \perp \overline{MN}$; $MJ = NJ$
    *Prove:* $MK = NK$

20. *Given:* $\overline{JK} \perp \overline{MN}$; $\angle 3 = \angle 4$
    *Prove:* $MJ = NJ$

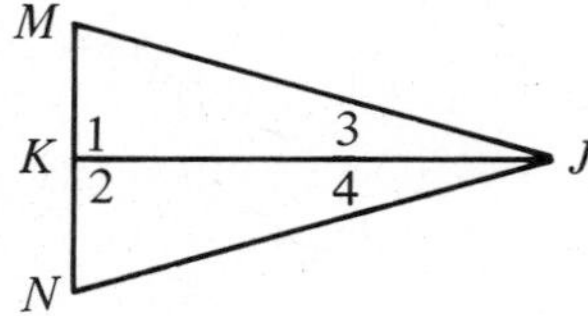


21. *Given:* $\angle 1 = \angle 2$; $AY = BX$
    *Prove:* $\angle A = \angle B$

22. *Given:* $\angle 1 = \angle 2$; $\angle 3 = \angle 4$
    *Prove:* $AX = BY$

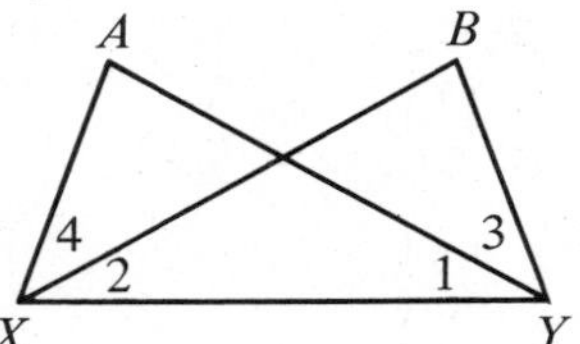


## Puzzles & Things

Sid and Gregory were hiking in the woods when they came to the Red Hawk River. Sid challenged Gregory to guess the width of the river. This is what Gregory did:

He stood at $B$ and looked out across the river. He then adjusted his cap until the tip of his visor was in line with his eye and point $X$. Keeping his neck stiff, he turned and noted the point $Z$, on the ground, that was in line with his eye and the tip of the visor.
By pacing, he found that the distance $BZ$ was about 12 m.
He claimed, "The river is about 12 m wide."
Explain why Gregory was right. $\triangle ABZ \cong \triangle ABX$ by the ASA Post.

## 2 • Congruent Triangles and Constructions

In this section, we shall use congruent triangles to show that our construction methods are correct.

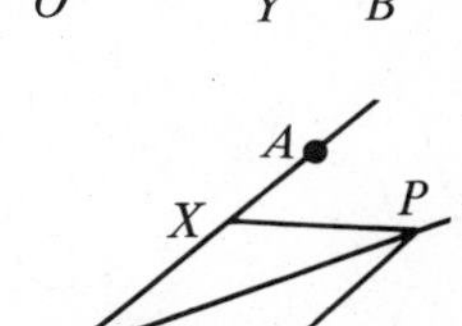


**Bisecting an Angle** (Construction 1, page 21)

To show that $\angle AOB$ really is bisected, draw $\overline{XP}$ and $\overline{YP}$. Then:

| | |
|---|---|
| 1. $OX = OY$ | by construction |
| 2. $XP = YP$ | by construction |
| 3. $OP = OP$ | from algebra |
| 4. $\triangle XOP \cong \triangle YOP$ | SSS Postulate |
| 5. $\angle XOP = \angle YOP$ | Corr. parts of $\cong$ ⚠ are $=$. |

Therefore, $\angle AOB$ is bisected.

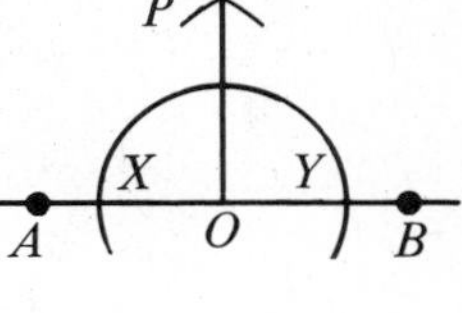


**Constructing a Perpendicular at a Point on a Line**
(Construction 2, page 22)

To show that $\overrightarrow{OP}$ really is perpendicular to $\overleftrightarrow{AB}$, draw $\overline{XP}$ and $\overline{YP}$. Use the SSS Postulate to show that $\triangle XOP \cong \triangle YOP$. Then you know that $\angle XOP = \angle YOP$. You can show that $\angle XOP$ and $\angle YOP$ are right angles (see Written Exercise 8). Therefore, $\overrightarrow{OP} \perp \overleftrightarrow{AB}$.

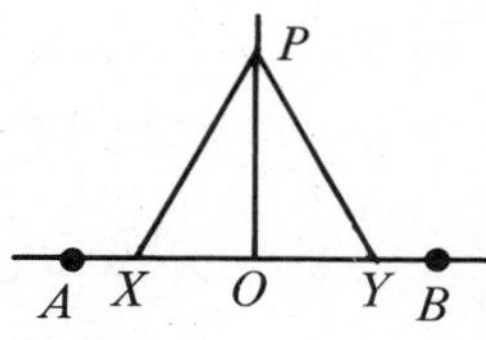


After a construction has been proved to be correct, the construction may be used in proofs. See, for example, Step 1 of Theorem 3 on page 153.

### *Classroom Practice*

Anna started out, in the usual way, to bisect $\angle AOB$. But Anna likes to experiment. So she set her compass for a good-sized radius, used $X$ and $Y$ as centers, and drew arcs to get point $P$ as shown. Finally she drew $\overline{OP}$ and claimed: $\overline{OP}$ bisects $\angle AOB$.

1. Was Anna's statement correct? yes Explain. (See Solution Key.)
2. How could Anna add to her diagram, without using a compass, so that she would clearly show a bisector of $\angle AOB$? Draw $\overrightarrow{PO}$.

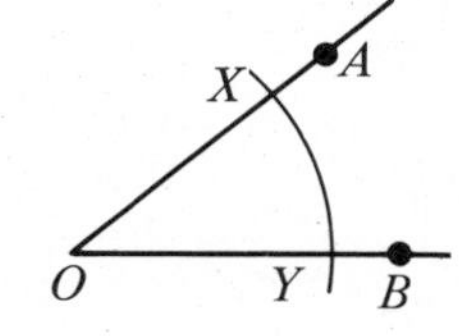


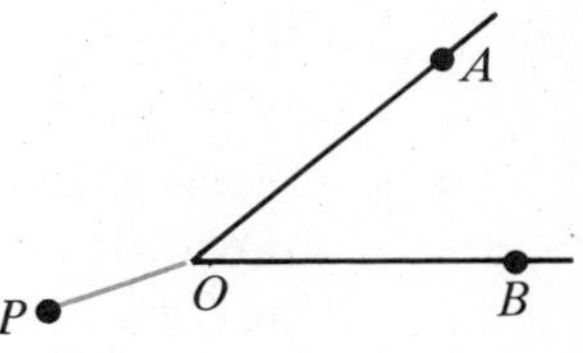

## Written Exercises

**On your paper, draw an acute $\triangle XYZ$ roughly like, but much larger than, the one shown. Use your triangle in Exercises 1–3.**

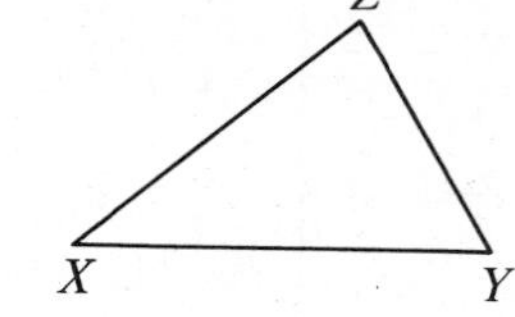


A **1. a.** Draw a line. On it choose a point $D$.
**b.** Set your compass for a radius equal to $XY$.
Then with $D$ as center, draw an arc that intersects the line at a point $E$.
**c.** At $D$, copy $\angle X$.
**d.** At $E$, copy $\angle Y$.
**e.** Use $F$ to label the point at which the new sides of $\angle D$ and $\angle E$ intersect.
**f.** Explain why $\triangle DEF \cong \triangle XYZ$. ASA Postulate

**2. a.** Draw a line. On it choose a point $G$.
**b.** Set your compass for a radius equal to $XY$.
Then with $G$ as center, draw an arc that intersects the line at a point $H$.
**c.** At $G$, copy $\angle X$.
**d.** Set your compass for a radius equal to $XZ$.
On the new side of $\angle G$, draw an arc.
**e.** Use $J$ to label the point at which the arc intersects the side of $\angle G$. Draw $\overline{JH}$.
**f.** Explain why $\triangle GHJ \cong \triangle XYZ$. SAS Postulate

**3. a.** Draw a line. On it choose a point $K$.
**b.** Set your compass for a radius equal to $XY$.
Then with $K$ as center, draw an arc that intersects the line at a point $M$.
**c.** Set your compass for a radius equal to $XZ$.
Use $K$ as center and draw an arc.
**d.** Set your compass for a radius equal to $YZ$.
Use $M$ as center and draw an arc.
**e.** Use $N$ to label the point at which the arcs intersect.
**f.** Draw $\overline{KN}$ and $\overline{MN}$.
**g.** Explain why $\triangle KMN \cong \triangle XYZ$. SSS Postulate

**4–6.** On your paper, draw an obtuse $\triangle XYZ$ roughly like, but much larger than, the one shown. Using $\triangle XYZ$, repeat Exercises 1–3.
4f. ASA Postulate
5f. SAS Postulate
6f. SSS Postulate

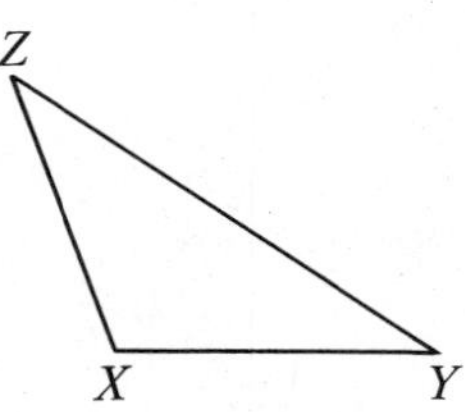

B **7.** The diagram at the left, below, illustrates Construction 3 on page 22. When $\overline{RS}$, $\overline{RT}$, $\overline{US}$, and $\overline{UT}$ are drawn, we have the diagram at the right.

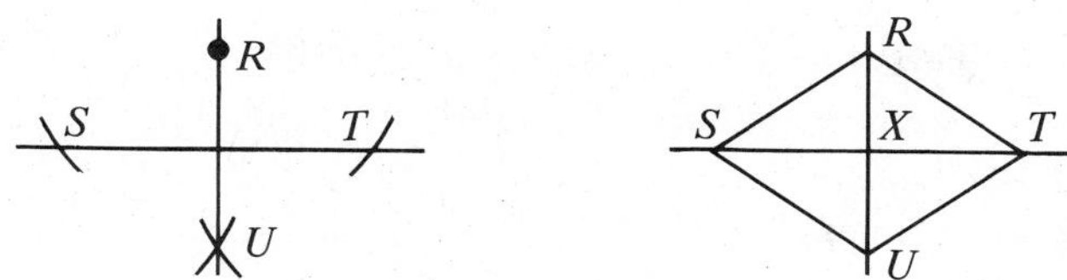


The steps below are the main ones in the proof that $\overleftrightarrow{RU} \perp \overleftrightarrow{ST}$. Complete each statement.

**a.** $\triangle RSU \cong \triangle RTU$ by $\underline{\quad ? \quad}$ (SSS/SAS/ASA/AAS). SSS

**b.** Then $\angle SRU = \angle TRU$ because $\underline{\ ?\ }$. Corr. parts of $\cong$ ⚠ are $=$.

**c.** Using $\triangle RXS$ and $\triangle RXT$:
$RS = RT$ by $\underline{\quad ? \quad}$ (algebra/construction); construction
$\angle SRX = \angle TRX$ because $\angle SRU = \angle TRU$ (see step **b**);
$RX = RX$ by $\underline{\ ?\ }$; algebra
$\triangle RXS \cong \triangle RXT$ by $\underline{\ ?\ }$. SAS

**d.** $\angle RXS = \angle RXT$ because $\underline{\ ?\ }$. Corr. parts of $\cong$ ⚠ are $=$.

**e.** Since $\angle RXS = \angle RXT$ and $\angle RXS + \angle RXT = 180°$, both $\angle RXS$ and $\angle RXT$ have measure $\underline{\ ?\ }°$. Then $\overleftrightarrow{RU} \perp \overleftrightarrow{ST}$.

**8.** Refer to the construction at the right, which illustrates Construction 2 on page 22. Explain why $\overrightarrow{OP} \perp \overleftrightarrow{XY}$.

(*Hint:* See step **e**, above.) $\triangle XOP \cong \triangle YOP$ by SSS; hence $\angle XOP = \angle YOP$; from step e above, $\overleftrightarrow{OP} \perp \overleftrightarrow{XY}$.

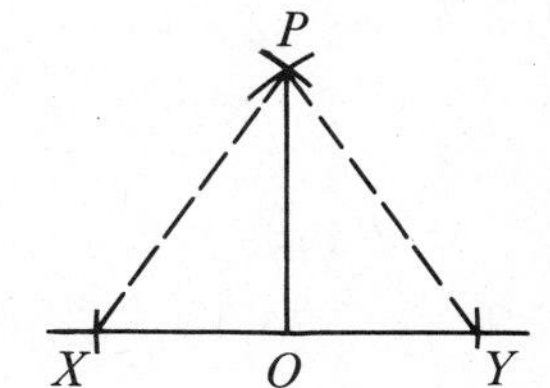


**9.** In the diagram at the right, $\angle A$ was given. $\angle O$ was constructed using Construction 4 on page 71. Explain why $\angle O = \angle A$.
$\triangle AXY \cong \triangle OBC$ by SSS; $\angle O = \angle A$ since corresponding parts of $\cong$ ⚠ are $=$.

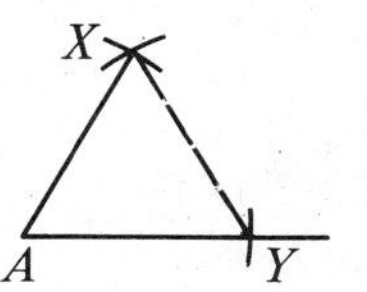


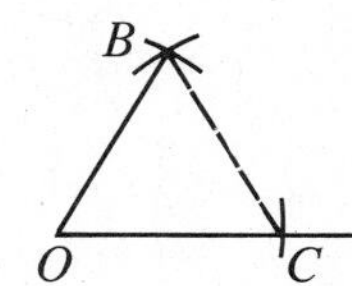

**10.** On your paper, draw a $\triangle DEZ$ with $DZ$ clearly shorter than $EZ$. Construct the bisector of $\angle Z$. Use $V$ to label the point where the bisector meets $\overline{DE}$. Is $\triangle DVZ \cong \triangle EVZ$? No
Explain. We have only two pairs of corr. parts.

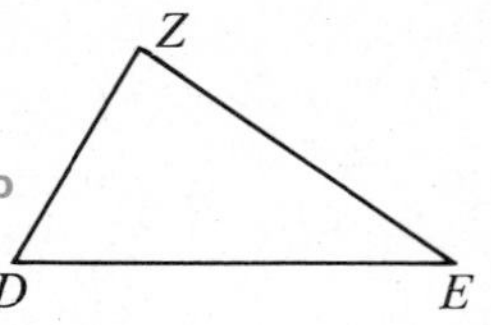


**11.** Draw a segment $\overline{DE}$. Using one setting of your compass, construct two arcs, one with center at $D$ and the other with center at $E$. $Z$ is the point where the arcs meet. isosceles;

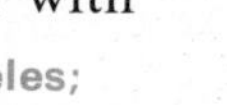

**a.** What kind of triangle is $\triangle DEZ$? Explain. by construction

**b.** Construct the bisector of $\angle Z$. Use $V$ to label the point where the bisector meets $\overline{DE}$.

**c.** Is $\triangle DVZ \cong \triangle EVZ$? Explain. Yes; SAS Postulate

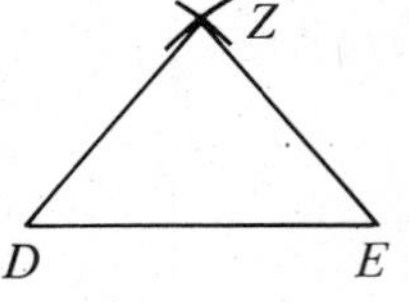


C **12.** Using a straightedge and lined paper, draw (you need not construct) a rectangle $ABCD$ that is clearly longer than it is wide. Construct the bisector of $\angle A$ and the bisector of $\angle B$. Use $M$ to label the point where the bisectors intersect. Explain why $\triangle AMB$ is a right triangle. (*Hint:* Each angle of a rectangle is a right angle.) $\angle BMA = 180° - \frac{1}{2}\angle A - \frac{1}{2}\angle B = 180° - 45° - 45° = 90°$

**13.** As in Exercise 12, draw a rectangle $ABCD$ that is clearly longer than it is wide. Construct the bisector of $\angle A$ and the bisector of $\angle C$. Explain why the bisectors are parallel. (*Hint:* Label the angle measures in your diagram. If necessary, glance back at Section 6 of Chapter 2.) $\overline{DC}$ is a transversal of both bisectors. Corr. angles are equal (45°). Hence the bisectors are parallel.

**14.** Draw a quadrilateral $ABCD$ roughly like the one shown, but much larger. Draw $\overline{AC}$.
Construct a $\triangle A'B'C'$ that is congruent to $\triangle ABC$.
Building on $\overline{A'C'}$, construct a $\triangle A'C'D'$ that is congruent to $\triangle ACD$.
Does each side and each angle of quadrilateral $A'B'C'D'$ equal the corresponding part of quadrilateral $ABCD$? Yes

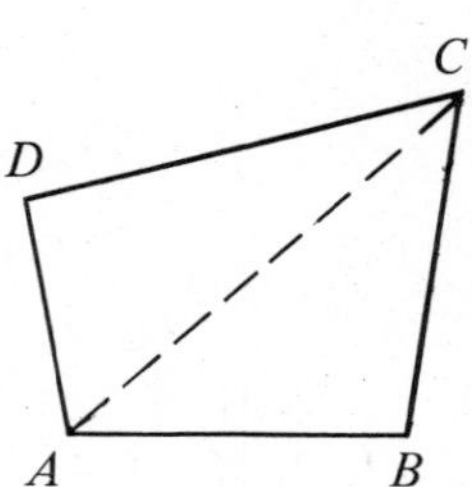


**15.** Draw a pentagon $ABCDE$. Draw diagonals $\overline{AC}$ and $\overline{AD}$. Construct a pentagon $A'B'C'D'E'$ that is congruent to pentagon $ABCDE$.

**16.** Draw a pentagon $RSTVW$. Choose any point $P$ inside the pentagon. Draw $\overline{PR}$, $\overline{PS}$, $\overline{PT}$, $\overline{PV}$, and $\overline{PW}$. Construct a pentagon $R'S'T'V'W'$ that is congruent to pentagon $RSTVW$.

## SELF-TEST

**Write proofs in two-column form.**

1. *Given:* $RM = TM$
   $UM = SM$
   *Prove:* $RU = TS$

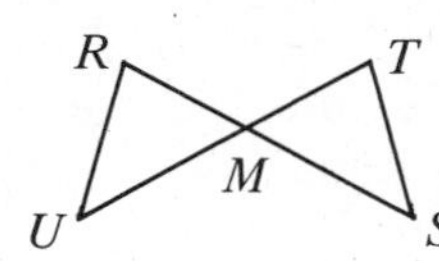


2. *Given:* $AX = AY$
   $\angle X = \angle Y = 90°$
   *Prove:* $\angle 1 = \angle 2$

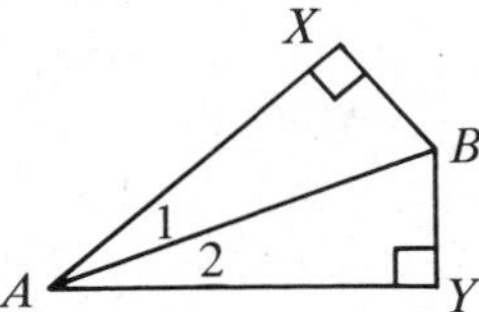


3. Suppose you want to prove that your construction of a perpendicular from $P$ to $m$ is correct.
   What postulate supports the statement:
   $\triangle PET \cong \triangle PIT$? SSS Postulate

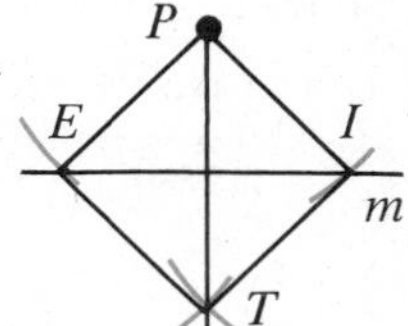


## CONSUMER CORNER

### *Life Insurance*

Many different life insurance policies are offered by many different companies. There are two general types of life insurance with which you should be familiar.

*Permanent* life insurance is the kind most people know. This type of insurance is part financial protection in case of death and part savings plan. The face amount of the policy is paid out by the insurance company either when the insured person dies or when the insured person reaches an age (often 65 or 70) specified in the policy.

*Term* life insurance does not provide a savings feature. The principal is paid out by the insurance company only if the insured person dies within the term of years specified in the policy.

Which type of insurance is better? Term insurance costs less, but there is no guarantee of ever collecting any money from the insurance company. Permanent life insurance costs more, but provides a savings plan in addition to financial protection against sudden death. Before you buy insurance, you should consult an insurance broker or a banker.

## 3 • Segment Bisectors

Suppose that $M$ is the midpoint of $\overline{YZ}$. Any segment, ray, or line that passes through $M$ *bisects* $\overline{YZ}$ and is a **bisector** of $\overline{YZ}$. The diagram suggests that a segment has an unlimited number of bisectors.

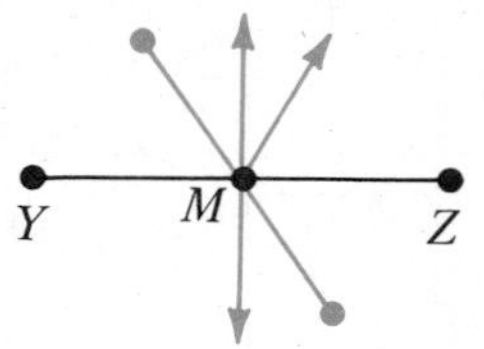


A bisector of a segment that is perpendicular to the segment is called a **perpendicular bisector** of the segment. As shown at the right, $YM = MZ$ and $\overline{LM} \perp \overline{YZ}$, so $\overline{LM}$ is a perpendicular bisector of $\overline{YZ}$. You may wish to refer to $\overline{LM}$ as *the* perpendicular bisector of $\overline{YZ}$.

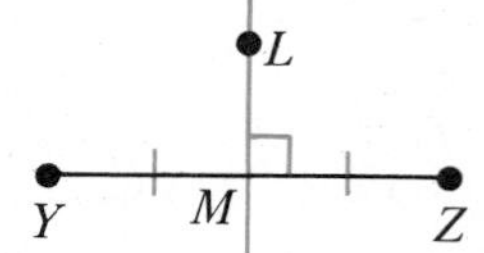

**CONSTRUCTION 6** *Given:* A segment
*Construct:* A perpendicular bisector of the segment

Follow these steps:

**1.**

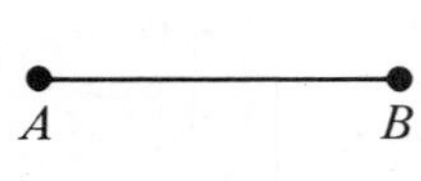


You are given $\overline{AB}$.

**2.**

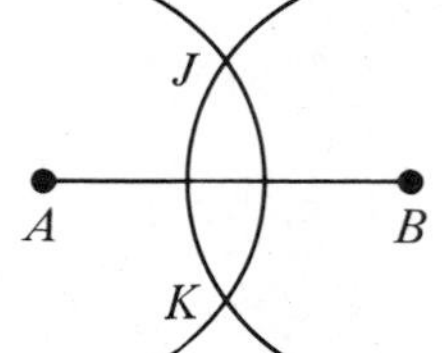


Set your compass for a convenient radius. Using $A$ and $B$ as centers, draw arcs that meet at $J$ and $K$.

**3.**

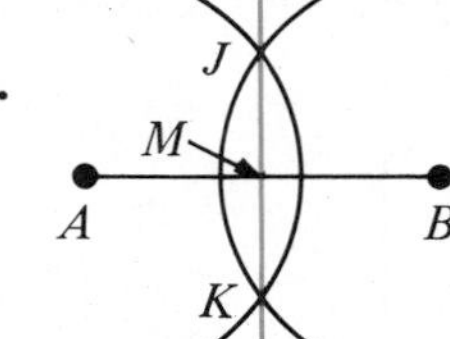


Draw $\overleftrightarrow{JK}$.
$\overleftrightarrow{JK}$ is a perpendicular bisector of $\overline{AB}$. $M$ is the midpoint of $\overline{AB}$.

A segment, $\overline{CD}$, and its perpendicular bisector are shown at the right. Is point $R$ closer to point $C$ or to point $D$? Neither one, it seems. $RC = RD$, and we say that $R$ is *equidistant* from $C$ and $D$. Point $S$ is also equidistant from $C$ and $D$ because $SC = SD$.

R
S
C M D
T
l

Any point on $l$ is equidistant from $C$ and $D$.

**THEOREM 1**

Any point on the perpendicular bisector of a segment is equidistant from the endpoints of the segment.

*Given:* $\overleftrightarrow{RM}$ is the perpendicular bisector of $\overline{CD}$.

*Prove:* $RC = RD$

See if you can supply the reasons for the proof.

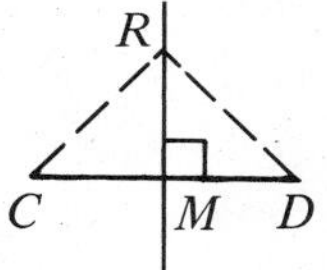


| STATEMENTS | REASONS |
|---|---|
| 1. $\overleftrightarrow{RM} \perp \overline{CD}$ | 1. __?__ Given |
| 2. $\angle RMC$ and $\angle RMD$ are right angles. | 2. __?__ Def. of *perpendicular* |
| 3. $\angle RMC = \angle RMD$ | 3. __?__ All right angles are =. |
| 4. $CM = DM$ | 4. __?__ *Given:* $\overleftrightarrow{RM}$ bisects $\overline{CD}$ |
| 5. $RM = RM$ | 5. __?__ From algebra |
| 6. $\triangle RMC \cong \triangle RMD$ | 6. __?__ SAS Postulate |
| 7. $RC = RD$ | 7. __?__ Corresponding parts |

Theorem 2 is the converse of Theorem 1. The proof is left as Exercise 16 on page 143.

**THEOREM 2**

Any point that is equidistant from the endpoints of a segment is on the perpendicular bisector of the segment.

## *Classroom Practice*

**In Exercises 1–7, line *l* is a perpendicular bisector of $\overline{AB}$. Classify each statement as true or false.**

True **1.** $M$ is the midpoint of $\overline{AB}$.

**2.** $\angle 1$ is an acute angle. False

**3.** $l \perp \overline{AB}$ True

**4.** $AD = BD$ True

**5.** $AB = CD$ False

**6.** $\angle 1 = \angle 2$ True

**7.** Any point on $\overline{CD}$ is equidistant from $A$ and $B$. True

8. A student tried to construct a perpendicular bisector as shown. What went wrong? The arcs do not intersect. The student must use a larger radius.

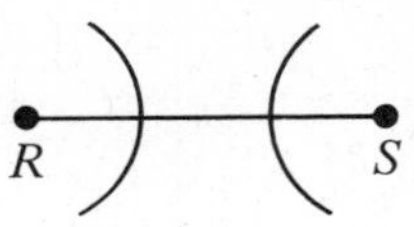


9. Think of the perpendicular bisector of $\overline{XY}$ and the perpendicular bisector of $\overline{YZ}$. Do the two perpendicular bisectors intersect? Explain. No, they are parallel by Theorem 8, page 66.

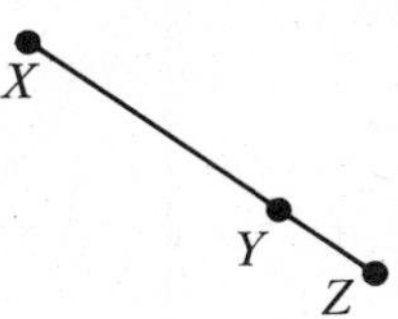


## *Written Exercises*

**In Exercises 1–5, $JK = KL$. Complete each statement.**

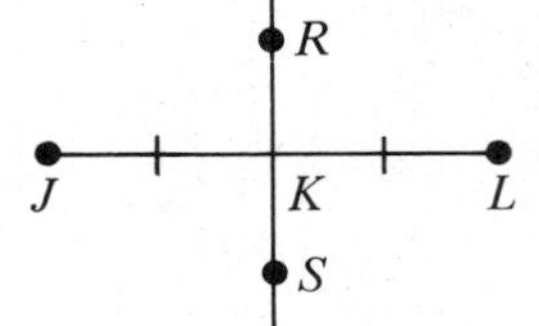


A 1. $K$ is the __?__ of $\overline{JL}$. midpoint

2. Since $\overleftrightarrow{RS}$ passes through $K$, $\overleftrightarrow{RS}$ is a __?__ of $\overline{JL}$. bisector

3. If $\overline{RK} \perp \overline{JL}$, then $\overline{RK}$ is a __?__ of $\overline{JL}$. perp. bisector

4. If $SJ = SL$, then $S$ is __?__ from $J$ and $L$. equidistant

5. Suppose $\overleftrightarrow{RS}$ is the perpendicular bisector of $\overline{JL}$. State the theorem that allows you to conclude that $RJ = RL$. Thm. 1: Any point on the perp. bis. of a segment is equidistant from the endpoints of the segment.

**In Exercises 6–11, draw a figure roughly like the one shown. Then construct the indicated perpendicular.**

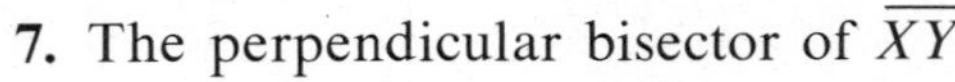

6. The perpendicular bisector of $\overline{AB}$

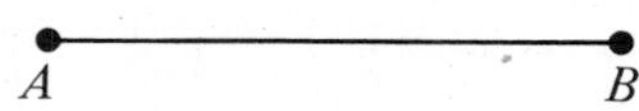


7. The perpendicular bisector of $\overline{XY}$

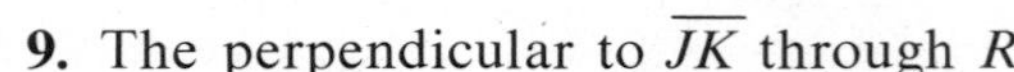

8. The perpendicular to $\overline{CD}$ at $P$

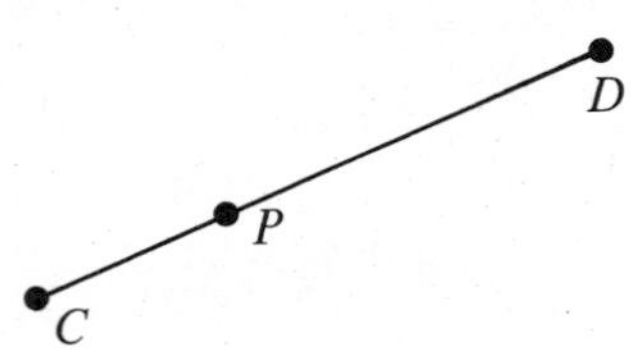


9. The perpendicular to $\overline{JK}$ through $R$

10. The perpendicular bisector of $\overline{PQ}$

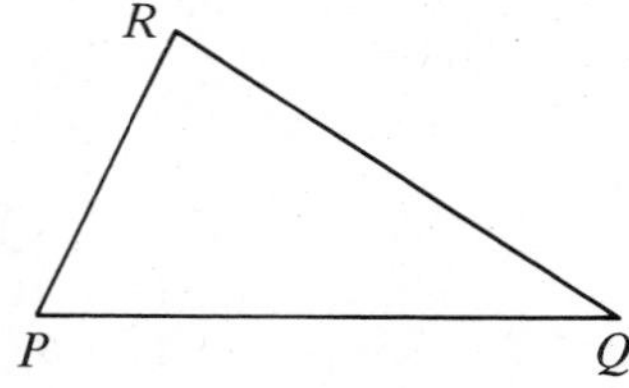


11. The perpendicular bisector of $\overline{BD}$

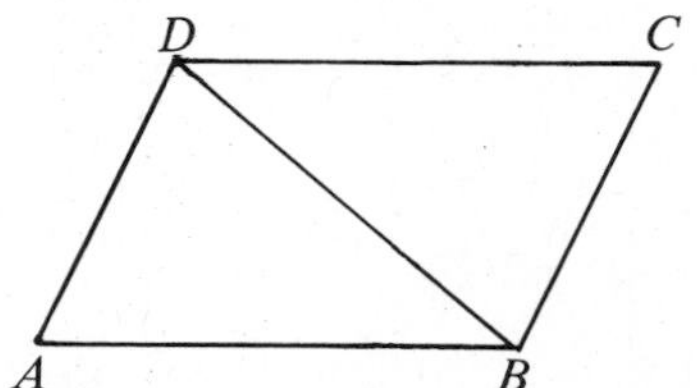

B **12.** Construct a 90° angle. Then draw a segment to form a right triangle. Construct the perpendicular bisector of each leg of the right triangle. midpoint of hypotenuse
Where do the perpendicular bisectors appear to meet?

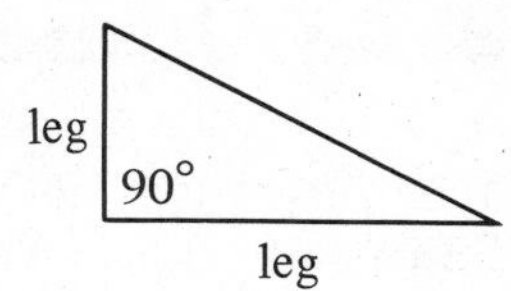


**13.** Repeat Exercise 12, using a different-looking right triangle.
Complete the statement: The perpendicular bisectors of the legs of a right triangle appear to meet at __?__. the midpt. of the hypotenuse

**14.** Construct a large isosceles triangle, using the method outlined in Exercise 11 on page 138. Then construct the perpendicular bisector of the base.
Through what point does the perpendicular bisector seem to pass? the vertex

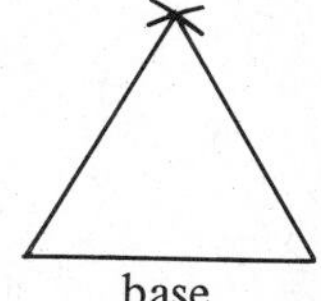


**15.** Repeat Exercise 14, using a different-looking isosceles triangle. Complete the statement: The perpendicular bisector of the base of an isosceles triangle appears to pass through __?__. the vertex

C **16.** One way to prove Theorem 2 is suggested below. Write the proof.

*Given:* $RC = RD$

$M$ is the midpoint of $\overline{CD}$.

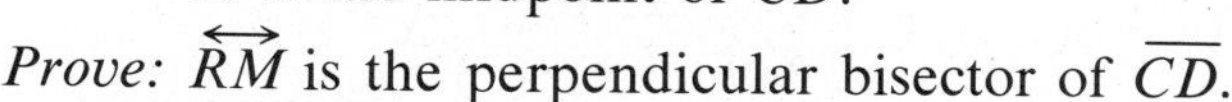

*Prove:* $\overleftrightarrow{RM}$ is the perpendicular bisector of $\overline{CD}$.

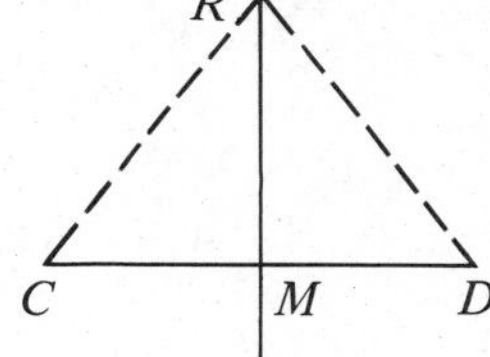


*Strategy for proof:*

A. Prove that $\triangle CRM \cong \triangle DRM$.

B. Prove that $\angle RMC$ and $\angle RMD$ are equal and are right angles.

C. Use the right angles to prove that $\overline{RM} \perp \overline{CD}$.

**17.** Use congruent triangles to show that Construction 6 does produce the perpendicular bisector of a segment.

*Given:* $JA = JB$; $KA = KB$

*Prove:* $AM = MB$; $\overleftrightarrow{JK} \perp \overline{AB}$

*Strategy for proof:*

A. Prove that $\triangle AJK \cong \triangle BJK$.

B. Prove that $\angle AJM = \angle BJM$.

C. Prove that $\triangle AJM \cong \triangle BJM$.

D. Prove that $AM = MB$ and $\angle AMJ = \angle BMJ$.

E. Use right angles to prove that $\overleftrightarrow{JK} \perp \overline{AB}$.

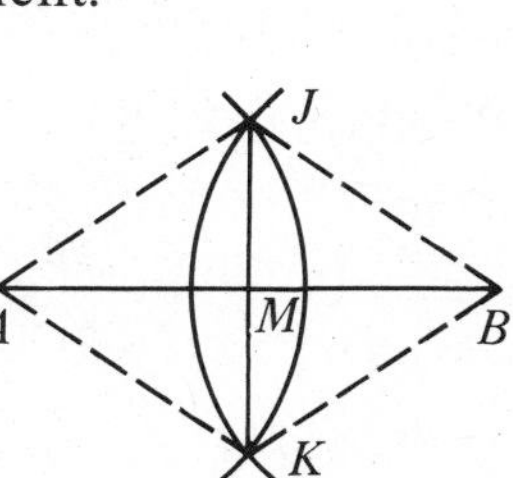

# 4 • Altitudes and Medians of a Triangle

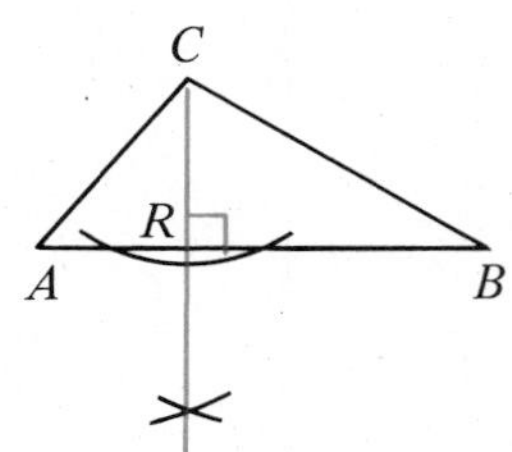


The diagram at the right shows how Construction 3 can be used to construct a perpendicular to side $\overline{AB}$ through vertex $C$. We call $\overline{CR}$ the *altitude* of $\triangle ABC$ drawn to side $\overline{AB}$. In general, an **altitude** of a triangle is a segment, drawn from any vertex, perpendicular to the line that contains the opposite side.

Every triangle has three altitudes, one from each vertex.

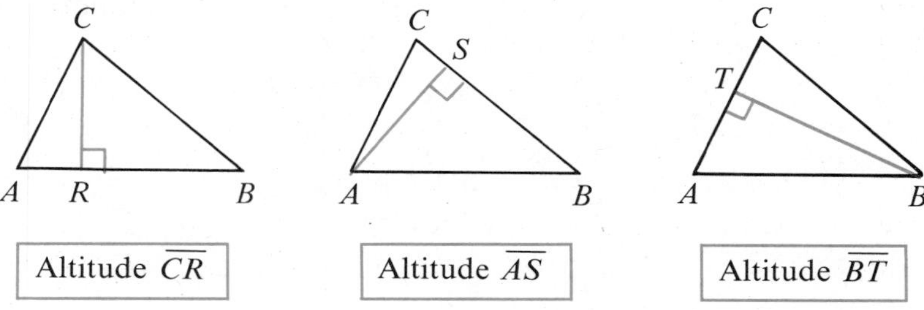


Sometimes it isn't so easy to draw an altitude. Here the altitude from $F$ doesn't intersect *segment* $DE$. But it does intersect *line* $DE$.

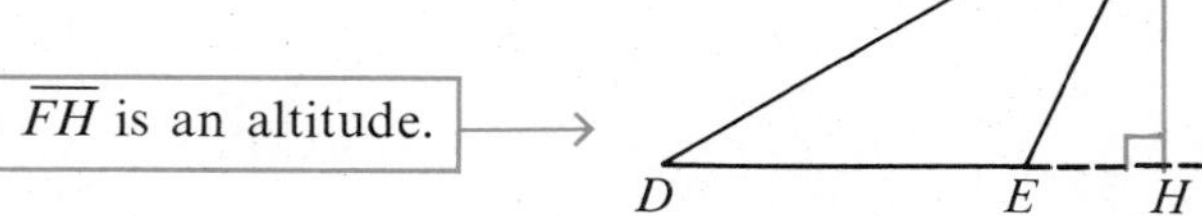


In any triangle, the three lines containing the altitudes meet in one point.

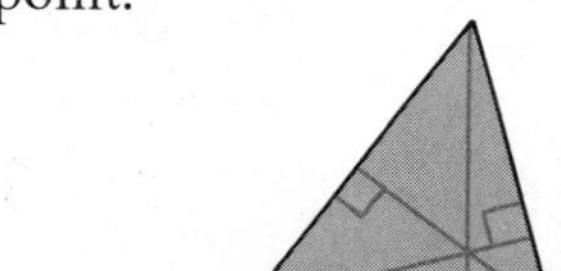

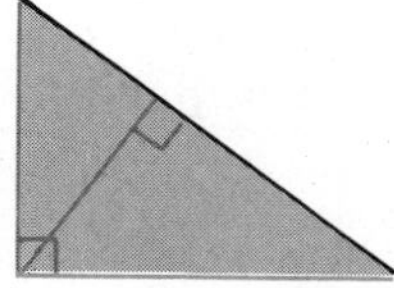

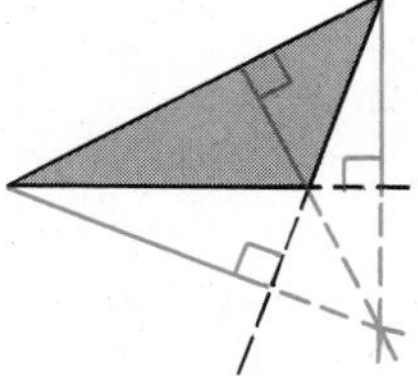

| **Acute triangle** | **Right triangle** | **Obtuse triangle** |
|---|---|---|
| The lines meet inside the triangle. | The lines meet at the vertex of the right angle. | The lines meet outside the triangle. |

Let's look at $\triangle ABC$ once again. Since $M$ is the midpoint of side $\overline{AB}$, $\overline{CM}$ is a *median* of the triangle. A **median** is a segment that joins a vertex of the triangle to the midpoint of the opposite side.

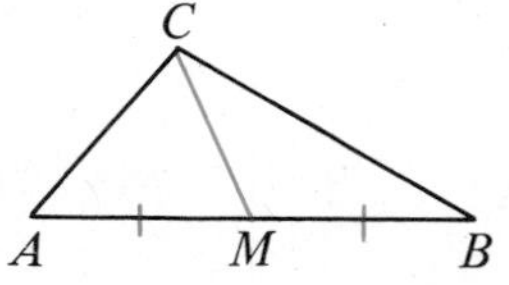

Every triangle has three medians, and they always meet inside the triangle.

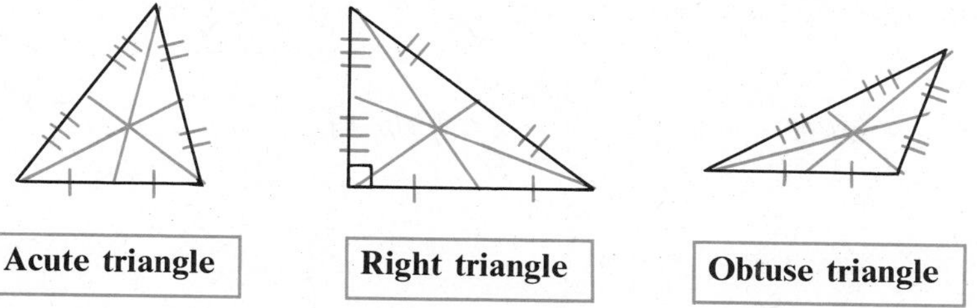


Compare the altitudes and the medians of the triangles shown. Notice that, in general, the altitude and the median to a side of a triangle are *different* segments.

## Classroom Practice

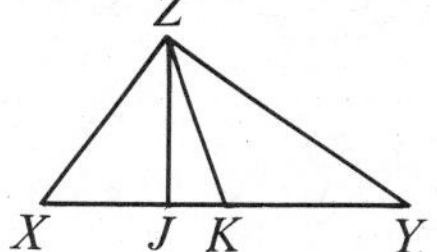


**1.** Point $K$ is the midpoint of $\overline{XY}$, and $\overline{ZJ} \perp \overline{XY}$.

**a.** The altitude shown is segment _?_. ZJ

**b.** The median shown is segment _?_. ZK

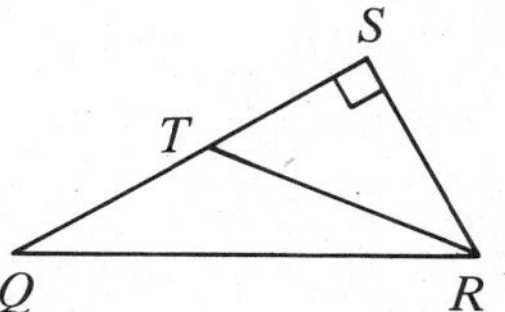


**2.** Point $T$ is the midpoint of leg $\overline{SQ}$ in right $\triangle QRS$.

**a.** The altitude to side $\overline{SQ}$ is segment _?_. RS

**b.** The median to side $\overline{SQ}$ is segment _?_. RT

**For each exercise, think of the three altitudes of the triangle shown. (Do not draw in your book.) Tell whether each altitude lies inside, on, or outside the triangle.**

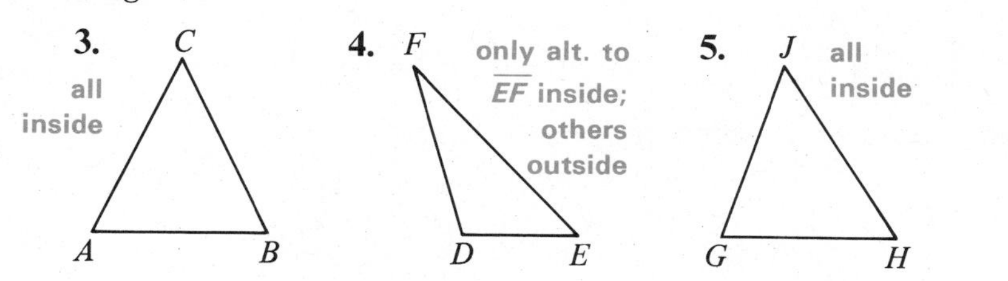


**3.** all inside

**4.** only alt. to $\overline{EF}$ inside; others outside

**5.** all inside

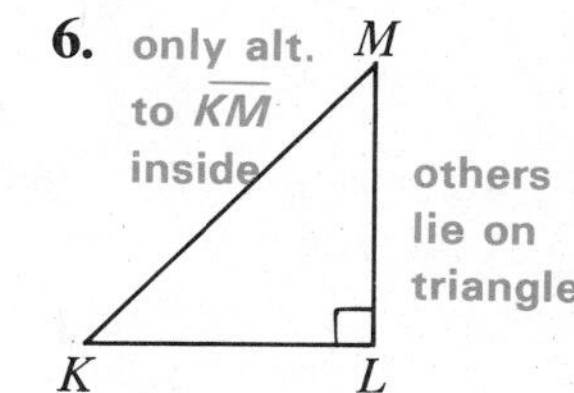


**6.** only alt. to $\overline{KM}$ inside; others lie on triangle

**7–10.** Use the figures for Exercises 3–6. Think of the three medians of the triangle shown. Tell whether each median lies inside, on, or outside the triangle. All medians lie inside.

**11.** You know that, in general, the altitude and the median to a side of a triangle are different segments. Describe a triangle in which an altitude and a median are the very same segment.
The altitude and median from the vertex of an isosceles triangle are the same segment.

## Written Exercises

**Draw a triangle roughly like the one shown, but larger. Draw and label the altitude to side $\overline{AB}$.**

A **1.**

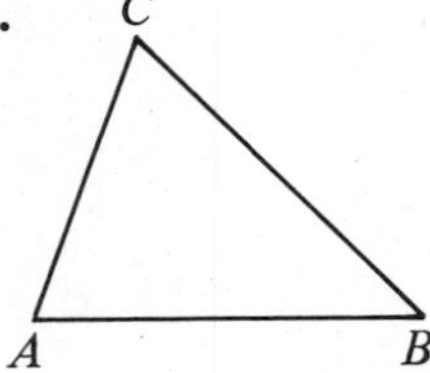


**2.**

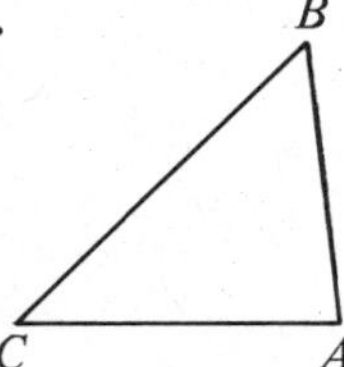


**3.**

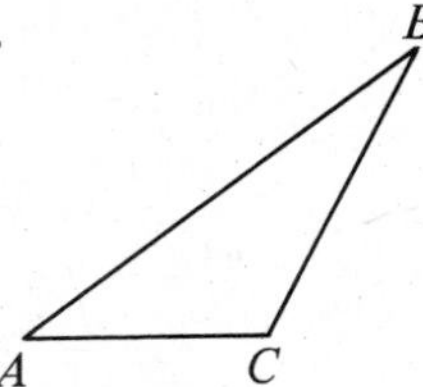


**Draw a triangle roughly like the one shown, but larger. Construct and label the midpoint of side $\overline{YZ}$. Then draw the median to $\overline{YZ}$.**

**4.**

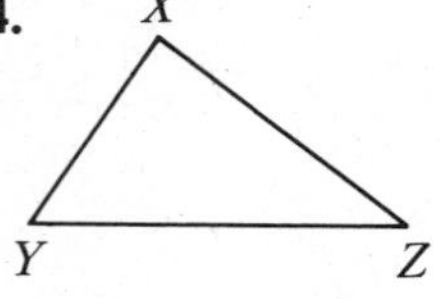


**5.**

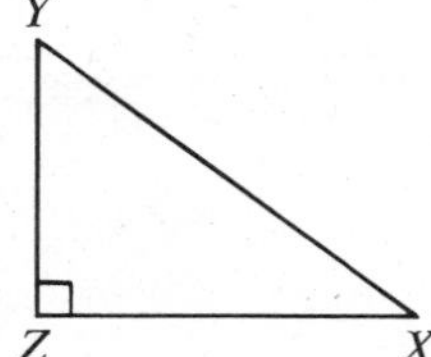


**6.**

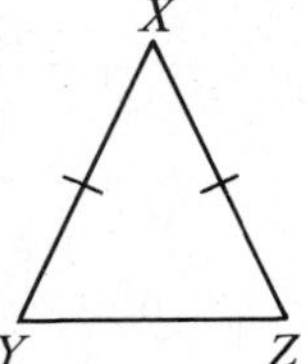


**7.** Draw a triangle roughly like $\triangle RST$, but larger. Then draw each of the following (you need not construct):

**a.** The altitude from $R$

**b.** The median from $R$

**c.** The perpendicular bisector of $\overline{ST}$

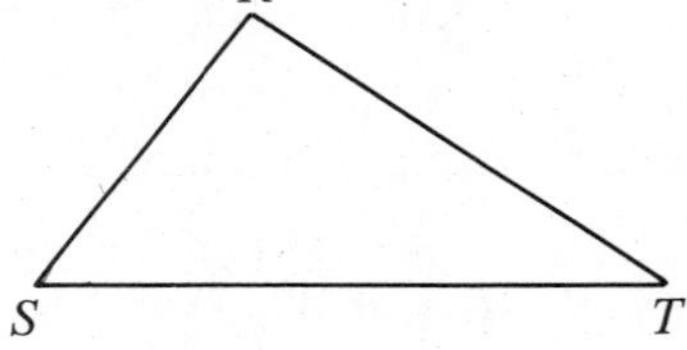


**8.** Repeat Exercise 7, using an isosceles $\triangle RST$ with $RS = RT$. What do you notice? All three segments are the same.

**Draw a triangle roughly like the one shown, but larger. Construct the three altitudes of the triangle.**

**9.**

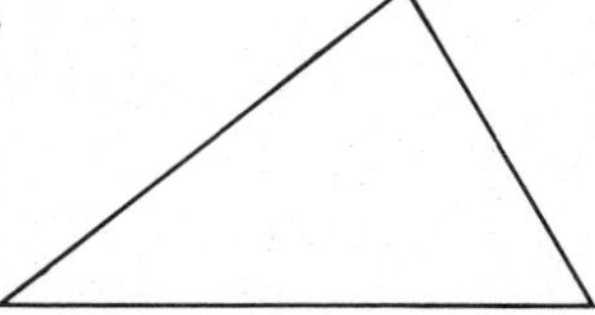

**10.**

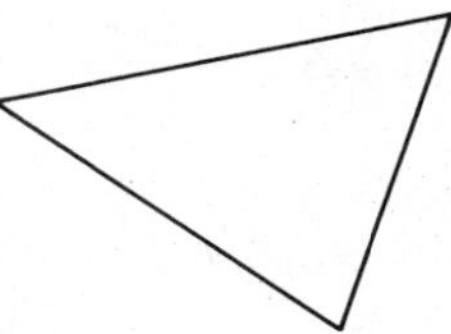

**11. a.** Draw an acute triangle.

**b.** Use Construction 6 to locate the midpoint of each side.

**c.** Draw the three medians of the triangle.

12. **a.** Construct a right angle.
**b.** Draw a segment to form a right triangle.
**c.** Use Construction 6 to locate the midpoint of each side.
**d.** Draw the three medians of the triangle.

13. **a.** Draw a large acute $\triangle ABC$.
**b.** Construct: the midpoint $M$ of $\overline{BC}$; the midpoint $N$ of $\overline{AC}$; the midpoint $K$ of $\overline{AB}$.
**c.** Draw the three medians. Use $P$ to label the point of intersection.
**d.**

| *By measurement* | | *By arithmetic* |
|---|---|---|
| $AP =$ ? | $AM =$ ? | $\frac{2}{3}(AM) =$ ? |
| $BP =$ ? | $BN =$ ? | $\frac{2}{3}(BN) =$ ? |
| $CP =$ ? | $CK =$ ? | $\frac{2}{3}(CK) =$ ? |

Measurements will vary; first and third columns should be the same.

14. Repeat Exercise 13 using an obtuse triangle. same relationships

15. Examine part **d** of Exercises 13 and 14.
What do you observe about the first and third columns? They are the same.
Complete: The medians of a triangle meet in a point which is ___?___ of the way from any vertex to the opposite side. two-thirds

C 16. **a.** Draw a large obtuse triangle.
**b.** Construct the three altitudes of the triangle.
**c.** If you extend the altitudes, will they meet in a point? Yes

17. Repeat Exercise 16, using a different-looking obtuse triangle. Yes

18. The goal is to prove that *corresponding altitudes of congruent triangles are equal.* Copy what is shown and write a proof in two-column form.

*Given:* $\triangle RST \cong \triangle XYZ$
$\overline{TV} \perp \overline{RS}$; $\overline{ZW} \perp \overline{XY}$

*Prove:* $TV = ZW$

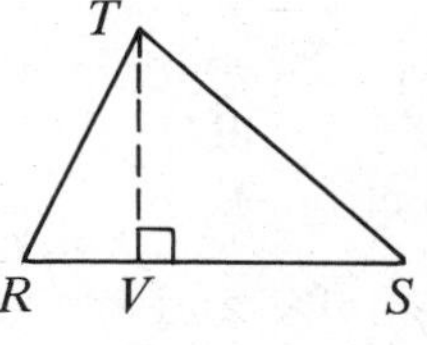


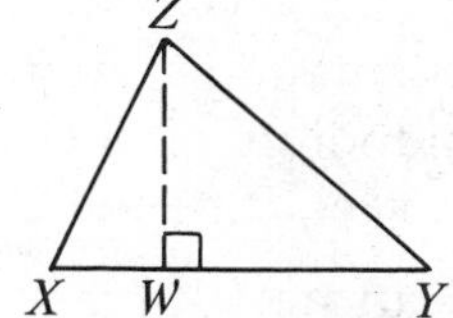


*Strategy for proof:*

A. Use the congruent triangles to prove $RT = XZ$ and $\angle R = \angle X$.

B. Use perpendicular lines to prove $\angle RVT = \angle XWZ$.

C. Prove $\triangle RVT \cong \triangle XWZ$.

D. Use the fact that corr. parts of $\cong$ $\triangle$s are $=$.

## Experiments

### EXPERIMENT 1

1. Take a large sheet of paper and fold it down the middle. Cut from the corner to any point on the fold as shown. Unfold.
2. What kind of triangle did you form? isosceles
3. Explain why the fold is both an altitude and a median. (see below)
4. Complete: The median and the altitude to the base of an ___?___ triangle are the same segment. isosceles

fold
cut

3. The fold is the perp. bisector of the base.

### EXPERIMENT 2

1. Plot points $A(0, 0)$, $B(6, 12)$, and $C(12, 0)$ on graph paper. Draw $\triangle ABC$.
2. Draw dots at the midpoints of the sides of $\triangle ABC$. Draw the three medians. Use $P$ to label the point where the medians meet. Use $M$ to label the midpoint of $\overline{BC}$.
3. $M$ is point (___?___, ___?___) and $P$ is point (___?___, ___?___). $M(9, 6)$ $P(6, 4)$
4. Measure $AP$ and $AM$ with your ruler. If you worked carefully, $AP = \frac{2}{3}(AM)$.

### EXPERIMENT 3

Repeat Experiment 2, using points $A(0, 0)$, $B(0, 6)$, and $C(12, -12)$. $M(6, -3)$ $P(4, -2)$

Experiments 2 and 3 suggest this property: The medians of a triangle intersect in a point which is two-thirds of the way along each median.

See Suggested Extension to Chapter 12, Section 7 on page T126.

## Puzzles & Things

### A Balancing Point

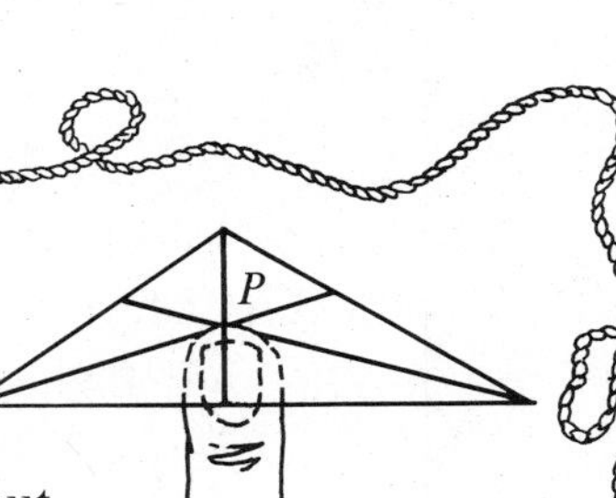


Draw a large triangle on cardboard. Construct the midpoints of the three sides. Draw the medians and let $P$ be the intersection point. Cut the triangle out.

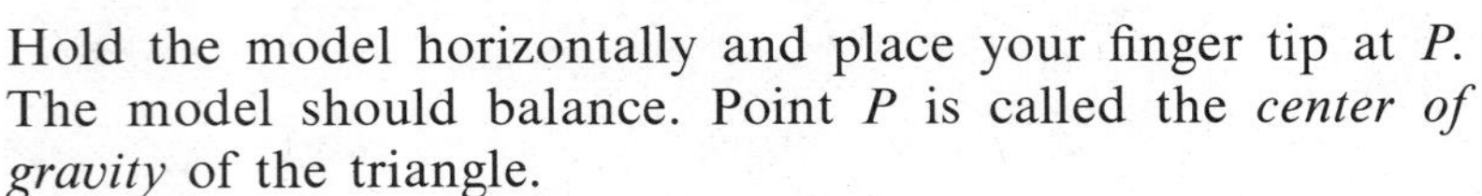
Hold the model horizontally and place your finger tip at $P$. The model should balance. Point $P$ is called the *center of gravity* of the triangle.

Try this experiment with other triangles.

## 5 • Inscribed and Circumscribed Circles

We know that the medians of a triangle meet in a point. So do the lines containing the altitudes. What about the perpendicular bisectors of the sides?

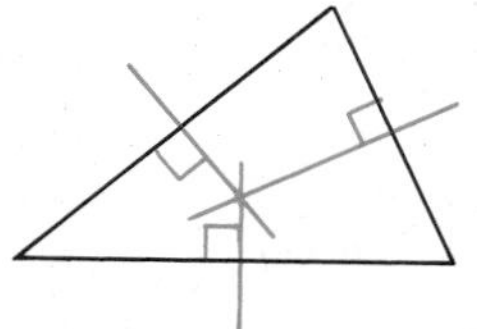

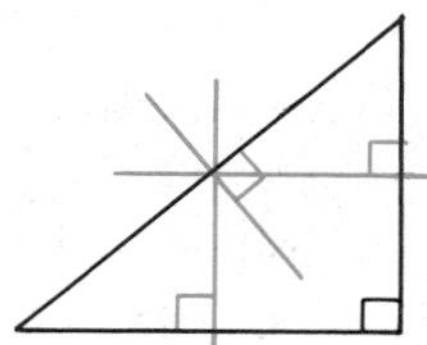

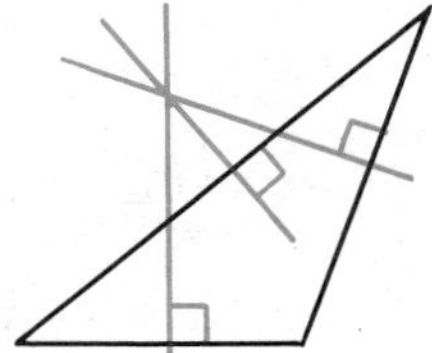

| **Acute triangle** | **Right triangle** | **Obtuse triangle** |
|---|---|---|
| ⊥ bisectors meet inside triangle. | ⊥ bisectors meet on triangle. | ⊥ bisectors meet outside triangle. |

This special point in which the perpendicular bisectors meet is used in the following construction.

CONSTRUCTION 7 *Given:* A triangle

*Construct:* A circle passing through the vertices of the triangle.

**1.**

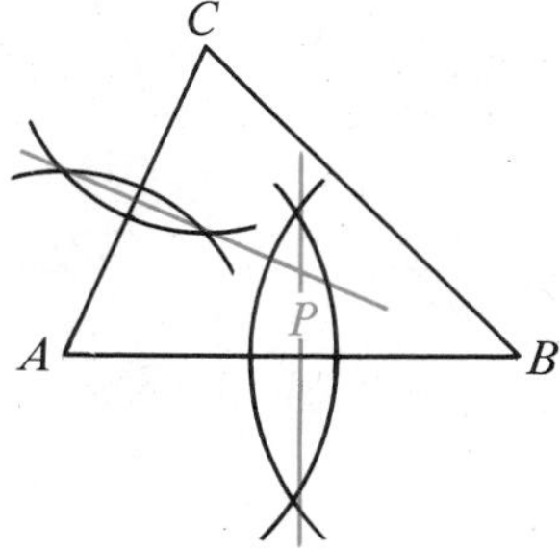


Given $\triangle ABC$, construct the perpendicular bisectors of any two sides. Label the meeting point $P$.

**2.**

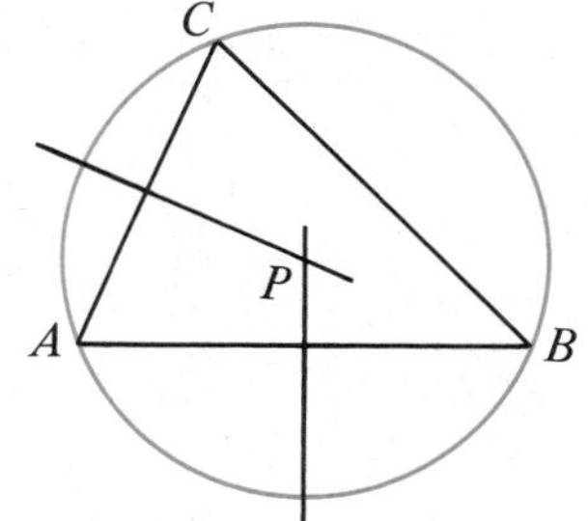


Using $P$ as center and $PA$ as radius, draw a circle. The circle should pass through $A$, $B$, and $C$.

When each vertex of a triangle is a point on a circle, we say that the circle is **circumscribed about** the triangle. In the construction above, for example, the circle shown is circumscribed about $\triangle ABC$. The figure at the right shows another **circumscribed circle.**

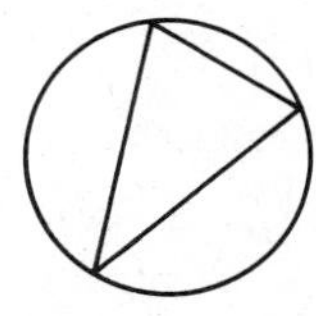

A circumscribed circle fits exactly *around* a triangle. On the other hand, an **inscribed circle** (see page 330) fits exactly *inside* a triangle. Here are some inscribed circles.

Suppose you are given a triangle, $\triangle DEF$. To find the center of the circle which can be inscribed in $\triangle DEF$, we use this fact: The angle bisectors of a triangle meet in a point which is the center of the inscribed circle.

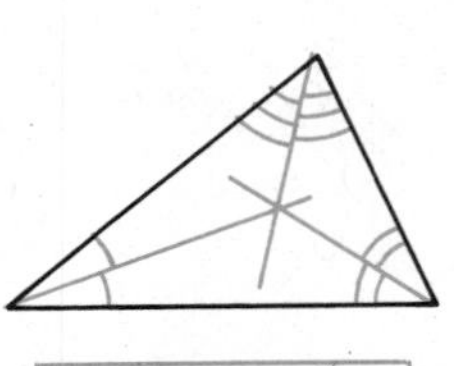

**Acute triangle**

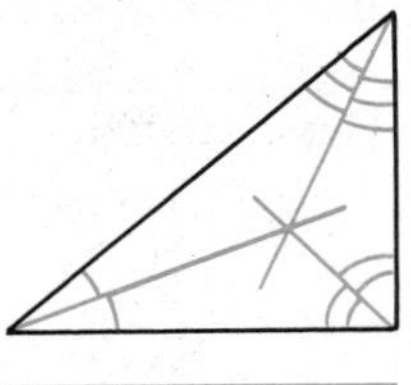

**Right triangle**

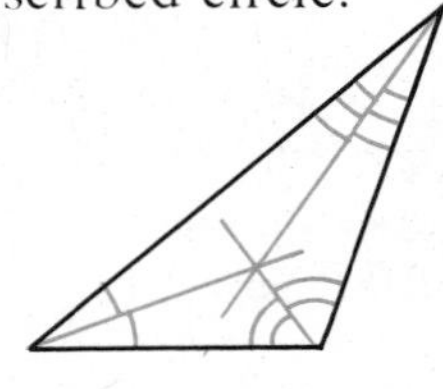

**Obtuse triangle**

CONSTRUCTION 8 *Given:* A triangle

*Construct:* An inscribed circle

**1.**

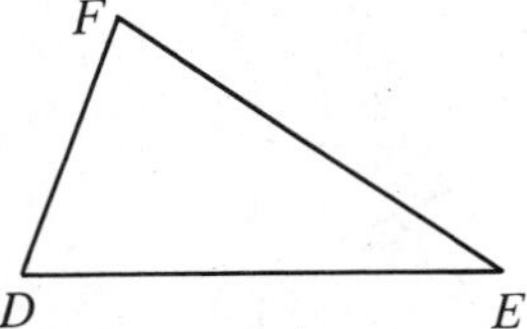


You are given $\triangle DEF$.

**2.**

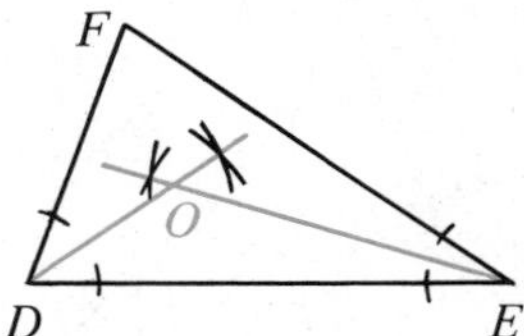


Construct the angle bisectors of any two angles. Label the meeting point $O$.

**3.**

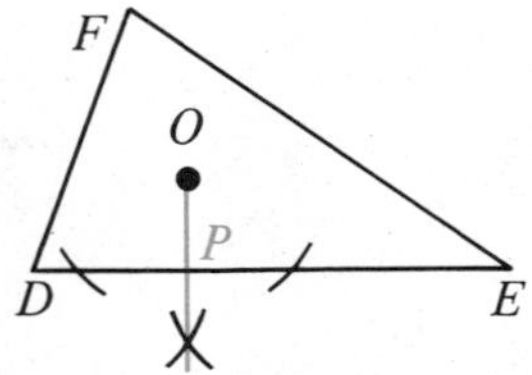


Construct a perpendicular from $O$ to $\overline{DE}$. Label the meeting point $P$.

**4.**

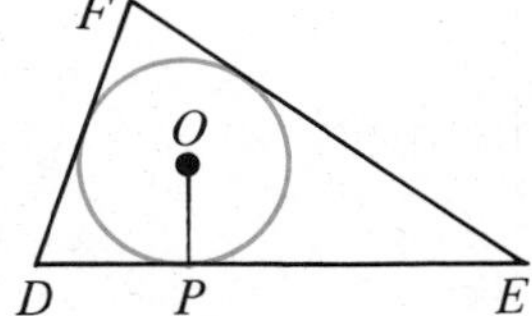


With $O$ as center and $OP$ as radius, draw a circle. The circle should just touch each side of $\triangle DEF$.

## Classroom Practice

1. Which of the diagrams below show a circle circumscribed about a triangle? b., d.

a. 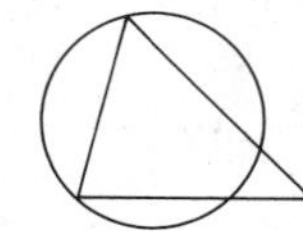 b. 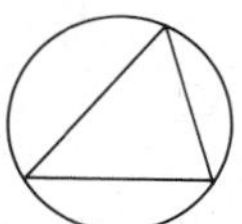 c. 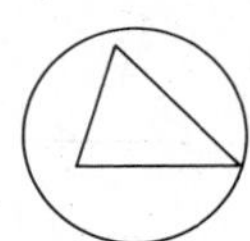

d. 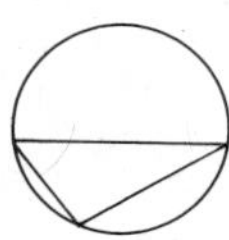 e.  f. 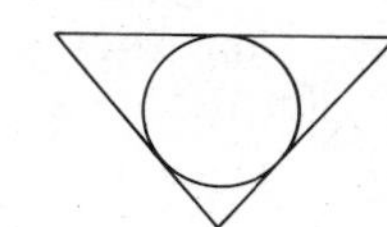

2. Which of the diagrams above show a circle inscribed in a triangle? e., f.

3. Complete: The center of a circle inscribed in a triangle is the point at which __?__. the angle bisectors meet

4. Complete: The center of a circle circumscribed about a triangle is the point at which __?__. the perp. bis. of the sides meet

5. The perpendicular bisector of $\overline{AC}$ and the perpendicular bisector of $\overline{BC}$ intersect at point $X$. We wish to show that $X$ lies on the perpendicular bisector of $\overline{AB}$. Supply the required reasons.

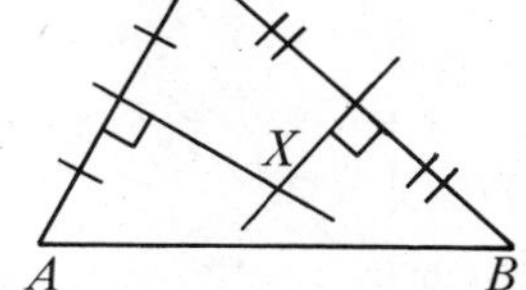


a. Draw $\overline{AX}$, $\overline{BX}$, and $\overline{CX}$.

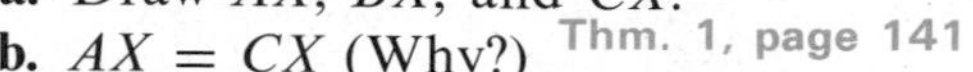

b. $AX = CX$ (Why?) Thm. 1, page 141

c. $BX = CX$ (Why?) Thm. 1, page 141

d. Then $AX = BX$. (Why?) Substitution Post.

e. $X$ is equidistant from $A$ and $B$. (Why?) (see below)

f. $X$ lies on the perpendicular bisector of $\overline{AB}$. (Why?) Thm. 2, page 141

Thus the perpendicular bisectors of the three sides of a triangle intersect in one point.

e. Definition of *equidistant*

## Written Exercises

**Sketch each of the following. You need not construct.**

A 1. A circle inscribed in an isosceles triangle

2. A circle inscribed in a scalene triangle

3. A circle circumscribed about an acute triangle

4. A circle circumscribed about an isosceles right triangle

**In Exercises 5–7, draw a triangle roughly like the one shown, but much larger. Use Construction 7 to circumscribe a circle about the triangle.**

**5.**

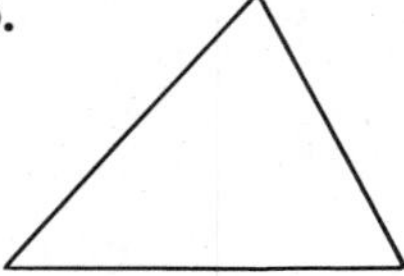

**6.**

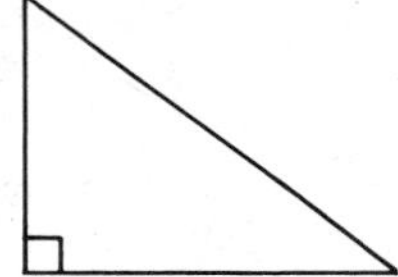

**7.**

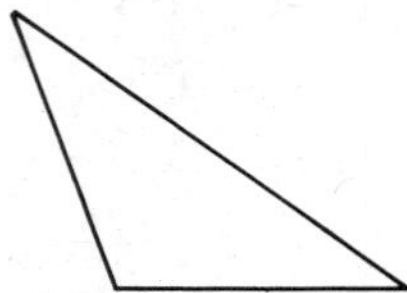

**In Exercises 8–10, draw a triangle roughly like the one shown, but much larger. Use Construction 8 to inscribe a circle in the triangle.**

**8.**

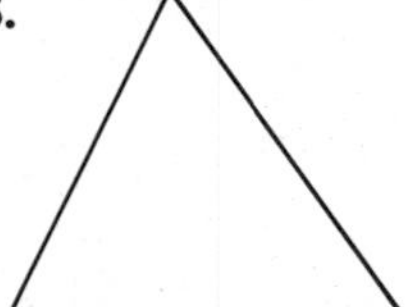

**9.**

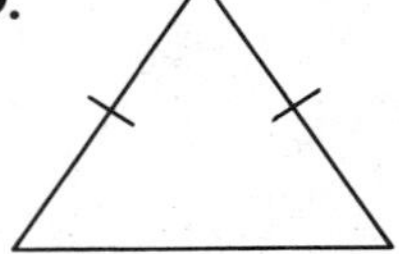

**10.**

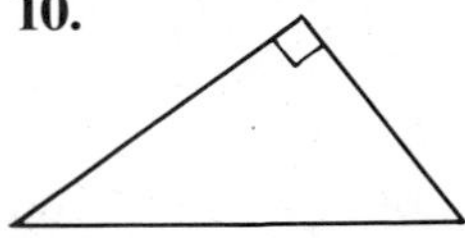

B **11.** Draw three noncollinear points on your paper and label them $X$, $Y$, and $Z$. Construct a circle that passes through the three points.

**12.** Repeat Exercise 11, using three different points.

**13.** Draw a scalene $\triangle ABC$. Circumscribe a circle about $\triangle ABC$ and inscribe a circle in $\triangle ABC$.

**14.** Repeat Exercise 13, using an isosceles $\triangle ABC$.

C **15.** Draw an obtuse $\triangle XYZ$. Construct a circle that passes through $Y$, $Z$, and the midpoint of $\overline{XZ}$.

## SELF-TEST

**Draw three triangles roughly like, but much larger than, the ones shown.**

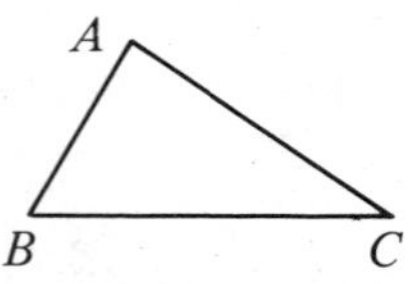


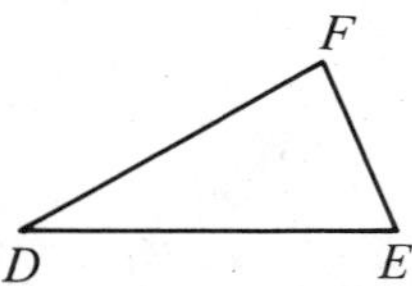


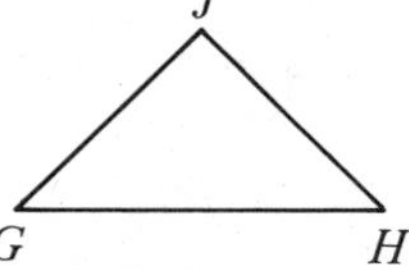


**1.** In $\triangle ABC$, construct the altitude from $C$.

**2.** In $\triangle ABC$, construct the median from $A$.

**3.** Circumscribe a circle about $\triangle DEF$.

**4.** Find, by construction, the point which would be the center of the circle inscribed in $\triangle GHJ$.

# 6 • Triangles with Two Equal Sides

## Explorations

1. Draw a large isosceles $\triangle ABC$, with $AC = BC$. Cut out the triangle.
2. Make a fold that bisects $\angle C$.
3. Does vertex $A$ fold onto vertex $B$? yes
4. Does $\angle A$ have the same measure as $\angle B$? yes

If you worked carefully, your answers to parts 3 and 4 were *yes*. Here's a picture statement of the theorem suggested by the exploration. If , then .

The exploration also suggests a proof involving a "line down the middle."

**THEOREM 3** "Base angles of an isosceles triangle are equal."

If two sides of a triangle are equal, then the angles opposite those sides are equal.

*Given:* $AC = BC$

*Prove:* $\angle A = \angle B$

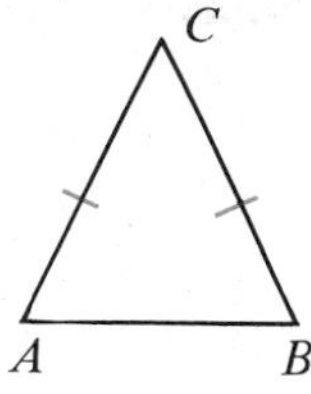


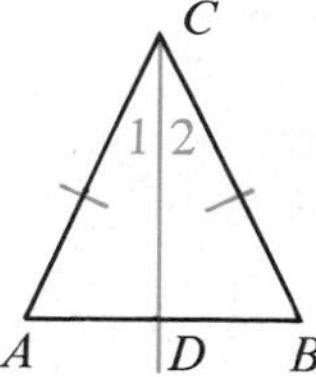


| STATEMENTS | REASONS |
|---|---|
| 1. Draw the bisector of $\angle C$. | 1. Every angle has a bisector. (Recall Construction 1.) |
| 2. $\angle 1 = \angle 2$ | 2. Definition of angle bisector |
| 3. $AC = BC$ | 3. Given |
| 4. $CD = CD$ | 4. From algebra |
| 5. $\triangle ADC \cong \triangle BDC$ | 5. SAS Postulate |
| 6. $\angle A = \angle B$ | 6. Corr. parts of $\cong$ $\triangle$s are $=$. |

**COROLLARY** An equilateral triangle is also equiangular, and each angle has measure 60°.

See Exercise 21 on page 157 for a proof.

We often use special terms to refer to parts of isosceles triangles.

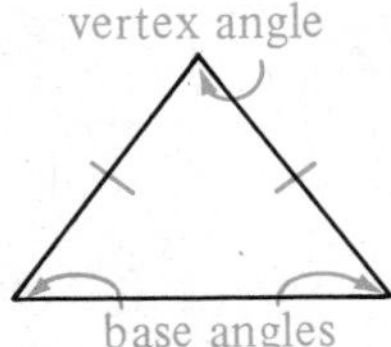


Some people like to state Theorem 3 in this form:

Base angles of an isosceles triangle are equal.

**Ways to Prove Two Angles Are Equal**

1. Show that they are corresponding parts of congruent triangles.
2. Show that they are opposite two equal sides of a triangle.
3. Show that they are corresponding angles or alternate interior angles of parallel lines.

## Classroom Practice

**Exercises 1–6 refer to isosceles $\triangle ABC$.**

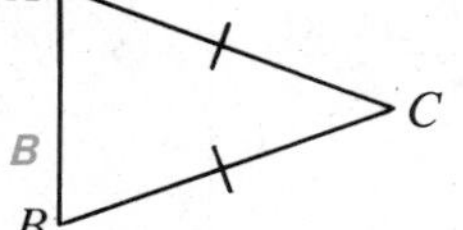


1. Name the base. $\overline{AB}$
2. Name the vertex angle. $\angle C$
3. Name the legs. $\overline{AC}$, $\overline{BC}$
4. Name the base angles. $\angle A$, $\angle B$
5. Name the vertices. $A$, $B$, $C$
6. Name *the* vertex. $C$

**In Exercises 7–12, name the angles that must be equal.**

7. $\angle A$, $\angle T$

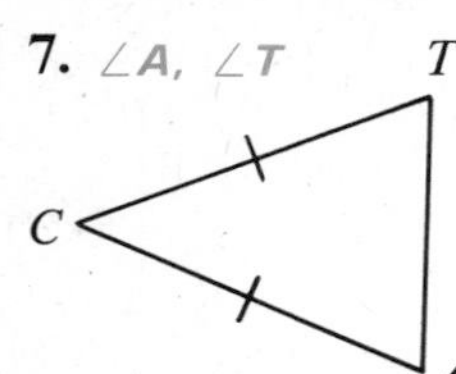


8. $\angle R$, $\angle D$

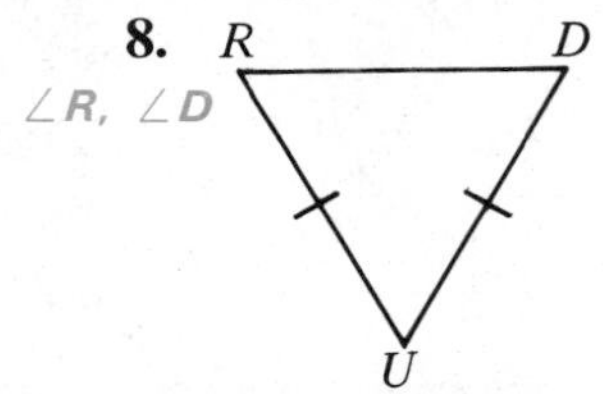


9. $\angle G$, $\angle S$

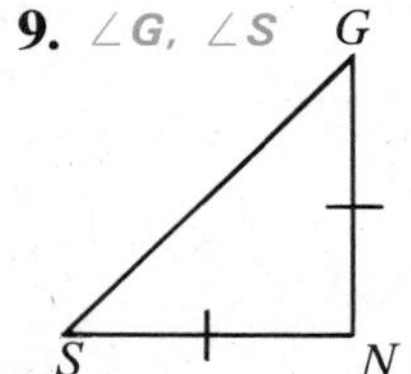


10. $\angle 1$, $\angle 2$

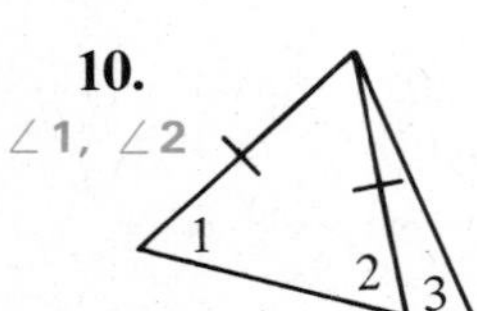


11. $\angle 1$, $\angle 2$

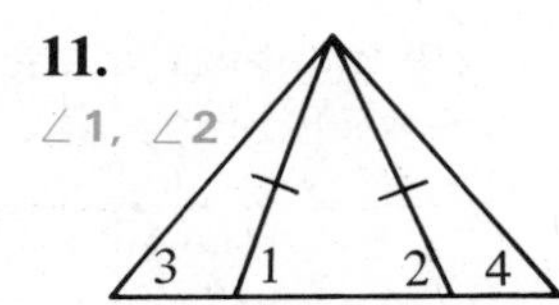


12. $\angle 3$, $\angle 4$

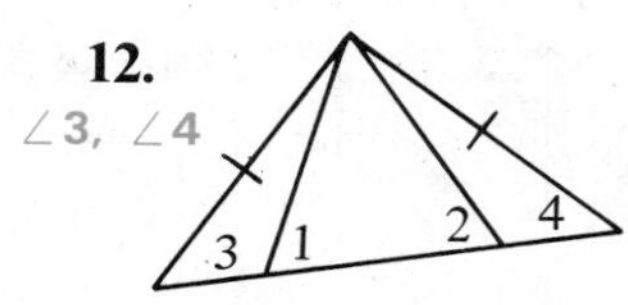

13. In the diagram for Exercise 7, you could say $CA = CT$, given. Then you could conclude: $\angle A = \angle T$. State the theorem that supports the conclusion. (see below)

14. In the diagram for Exercise 9, suppose $\angle N = 90°$. Then $\angle S = \underline{\ ?\ }°$. 45

15. In the diagram for Exercise 8, suppose that $DU = DR = RU$. Then $\angle D = \underline{\ ?\ }°$. 60

**In Exercises 16–18, $XZ = YZ$ and $\overline{ZE}$ is drawn in the way described. State the method you would use to prove that $\triangle XEZ \cong \triangle YEZ$.**

16. *Given:* $XZ = YZ$
$\overrightarrow{ZE}$ bisects $\angle XZY$.
*Prove:* $\triangle XEZ \cong \triangle YEZ$ SAS

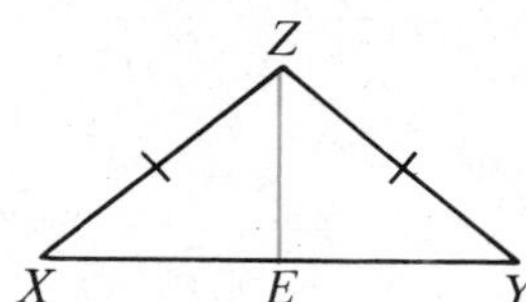


17. *Given:* $XZ = YZ$
$\overline{ZE}$ is a median.
*Prove:* $\triangle XEZ \cong \triangle YEZ$ SSS

18. *Given:* $XZ = YZ$
$\overline{ZE}$ is an altitude.
*Prove:* $\triangle XEZ \cong \triangle YEZ$ HL

13. Thm. 3: If two sides of a triangle are equal, then the angles opposite those sides are equal.

## *Written Exercises*

**In Exercises 1–10, use the diagram. Complete each row of the table.** (See page T127.)

| | | $\angle 1$ | $\angle 2$ | $\angle 3$ | $\angle 4$ | $\angle 5$ | |
|---|---|---|---|---|---|---|---|
| A | 1. | 65° | ? | ? | ? | ? | |
| | 2. | ? | ? | 120° | ? | ? | |
| | 3. | ? | ? | ? | 116° | ? | |
| | 4. | ? | 70° | ? | ? | ? | |
| | 5. | 68° | ? | ? | ? | ? | |
| | 6. | ? | ? | 112° | ? | ? | |
| | 7. | ? | ? | ? | ? | 42° | ← *Hint:* $\angle 1 + \angle 2 = \underline{\ ?\ }°$ |
| | 8. | ? | ? | ? | ? | 50° | |
| | 9. | $j°$ | ? | ? | ? | ? | ← Your answers will involve $j$. |
| | 10. | $k°$ | ? | ? | ? | ? | ← Your answers will involve $k$. |

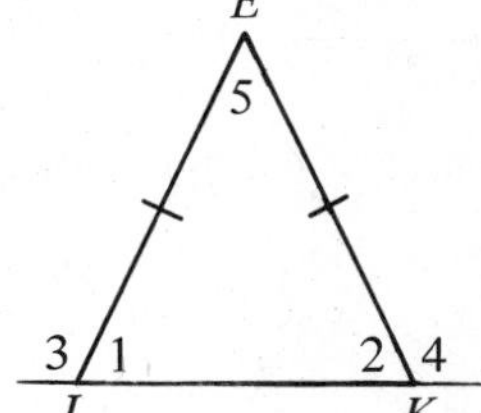

**In Exercises 11–19, equal sides are marked. Find the value of $x$.**

Sample

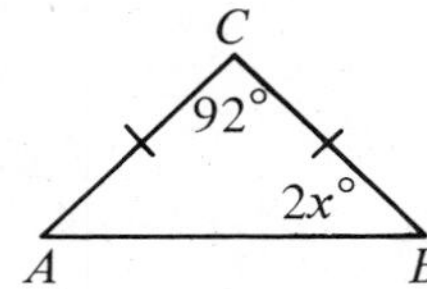


$$\angle A + \angle B + \angle C = 180°$$
$$2x° + 2x° + 92° = 180° \leftarrow \boxed{\angle A = \angle B = 2x°}$$
$$4x° + 92° = 180°$$
$$4x° = 88°$$
$$x° = 22°$$

**11.** 55

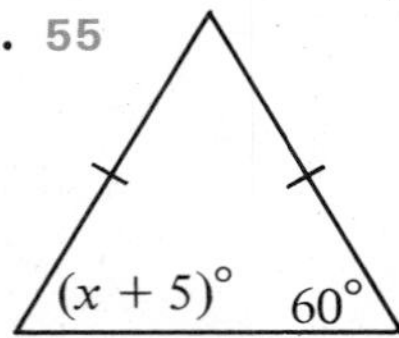


**12.** 45

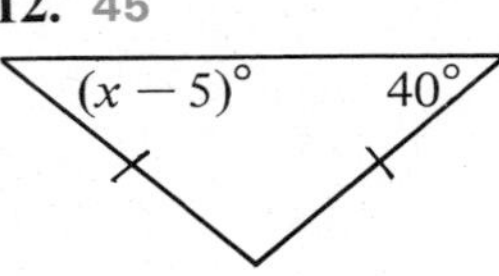


**13.** 9

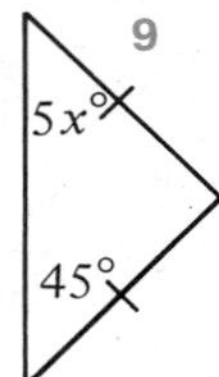


**14.** 140

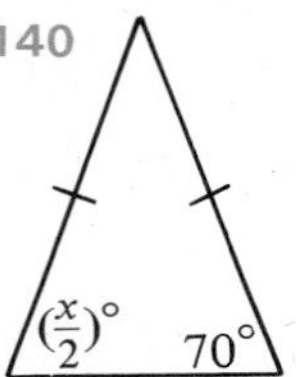


**15.** 6

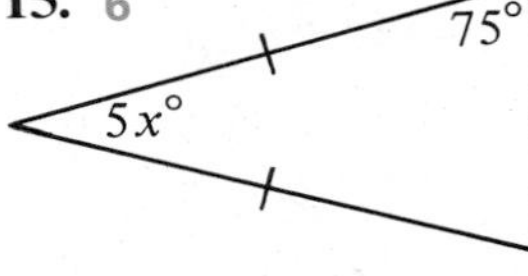


**16.** 10

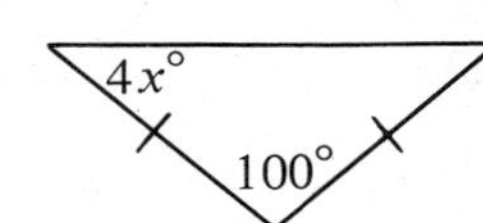


**17.** 25

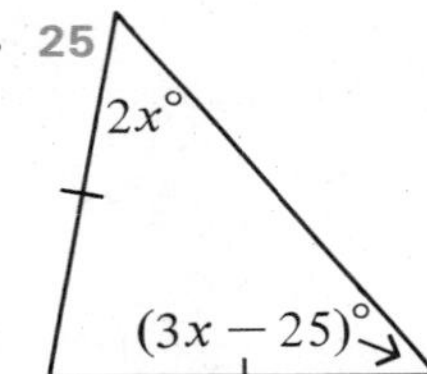


**18.** 40

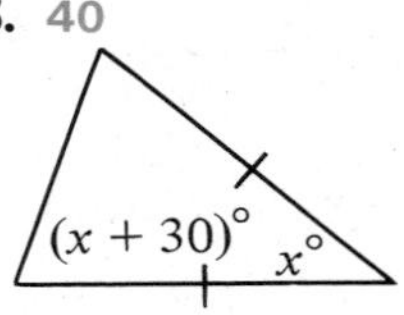


**19.** 180

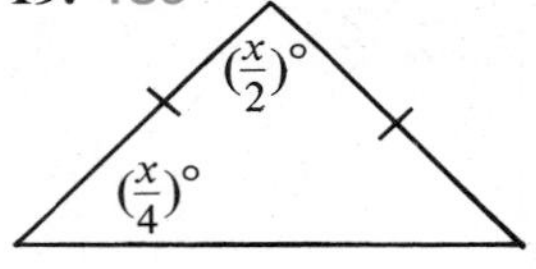


**In Exercises 20–22, complete the proofs by supplying the reasons.**

**20.** *Given:* $AC = BC$

*Prove:* $\angle 1 = \angle 3$

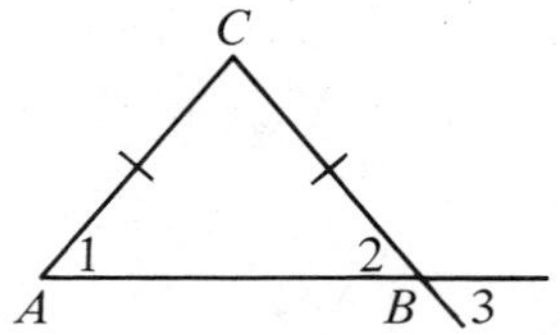


| STATEMENTS | REASONS |
|---|---|
| 1. $AC = BC$ | 1. ? Given |
| 2. $\angle 1 = \angle 2$ | 2. ? Thm. 3, page 153 |
| 3. $\angle 3 = \angle 2$ | 3. ? Vertical angles are =. |
| 4. $\angle 1 = \angle 3$ | 4. ? Substitution Post. |

B **21.** Complete this proof of the corollary to Theorem 3: An equilateral triangle is also equiangular, and each angle has measure $60°$.

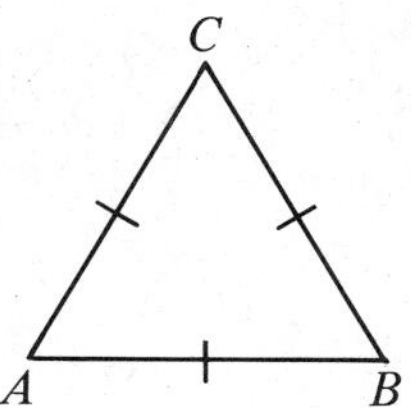


*Given:* $AB = BC = AC$

*Prove:* $\angle A = \angle B = \angle C = 60°$

| STATEMENTS | REASONS |
|---|---|
| 1. $AC = BC$; $AB = AC$; $AB = BC$ | 1. ? Given |
| 2. $\angle A = \angle B$; $\angle B = \angle C$; $\angle C = \angle A$ | 2. ? Thm. 3, page 153 |
| 3. $\angle A = \angle B = \angle C$ | 3. ? Substitution Post. |
| 4. $\angle A + \angle B + \angle C = 180°$ | 4. ? Angle sum of a △ |
| 5. $\angle A + \angle A + \angle A = 180°$, or $3 \cdot \angle A = 180°$ | 5. ? Substitution Post. |
| 6. $\angle A = 60°$ | 6. ? Division Post. |
| 7. $\angle A = \angle B = \angle C = 60°$ | 7. ? Substitution Post. |

**22.** *Given:* $AX = DX$; $AB = DC$

*Prove:* $\angle 1 = \angle 2$

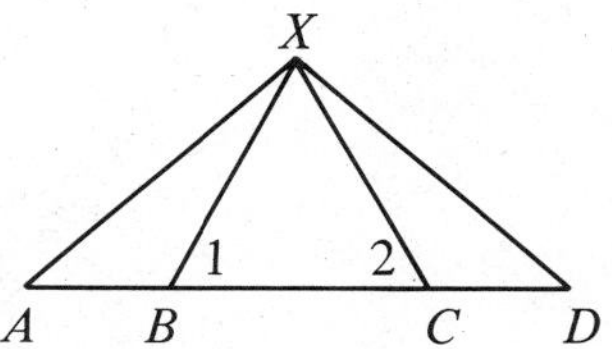


*Strategy for proof:*

A. Using isosceles $\triangle AXD$, prove that $\angle A = \angle D$.

B. Prove that $\triangle AXB \cong \triangle DXC$, and conclude that $BX = CX$.

C. Using isosceles $\triangle BXC$, prove that $\angle 1 = \angle 2$.

| STATEMENTS | REASONS |
|---|---|
| 1. $AX = DX$ | 1. ? Given |
| 2. $\angle A = \angle D$ | 2. ? Thm. 3, page 153 |
| 3. $AB = DC$ | 3. ? Given |
| 4. $\triangle AXB \cong \triangle DXC$ | 4. ? SAS Postulate |
| 5. $BX = CX$ | 5. ? Corresponding parts |
| 6. $\angle 1 = \angle 2$ | 6. ? Thm. 3, page 153 |

# 7 • Triangles with Two Equal Angles

In Section 6 you saw that when a triangle has two equal sides, it also has two equal angles. Experience suggests that when a triangle has two equal angles, it must also have two equal sides. Expressing this by diagram, we write:

**Theorem 3** If , then .

**Converse of Theorem 3** If , then .

We shall treat the converse as a theorem.

**THEOREM 4**

If two angles of a triangle are equal, then the sides opposite those angles are equal.

*Given:* $\angle A = \angle B$

*Prove:* $AC = BC$

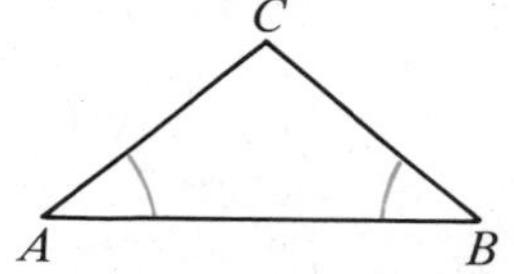


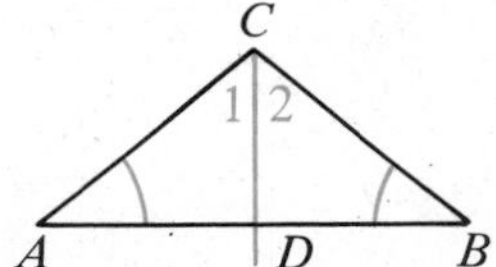


See if you can supply the reasons in the proof below.

| STATEMENTS | REASONS |
|---|---|
| 1. Draw the bisector of $\angle C$. | 1. Every angle has a bisector. (Recall Construction 1.) |
| 2. $\angle 1 = \angle 2$ | 2. ___?___ Def. of *bisector* |
| 3. $\angle A = \angle B$ | 3. ___?___ Given |
| 4. $CD = CD$ | 4. ___?___ From algebra |
| 5. $\triangle ACD \cong \triangle BCD$ | 5. ___?___ AAS Theorem |
| 6. $AC = BC$ | 6. ___?___ Corresponding parts |

**COROLLARY**

If a triangle is equiangular, it is also equilateral.

The proof is left as Exercise 11 on page 161.

The corollary on page 153 states that an equilateral triangle is also equiangular, and that each angle has measure 60°. We can use this fact to construct a 60° angle.

**CONSTRUCTION 9** *Construct:* A 60° angle

**1.**

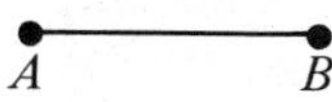


Draw a segment, $\overline{AB}$.

**2.**

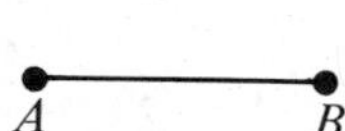


Set your compass for a radius of $AB$. Draw two arcs, one with $A$ as center, and one with $B$ as center.

**3.**

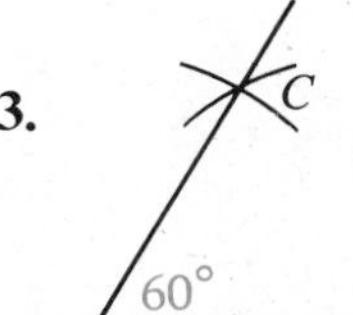


Draw $\overrightarrow{AC}$.
$\angle A$ is a 60° angle.

Can you explain why $\angle A$ must have measure 60°? Try this:

1. Draw $\overline{BC}$.
2. $AB = BC = AC$ by construction.
3. $\angle A = \angle B = \angle C = 60°$ (Why?) Thm. 3 (twice) and Subst. Post.

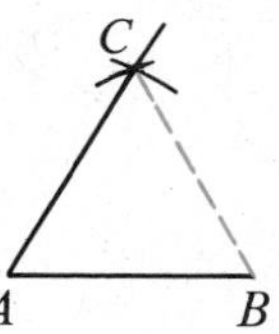


**Ways to Prove Two Segments Are Equal**

1. Show that they are corresponding parts of congruent triangles.
2. Show that they are opposite two equal angles of a triangle.

## Classroom Practice

**In Exercises 1–6, name the sides that must be equal.**

**1.** OA = OB

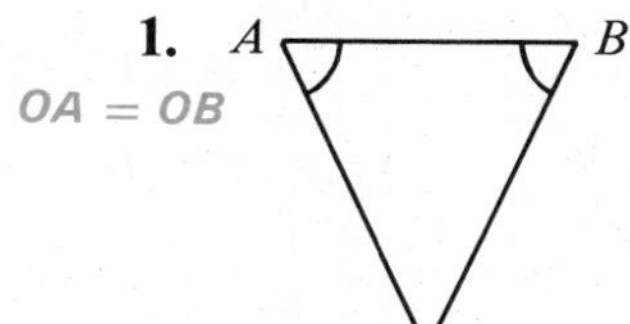


**2.** JC = JT

T
C
J

**3.** RE = RH

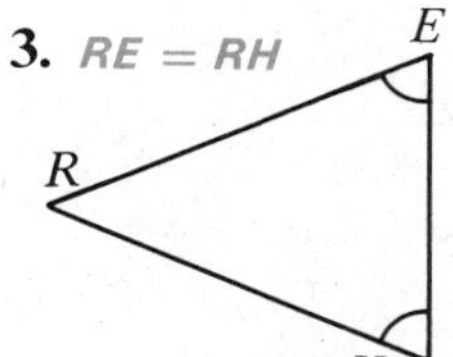

**Name the sides that must be equal.**

**4.** $ZX = ZY$

**5.** $TA = TB$

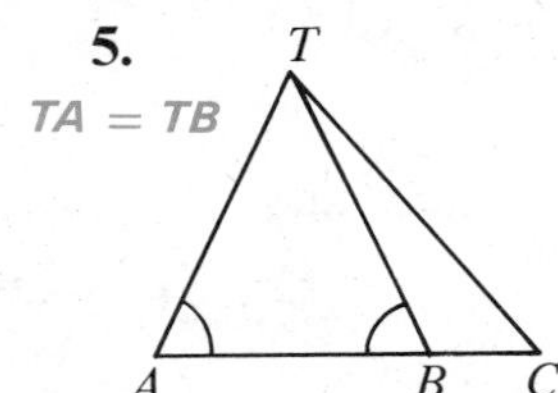


**6.** $HD = HG$
$HE = HF$

**7.** If you know that $AX = AY$, then you can conclude that $\angle X = \angle Y$. State the theorem that supports the conclusion.
Theorem 3, page 153

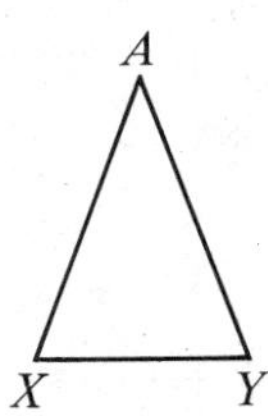


**8.** If you know that $\angle X = \angle Y$, then you can conclude that $AX = AY$. State the theorem that supports the conclusion.
Theorem 4, page 158

**9.** One student decided to try to prove $RT = ST$ as follows:

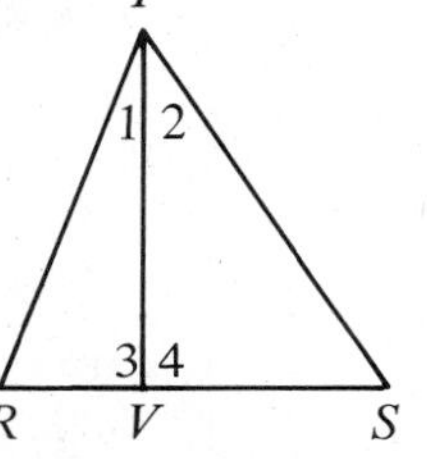


**a.** Bisect $\angle RTS$ with a segment that is perpendicular to $\overline{RS}$.
**b.** $\angle 1 = \angle 2$
**c.** $\angle 3 = \angle 4$ (Each has measure 90°.)
**d.** $TV = TV$
**e.** $\triangle RVT \cong \triangle SVT$
**f.** $RT = ST$

What is wrong with this reasoning? (see below)

**10. a.** Construct a 60° angle.
**b.** Use your construction from part **a** to construct a 120° angle.

9. The segment which is $\perp$ to $\overline{RS}$ does not necessarily bisect $\angle RTS$.

## Written Exercises

**Equal angles are marked. Find the value of $x$.**

Sample

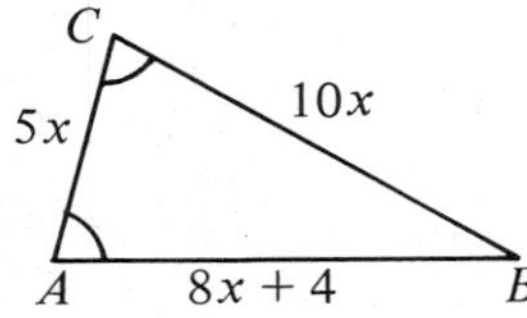


$$BC = BA$$
$$10x = 8x + 4$$
$$2x = 4$$
$$x = 2$$

A **1.** 6

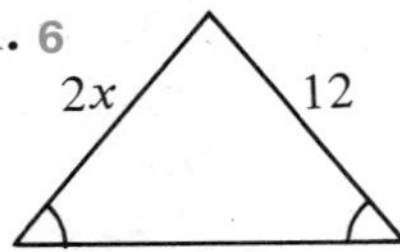


**2.** 11

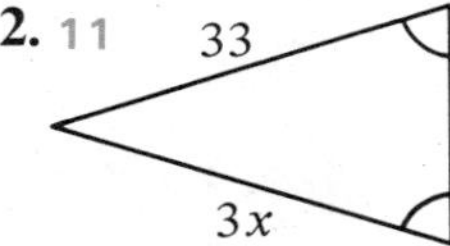


**3.** 6

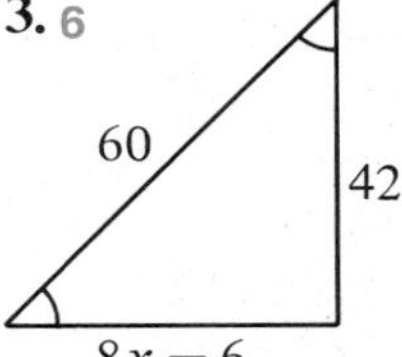

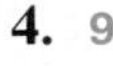

**4.** 9

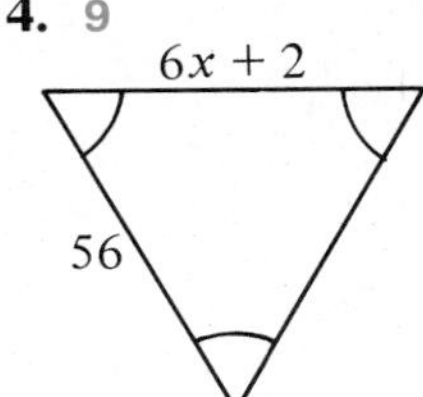


**5.** 9

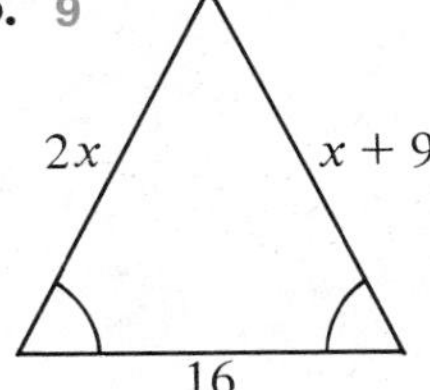


**6.** 7

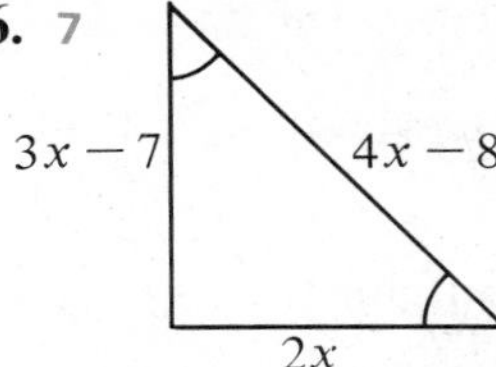


**7.** 10

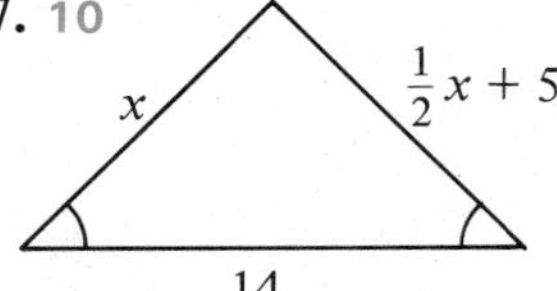


**8.** 3

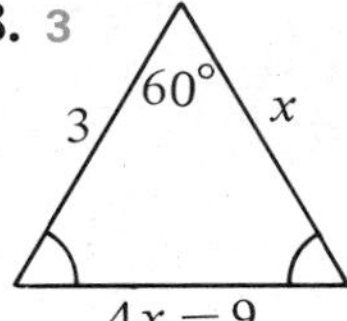


**9.** 8

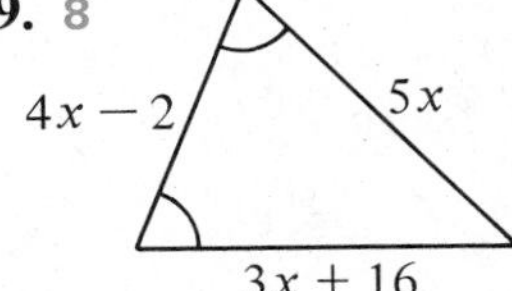


**10.** Complete the proof by supplying the reasons.

*Given:* $\angle 1 = \angle 2$

*Prove:* $AC = BC$

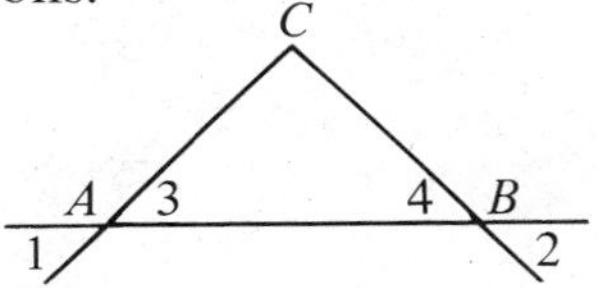


| STATEMENTS | REASONS |
|---|---|
| 1. $\angle 3 = \angle 1$; $\angle 4 = \angle 2$ | 1. ? Vertical angles are =. |
| 2. $\angle 1 = \angle 2$ | 2. ? Given |
| 3. $\angle 3 = \angle 4$ | 3. ? Substitution Post. |
| 4. $AC = BC$ | 4. ? Thm. 4, page 158 |

**11.** Complete this proof of the corollary of Theorem 4: If a triangle is equiangular, it is also equilateral.

*Given:* $\angle A = \angle B = \angle C$

*Prove:* $AB = BC = CA$

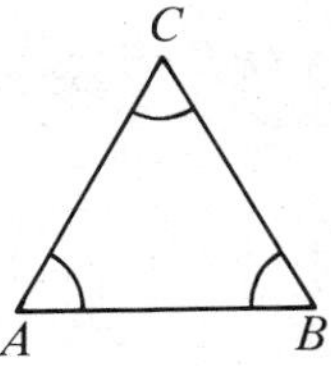


| STATEMENTS | REASONS |
|---|---|
| 1. $\angle A = \angle C$; $\angle A = \angle B$; $\angle B = \angle C$ | 1. ? Given |
| 2. $AB = BC$; $BC = CA$; $CA = AB$ | 2. ? Thm. 4, page 158 |
| 3. $AB = BC = CA$ | 3. ? Substitution Post. |

**12.** Construct a 60° angle.

**13.** Use your construction from Exercise 12. Construct a 30° angle.

**14.** Use your construction from Exercises 12 and 13. Construct a 15° angle.

**In Exercises 15–17, refer to the sample on page 74.**

B **15.** Construct a 150° angle. Select a strategy.
*One choice:* Use the fact that 150° = 180° − 30°.
*Another choice:* Use the fact that 150° = 90° + 60°.

**16.** Construct a 105° angle.

**17.** Construct a 75° angle.

**Equal angles are marked. Find the value of $x$.**

**18.** 12

$\frac{3}{2}x - 8$

$x$

$\frac{1}{3}x + 8$

**19.** 11

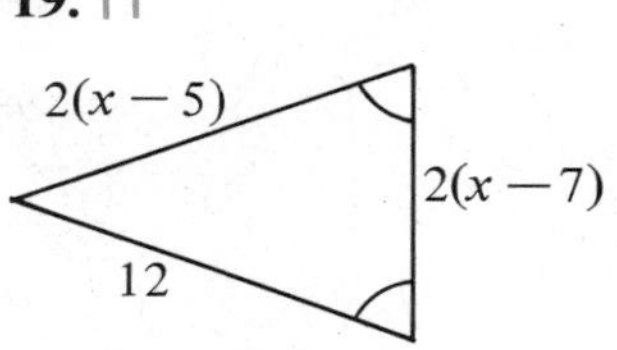


**20.** 10

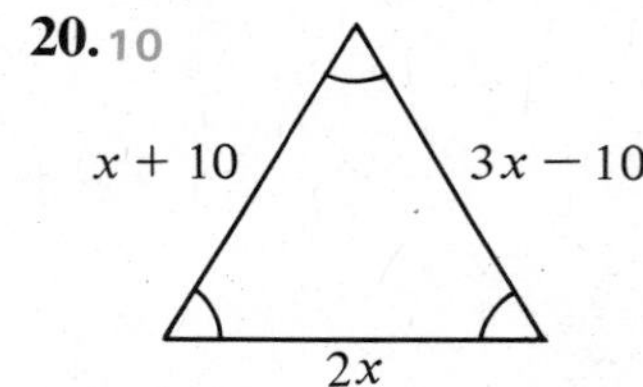


**Copy what is shown. Then write a proof in two-column form.**

**21.** *Given:* $JK = NM$; $\angle J = \angle N$

*Prove:* $\angle 5 = \angle 6$

*Strategy for proof:*

A. Think of $\angle J$ and $\angle N$ as angles of $\triangle JPN$. Prove that $PJ = PN$.

B. Prove that $\triangle JPK \cong \triangle NPM$ and conclude that $\angle 5 = \angle 6$.

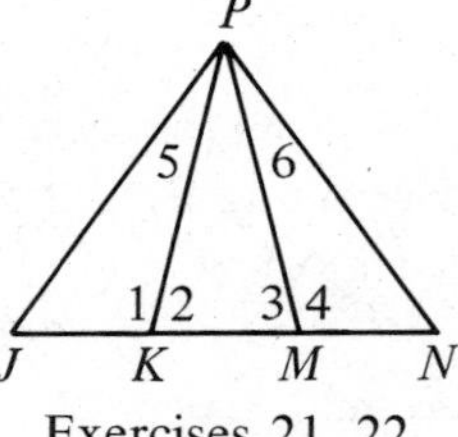

Exercises 21, 22

**22.** *Given:* $\angle 1 = \angle 4$

*Prove:* $\triangle PKM$ is an isosceles triangle.

C **23.** The goal of this exercise is to prove the statement: In an isosceles triangle, the bisector of the vertex angle bisects the base and is perpendicular to the base.

**a.** Draw and label an appropriate diagram.

**b.** List what you are given and what you are to prove in terms of your diagram.

**c.** Write a proof in two-column form.

## Experiments

### Counting Triangles You Cannot Draw

**Begin with a very large equilateral triangle.**

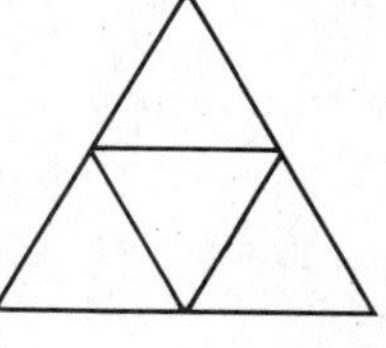

1. Join the midpoints of the three sides. How many equilateral triangles are shown now? 5

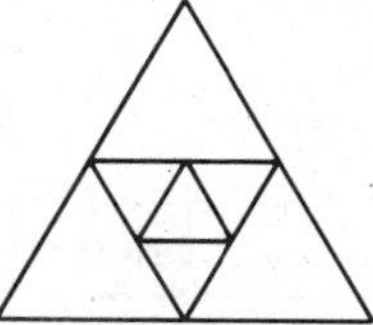

2. Using the "inside" triangle, again join the midpoints of the sides. How many equilateral triangles are there now? 9

3. Repeat this process and complete the table.

| Step | | 1 | 2 | 3 | 4 | 5 |
|---|---|---|---|---|---|---|
| No. of △ | 1 | 5 | 9 | ? 13 | ? 17 | ? 21 |

4. Look at your completed table. Each time you join the midpoints of a triangle, how many new triangles are formed? 4

5. How many triangles would be formed if you joined midpoints eight times? 33

## SELF-TEST

1. Suppose you know that $TA = TE$. Write the theorem that supports the statement:

$$\angle A = \angle E.$$ (see below)

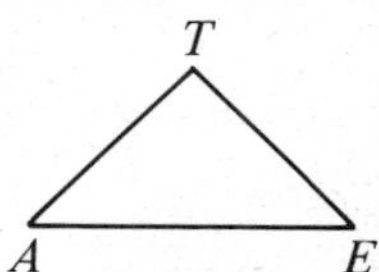


**In each diagram, equal angles are marked. Find $x$.**

2. 5

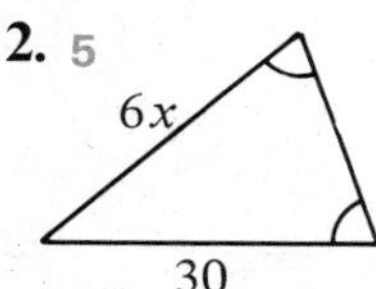


3. 4

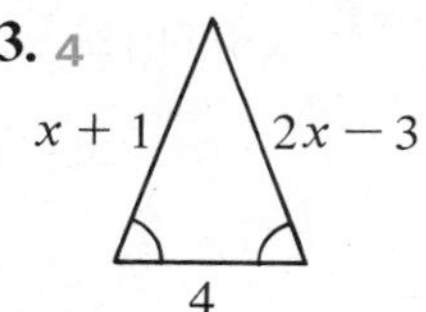


4. 12

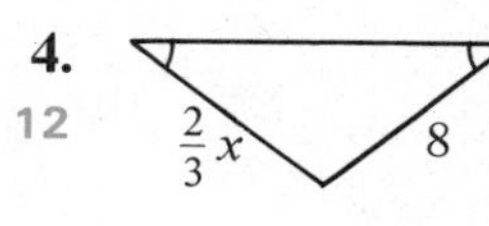


**In each diagram, equal sides are marked. Find $y$.**

5. 60

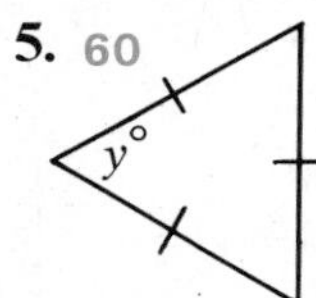


6. 40

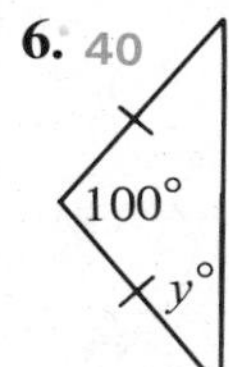


7. 44

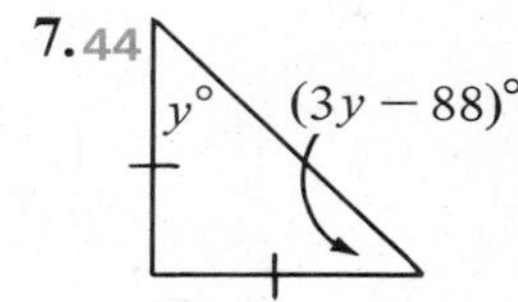


1. Thm. 3: If two sides of a triangle are equal, the angles opposite those sides are equal.

## Reviewing Arithmetic Skills

**Add or subtract. Be sure to keep the decimal points in line.**

**1.** 5.372 + 2.197 7.569 **2.** 91.08 − 16.37 74.71 **3.** 7.65 + 0.829 8.479 **4.** 56.7 − 29.54 27.16

**5.** 26.03 + 62.9 88.93 **6.** 5.003 − 1.315 3.688 **7.** 1.62 + 4.7 6.32 **8.** 9.666 − 7.209 2.457

**Multiply.**

Sample 39.6 × 2.04 = 80.784

1 decimal place | 2 decimal places | 3 decimal places

**9.** 4 × 39.48 157.92 **10.** 100 × 61.2 6120.0 **11.** 0.2 × 9.3 1.86 **12.** 5.9 × 0.766 4.5194

**13.** 0.16 × 365 58.40 **14.** 35.27 × 7.75 273.3425 **15.** 1.3 × 8.909 11.5817 **16.** 81 × 3.14 254.34

**Divide. If the division does not "come out even," round the answer to two decimal places.**

Sample $0.51\overline{)4.7} \rightarrow 0.51\overline{)4.70000}$ = 9.215 Round up *Answer:* 9.22

**17.** $1.5\overline{)135}$ 90 **18.** $0.7\overline{)2.93}$ 4.19 **19.** $0.34\overline{)69.7}$ 205 **20.** $0.8\overline{)11}$ 13.75

**21.** $6.1\overline{)0.437}$ 0.07 **22.** $0.03\overline{)12.8}$ 426.67 **23.** $0.075\overline{)5}$ 66.67 **24.** $9.4\overline{)6.18}$ 0.66

**Write as a percent.**

Samples $\frac{9}{25} = \frac{36}{100} = 36\%$ $0.9 = 0.90 = 90\%$ $\frac{3}{8} = 3 \div 8 = 0.375 = 37.5\%$

**25.** $\frac{3}{4}$ 75% **26.** 0.27 27% **27.** 0.6 60% **28.** $\frac{4}{5}$ 80%

**29.** $\frac{7}{8}$ 87.5% **30.** $0.33\frac{1}{3}$ $33\frac{1}{3}\%$ **31.** $\frac{1}{2}$ 50% **32.** $\frac{7}{10}$ 70%

**Complete.**

**33.** 80% of 1125 is __?__. 900 **34.** 17 is __?__% of 51. $33\frac{1}{3}\%$

**35.** 25% of __?__ is 96. 384 **36.** 30% of 15.8 is __?__. 4.74

**37.** 13 is __?__% of 65. 20 **38.** __?__ is 97% of 482. 467.54

# applications

## *The Triangle Inequality*

Suppose we are given the lengths of three line segments. Can we build a triangle with these segments? The SSS Postulate tells us that if we can, there is only one triangle possible.

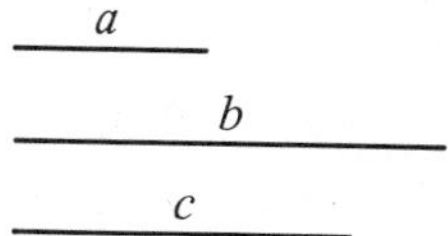


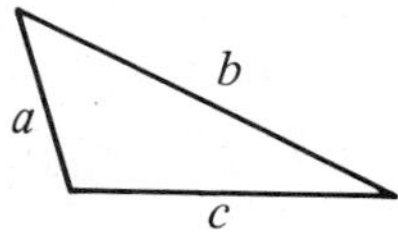


It may not be possible to make any triangle at all. Can you see that there is no triangle with sides of lengths 2, 5, and 10?

2

5

10

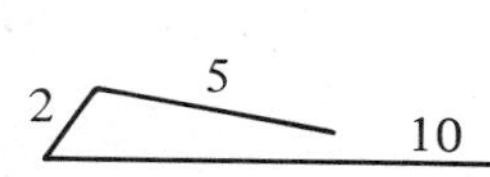


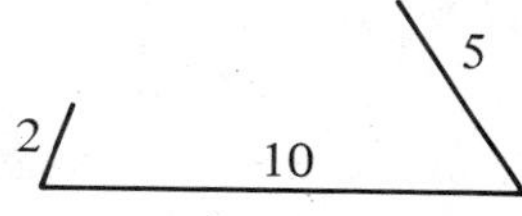


The triangle inequality is a rule which tells us whether three lengths can form the sides of a triangle.

> The Triangle Inequality: In a triangle, the sum of the lengths of any two sides must be greater than the length of the third side.

In the example above, the sum of 2 and 5 is not greater than 10. Therefore, we cannot make a triangle from these lengths.

Some people think of the triangle inequality as a special way of saying "the shortest path between two points is a straight line." You have probably used this idea yourself if you have ever taken a short cut across a corner. Look at $\triangle ABC$. If the triangle inequality were not true, the "short cut" from $A$ to $B$ would be longer than the "detour" through $C$!

**Exercises**

Can you draw a triangle using these lengths for the sides?

**1.** 3, 4, 5 Yes　　**2.** 3, 4, 1 No　　**3.** 3, 4, 20 No

**4.** 7, 7, 7 Yes　　**5.** 7, 7, 14 No　　**6.** 7, 7, 0.001 Yes

# Reviewing the Chapter

## Chapter Summary

1. One way to prove that two segments or two angles are equal is to show that they are corresponding parts of congruent triangles.

2. Congruent triangles can sometimes be used to show that constructions are correct.

3. Any segment, ray, or line that passes through the midpoint of a line segment is a bisector of the segment.

4. Any point on the perpendicular bisector of $\overline{AB}$ is equidistant from $A$ and $B$. Any point that is equidistant from $A$ and $B$ must lie on the perpendicular bisector of $\overline{AB}$.

5. Every triangle has three altitudes. Every triangle has three medians.

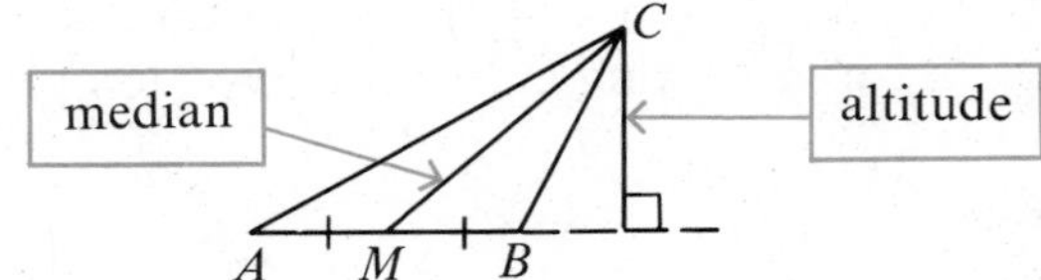


6. Given a triangle, a circle can be circumscribed about the triangle (Construction 7) and a circle can be inscribed in the triangle (Construction 8).

7. If two sides of a triangle are equal, then the angles opposite those sides are equal. An equilateral triangle is also equiangular, and each angle has measure 60°.

8. If two angles of a triangle are equal, then the sides opposite those angles are equal. If a triangle is equiangular, it is also equilateral.

9. Construction 9 tells how to construct a 60° angle.

## Chapter Review Test

**Supply reasons to complete the proof.** *(See pp. 130–134.)*

**1.** *Given:* $CM = DM$; $EM = FM$

*Prove:* $\overline{EC} \parallel \overline{DF}$

C, M, F, E, D, 1, 2, 3, 4, 5, 6

1. $CM = DM$; $EM = FM$ Given
2. $\angle 1 = \angle 4$ Vert. $\angle$s are =.
3. $\triangle CME \cong \triangle DMF$ SAS Postulate
4. $\angle 3 = \angle 6$ Corr. parts of $\cong$ ▵s are =.
5. $\overline{EC} \parallel \overline{DF}$ If two lines and a transversal form equal alternate interior angles, then the lines are parallel.

**Supply reasons to complete a proof that the following construction is correct.** (*See pp. 135–138.*)

**2.** Angle $A$ was given, and angle $B$ was constructed to be equal to angle $A$.  1., 2. By construction

1. $BT = AR$ and $BU = AS$
2. $TU = RS$
3. $\triangle UBT \cong \triangle SAR$ SSS Post.
4. $\angle B = \angle A$ Corresponding parts

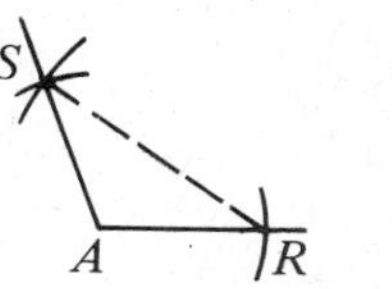


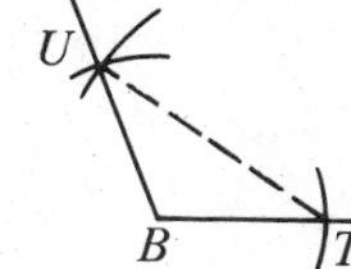


**Draw a segment $\overline{CD}$.** (*See pp. 140–143.*)

**3.** Construct the perpendicular bisector of $\overline{CD}$, and label it $k$.

**4.** Refer to Exercise 3. Suppose you know, for some point $X$, that $CX = DX$. Where must $X$ lie? on line $k$

**5.** Suppose $Z$ is a point on $k$. What can you say about $Z$ with respect to $C$ and $D$? $Z$ is equidistant from $C$ and $D$.

**Refer to the figure shown.** (*See pp. 144–147.*)

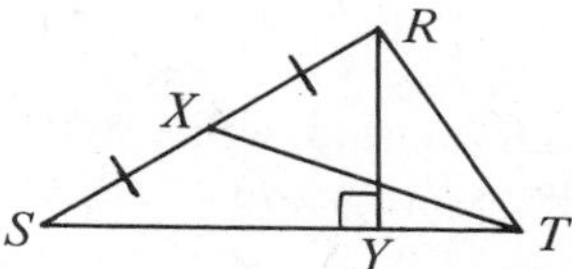


**6.** Name an altitude shown. $\overline{RY}$

**7.** Name a median shown. $\overline{TX}$

**8.** Draw a large acute triangle, $\triangle MNO$. Construct the altitude from $M$.

**Draw two large figures, an obtuse $\triangle ABC$ and an acute $\triangle DEF$.** (*See pp. 149–152.*)

**9.** Circumscribe a circle about $\triangle ABC$.

**10.** Inscribe a circle in $\triangle DEF$.

**Write a proof of the theorem.** (*See pp. 153–157.*)

**11.** If two sides of a triangle are equal, then the angles opposite those sides are equal.

*Given:* $KX = KY$

*Prove:* $\angle X = \angle Y$

(*Hint:* Begin your proof by drawing the bisector of $\angle K$.)

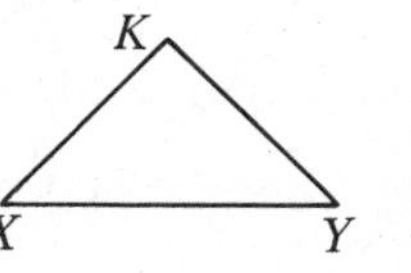


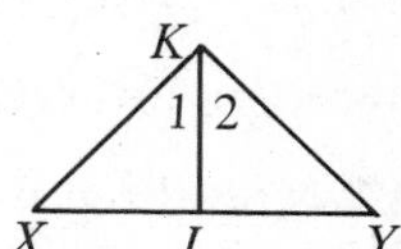


**Equal angles are marked. Find $x$.** (*See pp. 158–162.*)

**12.** 9

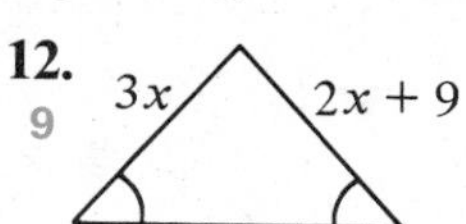


**13.** 7

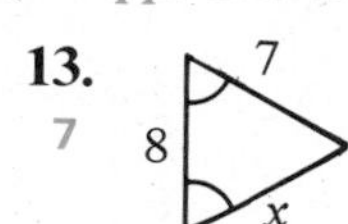


**14.** 6

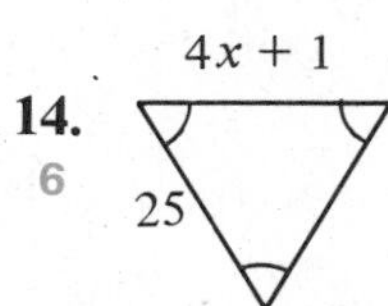

# Cumulative Review / Unit B

**Complete.**

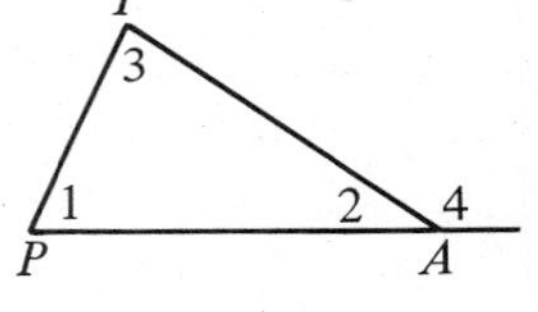


1. In $\triangle PAT$ at the right, $\angle 4 = \angle$ __?__ 1 $+ \angle$ __?__ 3.
2. A triangle with no equal sides is called __?__. scalene
3. A triangle with two equal sides is called __?__. isosceles
4. If a triangle has two 40° angles, the third angle equals __?__°. 100
5. If a triangle has a 110° angle, then the triangle is called __?__. obtuse
6. In a right triangle, the side opposite the right angle is called the __?__. hypotenuse
7. If $\triangle AUK \cong \triangle JOE$, then $\angle A = \angle$ __?__. $J$
8. If $\triangle DOG \cong \triangle AKC$, then $DO =$ __?__. $AK$

**Using the given information, write SSS, SAS, ASA, AAS, or HL to tell which method you could use to prove $\triangle LUB \cong \triangle LIB$.**

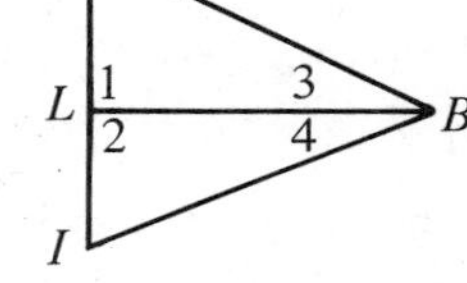


HL 9. $\overline{BL} \perp \overline{UI}$; $BU = BI$

10. $BU = BI$; $UL = IL$

ASA 11. $\angle 1 = \angle 2$; $\angle 3 = \angle 4$

12. $\angle U = \angle I$; $\angle 3 = \angle 4$

AAS 13. $\angle 1 = 90°$; $\angle U = \angle I$

14. $BU = BI$; $\angle 3 = \angle 4$

10. SSS 12. AAS 14. SAS

**Classify each statement as true or false.**

15. A segment has exactly one bisector. False
16. If point $A$ is on a perpendicular bisector of $\overline{CD}$, then $AC = AD$. True
17. The three lines containing the altitudes of a triangle intersect in a point. True
18. Medians and altitudes are always the same segments. False
19. In $\triangle ABC$, if $AB = AC$, then $\angle B = \angle C$. True
20. An equilateral triangle is also equiangular. True

21. Construct an equiangular triangle.
22. Draw an acute $\triangle DEF$. Circumscribe a circle about $\triangle DEF$.

# UNIT C

## *Here's what you'll learn in this chapter:*

1. To classify polygons.
2. To find the interior and exterior angle sums of a convex polygon.
3. To use the properties of parallelograms, rectangles, rhombuses, and squares.
4. To prove that a quadrilateral is a parallelogram.
5. To use properties of trapezoids.
6. To apply the Midpoints Theorem.

# Chapter 5

# Polygons

# 1 • Introducing Polygons

The word *polygon* comes from the Greek words meaning *many angles*. The polygons shown in the first row below are called **convex polygons.** Do you see how they are different from the polygons in the second row?

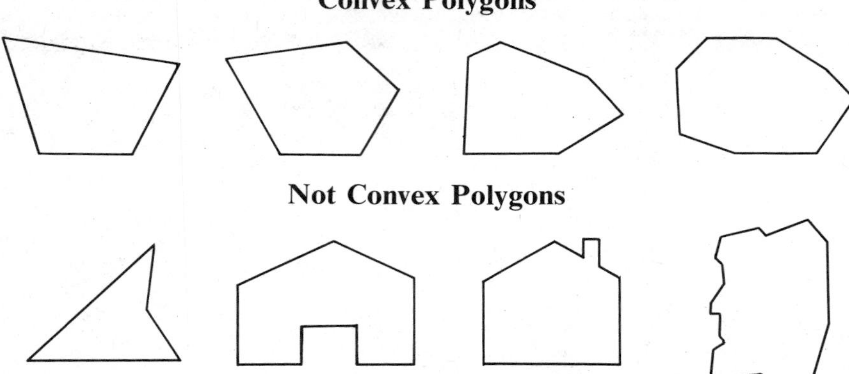


One way to tell whether or not a polygon is convex is to imagine fitting a rubber band along the edges of the figure. If the rubber band fits snugly, then the polygon is convex. Otherwise, the polygon is not convex.

The figures above should suggest what a polygon is. Even so, it is difficult to write a definition of *polygon*. Perhaps you and your class would like to try to write one. The figures below are *not* polygons and should not satisfy your definition. See page T69 for a definition.

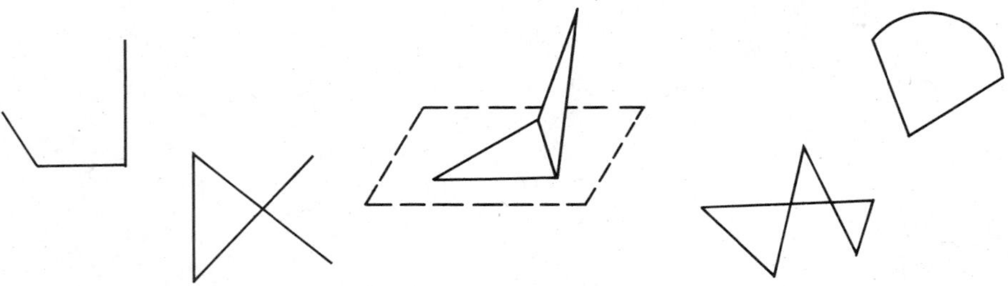

When referring to a polygon, we name its consecutive vertices in order. The *quadrilateral* shown at the top of the next page can be called, for example, *ABCD*, *DCBA*, or *BADC*. A polygon is classified according to the number of sides it has. The table at the right lists some special names.

| Number of Sides | Name of Polygon |
|---|---|
| 3 | triangle |
| 4 | quadrilateral |
| 5 | pentagon |
| 6 | hexagon |
| 8 | octagon |
| 10 | decagon |

The simplest polygon is a triangle. The terms which we defined for triangles (such as *sides, vertices,* and *angles*) also apply to other polygons.

Two sides which intersect are called **consecutive sides.** The endpoints of a side are called **consecutive vertices.** A segment which joins nonconsecutive vertices is called a **diagonal** of the polygon.

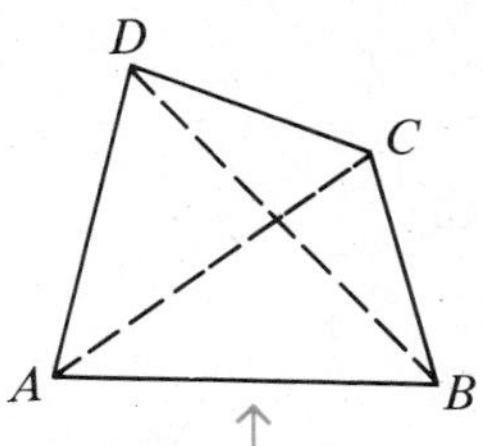


$\overline{AB}$ and $\overline{BC}$ are consecutive sides.
$A$ and $B$ are consecutive vertices.
$\overline{AC}$ and $\overline{BD}$ are diagonals.

Polygons can be equiangular, equilateral, or both as shown below.

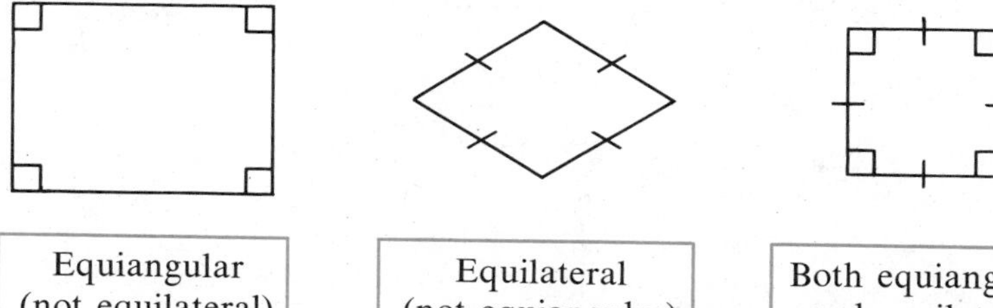

| Equiangular (not equilateral) | Equilateral (not equiangular) | Both equiangular and equilateral |
|---|---|---|

If a polygon is both equiangular and equilateral, it is called a **regular polygon.** A regular pentagon is shown at the right. The angle measures for regular polygons are explained in the next section.

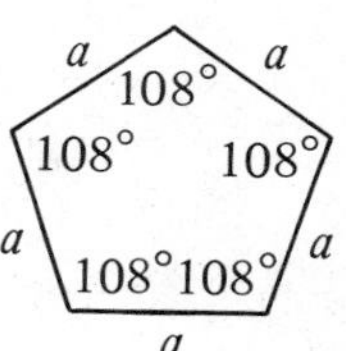


## Classroom Practice

**For each figure shown, decide:**
**a. if the figure is a polygon;**
**b. if the figure is a convex polygon.**

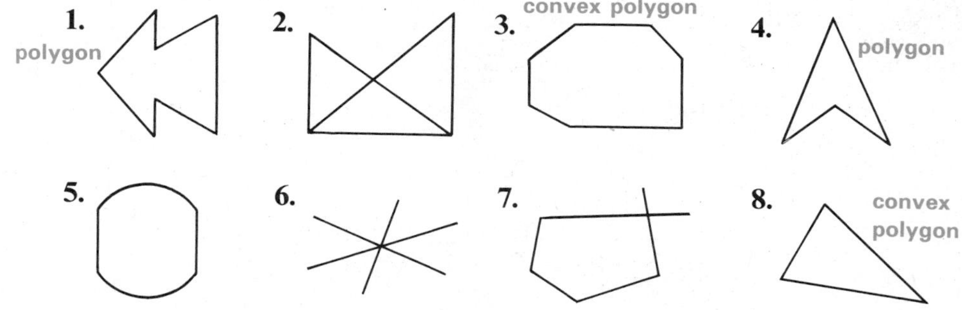

**Which of the following are acceptable names for the pentagon shown?**

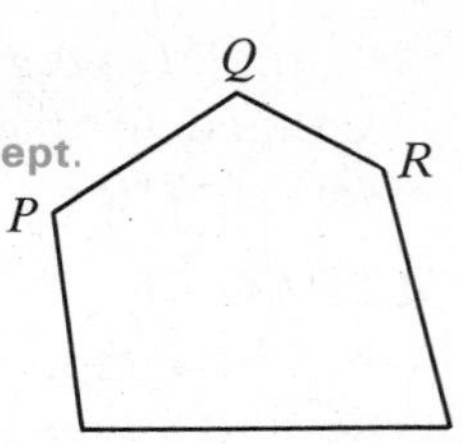


**9.** *PQRST* accept. **10.** *PTQRS* not accept. **11.** *SRQPT* accept.

**12.** Name any two consecutive sides of the pentagon.

**13.** Name any two consecutive vertices of the pentagon.

**14.** Name as many diagonals as you can. $\overline{QT}$, $\overline{QS}$, $\overline{RP}$, $\overline{RT}$, $\overline{SP}$

**15.** A regular polygon with four sides is usually called a ___?___. square

## Written Exercises

**Is the polygon shown a convex polygon?**

A **1.** Yes

**2.** No

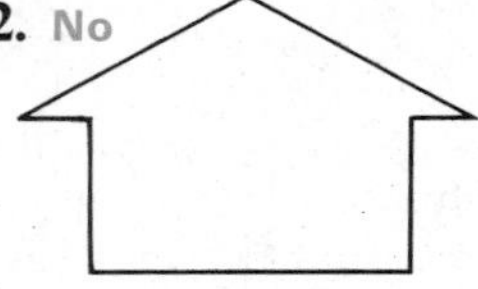

**3.** Yes

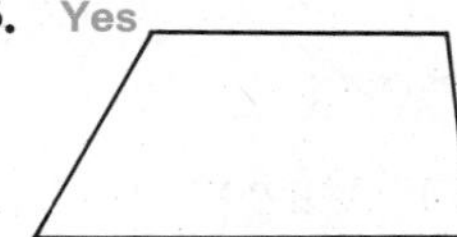

**4.** Yes

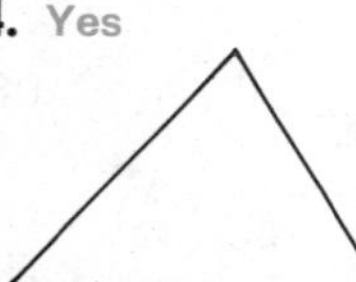

**5.** No

**6.** Yes

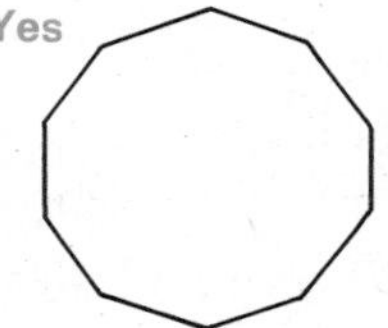

**Which of the following are acceptable names for the hexagon shown?**

**7.** *ABCDEF* acceptable **8.** *DCBAFE* acceptable **9.** *CDFEAB* not acceptable

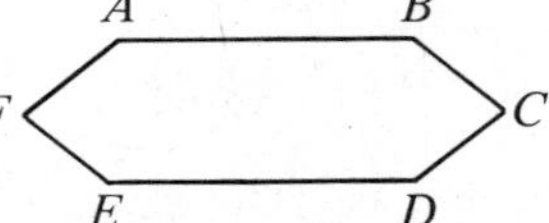


**10.** How many diagonals can you draw from vertex *A*? 3

**11.** How many diagonals can you draw from vertex *F*? 3

**12.** $\overline{DE}$ and ___?___ are consecutive sides. $\overline{EF}$ or $\overline{CD}$
(Two answers are possible.)

**Classify each polygon as equiangular, equilateral, or regular.**

**13.**

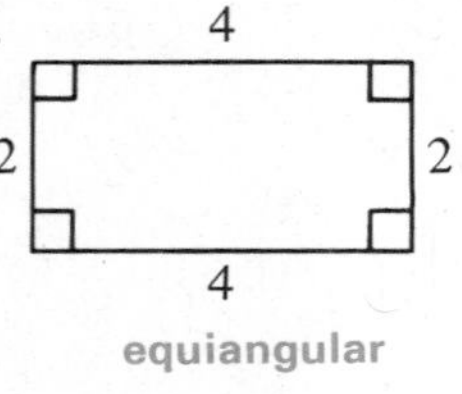


equiangular

**14.**

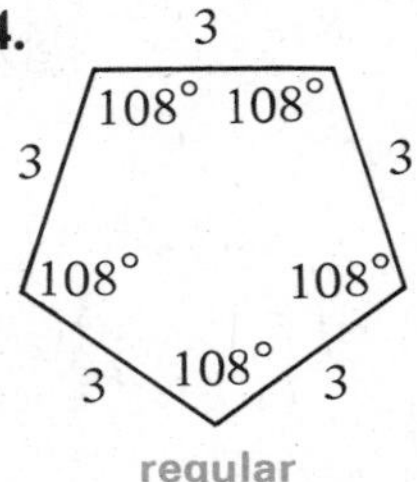


regular

**15.**

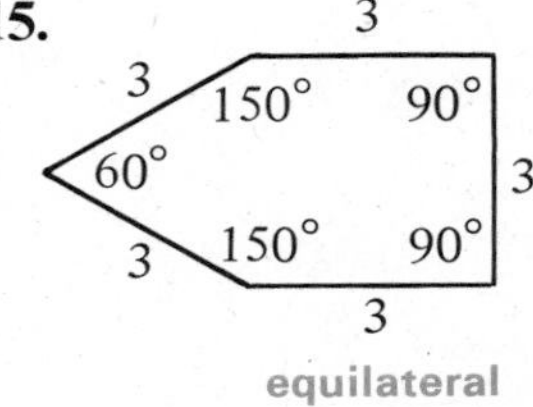


equilateral

**Draw a convex polygon which satisfies the conditions.**

**16.** A quadrilateral which is equiangular but not equilateral

**17.** A quadrilateral which is equilateral but not equiangular

**18.** A regular triangle

**19.** A regular hexagon

B **20.** A hexagon which is equilateral but not equiangular

**21.** A hexagon which is equiangular but not equilateral

**In a convex pentagon, you can draw two diagonals from each vertex. This information is given in the table below. Copy and complete the table.**

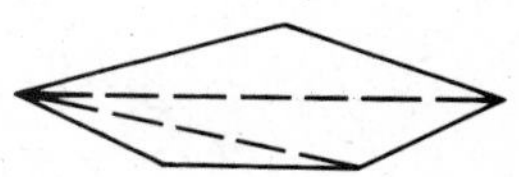

| | **22.** | | **23.** | **24.** | **25.** | **26.** | **27.** |
|---|---|---|---|---|---|---|---|
| Number of sides of a convex polygon | 4 | 5 | 6 | 7 | 8 | 20 | $n$ |
| Number of diagonals from each vertex | 1 ? | 2 | 3 ? | 4 ? | 5 ? | 17 ? | $n - 3$ ? |

**Copy and complete the table below.**
**(*Hint:* Draw a diagram for each exercise.)**

C

| | **28.** | **29.** | **30.** | **31.** | **32.** |
|---|---|---|---|---|---|
| Number of sides of a convex polygon | 4 | 5 | 6 | 7 | 8 |
| Total number of diagonals | ? | ? | ? | ? | ? |
| | 2 | 5 | 9 | 14 | 20 |

## *Experiments*

Cut out a strip of paper. A strip two or three centimeters wide cut from the long side of a sheet of notebook paper is convenient.

Figure 1

Begin to "tie" the paper as you would to form an ordinary overhand knot (see Figure 1).

Carefully press the folds flat. Trim off the excess paper labeled $L$ and $R$ in Figure 2. The polygon formed is a regular pentagon!

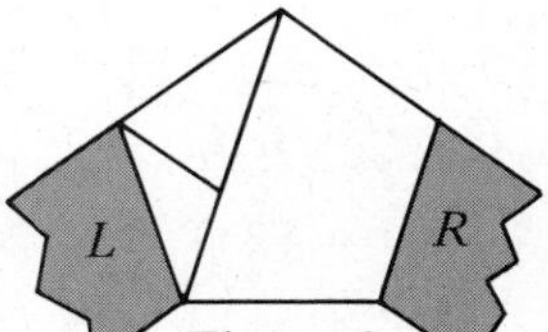

L R

Figure 2

## 2 • Angle Sums of Polygons

In Section 1 of Chapter 3 we proved that the angle sum of any triangle is 180°. In fact, we can find the angle sum of any convex polygon if we know how many sides the polygon has. The diagrams below suggest a way to find this sum. See page T71 for an alternative method.

**Angle Sum of a Quadrilateral**

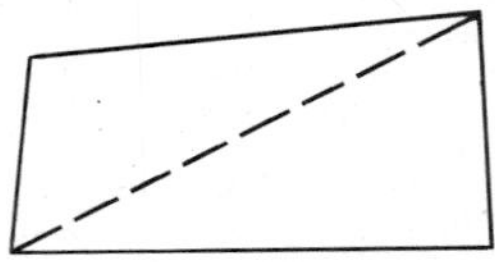

Angle sum of each triangle = 180°
Angle sum of quadrilateral = 2 × 180°
= 360°

**Angle Sum of a Pentagon**

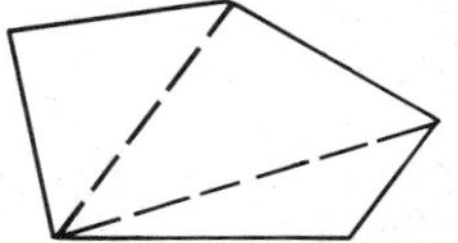

Angle sum of each triangle = 180°
Angle sum of pentagon = 3 × 180°
= 540°

Before reading further, try to find the angle sums of convex polygons with six and seven sides. Check your answers in the table below.

| Number of sides of polygon | Number of triangles formed by drawing all the diagonals from one vertex | Angle sum of polygon |
|---|---|---|
| 4 | 2 | 2 × 180° or 360° |
| 5 | 3 | 3 × 180° or 540° |
| 6 | 4 | 4 × 180° or 720° |
| 7 | 5 | 5 × 180° or 900° |
| 8 | 6 | 6 × 180° or 1080° |

Do you see that if a convex polygon has $n$ sides, you can form $n - 2$ triangles by drawing all the diagonals from one vertex? Therefore, the angle sum of the polygon is the same as the angle sum for $n - 2$ triangles. We state this as our next theorem.

**THEOREM 1**

If a convex polygon has $n$ sides, then its angle sum is given by the formula

$$S = (n - 2) \times 180°.$$

EXAMPLE A regular polygon has 12 sides.

**a.** Find its angle sum.

**b.** Find the measure of each angle of the polygon.

**a.** $S = (n - 2) \times 180° = (12 - 2) \times 180° = 1800°$

**b.** Since the polygon is regular, all 12 angles are equal.

The measure of each angle is $\frac{1}{12} \times 1800° = 150°$.

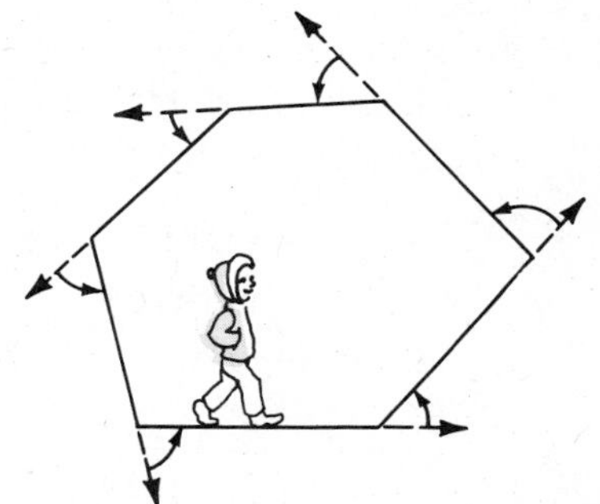

The angle sum of a polygon is sometimes called the *interior angle sum* to distinguish it from the *exterior angle sum* of the polygon. The exterior angle sum for the hexagon shown is the sum of the measures of the six indicated angles. (Notice that we consider only one of the two exterior angles at each vertex.) To find this sum, imagine yourself walking along the sides of the polygon. As you reach each vertex, you turn through the number of degrees in an exterior angle. When you return to your starting point, you will have turned through 360°. Do you see that given *any* convex polygon with any number of sides, you will turn through 360°? This fact is stated in Theorem 2. A more formal proof is suggested by Exercise 22, page 179.

**THEOREM 2**

The exterior angle sum of any convex polygon, one angle at each vertex, is 360°.

## Classroom Practice

**Copy and complete the table for convex polygons.**

| | Sample | 1. | 2. | 3. | 4. | 5. | 6. |
|---|---|---|---|---|---|---|---|
| Number of sides | 5 | 6 | 8 | 10 | 12 | ___?___ 13 | ___?___ 22 |
| Interior angle sum | $3 \times 180°$ | (See below.) ___?___ | ___?___ | ___?___ | ___?___ | $11 \times 180°$ | $20 \times 180°$ |
| Exterior angle sum | 360° | 360° ___?___ | 360° ___?___ | 360° ___?___ | 360° ___?___ | 360° ___?___ | 360° ___?___ |

1. $4 \times 180°$ 2. $6 \times 180°$ 3. $8 \times 180°$ 4. $10 \times 180°$

## Written Exercises

Interior angle sum: 1. 2 × 180°  2. 7 × 180°  3. 9 × 180°  4. 20 × 180°

**Copy and complete the table for convex polygons.** Ext. angle sum is always 360°.

A

| | **1.** | **2.** | **3.** | **4.** | **5.** | **6.** |
|---|---|---|---|---|---|---|
| Number of sides | 4 | 9 | 11 | 22 | ? 12 | ? 17 |
| Interior angle sum | ? | ? | ? | ? | 10 × 180° | 15 × 180° |
| Exterior angle sum | ? | ? | ? | ? | ? | ? |

**7.** In a regular triangle each interior angle has measure ___?___, and each exterior angle has measure ___?___. 60° 120°

**8. a.** In a regular quadrilateral each interior angle has measure ___?___, and each exterior angle has measure ___?___. 90° 90°

**b.** A regular polygon with four sides is called a ___?___. square

**In Exercises 9–11, the polygon shown is a regular polygon.**
**a. Name the polygon.**
**b. Find the interior angle sum and the measure of each interior angle.**
**c. Find the exterior angle sum and the measure of each exterior angle.**

**9.** a. pentagon

b. 540°; 108°
c. 360°; 72°

**10.** a. hexagon

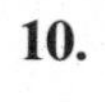

b. 720°; 120°
c. 360°; 60°

**11.** a. octagon

STOP

b. 1080°; 135°
c. 360°; 45°

**Copy and complete the table for regular convex polygons.**

B

| | **12.** | **13.** | **14.** | **15.** | **16.** |
|---|---|---|---|---|---|
| Number of sides | 12 | ? 6 | ? 9 | ? 18 | ? 36 |
| Each interior angle | ? | 120° | 140° | ? | ? |
| Each exterior angle | ? 30° | ? 60° | ? 40° | 20° | 10° |

interior angle:
12. 150°
15. 160°
16. 170°

**17.** The face of a honeycomb consists of interlocking regular hexagons. Can you interlock STOP signs as you can hexagons? Use the results of Exercise 11 to explain your answer. No, 135 is not a factor of 360.

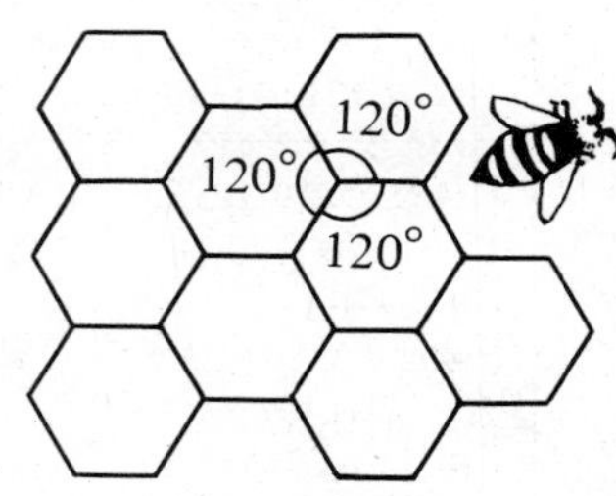


**18.** Can you tile a kitchen floor with regular pentagons? Use the results of Exercise 9 to explain your answer. No, 108 is not a factor of 360.

19. *Given:* Quadrilateral $ABCD$

$\angle A = \angle C = x°$

$\angle B = \angle D = y°$

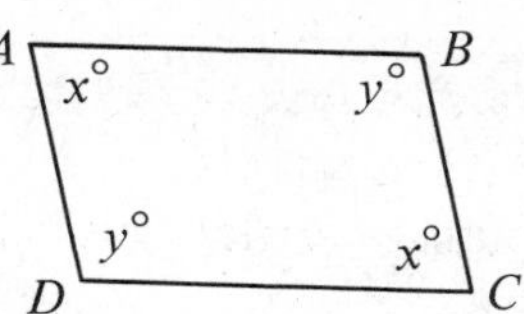


a. $2x° + 2y° = \underline{\ ?\ }°$ 360 **b.** $x° + y° = \underline{\ ?\ }°$ 180

c. $\overline{AD} \parallel \overline{BC}$ because same-side interior angles are ___?___. supplementary

d. $\overline{AB} \parallel \overline{CD}$ because ___?___. same-side interior $\angle$s are supplementary

20. Construct a regular hexagon, using compass and straightedge.

C 21. A regular pentagon and two diagonals are shown. Find the measure of $\angle 1$. 36°

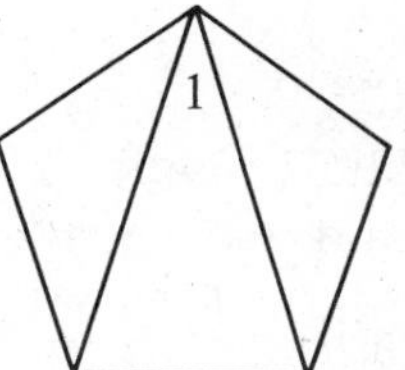


22. The diagram at the right shows part of a polygon with $n$ sides. Complete each statement.

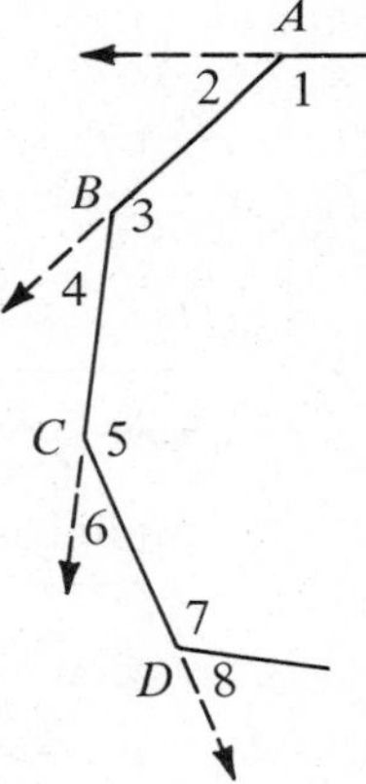


a. At vertex $A$, $\angle 1 + \angle 2 = \underline{\ ?\ }°$. 180

b. At vertex $B$, $\angle 3 + \angle 4 = \underline{\ ?\ }°$. 180

c. At any vertex, the sum of an interior and an exterior angle is ___?___°. 180

d. If the polygon has $n$ sides, then it has ___?___ $n$ vertices. The sum of the interior and the exterior angles at all the vertices is (___?___ × ___?___)°. $n \times 180$

e. From Theorem 1, the sum of the interior angles is ___?___°. $(n - 2) \times 180$

f. By subtracting your answer in part **e** from your answer in **d**, show that the sum of the exterior angles, one angle at each vertex, is 360°.

## SELF-TEST

1. Draw a quadrilateral which is not convex.
2. Draw a pentagon which is equilateral but not equiangular.
3. Draw a regular hexagon.
4. Find the measure of each interior angle of the hexagon. 120°
5. Find the measure of each exterior angle of the hexagon. 60°

# 3 • Special Quadrilaterals

Some special quadrilaterals are defined below.

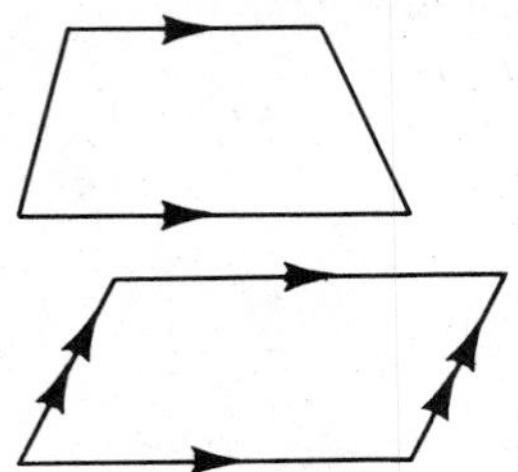

A **trapezoid** is a quadrilateral with just one pair of opposite sides parallel.

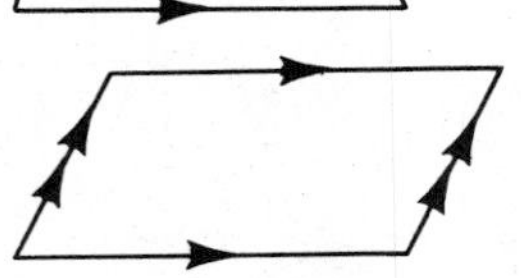

A **parallelogram** is a quadrilateral with both pairs of opposite sides parallel.

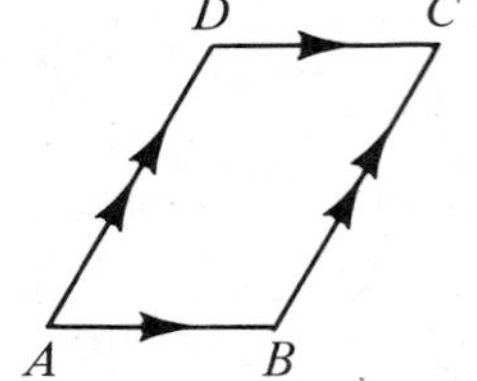


The symbol ▱ stands for parallelogram. In ▱$ABCD$, $\overline{AD} \parallel \overline{BC}$. Thus $\angle A$ and $\angle B$ must be supplementary angles. Also, $\angle B$ and $\angle C$ are supplementary because $\overline{AB} \parallel \overline{DC}$.

Three other special quadrilaterals are shown below with their definitions.

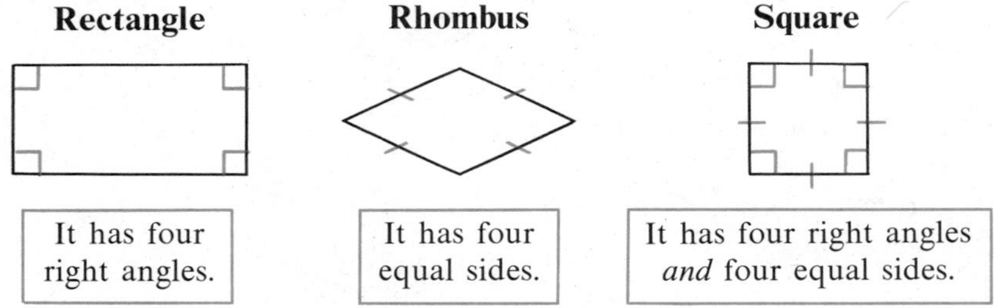


You can show that rectangles, rhombuses, and squares are all parallelograms (see Exercises 13–15). The diagram below illustrates how the special quadrilaterals relate to one another. Notice that every square is both a rectangle and a rhombus.

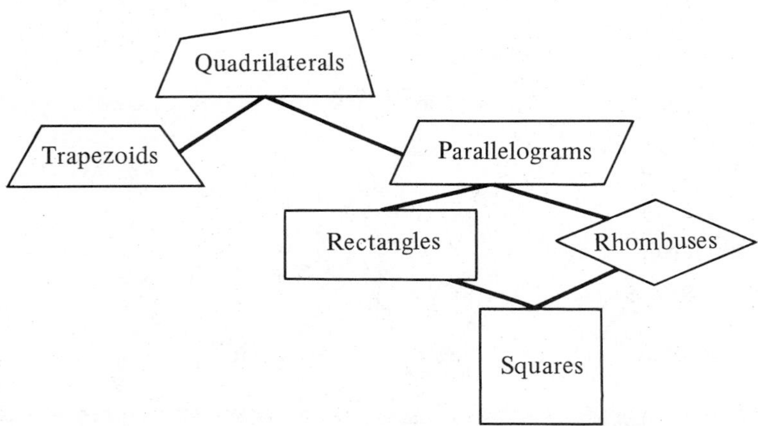

## Classroom Practice

**Classify each statement as true or false. Refer to the diagram at the bottom of page 180.**

True **1.** Every trapezoid is a quadrilateral.

**2.** Every rectangle is a quadrilateral. True

False **3.** Every parallelogram is a square.

**4.** Every square is a rhombus. True

False **5.** Every trapezoid is a parallelogram.

**6.** Every rectangle is a parallelogram. True

**7.** List each quadrilateral below which appears to be:

(See below.) **a.** a parallelogram.

1, 6, 9 **b.** a trapezoid.

3, 5, 12 **c.** a rectangle.

3, 7, 11, 12 **d.** a rhombus.

3, 12 **e.** a square.

a. 2, 3, 5, 7, 8, 11, 12

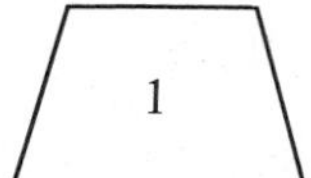

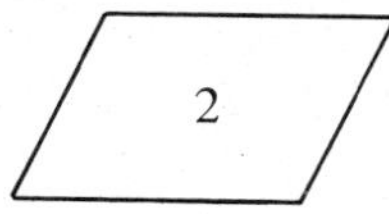

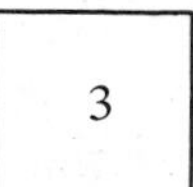

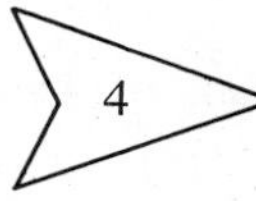

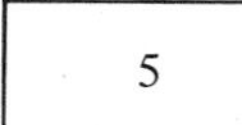

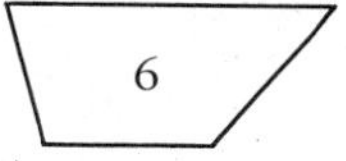

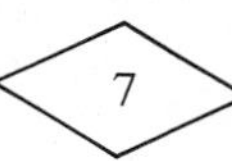

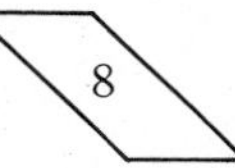

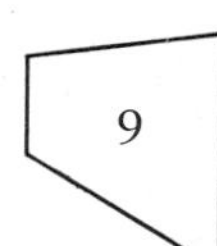

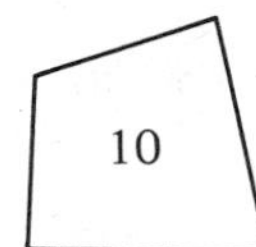

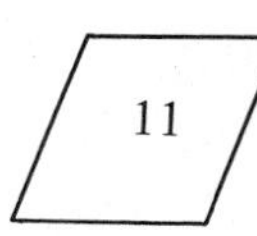

3, 12 **8.** List each figure above which is *both* a rectangle *and* a rhombus.

5 **9.** List each figure above which is a rectangle but not a square.

7, 11 **10.** List each figure above which is a rhombus but not a square.

**In Exercises 11–14, assume that lines that appear to be parallel *are* parallel. Name all quadrilaterals that are parallelograms.**

**11.** D E C / A F B

ADEF
EFBC
ABCD

**12.**

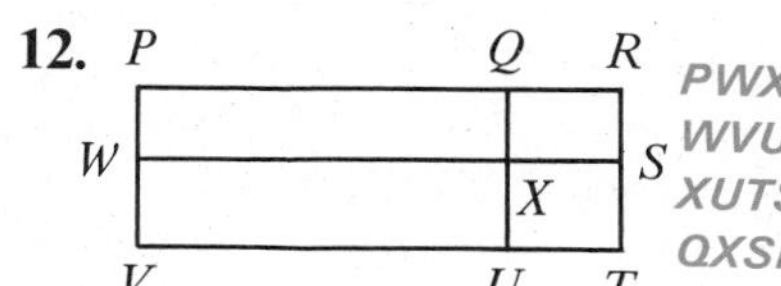


PWXQ, WVUX, XUTS, QXSR, PWSR, WVTS, PVUQ, QUTR, PVTR

**13.**

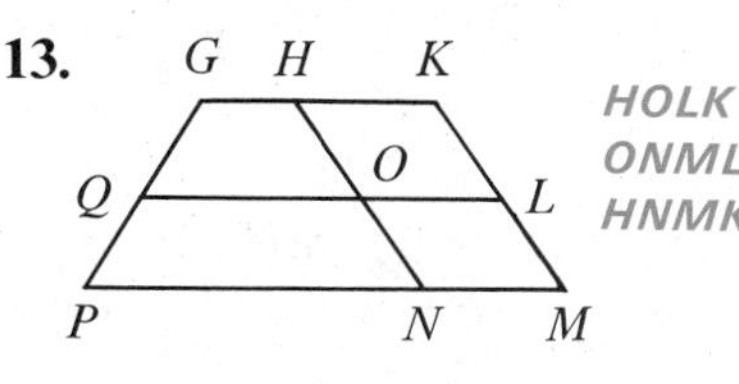


HOLK
ONML
HNMK

**14.**

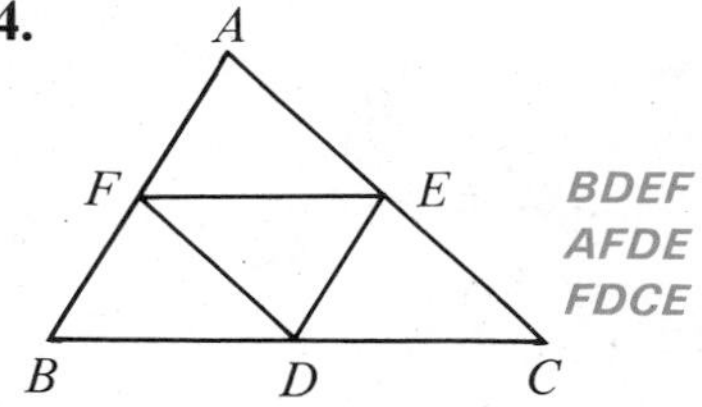


BDEF
AFDE
FDCE

GQOH, GPMK, GQLK, GPNH, QONP, QPML

**15.** Refer to the figure for Exercise 13. Name all trapezoids shown.

**16.** Refer to the figure for Exercise 14. Name all trapezoids shown.
FBCE, FDCA, ABDE

## Written Exercises

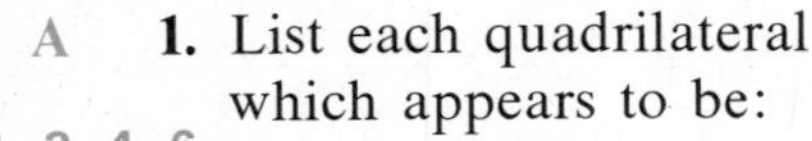

A **1.** List each quadrilateral which appears to be:

1, 3, 4, 6, 8, 10, 11 **a.** a parallelogram.

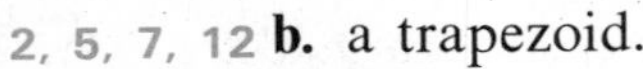

2, 5, 7, 12 **b.** a trapezoid.

3, 6, 10 **c.** a rectangle.

4, 6, 11 **d.** a rhombus.

6 **e.** a square.

6 **f.** both a rectangle and a rhombus.

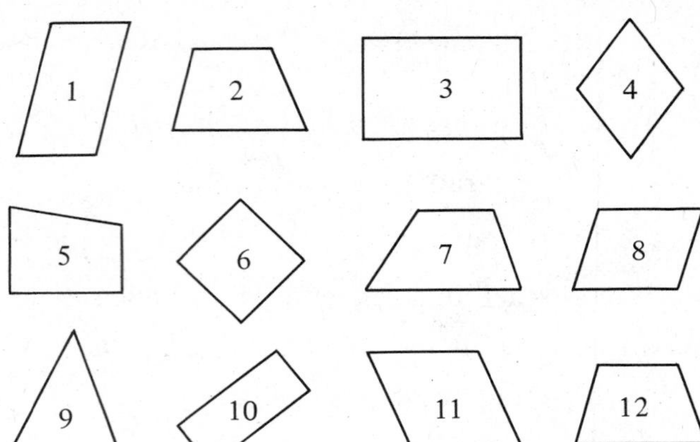


**True or False?**

**2.** All squares are rectangles. True

**3.** All rectangles are squares. False

**4.** All squares are rhombuses. True

**5.** All rhombuses are squares. False

**6.** Imagine pushing against a rectangle with a fixed base to form a parallelogram.

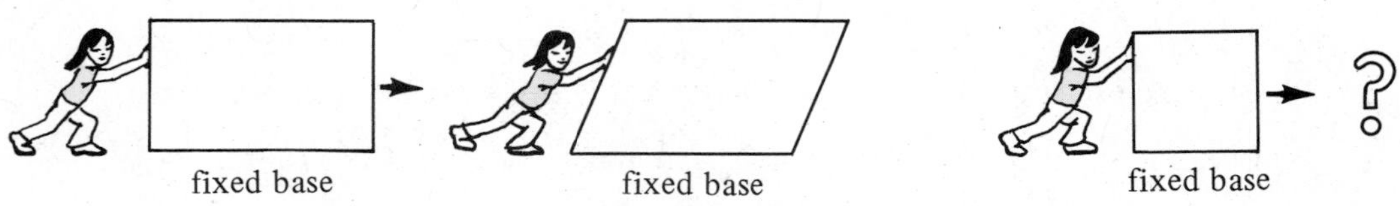


If you push against a square with a fixed base, what figure is formed? rhombus

**7.** There are seven parallelograms in the figure below. Name as many as you can.

APTS, STQB, PDVU, UVCQ, APQB, PDCQ, ADCB

**8.** Name three parallelograms in the figure below.

WGOE, EOHX, WGHX

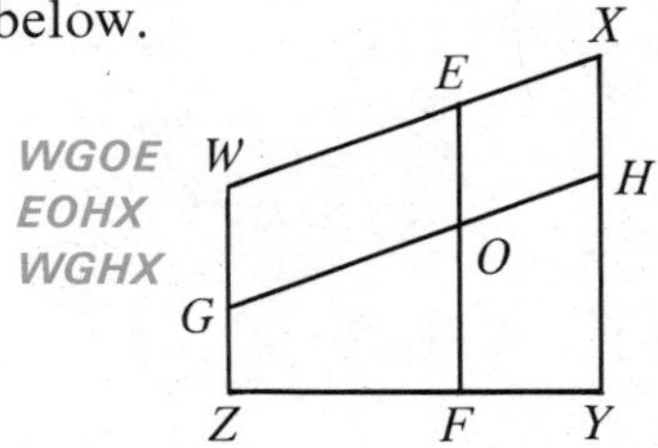


**9.** Refer to the figure for Exercise 7. Name two parallelograms which appear to be rhombuses. *APTS, UVCQ*

**10.** Refer to the figure for Exercise 8. Name six trapezoids. *GZFO, FYHO, GZYH, ZFEW, FYXE, ZYXW*

**11.** In the figure for Exercise 7, $\angle D = 70°$. Name four other angles with the same measure.
$\angle B$, $\angle PUV$, $\angle UVC$, $\angle UQC$, $\angle QTS$, $\angle AST$, $\angle APT$

**12.** In the figure for Exercise 8, $\angle W = 110°$. Find the measure of: **a.** $\angle X$. **b.** $\angle XHO$. **c.** $\angle HOE$.
70° 110° 70°

B **13.** Our goal is to show that a rhombus must be a parallelogram. Supply the reasons to complete the proof.

*Given:* $ABCD$ is a rhombus.

*Prove:* $ABCD$ is a ▱.

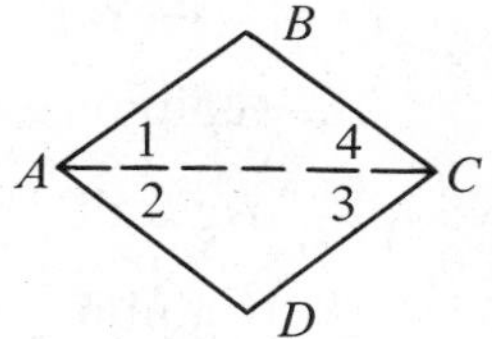


| STATEMENTS | REASONS |
|---|---|
| 1. $AB = CD$; $BC = DA$ | 1. ? Given: ABCD is a rhombus. |
| 2. $AC = AC$ | 2. ? From algebra |
| 3. $\triangle ABC \cong \triangle CDA$ | 3. ? SSS Postulate |
| 4. $\angle 1 = \angle 3$; $\angle 2 = \angle 4$ | 4. ? Corr. parts |
| 5. $\overline{AB} \parallel \overline{DC}$; $\overline{AD} \parallel \overline{BC}$ | 5. ? Thm. 6, page 66 |
| 6. $ABCD$ is a ▱. | 6. ? Def. of *parallelogram* |

**14.** Our goal is to show that a rectangle must be a parallelogram. Supply the reasons to complete the proof.

*Given:* $ABCD$ is a rectangle.

*Prove:* $ABCD$ is a ▱.

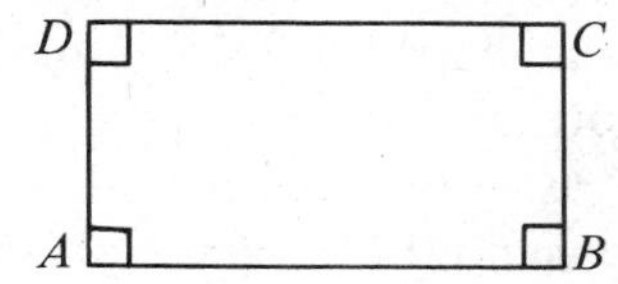


| STATEMENTS | REASONS |
|---|---|
| 1. $\angle A = 90°$; $\angle B = 90°$ | 1. ? Given: ABCD is a rectangle. |
| 2. $\overline{AD} \perp \overline{AB}$; $\overline{BC} \perp \overline{AB}$ | 2. ? Def. of *perpend. lines* |
| 3. $\overline{AD} \parallel \overline{BC}$ | 3. In a plane, if 2 lines are each $\perp$ to a third line, then ? . they are $\parallel$ |
| 4. $\angle B = 90°$; $\angle C = 90°$ | 4. ? same as 1. |
| 5. $\overline{AB} \perp \overline{BC}$; $\overline{DC} \perp \overline{BC}$ | 5. ? same as 2. |
| 6. $\overline{AB} \parallel \overline{DC}$ | 6. ? same as 3. |
| 7. $ABCD$ is a ▱. | 7. ? Def. of *parallelogram* |

Since a square is a rectangle, it has the properties of a rectangle.

**15.** Explain why Exercise 14 lets you conclude that a square must be a parallelogram.

**16.** Construct a rectangle, using straightedge and compass.

**17.** Construct a trapezoid, using straightedge and compass.

**18.** Draw a quadrilateral $ABCD$ and locate the midpoint of each side. Join the midpoints to form a quadrilateral $EFGH$. What special kind of quadrilateral does $EFGH$ appear to be? parallelogram

**19.** Repeat Exercise 18, beginning with a rectangle $ABCD$. rhombus

**20.** Repeat Exercise 18, beginning with a rhombus $ABCD$. rectangle

**21.** Repeat Exercise 18, beginning with a square $ABCD$. square

C **22.** Using straightedge and compass, construct a rhombus which has a 60° angle.

**23.** Using straightedge and compass, construct a parallelogram which has a 45° angle.

# CAREER NOTES

## *Aircraft Assembly Technician*

Suppose someone gave you a model airplane kit with forty parts inside. How long do you think it would take you to put it together? Four hours? Eight hours? Two days? Can you imagine how long it would take you to assemble an actual airplane with its thousands or even millions of parts?

Teams of aircraft assembly technicians divide the job of airplane construction into a large variety of highly specialized tasks. Some assembly technicians join complete sections of the aircraft. For example, they may use bolts, rivets, drills, and solder to join the landing gear to the fuselage. Other technicians work on a smaller scale, assembling engine or auxiliary component parts. Still others specialize in electronic equipment including tiny circuits and modules.

All aircraft assembly technicians must interpret engineering specifications on blueprints for both mechanical and electronic assemblies. Skilled assemblers need high school or vocational training plus about two to four years of plant experience to fully master assembly skills.

# 4 • Properties of Parallelograms

Parallelograms have several special properties. Try the explorations below, and see how many properties you can find.

## Explorations

Carefully draw a very large parallelogram $ABCD$ which is neither a rectangle nor a rhombus. (Side $\overline{AB}$ should be at least 12 cm long.) Use your parallelogram for the exercises that follow.

### A. The Angles of a Parallelogram

1. Carefully measure the four angles of $\square ABCD$.
2. Compare the measures of consecutive angles:
   $\angle A$ and $\angle B$, $\angle B$ and $\angle C$, and so on.
3. Compare the measures of opposite angles:
   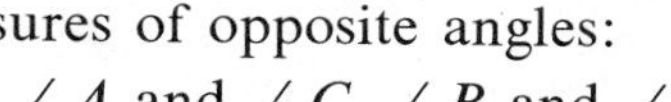
   $\angle A$ and $\angle C$, $\angle B$ and $\angle D$.

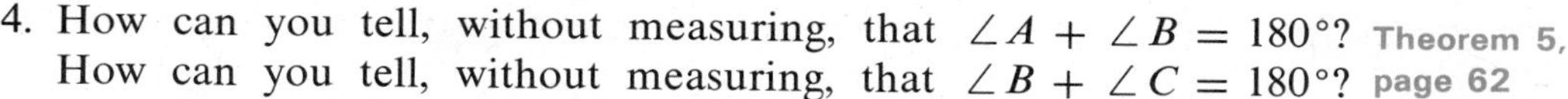

4. How can you tell, without measuring, that $\angle A + \angle B = 180°$? How can you tell, without measuring, that $\angle B + \angle C = 180°$? Theorem 5, page 62
5. How can you tell that $\angle A = \angle C$, using the two equations from Exercise 4? Subtraction and Substitution Postulates

### B. The Sides of a Parallelogram

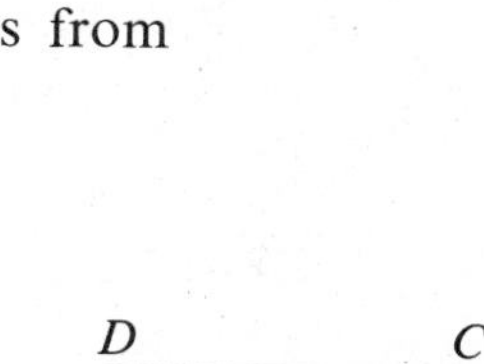


1. Carefully measure the four sides of $\square ABCD$.
2. Compare the lengths of opposite sides: They are equal.
   $\overline{AB}$ and $\overline{CD}$, $\overline{BC}$ and $\overline{DA}$.
3. 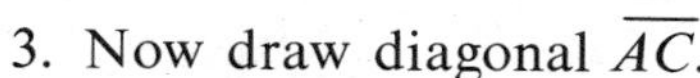 Now draw diagonal $\overline{AC}$.
4. What appears to be true about the two triangles formed? They are congruent.
5. How do you know that $\triangle ABC \cong \triangle CDA$? ASA Postulate
6. Use the fact that $\triangle ABC \cong \triangle CDA$ to show that the opposite sides of $\square ABCD$ are equal.

### C. The Diagonals of a Parallelogram

1. Draw the other diagonal, $\overline{BD}$. Let $O$ be the intersection point of the diagonals.
2. Carefully measure both diagonals. Is $AC = BD$? no
3. Carefully measure $\overline{AO}$ and $\overline{OC}$. Is $AO = OC$? yes
4. Carefully measure $\overline{BO}$ and $\overline{OD}$. Is $BO = OD$? yes
5. Would you say that the diagonals bisect each other? yes

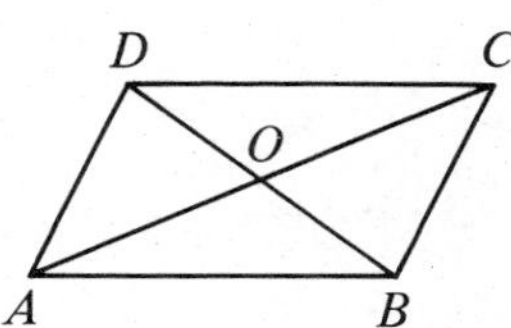

By now, you have probably discovered many properties of parallelograms. Perhaps you have even proved some of these properties. A summary of them is given below. Proofs of the theorems are left as exercises.

**Properties of a Parallelogram**

| | |
|---|---|
| By Definition: | Opposite sides of a parallelogram are parallel. |
| THEOREM 3 | Opposite sides of a parallelogram are equal. |
| THEOREM 4 | Opposite angles of a parallelogram are equal. |
| THEOREM 5 | Consecutive angles of a parallelogram are supplementary. |
| THEOREM 6 | Diagonals of a parallelogram bisect each other. |

*Warning:* The diagonals of a parallelogram are not usually equal.

## *Classroom Practice*

***PQRS*** **is a ▱. State the definition or theorem that justifies each statement.**

**1.** $\overline{PQ} \parallel \overline{SR}$ Definition

**2.** $PQ = SR$ Theorem 3

**3.** $SO = OQ$ Theorem 6

**4.** $\angle PSR = \angle PQR$ Thm. 4

**5.** $\angle SPQ + \angle PQR = 180°$ Thm. 5

**6.** $SP = RQ$ Thm. 3

**7.** $\overline{SP} \parallel \overline{RQ}$ Definition

**8.** $\overline{SQ}$ bisects $\overline{PR}$. Thm. 6

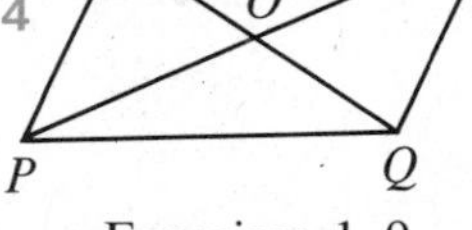

Exercises 1–9

**9.** There are four pairs of congruent triangles in the figure above. Name them. $\triangle SPQ \cong \triangle QRS$; $\triangle PQR \cong \triangle RSP$; $\triangle POQ \cong \triangle ROS$; $\triangle SOP \cong \triangle QOR$

**In Exercises 10–17: *ACEF* is a ▱;**
***BCDG*** **is a ▱.**

**Find the measure of each angle.**

**10.** $\angle C$ 70°

**11.** $\angle G$ 70°

**12.** $\angle GDC$ 110°

**13.** $\angle GBC$ 110°

**Find each length.**

**14.** $FE$ 14

**15.** $AF$ 7

**16.** $BG$ 4

**17.** $GD$ 6

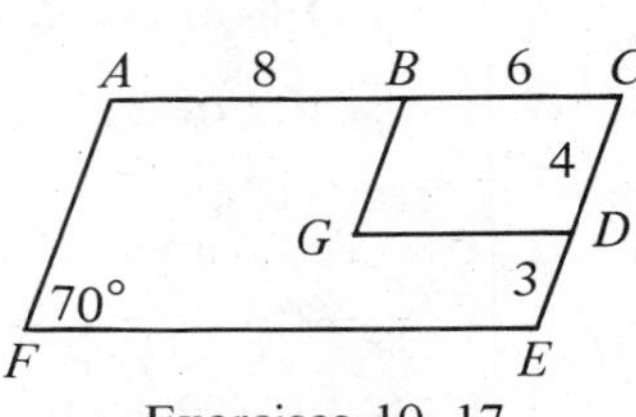

Exercises 10–17

## Written Exercises

*Given:* **PQRS is a ▱.**
**Find each length and angle measure.**

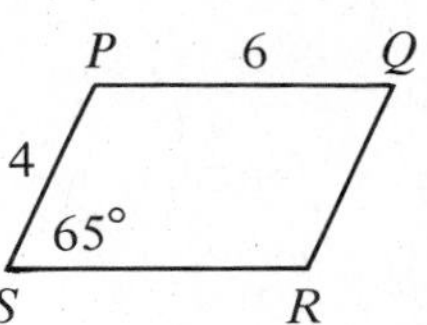


A **1.** $SR$ 6 **2.** $RQ$ 4 **3.** $\angle R$ 115° **4.** $\angle Q$ 65°

*Given:* **▱MECO and rectangle EXIC lie in the same plane.**
**Find each length and angle measure.**

**5.** $OC$ 10 **6.** $CI$ 8 **7.** $XI$ 4

**8.** $\angle I$ 90° **9.** $\angle M$ 110° **10.** $\angle XEM$ 160°

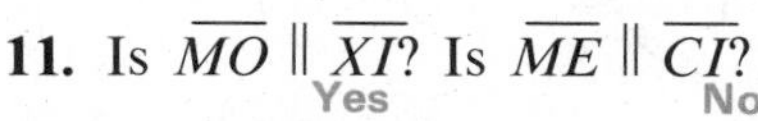

**11.** Is $\overline{MO} \parallel \overline{XI}$? Yes Is $\overline{ME} \parallel \overline{CI}$? No

*Given:* **▱ABCD; ▱AEFG**
**Find each length and angle measure.**

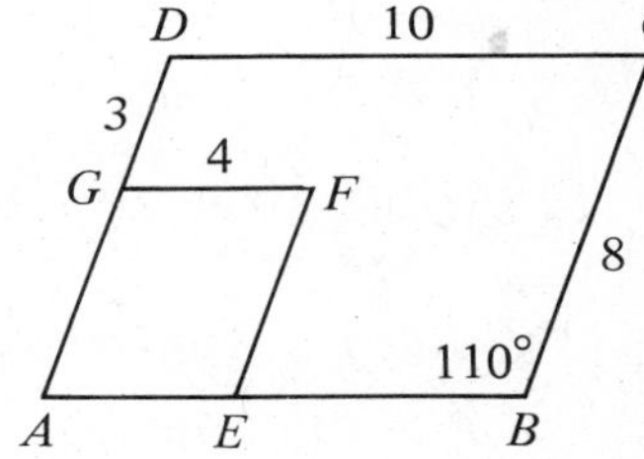


**12.** $AG$ 5 **13.** $AE$ 4 **14.** $BE$ 6

**15.** $\angle C$ 70° **16.** $\angle A$ 70° **17.** $\angle F$ 70°

**18.** Is $\overline{GF} \parallel \overline{DC}$? Yes Is $\overline{FE} \parallel \overline{CB}$? Yes

*Given:* **▱SALT**
**Find each angle measure.**

**19.** $\angle ALS$ 86° **20.** $\angle TLS$ 39° **21.** $\angle LAS$ 55°

**Suppose that $LO = 9$ and $AO = 16$.**
**Find each length.**

**22.** $SO$ 9 **23.** $OT$ 16 **24.** $SL$ 18

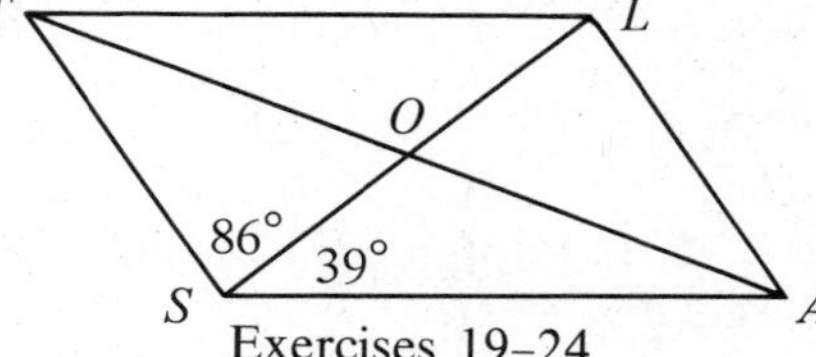

Exercises 19–24

**25.** $ABCD$ is a parallelogram. $AB = 8$ and $BC = 10$. Find the perimeter of the parallelogram. (*Hint:* The perimeter is the sum of the lengths of the sides.) 36

**26.** The length and width of a rectangle are 7 and 5. Find the perimeter of the rectangle. 24

*Given:* **▱RAFT**

B **27.** Find the value of $x$. 3

**28.** Find the value of $y$. 4

**29.** Find the value of $z$. 5

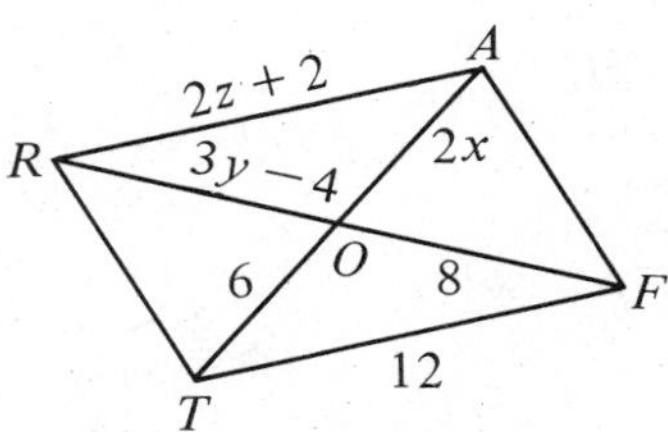

**The purpose of Exercises 30–32 is to prove Theorems 3 and 4.**

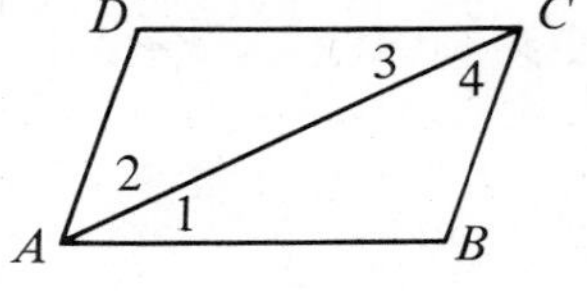


**30.** Supply the reasons to complete the proof.

*Given:* ▱$ABCD$

*Prove:* $\triangle ABC \cong \triangle CDA$

| STATEMENTS | REASONS |
|---|---|
| 1. $ABCD$ is a ▱. | 1. ? Given |
| 2. $\overline{AB} \parallel \overline{DC}$; $\overline{AD} \parallel \overline{BC}$ | 2. ? Def. of *parallelogram* |
| 3. $\angle 1 = \angle 3$; $\angle 2 = \angle 4$ | 3. ? Thm. 4, page 62 |
| 4. $AC = AC$ | 4. ? From algebra |
| 5. $\triangle ABC \cong \triangle CDA$ | 5. ? ASA Postulate |

**31.** *Given:* ▱$ABCD$

*Prove:* $AB = CD$; $BC = DA$

(*Hint:* Draw $\overline{AC}$. Then use the result of Exercise 30.)

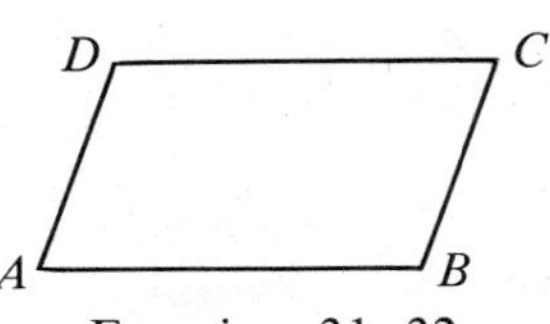

Exercises 31, 32

**32.** *Given:* ▱$ABCD$

*Prove:* $\angle B = \angle D$; $\angle A = \angle C$

(*Hint:* To prove that $\angle B = \angle D$, draw $\overline{AC}$ and use the result of Exercise 30. To prove that $\angle A = \angle C$, draw $\overline{BD}$.)

**33.** Complete this proof of Theorem 6 by supplying the reasons.

*Given:* ▱$EFGH$ with diagonals meeting at $O$

*Prove:* $EO = GO$; $FO = HO$

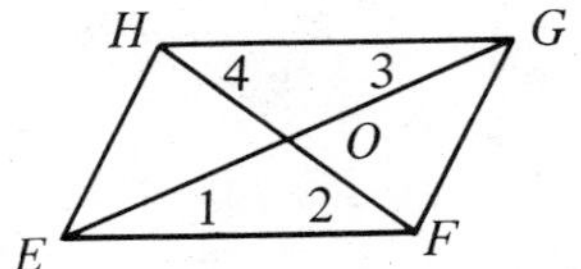


| STATEMENTS | REASONS |
|---|---|
| 1. $EFGH$ is a ▱. | 1. ? Given |
| 2. $\overline{EF} \parallel \overline{GH}$ | 2. ? Def. of *parallelogram* |
| 3. $\angle 1 = \angle 3$; $\angle 2 = \angle 4$ | 3. ? Thm. 4, page 62 |
| 4. $EF = GH$ | 4. ? Opp. sides of a ▱ are =. |
| 5. $\triangle EOF \cong \triangle GOH$ | 5. ? ASA Postulate |
| 6. $EO = GO$; $FO = HO$ | 6. ? Corresponding parts |

**34.** Write a proof of Theorem 5.

*Given:* ▱$WXYZ$

*Prove:* $\angle W$ and $\angle X$ are supplements.
$\angle W$ and $\angle Z$ are supplements.

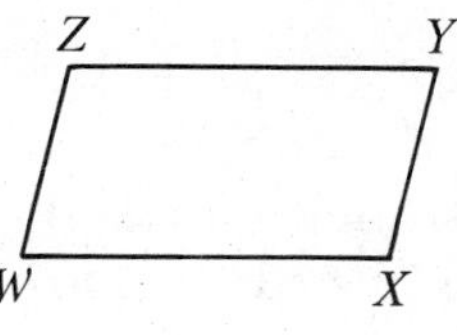


C **35.** *Given:* ▱$ABCD$

*Prove:* $RE = SE$

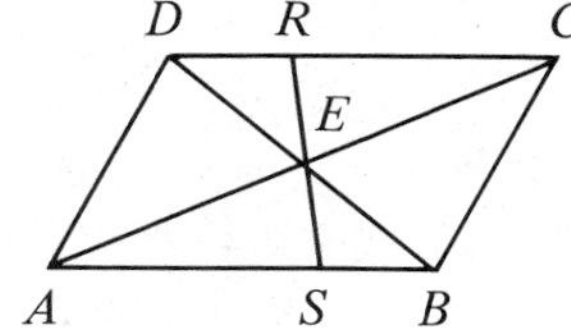


**36.** Our goal is to show that the distance between two parallel lines is always the same. To show this, we choose any two points on one line and prove that the points are the same distance from the other line. (The distance from a point to a line is defined to be the length of the *perpendicular* segment from the point to the line.)

*Given:* $l \parallel m$; $\overline{AX} \perp m$; $\overline{BY} \perp m$

*Prove:* $AX = BY$

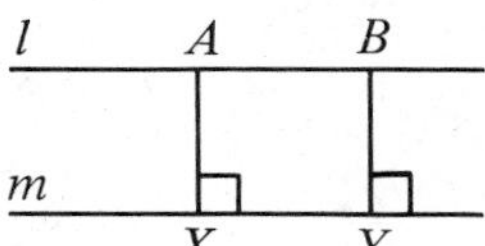


## SELF-TEST

**Define each of the following special quadrilaterals.** (See Glossary.)

**1.** Parallelogram **2.** Trapezoid **3.** Rhombus

**4.** Rectangle **5.** Square

***ABCD* is a parallelogram. Complete each statement.**

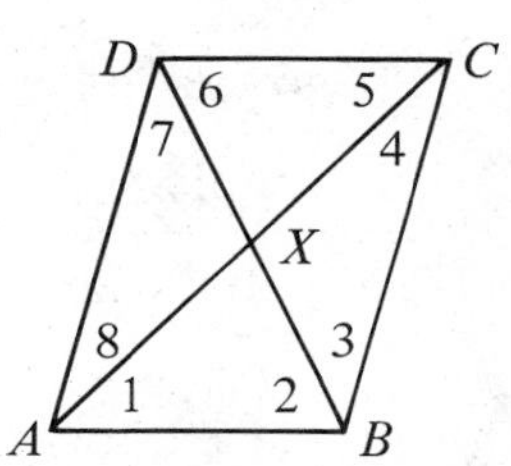


**6.** $AB = \underline{\ ?\ }$ CD **7.** $\overline{BC} \parallel \underline{\ ?\ }$ $\overline{AD}$

**8.** $DX = \underline{\ ?\ }$ BX **9.** $\angle 1 = \angle \underline{\ ?\ }$ 5

**10.** $\angle DAB = \angle \underline{\ ?\ }$ BCD **11.** $\angle 7 = \angle \underline{\ ?\ }$ 3

**12.** $\angle ABC$ and $\angle \underline{\ ?\ }$ are supplementary angles.
BCD or DAB

## 5 • Properties of Special Parallelograms

Since rectangles, rhombuses, and squares are parallelograms, they have all the properties listed on page 186. But because they are *special* parallelograms, they have other properties as well. Try the explorations below and see if you can discover what these properties are.

### *Explorations*

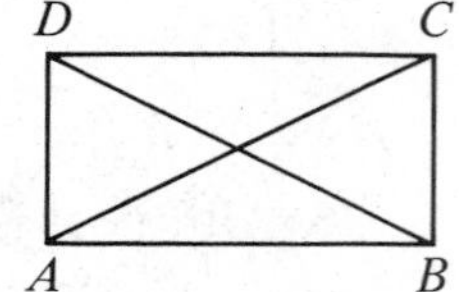


A. Carefully draw a very large rectangle that is not a square. Draw the two diagonals.

1. Measure the diagonals. Are they equal? yes
2. Are the diagonals perpendicular? no
3. Does each diagonal bisect two angles of the quadrilateral? (For example, in rectangle $ABCD$, does $\overline{BD}$ bisect $\angle ABC$ and $\angle ADC$?) no

Draw a different-looking rectangle and see whether your answers to questions 1–3 are the same.

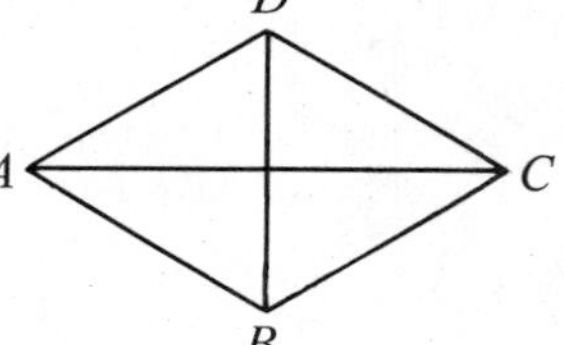


B. Carefully draw a very large rhombus that is not a square. Draw the two diagonals. Answer questions 1–3 in part A. Repeat this experiment with a different-looking rhombus.
1. no 2. yes 3. yes

C. Carefully draw a large square and its two diagonals. Answer questions 1–3 in part A.
Repeat this experiment with a different square.
1. yes 2. yes 3. yes

D. Now copy and complete the table.
In each space write $Y$ for *yes* or $N$ for *not necessarily.*

| | **Rectangle** | **Rhombus** | **Square** |
|---|---|---|---|
| Diagonals are equal. | Y | N | Y |
| Diagonals are perpendicular. | N | Y | Y |
| Each diagonal bisects two angles. | N | Y | Y |

If you did the exploration exercises carefully, then you will not be surprised by the following theorems. Proofs of these theorems are left as exercises.

**THEOREM 7**

The diagonals of a rectangle are equal.

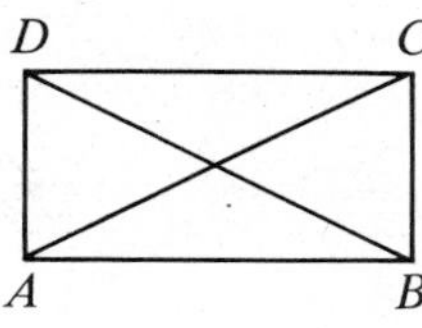


$AC = BD$

**THEOREM 8**

The diagonals of a rhombus are perpendicular, and they bisect the angles of the rhombus.

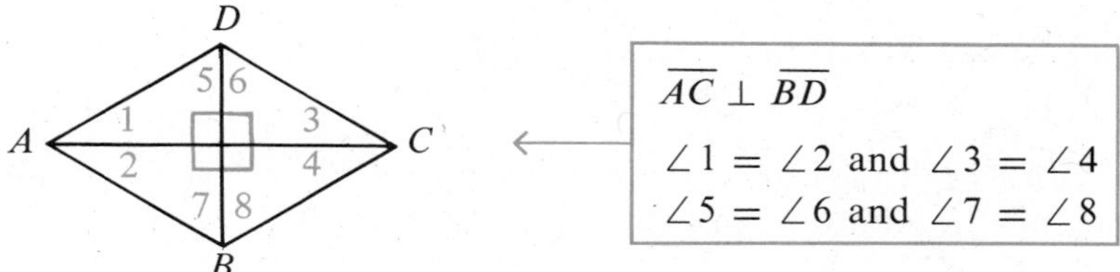


$\overline{AC} \perp \overline{BD}$

$\angle 1 = \angle 2$ and $\angle 3 = \angle 4$

$\angle 5 = \angle 6$ and $\angle 7 = \angle 8$

Both of these theorems apply to a square because a square is both a rectangle and a rhombus.

**EXAMPLE** In rectangle $WXYZ$, $WY = 8$. Find $WO$, $XO$, $YO$, and $ZO$.

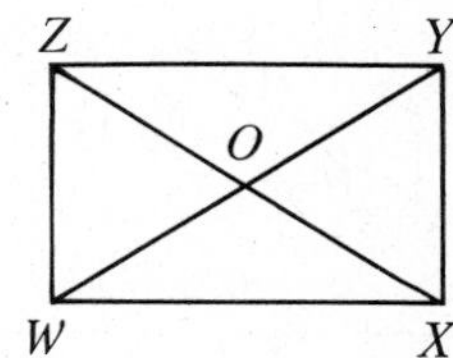


Since the diagonals of a rectangle are equal, $WY$ and $XZ$ both equal 8.

Since the diagonals of a parallelogram bisect each other, $WO = \frac{1}{2} \times 8 = 4$.

Likewise, $XO$, $YO$, and $ZO$ are equal to 4.

If half of rectangle $WXYZ$ is removed, we are left with a right triangle. Notice that $O$ is the midpoint of hypotenuse $\overline{WY}$. The fact that $WO = XO = YO$ suggests the following theorem.

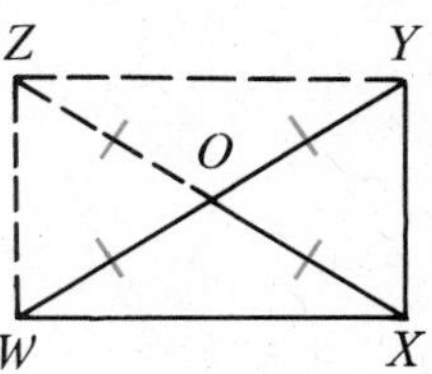

**THEOREM 9**

The midpoint of the hypotenuse of a right triangle is equidistant from the three vertices.

## Classroom Practice

***ABCD* is a rhombus.**

1. Suppose $\angle 1 = 20°$. Find the measure of each numbered angle. $\angle 2 = 20°$; $\angle 3 = \angle 4 = 70°$; $\angle 5 = 90°$
2. Suppose $\angle 1 = 30°$. Find the measure of each numbered angle. $\angle 2 = 30°$; $\angle 3 = \angle 4 = 60°$; $\angle 5 = 90°$

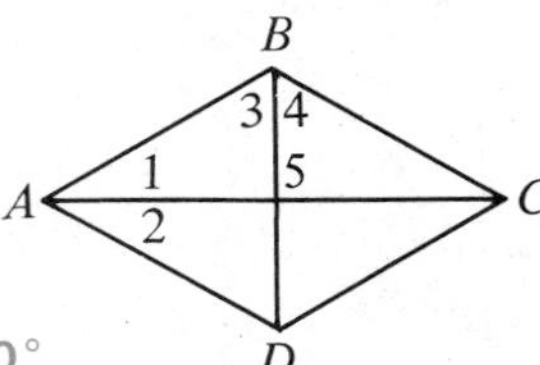


***PQRS* is a rectangle.**

3. Suppose $SQ = 10$. Find $SO$, $OQ$, $PO$, and $OR$. 5, 5, 5, 5
4. Suppose $\angle 1 = 62°$. Find the measure of each numbered angle. $\angle 2 = \angle 3 = 28°$; $\angle 4 = 62°$

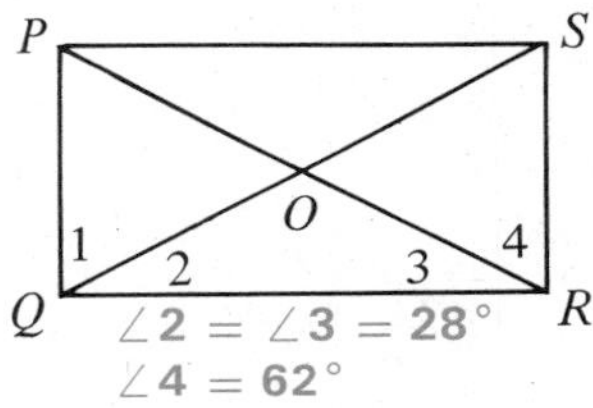


**$\triangle POR$ is a right triangle.**
***O* is the midpoint of the hypotenuse.**

5. $\overline{QO}$ is called a(n) median ___?___ (median/angle bisector/altitude).
6. Suppose $PR = 10$. Find $PO$, $OR$, and $OQ$. 5, 5, 5
7. Suppose $QO = 6$. Find $PO$ and $PR$. 6, 12

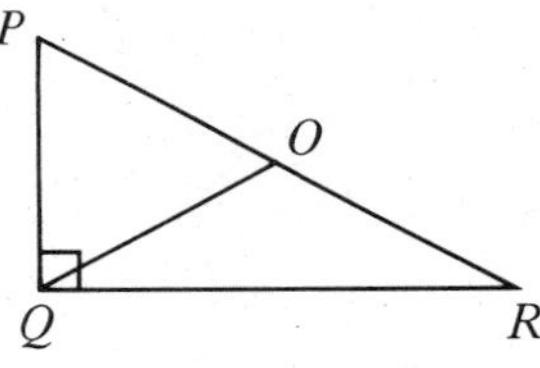


## Written Exercises

**In Exercises 1–10, refer to the quadrilaterals shown. For each exercise, state which quadrilaterals satisfy the given condition.**

**a.** Parallelogram **b.** Rectangle **c.** Rhombus **d.** Square

A **1.** All angles are right angles. **2.** Opposite sides are equal.

**3.** Diagonals are equal. **4.** Diagonals bisect each other.

1. b., d.
2. a., b., c., d.
3. b., d.
4. a., b., c., d.

a., b., c., d.
**5.** Opposite angles are equal.

c., d.
**6.** Diagonals are perpendicular.

c., d. **7.** Each diagonal bisects two angles.

**8.** All sides are equal. c., d.

**9.** Diagonals are perpendicular bisectors of each other. c., d.

**10.** When a diagonal is drawn, two congruent triangles are formed. a., b., c., d.

***STAR* is a rhombus.**

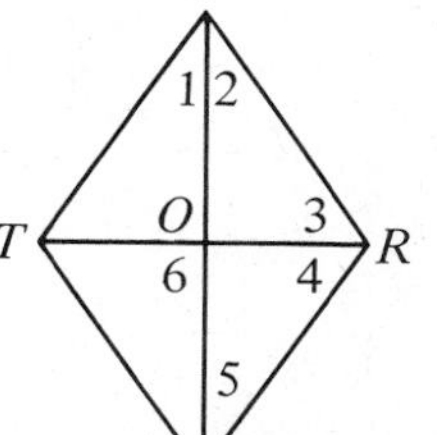


**11.** Suppose $\angle 1 = 25°$. $\angle 2 = 25°$; $\angle 3 = \angle 4 = 65°$; $\angle 5 = 25°$; $\angle 6 = 90°$
Find the measure of each numbered angle.

**12.** Suppose $\angle 5 = 32°$. $\angle 1 = \angle 2 = 32°$; $\angle 3 = \angle 4 = 58°$; $\angle 6 = 90°$
Find the measure of each numbered angle.

**13.** Suppose $SA = 8$ and $TR = 6$.
Find $SO$ and $TO$.
4 3

**14.** Suppose $RA = 10$. Find the perimeter of *STAR*. 40
(*Note:* The perimeter of a polygon is the sum of the lengths of its sides.)

***FLAT* is a rectangle.**

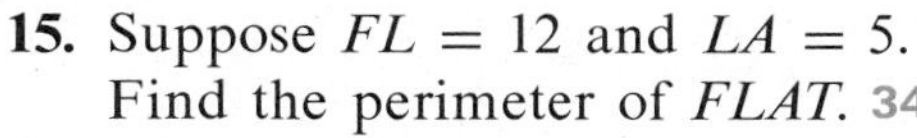

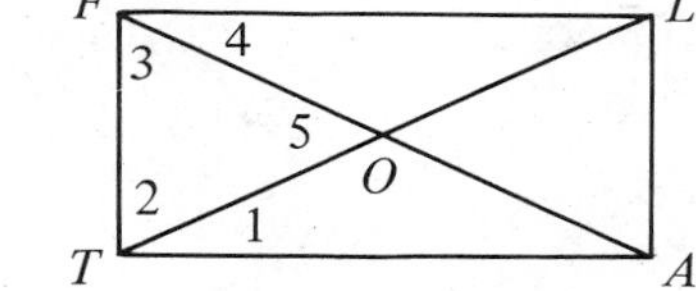


**15.** Suppose $FL = 12$ and $LA = 5$.
Find the perimeter of *FLAT*. 34

**16.** Suppose $FA = 13$. Find $TL$. 13

**17.** Suppose $FA = 14$. Find $FO$ and $TO$.
7 7

**18.** Suppose $\angle 1 = 20°$.
Find the measure of each numbered angle. $\angle 2 = \angle 3 = 70°$; $\angle 4 = 20°$; $\angle 5 = 40°$

**19.** Suppose $\angle 2 = 75°$.
Find the measure of each numbered angle. $\angle 1 = \angle 4 = 15°$; $\angle 3 = 75°$; $\angle 5 = 30°$

**20.** Suppose $\angle 5 = 24°$.
Find the measure of each numbered angle. $\angle 1 = \angle 4 = 12°$; $\angle 2 = \angle 3 = 78°$

***DEFG* is a square.**

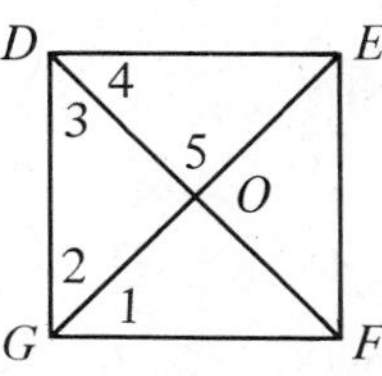


$\angle 1 = \angle 2 = \angle 3 = \angle 4 = 45°$
$\angle 5 = 90°$

**21.** Find the measure of each numbered angle.

**22.** If $DO = 8$, find $GE$. 16

***M* is the midpoint of the hypotenuse of right $\triangle SEN$.**

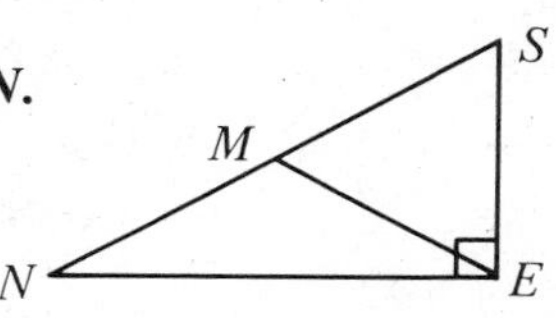


**23.** If $SN = 10$, find $ME$. 5

**24.** If $ME = 7$, find $SM$ and $SN$.
7 14

**B** **25.** The purpose of this exercise is to prove Theorem 7. Supply the reasons needed to complete the proof.

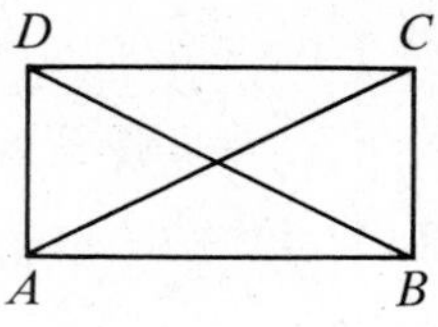


*Given:* Rectangle $ABCD$ with diagonals $\overline{AC}$ and $\overline{BD}$

*Prove:* $AC = BD$

| STATEMENTS | REASONS |
|---|---|
| 1. $ABCD$ is a rectangle. | 1. ___?___ Given |
| 2. $AD = BC$ | 2. ___?___ Opp. sides of a ▱ are =. |
| 3. $\angle DAB = \angle ABC = 90°$ | 3. ___?___ Def. of *rectangle* |
| 4. $AB = AB$ | 4. ___?___ From algebra |
| 5. $\triangle DAB \cong \triangle CBA$ | 5. ___?___ SAS Postulate |
| 6. $AC = BD$ | 6. ___?___ Corresponding parts |

**The purpose of Exercises 26 and 27 is to prove Theorem 8.**

**26.** Supply the reasons needed to complete the proof.

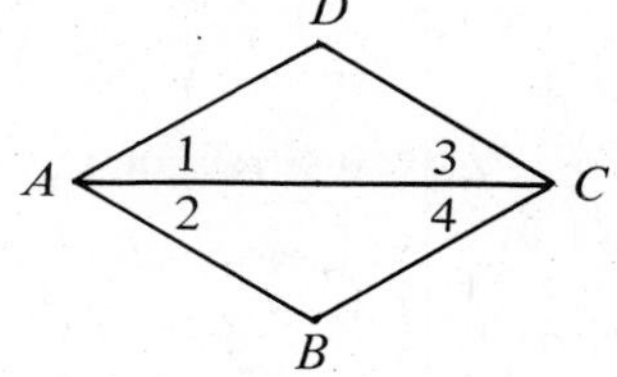


*Given:* Rhombus $ABCD$ with diagonal $\overline{AC}$

*Prove:* $\angle 1 = \angle 2$ and $\angle 3 = \angle 4$

| STATEMENTS | REASONS |
|---|---|
| 1. $ABCD$ is a rhombus. | 1. ___?___ Given |
| 2. $AB = AD$; $BC = DC$ | 2. ___?___ Def. of *rhombus* |
| 3. $AC = AC$ | 3. ___?___ From algebra |
| 4. $\triangle ABC \cong \triangle ADC$ | 4. ___?___ SSS Postulate |
| 5. $\angle 1 = \angle 2$ and $\angle 3 = \angle 4$ | 5. ___?___ Corresponding parts |

**C** **27.** Copy what is shown and write a two-column proof.

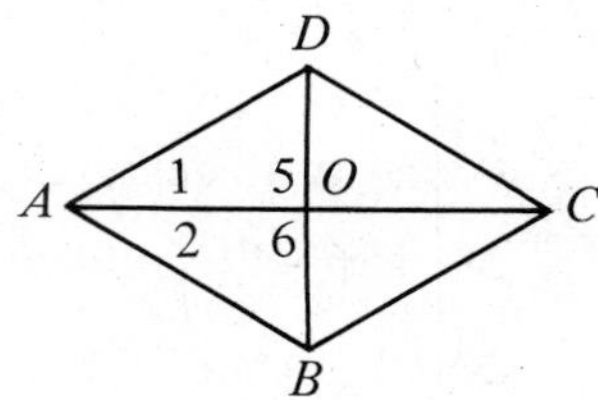


*Given:* Rhombus $ABCD$
Diagonals $\overline{AC}$ and $\overline{BD}$ meet at $O$.

*Prove:* $\overline{AC} \perp \overline{BD}$

(*Hint:* You know that $\angle 1 = \angle 2$ from Exercise 26. Show that $\triangle AOD \cong \triangle AOB$.)

**28.** Construct a rhombus and draw its diagonals. Then use a protractor to check that the diagonals are perpendicular.

# 6 • Proving Figures Are Parallelograms

How can you show that quadrilateral $ABCD$ is a parallelogram? Of course, one way is to show that its opposite sides are parallel. But there are other ways of showing that $ABCD$ is a parallelogram. See if you can decide what these are by trying the explorations below.

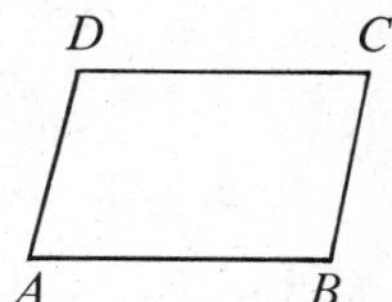


## Explorations

1. Use lined paper to draw two segments, $\overline{AB}$ and $\overline{DC}$, which are both parallel and equal.

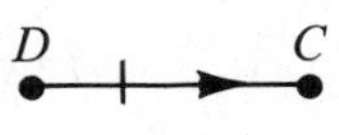


2. Draw $\overline{AD}$ and $\overline{BC}$.
   Do $\overline{AD}$ and $\overline{BC}$ appear to be parallel? yes

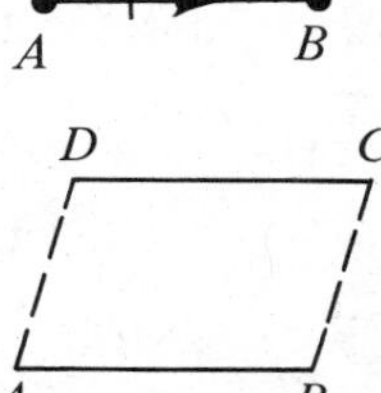


3. What kind of quadrilateral is $ABCD$? parallelogram

Repeat steps 1–3 using other segments which are both parallel and equal.

**THEOREM 10**

If a quadrilateral has one pair of opposite sides that are both parallel and equal, then the quadrilateral is a parallelogram.

*Given:* $\overline{AB} \parallel \overline{DC}$
$AB = DC$

*Prove:* $ABCD$ is a $\square$.

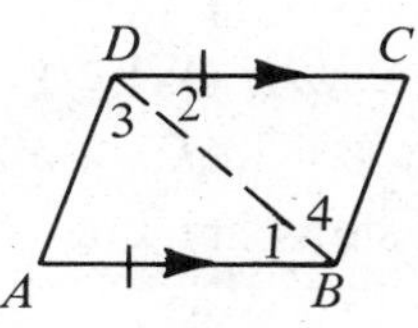


Here are the key steps:

1. Draw $\overline{DB}$. Then $\angle 1 = \angle 2$. (Why?) Thm. 4, p. 62
2. $\triangle ABD \cong \triangle CDB$ (Why?) SAS Postulate
3. $\angle 3 = \angle 4$ (Why?) Corresponding parts
4. $\overline{AD} \parallel \overline{BC}$ (Why?) Thm. 6, p. 66
5. $ABCD$ is a $\square$. (Why?) Def. of *parallelogram*

## Explorations

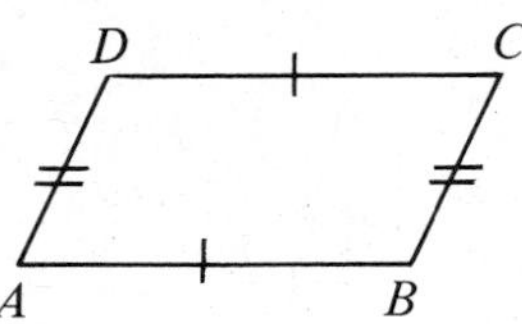


If $ABCD$ is a parallelogram, we know that $AB = DC$ and $AD = BC$. Now let's look at the converse situation.

Suppose $AB = DC$ and $AD = BC$.
Can we conclude that $ABCD$ is a ▱? yes

Follow the steps below to see how.

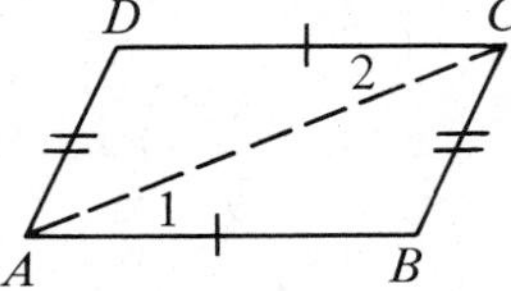


1. Draw $\overline{AC}$.
2. $\triangle ABC \cong \triangle CDA$ (Why?) SSS Postulate
3. $\angle 1 = \angle 2$ (Why?) Corresponding parts
4. $\overline{DC} \parallel \overline{AB}$ (Why?) Thm. 6, p. 66
5. $ABCD$ is a ▱. (Why?) ← *Hint:* The answer is not *By definition.*
   Theorem 10, p. 195

These five steps are the key ones in the proof of Theorem 11.

THEOREM 11

If a quadrilateral has both pairs of opposite sides equal, then the quadrilateral is a parallelogram.

## Explorations

We know that when $ABCD$ is a parallelogram, diagonals $\overline{AC}$ and $\overline{BD}$ bisect each other. Is the converse true? Follow these steps.

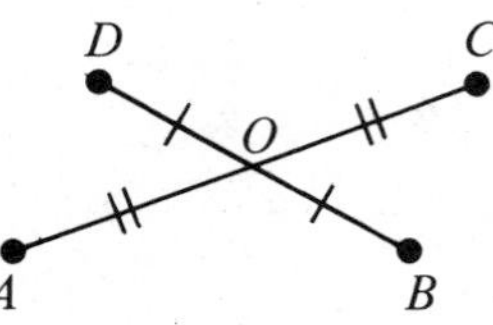


1. Draw two unequal segments, $\overline{AC}$ and $\overline{BD}$, which bisect each other at point $O$.
2. Draw quadrilateral $ABCD$.
3. $\triangle AOB \cong \triangle$ __?__ and $\triangle AOD \cong \triangle$ __?__ COD; COB
4. $AB = DC$ (Why?) Corresponding parts
   $AD = BC$ (Why?)
5. $ABCD$ is a ▱. (Why?) Thm. 11

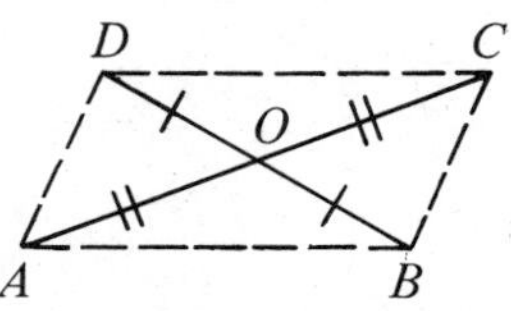


These steps are the key ones in the proof of Theorem 12.

THEOREM 12

If a quadrilateral has diagonals that bisect each other, then the quadrilateral is a parallelogram.

We now have four ways to show that a quadrilateral is a parallelogram.

1. Show that both pairs of opposite sides are parallel. (Definition of ▱)

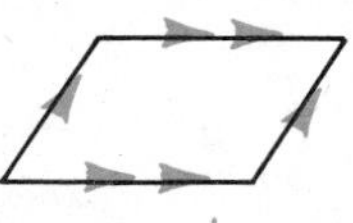

2. Show that one pair of opposite sides are parallel and equal.

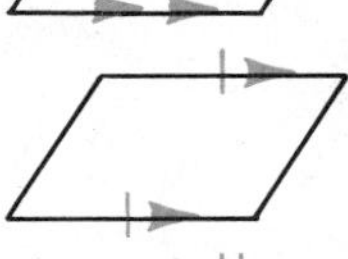

3. Show that both pairs of opposite sides are equal.

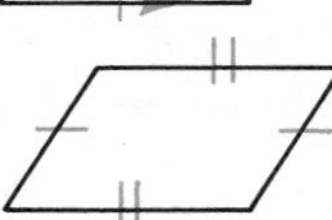

4. Show that the diagonals bisect each other.

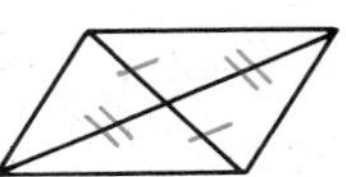

## Classroom Practice

**State the definition or theorem that allows you to conclude that *CDEF* is a parallelogram.**

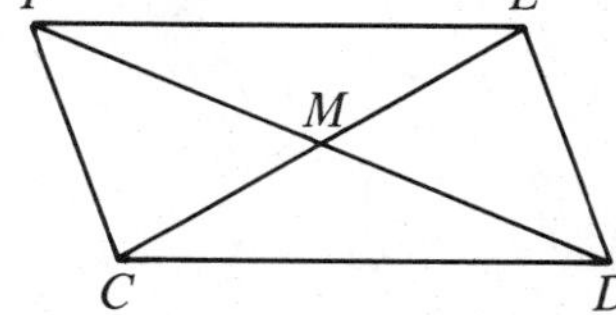


1. $CD = EF$; $DE = CF$ Thm. 11
2. $\overline{CD} \parallel \overline{EF}$; $\overline{DE} \parallel \overline{CF}$ (see below)
3. $CM = ME$; $DM = MF$ Thm. 12
4. $CF = DE$; $\overline{CF} \parallel \overline{DE}$ Thm. 10
5. $M$ is the midpoint of $\overline{CE}$ and $\overline{DF}$. Thm. 12
6. $CD = EF$; $\angle CDE = 70°$; $\angle DEF = 110°$ Thm. 10

2. A parallelogram is a quadrilateral with both pairs of opposite sides parallel.

## Written Exercises

**In Exercises 1–4, write the definition or theorem which supports the statement "*ABCD* is a ▱."**

A 1.

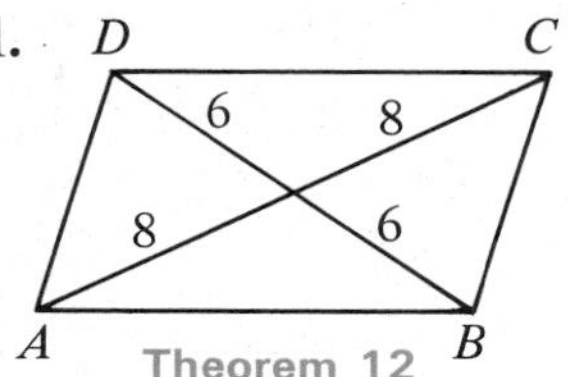


Theorem 12

2. D 11 C, 7, 7, A 11 B

Theorem 11

**Write the definition or theorem which supports the statement "*ABCD* is a ▱."**

**3.**

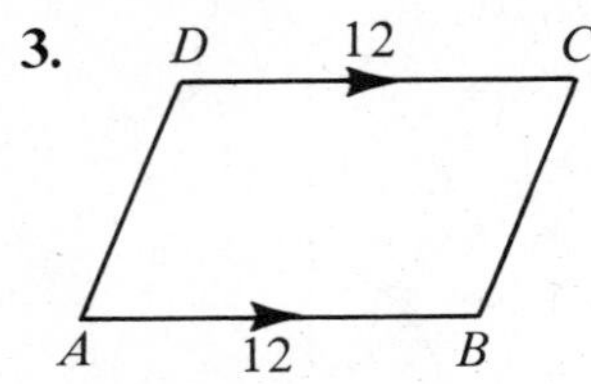


Theorem 10

**4.**

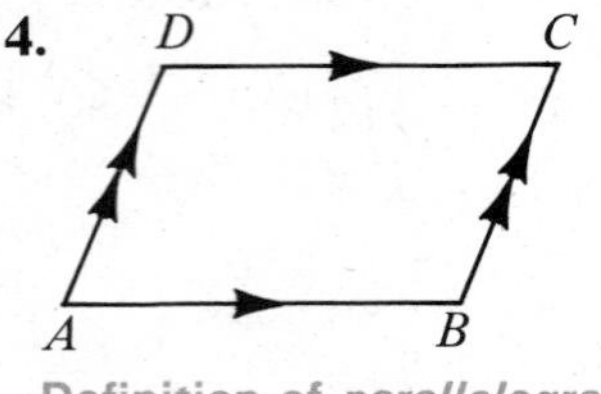


Definition of *parallelogram*

**In Exercises 5-7, supply the reasons to complete the proofs.**

**5.** *Given:* $PQ = ST$

$PS = QR$

$\angle 1 = \angle 2$

*Prove:* *PQTS* is a ▱.

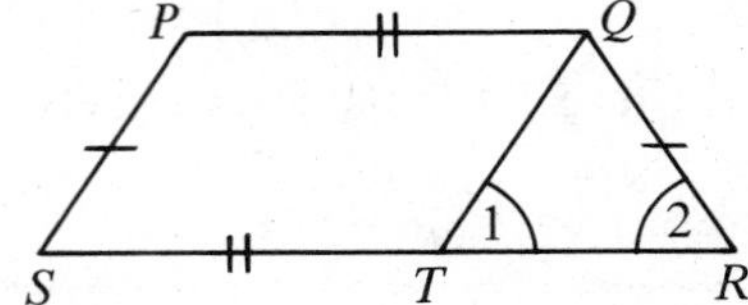


| STATEMENTS | REASONS |
|---|---|
| 1. $\angle 1 = \angle 2$ | 1. ? Given |
| 2. $QT = QR$ | 2. ? Thm. 4, page 158 |
| 3. $PS = QR$ | 3. ? Given |
| 4. $QT = PS$ | 4. ? Substitution Post. |
| 5. $PQ = ST$ | 5. ? Given |
| 6. *PQTS* is a ▱. | 6. ? Thm. 11, page 196 |

**6.** *Given:* *WXYZ* is a ▱.

*M* is the midpoint of $\overline{ZY}$.

*N* is the midpoint of $\overline{WX}$.

*Prove:* *WNYM* is a ▱.

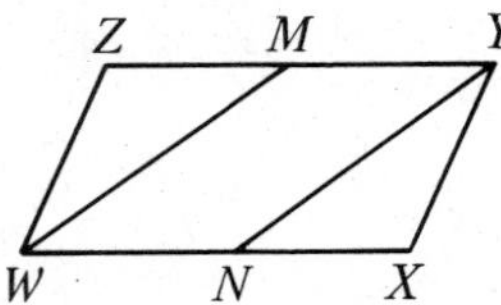


| STATEMENTS | REASONS |
|---|---|
| 1. $WX = ZY$ | 1. ? Opp. sides of a ▱ are =. |
| 2. $\frac{1}{2}WX = \frac{1}{2}ZY$ | 2. ? Multiplication Post. |
| 3. $WN = \frac{1}{2}WX$; $MY = \frac{1}{2}ZY$ | 3. ? *Given: M* is midpt. of $\overline{ZY}$ and *N* is midpt. of $\overline{WX}$ |
| 4. $WN = MY$ | 4. ? Substitution Postulate |
| 5. $\overline{WX} \parallel \overline{ZY}$ (and thus $\overline{WN} \parallel \overline{MY}$) | 5. ? Def. of *parallelogram* |
| 6. *WNYM* is a ▱. | 6. ? Thm. 10, page 195 |

B **7.** *Given:* $ABCD$ is a ▱.
$P$ is the midpoint of $\overline{AO}$.
$Q$ is the midpoint of $\overline{CO}$.

*Prove:* $PBQD$ is a ▱.

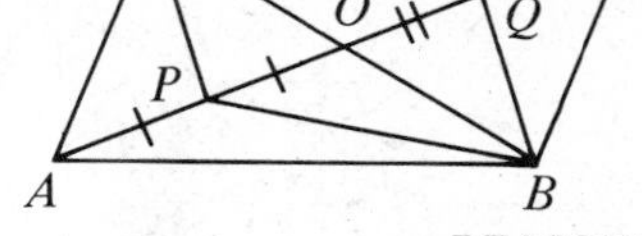


| STATEMENTS | REASONS |
|---|---|
| 1. $AO = CO$ | 1. ? Diags. of a ▱ bisect each oth. |
| 2. $\frac{1}{2}AO = \frac{1}{2}CO$ | 2. ? Multiplication Post. |
| 3. $PO = \frac{1}{2}AO$; $QO = \frac{1}{2}CO$ | 3. ? Given: $P$ is midpt. of $\overline{AO}$ and $Q$ is midpt. of $\overline{CO}$ |
| 4. $PO = QO$ | 4. ? Substitution Postulate |
| 5. $BO = DO$ | 5. ? Diags. of a ▱ bisect each oth. |
| 6. $PBQD$ is a ▱. | 6. ? Thm. 12, page 196 |

**8.** The quadrilaterals numbered 1, 2, 3, and 4 in the diagram are parallelograms. If you wanted to show that quadrilateral 5 is also a parallelogram, which method would you use? (*Hint:* If two lines are parallel to a third line, then they are parallel to each other.) Show that one pair of opposite sides are parallel and equal.

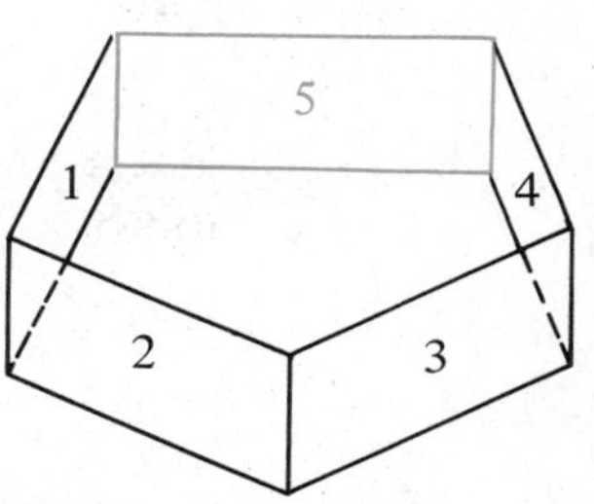


**9.** Draw a segment $\overline{AB}$ and its midpoint $M$. Draw a nonperpendicular segment $\overline{XY}$ that has $M$ as its midpoint and is equal in length to $\overline{AB}$. Draw quadrilateral $AXBY$. What kind of quadrilateral is it? Explain. parallelogram (Theorem 12, page 196)

**10.** Draw a segment $\overline{AB}$ and its midpoint $M$. Draw a perpendicular segment $\overline{XY}$ that has $M$ as its midpoint but is unequal to $\overline{AB}$. Draw quadrilateral $AXBY$. What kind of quadrilateral is it? Explain. rhombus Use SAS to show that four △s, hence four sides, are equal.

**11.** Draw a segment $\overline{AB}$ and its midpoint $M$. Draw a perpendicular segment $\overline{XY}$ that has $M$ as its midpoint and is equal to $\overline{AB}$. Draw quadrilateral $AXBY$. What kind of quadrilateral is it? Explain. square The sides are equal (see Ex. 10) and ⊥.

**12.** The legs of an ironing board are built so that $PO = QO = RO = SO$. No matter how the legs are adjusted, the top of the ironing board is parallel to the floor. Explain why. $\overline{RS}$ and $\overline{PQ}$ always bisect each other. Hence $PRQS$ is always a parallelogram, and $\overline{RQ} \parallel \overline{PS}$.

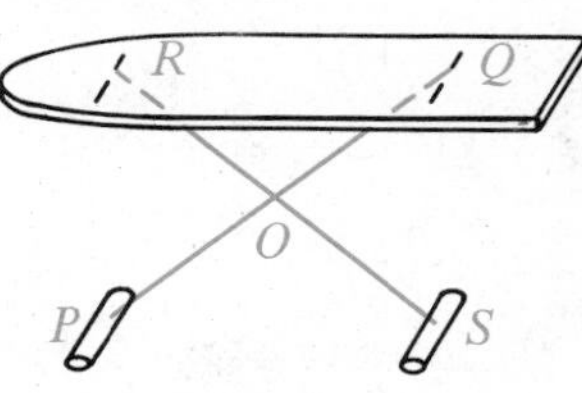

C **13.** Explain why the jaws of the pliers shown are always parallel.

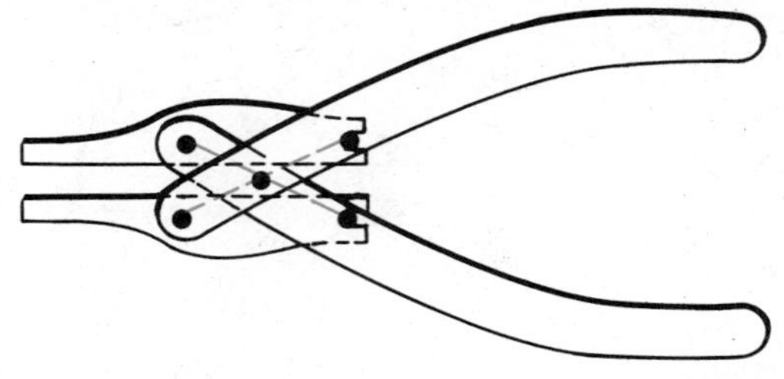

The four outer bolts always form a rectangle. The jaws are extensions of opposite, parallel sides.

**14.** *Given:* $ABCD$ is a ▱.
$\overline{DE} \perp \overline{AC}$
$\overline{BF} \perp \overline{AC}$

*Prove:* $BEDF$ is a ▱.

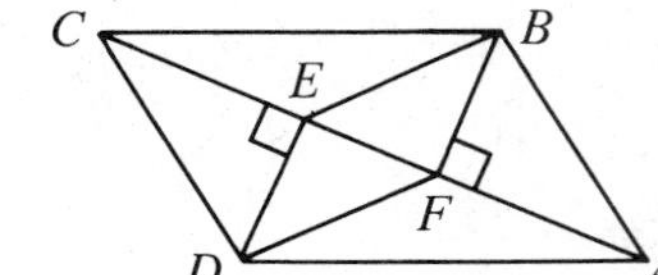


**15.** Prove that if a quadrilateral has equal opposite angles, then the quadrilateral is a parallelogram.
(*Note:* This exercise provides a fifth way to show that a quadrilateral is a parallelogram.)

**16.** Prove that a parallelogram with perpendicular diagonals must be a rhombus. (*Hint:* Show that all four sides are equal.)

**17.** Prove that a parallelogram with equal diagonals must be a rectangle. (*Hint:* Show that all four angles are right angles.)

## SELF-TEST

**1.** The diagonals of rectangle $ABCD$ meet at $E$. If $AC = 12$, find 12 $BD$ and $BE$. 6

**2.** $CROK$ is a rhombus with $\angle RCO = 25°$. Find the measures of $\angle 1$, $\angle 2$, $\angle 3$, and $\angle 4$. (Answers at right.)

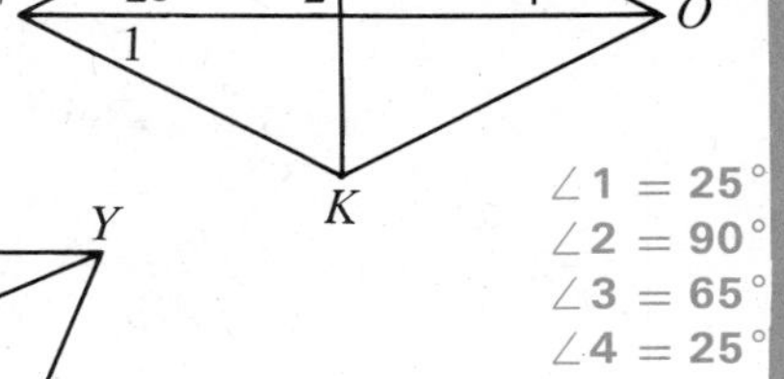


$\angle 1 = 25°$
$\angle 2 = 90°$
$\angle 3 = 65°$
$\angle 4 = 25°$

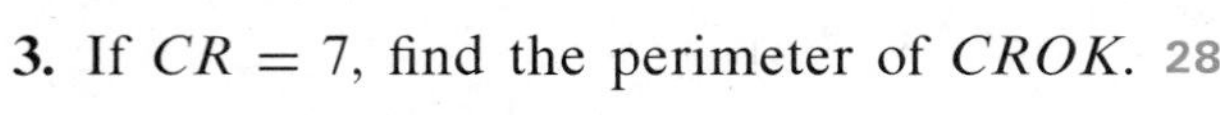

**3.** If $CR = 7$, find the perimeter of $CROK$. 28

**4.** *Given:* $WZ = XY$
$\angle 1 = \angle 2$

*Prove:* $WXYZ$ is a ▱.

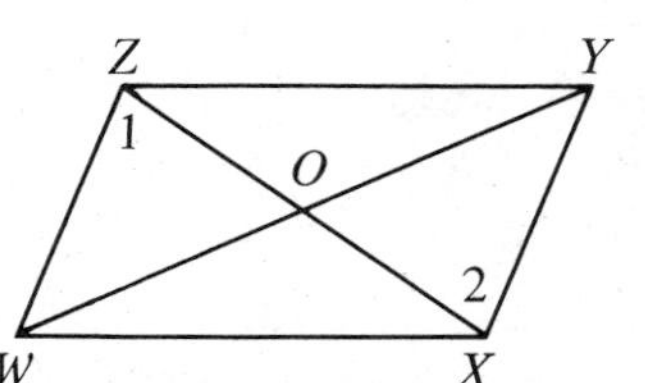

# 7 • Properties of Trapezoids

Recall that a trapezoid is a quadrilateral with just one pair of parallel sides. These parallel sides are called **bases.** The other sides are called **legs.** If the legs are equal, the trapezoid is an **isosceles trapezoid.**

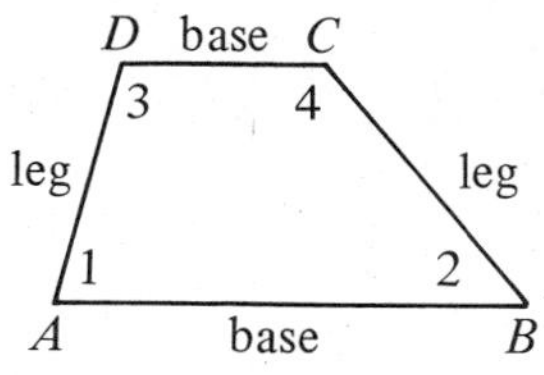


Trapezoid $ABCD$
$\angle 1$ and $\angle 2$ are base angles.
So are $\angle 3$ and $\angle 4$.

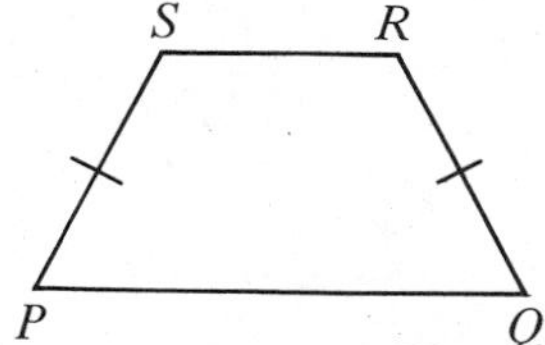


Isosceles trapezoid $PQRS$ has equal legs, $\overline{PS}$ and $\overline{QR}$.

The two angles that include a base are called **base angles.** Every trapezoid has two pairs of base angles.

Try the following explorations and see if you can discover the special properties of trapezoids and isosceles trapezoids.

## *Explorations*

Draw two large trapezoids, $ABCD$ which is not isosceles and $PQRS$ which is isosceles.

### A. The Angles of a Trapezoid

1. Measure base angles, $\angle A$ and $\angle B$, of trapezoid $ABCD$. Also measure $\angle C$ and $\angle D$.
2. Measure base angles, $\angle P$ and $\angle Q$, of trapezoid $PQRS$. Also measure $\angle R$ and $\angle S$.
3. What can you say about the base angles of an isosceles trapezoid? They are equal.

### B. The Median of a Trapezoid

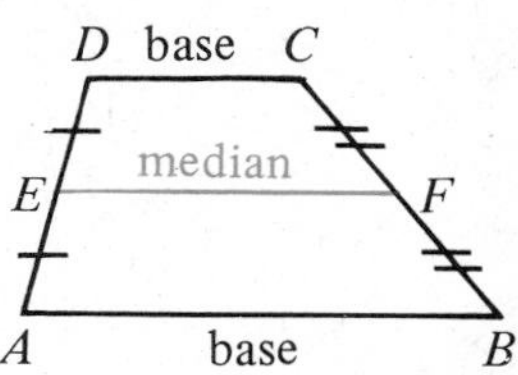


The segment joining the midpoints of the legs of a trapezoid is called the **median** of the trapezoid.

1. Draw the median, $\overline{EF}$, of trapezoid $ABCD$.
2. Does it appear that the median is parallel to the bases? yes
3. Measure $\overline{AB}$, $\overline{DC}$, and the median $\overline{EF}$.
   How does $EF$ compare with $AB + DC$? $EF = \frac{1}{2}(AB + DC)$

Repeat steps 1–3, using trapezoid $PQRS$.

By now, you may have discovered the following two theorems.

**THEOREM 13**

The base angles of an isosceles trapezoid are equal.

*Given:* $PQRS$ is a trapezoid with $SP = RQ$.

*Prove:* $\angle P = \angle Q$ and $\angle PSR = \angle QRS$

*Key ideas of proof:*

1. Draw $\overline{SX} \perp \overline{PQ}$ and $\overline{RY} \perp \overline{PQ}$.
2. $SX = RY$ because the distance between two parallel lines is always the same. (See Exercise 36 on page 189.)
3. $\triangle SPX \cong \triangle RQY$ (Why?) HL Theorem
4. Then $\angle P = \angle Q$.
5. $\angle PSR = \angle QRS$ (Supplements of equal angles are equal.)

**THEOREM 14**

The median of a trapezoid has two properties:

(1) It is parallel to the bases.
(2) Its length equals half the sum of the base lengths.

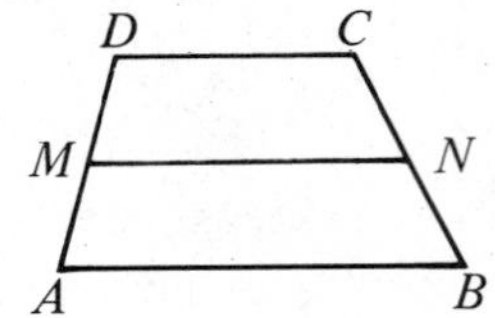


*Given:* Trapezoid $ABCD$ with median $\overline{MN}$

*Prove:* (1) $\overline{MN} \parallel \overline{AB}$ and $\overline{MN} \parallel \overline{DC}$

(2) $MN = \frac{1}{2}(AB + DC)$

At this stage of our work, a proof of Theorem 14 would be difficult. A proof using coordinate geometry is included in Chapter 12.

Two trapezoids and their medians are shown. For each, find the value of $x$.

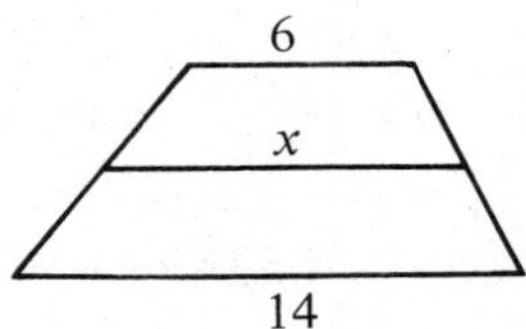


| | |
|---|---|
| $x = \frac{1}{2}(14 + 6)$ | $7 = \frac{1}{2}(10 + x)$ |
| $x = \frac{1}{2}(20)$ | $14 = 10 + x$ |
| $x = 10$ | $4 = x$ |

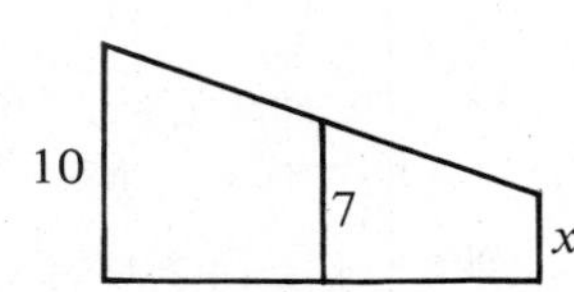

## Classroom Practice

1. $ABCD$ is a trapezoid.

   b. $\angle A$ and $\angle B$; $\angle C$ and $\angle D$

   a. Name its two bases. $\overline{AB}$, $\overline{DC}$

   b. Name two pairs of base angles.

   c. Name its legs. $\overline{AD}$, $\overline{BC}$

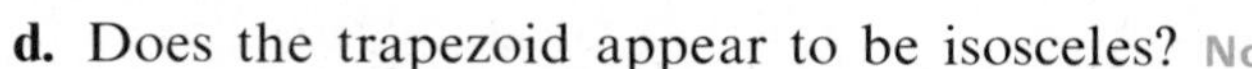

   d. Does the trapezoid appear to be isosceles? No

   e. The median of the trapezoid joins the midpoint of __?__ $\overline{AD}$ and the midpoint of __?__. $\overline{BC}$

   f. The median of the trapezoid is parallel to __?__ $\overline{AB}$ and __?__ $\overline{DC}$.

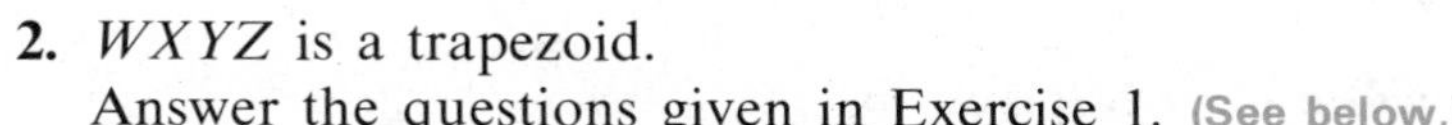

2. $WXYZ$ is a trapezoid.
   Answer the questions given in Exercise 1. (See below.)

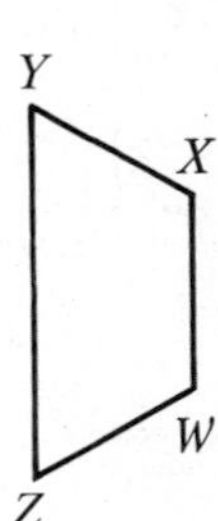


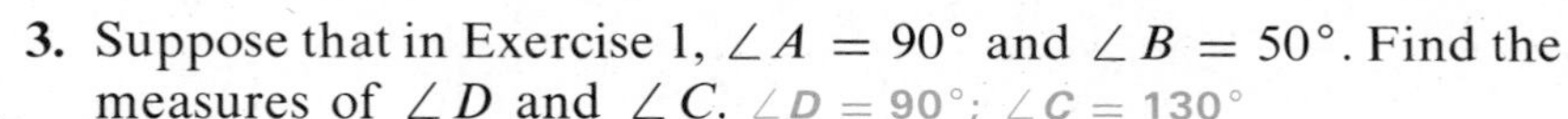

3. Suppose that in Exercise 1, $\angle A = 90°$ and $\angle B = 50°$. Find the measures of $\angle D$ and $\angle C$. $\angle D = 90°$; $\angle C = 130°$

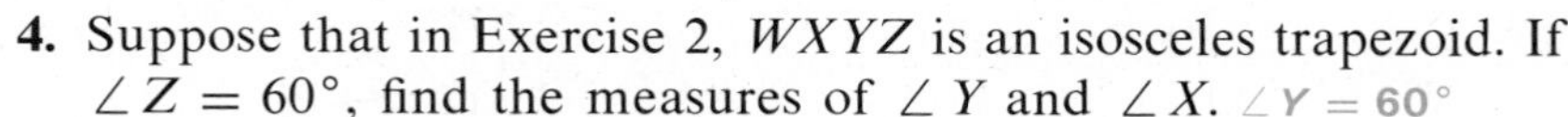

4. Suppose that in Exercise 2, $WXYZ$ is an isosceles trapezoid. If $\angle Z = 60°$, find the measures of $\angle Y$ and $\angle X$. $\angle Y = 60°$ $\angle X = 120°$

2. a. $\overline{XW}$, $\overline{YZ}$ b. $\angle X$ and $\angle W$; $\angle Y$ and $\angle Z$
   c. $\overline{XY}$, $\overline{WZ}$ d. Yes e. $\overline{XY}$, $\overline{WZ}$ f. $\overline{XW}$, $\overline{YZ}$

**Find the length of the median of each trapezoid.**

**5.** 8 (6, 10)

**6.** 9 (12, 6)

**7.** 14

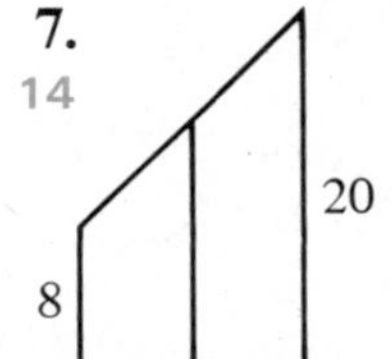


8. You can cut two congruent trapezoids out of cardboard and slide them together as shown.

   What kind of figure appears to be formed?

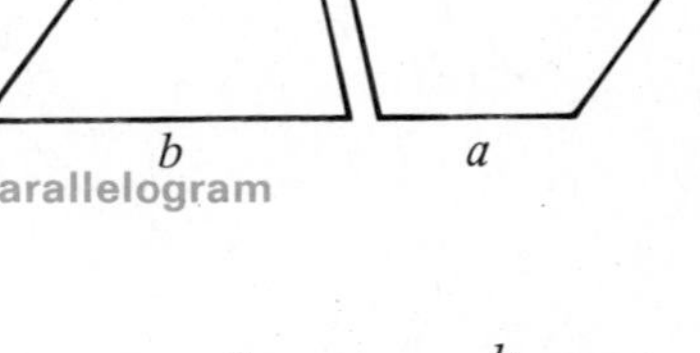


parallelogram

9. $P$ and $R$ are the midpoints of the opposite sides of the parallelogram shown.

   a. Do $\overline{PQ}$ and $\overline{QR}$ appear to be the medians of the two trapezoids? Yes

   b. Does the diagram suggest that $2m = a + b$? Yes

   c. Why is $m = \frac{1}{2}(a + b)$? Multiplication Postulate

   d. To what theorem is this result related? Theorem 14

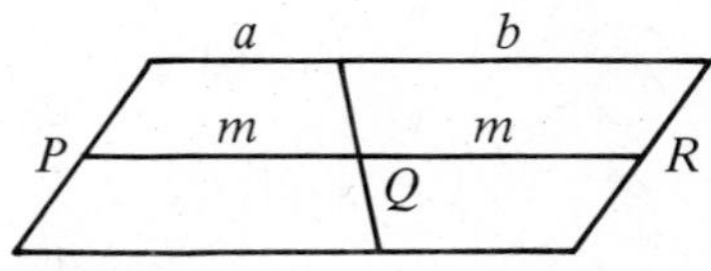

## Written Exercises

**PQRS is an isosceles trapezoid.**

A 1. If $\angle P = 50°$, find the measures of $\angle Q$, $\angle R$, and $\angle S$. 50° 130° 130°

2. If $\angle P = 60°$, find the measures of $\angle Q$, $\angle R$, and $\angle S$.

3. If $\angle S = 100°$, find the measures of $\angle P$, $\angle Q$, and $\angle R$.

4. If $\angle R = 110°$, find the measures of $\angle P$, $\angle Q$, and $\angle S$.

S R
P Q

2. 60°, 120°, 120°
3. 80°, 80°, 100°
4. 70°, 70°, 110°

5. The median of the trapezoid joins the midpoints of _?_ and _?_. $\overline{SP}$, $\overline{RQ}$

6. If $SR = 8$ and $PQ = 16$, find the length of the median. 12

**Find the length of the median of each trapezoid.**

7. 13

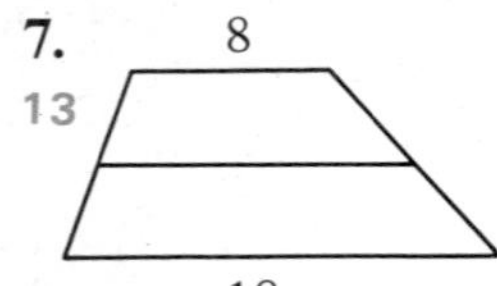


8. 18

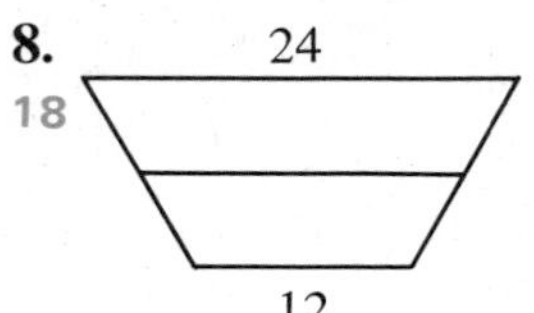


9. 12

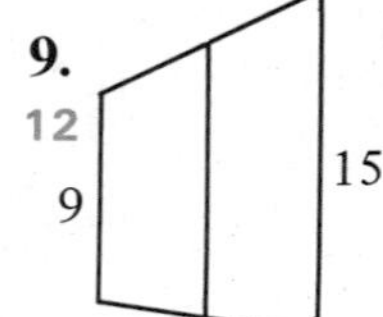


10. 16

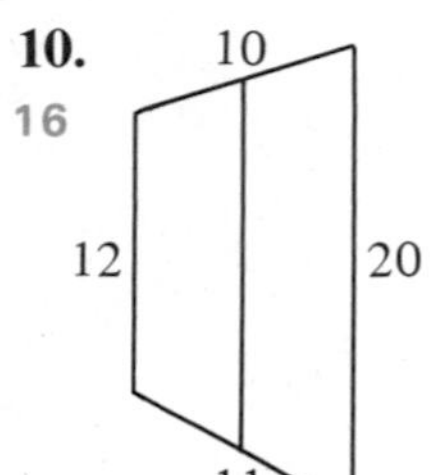


11. 13

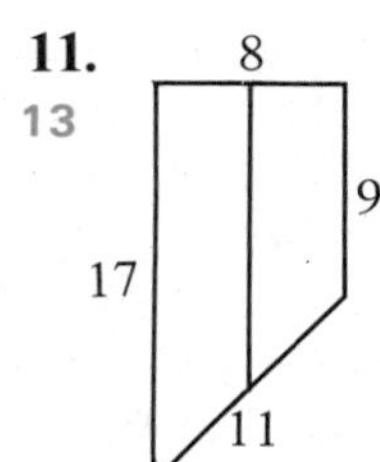


12. 14

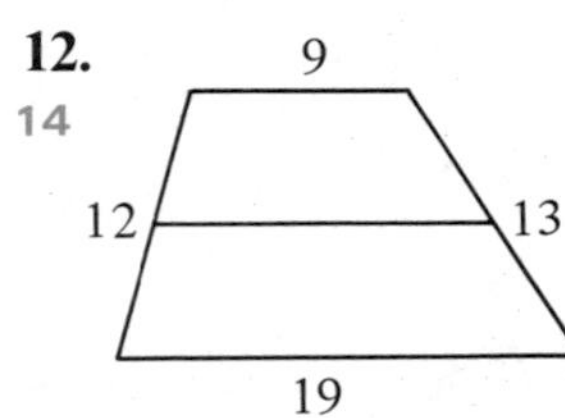


**In Exercises 13–21, a trapezoid and its median are shown. Find the value of $x$.**

13. 5

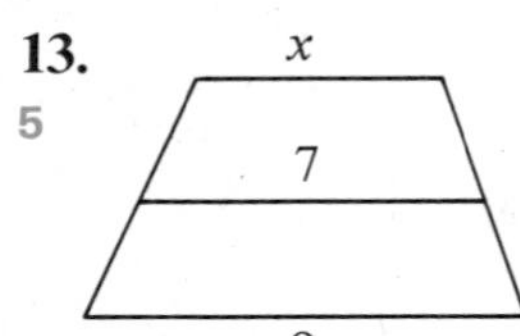


14. 16

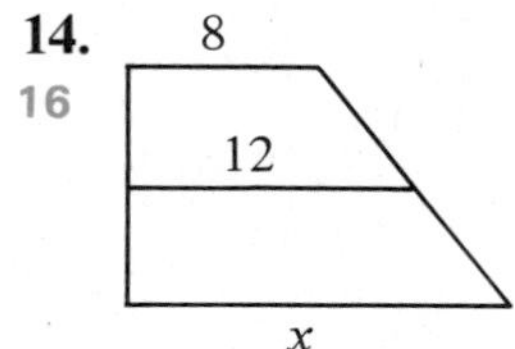


15. 4

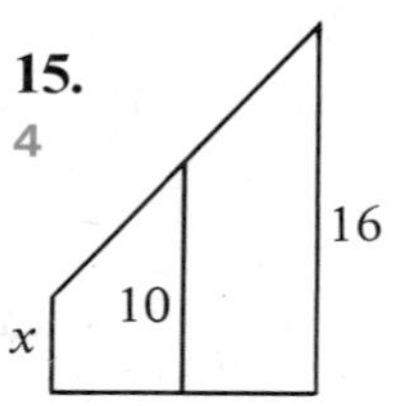


B 16. 2.1

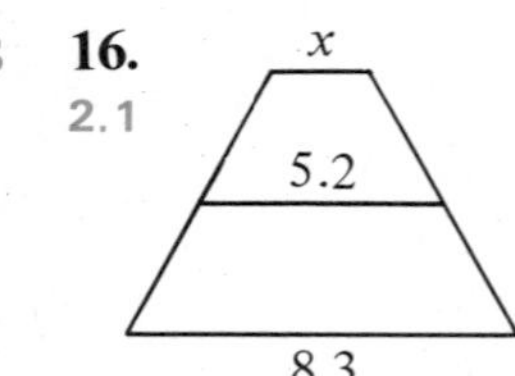


17. 4.7

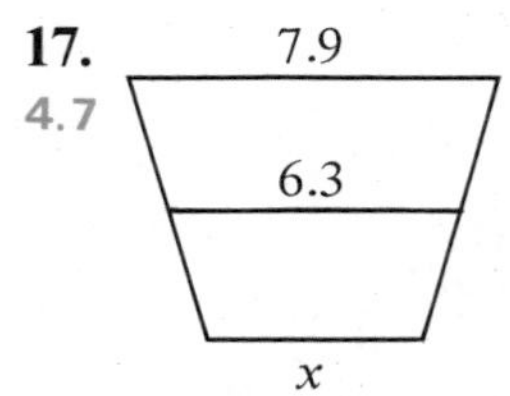


18. 4

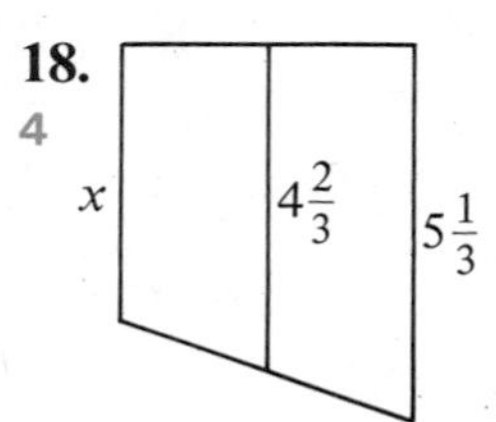

**19.** 4

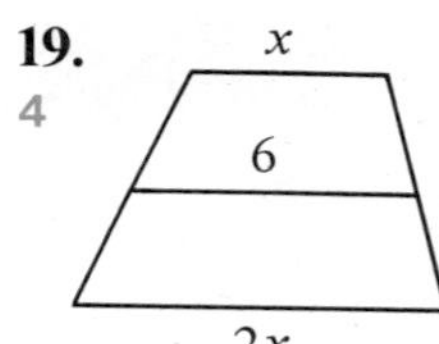


**20.** 9

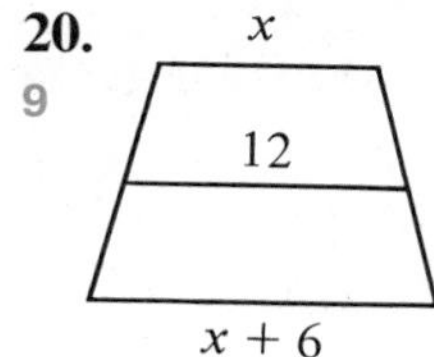


**21.** 6

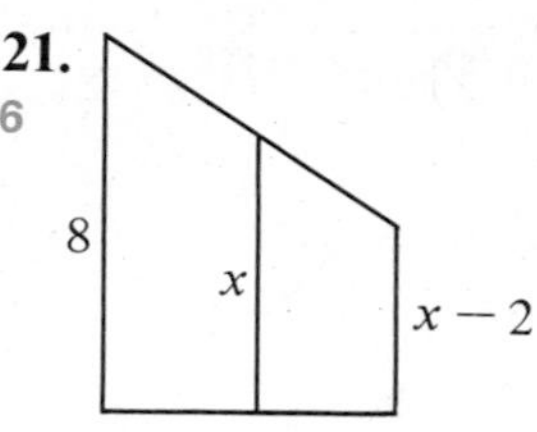


**22. a.** Theorem 13 can be expressed this way: If a trapezoid is isosceles, then __?__. the base angles are equal

**b.** What is the converse of the statement in part a? (See below.)

**c.** Do you think that the converse is a true statement? Yes

C **23.** Is it possible for the bases of a trapezoid to be equal? Explain. No; it would be a ▱. (Thm. 10, p. 195)

**24.** Is it possible for the diagonals of a trapezoid to bisect each other? Explain. No; it would be a ▱. (Thm. 12, p. 196)

**25.** Construct an isosceles trapezoid. Measure the base angles with a protractor.

**26.** Our goal is to prove that the diagonals of an isosceles trapezoid are equal.

*Given:* Trapezoid $ABCD$ with $AD = BC$

*Prove:* $AC = BD$

(*Hint:* Use Theorem 13.)

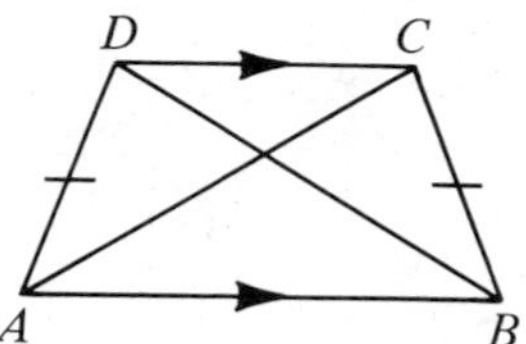


22. b. If the base angles of a trapezoid are equal, then the trapezoid is isosceles.

## Puzzles & Things

Here is another way to show that the sum of the angles of a triangle equals 180°. Draw a triangle $ABC$ and construct the inscribed circle. Cut out the triangle and fold $\angle A$, $\angle B$, and $\angle C$ to the center of the circle. There are six angles at the center, the three original angles and three vertical angles.

$2\angle A + 2\angle B + 2\angle C = 360°$,

so $\angle A + \angle B + \angle C = 180°$.

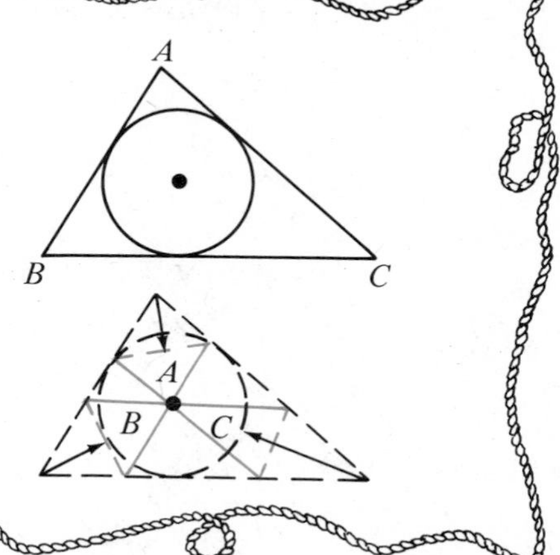

# 8 • The Midpoints Theorem

As you study the figures below from left to right, what do you notice? The base $\overline{DC}$ of trapezoid $ABCD$ becomes smaller and smaller. Finally, in figure (d), $\overline{DC}$ has shrunk to a single point and trapezoid $ABCD$ has become $\triangle ABC$.

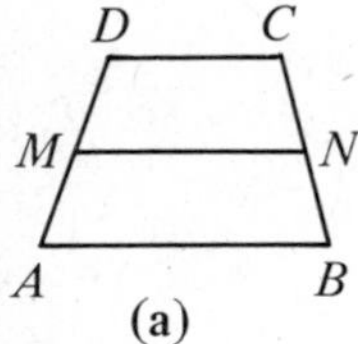

(a)

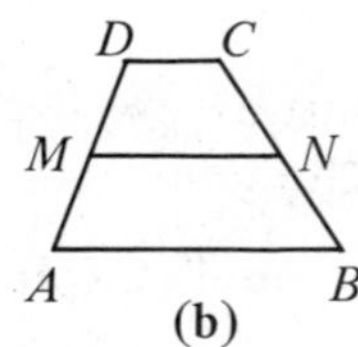

(b)

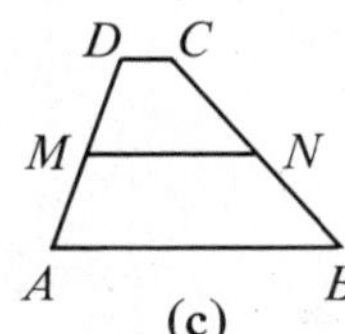

(c)

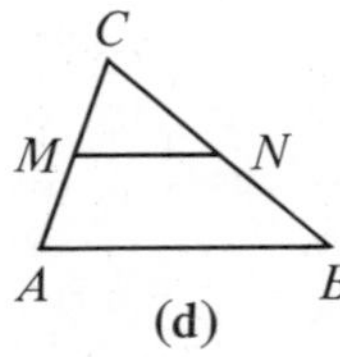

(d)

If we apply Theorem 14 to figures (a), (b), and (c) we have the following results for each figure:

(1) $\overline{MN} \parallel \overline{AB}$

(2) $MN = \frac{1}{2}(AB + DC)$

Theorem 14 can also suggest some information about figure (d). If we think of $\triangle ABC$ as a trapezoid $ABCD$ with $DC = 0$, we have

(1) $\overline{MN} \parallel \overline{AB}$

(2) $MN = \frac{1}{2}(AB + 0) = \frac{1}{2}AB$

These results are stated in the following theorem.

**THEOREM 15 (The Midpoints Theorem)**

The segment joining the midpoints of two sides of a triangle is parallel to the third side and half as long.

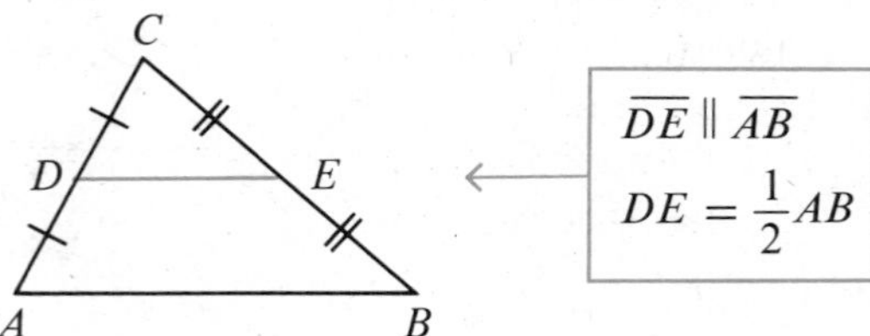


**EXAMPLE** $M$, $N$, and $O$ are the midpoints of the sides of $\triangle ABC$.
Find $MN$, $NO$, and $MO$.

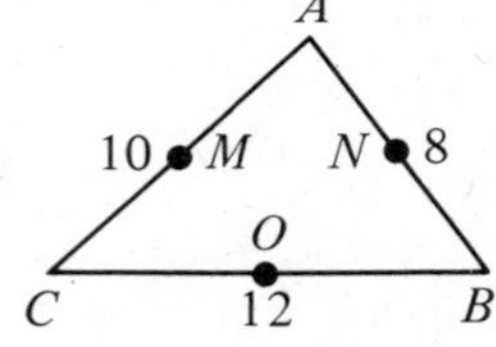

Use the Midpoints Theorem three times.

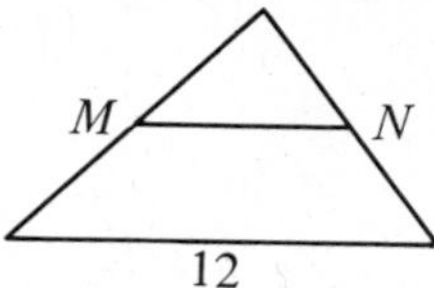


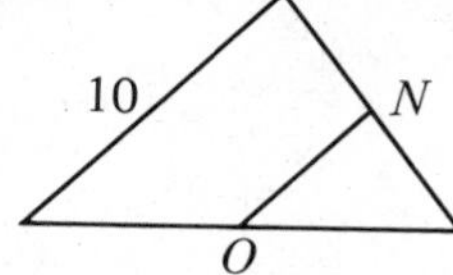


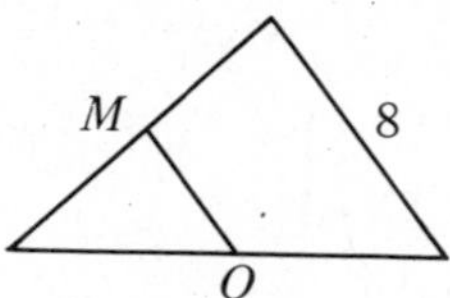


$MN = \frac{1}{2} \times 12 = 6 \qquad NO = \frac{1}{2} \times 10 = 5 \qquad MO = \frac{1}{2} \times 8 = 4$

## Classroom Practice

**$M$, $N$, and $O$ are the midpoints of the sides of $\triangle ABC$. Complete each statement.**

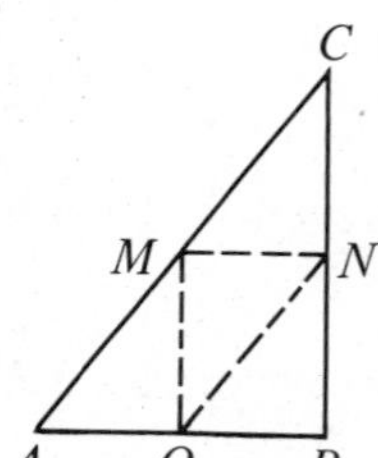


1. If $AB = 8$, then $MN =$ _?_. 4
2. If $AC = 14$, then $NO =$ _?_. 7
3. If $BC = 10$, then $MO =$ _?_. 5
4. If $MN = 11$, then $AB =$ _?_. 22
5. If $NO = 15$, then $AC =$ _?_. 30
6. If $MO = x$, then $BC =$ _?_. $2x$
7. Explain why $AMNO$ must be a parallelogram. Opposite sides are parallel.
8. Name parallelograms, other than $AMNO$, that are shown in the figure. *OMNB, OMCN*

## Written Exercises

**$M$ and $N$ are the midpoints of $\overline{XZ}$ and $\overline{YZ}$. Complete each statement.**

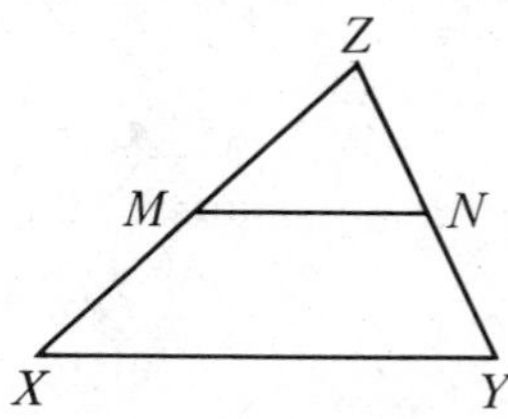


A

1. $\overline{MN} \parallel$ _?_. $\overline{XY}$
2. If $XY = 12$, then $MN =$ _?_. 6
3. If $XY = 20$, then $MN =$ _?_. 10
4. If $MN = 7$, then $XY =$ _?_. 14
5. If $ZM = 10$, $MN = 12$, and $ZN = 7$, find the perimeter of $\triangle XYZ$. 58

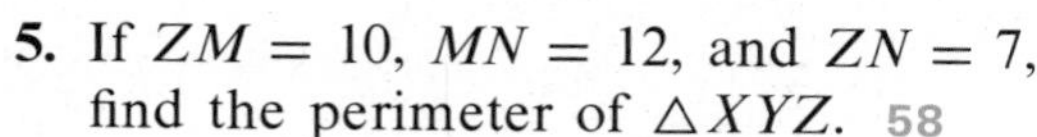

6. If $XM = 6$, $MN = 7$, and $NY = 4$, find the perimeter of $\triangle XYZ$. 34

**$R$, $S$, and $T$ are midpoints of the sides of $\triangle ABC$. Copy and complete the table.**

| | $AB$ | $BC$ | $AC$ | $ST$ | $RT$ | $RS$ | Perimeter of $\triangle ABC$ | Perimeter of $\triangle RST$ |
|---|---|---|---|---|---|---|---|---|
| **7.** | 8 | 10 | 12 | 4 ? | 5 ? | 6 ? | 30 ? | 15 ? |
| **8.** | 10 | 10 | 14 | 5 ? | 5 ? | 7 ? | 34 ? | 17 ? |
| **9.** | 8 ? | 12 ? | 10 ? | 4 | 6 | 5 | 30 ? | 15 ? |
| **10.** | 12 ? | 10 ? | 14 ? | 6 | 5 | 7 | 36 ? | 18 ? |
| **11.** | 14 | 12 ? | 8 ? | 7 ? | 6 | 4 | 34 ? | 17 ? |
| **12.** | 12 ? | 10 | 16 | 6 | 5 ? | 8 ? | 38 ? | 19 ? |

**13.** If the perimeter of $\triangle ABC$ is 32, then the perimeter of $\triangle RST$ is ___?___. 16

**14.** If the perimeter of $\triangle RST$ is 25, then the perimeter of $\triangle ABC$ is ___?___. 50

**In Exercises 15–18, exactly one of the lengths represented by $x$, $y$, and $z$ can be found. Find that length.**

**15.**

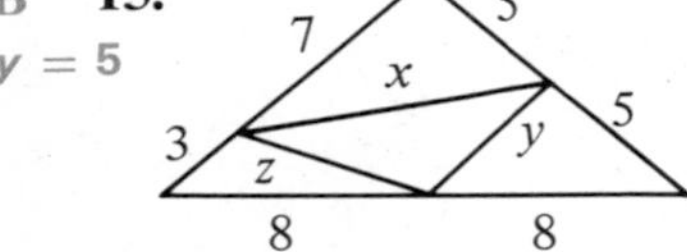


**16.** z = 10

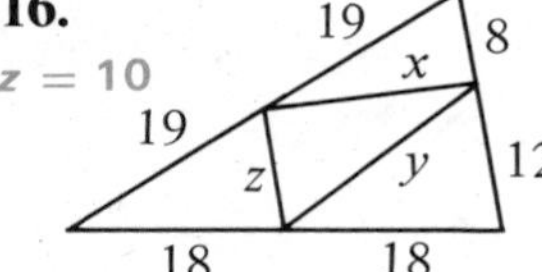


**17.** y = 13

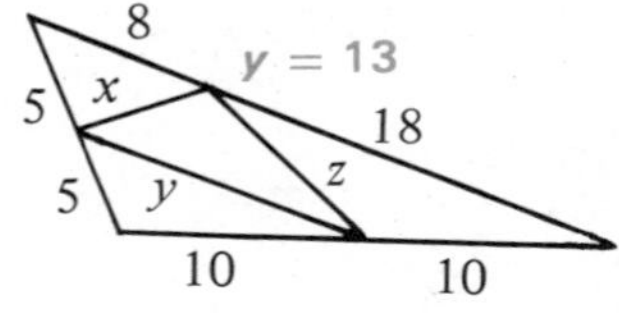


**18.** x = 8

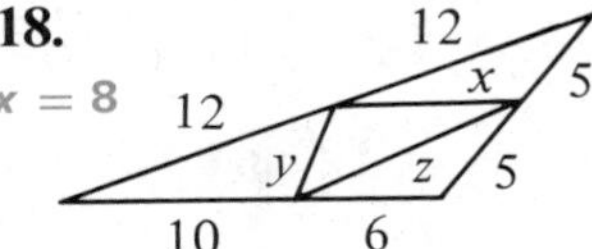


**$P$, $Q$, and $R$ are the midpoints of the sides of $\triangle XYZ$.**

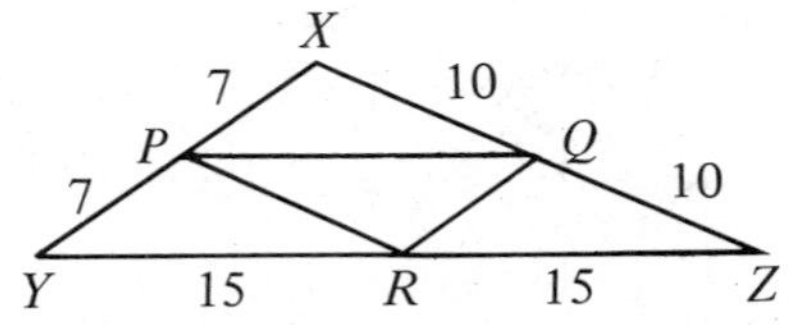


**19.** Find the perimeter of ▱$PQRY$. 44

**20.** Find the perimeter of ▱$XQRP$. 34

**21. a.** Name a parallelogram in the figure, other than $PQRY$ or $XQRP$. PRZQ

**b.** Find the perimeter of this parallelogram. 50

**22.** Draw a right $\triangle ABC$ with $\angle C = 90°$.
Let $X$ be the midpoint of $\overline{AC}$.
Let $Y$ be the midpoint of $\overline{BC}$.
Let $Z$ be the midpoint of $\overline{AB}$.

**a.** What kind of quadrilateral is $CXZY$? rectangle

**b.** If $CZ = 10$, find $XY$ and $AB$. 10 20

C **23.** Points $M$, $N$, and $O$ are the midpoints of the sides of a triangle, $\triangle DEF$. Copy the figure shown and construct $\triangle DEF$.

$M$ • $N$ • $O$ •

**24.** $ABCD$ is a trapezoid with median $\overline{MN}$.

Find the values of $x$, $y$, and $z$. $x = 4$ $y = 6$ $z = 4$

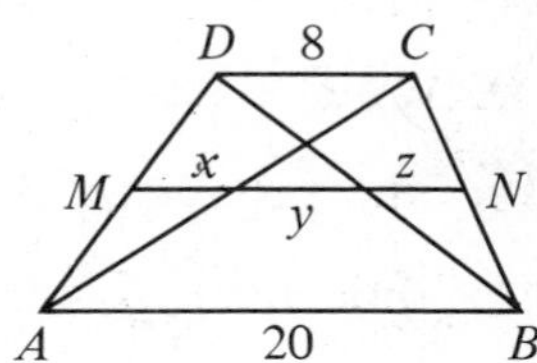


**25.** Let $W$, $X$, $Y$, and $Z$ be the midpoints of the sides of any quadrilateral $EFGH$.

*Prove:* $WXYZ$ is a ▱.

(*Hint:* Draw $\overline{EG}$.)

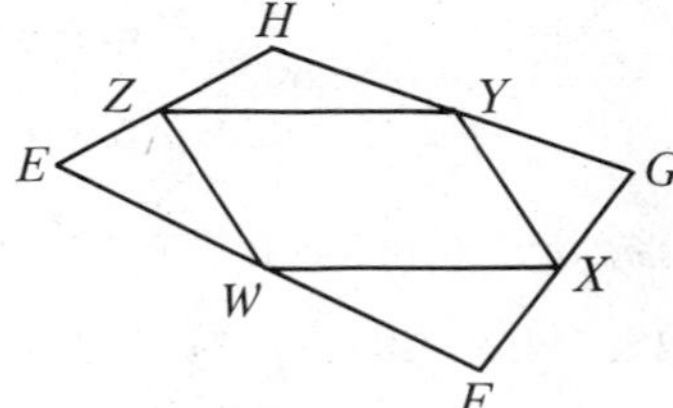


## SELF-TEST

***GOAT* is an isosceles trapezoid.**

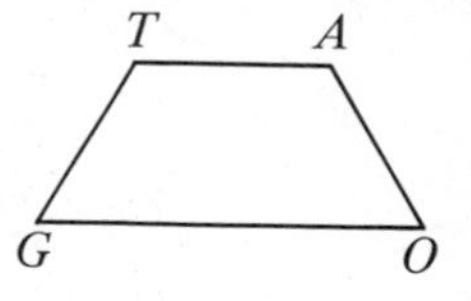


**1.** If $GO = 12$ and $TA = 6$, find the length of the median. 9

**2.** If $\angle T = 120°$, find the measures of $\angle G$, $\angle O$, and $\angle A$. 60° 60° 120°

**In the diagram, *P*, *K*, and *T* are the midpoints of the sides of $\triangle SAL$.**

**3.** Name three parallelograms shown. PTKL, SPKT, PKAT

**4.** If $PT = 5$, then $LA =$ __?__. 10

**5.** If the perimeter of $\triangle SAL = 18$, then the perimeter of $\triangle PKT =$ __?__. 9

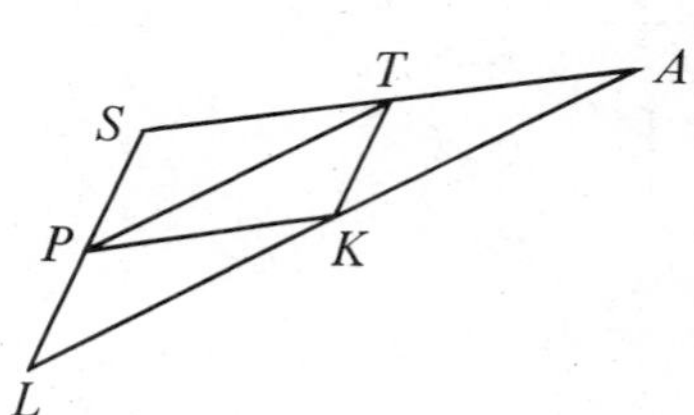

## Reviewing Algebraic Skills

**Write an expression using the given variable or variables.**

1. The quotient when 86 is divided by $n$ $\frac{86}{n}$
2. The third power of $k$ $k^3$
3. The sum of 13 and three times $x$ $13 + 3x$
4. The product of 4, $a$, and $b$ $4ab$
5. 18 subtracted from half of $c$ $\frac{1}{2}c - 18$
6. $m$ increased by 41 $m + 41$
7. $(a + b)$ multiplied by 7 $7(a + b)$
8. The ratio of 15 to $w$ $\frac{15}{w}$

**Write an equation or an inequality for each statement. Let *n* be the variable.**

9. When 34 is subtracted from some number, the difference is 12. $n - 34 = 12$
10. The product of some number and 4 is not equal to zero. $4n \neq 0$
11. One third of some number, plus 16, is equal to 27. $\frac{1}{3}n + 16 = 27$
12. When 6 is subtracted from half of some number, the difference is 24. $\frac{1}{2}n - 6 = 24$
13. Twice some number is less than 12. $2n < 12$
14. The fourth power of some number, decreased by 10, is 71. $n^4 - 10 = 71$
15. The sum of some number and 35 is greater than 60. $n + 35 > 60$
16. 25 is the quotient when 275 is divided by some number. $\frac{275}{n} = 25$

**Solve.**

Sample

$$2x - 3 = 7$$
$$2x - 3 + 3 = 7 + 3 \leftarrow \text{Add 3 to both sides.}$$
$$2x = 10$$
$$x = 5 \leftarrow \text{Divide both sides by 2 to get } x = 5.$$

17. $b + 17 = 41$ 24
18. $x - 9 = -12$ $-3$
19. $14 = n - 36$ 50
20. $8y = 72$ 9
21. $12m = -48$ $-4$
22. $-5z = 95$ $-19$
23. $16 + x = 3$ $-13$
24. $63 = 7g$ 9
25. $\frac{t}{6} = -4$ $-24$
26. $\frac{s}{12} = 30$ 360
27. $\frac{a}{51} = 0$ 0
28. $3x + 4 = 19$ 5
29. $38 = 4k - 6$ 11
30. $\frac{a}{6} + 2 = 7$ 30
31. $-13 = \frac{k}{2} - 1$ $-24$

# applications

## Golden Rectangle

Even though all rectangles have four right angles, not all rectangles are similar. Some are much longer than they are wide, while others (squares) are exactly as long as they are wide. In one type of rectangle, the golden rectangle, the length divided by the width will always equal $\frac{1 + \sqrt{5}}{2}$, about 1.6. Ancient Greek geometers and architects thought this rectangular shape was the most beautiful.

This photo of the Parthenon shows how closely the dimensions fit within a golden rectangle. The dashed line indicates the original outline of this famous Greek temple.

You can construct a golden rectangle by following the steps outlined here:

Construct square $ABCD$.

Find the midpoint $M$ of $\overline{AB}$.

Using $M$ as center and $MC$ as radius, draw an arc intersecting $\overleftrightarrow{AB}$ at $E$.

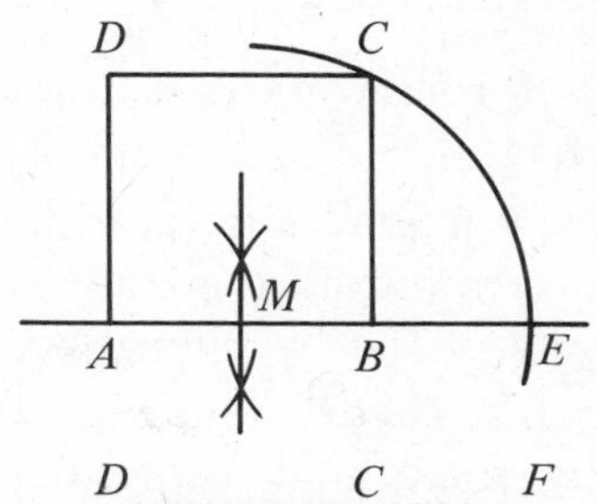


Construct a perpendicular to $\overleftrightarrow{AB}$ at point $E$.

Extend $\overline{DC}$ to meet the perpendicular at $F$.

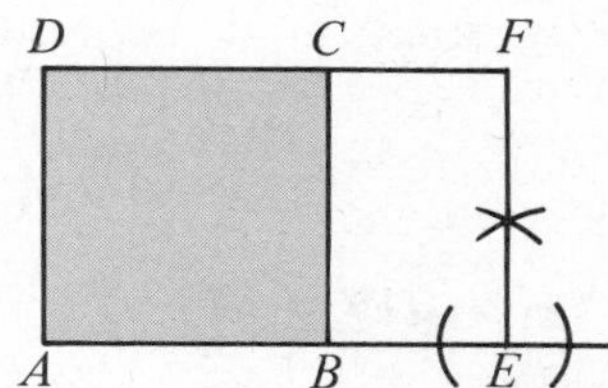


$AEFD$ is a golden rectangle. If we remove the original square $ABCD$, the remaining rectangle $BEFC$ is also a golden rectangle.

Construct a golden rectangle, measure the sides, and divide the length by the width. Is your result about 1.6?

## Reviewing the Chapter

### Chapter Summary

1. A polygon is classified according to the number of sides it has. A regular polygon is both equilateral and equiangular.
2. In a convex polygon with $n$ sides, the interior angle sum is $(n - 2) \times 180°$. The exterior angle sum of any convex polygon, one angle at each vertex, is $360°$.
3. The properties of some special quadrilaterals are summarized below.

| | parallelogram | rectangle | rhombus | square |
|---|---|---|---|---|
| opposite sides parallel | x | x | x | x |
| opposite sides equal | x | x | x | x |
| opposite angles equal | x | x | x | x |
| consecutive angles supplementary | x | x | x | x |
| diagonals bisect each other | x | x | x | x |
| diagonals equal | | x | | x |
| diagonals perpendicular | | | x | x |
| diagonals bisect angles | | | x | x |

4. Four ways for showing that a quadrilateral is a parallelogram are given on page 197.
5. A trapezoid is a quadrilateral with just one pair of parallel sides. The median of a trapezoid is parallel to the bases and its length equals half the sum of the base lengths.
6. The Midpoints Theorem states that the segment joining the midpoints of two sides of a triangle is parallel to the third side and half as long.

### Chapter Review Test

**Refer to the figure at the right.** (*See pp. 172–175.*)

**1.** Is the polygon convex? Yes

**2.** Does the polygon appear to be equilateral? Yes

**3.** Does the polygon appear to be equiangular? No

**4.** Is the polygon regular? No

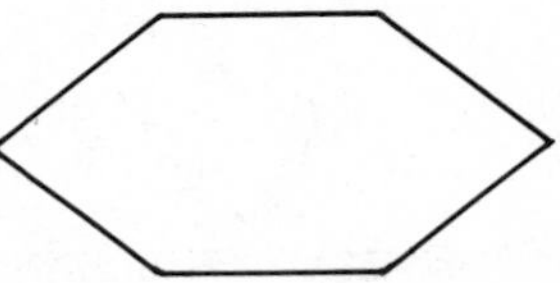

**Solve.** *(See pp. 176–179.)*

5. Find the interior angle sum of a pentagon. 540°
6. Find the exterior angle sum of a pentagon. 360°
7. Find the measure of each angle of a regular octagon. 135°

**Classify each statement as true or false.** *(See pp. 180–184.)*

False 8. Every rhombus is a square. 9. Every square is a parallelogram. True

10. Every parallelogram is a rectangle. False

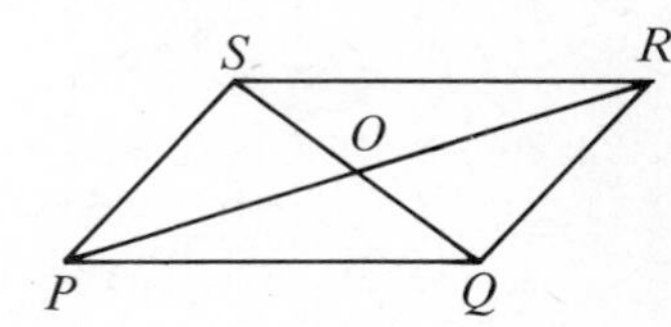


**Given ▱*PQRS*.** *(See pp. 185–189.)*

11. If $\angle RPQ = 18°$ and $\angle SPR = 30°$, find the measures of $\angle PRQ$ and $\angle PQR$. 30° 132°
12. If $PO = 12$ and $QO = 7$, find the lengths of $\overline{OS}$ and $\overline{PR}$. 7 24

**Given rectangle *KNRX* and rhombus *SLFG*.** *(See pp. 190–194.)*

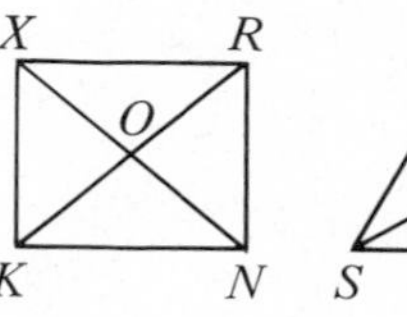


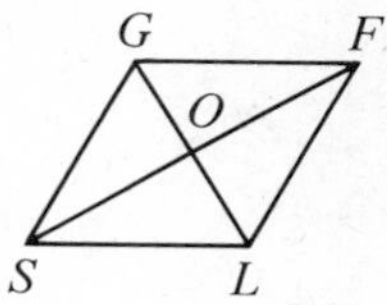


13. If $RK = 20$, then $ON =$ _?_. 10
14. If $\angle RKN = 40°$, find the measures of $\angle RKX$ and $\angle KXN$. 50° 50°
15. If $\angle LSG = 60°$, find the measures of $\angle FSG$ and $\angle LOF$. 90° 30°

**Write the definition or theorem that supports the statement "*ABCD* is a parallelogram."** *(See pp. 195–200.)*

16. Thm. 12, p. 196

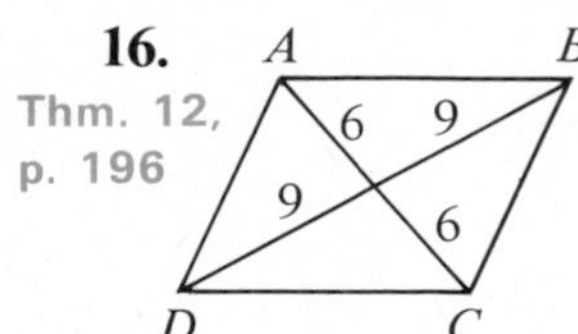


17. Thm. 10, p. 195

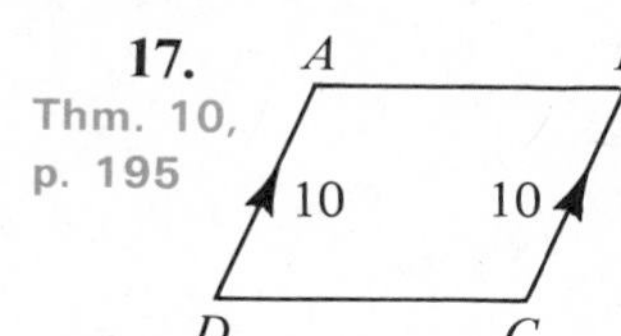


18. Thm. 11, p. 196

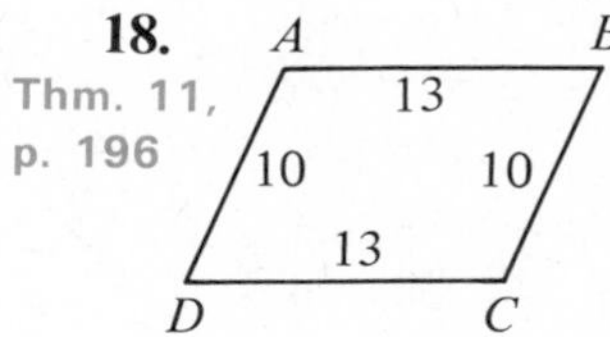


***LIFE* is an isosceles trapezoid with bases $\overline{LI}$ and $\overline{EF}$. $LE = FI = 6$, $EF = 8$, and $LI = 14$.** *(See pp. 201–205.)*

19. Find the length of the median of *LIFE*. 11
20. If $\angle L = 60°$, find the measures of $\angle I$, $\angle F$, and $\angle E$. 60°, 120°, 120°

***M*, *N*, and *O* are the midpoints of the sides of △*RAT*. $RA = 14$, $AT = 6$, and $TR = 12$.** *(See pp. 206–209.)*

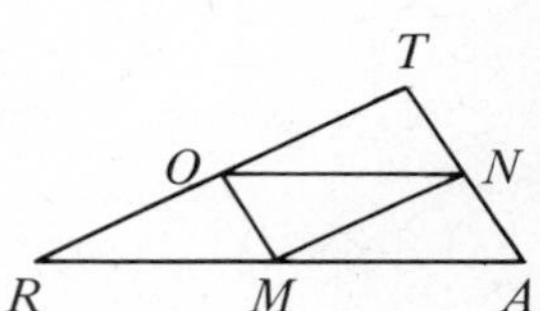


21. $MN =$ _?_ 6
22. The perimeter of △*NOM* is _?_. 16

## *Here's what you'll learn in this chapter:*

1. To find the area of a rectangle, a square, and a parallelogram.
2. To find the area of a triangle.
3. To find the area of a trapezoid.
4. To use the Pythagorean Theorem and its converse.
5. To find the circumference and the area of a circle.

# Chapter 6

# Areas

## 1 • Areas of Rectangles

Which of the rectangles shown at the right covers more surface? Count the squares to see.

The square covers more surface.

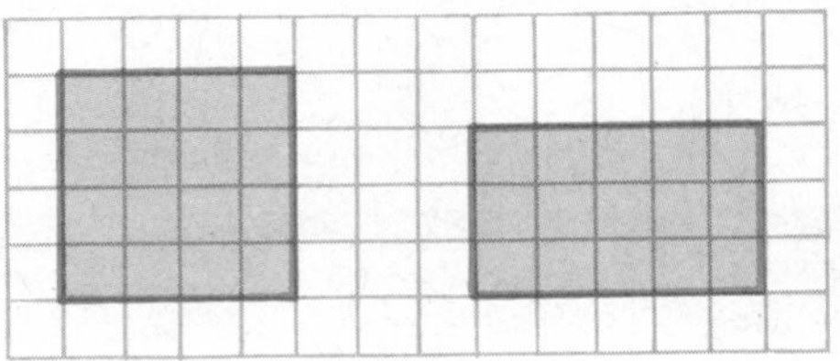

The $4 \times 4$ rectangle is made up of 16 squares. The $5 \times 3$ rectangle is made up of 15 squares. We say that the $4 \times 4$ rectangle has the greater *area*. The amount of surface in a region is its **area.**

A square with sides one unit long has an area of *one square unit*. A common unit of area is the square centimeter.

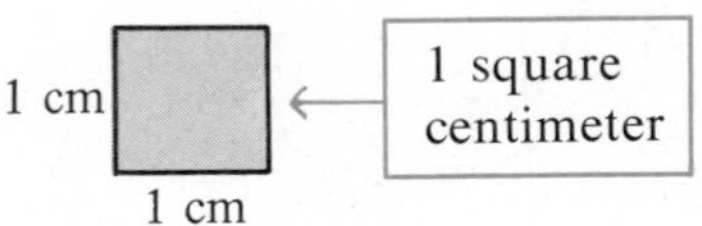


Rectangle *ABCD* has a *base* 5 cm long. Its *height* is 2 cm. Since the rectangle is made up of 10 square centimeters, its area is 10 square centimeters (written 10 cm²). Notice that the area is the product of the lengths of the sides:

$$10 = 5 \times 2.$$

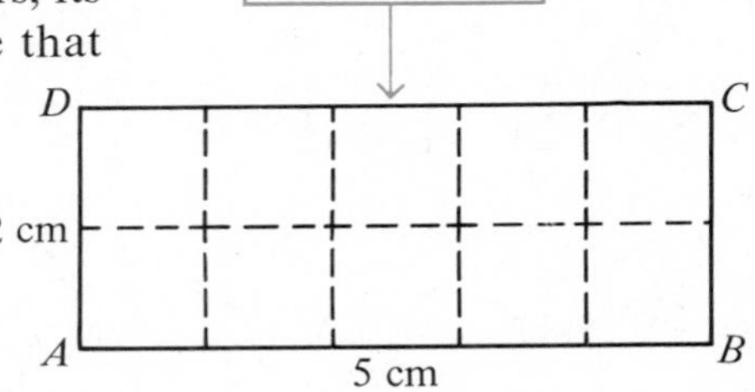


This example suggests the following postulate.

**POSTULATE 12**

The area of a rectangle is given by the formula:

**A**rea = **b**ase × **h**eight

**EXAMPLE 1** Find the area of a rectangle with base length 12 and height 6.

(Rectangle with base 12 and height 6)

$A = bh$

$= 12 \times 6$

$= 72$

*Answer:* 72 square units

**EXAMPLE 2** What is the area of a rectangle 2 m long and 40 cm wide?

*When the unit of length is 1 centimeter:*

Instead of using 2 m, use $2 \times 100 = 200$ cm.

$$A = bh$$
$$= 200 \times 40 = 8000$$

*Answer:* 8000 $\text{cm}^2$

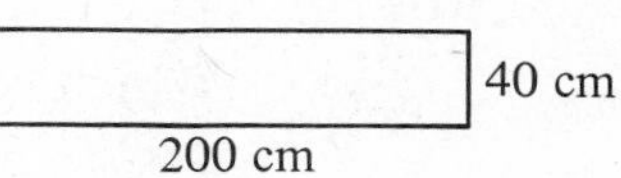


*When the unit of length is 1 meter:*

Instead of using 40 cm, use $\frac{40}{100} = 0.4$ m.

$$A = bh$$
$$= 2 \times 0.4 = 0.8$$

*Answer:* 0.8 $\text{m}^2$

0.4 m

2 m

You should see that 8000 $\text{cm}^2$ is the same amount of area as 0.8 $\text{m}^2$.

> Recall:
>
> Since 1 m = 100 cm, $1 \text{ m}^2 = 100 \text{ cm} \times 100 \text{ cm} = 10{,}000 \text{ cm}^2$.

Every square is a rectangle, so the formula $A = bh$ applies to squares. In a square, $b$ and $h$ are equal. By substituting $s$ for both $b$ and $h$ in the formula of Postulate 12, we obtain Theorem 1.

**THEOREM 1**

The area of a square is given by the formula:

Area = side squared

**EXAMPLE 3** Find the area of a square with sides of length 8.

8

8

$$A = s^2$$
$$= 8^2 = 8 \times 8 = 64$$

*Answer:* 64 square units

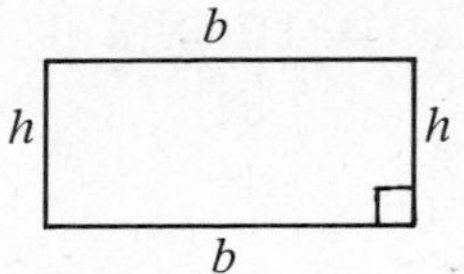


*Remember:* The distance around a region is its **perimeter.** To find the perimeter of a rectangle, use the formula $p = 2b + 2h$.

**EXAMPLE 4** The perimeter of each rectangle shown below is 100. Which rectangle has the greatest area?

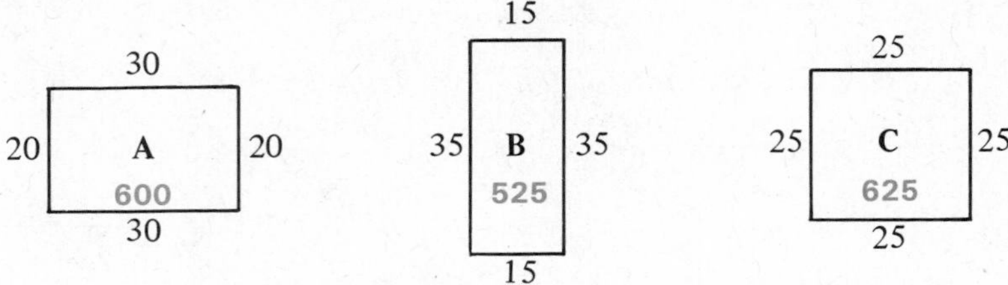


You should be able to show that rectangle C has the greatest area.

## Classroom Practice

1. Find the perimeter of the rectangle shown. 26
2. Find the area of the rectangle shown. 40

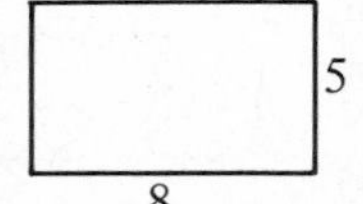


3. Each rectangle in Example 4 has perimeter 100.
   a. Draw two different rectangles, each with perimeter 100.
   b. Find the area of each rectangle you drew. Answers may vary.
4. Do you believe that you could draw a rectangle with perimeter 100 and an area as small as you please? Yes
5. Draw a square with sides 1 m long on the chalkboard. The area = __?__ $m^2$. 1
6. Use the figure of Exercise 5. Each side is __?__ cm long. 100 The area = __?__ $cm^2$. 10,000
7. Large regions are often measured in square kilometers ($km^2$). A memorial park is in the form of a square, 1.5 km on each side.
   a. The area of the park = __?__ $km^2$. 2.25
   b. The area of the park = __?__ $m^2$. (1 km = 1000 m) 2,250,000
8. a. Suppose two rectangles have equal areas. Must the bases have the same length? No
   b. Suppose two squares have equal areas. Must the sides of the squares have the same length? Yes

## Written Exercises

**Find the area of each rectangle.**

A **1.**

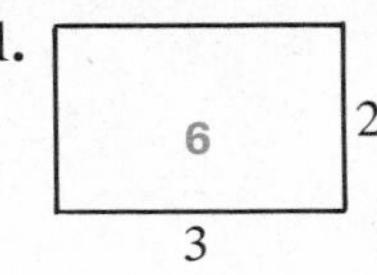


**2.**

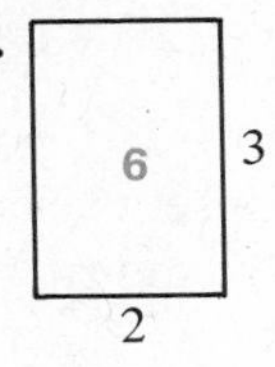


**3.**

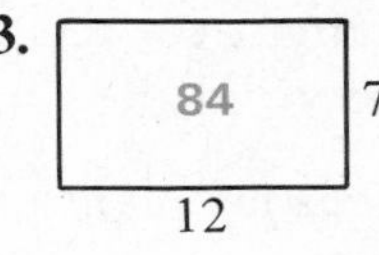


**4.**

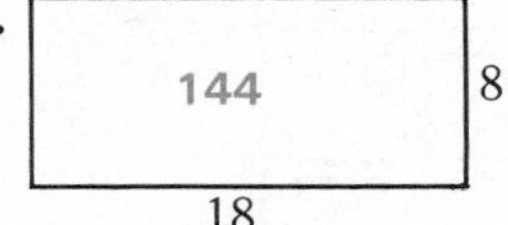


**5.**

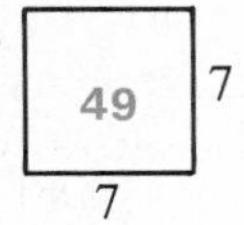


**6.**

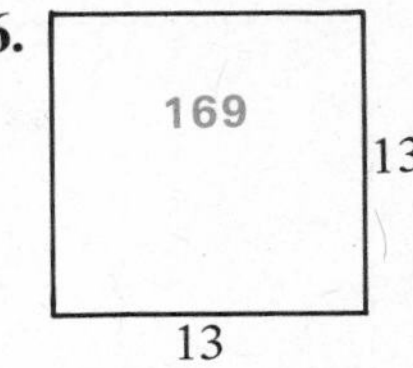


**In Exercises 7–12, find the perimeter and the area of a rectangle with base length *b* and height *h*.** (Perimeter listed first, then area.)

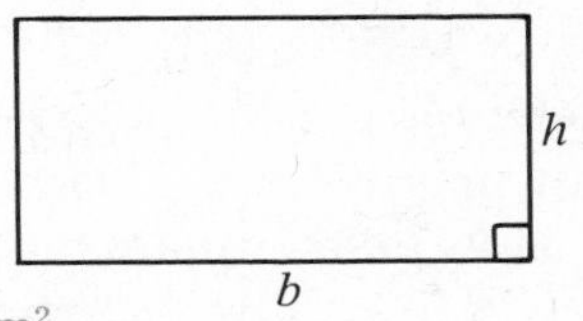


16; 12 **7.** $b = 6,\ h = 2$

**8.** $b = 10,\ h = 7$ 34; 70

**9.** $b = 4,\ h = 3.2$
14.4; 12.8

**10.** $b = 9.6,\ h = 4$
27.2; 38.4

**11.** $b = 7\frac{2}{5},\ h = 6$
$26\frac{4}{5}$; $44\frac{2}{5}$

**12.** $b = j$ cm, $h = k$ cm
$2j + 2k$ cm; $jk$ cm$^2$

**In Exercises 13–18, find the perimeter and the area of a square with sides of length *s*.** (Perimeter listed first; then area.)

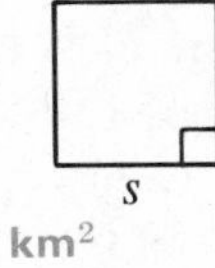


4; 1 **13.** $s = 1$

**14.** $s = 2$ 8; 4

**15.** $s = 3$ 12; 9

16; 16 **16.** $s = 4$

**17.** $s = 5$
20; 25

**18.** $s = j$ km
$4j$ km; $j^2$ km$^2$

**Copy and complete the table about squares. In Exercises 23 and 24, express your answers in terms of *k*.**

B

| | 19. | 20. | 21. | 22. | 23. | 24. | |
|---|---|---|---|---|---|---|---|
| side $s$ | 9 ? | 5 ? | 7 ? | 8 ? | $2k$ | $k + 3$ | |
| perimeter $p$ | 36 | 20 | 28 ? | 32 ? | $8k$ ? | ? | $4k + 12$ |
| Area $A$ | 81 ? | 25 ? | 49 | 64 | $4k^2$ ? | ? | $k^2 + 6k + 9$ |

**Find the area: a. in square centimeters; b. in square meters.**

**25.** A square with sides 60 cm long

**26.** A square with sides 0.9 m long

**27.** A rectangle 3 m long and 50 cm wide a. 15,000 cm$^2$ b. 1.5 m$^2$

**28.** A rectangle 5 m long and 70 cm wide a. 35,000 cm$^2$ b. 3.5 m$^2$

25. a. 3600 cm$^2$ b. 0.36 m$^2$

26. a. 8100 cm$^2$ b. 0.81 m$^2$

**29.** A manufacturer plans to cut rectangular greeting cards. Each card will have an area of 66 cm² and a length of 12 cm. How wide will the cards be? 5.5 cm

**30.** The area of a rectangular desk top is 2700 cm². The width is 45 cm. Find the length. 60 cm

**31.** The Sasons plan to recarpet their house, except for the shaded regions shown in the diagram. How many square meters of carpeting will be needed? about 162 m²

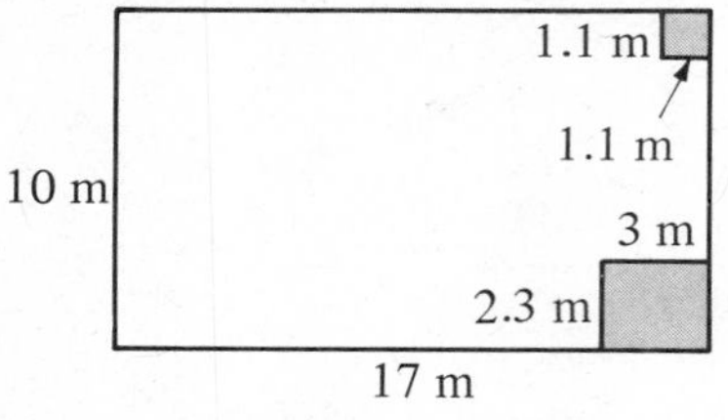

Exercise 31

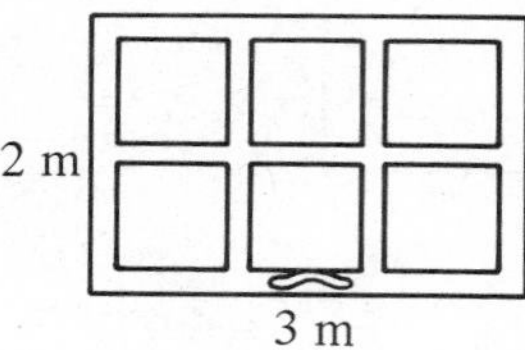

Exercise 32

C **32.** Some pleated draperies must be twice as wide as the window that they cover.

**a.** How many square meters of material are needed to cover the window shown? 12 m²

**b.** The drapery material is sold from a bolt of cloth 1.5 m wide. What length of material should be cut from the bolt? 8 m

**33.** A piece of sheet metal is cut and bent to form the box shown. The box has no top. Find the area of:

**a.** the bottom 72 cm² **b.** the two shaded sides 24 cm² **c.** the other two sides 108 cm²

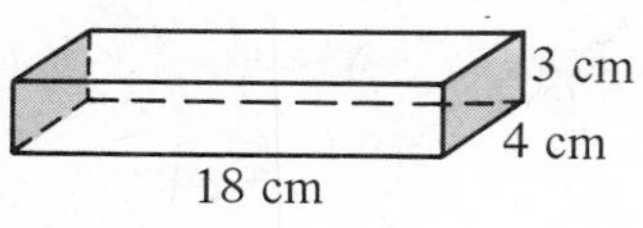

Exercise 33

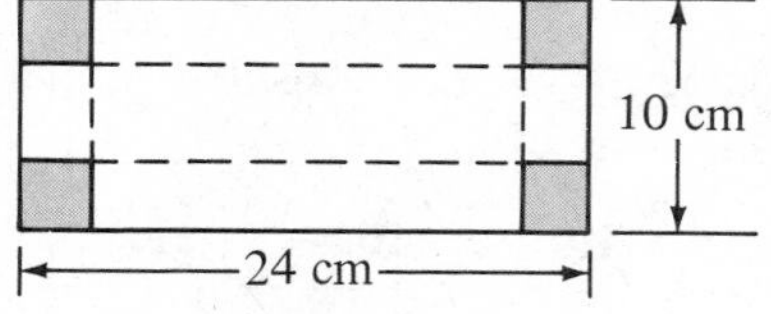

Exercise 34

**34.** The metal used for the box in Exercise 33 is 24 cm long and 10 cm wide. The dashed lines indicate folds. The shaded regions indicate wasted sheet metal. How much metal is wasted? 36 cm²

**35.** The roof of an A-frame cabin is to be shingled at a cost of $70 a square. (A *square,* in shingling, is a region with an area of 100 square feet.) Find the cost of shingling the roof of the cabin shown. $1008

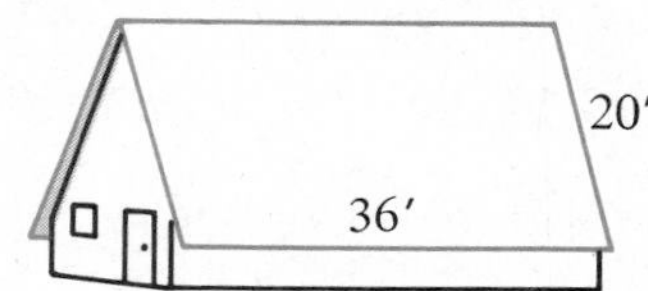

## 2 • Areas of Parallelograms

Suppose you are given the four sticks shown.

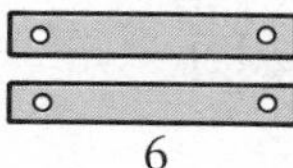


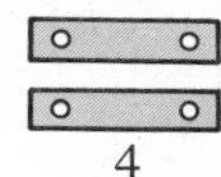


You can join the sticks, with equal sides opposite each other, to form a quadrilateral. The quadrilateral has to be a parallelogram. It can be, but does not have to be, a rectangle.

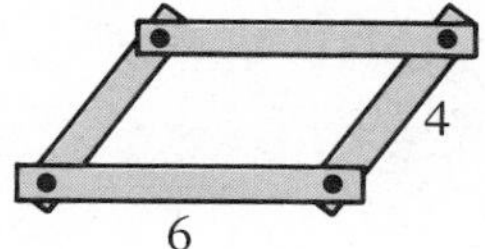


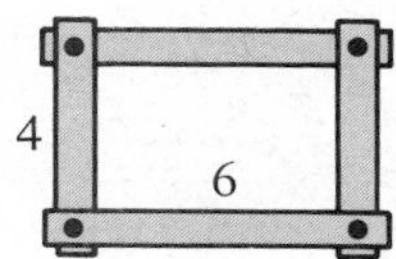


The area of the rectangle is 24, but the area of the parallelogram at the left is less than 24.

*The area of a parallelogram is* ***not*** *equal to the product of two consecutive sides, unless the parallelogram happens to be a rectangle.*

The area of the stick parallelogram depends on its *height*. The **height** of a parallelogram is the length of an *altitude*. This is a segment between, and perpendicular to, the lines containing the bases. Two altitudes are drawn to bases $\overline{AB}$ and $\overline{CD}$ in $\square ABCD$. Notice that these altitudes are equal.

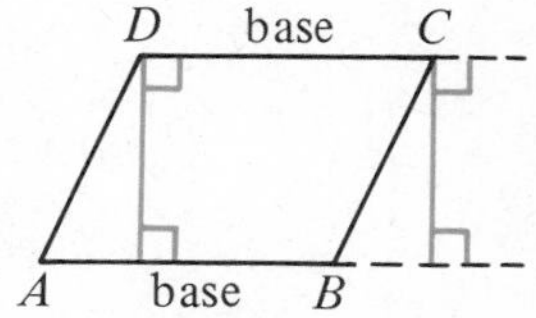


In any parallelogram, either pair of opposite sides may be considered the bases. If $\overline{AD}$ and $\overline{BC}$ are taken as bases, then the green segment is an altitude to those bases.

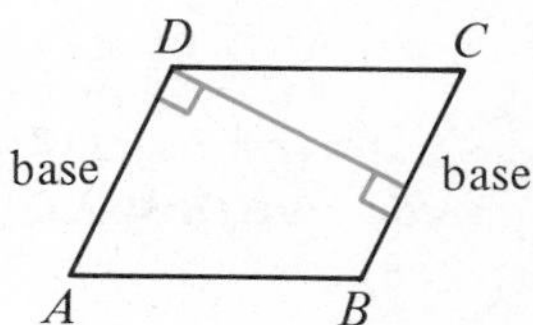


### Explorations

Cut a parallelogram out of cardboard.

Cut along the indicated altitude, $h$.

Move the triangle as shown to form a rectangle.

The area of the rectangle equals $bh$. Therefore the area of the original parallelogram is also equal to $bh$.

This exploration suggests the theorem stated on page 222.

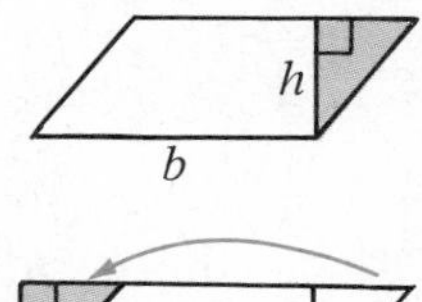


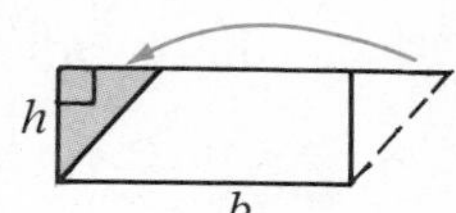

**THEOREM 2**

The area of a parallelogram is given by the formula:

**A**rea = **b**ase × **h**eight

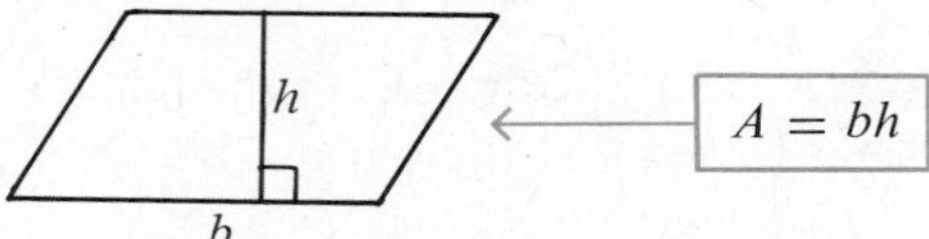


## *Classroom Practice*

**Find the area of each parallelogram.**

**1.** 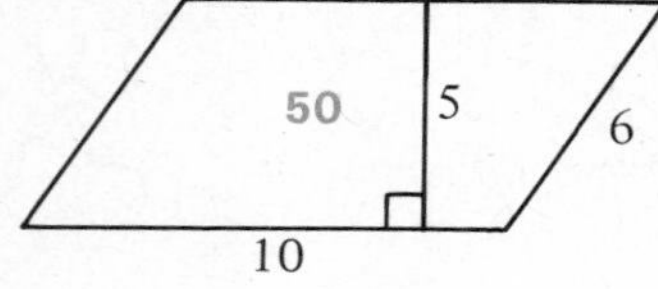


**2.** 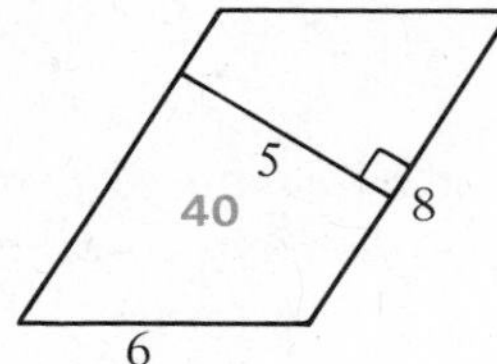


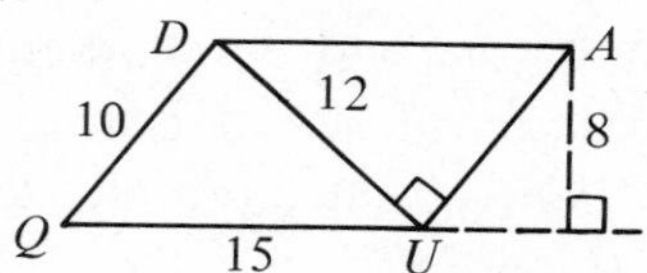


**3.** Take $\overline{QU}$ as a base of $\square QUAD$.
Area of $\square QUAD = 15 \times$ _?_ 8 = _?_ 120.

**4.** Take $\overline{UA}$ as a base of $\square QUAD$.
Area of $\square QUAD = 10 \times$ _?_ 12 = _?_ 120.

**Exercises 5 and 6 refer to $\square ABCD$ shown below. The parallelogram is constructed so that its shape may be changed.**

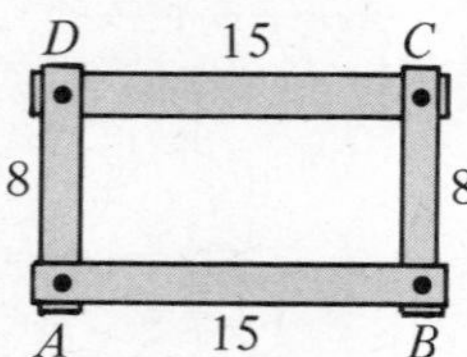


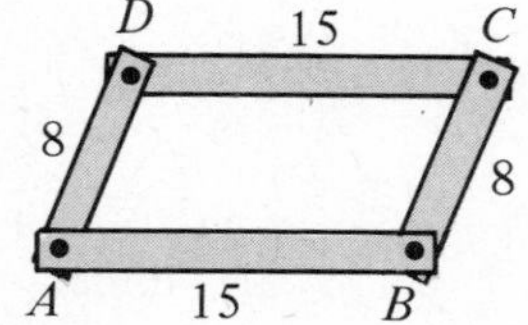


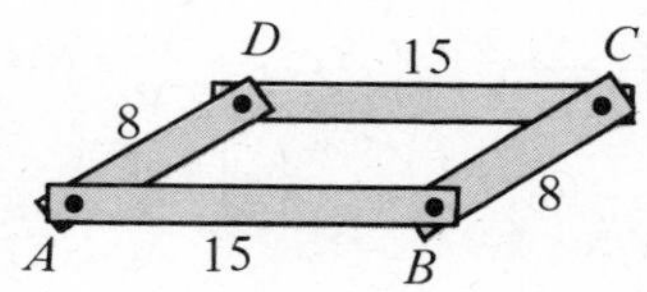


**5.** Find the greatest possible area that $\square ABCD$ can have. 120

**6.** As the height of $\square ABCD$ decreases, what happens to the area of the parallelogram? The area decreases.

**7.** For the parallelogram at the right:
**a.** Find the perimeter in meters; 8 m
**b.** Find the area in square meters. 21 m²

1 m
70 cm
3 m

## Written Exercises

**Find the area of each parallelogram.**

A **1.** 45

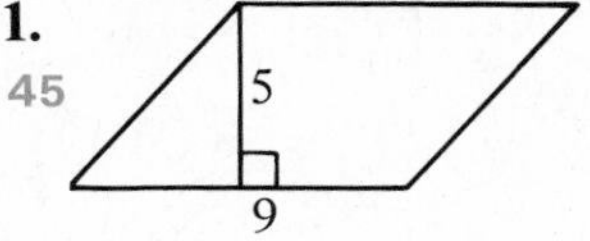


**2.** 72

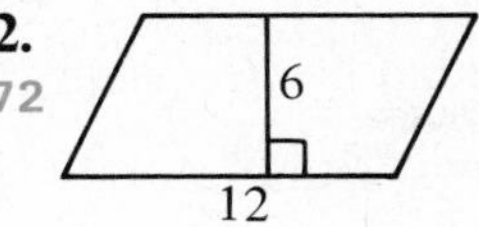


**3.** 28

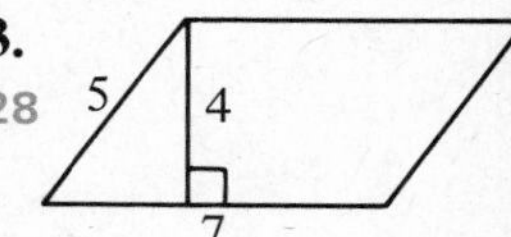


**4.** 60

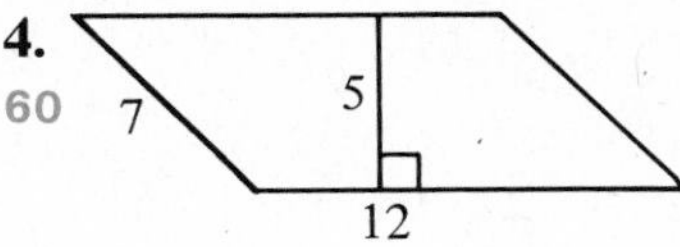


**5.** 56

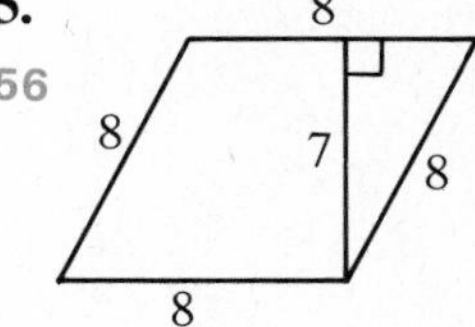


**6.** 69

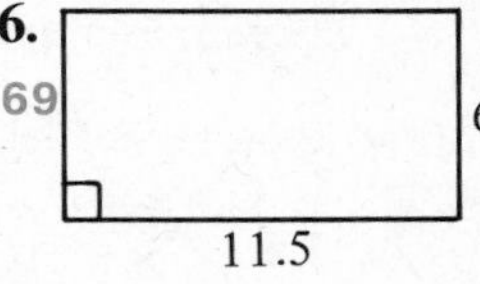


**7.** 84

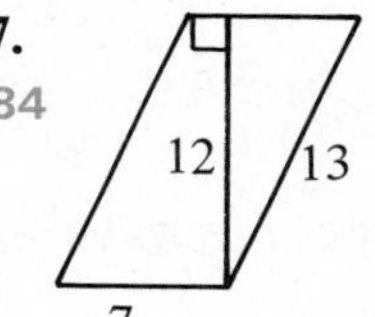


**8.** 286

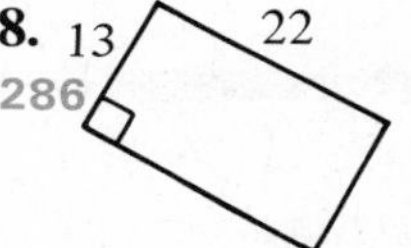


**9.** 30.4

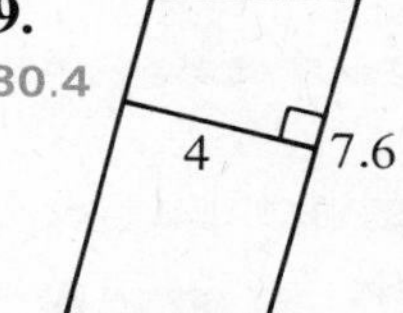


**Find the perimeter and the area of each parallelogram. Express your answers in terms of *k*.**

B **10.** $p = 6k + 2$ $A = 2k^2$

$k$ $k + 1$ $2k$

**11.** $p = 4k + 14$ $A = k^2 + 5k$

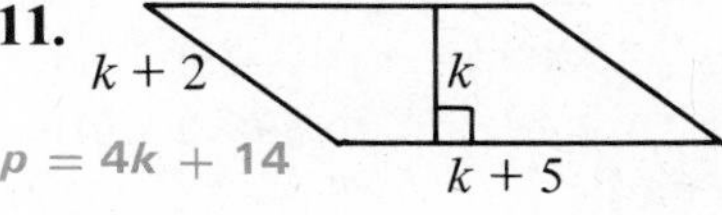


**12.** $p = \frac{16}{15}k$ $A = \frac{1}{15}k^2$

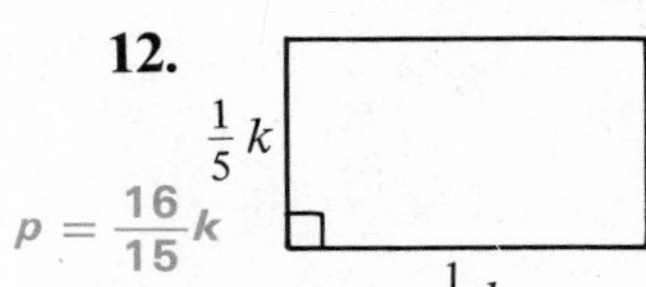


**13.** $p = 16k$ $A = 5k^2 + 20k$

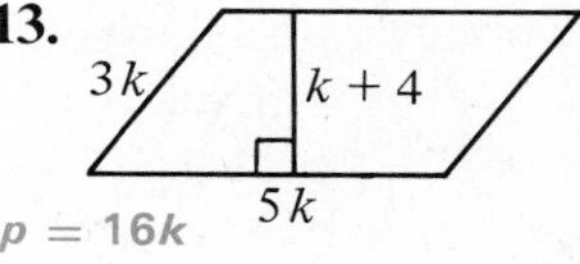


C **14.** The area of rectangle *CEFD* is 96. Find the area of ▱*ABCD*. 84

**15.** Construct a parallelogram *PQRS*. Then construct a rectangle *WXYZ* so that the area of the rectangle equals the area of the parallelogram.

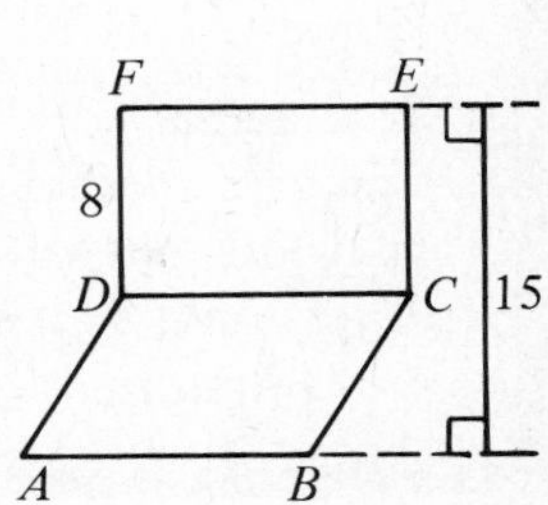

## SELF-TEST

1. The sides of a rectangle have lengths 10 and 3.

   a. The perimeter of the rectangle is ___?___. 26

   b. The area of the rectangle is ___?___. 30

2. The area of a square is 25 cm$^2$.

   a. The length of a side of the square is ___?___. 5

   b. The perimeter of the square is ___?___. 20

**Find the area of each parallelogram.**

**3.** 48

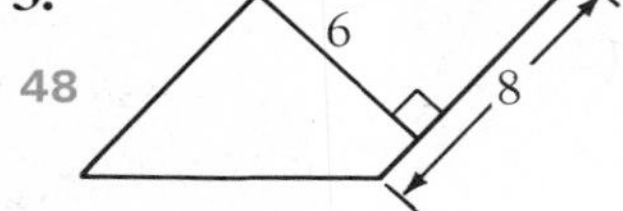


**4.** 60

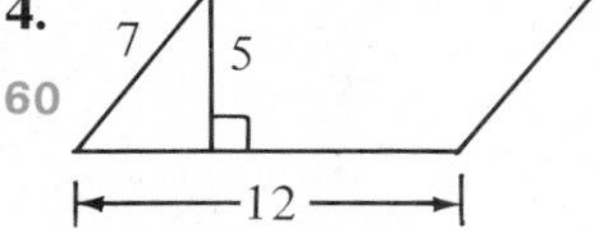


# CAREER NOTES

## *Actuary*

Did you know that in a recent year, there were 101,600 fires in the United States caused by faulty electrical wiring? In the same year, there were 14,782 fires of a similar nature in Canada.

Actuaries use information like that given above to establish the policy rates charged by insurance companies. They analyze data on the probability and actual frequency of certain types of losses. After they have analyzed the necessary statistical data, they develop policy-rate scales based on their estimations of anticipated losses.

Most actuaries have at least a bachelor's degree in mathematics, statistics, economics, or business administration. To gain full professional status, they must pass a series of examinations.

## 3 • Areas of Triangles

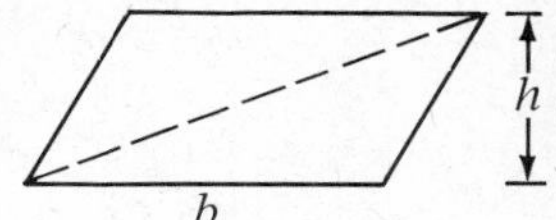


Given any parallelogram, you can separate it into two congruent triangles. You simply draw a diagonal. Since congruent triangles have equal areas:

$$\text{Area of each triangle} = \frac{1}{2}(\text{Area of parallelogram})$$
$$= \frac{1}{2}bh$$

The diagrams below suggest that any triangle is "half" of a parallelogram that can be built on the triangle. The parallelogram has the same base length and height as the triangle.

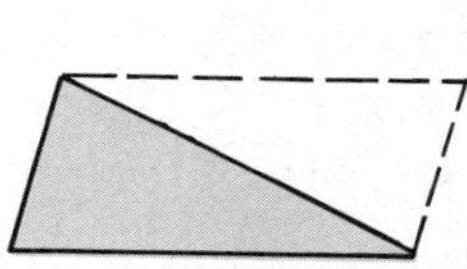

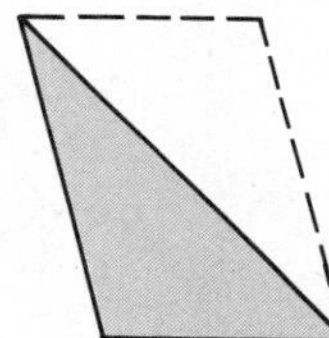

The discussion above contains the key ideas of the proof of Theorem 3.

**THEOREM 3**

The area of a triangle is given by the formula:

$$\text{Area} = \frac{1}{2} \times \text{base} \times \text{height}$$

**EXAMPLE** Find the area of each triangle.

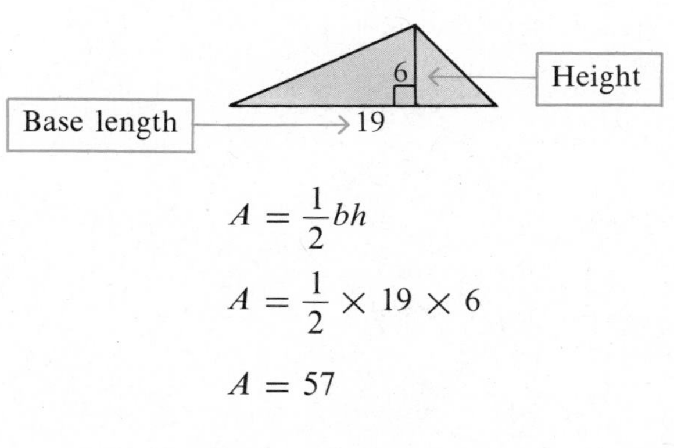


$A = \frac{1}{2}bh$

$A = \frac{1}{2} \times 19 \times 6$

$A = 57$

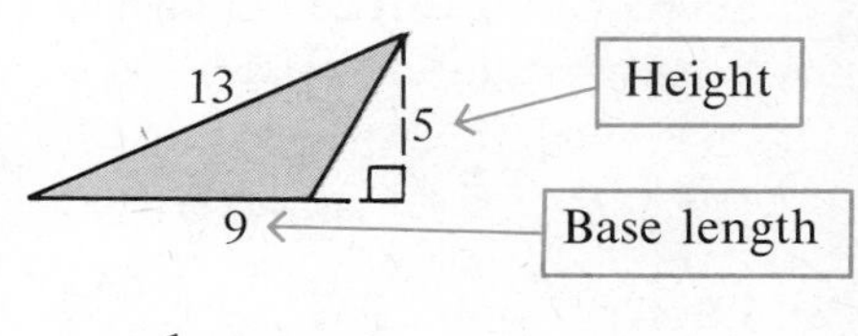


$A = \frac{1}{2}bh$

$A = \frac{1}{2} \times 9 \times 5$

$A = \frac{45}{2}$, or 22.5

## Classroom Practice

1. $\overline{DE}$ is taken as the base of $\triangle DEF$. Name the altitude to $\overline{DE}$. $\overline{FZ}$

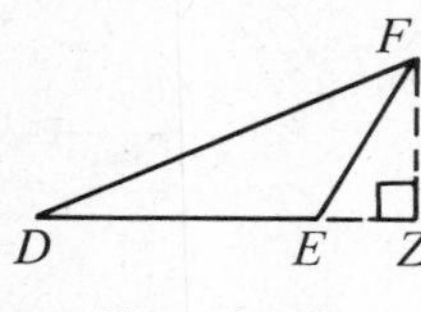

Exercise 1

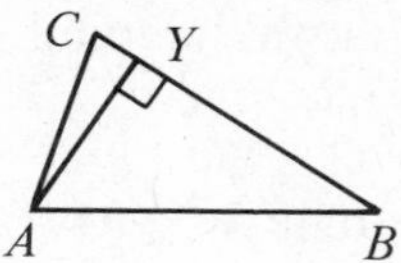

Exercise 2

2. $\overline{BC}$ is taken as the base of $\triangle ABC$. Name the altitude to $\overline{BC}$. $\overline{AY}$

**Exercises 3–5 refer to right $\triangle JKM$.**

3. Name the altitude to $\overline{MK}$. $\overline{JM}$
4. Name the altitude to $\overline{MJ}$. $\overline{KM}$
5. Name the altitude to $\overline{JK}$. $\overline{MN}$

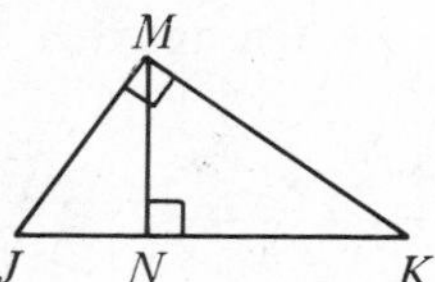


**In Exercises 6–10, use the diagram shown.**

6. The area of rectangle $ABCD$ is __?__. 24
7. The area of $\triangle AEB$ is __?__. 4
8. The area of $\triangle ECF$ is __?__. 4
9. The area of $\triangle FDA$ is __?__. 6
10. Subtract the areas of these triangles from the area of the rectangle. The area of $\triangle AEF$ is __?__. 10

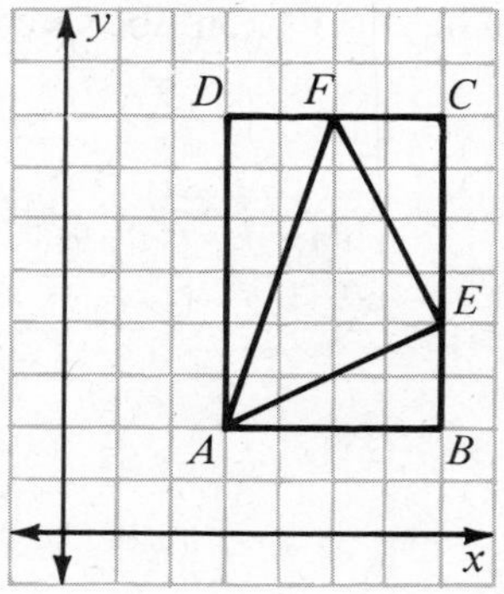


**Exercises 11–13 refer to rhombus $ABCD$ with $AC = 12$ and $BD = 20$. Recall that the diagonals of a rhombus are perpendicular bisectors of each other.**

11. $MC =$ __?__ 6 and $MD =$ __?__ 10
12. Area of $\triangle DMC =$ __?__ 30
13. Notice that the rhombus is separated into four congruent triangles.

    Area of rhombus $ABCD =$ __?__ 120

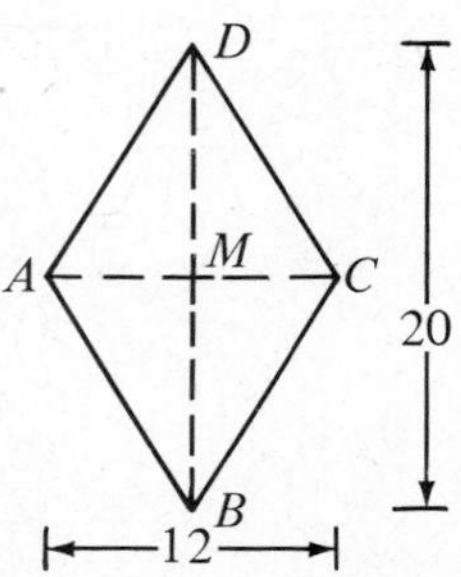

## Written Exercises

**Find the area of the shaded triangle.**

A **1.** 14

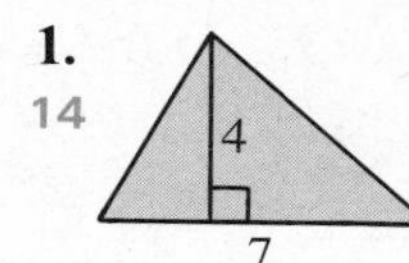


**2.** 30

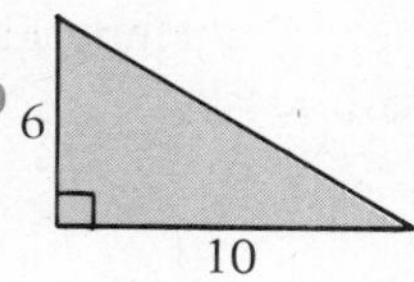


**3.** 32 m²

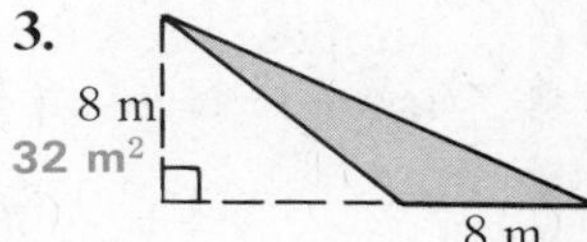


**4.** 31.5 cm²

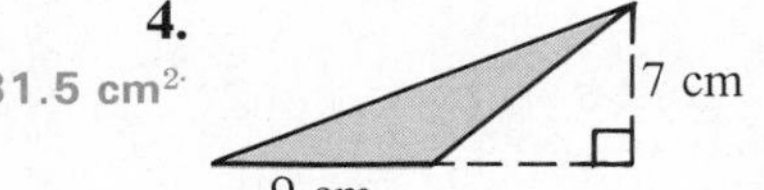


**5.** 56

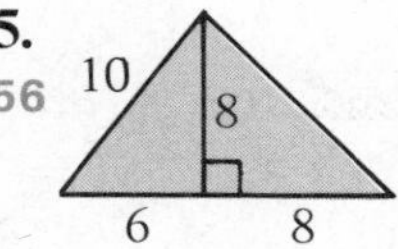


**6.** 90

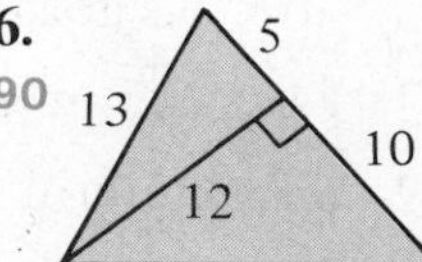


**7.** 8

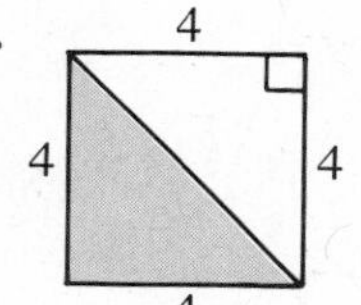


**8.** 72

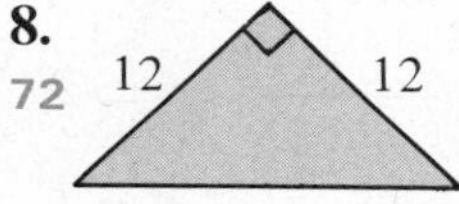


**9.** 20 m²

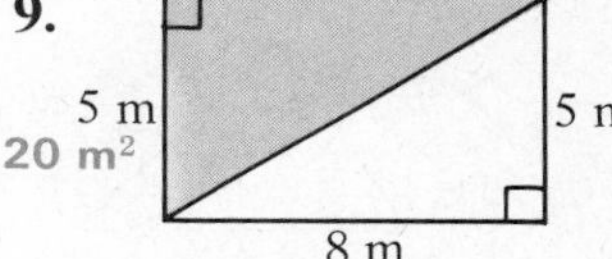


B **10.** 43.05

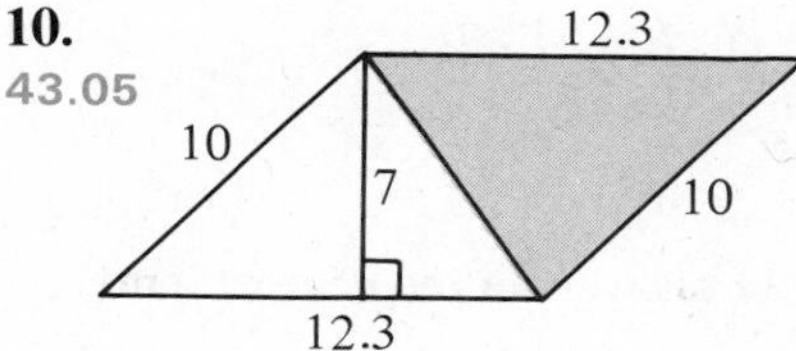


**11.** 24

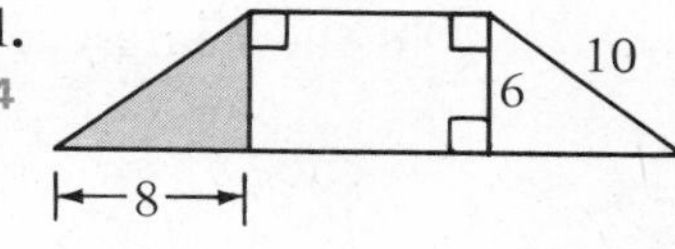


**Express the area in terms of *t*.**

**12.** $20t^2$

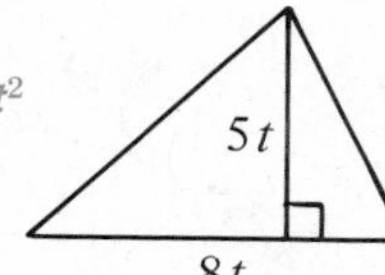


**13.** $\frac{3t^2 - 5t}{2}$

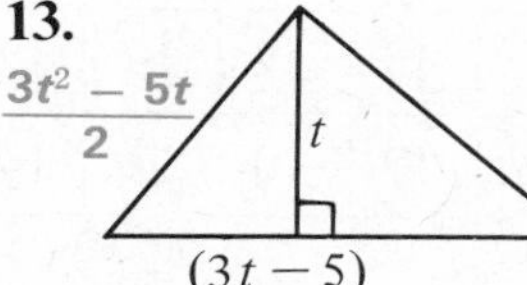


**14.** $\frac{t^2 - 49}{2}$

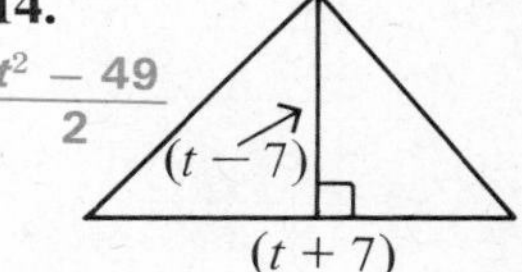


C **15.** Draw a triangle $ABC$. Then construct a rectangle $WXYZ$ so that the area of the rectangle equals the area of the triangle.

*Strategy:*

A. Construct $\overline{WX}$ so that $WX = \frac{1}{2}AB$.

B. Construct a line perpendicular to $\overline{WX}$ at $W$.

C. Mark off $Z$ on the perpendicular so that $WZ$ equals the length of the altitude from $C$ in $\triangle ABC$.

D. Complete rectangle $WXYZ$.

# CALCULATOR CORNER

Suppose the sides of a triangle have lengths $a$, $b$, and $c$. The area of the triangle is given by the formula

$$A = \sqrt{s(s-a)(s-b)(s-c)} \text{ where } s = \frac{a+b+c}{2}.$$

To use this formula:

1. First compute $s$. Then compute $s - a$, $s - b$, and $s - c$.
2. Substitute in the formula $\sqrt{s(s-a)(s-b)(s-c)}$.

**EXAMPLE** Find the area.

$a = 5$, $b = 6$, $c = 7$

1. $s = \frac{5+6+7}{2}$; $s = 9$

   $s - a = 4 \quad s - b = 3 \quad s - c = 2$

2. $\sqrt{s(s-a)(s-b)(s-c)} = \sqrt{9 \times 4 \times 3 \times 2}$

   $\doteq 14.696938$

To the nearest tenth, the area is 14.7.

**Find the area of the triangle specified. Round your answers to the nearest tenth.**

| | 1. | 2. | 3. | 4. | 5. | 6. | 7. | 8. |
|---|---|---|---|---|---|---|---|---|
| $a$ | 6 | 7 | 6 | 8 | 11 | 21 | 16 | 13.1 |
| $b$ | 8 | 5 | 6 | 6 | 15 | 17 | 19 | 12.0 |
| $c$ | 10 | 10 | 6 | 6 | 17 | 10 | 12 | 14.8 |

1. 24 5. 81.3
2. 16.2 6. 84
3. 15.6 7. 95.5
4. 17.9 8. 74.8

**9.** The formula for the area of an equilateral triangle with side $e$ is:

$$A = \frac{e^2}{4}\sqrt{3}.$$

Use this formula to compute the area of an equilateral triangle with sides 6 units long. How does your answer compare with the answer you got in Exercise 3 above? same

**10.** Use the formula to compute the area of an equilateral triangle with a side: **a.** 8 units long; **b.** 1.5 units long. a. 27.7 b. 1.0

## 4 • Areas of Trapezoids

The explorations below lead to a theorem about the area of a trapezoid.

### Explorations

Cut out three congruent trapezoids shaped roughly like trapezoid $RSTV$. The bases of your trapezoids should be 11 cm and 21 cm long. The altitudes should be 8 cm long.

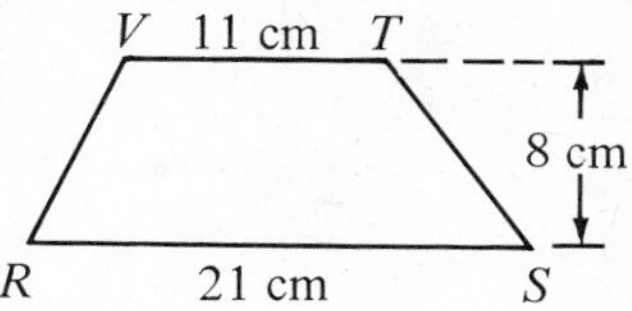


A. Cut along $\overline{VX}$ and $\overline{TY}$.
Since $RS = 21$ and $XY = 11$,

$$RX + YS = 21 - 11$$
$$= 10.$$

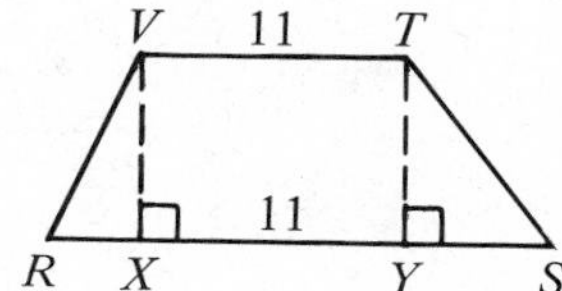


Place the two triangles alongside each other. Notice that rectangle $XYTV$ and $\triangle RSZ$ both have altitudes 8 cm long.

Add the area of rectangle $XYTV$ and the area of $\triangle RSZ$ to find the area of trapezoid $RSTV$. $88 + 40 = 128$

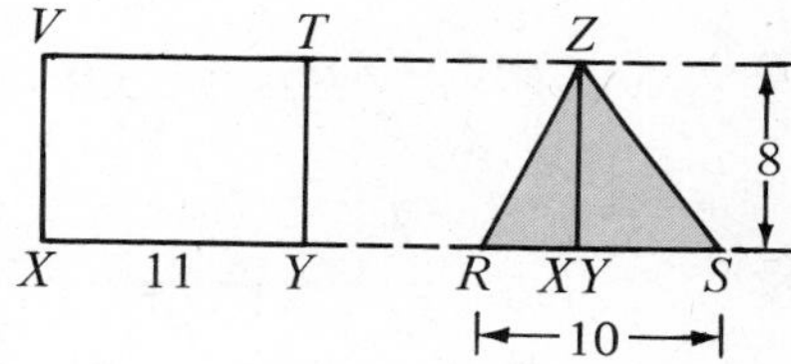


B. Take another copy of trapezoid $RSTV$. Cut along $\overline{VS}$.

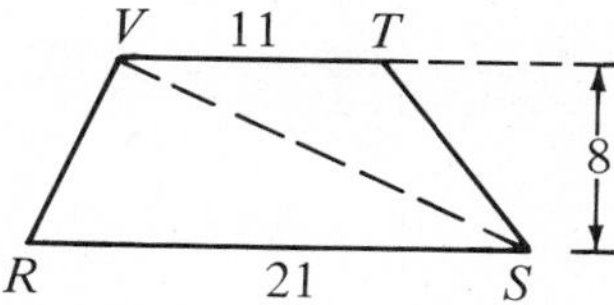


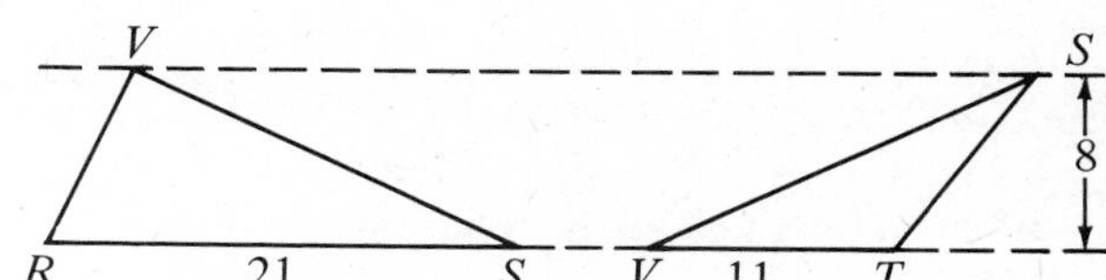


Place the triangles as shown above. Then add the areas of the triangles to find the area of the trapezoid. $84 + 44 = 128$

C. Take the third copy of the trapezoid.

Draw median $\overline{MN}$. Using Theorem 14 on page 202:

$$MN = \frac{1}{2}(21 + 11) = \frac{1}{2}(32) = 16.$$

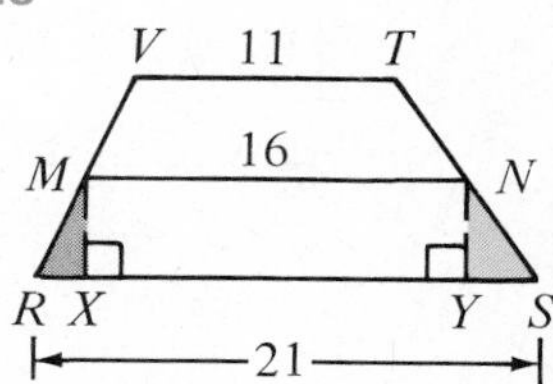


Cut along $\overline{MX}$ and $\overline{NY}$.

Move the triangles as shown. Find the area of trapezoid $RSTV$ by computing the area of the rectangle formed. $16 \times 8 = 128$

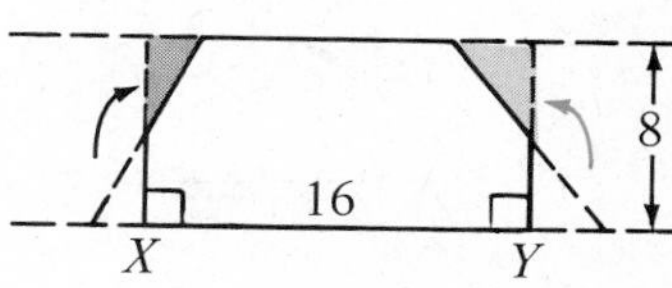

Each of the explorations suggests a way to prove Theorem 4.

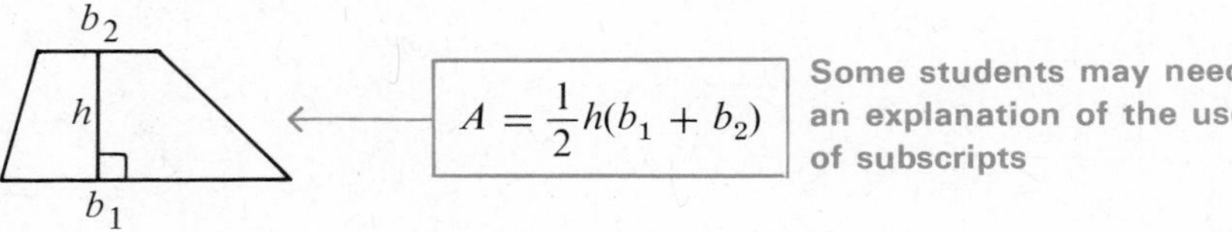

THEOREM 4

The area of a trapezoid is given by the formula:

$$\text{Area} = \frac{1}{2} \times \text{height} \times \text{sum of the bases}$$

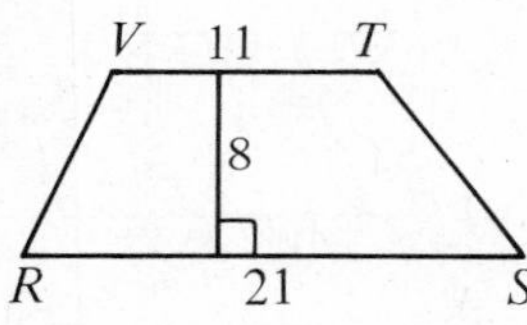


$$A = \frac{1}{2}h(b_1 + b_2)$$

Some students may need an explanation of the use of subscripts

EXAMPLE Find the area.

$$A = \frac{1}{2}h(b_1 + b_2)$$
$$= \frac{1}{2} \times 8 \times (21 + 11)$$
$$= 4 \times 32$$
$$= 128$$

Did you get this answer in Explorations A, B, and C?

## Classroom Practice

**Find the area of each trapezoid.**

**1.** 138

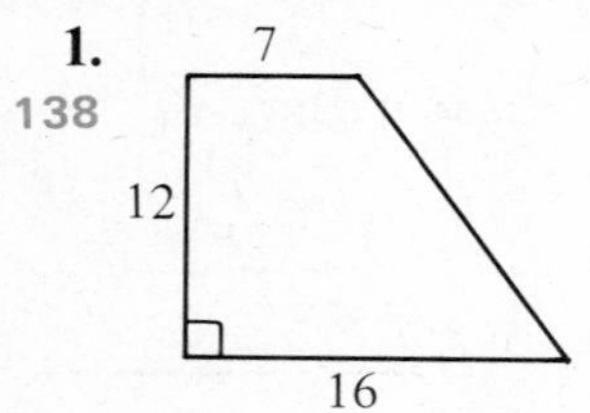


**2.** 138

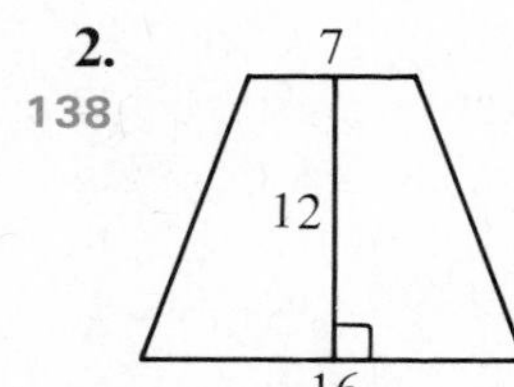


**3.** 138

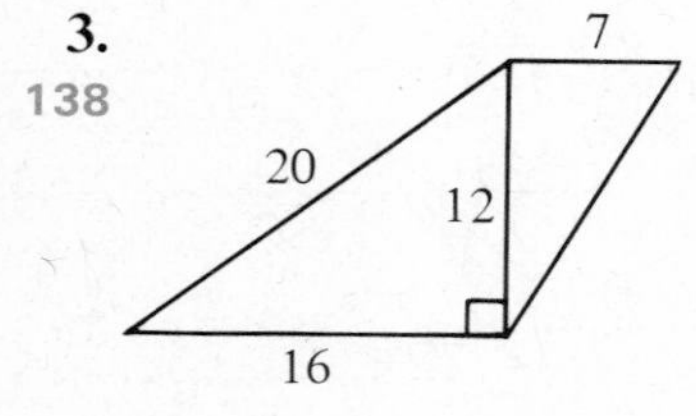


**4.** 138

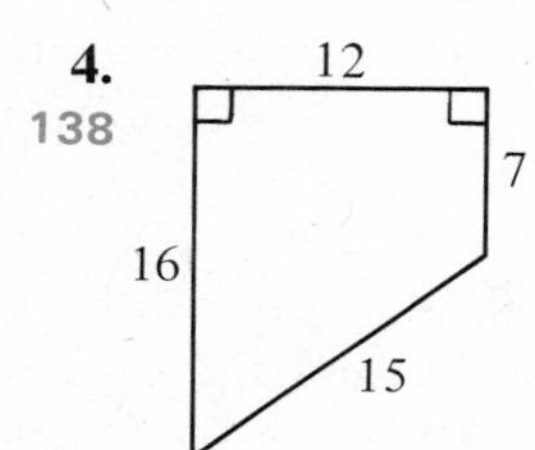

**The figure shows congruent trapezoids $ABEF$ and $DEBC$.**

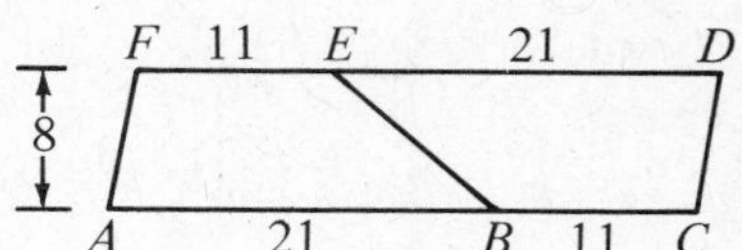


5. Why must quadrilateral $ACDF$ be a parallelogram? $\overline{AC} \parallel \overline{FD}$ and $AC = FD$

6. What is the area of parallelogram $ACDF$? 256

7. What is the area of trapezoid $ABEF$? 128

8. Refer to Explorations A–C. Which suggests that the area of a trapezoid equals the product of the median and the altitude? Expl. C

## Written Exercises

**Select the correct area formula from the column at the right.**

A

1. Triangle d. — a. $A = s^2$
2. Parallelogram c. — b. $A = \frac{1}{2}h(b_1 + b_2)$
3. Square a. — c. $A = bh$
4. Trapezoid b. — d. $A = \frac{1}{2}bh$

**Find the area of each trapezoid.**

5. 96

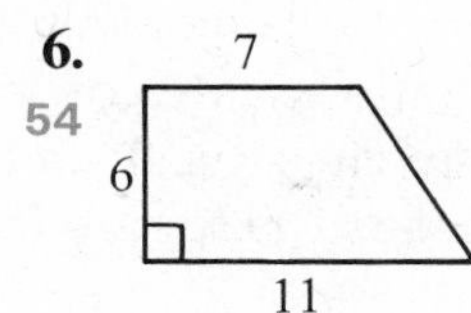


6. 54

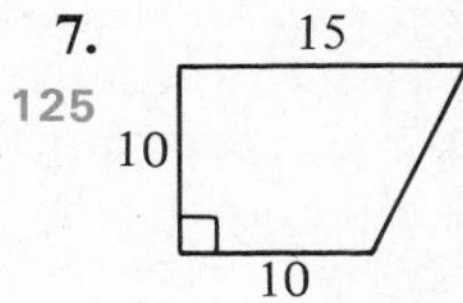


7. 125

15
10
10

8. 108.5

12
7
19

9. 87.5

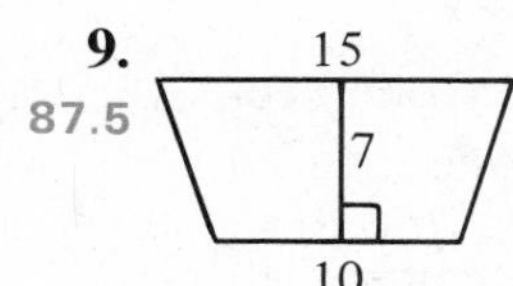


10. 24

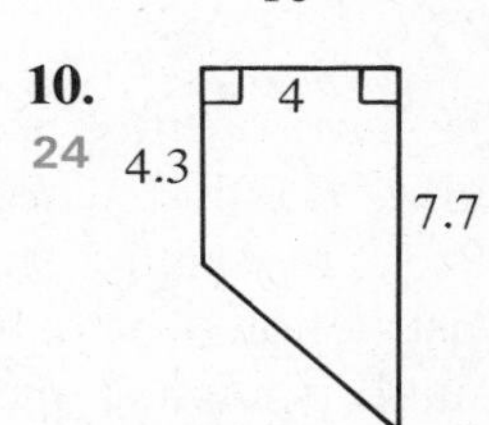


**In Exercises 11–16, find the area of each polygon.**

11. 28 cm$^2$

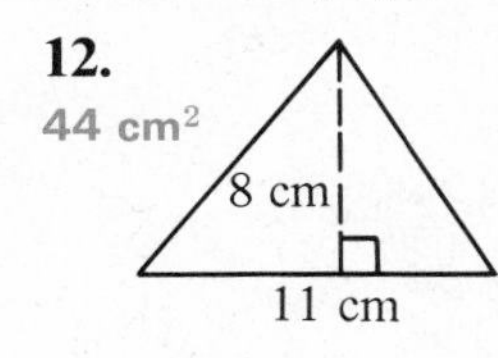


$\overline{HG} \parallel \overline{EF}$; $\overline{EH} \parallel \overline{FG}$

12. 44 cm$^2$

8 cm
11 cm

13. 54 cm$^2$

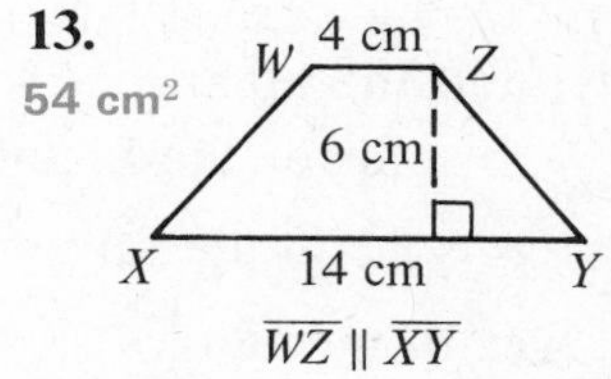


$\overline{WZ} \parallel \overline{XY}$

**Find the area of each polygon.**

**14.** 144 cm²

12 cm, 12 cm, 12 cm, 12 cm

**15.** 88 cm²

8 cm, 10 cm, 8 cm, 14 cm

**16.** 24 cm²

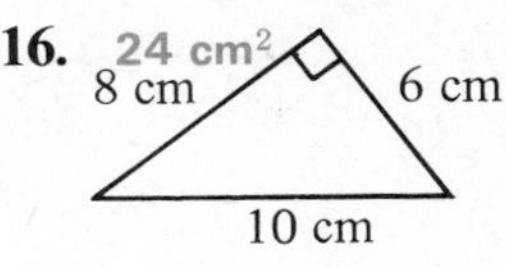


**Copy and complete the table about trapezoids.**

Sample $A = 30$, $b_1 = 7$, $b_2 = 3$. Find $h$.

$$A = \frac{1}{2}h(b_1 + b_2)$$

$$30 = \frac{1}{2}h(7 + 3)$$

$$60 = h(10)$$

$$6 = h$$

B

| | 17. | 18. | 19. | 20. | 21. (8) | 22. (10) | 23. (3) | 24. (17) |
|---|---|---|---|---|---|---|---|---|
| height $h$ | 7 | 8 | 7 | $j$ | ? | ? | 8 | 7 |
| base length $b_1$ | 10 | 10 | 12 | $k$ | 14 | 18 | 5 | ? |
| base length $b_2$ | 4 | 5 | 7 | $n$ | 6 | 12 | ? | 3 |
| Area $A$ | ? (49) | ? (60) | ? (66.5) | ? ($\frac{1}{2}j(k + n)$) | 80 | 150 | 32 | 70 |

C **25.** A *hip roof* consists of two isosceles trapezoids and two isosceles triangles. How many squares of shingles are needed for the roof shown? (Recall that in talk about roofs, one square means 100 square feet.) 20.4

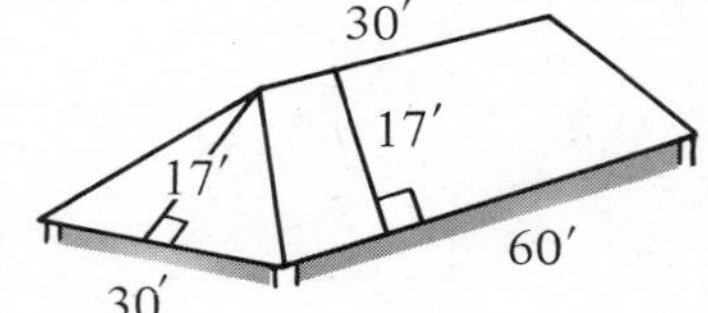


**26.** The Barry family used to farm one section of land. (A *section* is one square mile.) They sold a strip of land to permit construction of a highway. Then they sold a small triangular part that was awkward to reach.

To the nearest ten thousand square feet, find the area:

**a.** sold for the highway; 2,120,000 ft²

**b.** sold to the farmer; 1,330,000 ft²

**c.** in the Barrys' new farm. 24,430,000 ft²

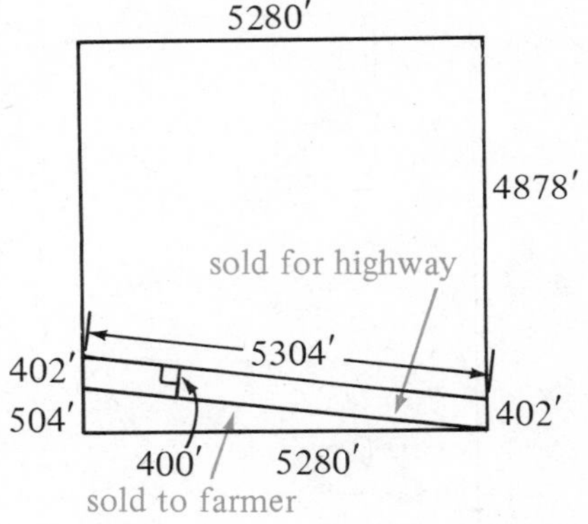

27. Carefully draw a trapezoid *EFGH*. Then construct a rectangle *WXYZ* so that the area of the rectangle equals twice the area of the trapezoid.

*Strategy:*

A. Construct $\overline{WX}$ so that *WX* equals the sum of the bases of trapezoid *EFGH*.

B. Construct a line perpendicular to $\overline{WX}$ at *W*.

C. Mark off *Z* on the perpendicular so that *WZ* equals the height of trapezoid *ABCD*.

D. Complete rectangle *WXYZ*.

## SELF-TEST

**Find the area of each triangle.**

**1.** 20

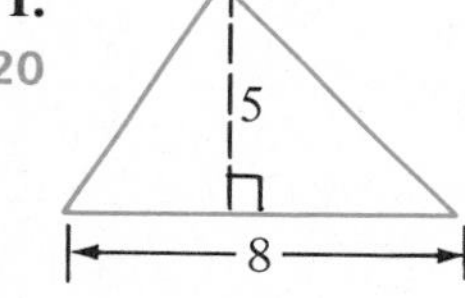


**2.** 12

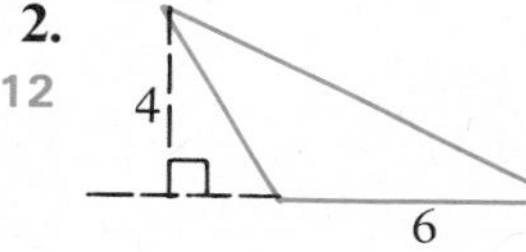


**3.** 84

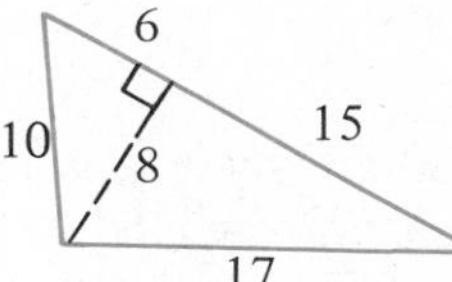


**Find the area of each trapezoid.**

**4.** 91

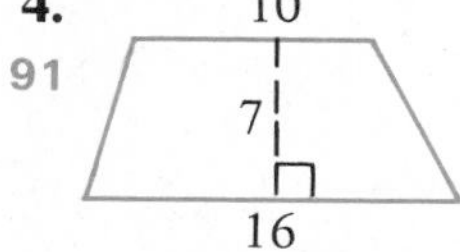


**5.** 26

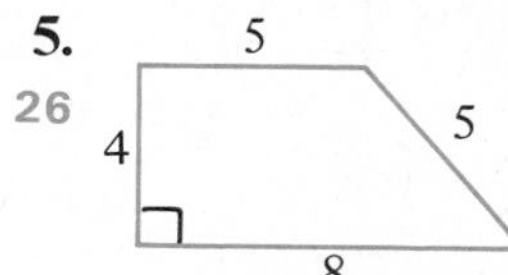


## Puzzles & Things

It is easy to join these sticks to form a rectangle with area 24.

How can you join the sticks to form a *nonrectangular* quadrilateral with area 24? Form diamond shape.

6

6

4

4

## 5 • The Pythagorean Theorem

### Explorations

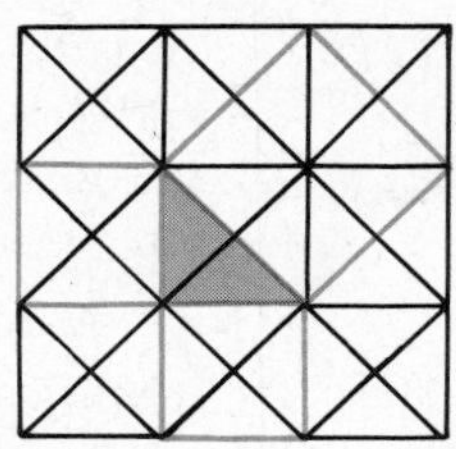

1. Part of a tiled floor is shown.
   Note the right triangle shaded in gray.
   Each side of that triangle is also the side of a square outlined in green.
   Count tiles to compare the area of the largest square with the sum of the areas of the smaller squares. equal

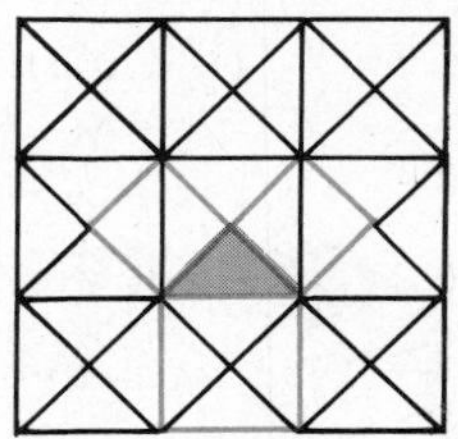

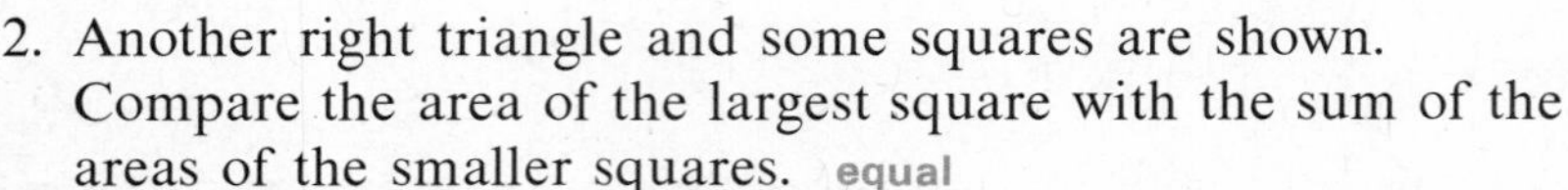

2. Another right triangle and some squares are shown.
   Compare the area of the largest square with the sum of the areas of the smaller squares. equal

The idea suggested above has often been expressed in this way: *The square on the hypotenuse of a right triangle is equal to the sum of the squares on the legs.*

The explorations above deal with special right triangles. The discussion that follows deals with *all* right triangles.

Begin with *any* right triangle.

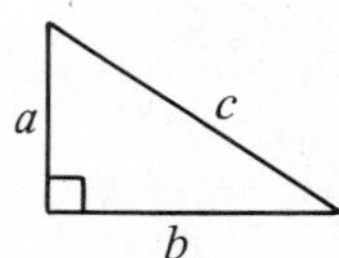


Draw a square, as shown, with sides of length $a + b$.

Locate two new points as shown.

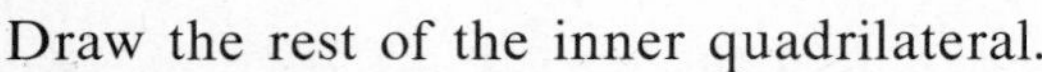

Draw the rest of the inner quadrilateral.

The four right triangles are congruent by the SAS Postulate.

Therefore, each hypotenuse has length $c$.

Each angle of the inner quadrilateral is a right angle (see Exercise 7 at the top of page 236).

The inner quadrilateral is a square with area $c^2$.

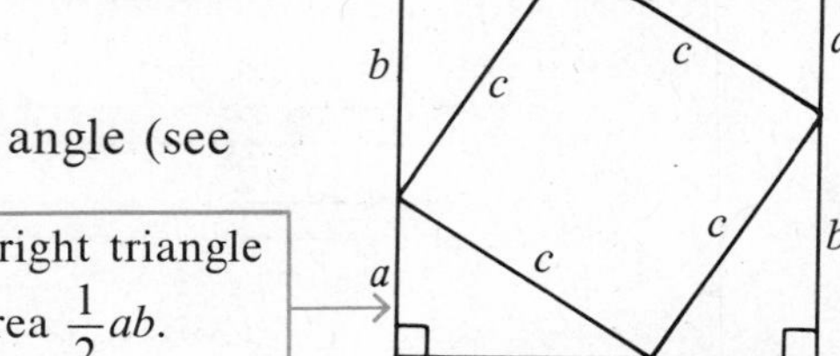

Area of larger square = Area of smaller square + Areas of four triangles

$$(a + b)^2 = c^2 + 4\left(\frac{1}{2}ab\right)$$

$$a^2 + 2ab + b^2 = c^2 + 2ab$$

$$a^2 + b^2 = c^2$$

**THEOREM 5 (The Pythagorean Theorem)**

In a right triangle, the square of the hypotenuse is equal to the sum of the squares of the legs.

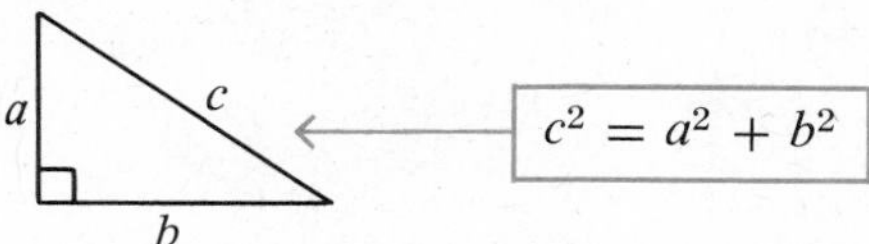


Theorem 5 is usually referred to as the **Pythagorean** (pi-**thag**-uh-**ree′**-an) **Theorem,** in honor of the Greek philosopher and mathematician Pythagoras. He is said to have written a proof of the theorem in the sixth century B.C.

**EXAMPLE** Find the value of $x$ for each right triangle. Remember: the hypotenuse is the longest side of a right triangle.

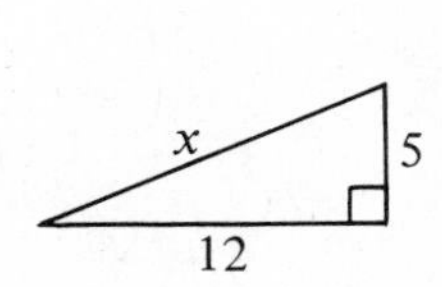


$$x^2 = 5^2 + 12^2$$
$$x^2 = 25 + 144$$
$$x^2 = 169$$
$$x = \sqrt{169}$$
$$x = 13$$

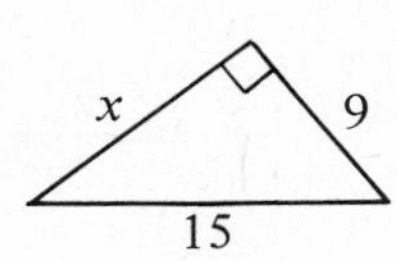


$$15^2 = x^2 + 9^2$$
$$225 = x^2 + 81$$
$$144 = x^2$$
$$\sqrt{144} = x$$
$$12 = x$$

## Classroom Practice

**Is each equation correctly written?**

**1.** $a^2 + b^2 = c^2$
Yes

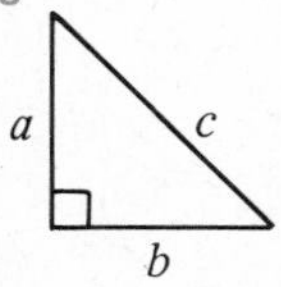


**2.** $c^2 = a^2 + b^2$
No

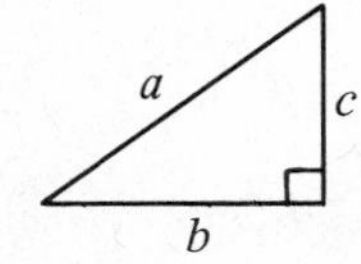


**3.** $r^2 = s^2 + t^2$
No

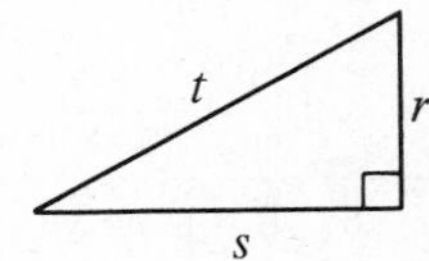

**Is each equation correctly written?**

**4.** $k^2 = l^2 - m^2$ Yes

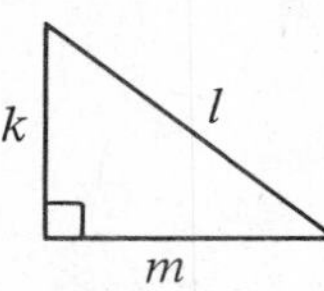


**5.** $d^2 = e^2 - f^2$ No

**6.** $p^2 = r^2 + q^2$ No

**7.** *Given:* $\angle 1$ and $\angle 5$ are right angles. Explain why $\angle 3$ must be a right angle.

(*Hint:* Use the fact that $\triangle RST \cong \triangle TUV$.)

$\angle 2 = \angle 6$ (Corresponding parts)
$\angle 4 + \angle 6 = 90°$, hence $\angle 4 + \angle 2 = 90°$
$\angle 3 + \angle 4 + \angle 2 = 180°$, hence $\angle 3 = 90°$

## *Written Exercises*

**In Exercises 1–6, write an equation you could use to find the value of $x$. Then solve the equation.**

A **1.** $x^2 = 3^2 + 4^2$; $x = 5$

**2.** $13^2 = x^2 + 12^2$; $x = 5$

**3.** $x^2 = 6^2 + 8^2$; $x = 10$

**4.**

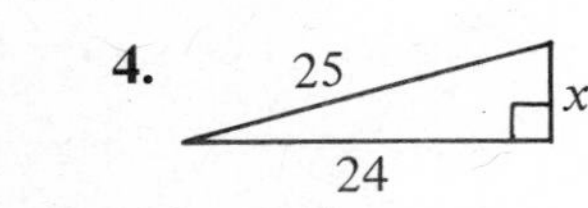


$25^2 = x^2 + 24^2$; $x = 7$

**5.**

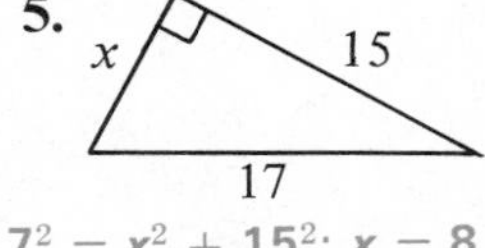


$17^2 = x^2 + 15^2$; $x = 8$

**6.**

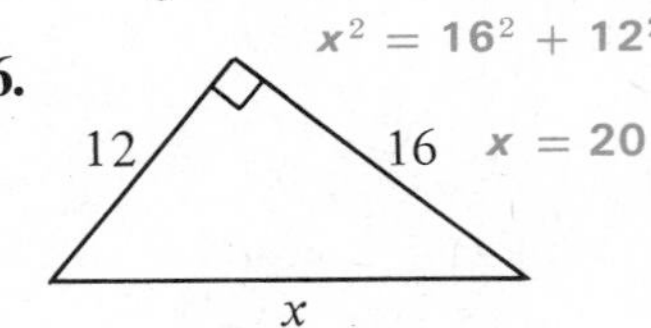


$x^2 = 16^2 + 12^2$; $x = 20$

**In Exercises 7–12, the lengths of two sides of a right triangle are given. Find the length of the third side.**

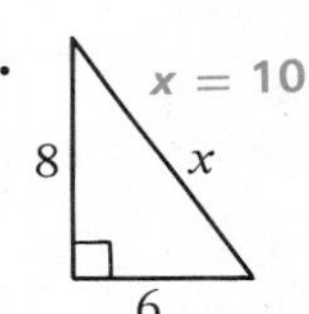


**7.** $a = 6, b = 8$ 10 **8.** $a = 5, b = 12$ 13 **9.** $a = 12, c = 15$ 9

**10.** $b = 4, c = 5$ 3 **11.** $a = 24, c = 26$ 10 **12.** $b = 16, c = 20$ 12

**In Exercises 13–21, use the square root table on page 465 to write an approximation for $x$ to the nearest tenth.**

**Sample**

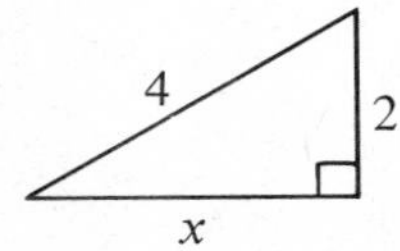


$4^2 = 2^2 + x^2$
$16 = 4 + x^2$
$12 = x^2$
$x = \sqrt{12} \doteq 3.5$

B **13.** 6.4

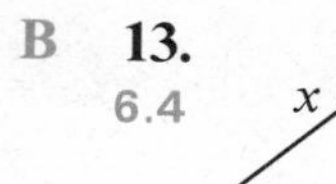


**14.** 5.3

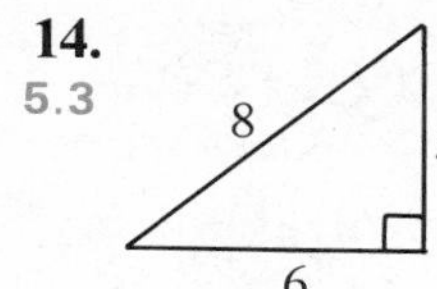


**15.** 7.8

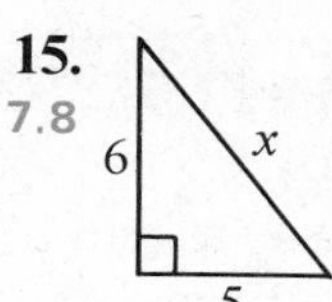


**16.** 5.7

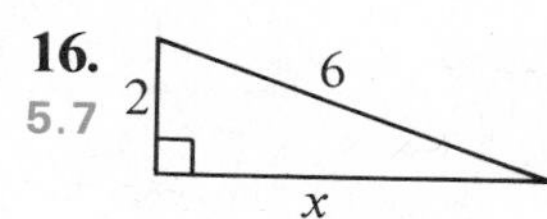


**17.** 5.2

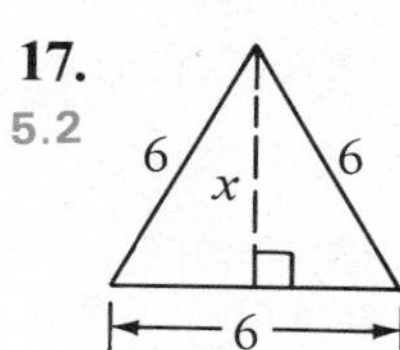


**18.** 6.9

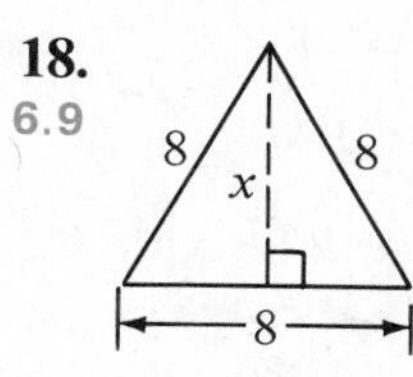


**19.** 7.1

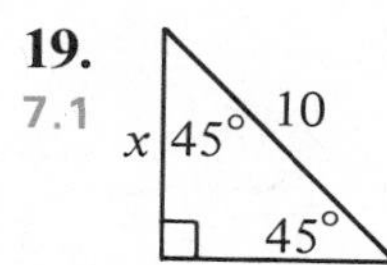


**20.** 8.5

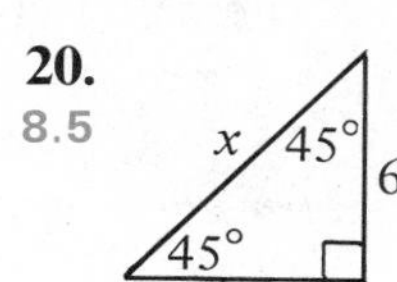


**21.** 7.2

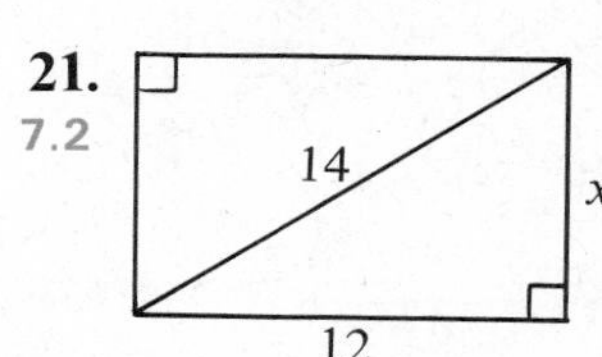


**In Exercises 22–27, use the square root table on page 465 to find an approximation for $x$ that is correct to the nearest tenth. Then find the area of each region.**

C **22.** $x \doteq 4.5$ $A \doteq 18$

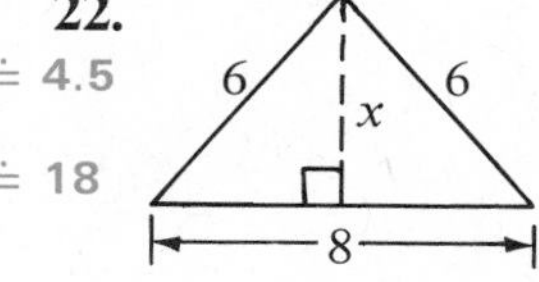


**23.** $x \doteq 7.2$ $A \doteq 86.4$

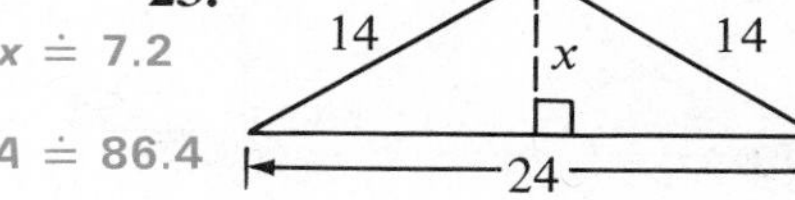


**24.** $x = 4$ $A = 32$

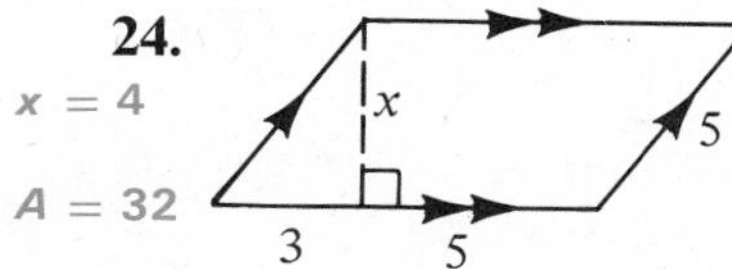


**25.** $x \doteq 6.4$ $A = 20$

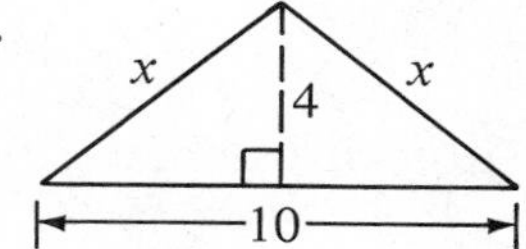


**26.** $x \doteq 7.4$ $A \doteq 33.3$

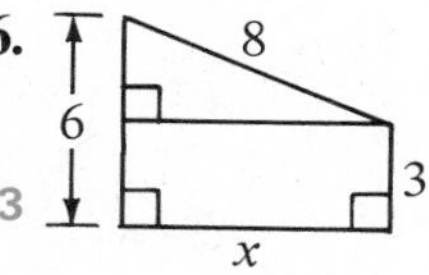


**27.** $x \doteq 3.9$ $A \doteq 66.3$

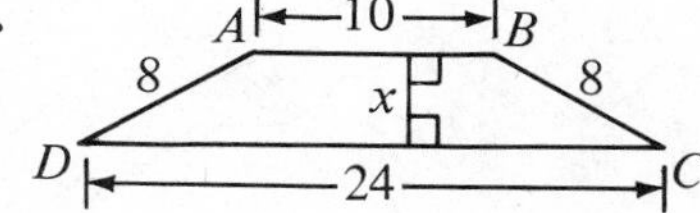


**28.** James A. Garfield (1831–1881), twentieth president of the United States, wrote a proof of the Pythagorean Theorem based on the diagram shown.

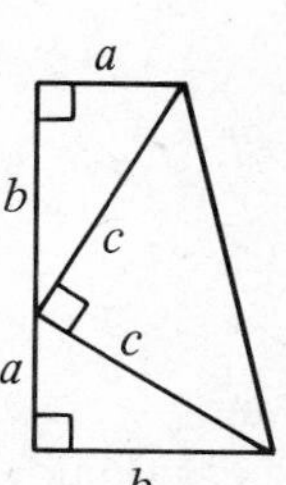


| Area of the trapezoid | = | Total area of 2 ≅ △s | + | Area of large rt. △ |
|---|---|---|---|---|
| ? | = | ? | + | ? |

Supply the missing measures in the equation above. Then simplify to show that $c^2 = a^2 + b^2$.

$\frac{1}{2}(a + b)(a + b) = 2\left(\frac{1}{2}ab\right) + \frac{1}{2}c^2$

# 6 • Converse of Pythagorean Theorem

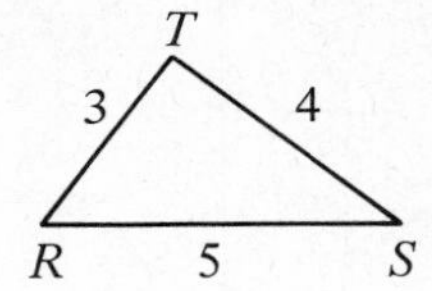


Suppose you are asked if $\triangle RST$, shown at the right, is a right triangle. You notice:

$$5^2 = 3^2 + 4^2 \text{ because}$$
$$25 = 9 + 16.$$

In order to conclude that $\triangle RST$ is a right triangle, you need to know whether the converse of the Pythagorean Theorem is true. Although some theorems have converses that are not true, the Pythagorean Theorem has a converse that *is* true. We omit the proof.

**THEOREM 6**

If the square of one side of a triangle is equal to the sum of the squares of the other two sides, then the triangle is a right triangle.

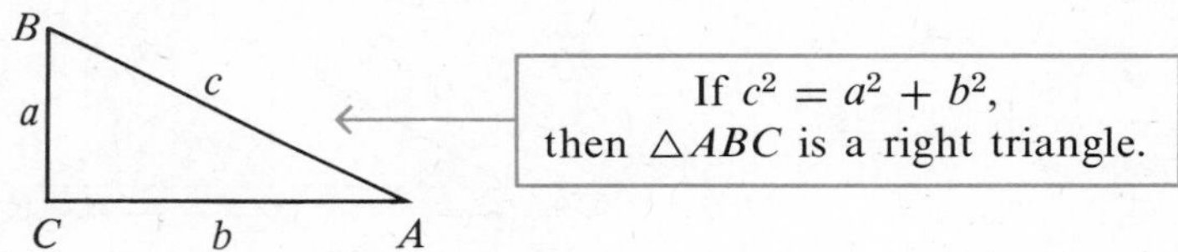


**EXAMPLE** Decide if each triangle shown is a right triangle.

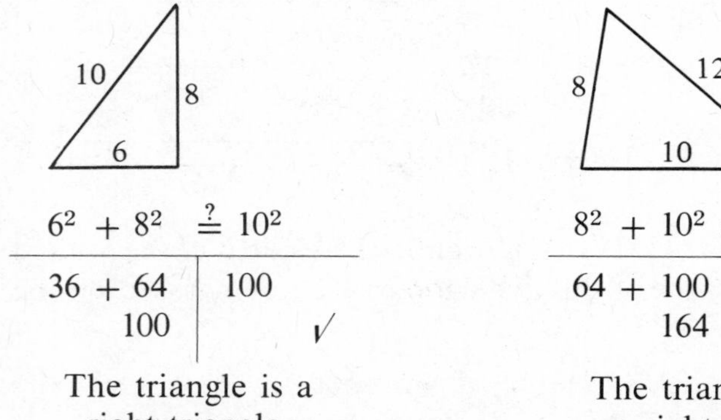


| $6^2 + 8^2 \stackrel{?}{=} 10^2$ | |
|---|---|
| $36 + 64$ | $100$ |
| $100$ | ✓ |

The triangle is a right triangle.

| $8^2 + 10^2 \stackrel{?}{=} 12^2$ | |
|---|---|
| $64 + 100$ | $144$ |
| $164$ | NO |

The triangle is not a right triangle.

When you know the lengths of the three sides of a triangle, you can easily decide whether the triangle is acute, right, or obtuse. Look at the strategy outlined on the next page.

### Strategy

1. Let $c$ be the longest side. Let $a$ and $b$ be the other two sides.
2. Compare $c^2$ to $a^2 + b^2$.
3. If $c^2 < a^2 + b^2$, then the triangle is acute.
   If $c^2 = a^2 + b^2$, then the triangle is a right triangle.
   If $c^2 > a^2 + b^2$, then the triangle is obtuse.

## *Classroom Practice*

**In each exercise, decide if the triangle is a right triangle. Explain your answers.**

**1.** Yes

40° 50°

**2.** No

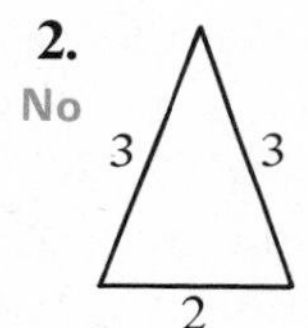


**3.** No

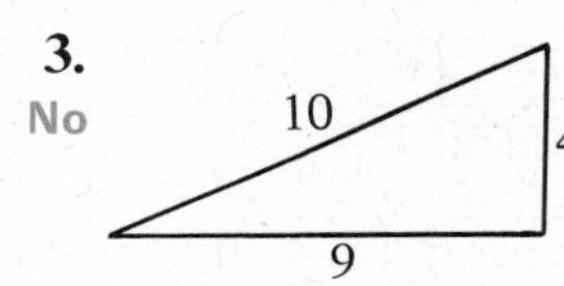


**4.** Yes

12 5 13

**5.** No

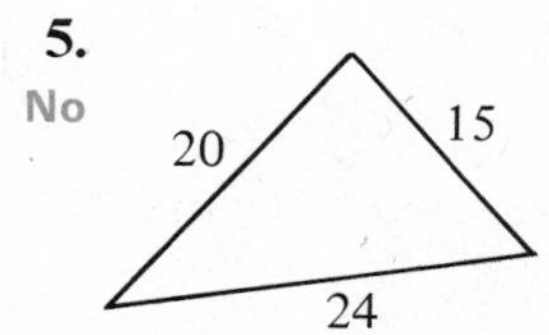


**6.** Yes

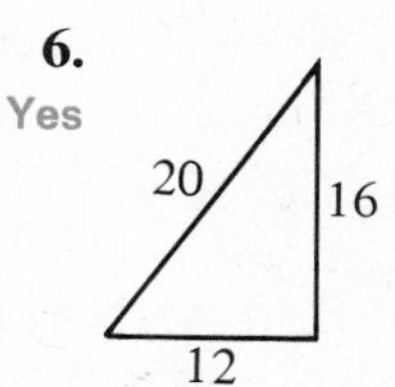


**In each exercise, decide if $\triangle ABC$ is a right triangle.**

**7.** $AB = 5$, $BC = 8$, $CA = 9$ No

**8.** $AB = 2$, $BC = 2$, $CA = 2$ No

**9.** $AB = 30$ cm, $BC = 40$ cm, $CA = 50$ cm Yes

**10.** To check the accuracy of a corner in a foundation you can measure 7 m out from $C$ to $A$, and 7 m out from $C$ to $B$. A string stretched from $A$ to $B$ should be about 10 cm less than 10 m long.

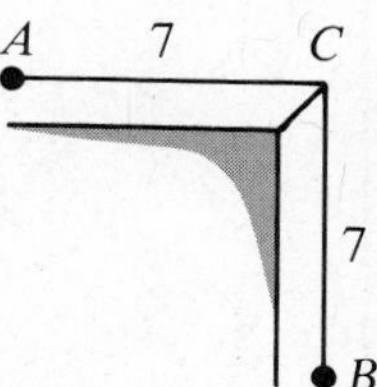


**a.** Suppose that $\overline{AB}$ is 10.1 m long. Is $\angle ACB$ an acute angle, a right angle, or an obtuse angle? obtuse

**b.** Suppose that $\overline{AB}$ is 9.8 m long. Is $\angle ACB$ an acute angle, a right angle, or an obtuse angle? acute

## Written Exercises

**Three sides of a triangle are given. Is the triangle a right triangle?**

A
1. 3, 4, 5 Yes
2. 30, 40, 50 Yes
3. 2, 3, 4 No
4. 4, 5, 6 No
5. 8, 15, 17 Yes
6. 4, 6, 8 No
7. 10, 15, 20 No
8. 7, 24, 25 Yes
9. 0.9, 1.2, 1.5 Yes
10. 0.5, 1.2, 1.3 Yes
11. 16, 21, 27 No
12. 14, 14, 20 No

**Three sides of a triangle are given. Classify the triangle as acute, right, or obtuse. (*Hint:* See the strategy on page 239.)**

B

| 13. | 14. | 15. | 16. | 17. | 18. | 19. |
|---|---|---|---|---|---|---|
| 6 | 7 | 10 | 7 | 11 | 15 | 12 |
| 8 | 7 | 10 | 11 | 60 | 16 | 21 |
| 10 | 10 | 14 | 16 | 61 | 21 | 25 |

13. right
14. obtuse
15. acute
16. obtuse
17. right
18. acute
19. obtuse

C
20. Suppose that $a$, $b$, and $c$ are the sides of a right triangle. Is a triangle with sides $7a$, $7b$, and $7c$ also a right triangle? Use algebra to show that your answer is correct. Yes

21. Repeat Exercise 20, using a triangle with sides $a + 7$, $b + 7$, and $c + 7$. No

22. Find the area of the quadrilateral shown. 36

23. Sketch $\square ABCD$ with $AB = 60$, $BC = 22$, and $AC = 64$. Which diagonal is longer: $\overline{AC}$ or $\overline{BD}$? $\overline{AC}$

24. Sketch $\square WXYZ$ with $WX = 5$, $WY = 6$, and $XZ = 8$. What special kind of parallelogram is $WXYZ$? rhombus

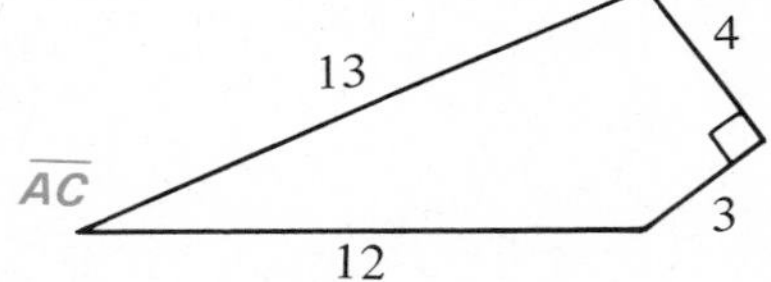


Exercise 22

FUNKY WINKERBEAN by Tom Batiuk. Reproduced through the courtesy of Field Newspaper Syndicate.

## SELF-TEST

**Find $x$.**

**1.** 10

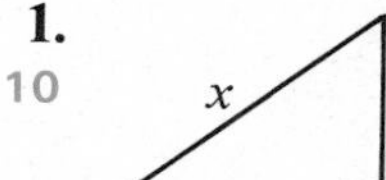


**2.** 4

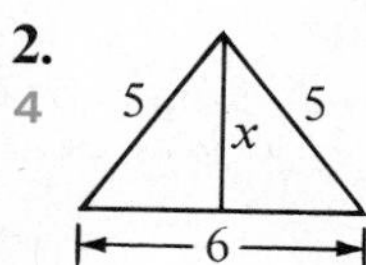


**3.** 10

26, $x$, 24

**4.** 50

40, 30, $x$

**The lengths of three sides of a triangle are given. Is the triangle a right triangle, an acute triangle, or an obtuse triangle?**

**5.** $a = 2, b = 3, c = 4$ obtuse

**6.** $a = 3, b = 4, c = 5$ right

**7.** $a = 6, b = 6, c = 6$ acute

**8.** $a = 2.1, b = 2.8, c = 3.5$ right

## Puzzles & Things

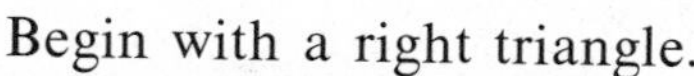

Begin with a right triangle.
Draw squares, as shown, and cut them out.

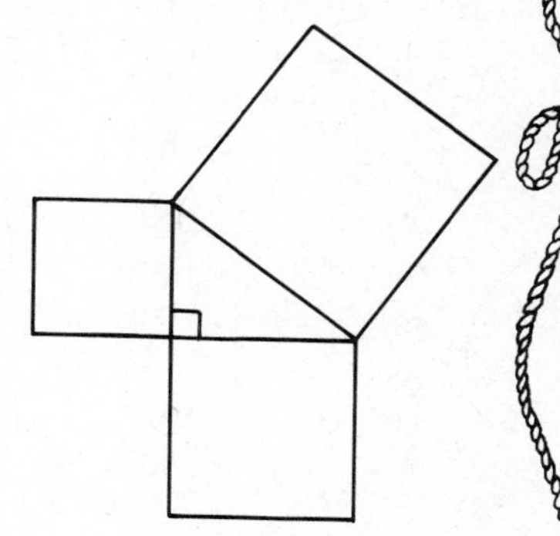

Place the two smaller squares next to one another.
Locate point $X$ so that $VX = AB$.
Cut along $\overline{AX}$ and $\overline{WX}$.
Try to rearrange the five pieces formed to cover the largest square.

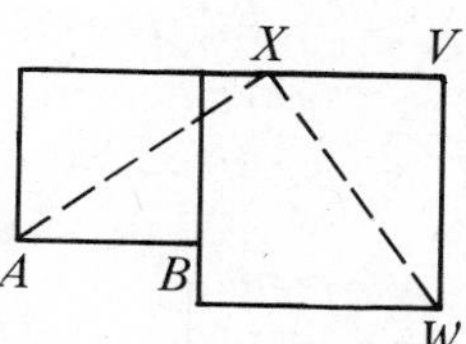

# 7 • Circumferences of Circles

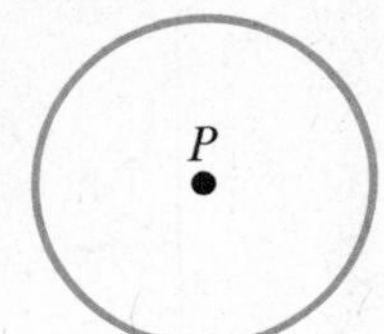


A **circle** is a figure, in a plane, whose points are all the same distance from a particular point in the plane. That point is called the **center** of the circle. Circle $P$ (written $\odot P$) is shown. The distance around $\odot P$ is called its **circumference.**

$\overline{PA}$, $\overline{PB}$, and $\overline{PC}$ are *radii* of $\odot P$. (The plural of radius is radii.) It follows from the definition of circle that *all radii of a circle are equal.*

$\overline{AC}$ is a *diameter* of $\odot P$. Can you see that any diameter of a circle is twice as long as a radius?

The words *radius* and *diameter* will refer sometimes to lengths of segments. We could say, for instance, that a circle has radius 5 and diameter 10.

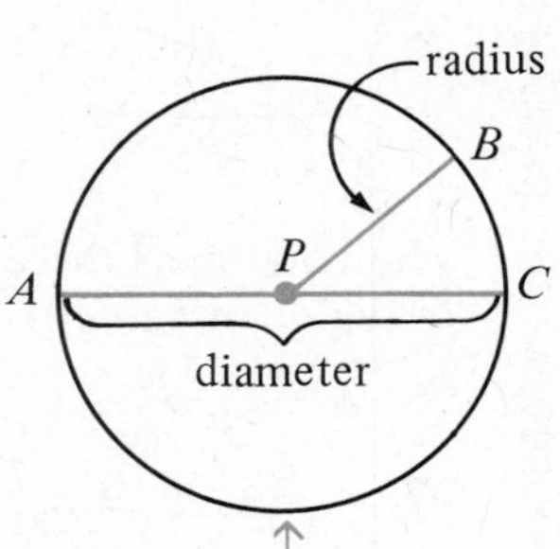


$PA = PB = PC; AC = 2(PA)$

A student measured the diameter of a half-dollar coin and reported: The diameter, $d$, is about 3.0 cm. Then she rolled the coin along a straight line until the coin had gone through one revolution.

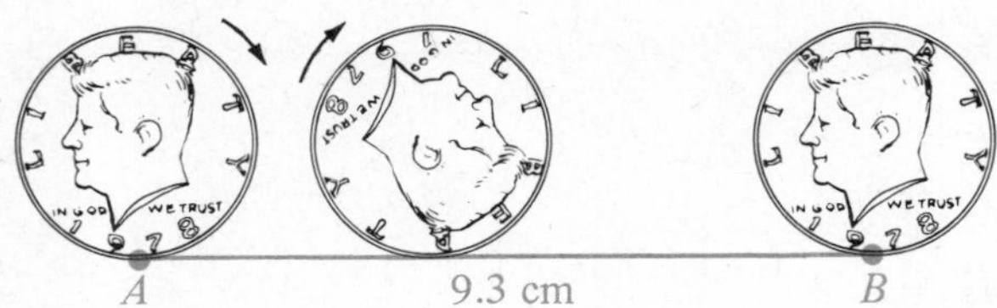


After measuring $\overline{AB}$ she reported: The circumference, $C$, is about 9.3 cm. Next she divided the circumference by the diameter, getting

$$\frac{9.3}{3.0}, \text{ or } 3.1. \leftarrow \boxed{\frac{C}{d} = 3.1}$$

Another student measured the diameter of a tin can. He found that the diameter was about 7.5 cm. The student then measured the distance around the rim of the can and said: The circumference is about 24.0 cm. In this case,

$$\frac{\text{circumference}}{\text{diameter}} = \frac{24.0}{7.5}, \text{ or } 3.2. \leftarrow \boxed{\frac{C}{d} = 3.2}$$

Notice that in the two cases on page 242 the values of $\frac{C}{d}$ are almost equal. Try this experiment yourself. Select some circular objects such as coins, plates, and wheels. For each object:

1. measure the diameter and the circumference;
2. divide the circumference by the diameter.

If you work carefully, you should find that $\frac{C}{d}$ is usually a little greater than 3. Mathematicians have shown that the quotient $\frac{C}{d}$ is *exactly* the same for all circles. This quotient is denoted by $\pi$, a Greek letter pronounced *pie*. By definition,

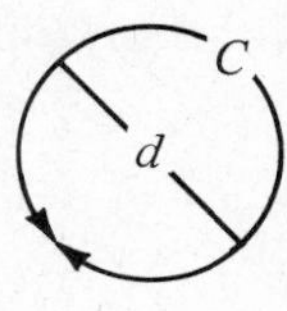


$$\pi = \frac{C}{d}.$$

The value of $\pi$ has been computed to thousands of decimal places. Some approximations in common use are the following:

$\pi \doteq 3.14$ $\quad\quad$ $\pi \doteq 3.1416$ $\quad\quad$ $\pi \doteq \frac{22}{7}$

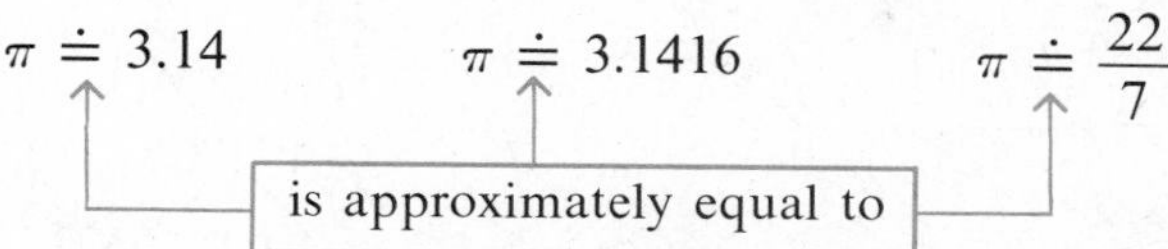


None of these is exact. Unless specified otherwise, you may use any approximation that is convenient.

In a circle with radius $r$, diameter $d$, and circumference $C$:

$$\frac{C}{d} = \pi$$
$$C = \pi d$$
$$C = \pi \times 2r \leftarrow \boxed{d = 2r}$$
$$C = 2\pi r$$

The circumference of a circle is given by the formula:

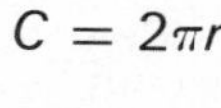

$$C = 2\pi r$$

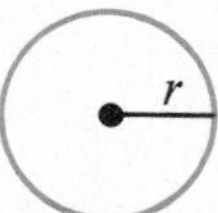

**EXAMPLE** Find the circumference of a circle with radius 4 cm. Round your answer to the nearest tenth.

$C = 2\pi r$

$C = 2\pi \times 4 = 8\pi$ ← Exact answer: $8\pi$ cm

$C = 8\pi \doteq 8 \times 3.14 = 25.12$ ← Approximate answer: 25.1 cm

Note that the exact circumference of a circle is expressed in terms of $\pi$. To find an approximate value, use an approximation of $\pi$.

## Classroom Practice

**Exercises 1–8 refer to the diagram below.**

1. Name the circle shown. $\odot O$
2. Name the center of the circle. $O$
3. Name all the radii shown. $\overline{OA}, \overline{OB}, \overline{OC}$
4. Name all the diameters shown. $\overline{AC}$
5. If $OC = 8$, then $OB =$ _?_. 8
6. If $OC = 3$, then $AC =$ _?_. 6
7. If $AC = 2x$, then $OB =$ _?_. $x$
8. If a radius of the circle is 2 cm long, then the circumference of the circle is _?_. $4\pi$

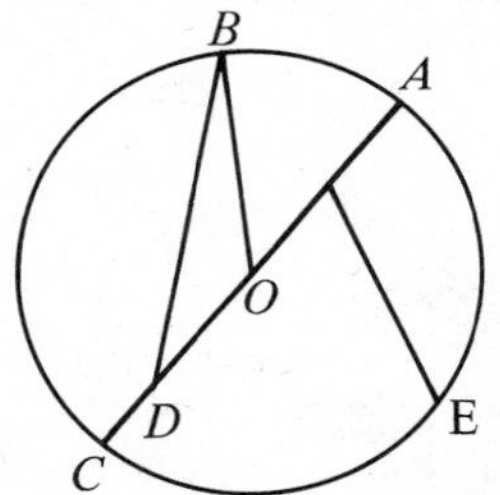


**Find the circumference of a circle with the given radius. Express your answers in terms of $\pi$.**

9.

| $r$ | 3 | 6 |
|---|---|---|
| $C$ | $6\pi$ | ? |

$12\pi$

10. $22\pi$ $44\pi$

| $r$ | 11 | 22 |
|---|---|---|
| $C$ | ? | ? |

11. $2j\pi$ $4j\pi$

| $r$ | $j$ | $2j$ |
|---|---|---|
| $C$ | ? | ? |

12. Complete the statement suggested by Exercises 9–11:
    If the radius of one circle is twice as. . . . great as that of a second circle, the circumference of the first circle is twice that of the second circle.

**Find the circumference of a circle with the given radius. Express your answers in terms of $\pi$.**

13.

| $r$ | 1 | 8 |
|---|---|---|
| $C$ | ? | ? |

$2\pi$ $16\pi$

14.

| $r$ | 1 | 13 |
|---|---|---|
| $C$ | ? | ? |

$2\pi$ $26\pi$

15.

| $r$ | 5 | $5k$ |
|---|---|---|
| $C$ | ? | ? |

$10\pi$ $10k\pi$

16. Complete the statement suggested by Exercises 13–15:
    If the radius of one circle is $k$ times as. . . . great as that of a second circle, the circumference of the first circle is $k$ times that of the second circle.

## Written Exercises

**In Exercises 1–4, the radius of a circle is given. Find the diameter.**

A **1.** 7 14 **2.** 12 m 24 m **3.** 5.1 cm 10.2 cm **4.** $x$ $2x$

**In Exercises 5–8, the diameter of a circle is given. Find the radius.**

**5.** 16 cm 8 cm **6.** 26 13 **7.** 21.6 10.8 **8.** $2y$ $y$

**In Exercises 9–17, find the circumference of a circle with the given radius *r* or diameter *d*. Express your answers in terms of $\pi$.**

Sample 1 $d = 4$ cm $C = \pi d$

$C = \pi \times 4 = 4\pi$

**9.** $d = 10$ $10\pi$ **10.** $d = 13$ $13\pi$ **11.** $r = 6$ $12\pi$

**12.** $d = 9.7$ m $9.7\pi$ m **13.** $d = 33$ m $33\pi$ m **14.** $r = 7.5$ cm $15\pi$ cm

**15.** $r = 0.4$ km $0.8\pi$ km **16.** $r = 16$ cm $32\pi$ cm **17.** $r = 18.4$ km $36.8\pi$ km

**In Exercises 18–23, find the radius of a circle with the given circumference.**

Sample 2 $C = 12\pi$ $C = 2\pi r$

$12\pi = 2\pi r$ ← Divide each side by $2\pi$.

$6 = r$

**18.** $C = 16\pi$ 8 **19.** $C = 2\pi$ 1 **20.** $C = 61\pi$ cm 30.5 cm

**21.** $C = 25\pi$ m 12.5 m **22.** $C = 46\pi$ cm 23 cm **23.** $C = 53\pi$ m 26.5 m

**In Exercises 24–29, find an approximation, correct to the nearest tenth, of the circumference of a circle with the given radius. Use 3.14 for $\pi$.**

B **24.** $r = 8$ cm 50.2 cm **25.** $r = 15$ m 94.2 m **26.** $r = 8.6$ cm 54.0 cm

**27.** $r = 2.1$ km 13.2 km **28.** $r = 37$ m 232.4 m **29.** $r = 6.5$ m 40.8 m

**In Exercises 30–35, find an approximation, correct to the nearest tenth, of the radius of a circle with the given circumference. Use 3.14 for $\pi$.**

**30.** $C = 31.4$ m 5 m **31.** $C = 314$ cm 50 cm **32.** $C = 1.57$ m 0.25 m

**33.** $C = 20$ cm 3.2 cm **34.** $C = 27.5$ cm 4.4 cm **35.** $C = 9.4$ km 1.5 km

**36.** Draw two circles. Then construct a circle whose circumference is equal to the sum of the circumferences of the given circles.

*Strategy:*

A. Let the radii of the given circles be $s$ and $t$.
B. $2\pi s + 2\pi t = 2\pi(s + t)$
C. Construct a segment with length $s + t$.
D. Construct a circle with radius $s + t$.

**In Exercises 37–39, use 3.14 for $\pi$. Write each answer correct to the nearest centimeter.**

C **37.** The radii of two circles are 10 cm and 11 cm. By how many centimeters is the circumference of the larger circle greater than the circumference of the smaller circle? 6.3 cm

**38.** Repeat Exercise 37, using circles with radii 100 cm and 101 cm. 6.3 cm

**39.** Wheels revolving in opposite directions have a drive belt as shown. Find the total length of the belt. 1074 cm

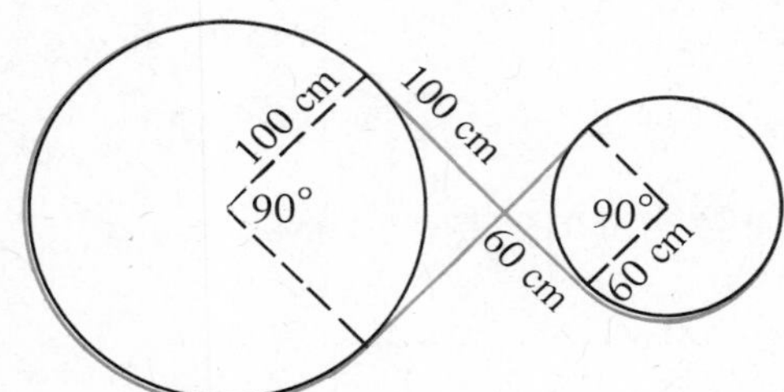


*Suggested strategy:*

A. $360° - 90° = 270°$

The belt covers $\frac{270}{360}$, or $\frac{3}{4}$ of the smaller wheel.

B. The belt covers $\frac{3}{4}$ of the larger wheel.

C. Add the parts to find the total length of the belt.

**40.** Look back at Experiment 2 on page 2 of Chapter 1. Now you can show that the distance between the earth and the stretched hoop is about 32 cm. Here is one way to do it.

**a.** Suppose the radius of the earth is $r$ meters.
Explain why the stretched hoop has circumference $2\pi r + 2$.

**b.** Let $R$ be the radius of the stretched hoop.
Explain why $2\pi R = 2\pi r + 2$.

**c.** Conclude that $2\pi(R - r) = 2$,

and that $$R - r = \frac{2}{2\pi} \doteq \frac{2}{2(3.14)} \doteq 0.32$$

0.32 m = __?__ cm, the distance between the earth and the hoop. 32

**d.** Make a sketch showing the stretched hoop around the earth. Show $R$, $r$, and $R - r$ on your sketch.

## 8 • Areas of Circles

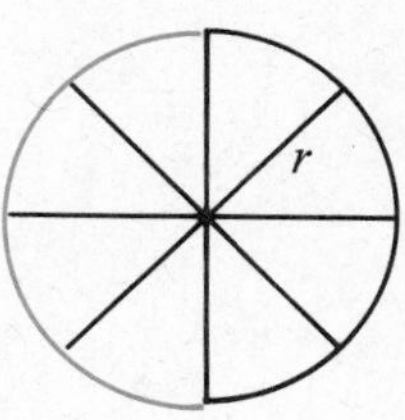


The diagram represents an apple pie cut into eight equal pieces. Suppose you rearrange these eight pieces as shown below. Notice that the figure formed resembles a parallelogram.

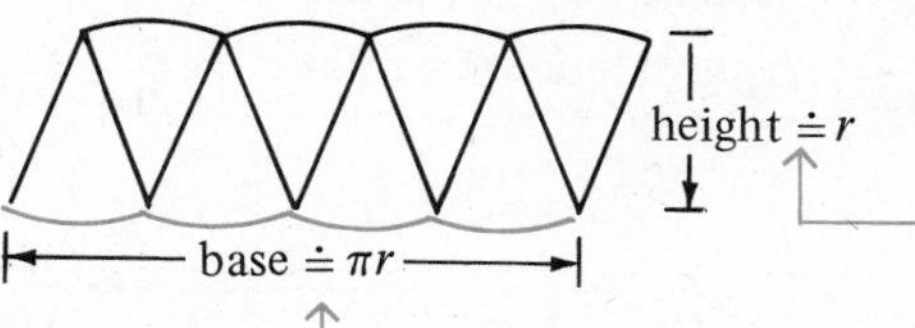


The "height" is approximately equal to $r$, the radius of the circular pie.

The "base" is approximately equal to half the circumference of the circular pie.

$$\begin{aligned} \text{Area of eight pieces of pie} &\doteq \text{Area of parallelogram} \\ &= \text{base} \times \text{height} \\ &\doteq \pi r \times r \\ &= \pi r^2 \end{aligned}$$

Now suppose you cut the pie into sixteen equal pieces, instead of eight.

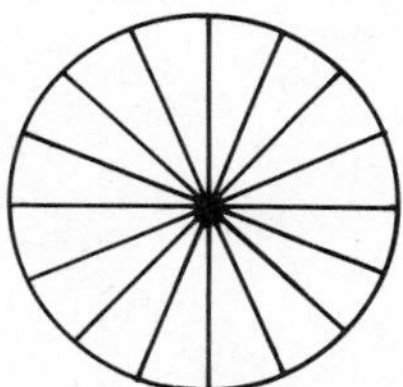

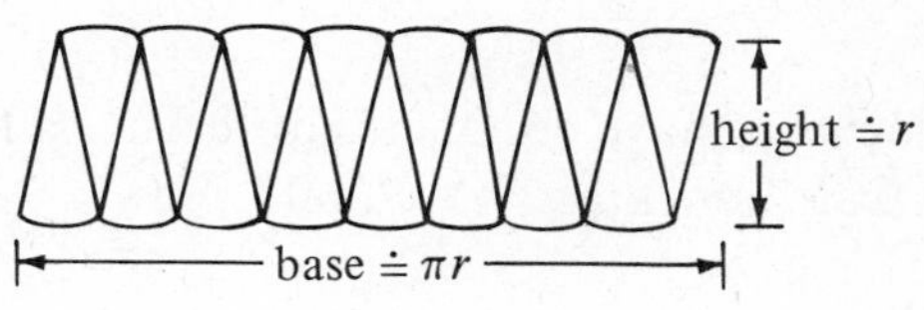


The figure formed looks even more like a parallelogram than the first one does. This means that the base is more nearly equal to $\pi r$. The area is more nearly equal to $\pi r^2$.

The discussion above suggests that $\pi r^2$ is approximately equal to the area of a circle with radius $r$. It can be proved, in an advanced geometry course, that $\pi r^2$ is the *exact* area.

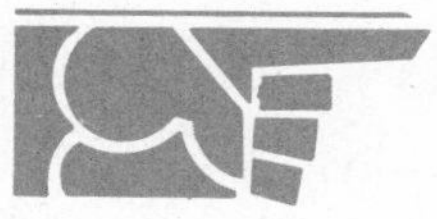

The area of a circle is given by the formula:

$$A = \pi r^2$$

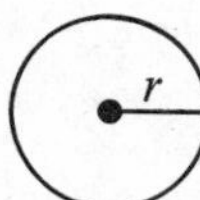

EXAMPLE Find an approximation, correct to tenths, of the area of a circle with diameter 6 m.

Since the diameter is 6 m, the radius is 3 m.

$A = \pi r^2$

$A = \pi \times 3^2 = \pi \times 9 = 9\pi$ ← Exact area: $9\pi$ m²

$A = 9\pi \doteq 9 \times 3.14 = 28.26$ ← Approximate area: 28.3 m²

## Classroom Practice

**Exercises 1–8 refer to a circle with radius $r$, diameter $d$, circumference $C$, and area $A$. Find the missing measures.** (See page T127.)

| | 1. | 2. | 3. | 4. | 5. | 6. | 7. | 8. |
|---|---|---|---|---|---|---|---|---|
| $r$ | 5 | 9 | ? | ? | ? | ? | ? | ? |
| $d$ | ? | ? | 8 | 16 | ? | ? | ? | ? |
| $C$ | ? | ? | ? | ? | $28\pi$ | $12\pi$ | ? | ? |
| $A$ | ? | ? | ? | ? | ? | ? | $4\pi$ | $\pi$ |

9. Suppose two circles have equal circumferences. Must their radii be equal? Must their areas be equal?
Yes Yes

## Written Exercises

**Find the area of a circle with the given radius or diameter. Express your answers in terms of $\pi$.**

A

1. $r = 5$ $25\pi$
2. $r = 9$ $81\pi$
3. $d = 6$ $9\pi$
4. $d = 8$ cm $16\pi$ cm²
5. $r = 1.2$ cm $1.44\pi$ cm²
6. $r = 3.5$ m $12.25\pi$ m²
7. $d = 7$ cm $12.25\pi$ cm²
8. $d = 2.6$ m $1.69\pi$ m²
9. $r = 5\frac{5}{6}$ $\frac{1225}{36}\pi$

**Find the radius of a circle with the given area.**

Sample 1 $A = 49\pi$ cm²

$$A = \pi r^2$$
$$49\pi = \pi r^2$$
$$49 = r^2$$
$$7 = r$$

*Answer:* 7 cm

10. $A = 36\pi$ 6
11. $A = 25\pi$ 5
12. $A = 9\pi\ m^2$ 3 m
13. $A = 81\pi\ cm^2$ 9 cm
14. $A = 100\pi\ cm^2$ 10 cm
15. $A = 64\pi\ cm^2$ 8 cm

**Find an approximation, to the nearest tenth, of the area of a circle with the given radius or diameter. Use 3.14 for $\pi$.**

B 16. $r = 6$ 113.0
17. $r = 7$ 153.9
18. $r = 3$ m 28.3 $m^2$
19. $r = 1.2$ cm 4.5 $cm^2$
20. $d = 1.4$ km 1.5 $km^2$
21. $d = 17$ cm 226.9 $cm^2$

**Find the exact area of a circle with the given circumference.**

Sample 2 $C = 8\pi$

1. Find $r$.

$$2\pi r = 8\pi$$
$$r = \frac{8\pi}{2\pi}$$
$$r = 4$$

2. Find the area.

$$A = \pi r^2$$
$$A = \pi(4^2) = 16\pi$$

22. $C = 14\pi$ $49\pi$
23. $C = 48\pi$ $576\pi$
24. $C = 16\pi$ $64\pi$
25. $C = 11\pi$ $30.25\pi$

26. The area of a circle is $4\pi\ m^2$. Find the circumference. $4\pi$ m

27. The area of a circle is $\frac{49}{4}\pi\ cm^2$. Find the circumference. $7\pi$ cm

**Find the area of the shaded region in terms of $\pi$.**

C 28. $16\pi$

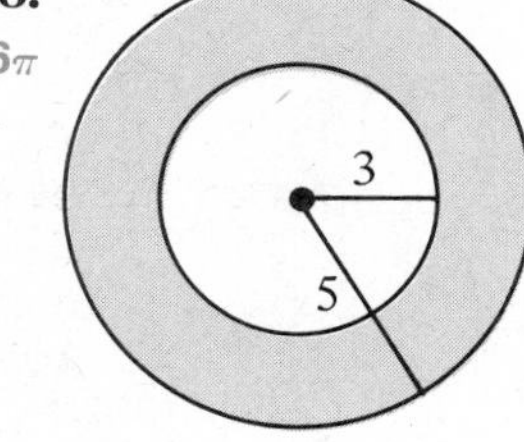


29. $25\pi - 50$

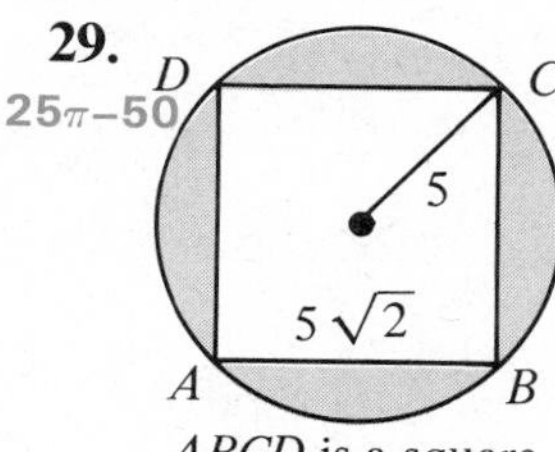

*ABCD* is a square.

30. $68 - 16\pi$

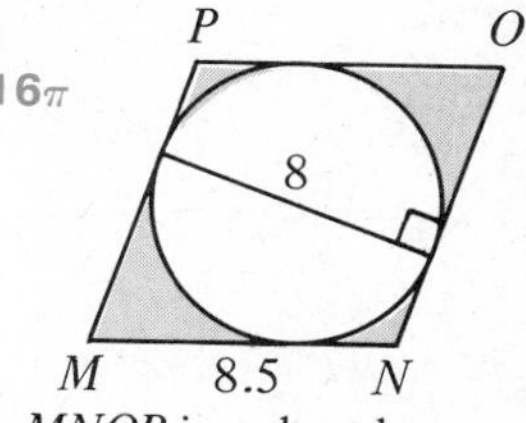

*MNOP* is a rhombus.

31. $15\pi$

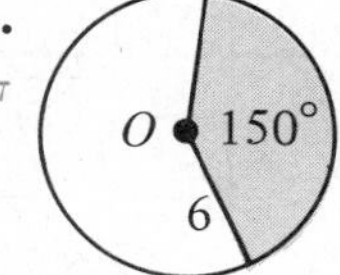


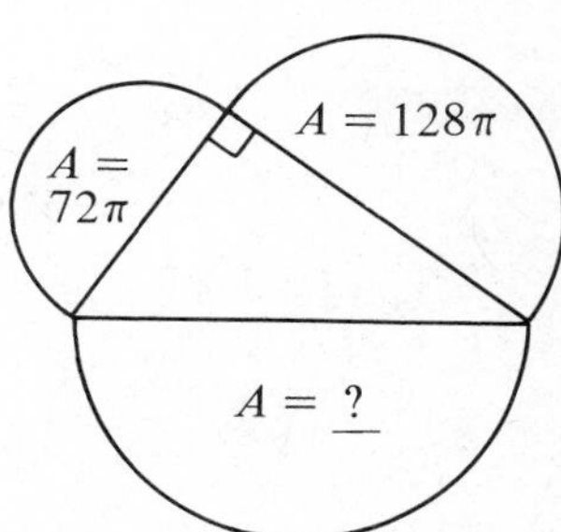


32. If $72\pi$ and $128\pi$ are the areas of the indicated semicircles, find the area of the largest semicircle. $200\pi$

**33.** Draw two circles. Then construct a circle whose area is equal to the sum of the areas of the given circles.

*Strategy:*

A. Let the radii of the given circles be $s$ and $t$.
B. $\pi s^2 + \pi t^2 = \pi(s^2 + t^2)$
C. Construct a right triangle with legs $s$ and $t$. Let the hypotenuse be $r$. Then $r^2 = s^2 + t^2$.
D. Construct a circle with radius $r$.

## SELF-TEST

**1.** Complete: By definition, $\pi = \frac{?}{?}$. $\frac{C}{d}$

**2.** Write an approximation for $\pi$ that is correct to the nearest hundredth. 3.14

**Copy and complete the table about circles. Some answers may be given in terms of $\pi$.**

| | **3.** | **4.** | **5.** | **6.** |
|---|---|---|---|---|
| radius $r$ | 5 | ? | ? | ? |
| diameter $d$ | ? | 16 | ? | ? |
| circumference $C$ | ? | ? | $20\pi$ | ? |
| area $A$ | ? | ? | ? | $36\pi$ |

3. $d = 10$; $C = 10\pi$; $A = 25\pi$
4. $r = 8$; $C = 16\pi$; $A = 64\pi$
5. $r = 10$; $d = 20$; $A = 100\pi$
6. $r = 6$; $d = 12$; $C = 12\pi$

## Reviewing Algebraic Skills

**Solve.**

Samples

$$\frac{2x}{5} + 1 = 9$$
$$\frac{2x}{5} + 1 - 1 = 9 - 1$$
$$\frac{2x}{5} = \frac{8}{1}$$
$$2x = 40$$
$$x = 20$$

$$0.12x = 3$$
$$100 \times 0.12x = 100 \times 3$$
$$12x = 300$$
$$x = 25$$

$$\frac{n}{2} + \frac{n}{5} = 7$$
$$\frac{5n}{10} + \frac{2n}{10} = 7$$
$$\frac{5n + 2n}{10} = 7$$
$$\frac{7n}{10} = \frac{7}{1}$$
$$7n = 70$$
$$n = 10$$

**Solve.**

1. $\frac{a}{9} + 3 = 13$ 90
2. $30 + \frac{d}{4} = 51$ 84
3. $\frac{b}{2} + 17 = 0$ $-34$
4. $0.6x = 42$ 70
5. $0.25y = 3.5$ 14
6. $78 = 1.3m$ 60
7. $\frac{2n}{3} = \frac{4}{7}$ $\frac{6}{7}$
8. $\frac{3x}{5} + 2 = 11$ 15
9. $\frac{5b}{2} - 12 = -7$ 2
10. $\frac{k}{2} + \frac{k}{4} = 9$ 12
11. $\frac{c}{3} - \frac{2c}{9} = \frac{1}{6}$ $\frac{3}{2}$
12. $\frac{3m}{10} - \frac{m}{2} = 4$ $-20$
13. $\frac{1}{4} + \frac{2}{3} = \frac{a}{6}$ $5\frac{1}{2}$
14. $\frac{2m}{3} + \frac{m}{2} = \frac{7}{2}$ 3
15. $\frac{4k}{5} - \frac{2k}{3} = -4$ $-30$

**Write an equation. Then solve.**

16. When half a number is subtracted from 3 times the number, the difference is 15. What is the number? 6
17. Bart is 97 cm tall. He is 4 cm more than $\frac{3}{5}$ as tall as his sister Lucy is. How tall is Lucy? 155 cm
18. One day the Corner Bookshop sold 17 cookbooks. This was $\frac{1}{8}$ of all the books sold that day. How many books did the shop sell in all? 136

# extra for experts

## *Line Symmetry*

Look at the letter A shown here. If we were to fold this letter along line *l*, one side would fit exactly on the other. We say that this letter has *symmetry* with respect to line *l*. We call line *l* an *axis of symmetry*.

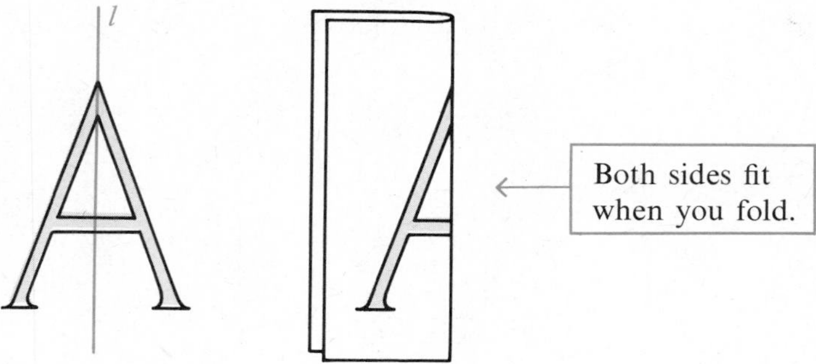


Not all types of lettering are alike. Let's consider a second letter A. Does this letter have an axis of symmetry? No. No matter what line we choose for our fold, we cannot make the opposite sides fit exactly.

Now consider the letter H shown here. Do you see that line *l* and line *m* are both axes of symmetry for this letter? We could fold the letter along either line and the opposite sides would fit. As you can see, some figures have more than one axis of symmetry.

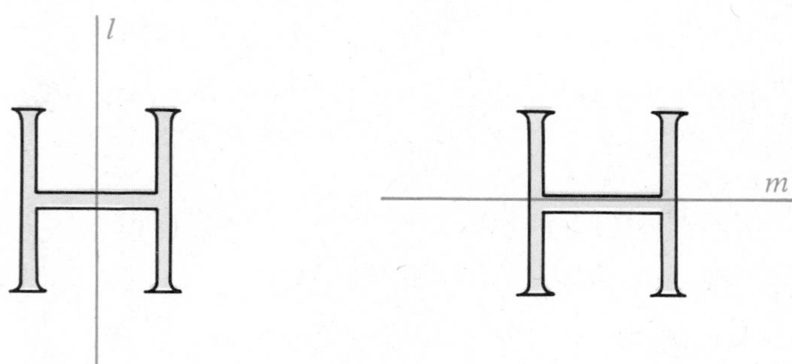

The examples of traditional Mexican art shown here were cut from folded, handmade paper. Notice the symmetry that results.

**Exercises**

These symbols were used by alchemists during the Middle Ages to represent copper, lead, and tin, respectively. How many axes of symmetry does each symbol have?

**1.** 2

**2.** 2
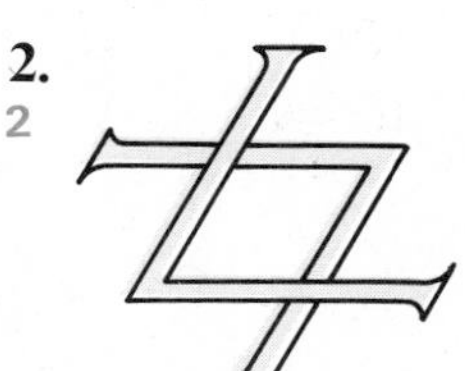

**3.** 2
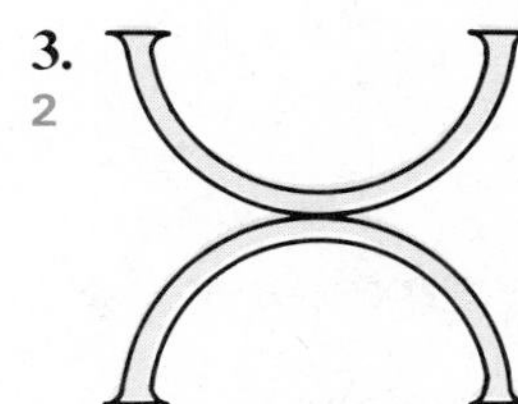

Does each of the following figures *always, sometimes,* or *never* have an axis of symmetry?

**4.** Triangle sometimes

**5.** Parallelogram sometimes

**6.** Rhombus always

**7.** Circle always

**8.** How many axes of symmetry does a regular hexagon have? 6

## Reviewing the Chapter

### Chapter Summary

1. The following formulas for area can be used.

**Rectangle**
$A = bh$

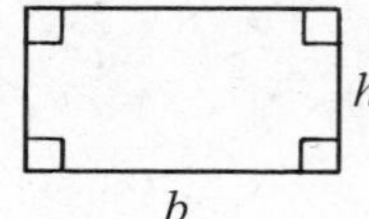


**Square**
$A = s^2$

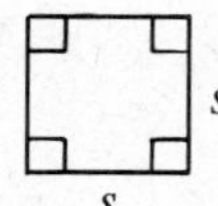


**Parallelogram**
$A = bh$

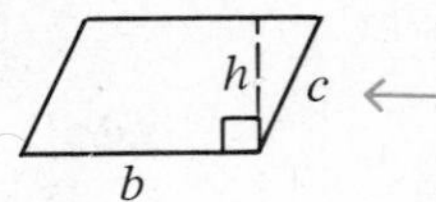


Unless a parallelogram is also a rectangle, $h \neq c$.

**Triangle**
$A = \frac{1}{2}bh$

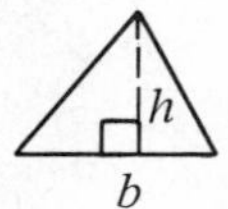


**Trapezoid**
$A = \frac{1}{2}h(b_1 + b_2)$

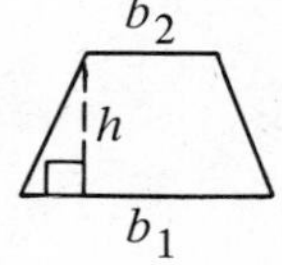


2. The Pythagorean Theorem states:
In any right triangle, the square of the hypotenuse is equal to the sum of the squares of the legs.
If $\triangle ABC$ is a right triangle, then $c^2 = a^2 + b^2$.

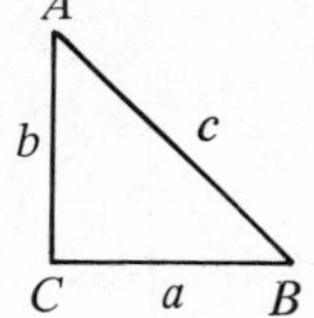


3. The converse of the Pythagorean Theorem is true.
If $c^2 = a^2 + b^2$, then $\triangle ABC$ is a right triangle.

4. For any circle: $C = 2\pi r$ and $A = \pi r^2$.

### Chapter Review Test

**Copy and complete the table about rectangles.** (*See pp. 216–220.*)

| | 1. | 2. | 3. | 4. |
|---|---|---|---|---|
| base $b$ | 5 | 30 | 7 | 7.2 |
| height $h$ | 2 | 20 | ? | 4 |
| perimeter $p$ | ? | ? | ? | ? |
| area $A$ | ? | ? | 49 | ? |

1. $p = 14$; $A = 10$
2. $p = 100$; $A = 600$
3. $h = 7$; $p = 28$
4. $p = 22.4$; $A = 28.8$

Find the area of the shaded region. (*See pp. 221–227.*)

**5.** 50

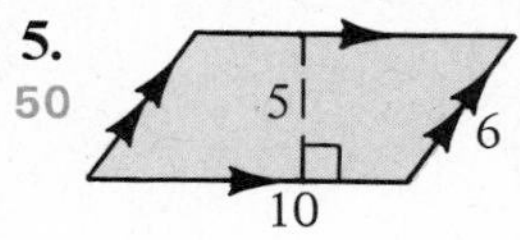


**6.** 42

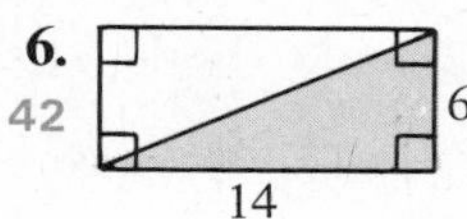


**7.** 45

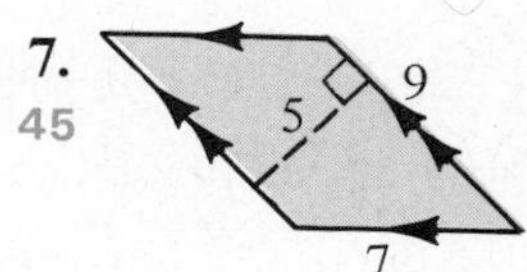


**8.** 36

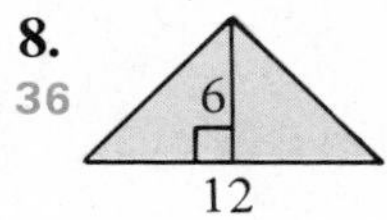


**9.** 44

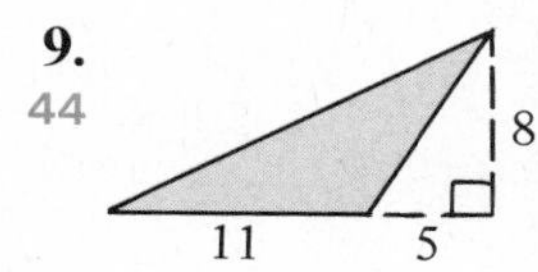


**10.** 96

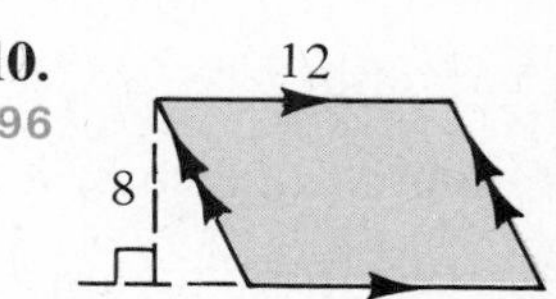


Copy and complete the table about trapezoids. (*See pp. 229–233.*)

| | **11.** | **12.** | **13.** | **14.** | |
|---|---|---|---|---|---|
| base length $b_1$ | 12 | 11 | 8.3 | 7 | |
| base length $b_2$ | 8 | 6 | 4.5 | 5 | |
| height $h$ | 5 | 4 | 5 | __?__ | 4 |
| area $A$ | __?__ | __?__ | __?__ | 24 | |
| | 50 | 34 | 32 | | |

In each exercise, find $x$. (*See pp. 234–237.*)

**15.** 10

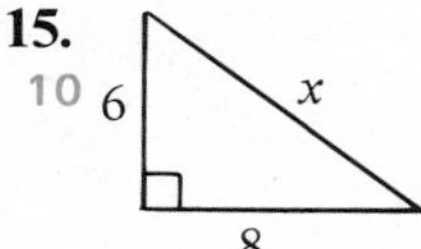


**16.** 9

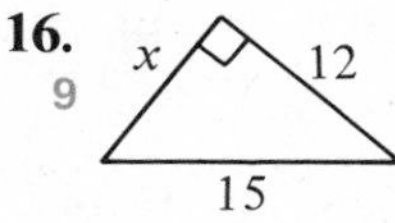


**17.** 3

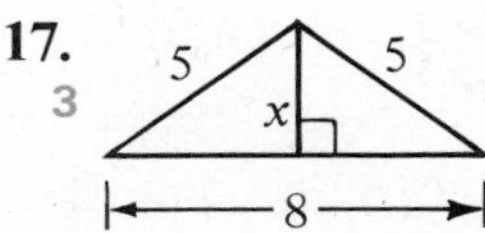


The lengths of the sides of a triangle are given. State whether the triangle is acute, right, or obtuse. (*See pp. 238–240.*)

**18.** 4, 5, 8 obtuse

**19.** 11, 60, 61 right

**20.** 8, 8, 8 acute

Complete the statements about circles. (*See pp. 242–250.*)

**21.** If $d = 12$, then $C =$ __?__. Answer in terms of $\pi$. $12\pi$

**22.** If $C = 18\pi$, then $r =$ __?__. 9

**23.** If $r = 5$, then $A =$ __?__. Answer in terms of $\pi$. $25\pi$

**24.** If $d = 8$, then $A =$ __?__. 50.2
Use 3.14 for $\pi$ and round your answer to tenths.

**25.** If $r = 12$, then $C =$ __?__. 75.4
Use 3.14 for $\pi$ and round your answer to tenths.

**26.** If $A = 81\pi$, then $r =$ __?__. 9

# Cumulative Review / Unit C

**Complete using *always, sometimes,* or *never*.**

1. An equilateral triangle is __?__ a regular polygon. always
2. The angle sum of a pentagon is __?__ 540°. always
3. A parallelogram is __?__ a square. sometimes
4. A rhombus is __?__ a parallelogram. always
5. Opposite angles of a quadrilateral are __?__ equal. sometimes
6. Consecutive angles of a parallelogram are __?__ complementary. never
7. The diagonals of a quadrilateral __?__ bisect each other. sometimes
8. The diagonals of a rectangle are __?__ equal. always

**Complete.**

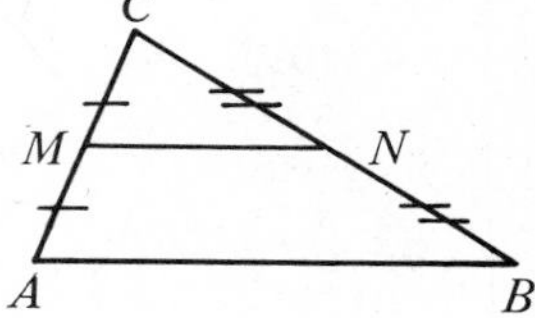


9. In rhombus $JKLM$, $\overline{MK}$ __?__ $\overline{LJ}$. ⊥
10. In $\triangle ABC$ at the right, $MN =$ __?__. $\frac{1}{2}AB$
11. In parallelogram $QRST$, $QR =$ __?__ TS and $QT =$ __?__ RS.
12. The median of a trapezoid is __?__ to the bases. parallel
13. If $M$ is the midpoint of hypotenuse $\overline{DE}$ in right $\triangle DEF$, then $MD =$ __?__ $=$ __?__. MF ME
14. A quadrilateral must be a parallelogram if one pair of opposite sides are both __?__ and __?__. parallel equal

**Find the area. Use 3.14 for $\pi$ and round to the nearest tenth.**

15. 78

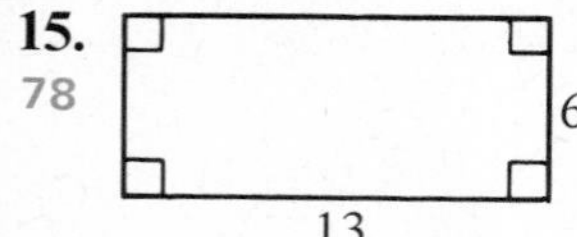


16. 17.6 cm²

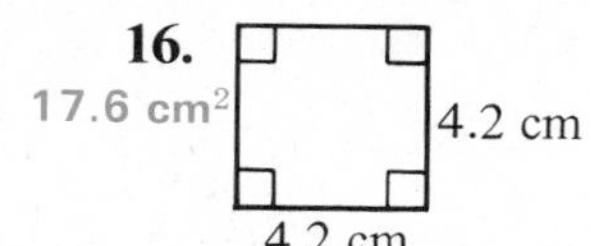


17. 40

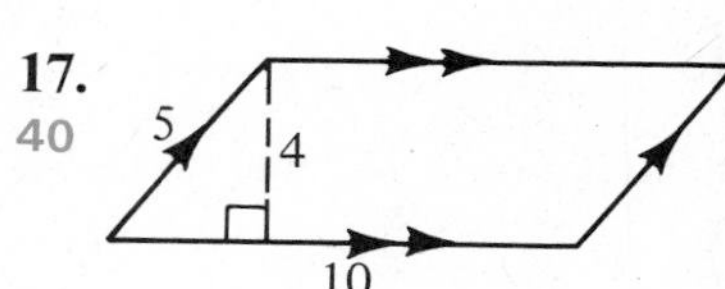


18. 125 m²

10 m

25 m

19. 48 m²

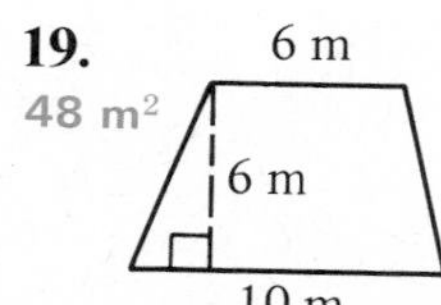


20. 379.9

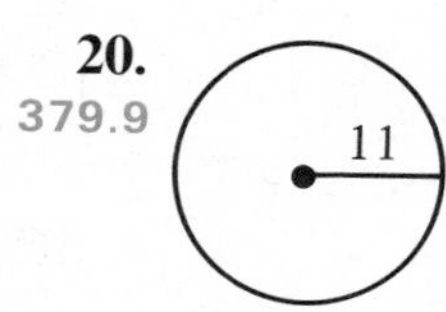


21. Is a triangle with sides 3 m, 4 m, and 6 m a right triangle? No (obtuse)
22. Find the exact circumference of a circle with radius 6 m. $12\pi$ m

# UNIT D

## *Here's what you'll learn in this chapter:*

1. To find the ratio of two numbers.
2. To write proportions in several forms.
3. To solve problems using proportions.
4. To make maps and scale drawings.

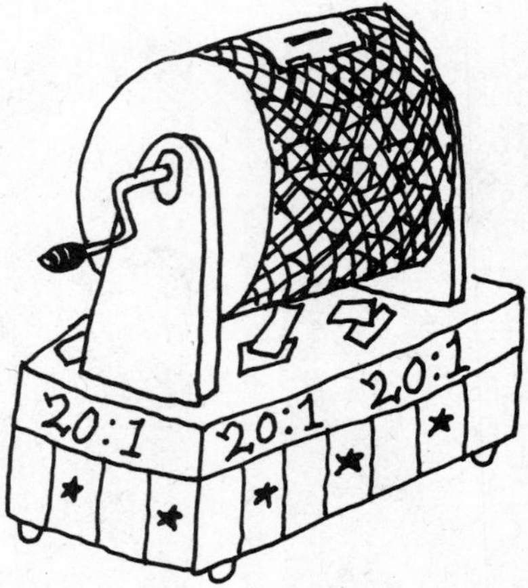

# Chapter 7

# Ratios and Proportions

## 1 • Ratios

In this chapter and the next, we'll see how ratios and proportions are used by mapmakers, technical artists, and commercial photographers. Before doing so, however, we must review what is meant by *ratio*. In the next section, we'll review proportions.

The **ratio** of two numbers is the quotient of the two numbers.

| Ratio | Written Forms |
|---|---|
| 2 to 3 | $\frac{2}{3}$ or 2:3 |
| 5 to 1 | $\frac{5}{1}$ or 5:1 |
| $a$ to $b$, $b \neq 0$ | $\frac{a}{b}$ or $a{:}b$ |

A ratio is usually expressed in *simplest form*.

$\frac{4}{8} = \frac{\mathbf{1}}{\mathbf{2}}$ ← simplest form

$\frac{2x^2}{2xy} = \frac{2 \cdot x \cdot x}{2 \cdot x \cdot y} = \frac{\boldsymbol{x}}{\boldsymbol{y}}$ ← simplest form

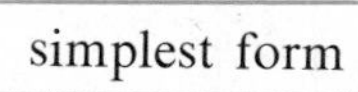

**EXAMPLE 1** There are 60 streetcars and 72 subway cars in the Santa Sofia Transportation System.

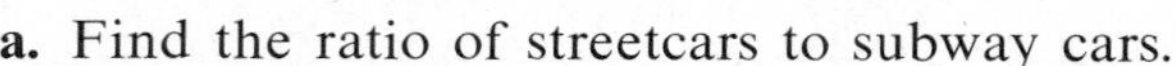

**a.** Find the ratio of streetcars to subway cars.

**b.** Find the ratio of subway cars to streetcars.

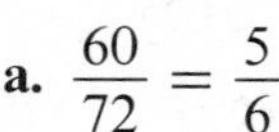

**a.** $\frac{60}{72} = \frac{5}{6}$ **b.** $\frac{72}{60} = \frac{6}{5}$

**EXAMPLE 2** A rectangle is 3 m long and 80 cm wide. Find the ratio of its length to its width.

**Method 1**

Express the length in centimeters.
3 m = 300 cm

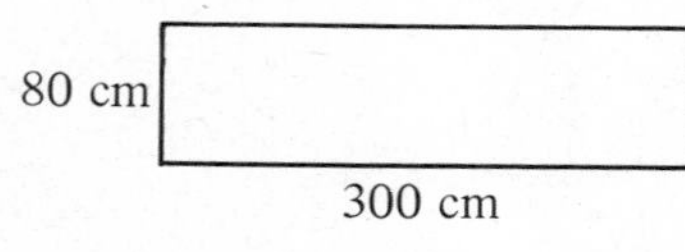


$$\frac{\text{length}}{\text{width}} = \frac{300}{80} = \frac{15}{4}$$

**Method 2**

Express the width in meters.
80 cm = 0.8 m

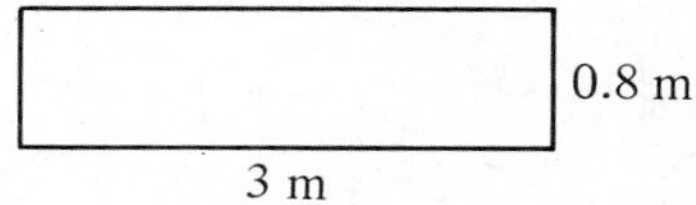


$$\frac{\text{length}}{\text{width}} = \frac{3}{0.8} = \frac{30}{8} = \frac{15}{4}$$

Notice that the ratio is 15:4, no matter which unit is used. Notice also that the ratio contains no units. The ratio is 15:4, and not 15:4 cm or 15:4 m.

In the preceding examples, ratios were used to compare two numbers. Ratios can also be used to compare three or more numbers. For example, in $\triangle ABC$ shown below, $a$, $b$, and $c$ are in the ratio 3 to 4 to 5. This means that

$$a:b = 3:4$$
$$a:c = 3:5$$
$$b:c = 4:5$$

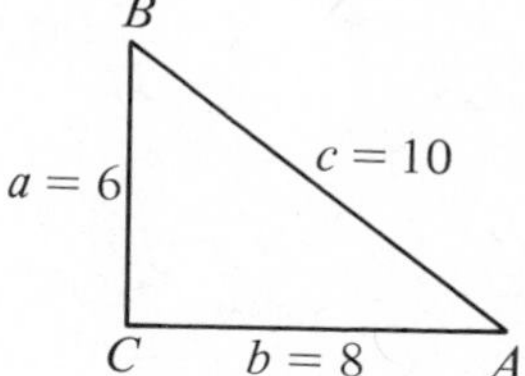


We combine these steps by writing

$$a:b:c = 3:4:5.$$

## Classroom Practice

**Express each ratio in simplest form.**

1. $\frac{5}{15}$ $\frac{1}{3}$
2. $\frac{10}{15}$ $\frac{2}{3}$
3. $\frac{9}{12}$ $\frac{3}{4}$
4. $\frac{500}{1000}$ $\frac{1}{2}$
5. 6:8 3:4
6. 20:25 4:5
7. 2:4:6 1:2:3
8. 30:40:50 3:4:5

**Given $a = 3$ and $b = 5$, find each ratio.**

9. $\frac{a}{b}$ $\frac{3}{5}$
10. $\frac{b}{a}$ $\frac{5}{3}$
11. $\frac{a}{a+b}$ $\frac{3}{8}$
12. $\frac{b}{a+b}$ $\frac{5}{8}$

**Use the figure to find each ratio in simplest form.**

13. $\frac{AB}{BC}$ $\frac{3}{2}$
14. $\frac{AB}{AC}$ $\frac{3}{5}$
15. $\frac{AC}{BC}$ $\frac{5}{2}$

6 4
A B C

## Written Exercises

**Express each ratio in simplest form.**

A
1. $\frac{6}{12}$ $\frac{1}{2}$
2. $\frac{6}{9}$ $\frac{2}{3}$
3. $\frac{18}{24}$ $\frac{3}{4}$
4. $\frac{36}{72}$ $\frac{1}{2}$
5. 21:28 3:4
6. 25:45 5:9
7. 10:20:30 1:2:3
8. 15:25:35 3:5:7

**Given $a = 2$ and $b = 3$, find each ratio.**

9. $\frac{a}{b}$ $\frac{2}{3}$
10. $\frac{b}{a}$ $\frac{3}{2}$
11. $\frac{a}{a+b}$ $\frac{2}{5}$
12. $\frac{b}{a+b}$ $\frac{3}{5}$

**Given $c = 4$ and $d = 5$, find each ratio.**

**13.** $\frac{c}{d}$ $\frac{4}{5}$ **14.** $\frac{d}{c}$ $\frac{5}{4}$ **15.** $\frac{d}{c + d}$ $\frac{5}{9}$ **16.** $\frac{d - c}{d + c}$ $\frac{1}{9}$

**Use the figures below to find each ratio in simplest form.**

**17.** $\frac{AD}{DB}$ $\frac{2}{1}$ **18.** $\frac{AD}{AB}$ $\frac{2}{3}$ **19.** $\frac{DB}{AB}$ $\frac{1}{3}$

**20.** $\frac{AE}{AC}$ $\frac{2}{3}$ **21.** $\frac{AC}{AE}$ $\frac{3}{2}$ **22.** $\frac{EC}{AC}$ $\frac{1}{3}$

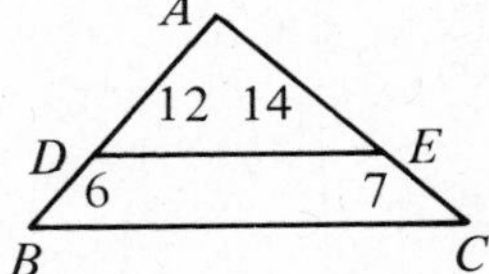


**23.** $\frac{PO}{OS}$ $\frac{3}{5}$ **24.** $\frac{PO}{PS}$ $\frac{3}{8}$ **25.** $\frac{OS}{PS}$ $\frac{5}{8}$

**26.** $\frac{OR}{QO}$ $\frac{5}{3}$ **27.** $\frac{OR}{QR}$ $\frac{5}{8}$ **28.** $\frac{QR}{PS}$ $\frac{3}{2}$

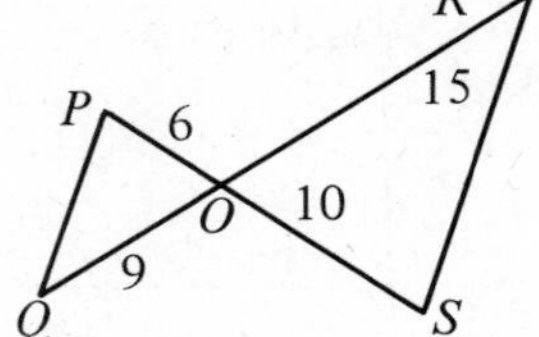


**29.** $\frac{\text{length of } A}{\text{length of } B}$ $\frac{3}{2}$ **30.** $\frac{\text{width of } A}{\text{width of } B}$ $\frac{2}{3}$

**31.** $\frac{\text{area of } A}{\text{area of } B}$ $\frac{1}{1}$ **32.** $\frac{\text{perimeter of } A}{\text{perimeter of } B}$ $\frac{8}{7}$

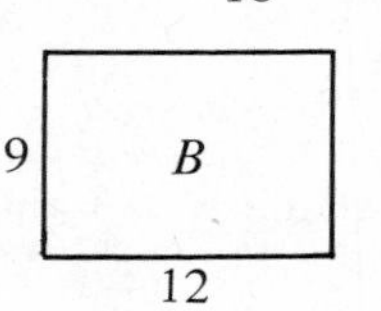


**In Exercises 33–36, find, in simplest form:**
**a. the ratio of the area of the shaded part to the area of the unshaded part;**
**b. the ratio of the area of the shaded part to the total area.**

B **33.**

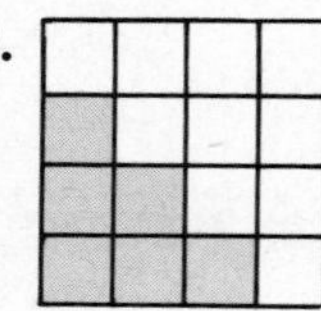

**34.** a. $\frac{1}{2}$ b. $\frac{1}{3}$
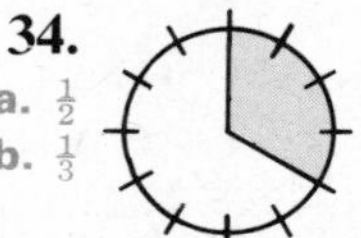

**35.** a. $\frac{1}{3}$ b. $\frac{1}{4}$
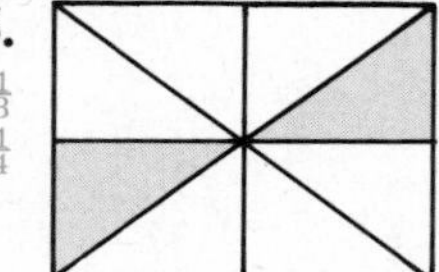

**36.** a. $\frac{1}{5}$ b. $\frac{1}{6}$
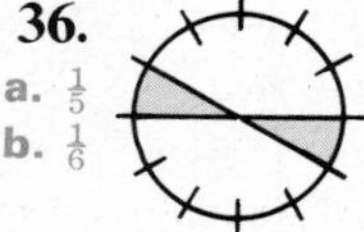

**Express each ratio in simplest form.**

**37.** $\frac{30 \text{ cm}}{1 \text{ m}}$ $\frac{3}{10}$ **38.** $\frac{4 \text{ mm}}{10 \text{ m}}$ $\frac{1}{2500}$ **39.** $\frac{2 \text{ m}}{3 \text{ km}}$ $\frac{1}{1500}$

C **40.** The measures of the angles of a triangle are in the ratio 3:4:5. Find the measures of the angles. (*Hint:* Let $3x$ represent the measure of the smallest angle.) 45°, 60°, 75°

## 2 • Proportions

A **proportion** is an equation which states that two ratios are equal. Here are some examples of proportions.

$$\frac{4}{6} = \frac{2}{3} \qquad 1:5 = 6:30 \qquad \frac{a}{b} = \frac{c}{d} \quad (b \neq 0,\ d \neq 0)$$

The first and last numbers in a proportion are called the *extremes*. The middle numbers are called the *means*.

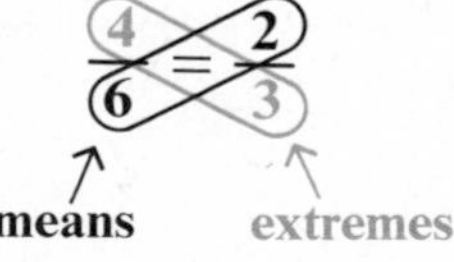


$1:5 = 6:30$

means

extremes

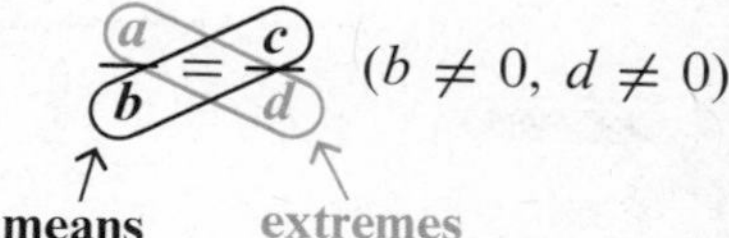


It is sometimes helpful to change a proportion from one form to another. The following properties, based on the postulates of equality, provide ways of changing proportions. The variables used in each property represent nonzero numbers.

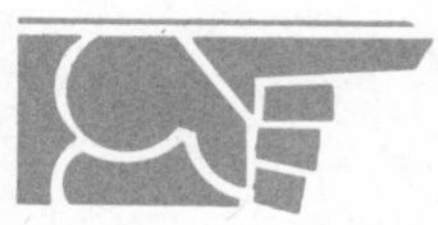

**PROPERTY 1 (The Cross-Multiplying Property)**

In a proportion, the product of the means equals the product of the extremes.

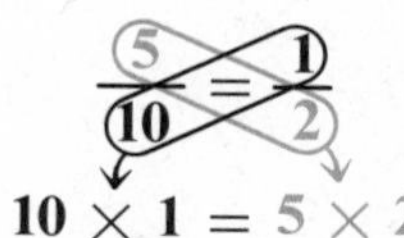

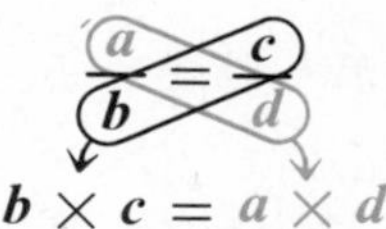

$10 \times 1 = 5 \times 2 \qquad b \times c = a \times d$

**PROPERTY 2 (The Switching Property)**

In a proportion, the means (or the extremes) may be switched.

switch the means

$$\frac{5}{10} = \frac{1}{2} \qquad \frac{5}{1} = \frac{10}{2}$$

$$\frac{a}{b} = \frac{c}{d} \qquad \frac{d}{b} = \frac{c}{a}$$

switch the extremes

**PROPERTY 3 (The Overturning Property)**

In a proportion, the ratios may be turned upside-down.

$$\frac{5}{10} = \frac{1}{2} \qquad \frac{a}{b} = \frac{c}{d}$$

$$\frac{10}{5} = \frac{2}{1} \qquad \frac{b}{a} = \frac{d}{c}$$

**PROPERTY 4 (The Numerator-Changing Property)**

If $\frac{a}{b} = \frac{c}{d}$, then $\frac{a+b}{b} = \frac{c+d}{d}$.

Also, if $\frac{a+b}{b} = \frac{c+d}{d}$, then $\frac{a}{b} = \frac{c}{d}$.

In the following exercises, all variables represent nonzero numbers.

## Classroom Practice

**Tell whether each of the following is a proportion.**

**1.** $3:6 = 1:2$ Yes **2.** $\frac{2}{5} = \frac{4}{10}$ Yes **3.** $\frac{5}{6} = \frac{1}{2} + \frac{1}{3}$ No **4.** $\frac{1}{3} = \frac{3}{9}$ Yes

**Use the Cross-Multiplying Property to complete each statement.**

**5.** If $\frac{6}{8} = \frac{3}{4}$, then $8 \times 3 =$ ___?___. $6 \times 4$

**6.** If $\frac{1}{7} = \frac{2}{14}$, then ___?___ $= 1 \times 14$. $7 \times 2$

**7.** If $\frac{a}{b} = \frac{c}{d}$, then $bc =$ ___?___. $ad$

**8.** If $\frac{x}{y} = \frac{p}{q}$, then $py =$ ___?___. $qx$

**Use the Switching Property to complete each statement.**

**9.** If $\frac{4}{6} = \frac{2}{3}$, then $\frac{4}{2} =$ ___?___ $\frac{6}{3}$ and $\frac{3}{6} =$ ___?___. $\frac{2}{4}$

**10.** If $\frac{1}{4} = \frac{2}{8}$, then $\frac{1}{2} =$ ___?___ $\frac{4}{8}$ and $\frac{8}{4} =$ ___?___. $\frac{2}{1}$

**Use the Overturning Property to complete each statement.**

**11.** If $\frac{a}{b} = \frac{2}{3}$, then $\frac{b}{a} = $ ___?___. $\frac{3}{2}$

**12.** If $\frac{2}{9} = \frac{x}{6}$, then $\frac{9}{2} = $ ___?___. $\frac{6}{x}$

**Use the Numerator-Changing Property to complete each statement.**

**13.** If $\frac{7}{3} = \frac{x}{6}$, then $\frac{7+3}{3} = $ ___?___. $\frac{x+6}{6}$

**14.** If $\frac{w}{x} = \frac{y}{z}$, then $\frac{w+x}{x} = $ ___?___. $\frac{y+z}{z}$

**Find the value of $x$.**

**15.** $\frac{2}{5} = \frac{x}{20}$
$5x = $ ___?___ 40
$x = $ ___?___ 8

**16.** $\frac{5}{6} = \frac{x}{12}$
$6x = $ ___?___ 60
$x = $ ___?___ 10

**17.** $\frac{3}{8} = \frac{x}{10}$
$8x = $ ___?___ 30
$x = $ ___?___ $3\frac{3}{4}$

**18.** $\frac{6}{x} = \frac{9}{6}$
$9x = $ ___?___ 36
$x = $ ___?___ 4

## Written Exercises

**Complete each statement.**

A

**1.** If $\frac{a}{2} = \frac{b}{3}$, then $2b = $ ___?___. $3a$

**2.** If $\frac{x}{y} = \frac{3}{4}$, then $3y = $ ___?___. $4x$

**3.** If $\frac{5}{r} = \frac{3}{5}$, then ___?___ $= 25$. $3r$

**4.** If $\frac{7}{c} = \frac{d}{5}$, then ___?___ $= 35$. $cd$

**5.** If $\frac{a}{3} = \frac{b}{4}$, then $\frac{a}{b} = $ ___?___. $\frac{3}{4}$

**6.** If $\frac{p}{q} = \frac{5}{6}$, then $\frac{6}{q} = $ ___?___. $\frac{5}{p}$

**7.** If $\frac{r}{s} = \frac{2}{3}$, then $\frac{r+s}{s} = $ ___?___. $\frac{5}{3}$

**8.** If $\frac{y}{z} = \frac{7}{9}$, then ___?___ $= \frac{9}{7}$. $\frac{z}{y}$

**9.** If $\frac{x}{12} = \frac{3}{4}$, then $\frac{x}{3} = $ ___?___. $\frac{12}{4}$, or $\frac{3}{1}$

**10.** If $\frac{1}{8} = \frac{9}{x}$, then ___?___ $= \frac{9+x}{x}$. $\frac{9}{8}$

**11.** If $\frac{e}{f} = \frac{8}{5}$, then $5e = $ ___?___. $8f$

**12.** If $\frac{k}{j} = \frac{9}{4}$, then $4k = $ ___?___. $9j$

**Suppose $\frac{a}{b} = \frac{3}{4}$ and $\frac{c}{d} = \frac{5}{7}$. Find each ratio in simplest form.**

**13.** $\frac{b}{a}$ $\frac{4}{3}$

**14.** $\frac{a+b}{b}$ $\frac{7}{4}$

**15.** $\frac{a+b}{a}$ $\frac{7}{3}$

**16.** $\frac{2a}{2b}$ $\frac{3}{4}$

**17.** $\frac{d}{c}$ $\frac{7}{5}$

**18.** $\frac{c+d}{d}$ $\frac{12}{7}$

**19.** $\frac{c-d}{c}$ $-\frac{2}{5}$

**20.** $\frac{3d}{3c}$ $\frac{7}{5}$

**In each exercise, find the value of $x$.**

**21.** $\frac{x}{6} = \frac{1}{2}$ 3 **22.** $\frac{4}{3} = \frac{16}{x}$ 12 **23.** $\frac{1}{3} = \frac{10}{x}$ 30 **24.** $\frac{9}{x} = \frac{9}{7}$ 7

**25.** $3:8 = x:16$ 6 **26.** $9:x = 3:1$ 3 **27.** $x:10 = 4:5$ 8 **28.** $3:5 = 24:x$ 40

B **29.** $\frac{10}{3x} = \frac{5}{6}$ 4 **30.** $\frac{5}{2x} = \frac{25}{1}$ 0.1 **31.** $\frac{1}{2} = \frac{x+1}{8}$ 3 **32.** $\frac{x-5}{6} = \frac{4}{9}$ $7\frac{2}{3}$

**Find the value of $x$.**

C **33.** $\frac{3x-2}{4} = \frac{x}{3}$ $\frac{6}{5}$ **34.** $\frac{1}{2} = \frac{5x+4}{3}$ $-\frac{1}{2}$ **35.** $\frac{x}{3} = \frac{x+2}{5}$ 3

**36.** $\frac{x-5}{x} = \frac{3}{4}$ 20 **37.** $\frac{x+2}{x-1} = \frac{x+3}{x-3}$ $-1$ **38.** $\frac{(2x-3)^2}{(2x+1)(x-3)} = \frac{2}{1}$ $7\frac{1}{2}$

# CAREER NOTES

## *Auto Mechanic*

In 1972, the number of passenger cars in use around the world was about 216,000,000 and in 1973 the number rose to about 233,000,000. Guess how many are in use today. Can you imagine the amount of work involved in keeping these cars running well?

Auto mechanics maintain and repair many different kinds of automobiles. They periodically examine, adjust, and replace car parts. They clean carburetors, balance wheels, replace spark plugs and distributor points, and grind valves.

Auto mechanics may work with sophisticated testing equipment or simple hand tools. Since parts for many cars are measured in metric units, mechanics must be familiar with both metric and nonmetric tools.

It takes three or four years of formal apprenticeship to become a senior auto mechanic. Some senior mechanics work for companies or repair garages. Others operate their own businesses. Mechanics may specialize in repairing particular car components or particular types of cars.

## 3 • Using Proportions

Proportions can be used to solve many kinds of problems. You probably remember, from your study of algebra, how to solve Example 1.

**EXAMPLE 1** Four cans of paint cost \$30.
How much will six cans of paint cost?

**1.** Summarize your data.

| Number of cans | 4 | 6 |
|---|---|---|
| Cost | \$30 | \$$x$ |

**2.** Write a proportion.

$$\frac{4}{30} = \frac{6}{x}$$
$$4x = 180$$
$$x = 45$$

**3.** *Answer:* \$45

**EXAMPLE 2** Bob Allard's summer job is painting houses and barns. He has just used three cans of paint to paint the front of the barn shown. How much more paint will he need for the remaining sides?

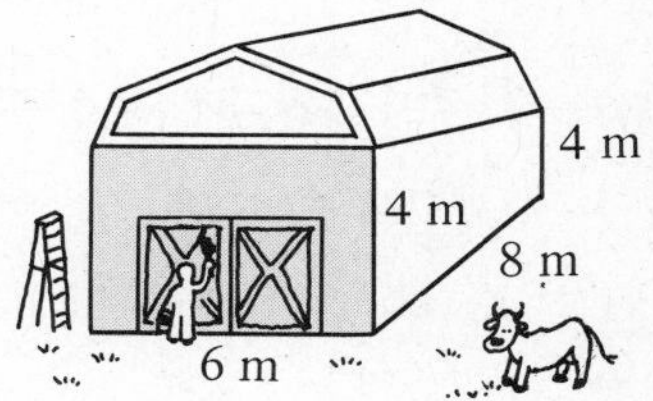


**1.** Estimate the area of the painted and unpainted sides. (Ignore the areas of windows and doors.)

Area of painted side $= 6 \times 4 = 24\ \text{m}^2$

Area of unpainted sides $= \underbrace{8 \times 4}_{\text{side}} + \underbrace{6 \times 4}_{\text{back}} + \underbrace{8 \times 4}_{\text{side}} = 88\ \text{m}^2$

**2.** Summarize your data.

| | Area | Number of cans |
|---|---|---|
| Painted | $24\ \text{m}^2$ | 3 |
| Unpainted | $88\ \text{m}^2$ | $x$ |

**3.** Write a proportion.

$$\frac{24}{88} = \frac{3}{x}$$
$$24x = 264$$
$$x = 11$$

**4.** *Answer:* He will need about 11 more cans of paint.

## Classroom Practice

**Make up a problem to go with each table below.**
**Then write a proportion which can be solved for $x$.** Answers will vary.

**1.**

| Number of cans | 4 | 6 |
|---|---|---|
| Cost | \$21 | \$$x$ |

$\frac{4}{21} = \frac{6}{x}$

**2.**

| Number of boxes | 8 | 20 |
|---|---|---|
| Cost | \$3 | \$$x$ |

$\frac{8}{3} = \frac{20}{x}$

**3.**

| Painted area | 10 m² | 65 m² |
|---|---|---|
| Cost | \$4 | \$$x$ |

$\frac{10}{4} = \frac{65}{x}$

**4.**

| Cost of gasoline | \$6 | \$9 |
|---|---|---|
| Distance traveled | 300 km | $x$ km |

$\frac{6}{300} = \frac{9}{x}$

**5.** Six grapefruits cost 98¢. How many can you buy for \$2.45? 15

**6.** Four tickets to a track meet cost \$5. How many can you buy for \$7.50? 6

## Written Exercises

A **1.** Four cans of paint cost \$30. How much will five cans cost? \$37.50

**2.** Three cans of soup cost 84¢. How much will ten cans cost? \$2.80

**3.** Three boxes of cereal cost \$1.98. How much will seven boxes cost? \$4.62

**4.** Four bottles of root beer cost \$1.56. How much will twelve bottles cost? \$4.68

**5.** Two loaves of whole wheat bread cost \$1.15. How many loaves can you buy for \$3.45? 6

**6.** Two packages of Crispy Crackers cost \$1.39. How many packages can you buy for \$3.50? 5

**7.** It costs \$9 to paint the front of the barn shown. How much will it cost to paint the right side? \$13.50

**8.** Two cans of paint are needed to paint the front of the barn shown. How much paint is needed to paint the other three sides? 8 cans

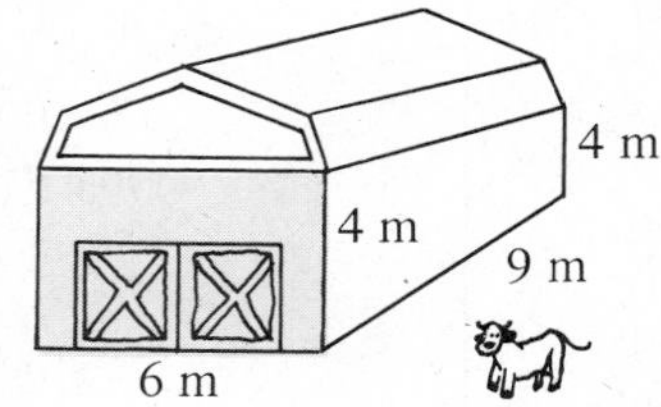


B **9.** The Feldons would like to redo their kitchen floor. They find that linoleum will cost \$4 per square meter. Carpeting will cost \$9 per square meter. The new kitchen floor will cost \$60 if linoleum is used. How much will it cost if carpeting is used? \$135

10. It has taken Paula 45 minutes to mow a 5 m by 34 m strip of lawn. How much more time will she need to finish the job? (Assume that she mows at a constant rate.) 99 minutes

11. The McHale Construction Company is laying the foundation for a house. Seven rows of cement blocks have been installed. Three more rows are needed to complete the job. If 840 blocks have already been used, how many blocks will be used for the entire job? 1200

## SELF-TEST

**Express each ratio in simplest form.**

1. $\frac{8}{12}$ $\frac{2}{3}$
2. $\frac{25}{15}$ $\frac{5}{3}$
3. 25:40 5:8
4. 9:18:27 1:2:3

**Find the value of *x*.**

5. $\frac{x}{6} = \frac{7}{3}$ 14
6. $\frac{10}{x} = \frac{8}{12}$ 15
7. $\frac{4}{6} = \frac{6}{x}$ 9
8. $x:6 = 3:9$ 2

**Solve.**

9. Three loaves of bread cost $1.92. How much will 5 loaves cost? $3.20
10. A rug 3 m wide and 4 m long costs $132. How much would a 4 m by 5 m rug of the same material cost? $220

# 4 • Maps and Scale Drawings

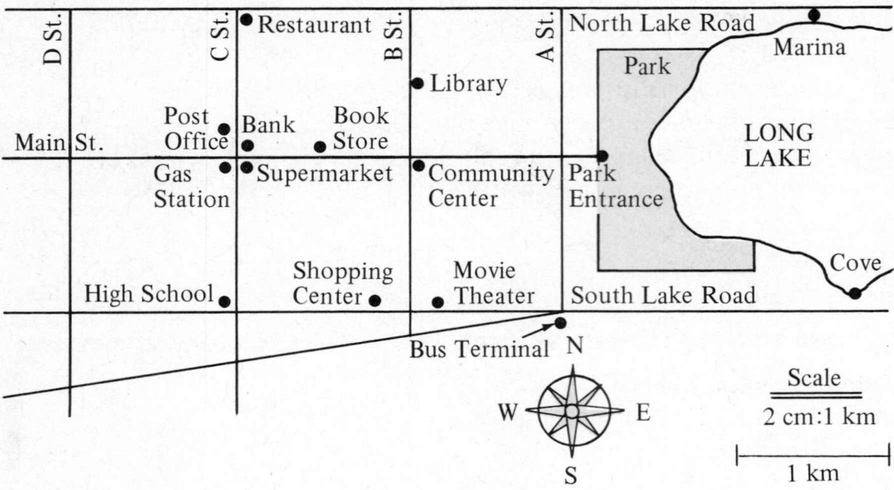


The map above shows part of the town of Lakeville. Notice that the **scale** of the map is

$$2\text{ cm} : 1\text{ km}.$$

This means that a distance of 2 cm *on the map* represents an *actual* distance of 1 km in Lakeville. For example, the distance between the high school and the post office is about 2.4 cm. To find the actual distance, we write a proportion:

$$\frac{2\text{ cm}}{1\text{ km}} = \frac{2.4\text{ cm}}{x\text{ km}}$$

$$\frac{2}{1} = \frac{2.4}{x}$$

$$2x = 2.4$$

$$x = 1.2$$

← The actual distance is about 1.2 km.

A *scale drawing* of a plot of land is very much like a map. So is the floor plan of a house. In the floor plan on the next page, the scale is listed as 1:200. This means that

$$\frac{\text{distance in drawing}}{\text{corresponding distance in house}} = \frac{1}{200}.$$

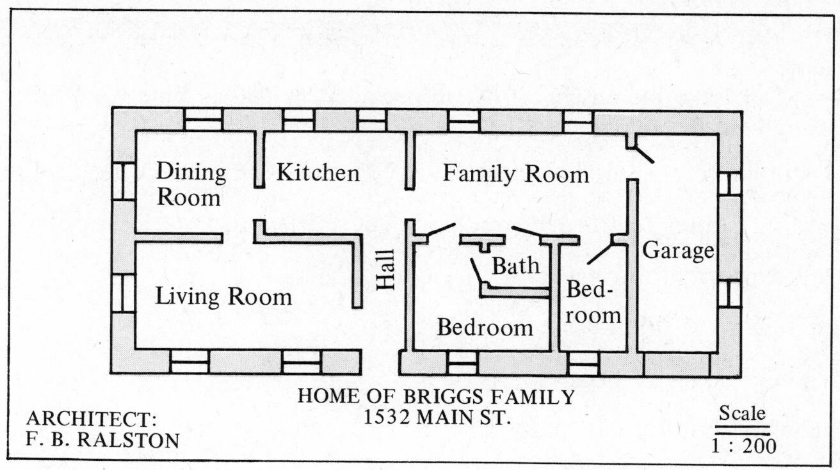


## *Classroom Practice*

**Refer to the map of Lakeville on page 270. Use a ruler to find the distances referred to in the first row of the table. Measure to the nearest centimeter. Then copy and complete the table.**

| | | Post Office to Park Entrance | Gas Station to Marina | Community Center to High School |
|---|---|---|---|---|
| **1.** | Distance on the map in cm | ? 5 | ? 10 | ? 5 |
| **2.** | Actual distance when scale is 2 cm : 1 km | ? 2.5 | ? 5 | ? 2.5 |

**Exercises 3–7 refer to the floor plan above.**

**3.** A scale of 1 : 200 means that

1 cm in the floor plan = 200 cm in the house.

Then 1 cm in the floor plan = ___?___ m in the house. 2

**Use a ruler to find each distance to the nearest centimeter. Then find the actual distance in the house.**

**4.** The length and the width of the living room 6 m × 4 m

**5.** The perimeter of the living room 20 m

**6.** The length and the width of the family room 6 m × 2 m

**7.** The perimeter of the entire house 52 m

## Written Exercises

**Use the map of Lakeville on page 270, with scale 1 cm:800 m. Find each actual distance in the town.**

A 1. Gas station to community center 2080 m

2. Bus terminal to movie theater 1360 m

3. Shopping center to library 2960 m

4. Park entrance to supermarket 3760 m

5. Restaurant to shopping center by car 4880 m

6. High school to book store by car 2480 m

7. Marina to cove by boat 3120 m

8. Marina to cove by car 8400 m

**Use the floor plan on page 271. Find the actual length, width, perimeter, and area of each room. Use the scale 1:250.**

9. Dining room

9. $l = 4$ m, $w = 3.75$ m, $p = 15.5$ m, $A = 15$ m$^2$

10. The smaller bedroom

10. $l = 2.25$ m, $w = 3.75$ m, $p = 12$ m, $A = 8.4$ m$^2$

11. Kitchen $l = 4.75$ m; $w = 3.5$ m; $p = 16.5$ m; $A = 16.6$ m$^2$

12. Garage $l = 2.5$ m; $w = 7.75$ m; $p = 20.5$ m; $A = 19.4$ m$^2$

**Use the map of Illinois to find the approximate distance between the following cities.**

B 13. Chicago and Springfield 300 km

14. Decatur and Rockford 270 km

15. St. Louis and Chicago 440 km

16. Peoria and Indianapolis 310 km

17. The diagram shows three cities in Canada.
    a. Measure the map distances between the cities to the nearest millimeter.
    b. Write a proportion to find the actual distance between Montreal and North Bay. (Round the distance to the nearest 10 km.)
    c. Find the distance between Toronto and North Bay. (Round the distance to the nearest 10 km.)

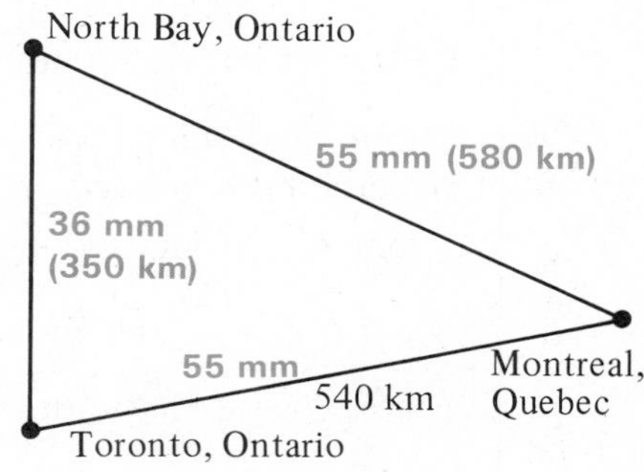

# 5 • Making Maps and Scale Drawings

When making a map or a scale drawing, you must first decide on the scale you are going to use. For example, suppose you are making a scale drawing of your classroom.

Suppose your classroom is 10 m long and you choose to represent this distance by a line segment 20 cm long. Then your scale is:

$$\frac{\text{length of classroom in drawing}}{\text{actual length of classroom}} = \frac{20\text{ cm}}{10\text{ m}} = \frac{20\text{ cm}}{1000\text{ cm}} = \frac{1}{50}$$

Measure the width and other distances in meters. Express these measurements in centimeters and multiply each by the *scale ratio,* $\frac{1}{50}$, to find the corresponding distance in your drawing.

## Classroom Practice

1. Make a scale drawing of your classroom. Follow the instructions above. Suggested scale: 1 cm : 1 m or $\frac{1}{100}$

## Written Exercises

A 1. Make a scale drawing of an Olympic-sized swimming pool which is 50 m long and 21 m wide. Suggested scale: 1 cm : 5 m or $\frac{1}{500}$

2. Make a scale drawing of the cover of this book, using the scale 1 : 2. Drawing should be 9.6 cm × 12 cm.

3. Repeat Exercise 2, using the scale 1:4. Drawing should be 4.8 cm × 6 cm.

4. In the town of Adams, the high school is 4 km south of the post office.
The supermarket is 3 km east of the post office and is 5 km from the high school.
Draw a map showing the school, the post office, and the supermarket.
Be sure to include the scale on your map.

5. A photograph of the Fabrizio family measured 24 cm by 18 cm. The frame was a strip of wood 1.5 cm wide.
Make a scale drawing of the photograph and its frame, using the scale 1:3.

6. Town *A* is 8 km south of city *B*.
City *C* is 4 km northwest (NW) of *A*.
Find the distance, to the nearest kilometer, from *B* to *C*. 6 km

7. Allentown is 5 km north of Belleville.
Canton is 8 km southeast (SE) of Belleville.
Make a scale drawing and find the distance, to the nearest kilometer, from Allentown to Canton. 12 km

B 8. Dallas, Texas, is located about 300 km west of Shreveport, Louisiana.
San Antonio, Texas, is located about 620 km southwest (SW) of Shreveport.
To the nearest 50 km, how far is it from Dallas to San Antonio? 500 km

9. Firetower *A* is 8 km north of firetower *B*.
From *A*, a fire is sighted on a bearing of 60°.
From *B*, the same fire is sighted on a bearing of 25°.

a. To the nearest kilometer, how far is it from *A* to the fire? 6 km
b. To the nearest kilometer, how far is it from *B* to the fire? 12 km

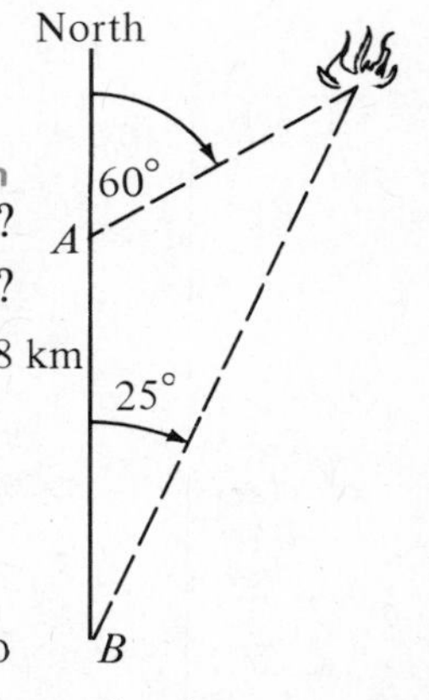


10. Firetower *A* is 5 km north of firetower *B*.
From *A*, a fire is sighted at a point *F*, directly east of *A*.
From *B*, the same fire is sighted on a bearing of 55°.

a. Make a scale drawing showing *A*, *B*, and *F*.
b. Find the distances to the nearest kilometer from *A* and *B* to the fire. from A: 7 km from B: 9 km

C 11. Make a scale drawing of your bedroom. Include the furniture.

## SELF-TEST

**Use the diagram at the right.**

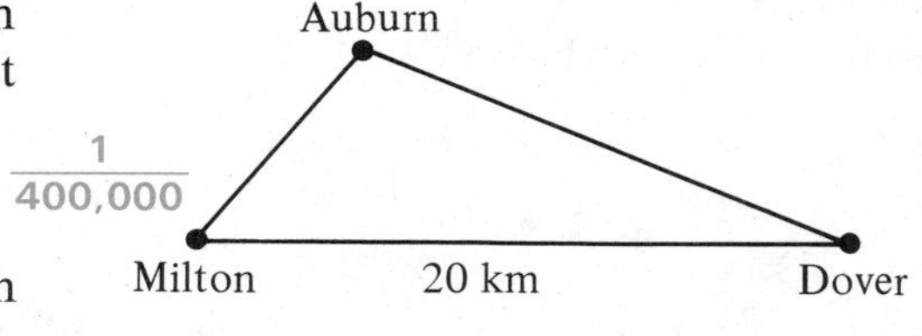


1. Measure the map distance between Dover and Milton to the nearest centimeter. 5 cm
   Then give the scale of the map. $\frac{1}{400,000}$
2. Find the actual distance between Dover and Auburn. 16 km
3. Find the actual distance between Auburn and Milton. 8 km
4. Make a scale drawing of a basketball court 26 m long and 14 m wide. Suggested scale: 1 cm : 4 m or $\frac{1}{400}$

## CONSUMER CORNER

### *The Consumer Price Index*

Few consumers like the word "inflation." It means that things cost more now than they used to. Of course, not everything is more expensive today. (The cost of an electronic calculator is much less than it was 5 years ago.) But on the average, prices are going up.

The Consumer Price Index (CPI) is a number which keeps track of inflation. It takes into account the cost of food, clothing, housing, transportation, medical care, and other goods and services used by consumers. The CPI compares the *total price now* for a selection of typical consumer purchases to the *former price* during a base year.

The CPI is 175. ← This means that the current total price of a selection of typical consumer purchases is 175% of the total price during the base year.

**Exercise**

Consult a newspaper or your library to find out the current CPI. What year is used as the base year? Get a copy of your family's last grocery bill. About how much would the bill have been during the base year?

## Reviewing Algebraic Skills

**Simplify. Use the distributive property.**

Sample $3(2 + 4x) - 8x + 1$

$6 + 12x - 8x + 1$

$4x + 7$

**1.** $5(x + 8) + 3x - 7$ $8x + 33$

**2.** $2(3 - 6k^2) + 9k^2$ $6 - 3k^2$

**3.** $-(a + 9 - 6a) - 4a$ $a - 9$

**4.** $8b^3 + 4(6 - 2b^3)$ $24$

**5.** $5 - 3(n + 1) - 6n$ $2 - 9n$

**6.** $x^2 - (12 - x^2) + 16$ $2x^2 + 4$

**7.** $0.2(5 - 3m) + m$ $1 + 0.4m$

**8.** $4(9 - 1.75x) + 7x$ $36$

**9.** $10(1.5a + 6.13) - 7a$ $8a + 61.3$

**Solve.**

Sample $5(m + 4) = 35$

$5m + 20 = 35$

$5m = 15$

$m = 3$

**10.** $2(x - 10) = 6$ $13$

**11.** $5(w + 3) = 45$ $6$

**12.** $3(2n + 1) = 21$ $3$

**13.** $11(a + 7) = 0$ $-7$

**14.** $7x = 4(x - 9)$ $-12$

**15.** $6(3b - 4) = 12$ $2$

**16.** $39 = 13(x + 4)$ $-1$

**17.** $3(4 + 2m) = 3m$ $-4$

**18.** $6(2k + 1) - 9k = 0$ $-2$

**19.** $9y = 4(2y - 12)$ $-48$

**20.** $7(9 + 2c) = 5c$ $-7$

**21.** $13 + 10d = 9(d + 5)$ $32$

**22.** $5(32 - x) = 3x$ $20$

**23.** $a + 7 = 2(5a - 1)$ $1$

**24.** $7x - 3(5x + 1) = 13$ $-2$

**Write an equation. Then solve.**

**25.** The perimeter of a square is 76. The length of a side is $2n + 3$. Find the value of $n$. 8

**26.** At the Book Fair, Sue bought 3 books that cost $(5x - 1)$ cents each. She spent \$7.62 in all. What was the cost of each book? \$2.54

**27.** A rectangle has length and width as shown. The perimeter is 28 cm. How many centimeters long is the rectangle? How many centimeters wide?
length: 8 cm width: 6 cm

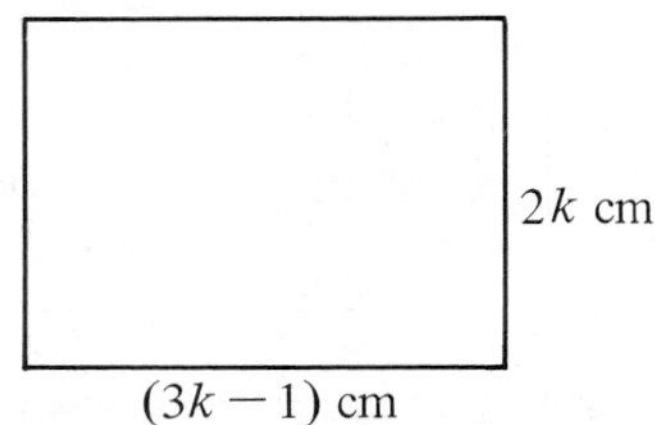

# applications

## *Mechanical Drawing*

Technical artists prepare mechanical drawings for architects and machinists. Many mechanical drawings show a building, a machine, or a tool, as seen from different views. For example, a calculator might be drawn like this.

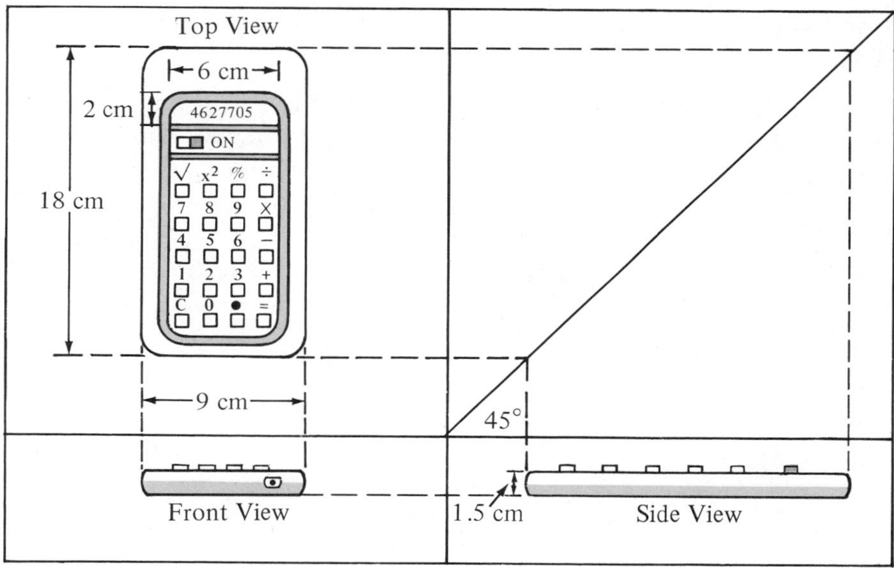


Each length in a mechanical drawing is drawn to scale. Suppose the actual calculator is 9 cm wide. If this width is represented by a segment 3 cm long, then the scale is 3:9, or 1:3.

**Exercises**

Sketch each object as seen from the top, front, and side.

**1.**  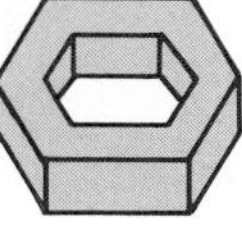

**2.** 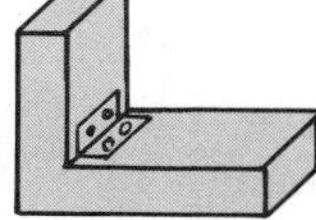

**3.** 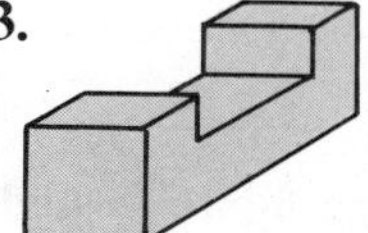

**4.** Make a mechanical drawing of a milk container, showing the top, the front, and the side.

## Reviewing the Chapter

### Chapter Summary

1. A ratio is a quotient of two numbers. The ratio of 2 to 3 is written $\frac{2}{3}$ or 2:3.
2. To find the ratio of two measures, first express both measures in terms of the same unit. Note that there are *no* units in the final answer.
3. A proportion is an equation which states that two ratios are equal. The first and the last numbers in a proportion are called the extremes. The middle numbers are called the means.
4. There are four helpful properties for changing the form of a proportion: The Cross-Multiplying Property, The Switching Property, The Overturning Property, and The Numerator-Changing Property.
5. Proportions are used in problem solving.
6. Proportions are used in making and reading maps and scale drawings. The scale of a map is the ratio of the map distance to the actual distance.

### Chapter Review Test

**Express each ratio in simplest form.** (*See pp. 260–262.*)

**1.** $\frac{9}{15}$ $\frac{3}{5}$

**2.** $\frac{56}{16}$ $\frac{7}{2}$

**3.** $\frac{24x}{9x}$ $\frac{8}{3}$

**4.** 21:14 3:2

**5.** $ab:ac$ $b:c$

**6.** 48:30:24 8:5:4

**7.** 8 m:40 cm 20:1

**8.** 20 m:2 km 1:100

**9.** 20 min to 3 h 1:9

**Use the figure to find each ratio in simplest form.** (*See pp. 260–262.*)

**10.** $\frac{AB}{DC}$ $\frac{9}{5}$

**11.** $\frac{AE}{ED}$ $\frac{1}{2}$

**12.** $\frac{ED}{FC}$ $\frac{3}{4}$

**13.** $\frac{AD}{BC}$ $\frac{3}{4}$

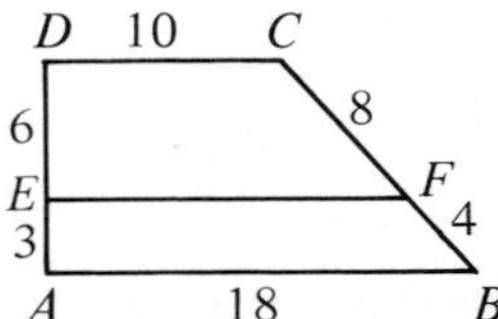

Complete each statement. All variables represent nonzero numbers. (See pp. 263–266.)

14. If $\frac{a}{4} = \frac{b}{5}$, then $\frac{a}{b} = $ __?__. $\frac{4}{5}$

15. If $\frac{m}{6} = \frac{3}{2}$, then __?__ $= 18$. $2m$

16. If $\frac{p}{4} = \frac{2}{5}$, then $\frac{p+4}{4} = $ __?__. $\frac{7}{5}$

17. If $\frac{x}{9} = \frac{4}{y}$, then $\frac{9}{x} = $ __?__. $\frac{y}{4}$

Find the value of $x$. (See pp. 263–266.)

18. $\frac{x}{8} = \frac{3}{4}$ 6

19. $\frac{5}{6} = \frac{x}{18}$ 15

20. $x:8 = 5:2$ 20

Solve. (See pp. 267–269.)

21. Three boxes of cereal cost $2.60. How much will 6 boxes cost? $5.20

22. It costs $6.60 to paint a fence 2 m high and 15 m long. How much will it cost to paint another fence of the same type if it is 3 m high and 25 m long? $16.50

Use the diagram at the right. (See pp. 270–272.)

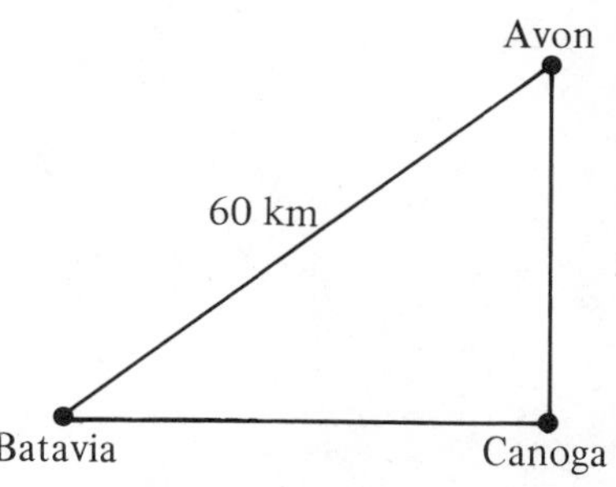


23. Measure the map distance between Avon and Batavia to the nearest centimeter. Then give the scale of the map. $\frac{1}{1{,}200{,}000}$

24. Find the actual distance between Batavia and Canoga. 48 km

25. Find the actual distance between Avon and Canoga. 36 km

Draw a map. Be sure to include the scale. (See pp. 273–275.)

26. The Liberty School is 1 km north of the post office, and the local business district is 3 km east of the school. Draw a map showing the school, post office, and business district.

## *Here's what you'll learn in this chapter:*

1. To tell whether two polygons are similar.
2. To find missing parts of similar triangles.
3. To use properties related to parallel lines.
4. To find the perimeters and areas of two similar polygons.

# Chapter 8

# Similar Polygons

## 1 • Defining Similar Polygons

Two polygons with the same shape are called *similar* polygons. Quadrilaterals $ABCD$ and $WXYZ$ are similar polygons.

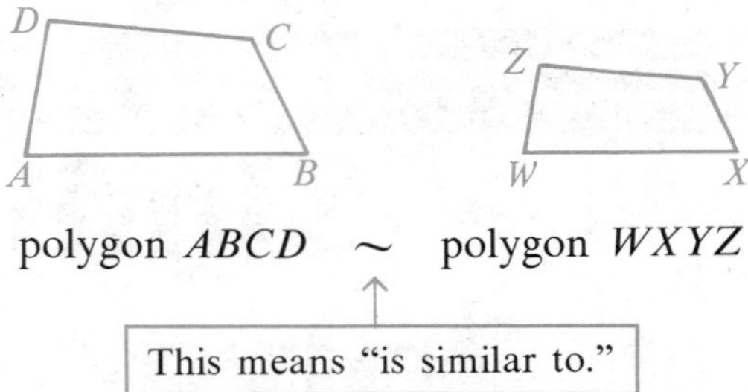


Recall that we name congruent polygons by listing their vertices in corresponding order. We name similar polygons the same way:

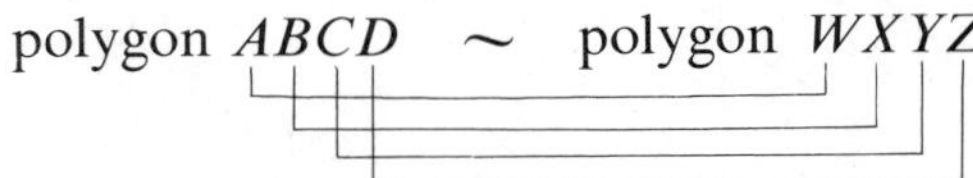

When two polygons are similar, the following are true:
1. Corresponding angles are equal.
2. Corresponding sides are in proportion (have equal ratios).

Since quadrilateral $ABCD \sim$ quadrilateral $WXYZ$, we can conclude:

1. $\angle A = \angle W$, $\angle B = \angle X$, $\angle C = \angle Y$, $\angle D = \angle Z$
2. $\frac{AB}{WX} = \frac{BC}{XY} = \frac{CD}{YZ} = \frac{DA}{ZW}$

Suppose that you wish to show that two polygons are similar. To do this, you must show that *both* conditions of the definition are true.

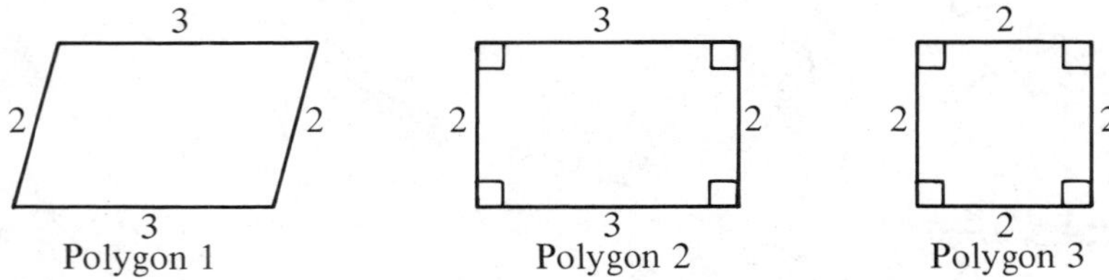


The corresponding sides of Polygons 1 and 2 are in proportion. However, corresponding angles are not equal. Therefore the polygons are not similar.

The corresponding angles of Polygons 2 and 3 are equal. However, their corresponding sides are not in proportion. Therefore Polygons 2 and 3 are not similar.

**EXAMPLE** $\triangle PQR \sim \triangle STU$.
Find the values of $x$ and $y$.

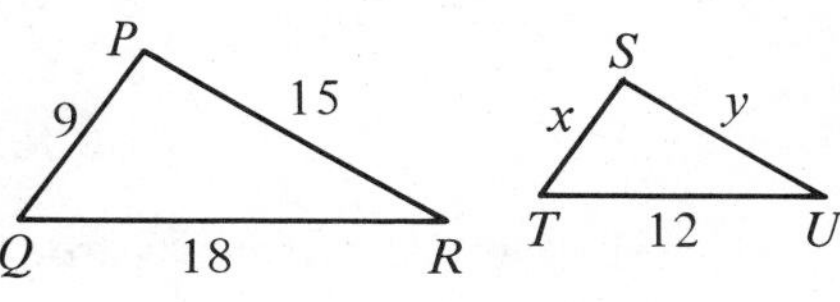


Since corresponding sides are in proportion:

$$\frac{PQ}{ST} = \frac{QR}{TU} = \frac{RP}{US}$$

$$\frac{9}{x} = \frac{18}{12} = \frac{15}{y}$$

$$\frac{9}{x} = \frac{3}{2} = \frac{15}{y}$$

$$\frac{9}{x} = \frac{3}{2} \qquad\qquad \frac{3}{2} = \frac{15}{y}$$

$$18 = 3x \qquad\qquad 3y = 30$$

$$6 = x \qquad\qquad y = 10$$

If two polygons are similar, the ratio of two corresponding sides is called the *scale factor*. The scale factor of $\triangle ABC$ to $\triangle DEF$ is $\frac{5}{10}$, or $\frac{1}{2}$. Likewise, the scale factor of $\triangle DEF$ to $\triangle ABC$ is $\frac{2}{1}$. Notice that the ratio of the perimeters of these triangles is equal to the scale factor:

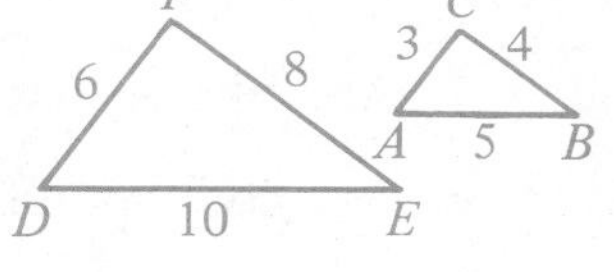


$$\frac{\text{perimeter of } \triangle DEF}{\text{perimeter of } \triangle ABC} = \frac{10 + 8 + 6}{5 + 4 + 3} = \frac{24}{12} = \frac{2}{1}.$$

## Classroom Practice

**In Exercises 1–3, state why the two polygons are, or are not, similar.**

**1.** Yes; corr. ∠s =; corr. sides in proportion

**2.** No; corr. sides not in proportion

**3.** No; corr. ∠s not equal

$\triangle ABC \sim \triangle DEF$. **Complete each statement.**

4. The scale factor of $\triangle ABC$ to $\triangle DEF$ is ___?___. $\frac{2}{3}$

5. $\frac{x}{9} = \frac{10}{?}$ $\frac{10}{15}$

6. $\frac{8}{y} = \frac{x}{?}$ $\frac{x}{9}$

7. $\angle C = \angle$ ___?___ $\angle F$

8. $\angle$ ___?___ $= \angle D$ $\angle A$

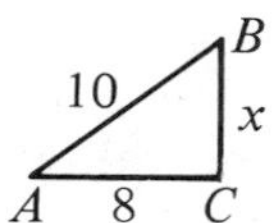


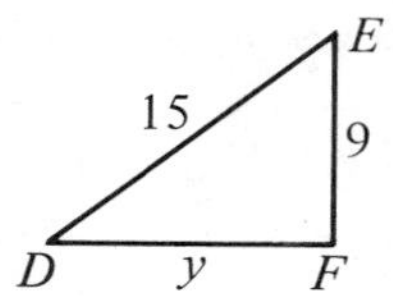


**Classify each statement as true or false.**

9. All squares are similar. True

10. All rectangles are similar. False

11. All equilateral triangles are similar. True

12. All isosceles triangles are similar. False

13. All rhombuses are similar. False

14. Every polygon is similar to itself. True

15. Two congruent polygons are always similar. True

## Written Exercises

**Match the vertices of rectangles *ABCD* and *WXYZ* like this:**

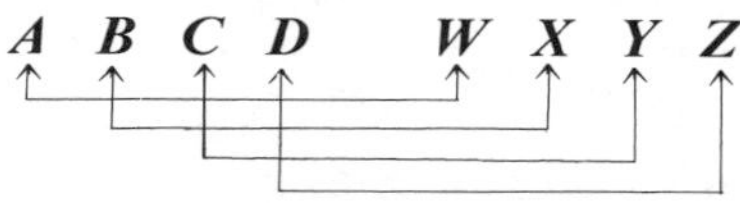


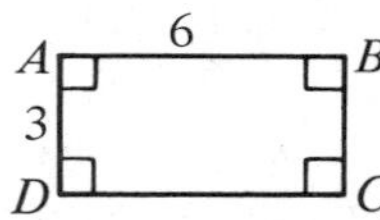


A 1. Are corresponding angles equal? Yes

2. Are corresponding sides in proportion? No

3. Are the rectangles similar? No

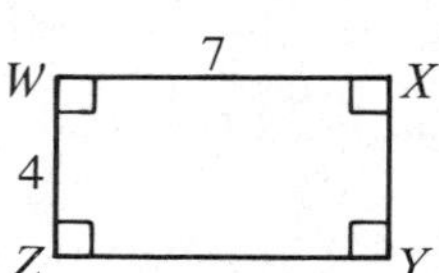


**Match the vertices of quadrilaterals *EFGH* and *PQRS* like this:**

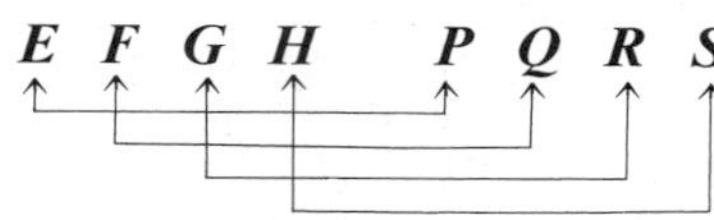


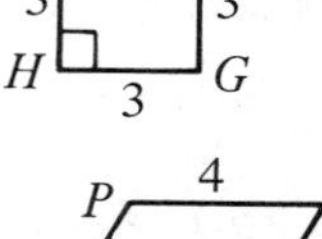


4. Are corresponding angles equal? No

5. Are corresponding sides in proportion? Yes

6. Are the quadrilaterals similar? No

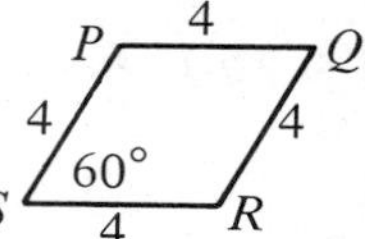


**In Exercises 7–9, state why the two polygons are, or are not, similar.**

7.

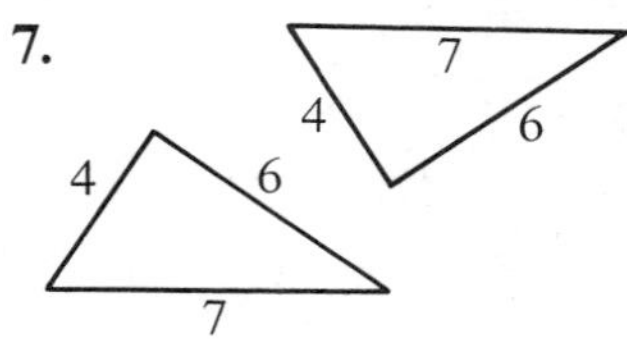


Yes; polygons ≅

8.

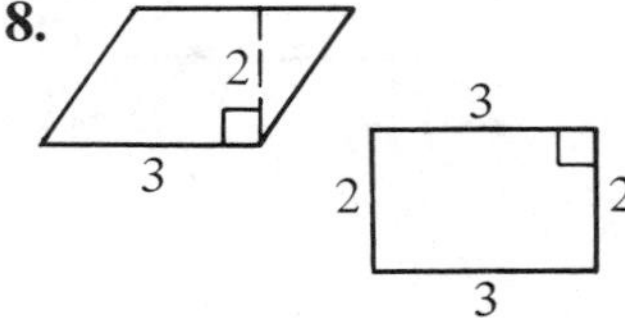


No; corr. ∠s not =

9.

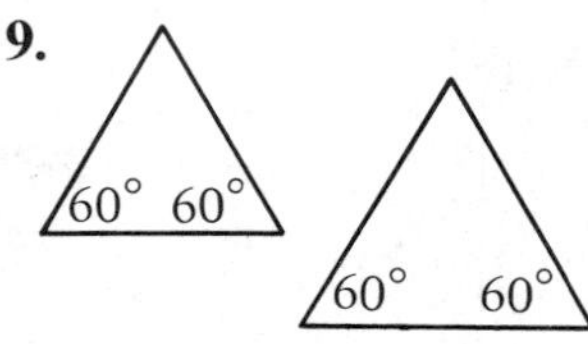


Yes; both equiangular and equilateral

**In Exercises 10–12, the two polygons are similar. Complete each statement.**

**10.** 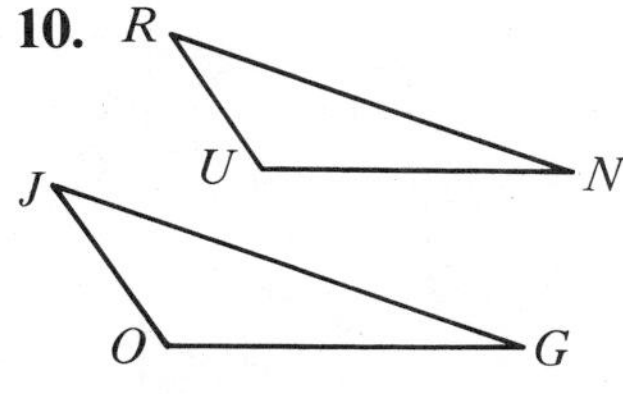


$\triangle RUN \sim$ __?__ $\triangle JOG$

$\frac{RU}{JO} = \frac{UN}{?} = \frac{NR}{?}$ OG GJ

**11.** 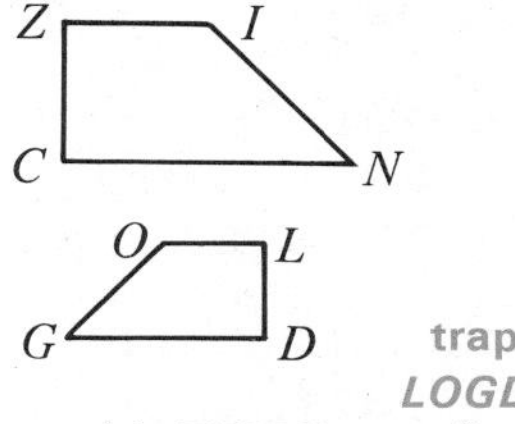


trapezoid $ZINC \sim$ __?__ trap. LOGD

$\frac{ZI}{LO} = \frac{IN}{?} = \frac{NC}{?}$ OG GD

**12.** 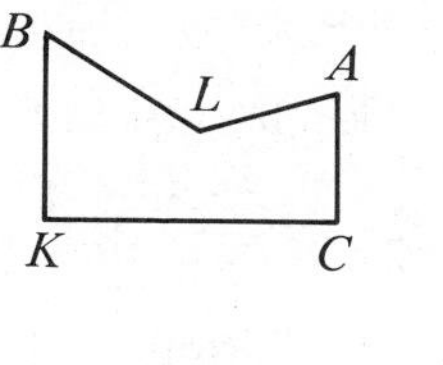


pentagon $BLACK \sim$ __?__ pent. TEWHI

$\angle A = \angle$ __?__ ; $\angle W$ $\frac{CK}{?} = \frac{KB}{?}$ HI IT

**13.** Are rectangles 1 and 2 similar? Yes

**14.** What is the scale factor of rectangle 1 to rectangle 2? $\frac{2}{3}$

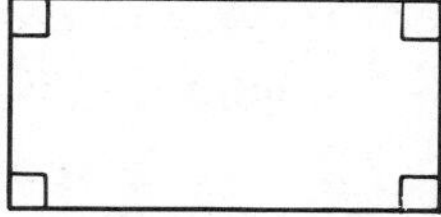


Rectangle 1

**15. a.** $\frac{\text{perimeter of rectangle 1}}{\text{perimeter of rectangle 2}} = \frac{2 + 4 + 2 + 4}{? + ? + ? + ?} = \frac{12}{?}$ 3 + 6 + 3 + 6; 18

**b.** Is the ratio of the perimeters equal to the scale factor? Yes

6

3

Rectangle 2

**16. a.** $\frac{\text{area of rectangle 1}}{\text{area of rectangle 2}} = \frac{8}{?}$ $\frac{8}{18}$

**b.** Is the ratio of the areas equal to the scale factor? No

**In Exercises 17–19, the two polygons shown are similar. Find the values of *x*, *y*, and *z*.**

B **17.** 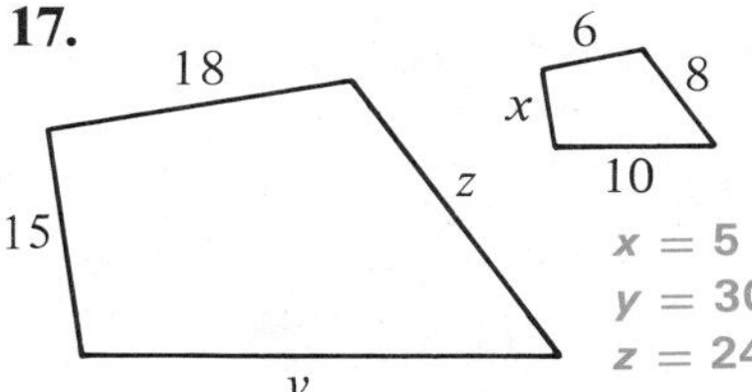


$x = 5$ $y = 30$ $z = 24$

**18.** 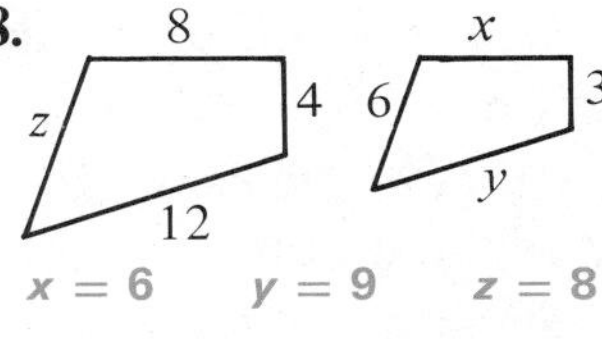


$x = 6$ $y = 9$ $z = 8$

**19.** 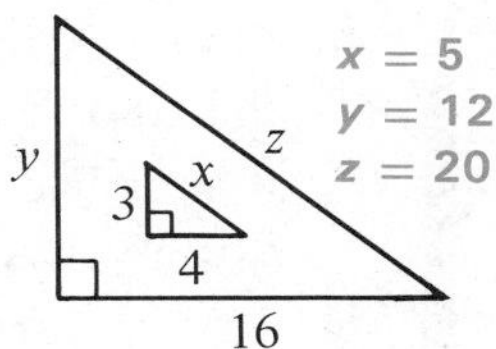


$x = 5$ $y = 12$ $z = 20$

**20.** The length and width of a rectangle are 18 and 12. A similar rectangle has length 27. What is its width? 18

**21.** The sides of a triangle are 6 cm, 8 cm, and 9 cm long. The shortest side of a similar triangle is 15 cm long. How long are its other sides? 20 cm, 22.5 cm

**22. a.** Plot points $A(-4, 8)$, $B(-4, 2)$, and $C(5, 2)$ on graph paper. Draw $\triangle ABC$.

**b.** Plot points $D(5, -3)$ and $E(5, -5)$ on the same graph.

**c.** Locate a point $F$ so that $\triangle ABC \sim \triangle DEF$. (More than one answer is possible.) $F_1(8, -5)$; $F_2(2, -5)$

**23.** Repeat Exercise 22, using points $A(4, 10)$, $B(4, 4)$, $C(0, 4)$, $D(6, 1)$, and $E(6, 13)$. $F_1(14, 13)$; $F_2(-2, 13)$

C **24.** The length and width of a rectangle are represented by $x$ and $y$ $(x \neq y)$. The length and width of another rectangle are represented by $x + 2$ and $y + 2$. Are the rectangles similar? No

**25.** The length and width of a rectangle are represented by $x$ and $y$ $(x \neq y)$. The length and width of another rectangle are represented by $2x$ and $2y$. Are the rectangles similar? Yes

**26.** When a card 8 cm long is cut in half, each piece has the same shape as the original card. Find the *exact* value of $x$. (The answer involves a square root.) $x = \sqrt{32} = 4\sqrt{2}$

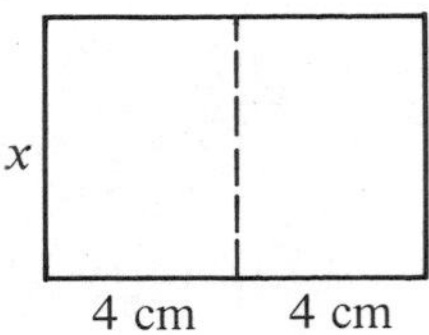


## *Encounter—A game for two people*

1. Encounter is a game that is played on graph paper. The players choose any two starting points, *A* and *B*, on the grid.
2. Player A draws a horizontal segment from point *A* to any other point of the grid. (The segment should not be very long.)
3. Player B starts at point *B* and draws a segment in the same direction as player A's segment, but twice as long.
4. Player A joins a vertical segment to the end of the first segment drawn.
5. Player B draws a segment in the same direction as player A's second segment, but twice as long.
6. Taking turns, the players draw horizontal segments. Then they both draw vertical segments. Each time, player B draws a segment in the same direction as player A's, but twice as long.

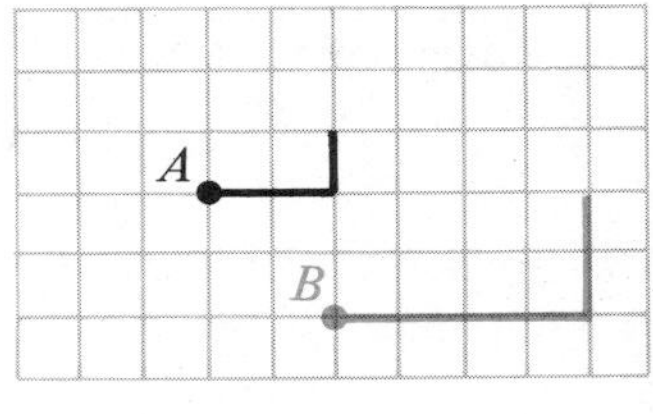


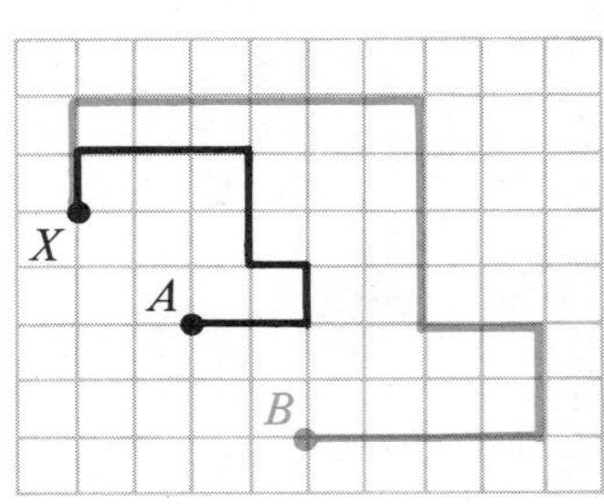


The object of the game is for player A to move, in as few moves as possible, to a point *X* that will force B to move to the same point.

Play the game and discover the answers to the questions below!

**1.** Will there always be a winning point *X*? Yes

**2.** How is the winning point *X* related to the starting points? *A* is midpt. of $\overline{XB}$.

**3.** What is the fewest number of moves that player A can make and *always* win? 2 moves

## 2 • The AA Postulate

You can prove that two polygons are similar by using the definition of *similar*. That is, by showing that

(1) corresponding angles are equal, and
(2) corresponding sides are in proportion.

There is, however, a more direct method for proving two *triangles* similar. The exploration below should help you discover this method.

### *Explorations*

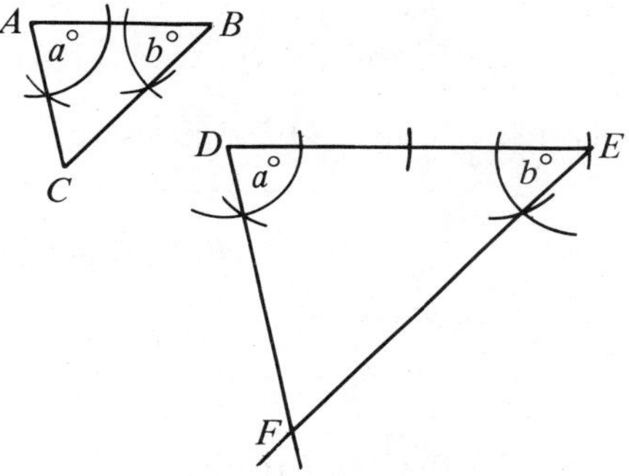


1. Draw any scalene $\triangle ABC$.
2. Construct $\overline{DE}$ with length $2(AB)$.
3. Copy $\angle A$ at $D$. Copy $\angle B$ at $E$. Let $F$ be the point shown.
4. Measure $\overline{AC}$ and $\overline{DF}$. Then measure $\overline{BC}$ and $\overline{EF}$.

   Remember that $\frac{AB}{DE} = \frac{1}{2}$.

   Is $\frac{AC}{DF} \doteq \frac{1}{2}$? Is $\frac{BC}{EF} \doteq \frac{1}{2}$? Yes; Yes

   Do you think that corresponding sides are in proportion? Yes
5. Remember that $\angle A = \angle D$ and $\angle B = \angle E$. Is $\angle C = \angle F$? Yes
   Do you think that corresponding angles are equal? Yes
6. Does it seem that $\triangle ABC \sim \triangle DEF$? Yes

If you repeat the exploration using different-looking triangles, you will obtain the same result.

**POSTULATE 13 (The AA Postulate)**

If two angles of one triangle are equal to two angles of another triangle, then the triangles are similar.

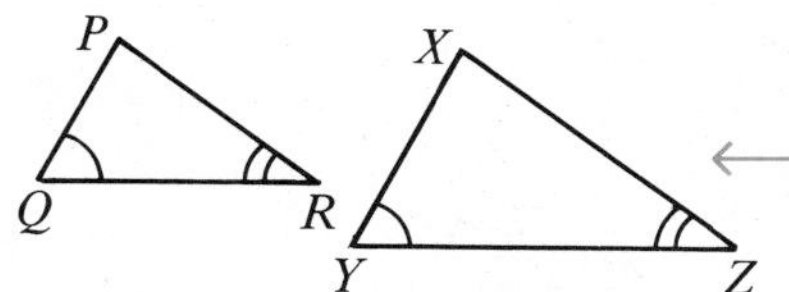


If $\angle Q = \angle Y$ and $\angle R = \angle Z$, then $\triangle PQR \sim \triangle XYZ$.

**EXAMPLE** *Given:* $\angle B = \angle E$

*Prove:* $\triangle ABC \sim \triangle DEC$

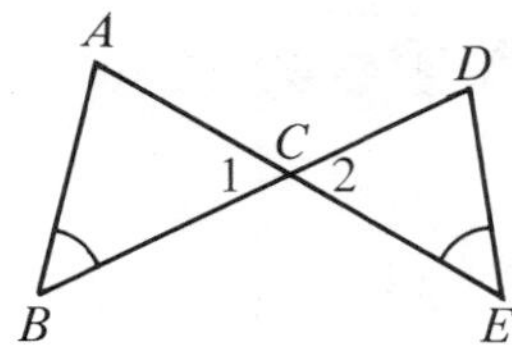


| STATEMENTS | REASONS |
|---|---|
| 1. $\angle B = \angle E$ | 1. Given |
| 2. $\angle 1 = \angle 2$ | 2. Vertical angles are equal. |
| 3. $\triangle ABC \sim \triangle DEC$ | 3. AA Postulate |

Suppose, in the proof above, we were asked to prove $\frac{AB}{DE} = \frac{BC}{EC}$. We would need just one additional step:

| | |
|---|---|
| 4. $\frac{AB}{DE} = \frac{BC}{EC}$ | 4. Corresponding sides of $\sim$ ⚠s are in proportion. |

The definition of similar triangles may be used in a proof in much the same way that the definition of congruent triangles was used.

> The definition of congruent triangles tells us:
> 1. Corresponding angles of congruent triangles are equal.
> 2. Corresponding sides of congruent triangles are equal.
>
> The definition of similar triangles tells us:
> 1. Corresponding angles of similar triangles are equal.
> 2. Corresponding sides of similar triangles are in proportion.

## Classroom Practice

**In each exercise, state whether the two triangles are, or are not, similar.**

**1.** Yes

40° 50°

40° 50°

**2.** Yes

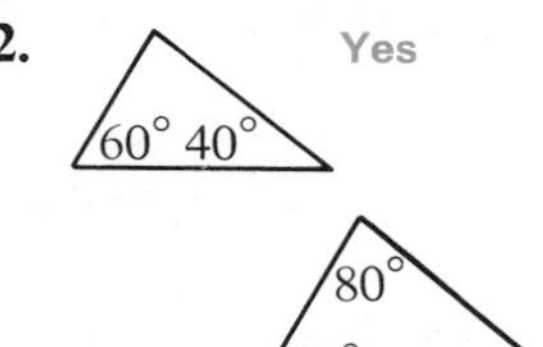


**3.** No

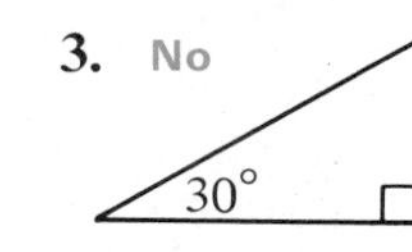


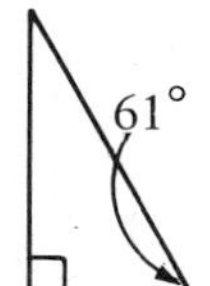

4. Yes

5. No

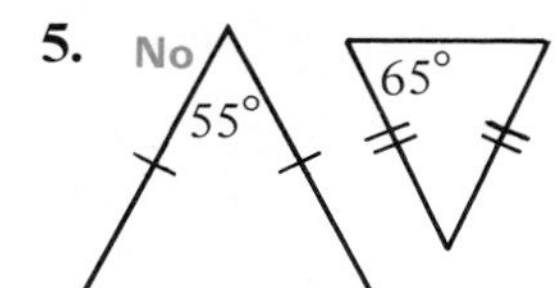


6. Yes

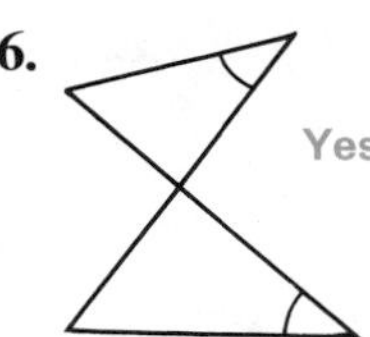

7. Complete the statement suggested by Exercise 4 above: If the vertex angles of two isosceles triangles __?__. are equal, the triangles are similar.

**Complete each proportion.**

8. $\triangle ABC \sim \triangle DEF$

$\frac{AB}{?} = \frac{BC}{?} = \frac{AC}{?}$ DE EF DF

9. $\triangle RST \sim \triangle XYZ$

$\frac{XY}{?} = \frac{XZ}{?} = \frac{YZ}{?}$ RS RT ST

10. $\triangle KLM \sim \triangle RST$

$\frac{?}{KL} = \frac{?}{LM} = \frac{?}{KM}$ RS ST RT

11. Supply the reasons to complete the proof.

*Given:* $\angle 1 = \angle 2$

*Prove:* $\frac{AB}{AD} = \frac{AC}{AE}$

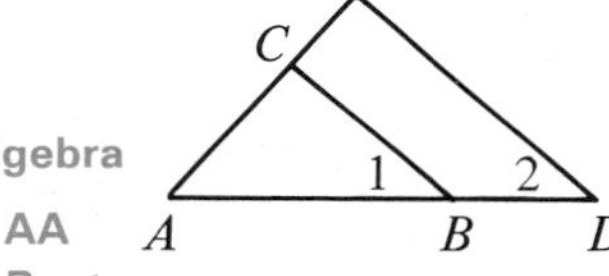


1. $\angle 1 = \angle 2$ Given
2. $\angle A = \angle A$ From algebra
3. $\triangle ABC \sim \triangle ADE$ AA Post.
4. $\frac{AB}{AD} = \frac{AC}{AE}$ Corr. parts of similar triangles are in proportion.

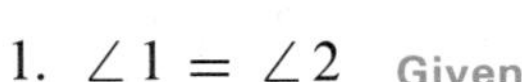

**Use the figure from Exercise 11. Assume that $\triangle ABC \sim \triangle ADE$.**

12. If $AB = 8$, $AD = 12$, and $BC = 6$, find $DE$. 9

13. If $AB = 15$, $AC = 9$, and $AE = 15$, find $AD$. 25

## Written Exercises

**In each exercise, state whether the two triangles are, or are not, similar.**

A 1. No

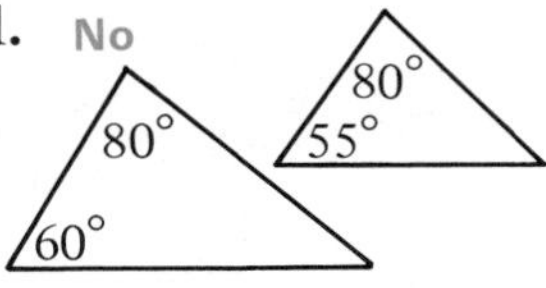


2. No

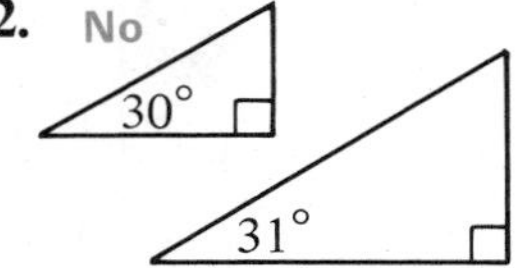


3. Yes

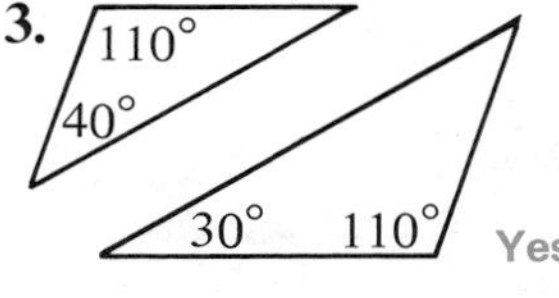


4. Yes

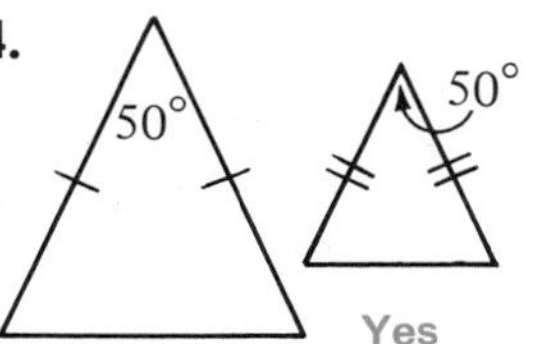


5. No

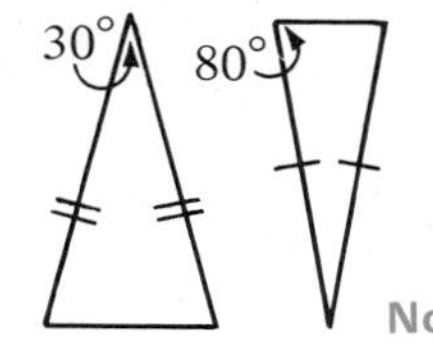


6. Yes

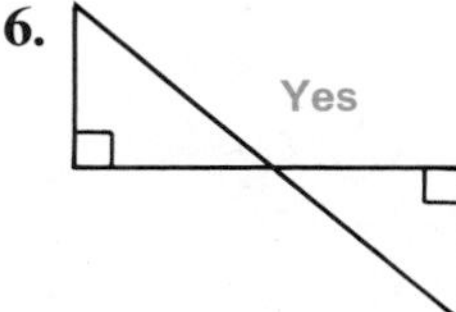

**State whether the two triangles are, or are not, similar.**

7. 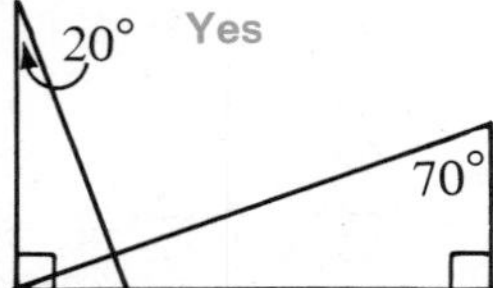


8. 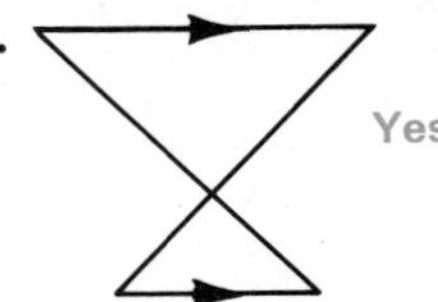


9. 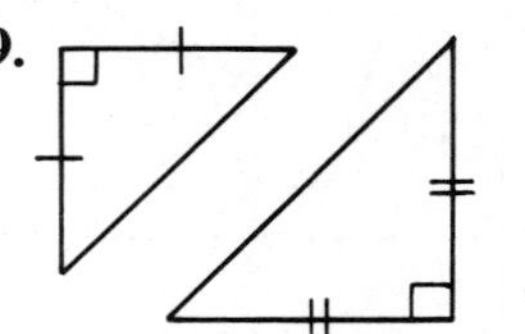


**Complete each statement.**

10. 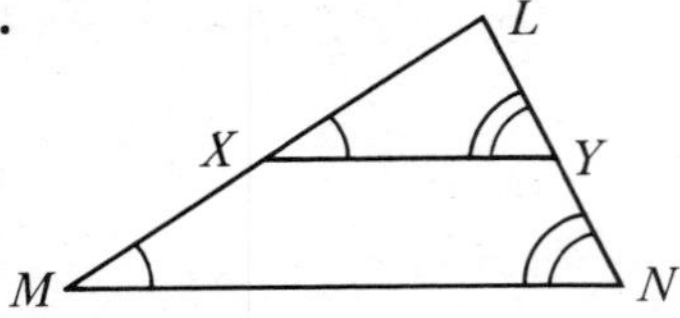


a. $\triangle LMN \sim \triangle$ _?_ $\triangle LXY$

b. $\frac{LX}{LM} = \frac{LY}{?} = \frac{XY}{?}$ $LN$ $MN$

11. 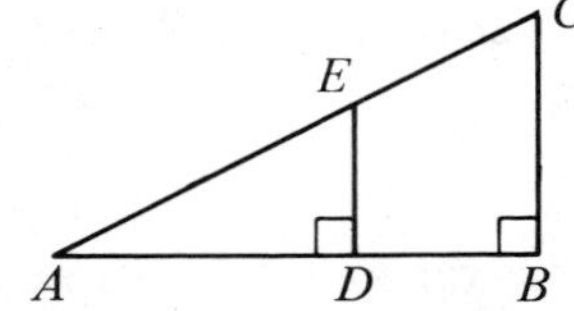


a. $\triangle ABC \sim \triangle$ _?_ $\triangle ADE$

b. $\frac{AB}{AD} = \frac{BC}{?} = \frac{CA}{?}$ $DE$ $EA$

12. 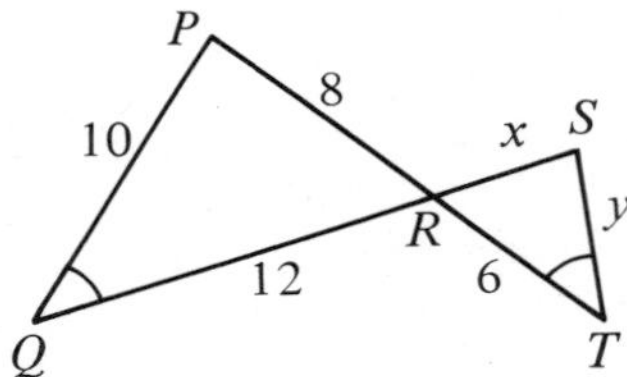


a. $\triangle PQR \sim \triangle$ _?_ $\triangle STR$

b. $\frac{12}{6} = \frac{?}{x}$ and $\frac{12}{6} = \frac{?}{y}$ $\frac{8}{x}, \frac{10}{y}$

c. $x =$ _?_ and $y =$ _?_ 4 5

13. 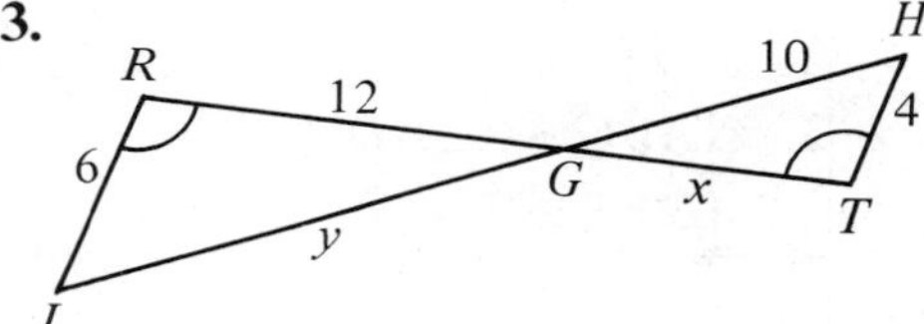


a. $\triangle RIG \sim \triangle$ _?_ $\triangle THG$

b. $\frac{4}{6} = \frac{x}{?}$ and $\frac{4}{6} = \frac{?}{y}$ $\frac{x}{12}, \frac{10}{y}$

c. $x =$ _?_ and $y =$ _?_ 8 15

14. 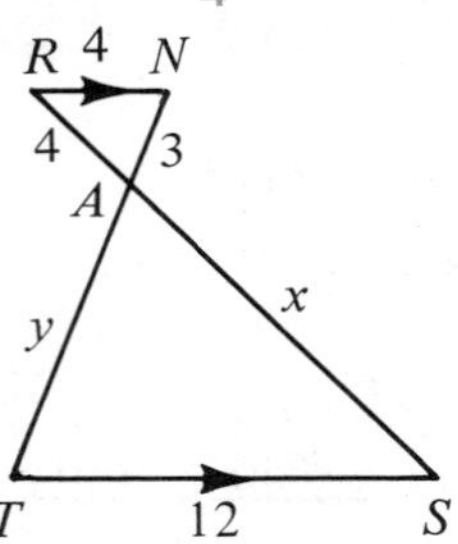


a. $\triangle SAT \sim \triangle$ _?_ $\triangle RAN$

b. $x =$ _?_ 12

c. $y =$ _?_ 9

15. 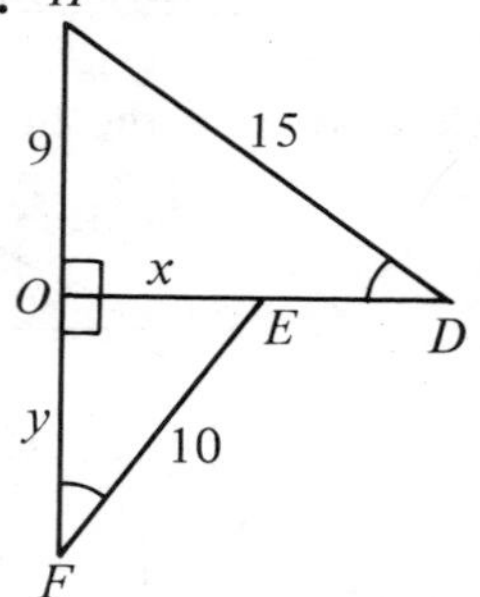


a. $\triangle FOE \sim \triangle$ _?_ $\triangle DOH$

b. $x =$ _?_ 6

c. $y =$ _?_ 8

**Supply the reasons to complete each proof.**

B **16.**

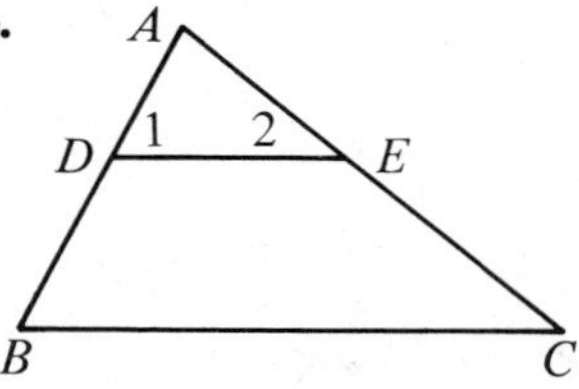


*Given:* $\overline{DE} \parallel \overline{BC}$

*Prove:* $\frac{AD}{AB} = \frac{DE}{BC}$

1. $\overline{DE} \parallel \overline{BC}$ Given
2. $\angle B = \angle 1$ Corr. angles
3. $\angle C = \angle 2$ Corr. angles
4. $\triangle ADE \sim \triangle ABC$ AA Postulate
5. $\frac{AD}{AB} = \frac{DE}{BC}$ Corr. sides of $\sim$ △s are in proportion.

**17.**

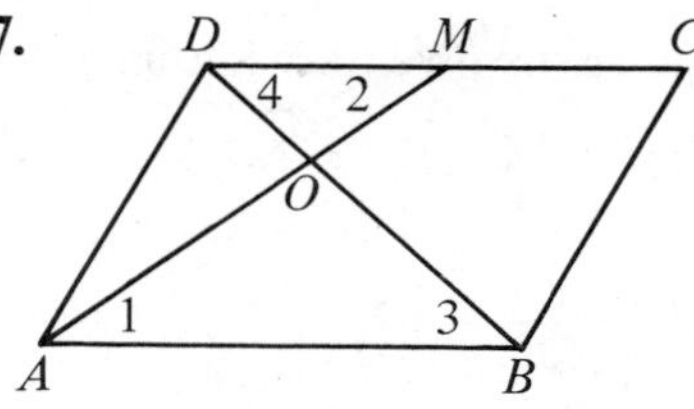


*Given:* $ABCD$ is a ▱.

*Prove:* $\frac{AO}{MO} = \frac{AB}{MD}$

1. $ABCD$ is a ▱. Given
2. $\overline{DM} \parallel \overline{AB}$ Opp. sides of a ▱ are ∥.
3. $\angle 1 = \angle 2$; $\angle 3 = \angle 4$ Alt. interior ∠s
4. $\triangle AOB \sim \triangle MOD$ AA Postulate
5. $\frac{AO}{MO} = \frac{AB}{MD}$ Corr. sides of $\sim$ △s are in proportion.

**In the figure shown, *ABCD* is a parallelogram.**

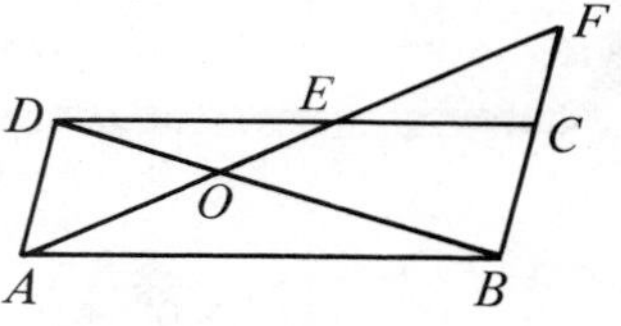


**18.** $\triangle ABO \sim \triangle$ ___?___ $\triangle EDO$

**19.** $\triangle DOA \sim \triangle$ ___?___ $\triangle BOF$

**20.** $\triangle AFB \sim \triangle$ ___?___ $\triangle EAD$; also $\triangle AFB \sim \triangle$ ___?___ $\triangle EFC$

**21.** $\triangle AED \sim \triangle$ ___?___ $\triangle FAB$; also $\triangle AED \sim \triangle$ ___?___ $\triangle FEC$

**22.** *Given:* $\angle X = \angle Y$

*Prove:* $\frac{XS}{YS} = \frac{ST}{SR}$

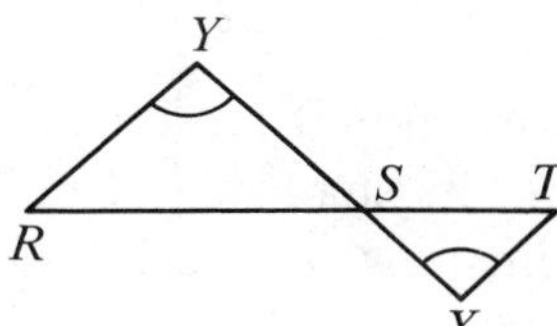


C **23.** *Given:* $\overline{EA} \parallel \overline{PL}$

*Prove:* $\frac{SE}{SA} = \frac{SP}{SL}$

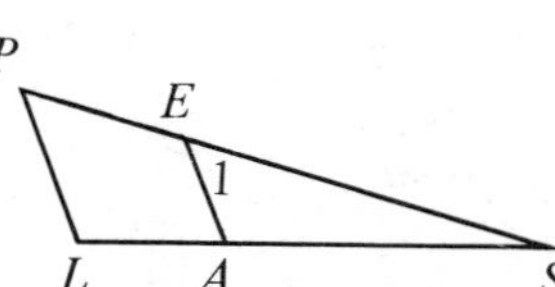


**24.** This exercise proves the following: If two similar triangles have scale factor $k$, then their corresponding altitudes have scale factor $k$.

*Given:* $\triangle ABC \sim \triangle DEF$; $\frac{AC}{DF} = k$

$\overline{CX}$ and $\overline{FY}$ are corresponding altitudes.

*Prove:* $\frac{CX}{FY} = k$

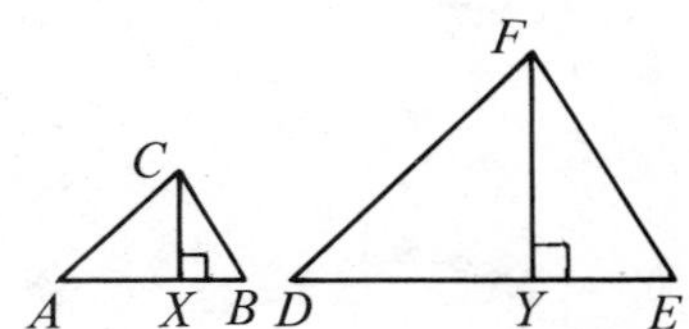

## SELF-TEST

**The two polygons given are similar. Complete each statement.**

1. $\triangle PUN \sim \triangle$ _?_ $\triangle JOK$

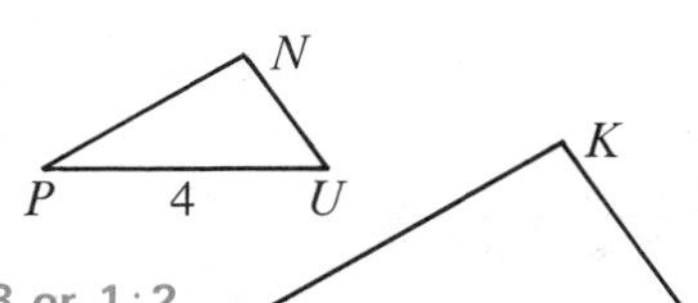


2. $\frac{PU}{JO} = \frac{UN}{?} = \frac{NP}{?}$ OK KJ

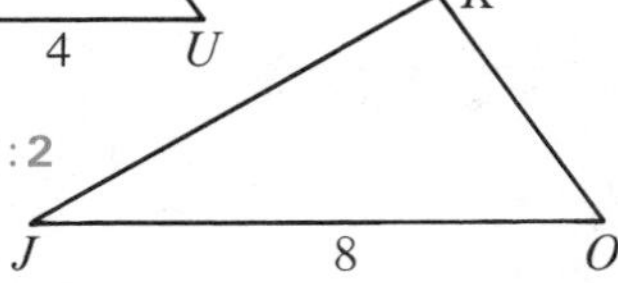


3. The scale factor is _?_ : _?_. 4:8 or 1:2

4. $\angle P = \angle$ _?_ $\angle J$

**State whether the two polygons are, or are not, similar.**

5. 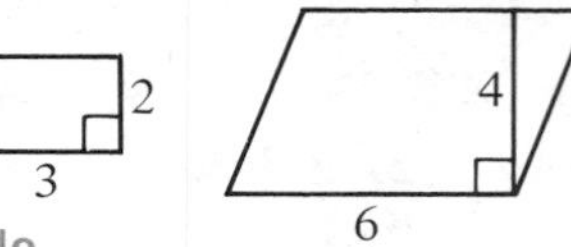


No

6. 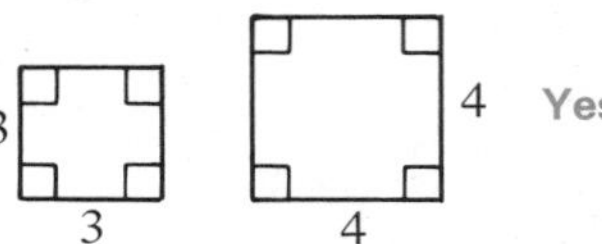


Yes

7. 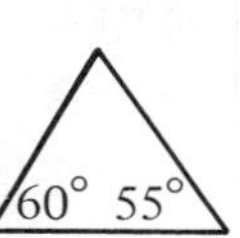

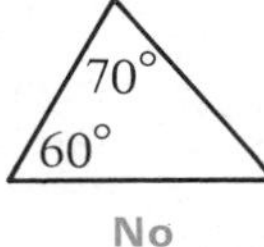


No

8. 

Yes

## Puzzles & Things

Sam stared at a cactus in the Painted Desert until he lost his memory. The cactus is 0.5 m high and its shadow is 1 m long. Sam's shadow is 3.5 m long. Can you tell him how tall he is? 1.75 m

# 3 • A Special Case of Similar Triangles

In the figure at the right, $\overline{DE} \parallel \overline{BC}$. Do you see that $\triangle ADE \sim \triangle ABC$? (For a proof, see Exercise 16 on page 291.) Since corresponding sides of these triangles are in proportion, we can find the values of $x$ and $y$.

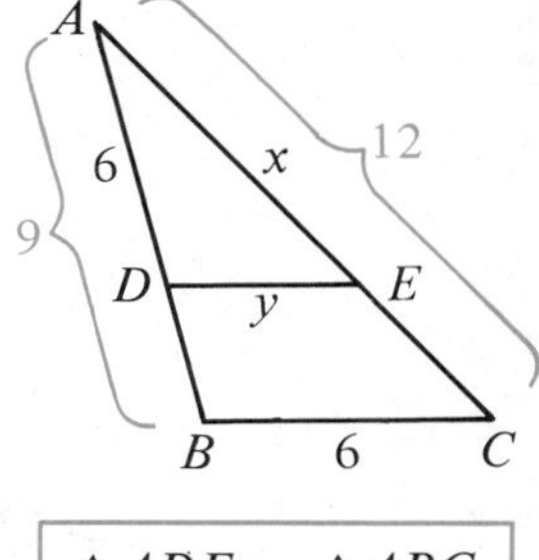


| | |
|---|---|
| $\frac{AD}{AB} = \frac{AE}{AC}$ | $\frac{AD}{AB} = \frac{DE}{BC}$ |
| $\frac{6}{9} = \frac{x}{12}$ | $\frac{6}{9} = \frac{y}{6}$ |
| $72 = 9x$ | $36 = 9y$ |
| $8 = x$ | $4 = y$ |

## Classroom Practice

**Complete each statement. Then find the values of $x$ and $y$.**

**1.**

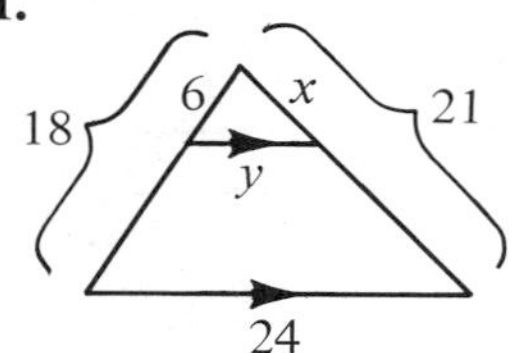


$\frac{6}{18} = \frac{x}{?} = \frac{y}{?}$ $\quad \frac{x}{21} = \frac{y}{24}$

$x = 7$; $y = 8$

**2.**

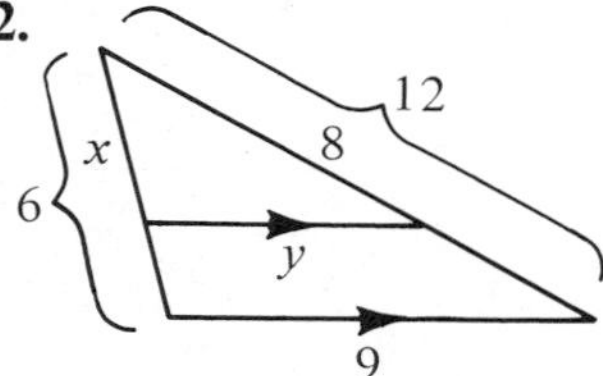


$\frac{x}{6} = \frac{8}{?} = \frac{y}{?}$ $\quad \frac{8}{12} = \frac{y}{9}$

$x = 4$; $y = 6$

**3.**

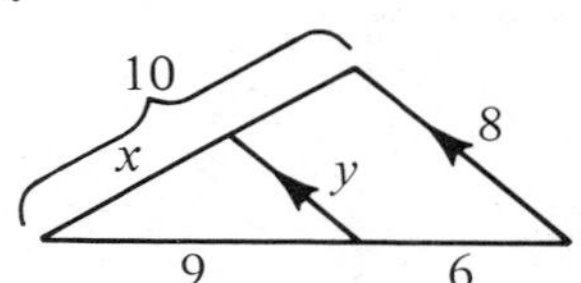


$\frac{10}{x} = \frac{15}{?} = \frac{?}{y}$ $\quad \frac{15}{9} = \frac{8}{y}$

$x = 6$; $y = 4.8$

## Written Exercises

**Complete each statement. Then find the values of $x$ and $y$.**

A **1.**

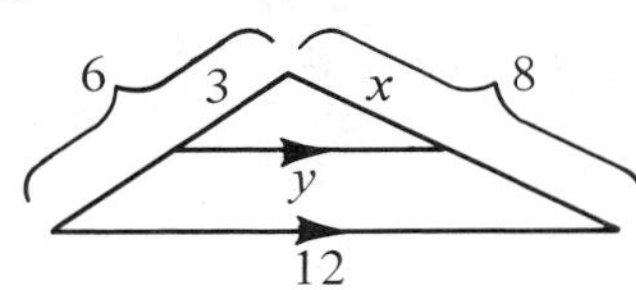


$\frac{3}{6} = \frac{x}{?} = \frac{y}{?}$ $\quad \frac{x}{8} = \frac{y}{12}$

$x = 4$; $y = 6$

**2.**

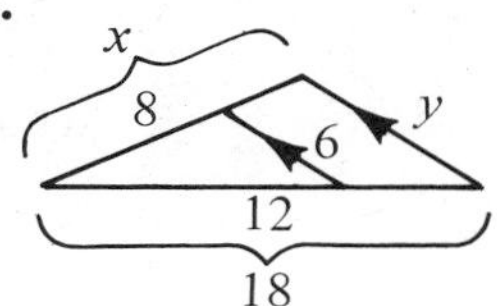


$\frac{18}{12} = \frac{x}{?} = \frac{y}{?}$ $\quad \frac{x}{8} = \frac{y}{6}$

$x = 12$; $y = 9$

**3.**

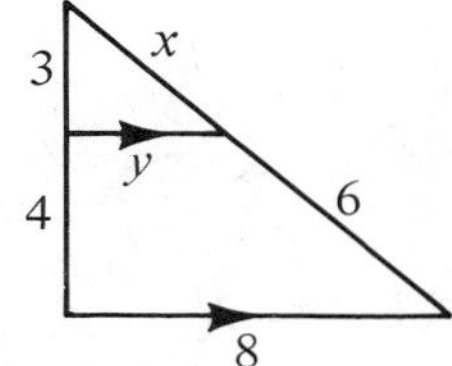


$\frac{x}{x+6} = \frac{3}{?} = \frac{y}{?}$ $\quad \frac{3}{7} = \frac{y}{8}$

$x = 4\frac{1}{2}$; $y = 3\frac{3}{7}$

**Find the values of $x$ and $y$.**

**4.**

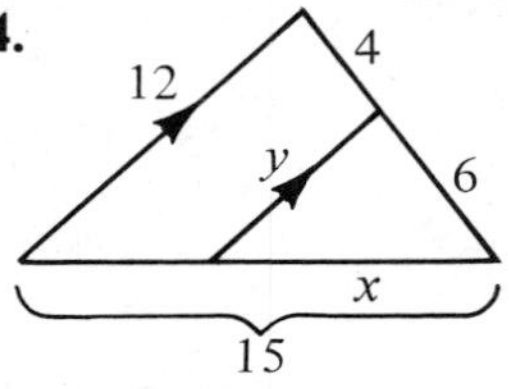


$x = 9$; $y = 7.2$

**5.**

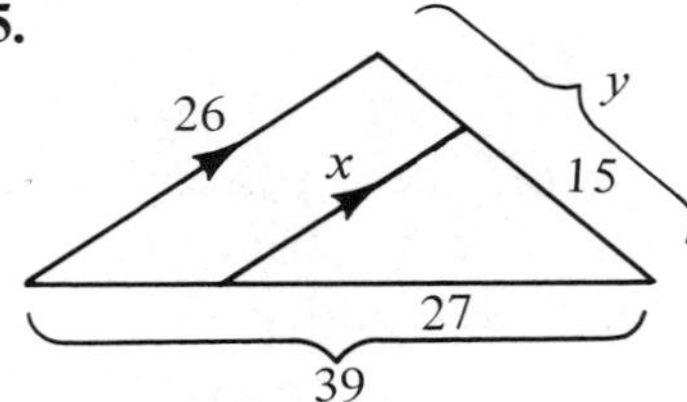


$x = 18$; $y = 21\frac{2}{3}$

**6.**

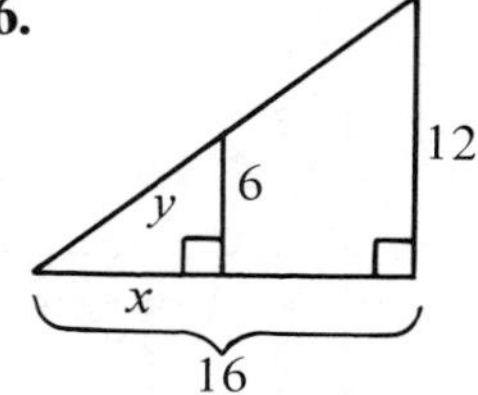


$x = 8$; $y = 10$

**7.**

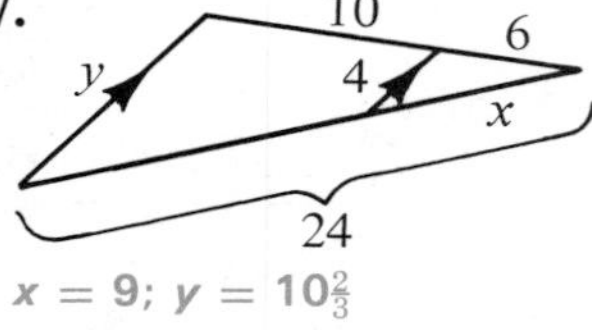


$x = 9$; $y = 10\frac{2}{3}$

**8.**

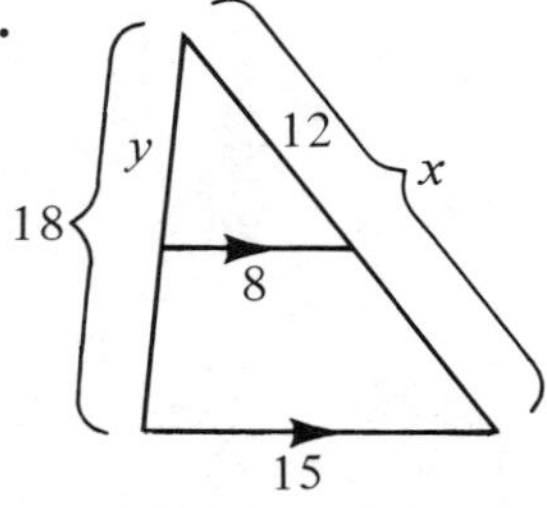


$x = 22.5$; $y = 9.6$

**9.**

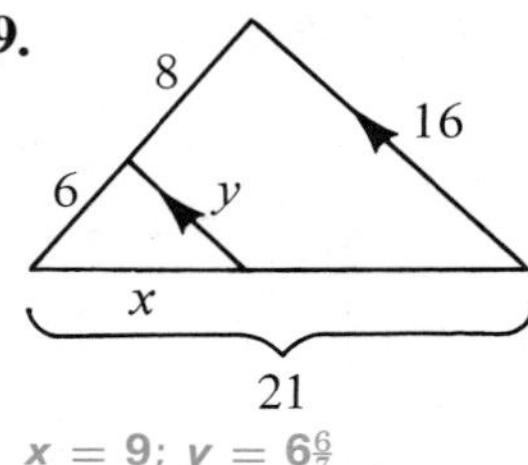


$x = 9$; $y = 6\frac{6}{7}$

**In each exercise, find the value of $x$.**

B **10.**

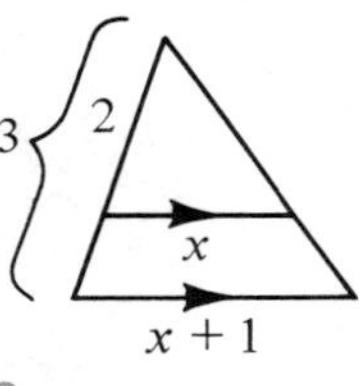


2

**11.**

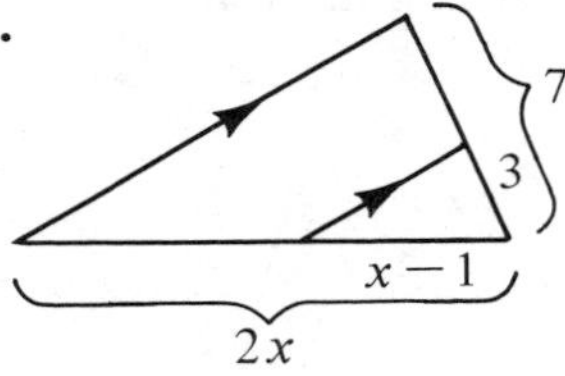


7

**12.**

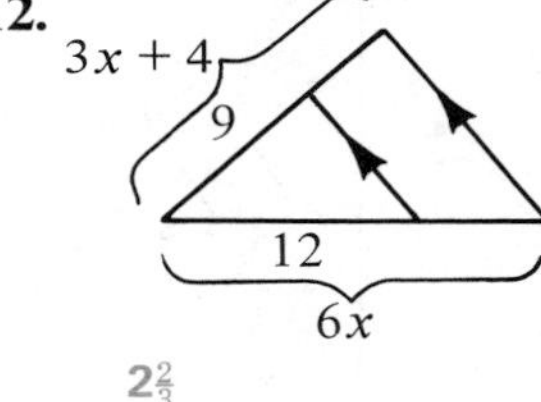


$2\frac{2}{3}$

## Puzzles & Things

Try to draw each figure below without lifting your pencil from the paper and without retracing any line. It is impossible to do this for one of the figures shown. Which one? The center figure

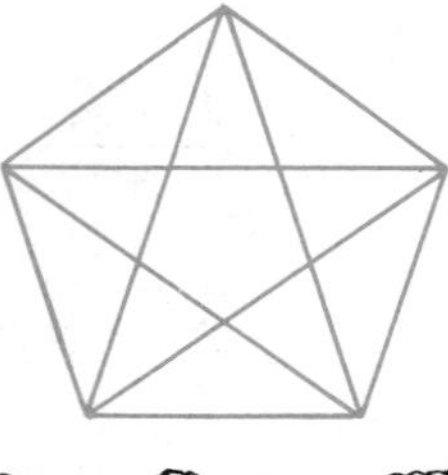

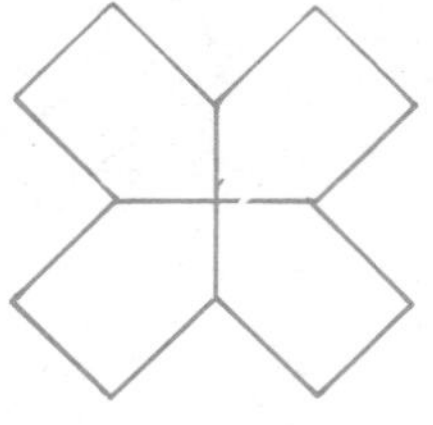

## 4 • The Triangle Proportionality Theorem

In the figure at the right, $\overline{PQ} \parallel \overline{YZ}$. We have seen that this means that $\triangle XYZ \sim \triangle XPQ$. Since corresponding sides of these similar triangles are in proportion,

$$\frac{XY}{XP} = \frac{XZ}{XQ}$$

$$\text{or } \frac{a+b}{a} = \frac{c+d}{c}$$

$$\frac{b}{a} = \frac{d}{c}$$

$$\frac{a}{b} = \frac{c}{d}$$

Use properties of proportions.

The discussion above proves the following useful theorem.

**THEOREM 1 (The Triangle Proportionality Theorem)**

If a line intersects a triangle and is parallel to one side, then it divides the other two sides proportionally.

If [triangle with sides $a$, $b$ and $c$, $d$], then $\frac{a}{b} = \frac{c}{d}$.

**EXAMPLE** Find the values of $x$ and $y$.

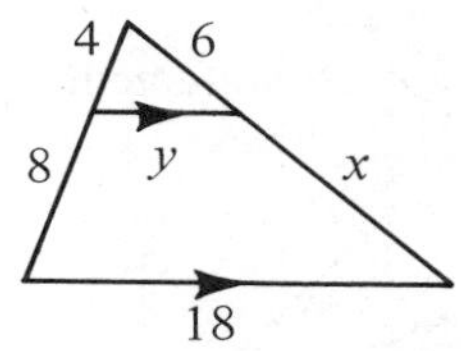


$$\frac{4}{8} = \frac{6}{x} \qquad \frac{4}{4+8} = \frac{y}{18}$$

$$4x = 48 \qquad 72 = 12y$$

$$x = 12 \qquad 6 = y$$

Caution! Notice that $\frac{4}{8} = \frac{6}{x}$, but $\frac{4}{8} \neq \frac{y}{18}$.

Using properties of proportions, it can be shown that the following proportions are true when $\overline{PQ} \parallel \overline{YZ}$:

$$\frac{XP}{XY} = \frac{XQ}{XZ} \qquad \frac{XP}{PY} = \frac{XQ}{QZ} \qquad \frac{PY}{XY} = \frac{QZ}{XZ}$$

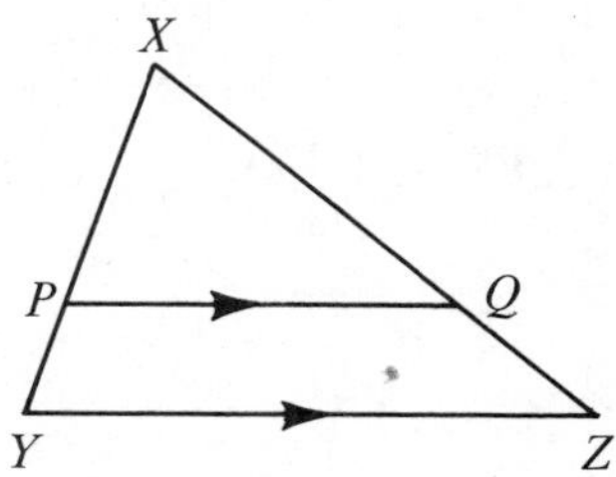


We shall agree that Theorem 1 may be used to justify each of these proportions.

Theorem 1 has a corollary. For a proof, see Exercise 19.

**COROLLARY**

If three parallel lines intersect two transversals, they divide the transversals proportionally.

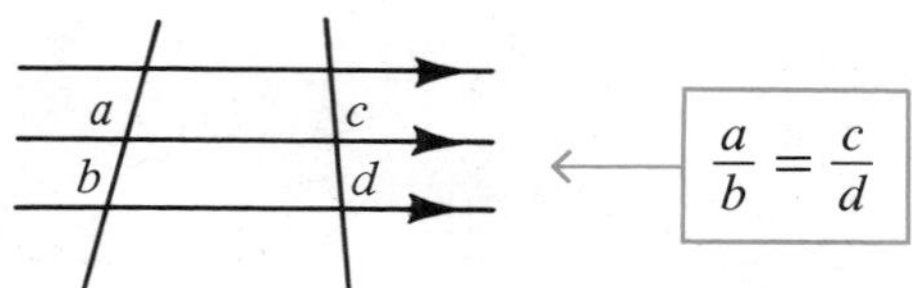


$$\frac{a}{b} = \frac{c}{d}$$

## *Classroom Practice*

**Complete each statement.**

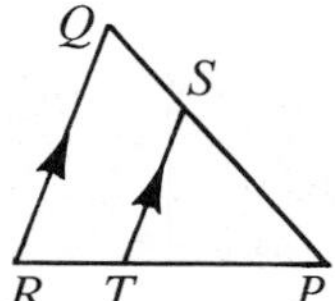


1. $\frac{PS}{SQ} = \frac{PT}{?}$ TR
2. $\frac{PQ}{PS} = \frac{PR}{?}$ PT
3. $\frac{ST}{QR} = \frac{PS}{?}$ PQ
4. $\frac{SQ}{PQ} = \frac{TR}{?}$ PR

**Use the figure below to find the value of each of the following.**

5. $\frac{BD}{BA}$ $\frac{2}{5}$
6. $\frac{BE}{EC}$ $\frac{2}{3}$
7. $\frac{BE}{BC}$ $\frac{2}{5}$
8. $\frac{EC}{BC}$ $\frac{3}{5}$
9. $\frac{DE}{AC}$ $\frac{2}{5}$
10. $\frac{BA}{DA}$ $\frac{5}{3}$

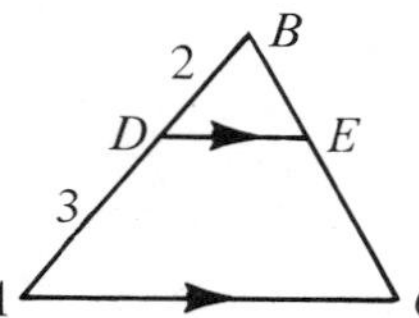


**Complete each statement. Then find the values of $x$ and $y$.**

11.

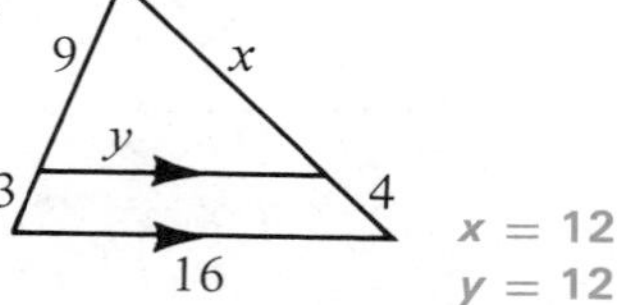


$x = 12$
$y = 12$

$\frac{x}{4} = \frac{9}{?}$ and $\frac{y}{16} = \frac{9}{?}$ 3 12

12.

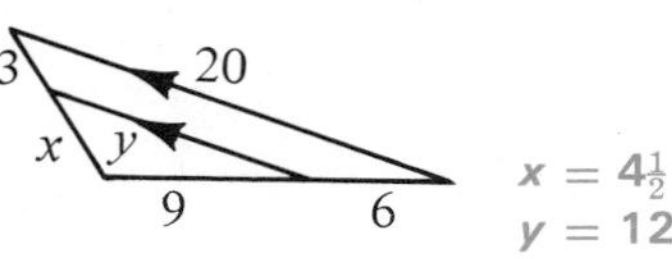


$x = 4\frac{1}{2}$
$y = 12$

$\frac{x}{3} = \frac{9}{?}$ and $\frac{y}{20} = \frac{9}{?}$ 6 15

13. If $\frac{AB}{BC} = \frac{5}{7}$, then $\frac{DE}{EF} = $ __?__. $\frac{5}{7}$

14. If $\frac{AB}{BC} = \frac{5}{7}$, then $\frac{DF}{DE} = $ __?__. $\frac{12}{5}$

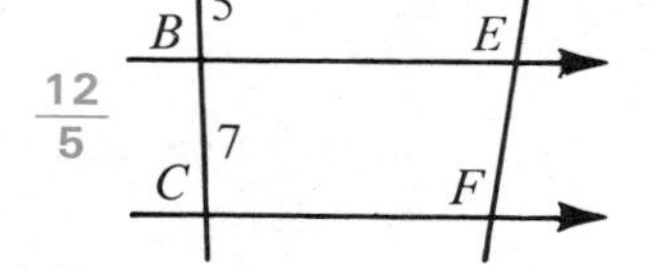

## Written Exercises

For each figure below, complete the statement: $\frac{a}{b} = \frac{?}{?}$.

A **1.**

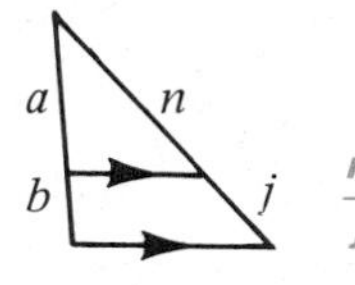


$\frac{n}{j}$

**2.**

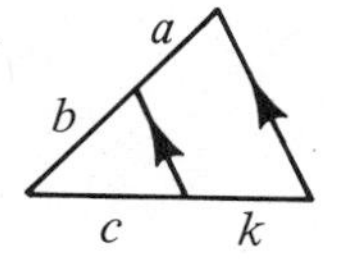


$\frac{k}{c}$

**3.**

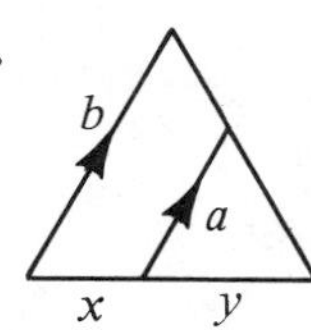


$\frac{y}{x + y}$

**4.**

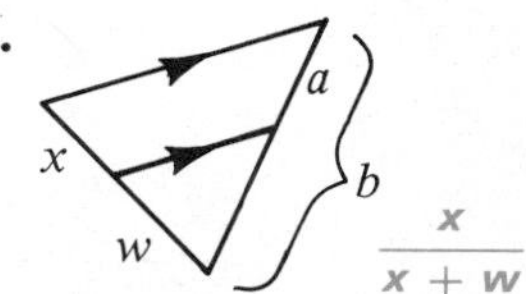


$\frac{x}{x + w}$

**Complete each statement.**

**5.** $\frac{AX}{XB} = \frac{AY}{?}$ $YC$

**6.** $\frac{AX}{AB} = \frac{AY}{?}$ $AC$

**7.** $\frac{XY}{BC} = \frac{AY}{?}$ $AC$

**8.** $\frac{XB}{AB} = \frac{YC}{?}$ $AC$

A, X, Y, B, C

**Find the values of $x$ and $y$ in each figure below.**

**9.**

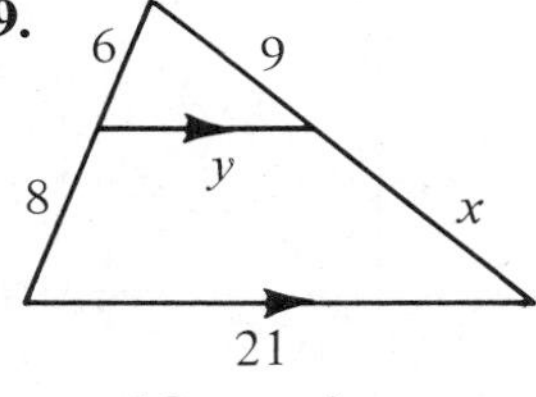


$x = 12$; $y = 9$

**10.**

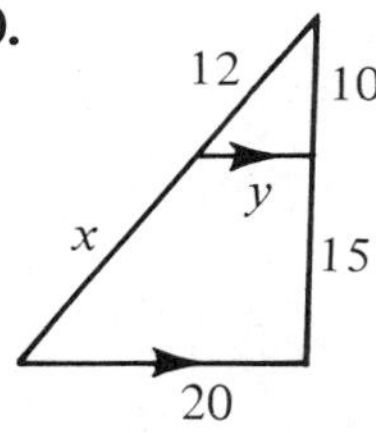


$x = 18$; $y = 8$

**11.**

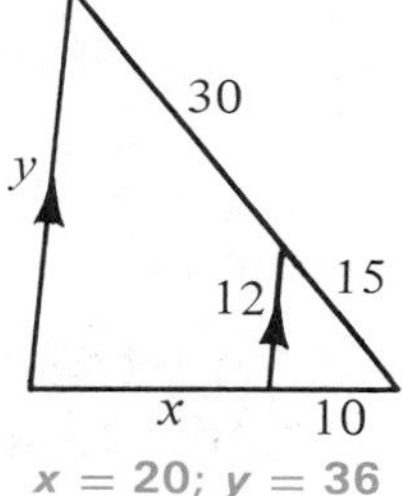


$x = 20$; $y = 36$

**12.**

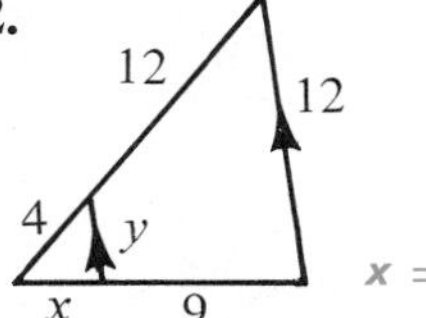


$x = 3$; $y = 3$

**13.**

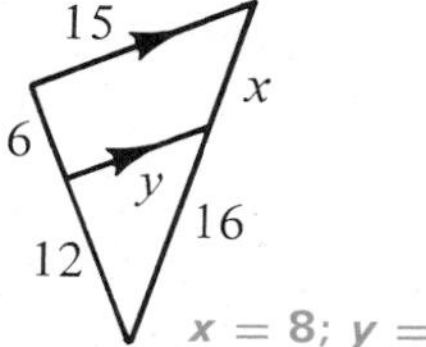


$x = 8$; $y = 10$

**14.**

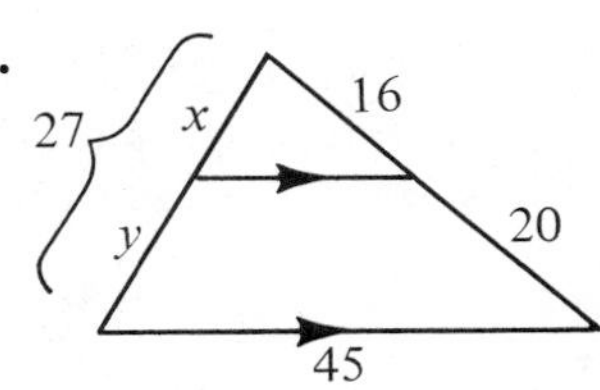


$x = 12$; $y = 15$

**In each figure, find the value of $x$.**

B **15.** 18

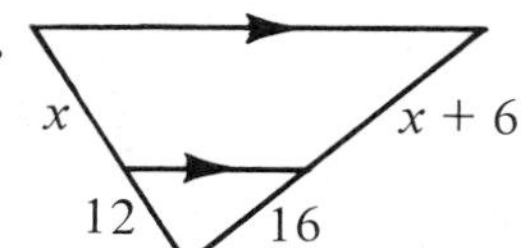


**16.** $18\frac{2}{3}$

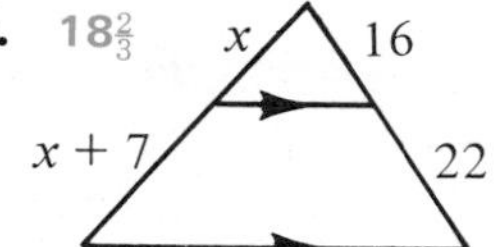


**17.** $13\frac{1}{3}$

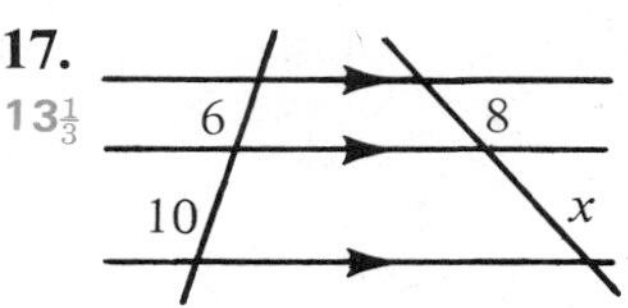


**18.** 18

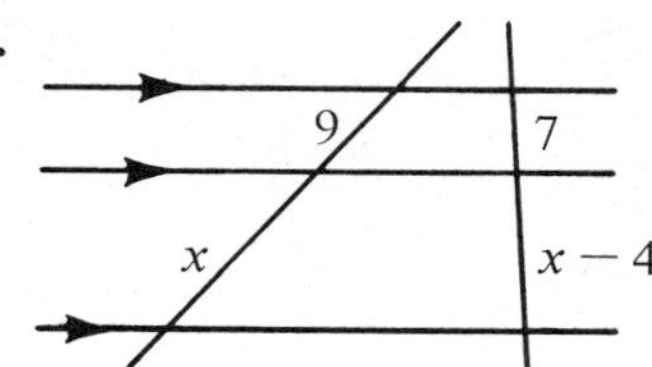

**19.** Supply the reasons for the following proof of the Corollary to Theorem 1.

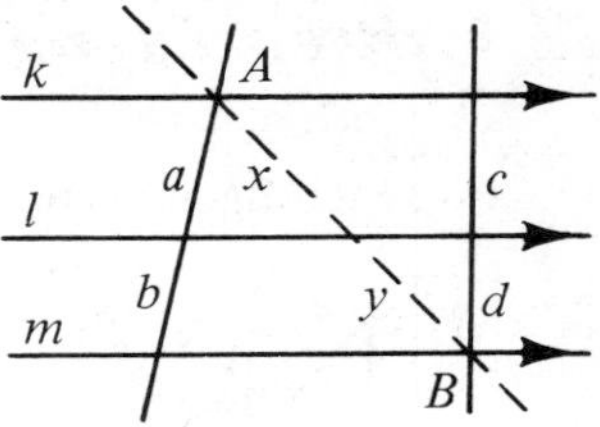


*Given:* $k \parallel l \parallel m$

*Prove:* $\frac{a}{b} = \frac{c}{d}$

| STATEMENTS | REASONS |
|---|---|
| 1. $k \parallel l \parallel m$ | 1. ? Given |
| 2. Draw $\overleftrightarrow{AB}$. | 2. Through any two points there is ? . exactly one line |
| 3. $\frac{a}{b} = \frac{x}{y}$; $\frac{x}{y} = \frac{c}{d}$ | 3. ? Thm. 1, p. 295 |
| 4. $\frac{a}{b} = \frac{c}{d}$ | 4. ? Substitution |

**20.** As shown, lots $A$ and $B$ are bounded at the front and back by Maple Street and Elm Street, respectively. Use the diagram to find $x$ and $y$, the distance each lot has along Elm Street. $x = 100$, $y = 150$

**21.** Which lot has the greater area? How much greater? *B* has the greater area by 1800 m$^2$.

**In Exercises 22 and 23, use the statement: The bisector of an angle of a triangle divides the opposite side in the same ratio as the other two sides of the triangle.**

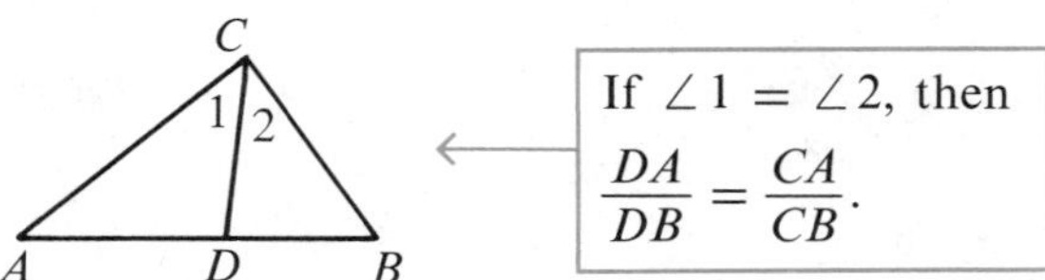


**Complete each statement. Then find the value of *x*.**

C **22.**

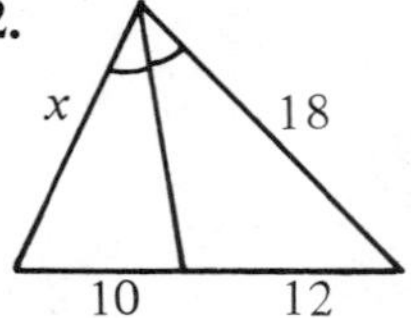


$\frac{10}{12} = \frac{x}{?}$ $\frac{x}{18}$, $x = 15$

**23.**

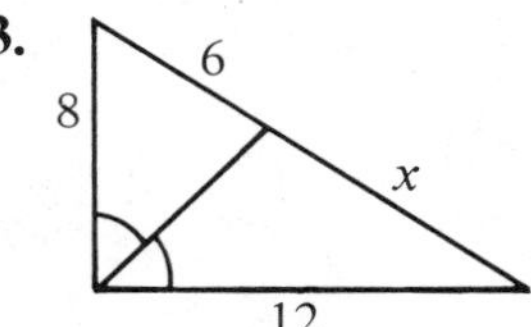


$\frac{x}{6} = \frac{?}{?}$ $\frac{12}{8}$, $x = 9$

## Experiments

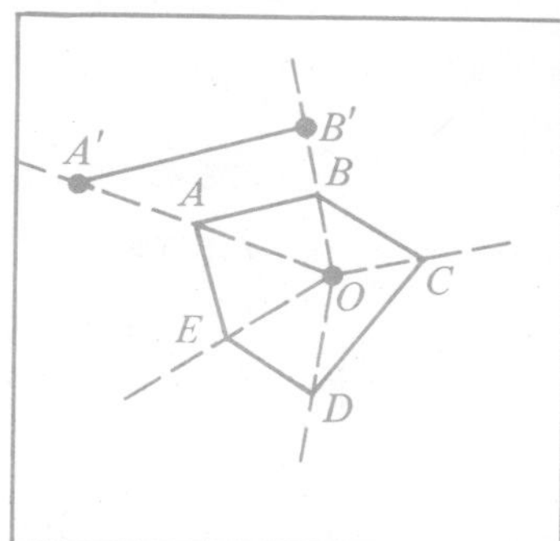


1. Draw a small pentagon $ABCDE$ near the center of a large sheet of paper.
2. Choose a point $O$ inside the pentagon. Draw dotted rays from $O$ through each vertex.
3. As shown, locate point $A'$ on $\overrightarrow{OA}$ so that
$$OA' = 2(OA).$$
Locate point $B'$ on $\overrightarrow{OB}$ so that $OB' = 2(OB)$. Locate points $C'$, $D'$, and $E'$ in the same way.
4. Draw pentagon $A'B'C'D'E'$.
5. Using a protractor, compare the measures of corresponding angles of the pentagons.
6. Using a ruler, compare the lengths of corresponding sides of the pentagons.
7. What can you conclude about pentagons $ABCDE$ and $A'B'C'D'E'$? Can you prove your conclusion? They are similar.

# CAREER NOTES

### Helicopter Pilot

Helicopter pilots work in many different situations. For example, they deliver mail, herd cattle, transport building materials and fully assembled towers, rescue people from mountains and jungles, drop food and medical aid to flood and disaster victims, and broadcast traffic reports. Helicopters perform important tasks in farming. For example, helicopters are used to seed and to fertilize large areas of land.

Helicopters are very maneuverable. They can be flown straight up or down, forward, backward, or sideways. They can also hover over one spot and turn completely around.

Because of the complexity of flight and the responsibility involved, helicopter pilots must obtain pilots' certificates with helicopter ratings.

## 5 • Perimeters and Areas

Have you ever seen a billboard like this one?

The increased amount of litter is represented by two similar trash cans. The dimensions of the larger can are *twice* the corresponding dimensions of the smaller one. Yet the larger can seems huge in comparison with the smaller one. This is because its area is *four times as great*. Do you see why?

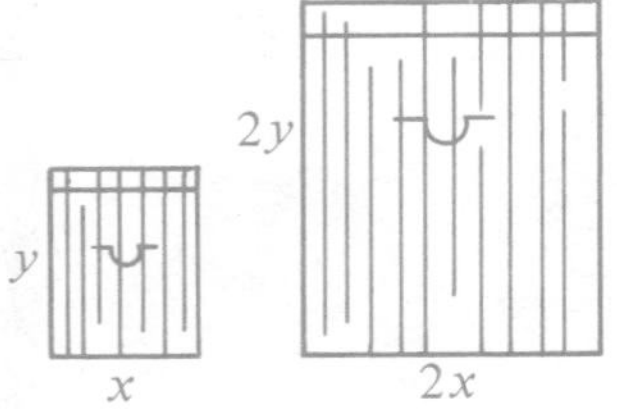


$$\begin{aligned}
\text{Area of a rectangle} &= \text{base} \times \text{height} \\
\text{Area of smaller rectangle} &= xy \\
\text{Area of larger rectangle} &= (2x)(2y) \\
&= 4xy \\
&= 4(\text{area of smaller rectangle})
\end{aligned}$$

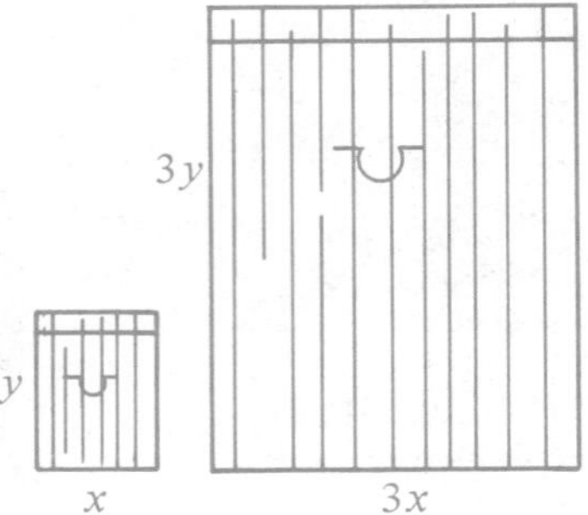


Suppose that the dimensions of the larger trash can were three times those of the smaller trash can. Then the larger area would be *nine* times the smaller one:

$$\begin{aligned}
\text{Area of smaller rectangle} &= xy \\
\text{Area of larger rectangle} &= (3x)(3y) \\
&= 9xy \\
&= 9(\text{area of smaller rectangle})
\end{aligned}$$

Our work in Section 1 suggested that the perimeters of similar polygons are related in a special way. The discussion above suggests that the areas of similar polygons are also related.

**THEOREM 2**

If two similar polygons have a scale factor $a:b$, then
(1) the ratio of their perimeters is $a:b$;
(2) the ratio of their areas is $a^2:b^2$.

Theorem 2 is true, not only for polygons, but for figures such as circles, which are not polygons.

**EXAMPLE** The similar figures below have the scale factor 3:2. Find
**a.** the ratio of their perimeters;
**b.** the ratio of their areas.

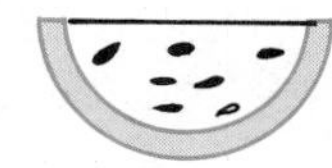

Using Theorem 2:
**a.** the ratio of their perimeters is 3:2;
**b.** the ratio of their areas is $3^2:2^2$, or 9:4.

## *Classroom Practice*

**Each exercise of the table refers to two similar figures.** (Answers are *above* blanks.)
**Copy and complete the table.**

| | | | | | 2:3 | 3:8 | 1:2 | 6:5 |
|---|---|---|---|---|---|---|---|---|
| | **1.** | **2.** | **3.** | **4.** | **5.** | **6.** | **7.** | **8.** |
| Scale factor | 1:4 | 1:5 | 2:5 | 3:7 | ? | ? | ? | ? |
| Ratio of perimeters | 1:4<br>? | 1:5<br>? | 2:5<br>? | 3:7<br>? | 2:3 | 3:8 | 1:2<br>? | 6:5<br>? |
| Ratio of areas | 1:16<br>? | 1:25<br>? | 4:25<br>? | 9:49<br>? | 4:9<br>? | 9:64<br>? | 1:4 | 36:25 |

**The purpose of Exercises 9 and 10 is to prove Theorem 2 for similar triangles. The triangles shown have the scale factor *a*:*b*.**

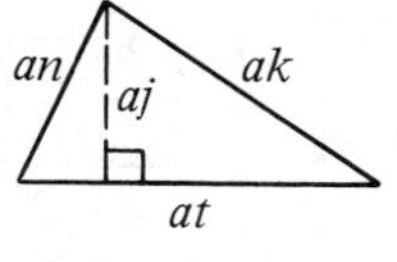

Triangle 1

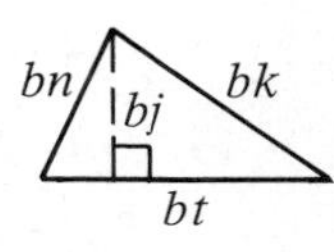

Triangle 2

**9.** $\dfrac{\text{perimeter of triangle 1}}{\text{perimeter of triangle 2}} = \dfrac{at + ak + an}{bt + bk + bn}$
Show that this ratio is equal to $a:b$.

**10.** Recall from Exercise 24, page 291, that corresponding altitudes of similar triangles have the same ratio as corresponding sides. Write an expression for the ratio of the areas, and show that this ratio is equal to $a^2:b^2$.

## Written Exercises

**Each exercise refers to two similar figures. If the given ratio is the scale factor, find the ratio of the perimeters and the ratio of the areas.**

| | p | A |
|---|---|---|
| 1. | 1:2 | 1:4 |
| 2. | 1:3 | 1:9 |
| 3. | 2:3 | 4:9 |
| 4. | 5:4 | 25:16 |

A **1.** 1:2 **2.** 1:3 **3.** 2:3 **4.** 5:4

**Each exercise refers to two similar figures. Copy and complete the table.**

| | 5. | 6. | 7. | 8. | 9. | 10. |
|---|---|---|---|---|---|---|
| Scale factor | ? | ? | ? | ? | ? | ? |
| Ratio of perimeters | 3:5 3:5 | 7:4 7:4 | 2:3 ? | 9:5 ? | 3:7 ? | 10:1 ? |
| Ratio of areas | ? | ? | 2:3 4:9 | 9:5 81:25 | 3:7 9:49 | 10:1 100:1 |
| | 9:25 | 49:16 | | | | |

(Answers are *below* blanks.)

**By measuring each pair of similar figures, find:**
**a. their scale factor; b. the ratio of their perimeters;**
**c. the ratio of their areas.**

**11.**

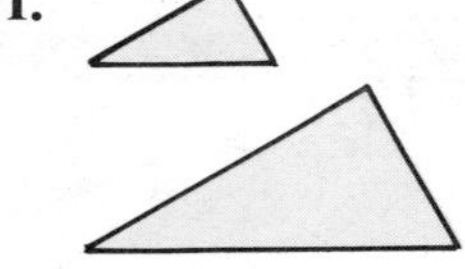

a. 1:2
b. 1:2
c. 1:4

**12.**

a. 1:3
b. 1:3
c. 1:9

**13.**

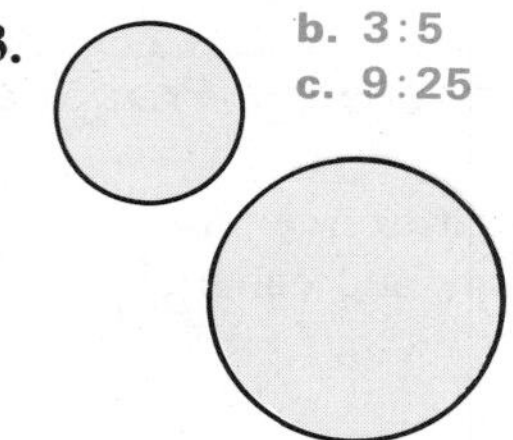

a. 3:5
b. 3:5
c. 9:25

B **14.** Refer to the floor plan of a house on page 271. Find the ratio of the floor area in the actual house to the corresponding area in the drawing. 40,000:1

**15.** The widths of two similar rectangles are 15 and 25. Find the ratio of their perimeters and the ratio of their areas. p—3:5 A—9:25

**16.** The bases of two similar triangles are 18 and 27. Find the ratio of their perimeters and the ratio of their areas. p—2:3 A—4:9

**17.** *Given:* $\triangle ABC \sim \triangle DEF$ with scale factor 3:4.

**a.** If $\triangle ABC$ has perimeter 15, then $\triangle DEF$ has perimeter __?__. 20

**b.** If $\triangle ABC$ has area 18, then $\triangle DEF$ has area __?__. 32

**18.** *Given:* $\triangle PQR \sim \triangle XYZ$ with scale factor 3:5.

**a.** If $\triangle PQR$ has perimeter 30, then $\triangle XYZ$ has perimeter __?__. 50

**b.** If $\triangle PQR$ has area 36, then $\triangle XYZ$ has area __?__. 100

**19.** *Given:* $\triangle LMN$; $O$ is the midpoint of $\overline{LN}$; $P$ is the midpoint of $\overline{MN}$.

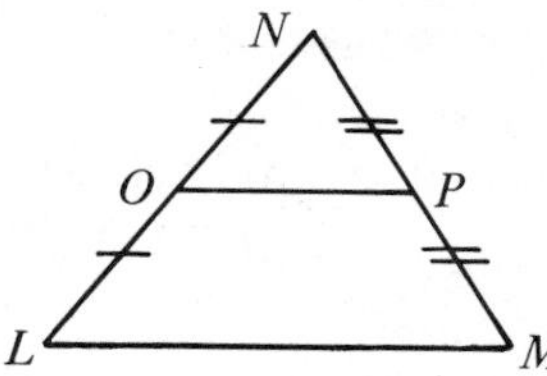


**a.** $\dfrac{\text{perimeter of } \triangle OPN}{\text{perimeter of } \triangle LMN} = \underline{\ ?\ }$ $\frac{1}{2}$

**b.** $\dfrac{\text{area of } \triangle OPN}{\text{area of } \triangle LMN} = \underline{\ ?\ }$ $\frac{1}{4}$

**20.** The floors of two rooms are similar rectangles with scale factor 3:4. It costs \$9 to paint the floor of the smaller room. How much does it cost to paint the floor of the larger room? \$16

C **21.** The perimeters of two similar hexagons are in the ratio 1:2. The sum of the areas of the hexagons is 80 $cm^2$. Find the area of each hexagon. 16 $cm^2$, 64 $cm^2$

**22.** The areas of two similar pentagons are 27 $cm^2$ and 48 $cm^2$. The sum of the perimeters of the pentagons is 42 cm. Find the perimeter of each pentagon. 18 cm, 24 cm

## SELF-TEST

**Find the values of $x$ and $y$.**

**1.**

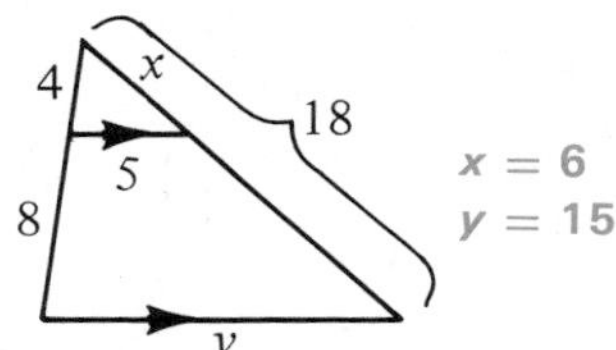


$x = 6$
$y = 15$

**2.**

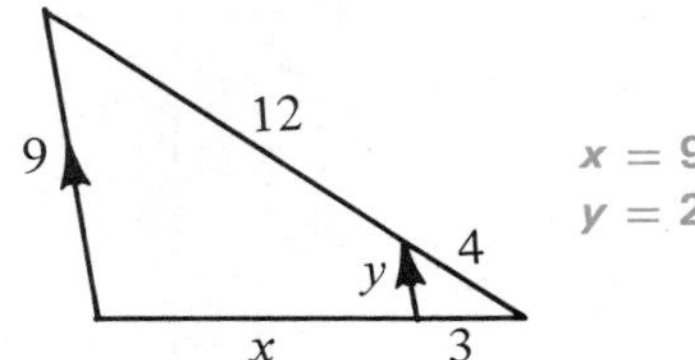


$x = 9$
$y = 2\frac{1}{4}$

**The table refers to two similar figures. Copy and complete the table.**

| | 3. | 4. 3:7 | 5. 5:6 |
|---|---|---|---|
| Scale factor | 1:3 | ? | ? |
| Ratio of perimeters | 1:3 ? | 3:7 | 5:6 ? |
| Ratio of areas | 1:9 ? | 9:49 ? | 25:36 |

(Answers are *above* blanks.)

## CALCULATOR CORNER

Can you see that any two equilateral triangles are similar polygons?

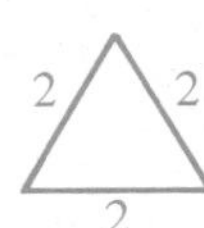

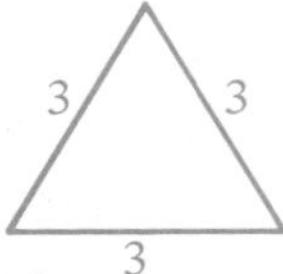


The area of an equilateral triangle is given by the formula

$$A = \frac{s^2\sqrt{3}}{4}$$ where $s$ is the length of a side.

Use your calculator to compute the perimeter and area of each triangle described. ($\sqrt{3} \doteq 1.732$) Round each area to the nearest tenth.

| $s$ | 1 | 2 | 3 | 4 | 5 | 6 | 7 |
|---|---|---|---|---|---|---|---|
| perimeter | 3 | ? 6 | ? 9 | ? 12 | ? 15 | ? 18 | ? 21 |
| area | 0.4 | ? | ? | ? | ? | ? | ? |
| | | 1.7 | 3.9 | 6.9 | 10.8 | 15.6 | 21.2 |

Now copy and complete each graph.

(See Solution Key.)

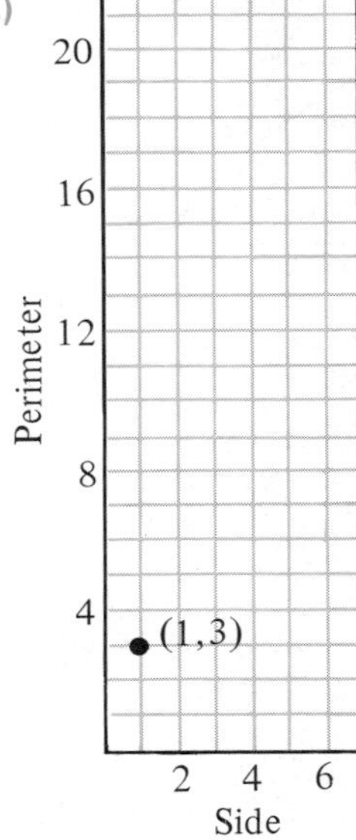


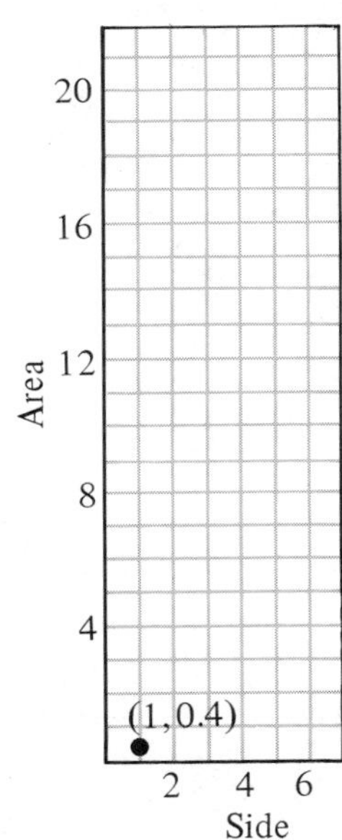

# Reviewing Algebraic Skills

$5^2 = 25$ ← square of 5

$\sqrt{25} = 5$ ← positive square root of 25

$(-5)^2 = 25$ ← square of $-5$

$-\sqrt{25} = -5$ ← negative square root of 25

**Complete the table.**

| | Number | Positive Square Root | Negative Square Root |
|---|---|---|---|
| **1.** | 64 | 8 | ? $-8$ |
| **2.** | 121 | ? 11 | $-11$ |
| **3.** | 49 | ? 7 | ? $-7$ |
| **4.** | 81 | ? 9 | ? $-9$ |
| **5.** | 169 | 13 | ? $-13$ |
| **6.** | 36 | ? 6 | ? $-6$ |
| **7.** | 100 | ? 10 | ? $-10$ |
| **8.** | 144 | ? 12 | ? $-12$ |

**Find the value. Leave your answer in simplest radical form if the number is not a perfect square. Assume that variables represent numbers greater than zero.**

Sample 1 $\sqrt{900} = \sqrt{9 \cdot 100}$
$= \sqrt{9} \cdot \sqrt{100}$
$= 3 \cdot 10$
$= 30$

Sample 2 $\sqrt{72x^2} = \sqrt{36 \cdot 2 \cdot x^2}$
$= \sqrt{36} \cdot \sqrt{2} \cdot \sqrt{x^2}$
$= 6 \cdot \sqrt{2} \cdot x$
$= 6x\sqrt{2}$

**9.** $\sqrt{225}$ 15 **10.** $\sqrt{18}$ $3\sqrt{2}$ **11.** $\sqrt{49n^2}$ $7n$ **12.** $\sqrt{75}$ $5\sqrt{3}$ **13.** $\sqrt{63}$ $3\sqrt{7}$

**14.** $\sqrt{16y^2}$ $4y$ **15.** $\sqrt{400}$ 20 **16.** $\sqrt{125}$ $5\sqrt{5}$ **17.** $\sqrt{128}$ $8\sqrt{2}$ **18.** $\sqrt{50a^2}$ $5a\sqrt{2}$

**19.** $\sqrt{98}$ $7\sqrt{2}$ **20.** $\sqrt{20k^2}$ **21.** $\sqrt{196}$ 14 **22.** $\sqrt{162}$ $9\sqrt{2}$ **23.** $\sqrt{700}$ $10\sqrt{7}$

**24.** $\sqrt{32b^2}$ **25.** $\sqrt{324}$ 18 **26.** $\sqrt{45}$ $3\sqrt{5}$ **27.** $\sqrt{256}$ 16 **28.** $\sqrt{147}$ $7\sqrt{3}$

$4b\sqrt{2}$ 20. $2k\sqrt{5}$

**29.** A square has the area given in the figure. What is the length of a side? $4\sqrt{3}$ units

48 square units

**30.** What is the negative square root of 128? $-8\sqrt{2}$

# applications

## *Art and Geometry*

In the period between 1400 and 1700, artists began to use geometric ideas to make their paintings more realistic. The sketch below illustrates some of their techniques.

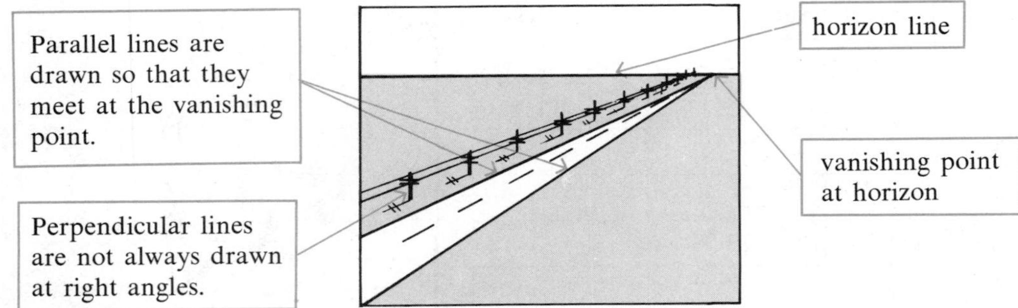


Baldassare Peruzzi, a sixteenth century Italian architect and painter, drew this picture of ancient Roman monuments. Notice his use of the vanishing point.

**Exercises**

1. Draw the tiled hallway shown by following these steps:

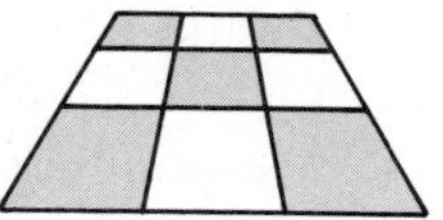

   (1) Draw the horizon and three vanishing points $A$, $B$, and $C$ with $AB = BC$.
   (2) Draw $DEFG$ with $DE = EF = FG$. Draw $\overline{BD}$, $\overline{BE}$, $\overline{BF}$, and $\overline{BG}$.
   (3) Draw $\overline{DC}$ and $\overline{GA}$, marking the points in which they intersect $\overline{BD}$, $\overline{BE}$, $\overline{BF}$, and $\overline{BG}$.

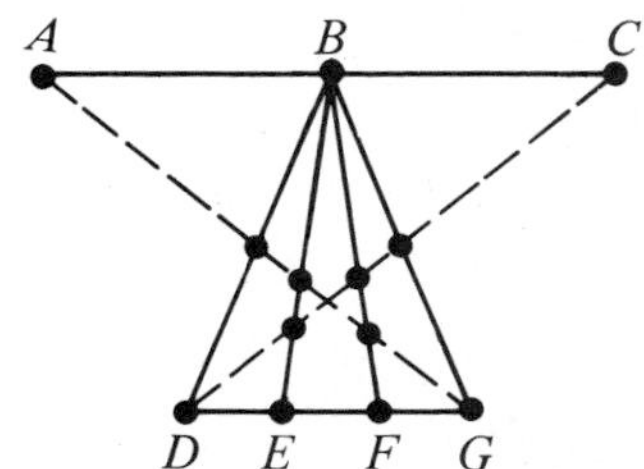


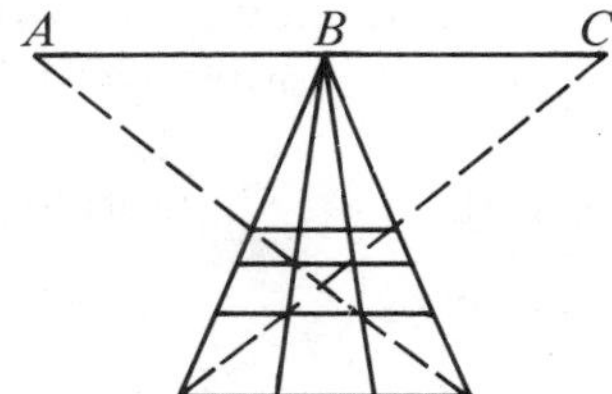


   (4) Draw horizontal lines through the intersection points.
   (5) Erase the construction lines and shade every other square.

2. Cut a picture from a magazine or newspaper and enlarge it by the method described below.

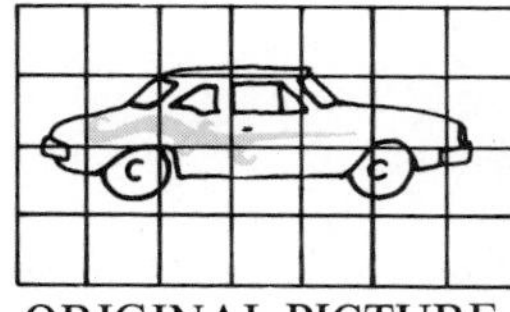

ORIGINAL PICTURE

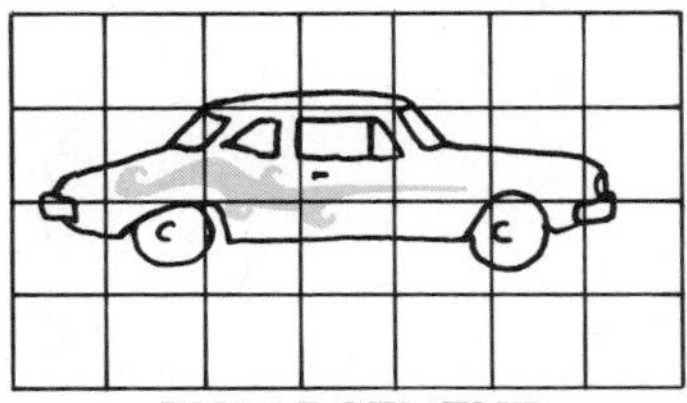

ENLARGEMENT

   (1) Draw a rectangular grid on the picture.
   (2) Draw a larger rectangular grid.
   (3) Copy each square of the picture in the corresponding square of the larger grid.

3. The humorous picture at the right is called "False Perspective." It was created in 1753 by the famous British artist William Hogarth. Describe some of the false perspectives in this work.

## Reviewing the Chapter

### Chapter Summary

1. If two figures have the same shape, they are similar. Two things are true of similar polygons:
   (a) Corresponding angles are equal.
   (b) Corresponding sides are in proportion (have equal ratios).

2. To show that two polygons are similar, you must show that both (a) and (b) above are true. However, to show that two *triangles* are similar, you only need to show that two angles of one triangle are equal to two angles of the other triangle.

3. The Triangle Proportionality Theorem states:
   If [triangle with sides a, b, c, d and parallel segment], then $\frac{a}{b} = \frac{c}{d}$.

4. If three parallel lines intersect two transversals, they divide the transversals proportionally.

5. The scale factor of the similar figures shown is 3:2. This is the ratio of a pair of corresponding sides. The ratio of the perimeters is also 3:2. The ratio of the areas is $3^2:2^2$, or 9:4.

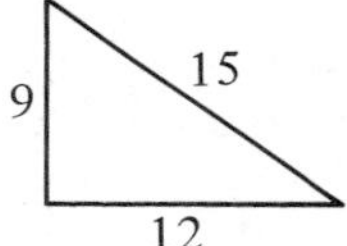

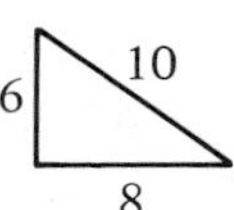


### Chapter Review Test

**In Exercises 1–6, the two polygons given are similar. Complete each statement.**
*(See pp. 282–286.)*

1. $\triangle LAF \sim \triangle$ _?_ $\triangle JIG$
2. $\frac{LA}{JI} = \frac{LF}{?} = \frac{AF}{?}$ $JG$; $IG$
3. $\angle A = \angle$ _?_ $\angle I$

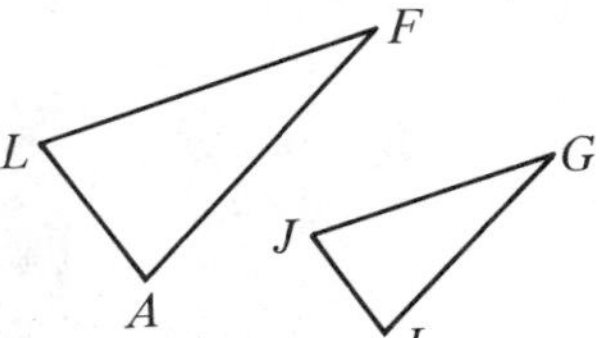


4. Trapezoid $SKON \sim$ trapezoid _?_ FLAP
5. The scale factor is _?_:_?_. 2:3
6. $\frac{14}{21} = \frac{x}{?}$ 27

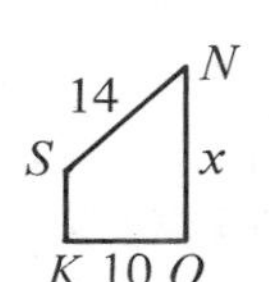

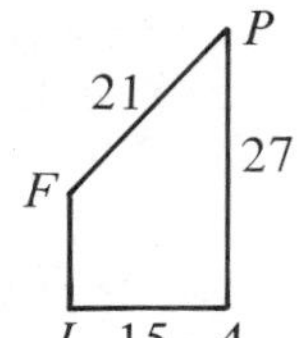

**In the diagram at the right, $\overline{UV} \parallel \overline{RS}$. Complete each statement.** *(See pp. 287–291.)*

7. $\angle R = \angle$ _?_ and $\angle S = \angle$ _?_ V U

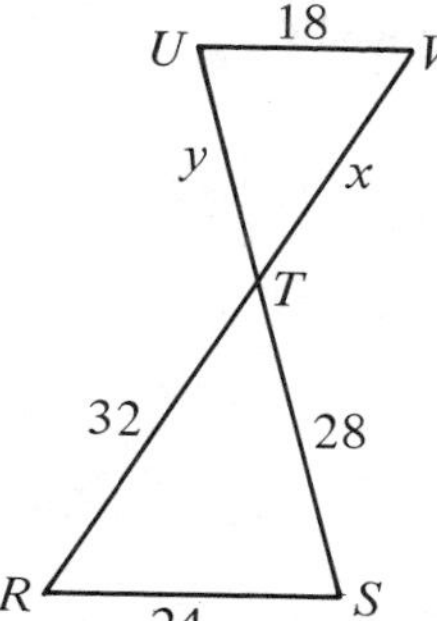


8. $\triangle RST \sim \triangle$ _?_ $\triangle VUT$

9. $\frac{18}{24} = \frac{x}{?}$ 32

10. $x =$ _?_ 24

11. $y =$ _?_ 21

**For each figure, complete the statement $\frac{a}{b} = \frac{?}{?}$.** *(See pp. 293–294.)*

12.

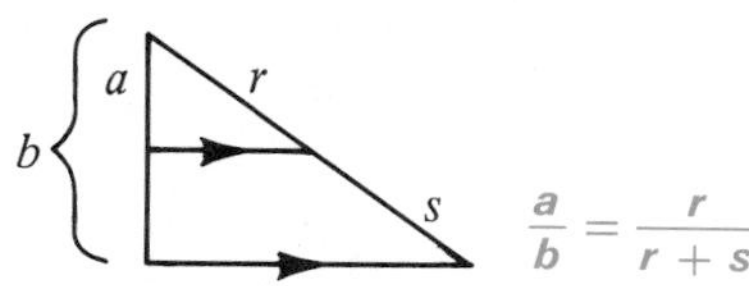


$\frac{a}{b} = \frac{r}{r + s}$

13.

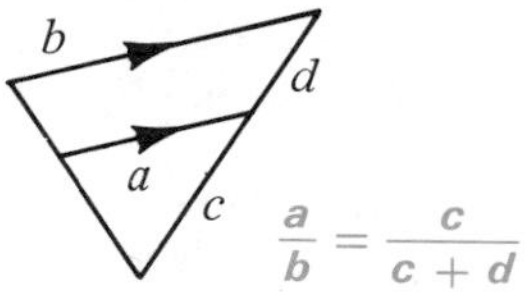


$\frac{a}{b} = \frac{c}{c + d}$

**For each figure, find the value of $x$.** *(See pp. 295–298.)*

14. 18

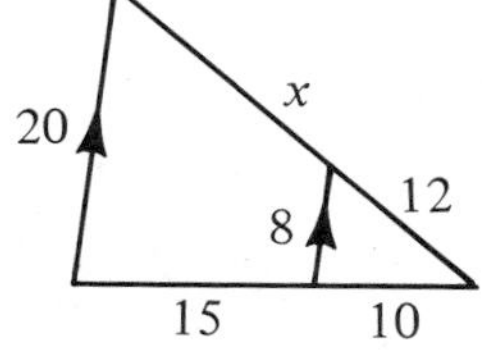


15. 4

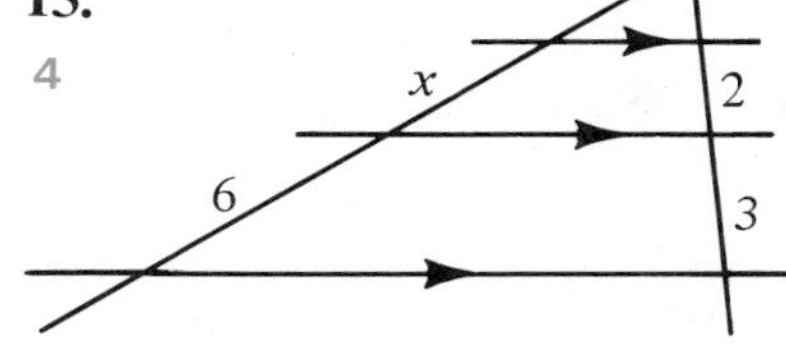


**For the pair of similar rectangles shown, complete each statement.** *(See pp. 300–303.)*

16. The scale factor is _?_ : _?_. 6:5

17. The ratio of their perimeters is _?_ : _?_. 6:5

18. The ratio of their areas is _?_ : _?_. 36:25

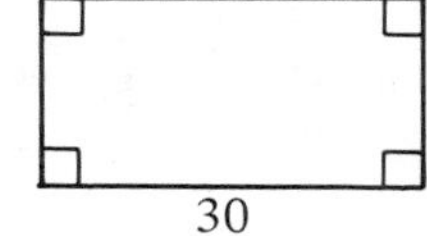


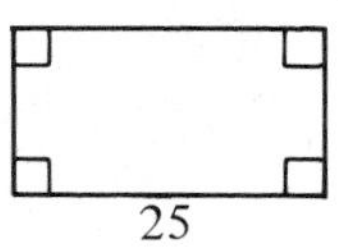

# Cumulative Review / Unit D

**Express each ratio in simplest form.**

1. $\frac{11}{77}$ $\frac{1}{7}$
2. $\frac{45}{100}$ $\frac{9}{20}$
3. $\frac{20 \text{ cm}}{4 \text{ m}}$ $\frac{1}{20}$
4. $8:16:24$ 1:2:3

**Find the value of $x$.**

5. $\frac{x}{2} = \frac{6}{3}$ 4
6. $\frac{1}{7} = \frac{2}{x}$ 14
7. $\frac{2}{x} = \frac{4}{22}$ 11
8. $10:15 = x:3$ 2

9. Three 8-track tapes cost $24. How much will five tapes cost? $40

10. In a shopping mall, the hobby store is 50 m north of Elmo's Market. The bicycle shop is 60 m west of Elmo's. Draw a map showing the hobby store, the bicycle shop, and Elmo's Market. Be sure to include the scale.

**State whether the two polygons are, or are not, similar.**

11. No

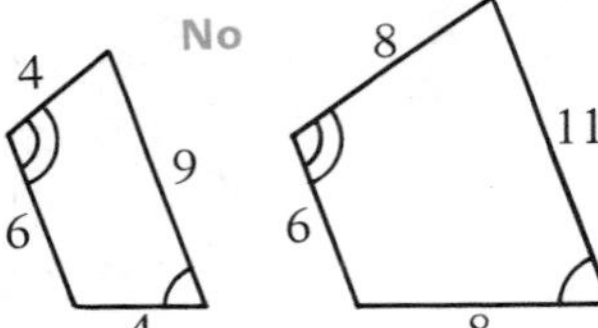


12. Yes

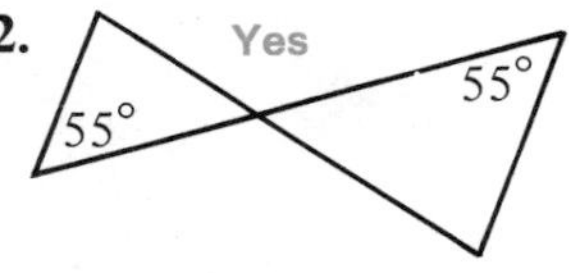


13. Yes

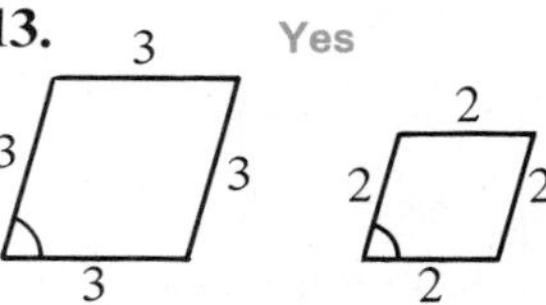


**In the diagram, $\overline{OS} \parallel \overline{HE}$. Complete each statement.**

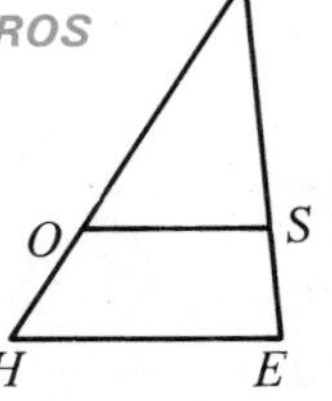


14. $\triangle ROS \sim \triangle$ _?_ $\triangle RHE$

15. $\angle RHE = \angle$ _?_ $\angle ROS$

16. $\frac{?}{RH} = \frac{RS}{RE}$ $\frac{RO}{RH} = \frac{RS}{RE}$

17. $\frac{RO}{OH} = \frac{RS}{?}$ $SE$

18. If $RS = 8$, $SE = 4$, and $OS = 6$, then $HE =$ _?_. 9

**The quadrilaterals shown are similar. Complete each statement.**

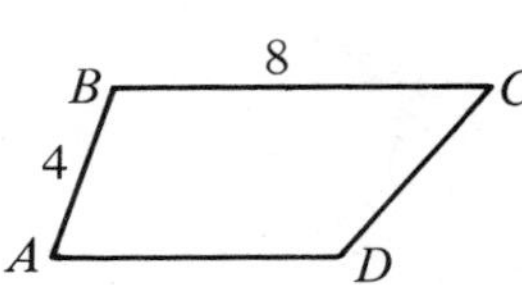


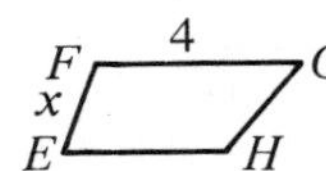


19. $\angle E = \angle$ _?_ $\angle A$

20. The scale factor is _?_:_?_. 2:1

21. $x =$ _?_ 2

22. The ratio of the perimeters is _?_:_?_. 2:1

23. The ratio of the areas is _?_:_?_. 4:1

# UNIT E

## *Here's what you'll learn in this chapter:*

1. To define a circle and the points, lines, and segments related to circles.
2. To apply theorems relating tangents and radii.
3. To construct a tangent to a circle at a given point on the circle.
4. To classify and measure arcs.
5. To use theorems involving the chords of a circle.
6. To draw a circle inscribed in a polygon and a circle circumscribed about a polygon.
7. To use theorems relating angle measure and arc measure.

# Chapter 9

# Circles

# 1 • Basic Terms

Set your compass for a radius of 2 cm.
Now draw a complete curve.
You know, of course, that the curve is a *circle.*
The pin point is the *center* of the circle.

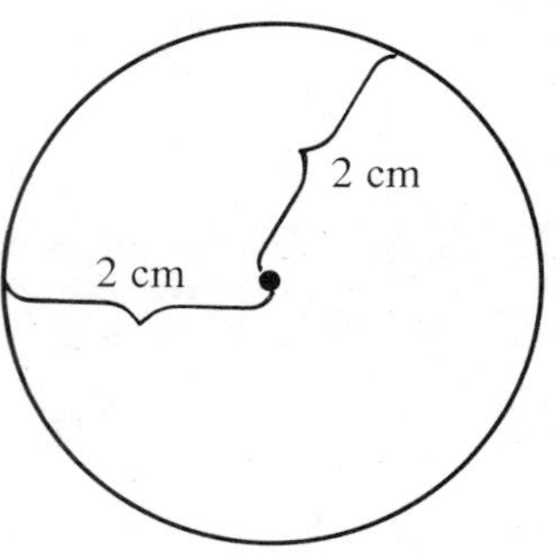


This experiment should remind you that a **circle** is a figure, in a plane, whose points are the same distance from a particular point in the plane. The table below shows some important definitions relating to circles.

| | |
|---|---|
| **radius** | 1. a segment that joins the center and a point on the circle<br>2. the length of such a segment |
| **chord** | a segment that joins two points on the circle |
| **diameter** | 1. a chord that passes through the center<br>2. the length of such a chord |
| **secant** | a line that contains a chord |
| **tangent** | a line, in the plane of the circle, that intersects the circle in exactly one point |
| **point of tangency** | the point in which a tangent intersects the circle |

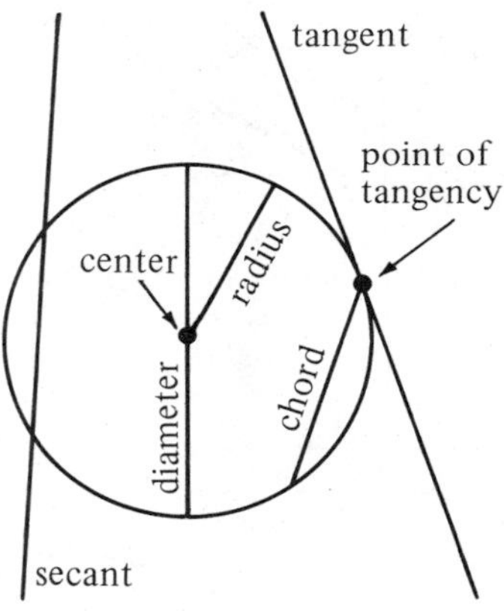


From the definition of a circle, you can see that:

(1) All radii of a circle are equal.

(2) All diameters of a circle are equal.

Many of the terms used for circles are also used for *spheres*. A **sphere** is a figure in space whose points are the same distance from a particular point. That point is called the *center* of the sphere.

$\overline{PA}$, $\overline{PB}$, and $\overline{PC}$ are radii of the sphere.

$\overline{BC}$ is a diameter.

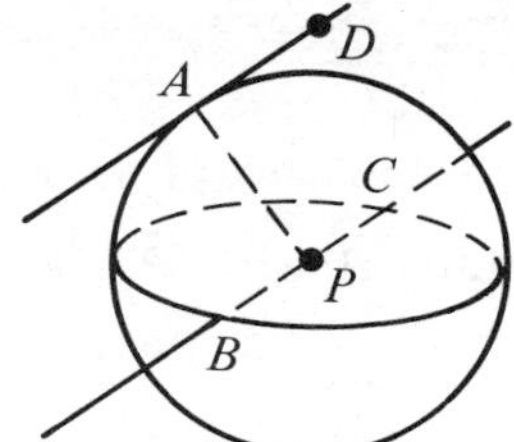


$\overleftrightarrow{BC}$ is a secant.

$\overleftrightarrow{AD}$ is a tangent.

## Classroom Practice

**Exercises 1–10 refer to $\odot O$ (circle with center $O$) in the diagram.**

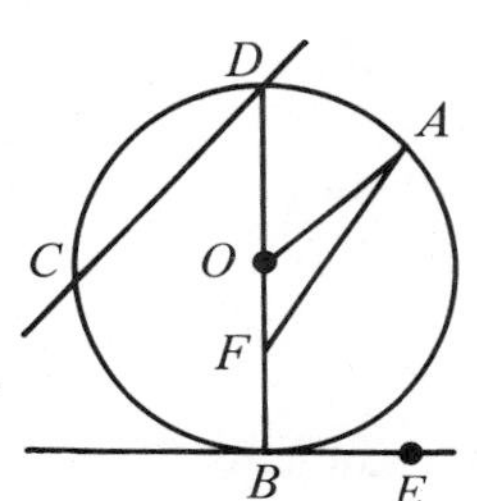


1. Name all the radii shown. $\overline{OD}$, $\overline{OA}$, $\overline{OB}$
2. Name a secant shown. $\overleftrightarrow{CD}$
3. Is $\overleftrightarrow{CD}$ a chord? No
4. Is $\overline{CD}$ a chord? Yes
5. Explain why $\overline{AF}$ is not a chord. F is not on the circle.
6. Name a tangent to $\odot O$. $\overleftrightarrow{BE}$
7. Is $\overline{BD}$ a chord? a diameter? Yes; Yes
8. Name a point of tangency. B
9. How many diameters that contain point $C$ can be drawn? that contain point $O$? One; an infinite number
10. How many secants that contain both $A$ and $C$ can be drawn? One
11. State a definition of a radius of a sphere.
    A segment joining the center and a point on the sphere
12. State a definition of a tangent to a sphere.
    A line or plane that intersects the sphere in exactly one point
13. Set a basketball on top of a desk and you see a sphere that is tangent to a plane. Hold a piece of cardboard to illustrate another plane tangent to the sphere. In how many positions can you hold the cardboard to show a tangent plane? An infinite number
14. Refer to Exercise 13. Hold the piece of cardboard so that it is both tangent to the ball and parallel to the desk top. Consider the point where the cardboard touches the ball and the point where the desk top touches the ball. What can you say about the segment that joins these two points? It is a diameter of the sphere.

## Written Exercises

**Exercises 1–10 refer to the diagram. Name each of the following.**

A **1.** A circle ⊙$A$ **2.** Four radii $\overline{AR}$, $\overline{AC}$, $\overline{AB}$, $\overline{AD}$

**3.** Two diameters $\overline{RB}$, $\overline{CD}$ **4.** Two tangents $\overleftrightarrow{GE}$, $\overleftrightarrow{BF}$

**5.** A chord that is not a diameter $\overline{BC}$

**6.** Two secants, each containing a diameter $\overleftrightarrow{RB}$, $\overleftrightarrow{CD}$

**7.** A secant that does not contain a diameter $\overleftrightarrow{BC}$

**8.** Two points of tangency $R$, $B$

**9.** How many tangents containing both point $A$ and point $D$ can be drawn? None

**10.** How many chords containing both point $R$ and point $C$ can be drawn? One

**The length of a radius is given. Find the length of a diameter.**

**11.** 19 38 **12.** 5.3 10.6 **13.** $7\frac{1}{2}$ 15 **14.** $3k$ $6k$

**The length of a diameter is given. Find the length of a radius.**

**15.** 26 13 **16.** 2.4 1.2 **17.** $8\frac{1}{2}$ $4\frac{1}{4}$ **18.** $5k$ $2.5k$

**Refer to the diagram of the sphere with center $O$. Name each of the following.**

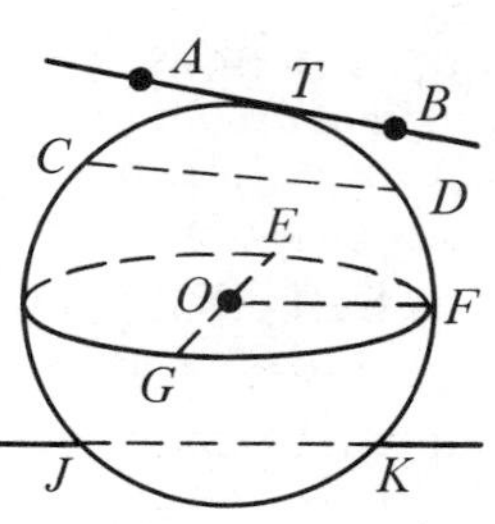

B **19.** Eight points on the sphere $J, K, E, F, G, C, D, T$

**20.** Three radii of the sphere $\overline{OE}$, $\overline{OG}$, $\overline{OF}$

**21.** A diameter of the sphere $\overline{EG}$

**22.** Three chords of the sphere $\overline{JK}$, $\overline{EG}$, $\overline{CD}$

**23.** A secant of the sphere $\overleftrightarrow{JK}$

**24.** A tangent to the sphere $\overleftrightarrow{AB}$

**25.** Write a definition of a diameter of a sphere. A chord that passes through the center of the sphere

**26.** Write a definition of a chord of a sphere.
A segment that joins two points on the sphere

**For each exercise draw a circle with radius 8. Draw two points *R* and *S* that satisfy the conditions stated. If the conditions cannot be satisfied, write *not possible.***

C **27.** $\overline{RS}$ is a chord and $RS = 10$. (Drawings omitted)

**28.** $R$ and $S$ both lie inside the circle and $RS = 17$. Not possible

**29.** $R$ and $S$ both lie outside the circle and $RS = 7$.

**30.** $R$ lies inside the circle, $S$ lies outside the circle, and $\overleftrightarrow{RS}$ intersects the circle in exactly one point. Not possible

**31.** $\overline{OA}$ and $\overline{OB}$ are radii.
$\angle A = 5x - 3$; $\angle B = 3x + 17$.
Find $x$. 10

**32.** Point $P$ is the center of the circle.
Find the measure of $\angle E$. 25°

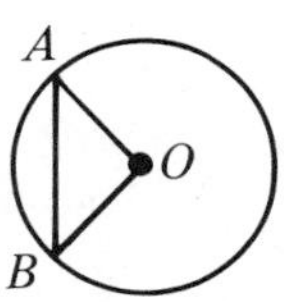

Exercise 31

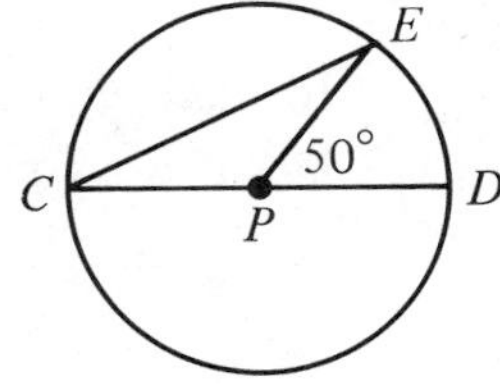

Exercise 32

## Experiments

1. Copy the diagram shown.
2. Construct a line, through $O$, perpendicular to chord $\overline{AB}$. Let $C$ be the point of intersection with $\overline{AB}$.
3. What appears to be true about $AC$ and $BC$? $AC = BC$
4. Prove that your conclusion is true.

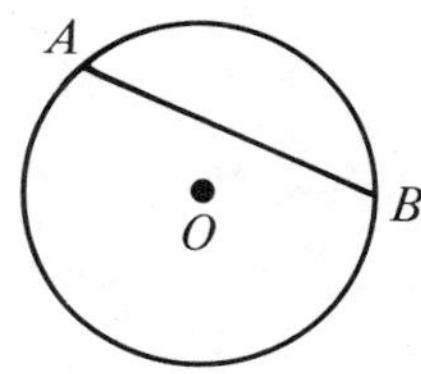

"Mary! Mary!"

## 2 • Tangents

### Explorations

1. Draw circles and tangents like those shown.

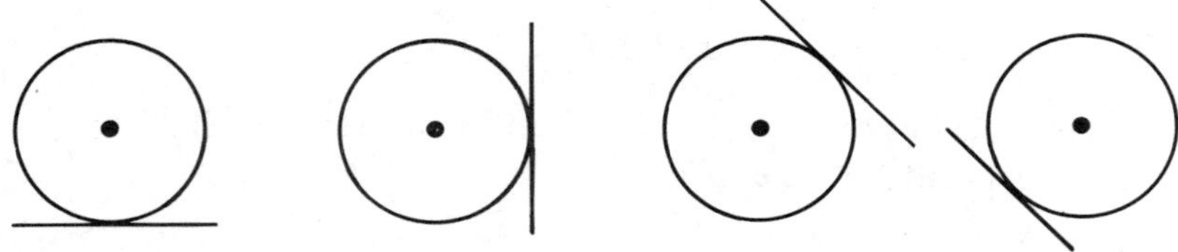

In each case draw the radius to the point of tangency.
What do you observe? **The radii are ⊥ to the tangents.**

2. Draw circles and radii like those shown.

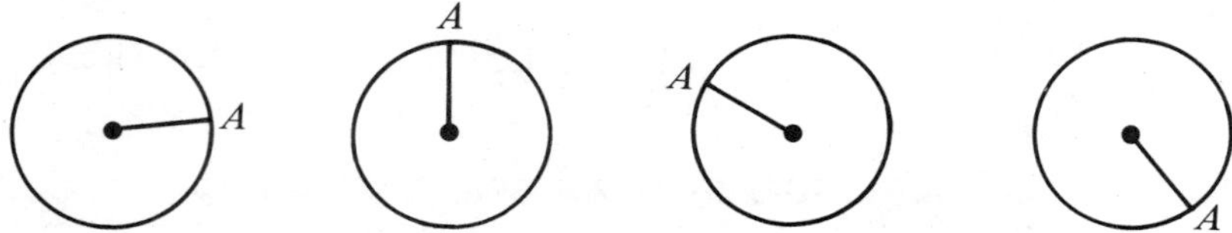


In each case draw a line that passes through $A$ and is perpendicular to the radius.
What do you observe? **These lines are tangents.**

These explorations suggest two theorems that we state but do not prove.

**THEOREM 1**

A radius drawn to a point of tangency is perpendicular to the tangent.

**THEOREM 2**

If a line lies in the plane of a circle and is perpendicular to a radius at its outer endpoint, the line is tangent to the circle.

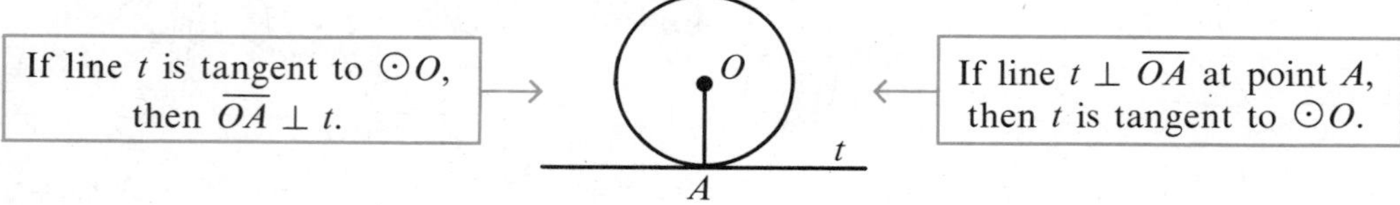

A tangent to a circle has been defined as a line. However, we sometimes say that a *segment* is tangent to a circle. For example, since $\overleftrightarrow{PX}$ is tangent to the circle at $X$, $\overline{PX}$ may also be called a tangent to the circle.

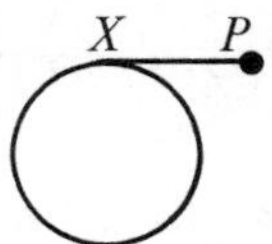


A line that is tangent to each of two coplanar circles is called a **common tangent.**

A common *internal* tangent intersects the segment joining the centers.

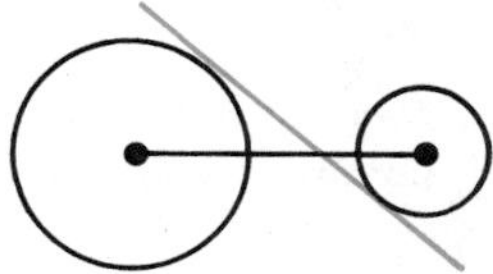

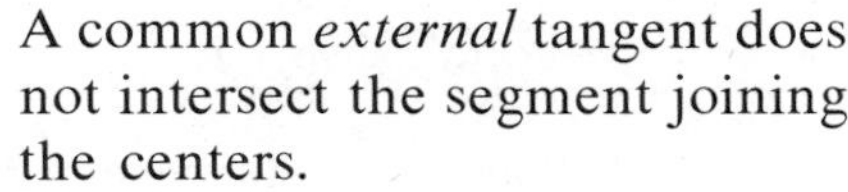
A common *external* tangent does not intersect the segment joining the centers.

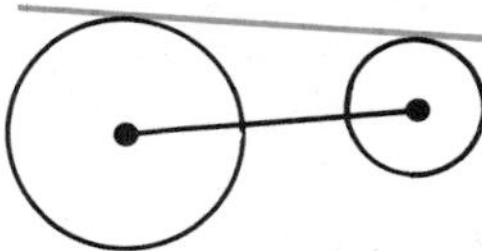

When two coplanar circles are tangent to a line at one point, we say that the *circles are tangent to each other.*

Circles $R$ and $S$ are *externally* tangent. Line $l$ is a common internal tangent.

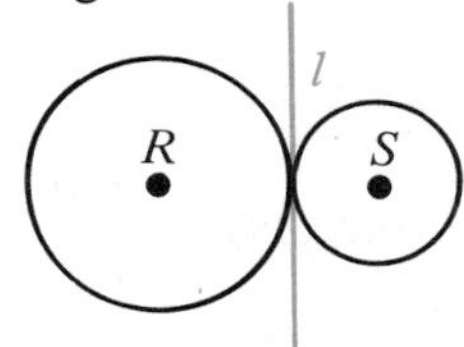


Circles $O$ and $P$ are *internally* tangent. Line $m$ is a common external tangent.

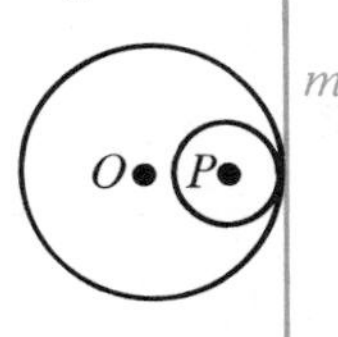

**CONSTRUCTION 10** *Given:* Point $A$ on $\odot O$

*Construct:* A tangent to $\odot O$ at point $A$

1. You are given $\odot O$ with point $A$.

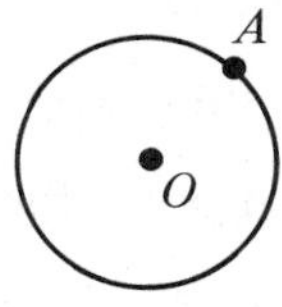


2. Draw $\overrightarrow{OA}$.
   Using Construction 2, page 22, construct a line perpendicular to $\overrightarrow{OA}$ at point $A$. Call the line $l$.
3. Line $l$ is tangent to $\odot O$.

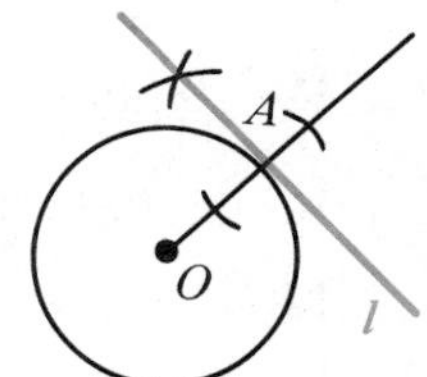

## Classroom Practice

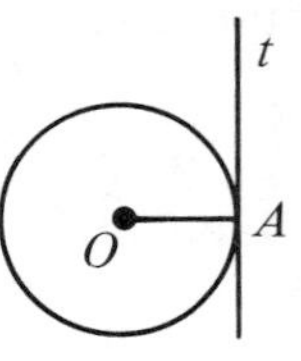


1. If line $t$ is tangent to $\odot O$ at point $A$, what must be true about $\overline{OA}$ and line $t$? State the theorem that supports your conclusion. $\overline{OA} \perp t$; Thm. 1
2. If line $t$ and $\odot O$ lie in the same plane, and if line $t$ is perpendicular to $\overline{OA}$, what must be true about line $t$ and $\odot O$? State the theorem that supports your conclusion. $t$ is a tangent to $\odot O$; Thm. 2

**In each diagram, which lines are common external tangents and which are common internal tangents?**

3. 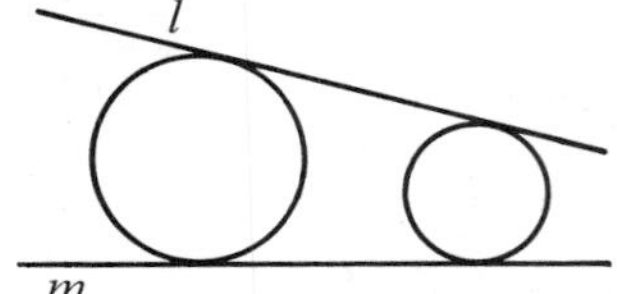


4. 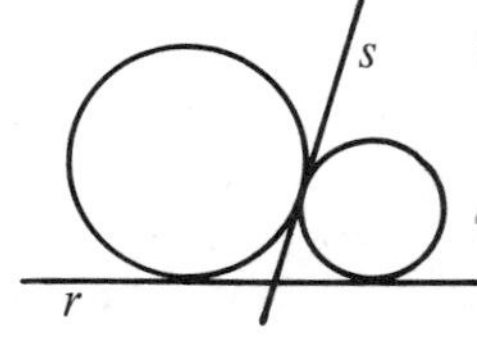


5. 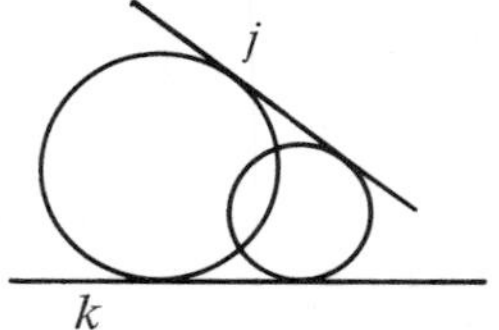


6. 

3. $l$ and $m$ both are common external tangents.
4. $s$ is a common internal tangent. $r$ is a common external tangent.
5. $j$ and $k$ both are common external tangents
6. $t$ is a common external tangent

7. In the figures for Exercises 3–6, state whether the two circles are externally tangent, internally tangent, or are not tangent.

**Draw a circle $O$ on the chalkboard. Choose a point $P$ outside the circle. Draw tangents, $\overline{PX}$ and $\overline{PY}$, to the circle.**

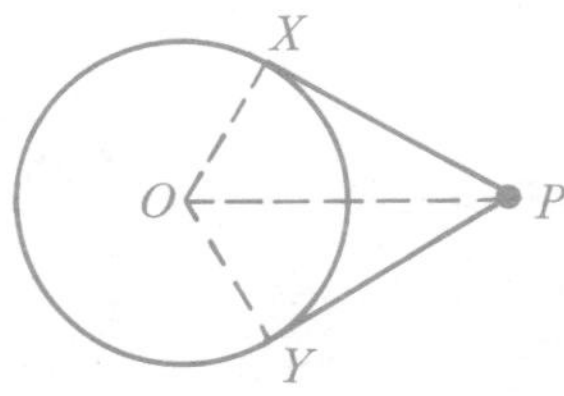

Exercises 8–14

8. What appears to be true about $PX$ and $PY$? They are equal.
9. Complete the listing of what is given.
   *Given:* $\odot O$; $\overline{PX}$ and $\overline{PY}$ are . . . tangents to $\odot O$ at $X$ and $Y$ respectively.
   *Prove:* $PX = PY$

**By drawing $\overline{OX}$, $\overline{OY}$, and $\overline{OP}$, we form two triangles that appear to be congruent.**

10. State a theorem that supports the statements: $\overline{OX} \perp \overline{PX}$; $\overline{OY} \perp \overline{PY}$. Thm. 1, p. 318
11. State a reason that supports the statement: $OX = OY$. Radii of a circle are =.
12. Explain why right $\triangle PXO \cong$ right $\triangle PYO$. HL Theorem
13. State a reason that supports the statement: $PX = PY$. Corr. parts of $\cong$ ⚠ are =.
14. Complete this statement of the theorem that has just been proved: If two tangent segments are drawn to . . . a circle from an exterior point, then the segments are equal.

## Written Exercises

**In each exercise, state the number of common internal tangents and the number of common external tangents that can be drawn to the two circles.**

A **1.** 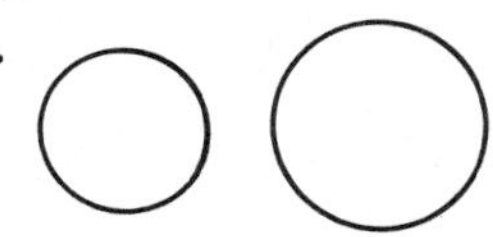
internal: 2; external: 2

**2.** internal: 1; external: 2

**3.** 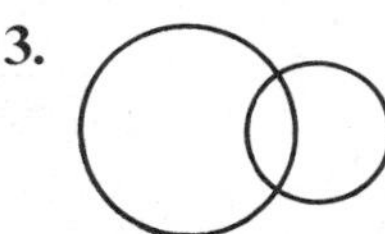
internal: none; external: 2

**4.** internal: none; external: 2

**5.** 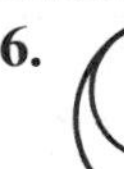
internal: none; external: none

**6.** internal: none; external: 2

**7.** Which of the six diagrams above shows two circles that are externally tangent? two circles that are internally tangent? ext: Ex. 2 int: Ex. 6

**8.** Draw a figure showing two circles that are tangent to a third circle but are not tangent to each other.

**In Exercises 9–12, line *t* lies in the plane of the three circles and intersects each of the circles in exactly one point, *X*. Classify each statement as true or false.**

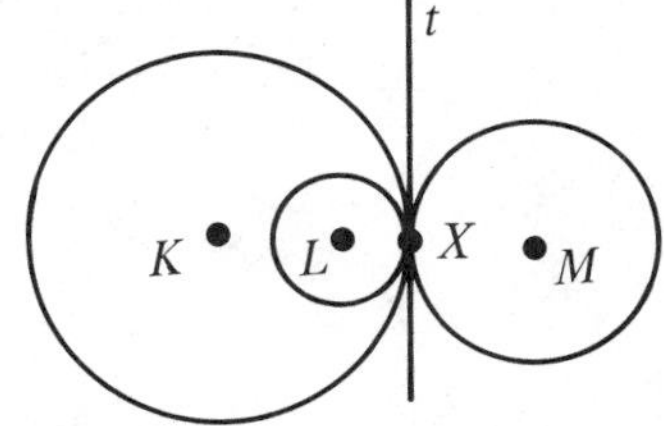


**9.** Line $t$ is a common tangent of $\odot L$ and $\odot M$. True

**10.** Line $t$ is a common external tangent of $\odot L$ and $\odot M$. False

**11.** Line $t$ is a common external tangent of $\odot K$ and $\odot L$. True

**12.** $\odot M$ and $\odot K$ are internally tangent circles. False

**In Exercises 13 and 14, draw a figure roughly like the one shown, but larger.**

**13.** Construct a line tangent to $\odot P$ at point $X$.

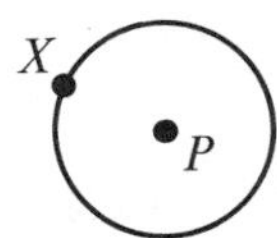


**14.** Construct lines tangent to $\odot O$ at points $D$ and $E$.

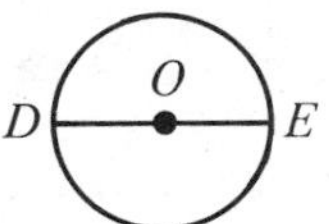


**If possible, draw a diagram to illustrate the conditions.** (Drawings omitted)

B **15.** Two circles with five common tangents Not possible

**16.** Two tangent circles with three common tangents

**17.** Two externally tangent circles with two common internal tangents Not possible

**18.** Two internally tangent circles with one common external tangent

**Find the required length.**

**19.**

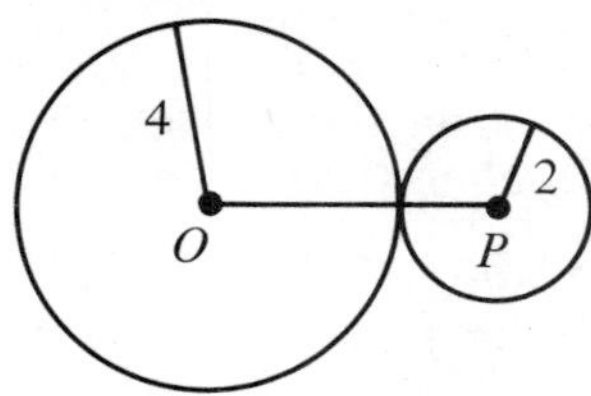


$OP = \underline{\ ?\ }$ 6

**20.**

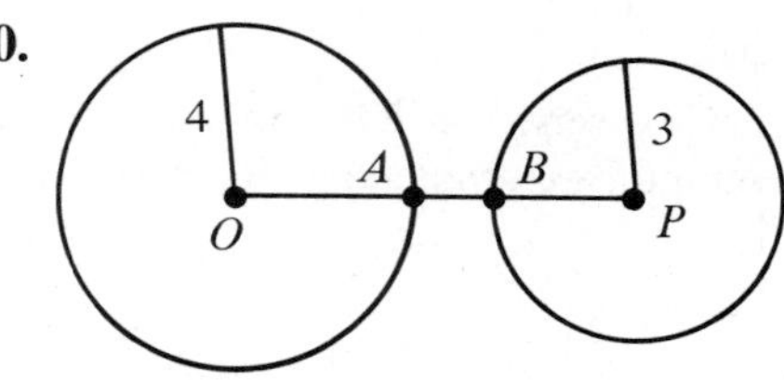


$OP = 9$ $AB = \underline{\ ?\ }$ 2

**21.**

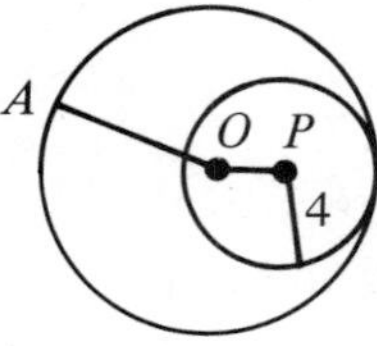


$OA = 7$ $OP = \underline{\ ?\ }$ 3

**22.**

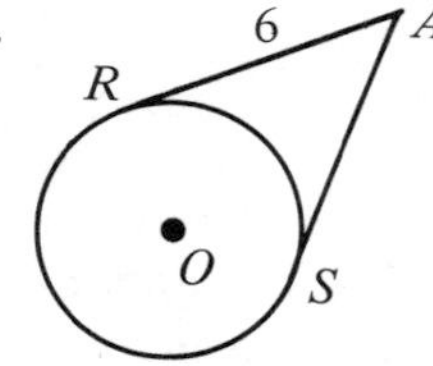


$AS = \underline{\ ?\ }$ 6
(*Hint:* See Exercise 14, page 320.)

C **23.**

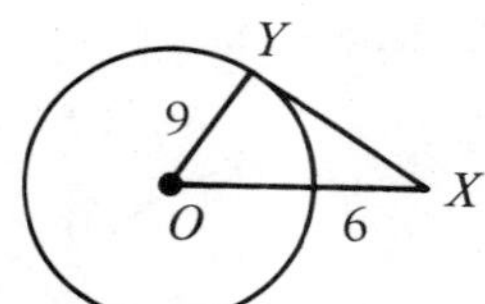


$XY = \underline{\ ?\ }$ 12

**24.**

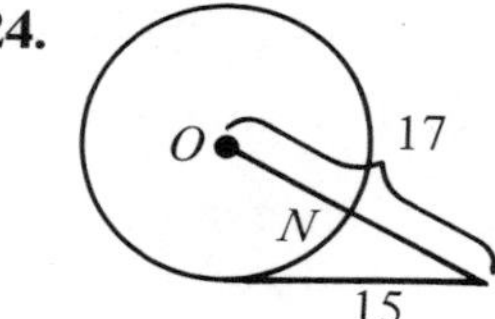


$ON = \underline{\ ?\ }$ 8

**25.** Refer to the diagram at the bottom of page 319. Explain why line $l$ must be tangent to $\odot O$. *l* is a line in the plane of the circle that is perpendicular to a radius ($\overline{OA}$) at its outer endpoint ($A$). By Thm. 2, p. 318, *l* is tangent to $\odot O$.

## Puzzles & Things

Using ordinary household waxed paper, cut out a circle with as large a radius as convenient. Mark the center. Fold the paper so that some point of the circle falls on the center $O$. Make a sharp crease, then unfold. Make about twenty different creases in the same way. Hold the paper at arm's length. The creases should suggest a circle!

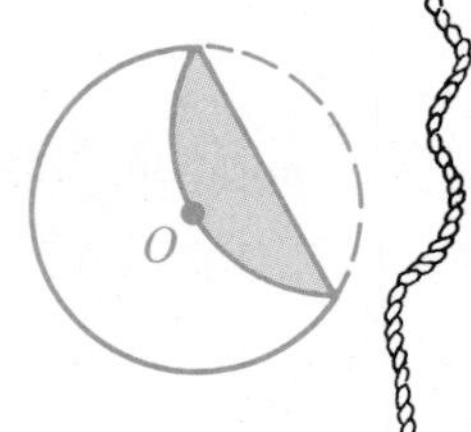

## 3 • Arcs and Central Angles

An *arc* is part of a circle.

### Classifying Arcs

**Semicircle**

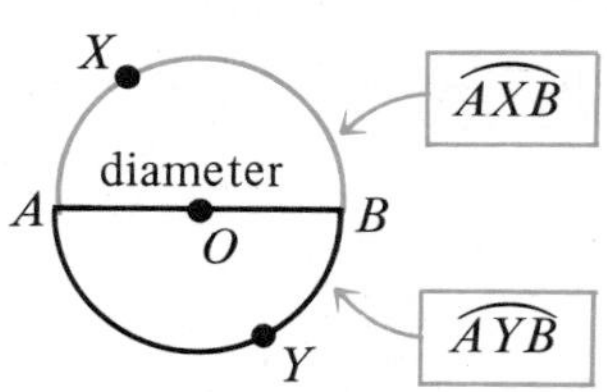


Exactly half a circle

**Minor Arc** | **Major Arc**

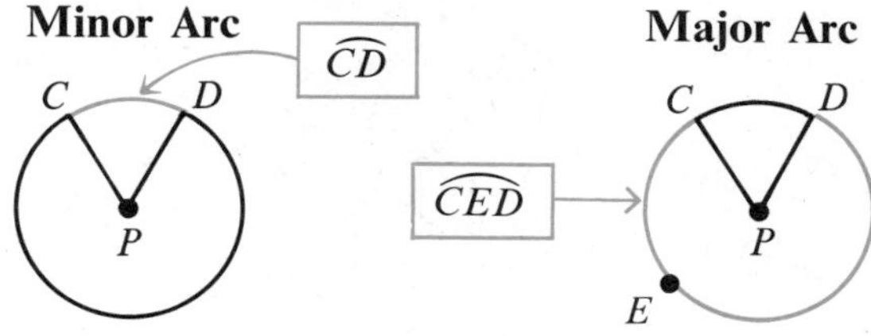


Less than a semicircle

Greater than a semicircle

Notice that you need three letters to name a semicircle or a major arc. $\widehat{AXB}$ is read "arc $AXB$."

A **central angle** of a circle is an angle whose vertex is the center of the circle.

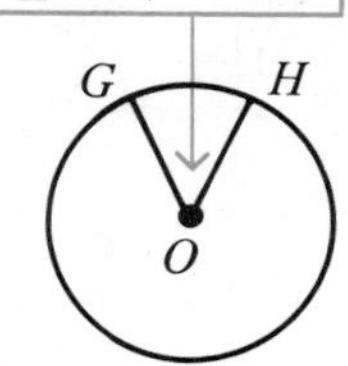

The degree measure of a minor arc is defined to be the measure of its central angle.

By definition, $\angle GOH = \widehat{GH}$. You may read this as "angle $GOH$ equals arc $GH$." Just remember that this means that the *measure* of the angle equals the *measure* of the arc.

### Finding the Measure of an Arc

**Semicircle**

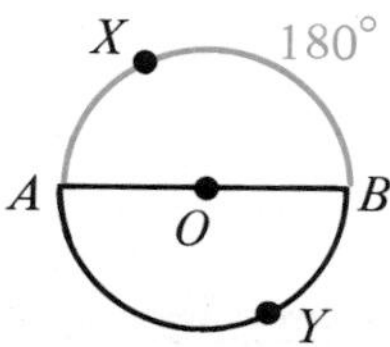


$\widehat{AXB} = \widehat{AYB} = 180°$

**Minor Arc**

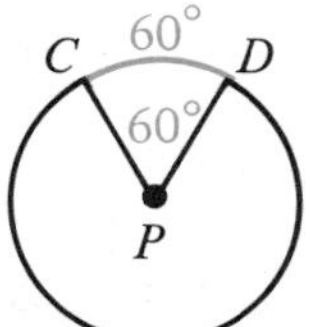


$\widehat{CD} = \angle CPD = 60°$

**Major Arc**

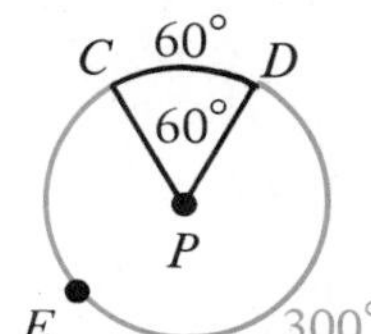


$\widehat{CED} = 360° - \widehat{CD} = 300°$

If two arcs of a circle have equal measures, they are called **equal arcs.** Thus, in the diagram, $\widehat{AB} = \widehat{CD}$ because each arc has measure 70°.

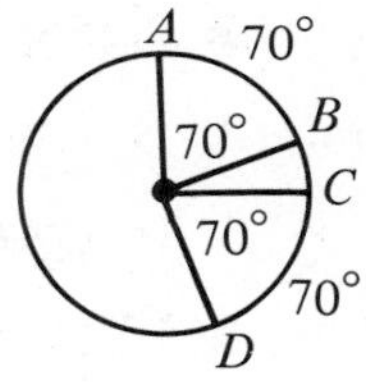

**THEOREM 3**

In a circle, equal central angles have equal minor arcs.

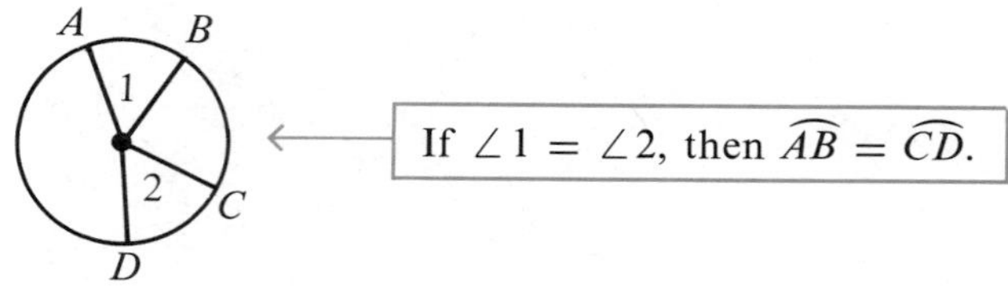


*Strategy for proof:* $\overset{\frown}{AB} = \angle 1$ (Why?)
$\angle 1 = \angle 2$ (Why?)
$\angle 2 = \overset{\frown}{CD}$ (Why?)
$\overset{\frown}{AB} = \overset{\frown}{CD}$

**THEOREM 4**

In a circle, equal minor arcs have equal central angles.

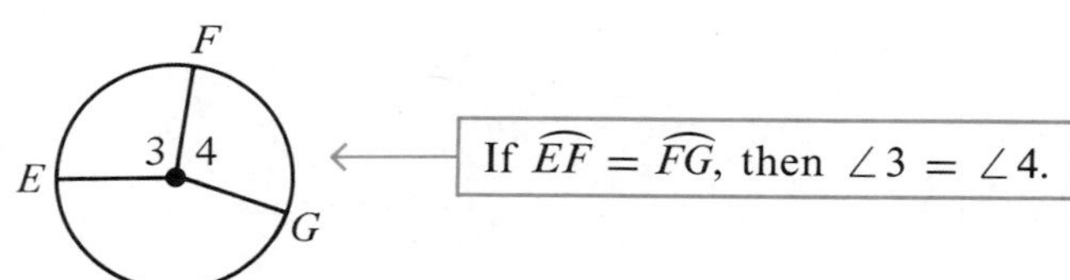


The proof is left as Exercise 26.

## Classroom Practice

**Exercises 1–6 refer to the diagram shown.**

$\overset{\frown}{AB}$, $\overset{\frown}{BC}$ **1.** Name a minor arc. **2.** Name a major arc. $\overset{\frown}{ACB}$, $\overset{\frown}{BAC}$

$\overset{\frown}{ABC}$ **3.** Name a semicircle. **4.** Name two central angles. ∠AOB, ∠BOC

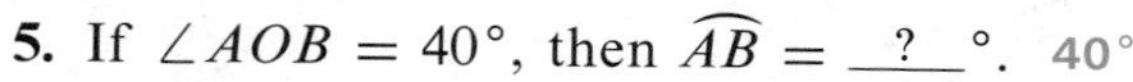

**5.** If $\angle AOB = 40°$, then $\overset{\frown}{AB} = $ _?_ °. 40°

**6.** If $\angle AOB = 40°$, then $\overset{\frown}{ACB} = $ _?_ °. 320°

**$\overline{AD}$ and $\overline{EC}$ are diameters of $\odot O$. $\overline{OB}$ is a radius.**
**Classify each statement as true or false.**

7. $\angle AOC = 100°$ True
8. $\angle AOE = 50°$ False
9. $\angle AOE$ is a central angle. True
10. $\widehat{ABC}$ is a minor arc. True
11. $\widehat{AED}$ is a semicircle. True
12. $\widehat{BCD}$ is a major arc. False
13. $\widehat{AB} = 50°$ True
14. $\widehat{ABD} = 180°$ True
15. $\widehat{AB} = \widehat{BC}$ True
16. $\widehat{BD} = 100°$ False
17. $\widehat{CDA}$ is a major arc. True
18. $\widehat{DC} = \widehat{EA}$ True

## Written Exercises

**In Exercises 1–9, radii, diameters, and chords of $\odot O$ are shown. State the measure of $\angle 1$.**

A

1. 110°

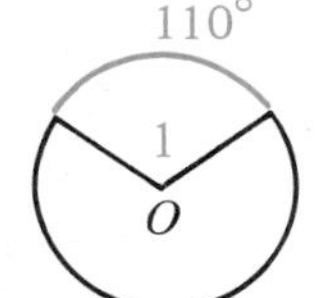


2. 45°

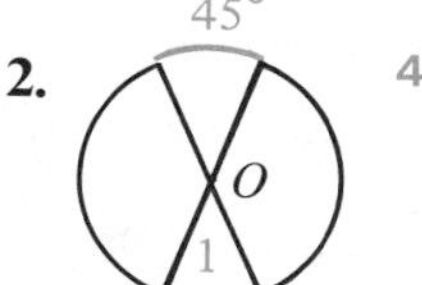


3. 58°

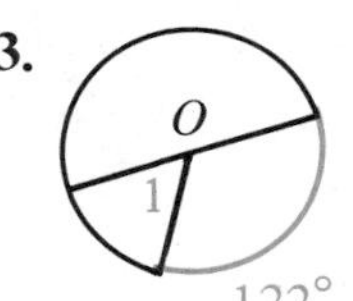


4. 47° 133°

5. 42½°

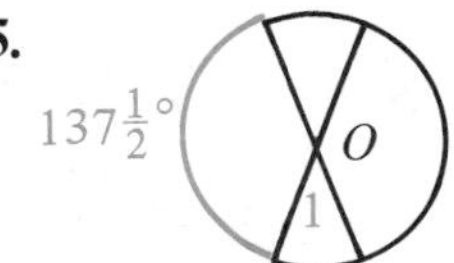


6. 67⅔°

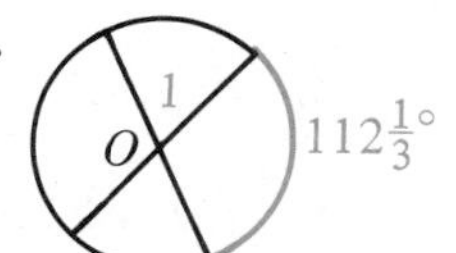


7. 120°

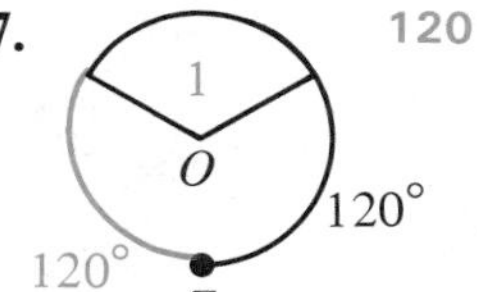


8. 60°

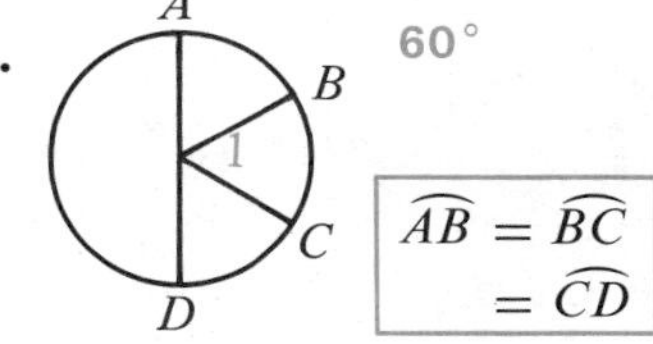


9. 45°

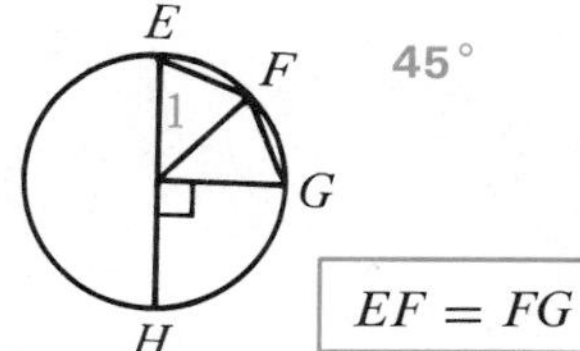


**In Exercises 10–12, find the measure of the indicated arc.**

10. $\widehat{AB} = \underline{\ ?\ }°$ 72°
11. $\widehat{JL} = \underline{\ ?\ }°$ 49°
12. $\widehat{RSQ} = \underline{\ ?\ }°$ 220°

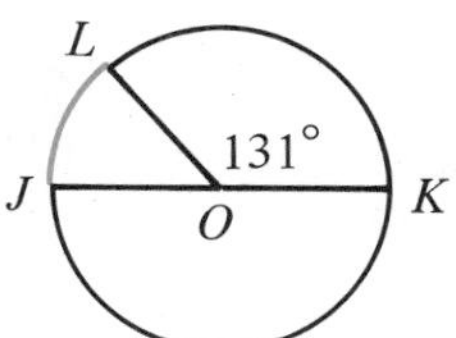


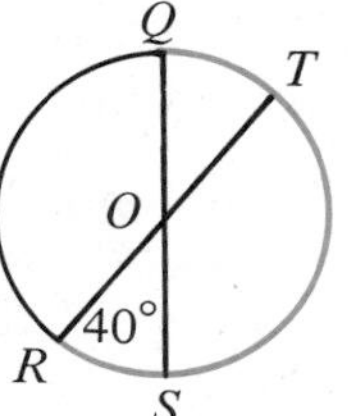

**In the figure for Exercises 13–16, diameter $\overline{XY}$ bisects acute angle $POQ$.**

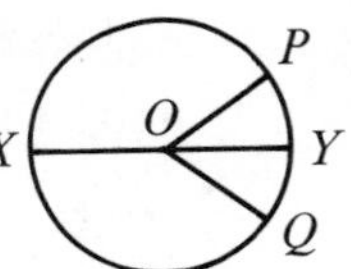


(See below) **13.** Name five minor arcs. **14.** Name five major arcs.

**15.** Name two semicircles. **16.** Name three *pairs* of equal arcs.

**In the figure, $\overline{BC}$ is a diameter of $\odot O$.**

B **17.** If $\angle 1 = 40°$, then $\widehat{AB} =$ _?_ °. 140°

**18.** If $\angle 1 = 36°$, then $\angle 3 =$ _?_ °. (*Hint:* $AO = BO$) 18°

**19.** If $\angle 1 = 42°$, then $\angle 2 =$ _?_ °. 21°

**20.** If $\angle 2 = 25°$, then $\angle 1 =$ _?_ °. 50°

**21.** If $\angle 3 = 28°$, then $\angle 1 =$ _?_ °. 56°

**22.** If $\angle 2 = 31°$, then $\widehat{ACB} =$ _?_ °. 242°

**In Exercises 23–25, $\overline{AB}$ is a diameter of $\odot O$.**

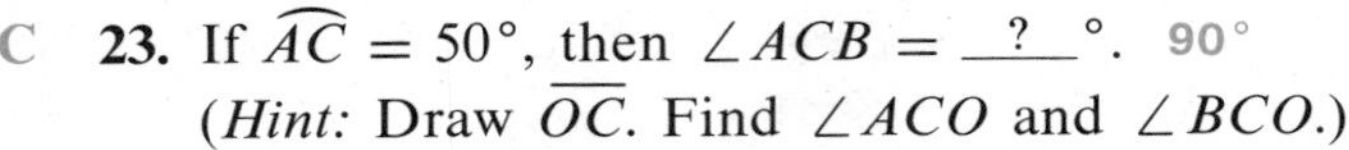

C **23.** If $\widehat{AC} = 50°$, then $\angle ACB =$ _?_ °. 90°
(*Hint:* Draw $\overline{OC}$. Find $\angle ACO$ and $\angle BCO$.)

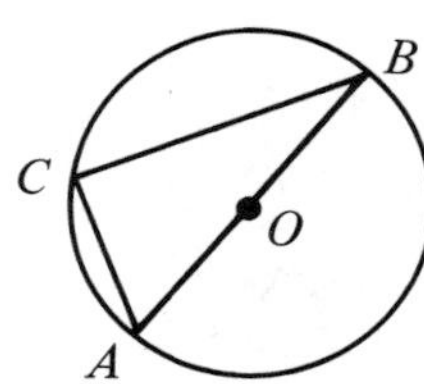


**24.** If $\widehat{BC} = 120°$, then $\angle ACB =$ _?_ °. 90°

**25.** If $\widehat{AC} = j°$, then $\angle ACB =$ _?_ °. 90°

**26.** Write a proof of Theorem 4.

13. $\widehat{XP}$, $\widehat{PY}$, $\widehat{PQ}$, $\widehat{YQ}$, $\widehat{QX}$

14. $\widehat{XPQ}$, $\widehat{PQX}$, $\widehat{YQP}$, $\widehat{QXP}$, $\widehat{QXY}$

15. $\widehat{XPY}$, $\widehat{XQY}$

16. $\widehat{PY} = \widehat{YQ}$; $\widehat{XP} = \widehat{XQ}$; $\widehat{XPY} = \widehat{XQY}$

The project on page 322 involved folding waxed paper to form a circle. You can fold paper to form other curves. For this project, use a rectangular sheet of waxed paper.

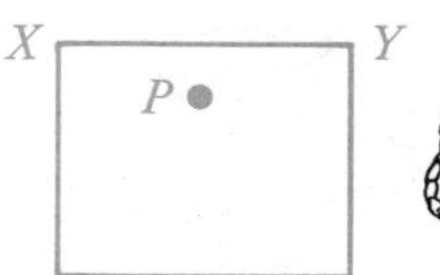


Select a side $\overline{XY}$ and a point $P$.

Fold the paper so that some point of $\overline{XY}$ falls on point $P$. Make a sharp crease, then unfold.

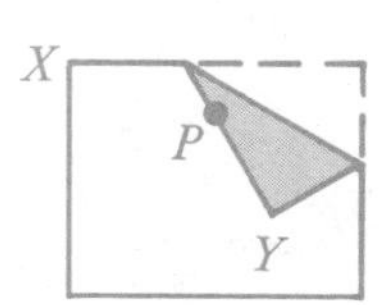


Make about twenty different creases in the same way.

Hold the paper at arm's length and the creases will suggest a *parabola*.

## SELF-TEST

**Name each of the following.**

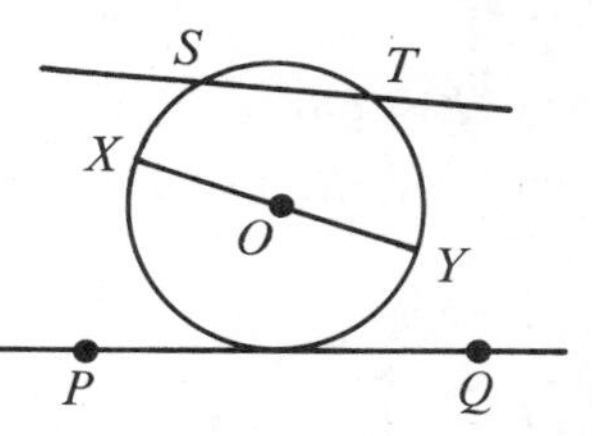


1. A radius $\overline{OX}$; $\overline{OY}$
2. A diameter $\overline{XY}$
3. A secant $\overleftrightarrow{ST}$
4. A tangent $\overleftrightarrow{PQ}$
5. A chord that is not a diameter $\overline{ST}$

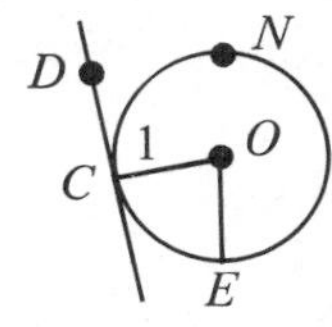

6. If $\angle 1 = 90°$, then $\overleftrightarrow{CD}$ is _?_ to $\odot O$. tangent
7. If $\widehat{CE} = 80°$, then $\angle COE =$ _?_ °. 80°
8. If $\widehat{CE} = 80°$, then $\widehat{CNE} =$ _?_ °. 280°

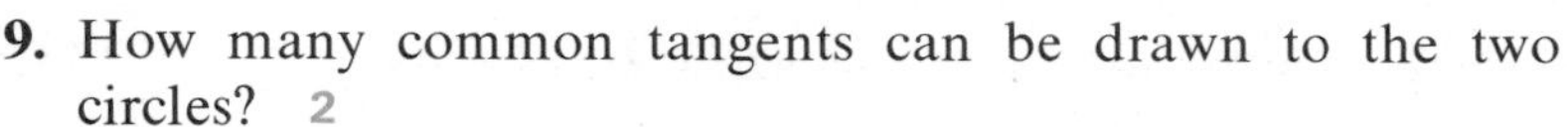

9. How many common tangents can be drawn to the two circles? 2

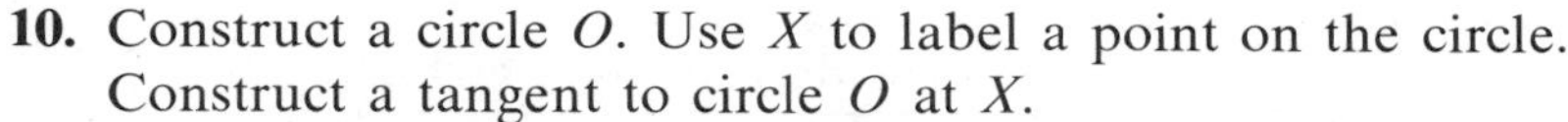

10. Construct a circle $O$. Use $X$ to label a point on the circle. Construct a tangent to circle $O$ at $X$.

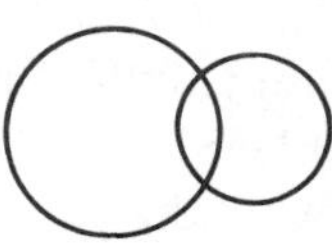

Exercise 9

# CAREER NOTES

### *Marine Dietician*

Have you ever tried tuna hot dogs or fish luncheon rolls? These are just two examples of food products that marine dieticians have developed. Marine dieticians are both nutrition experts and oceanographers. They analyze possible food sources in the oceans.

Most of the marine life that can be harvested is not considered desirable as human food. One of the most challenging problems facing marine dieticians is the conversion of such marine life into acceptable food products.

Some marine dieticians begin their careers as lab assistants after earning bachelor's degrees in related fields. Most jobs in research, however, require graduate training.

## 4 • Chords

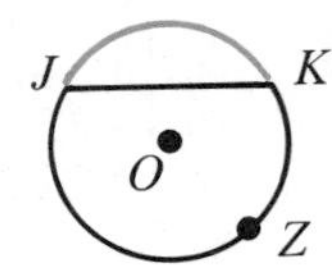


Chord $\overline{JK}$ separates $\odot O$ into two arcs: minor arc $JK$ and major arc $JZK$. We call $\widehat{JK}$ *the* arc of chord $\overline{JK}$.

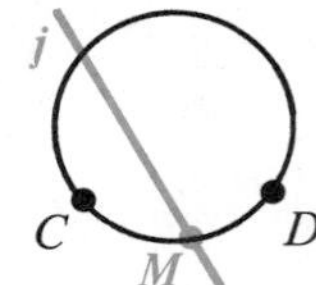


If $\widehat{CM} = \widehat{MD}$, then $M$ is the **midpoint** of $\widehat{CD}$. A line, ray, or segment that contains $M$ **bisects** $\widehat{CD}$. In the diagram, line $j$ bisects $\widehat{CD}$.

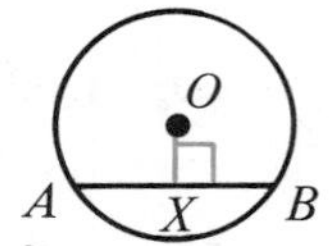


The *distance from center O to chord* $\overline{AB}$ is the length of the shortest segment that can be drawn from $O$ to a point on $\overline{AB}$. It can be shown that the shortest segment is always the *perpendicular* segment from the point to the line.

$OX$ is the distance from $O$ to $\overline{AB}$.

### Explorations

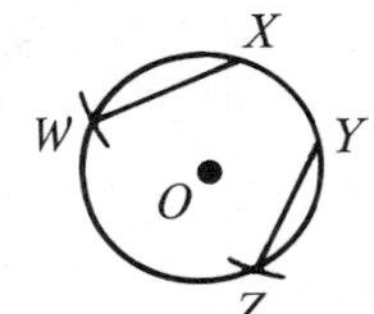


1. Draw a circle with center $O$. Then draw equal chords $\overline{WX}$ and $\overline{YZ}$ as shown. SSS Postulate
   Draw four additional segments and prove that $\triangle WOX \cong \triangle YOZ$. Then use corresponding angles of the congruent triangles to prove that $\widehat{WX} = \widehat{YZ}$.

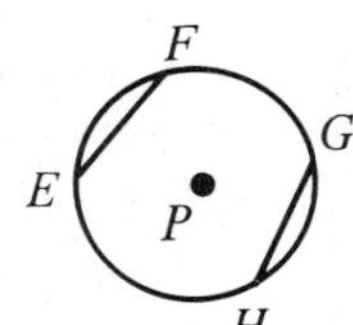


2. Draw a circle with center $P$. On $\odot P$ mark off an arc, $\widehat{EF}$. Choose a point $G$ on the circle, and then a point $H$ so that it looks as if $\widehat{GH} = \widehat{EF}$. Assume that $\widehat{GH}$ really does equal $\widehat{EF}$.
   Draw $\overline{EF}$ and $\overline{GH}$. Try to prove that $EF = GH$.
   Theorem 4, page 324; SAS Postulate; Corr. parts

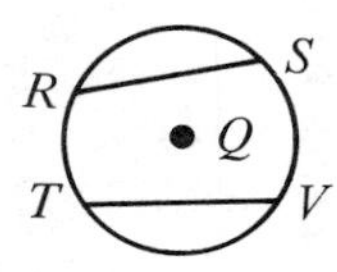


3. Draw a circle with center $Q$. Then draw equal chords $\overline{RS}$ and $\overline{TV}$. Draw a segment that will help you think of the distance from $Q$ to $\overline{RS}$. Also draw a segment that will remind you of the distance from $Q$ to $\overline{TV}$. What appears to be true about the segments that you have drawn? They have the same length.
4. Draw a large circle. Then draw a chord and the diameter that is perpendicular to the chord. Do you see any equal segments? any equal arcs? The chord is divided into equal segments. There are pairs of equal minor arcs and equal major arcs.

These explorations lead to the following theorems.

**THEOREM 5**

In a circle, equal chords have equal arcs and equal arcs have equal chords.

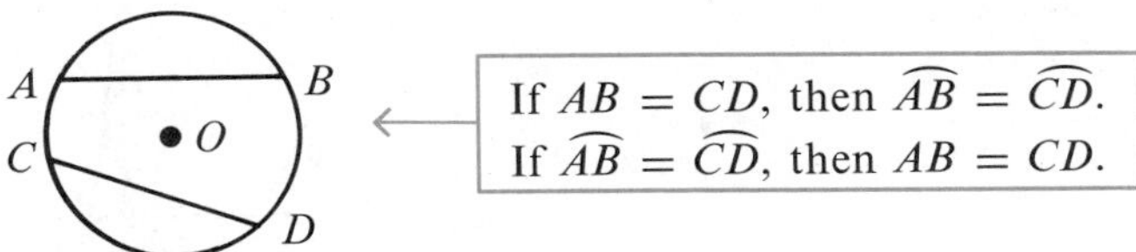


Do you see that Theorem 5 is a "double" theorem? It states both a theorem and its converse. Theorem 6 is also a "double" theorem.

**THEOREM 6**

In a circle, equal chords are equidistant from the center.

Chords that are equidistant from the center are equal.

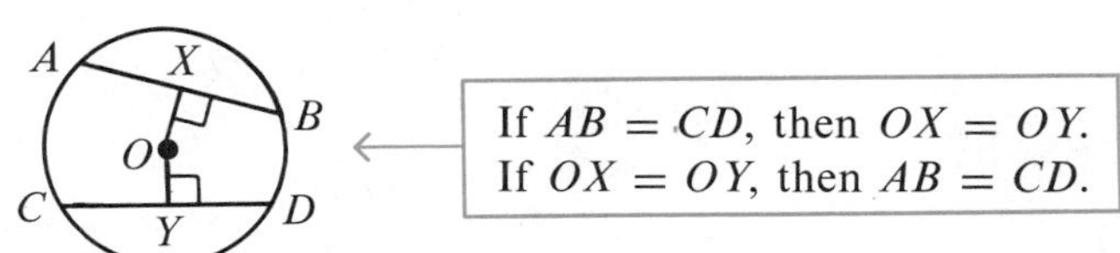


We omit the proof.

**THEOREM 7**

A diameter that is perpendicular to a chord bisects the chord and its arc.

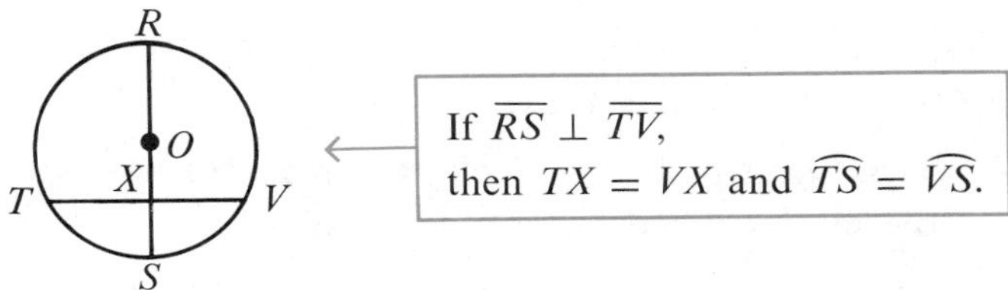


The strategy for a proof is left as Exercise 30.

We have used the terms *inscribed* and *circumscribed* with respect to triangles and circles. As the diagrams show, the terms are applied to other polygons, too.

A polygon is inscribed in a circle when each vertex lies on the circle.

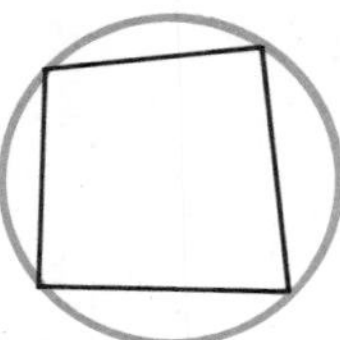

Quadrilateral inscribed in a circle
Circle circumscribed about a quadrilateral

A polygon is circumscribed about a circle when each side is tangent to the circle.

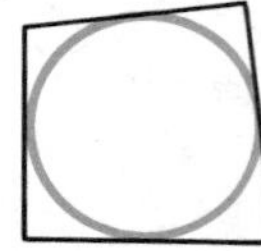

Quadrilateral circumscribed about a circle
Circle inscribed in a quadrilateral

## Classroom Practice

**$\overline{AB}$ is a diameter of $\odot O$. $\overline{AB} \perp \overline{XY}$.**

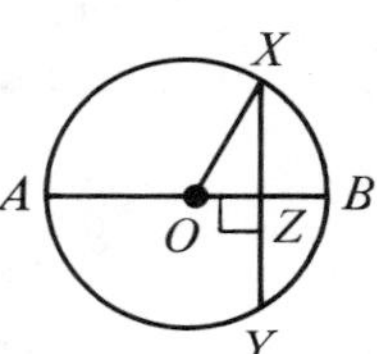

1. $XZ =$ _?_ $ZY$

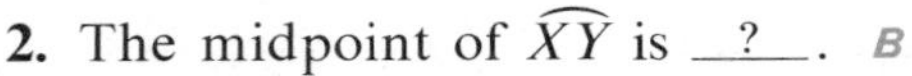

2. The midpoint of $\widehat{XY}$ is _?_. $B$

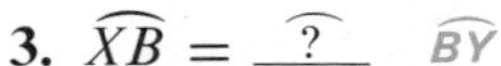

3. $\widehat{XB} =$ _?_ $\widehat{BY}$

4. $\widehat{AX} = 180° -$ _?_ $\widehat{XB}$ $\widehat{AY} = 180° -$ _?_ $\widehat{BY}$

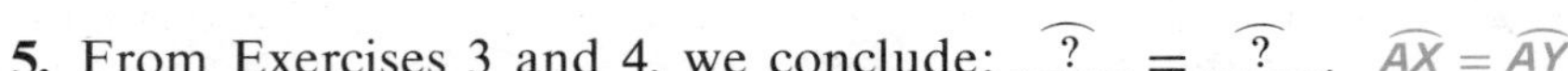

5. From Exercises 3 and 4, we conclude: _?_ = _?_. $\widehat{AX} = \widehat{AY}$

**Exercises 6–10 refer to the figure.**

6. $\overline{PM}$ is a _?_ of $\overline{RS}$. bisector
7. If $PJ = PK$, then $RS =$ _?_. $TV$
8. Which is longer: $\overline{PS}$ (not drawn) or $\overline{JS}$? $\overline{PS}$

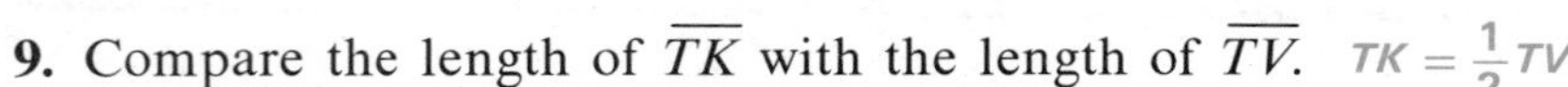

9. Compare the length of $\overline{TK}$ with the length of $\overline{TV}$. $TK = \frac{1}{2}TV$
10. If $RS = TV$, then $\widehat{RS} =$ _?_. $\widehat{TV}$

**Classify each statement as true or false.**

11. If a polygon is inscribed in a circle, the sides of the polygon are chords of the circle. True
12. If a rectangle is circumscribed about a circle, then the rectangle must be a square. True

13. A triangle inscribed in a circle must be isosceles. False

14. It is possible to draw an inscribed quadrilateral in such a way that one of its sides is a diameter of the circle. True

## Written Exercises

**State whether the polygon is inscribed in the circle, is circumscribed about the circle, or neither.**

A **1.** inscribed **2.** circumscribed **3.**  circumscribed

**4.** 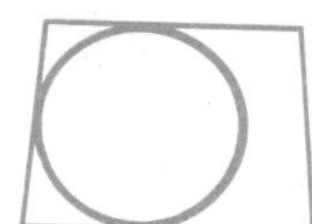 neither **5.**  neither **6.**  inscribed

**Exercises 7–12 refer to $\odot O$ with $\overline{OR} \perp \overline{AB}$.**

**7.** If $RB = 5$, $AB = \underline{\ ?\ }$. 10

**8.** If $AB = 14$, $AR = \underline{\ ?\ }$. 7

**9.** If $RB = 4$ and $OR = 3$, $OB = \underline{\ ?\ }$. 5

**10.** If $OB = 10$ and $RB = 8$, $OR = \underline{\ ?\ }$. 6

**11.** If $OB = 10$ and $AR = 6$, $OR = \underline{\ ?\ }$. 8

**12.** If $OB = 17$ and $AB = 30$, $OR = \underline{\ ?\ }$. 8

**In each exercise, a circle $O$ is shown. Can you conclude that $\widehat{AB} = \widehat{BC}$? Write *yes* or *no*.**

**13.** 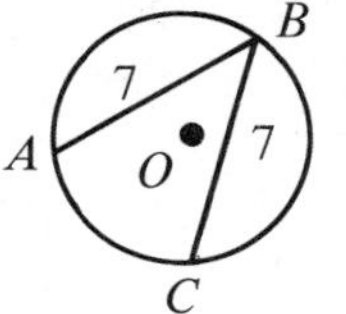

Yes

**14.** 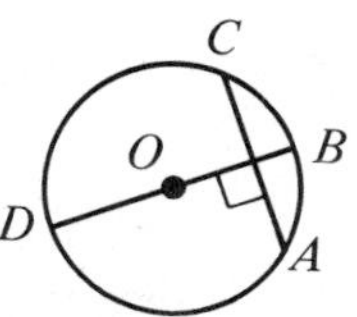

Yes

**15.** 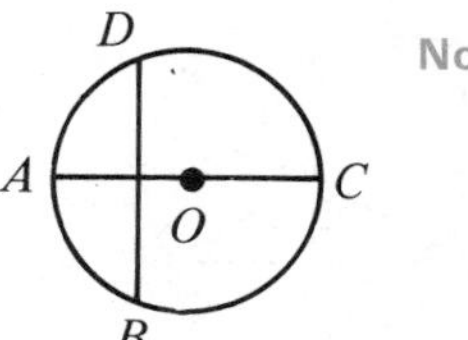

No

**16.** 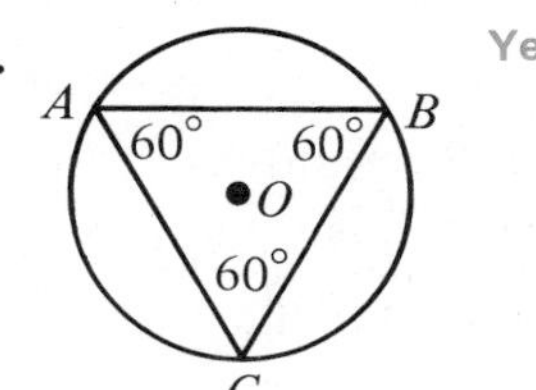

Yes

B **17.** Here is a way to construct an inscribed regular hexagon:

**a.** Construct a circle.

**b.** Without changing your compass, mark off points around the circle. You should end up at the starting point.

**c.** Draw the hexagon.

**18.** Construct a circle. Inscribe an equilateral triangle in the circle. (*Hint:* See Exercise 17.)

**19.** Construct a circle. Inscribe a square in the circle. (*Hint:* Draw any diameter. Use Construction 2, page 22, to get a diameter that is perpendicular to the first one. Connect endpoints.)

**20.** Construct a circle. Inscribe a regular octagon in the circle. (*Hint:* Construct perpendicular diameters as in Exercise 19. Then construct two additional diameters that bisect central angles.)

**In each exercise, a circle *O* is shown. Find *ST*.**

**21.** 8

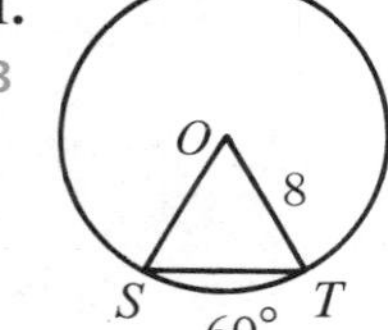


**22.** 4

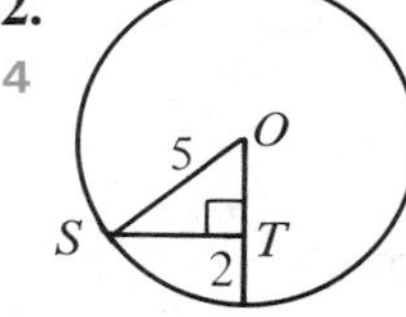


**23.** 10

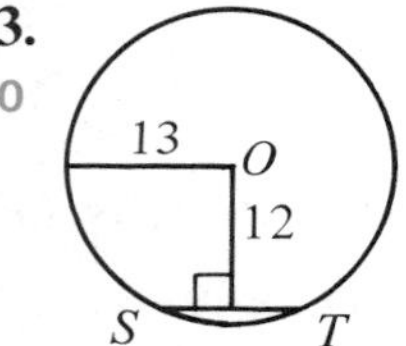


**Draw the figure described. If the figure cannot be drawn, write *not possible*. (You need not construct.)** (Drawings omitted)

**24.** A rectangle inscribed in a circle

**25.** A trapezoid circumscribed about a circle

**26.** A parallelogram, not a rectangle, inscribed in a circle Not possible

C **27.** Explain why the construction described in Exercise 17 works.

**28.** Construct a circle. Then construct a square that is circumscribed about the circle.

**29.** One student insisted: A diameter that bisects a chord must be perpendicular to the chord. Draw a figure that would show that the student is mistaken.

**30.** *Given:* $\odot O$ with $\overline{RS} \perp \overline{TV}$.

State a strategy you could use to show that

$$TX = VX \quad \text{and} \quad \overset{\frown}{TS} = \overset{\frown}{VS}.$$

You need not write out the proof.

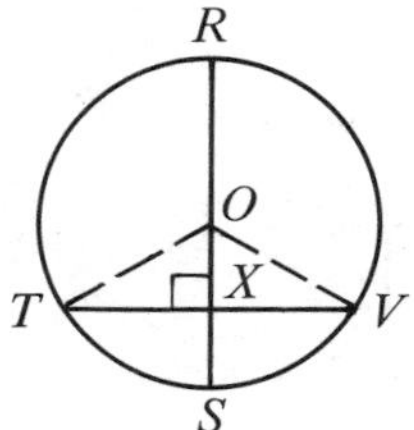

# 5 • Inscribed Angles

An angle is *inscribed in* a circle and is an **inscribed angle** if its vertex lies on the circle and its sides are chords of the circle. Each diagram below shows an $\angle C$ inscribed in $\odot O$.

**Inscribed Angles**

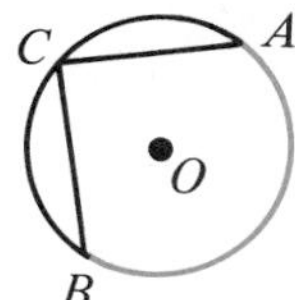


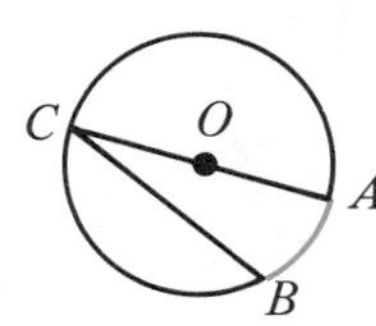


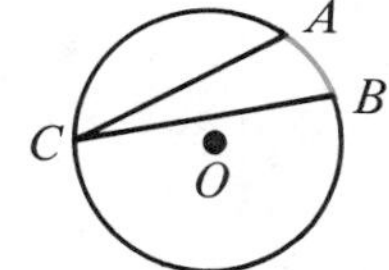


In each case, $\angle C$ **intercepts** an arc, $\widehat{AB}$.

## *Explorations*

Draw a circle $O$ with a radius at least 5 cm long. Choose three points $A$, $B$, and $C$ on the circle so that $\widehat{ACB}$ is a major arc.

Draw $\overline{CA}$ and $\overline{CB}$.

Use a protractor to measure $\angle ACB$.

Draw $\overline{OA}$ and $\overline{OB}$.

Use a protractor to measure $\angle AOB$.

How does the measure of $\angle ACB$ compare with the measure of $\angle AOB$? $\angle ACB = \frac{1}{2}\angle AOB$

Recall that $\angle AOB = \widehat{AB}$.

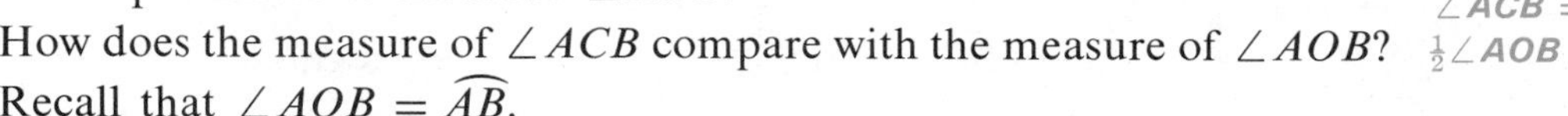

How does the measure of $\angle ACB$ compare with the measure of $\widehat{AB}$? $\angle ACB = \frac{1}{2}\widehat{AB}$

Even if your angle measures are not exact, your results should suggest the following theorem.

**THEOREM 8**

An inscribed angle is equal to half its intercepted arc.

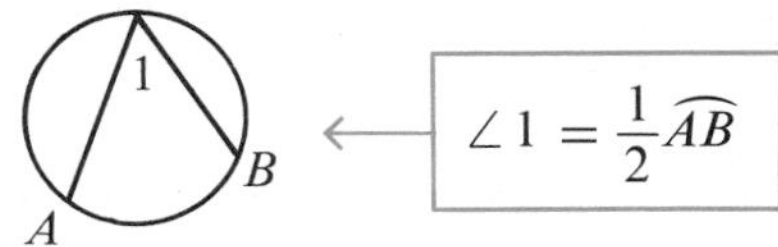


See Exercises 31–33.

**EXAMPLE** Find the measures of $\angle 1$, $\angle 2$, and $\angle 3$.

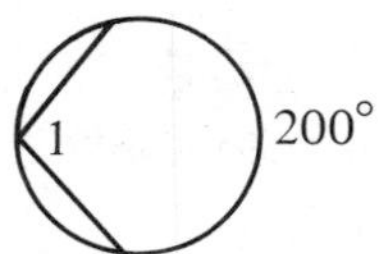


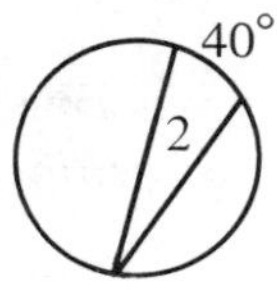


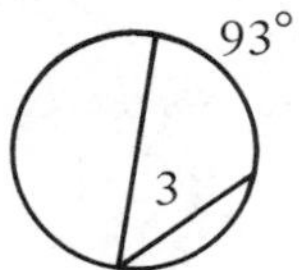


$\angle 1 = \frac{1}{2}(200°) = 100°$ $\quad \angle 2 = \frac{1}{2}(40°) = 20°$ $\quad \angle 3 = \frac{1}{2}(93°) = 46.5°$

In the first three figures below, $\angle A$ is an inscribed angle formed by chords $\overline{AX}$ and $\overline{AY}$. As point $Y$ moves along $\widehat{XA}$ toward point $A$, $\overline{AY}$ becomes more and more like a tangent to the circle.

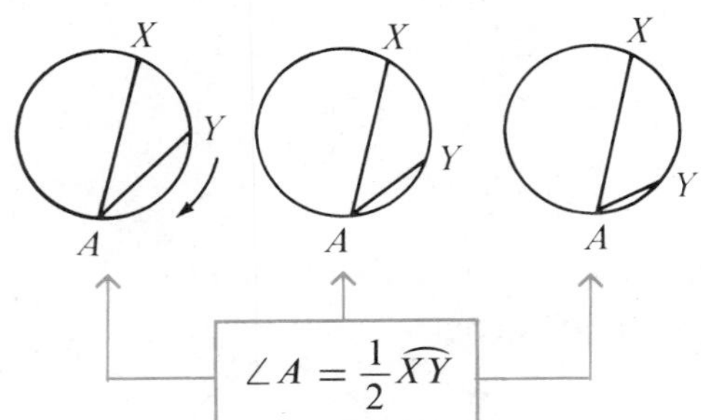


$\angle A = \frac{1}{2}\widehat{XY}$

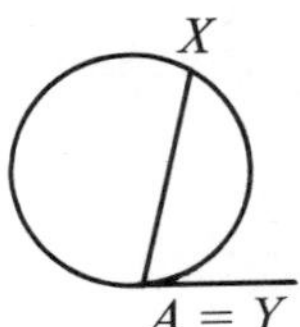


What seems to be true about the measure of $\angle A$?
$\angle A = \frac{1}{2}\widehat{XA}$

**THEOREM 9**

An angle formed by a chord and a tangent is equal to half its intercepted arc.

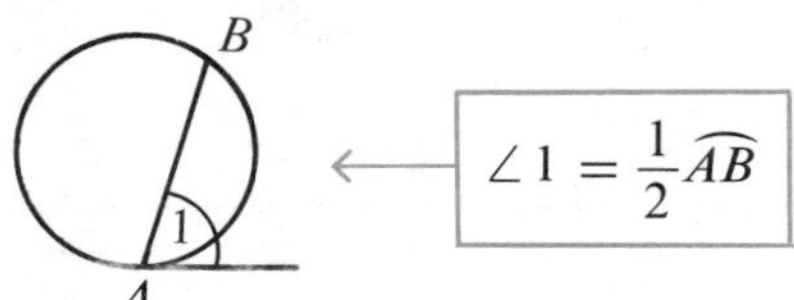


$\angle 1 = \frac{1}{2}\widehat{AB}$

## *Classroom Practice*

**State whether or not $\angle 1$ is an inscribed angle.**

**1.** 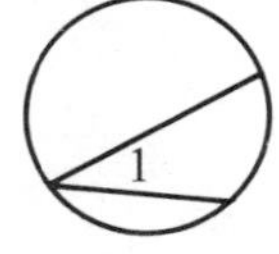

Yes

**2.** 

Yes

**3.** 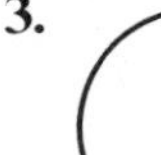

No

4. No

5. 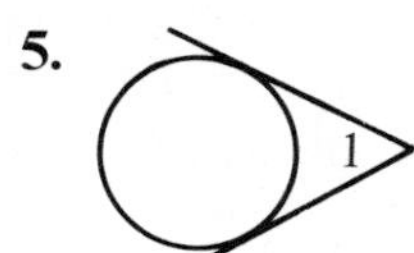

No

6. 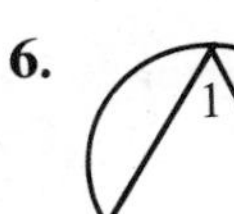

Yes

**In the diagram, $\overrightarrow{CD}$ is a tangent. Complete each statement.**

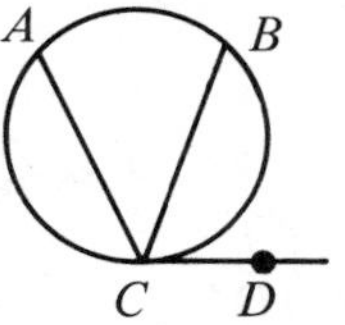


7. The inscribed angle pictured is $\angle$ ___?___. $\angle ACB$
8. $\angle ACB$ intercepts $\widehat{\phantom{?}}$ ___?___. $\widehat{AB}$
9. $\angle BCD$ intercepts $\widehat{\phantom{?}}$ ___?___. $\widehat{BC}$

10. $\angle ACB = \frac{1}{2}\widehat{\,?\,}$ $\widehat{AB}$ 11. $\angle BCD = \frac{1}{2}\widehat{\,?\,}$ $\widehat{BC}$ 12. $\angle ACD = \frac{1}{2}\widehat{\,?\,}$ $\widehat{ABC}$

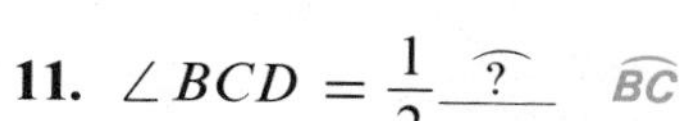

## Written Exercises

**In Exercises 1–8, use the diagram.**

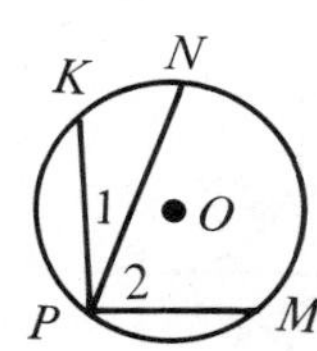


A 1. If $\widehat{KN} = 50°$, then $\angle 1 =$ ___?___°. 25°
2. If $\widehat{NM} = 110°$, then $\angle 2 =$ ___?___°. 55°
3. If $\widehat{KN} = 70°$ and $\widehat{NM} = 115°$, then $\widehat{KNM} =$ ___?___°. 185°
4. If $\widehat{KPM} = 170°$ and $\widehat{KP} = 100°$, then $\widehat{PM} =$ ___?___°. 70°
5. If $\angle 1 = 28°$, then $\widehat{KN} =$ ___?___°. 56°
6. If $\angle 2 = 76°$, then $\widehat{NM} =$ ___?___°. 152°
7. If $\angle 1 = 24°$ and $\angle 2 = 68°$, then $\widehat{KNM} =$ ___?___°. 184°
8. If $\angle 1 = 28°$ and $\angle 2 = 69°$, then $\widehat{KPM} =$ ___?___°. 166°

**In the diagram, $\overleftrightarrow{DE}$ is tangent to $\odot O$ at point $A$.**

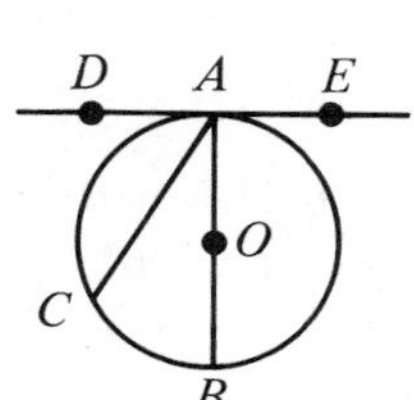


9. $\angle BAE =$ ___?___° 90°
10. $\angle DAB =$ ___?___° 90°
11. If $\angle CAB = 30°$, then $\angle DAC =$ ___?___°. 60°
12. If $\angle DAC = 55°$, then $\angle CAB =$ ___?___°. 35°
13. If $\angle CAB = 32°$, then $\widehat{BC} =$ ___?___°. 64°
14. If $\widehat{AC} = 100°$, then $\angle CAB =$ ___?___° 40°

**Exercises 15–20 refer to the diagram.**

B **15.** If $\widehat{AB} = 96°$, then $\angle D =$ 48 __?__° and $\angle C =$ __?__°. 48

**16.** If $\widehat{DC} = 118°$, then $\angle A =$ 59 __?__° and $\angle B =$ __?__°. 59

**17.** If $\angle D = 44°$, then $\widehat{AB} =$ 88 __?__° and $\angle C =$ __?__°. 44

**18.** If $\angle D = 47°$, then $\widehat{AB} =$ 94 __?__° and $\angle C =$ __?__°. 47

**19.** Is $\angle D = \angle C$? Is $\angle A = \angle B$? Yes; Yes

**20.** Is $\triangle ADR \sim \triangle BCR$? Yes

**In each diagram, find the measure of $\angle 1$.**

**21.** 51°

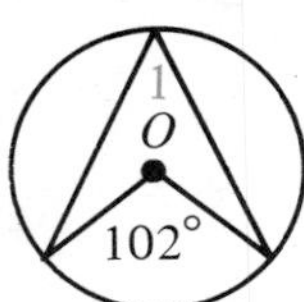


**22.** 40°

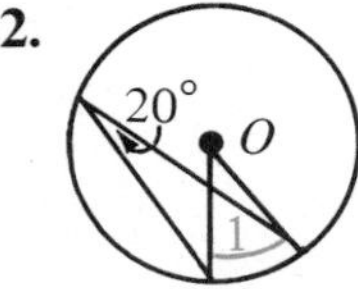


**23.** 37°

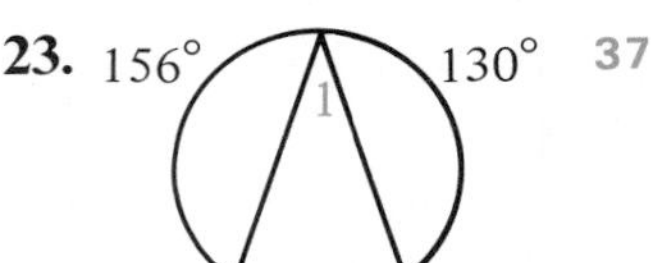


**24.** 43°

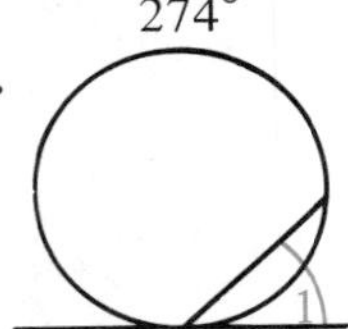


**25.** 94°

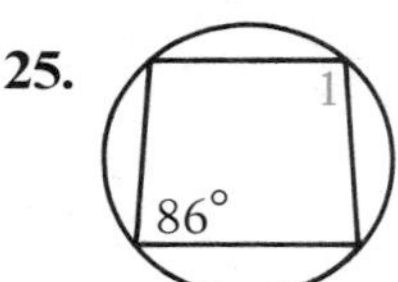


**26.** 70°

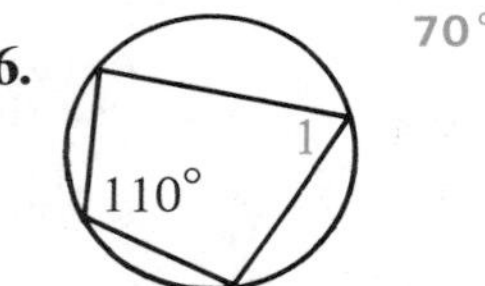


**$\triangle CAB$ is isosceles with $AC = AB$.**

**27.** If $\angle A = 55°$, then $\widehat{AB} =$ __?__°. 125

**28.** If $\widehat{CB} = k°$, then $\angle B =$ __?__°. $90 - \frac{k}{4}$
(Answer in terms of $k$.)

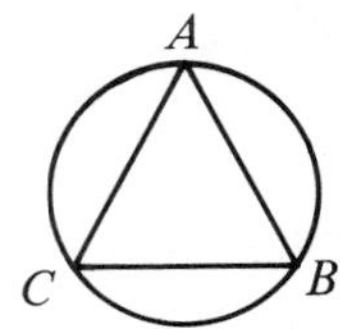


**29.** $DEFGH$ is a regular pentagon.

**a.** $\widehat{DE} =$ __?__° and $\widehat{EF} =$ __?__° 72; 72

**b.** Find the measure of each numbered angle.
$\angle 1 = 36°$; $\angle 2 = 36°$; $\angle 3 = 36°$
$\angle 4 = 108°$

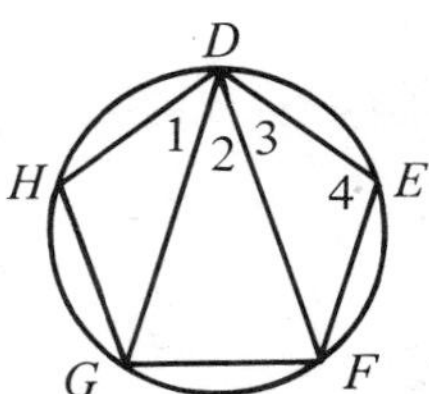


C **30.** Explain why the opposite angles of a quadrilateral inscribed in a circle must be supplementary.
These angles are inscribed in arcs which sum to 360°.
By Theorem 8, the angles sum to $\frac{1}{2}(360°) = 180°$.

**In Exercises 31–33, write a strategy for proving the three cases of Theorem 8. In each case, $\overline{CA}$ and $\overline{CB}$ are chords of $\odot O$. Show that $\angle ACB = \frac{1}{2}\widehat{AB}$. You need not write out the proof.**

**31.** *Case 1*

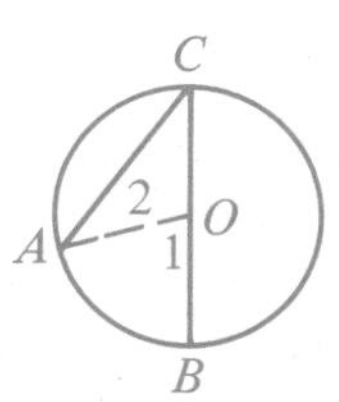


*Hint:*
$\angle ACB + \angle 2 = \angle 1$

$\angle ACB = \angle 2$

$2(\angle ACB) = \angle 1 = \widehat{AB}$

$\angle ACB = \frac{1}{2}\widehat{AB}$

**32.** *Case 2*

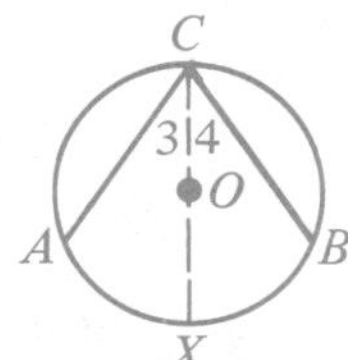


*Hint:* Use Case 1.
$\widehat{AB} = \widehat{AX} + \widehat{XB}$

$\angle 3 = \frac{1}{2}\widehat{AX}$; $\angle 4 = \frac{1}{2}\widehat{XB}$

$\angle 3 + \angle 4 = \frac{1}{2}(\widehat{AX} + \widehat{XB})$

$\angle ACB = \frac{1}{2}\widehat{AB}$

**33.** *Case 3*

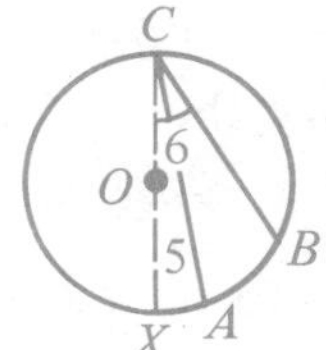


*Hint:* Use Case 1.
$\widehat{AB} = \widehat{XB} - \widehat{XA}$

$\angle 6 = \frac{1}{2}\widehat{XB}$; $\angle 5 = \frac{1}{2}\widehat{XA}$

$\angle 6 - \angle 5 = \frac{1}{2}(\widehat{XB} - \widehat{XA})$

$\angle ABC = \frac{1}{2}\widehat{AB}$

## SELF-TEST

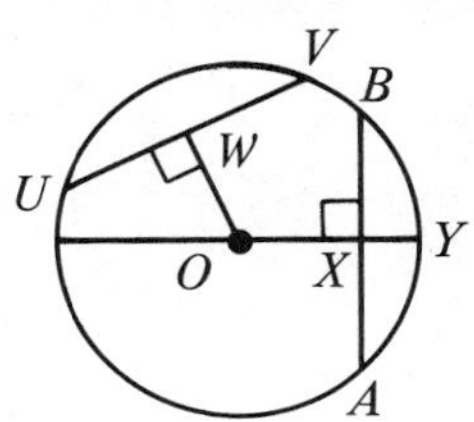


**1.** If $AB = 12$, then $AX =$ __?__. 6

**2.** If $\widehat{BY} = 32°$, then $\widehat{AY} =$ __?__°. 32

**3.** If $AB = 12$ and $OW = OX$, then $UV =$ __?__. 12

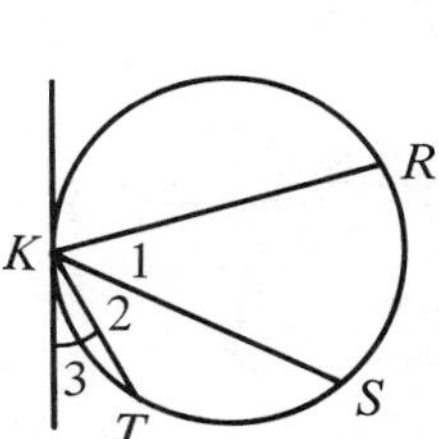


**4.** If $\widehat{RS} = 80°$, then $\angle 1 =$ __?__°. 40

**5.** If $\angle 2 = 38°$, then $\widehat{ST} =$ __?__°. 76

**6.** If $\angle 1 = 42°$ and $\angle 2 = 36°$, then $\widehat{RST} =$ __?__° and $\widehat{RKT} =$ __?__°. 156, 204

**7.** If $\widehat{TK} = 60°$, then $\angle 3 =$ __?__°. 30

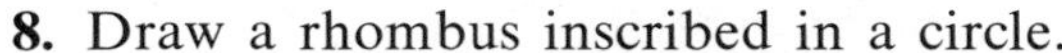

**8.** Draw a rhombus inscribed in a circle.

# 6 • Other Angles

## Explorations

**1.** We wish to find the measure of $\angle 1$ without using a protractor. Draw $\overline{AD}$. You can easily find the measures of $\angle ADC$ and $\angle DAB$.

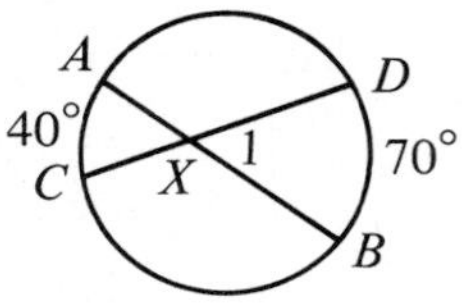


Notice that $\angle 1$ is an exterior angle of $\triangle AXD$.

$\angle 1 = \underline{\ \ ?\ \ }° + \underline{\ \ ?\ \ }°$

35 20

**2.** We wish to find the measure of $\angle P$ without using a protractor.

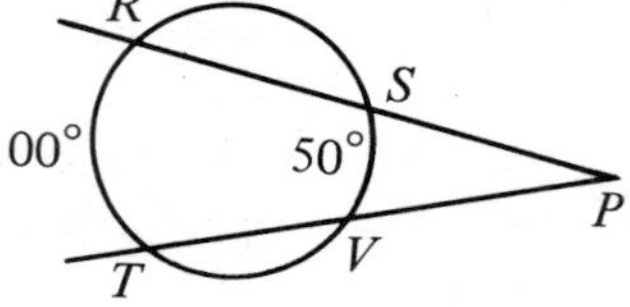


Draw $\overline{ST}$. You can easily find the measures of $\angle RST$ and $\angle STV$.

Notice that $\angle RST$ is an exterior angle of $\triangle TSP$.

$\angle P = \underline{\ \ ?\ \ }° - \underline{\ \ ?\ \ }°$

50 25

These explorations suggest two theorems—and proofs of these theorems.

**THEOREM 10**

An angle formed by two chords is equal to half the sum of the intercepted arcs.

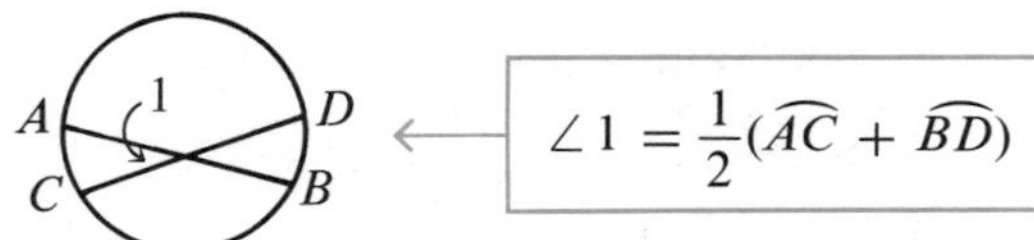

**THEOREM 11**

An angle formed by two secants is equal to half the difference of the intercepted arcs.

A B P D C

$\angle P = \frac{1}{2}(\widehat{AC} - \widehat{BD})$

**EXAMPLE** In each diagram, find the measure of $\angle 1$.

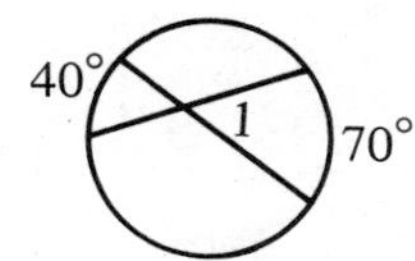


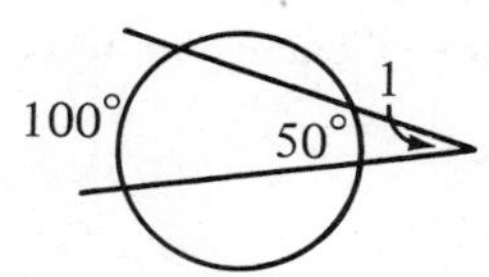


$$\angle 1 = \frac{1}{2}(40° + 70°) = \frac{1}{2}(110°) = 55°$$

$$\angle 1 = \frac{1}{2}(100° - 50°) = \frac{1}{2}(50°) = 25°$$

Did you get these answers when you tried the explorations on the previous page?

**Summary of Angle and Arc Relationships**

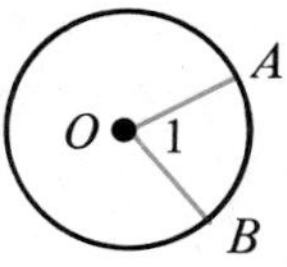


$\angle 1$ is a central angle.

$\angle 1 = \widehat{AB}$

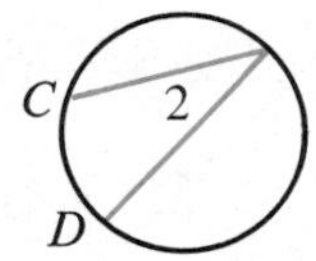


$\angle 2$ is an inscribed angle.

$\angle 2 = \frac{1}{2}\widehat{CD}$

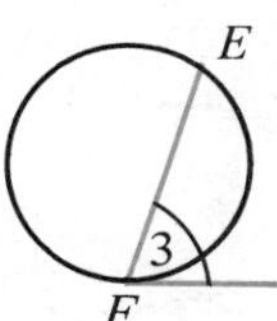


$\angle 3$ is formed by a chord and a tangent.

$\angle 3 = \frac{1}{2}\widehat{EF}$

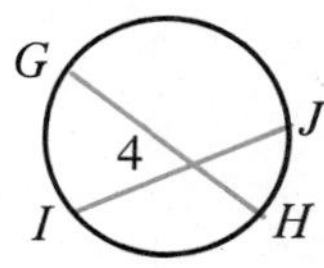


$\angle 4$ is formed by two chords.

$\angle 4 = \frac{1}{2}(\widehat{GI} + \widehat{JH})$

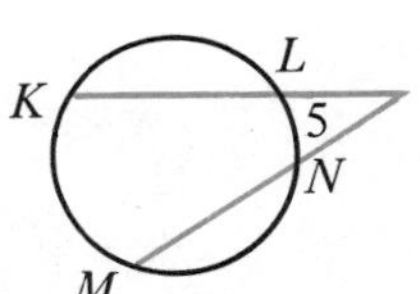


$\angle 5$ is formed by two secants.

$\angle 5 = \frac{1}{2}(\widehat{KM} - \widehat{LN})$

## Classroom Practice

**Find the measure of each numbered angle.**

**1.**

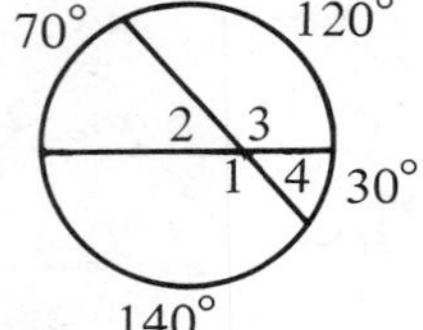


**2.**

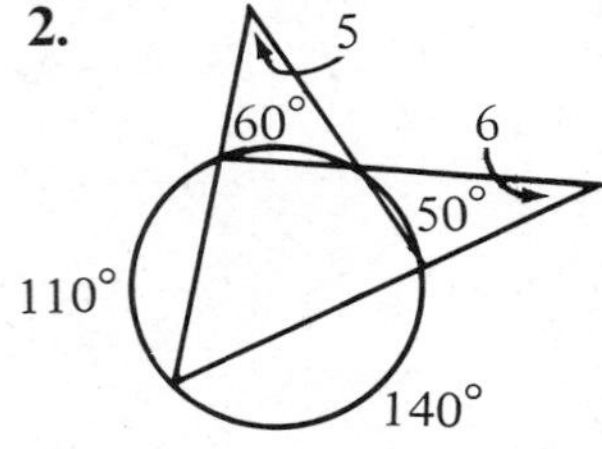


**3.**

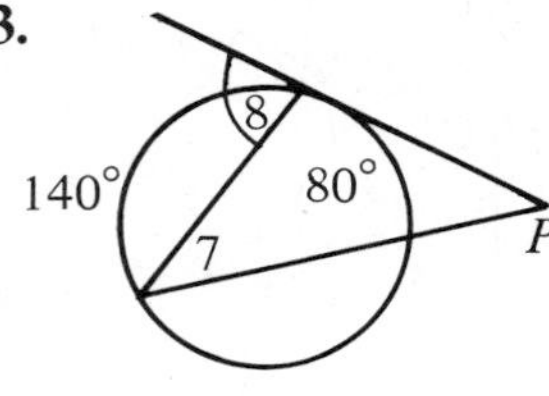


**4.** Using the diagram for Exercise 3, find $\angle P$. (*Hint:* $\angle 8$ is an exterior angle of the triangle.)

1. $\angle 1 = 130°$; $\angle 2 = 50°$; $\angle 3 = 130°$; $\angle 4 = 50°$
2. $\angle 5 = 40°$; $\angle 6 = 30°$
3. $\angle 7 = 40°$; $\angle 8 = 70°$
4. $\angle P = 30°$

## Written Exercises

**Find the measure of $\angle 1$.**

A **1.** 40°

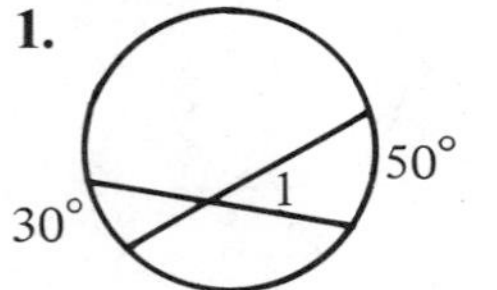


**2.** 44°

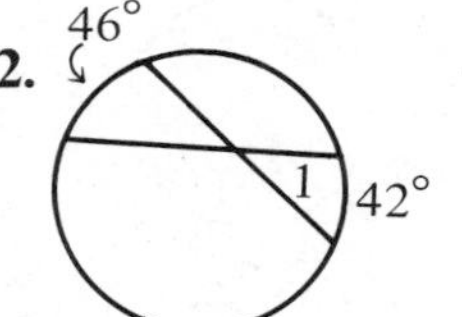


**3.** 38°

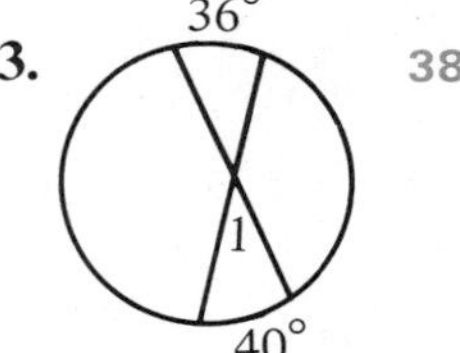


**4.** 110°

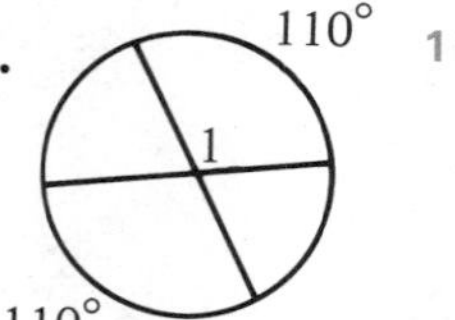


**5.** 80°

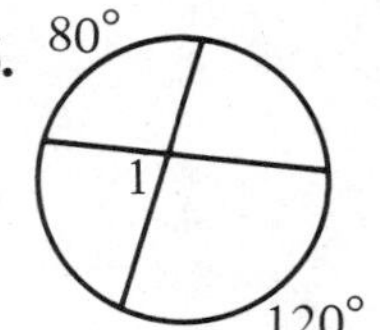


**6.** 70°

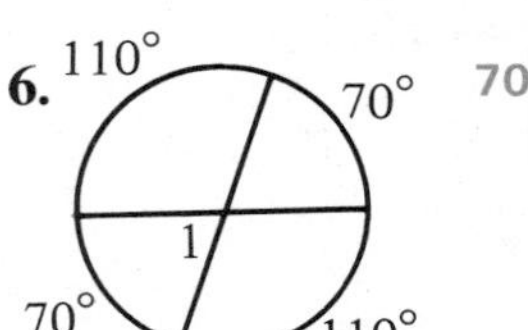


**7.** 35°

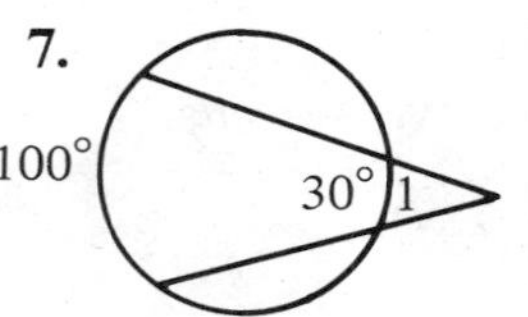


**8.** 50°

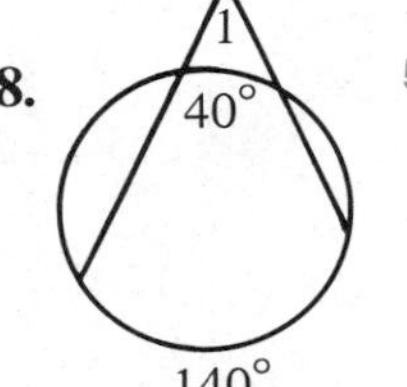


**9.** 59°

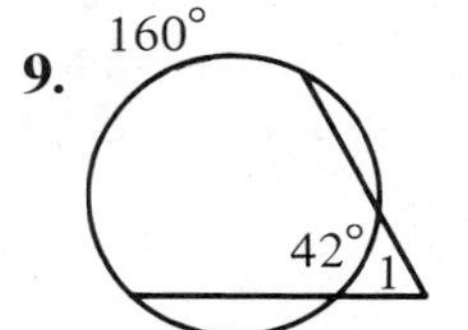
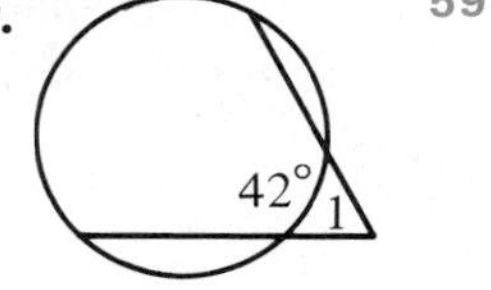

**10.** 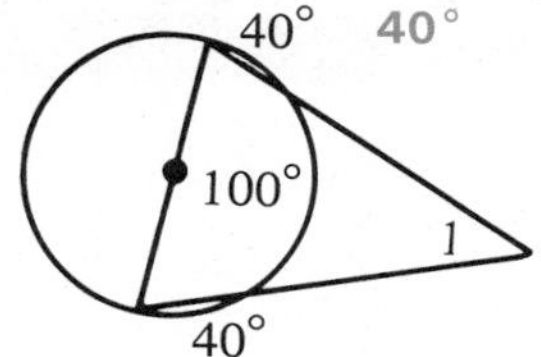

40°

**11.** 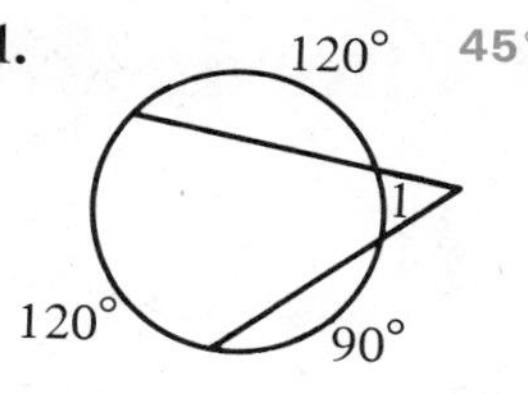

45°

**12.** 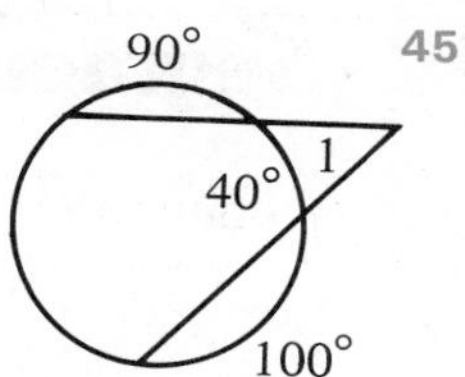

45°

**In each exercise find the value of $x$.**

Sample 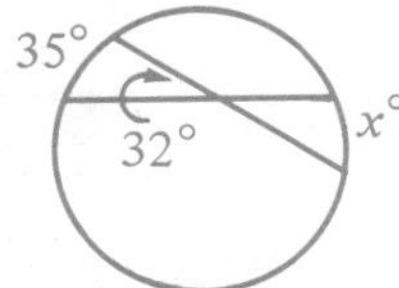


$$32 = \frac{1}{2}(35 + x)$$
$$64 = 35 + x$$
$$29 = x$$

B **13.** 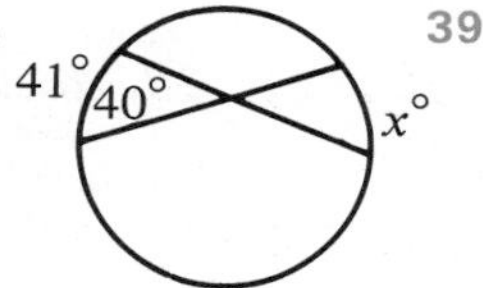

39

**14.** 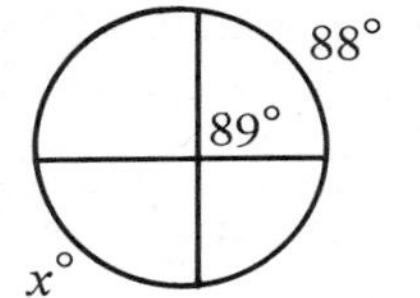

90

**15.** 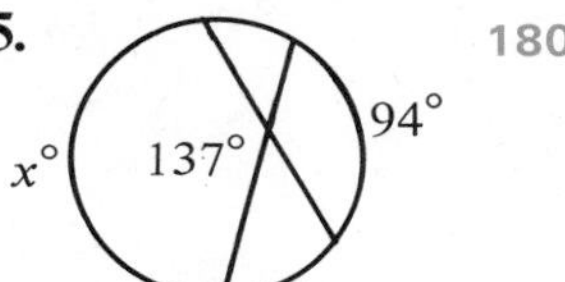

180

**16.** 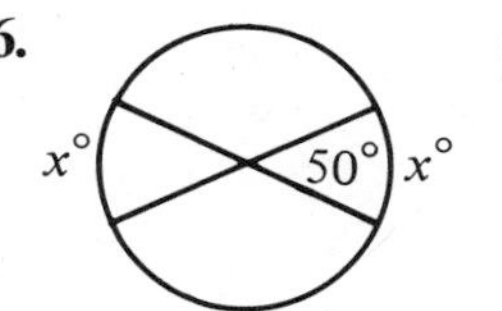

50

**17.** 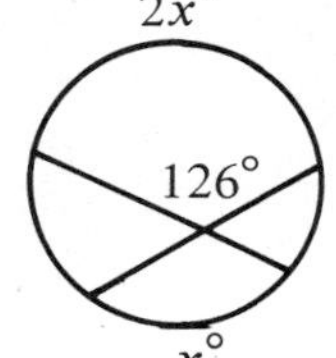

84

**18.** 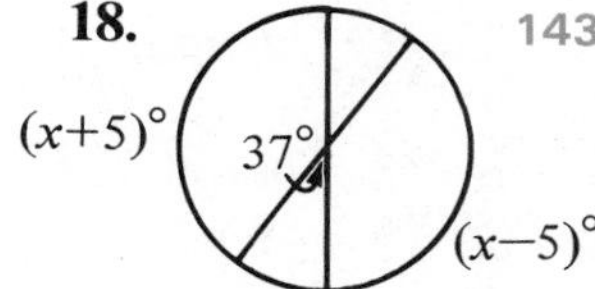

143

**19.** 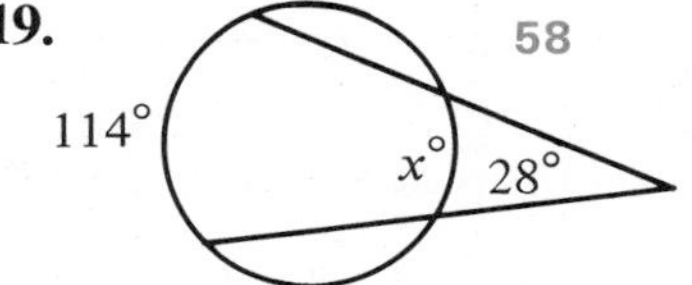

58

**20.** 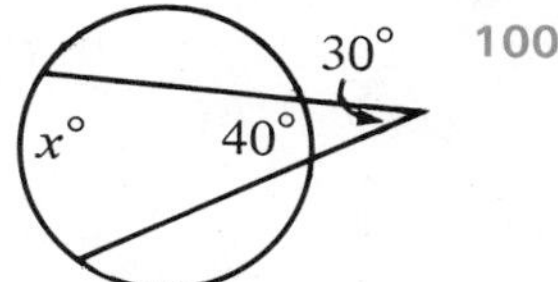

100

C **21.** 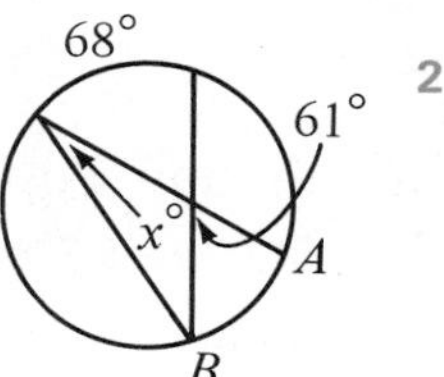

27

**22.** 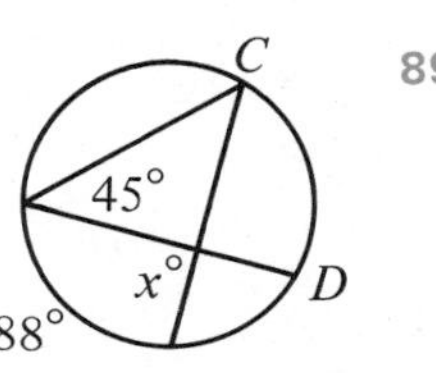

89

**23.** 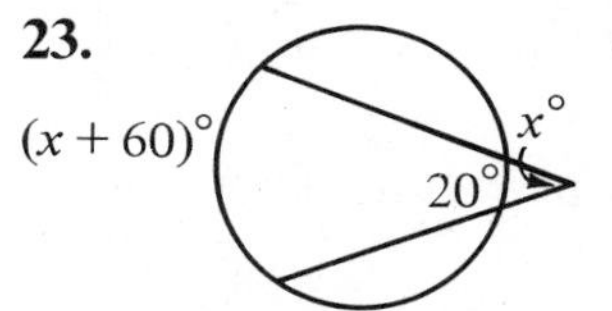

40

**24.** 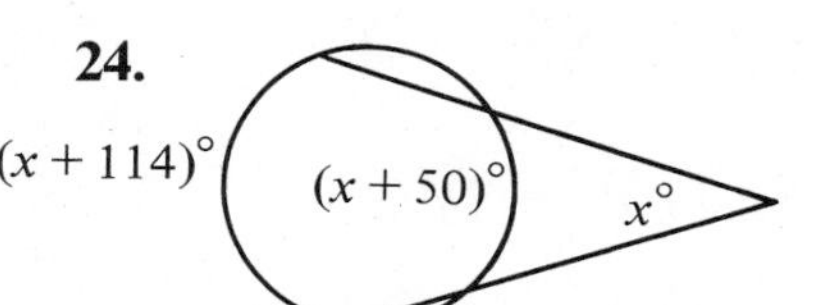

32

## 7 • Segments of Chords

Do you believe that the equation

$$AX \cdot XB = CX \cdot XD$$

can possibly be correct? Some people do not believe it until they see a proof.

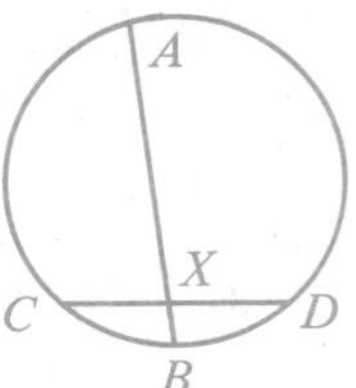

**THEOREM 12**

If two chords intersect inside a circle, the product of the lengths of the segments of one chord equals the product of the lengths of the segments of the other.

*Given:* Chords $\overline{AB}$ and $\overline{CD}$ intersect at point $X$ inside the circle.

*Prove:* $AX \cdot XB = CX \cdot XD$

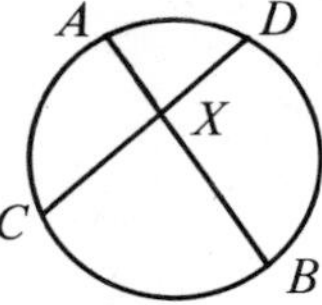


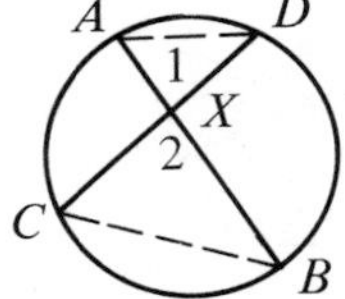


| STATEMENTS | REASONS |
|---|---|
| 1. Draw $\overline{AD}$ and $\overline{BC}$. | 1. Through any two points there is exactly one line. |
| 2. $\angle A = \frac{1}{2}\widehat{BD}$; $\angle C = \frac{1}{2}\widehat{BD}$ | 2. An inscribed angle is equal to _?_. half its intercepted arc |
| 3. $\angle A = \angle C$ | 3. Substitution Postulate |
| 4. $\angle 1 = \angle 2$ | 4. _?_ Vertical angles are equal. |
| 5. $\triangle AXD \sim \triangle CXB$ | 5. AA Postulate |
| 6. $\frac{AX}{CX} = \frac{XD}{XB}$ | 6. Corresponding sides of similar triangles are in proportion. |
| 7. $AX \cdot XB = CX \cdot XD$ | 7. A property of proportions |

Sometimes it is simpler to apply Theorem 12 by thinking of a figure like the one shown.

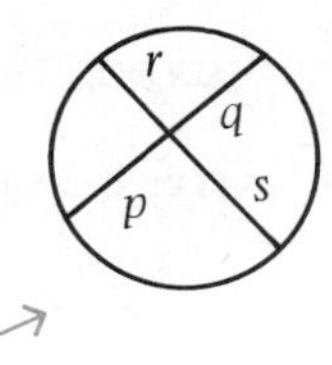


$p \times q = r \times s$

## Classroom Practice

**In each exercise, find the length $x$.**

**1.**

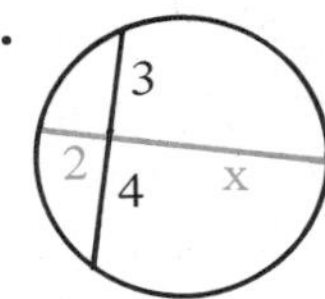


$2x = \underline{\ ?\ }$ 12

$x = \underline{\ ?\ }$ 6

**2.**

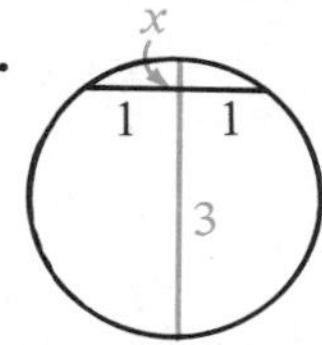


$3x = \underline{\ ?\ }$ 1

$x = \underline{\ ?\ }$ $\frac{1}{3}$

**3.**

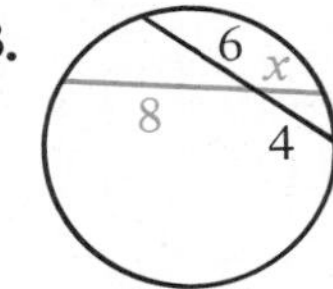


$8x = \underline{\ ?\ }$ 24

$x = \underline{\ ?\ }$ 3

**Exercises 4–7 lead to a formula about the lengths associated with secants to a circle from an outside point.**

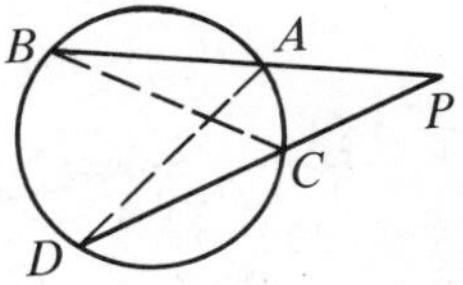


**4.** Name two angles of $\triangle PBC$ that are equal to two angles of $\triangle PDA$. $\angle P = \angle P$, $\angle B = \angle D$

**5.** Complete: $\triangle PBC \sim \triangle \underline{\ ?\ }$. $\triangle PDA$

**6.** Write a proportion that involves $PB$, $PA$, $PD$, and $PC$. $\frac{PB}{PD} = \frac{PC}{PA}$

**7.** Complete: $PB \cdot \underline{\ ?\ } = PD \cdot \underline{\ ?\ }$. $PA$ $PC$

**8.** Look at the figures below. As point $B$ moves along $\overset{\frown}{BA}$ toward point $A$, $\overrightarrow{PB}$ becomes more and more like a tangent to the circle.

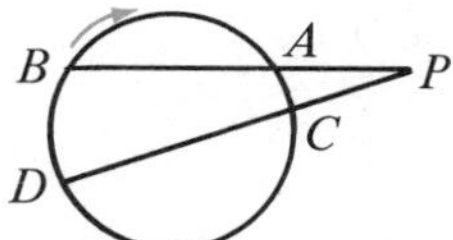


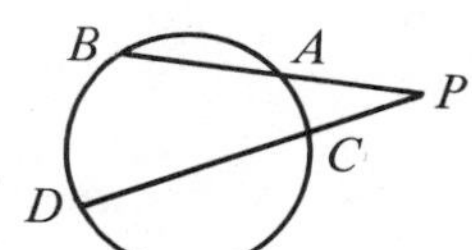


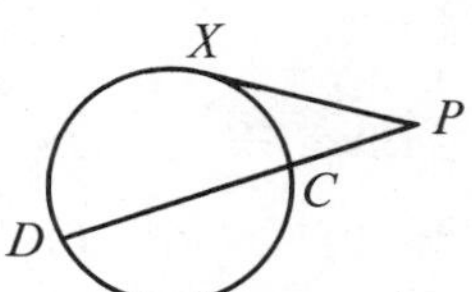


In the third diagram, $A$ and $B$ have become the same point, $X$. Look at the equation in Exercise 7. Suggest an equation involving $PX$, $PC$, and $PD$. $(PX)^2 = PC \cdot PD$

## Written Exercises

**In each exercise, find the length $x$.**

Sample

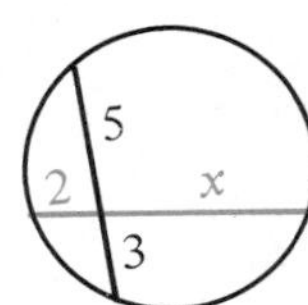


$$2x = 3 \cdot 5$$
$$2x = 15$$
$$x = \frac{15}{2} = 7\frac{1}{2}$$

A

1. 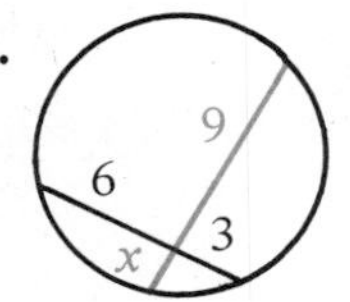

2

2. 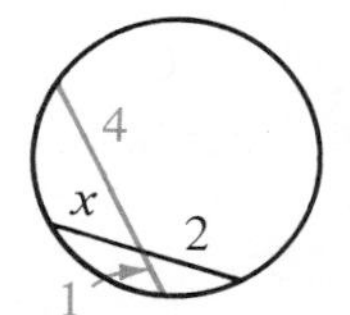

2

3. 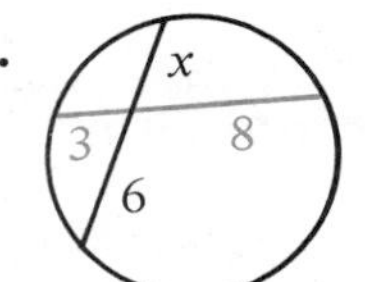

4

4. 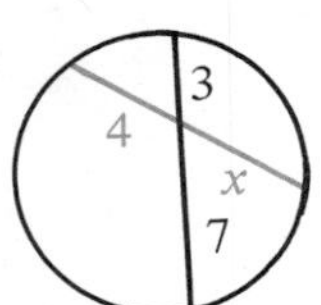

$5\frac{1}{4}$

5. 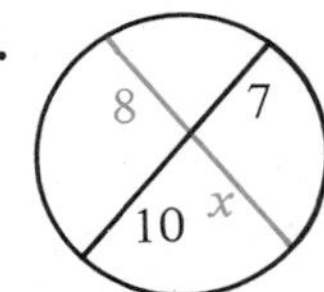

$8\frac{3}{4}$

6. 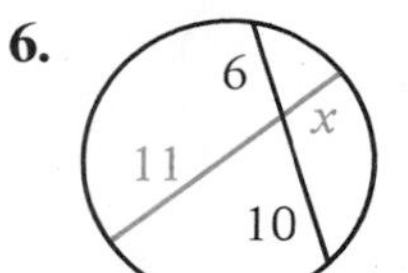

$5\frac{5}{11}$

7. 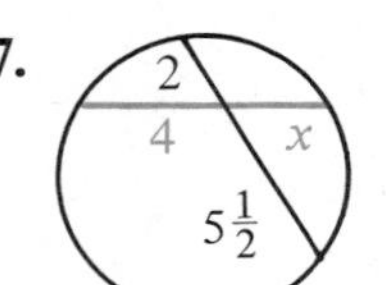

$2\frac{3}{4}$

8. 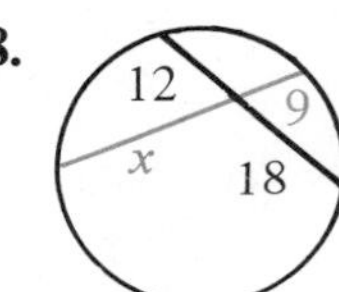

24

9. 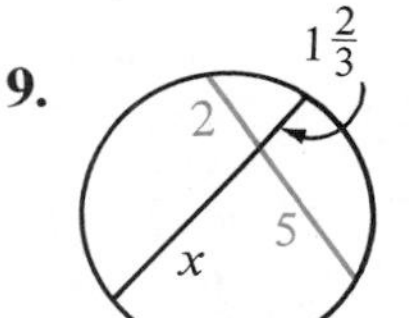

6

B

10. 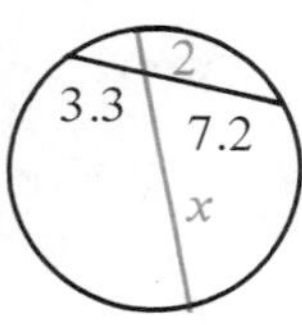

11.88

11. 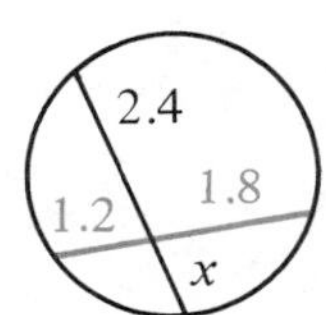

.9

12. 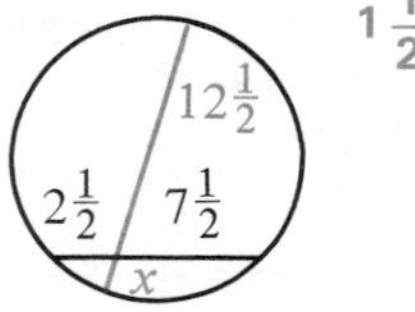

$1\frac{1}{2}$

**Exercises 13–16 lead to the same equation that was developed in Exercise 8, page 343. In the diagram, $\overline{PX}$ is a tangent segment and $\overleftrightarrow{PD}$ is a secant.**

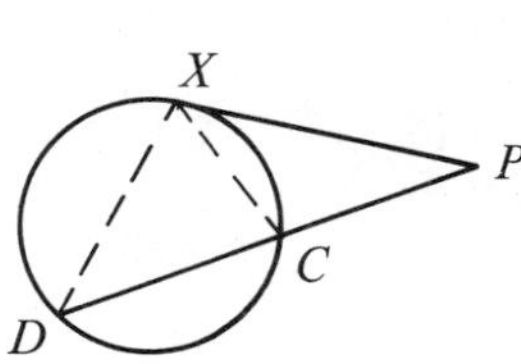


13. $\angle PXC = \frac{1}{2}\underline{\ ?\ }$ $\widehat{XC}$; $\angle PDX = \frac{1}{2}\underline{\ ?\ }$ $\widehat{XC}$

$\angle PXC = \angle PDX$; $\angle P = \angle P$

14. $\triangle PXC \sim \triangle\underline{\ ?\ }$ PDX

15. $\frac{PX}{?} = \frac{PC}{?}$ PD PX

16. $PX \times \underline{\ ?\ } = PC \times \underline{\ ?\ }$ PX PD

**Secants and tangents of circles are shown. Find $x$.**

C **17.** 6

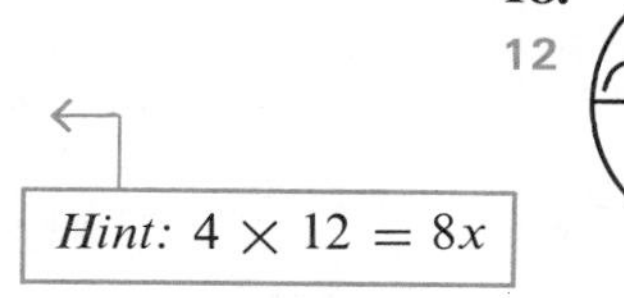


**18.** 12

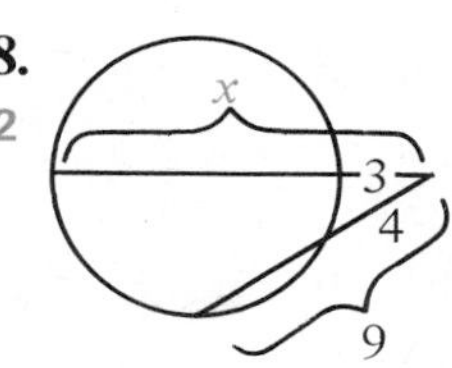


**19.** 6

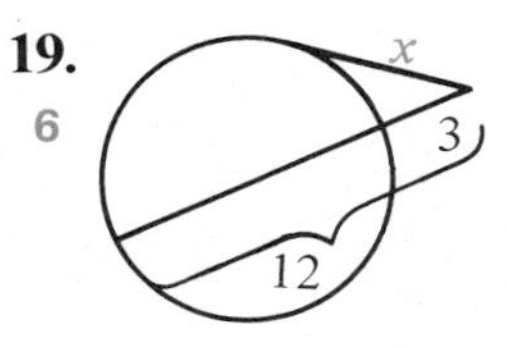


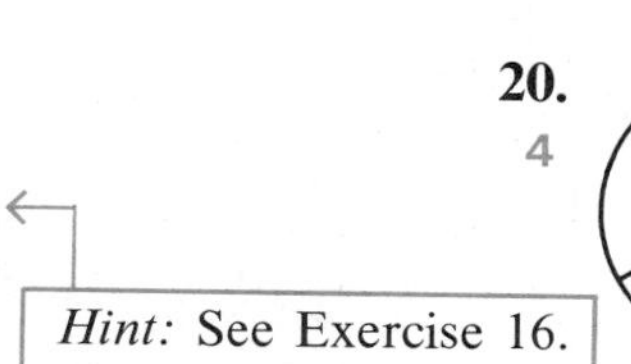


**20.** 4

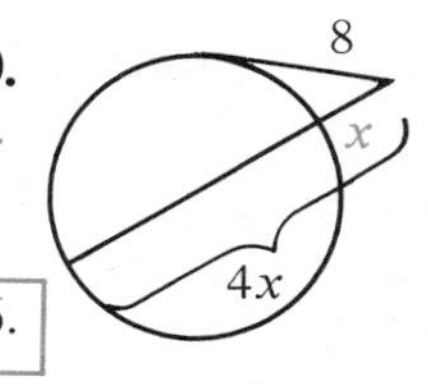


## Using Circles to Set Up Schedules

Five teams enter a tournament. Each team is to play each other team once. Begin arranging a schedule by dividing a circle into five equal arcs. Call the points, and the teams, $A$, $B$, $C$, $D$, and $E$.

FIRST ROUND

Draw the diameter containing $A$.

Connect other points as shown.

*Games:* $A$-bye $B$-$E$ $C$-$D$

*Bye* means that the team does not play.

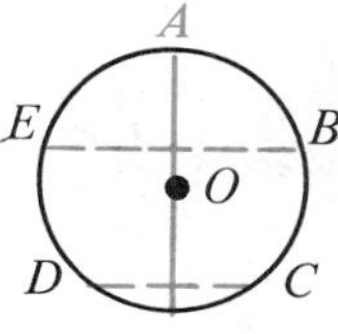


SECOND ROUND

Draw the diameter containing $B$.

*Games:* $B$-bye $C$-$A$ $D$-$E$

THIRD, FOURTH, AND FIFTH ROUNDS

Draw diameters containing $C$, $D$, and $E$.

In the five rounds there will be a total of ten games, not counting byes.

For a tournament of six teams, use five equal arcs as above. But when you draw the diameter containing $A$, let that mean that $A$ will play the sixth team, $O$. There won't be any byes. In the five rounds there will be a total of fifteen games.

For a tournament of seven teams—or of eight teams—use seven equal arcs. You should get 21 games and 28 games, respectively.

## SELF-TEST

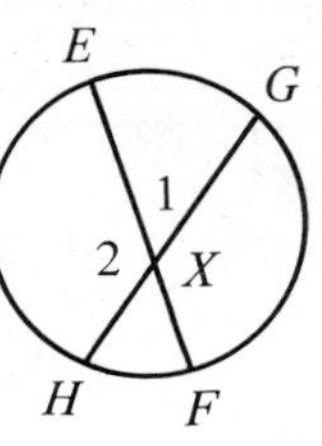


1. If $\widehat{GE} = 60°$ and $\widehat{HF} = 40°$, then $\angle 1 =$ _?_°. 50
2. If $\widehat{GE} = 67°$ and $\widehat{HF} = 41°$, then $\angle 2 =$ _?_°. 126
3. If $\angle 2 = 130°$ and $\widehat{EH} = 140°$, then $\widehat{GF} =$ _?_°. 130
4. If $EX = 15$, $XF = 8$, and $GX = 12$, then $XH =$ _?_. 10
5. If $GX = 9$, $XH = 8$, and $EX = 12$, then $FX =$ _?_. 6
6. If $\widehat{JM} = 100°$ and $\widehat{KN} = 50°$, then $\angle 3 =$ _?_°. 25
7. If $\widehat{JK} = 108°$, $\widehat{JM} = 96°$, and $\widehat{MN} = 94°$, then $\angle 3 =$ _?_°. 17°
8. If $\angle 3 = 40°$ and $\widehat{KN} = 30°$, then $\widehat{JM} =$ _?_°. 110

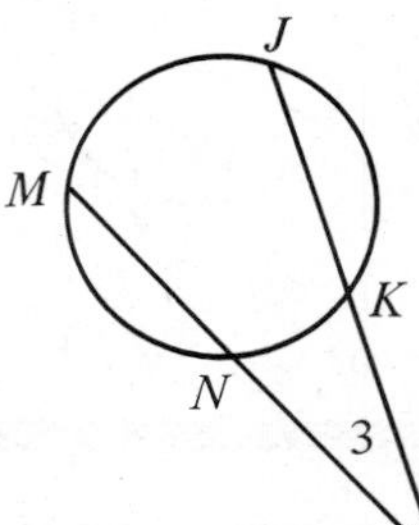


## Puzzles & Things

### Constructing the Center of a Circle

Suppose you have a circle, but have lost track of its center. How can you find the center?

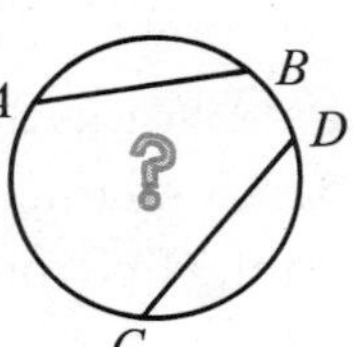


Draw two chords, $\overline{AB}$ and $\overline{CD}$.
Construct the perpendicular bisector of each chord.
The two perpendicular bisectors intersect at the center of the circle.

Try the construction when $\overline{AB}$ and $\overline{CD}$ are parallel. Why doesn't the construction work?

Return to the original problem. Can you discover a different way to construct the center?

## Reviewing Algebraic Skills

Do you remember this rule? $\sqrt{\frac{a}{b}} = \frac{\sqrt{a}}{\sqrt{b}}$ and $\frac{\sqrt{a}}{\sqrt{b}} = \sqrt{\frac{a}{b}}$

**Find the square root. Express the result in simplest form. Assume that any variable represents a number greater than zero.**

Samples $\sqrt{\frac{100}{49}} = \frac{\sqrt{100}}{\sqrt{49}} = \frac{10}{7}$ *or* $1\frac{3}{7}$ $\qquad \sqrt{\frac{5}{64}} = \frac{\sqrt{5}}{\sqrt{64}} = \frac{\sqrt{5}}{8}$ $\qquad \sqrt{\frac{8n^2}{9}} = \frac{\sqrt{4 \cdot 2 \cdot n^2}}{\sqrt{9}} = \frac{2n\sqrt{2}}{3}$

1. $\sqrt{\frac{1}{81}}$ $\frac{1}{9}$
2. $\sqrt{\frac{4}{49}}$ $\frac{2}{7}$
3. $\sqrt{\frac{121}{36}}$ $\frac{11}{6}$
4. $\sqrt{\frac{9}{25}}$ $\frac{3}{5}$
5. $\sqrt{\frac{169}{16}}$ $\frac{13}{4}$
6. $\sqrt{\frac{2}{49}}$ $\frac{\sqrt{2}}{7}$
7. $\sqrt{\frac{3}{100}}$ $\frac{\sqrt{3}}{10}$
8. $\sqrt{\frac{7}{36}}$ $\frac{\sqrt{7}}{6}$
9. $\sqrt{\frac{5}{16}}$ $\frac{\sqrt{5}}{4}$
10. $\sqrt{\frac{11}{64}}$ $\frac{\sqrt{11}}{8}$
11. $\sqrt{\frac{36x^2}{25}}$ $\frac{6x}{5}$
12. $\sqrt{\frac{4b^2}{81}}$ $\frac{2b}{9}$
13. $\sqrt{\frac{2c^2}{100}}$ $\frac{c\sqrt{2}}{10}$
14. $\sqrt{\frac{7a^2}{16}}$ $\frac{a\sqrt{7}}{4}$
15. $\sqrt{\frac{18n^2}{49}}$ $\frac{3n\sqrt{2}}{7}$
16. $\sqrt{\frac{20k^2}{81}}$ $\frac{2k\sqrt{5}}{9}$
17. $\sqrt{\frac{75x^2}{36}}$ $\frac{5x\sqrt{3}}{6}$
18. $\sqrt{\frac{28a^2}{25}}$ $\frac{2a\sqrt{7}}{5}$
19. $\sqrt{\frac{45d^2}{144}}$ $\frac{d\sqrt{5}}{4}$
20. $\sqrt{\frac{32b^2}{49}}$ $\frac{4b\sqrt{2}}{7}$

**Express in simplest radical form.**

Sample $\frac{\sqrt{2}}{\sqrt{5}} = \frac{\sqrt{2} \cdot \sqrt{5}}{\sqrt{5} \cdot \sqrt{5}} = \frac{\sqrt{10}}{5}$ *or* $\frac{1}{5}\sqrt{10}$ ← Multiply the numerator and denominator by a number that will make the denominator a whole number.

21. $\frac{\sqrt{3}}{\sqrt{7}}$ $\frac{\sqrt{21}}{7}$
22. $\frac{\sqrt{6}}{\sqrt{3}}$ $\sqrt{2}$
23. $\frac{\sqrt{5}}{\sqrt{8}}$ $\frac{\sqrt{10}}{4}$
24. $\frac{\sqrt{11}}{\sqrt{2}}$ $\frac{\sqrt{22}}{2}$
25. $\frac{\sqrt{7}}{\sqrt{5}}$ $\frac{\sqrt{35}}{5}$
26. $\sqrt{\frac{1}{8}}$ $\frac{\sqrt{2}}{4}$
27. $\sqrt{\frac{4}{11}}$ $\frac{2\sqrt{11}}{11}$
28. $\sqrt{\frac{16}{7}}$ $\frac{4\sqrt{7}}{7}$
29. $\sqrt{\frac{3}{2}}$ $\frac{\sqrt{6}}{2}$
30. $\sqrt{\frac{2}{5}}$ $\frac{\sqrt{10}}{5}$
31. $\frac{5\sqrt{6}}{\sqrt{3}}$ $5\sqrt{2}$
32. $\frac{3\sqrt{8}}{\sqrt{2}}$ 6
33. $\frac{6\sqrt{5}}{\sqrt{3}}$ $2\sqrt{15}$
34. $\frac{10\sqrt{2}}{\sqrt{5}}$ $2\sqrt{10}$
35. $\frac{4\sqrt{7}}{\sqrt{2}}$ $2\sqrt{14}$
36. The area of a rectangle is 10 square units. The width of the rectangle is $\sqrt{2}$ units. What is the length? $5\sqrt{2}$ units

# extra for experts

## *Indirect Proof*

The method we have been using to prove statements is called *direct proof.* Sometimes a direct proof is very difficult or impossible to use, so we use an indirect method of reasoning instead. We call this method of reasoning *indirect proof.* We often use it in everyday situations.

Suppose you are watching the basketball playoffs on television. The Pivots lead the Chargers by one point in the final seconds of the game. One of the Chargers takes a shot and misses. A teammate tips up the rebound for a basket just as the final buzzer goes off. No fouls are called, but suddenly the television goes blank. Did the final basket count?

Later you learn that the Pivots won the game. You conclude that the final basket did not count.

First, assume that the final basket counts. That basket puts the Chargers ahead by one point, and they win the game. This result contradicts the fact that the Pivots won the game. Our assumption must be incorrect. We conclude that the final basket did not count.

> To write an indirect proof:
>
> Begin by assuming that what you wish to prove is not true. Reason logically until you reach a contradiction of a known fact. Conclude that your assumption is *false* and that what you wish to prove is *true*.

### Example 1

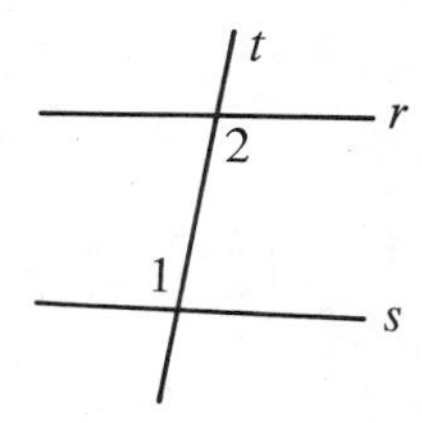


*Given:* Lines $r$ and $s$ with transversal $t$, $\angle 1 \neq \angle 2$.

*Prove:* $r$ is not parallel to $s$.

*Proof:* Assume that $r$ is parallel to $s$. Then, since $\angle 1$ and $\angle 2$ are alternate interior angles, $\angle 1 = \angle 2$. This contradicts the given information, $\angle 1 \neq \angle 2$. Our assumption, $r$ is parallel to $s$, must be false. We conclude that $r$ is not parallel to $s$.

### Example 2

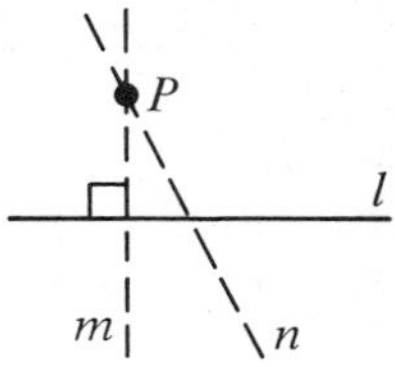


*Given:* line $l$ and point $P$.

*Prove:* There is only one line through $P$ perpendicular to $l$.

*Proof:* We know from Construction 3, page 22, that we can draw a line through $P$ perpendicular to $l$.

Assume that there is another line $n$ through $P$ perpendicular to $l$.

If two lines are perpendicular to a third line, they are parallel to each other, so line $m$ is parallel to line $n$. But $m$ and $n$ intersect at $P$. This contradicts the fact that $m$ is parallel to $n$.

We conclude that there is only one line through $P$ perpendicular to $l$.

Notice that an indirect proof depends on our ability to reason until we have found a contradiction. Indirect proof is sometimes called proof by contradiction.

## Exercises

Write an indirect proof for the following.

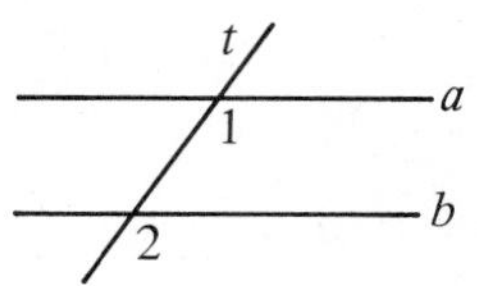


1. *Given:* Lines $a$ and $b$ with transversal $t$; $\angle 1 \neq \angle 2$.
   *Prove:* $a$ is not parallel to $b$.

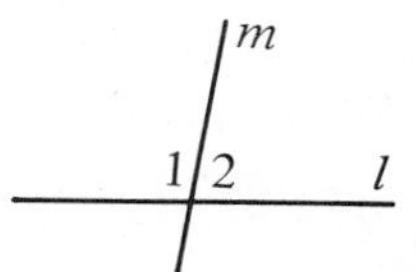


2. *Given:* Lines $l$ and $m$; $l$ is not perpendicular to $m$.
   *Prove:* $\angle 1 \neq \angle 2$

## Reviewing the Chapter

### Chapter Summary

1. Many of the terms used with circles are discussed on page 314.
2. If line $t$ is tangent to $\odot O$ at point $A$, then $\overline{OA} \perp t$.
   If line $t \perp \overline{OA}$ at point $A$, then $t$ is tangent to $\odot O$.
   Construction 10 shows how to construct a tangent to a circle at a given point.

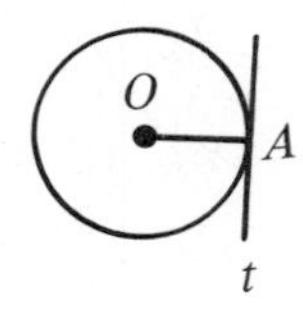


3. Given two circles, a common internal tangent intersects the segment joining the centers, and a common external tangent does not. Two circles may be externally tangent or internally tangent.
4. Arcs are classified on page 323.
5. In a circle, equal central angles have equal arcs, and equal minor arcs have equal central angles.
6. Given the figure at the right. When any one of these three statements is true, both of the others are also true.
   $QR = ST$ $\qquad$ $\widehat{QR} = \widehat{ST}$ $\qquad$ $OJ = OK$

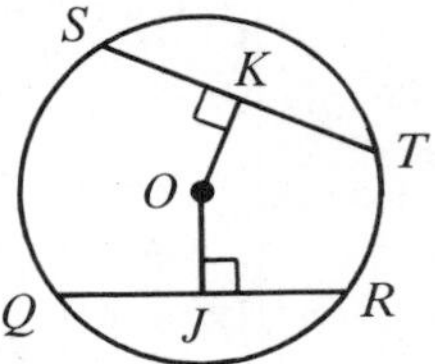


7. A diameter that is perpendicular to a chord bisects the chord and its arc.
8. A polygon is inscribed in a circle when each vertex lies on the circle. A polygon is circumscribed about a circle when each side is tangent to the circle.
9. A summary of angle and arc relationships is given on page 339.
10. If two chords intersect inside a circle, then the product of the lengths of the segments of one chord equals the product of the lengths of the segments of the other.

### Chapter Review Test

**Refer to the figure and use letters to name the following.** *(See pp. 314–317)*

**1.** A radius $\overline{OB}$ or $\overline{OC}$ **2.** A diameter $\overline{CB}$

**3.** A secant $\overleftrightarrow{BC}$ **4.** A tangent $\overleftrightarrow{BE}$

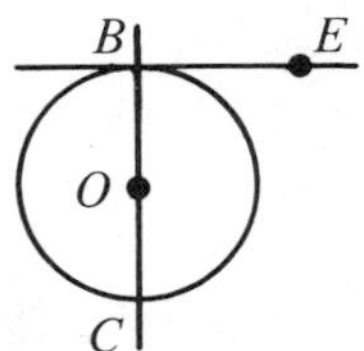

**Refer to the diagram and complete the statement.** (*See pp. 318–322*)

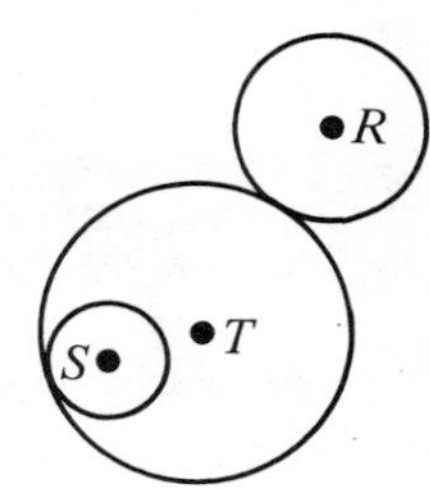


5. The number of common external tangents that can be drawn to $\odot R$ and $\odot S$ is _?_. 2
6. The number of common internal tangents that can be drawn to $\odot R$ and $\odot S$ is _?_. 2
7. $\odot T$ and $\odot$ _?_ are externally tangent. R
8. $\odot T$ and $\odot$ _?_ are internally tangent. S

**Write numerical values to complete the statements.** (*See pp. 323–326.*)

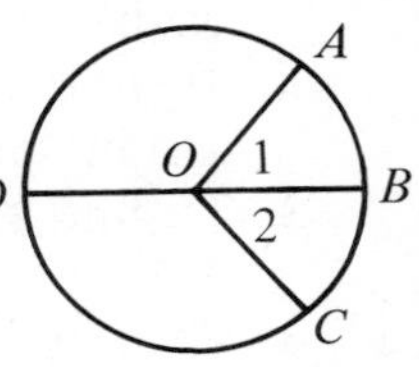


9. $\widehat{DAB}$ = _?_° 180
10. If $\angle 1 = 50°$, $\widehat{AB}$ = _?_°. 50
11. If $\widehat{BC} = 48°$, $\angle 2$ = _?_°. 48
12. If $\widehat{AD} = 126°$, $\angle 1$ = _?_°. 54
13. If $\widehat{AB} = \widehat{BC}$ and $\angle 1 = 47°$, then $\angle 2$ = _?_°. 47

**Write numerical values to complete the statements.** (*See pp. 328–332.*)

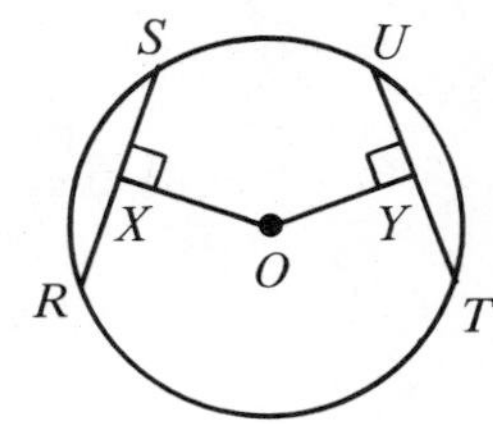


14. If $TU = 7$ and $\widehat{RS} = \widehat{TU}$, then $RS$ = _?_. 7
15. If $\widehat{RS} = 70°$ and $TU = RS$, then $\widehat{TU}$ = _?_°. 70
16. If $RS = TU$ and $OX = 5$, then $OY$ = _?_. 5
17. If $OX = OY$ and $TU = 4$, then $RS$ = _?_. 4

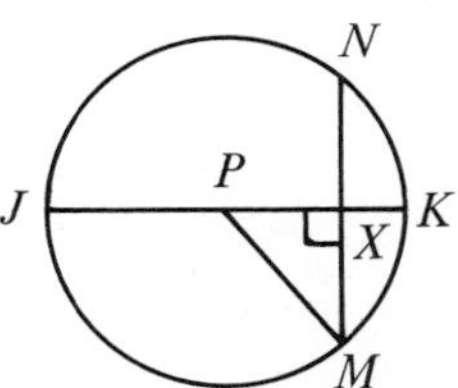


18. If $\widehat{MN} = 100°$, $\widehat{MK}$ = _?_°. 50
19. If $\widehat{MK} = 48°$, $\widehat{JM}$ = _?_°. 132
20. If $MN = 14$, $MX$ = _?_. 7
21. If $MN = 16$ and $PX = 6$, $MP$ = _?_. 10

**State the numerical value of *x*.** (*See pp. 333–345.*)

22. 35

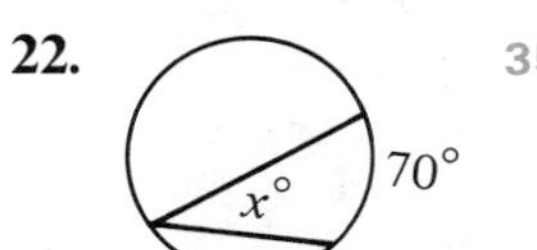


23. 80

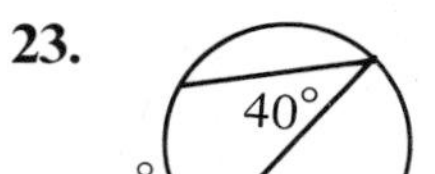


24. 55

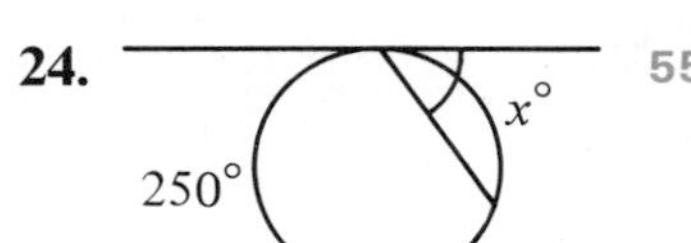


25. 45

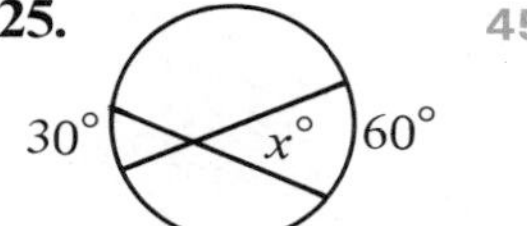


26. 30

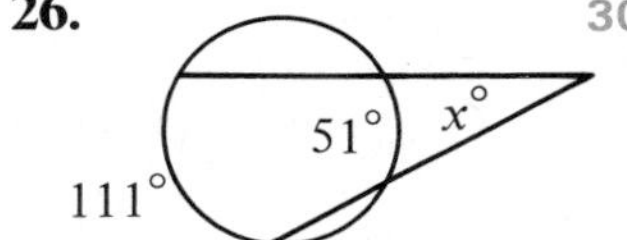


27. 6

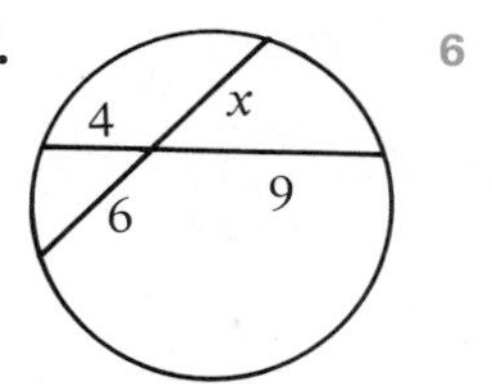

## *Here's what you'll learn in this chapter:*

1. To state the positions of points and lines with respect to each other.
2. To find the lateral area, total area, and volume of a right prism.
3. To find the lateral area, total area, and volume of a right circular cylinder.
4. To find the lateral area, total area, and volume of a regular pyramid.
5. To find the lateral area, total area, and volume of a right circular cone.
6. To find the area and volume of a sphere.

# Chapter 10

# Areas and Volumes of Solids

## 1 • Lines and Planes in Space

Look at lines *l* and *m* in the diagram. The lines do not meet, but they are not parallel. They are *skew* lines. **Skew lines** are two lines that do not lie in any one plane.

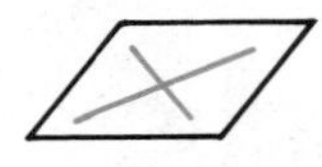

Intersecting lines are coplanar.

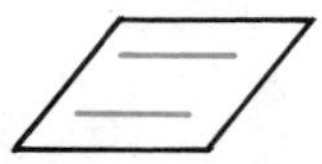

Parallel lines are coplanar.

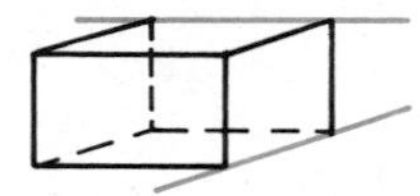

Skew lines are not coplanar.

Look at line *t* and plane *P*. The line and the plane are *parallel*. A line and a plane are **parallel** when they do not have any point in common. Any segment of the line is also said to be parallel to the plane.

**Possible positions of a line and a plane**

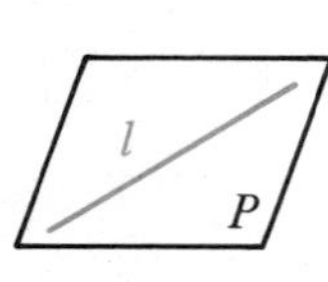


*l* lies in *P*.
*P* contains *l*.

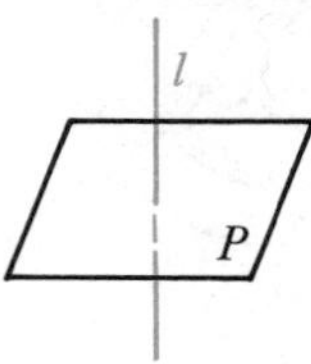


*l* intersects *P*.
*P* intersects *l*.

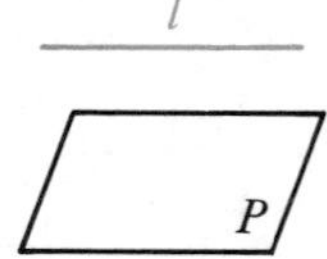


*l* and *P* are parallel.
$l \parallel P$

A line and a plane can intersect in a special way. Notice in the diagram that an axle is perpendicular to each spoke of a wagon wheel. The diagram suggests a line *perpendicular* to a plane.

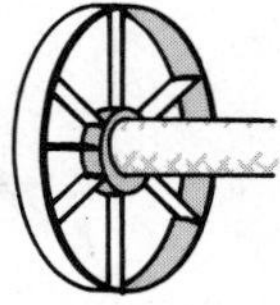

$l \perp P$

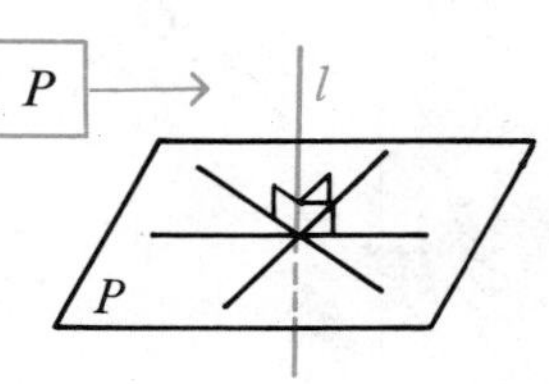


Line *l* is **perpendicular** to plane *P* when *l* is perpendicular to *every* line in *P* that passes through the point of intersection.

Suppose that $l \perp P$ and that plane $M$ contains line $l$. Then plane $M$ is said to be **perpendicular** to plane $P$. Perpendicular planes are one special kind of intersecting planes.

If $l \perp P$, then $M \perp P$.

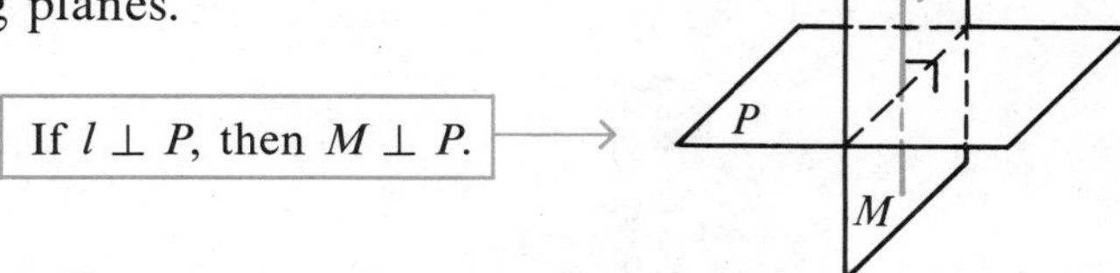


**Possible positions of two planes**

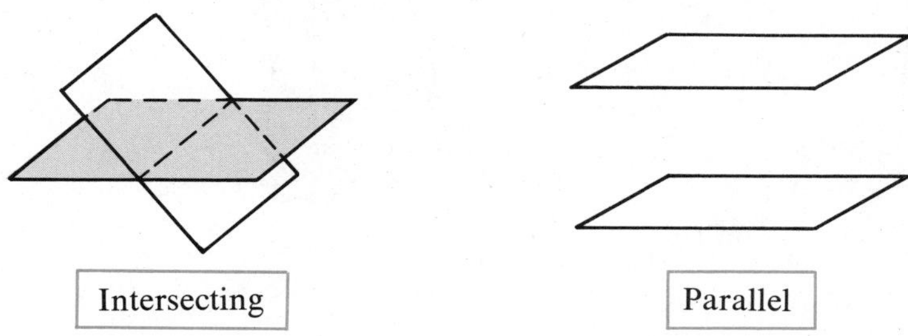

Intersecting

Parallel

## *Classroom Practice*

**Use your classroom and its furnishings to find examples that suggest each figure named.** Examples:

1. Two lines that intersect the corner of a room
2. Two lines that are parallel top and bottom edges of a wall
3. Two lines that are skew side edge of floor and top edge of front wall
4. Two planes that intersect wall and ceiling
5. Two planes that are parallel ceiling and floor
6. Two planes that are perpendicular floor and front wall
7. A line and a plane such that the line Answers on page T127
   - **a.** lies in the plane
   - **b.** intersects the plane and is perpendicular to the plane
   - **c.** intersects the plane but is not perpendicular to the plane
   - **d.** is parallel to the plane
8. **a.** Four points that all lie in one plane
   **b.** Four points that do not all lie in any one plane
9. Two parallel planes that are intersected by a third plane the floor and ceiling and a wall
10. Two lines that are both perpendicular to a third line and
    **a.** are parallel to each other **b.** are perpendicular to each other
11. Alonzo said: "If two planes are perpendicular, every line in one of the planes must be perpendicular to the other plane." Explain why Alonzo was wrong. Any 2 points determine a line, so some lines in one plane will be parallel to the second plane, while others will intersect the plane but not be perpendicular to it.

12. Lee wanted to set a pole upright, and said to a friend: "Stand over there and tell me when it's straight up." Could the friend tell for sure that the pole was upright? No

## Written Exercises

**Use a straightedge to draw each figure.**

A

1. A line in a plane
2. A line intersecting a plane
3. A line parallel to a plane
4. A line perpendicular to a plane

**A rectangular solid is shown. Name the figures described. In some cases, more than one answer is possible.**

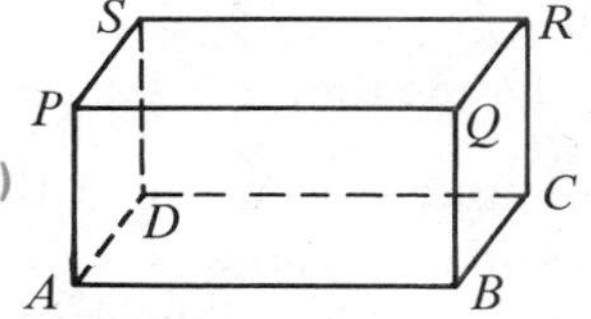


Exercises 5–14

5. Three lines parallel to $\overleftrightarrow{AB}$ $\overleftrightarrow{PQ}$, $\overleftrightarrow{SR}$, $\overleftrightarrow{DC}$
6. Four lines perpendicular to $\overleftrightarrow{BQ}$ (see below)
7. Four lines skew to $\overleftrightarrow{AD}$ $\overleftrightarrow{PQ}$, $\overleftrightarrow{SR}$, $\overleftrightarrow{QB}$, $\overleftrightarrow{RC}$
8. A plane parallel to plane $ADSP$ plane $BCRQ$
9. Four planes, each one perpendicular to plane $ADSP$ planes $PQRS$, $SDCR$, $ABCD$, $ABQP$
10. Two lines that are perpendicular to $\overleftrightarrow{PS}$ and are parallel to each other $\overleftrightarrow{PA}$ and $\overleftrightarrow{SD}$ (or $\overleftrightarrow{SR}$ and $\overleftrightarrow{PQ}$)
11. Two lines that are perpendicular to $\overleftrightarrow{PS}$ and are skew to each other $\overleftrightarrow{PQ}$ and $\overleftrightarrow{SD}$ or $\overleftrightarrow{SR}$ and $\overleftrightarrow{PA}$
12. Two lines that are perpendicular to $\overleftrightarrow{PS}$ and are perpendicular to each other $\overleftrightarrow{PQ}$ and $\overleftrightarrow{PA}$ or $\overleftrightarrow{SR}$ and $\overleftrightarrow{SD}$
13. $\overleftrightarrow{BD}$ and $\overleftrightarrow{QS}$ (not drawn) are __?__ lines. parallel
14. $\overleftrightarrow{PA}$ and $\overleftrightarrow{AC}$ are __?__ lines. perpendicular

6. $\overleftrightarrow{PQ}$, $\overleftrightarrow{AB}$, $\overleftrightarrow{RQ}$, $\overleftrightarrow{BC}$

**Quadrilateral $JKLM$ is a square. The lengths of $\overline{VJ}$, $\overline{VK}$, $\overline{VL}$, and $\overline{VM}$ are equal. Tell whether each statement is true or false.**

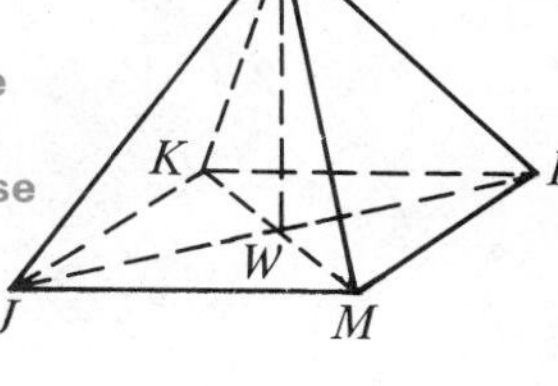


15. $JW = WL$ True
16. $JW = KW$ True
17. $\angle JKL > 90°$ False
18. $\angle VJM < \angle VMJ$ False
19. $\overleftrightarrow{JL}$ and $\overleftrightarrow{VK}$ are skew. True
20. $\triangle MVL \cong \triangle WVL$ False
21. $\angle JWM > 90°$ False
22. $\triangle VKJ$ is a right $\triangle$. False
23. $VM = VW$ False
24. $\overline{VW} \perp$ plane $JKLM$ True

**Draw a figure to illustrate each statement.**
**Some statements have more than one solution.**

B 25. Two lines that are perpendicular to the same line $l$ do not have to be parallel to each other.

26. Two lines that are skew to the same line $l$ do not have to be skew to each other.

27. Line $j$ lies in a plane $P$ and line $k$ lies in a plane $Q$, but lines $j$ and $k$ do not have to be skew lines.

28. Two planes both perpendicular to plane $X$ do not have to be parallel to each other.

29. A line that is perpendicular to a line in a plane does not have to be perpendicular to the plane.

**Line $b$ and plane $Q$ have the positions described. Tell how many planes can be drawn that contain line $b$ and are, at the same time, perpendicular to plane $Q$.**

30. $b$ lies in $Q$. one
31. $b \parallel Q$ one
32. $b \perp Q$ an indefinite number
33. $b$ intersects $Q$, but $b$ is not $\perp$ to $Q$. one

C 34. In the figure:
$j \parallel X$; $V$ contains $j$;
$V$ intersects $X$ in $k$.
Explain why $j$ and $k$ must be parallel lines. (see below)

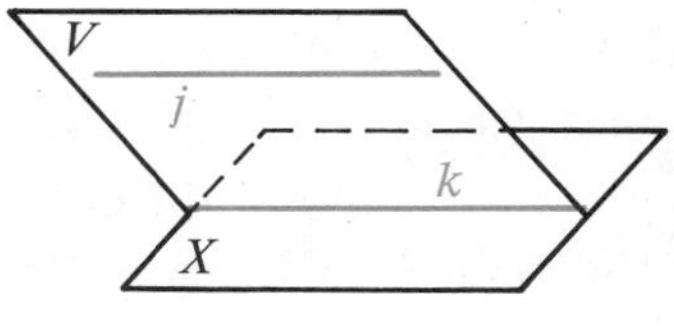


35. In the figure:
$P \parallel Q$; $R$ intersects $P$ in $l$, and $Q$ in $m$.
Explain why $l$ and $m$ must be parallel lines.
No line in $P$ intersects a line in $Q$, so $l$ and $m$ do not intersect. Since they are coplanar, $l \parallel m$.

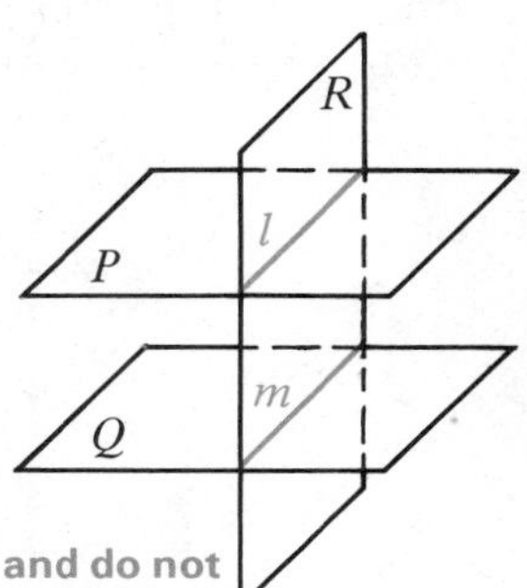


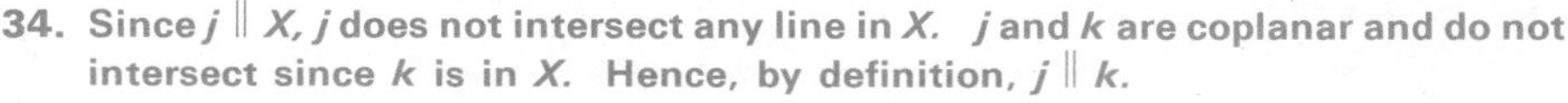
34. Since $j \parallel X$, $j$ does not intersect any line in $X$. $j$ and $k$ are coplanar and do not intersect since $k$ is in $X$. Hence, by definition, $j \parallel k$.

## *Experiments*

To make an interesting surface like the one pictured above, take a long strip of paper.

A X
B Y

Give the strip a half-twist.

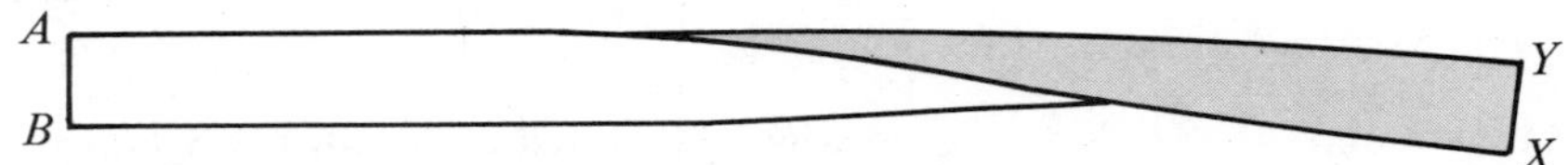


Tape the ends together, joining *X* and *B*, *Y* and *A*. The resulting figure is called a *Möbius band.*

**1.** Draw a pencil line down the middle. Do you return to your starting point? How many sides does the band have? one

**2.** Cut along your pencil line. What happens to the band? It is still a single strip.

**3.** Take another long strip of paper. Give the paper a full twist and tape the ends together. Then cut the band down the middle, as before. What happens to the band? It becomes 2 interlocked strips.

> A mathematician confided
> That a Möbius band is one-sided.
> And you'll get quite a laugh
> If you cut one in half
> For it stays in one piece when divided.

## 2 • Right Prisms

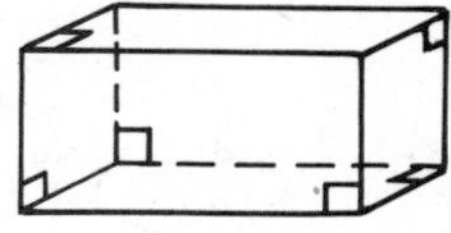

The figure shows a *rectangular solid.* You probably see many rectangular solids every day, for example, bricks and cereal boxes.

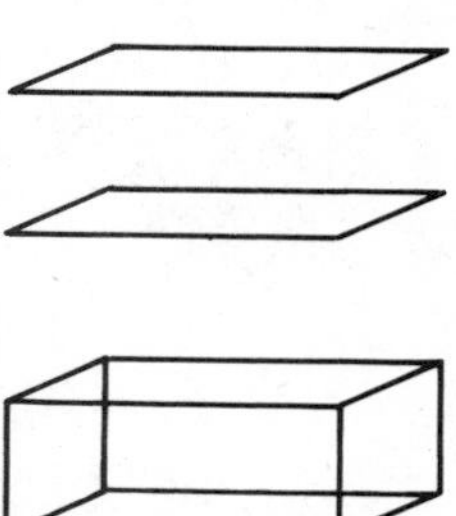

Some people have trouble drawing rectangular solids. One way to proceed is this:

Draw a parallelogram.

Draw a second parallelogram directly above the first one.

Draw four vertical segments.

When you look at a box you cannot see some of the edges. Because of this fact, some people draw dashed lines to show hidden segments. Other people don't show the hidden edges at all.

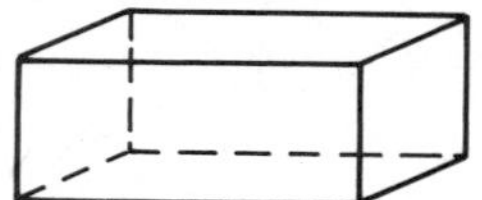

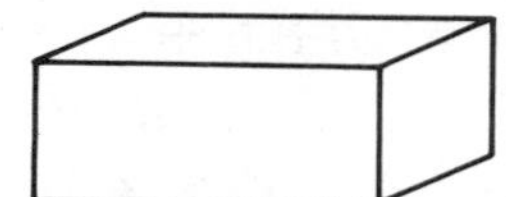

A rectangular solid is the most common kind of **right prism.** Two other right prisms are pictured below. The shaded *faces,* called *bases,* are congruent and parallel. The other faces of each prism are called *lateral faces.* Other parts of a prism are named as shown.

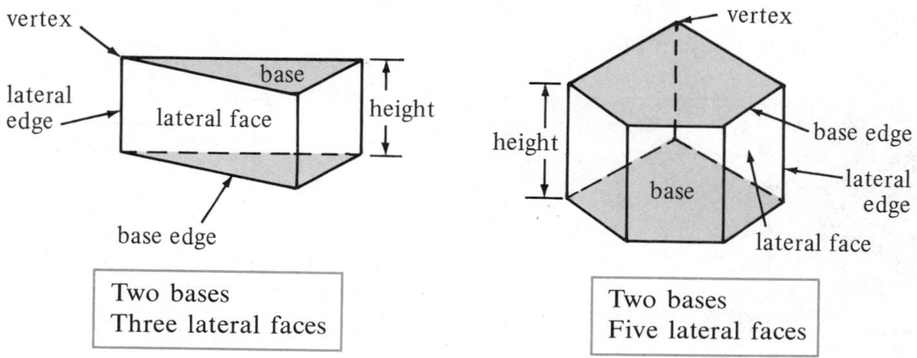


In a right prism, each lateral edge is perpendicular to the bases. Any segment, such as a lateral edge, that is perpendicular to the bases and has an endpoint on each base is called an *altitude* of the prism. The length of an altitude is the *height, h,* of the prism.

The **lateral area** (L.A.) of a prism is the sum of the areas of the lateral faces. Can you see that the lateral area of the prism shown is the sum of the areas of six rectangles?

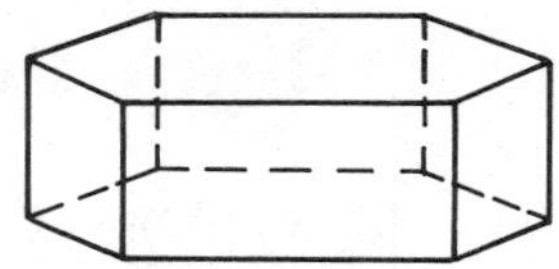

The total area (T.A.) of a prism is the sum of the areas of all the faces. Using $B$ to represent the area of a base,

**Total Area = Lateral Area + 2 × Area of a Base**

$$\text{T.A.} = \text{L.A.} + 2B$$

**EXAMPLE 1** The base of a right prism is a 5 by 3 rectangle. The height is 2. Find:

**a.** the lateral area;
**b.** the total area.

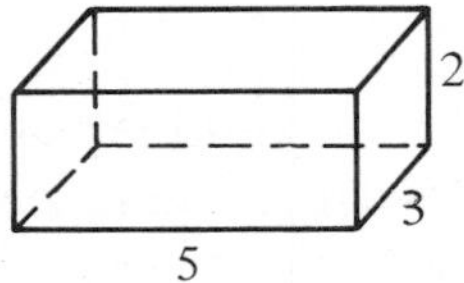


**a.** The area of the closest face is $5 \times 2 = 10$.
The area of an end face is $3 \times 2 = 6$.
$\text{L.A.} = 10 + 6 + 10 + 6 = 32$

**b.** $\text{T.A.} = \text{L.A.} + 2B$
$\text{T.A.} = 32 + 2(5 \times 3) = 32 + 30 = 62$

A prism has *volume* as well as area. When each edge of a rectangular solid is one unit long, the volume of the solid is one cubic unit. Can you see that the rectangular solid shown below can be filled with blocks that are 1 cm cubes?

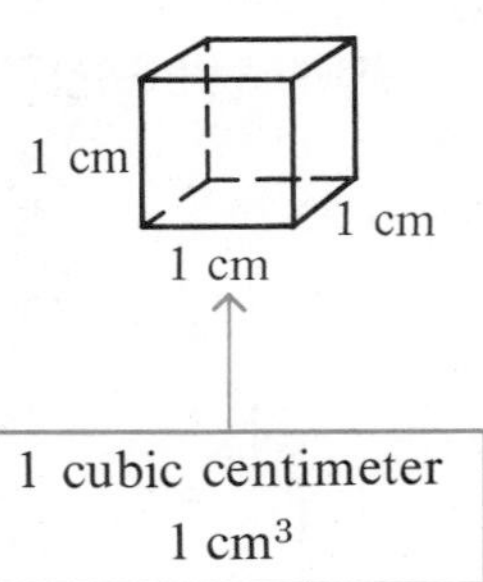


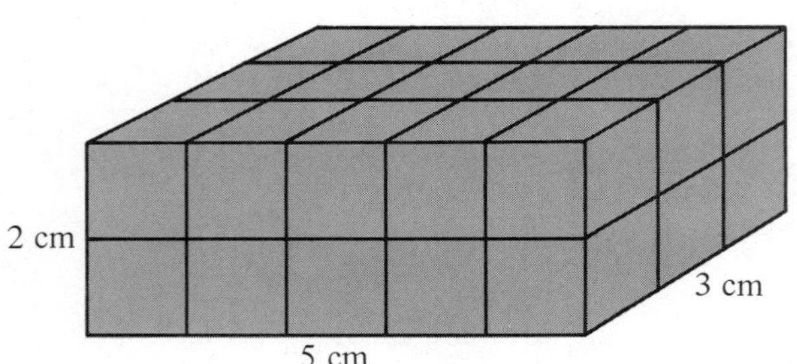


Fifteen blocks form a bottom layer, fifteen more a top layer. The box can be filled with 30 blocks, and the volume, $V$, is 30 $\text{cm}^3$. Notice that the volume is the product of the base area, $B$, and the height, $h$:

$$V = 15 \times 2$$

In any right prism:

**Volume = Base × height**

$$V = Bh$$

**EXAMPLE 2** The base of a rectangular solid is a 6 cm square. The height of the solid is 10 cm. Find the volume.

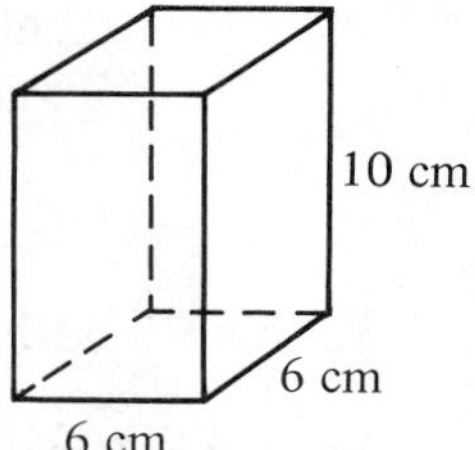


$B = s^2 = 6^2 = 36$

$V = Bh$

$V = 36 \times 10 = 360$

*Answer:* 360 $\text{cm}^3$

## Classroom Practice

**For each right prism, state the number of:**

**a. lateral edges** **b. lateral faces** **c. bases**
**d. base edges** **e. faces** **f. vertices**

**1.**

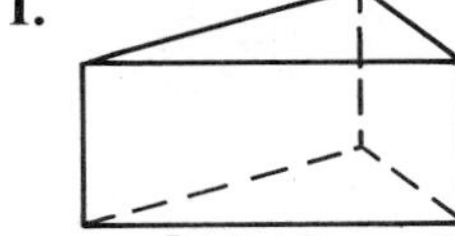

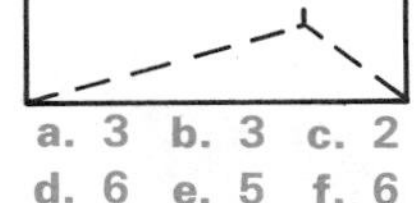

a. 3 b. 3 c. 2
d. 6 e. 5 f. 6

**2.**

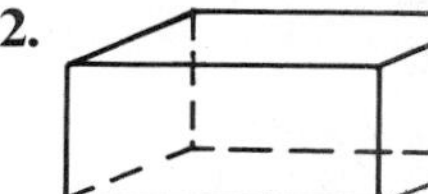

a. 4 b. 4 c. 2
d. 8 e. 6 f. 8

**3.**

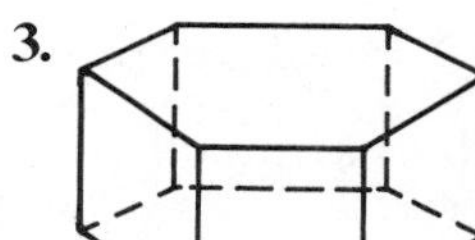

a. 6
b. 6
c. 2
d. 12
e. 8
f. 12

**Tell why the solid pictured is not a right prism.**

**4.**

bases not parallel

**5.**

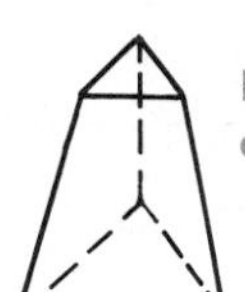

bases not congruent

**6.**

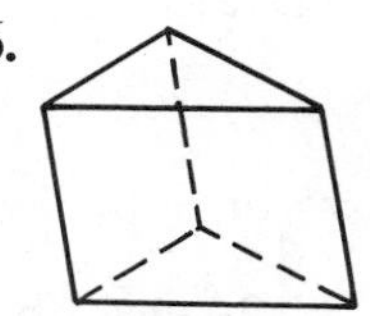

lateral edge not perpendicular to base

**7.** One student said that the diagram at the left shows a right prism, but the one at the right does not. Was the student correct? Explain.

No; the prism is still a right prism when tipped on its side.

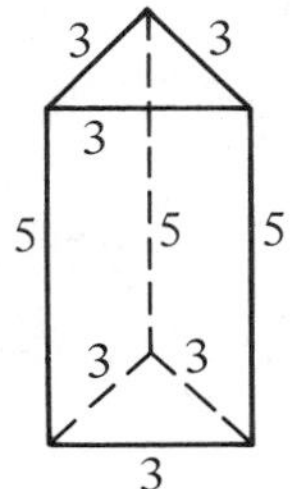


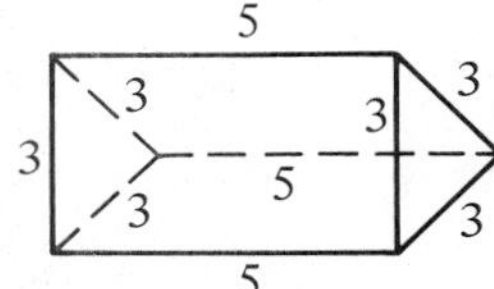

8. The bases of the right prism shown are isosceles trapezoids. Find the lateral area, the total area, and the volume of the prism. L.A. = 60; T.A. = 100; $V = 60$

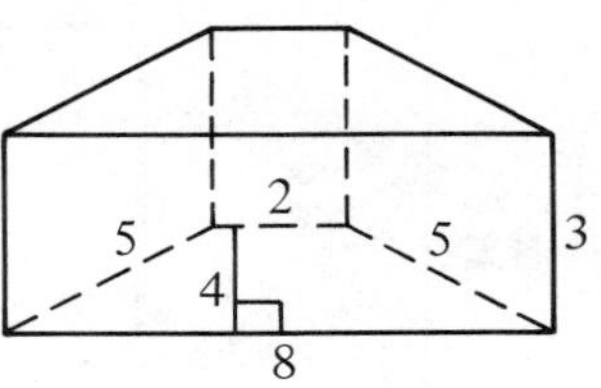


**Classify each statement as true or false.**

9. Every right prism has two bases. True

10. Every right prism has a rectangular base. False

11. Each base of a right prism must have at least four edges. False

12. Every lateral face of a right prism must be a rectangle. True

13. The length of an altitude of a prism is called its height. True

14. In any right prism, T.A. = 2(L.A.) + $B$. False

## *Written Exercises*

**Exercises 1–10 refer to the rectangular solid.**

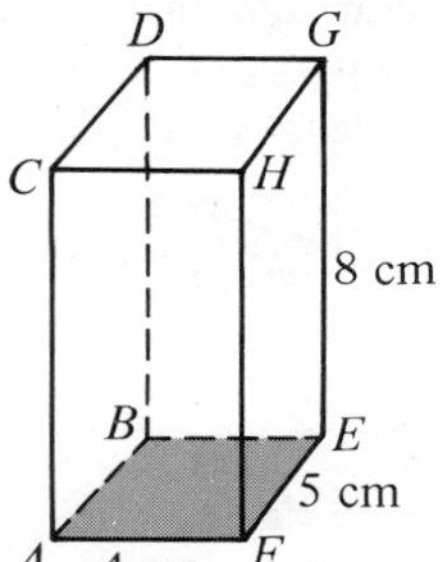


A 1. $BE$ = __?__ 4 cm 2. $DG$ = __?__ 4 cm

3. $DB$ = __?__ 8 cm 4. $AB$ = __?__ 5 cm

5. The perimeter of quadrilateral $AFHC$ = __?__. 24 cm

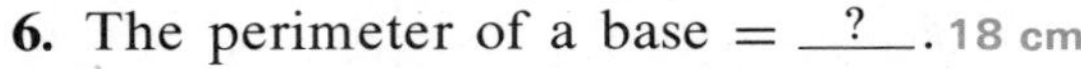

6. The perimeter of a base = __?__. 18 cm

7. The area of a base = __?__. 20 $\text{cm}^2$

8. The lateral area of the prism = __?__. 144 $\text{cm}^2$

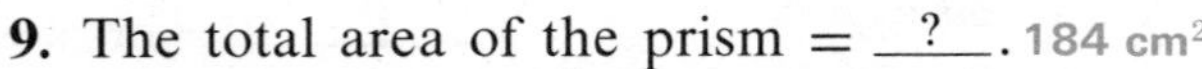

9. The total area of the prism = __?__. 184 $\text{cm}^2$

10. The volume of the prism = __?__. 160 $\text{cm}^3$

**Exercises 11–14 deal with right prisms. The number of sides in the base is not specified. Complete the table.**

| | $B$ | $h$ | $V$ | |
|---|---|---|---|---|
| **11.** | 30 $\text{cm}^2$ | 4 cm | __?__ | 120 $\text{cm}^3$ |
| **12.** | __?__ | 5 cm | 100 $\text{cm}^3$ | 20 $\text{cm}^2$ |
| **13.** | __?__ | 2 cm | 100 $\text{cm}^3$ | 50 $\text{cm}^2$ |
| **14.** | 64 $\text{cm}^2$ | __?__ | 256 $\text{cm}^3$ | 4 cm |

**Exercises 15–18 deal with a rectangular solid having dimensions $l$, $w$, and $h$. Draw a figure if you need one. Complete the table.**

| | $l$ | $w$ | $h$ | L.A. | T.A. | $V$ | |
|---|---|---|---|---|---|---|---|
| B **15.** | 6 | 2 | 3 | ? 48 | ? 72 | ? 36 | |
| **16.** | 8 | 3 | 4 | ? 88 | ? | ? 96 | T.A. = 136 |
| **17.** | 10 | 4 | ? 3 | ? 84 | ? | 120 | T.A. = 164 |
| **18.** | ? 15 | 6 | 6 | ? | ? | 540 | |
| | | | | 252 | 432 | | |

**Exercises 19–22 deal with *cubes.* A cube is a rectangular solid with all edges equal. Complete the table.**

| | Edge | $B$ | L.A. | T.A. | $V$ |
|---|---|---|---|---|---|
| **19.** | 2 | ? 4 | ? 16 | ? 24 | ? 8 |
| **20.** | ? 4 | 16 | ? 64 | ? 96 | ? 64 |
| **21.** | 5 | ? 25 | ? | ? | ? |
| **22.** | ? 10 | ? | ? | ? | 1000 |
| | | 100 | 400 | 600 | |

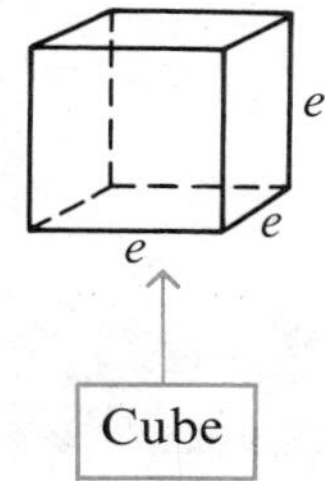


21. L.A. = 100; T.A. = 150; V = 125

**23.** Examine your answers for Exercises 19 and 20 as a pair. Then look at those for Exercises 21 and 22 as a pair. These exercises suggest that when each edge of a cube is doubled:

**a.** the area is multiplied by _?_; 4

**b.** the volume is multiplied by _?_. 8

C **24.** One cube has edges 10 cm long. Another cube has edges 30 cm long. Find the ratio:

**a.** of the total area of the smaller cube to that of the larger cube; $\frac{1}{9}$

**b.** of the volume of the smaller cube to that of the larger cube. $\frac{1}{27}$

**25.** When you buy a *two-by-four* at a lumber yard, the end doesn't measure 2 inches by 4 inches. It measures about $1\frac{1}{2}$ inches by $3\frac{1}{2}$ inches. Suppose the rough-cut lumber has a 2-inch by 4-inch end before it is planed down. What percent of the wood is lost in planing? 34.4%

**26. a.** How many square centimeters of aluminum foil are needed to cover the block of cheese pictured? (Ignore overlap.) $4000\text{ cm}^2$

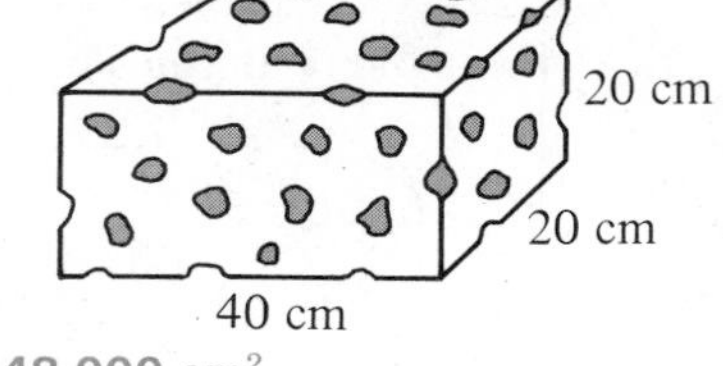


**b.** Suppose the block is cut into cubes with 2 cm edges. How many square centimeters of foil are needed to wrap all the individual cubes? $48{,}000\text{ cm}^2$

**27.** How many liters of water are needed to fill the family swimming pool shown? 98,750 L
(*Hints:* Think of *PQRST* as the base of a right prism. 1 $m^3$ contains 1000 L.)

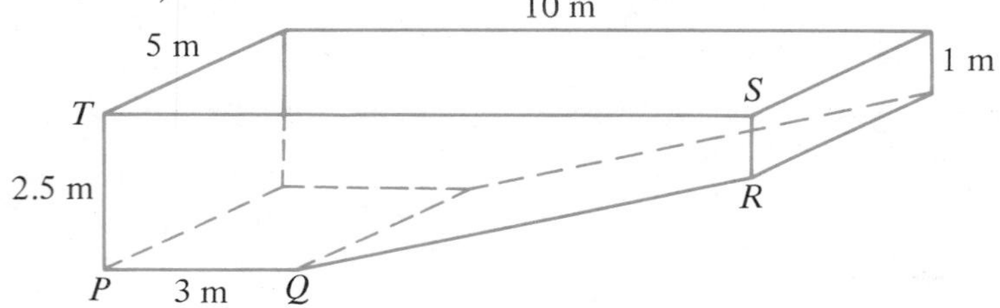


## CONSUMER CORNER

### *Do You Get What You Pay For?*

Consumers often have to decide, "Which one should I buy?" For example, you may have to decide among two, three, or a dozen different radios. Several different winter coats may look attractive. Occasionally, you may find an unusual bargain and be able to buy the best product at the lowest price. More often, however, you have to pay a higher price for a better quality item.

Is the extra expense worth it? The answer depends on your own needs, tastes, and financial resources. The radio which costs an extra $15 may produce a much better sound. The camera which costs twice as much may last three times longer. Sometimes, however, extra dollars only buy extra features or frills which are of no use.

Here are some common-sense suggestions for making wise purchases:

**(1)** Decide exactly what you want and how long you want it to last.
**(2)** Talk with people who have bought a similar item.
**(3)** Consult a trade magazine or a consumer magazine.
**(4)** Compare prices in several different stores before you buy.

## 3 • Right Circular Cylinders

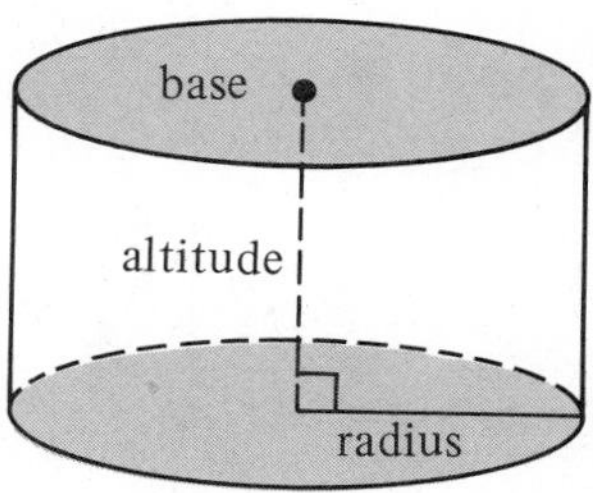

**Right Circular Cylinder**

A **right circular cylinder** is like a right prism except that its bases are congruent circles instead of congruent polygons. The *radius* of a base is also called the radius of the cylinder.

As in right prisms, an *altitude* of a right circular cylinder is a segment that is perpendicular to the bases and has an endpoint in each base. The length of an altitude is the *height, h,* of the cylinder. We'll use the word *cylinder* to mean a right circular cylinder.

To find the lateral area of a cylinder, imagine that the diagram shows a tin can with its ends removed. If you cut along $\overline{AB}$, you can unroll the metal and lay it out flat.

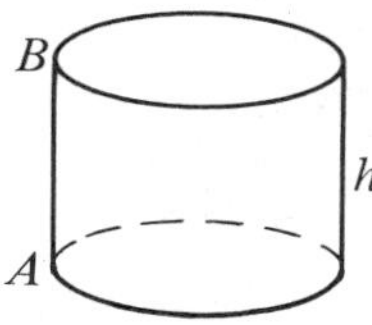


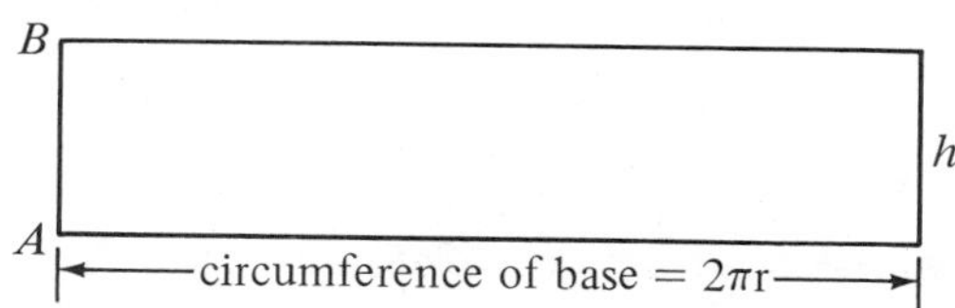


The lateral surface of the cylinder becomes a rectangular region.

$$\begin{aligned}\text{L.A. of cylinder} &= \text{area of rectangle}\\ &= 2\pi r \times h\\ &= 2\pi rh\end{aligned}$$

The formula for the total area of a cylinder is much like the formula for the total area of a right prism:

$$\text{T.A.} = \text{L.A.} + 2B$$

$$\text{T.A.} = 2\pi rh + 2 \times \pi r^2$$

You can find the volume of a cylinder in a similar way:

$$V = Bh$$

$$V = \pi r^2 \times h$$

In any (right circular) cylinder:

| | | |
|---|---|---|
| | T.A. = L.A. + 2B | $V = Bh$ |
| **L.A. =** $\mathbf{2\pi rh}$ | **T.A. =** $\mathbf{2\pi rh + 2\pi r^2}$ | $\mathbf{V = \pi r^2 h}$ |

**EXAMPLE** A cylinder has a radius of 3 cm and a height of 4 cm. Find: **a.** the lateral area **b.** the total area **c.** the volume.

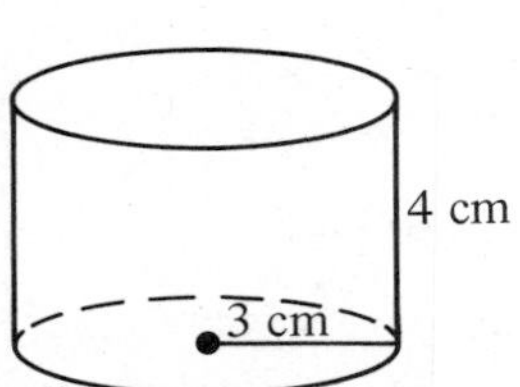


**a.** L.A. $= 2\pi rh$
L.A. $= 2\pi \times 3 \times 4 = 24\pi \text{ cm}^2$

**b.** T.A. $=$ L.A. $+ 2B$
T.A. $= 24\pi + 2\pi r^2$
T.A. $= 24\pi + (2\pi \times 3^2)$
$= 24\pi + 18\pi = 42\pi \text{ cm}^2$

**c.** $V = \pi r^2 h$
$V = \pi \times 3^2 \times 4$
$= 36\pi \text{ cm}^3$

## *Classroom Practice*

1. When you use the formula T.A. $=$ L.A. $+ 2B$, what should you substitute for L.A.? (Use the figure shown.) $2\pi rh$

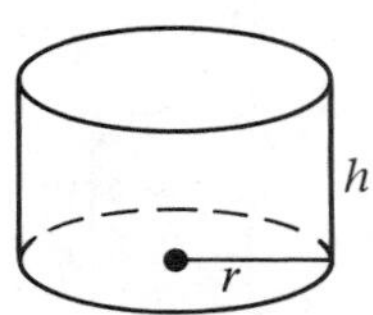


2. When you use the formula $V = Bh$, what formula do you use to find $B$? (Use the figure shown.) $\pi r^2$
3. The lateral area of a new piece of chalk is much greater than the area of a base. Name an object, shaped like a cylinder, in which:
   **a.** the area of a base is much greater than the lateral area; for example, a coin
   **b.** the area of a base is roughly equal to the lateral area. any object where $r = h$, such as a can of tuna
4. Why is it incorrect to call the solid shown a cylinder? The bases are not congruent.
5. Why is it incorrect to call the solid shown a right cylinder? (see below)

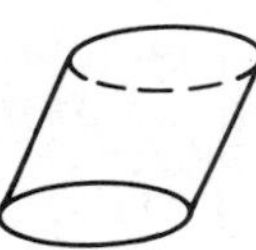

6. For the cylinder shown, find:
   **a.** the lateral area; $12\pi$
   **b.** the total area; $30\pi$
   **c.** the volume. $18\pi$

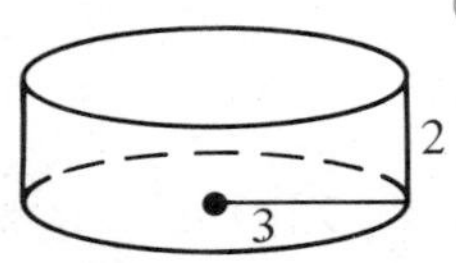


5. The sides are not perpendicular to the bases.

## *Written Exercises*

**Find the indicated values for the cylinder shown.**

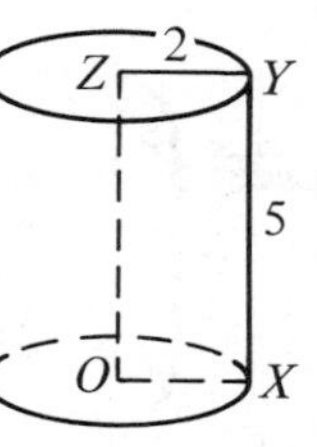


A
1. $OX$ 2
2. $OZ$ 5
3. Height of cylinder 5
4. Circumference of base $4\pi$
5. Area of base $4\pi$
6. Lateral area $20\pi$
7. Total area $28\pi$
8. Volume $20\pi$

**Complete the table, which refers to cylinders.**
**$C$ represents the circumference of a base.**

| | | $r$ | $h$ | $C$ | $B$ | L.A. | T.A. | $V$ | |
|---|---|---|---|---|---|---|---|---|---|
| | **9.** | 5 | 2 | ? | ? | ? | ? | ? | $10\pi$; $25\pi$; $20\pi$; $70\pi$; $50\pi$ |
| | **10.** | 8 | 3 | ? | ? | ? | ? | ? | $16\pi$; $64\pi$; $48\pi$; $176\pi$; $192\pi$ |
| | **11.** | 1 | 6 | ? | ? | ? | ? | ? | $2\pi$; $\pi$; $12\pi$; $14\pi$; $6\pi$ |
| | **12.** | 6 | 1 | ? | ? | ? | ? | ? | $12\pi$; $36\pi$; $12\pi$; $84\pi$; $36\pi$ |
| B | **13.** | ? 3 | 2 | $6\pi$ | ? $9\pi$ | ? | ? | ? | $12\pi$; $30\pi$; $18\pi$ |
| | **14.** | ? 6 | 4 | ? | $36\pi$ | ? | ? | ? | $12\pi$; $48\pi$; $120\pi$; $144\pi$ |
| | **15.** | 3 | ? 4 | ? $6\pi$ | ? $9\pi$ | ? | ? | $36\pi$ | $24\pi$; $42\pi$ |
| | **16.** | ? 2 | 5 | ? $4\pi$ | ? $4\pi$ | ? | ? | $20\pi$ | |
| | | | | | | $20\pi$ | $28\pi$ | | |

**Use 3.14 for $\pi$. Write your answers correct to the nearest integer.**

**17.** In a cylinder: $d = 6$; $h = 8$. $V =$ ? 226

**18.** In a cylinder: $r = 10$; $h = 3$. T.A. $=$ ? 816

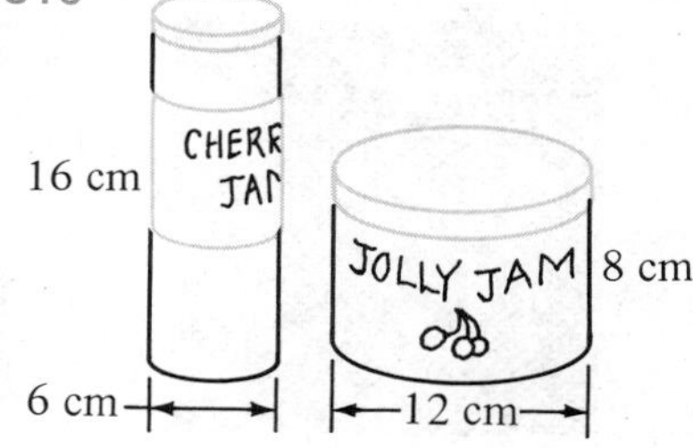


**19.** One jar of jam is twice as tall as another, but only half as wide. Which jar holds more jam? the shorter jar

**20.** If the jar on the left costs 99¢ and the one on the right costs \$1.80, which is the better buy? the jar on the right

C **21.** A chemical company has developed an additive that cuts down on friction, permitting water to flow through a hose twice as fast. Using this additive, a fire department can replace 7 cm hose with 5 cm hose, handle a hose considerably lighter, yet deliver the same amount of water. Show that the amount of water in a 7 cm hose is about twice the amount in a 5 cm hose. (Use the same length for each hose.) The ratio is 49 : 25, or approximately 2.

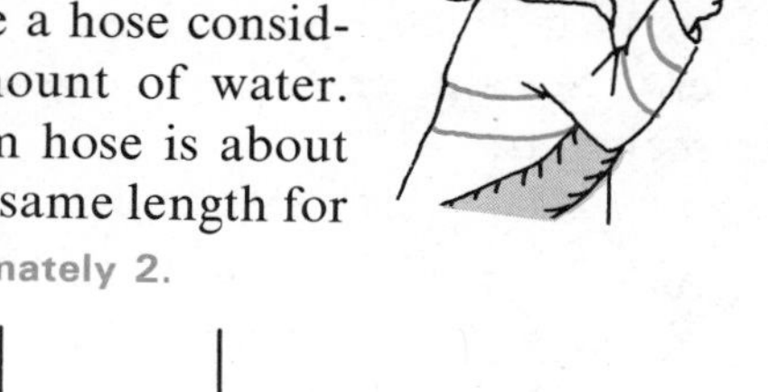

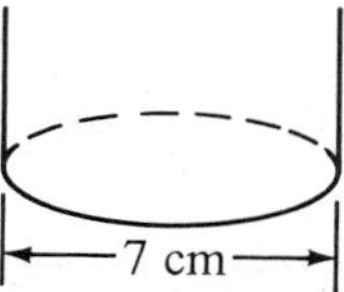


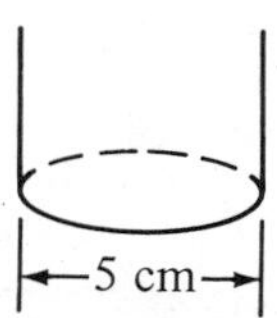

## SELF-TEST

**Refer to the rectangular solid shown.** 1. planes *TUFE, TEDS* 2. planes *CDSR, FETU*

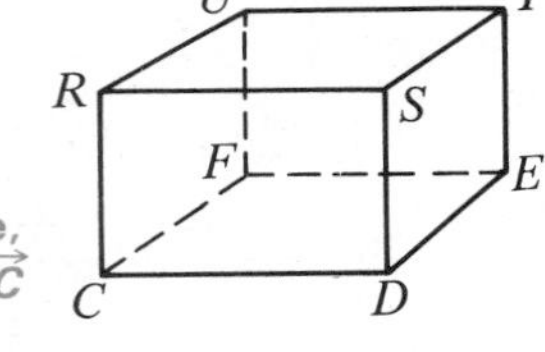


1. Name two planes that are parallel to $\overline{CR}$.
2. Name two planes that are perpendicular to $\overline{DE}$.
3. Name any line shown that is skew to $\overleftrightarrow{UT}$. for example, $\overleftrightarrow{FC}$

**In the rectangular solid shown, let $CD = 8$, $DE = 5$, and $DS = 4$.**

4. Total area = __?__ 184
5. Volume = __?__ 160

**In a certain cylinder, $r = 8$ and $h = 4$.**
**Find the indicated values in terms of $\pi$.**

6. L.A. = __?__ $64\pi$
7. T.A. = __?__ $192\pi$
8. $V$ = __?__ $256\pi$

### *Some Shapes in Nature*

Many of the shapes you have studied in this course occur in nature. Here are a few examples.

**1.** 

**2.** 

**3.** 

1. Did you guess that this is a much-enlarged picture of a snowflake? A snowflake is sometimes described as *hexagonal.*
2. A crystal of Iceland spar has the form of a *parallelepiped* (a solid with six faces, each a parallelogram). The crystal has an interesting property. Set a piece of Iceland spar over one segment and you see two segments.

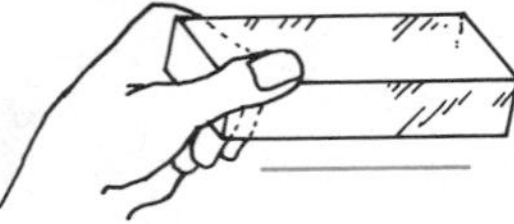
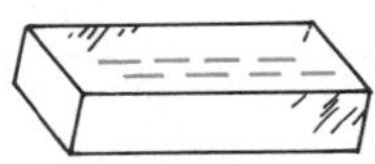

3. Quartz crystals suggest plane surfaces bounded by various kinds of polygons.

## 4 • Regular Pyramids

The ancient Egyptians built *pyramids* that still stand. Because the bases are squares, the pyramids are called *square* pyramids. We say that a pyramid is *regular* if its base is a regular polygon and the top lies directly over the center of the base.

The table and diagram below explain some of the terms used for regular pyramids.

| | |
|---|---|
| **vertices** | points $A$, $B$, $C$, $D$, and $V$ |
| **the vertex** | point $V$ |
| **the base** | square $ABCD$ |
| **lateral edges** | $\overline{VA}$, $\overline{VB}$, $\overline{VC}$, and $\overline{VD}$ |
| **base edges** | $\overline{AB}$, $\overline{BC}$, $\overline{CD}$, and $\overline{DA}$ |
| **faces** | $\triangle VDC$ is one of four congruent lateral faces. Base $ABCD$ is also a face. |
| **center of base** | point $T$ |
| **altitude** | $\overline{VT}$ (Note: $\overline{VT} \perp$ plane $ABCD$) |
| **height** | $VT$, also $h$, the length of $\overline{VT}$ |
| **slant height** | $VM$, also $l$, the length of $\overline{VM}$ (Note: $\overline{VM} \perp \overline{CD}$; $M$ is the midpoint of $\overline{CD}$.) |

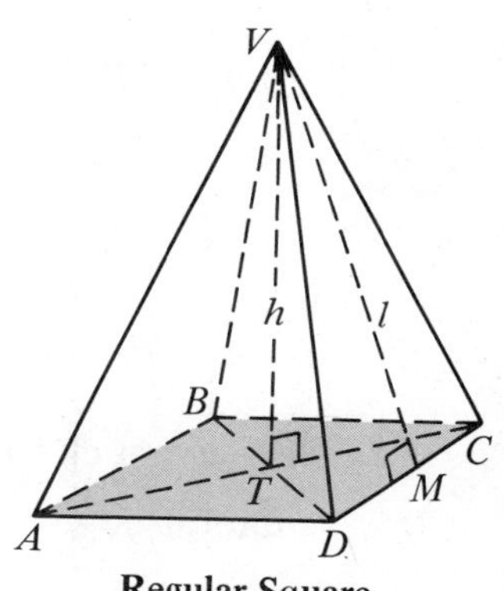


**Regular Square Pyramid**

The lateral faces of a pyramid are always triangular. To find the lateral area of a pyramid, use the formula for the area of a triangle. To find the total area, you simply add the lateral area and the area of the base. To find the volume, use the formula that we state without proof.

In any regular pyramid:

$$\text{T.A.} = \text{L.A.} + B \qquad V = \frac{1}{3}Bh$$

**EXAMPLE** The base of a regular square pyramid has edges of length 6. The height of the pyramid equals 4 and the slant height equals 5. Find:

**a.** the lateral area; **b.** the total area; **c.** the volume.

Draw a diagram.

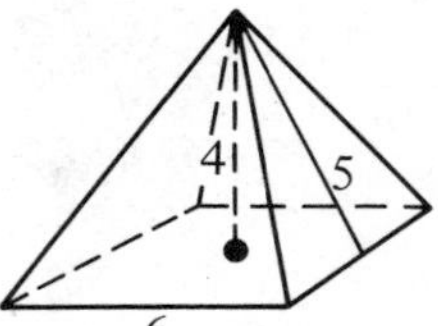


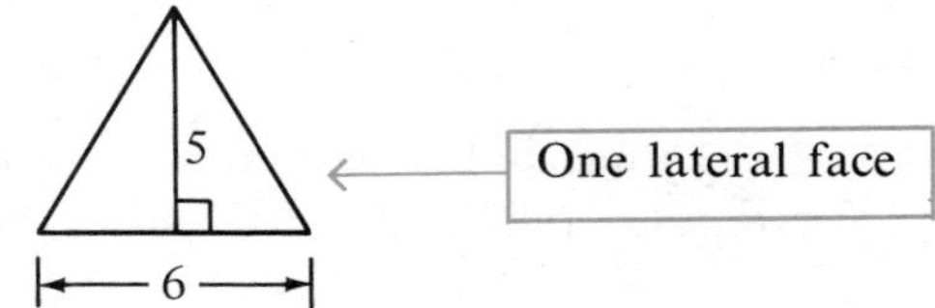


**a.** The area of one lateral face $= \frac{1}{2} \times 6 \times 5 = 15$

L.A. $= 4 \times 15 = 60$

**b.** $B = 6^2 = 36$

T.A. = L.A. + $B$

T.A. $= 60 + 36 = 96$

**c.** $V = \frac{1}{3}Bh$

$V = \frac{1}{3} \times 36 \times 4 = 48$

## Classroom Practice

**Use the diagram of a regular triangular pyramid to name:** 1. $\overline{VX}$, $\overline{VY}$, or $\overline{VZ}$

1. A lateral edge
2. The vertex $V$
3. The altitude $\overline{VW}$
4. The base $\triangle XYZ$
5. A slant height $\overline{VM}$
6. A lateral face

6. $\triangle VXY$, $\triangle VYZ$, or $\triangle VXZ$

7. Name all the edges that equal $\overline{VY}$. $\overline{VX}$, $\overline{VZ}$
8. Which is longer: $\overline{VW}$ or $\overline{VM}$? $\overline{VM}$
9. Which is longer: $\overline{VM}$ or $\overline{VX}$? $\overline{VX}$
10. Name the hypotenuse of right $\triangle YVM$. $\overline{VY}$
11. Does $\triangle VYZ$ have to be isosceles? equilateral? yes; no
12. $\angle XYZ =$ ___?___ ° (60) $\angle XWY =$ ___?___ ° (120) $\angle WXY =$ ___?___ ° (30)

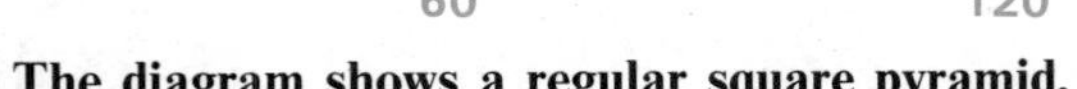

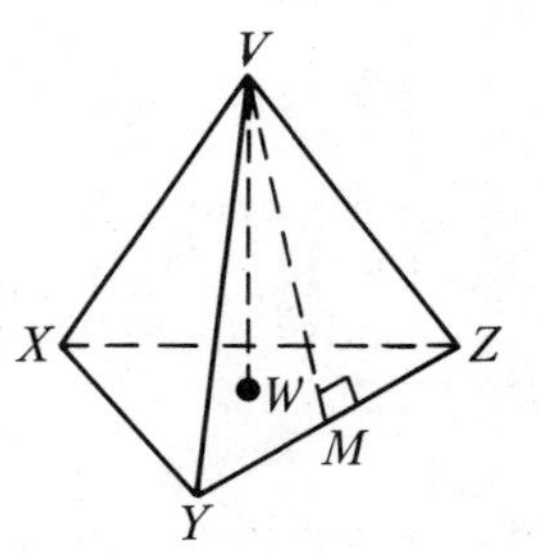


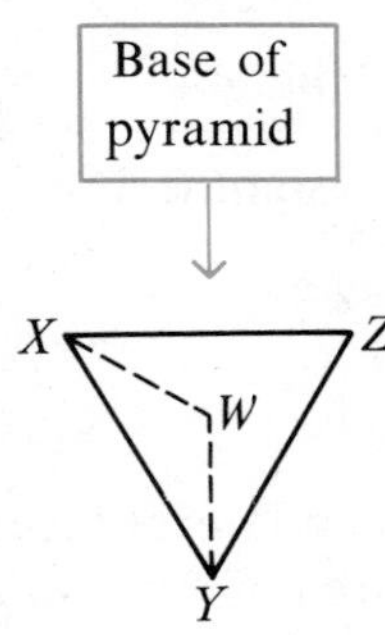


Exercise 12

**The diagram shows a regular square pyramid.**

13. Find the lateral area. 320 square units
14. Find the total area. 576 square units
15. Find the volume. 512 cubic units

## Written Exercises

**Refer to the regular square pyramid shown. Tell whether each statement is true or false.**

A 1. The pyramid has five faces. True

2. All eight edges of the pyramid must be equal. False

3. $VM$ is the height of the pyramid. False

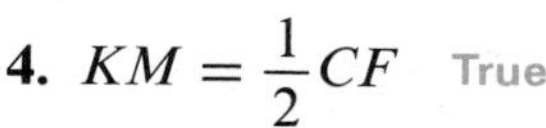

4. $KM = \frac{1}{2}CF$ True

5. $KM = ME$ True

6. If $\overline{KC}$ were drawn, $\angle VKC$ would be a right angle. True

7. L.A. $= 4 \times$ area of quadrilateral $CDEF$ False

8. T.A. $=$ L.A. $+ 2B$ False

9. $VM$ must be greater than $VK$. True

10. $VM$ must be greater than $KM$. True

**Draw a regular pyramid whose base is the polygon named.**

11. Triangle
12. Square
13. Pentagon
14. Hexagon

**Exercises 15–20 refer to a regular pyramid whose base is an 8 by 8 square. The height equals 3 and the slant height equals 5.**

15. Draw a figure.
16. Perimeter of the base = __?__ 32
17. Area of the base = __?__ 64
18. Lateral area of the pyramid = __?__ 80
19. Total area of the pyramid = __?__ 144
20. Volume of the pyramid = __?__ 64

**In Exercises 21 and 22, a regular pyramid is described. Find the lateral area, the total area, and the volume.**

B 21. The base is a 12 cm by 12 cm square. The height equals 8 cm. The slant height equals 10 cm. L.A. = 240 cm$^2$; T.A. = 384 cm$^2$; $V$ = 384 cm$^3$

22. The base is a 16 cm by 16 cm square. The height equals 15 cm. The slant height equals 17 cm. L.A. = 544 cm$^2$; T.A. = 800 cm$^2$; $V$ = 1280 cm$^3$

23. The base of a regular pyramid is a hexagon with sides 4 m long. The slant height equals 10 m. Find the lateral area. 120 m$^2$

24. In a certain regular pyramid: $B = 52$; $h = 6$; $l = 7$.
Decide which you can find, the lateral area or the volume. Then find it. $V = 104$

C 25. A cube has a 6 cm edge. A pyramid is formed by joining the vertices of one face to $X$, the center of the opposite face. Draw a figure. Find the volume of the pyramid. 72 cm³

26. Repeat Exercise 25, but use $Y$, the center of the cube, instead of $X$. 36 cm³

## *A Class Experiment*

The purpose of this experiment is to find a relation between the number of vertices, the number of faces, and the number of edges that a solid has. Divide the class into ten committees. Each committee can work with one of the solids below.

1. prism with triangular base
2. pyramid with triangular base
3. prism with square base
4. pyramid with square base
5. prism with hexagonal base
6. pyramid with hexagonal base

7. 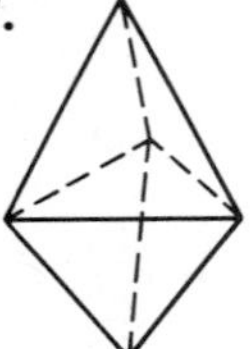

8. 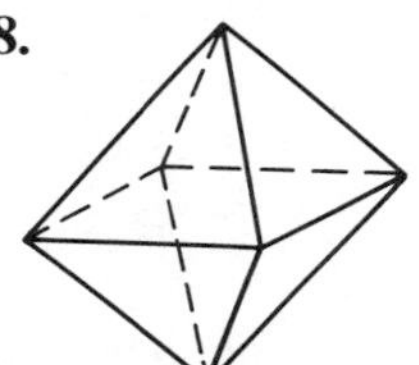

9. 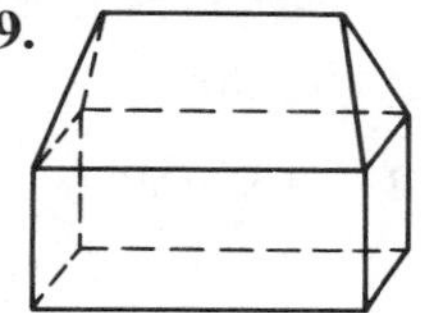

10. 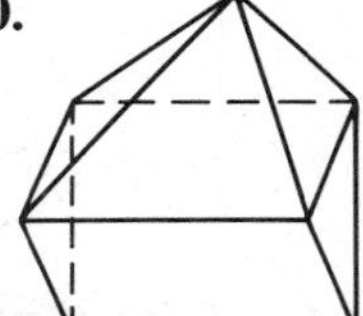

For each figure, count:
$V$, the number of vertices;
$F$, the number of faces;
$E$, the number of edges.

Copy and complete the table at the chalkboard.

| | 1. | 2. | 3. | 4. | 5. | 6. | 7. | 8. | 9. | 10. |
|---|---|---|---|---|---|---|---|---|---|---|
| $V$ | ? 6 | ? 4 | ? 8 | ? 5 | ? 12 | ? 7 | ? 5 | ? 6 | ? 10 | ? 7 |
| $F$ | ? 5 | ? 4 | ? 6 | ? 5 | ? 8 | ? 7 | ? 6 | ? 8 | ? 9 | ? 8 |
| $E$ | ? 9 | ? 6 | ? 12 | ? 8 | ? 18 | ? 12 | ? 9 | ? 12 | ? 17 | ? 13 |

Study the columns. Find a formula that tells how $V$, $F$, and $E$ are related. $E = V + F - 2$

# 5 • Right Circular Cones

A **right circular cone** is very much like a regular pyramid. Notice that the base of a cone is circular. As the diagram shows, we use many of the same terms to describe a cone as we use for other solids.

vertex
slant height
altitude
radius
base

**Right Circular Cone**

The formula for the volume of a pyramid suggests the formula for the volume of a cone:

$$V = \frac{1}{3}Bh; \; V = \frac{1}{3} \times \pi r^2 \times h$$

The formula, stated below, for the lateral area of a cone will be verified in the exercises.

In any right circular cone:

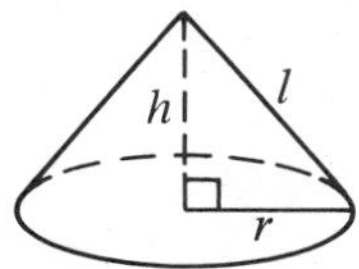


T.A. = L.A. + $B$ $\qquad V = \frac{1}{3}Bh$

**L.A.** $= \pi \boldsymbol{rl}$ $\qquad$ **T.A.** $= \pi \boldsymbol{rl} + \pi \boldsymbol{r}^2$ $\qquad \boldsymbol{V} = \frac{\mathbf{1}}{\mathbf{3}}\pi \boldsymbol{r}^2\boldsymbol{h}$

In the remainder of the course, the word *cone* will mean right circular cone.

**EXAMPLE** For the cone pictured, find:

**a.** the lateral area
**b.** the total area
**c.** the volume

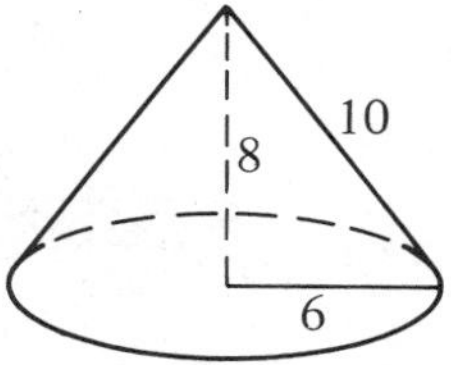


**a.** L.A. $= \pi rl$
$= \pi \times 6 \times 10 = 60\pi$

**b.** T.A. = L.A. + $B$
$= 60\pi + \pi r^2$
$= 60\pi + (\pi \times 6^2)$
$= 60\pi + 36\pi = 96\pi$

**c.** $V = \frac{1}{3}Bh$
$= \frac{1}{3} \times \pi r^2 \times h$
$= \frac{1}{3} \times 36\pi \times 8 = 96\pi$

## Classroom Practice

1. In the example on page 373, the number of cubic units in the volume is equal to the number of square units in the total area. Do you think that this is true for all cones? Find the lateral area, the total area, and the volume for a cone with $r = 8$, $h = 6$, and $l = 10$. No; L.A. $= 80\pi$; T.A. $= 144\pi$; $V = 128\pi$

**Draw a circle whose radius is actually 6 cm.**
**Draw two radii that form a 120° angle.**

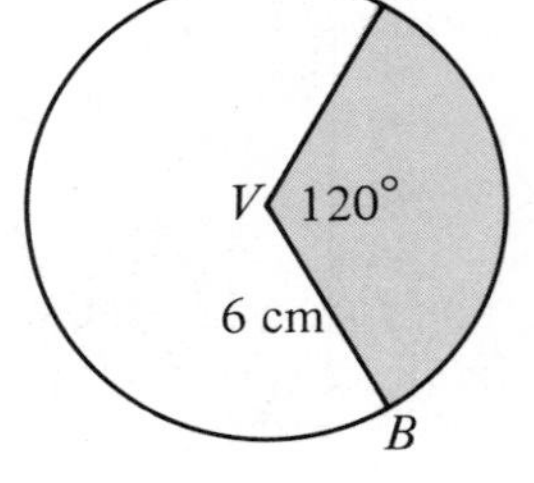


2. The area of the shaded region is what fractional part of the area of the circle? $\frac{1}{3}$

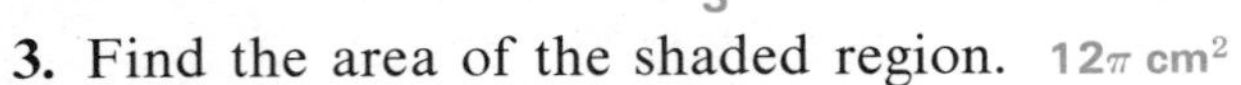

3. Find the area of the shaded region. $12\pi$ cm$^2$

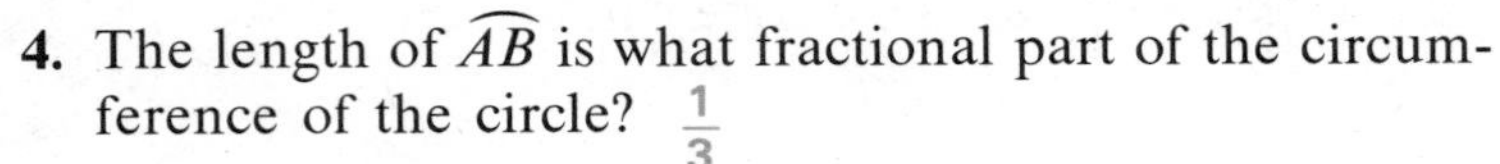

4. The length of $\widehat{AB}$ is what fractional part of the circumference of the circle? $\frac{1}{3}$
5. Find the length of $\widehat{AB}$. $4\pi$ cm

**Cut out the shaded region. Curve the paper to form a cone, letting $\overline{VA}$ and $\overline{VB}$ come together.**

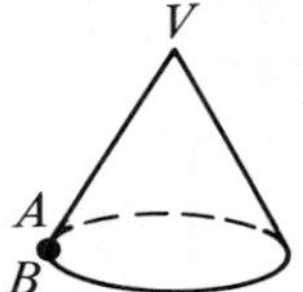


6. The slant height of the cone equals __?__. 6 cm
7. The lateral area of the cone equals __?__. $12\pi$ cm$^2$ (Answer this the easy way. See Exercise 3.)
8. The circumference of the base of the cone equals __?__. (Again, the answer is easy. See Exercise 5.) $4\pi$ cm
9. Use your answer for Exercise 8 to find the radius of the base of the cone. 2
10. Show that your answers for Exercises 6, 7, and 9 satisfy the formula L.A. $= \pi rl$. L.A. $= \pi rl = \pi \cdot 2 \cdot 6 = 12\pi$, which agrees with the answer for Exercise 7

## Written Exercises

**Find the lateral area of each cone.**

A

1. $54\pi$

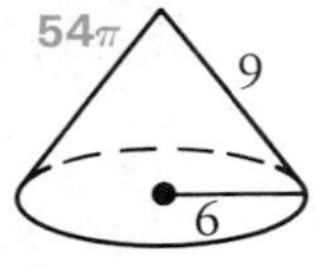


2. $16\pi$

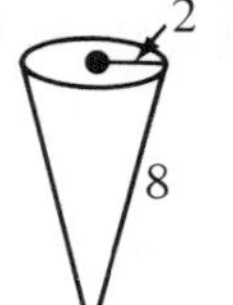


3. $30\pi$

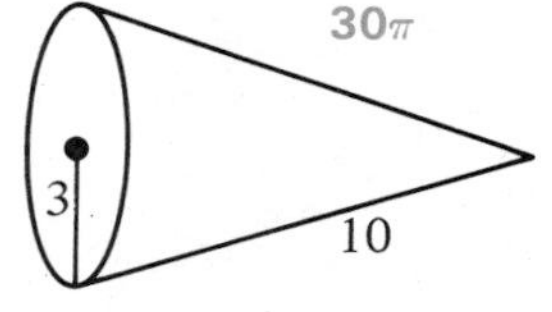


**4–6.** Find the total areas of the cones shown in Exercises 1–3.
4. $90\pi$ 5. $20\pi$ 6. $39\pi$

**Find the volume of each cone.**

7. 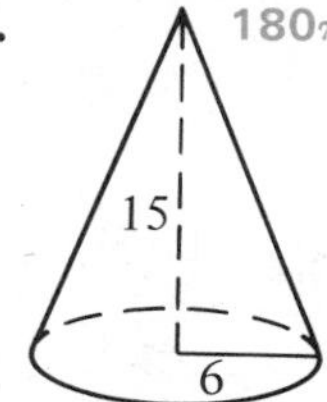

180π

8. 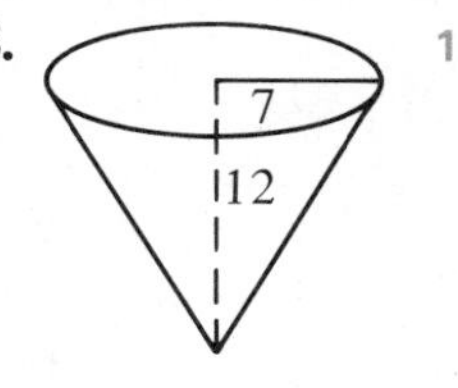

196π

9. 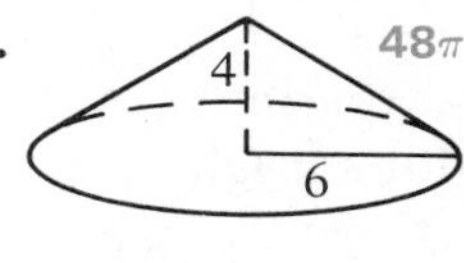

48π

**Copy and complete the table, which deals with cones.**
**($C$ represents the circumference of the base.)** Answers on page T128

| | $r$ | $C$ | $B$ | $h$ | $l$ | L.A. | T.A. | $V$ |
|---|---|---|---|---|---|---|---|---|
| **10.** | 3 | ? | ? | 4 | 5 | ? | ? | ? |
| **11.** | 12 | ? | ? | 9 | 15 | ? | ? | ? |
| **12.** | 8 | ? | ? | 15 | 17 | ? | ? | ? |
| B **13.** | ? | $12\pi$ | ? | 8 | 10 | ? | ? | ? |
| **14.** | ? | ? | $16\pi$ | 3 | 5 | ? | ? | ? |
| **15.** | 5 | ? | ? | ? | ? | ? | ? | $100\pi$ |

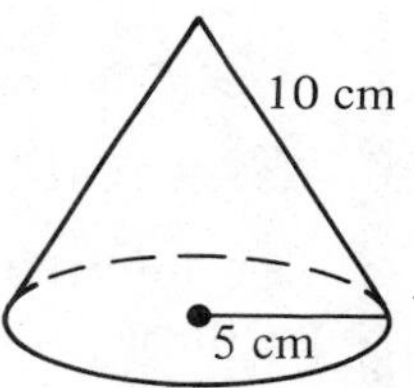


**16.** A piece of sheet metal is cut and formed into the lateral surface of the cone pictured. There are 0.24 g in 1 cm² of the metal. Find the total number of grams of metal. (Use 3.14 for $\pi$.) 37.68 g

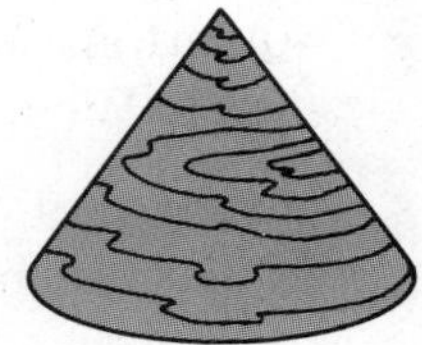

C **17.** The solid hardwood cone pictured has a 16 cm radius and a 35 cm altitude. There are 0.62 g of wood in 1 cm³ of the hardwood used. Find the total number of grams of wood, to the nearest 10 g. (Use 3.14 for $\pi$.) 5810 g

**Refer to the diagram below of a cone and a regular square pyramid.**

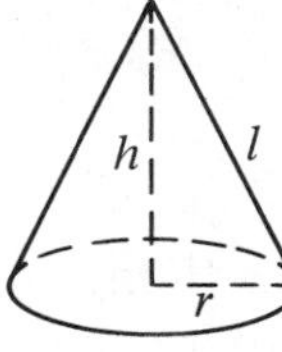


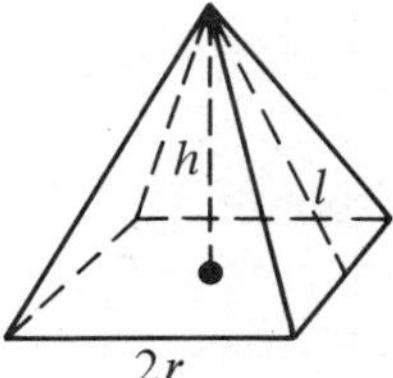


**18.** Find the ratio of the lateral areas of the solids. $\frac{\pi}{4}$

**19.** Find the ratio of the total areas of the solids. $\frac{\pi}{4}$

**20.** Find the ratio of the volumes of the solids. $\frac{\pi}{4}$

For this experiment you need a small piece of cardboard with a bright, solid-colored surface. Close your left eye. Gaze straight ahead. Hold the card in your right hand with your right arm stretched out to the side. The color of the card cannot be accurately judged. Slowly move your unbent arm forward. At a certain stage you begin to see the color clearly. Why?

The back of the retina of your eye is lined with *rods* and *cones*. The rods—long, thin cylinders—register only in black and white. An object viewed from the side is seen primarily by the rods. The cones, which are able to distinguish color, are concentrated near the center of your eye.

## CAREER NOTES

### Stock Clerk

An umbrella company orders and receives a large shipment of assorted umbrella parts. However, mixed in with the order are 40 cartons, each containing 50 toy rubber ducks. What will happen to the shipment?

It is the job of stock clerks to receive and unpack the merchandise, inspect and count the goods received, and check each item against outgoing orders. They report articles that have been damaged, lost, or sent by mistake.

Stock clerks organize merchandise for storage and for display. They mark the goods with identifying codes and prices and arrange them on shelves or in bins. By taking frequent tallies of the items, stock clerks keep records of goods entering and leaving the stockroom.

Stock clerks may acquire their skills by training received on the job. However, applicants should have a high school diploma.

# CALCULATOR CORNER

Solid metal cones are to be made of various metals. How many cones of the size specified can be made from 10 kg (10,000 g) of the metal named? Round your answer to the nearest 10 cones.

**EXAMPLE** Bronze cones: $r = 1.5$ cm; $h = 4$ cm.
There are 8.8 g in 1 $cm^3$ of bronze.

$$\text{Number of cones} = \begin{pmatrix}\text{total number of}\\ \text{grams of metal}\end{pmatrix} \div \begin{pmatrix}\text{total number of}\\ \text{grams in one cone}\end{pmatrix}$$

$$\text{Number of cones} = 10{,}000 \div \left(\frac{1}{3}\pi r^2 h \times 8.8\right)$$

$$= 10{,}000 \div \left(\frac{1}{3}\pi \times 1.5^2 \times 4 \times 8.8\right) \doteq 120$$

Copy and complete the table.

| | $r$ (in cm) | $h$ (in cm) | Grams in 1 $cm^3$ | No. of cones |
|---|---|---|---|---|
| Aluminum | 2 | 3 | 2.7 | ? 290 |
| Brass | 2.6 | 4 | 8.6 | ? 40 |
| Iron | 5.2 | 7.6 | 7.9 | ? 10 |
| Magnesium | 3.2 | 4.1 | 1.7 | ? 130 |
| Nickel | 3 | 8 | 8.9 | ? 10 |

The Boston Phoenix

## 6 • Spheres

Look at the circle and the sphere. Each has radius $r$.

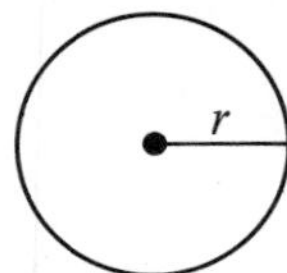


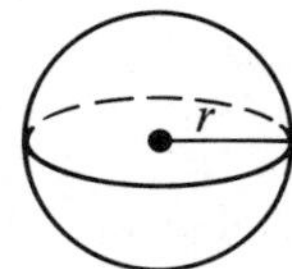


Recall that the area of the circle equals $\pi r^2$. It happens that the surface area of the sphere is four times the area of the circle, or $4\pi r^2$.

The formula for the volume of a sphere is stated without proof.

In any sphere:

$$A = 4\pi r^2 \qquad V = \frac{4}{3}\pi r^3$$

**EXAMPLE** The diameter of a sphere is 8.

**a.** Find the area and the volume in terms of $\pi$.

**b.** Find approximations for the area and the volume. Round your answers to the nearest integer.

Since $d = 8$, $r = 4$.

**a.** $A = 4\pi r^2$ $\qquad$ $V = \frac{4}{3}\pi r^3$

$= 4\pi \times 4^2$ $\qquad$ $= \frac{4}{3}\pi \times 4^3$

$= 64\pi$ $\qquad$ $= \frac{256\pi}{3}$

The area is $64\pi$, and the volume is $\frac{256\pi}{3}$.

**b.** $A = 64\pi$ $\qquad$ $V = \frac{256\pi}{3}$

$A \doteq 64 \times 3.14 = 200.96$ $\qquad$ $V \doteq \frac{256 \times 3.14}{3} = 267.95$

$A \doteq 201.$ $\qquad$ $V \doteq 268$

To the nearest integer, the area is 201, and the volume is 268.

## Classroom Practice

**Find the area and the volume of a sphere with the given radius. Express your answers in terms of $\pi$.**

1. $r = 2$ cm (see below)  2. $r = 5$ cm  3. $r = 0.1$ cm  4. $r = \frac{1}{4}$  $A = \frac{\pi}{4}$; $V = \frac{1}{48}\pi$

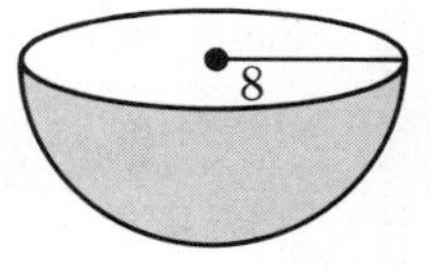


5. If the area of a sphere is $36\pi$, what is its radius? 3

6. "Half" of a sphere is called a *hemisphere*. Find the area and the volume of the hemisphere shown. $A = 128\pi$; $V = 341\frac{1}{3}\pi$

1. $A = 16\pi$; $V = \frac{32}{3}\pi$  2. $A = 100\pi$; $V = \frac{500}{3}\pi$  3. $A = 0.04\pi$; $V = \frac{0.004}{3}\pi$

## Written Exercises

1. $A = 144\pi$; $V = 288\pi$
2. $A = 576\pi$; $V = 2304\pi$
3. $A = 256\pi$; $V = \frac{2048}{3}\pi$
4. $A = \pi$; $V = \frac{\pi}{6}$

**Find the area and the volume of a sphere with the given radius. Express your answers in terms of $\pi$.**

A 1. $r = 6$  2. $r = 12$  3. $r = 8$  4. $r = \frac{1}{2}$

**Find the area and the volume of a sphere with the given diameter. Use 3.14 for $\pi$. Round your answers to the nearest integer.**

5. $d = 18$  6. $d = 2$ m  7. $d = 12$ cm  8. $d = 0.6$

5. $A \doteq 1017$; $V \doteq 3052$
6. $A \doteq 13\ m^2$; $V \doteq 4\ m^3$
7. $A \doteq 452\ cm^2$; $V \doteq 904\ cm^3$
8. $A \doteq 1$; $V \doteq 0.1$

**Copy and complete the table about spheres. Write your answers in terms of $\pi$.**

B

| | 9. | 10. | 11. | 12. | 13. | 14. | 15. | 16. |
|---|---|---|---|---|---|---|---|---|
| $r$ | $\frac{1}{8}$ | ? | ? | ? | $\frac{3}{2}$ | ? | ? | ? |
| $d$ | ? | $\frac{3}{4}$ | ? | ? | ? | ? | ? | $2\sqrt{3}$ |
| $A$ | ? | ? | $100\pi$ | ? | ? | $144\pi$ | ? | ? |
| $V$ | ? | ? | ? | $288\pi$ | ? | ? | $\frac{1372\pi}{3}$ | ? |

Answers on page T128

**A sphere fits inside a cylinder as shown.**

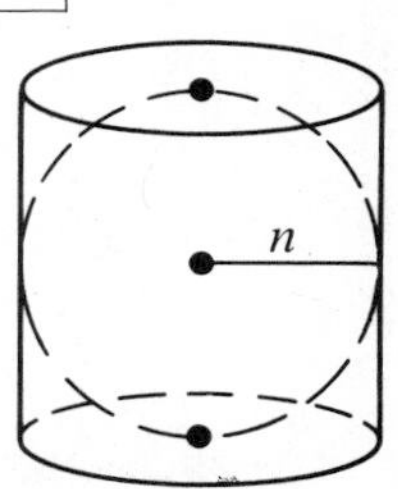


C 17. Show that the area of the sphere equals the lateral area of the cylinder. $A = 4\pi n^2 = 2\pi n \cdot 2n =$ L.A.

18. Find the ratio of the volume of the sphere to the volume of the cylinder. $\frac{2}{3}$

## SELF-TEST

**Exercises 1-4 refer to a regular pyramid whose base is an 18 by 18 square. The height equals 12 and the slant height equals 15.**

1. Draw a figure.
2. L.A. = ___?___ 540
3. T.A. = ___?___ 864
4. $V$ = ___?___ 1296

**Refer to the cone shown. Answer in terms of $\pi$.**

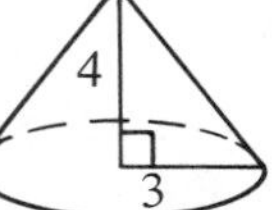


5. Slant height = ___?___ 5
6. L.A. = ___?___ $15\pi$
7. T.A. = ___?___ $24\pi$
8. $V$ = ___?___ $12\pi$

**The radius of a certain sphere is 4. Use 3.14 for $\pi$.**

9. $A$ = ___?___ 200.96
10. $V$ = ___?___ 268

## CALCULATOR CORNER

A jewelry designer plans to make earrings that are hollow spheres. Find the total number of grams in each earring described. Round your answers to the nearest tenth of a gram.

**EXAMPLE** The outer diameter is 1 cm, and the inner diameter is 0.9 cm. The alloy to be used has 8.6 g/cm³.

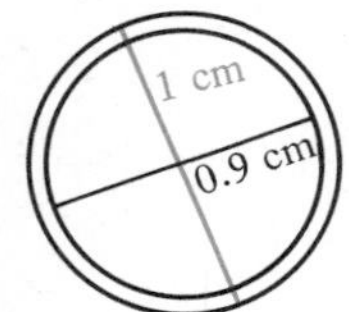


$$\text{Total number of grams} = \left[\frac{4}{3}\pi(0.5)^3 - \frac{4}{3}\pi(0.45)^3\right]8.6$$
$$\doteq 1.2$$

Copy and complete the table.

| Metal | Outer diam. (in cm) | Inner diam. (in cm) | Grams in 1 cm³ | Total no. of grams |
|---|---|---|---|---|
| Bronze | 0.8 | 0.6 | 8.8 | ___?___ 1.4 |
| German Silver | 0.8 | 0.66 | 8.3 | ___?___ 1.0 |
| Silver | 0.8 | 0.65 | 10.5 | ___?___ 1.3 |
| Gold | 0.7 | 0.54 | 19.3 | ___?___ 1.9 |

## 7 • Similar Solids (Optional)

Two solids are called *similar solids* if they have the same shape. The triangular prisms below are similar.

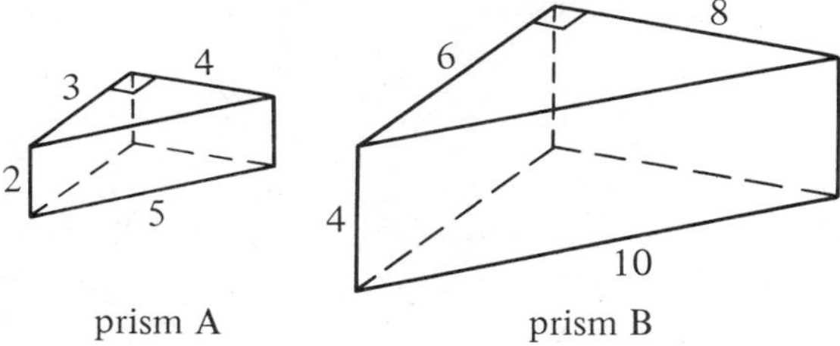


Notice that in similar solids:
(1) corresponding angles are equal;
(2) corresponding segments are in proportion.

### Explorations

Recall, from Chapter 8, that the perimeters and areas of similar figures are related. Let's see whether the surface areas and volumes of similar solids are related. Use the similar triangular prisms shown above. Copy and complete the table.

| | prism A | prism B | ratio in simplest form |
|---|---|---|---|
| hypotenuse of base | 5 | 10 | 1:2 |
| height | ? 2 | ? 4 | ? 1:2 |
| base area | ? 6 | ? 24 | ? 1:4 |
| lateral area | ? 24 | ? 96 | ? 1:4 |
| total area | ? 36 | ? 144 | ? 1:4 |
| volume | ? 12 | ? 96 | ? 1:8 |

You should have found that corresponding lengths are in the ratio 1:2. Now notice: the base areas, lateral areas, and total areas are all in the ratio 1:4, or $1^2:2^2$. The volumes are in the ratio 1:8, or $1^3:2^3$.

This exploration suggests the following theorem.

**THEOREM 1**

Suppose two similar solids have scale factor $a:b$. Then:
(1) the ratio of corresponding segments is $a:b$;
(2) the ratio of the areas is $a^2:b^2$;
(3) the ratio of the volumes is $a^3:b^3$.

**EXAMPLE** Suppose the two right cylinders shown are similar. Find:

**a.** the scale factor
**b.** the height of the larger cylinder
**c.** the ratio of the base areas
**d.** the ratio of the lateral areas
**e.** the ratio of the volumes

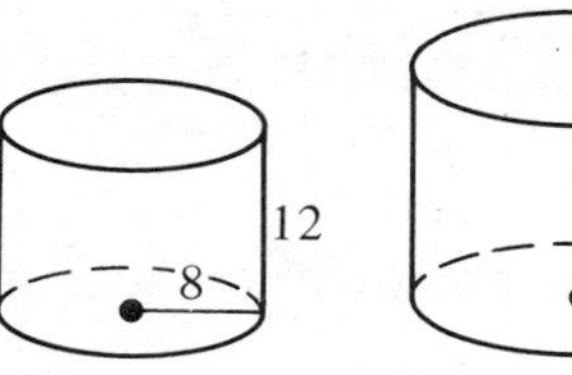

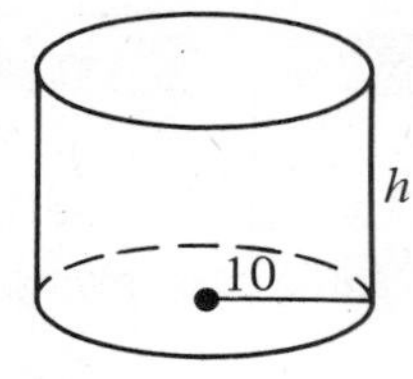


**a.** The scale factor is 8:10, or 4:5
**b.** Write a proportion and solve for $h$. Then $h = 15$.
**c.** ratio of base areas $= 4^2:5^2 = 16:25$
**d.** ratio of lateral areas $= 16:25$
**e.** ratio of volumes $= 4^3:5^3 = 64:125$

$$\frac{4}{5} = \frac{12}{h}$$
$$4h = 60$$
$$h = 15$$

## Classroom Practice

**Refer to the similar pyramids shown.**

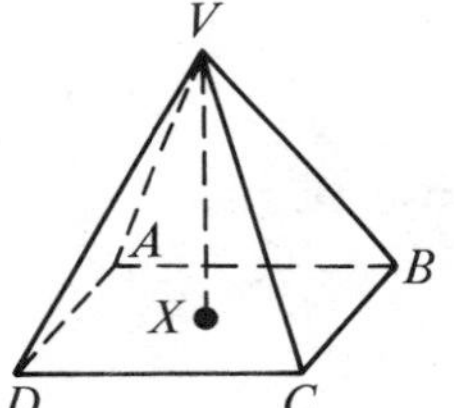

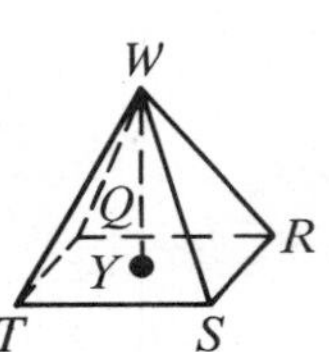


1. $\angle DVC$ corresponds to $\angle$ _?_. *TWS*
2. $\overline{BC}$ and _?_ are corresponding segments. $\overline{RS}$
3. $\frac{VC}{WS} = \frac{DA}{?}$ *TQ*
4. $\frac{AB}{QR} = \frac{?}{WY}$ *VX*
5. Suppose the pyramids have scale factor 10:7. Find the ratio of:
   **a.** the base areas **b.** the total areas
   **c.** the volumes.
   a. $\frac{100}{49}$ b. $\frac{100}{49}$ c. $\frac{1000}{343}$

## Written Exercises

**Copy and complete the table which deals with lengths, areas, and volumes of similar solids.**

A

| | 1. | 2. | 3. | 4. | 5. | 6. | 7. | 8. |
|---|---|---|---|---|---|---|---|---|
| ratio of corresponding segments | 3:4 | 4:3 | 1:6 | 7:9 | 2:5 ? | 3:2 ? | 1:4 ? | 10:1 ? |
| ratio of areas | ? | ? | ? | ? | 4:25 | ? | ? | 100:1 |
| ratio of volumes | ? | ? | ? | ? | ? | 27:8 | 1:64 | ? 1000:1 |

areas: 1. 9:16 2. 16:9 3. 1:36 4. 49:81 5. — 6. 9:4 7. 1:16
volumes: 27:64 64:27 1:216 343:729 8:125 — —

**Exercises 9–11 refer to two similar prisms which have scale factor 3:5.**

B **9.** The shortest edge of the smaller prism is 6 cm long. How long is the shortest edge of the larger prism? 10 cm

**10.** The base area of the larger prism is 50 cm$^2$. Find the base area of the smaller prism. 18 cm$^2$

**11.** The volume of the smaller prism is 216 cm$^3$. Find the volume of the larger prism. 1000 cm$^3$

**12.** The total areas of two similar cones have the ratio 9:4. Find the ratio of their volumes. 27:8

**13.** Any two spheres are similar solids. The volumes of two spheres are $288\pi$ and $7776\pi$, respectively. Find the ratios of their areas. 1:9

**A town has two water towers that are similar solids. Two corresponding lengths are labeled.**

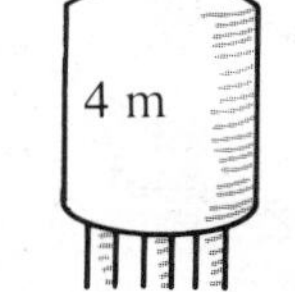


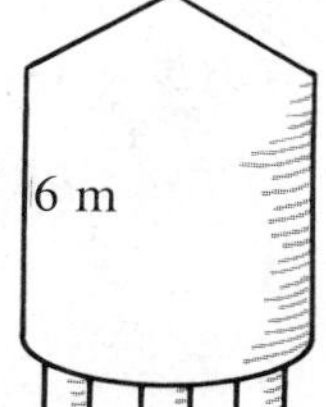


C **14.** Twenty liters of paint were needed to paint the smaller tower. How much paint is needed for the larger tower? 45 L

**15.** The capacity of the larger tank is 180,000 liters. What is the capacity of the smaller tank? 53,333 L

**16.** For two spheres with scale factor $a:b$, prove:

**a.** the ratio of their areas is $a^2:b^2$;

**b.** the ratio of their volumes is $a^3:b^3$.

**17.** A leg bone of a certain animal has a cross-section area of 15 cm$^2$. The bone supports about 50 kg. Imagine a similar, but larger, animal with a scale factor 10:1.

**a.** In the smaller animal, the bone supports __?__ kg/cm$^2$. $3\frac{1}{3}$

**b.** In the larger animal, the corresponding bone would have a cross-section area of __?__, and the bone would have to support 1500 cm$^2$

50,000 __?__ kg. Thus it would have to support __?__ kg/cm$^2$. $33\frac{1}{3}$

**c.** Comparing (a) and (b), comment on the statement "Bigger is better." In this case, bigger is not better. The bones of the larger animal would be under 10 times as much strain.

## Reviewing Algebraic Skills

**Multiply. The samples will help you remember some patterns.**

Samples

1. $2x^2(x - 3y) = (2x^2)(x) - (2x^2)(3y) = 2x^3 - 6x^2y$
2. $(a - 4b)(2a + 9b) = 2a^2 + 9ab - 8ab - 36b^2 = 2a^2 + ab - 36b^2$
3. $(c + 7d)(c + 7d) = c^2 + 7cd + 7cd + 49d^2 = c^2 + 14cd + 49d^2$
4. $(12 + 2k)(12 - 2k) = 144 - 24k + 24k - 4k^2 = 144 - 4k^2$

1. $a^3(3a^2 - ab - b^2)$ $3a^5 - a^4b - a^3b^2$
2. $(a + 5)(a - 3)$ $a^2 + 2a - 15$
3. $(r + 4)(r + 4)$ $r^2 + 8r + 16$
4. $(m + 8)(m - 8)$ $m^2 - 64$
5. $(10 - 3x)(10 - 3x)$ $100 - 60x + 9x^2$
6. $c^2d^3(cd^2 - 7cd)$ $c^3d^5 - 7c^3d^4$
7. $(b - 13)(b - 13)$ $b^2 - 26b + 169$
8. $(m + 2n)(m - n)$ $m^2 + mn - 2n^2$
9. $(6w + 2x)(6w - 2x)$ $36w^2 - 4x^2$
10. $(x - 6)(x - 9)$ $x^2 - 15x + 54$
11. $-6k(5h + 4hk - k^4)$ $-30hk - 24hk^2 + 6k^5$
12. $(2d + 7c)(2d + 7c)$ $4d^2 + 28cd + 49c^2$
13. $(a + 12b)(a - 12b)$ $a^2 - 144b^2$
14. $(3y + 4z)(5y + 7z)$ $15y^2 + 41yz + 28z^2$
15. $(8k - h)(3k + 2h)$ $24k^2 + 13hk - 2h^2$
16. $(2b + 6)(b - 5)$ $2b^2 - 4b - 30$
17. $(3m + 2n)(3m - 2n)$ $9m^2 - 4n^2$
18. $-ab^4(2a^2b^2 - 5b^3)$ $-2a^3b^6 + 5ab^7$

**Factor.**

Samples

1. $4d^6 + 14cd^8 = 2d^6(2 + 7cd^2)$
2. $n^2 - 11n - 26 = (n - 13)(n + 2)$
3. $x^2 - 6x + 9 = (x - 3)(x - 3)$, or $(x - 3)^2$
4. $100c^2 - 9d^2 = (10c + 3d)(10c - 3d)$

19. $15a^2x - 10ax^2$ $5ax(3a - 2x)$
20. $x^2 + 6x + 8$ $(x + 4)(x + 2)$
21. $y^2 - 20y + 100$ $(y - 10)(y - 10)$ or $(y - 10)^2$
22. $4m^2 - 9$ $(2m - 3)(2m + 3)$
23. $a^2 + 2a - 35$ $(a + 7)(a - 5)$
24. $14b^7 - 7b^6 + 28b^5$ $7b^5(2b^2 - b + 4)$
25. $k^2 + 14k + 49$ $(k + 7)(k + 7)$, or $(k + 7)^2$
26. $m^2 + 17m + 16$ $(m + 16)(m + 1)$
27. $c^2 - 13c + 30$ $(c - 10)(c - 3)$
28. $25x^2 - 121y^2$ $(5x - 11y)(5x + 11y)$
29. $27a^3b^3 + 6ab^2c$ $3ab^2(9a^2b + 2c)$
30. $b^2 - 8b + 12$ $(b - 6)(b - 2)$
31. $144 + 24n + n^2$ $(12 + n)(12 + n)$, or $(12 + n)^2$
32. $1 - 36x^2y^2$ $(1 - 6xy)(1 + 6xy)$
33. $h^2 + 6h - 16$ $(h + 8)(h - 2)$
34. $r^2 - 16r + 64$ $(r - 8)(r - 8)$, or $(r - 8)^2$
35. $n^2 - 12n + 27$ $(n - 9)(n - 3)$
36. $a^2 - a - 72$ $(a - 9)(a + 8)$
37. $k^2 - 9k - 22$ $(k - 11)(k + 2)$
38. $c^2 + 18c + 81$ $(c + 9)(c + 9)$, or $(c + 9)^2$
39. $r^2 + 11r + 28$ $(r + 7)(r + 4)$
40. $144 - 25y^2$ $(12 - 5y)(12 + 5y)$
41. $d^2 - 20d + 19$ $(d - 19)(d - 1)$
42. $m^2 - 2m - 63$ $(m - 9)(m + 7)$

# applications

## *Surface Area and Volume*

Geometry tells us that, in general, a small object has more surface area *per unit of volume* than a large object has. Let us compare a baseball with radius 3.5 cm and a basketball with radius 12.4 cm.

Baseball

$$\frac{\text{Surface area}}{\text{Volume}} \doteq \frac{153.9}{179.5} \doteq 0.86$$

Basketball

$$\frac{\text{Surface area}}{\text{Volume}} \doteq \frac{1931.2}{7982.4} \doteq 0.24$$

Now let us see how this principle affects a relatively small animal, a mouse, and a larger animal, a human being. Having more skin area per unit of volume, a mouse loses body heat faster than a person does. Just to keep warm, a mouse must eat and burn more food relative to its size. A mouse needs to eat about one half of its weight in food each day. How much food would you have to consume if you ate at that rate?

The relationship between surface area and volume also helps to explain the difference between a mouse's lung and a human lung. In order to do its job well, the lung must have enough surface area in its air sacs. A small animal like a mouse needs only a simple lung to provide enough air-sac surface. A larger animal like a human being needs a more complex lung to provide enough surface area for breathing. A giant mouse with a simple lung could not breathe enough oxygen to keep it alive.

**Exercise**

Compute and compare the ratio of total surface area to volume for a small cube with edges 2 cm long and a larger cube with edges 60 cm long. small cube: $\frac{3}{1}$; larger cube: $\frac{1}{10}$

# Reviewing the Chapter

## Chapter Summary

1. Two lines can intersect, be parallel, or be skew. A line can lie in a plane, intersect the plane, or be parallel to the plane. Two planes intersect, or else they are parallel.

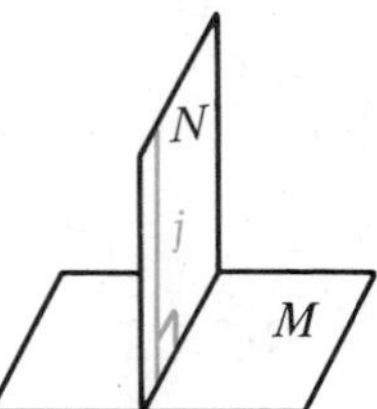


If line $j \perp$ plane $M$, and if plane $N$ contains line $j$, then $N \perp M$.

2. In any right prism:
   L.A. = sum of the areas of the lateral faces
   T.A. = L.A. + $2B$
   $V = Bh$

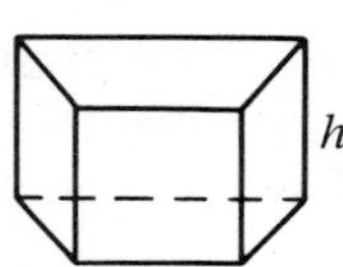


3. In any right circular cylinder:
   L.A. = $2\pi rh$
   T.A. = L.A. + $2B = 2\pi rh + 2\pi r^2$
   $V = Bh = \pi r^2 h$

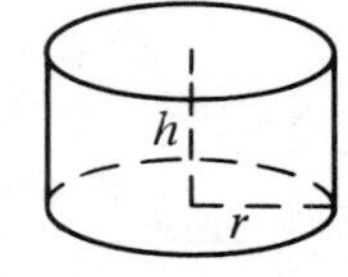


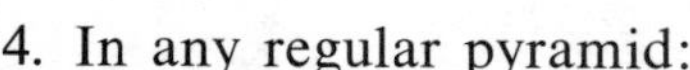

4. In any regular pyramid:
   L.A. = sum of the areas of the lateral faces
   T.A. = L.A. + $B$
   $V = \frac{1}{3}Bh$

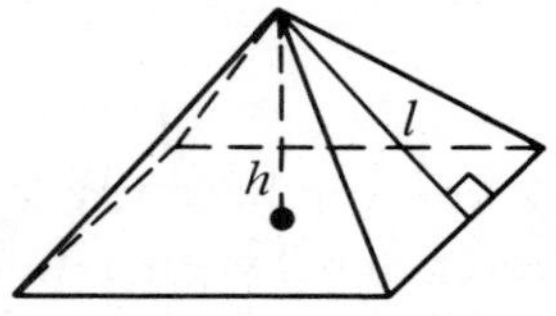


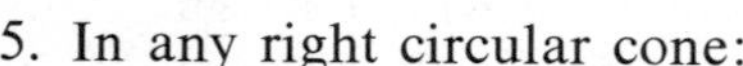

5. In any right circular cone:
   L.A. = $\pi rl$
   T.A. = L.A. + $B = \pi rl + \pi r^2$
   $V = \frac{1}{3}Bh = \frac{1}{3}\pi r^2 h$

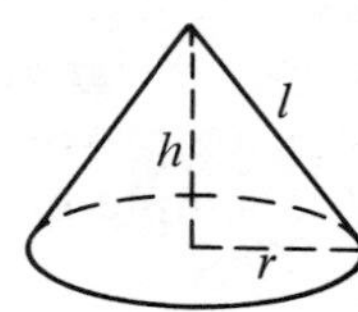


6. In any sphere:
   $A = 4\pi r^2$
   $V = \frac{4}{3}\pi r^3$

## Chapter Review Test

**Tell whether the statements are true or false.** (*See pp. 354–357.*)

1. If two planes do not intersect, they must be parallel. True
2. If two lines do not intersect, they must be parallel. False
3. If a line does not lie in a plane, the line must be parallel to the plane. False
4. If line $\overleftrightarrow{AB}$ is perpendicular to plane $R$, then $\overleftrightarrow{AB}$ is perpendicular to every line in $R$. False

**Refer to the right prism shown.** (*See pp. 359–364.*)

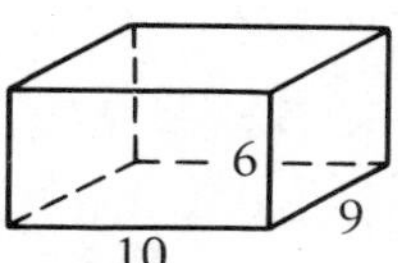


5. $B =$ __?__ 90 6. L.A. = __?__ 228
7. T.A. = __?__ 408 8. $V =$ __?__ 540

**Refer to the cylinder shown. Answer in terms of $\pi$.** (*See pp. 365–367.*)

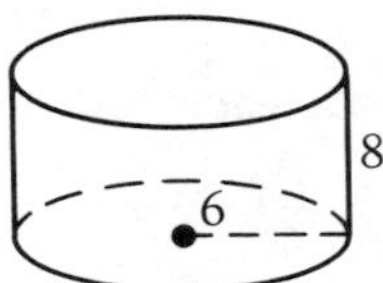


9. $C =$ __?__ $12\pi$ 10. L.A. = __?__ $96\pi$
11. T.A. = __?__ $168\pi$ 12. $V =$ __?__ $288\pi$

**Refer to the regular square pyramid shown.** (*See pp. 369–372.*)

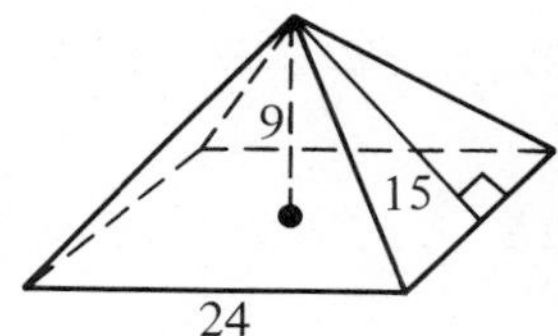


13. $B =$ __?__ 576 14. L.A. = __?__ 720
15. T.A. = __?__ 1296 16. $V =$ __?__ 1728

**Refer to the right circular cone shown. Answer in terms of $\pi$.** (*See pp. 373–375.*)

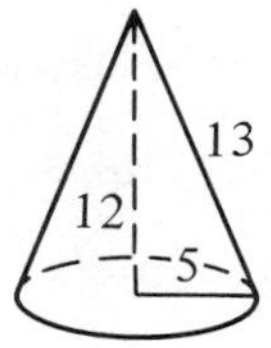


17. $C =$ __?__ $10\pi$ 18. L.A. = __?__ $65\pi$
19. T.A. = __?__ $90\pi$ 20. $V =$ __?__ $100\pi$

**Answer the questions about spheres in terms of $\pi$.** (*See pp. 378–379.*)

21. When $r = 5$, $A =$ __?__. $100\pi$ 22. When $d = 8$, $V =$ __?__. $\frac{256}{3}\pi$

# Cumulative Review / Unit E

**Complete.**

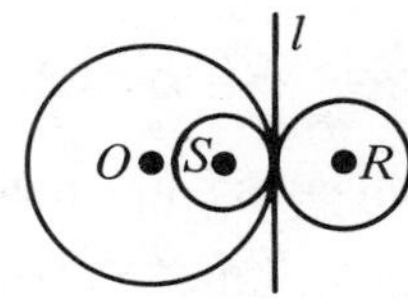


1. Line $l$ is a common internal tangent of $\odot S$ and ___?___. $\odot R$

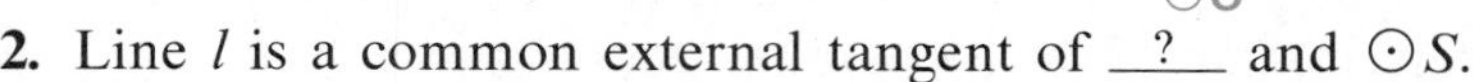

2. Line $l$ is a common external tangent of ___?___ and $\odot S$. $\odot O$

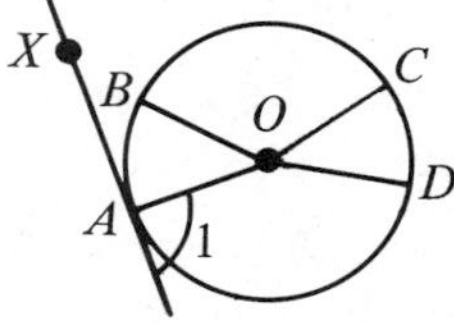


3. If $\overleftrightarrow{AX}$ is a tangent of $\odot O$, then $\angle 1 =$ ___?___°. 90
4. If $\angle AOD = 150°$, then $\widehat{AD} =$ ___?___°. 150
5. If $\angle BOA = \angle COD$ and $\widehat{AB} = 47°$, then $\widehat{CD} =$ ___?___°. 47

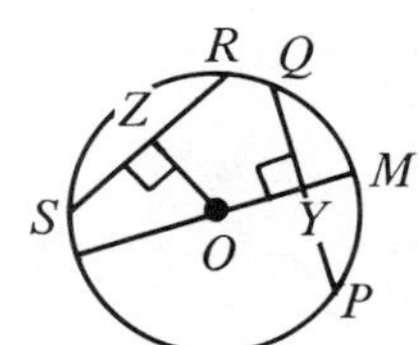


6. If $PQ = RS$ and $\widehat{RS} = 100°$, then $\widehat{PQ} =$ ___?___°. 100
7. If $OY = OZ$, then $PQ =$ ___?___. RS
8. If $RS = 10$, then $RZ =$ ___?___. 5
9. If $\widehat{PQ} = 98°$, then $\widehat{PM} =$ ___?___°. 49

**Classify each statement as true or false.**

10. If $\widehat{CF} = 60°$, then $\angle CEF = 30°$. True
11. If $\angle CEA = 70°$, then $\widehat{EBC} = 140°$. True
12. $\angle BDE = \frac{1}{2}(\widehat{BE} + \widehat{EF})$ False
13. $\angle EAF = \frac{1}{2}(\widehat{EF} - \widehat{BE})$ True
14. $BD \cdot DF = ED \cdot DC$ True

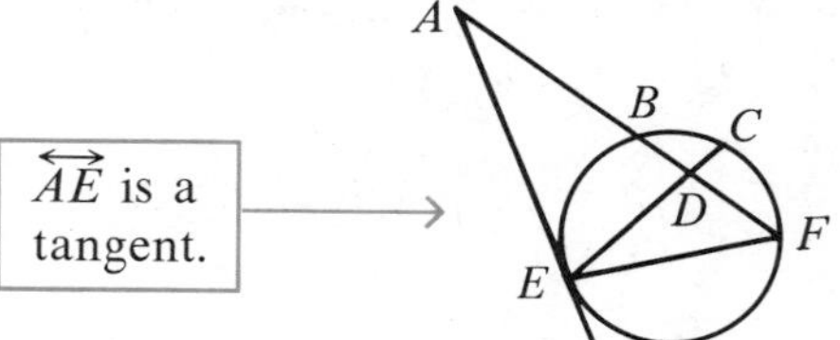


Exercises 10–15

15. $\triangle DEF$ is inscribed in the circle. False

16. Skew lines sometimes intersect. False
17. Two intersecting lines must be coplanar. True
18. Find the volume of a right prism with base area 25 and height 7. 175
19. Find the lateral area of a cylinder with radius 4 and height 7. $56\pi$
20. A regular square pyramid has base edges that are 4 m long. The height is 6 m. Find the volume of the pyramid. 32 $m^3$
21. Find the total area of a cone with radius 3 and slant height 5. $24\pi$
22. Find the area and volume of a sphere with radius 3 cm. $36\pi$

# UNIT F

## *Here's what you'll learn in this chapter:*

1. To solve problems involving some common right triangle lengths.
2. To apply theorems about 45°-45°-90° triangles and 30°-60°-90° triangles.
3. To find the length of the diagonal of a rectangular solid.
4. To use right triangles to solve problems involving pyramids and cones.
5. To use the tangent, sine, and cosine ratios of an acute angle of a right triangle.

# Chapter 11

# Right Triangles

# 1 • Reviewing Right Triangles

In this section, we shall review right triangles. The Pythagorean Theorem and its converse are the most important statements to remember when working with right triangles. Certain right triangles appear often in geometry and are listed below.

| Some Common Right Triangle Lengths | | |
|---|---|---|
| 3-4-5 | 5-12-13 | 8-15-17 |
| 6-8-10 | | |
| 9-12-15 | | |

The first entry in the table, 3-4-5, represents the triangle shown. Remember: The triangle must be a right triangle because

$$3^2 + 4^2 = 5^2.$$

**EXAMPLE** Find the exact values of $x$ and $y$ in the diagram.

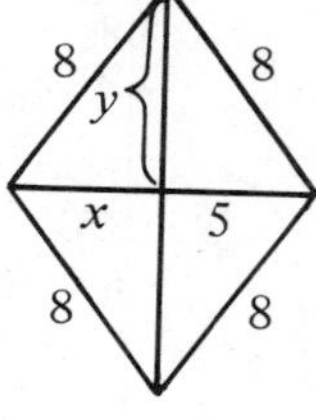


1. Since the four sides are equal, the quadrilateral is a rhombus.
2. The diagonals of a rhombus bisect each other. Therefore $x = 5$.
3. The diagonals of a rhombus are perpendicular. Therefore:

$$5^2 + y^2 = 8^2$$
$$25 + y^2 = 64$$
$$y^2 = 39$$
$$y = \sqrt{39}$$

Take the square root of both sides. →

## *Classroom Practice*

**Show that each equation is true.**

**1.** $6^2 + 8^2 = 10^2$ **2.** $5^2 + 12^2 = 13^2$ **3.** $8^2 + 15^2 = 17^2$

**Find the exact value of $x$.**

**4.**

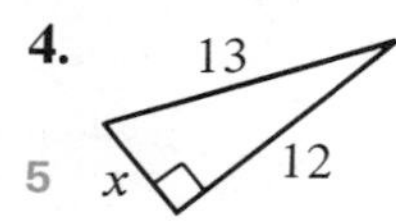


**5.** 4, 3 $x$, 5

**6.**

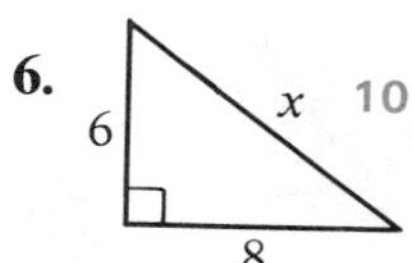

7. 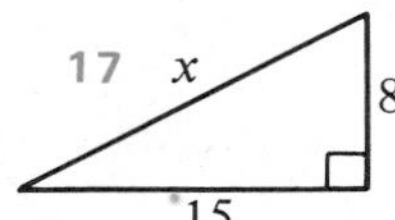


8. 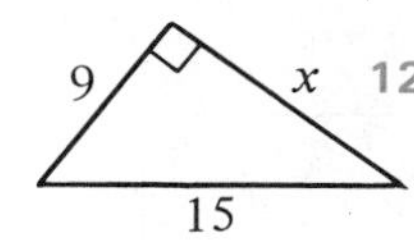


9. 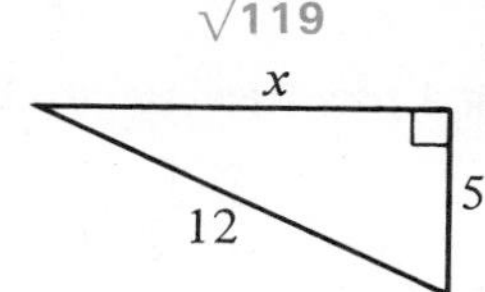


Find the exact values of $x$ and $y$.

10. $x = 13$, $y = 15$

11. 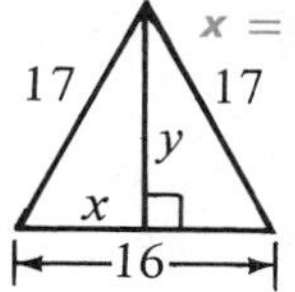


$x = 8$, $y = 15$

12. 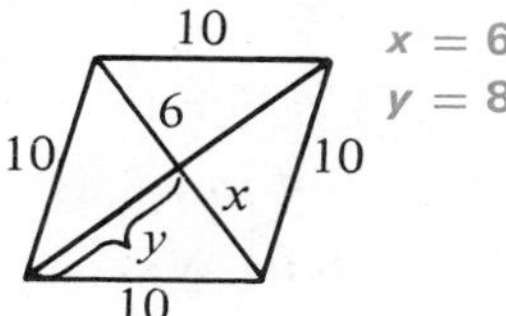


$x = 6$, $y = 8$

## Written Exercises

Find the exact value of $x$.

A 1. 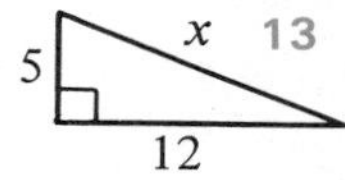


2. 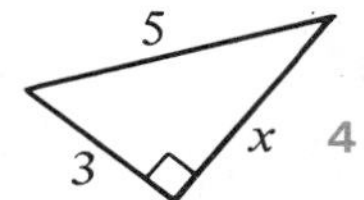


3. 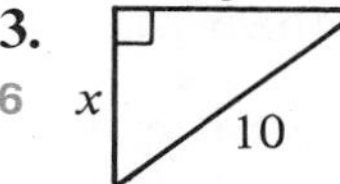


4. 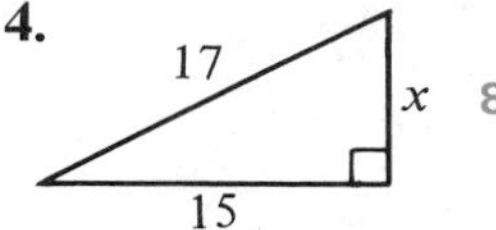


5. 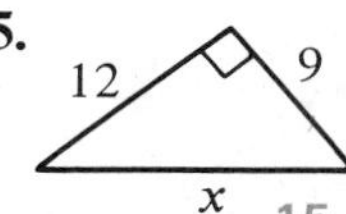


6. $x$ $\sqrt{7}$, 4, 3

Find the exact values of $x$ and $y$.

7. $x = 8$, $y = \sqrt{37}$

8. 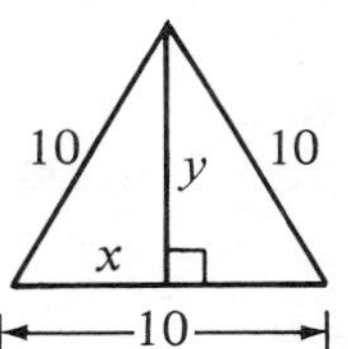


$x = 5$, $y = 5\sqrt{3}$

9. 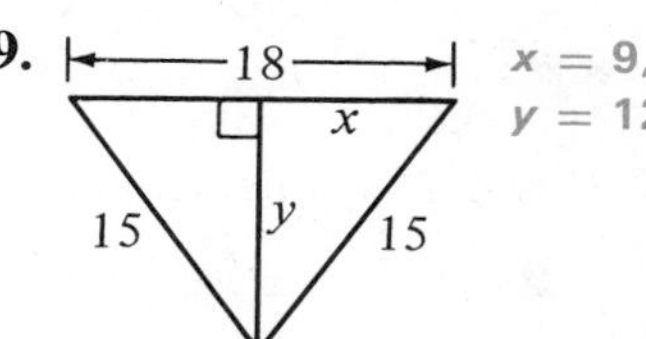


$x = 9$, $y = 12$

10. 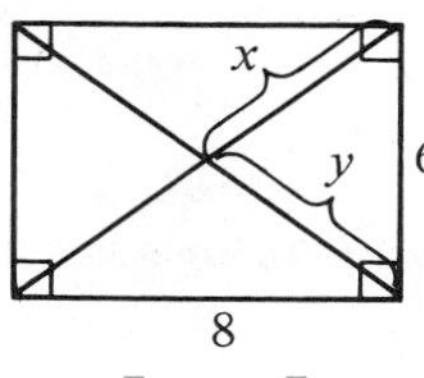


$x = 5$, $y = 5$

11. 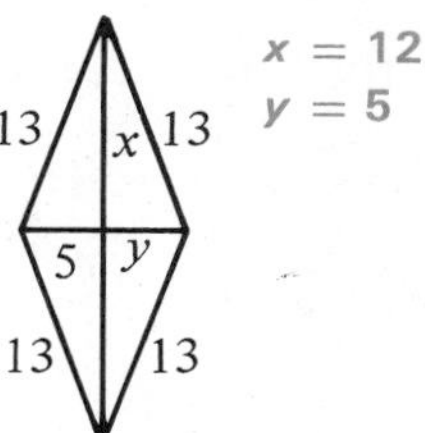


$x = 12$, $y = 5$

12. 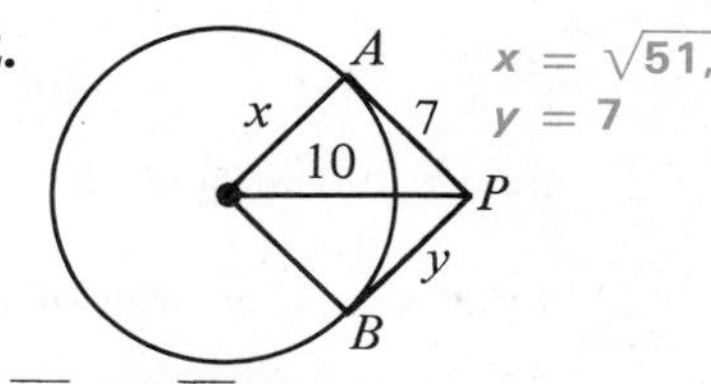


$\overline{PA}$ and $\overline{PB}$ are tangents.

$x = \sqrt{51}$, $y = 7$

13. 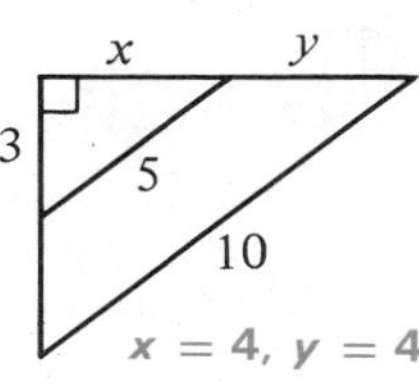


$x = 4$, $y = 4$

14. 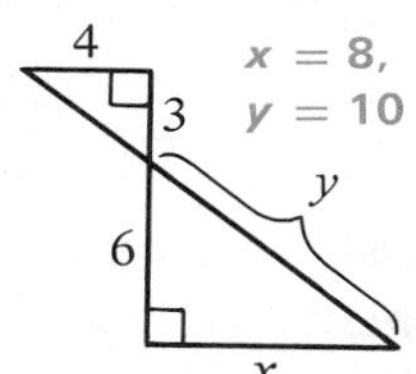


$x = 8$, $y = 10$

15. 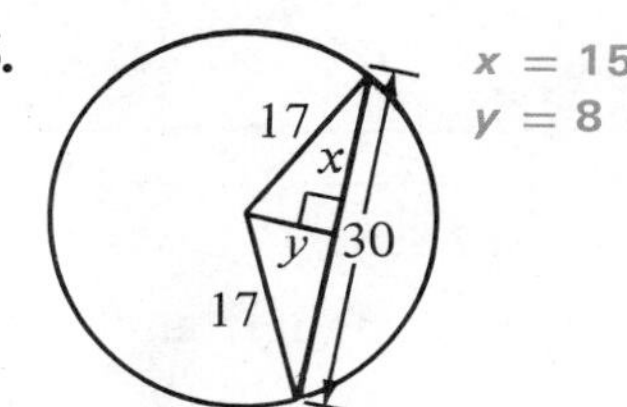


$x = 15$, $y = 8$

**Find the area. (*Hint:* First find $x$.)**

16. 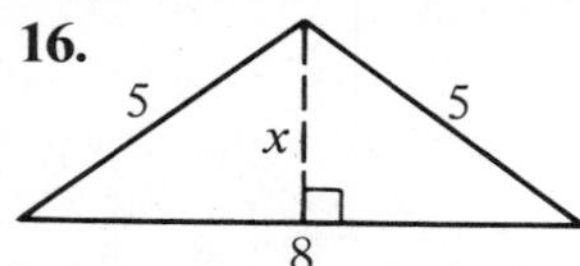


$x = 3$, $A = 12$ square units

17. 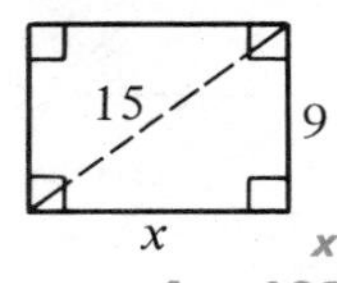


$x = 12$, $A = 108$ square units

18. 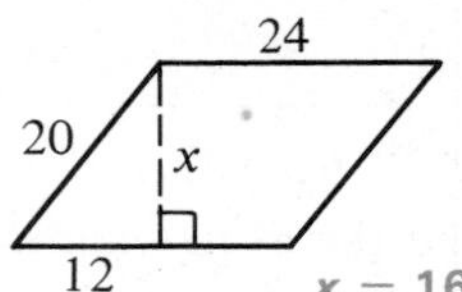


$x = 16$, $A = 384$ square units

B 19. Is $\angle C$ a right angle? Explain. yes

20. Why must $\overline{AB}$ be a diameter of the circle? (*Hint:* What is the measure of $\widehat{ADB}$?) 180°

21. What is the area of the circle? $25\pi$

22. What is the circumference of the circle? $10\pi$

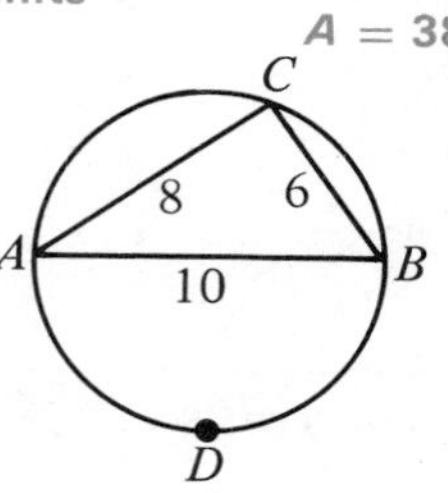


$p = 20$, $q = 15$

23. Find the values of $p$ and $q$.

24. Is $p^2 + q^2 = r^2$? Yes

25. Is $\triangle JKL$ a right triangle? Yes

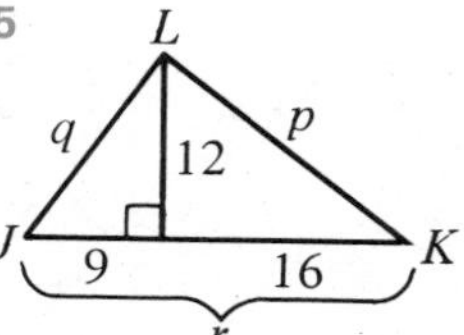


$x = 10$, $y = 17$

26. Find the values of $x$ and $y$.

27. Is $x^2 + y^2 = z^2$? No

28. Is $\triangle STU$ a right triangle? No

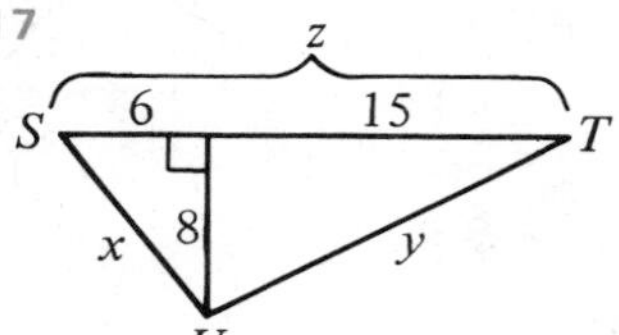


***ABCD* is a parallelogram. $AB = 15$, $AC = 24$, and $BD = 18$.**

29. $AO =$ _?_ 12

30. $BO =$ _?_ 9

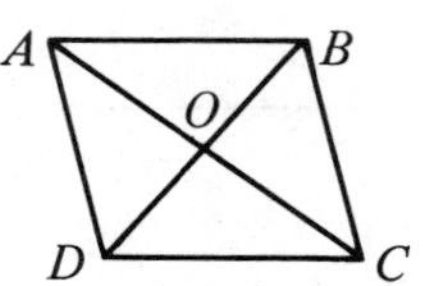


31. Is $\triangle AOB$ a right triangle? Explain. Yes; $12^2 + 9^2 = 15^2$

32. What special kind of parallelogram is $ABCD$? Explain. rhombus; the diagonals are perpendicular

**Find the exact area of each shaded region.**

C 33. 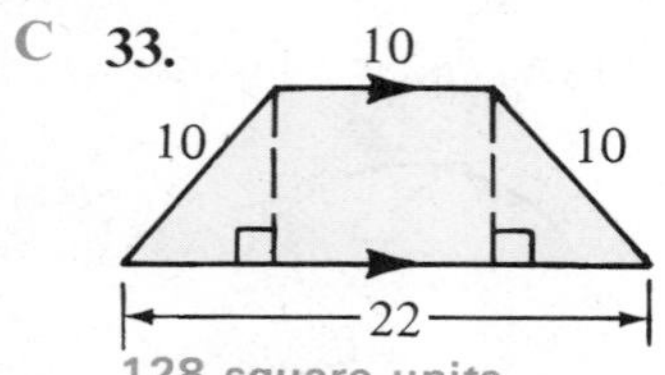


128 square units

34. 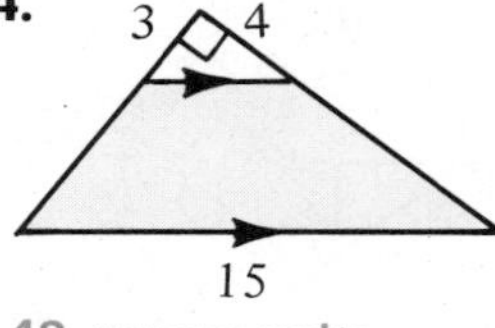


48 square units

35. 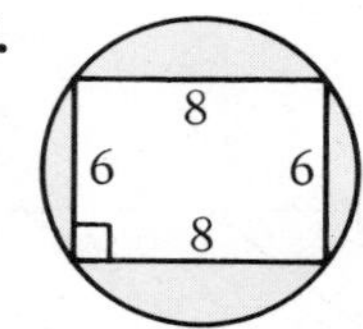


$25\pi - 48$ square units

36. A right triangle has legs of length 30 and 40. How long is the median drawn to the hypotenuse? 25

## 2 • Special Right Triangles

The triangles shown below are special right triangles. The one at the left is an isosceles right triangle. It is often called a 45°-45°-90° triangle. The other special triangle is a 30°-60°-90° triangle.

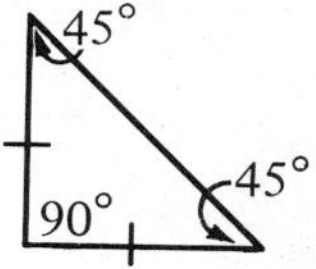


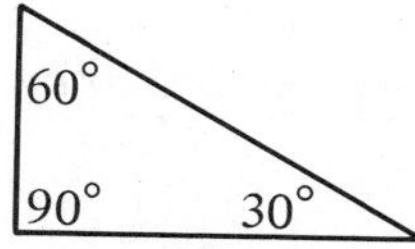


The Pythagorean Theorem can be used to prove two theorems about these special triangles.

**THEOREM 1**

In a 45°-45°-90° triangle, the hypotenuse is $\sqrt{2}$ times as long as a leg.

*Given:* A 45°-45°-90° triangle

*Prove:* $h = l\sqrt{2}$

*Proof:*
$$h^2 = l^2 + l^2$$
$$h^2 = 2l^2$$
$$h = \sqrt{2l^2}$$
$$h = l\sqrt{2}$$

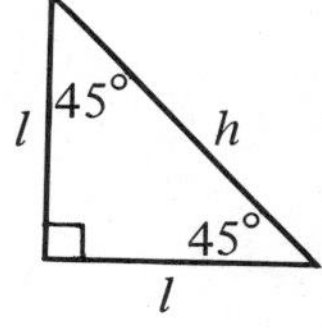


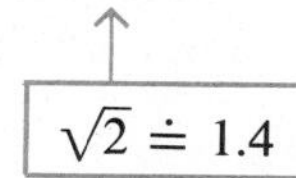


**EXAMPLE 1** For each diagram below, find the value of $t$.

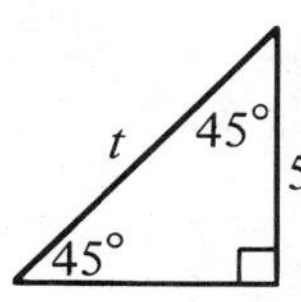


hypotenuse = leg × $\sqrt{2}$
$t = 5\sqrt{2}$

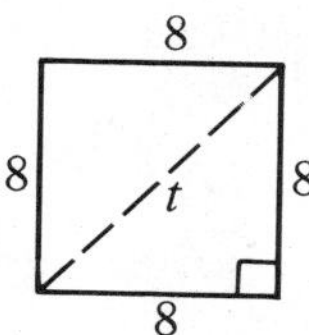


hypotenuse = leg × $\sqrt{2}$
$t = 8\sqrt{2}$

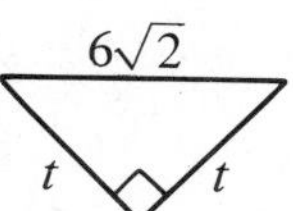


hypotenuse = leg × $\sqrt{2}$
$6\sqrt{2} = t\sqrt{2}$
$6 = t$

**THEOREM 2**

In a 30°-60°-90° triangle,

**a.** the hypotenuse is twice as long as the shorter leg;

**b.** the longer leg is $\sqrt{3}$ times as long as the shorter leg.

*Given:* A 30°-60°-90° triangle

*Prove:* **a.** $h = 2s$

**b.** $l = s\sqrt{3}$

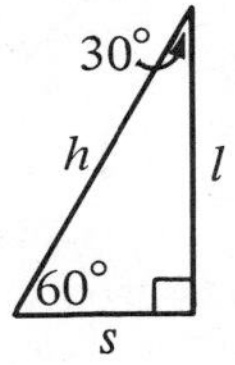


*Proof:*

Notice that a 30°-60°-90° triangle is "half" of an equilateral triangle.

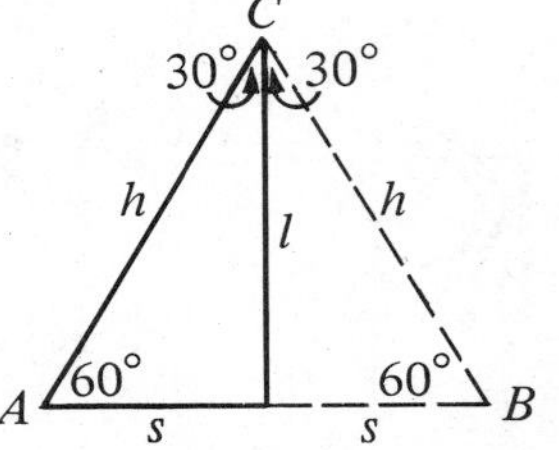


**a.** Since $\triangle ABC$ is equilateral, $h = 2s$.

**b.** To find $l$, use the Pythagorean Theorem.

$$l^2 + s^2 = h^2$$
$$l^2 + s^2 = (2s)^2$$
$$l^2 + s^2 = 4s^2$$
$$l^2 = 3s^2$$
$$l = \sqrt{3s^2}$$
$$l = s\sqrt{3}$$

$\sqrt{3} \doteq 1.7$

EXAMPLE 2 In each triangle below, the length of one side is given. Find the lengths of the other two sides.

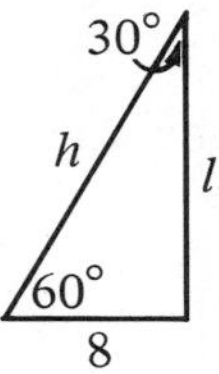


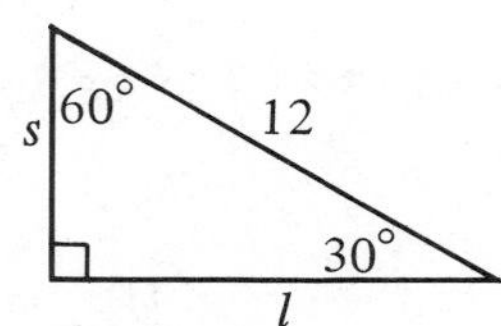


hypotenuse = 2 × shorter leg

$h = 2 \times 8$

$h = 16$

longer leg = shorter leg × $\sqrt{3}$

$l = 8\sqrt{3}$

hypotenuse = 2 × shorter leg

$12 = 2s$

$6 = s$

longer leg = shorter leg × $\sqrt{3}$

$l = 6\sqrt{3}$

## Classroom Practice

**$\triangle ABC$ is an isosceles right triangle.**

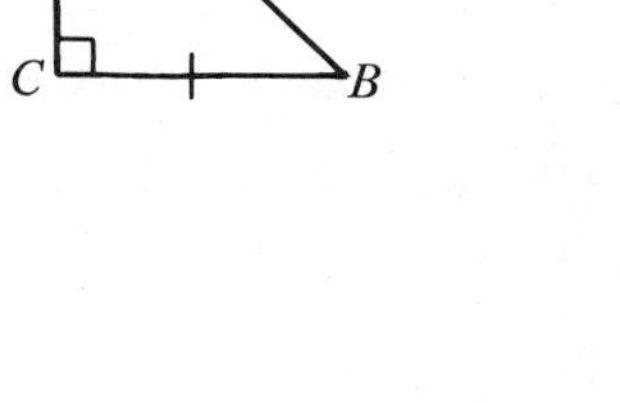


1. $\angle A = \underline{\ \ ?\ \ }^\circ$ 45
2. $\angle B = \underline{\ \ ?\ \ }^\circ$ 45
3. If $AC = 3$, then $BC = \underline{\ \ ?\ \ }$ and $AB = \underline{\ \ ?\ \ }$. 3; $3\sqrt{2}$
4. If $AC = 4$, then $BC = \underline{\ \ ?\ \ }$ and $AB = \underline{\ \ ?\ \ }$. 4; $4\sqrt{2}$
5. If $BC = 9$, then $AB = \underline{\ \ ?\ \ }$. $9\sqrt{2}$
6. If $AB = 7\sqrt{2}$, then $BC = \underline{\ \ ?\ \ }$. 7
7. If $AB = 2\sqrt{2}$, then $AC = \underline{\ \ ?\ \ }$. 2

**$\triangle XYZ$ is a 30°-60°-90° triangle.**

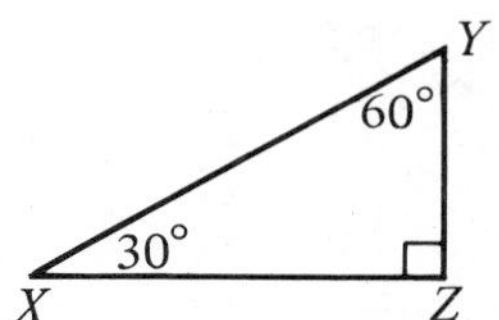


8. Which leg is the shorter leg? $\overline{YZ}$
9. In a 30°-60°-90° triangle, the shorter leg is *always* opposite the $\underline{\ \ ?\ \ }^\circ$ angle. 30

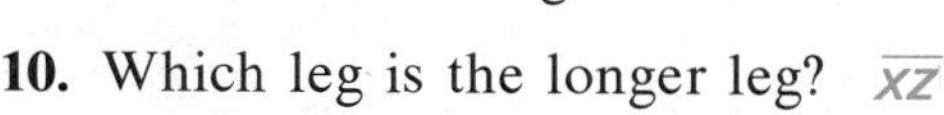

10. Which leg is the longer leg? $\overline{XZ}$

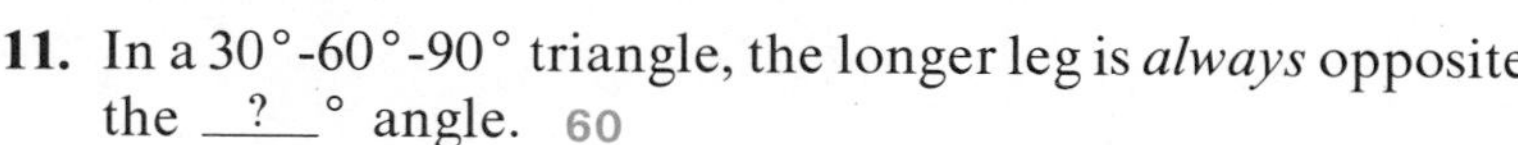

11. In a 30°-60°-90° triangle, the longer leg is *always* opposite the $\underline{\ \ ?\ \ }^\circ$ angle. 60
12. If $YZ = 5$, then $XY = \underline{\ \ ?\ \ }$ and $XZ = \underline{\ \ ?\ \ }$. 10; $5\sqrt{3}$
13. If $YZ = 6$, then $XY = \underline{\ \ ?\ \ }$ and $XZ = \underline{\ \ ?\ \ }$. 12; $6\sqrt{3}$
14. If $XY = 8$, then $YZ = \underline{\ \ ?\ \ }$ and $XZ = \underline{\ \ ?\ \ }$. 4; $4\sqrt{3}$
15. If $XY = 6$, then $YZ = \underline{\ \ ?\ \ }$ and $XZ = \underline{\ \ ?\ \ }$. 3; $3\sqrt{3}$

## Written Exercises

**In Exercises 1–9, find the exact values of $x$ and $y$.**

A

1. 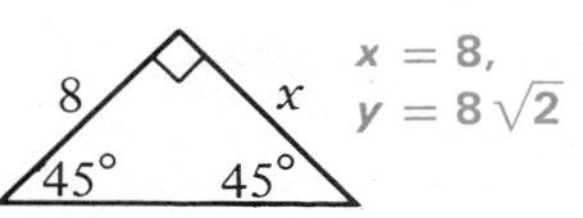

$x = 8$, $y = 8\sqrt{2}$

2. 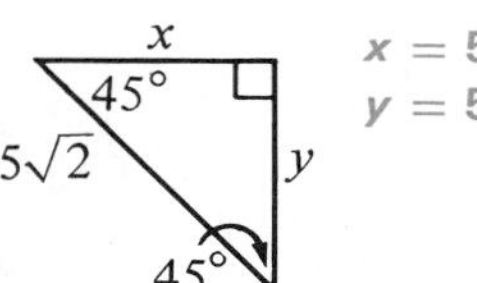

$x = 5$, $y = 5$

3. 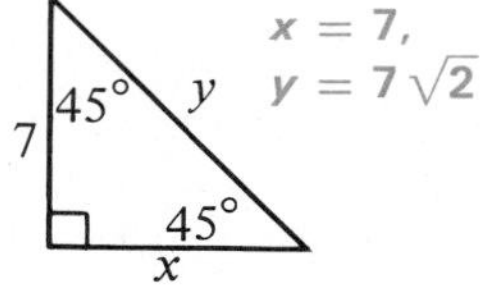

$x = 7$, $y = 7\sqrt{2}$

4. 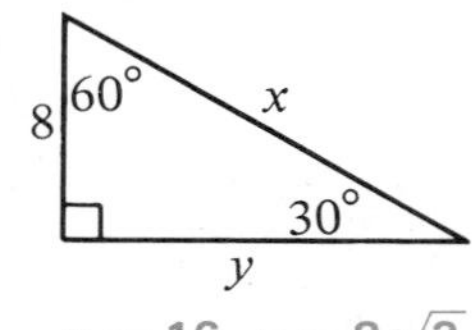

$x = 16$, $y = 8\sqrt{3}$

5. 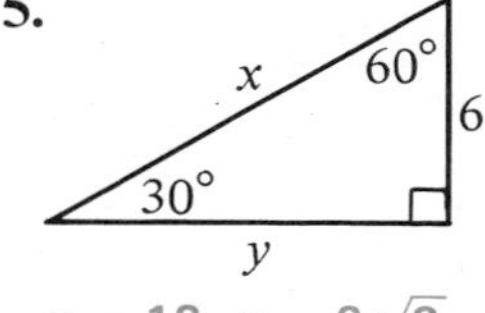

$x = 12$, $y = 6\sqrt{3}$

6. 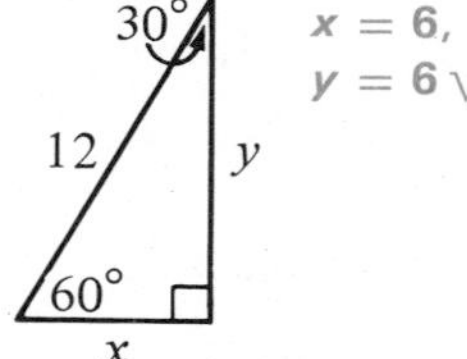

$x = 6$, $y = 6\sqrt{3}$

7. 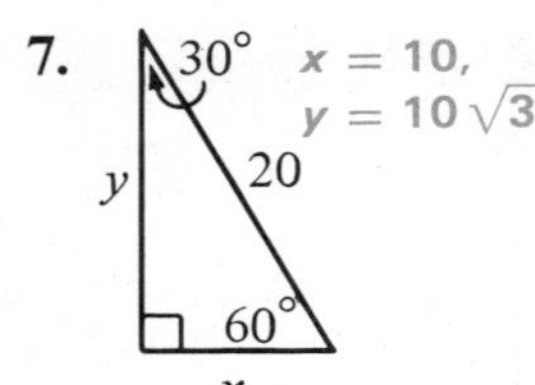

$x = 10$, $y = 10\sqrt{3}$

8. 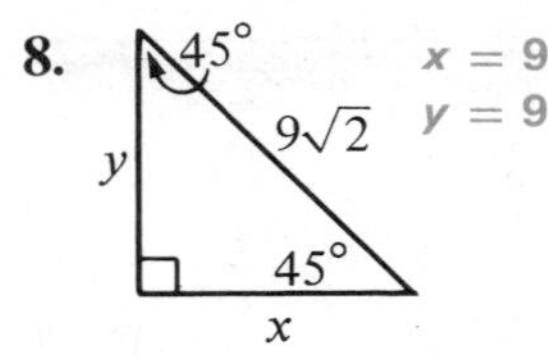

$x = 9$, $y = 9$

9. 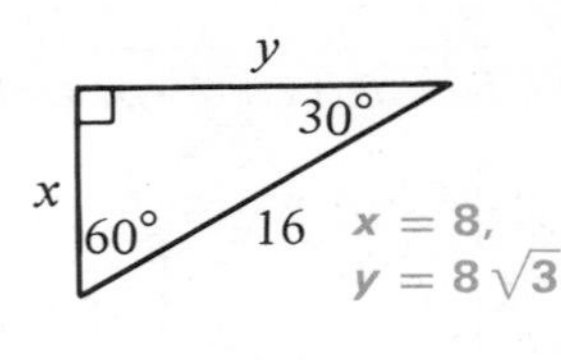

$x = 8$, $y = 8\sqrt{3}$

**In the diagram shown, $\triangle ABC$ is equilateral. $\overline{AD}$ is an altitude.**

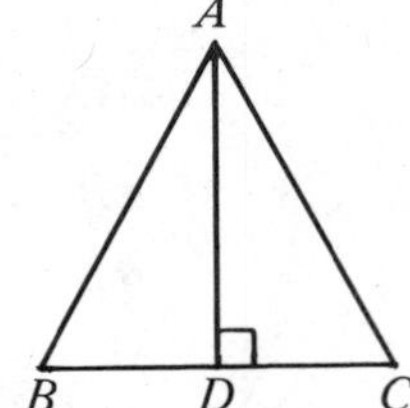


**10.** $\angle ABD =$ __?__° 60 **11.** $\angle ADB =$ __?__° 90

**12.** $\angle BAD =$ __?__° 30 **13.** $\angle CAD =$ __?__° 30

**Suppose $AB = 6$. Find:**

**14.** $BD$ 3 **15.** $AD$ $3\sqrt{3}$ **16.** Area of $\triangle ABC$ $9\sqrt{3}$

**In the diagram shown, $ABCD$ is a square. Suppose $AB = 6$. Find:**

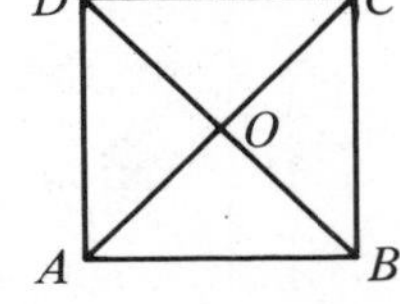


**17.** $AC$ $6\sqrt{2}$ **18.** $AO$ $3\sqrt{2}$ **19.** $BO$ $3\sqrt{2}$

**Suppose $AO = 4$. Find:**

**20.** $BO$ 4 **21.** Area of $\triangle AOB$ 8 **22.** Area of $ABCD$ 32

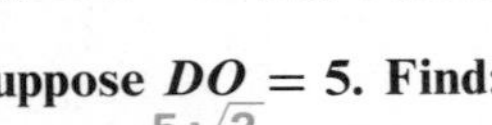

**Suppose $DO = 5$. Find:**

**23.** $DC$ $5\sqrt{2}$ **24.** Area of $\triangle DOC$ $12\frac{1}{2}$ **25.** Area of $ABCD$ 50

**In Exercises 26–28, find the exact value of $t$.**

Sample 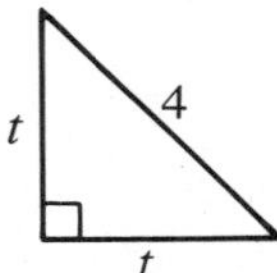


*Method 1*

hypotenuse = leg × $\sqrt{2}$ (Thm. 1)

$$4 = t\sqrt{2}$$

$$\frac{4}{\sqrt{2}} = t$$

Simplify.

$$t = \frac{4}{\sqrt{2}} = \frac{4 \cdot \sqrt{2}}{\sqrt{2} \cdot \sqrt{2}} = \frac{4\sqrt{2}}{2} = 2\sqrt{2}$$

*Method 2*

$$t^2 + t^2 = 4^2 \text{ (Pythagorean Thm.)}$$

$$2t^2 = 16$$

$$t^2 = 8$$

$$t = \sqrt{8}$$

Simplify.

$$t = \sqrt{8} = \sqrt{4 \times 2} = 2\sqrt{2}$$

B **26.** 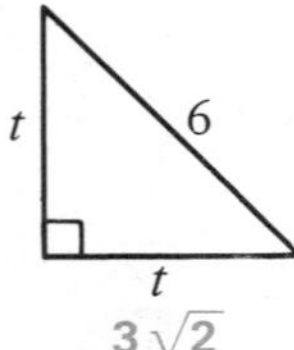

$3\sqrt{2}$

**27.** 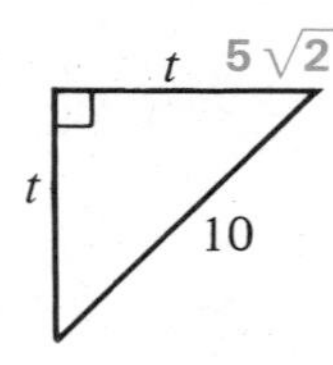

$5\sqrt{2}$

**28.** 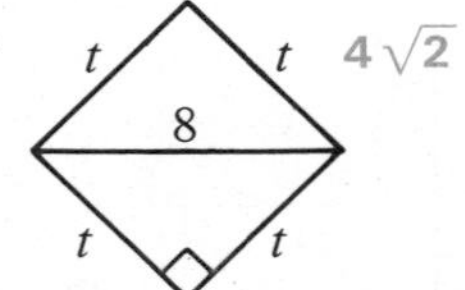

$4\sqrt{2}$

**29.** Each edge of the cube shown has length 6. Find the length of each side of the green triangle. $6\sqrt{2}$

**30.** What is the measure of each angle of the green triangle? $60°$

**$\triangle ABC$ is a $30°$-$60°$-$90°$ triangle. $\overline{CD}$ is an altitude. Copy and complete the table.**

Answers on page T128

|  | $AB$ | $BC$ | $AC$ | $CD$ | $AD$ | $DB$ |
|---|---|---|---|---|---|---|
| Sample | 4 | 2 | $2\sqrt{3}$ | $\sqrt{3}$ | 3 | 1 |
| **31.** | 12 | ? | ? | ? | ? | ? |
| **32.** | ? | 10 | ? | ? | ? | ? |
| **33.** | ? | ? | $4\sqrt{3}$ | ? | ? | ? |
| **34.** | ? | ? | ? | ? | ? | 3 |
| C **35.** | ? | ? | ? | $7\sqrt{3}$ | ? | ? |
| **36.** | ? | ? | ? | ? | 9 | ? |

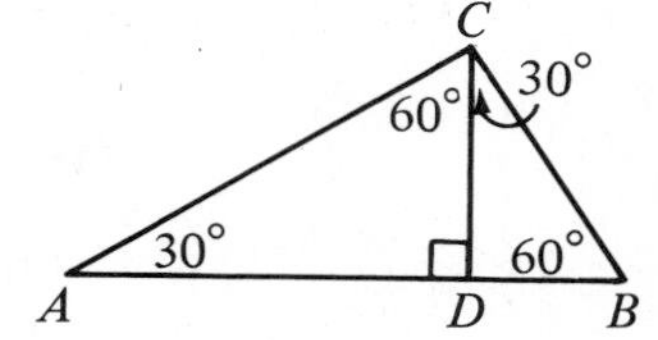


## CONSUMER CORNER

### Calling Long Distance

It's fun to make long distance calls to friends or family members, but a long distance call costs more than one across town. You can save on telephone bills by knowing how long distance rates vary at different times of the day. The chart below shows a sample rate structure for a long distance direct-dial call.

| BUSINESS HOURS (8 A.M.–5 P.M.) | | EVENINGS (5 P.M.–11 P.M.) | | NIGHTS (11 P.M.–8 A.M.) | |
|---|---|---|---|---|---|
| First min | Each add. min | First min | Each add. min | First min | Each add. min |
| \$0.41 | \$0.27 | \$0.26 | \$0.18 | \$0.16 | \$0.11 |

In general, you save money by calling late in the day or early in the morning. Discount rates may also apply all day on weekends. Check with your local telephone company for details.

# 3 • Using Special Right Triangles

In this section, we will apply the theorems about 45°-45°-90° triangles and 30°-60°-90° triangles to many figures you have studied in this course. Here is an example.

**EXAMPLE** Find the area of $\square ABCD$ if:
$\angle A = 60°$, $AD = 8$, and $AB = 10$.

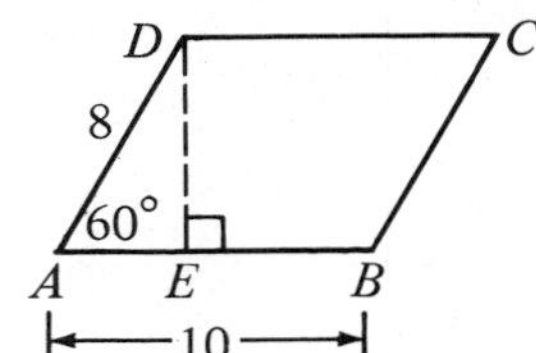


1. Draw altitude $\overline{DE}$.
2. Notice that $\triangle ADE$ is a 30°-60°-90° triangle.
3. $AE = \frac{1}{2} \times 8 = 4$
   $DE = 4\sqrt{3}$
4. Area = base × height
   $= 10 \times 4\sqrt{3}$
   $= 40\sqrt{3}$

## Classroom Practice

**Exercises 1–6 refer to the diagram.**

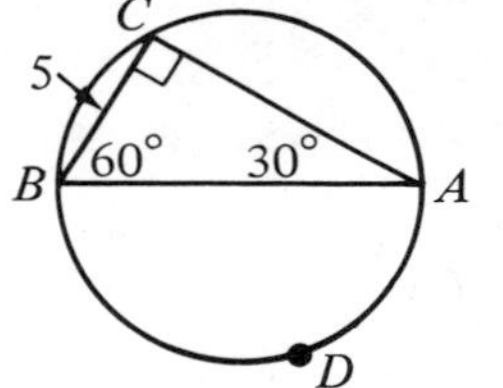


1. $\triangle ABC$ is a _?_°-_?_°-_?_° triangle. 30 60 90
2. Since $BC = 5$, $AB =$ _?_. 10
3. Since $\angle C = 90°$, $\widehat{BDA} =$ _?_°. 180
4. $\overline{AB}$ is a _?_ of the circle. diameter
5. Find the radius of the circle. 5
6. Find the area of the circle. $25\pi$

***WXYZ* is a rectangle. $XZ = 12$ and $\angle ZXW = 30°$. Find:**

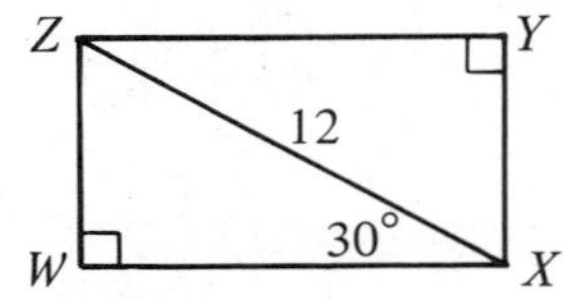


7. $ZW$ 6
8. $WX$ $6\sqrt{3}$
9. The area of rectangle $WXYZ$ $36\sqrt{3}$

## Written Exercises

**Find the area of each triangle.**

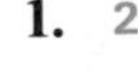

**1.** 2

45° 45° $2\sqrt{2}$

**2.** $8\sqrt{3}$

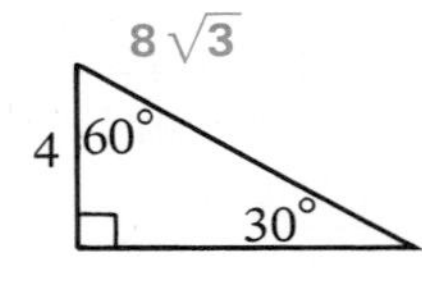


**3.** $50\sqrt{3}$

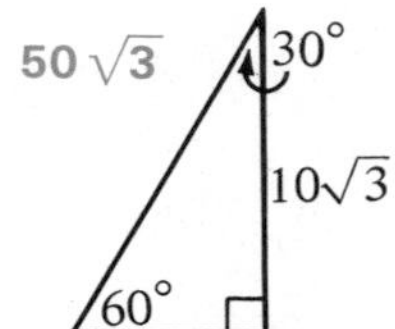

**Find the area of each parallelogram. Refer to the example, page 400.**

**4.** 60

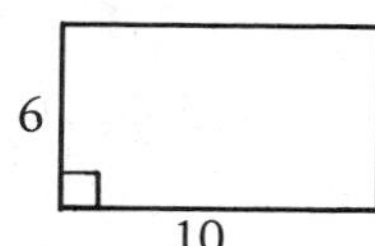


**5.** $30\sqrt{3}$

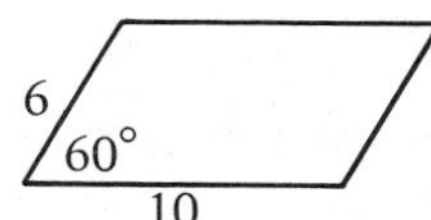


**6.** 30

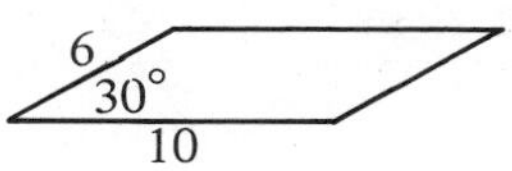


**For each triangle shown, find the value of $x$.**
**Then find the area of the triangle.**

**7.** $x = 2\sqrt{3}$, $A = 4\sqrt{3}$

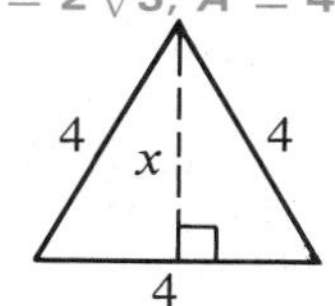


**8.** $x = 7$, $A = 49$

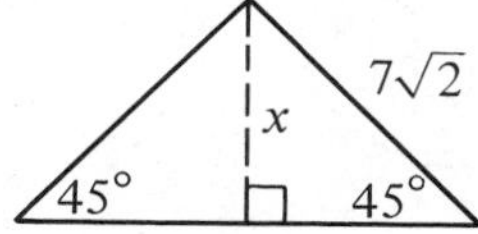


**9.** $x = 8$, $A = 64\sqrt{3}$

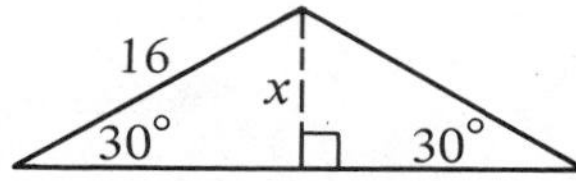

**$\overline{TA}$ and $\overline{TB}$ are tangents to $\odot O$.**
**$OA = 4$ and $\angle ATB = 60°$.**
**Find each of the following.**

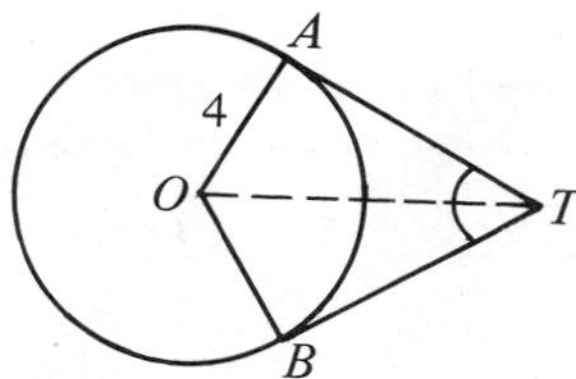


**10.** $\angle OAT$ 90° **11.** $\angle OTA$ 30°

**12.** $AT$ $4\sqrt{3}$ **13.** $BT$ $4\sqrt{3}$

**Study the diagram. Then find each of the following.**

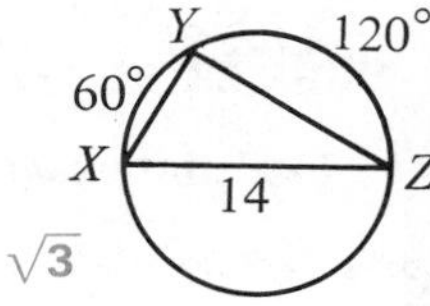


**14.** $\angle Z$ 30° **15.** $\angle X$ 60° **16.** $\angle Y$ 90°

**17.** $XY$ 7 **18.** $YZ$ $7\sqrt{3}$ **19.** The area of $\triangle XYZ$ $\frac{49}{2}\sqrt{3}$

**$PQRS$ is a rhombus. $\angle SPQ = 120°$ and $SP = 8$.**
**Find each of the following.**

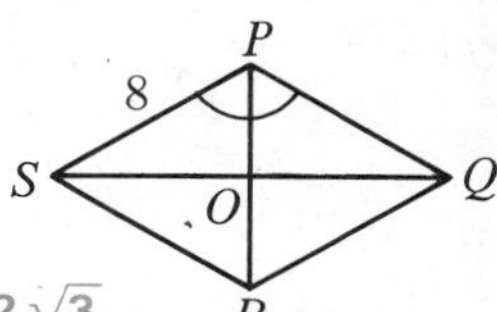


B **20.** $\angle SPO$ 60° **21.** $\angle POS$ 90° **22.** $\angle PSO$ 30°

**23.** $PO$ 4 **24.** $SO$ $4\sqrt{3}$ **25.** The area of $PQRS$ $32\sqrt{3}$

**26.** Is $\triangle EFG \sim \triangle HIJ$? Yes

**27.** What is the scale factor of $\triangle EFG$ to $\triangle HIJ$? 5:3

**28.** What is the ratio of their perimeters? 5:3

**29.** What is the ratio of their areas? 25:9

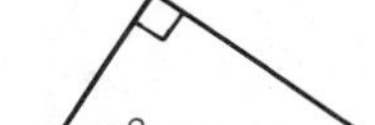


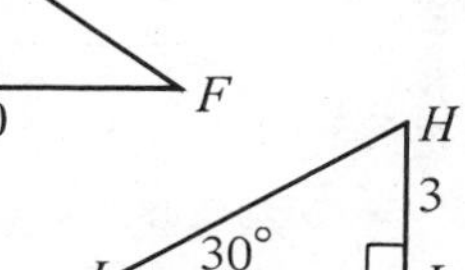

***QRST* is a square inscribed in ⊙*O*. The radius of ⊙*O* is 4.**

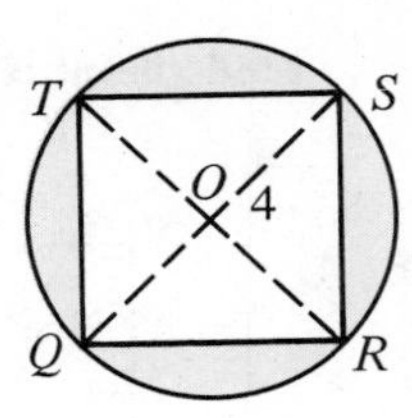


30. Find the area of the circle. $16\pi$

31. Find the area of the square. 32

32. Find the area of the shaded region. 18.24

C 33. Find the area of trapezoid *ABCD* if $\angle A = \angle B = 45°$, $AB = 16$, and $DC = 6$. 55

34. Find the area of a regular hexagon with sides 2 cm long. $6\sqrt{3}$

35. The wrench shown just fits the nut. Find the value of $x$. $\sqrt{3}$ cm

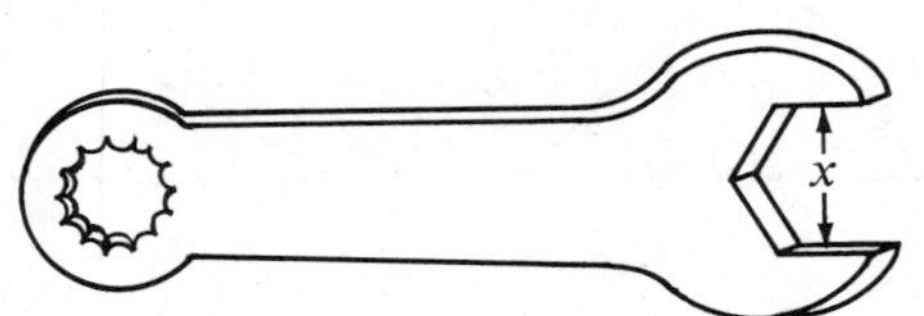


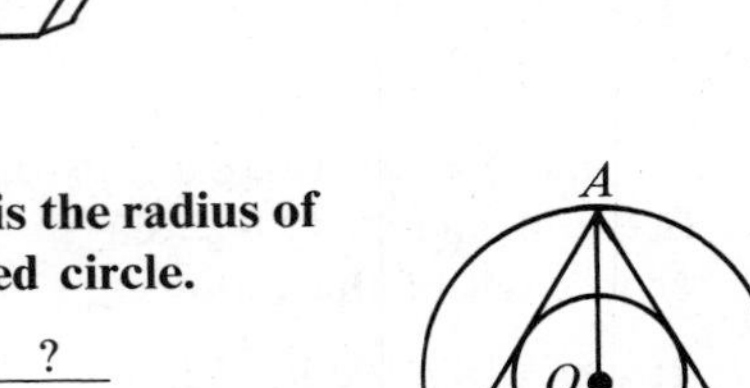


**$\triangle ABC$ is an equilateral triangle with sides 6 cm long. *OD* is the radius of the inscribed circle. *OA* is the radius of the circumscribed circle.**

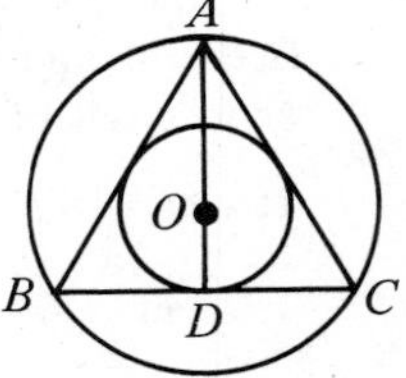


36. $AD = \underline{\ ?\ }$ $3\sqrt{3}$ 37. $OD = \underline{\ ?\ }$ $\sqrt{3}$ 38. $OA = \underline{\ ?\ }$ $2\sqrt{3}$

*Hint:* See the Experiments on page 148.

## SELF-TEST

**Find the exact values of $x$ and $y$.**

1. $x = 12$, $y = 9$

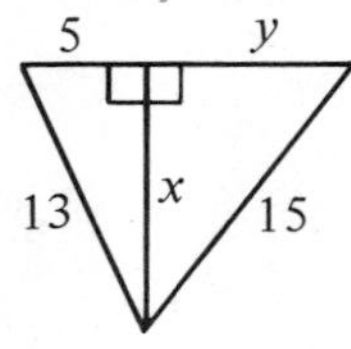


2. $x = 2$, $y = 2\sqrt{2}$

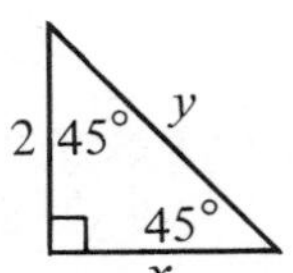


3. $x = 5$, $y = 5\sqrt{3}$

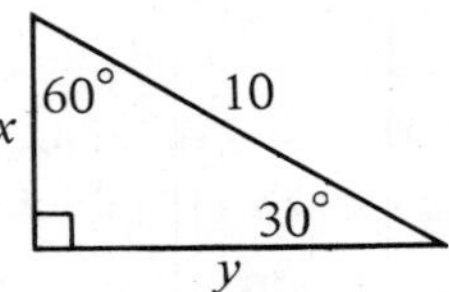


**Find the area of each polygon.**

4. 18

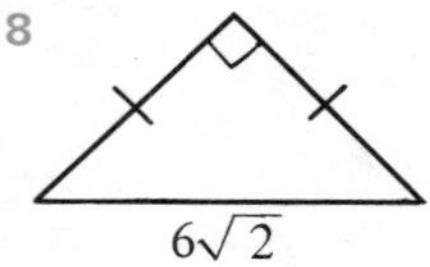


5. $27\sqrt{3}$

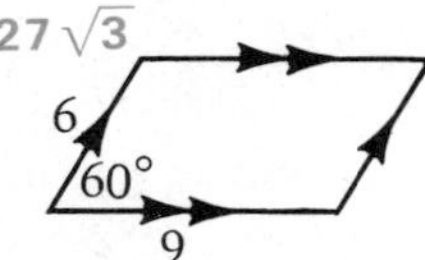


6. $27\sqrt{3}$

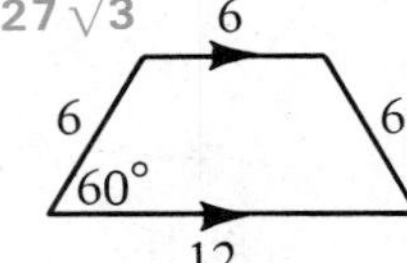

# 4 • Diagonals of Rectangular Solids

The rectangular solid shown is 3 cm long, 1 cm wide, and 2 cm high. $\overline{HB}$ is called a *diagonal* of the solid. A rectangular solid has four diagonals which are all equal in length. The other diagonals, not drawn in the figure, are $\overline{EC}$, $\overline{GA}$, and $\overline{FD}$.

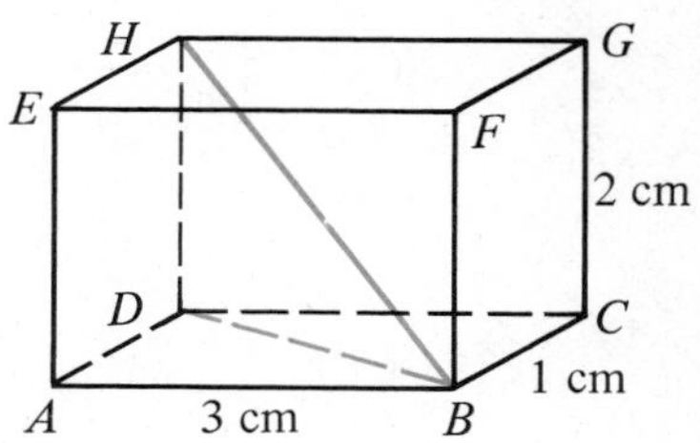


We can use the Pythagorean Theorem to find the length of $\overline{HB}$.

1. First study rectangle $ABCD$.

$$(DB)^2 = 1^2 + 3^2$$
$$(DB)^2 = 1 + 9 = 10$$
$$DB = \sqrt{10}$$

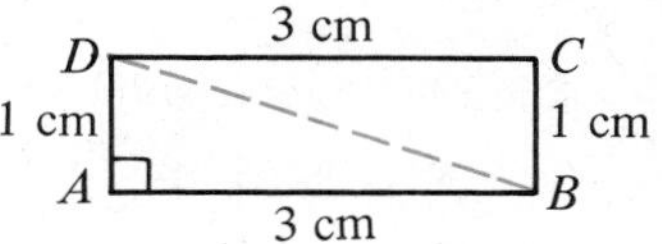


2. Now study right $\triangle HDB$. Notice:

$$(HB)^2 = (HD)^2 + (DB)^2$$
$$(HB)^2 = 2^2 + 10$$
$$(HB)^2 = 14$$

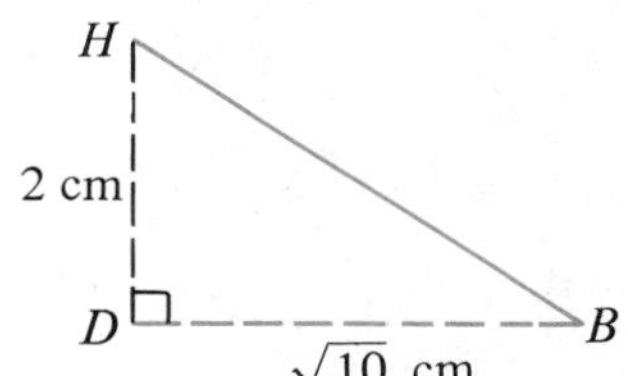


3. $\overline{HB}$ is exactly $\sqrt{14}$ cm long. If we use the square root table on page 465, we find that $\overline{HB}$ is approximately 3.742 cm long.

The method illustrated above can be used to find the length of a diagonal of any rectangular solid.

1. $x^2 = a^2 + b^2$
2. $d^2 = x^2 + c^2$

   $d^2 = (a^2 + b^2) + c^2$ ← Substitute using step 1.
3. $d = \sqrt{a^2 + b^2 + c^2}$

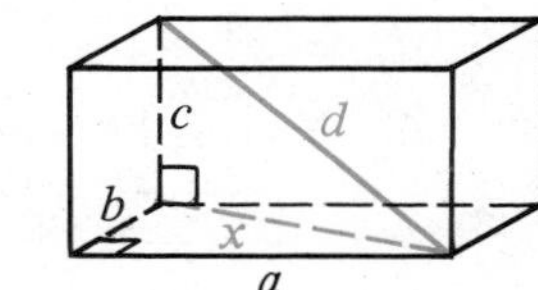

If a rectangular solid has dimensions $a$, $b$, and $c$, then a diagonal has length

$$d = \sqrt{a^2 + b^2 + c^2}.$$

**EXAMPLE** A rectangular solid is shown. Find the length of a diagonal of the solid.

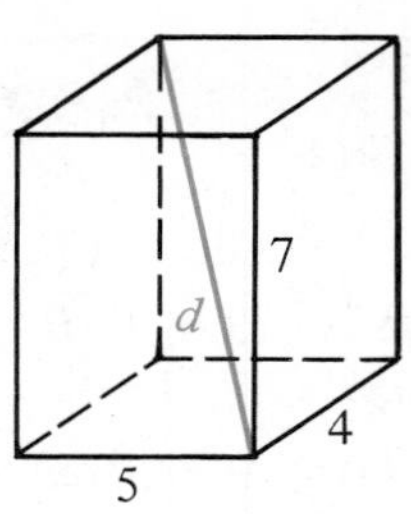


$$\begin{aligned} d &= \sqrt{5^2 + 4^2 + 7^2} \\ &= \sqrt{25 + 16 + 49} \\ &= \sqrt{90} \\ &= \sqrt{9 \cdot 10} \\ &= 3\sqrt{10} \end{aligned}$$

## Classroom Practice

**The rectangular solid shown has dimensions 4, 2, and 3.**

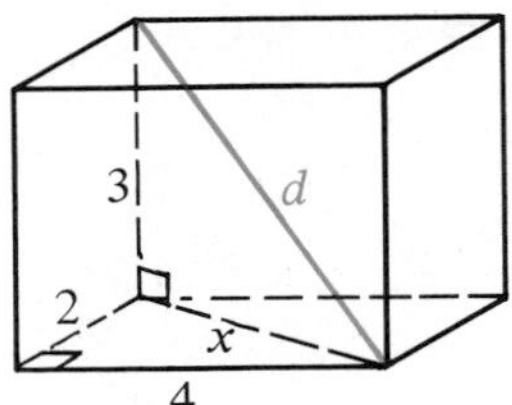


1. $x^2 = 2^2 + 4^2$
   $x^2 = \underline{\ ?\ }$ 20

2. $d^2 = 3^2 + x^2$
   $d^2 = \underline{\ ?\ }$ 9 $+ \underline{\ ?\ }$ 20

3. $d = \sqrt{\underline{\ ?\ }}$ 29

4. Using the formula for a diagonal of a rectangular solid:

$$d = \sqrt{\underset{2}{\underline{\ ?\ }}^2 + \underset{3}{\underline{\ ?\ }}^2 + \underset{4}{\underline{\ ?\ }}^2}$$

$$d = \sqrt{\underset{4}{\underline{\ ?\ }} + \underset{9}{\underline{\ ?\ }} + \underset{16}{\underline{\ ?\ }}}$$

$$d = \sqrt{\underset{29}{\underline{\ ?\ }}}$$

**The rectangular solid shown has dimensions 6, 2, and 3.**

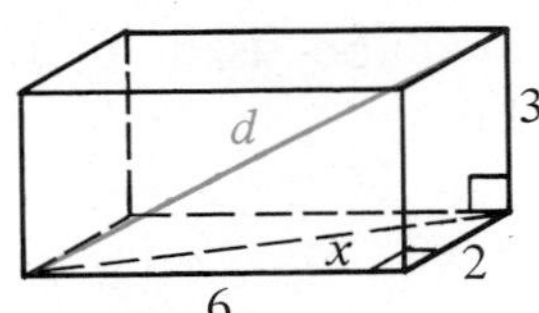


5. $x^2 = \overset{2}{\underline{\ ?\ }}^2 + \overset{6}{\underline{\ ?\ }}^2$
   $x^2 = \underline{\ ?\ }$ 40

6. $d^2 = x^2 + \overset{3}{\underline{\ ?\ }}^2$
   $d^2 = \underline{\ ?\ }$ 40 $+ \underline{\ ?\ }$ 9

7. $d = \sqrt{\underline{\ ?\ }}$ 49

8. Use the formula for a diagonal of a rectangular solid to show that your answer for Exercise 7 is correct. $d = \sqrt{6^2 + 2^2 + 3^2} = 7$

**Exercises 9–11 refer to the rectangular solid shown.**

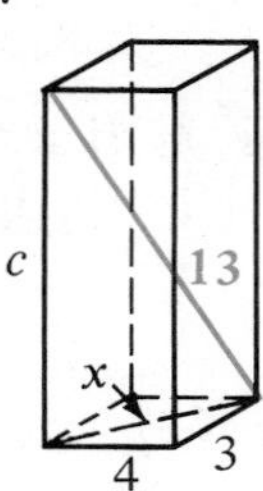


9. Find the value of $x$. 5

10. Find the height $c$. 12

11. Find the volume of the solid. 144

## Written Exercises

**Copy and complete the table, which refers to the rectangular solid shown.**

| | | $a$ | $b$ | $c$ | $x$ | $d$ |
|---|---|---|---|---|---|---|
| A | **1.** | 2 | 4 | 5 | ? $2\sqrt{5}$ | ? $3\sqrt{5}$ |
| | **2.** | 3 | 4 | 5 | ? 5 | ? $5\sqrt{2}$ |
| | **3.** | 2 | 1 | 3 | ? $\sqrt{5}$ | ? $\sqrt{14}$ |
| | **4.** | 3 | 2 | 6 | ? $\sqrt{13}$ | ? 7 |
| | **5.** | 5 | 2 | 6 | ? $\sqrt{29}$ | ? $\sqrt{65}$ |
| | **6.** | 6 | 2 | 5 | ? $2\sqrt{10}$ | ? $\sqrt{65}$ |
| B | **7.** | 9 | 12 | ? 8 | ? 15 | 17 |
| | **8.** | 3 | ? 4 | ? 12 | 5 | 13 |

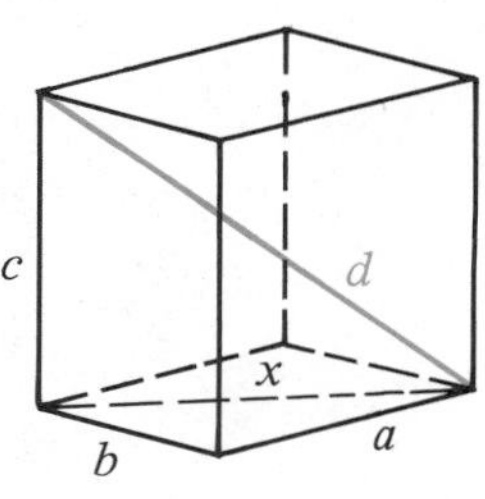


**The figure shows a cube with edges 1 cm long.**

**9.** Show that $x = \sqrt{2}$. $x^2 = 1^2 + 1^2$, so $x = \sqrt{2}$

**10.** Show that $d = \sqrt{3}$. $d = \sqrt{1^2 + 1^2 + 1^2} = \sqrt{3}$

**11.** A rectangular solid is 21 cm long, 20 cm wide, and 8 cm high. Find the length of a diagonal to the nearest tenth. 30.1

**12.** A rectangular solid is 20 cm long, 15 cm wide, and 10 cm high. Find the length of a diagonal to the nearest tenth. 26.9

C **13.** Will a very thin metal rod, 70 cm long, fit inside a box that is 51 cm long, 43 cm wide, and 21 cm high? Explain. No; the diagonal of the box is $d$, with $d = \sqrt{51^2 + 43^2 + 21^2} \doteq 69.936$

## Puzzles & Things

Make a 3-4-5 triangle with 12 straws of equal length.

**a.** By moving only 3 straws, make a polygon with area 4.

**b.** By moving only 2 straws, make a polygon with area 5.

## 5 • Right Triangles in Pyramids and Cones

In the previous section, we used right triangles to solve problems involving rectangular solids. In this section, we'll use right triangles to work with pyramids and cones.

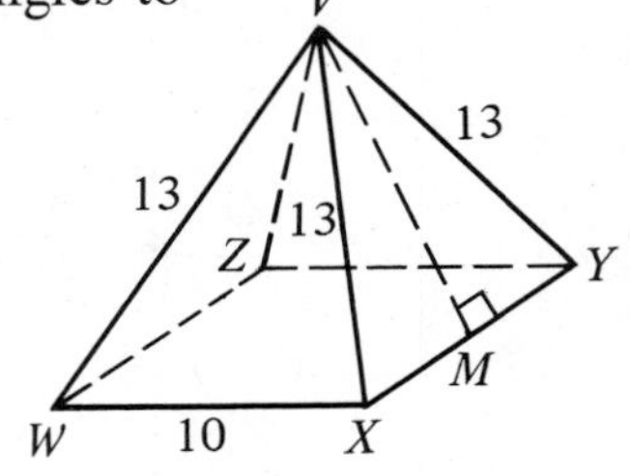


**EXAMPLE 1** For the regular pyramid shown, find:

**a.** the lateral area;

**b.** the total area;

**c.** the volume.

**a.** Notice that $\triangle VXM$ is a 5-12-13 right triangle with $VM = 12$.

The area of one lateral face $= \frac{1}{2} \times 10 \times 12$

$= 60$

L.A. $= 4 \times 60 = 240$

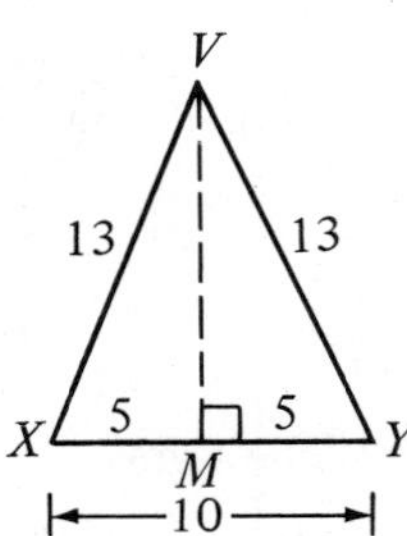


one lateral face

**b.** T.A. $=$ L.A. $+ B$

$= 240 + 10^2$

$= 340$

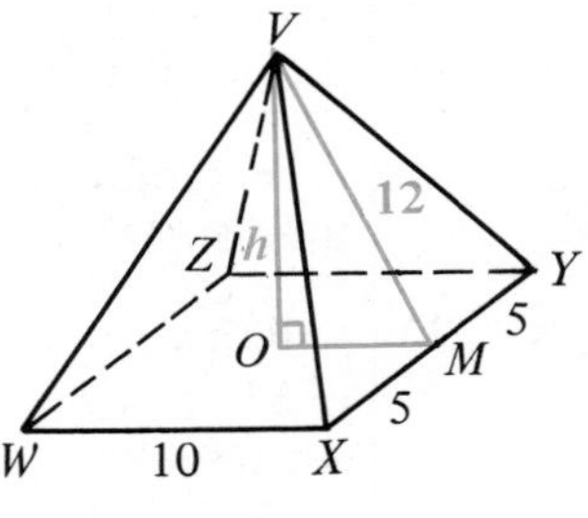


**c.** To find the volume, we need to find the height, $h$. To do this, we use right $\triangle VOM$. We know from part (a) that $VM = 12$. We also know that $OM = 5$. (Why?) Now we can use the Pythagorean Theorem to find $h$.

$$h^2 + 5^2 = 12^2$$
$$h^2 + 25 = 144$$
$$h^2 = 119$$
$$h = \sqrt{119}$$

Recall the formula for the volume of a pyramid:

$$V = \frac{1}{3}Bh$$
$$= \frac{1}{3} \times 10^2 \times \sqrt{119}$$
$$= \frac{100}{3}\sqrt{119}$$

**EXAMPLE 2** For the cone shown, find:

**a.** the lateral area;

**b.** the total area;

**c.** the volume.

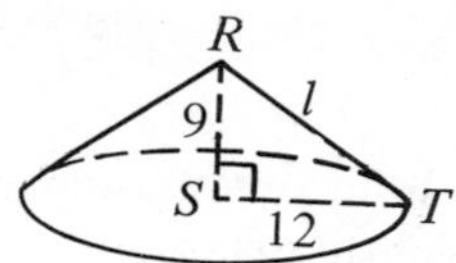


**a.** To find the lateral area, we must find $l$, the slant height of the cone. Notice that $\triangle RST$ is a 9-12-15 triangle with $l = 15$.

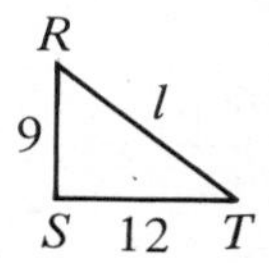


$$\begin{aligned} \text{L.A.} &= \pi r l \\ &= \pi \times 12 \times 15 \\ &= 180\pi \end{aligned}$$

**b.**
$$\begin{aligned} \text{T.A.} &= \text{L.A.} + B \\ &= 180\pi + \pi r^2 \\ &= 180\pi + (\pi \times 12^2) \\ &= 324\pi \end{aligned}$$

**c.**
$$\begin{aligned} V &= \frac{1}{3}Bh \\ &= \frac{1}{3}\pi r^2 h \\ &= \frac{1}{3}\pi \times 12^2 \times 9 \\ &= 432\pi \end{aligned}$$

## Classroom Practice

**Exercises 1–7 refer to the regular square pyramid shown.**

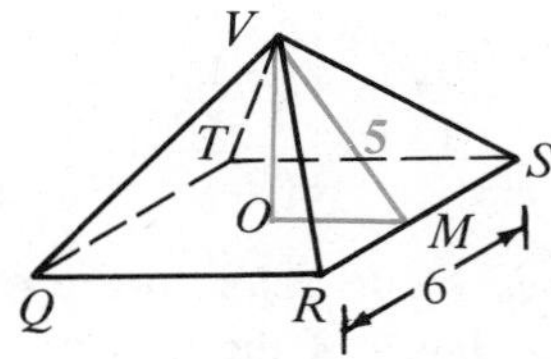


1. The area of lateral face $VRS$ = __?__. 15
2. The lateral area of the pyramid = __?__. 60
3. The area of the base = __?__. 36
4. The total area of the pyramid = __?__. 96
5. $OM$ = __?__ 3
6. The height, $VO$, of the pyramid = __?__. 4
7. The volume of the pyramid = __?__. 48

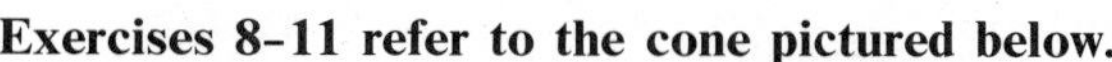

**Exercises 8–11 refer to the cone pictured below.**

8. The lateral area of the cone = __?__. $255\pi$
9. The total area of the cone = __?__. $480\pi$
10. The height, $h$, of the cone = __?__. 8
11. The volume of the cone = __?__. $600\pi$

## Written Exercises

**Exercises 1–6 refer to the regular square pyramid shown. Copy and complete the table. Draw an accurate diagram for each exercise if you wish.**

| | | $s$ | $h$ | $l$ | L.A. | T.A. | $V$ |
|---|---|---|---|---|---|---|---|
| A | **1.** | 8 | 3 | ? 5 | ? 80 | ? 144 | ? 64 |
| | **2.** | 10 | 12 | ? 13 | ? 260 | ? 360 | ? 400 |
| | **3.** | 12 | 8 | ? 10 | ? 240 | ? 384 | ? 384 |
| | **4.** | 24 | ? 5 | 13 | ? 624 | ? 1200 | ? 960 |
| | **5.** | 12 | ? 8 | 10 | ? 240 | ? 384 | ? 384 |
| | **6.** | ? $12\sqrt{3}$ | 6 | 12 | ? $288\sqrt{3}$ | ? T.A. $= 288\sqrt{3} + 432$ | ? 864 |

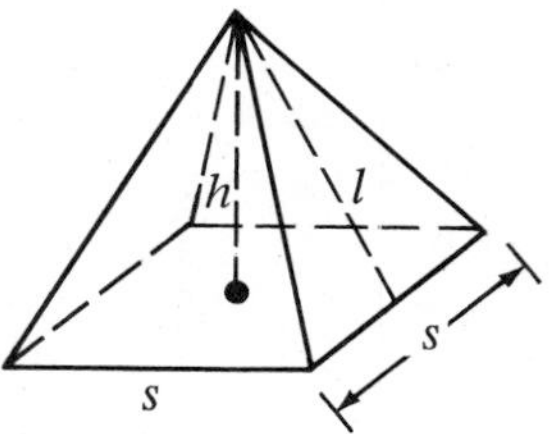


**Exercises 7–12 refer to the cone shown. Copy and complete the table. Draw an accurate diagram for each exercise if you wish.**

| | $r$ | $h$ | $l$ | L.A. | T.A. | $V$ |
|---|---|---|---|---|---|---|
| **7.** | 8 | 6 | ? 10 | ? $80\pi$ | ? $144\pi$ | ? $128\pi$ |
| **8.** | 5 | 12 | ? 13 | ? $65\pi$ | ? $90\pi$ | ? $100\pi$ |
| **9.** | 15 | 8 | ? 17 | ? $255\pi$ | ? $480\pi$ | ? $600\pi$ |
| **10.** | 9 | 12 | ? 15 | ? $135\pi$ | ? $216\pi$ | ? $324\pi$ |
| **11.** | ? 15 | 8 | 17 | ? $255\pi$ | ? $480\pi$ | ? $600\pi$ |
| **12.** | 1 | ? $\sqrt{3}$ | 2 | ? $2\pi$ | ? $3\pi$ | ? $\frac{\sqrt{3}}{3}\pi$ |

**Exercises 13–15 refer to the regular pyramid shown. The four faces of the pyramid are equilateral triangles.**

B **13.** Find the slant height $l$. $2\sqrt{3}$

**14.** Find the lateral area of the pyramid. $12\sqrt{3}$

**15.** Find the total area of the pyramid.
Remember: the four faces are congruent. $16\sqrt{3}$

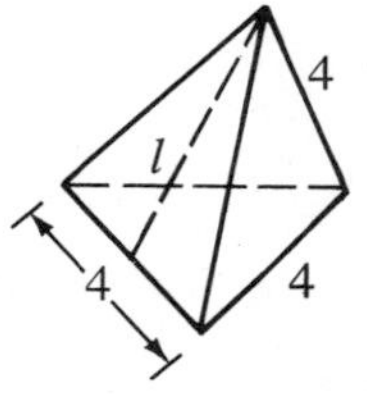


**A regular square pyramid has base edges that are 16 cm long and lateral edges that are 17 cm long. Find each of the following.**

**16.** The slant height of the pyramid 15 cm

**17.** The lateral area of the pyramid 480 cm$^2$

**18.** The total area of the pyramid 736 cm$^2$

**19.** The volume of the pyramid $\frac{256\sqrt{161}}{3}$ cm$^3$

20. A regular square pyramid has base edges that are 18 cm long and lateral edges that are 15 cm long. Find the lateral area, the total area, and the volume of the pyramid. L.A. $= 432$ cm$^2$; T.A. $= 756$ cm$^2$; $V = 324\sqrt{7}$ cm$^3$

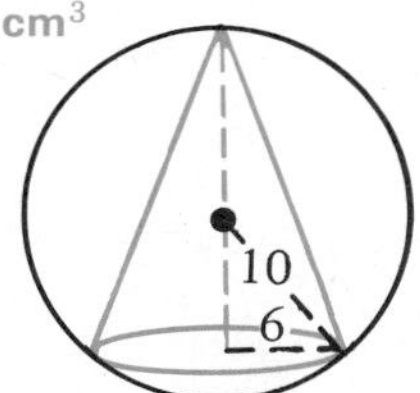


**A cone with radius 6 is inscribed in a sphere with radius 10.**

C 21. Find the height of the cone. 18

22. Find the volume of the cone. $216\pi$

23. Find the volume of the sphere. $\frac{4000}{3}\pi$

## SELF-TEST

1. A rectangular solid is 8 cm long, 8 cm wide, and 4 cm high. Find the length of a diagonal. 12
2. A cone has height 3 and slant height 5. What is its radius? 4
3. Find the volume of the cone described in Exercise 2. $16\pi$
4. A regular square pyramid has height 12 and base edges 10. Find its lateral area. 260

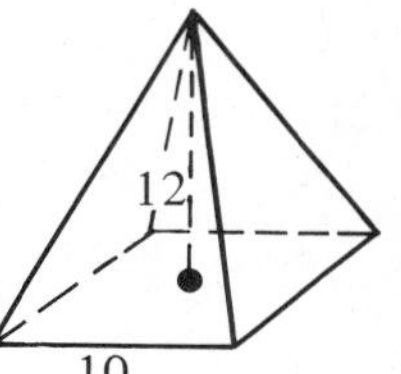


Exercise 4

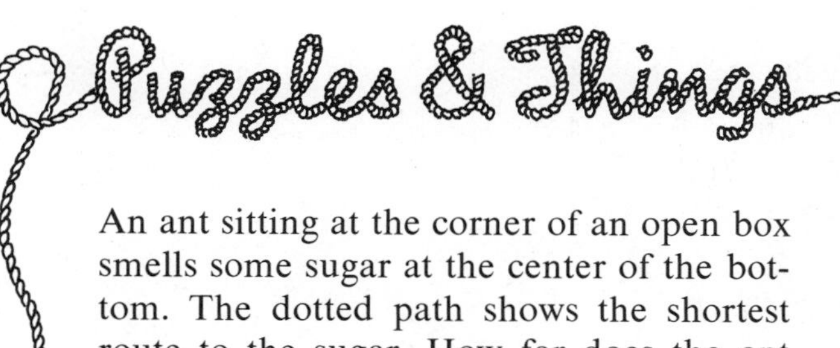


An ant sitting at the corner of an open box smells some sugar at the center of the bottom. The dotted path shows the shortest route to the sugar. How far does the ant have to crawl? 10

*Hint:* Imagine unfolding the box as shown.

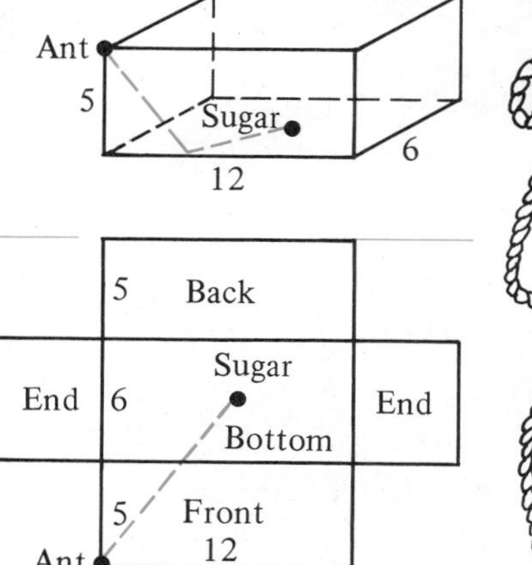

## 6 • The Tangent Ratio

The word *trigonometry* comes from Greek words which mean "triangle measurement." In this course, the study of trigonometry will be limited to *right* triangles.

In each right triangle below, an angle is marked in color. The diagram indicates the leg *adjacent to* (next to) this angle and the leg *opposite* this angle.

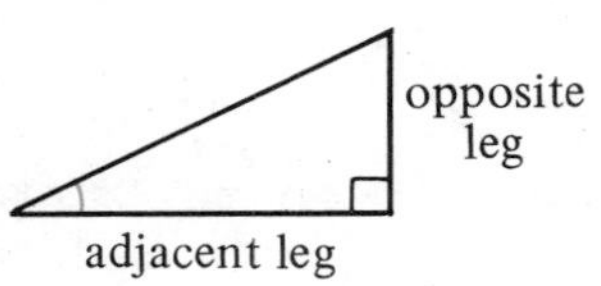


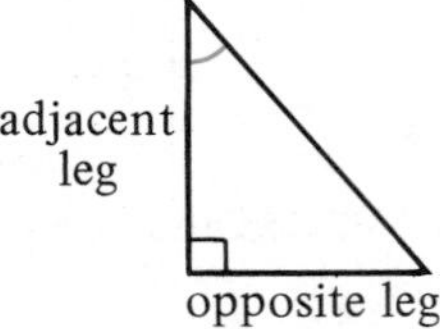


We are now ready to define the first important ratio of trigonometry.

$$\textbf{tangent} \text{ of } \angle A = \frac{\text{leg opposite } \angle A}{\text{leg adjacent to } \angle A}$$

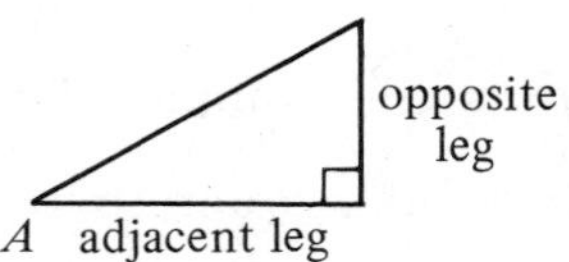


We can abbreviate this by writing:

$$\tan A = \frac{\text{opposite}}{\text{adjacent}}$$

**EXAMPLE 1** In the right triangle shown, find $\tan A$ and $\tan B$.

$$\tan A = \frac{\text{leg opposite } \angle A}{\text{leg adjacent to } \angle A} = \frac{3}{4}$$

$$\tan B = \frac{\text{leg opposite } \angle B}{\text{leg adjacent to } \angle B} = \frac{4}{3}$$

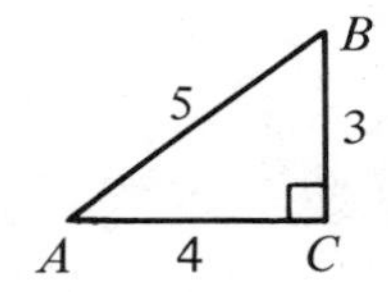


In the right triangles shown, $\angle R = \angle X$.
Do you see that $\triangle RST \sim \triangle XYZ$? (Why?)
Therefore,

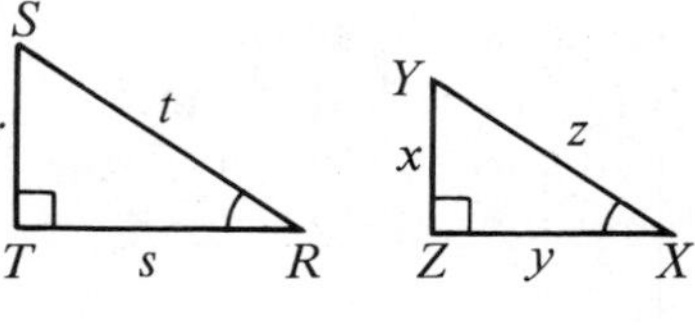


$$\frac{r}{x} = \frac{s}{y}$$ ← Corr. sides of ~ △ are proportional.

$$\frac{r}{s} = \frac{x}{y}$$ ← Use the Switching Property, page 263.

$$\tan R = \tan X$$

The discussion above shows that if $\angle R = \angle X$, then $\tan R = \tan X$. This means that the value of the tangent ratio does not depend on the size of a right triangle, but only on the size of an angle.

On page 418, there is a table that lists values of the tangent ratio for selected acute angles. Most of the values in the table are not exact. They are rounded to the nearest thousandth.

| Angle | Tangent |
|---|---|
| 5° | 0.087 |
| 10° | 0.176 |
| 15° | 0.268 |
| 20° | 0.364 |

Part of the table is shown at the right. Notice that:

$$\tan 15° = 0.268.$$

For convenience, we'll use = rather than ≐.

**EXAMPLE 2** Find the value of $y$ to the nearest tenth.

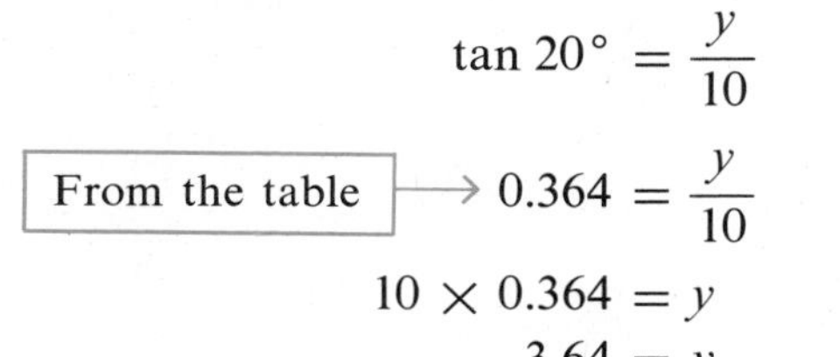

$$\tan 20° = \frac{y}{10}$$

From the table → $0.364 = \frac{y}{10}$

$$10 \times 0.364 = y$$

$$3.64 = y$$

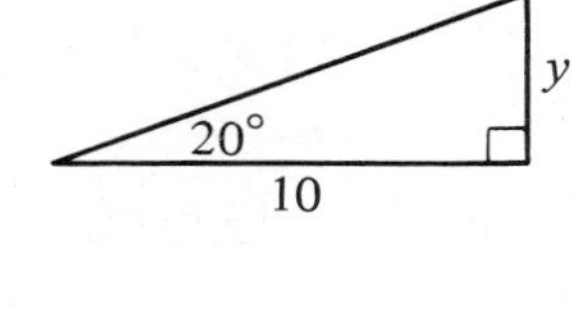


To the nearest tenth, $y = 3.6$.

## *Classroom Practice*

**Use the table on page 418 to complete the following.**

1. $\tan 15° =$ ___?___ 0.268
2. $\tan 30° =$ ___?___ 0.577
3. $\tan 65° =$ ___?___ 2.145
4. tan ___?___ $= 0.364$ 20°
5. tan ___?___ $= 1.732$ 60°
6. tan ___?___ $= 0.087$ 5°

**Use the definition of tangent to find the value of tan *A* for each right triangle shown. Express your answers in simplest form.**

7. $\frac{1}{2}$

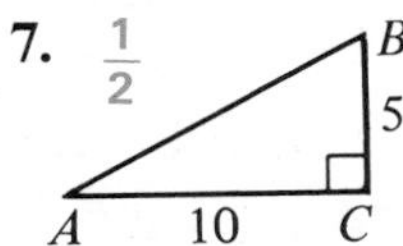


8. $\frac{5}{8}$

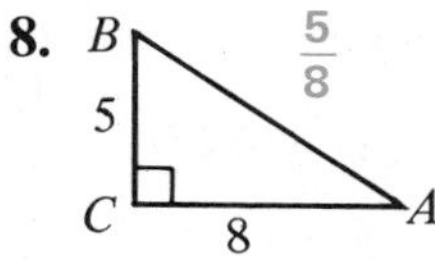


9. $\frac{4}{3}$

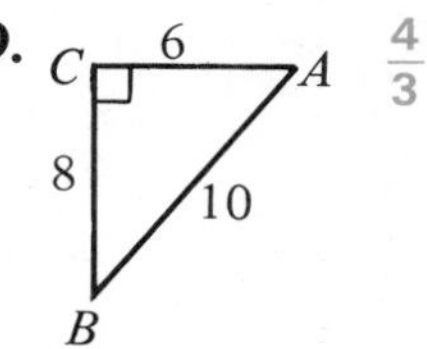


10–12. Find tan *B* for each right triangle above. Express your answers in simplest form. 10. 2 11. $\frac{8}{5}$ 12. $\frac{3}{4}$

13. What do you know about the legs of a 45°-45°-90° triangle? They are equal.

14. Without using the table, state the value of tan 45°. 1

**15.** The diagram shows a 30°-60°-90° triangle. The length of the longer leg is exactly $\sqrt{3}$. This is approximately 1.732.

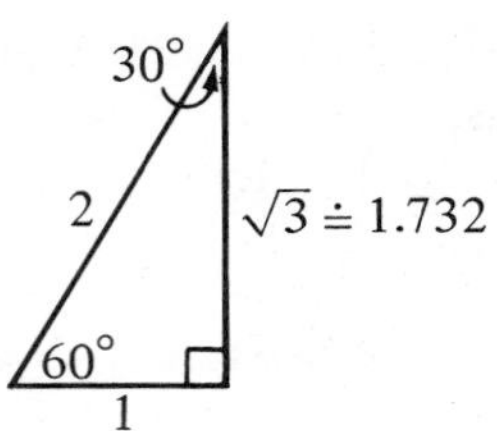


**a.** Using the diagram, find tan 60°. 1.732

**b.** Using the table, find tan 60°. 1.732

**There are two ways to find the value of *t*.**

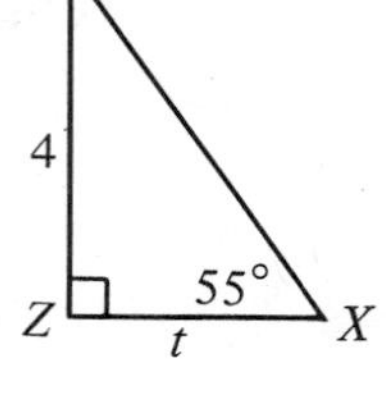


**16. a.** From the figure, $\tan 55° = \frac{?}{?}$. $\frac{4}{t}$

**b.** Use the table: tan 55° = _?_. 1.428

**c.** From parts (a) and (b) we have $1.428 = \frac{4}{t}$.

Then $1.428t = 4$, and $t = \frac{4}{1.428}$.

Correct to tenths, $t$ = _?_. 2.8

**17.** Here is an easier way to find the value of *t*.

**a.** Find the measure of $\angle Y$. 35°

**b.** From the figure, $\tan Y = \frac{?}{?}$. $\frac{t}{4}$

**c.** Use the table to find the value of tan *Y*. 0.700

**d.** From parts (b) and (c) we have $0.700 = \frac{t}{4}$.

Correct to tenths, $t$ = _?_. 2.8

**e.** Compare your answer for part (d) with your answer for Exercise 16, part (c). They are the same.

## *Written Exercises*

**Use the table on page 418 to complete the following.**

A **1.** tan 5° = _?_ 0.087 **2.** tan 25° = _?_ 0.466 **3.** tan 70° = _?_ 2.747

**4.** tan _?_ = 3.732 75° **5.** tan _?_ = 0.577 30° **6.** tan _?_ = 0.176 10°

**Find tan *A* and tan *B* for each right triangle shown. Express your answers in simplest form.**

**7.**

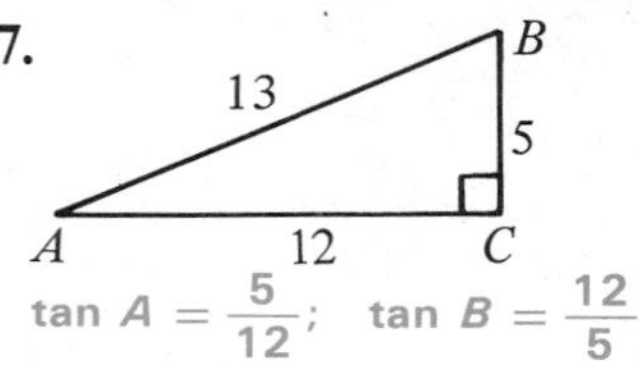


$\tan A = \frac{5}{12}$; $\tan B = \frac{12}{5}$

**8.**

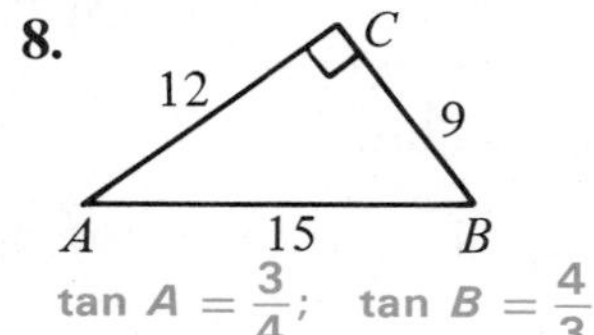


$\tan A = \frac{3}{4}$; $\tan B = \frac{4}{3}$

**9.** A 4 C, 4, $4\sqrt{2}$, B  tan $A = 1$; tan $B = 1$

**10.** 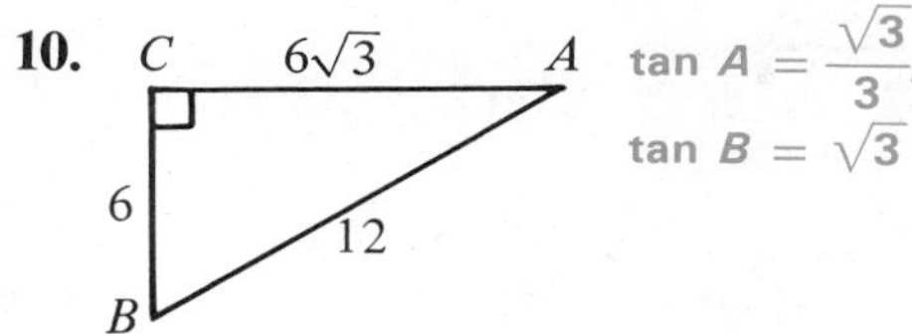

tan $A = \frac{\sqrt{3}}{3}$; tan $B = \sqrt{3}$

**Find the value of $y$ to the nearest tenth. Use the table on page 418.**

**11.** 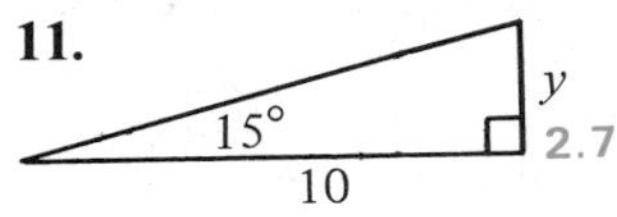

2.7

**12.** 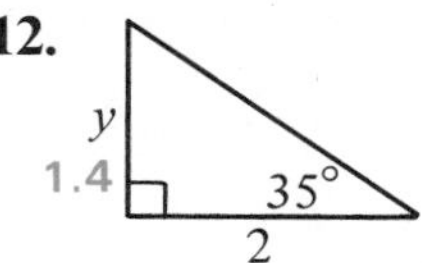

1.4

**13.** 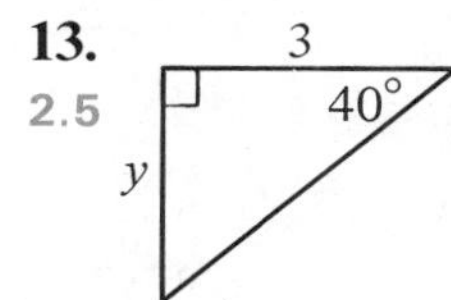

2.5

B **14.** 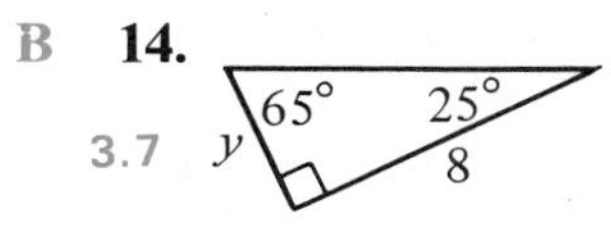

3.7

**15.** 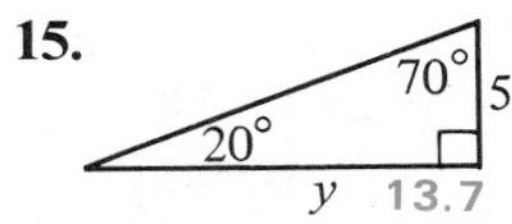

13.7

**16.** 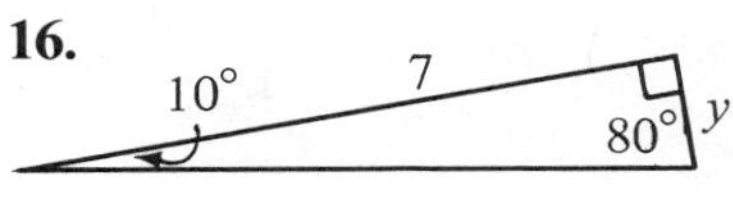


**17.** The diagram shows the path of an airplane after take-off. Find $x$, the altitude of the plane, to the nearest 10 m. 20 m

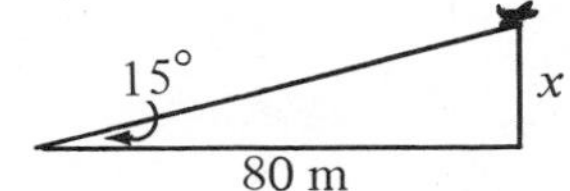


**18.** The shadow of a building is 40 m long. The angle between the ground and the line to the sun is 35°. Find $x$, the height of the building, to the nearest 10 m. 30 m

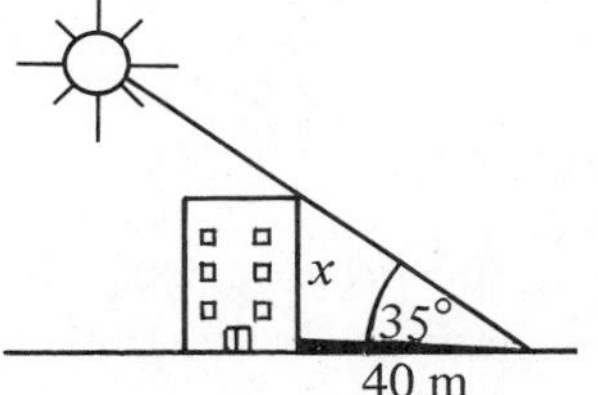


**For each right triangle shown, do three things:**

**a. find tan $A$ as a fraction;**

**b. find tan $A$ as a decimal;**

**c. find the measure of $\angle A$ to the nearest five degrees by using the table on page 418.**

C **19.** 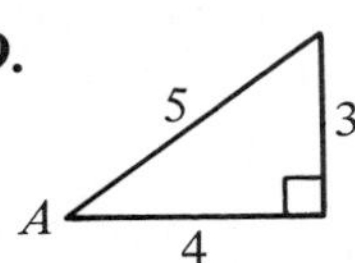

a. $\frac{3}{4}$ b. 0.75 c. 35°

**20.** 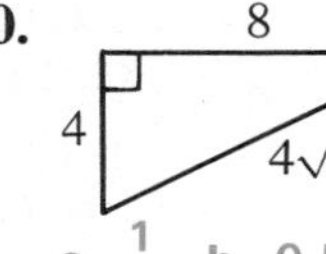
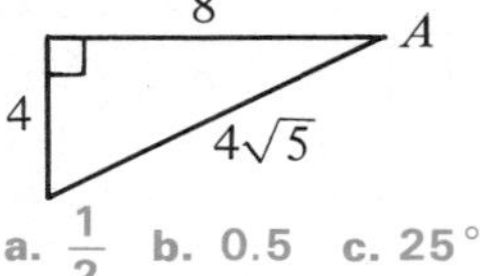

a. $\frac{1}{2}$ b. 0.5 c. 25°

**21.** 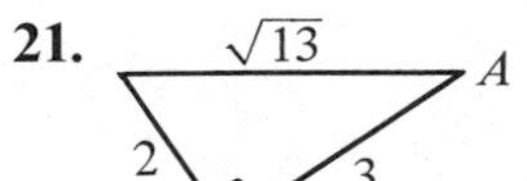
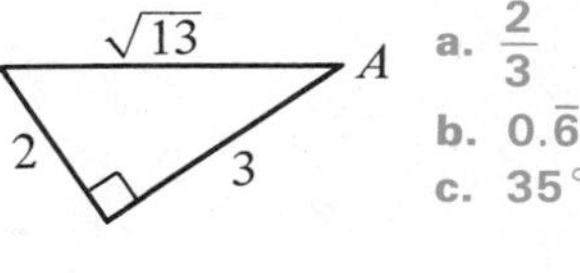

a. $\frac{2}{3}$ b. $0.\overline{6}$ c. 35°

**Exercises 22–24 refer to the rectangular solid shown.**

**22.** $x =$ _?_ 5

**23.** tan $\angle ABC =$ _?_ 0.4

**24.** To the nearest five degrees, $\angle ABC =$ _?_°. 20

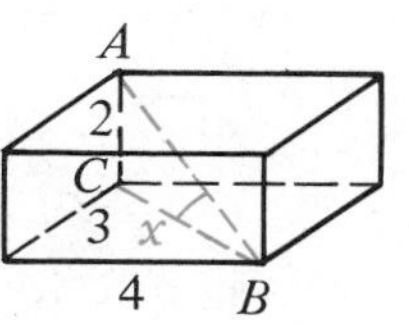

## 7 • The Sine and Cosine Ratios

The tangent ratio involves the two legs of a right triangle. Two other important trigonometric ratios involve the hypotenuse and a leg of a right triangle. These ratios are called the *sine* and the *cosine*.

**Trigonometric Ratios**

**tangent** of $\angle A = \dfrac{\text{leg opposite } \angle A}{\text{leg adjacent to } \angle A}$

**sine** of $\angle A = \dfrac{\text{leg opposite } \angle A}{\text{hypotenuse}}$

**cosine** of $\angle A = \dfrac{\text{leg adjacent to } \angle A}{\text{hypotenuse}}$

hypotenuse
opposite leg
A
adjacent leg

We write:

$$\tan A = \frac{\text{opposite}}{\text{adjacent}} \qquad \sin A = \frac{\text{opposite}}{\text{hypotenuse}} \qquad \cos A = \frac{\text{adjacent}}{\text{hypotenuse}}$$

In the previous section, we used the table on page 418 in our work with tangents. Notice that the table lists values of the sine ratio and the cosine ratio, in addition to those of the tangent ratio. Remember that most of the values are approximate. We shall use the trigonometric table in the examples which follow.

**EXAMPLE 1** Find the value of $y$ to the nearest tenth.

10
$y$
20°

$$\sin 20^\circ = \frac{\text{opposite}}{\text{hypotenuse}}$$

$$\sin 20^\circ = \frac{y}{10}$$

From the table → $0.342 = \dfrac{y}{10}$

$$10 \times 0.342 = y$$

$$3.42 = y$$

To the nearest tenth, $y = 3.4$.

**EXAMPLE 2** A guy wire is stretched from the top of a tower to a point 10 m from the base of the tower. The wire makes a 65° angle with the ground. Find $z$, the length of the wire, to the nearest meter.

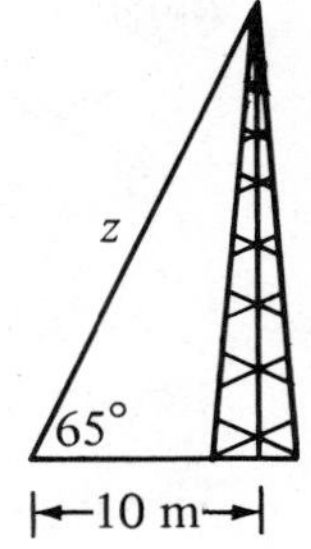


$$\cos 65° = \frac{\text{adjacent}}{\text{hypotenuse}}$$

$$0.423 = \frac{10}{z}$$

$$0.423z = 10$$

$$z = \frac{10}{0.423}$$

To the nearest meter, $z = 24$ m.

**EXAMPLE 3** Find the measure of $\angle A$ to the nearest five degrees.

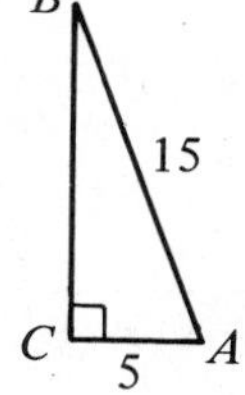


The given sides of the triangle are the leg adjacent to $\angle A$ and the hypotenuse. Therefore, we use the cosine ratio.

1. Find $\cos A$ as a fraction: $\cos A = \frac{\text{adjacent}}{\text{hypotenuse}}$

   $\cos A = \frac{5}{15} = \frac{1}{3}$

2. Express $\cos A$ as a decimal:

   $\cos A = 0.333\ldots$

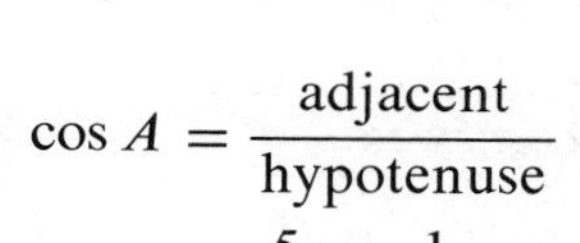


3. Look in the table under *Cosine* to find the entry closest to 0.333.

To the nearest five degrees, $\angle A = 70°$.

## Classroom Practice

**Match each name with the correct expression.**

**1.** sine b. **a.** $\frac{\text{opposite}}{\text{adjacent}}$

**2.** cosine c. **b.** $\frac{\text{opposite}}{\text{hypotenuse}}$

**3.** tangent a. **c.** $\frac{\text{adjacent}}{\text{hypotenuse}}$

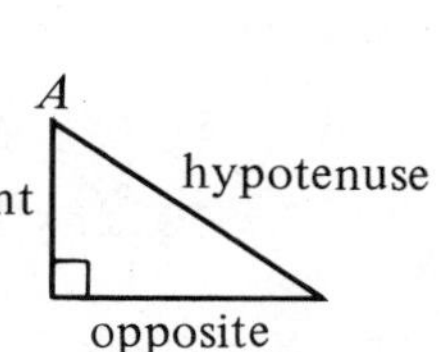

**Refer to $\triangle PQR$. Find each ratio.**

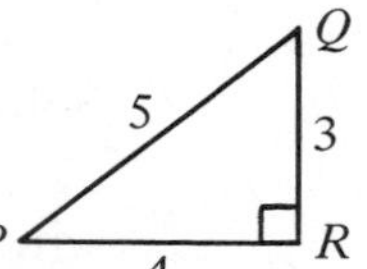


4. $\sin P$ $\frac{3}{5}$ 5. $\cos P$ $\frac{4}{5}$ 6. $\tan P$ $\frac{3}{4}$
7. $\sin Q$ $\frac{4}{5}$ 8. $\cos Q$ $\frac{3}{5}$ 9. $\tan Q$ $\frac{4}{3}$

**Use the table on page 418 to find the following.**

10. $\sin 25°$ 0.423 11. $\cos 40°$ 0.766 12. $\tan 75°$ 3.732 13. $\sin 50°$ 0.766

**Use the table on page 418 to find the measure of each angle to the nearest five degrees.**

14. $\sin A = 0.259$ 15° 15. $\cos P = 0.643$ 50° 16. $\tan R = 0.375$ 20° 17. $\sin S = 0.350$ 20°

**In each exercise, state an equation you could use to find the value of $x$.**

18.

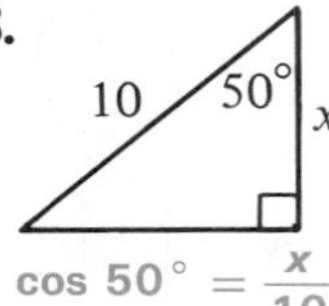


$\cos 50° = \frac{x}{10}$

19.

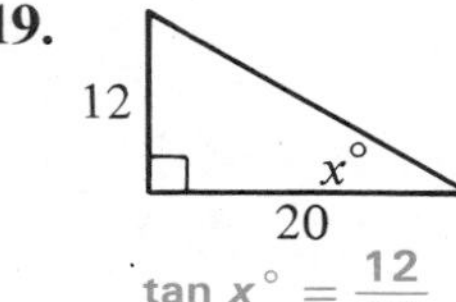


$\tan x° = \frac{12}{20}$

20.

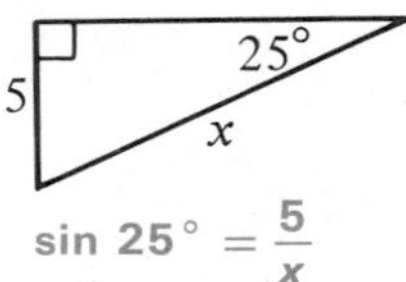


$\sin 25° = \frac{5}{x}$

## *Written Exercises*

**Use the table on page 418 to find the following.**

A 1. $\sin 5°$ 0.087 2. $\cos 15°$ 0.966 3. $\tan 45°$ 1 4. $\cos 80°$ 0.174

**Use the table on page 418 to find the measure of $\angle A$ to the nearest five degrees.**

5. $\sin A = 0.966$ 75° 6. $\cos A = 0.574$ 55° 7. $\tan A = 2.140$ 65° 8. $\cos A = 0.490$ 60°

**Refer to $\triangle ABC$. Find each ratio.**

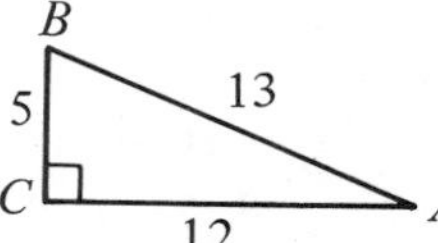


9. $\sin A$ $\frac{5}{13}$ 10. $\cos A$ $\frac{12}{13}$ 11. $\tan A$ $\frac{5}{12}$
12. $\sin B$ $\frac{12}{13}$ 13. $\cos B$ $\frac{5}{13}$ 14. $\tan B$ $\frac{12}{5}$

15. In $\triangle ABC$ above, $\tan B = \frac{12}{5} = 2.400$. Use the trigonometric table to find the measure of $\angle B$ to the nearest five degrees. 65°

**Refer to $\triangle XYZ$. Find each ratio.**

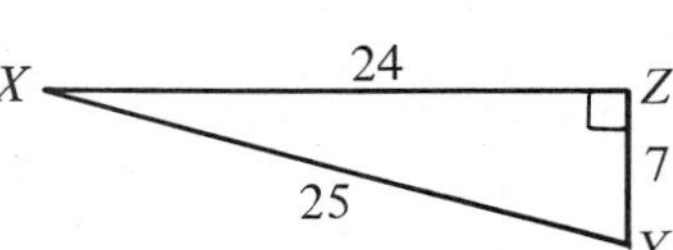


16. $\sin X$ $\frac{7}{25}$ 17. $\cos X$ $\frac{24}{25}$ 18. $\tan X$ $\frac{7}{24}$
19. $\sin Y$ $\frac{24}{25}$ 20. $\cos Y$ $\frac{7}{25}$ 21. $\tan Y$ $\frac{24}{7}$

22. In $\triangle XYZ$ above, $\sin X = \frac{7}{25} = 0.280$. Use the trigonometric table to find the measure of $\angle X$ to the nearest five degrees. 15°

**23.** Find sin $A$ as a fraction. $\frac{1}{2}$ **24.** Find sin $A$ as a decimal. 0.5

**25.** Use the table to find the measure of $\angle A$ to the nearest five degrees. $30°$

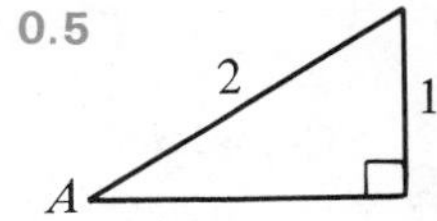


**26.** Find cos $B$ as a fraction. $\frac{9}{10}$ **27.** Find cos $B$ as a decimal. 0.9

**28.** Use the table to find the measure of $\angle B$ to the nearest five degrees. $25°$

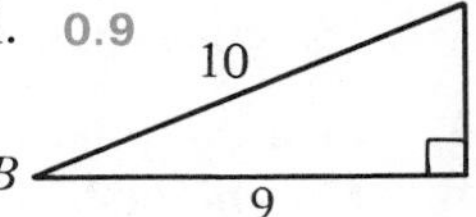


**Find the value of $y$ to the nearest tenth. Use the table on page 418.**

**29.**

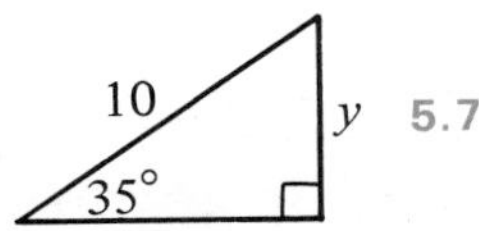


5.7

**30.**

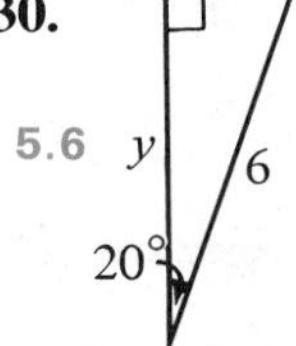


5.6

**31.**

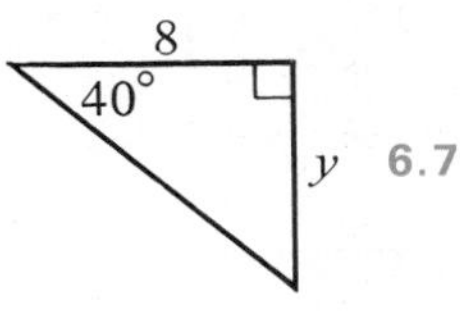


6.7

B **32.** 4.7

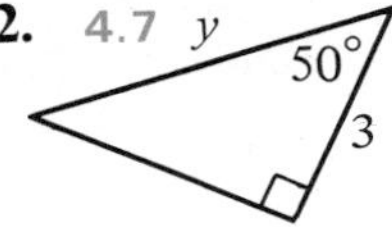


**33.**

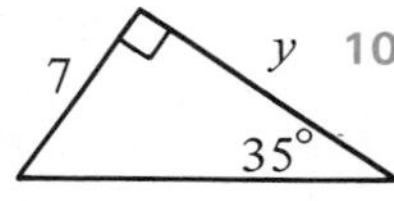


10

**34.**

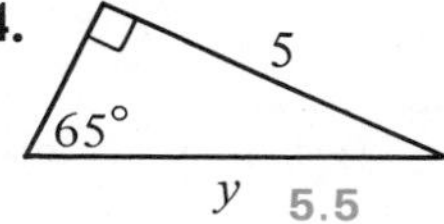


5.5

**35.** A ladder is 4 m long. It is leaning against a house at a $70°$ angle with the ground. How far up the side of the house does the ladder reach? 3.8 m

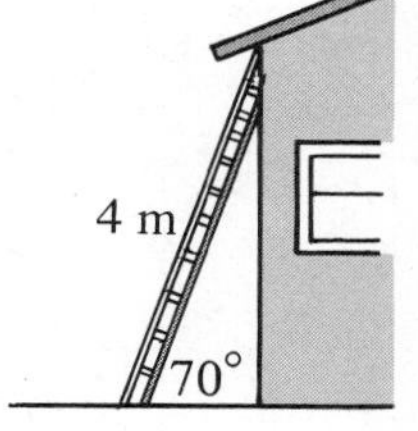


**36.** A golfer stands 100 m from the Number 7 hole. The golfer's aim is poor, and the ball goes $20°$ off course and lands at the right of the hole.

**a.** How far is the ball from the hole? 36.4 m

**b.** How far is the ball from the golfer? 106.4 m

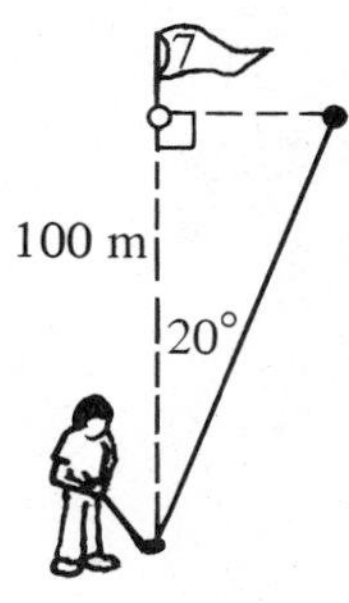


**Find the measure of $\angle A$ to the nearest five degrees.**

C **37.**

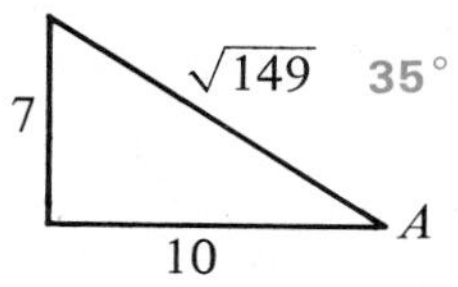


$35°$

**38.**

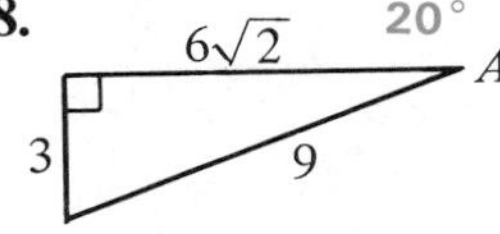


$20°$

**39.** $75°$

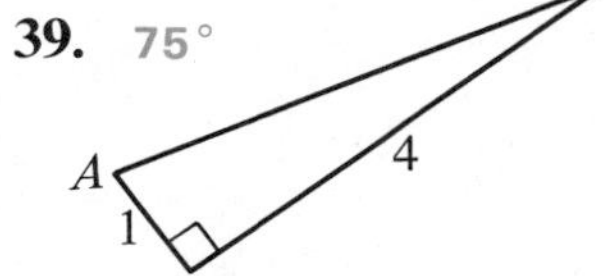

## SELF-TEST

**Complete.**

B, 8, 17, C, 15, A

1. tan $A$ = ___?___ $\frac{8}{15}$
2. sin $A$ = ___?___ $\frac{8}{17}$
3. cos $B$ = ___?___ $\frac{8}{17}$
4. sin $B$ = ___?___ $\frac{15}{17}$

**Find the values of $x$, $y$, and $z$ to the nearest tenth. Use the table below.**

**5.**

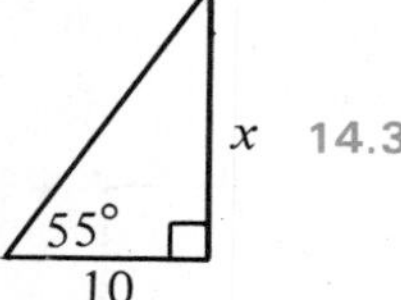


14.3

**6.**

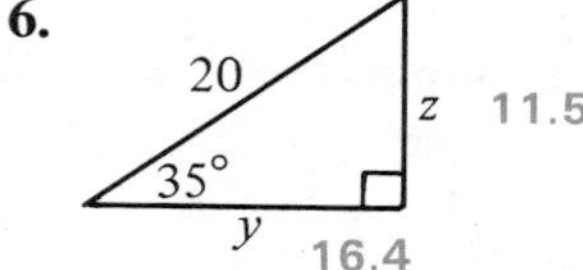


11.5

16.4

### Table of Trigonometric Ratios

| Angle | Sine | Cosine | Tangent |
|---|---|---|---|
| 5° | 0.087 | 0.996 | 0.087 |
| 10° | 0.174 | 0.985 | 0.176 |
| 15° | 0.259 | 0.966 | 0.268 |
| 20° | 0.342 | 0.940 | 0.364 |
| 25° | 0.423 | 0.906 | 0.466 |
| 30° | 0.500 | 0.866 | 0.577 |
| 35° | 0.574 | 0.819 | 0.700 |
| 40° | 0.643 | 0.766 | 0.839 |
| 45° | 0.707 | 0.707 | 1.000 |

| Angle | Sine | Cosine | Tangent |
|---|---|---|---|
| 50° | 0.766 | 0.643 | 1.192 |
| 55° | 0.819 | 0.574 | 1.428 |
| 60° | 0.866 | 0.500 | 1.732 |
| 65° | 0.906 | 0.423 | 2.145 |
| 70° | 0.940 | 0.342 | 2.747 |
| 75° | 0.966 | 0.259 | 3.732 |
| 80° | 0.985 | 0.174 | 5.671 |
| 85° | 0.996 | 0.087 | 11.430 |

## Reviewing Algebraic Skills

**Simplify.**

Samples $\frac{-5x^2}{20xy} = \frac{-1 \cdot 5 \cdot x \cdot x}{4 \cdot 5 \cdot x \cdot y} = \frac{-x}{4y}$ *or* $-\frac{x}{4y}$

$\frac{7x - 21}{x^2 - 9} = \frac{7(x - 3)}{(x + 3)(x - 3)} = \frac{7}{x + 3}$

**1.** $\frac{-3a^2b^2}{12ab^2}$ $-\frac{a}{4}$ **2.** $\frac{2h^4k^5}{10h^3k}$ $\frac{hk^4}{5}$ **3.** $\frac{11b^2c^4}{-33bc^2}$ $-\frac{bc^2}{3}$ **4.** $\frac{-4r^3s}{-16rt}$ $\frac{r^2s}{4t}$

**5.** $\frac{2m}{am + bm}$ $\frac{2}{a + b}$ **6.** $\frac{6x^2}{3xy - 9x^2}$ $\frac{2x}{y - 3x}$ **7.** $\frac{2a + 2b}{a^2 - b^2}$ $\frac{2}{a - b}$ **8.** $\frac{x + 4}{x^2 + 6x + 8}$ $\frac{1}{x + 2}$

**9.** $\frac{a^2 - 64}{a + 8}$ $a - 8$ **10.** $\frac{6r - 6s}{r^2 - s^2}$ $\frac{6}{r + s}$ **11.** $\frac{d^2 - 2d - 15}{13d + 39}$ $\frac{d - 5}{13}$ **12.** $\frac{3a - 21}{a^2 - 14a + 49}$ $\frac{3}{a - 7}$

**Multiply.**

Sample $\frac{a^2 - 2ab + b^2}{10} \cdot \frac{5}{a - b} = \frac{5(a^2 - 2ab + b^2)}{10(a - b)} = \frac{5(a - b)(a - b)}{2 \cdot 5(a - b)} = \frac{a - b}{2}$

**13.** $\frac{x}{y} \cdot \frac{5y}{2x}$ $\frac{5}{2}$ **14.** $\frac{8a^2}{b} \cdot \frac{b^2}{2a}$ $4ab$ **15.** $\frac{a + b}{3} \cdot \frac{9}{ab + b^2}$ $\frac{3}{b}$

**16.** $\frac{7x}{9y} \cdot \frac{18}{35x^2}$ $\frac{2}{5xy}$ **17.** $\frac{4}{x + 2} \cdot \frac{x^2 - 4}{12}$ $\frac{x - 2}{3}$ **18.** $\frac{7x - 21}{3} \cdot \frac{15}{x - 3}$ $35$

**19.** $\frac{x - 5}{y} \cdot \frac{y^3}{x^2 - 25}$ $\frac{y^2}{x + 5}$ **20.** $\frac{m - 3}{m + 3} \cdot \frac{3 + m}{3 - m}$ $-1$ **21.** $\frac{x^2 + 4x + 4}{28} \cdot \frac{7}{x + 2}$ $\frac{x + 2}{4}$

**Divide.**

Sample $\frac{a^3}{3} \div \frac{a^4}{3a^2 + 3} = \frac{a^3}{3} \cdot \frac{3a^2 + 3}{a^4} = \frac{a \cdot a \cdot a \cdot 3(a^2 + 1)}{3 \cdot a \cdot a \cdot a \cdot a} = \frac{a^2 + 1}{a}$

**22.** $\frac{b}{3} \div \frac{1}{9}$ $3b$ **23.** $\frac{m^2}{n^2} \div 2m$ $\frac{m}{2n^2}$ **24.** $3r^2s^2 \div \frac{12s^3}{5t^2}$ $\frac{5r^2t^2}{4s}$

**25.** $\frac{a + b}{12} \div \frac{a + b}{6b}$ $\frac{b}{2}$ **26.** $\frac{2\pi r - 2\pi s}{9} \div \frac{2\pi}{3}$ $\frac{r - s}{3}$ **27.** $\frac{4c - 12}{7} \div (c - 3)$ $\frac{4}{7}$

**28.** $\frac{n^2 - 64}{5} \div (n + 8)$ $\frac{n - 8}{5}$ **29.** $\frac{d^2 + d^3}{2c + 4} \div \frac{d^2}{6}$ $\frac{3(1 + d)}{c + 2}$ **30.** $\frac{3y}{y^2 - 49} \div \frac{1}{y + 7}$ $\frac{3y}{y - 7}$

# extra for experts

## *Finding Areas with Trigonometry*

If you know two sides and the included angle of a triangle, you can find its area using this formula:

**Area $= \frac{1}{2}$(product of two sides) × (sine of included angle)**

Examples

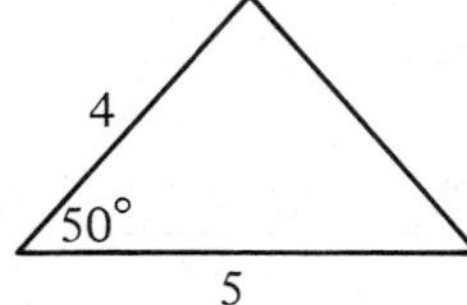


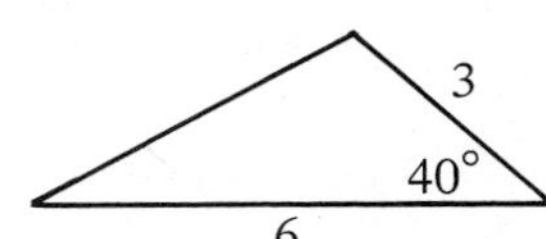


$$\text{Area} = \frac{1}{2}(4 \times 5)\sin 50^\circ = 10 \sin 50^\circ = 10(0.766) = 7.66$$

$$\text{Area} = \frac{1}{2}(6 \times 3)\sin 40^\circ = 9 \sin 40^\circ = 9(0.643) = 5.787$$

Let's see why this new formula works:

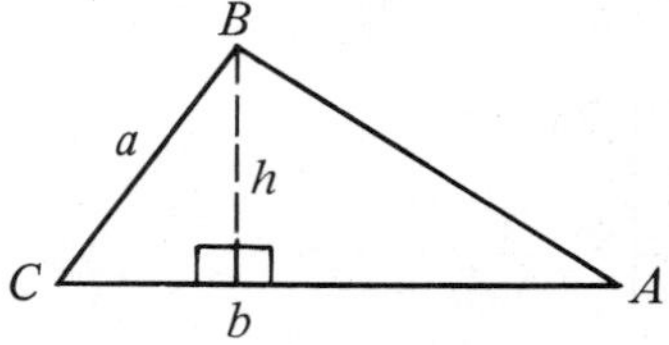


$\sin C = \frac{h}{a}$, so

$a \times \sin C = h$

$$\text{Area} = \frac{1}{2}bh$$

$$= \frac{1}{2}b(a \sin C) \longleftarrow \boxed{\text{Substitute}}$$

$$= \frac{1}{2}ab \sin C$$

$$= \frac{1}{2}(\text{product of sides}) \times (\text{sine of included angle})$$

This formula can be used to find the area of any regular polygon. For example, the area of a regular octagon may be found by circumscribing a circle about it. Then the center of the circle is joined to the vertices of the polygon as shown at the top of page 421. We have 8 isosceles triangles.

$$\text{This angle} = \frac{360°}{\text{number of sides}} = \frac{360°}{8}$$

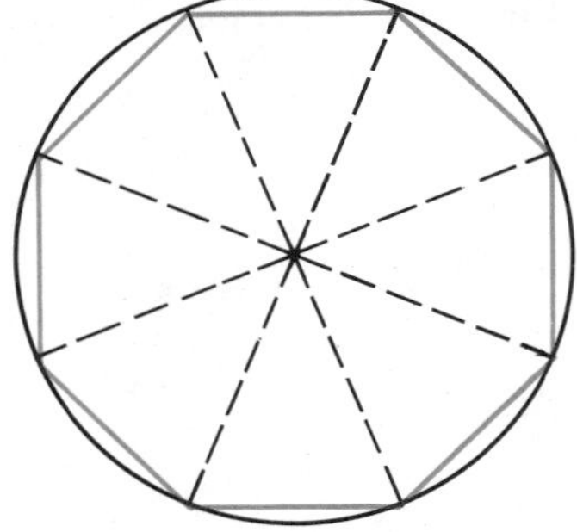

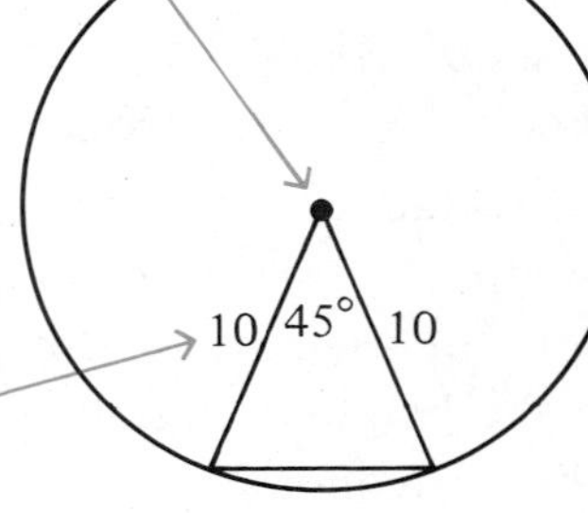


The sides of the triangle are radii of the circle.

Suppose the radius is 10.

$$\text{Area of one triangle} = \frac{1}{2}(\text{product of two sides}) \times (\text{sine of included angle})$$

$$= \frac{1}{2}(10 \times 10) \sin 45° = 50(0.707) = 35.35$$

$$\text{Area of octagon} = 8 \times \text{Area of one triangle}$$

$$= 8 \times 35.35 = 282.80$$

**Exercises**

1. Two sides of a triangle are 5 and 8 and the included angle is 30°. Find the area. 10
2. Two sides of a triangle are 6 and 10 and the included angle is 70°. Find the area. 28.20
3. A regular hexagon is inscribed in a circle with radius 10.

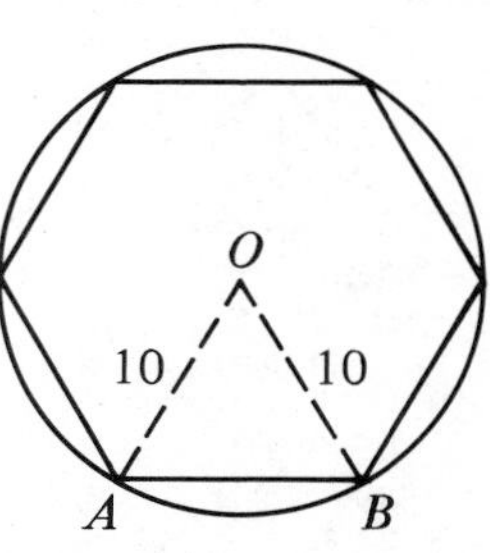


   **a.** Find the measure of $\angle AOB$. 60°
   **b.** Find the area of $\triangle AOB$. 43.3
   **c.** Find the area of the hexagon. 259.8
4. A regular polygon with 12 sides is inscribed in a circle with radius 2. Find the area of the polygon. 12
5. A regular polygon with 9 sides is inscribed in a circle with radius 1. Find the area of the polygon. 2.89

# Reviewing the Chapter

## Chapter Summary

1. Right triangle lengths you should know are included in the table on page 392.
2. In a 45°-45°-90° triangle, the hypotenuse is $\sqrt{2}$ times as long as a leg.
3. In a 30°-60°-90° triangle, the hypotenuse is twice as long as the shorter leg, and the longer leg is $\sqrt{3}$ times as long as the shorter leg.
4. If a rectangular solid has dimensions $a$, $b$, and $c$, then a diagonal has length $d = \sqrt{a^2 + b^2 + c^2}$.
5. You can often use the Pythagorean Theorem to find the slant height or the height of a regular pyramid or cone.
6. Three trigonometric ratios are defined for any acute angle of a right triangle as follows:

$$\tan A = \frac{\text{opposite}}{\text{adjacent}}$$

$$\sin A = \frac{\text{opposite}}{\text{hypotenuse}}$$

$$\cos A = \frac{\text{adjacent}}{\text{hypotenuse}}$$

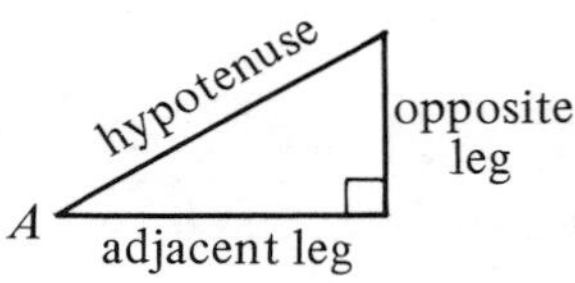


## Chapter Review Test

**Find the exact values of $x$ and $y$.** *(See pp. 392–399.)*

**1.**

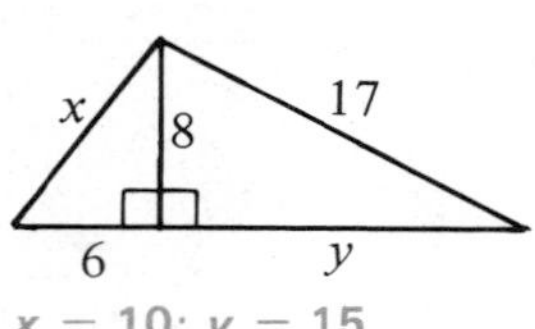


$x = 10$; $y = 15$

**2.**

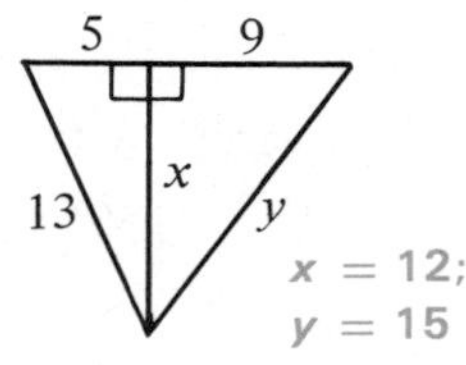


$x = 12$; $y = 15$

**3.**

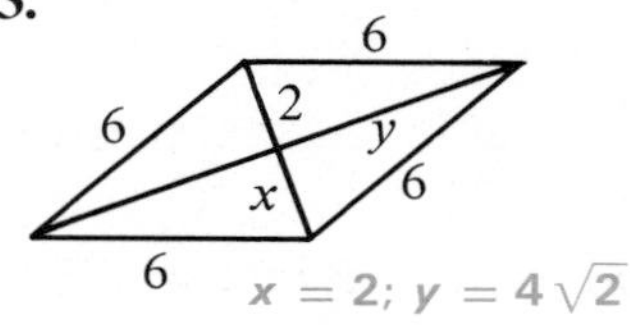


$x = 2$; $y = 4\sqrt{2}$

**4.**

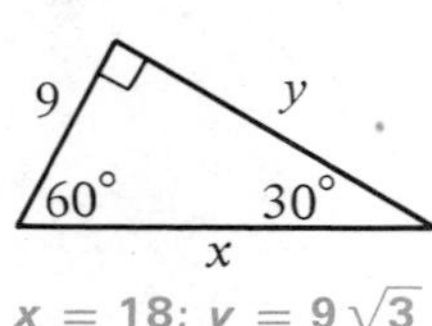


$x = 18$; $y = 9\sqrt{3}$

**5.**

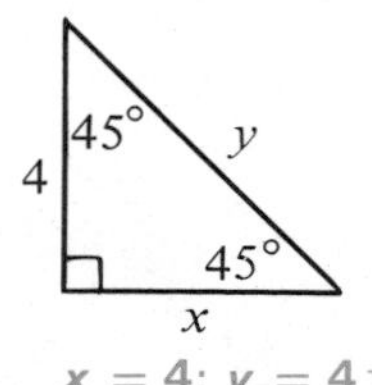


$x = 4$; $y = 4\sqrt{2}$

**6.**

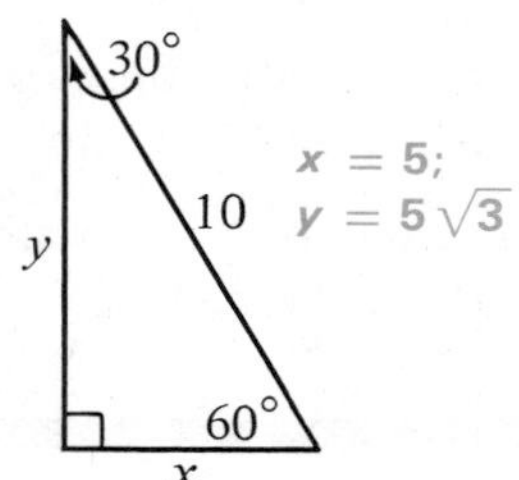


$x = 5$; $y = 5\sqrt{3}$

Find the exact area of each shaded figure. (See pp. 400–402.)

7. $18\sqrt{3}$

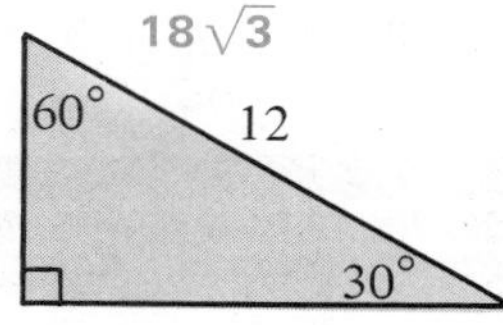


8. 18

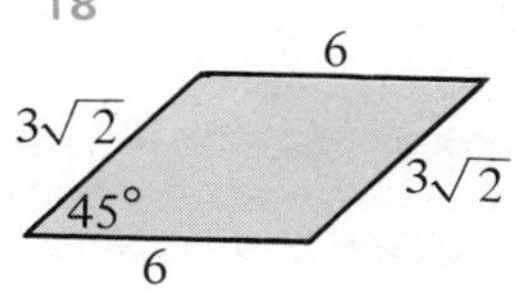


9. $25\sqrt{3}$

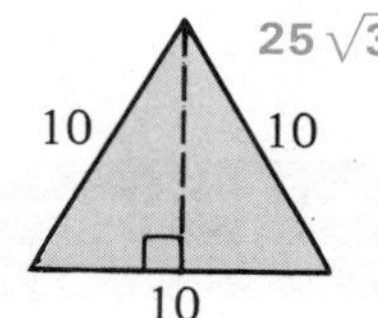


Refer to the rectangular solid shown. (See pp. 403–405.)

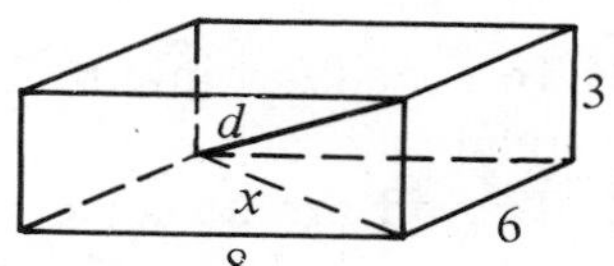


10. Find the value of $x$. 10

11. Find the length of the diagonal $d$. $\sqrt{109}$

Refer to the regular square pyramid and cone shown at the right. (See pp. 406–409.)

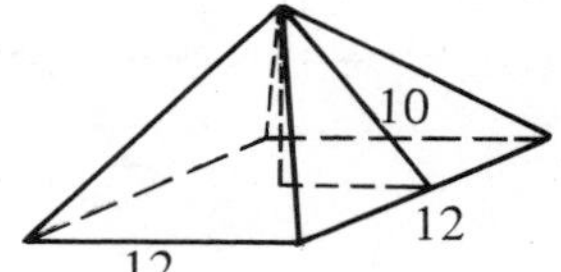


12. Find the lateral area of the pyramid. 240

13. Find the total area of the pyramid. 384

14. Find the height of the pyramid. 8

15. Find the volume of the pyramid. 384

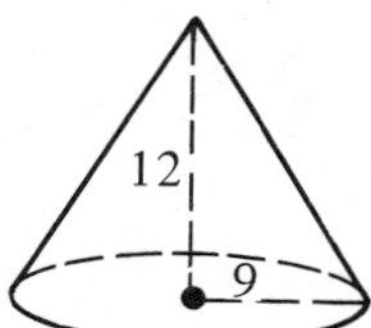


16. Find the slant height of the cone. 15

17. Find the lateral area of the cone. $135\pi$

18. Find the total area of the cone. $216\pi$

19. Find the volume of the cone. $324\pi$

Use the diagram to find the following. (See pp. 410–417.)

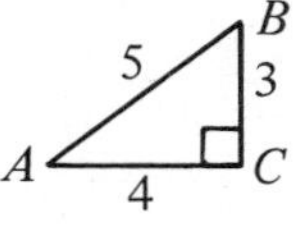


20. $\tan A$ $\frac{3}{4}$

21. $\cos A$ $\frac{4}{5}$

22. $\sin B$ $\frac{4}{5}$

23. $\tan B$ $\frac{4}{3}$

Find the value of $x$ to the nearest tenth. Use the table on page 418.

24. 1.5

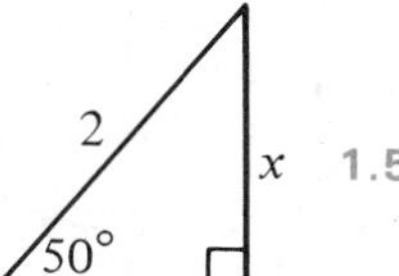


25. 4.7

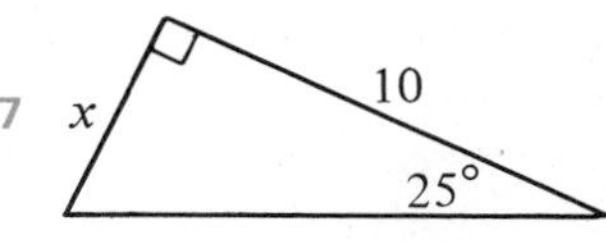


26. 5.6

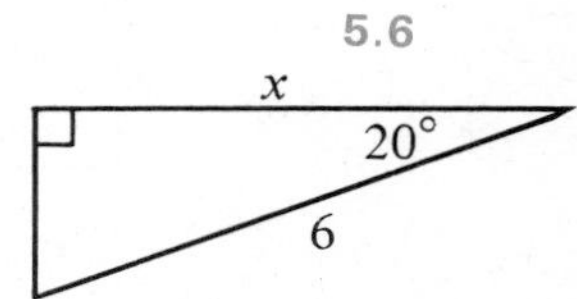

*Here's what you'll learn in this chapter:*

1. To specify points by their coordinates in the coordinate plane.
2. To find the distance between two points in the coordinate plane.
3. To apply the midpoint formula.
4. To find the slope of a line.
5. To find the slopes of parallel and perpendicular lines.
6. To graph the line specified by a given equation.
7. To prove theorems using coordinate geometry.

# Chapter 12

# Coordinate Geometry

# 1 • Points and Coordinates

The *coordinate plane* has an $x$-axis and a $y$-axis, as shown in the diagram. These **coordinate axes** (**ax**-eez) are number lines that intersect in a point called the origin, point $O$. The axes separate the plane into four quadrants.

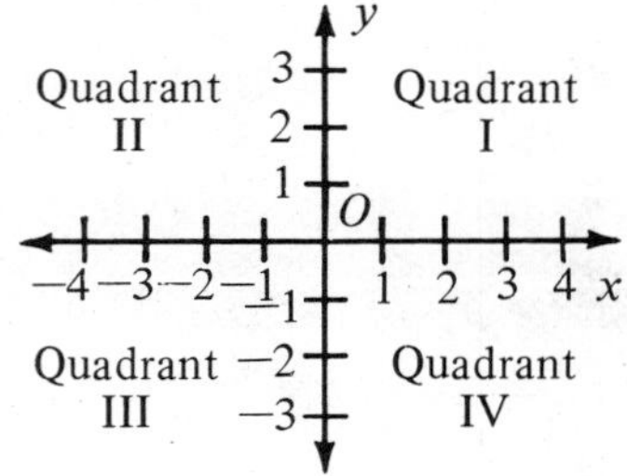


Every point in the coordinate plane can be named by two numbers, called the **coordinates** of the point. In the diagram, the **$x$-coordinate** of point $A$ is 2. The **$y$-coordinate** is 4. We can refer to point $A$ as the point (2, 4). Notice that the origin is the point (0, 0).

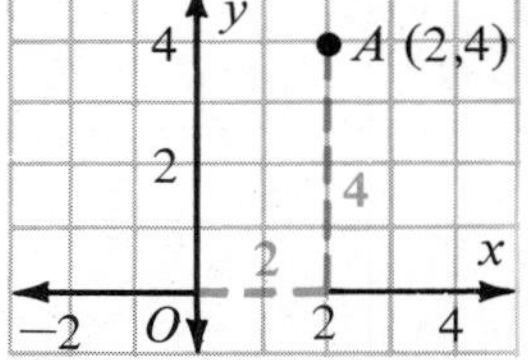


Point $B$, with coordinates $-2$ and 3, has been *plotted* (drawn) in this diagram. We can name point $B$ as the point $(-2, 3)$. Can you name the coordinates of points $C$ and $D$? (Remember that the $x$-coordinate is always named first.)

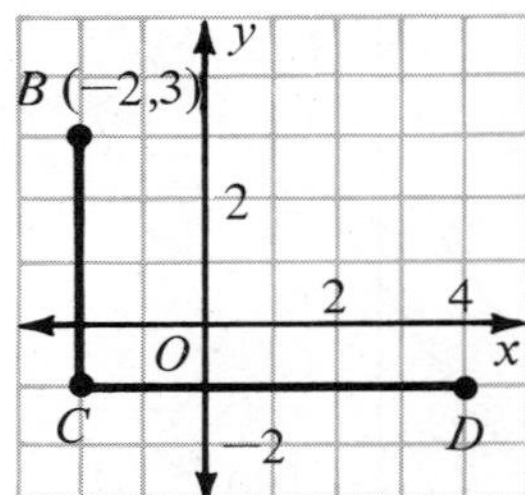


From the diagram you can conclude:

$$BC = 4$$
$$CD = 6$$
$$\angle BCD = 90°$$

## Classroom Practice

**Exercises 1–5 refer to points that are labeled in Figure 1.**

1. Point $B$ lies on an axis, not in a quadrant. Name two other points that do not lie in quadrants. *E, O*
2. Name the points that lie in:
   **a.** quadrant I. *D, A* **b.** quadrant II. *F, G*
   **c.** quadrant III. *H, J* **d.** quadrant IV. *C*
3. Name the points that have:
   **a.** $x$-coordinate 0. *E, O*
   **b.** a positive $x$-coordinate. *A, B, C, D*
   **c.** a negative $x$-coordinate. *F, G, H, J*

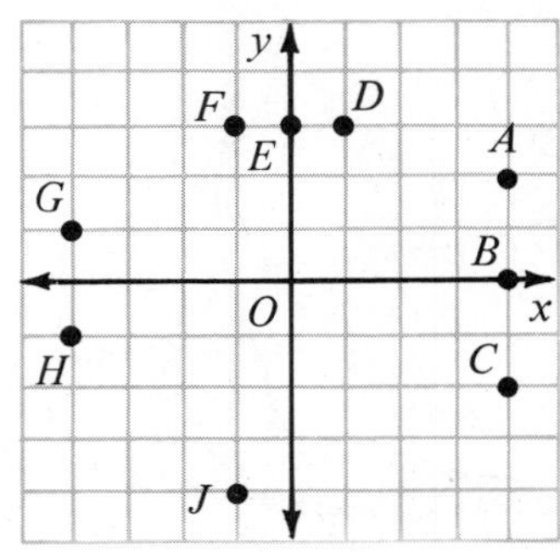


Figure 1

4. Name the points in Figure 1 that have:
   a. $y$-coordinate 0. *B, O*
   b. a positive $y$-coordinate. *A, D, E, F, G*
   c. a negative $y$-coordinate. *C, H, J*

5. State the coordinates of each point in Figure 1. (see below)

6. Think of all the points that lie on the $x$-axis. What can you say about the $y$-coordinate of each of those points? It is zero.

7. Think of all the points that have an $x$-coordinate equal to 0. What can you say about each of those points? They are on the $y$-axis.

8. From the diagram, what can you conclude about $ST$? about $\angle RTS$? $ST = 5$; $\angle RTS = 45°$

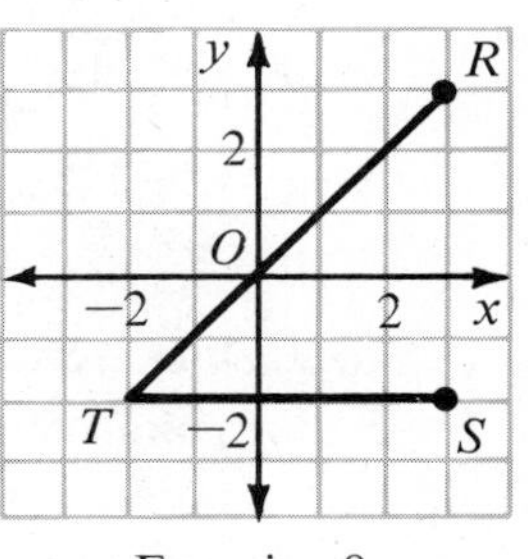

Exercise 8

**The legs of the right triangle are parallel to the coordinate axes. State the coordinates of point $C$.**

9.
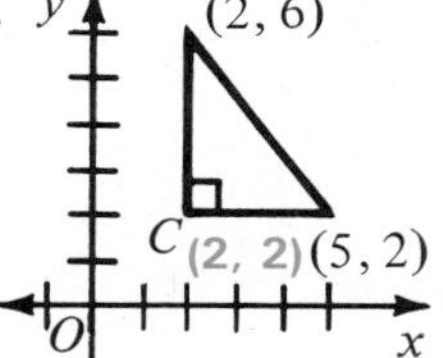


10.
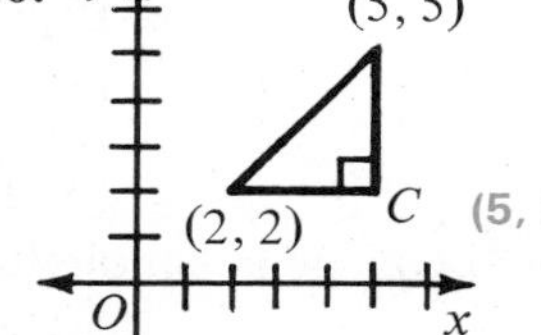


11.
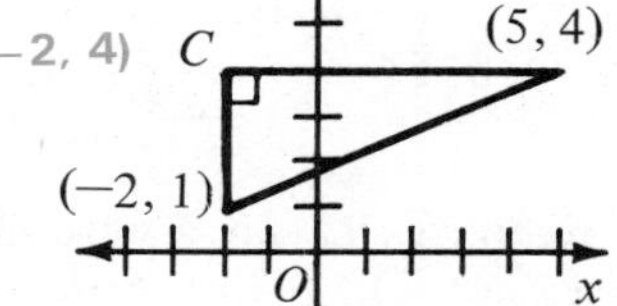


12.
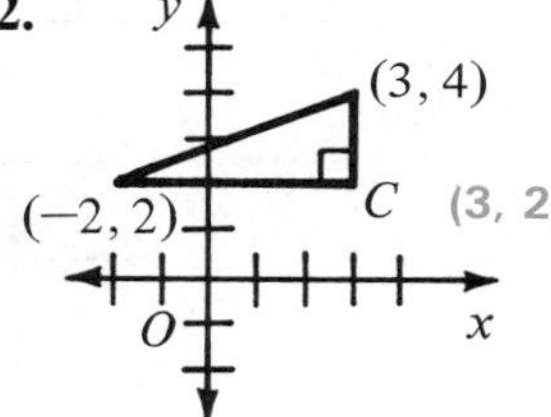


13.
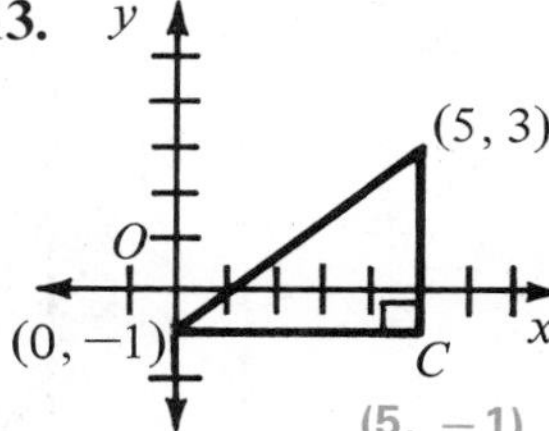


14.
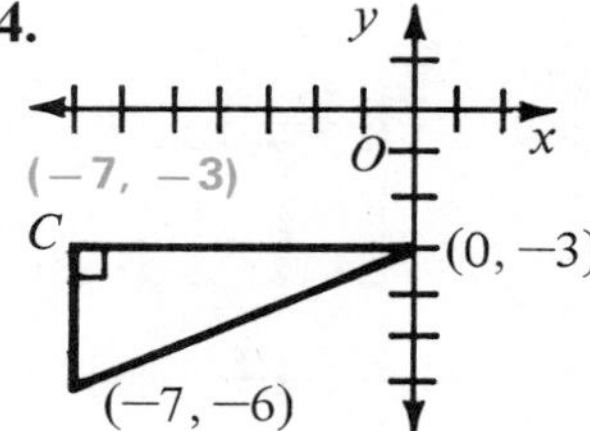


5. $A = (4, 2)$; $B = (4, 0)$; $C = (4, -2)$; $D = (1, 3)$; $E = (0, 3)$; $F = (-1, 3)$; $G = (-4, 1)$; $H = (-4, -1)$; $J = (-1, -4)$; $O = (0, 0)$

## Written Exercises

A 1. Point $(3, -1)$ lies in quadrant _?_ (IV), and point $(-3, 1)$ lies in quadrant _?_. II

2. Are $(-5, -4)$ and $(-4, -5)$ the same point? (No) Do the points lie in the same quadrant? Yes

3. If the $x$-coordinate and the $y$-coordinate of a point are both negative numbers, the point must lie in quadrant _?_. III

4. Point $(-4, 0)$ lies on the __?__ *x* -axis.

5. If the $x$-coordinate of a point is 0, the point must lie on the __?__ *y* -axis.

6. Use the diagram to find the coordinates of each of the labeled points. A(0, 3); B(2, 4); C(3, 1); D(1, 0); E(1, −3); F(3, −4); G(0, −4); H(−3, −2); J(−3, 0); K(−3, 3); L(−2, 2); M(−1, 4)

Sample  $Z(3, -2)$

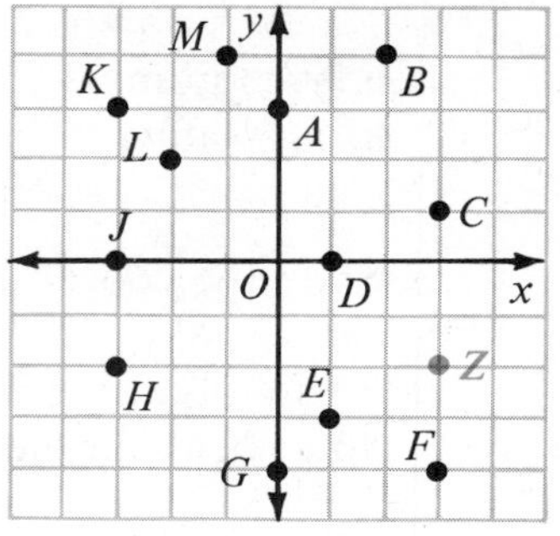

Exercise 6

**For each exercise, draw a pair of coordinate axes.**

**a. Plot points $R$ and $S$. Draw $\overleftrightarrow{RS}$.** **b. State which point ($A$, $B$, or $C$) lies on $\overleftrightarrow{RS}$.**

| | $R$ | $S$ | $A$ | $B$ | $C$ | |
|---|---|---|---|---|---|---|
| **7.** | $(-2, -3)$ | $(-2, 1)$ | $(2, 2)$ | $(4, -2)$ | $(-2, -2)$ | b. C |
| **8.** | $(0, 0)$ | $(-3, 2)$ | $(3, 2)$ | $(-6, 4)$ | $(1, 1)$ | b. B |
| **9.** | $(1, 1)$ | $(2, 2)$ | $(5, 0)$ | $(6, 7)$ | $(-3, -3)$ | b. C |
| **10.** | $(5, 5)$ | $(-5, 0)$ | $(-7, -1)$ | $(-2, 1)$ | $(7, 7)$ | b. A |

**In Exercises 11–16, a base of the rectangle is parallel to the $x$-axis. State the coordinates of points $J$ and $K$.**

**11.**

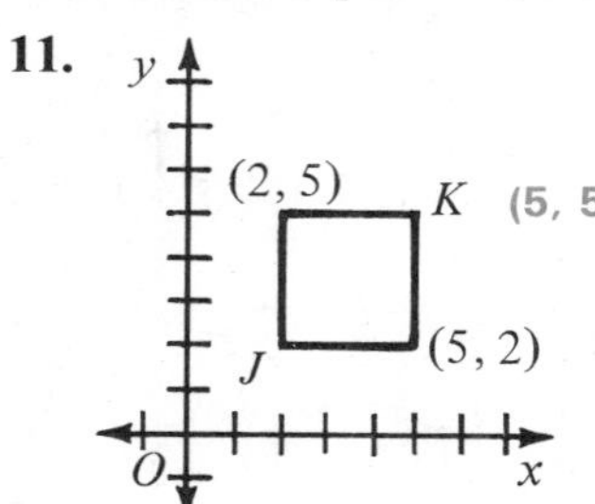


**12.**

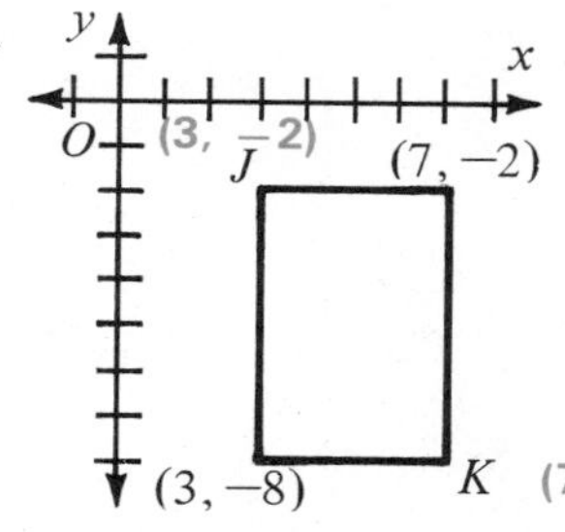


**13.**

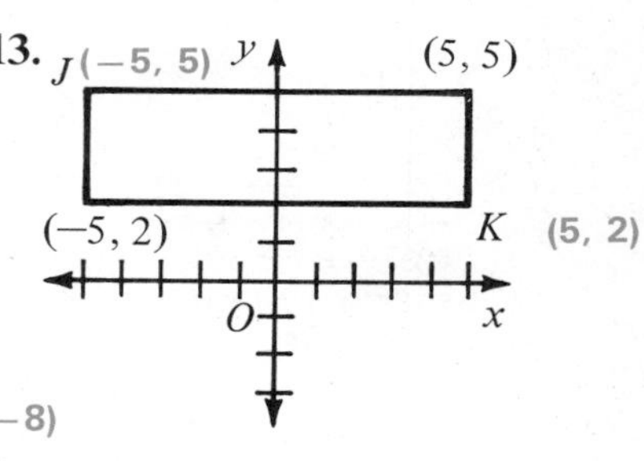


**14.**

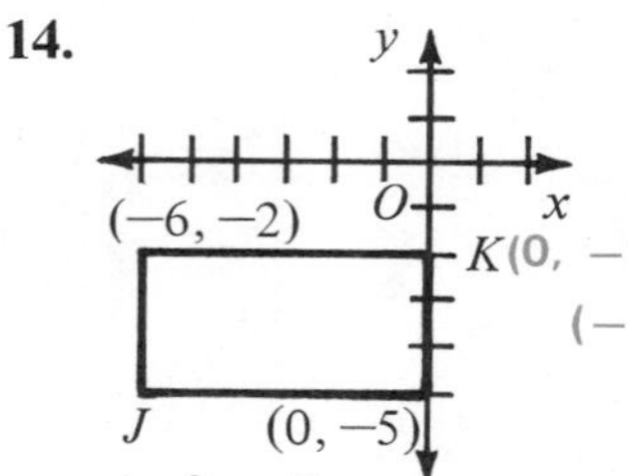


**15.**

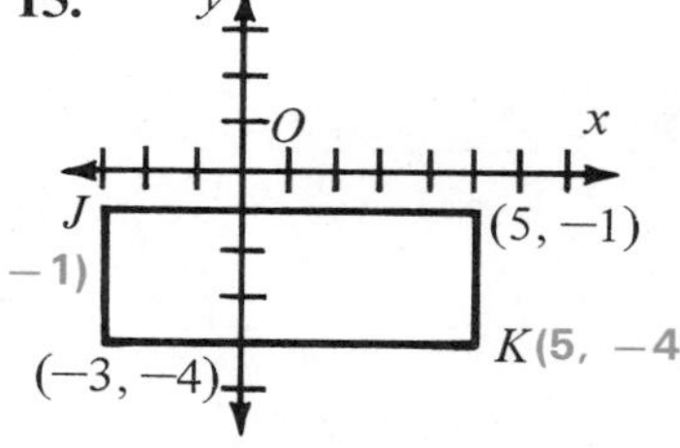


**16.**

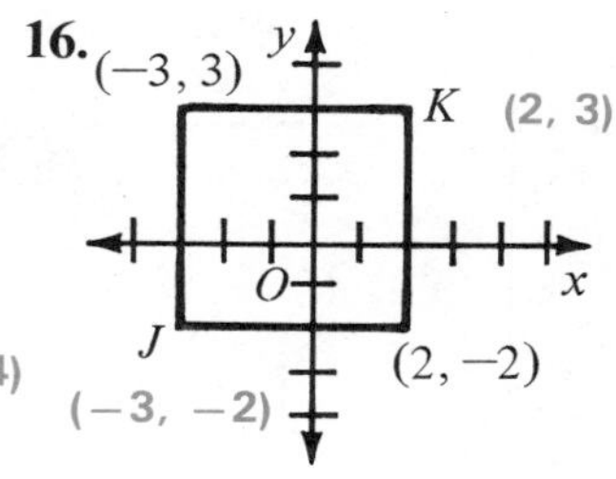


**In Exercises 17–22, find the distance between the points named.**

**17.** $(4, 0)$ and $(9, 0)$ 5 **18.** $(0, 7)$ and $(0, 2)$ 5 **19.** $(5, 2)$ and $(2, 2)$ 3

**20.** $(4, 1)$ and $(4, 6)$ 5 **21.** $(1, 3)$ and $(-5, 3)$ 6 **22.** $(-2, 4)$ and $(-2, -3)$ 7

**Plot the four points and draw quadrilateral $ABCD$. State whether the quadrilateral is a square, rectangle, parallelogram, or trapezoid. (Use the name that gives the best description of the figure.)**

| | $A$ | $B$ | $C$ | $D$ | |
|---|---|---|---|---|---|
| B **23.** | $(-3, -2)$ | $(6, -2)$ | $(5, 1)$ | $(-1, 1)$ | trapezoid |
| **24.** | $(2, 1)$ | $(6, 3)$ | $(6, 0)$ | $(2, -2)$ | parallelogram |
| **25.** | $(-1, -1)$ | $(1, 1)$ | $(5, -3)$ | $(3, -5)$ | rectangle |
| **26.** | $(3, 2)$ | $(5, -1)$ | $(8, 1)$ | $(6, 4)$ | square |

**Plot points $R$ and $S$ and draw $\overleftrightarrow{RS}$. Point $T$ is to lie on $\overleftrightarrow{RS}$, but only one coordinate of $T$ is given. Find the other coordinate of $T$.**

| | $R$ | $S$ | $T$ |
|---|---|---|---|
| **27.** | $(0, -2)$ | $(-3, 0)$ | $(-6, \underline{\ ?\ })$ 2 |
| **28.** | $(9, 9)$ | $(6, 4)$ | $(0, \underline{\ ?\ })$ −6 |
| **29.** | $(6, -5)$ | $(10, 5)$ | $(\underline{\ ?\ }, 0)$ 8 |
| **30.** | $(-6, -1)$ | $(9, -7)$ | $(\underline{\ ?\ }, -3)$ −1 |

C **31.** Points (0, 0), (0, 5), and (3, 4) are three of the vertices of a parallelogram. Find three possible positions for the fourth vertex. (−3, 1); (3, −1); (3, 9)

**32.** Repeat Exercise 31 but use points (−1, 2), (5, 0), and (7, 4). (1, 6); (13, 2); (−3, −2)

## Puzzles & Things

Estelle, George, Jim, Keiko, Laura, and Luis are in the middle of a race.
Estelle is 20 m ahead of Jim.
Jim is 50 m ahead of George.
George is 10 m behind Laura.
Laura is 50 m behind Keiko.
Luis is 30 m ahead of Keiko.
Who is winning the race? Who is second? Third? Fourth? Fifth? Last?
Luis is winning; 2nd: Estelle; 3rd: Keiko; 4th: Jim; 5th: Laura; George is last.

# 2 • Distance between Two Points

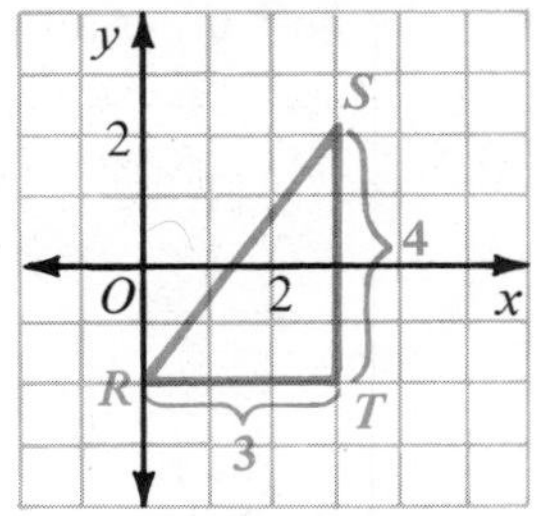


You can count squares to check the lengths of $\overline{RT}$ and $\overline{ST}$ marked in the diagram. You cannot find the length of $\overline{RS}$ by counting squares. However, you can think this way:

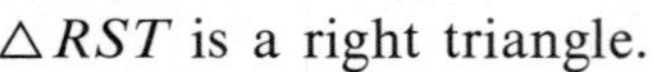

$\triangle RST$ is a right triangle.
The lengths of the legs are 3 and 4.
Thus, the length $RS$ of the hypotenuse must be 5.

**EXAMPLE** Find the distance between $A(-2, 2)$ and $B(5, -1)$.

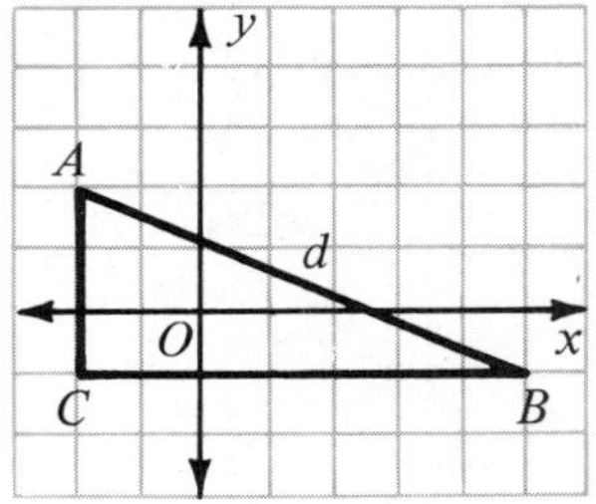


Plot points $A$ and $B$. Then draw horizontal and vertical segments to form right $\triangle ACB$. Find $AC$ and $BC$ by counting.

$AC = 3 \qquad BC = 7$

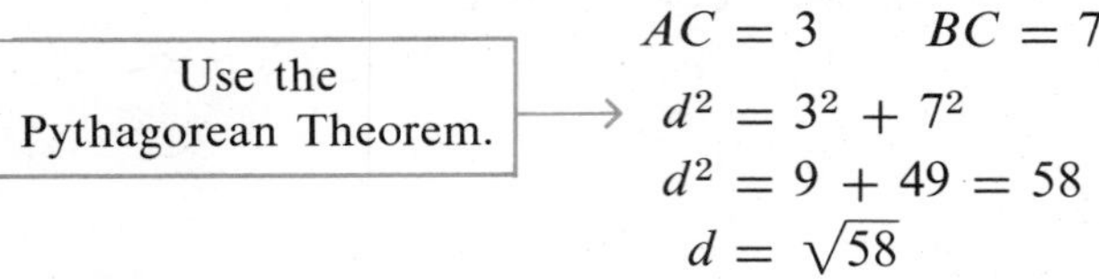


$$d^2 = 3^2 + 7^2$$
$$d^2 = 9 + 49 = 58$$
$$d = \sqrt{58}$$

By using the square root table on page 465, you can approximate $d$ to the nearest tenth.

$$d = \sqrt{58} \doteq 7.6$$

## Classroom Practice

**State the lengths of the two legs of the right triangle.**

**1.**
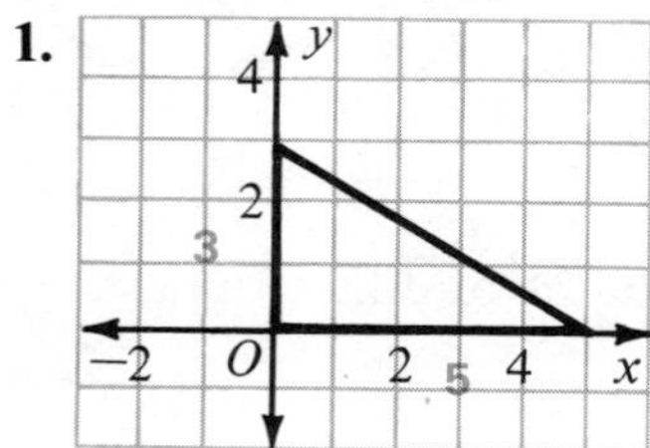

**2.**
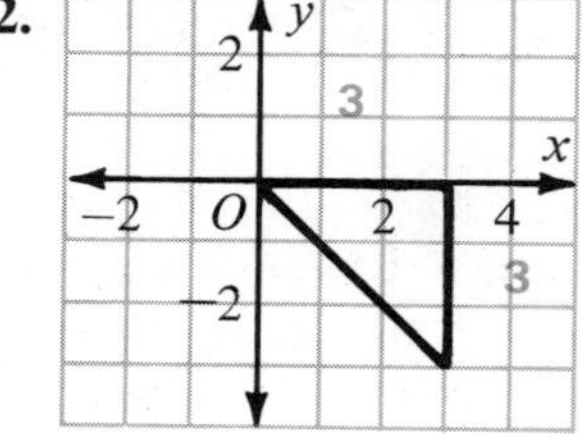

**3.**
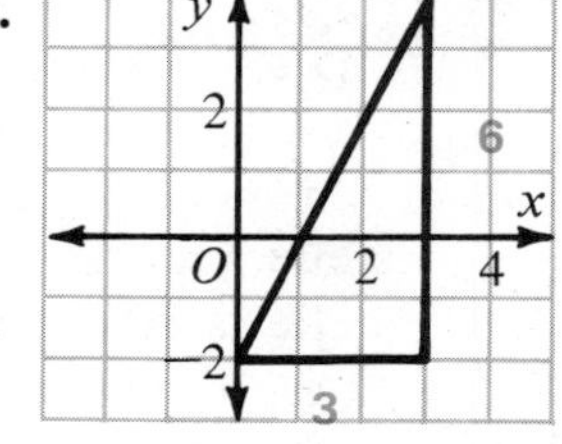

**4.**
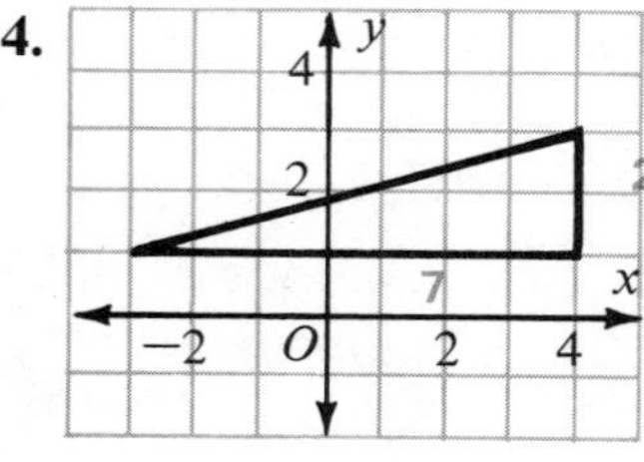

**5.**
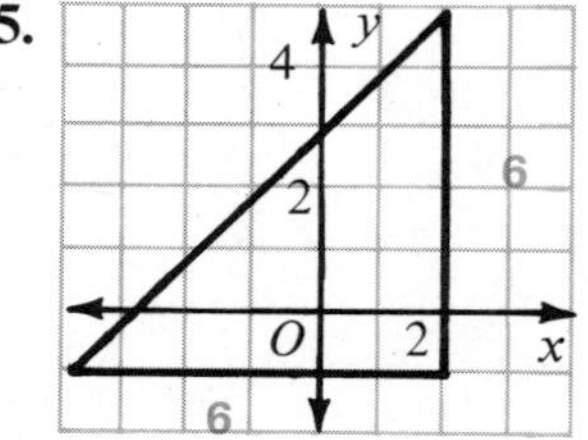

**6.**
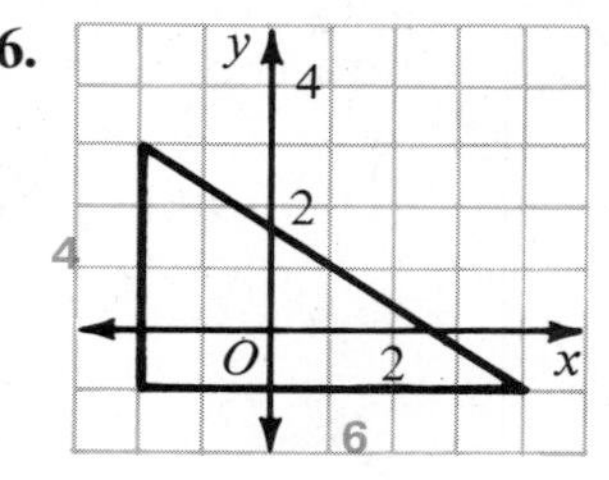

7. Leg $\overline{RT}$ of the right triangle is parallel to the $x$-axis. Answer in terms of $a$, $b$, and $c$.

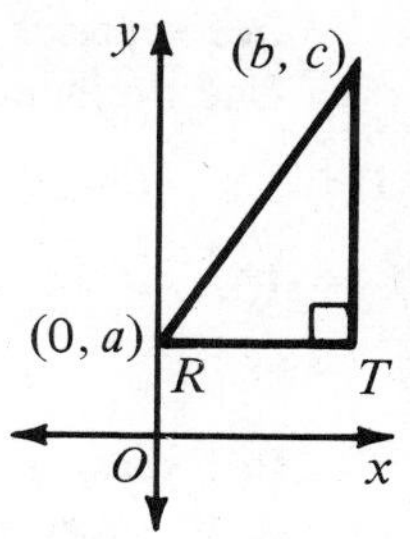


a. The $x$-coordinate of point $T$ is __?__. *b*

b. The $y$-coordinate of point $T$ is __?__. *a*

c. The length of $\overline{RT}$ is __?__. *b*

8. Leg $\overline{VW}$ of the right triangle is parallel to the $x$-axis. Answer in terms of $j$, $k$, $p$, and $q$.

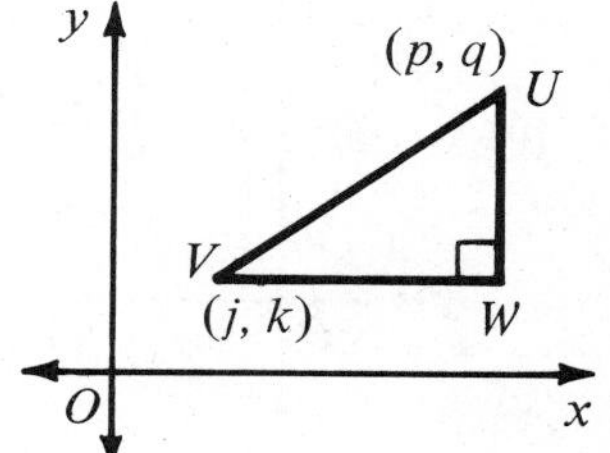


a. The $x$-coordinate of point $W$ is __?__. *p*

b. The length of $\overline{VW}$ is __?__. $p - j$

c. The $y$-coordinate of point $W$ is __?__. *k*

d. The length of $\overline{UW}$ is __?__. $q - k$

## Written Exercises

**In Exercises 1–12, draw axes and plot points $A$ and $B$. Then draw a right triangle you can use to find $AB$. Then find $AB$. Leave your answer in radical form if it isn't a whole number.**

Sample $A(-3, 1)$ and $B(5, 4)$

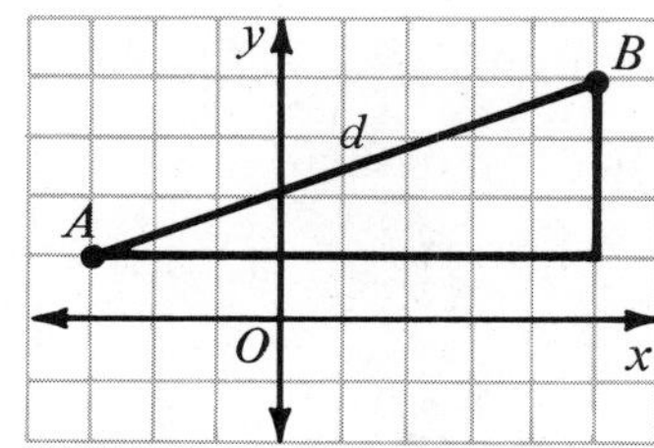


$$d^2 = 8^2 + 3^2$$
$$d^2 = 64 + 9$$
$$d^2 = 73$$
$$d = \sqrt{73}$$

A

1. $A(0, 4)$ and $B(5, 2)$ $d = \sqrt{29}$
2. $A(2, 2)$ and $B(6, 7)$ $d = \sqrt{41}$
3. $A(-2, -1)$ and $B(3, 5)$ $d = \sqrt{61}$
4. $A(-5, 3)$ and $B(4, -4)$ $d = \sqrt{130}$
5. $A(2, 1)$ and $B(4, 2)$ $d = \sqrt{5}$
6. $A(3, 5)$ and $B(5, 8)$ $d = \sqrt{13}$
7. $A(-2, 1)$ and $B(-5, 4)$ $d = 3\sqrt{2}$
8. $A(-6, 7)$ and $B(-4, -2)$ $d = \sqrt{85}$
9. $A(2, 4)$ and $B(-2, 1)$ $d = 5$
10. $A(-3, 3)$ and $B(1, 6)$ $d = 5$
11. $A(4, -2)$ and $B(-2, 3)$ $d = \sqrt{61}$
12. $A(-2, -3)$ and $B(1, 5)$ $d = \sqrt{73}$

**In Exercises 13–16, find the distance between points $A$ and $B$ correct to tenths. Use the square root table on page 465.**

B **13.** $A(-2, -2)$ and $B(3, 3)$ 7.1 **14.** $A(2, -2)$ and $B(-4, 4)$ 8.5

**15.** $A(-4, -3)$ and $B(-6, -7)$ 4.5 **16.** $A(0, 6)$ and $B(-4, -1)$ 8.1

**In Exercises 17–20, find:**
**a. the perimeter of the triangle. b. the area of the triangle.**

**17.**

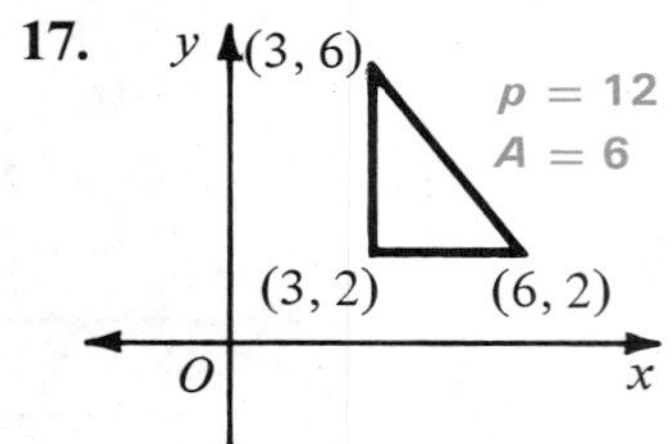


**18.**

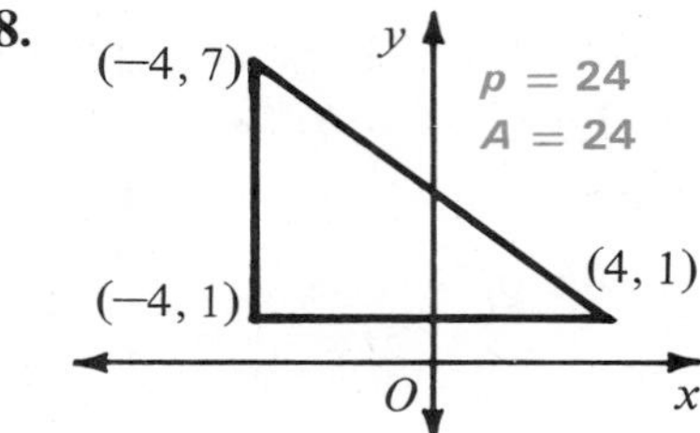


**19.**

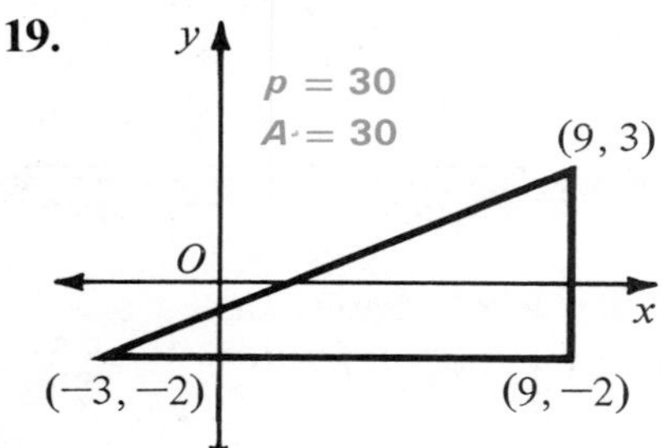


**20.**

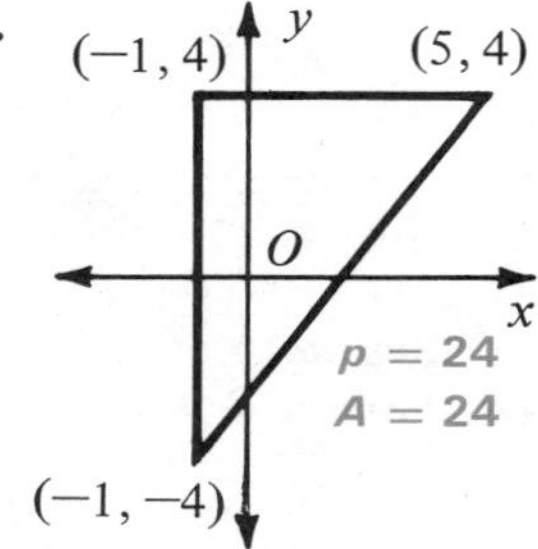


**Find the perimeter and the area of the square with the given vertices.**

C **21.** Vertices: (0, 0); (4, 3); (1, 7); (−3, 4) $p = 20$; $A = 25$

**22.** Vertices: (2, −1); (4, 1); (6, −1); (4, −3) $p = 8\sqrt{2}$; $A = 8$

**Find the perimeter and the area of the quadrilateral shown.**

**23.**

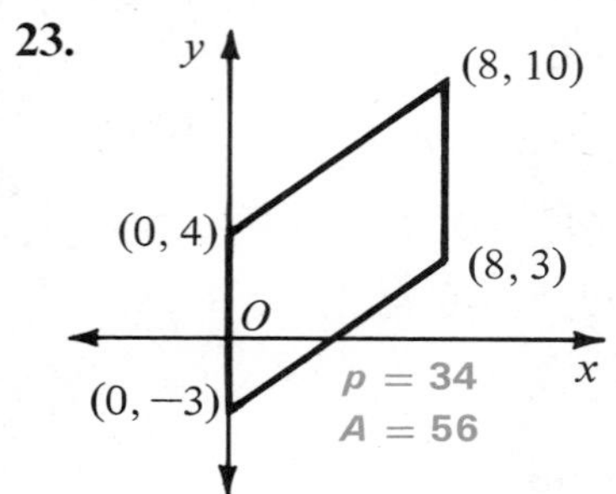


**24.**

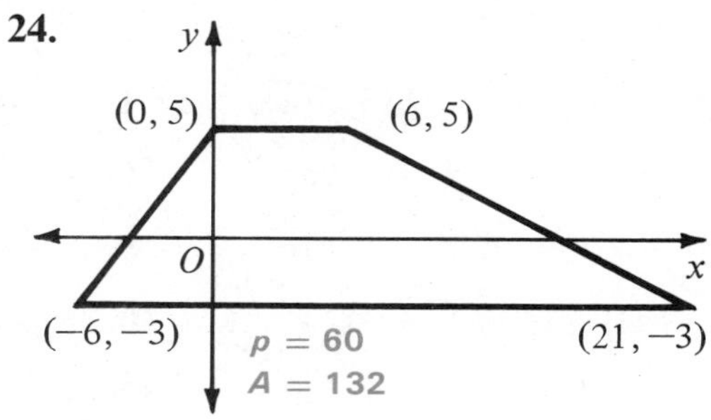

## 3 • Midpoint of a Segment

You should remember that the **average** of two numbers is equal to half the sum of the numbers.

EXAMPLE 1 The average of 4 and 10 is $\frac{4 + 10}{2} = \frac{14}{2} = 7$.

EXAMPLE 2 The average of 4 and $-10$ is $\frac{4 + (-10)}{2} = \frac{-6}{2} = -3$.

### Explorations

Part A

1. Points $R$ and $S$ lie on a number line. Find the coordinate of the midpoint of $\overline{RS}$.

a. 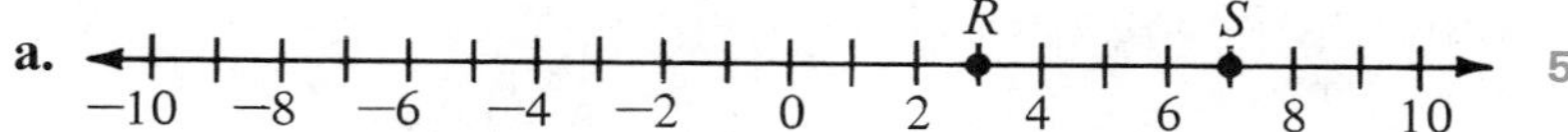

5

b. 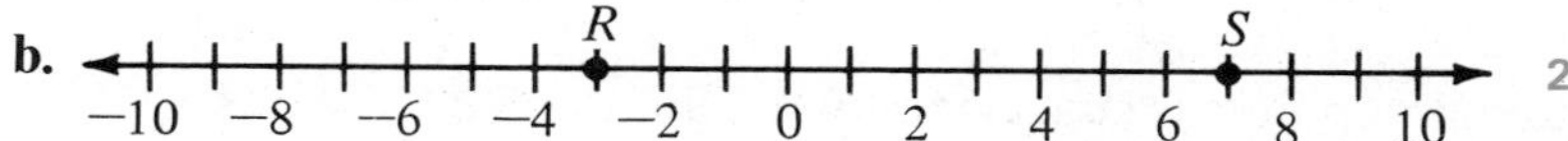

2

c. 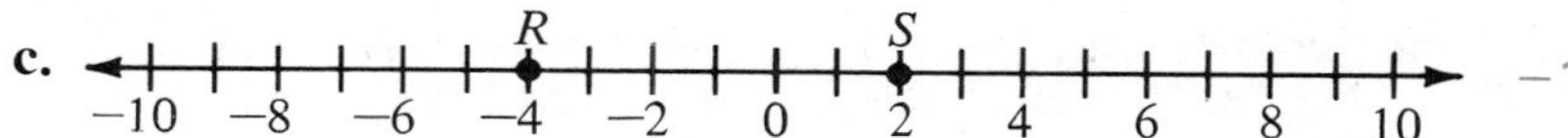

−1

d. 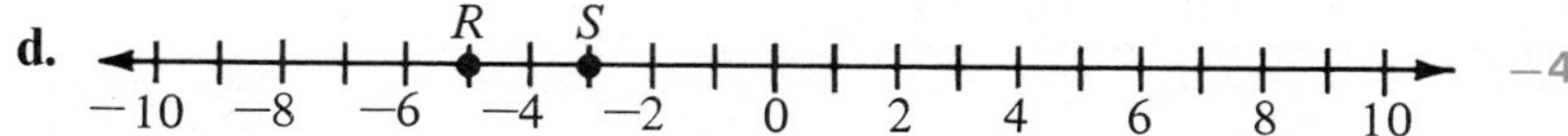

−4

2. Suppose, in Exercise 1, that each number line were vertical rather than horizontal. Would the answers be any different? If necessary, draw vertical number lines to check your answer. no

3. Find the average of each pair of numbers.
   **a.** 3 and 7 5 **b.** $-3$ and 7 2
   **c.** $-4$ and 2 $-1$ **d.** $-5$ and $-3$ $-4$

4. Compare your answers to Exercises 1 and 3. Complete the following statement about points $R$ and $S$ on a number line: The coordinate of the midpoint of $\overline{RS}$ is equal to the _?_ of the coordinates of $R$ and $S$. average

### Part B

*Given:* $\overline{AB}$ with midpoint $M$; the horizontal and vertical segments shown.

1. The $x$-coordinate of point $C$ is __?__ 5.
2. Because $S$ is the midpoint of $\overline{AC}$, the $x$-coordinate of $S$ is __?__ 3.
3. The $x$-coordinate of $M$ is __?__ 3.
4. You know that the $x$-coordinate of $A$ is 1, and the $x$-coordinate of $B$ is 5. Then what is a simple way of finding the $x$-coordinate of midpoint $M$? **The $x$-coordinate of $M$ is the average of 1 and 5.**
5. The $y$-coordinate of $A$ is 2 and of $B$ is 8. The $y$-coordinate of $M$ is 5 __?__. (*Hint:* Use point $T$.)

The explorations above suggest this strategy:

To find the coordinates of the midpoint of a segment when you know the coordinates of the endpoints:

Find the average of the $x$-coordinates.

Find the average of the $y$-coordinates.

A convenient way to name points is suggested by the diagram at the right.

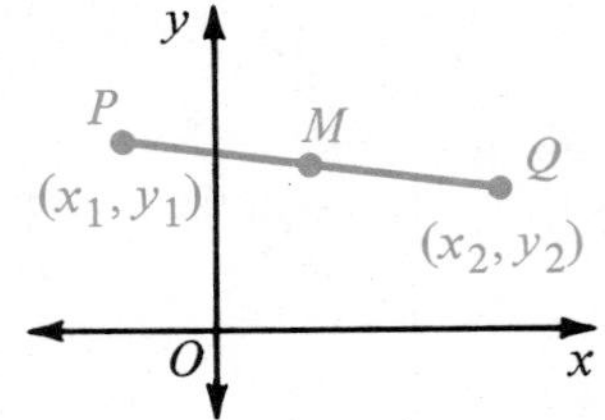


Point $P$ has coordinates $(x_1, y_1)$.

This is read "$x$-sub-1, $y$-sub-1."

**THE MIDPOINT FORMULA**

Let $P(x_1, y_1)$ and $Q(x_2, y_2)$ be any two points. Then the midpoint of $\overline{PQ}$ is the point $\left(\frac{x_1 + x_2}{2}, \frac{y_1 + y_2}{2}\right)$.

**EXAMPLE 1** Find the coordinates of the midpoint of the segment that joins points (1, 2) and (5, 8).

The coordinates are $\left(\frac{1 + 5}{2}, \frac{2 + 8}{2}\right)$, or (3, 5).

**EXAMPLE 2** Find the coordinates of the midpoint of the segment that joins points $(-2, 4)$ and $(-6, 7)$.

The coordinates are $\left(\frac{-2 + (-6)}{2}, \frac{4 + 7}{2}\right)$, or $\left(\frac{-8}{2}, \frac{11}{2}\right)$, or $\left(-4, 5\frac{1}{2}\right)$.

## Classroom Practice

1. State the $x$-coordinate of the midpoint of each segment.

a. 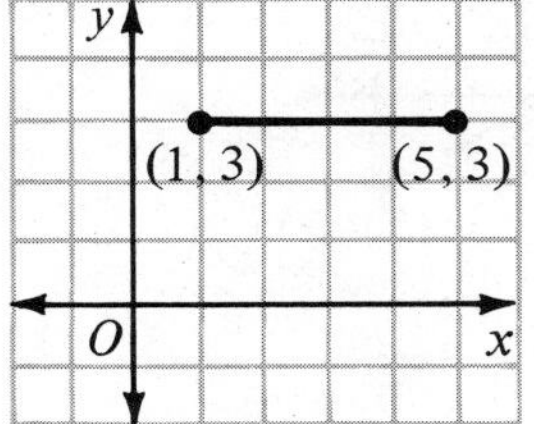

3

b. 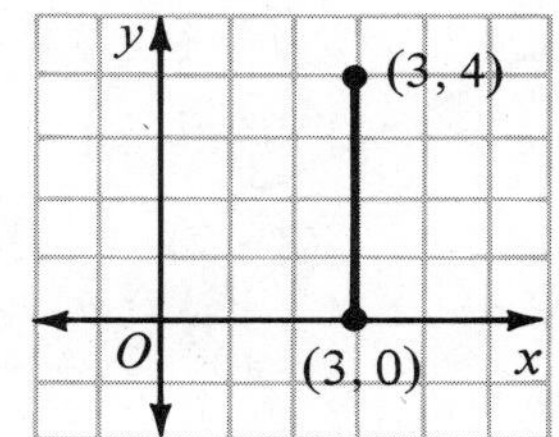

3

c. 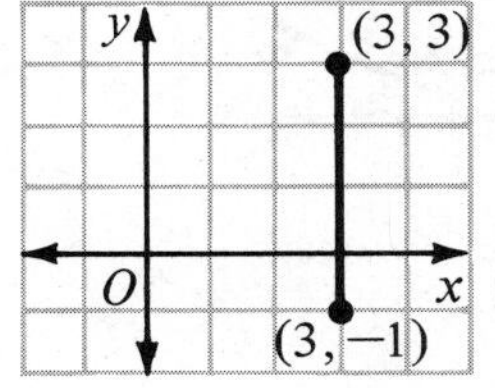

3

d. 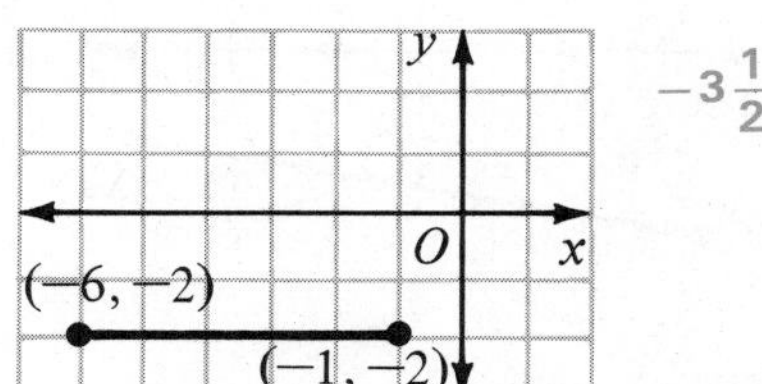

$-3\frac{1}{2}$

2. State the $y$-coordinate of the midpoint of each segment shown in Exercise 1. a. 3; b. 2; c. 1; d. −2

3. State the coordinates of the midpoint of each segment.

a. 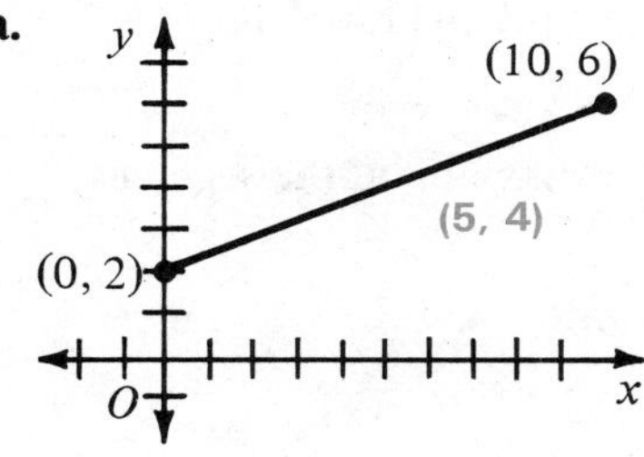

(5, 4)

b. 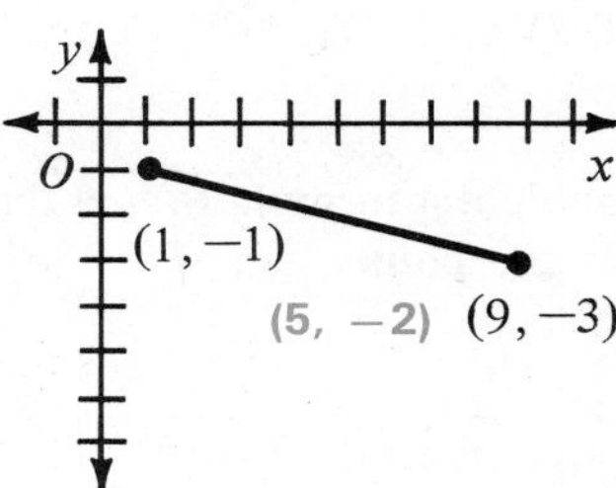

(5, −2)

c. 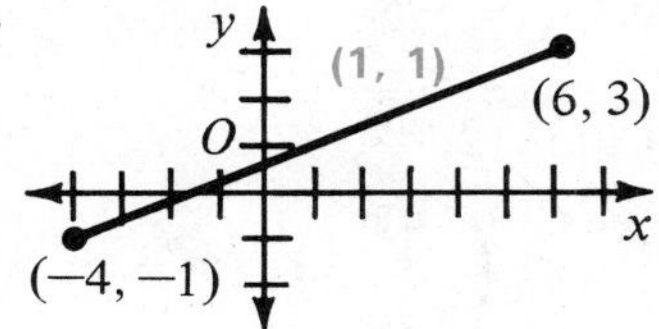

(1, 1)

d. 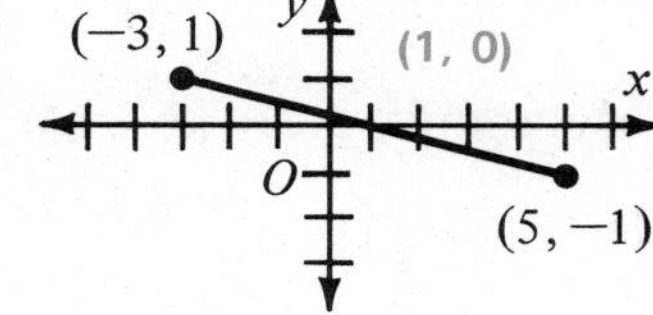

(1, 0)

## Written Exercises

**Plot points $C$ and $D$. Draw $\overline{CD}$. Mark the midpoint of $\overline{CD}$ and label it $M$. State the coordinates of $M$.**

A **1.** $C(2, 0)$ and $D(8, 6)$ $(5, 3)$ **2.** $C(3, 1)$ and $D(-7, 1)$ $(-2, 1)$

**3.** $C(-5, 2)$ and $D(3, 6)$ $(-1, 4)$ **4.** $C(0, 1)$ and $D(6, 6)$ $\left(3, 3\frac{1}{2}\right)$

**State the coordinates of the midpoint of the segment.**

**5.**

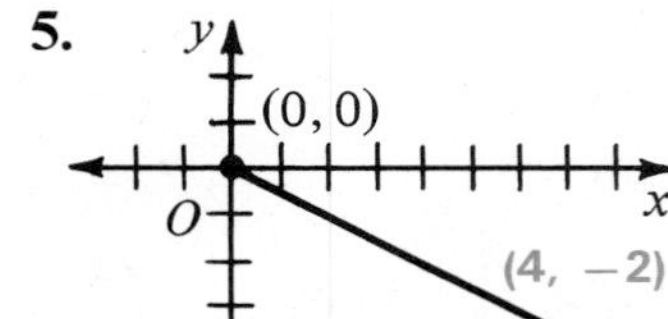


**6.**

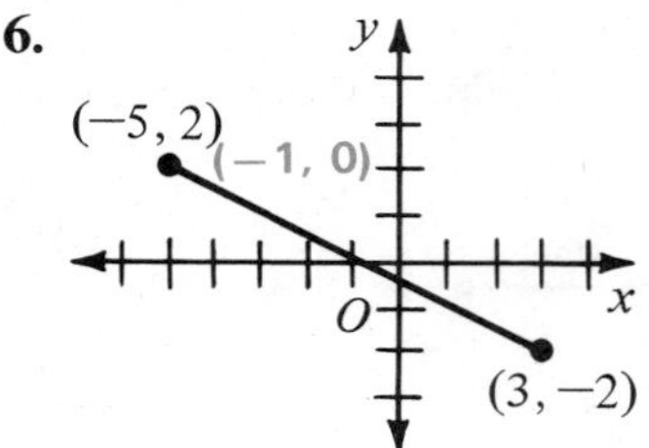


**7.**

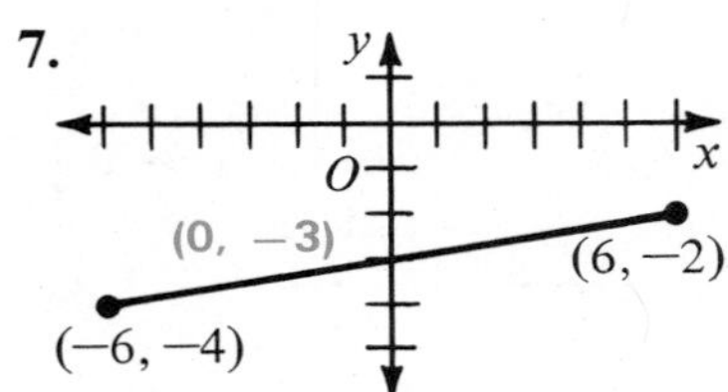


**8.**

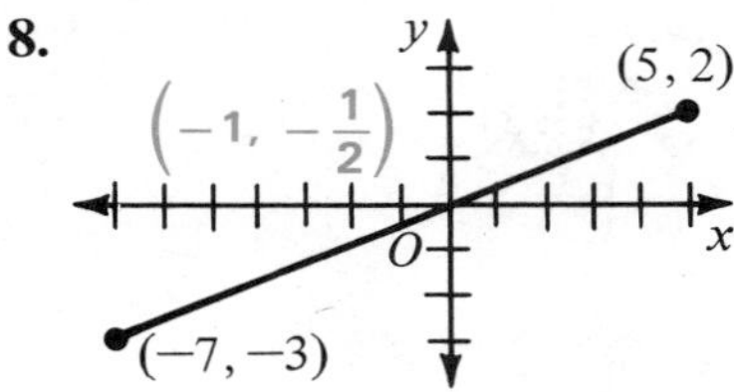


**Plot points $E$ and $M$ and draw $\overleftrightarrow{EM}$. Mark point $F$ in such a position that $M$ is the midpoint of $\overline{EF}$. From your drawing state the coordinates of $F$.**

**9.** $E(0, 3)$ and $M(4, 3)$ $(8, 3)$ **10.** $E(5, -1)$ and $M(5, 2)$ $(5, 5)$

**11.** $E(2, 2)$ and $M(5, 4)$ $(8, 6)$ **12.** $E(-2, 1)$ and $M(1, 0)$ $(4, -1)$

**Use the midpoint formula to find the coordinates of the midpoint of the segment that joins the points named.**

**13.** $(2, 5)$ and $(8, 1)$ $(5, 3)$ **14.** $(0, -6)$ and $(4, -2)$ $(2, -4)$

**15.** $(-3, -5)$ and $(7, -5)$ $(2, -5)$ **16.** $(11, 5)$ and $(-1, 7)$ $(5, 6)$

**17.** $(2, 1)$ and $(8, 8)$ $\left(5, 4\frac{1}{2}\right)$ **18.** $(0, 5)$ and $(-6, -8)$ $\left(-3, -1\frac{1}{2}\right)$

B **19.** $(1, 2.5)$ and $(5, 3.2)$ $(3, 2.85)$ **20.** $(-1, 1.6)$ and $(2, 6.4)$ $(.5, 4)$

**21.** $(0, -3)$ and $\left(1\frac{1}{2}, -7\right)$ $\left(\frac{3}{4}, -5\right)$ **22.** $\left(-\frac{1}{3}, 0\right)$ and $\left(4\frac{1}{3}, 5\right)$ $\left(2, 2\frac{1}{2}\right)$

**$M$ is the midpoint of $\overline{AB}$. The coordinates of $A$ and $M$ are given. Use the midpoint formula to find the coordinates of $B$.**

**Sample** $A(4, -3)$ and $M(6, 1)$

Let $(t, u)$ be the coordinates of $B$.

$$\frac{4 + t}{2} = 6 \qquad\qquad \frac{-3 + u}{2} = 1$$

$$4 + t = 12 \qquad\qquad -3 + u = 2$$

$$t = 8 \qquad\qquad u = 5$$

The coordinates of point $B$ are $(8, 5)$.

**23.** $A(0, 3)$ and $M(5, 4)$ $(10, 5)$ **24.** $A(-1, 1)$ and $M(2, 5)$ $(5, 9)$

**25.** $A(1, 5)$ and $M(2, 2)$ $(3, -1)$ **26.** $A(4, 1)$ and $M(2, 0)$ $(0, -1)$

B.C. by permission of Johnny Hart and Field Enterprises, Inc.

## SELF-TEST

**The sides of rectangle $RSTU$ are parallel to the coordinate axes.**

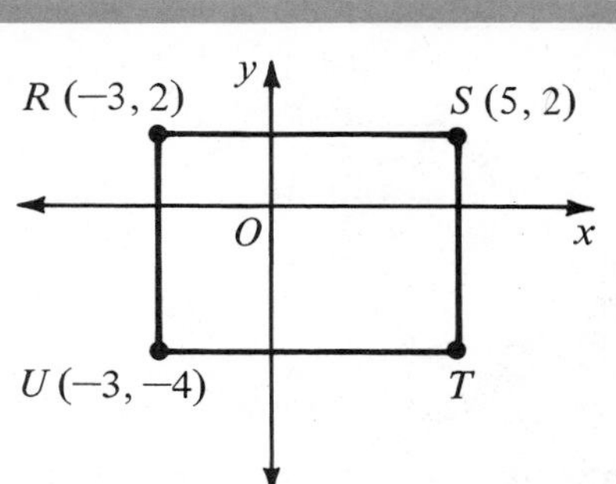


1. Point $T$ has coordinates (__?__, __?__). $5$, $-4$
2. The midpoint of $\overline{RS}$ has coordinates (__?__, __?__). $(1, 2)$
3. The midpoint of $\overline{SU}$ has coordinates (__?__, __?__). $(1, -1)$
4. $RU =$ __?__ $6$ 5. $SU =$ __?__ $10$

**In Exercises 6–8, use points $A(-9, -5)$ and $B(3, 0)$.**

6. The distance between the origin and point $B$ is __?__. $3$
7. The distance between $A$ and $B$ is __?__. $13$
8. The midpoint of $\overline{AB}$ has coordinates (__?__, __?__). $\left(-3, 2\frac{1}{2}\right)$

## 4 • Slope of a Line

A car can make the climb at the left, but not the climb at the right.

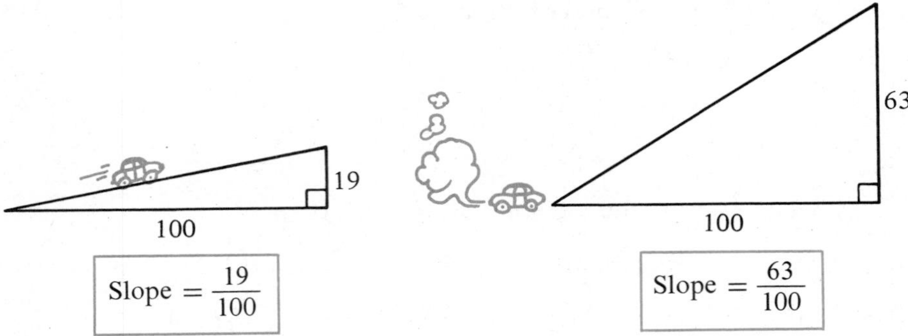


The *slope* of a road is the ratio of *rise* to *run*.

**Slope** $= \dfrac{\textbf{rise}}{\textbf{run}}$

Lines have slopes, too.

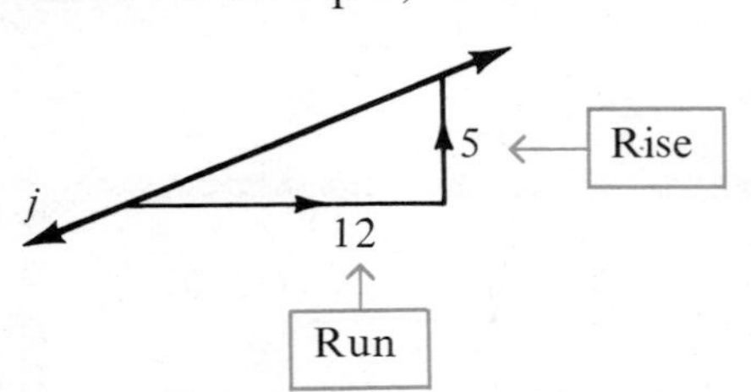


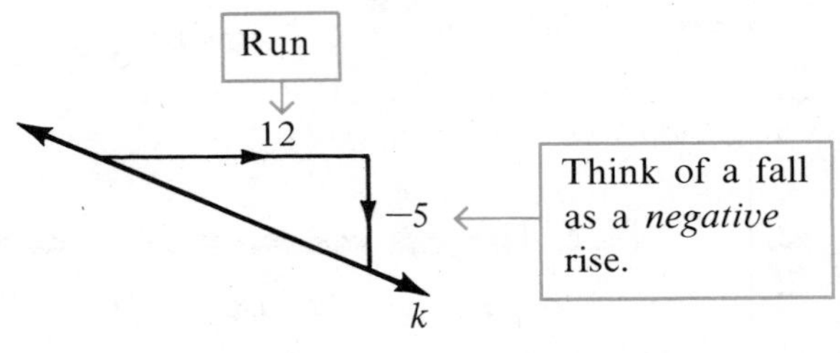


$$\text{Slope of } j = \frac{\text{rise}}{\text{run}} = \frac{5}{12}$$

$$\text{Slope of } k = \frac{\text{rise}}{\text{run}} = \frac{-5}{12} = -\frac{5}{12}$$

Count squares in this figure and you find that the rise is 4, the run is 3, and the slope is $\frac{4}{3}$. Instead of counting squares you can subtract coordinates, as shown in the figure.

$$\begin{aligned} \text{Slope} &= \frac{\text{rise}}{\text{run}} \\ &= \frac{6-2}{4-1} = \frac{4}{3} \end{aligned}$$

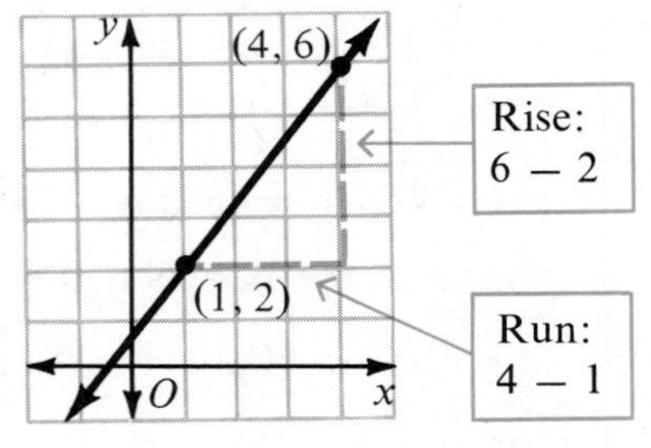

The slope of the line that joins points $(x_1, y_1)$ and $(x_2, y_2)$ is defined by

$$\text{Slope} = \frac{y_2 - y_1}{x_2 - x_1}$$

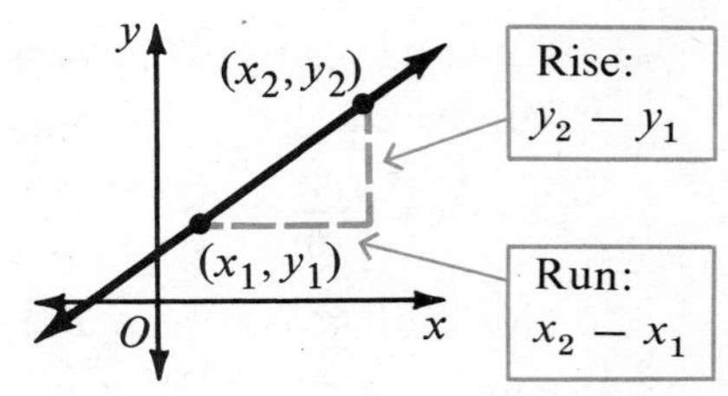


Here are some more facts that will help you understand the meaning of "slope."

**1.** When a line *rises from left to right,* the slope is a *positive* number.

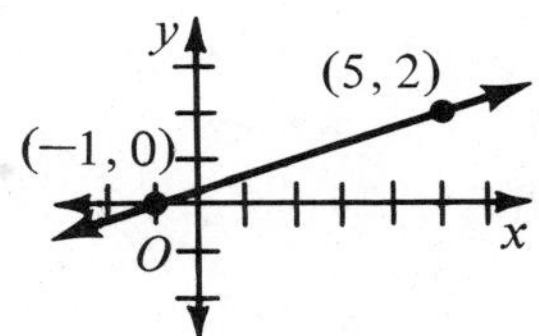


$$\frac{2 - 0}{5 - (-1)} = \frac{2}{6} = \frac{1}{3}$$

**2.** When a line *falls from left to right,* the slope is a *negative* number.

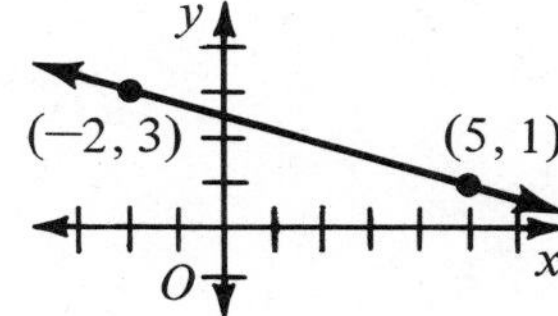


$$\frac{1 - 3}{5 - (-2)} = \frac{-2}{7} = -\frac{2}{7}$$

**3.** A *horizontal* line does not rise or fall. The slope of a horizontal line is zero.

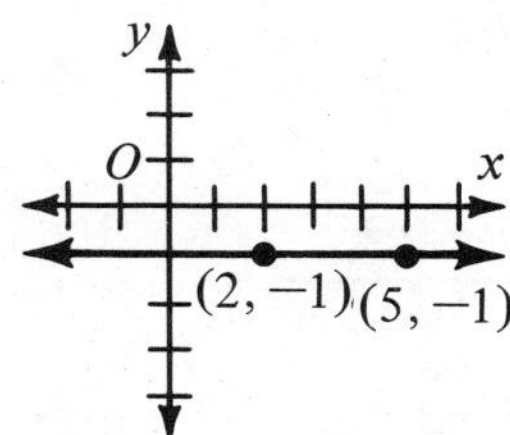


$$\frac{-1 - (-1)}{5 - 2} = \frac{0}{3} = 0$$

**4.** The word "slope" does not apply to a *vertical* line. We say that the slope of a vertical line is *not defined.*

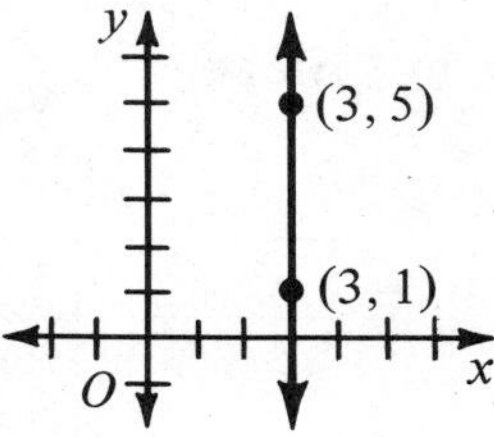


Note that the expression $\frac{5 - 1}{3 - 3}$ does not represent a number.

## Explorations

### Part A

1. Think of going from $A$ to $B$.
   Run = ___?___   Rise = ___?___ 4

   Slope $= \frac{\text{rise}}{\text{run}} =$ ___?___ $\frac{4}{5}$

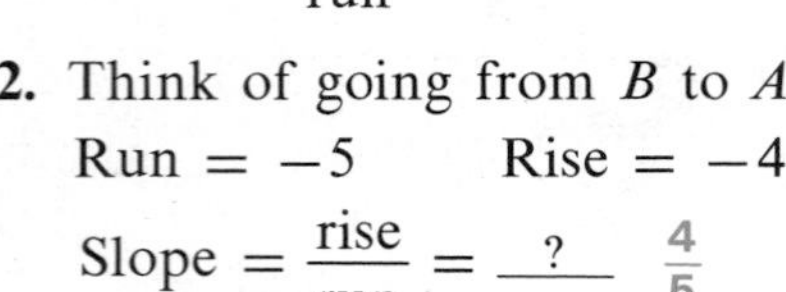

2. Think of going from $B$ to $A$.
   Run $= -5$   Rise $= -4$

   Slope $= \frac{\text{rise}}{\text{run}} =$ ___?___ $\frac{4}{5}$

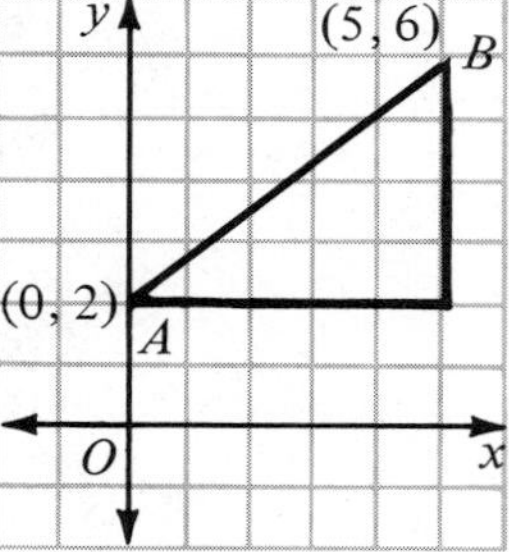


Part A suggests that when you compute the slope by using the ratio $\frac{\text{rise}}{\text{run}}$, you may start at *either* point. Test this with other points.

### Part B

Copy and complete the table.

| $(x_1, y_1)$ | $(x_2, y_2)$ | $y_2 - y_1$ | $x_2 - x_1$ | Slope |
|---|---|---|---|---|
| (0, 2) | (5, 6) | ? 4 | ? 5 | ? $\frac{4}{5}$ |
| (5, 6) | (0, 2) | ? $-4$ | ? $-5$ | ? $\frac{4}{5}$ |

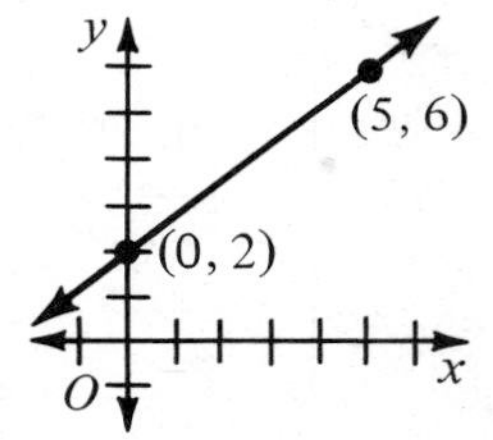


Part B suggests that when you compute the slope by using $\frac{y_2 - y_1}{x_2 - x_1}$, it doesn't matter which point you choose as $(x_2, y_2)$.

### Part C

Use the points named to compute the slope of the line.

all slopes: $-\frac{1}{2}$

| Points | Slope |
|---|---|
| 1. $R$ and $S$ | ? |
| 2. $R$ and $T$ | ? |
| 3. $R$ and $U$ | ? |
| 4. $R$ and $V$ | ? |
| 5. $S$ and $U$ | ? |
| 6. $S$ and $V$ | ? |

Part C suggests that when you compute the slope of a line, you may use *any* two points on the line.

## Classroom Practice

**For each diagram, think of going from point $R$ to point $S$.**

**a. Tell whether the rise is positive, negative, or zero.**

**b. Tell whether the run is positive, negative, or zero.**

**c. Tell whether the slope is positive, negative, zero, or not defined.**

**1.** 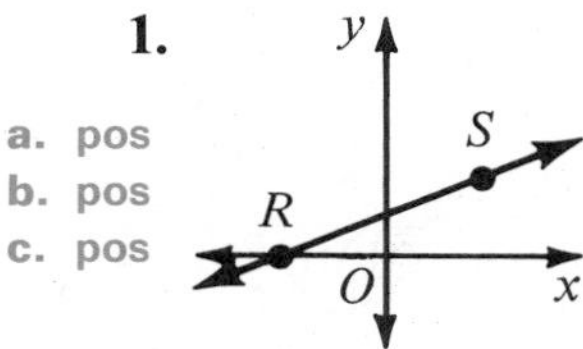


**2.** 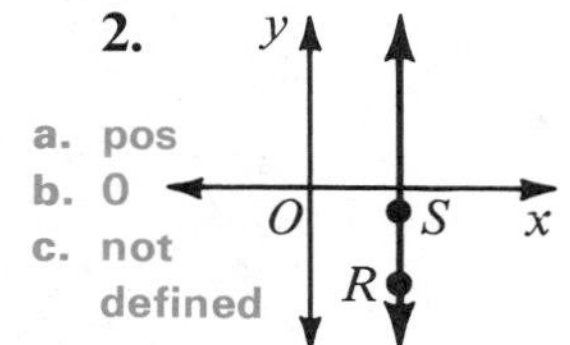


**3.** 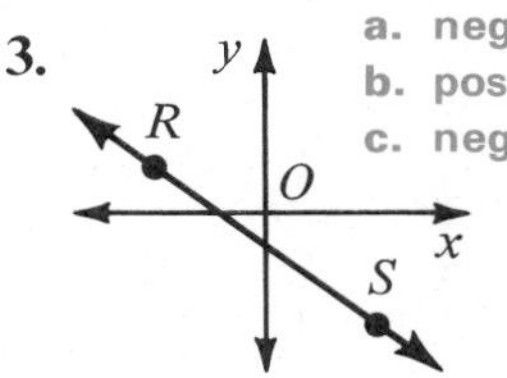


**4.** 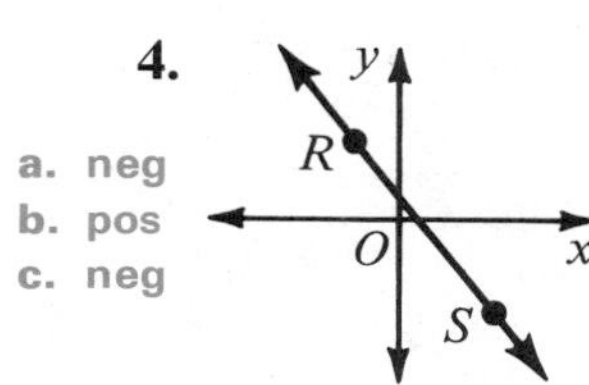


**5.** 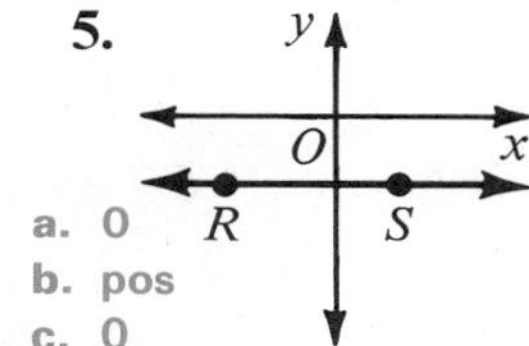


**6.** 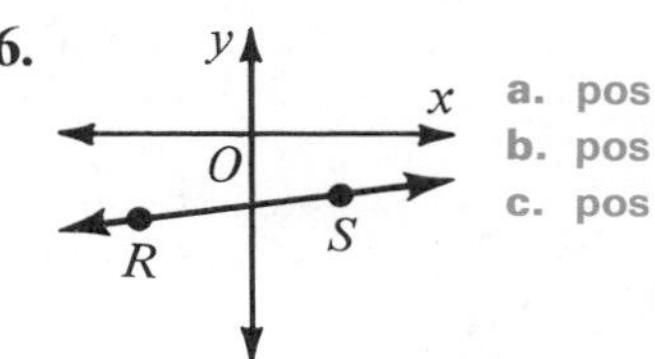


## Written Exercises

A **1.** Name the line that fits the description.

**a.** The slope is positive. *a*

**b.** The slope is zero. *c*

**c.** The slope is negative. *d*

**d.** Slope is not defined for the line. *b*

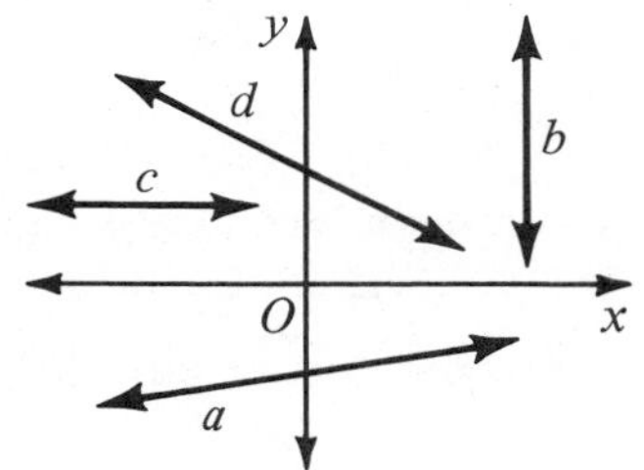

**State the slope of the line shown. If the slope is not defined for the line, write *Not defined.***

**2.** $\frac{3}{5}$ 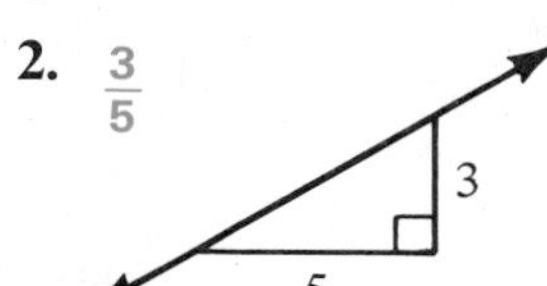

**3.** $\frac{1}{3}$ 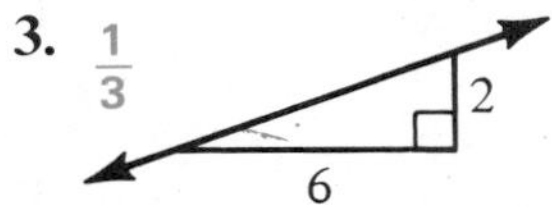

**4.** 0 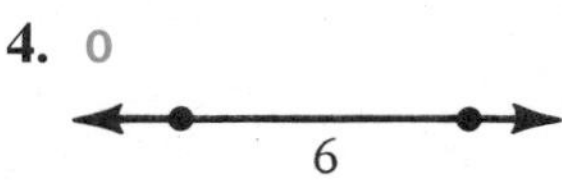

**5.** $-\frac{7}{3}$ 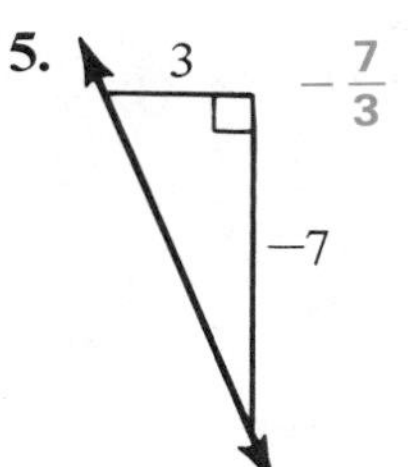

**6.** $-1$ 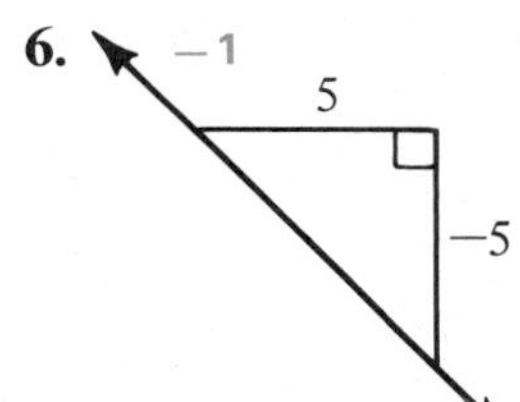

**7.** 6 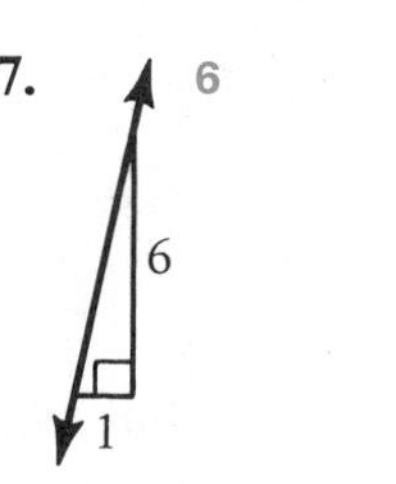

**Take $P$ as point $(x_1, y_1)$ and $Q$ as point $(x_2, y_2)$. Copy and complete the table. When $\overleftrightarrow{PQ}$ does not have a slope, write *Not defined.***

| | $P$ | $Q$ | $y_2 - y_1$ | $x_2 - x_1$ | Slope | |
|---|---|---|---|---|---|---|
| **8.** | (0, 0) | (6, 5) | ? 5 | ? 6 | ? | $\frac{5}{6}$ |
| **9.** | (0, 0) | (−3, −7) | ? −7 | ? −3 | ? | $\frac{7}{3}$ |
| **10.** | (2, 1) | (6, −2) | ? −3 | ? 4 | ? | $-\frac{3}{4}$ |
| **11.** | (6, −2) | (2, 1) | ? 3 | ? −4 | ? | $-\frac{3}{4}$ |
| **12.** | (−3, −1) | (−5, 4) | ? 5 | ? −2 | ? | $-\frac{5}{2}$ |
| **13.** | (−5, 4) | (−3, −1) | ? −5 | ? 2 | ? | $-\frac{5}{2}$ |

**The coordinates of the vertices of quadrilateral *ABCD* are given. State which sides of the quadrilateral have positive slopes.**

B **14.** $A(-5, 2)$; $B(4, 6)$; $C(2, -3)$; $D(-1, -2)$ $\overline{AB}$, $\overline{BC}$

**15.** $A(3, 4)$; $B(6, -5)$; $C(-7, -1)$; $D(-2, 6)$ $\overline{CD}$

**16.** $A(8, -10)$; $B(-6, -2)$; $C(-4, 6)$; $D(10, -2)$ $\overline{BC}$, $\overline{AD}$

**17.** $A(-5, 0)$; $B(1, 1)$; $C(1, 6)$; $D(-4, 5)$ $\overline{AB}$, $\overline{CD}$, $\overline{AD}$

**In Exercises 18–21, a line is described. State three points (any three points) that the line passes through. You may use graph paper, but write your answers in the form: Points (__?__, __?__), (__?__, __?__), and (__?__, __?__).** (Answers will vary.)

**18.** A line through the origin with slope equal to 1 For example: (1, 1), (2, 2) and (−3, −3)

**19.** A line through point (0, 4) with slope equal to 1 (1, 5), (2, 6), and (−1, 3)

**20.** A line containing points (2, 0) and (0, 3) (4, −3), (−2, 6), and (−4, 9)

**21.** A line through point (0, −4) with slope equal to 0 (−1, −4), (2, −4) and (6, −4)

C **22.** Rosalie says: "No matter how great a number you choose, I can find a line whose slope is equal to that number." Isabella chooses the number *one billion*. Rosalie could respond by saying: "Take the line that contains points (__?__, __?__) and (__?__, __?__)." (Answers will vary.) (1, 1 billion), (2, 2 billion)

**23.** You are given points $(a, b)$ and $(c, d)$ on a line. Show that you get the same value for the slope whether you choose $(a, b)$ to be $(x_1, y_1)$ or $(x_2, y_2)$.

*Suggested strategy:* Write two expressions for the slope.
Then use the algebraic property: $d - b = -(b - d)$.

## 5 • Parallel and Perpendicular Lines

The purpose of this section is to show how you can use the slopes of two lines to decide if the lines are parallel or perpendicular. Since vertical and horizontal lines are special, they will be considered in the exercises, rather than the lesson itself.

Suppose lines $p$ and $q$ are parallel.
Draw two vertical segments and label lengths as shown.

1. $\angle 1 = \angle 2$. Why?
2. The triangles are similar. Why?
3. $\frac{a}{c} = \frac{b}{d}$. Why?
4. $\frac{a}{b} = \frac{c}{d}$. Why?
5. Slope of line $p$ = slope of line $q$.

We have just shown that if two lines are parallel, then their slopes are equal. The converse is also true. (See Exercise 21.)

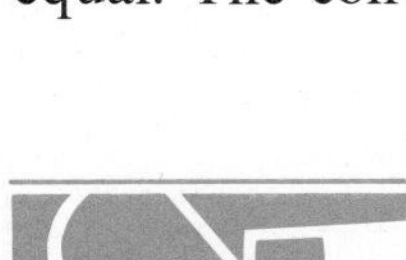

If two lines are parallel, then they have equal slopes.

If two lines have equal slopes, then they are parallel.

### *Explorations*

Draw a line through the origin and point (2, 3). If your line is carefully drawn, you will see that it also contains points (−2, −3), (4, 6), and (6, 9).

**1.** Use a compass to construct, or use a protractor to draw, lines perpendicular to the given line at points (−2, −3), (0, 0), (2, 3), (4, 6), and (6, 9).

**2.** On each of the perpendiculars choose a convenient point and label it with its coordinates.

**3.** Find the slope of each perpendicular.

**4.** If you worked carefully, you found that each perpendicular has slope $-\frac{2}{3}$. Notice that the given line has slope $\frac{3}{2}$. Describe a relation between the numbers $\frac{3}{2}$ and $-\frac{2}{3}$. $\frac{3}{2} \cdot \left(-\frac{2}{3}\right) = -1$

Suppose a line $p$ has slope $\frac{4}{5}$. From Exercises 1–4 on page 443, what would you guess to be the slope of a line perpendicular to $p$? The Explorations suggest that there is a simple relationship between the slopes of two perpendicular lines.

If two lines are perpendicular, then the product of their slopes is $-1$.

If the product of the slopes of two lines is $-1$, then the lines are perpendicular.

## Classroom Practice

**1.** Line $l$ has slope $\frac{2}{7}$.

**a.** The slope of any line parallel to $l$ equals __?__. $\frac{2}{7}$

**b.** The slope of any line perpendicular to $l$ equals __?__. $-\frac{7}{2}$

**2.** Line $j$ has slope $-5$.

**a.** The slope of any line parallel to $j$ equals __?__. $-5$

**b.** The slope of any line perpendicular to $j$ equals __?__. $\frac{1}{5}$

**3.** Suppose one line has slope $\frac{3}{11}$ and another line has slope $\frac{4}{11}$. Can the lines be parallel? Explain. No. $\frac{3}{11} \neq \frac{4}{11}$

**4.** Suppose one line has slope $\frac{2}{5}$ and another line has slope $\frac{5}{2}$. Are the lines perpendicular? Explain. No. $\frac{2}{5} \cdot \frac{5}{2} \neq -1$

**5.** *Given:* The slopes of two lines are 1 and $-1$. Are the lines parallel? Are they perpendicular? Explain. no, $1 \neq -1$; yes $1(-1) = -1$

**6.** *Given:* Points $A(0, 1)$, $B(3, 3)$, $C(6, 5)$, and $D(12, 9)$.

**a.** The slope of $\overleftrightarrow{AB}$ equals __?__. $\frac{2}{3}$

**b.** The slope of $\overleftrightarrow{CD}$ equals __?__. $\frac{2}{3}$

**c.** Do you think that $\overleftrightarrow{AB}$ and $\overleftrightarrow{CD}$ are parallel lines? Yes

**d.** Plot points $A$, $B$, $C$, and $D$. Do you need to change your answer to part (c)? Explain. They are the same line.

## Written Exercises

A **1.** A given line has slope $-\frac{5}{7}$.

**a.** Any line parallel to the given line has slope __?__. $-\frac{5}{7}$

**b.** Any line perpendicular to the given line has slope __?__. $\frac{7}{5}$

**2.** A given line has slope 2.

**a.** Any line parallel to the given line has slope __?__. 2

**b.** Any line perpendicular to the given line has slope __?__. $-\frac{1}{2}$

**3.** A given line is vertical.

**a.** The slope of the given line is $\underset{\text{0/not defined}}{\underline{\quad ? \quad}}$. not defined

**b.** The slope of a line perpendicular to the given line equals __?__. 0

**4.** A given line rises to the right.

**a.** The slope of the line is $\underset{\text{positive/negative}}{\underline{\quad ? \quad}}$. positive

**b.** The slope of a line perpendicular to the given line is $\underset{\text{positive/negative}}{\underline{\quad ? \quad}}$. negative

**The slopes of two lines are given. Are the lines parallel, perpendicular, or neither?**

**5.** $\frac{4}{8}$ and $\frac{1}{2}$ parallel

**6.** $\frac{7}{2}$ and $\frac{2}{7}$ neither

**7.** $-\frac{4}{3}$ and $\frac{3}{4}$ perpendicular

**8.** 3 and $-3$ neither

**Copy and complete the table.**

| | $A$ | $B$ | $C$ | $D$ | Slope of $\overleftrightarrow{AB}$ | Slope of $\overleftrightarrow{CD}$ | Is $\overleftrightarrow{AB} \parallel \overleftrightarrow{CD}$? | Is $\overleftrightarrow{AB} \perp \overleftrightarrow{CD}$? |
|---|---|---|---|---|---|---|---|---|
| Sample | $(-1, 1)$ | $(3, 5)$ | $(0, -2)$ | $(3, 2)$ | 1 | $\frac{4}{3}$ | No | No |
| **9.** | $(2, 2)$ | $(5, 2)$ | $(-4, 4)$ | $(0, 4)$ | ? 0 | ? 0 | ? Yes | ? No |
| **10.** | $(0, 0)$ | $(3, 4)$ | $(-1, -2)$ | $(2, 2)$ | ? $\frac{4}{3}$ | ? $\frac{4}{3}$ | ? Yes | ? No |
| **11.** | $(3, -1)$ | $(2, 1)$ | $(5, 0)$ | $(3, 4)$ | ? $-2$ | ? $-2$ | ? Yes | ? No |
| **12.** | $(0, 3)$ | $(2, 0)$ | $(0, 0)$ | $(6, -4)$ | ? $-\frac{3}{2}$ | ? $-\frac{2}{3}$ | ? No | ? No |

$\angle F$ **is a right angle. Find the slope of** $\overleftrightarrow{EF}$ **and the slope of** $\overleftrightarrow{FG}$**.**

B **13.**

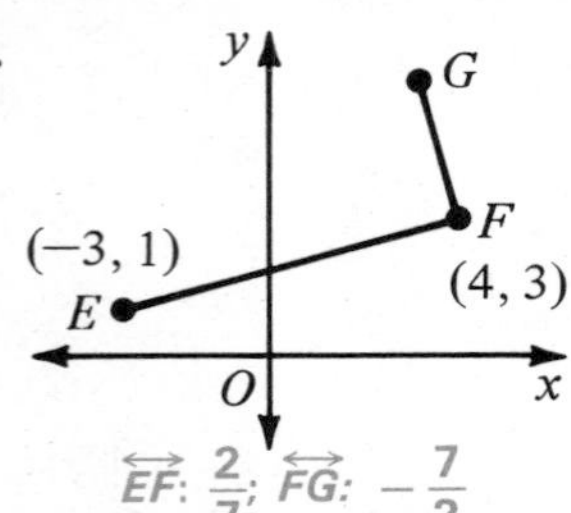


$\overleftrightarrow{EF}$: $\frac{2}{7}$; $\overleftrightarrow{FG}$: $-\frac{7}{2}$

**14.**

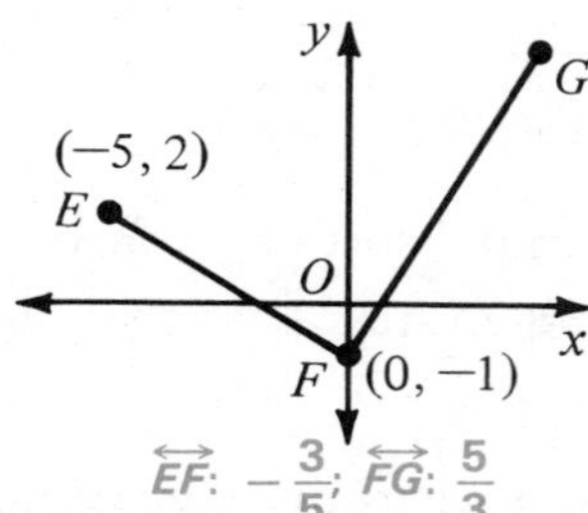


$\overleftrightarrow{EF}$: $-\frac{3}{5}$; $\overleftrightarrow{FG}$: $\frac{5}{3}$

**For Exercises 15–18, a strategy is: Draw a diagram. Then find and use slopes as necessary.**

**Determine if the diagonals of quadrilateral** ***RSTV*** **are perpendicular.**

**15.** $R(0, 0)$; $S(4, 3)$; $T(1, 7)$; $V(-3, 4)$ yes

**16.** $R(-2, 6)$; $S(5, 5)$; $T(7, -3)$; $V(-3, -4)$ no

**What special kind of figure is quadrilateral** ***ABCD*****?**

**17.** $A(-1, 0)$; $B(0, 3)$; $C(6, 3)$; $D(5, 0)$ parallelogram

**18.** $A(0, 0)$; $B(4, 2)$; $C(2, 3)$; $D(0, 2)$ trapezoid

C **19.** You are given the figure shown. $M$ and $N$ are the midpoints of $\overline{RV}$ and $\overline{ST}$.

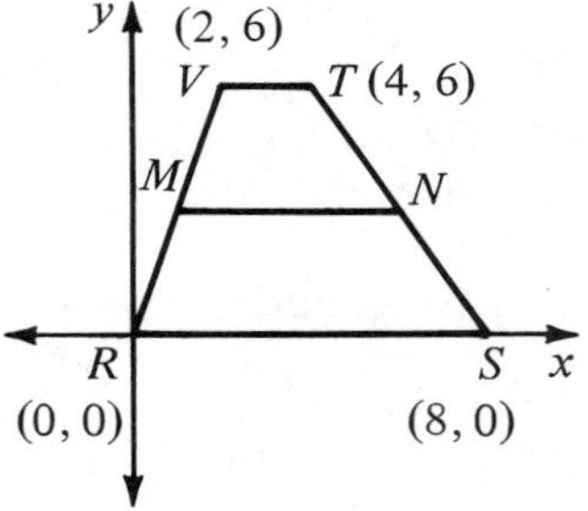


**a.** $M$ has coordinates (_?_, _?_). (1, 3)

**b.** $N$ has coordinates (_?_, _?_). (6, 3)

**c.** Slope of $\overline{MN}$ = _?_; slope of $\overline{RS}$ = _?_; slope of $\overline{VT}$ = _?_. 0; 0; 0

**d.** $\overline{MN} \parallel \overline{RS} \parallel \overline{VT}$. Why? Their slopes are equal.

**e.** $RS$ = _?_; $VT$ = _?_; $MN$ = _?_ 8; 2; 5

Does $MN = \frac{1}{2}(RS + VT)$? yes

**20.** *Given:* $\triangle ABC$. $M$ and $N$ are the midpoints of $\overline{AC}$ and $\overline{BC}$.

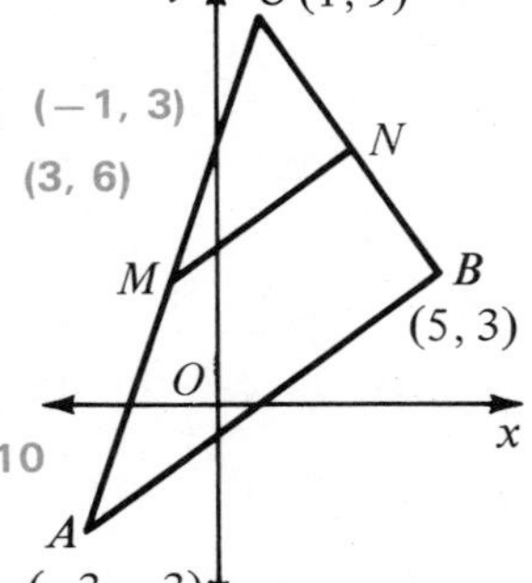


**a.** $M$ has coordinates (_?_, _?_). (−1, 3)

**b.** $N$ has coordinates (_?_, _?_). (3, 6)

**c.** Slope of $\overline{MN}$ = _?_; $\frac{3}{4}$

slope of $\overline{AB}$ = _?_. $\frac{3}{4}$

**d.** Is $\overline{MN} \parallel \overline{AB}$? Yes

**e.** $MN$ = _?_ and $AB$ = _?_ 5; 10

**f.** Does $MN = \frac{1}{2}AB$? Yes

**21.** Our goal is to show that: If two lines have equal slopes, then the lines are parallel.

*Given:* Lines $p$ and $q$
Slope of $p$ = slope of $q$

*Prove:* $p \parallel q$

*Suggested strategy:* Take points $B$ and $E$ so that $AB = DE$. Draw vertical segments $\overline{BC}$ and $\overline{EF}$.

Show that $\frac{BC}{AB} = \frac{EF}{DE}$ and conclude that $BC = EF$.

Prove that $\triangle ABC \cong \triangle DEF$.

Since $\angle 1 = \angle 2$, you can conclude that $p \parallel q$.

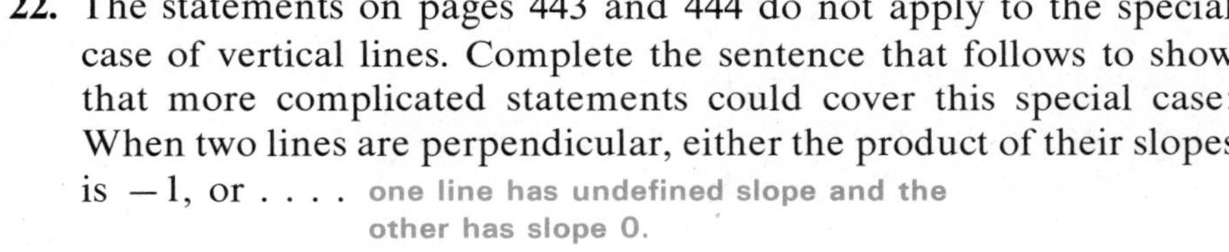

**22.** The statements on pages 443 and 444 do not apply to the special case of vertical lines. Complete the sentence that follows to show that more complicated statements could cover this special case: When two lines are perpendicular, either the product of their slopes is $-1$, or . . . . one line has undefined slope and the other has slope 0.

## SELF-TEST

1. The slope of a $\underline{\quad ? \quad}$ (horizontal/vertical) line equals 0. horizontal

2. The slope of a $\underline{\quad ? \quad}$ (horizontal/vertical) line is not defined. vertical

3. You are given point $A(2, 0)$ and point $B(5, 4)$. Find the slope of $\overleftrightarrow{AB}$. $\frac{4}{3}$

4. You are given point $B(5, 4)$ and point $C(8, -2)$. Find the slope of $\overleftrightarrow{BC}$. $-2$

5. If the slope of line $j$ equals $\frac{3}{7}$, then the slope of any line parallel to $j$ equals $\underline{\ ?\ }$. $\frac{3}{7}$

6. If the slope of line $k$ equals $-\frac{5}{2}$, then the slope of any line perpendicular to $k$ equals $\underline{\ ?\ }$. $\frac{2}{5}$

# 6 • Equations and Lines

Let's see how the line shown in the figure is related to the equation $2x + 3y = 12$. Do the coordinates of the four labeled points make the equation a true statement when they are substituted for $x$ and $y$?

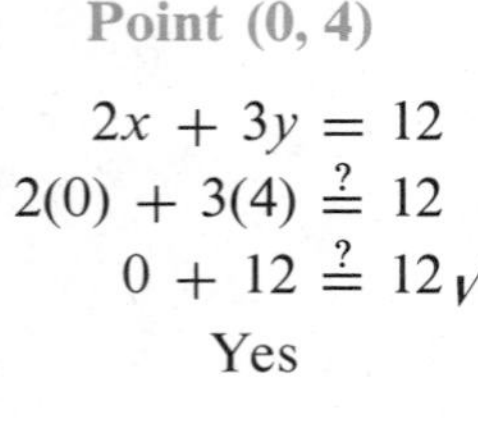

**Point (0, 4)**

$$2x + 3y = 12$$
$$2(0) + 3(4) \stackrel{?}{=} 12$$
$$0 + 12 \stackrel{?}{=} 12 \checkmark$$

Yes

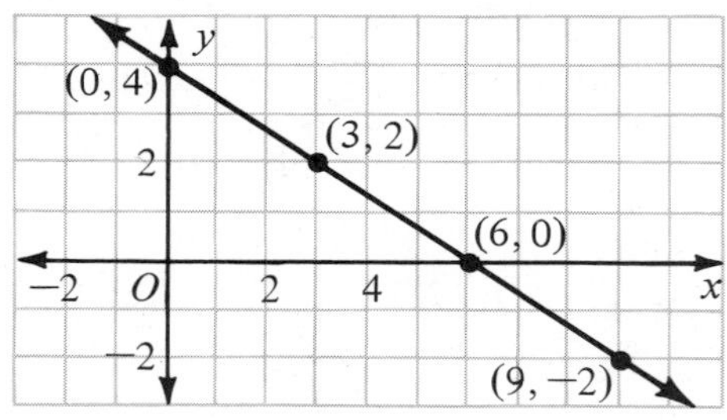


**Point (3, 2)**

$$2x + 3y = 12$$
$$2(3) + 3(2) \stackrel{?}{=} 12$$
$$6 + 6 \stackrel{?}{=} 12 \checkmark$$

Yes

**Point (6, 0)**

$$2x + 3y = 12$$
$$2(6) + 3(0) \stackrel{?}{=} 12$$
$$12 + 0 \stackrel{?}{=} 12 \checkmark$$

Yes

**Point (9, −2)**

$$2x + 3y = 12$$
$$2(9) + 3(-2) \stackrel{?}{=} 12$$
$$18 - 6 \stackrel{?}{=} 12 \checkmark$$

Yes

Suppose you kept on testing the coordinates of different points. You would find that the coordinates of any point on the line make the equation a true statement. The coordinates of any other point do not. The line is called the **graph** of the equation $2x + 3y = 12$.

In general, it is true that:

If a point lies on the graph of an equation, then its coordinates make the equation a true statement.

If the coordinates of a point make an equation a true statement, then the point lies on the graph of the equation.

The facts you discovered about the equation $2x + 3y = 12$ are true for every equation in the form $ax + by = c$.

If an equation can be written in the form $ax + by = c$, then the graph of the equation is a line. (Assume that $a$ and $b$ are not both equal to zero.)

The examples that follow show how to graph an equation that can be written in the form $ax + by = c$.

**EXAMPLE 1** Draw the graph of $2x + y = 6$.

Pick any three numbers to use for $x$ or for $y$. Find the coordinates of three points.

| Let $x = 0$: | Let $y = 0$: | Let $x = 1$: |
|---|---|---|
| $2x + y = 6$ | $2x + y = 6$ | $2x + y = 6$ |
| $2(0) + y = 6$ | $2x + 0 = 6$ | $2(1) + y = 6$ |
| $0 + y = 6$ | $2x = 6$ | $2 + y = 6$ |
| $y = 6$ | $x = 3$ | $y = 4$ |

Now plot the points:

(0, 6); (3, 0); (1, 4).

Then draw the line.

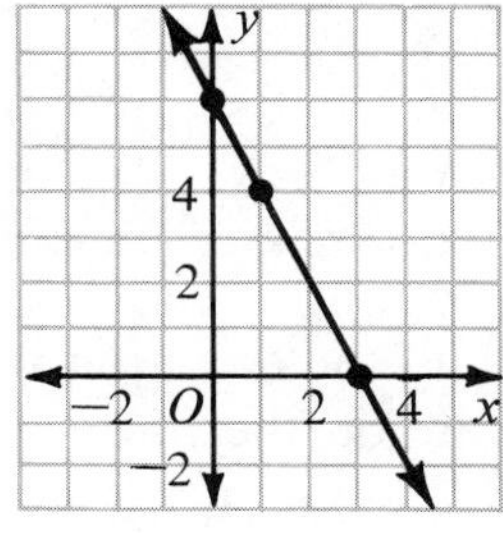


**EXAMPLE 2** Draw the graph of $x - 3y = 3$.

| Let $x = 0$: | Let $y = 0$: | Let $x = 7$: |
|---|---|---|
| $x - 3y = 3$ | $x - 3y = 3$ | $x - 3y = 3$ |
| $0 - 3y = 3$ | $x - 3(0) = 3$ | $7 - 3y = 3$ |
| $-3y = 3$ | $x - 0 = 3$ | $-3y = -4$ |
| $y = -1$ | $x = 3$ | $y = 1\frac{1}{3}$ |

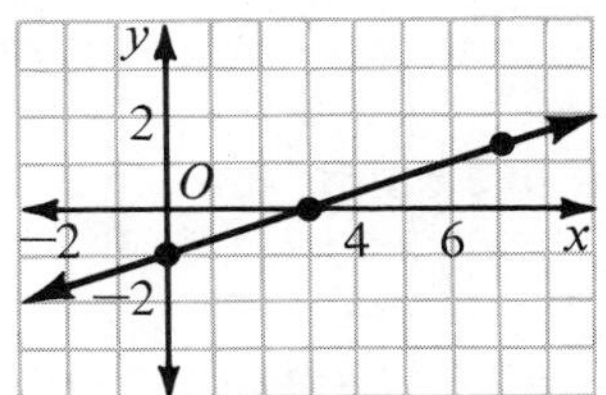


Notice that when you let $x = 7$, you get a fractional value for $y$. You have two choices: (1) estimate the position of $\left(7, 1\frac{1}{3}\right)$; or (2) forget that point and try other values for $x$ or $y$ until you get a pair of coordinates that doesn't involve fractions.

**EXAMPLE 3** Draw the graph of $x = 2$.

The equation can be rewritten in the form $x + 0y = 2$.

If you try to let $x$ be any number other than 2, you cannot find a value for $y$.

On the other hand, no matter what value you assign to $y$, the value of $x$ is always 2.

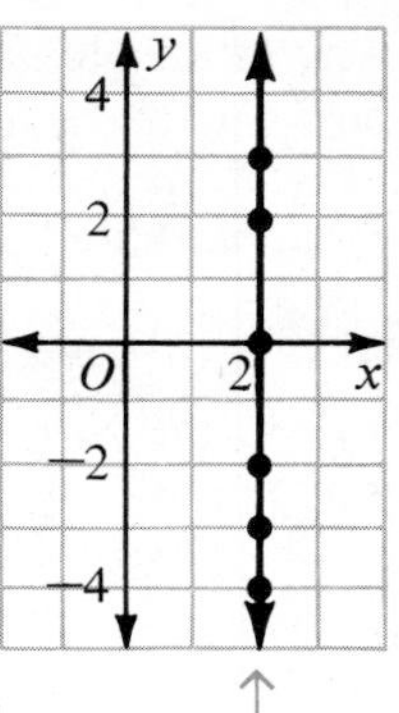


The graph of $x = 2$ is a vertical line.

## Classroom Practice

1. The graph of the equation $y = x - 2$ is shown. Does the point lie on the line?

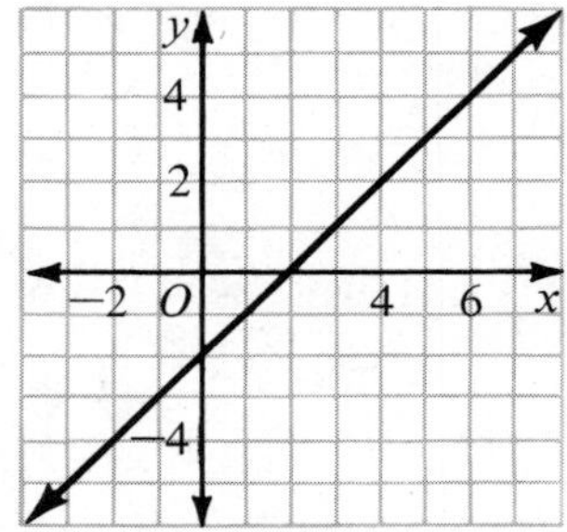


   a. (2, 0) Yes  b. (0, 2) No
   c. (3, 1) Yes  d. (1, 3) No
   e. (4, 4) No  f. (1, −1) Yes
   g. (−1, −3) Yes  h. $\left(2\frac{1}{2}, \frac{1}{2}\right)$ Yes

2. Do the coordinates of the point make the equation $2x - y = 4$ a true statement?

   a. (2, 2) No  b. (4, 0) No  c. (2, 0) Yes  d. (1, 1) No
   e. (10, 16) Yes  f. (0, −4) Yes  g. (−3, −10) Yes  h. (−2, 0) No

3. Name the coordinates of five points (any five) that lie on the graph of the equation $y = 2x$. For example: (−3, −6), (0, 0), (1, 2), (2, 4), (6, 12)

4. The equation $y = 5$ is given. Note that the equation can be written in the form $0x + y = 5$.

   a. When $x = 0$, $y =$ ___?___. 5
   b. When $x = -13$, $y =$ ___?___. 5
   c. No matter what value you assign to $x$, $y =$ ___?___. 5
   d. The graph of $y = 5$ is a $\frac{?}{\text{horizontal/vertical}}$ line. horizontal

## Written Exercises

A **1.** State the coordinates of four points (any four) that lie on the line at the left, below. For example: (0, −1), (3, −3), (−3, 1), (−6, 3)

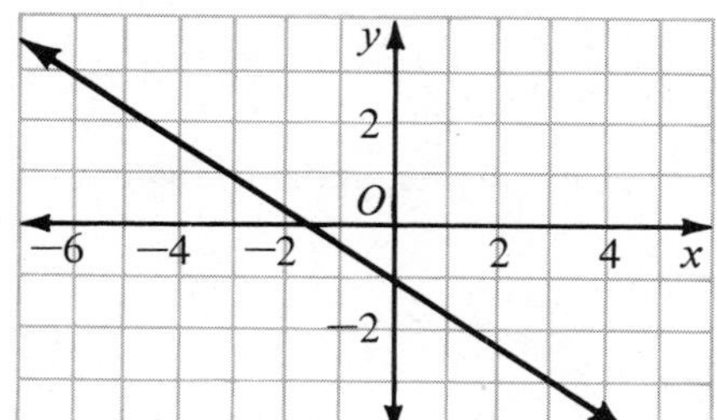


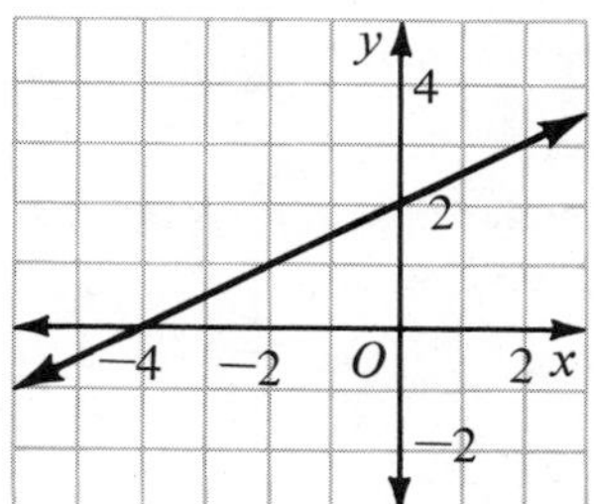


**2.** One of the points named does not lie on the line at the right, above. Which point?

(−4, 0) $\quad$ <u>(1, 3)</u> $\quad$ $\left(1, 2\frac{1}{2}\right)$ $\quad$ (0, 2)

**Copy and complete the table of values.**

**3.** $x + y = 6$

| $x$ | $y$ |
|---|---|
| 0 | ? 6 |
| 6 ? | 0 |
| 2 | ? 4 |

**4.** $x - y = 6$

| $x$ | $y$ |
|---|---|
| 0 | ? −6 |
| 6 ? | 0 |
| 4 | ? −2 |

**5.** $y = 3x$

| $x$ | $y$ |
|---|---|
| 0 | ? 0 |
| 0 ? | 0 |
| 3 | ? 9 |

**6.** $y = x + 4$

| $x$ | $y$ |
|---|---|
| 0 | ? 4 |
| −4 ? | 0 |
| 3 | ? 7 |

**7.** $2x - 3y = 12$

| $x$ | $y$ |
|---|---|
| 0 | ? −4 |
| 6 ? | 0 |
| 12 ? | 4 |

**8.** $3x - y = -6$

| $x$ | $y$ |
|---|---|
| 0 | ? 6 |
| −2 ? | 0 |
| −1 ? | 3 |

**9–14.** Draw the graphs of the equations in Exercises 3–8. If your points do not lie on a line, check the work you did earlier.

**15.** Draw the graph of $x = 5$. (*Hint:* See Example 3, page 450.)

**16.** Draw the graph of $y = -4$.

**Make a table of values for plotting three points. Plot the points and draw the graph of the equation.**

B **17.** $3x + 2y = 9$ $\qquad$ **18.** $x - 4y = 6$

**19.** $4x + 3y = 6$ $\qquad$ **20.** $2x - 3y = -12$

For each exercise, graph the two equations on the same pair of axes. Inspect your drawing and state the coordinates of the point where the graphs intersect.

**21.** $x + y = 6$ (4, 2)
$x - y = 2$

**22.** $y = x + 2$ (−1, 1)
$y = -x$

**23.** $2x + y = 6$ (2, 2)
$3x - y = 4$

**24.** $2x + y = -1$ (−2, 3)
$x + 2y = 4$

Graph the three equations on the same pair of axes. Find the area of the triangle formed by the three lines.

C **25.** $x = 1$ $A = 8$
$y = -1$
$y = x + 2$

**26.** $x = 2$ $A = 2$
$y = 2$
$x + y = 6$

**27.** $y = -1$ $A = 3$
$y = 3x + 2$
$3x + y = 2$

# CONSUMER CORNER

## *Energy Usage*

Every time you toast a piece of bread, use a hair dryer, or play the radio, you use energy. Some machines use more energy than others. The chart below lists this usage in terms of the length of time the machine would run if supplied with the amount of energy in a liter of gasoline.

| | | | |
|---|---|---|---|
| electric clock | 31 weeks | toaster | $8\frac{1}{2}$ hours |
| black & white television | $2\frac{3}{4}$ days | oven | 3 hours |
| color television | $1\frac{1}{2}$ days | electric fan | $2\frac{1}{4}$ days |

**Exercises**

1. Which of the machines in the chart uses the most energy? oven
2. Estimate the cost of running an electric clock for one year. (Assume that gasoline costs 30¢ per liter.) 50¢
3. On the average, how many hours do you spend each week watching television? Express the amount of energy used in terms of liters of gasoline.

# 7 • Coordinate Geometry Proofs

Recall Theorem 14 in Chapter 5:

> The median of a trapezoid has two properties.
> (1) It is parallel to the bases.
> (2) Its length equals half the sum of the base lengths.

This theorem was stated without proof. We are now able to prove the theorem by using coordinates.

*Given:* Trapezoid $ABCD$ with median $\overline{MN}$

*Prove:* 1. $\overline{MN} \parallel \overline{AB} \parallel \overline{DC}$

2. $MN = \frac{1}{2}(AB + DC)$

*Proof:*

Draw coordinate axes as shown. Then $A$ is point $(0, 0)$, and the $y$-coordinate of $B$ is 0. Assign coordinates to $B$, $C$, and $D$ as shown. (Because $\overline{DC}$ is horizontal, $D$ and $C$ must have equal $y$-coordinates.)

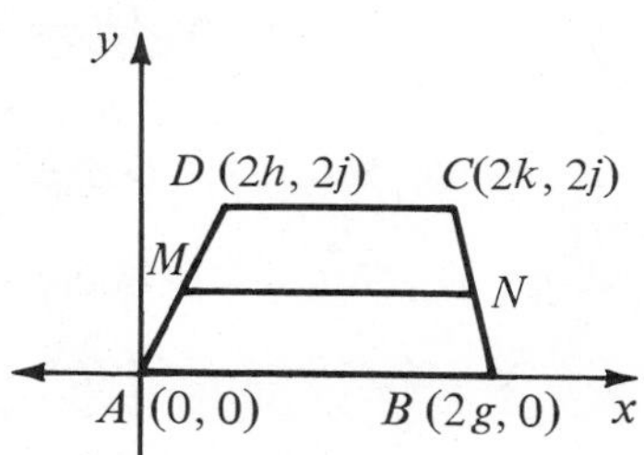


The coordinates of $M$ are $\left(\frac{2h + 0}{2}, \frac{2j + 0}{2}\right)$, or $(h, j)$.

The coordinates of $N$ are $\left(\frac{2g + 2k}{2}, \frac{0 + 2j}{2}\right)$, or $(g + k, j)$.

1. Slope of $\overline{MN} = \frac{j - j}{(g + k) - h} = \frac{0}{g + k - h} = 0.$
   Slope of $\overline{AB}$ = slope of $\overline{DC} = 0$.
   Therefore, $\overline{MN} \parallel \overline{AB} \parallel \overline{DC}$.

2. $MN = g + k - h$
   $AB = 2g - 0 = 2g$
   $DC = 2k - 2h$

   $AB + DC = 2g + 2k - 2h$, and $\frac{1}{2}(AB + DC) = g + k - h$.

   Because both $MN$ and $\frac{1}{2}(AB + DC)$ equal $g + k - h$,

   $MN = \frac{1}{2}(AB + DC)$.

## Classroom Practice

**The purpose of these exercises is to use coordinates to prove Theorem 15 from Chapter 5: The segment joining the midpoints of two sides of a triangle is parallel to the third side and half as long.**

*Given:* $\triangle ABC$;
midpoints $D$ and $E$ as shown

*Prove:* 1. $\overline{DE} \parallel \overline{AB}$

2. $DE = \frac{1}{2}AB$

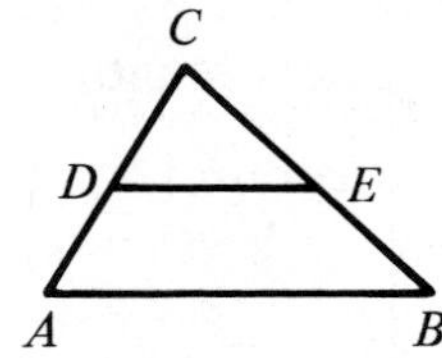


*Proof:*
Draw axes and assign coordinates as shown.

**1. a.** The coordinates of $D$ are ( ? , ? ). (h, j)

**b.** The coordinates of $E$ are ( ? , ? ). (h + g, j)

**c.** Slope of $\overline{AB} = \frac{0}{2g} =$ ? . 0

**d.** Slope of $\overline{DE} = \frac{j - j}{(g + h) - h} =$ ? . 0

**e.** $\overline{DE} \parallel \overline{AB}$ because ? . The slopes are equal.

**2. a.** $DE = (g + h) - h =$ ? . g **b.** Because $AB = 2g$, $\frac{1}{2}AB =$ ? . g

**c.** Because both $DE$ and $\frac{1}{2}AB$ equal ? g, $DE = \frac{1}{2}AB$.

## Written Exercises

A **1.** Axes have been drawn for a particular rectangle. Complete a proof that the diagonals are equal.

**a.** Because $\overline{VT}$ is horizontal, the $y$-coordinate of $T$ is ? . 5

**b.** Because $\overline{ST}$ is vertical, the $x$-coordinate of $T$ is ? . 4

**c.** In right $\triangle VRS$, $(VS)^2 = 5^2 + \text{?}^2$ (4), and $VS = \sqrt{\text{?}}$. $VS = \sqrt{41}$

**d.** In right $\triangle TSR$, $(RT)^2 = \text{?}^2 + \text{?}^2$ (5, 4), and $RT = \sqrt{\text{?}}$. $RT = \sqrt{41}$

**e.** Because both $VS$ and $RT$ equal ? ($\sqrt{41}$), $VS = RT$.

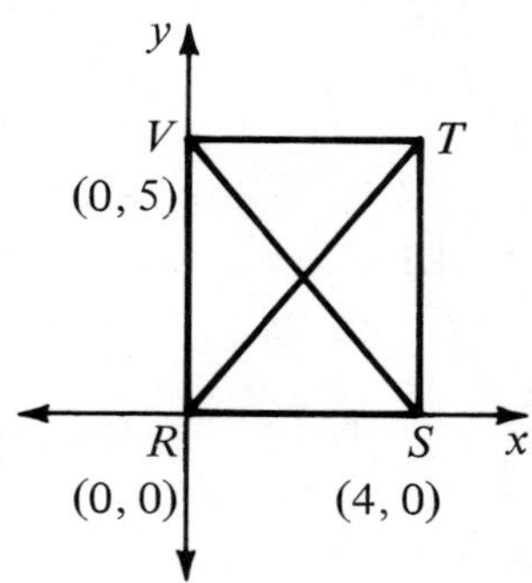

**2.** Axes have been drawn for a particular square. Complete a proof that the diagonals are perpendicular.

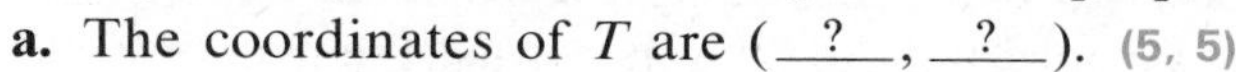

**a.** The coordinates of $T$ are ( ? , ? ). (5, 5)

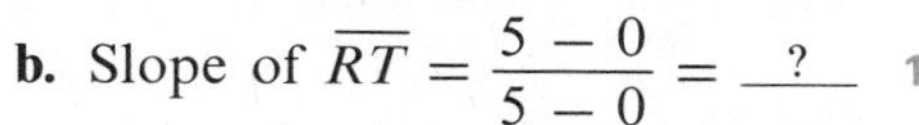

**b.** Slope of $\overline{RT} = \dfrac{5-0}{5-0} =$ ? 1

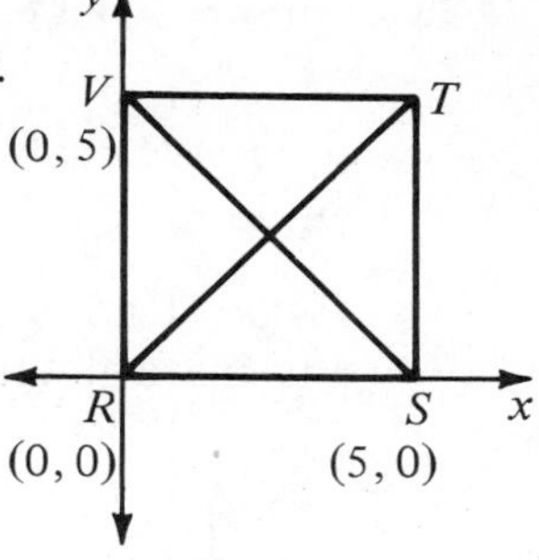



**c.** Slope of $\overline{VS} = \dfrac{0-5}{5-0} =$ ? −1

**d.** (Slope of $\overline{RT}$) · (Slope of $\overline{VS}$) = ? · ? = ? , so $\overline{RT} \perp \overline{VS}$.
1 −1 −1

**3.** Axes have been drawn for a particular right triangle. Complete a proof that the midpoint $M$ of the hypotenuse is equidistant from the three vertices.

**a.** The coordinates of $M$ are ( ? , ? ). (2, 3)

**b.** Draw horizontal and vertical segments from $M$ as shown.

**c.** The coordinates of $J$ are ( ? , ? ), and the coordinates of $K$ are ( ? , ? ). (0, 3) (2, 0)

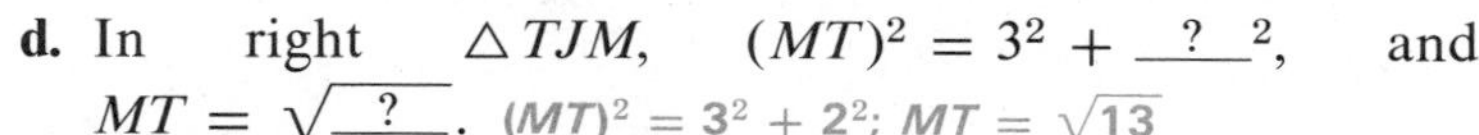

**d.** In right $\triangle TJM$, $(MT)^2 = 3^2 + \underline{\ ?\ }^2$, and $MT = \sqrt{\underline{\ ?\ }}$. $(MT)^2 = 3^2 + 2^2$; $MT = \sqrt{13}$

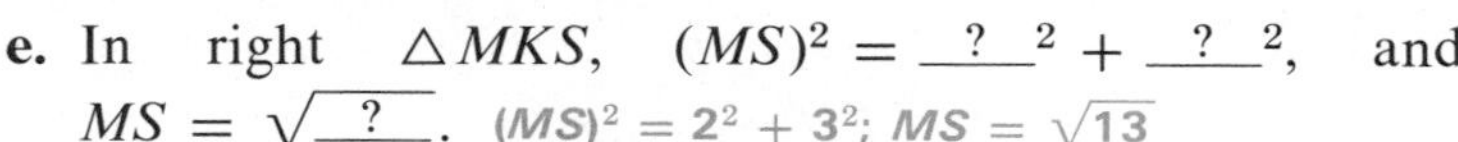

**e.** In right $\triangle MKS$, $(MS)^2 = \underline{\ ?\ }^2 + \underline{\ ?\ }^2$, and $MS = \sqrt{\underline{\ ?\ }}$. $(MS)^2 = 2^2 + 3^2$; $MS = \sqrt{13}$

**f.** In right $\triangle MKR$, $(MR)^2 = \underline{\ ?\ }^2 + \underline{\ ?\ }^2$, and $MR = \sqrt{\underline{\ ?\ }}$. $(MR)^2 = 3^2 + 2^2$; $MR = \sqrt{13}$

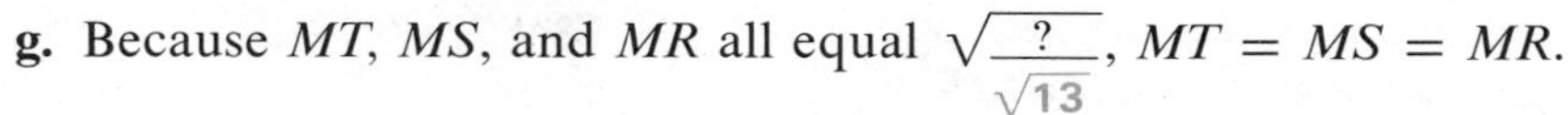

**g.** Because $MT$, $MS$, and $MR$ all equal $\sqrt{\underline{\ ?\ }}$, $MT = MS = MR$. $\sqrt{13}$

**In Exercises 4–6 copy the diagram shown. See Exercises 1–3 for ideas about proofs.**

B **4.** *Prove:* The diagonals of any rectangle are equal.

**5.** *Prove:* The diagonals of any square are perpendicular.

**6.** *Prove:* The midpoint of the hypotenuse of any right triangle is equidistant from the three vertices.

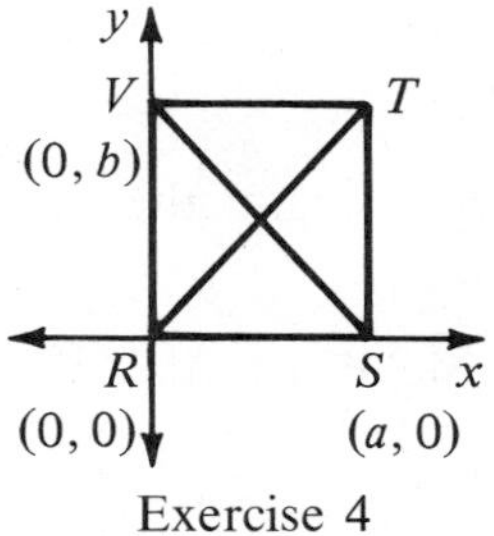



Exercise 4

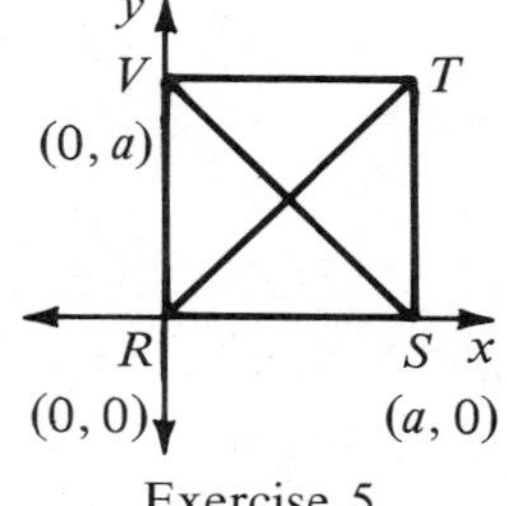



Exercise 5

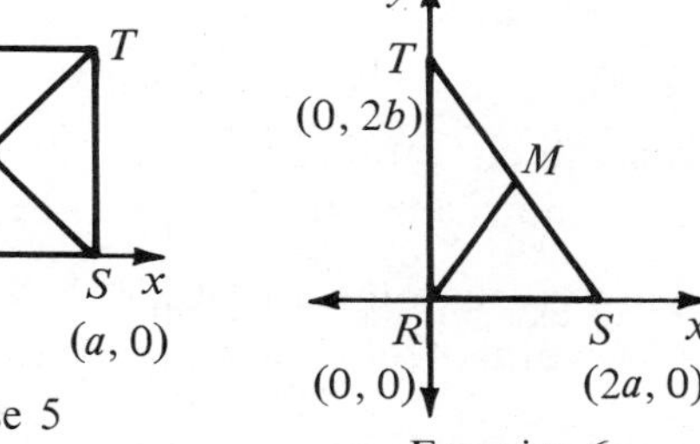



Exercise 6

**In Exercises 7 and 8, copy the diagrams shown.**

C 7. *Prove:* The medians drawn to the legs of an isosceles triangle are equal. (*Hint:* Notice the $x$-coordinate of $T$. What must the $x$-coordinate of $S$ be?)

8. *Prove:* The segments joining, in order, the midpoints of the sides of any quadrilateral form a parallelogram.

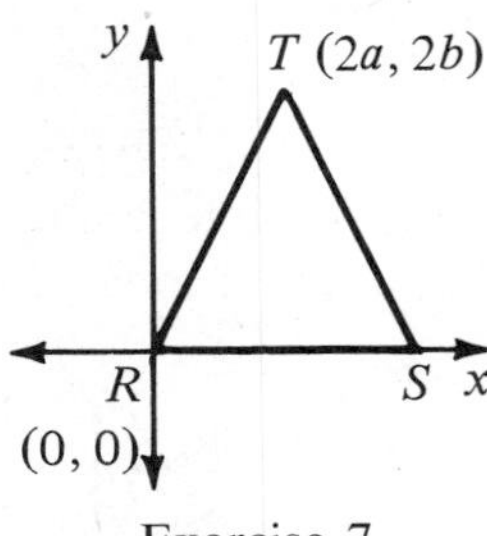


Exercise 7

y
V (2b, 2c) J T (2d, 2e)
K H
R G S x
(0, 0) (2a, 0)

Exercise 8

## SELF-TEST

1. Do the coordinates of the point $(5, -3)$ make the equation $2x - 3y = 1$ a true statement? No

**Copy and complete each table of values.**

2. $x + y = 8$

| $x$ | $y$ |
|---|---|
| 0 | ? 8 |
| 8 ? | 0 |
| 3 | ? 5 |

3. $4x - 3y = 12$

| $x$ | $y$ |
|---|---|
| 0 | ? $-4$ |
| 3 ? | 0 |
| 5 | ? $\frac{8}{3}$ |

4. Given the equation $2x + y = 10$, make a table of values, plot the points, and draw the graph of the equation.

5. You are given points $A(0, 0)$, $B(5, 0)$, $C(6, 4)$, and $D(1, 4)$. Prove that quadrilateral $ABCD$ is a parallelogram.

## Reviewing Algebraic Skills

**Simplify.**

Sample 1 $\frac{6ab}{cd} - \frac{3ab + 2}{cd} = \frac{6ab - (3ab + 2)}{cd}$ ← Be careful with signs!

The denominators are the same.

$= \frac{6ab - 3ab - 2}{cd}$

$= \frac{3ab - 2}{cd}$

1. $\frac{12x}{7} - \frac{8x}{7}$ $\frac{4x}{7}$
2. $\frac{2ab}{3z} + \frac{4ab}{3z}$ $\frac{2ab}{z}$
3. $\frac{4xy}{5} - \frac{9xy}{5}$ $-xy$
4. $\frac{11d^2}{2c} - \frac{9d^2}{2c}$ $\frac{d^2}{c}$
5. $\frac{6b^3}{a} + \frac{2b}{a}$ $\frac{6b^3 + 2b}{a}$
6. $\frac{-8k}{7} + \frac{3k}{7}$ $\frac{-5k}{7}$
7. $\frac{11}{x + y} - \frac{10}{x + y}$ $\frac{1}{x + y}$
8. $\frac{4x + 2}{k} - \frac{2 + 4x}{k}$ $0$
9. $\frac{4m - n}{5n} + \frac{n + m}{5n}$ $\frac{m}{n}$
10. $\frac{5h + 2k}{h + k} + \frac{h + 4k}{h + k}$ $6$
11. $\frac{b^2}{b + 1} - \frac{1}{b + 1}$ $b - 1$
12. $\frac{a^2 - 6a}{a - 3} + \frac{9}{a - 3}$ $a - 3$

Sample 2 $\frac{9}{8c} + \frac{5}{2d} =$ ← The denominators are different. First rename the fractions. The new denominator can be $8cd$.

$\frac{9d}{8cd} + \frac{20c}{8cd} =$

$\frac{9d + 20c}{8cd}$

13. $\frac{a}{5} + \frac{a}{2}$ $\frac{7a}{10}$
14. $\frac{x}{3} - \frac{x}{8}$ $\frac{5x}{24}$
15. $\frac{2a}{3} + \frac{a}{6}$ $\frac{5a}{6}$
16. $\frac{n}{10} + \frac{4n}{5}$ $\frac{9n}{10}$
17. $\frac{5}{2a} + \frac{1}{a}$ $\frac{7}{2a}$
18. $\frac{3}{h} - \frac{1}{3h}$ $\frac{8}{3h}$
19. $\frac{7}{ab} - \frac{5a}{b}$ $\frac{7 - 5a^2}{ab}$
20. $\frac{2}{d} + \frac{3}{d^2}$ $\frac{2d + 3}{d^2}$
21. $\frac{3m}{4} - \frac{2m}{3}$ $\frac{m}{12}$
22. $\frac{2a}{5} + \frac{a}{4}$ $\frac{13a}{20}$
23. $\frac{7}{x} + \frac{1}{2}$ $\frac{14 + x}{2x}$
24. $\frac{1}{y} - \frac{1}{z}$ $\frac{z - y}{zy}$
25. $\frac{4}{3n} - \frac{2}{n}$ $\frac{-2}{3n}$
26. $\frac{a^2c}{b} + \frac{a^2b}{c}$ $\frac{a^2c^2 + a^2b^2}{bc}$
27. $\frac{5x}{6} + \frac{x}{2}$ $\frac{4x}{3}$
28. $\frac{3m}{5} - \frac{m}{10}$ $\frac{m}{2}$

# applications

## *Latitude and Longitude*

When traveling over land, you can sometimes tell your location by noticing landmarks that are near you. In the middle of the ocean, this would be very difficult to do. One of the ways that air and sea navigators describe their exact location is by using the system of *latitude* and *longitude*. This system consists of a grid of imaginary lines, east-west lines of latitude and north-south lines of longitude. Each point on the earth is at the crossing of a particular line of latitude and a particular line of longitude. Most globes and large maps show some of these lines.

The *equator*, a line that divides the earth in half, is used as the line of zero latitude. Other lines of latitude, also called parallels of latitude, are marked to indicate degrees north and south of the equator. We measure 90° of latitude north of the equator and 90° of latitude south.

Lines of longitude, also called meridians, run vertically from the North Pole to the South Pole. These lines indicate degrees east or west of a zero line, called the prime meridian. We measure 180° of longitude west of the prime meridian and 180° of longitude east.

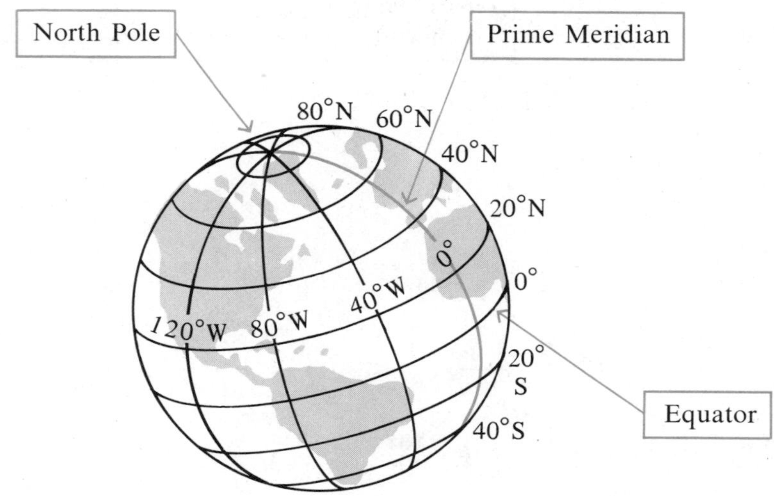

There is no natural location for the prime meridian as there is for the equator. Originally each nation used the line of longitude passing through its own national observatory. This led to some confusion, and in 1884, most nations agreed to use the meridian passing through Greenwich, England, as the prime meridian.

**Examples** Look at the illustration of a globe shown here. Do you see that 40°N, 40°W is near the middle of the North Atlantic Ocean?

Locate the spot labeled 20°S, 80°W. It is near the west coast of South America.

## Exercises

**Find a map or globe showing latitude and longitude.**

1. Name the ocean in which the following locations are found.
   **a.** 80° N, 160° W Arctic **b.** 5° S, 60° E Indian **c.** 30° S, 10° W S. Atl.
   **d.** 40° N, 150° W N. Pac. **e.** 50° N, 20° W N. Atl. **f.** 50° S, 160° W S. Pac.
2. Find the approximate latitude and longitude for the place where you live. Answers will vary
3. The location 0° latitude, 0° longitude is near what continent? Africa
4. Name the countries in Africa through which the equator passes.
   Gabon, Congo, Uganda, Kenya, Somali Republic

## Reviewing the Chapter

### Chapter Summary

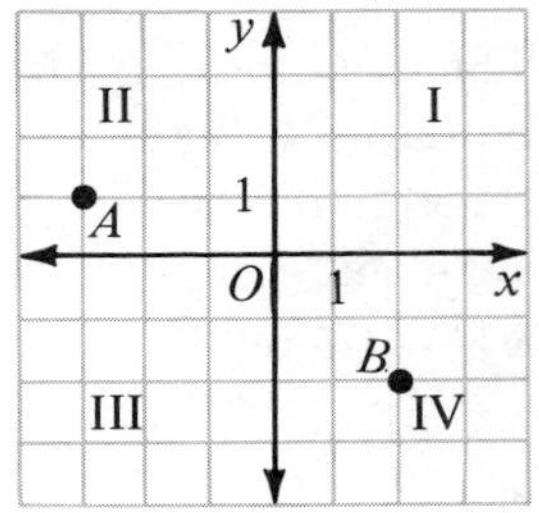


1. In the coordinate plane, the $x$-axis and the $y$-axis intersect at the origin, point (0, 0).

   Point $A(-3, 1)$ lies in Quadrant II.

   Point $B(2, -2)$ lies in Quadrant IV.

2. The Pythagorean Theorem can be used to find the distance between two points in the coordinate plane.
3. Given $P(x_1, y_1)$ and $Q(x_2, y_2)$. The midpoint $M$ of $\overline{PQ}$ has coordinates $\left(\frac{x_1 + x_2}{2}, \frac{y_1 + y_2}{2}\right)$.
4. The line that joins points $(x_1, y_1)$ and $(x_2, y_2)$ has slope $\frac{y_2 - y_1}{x_2 - x_1}$. The slope of a vertical line is not defined.
5. The following statements apply to nonvertical lines:
   If two lines are parallel, then their slopes are equal.
   If two lines have equal slopes, then they are parallel.
   If two lines are perpendicular, then the product of their slopes is $-1$. If the product of the slopes of two lines is $-1$, then the lines are perpendicular.
6. If an equation can be written in the form $ax + by = c$ ($a$ and $b$ not both 0), then its graph is a straight line. We find the graph by first preparing a table of values.
7. Coordinate geometry can be used to prove theorems.

### Chapter Review Test

**Refer to the diagram at the right.** (*See pp. 426–429.*)

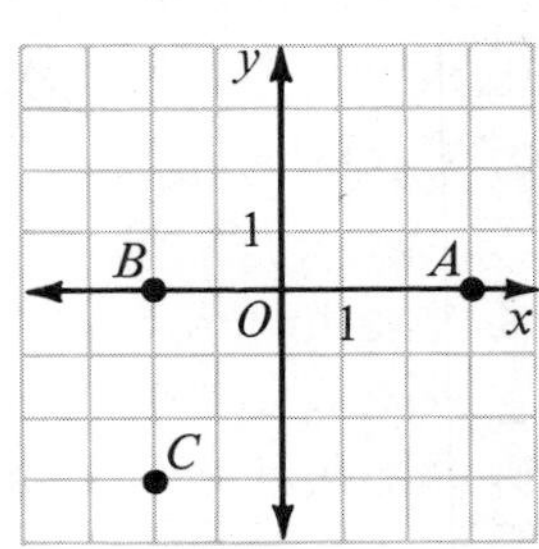


**1.** The coordinates of point $A$ are _?_. (3, 0)

**2.** The coordinates of point $B$ are _?_. (−2, 0)

**3.** Point $B$ lies on the _?_-axis. *x*

**4.** Suppose $D$ is located so that quadrilateral $ABCD$ is a rectangle. Point $D$ has coordinates (_?_, _?_). (3, −3)

**5.** Point $C$ lies in quadrant _?_. III

**Find the distance between the points named. Use graph paper if you wish.** (*See pp. 430–432.*)

**6.** (0, 0) and (6, 8) 10

**7.** (3, 0) and (3, 7) 7

**8.** (0, 2) and (4, 5) 5

**9.** (−1, −1) and (7, −7) 10

**State the coordinates of the midpoint of the segment that joins the points named.** (*See pp. 433–437.*)

**10.** (2, 0) and (6, 0) (4, 0)

**11.** (3, −8) and (3, 0) (3, −4)

**12.** (3, 4) and (5, −4) (4, 0)

**13.** (3, 4) and (−5, 1) $\left(-1, \frac{5}{2}\right)$

**State the slope of the line. If the slope is not defined for a particular line, write *not defined*.** (*See pp. 438–442.*)

**14.** $\overleftrightarrow{OA}$ $\frac{1}{2}$

**15.** $\overleftrightarrow{OB}$ $-\frac{3}{2}$

**16.** $\overleftrightarrow{BA}$ $-\frac{1}{2}$

**17.** $\overleftrightarrow{CD}$ 0

**18.** $\overleftrightarrow{CA}$ $\frac{3}{4}$

**19.** $\overleftrightarrow{CB}$ not defined

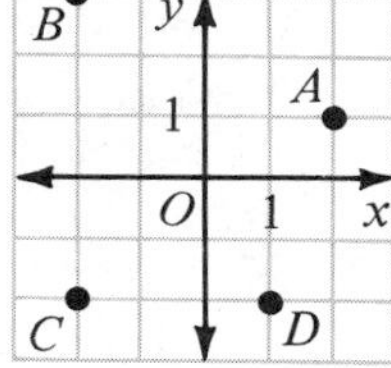


**A certain line *t* has slope $\frac{2}{3}$. Classify each statement as true or false.** (*See pp. 443–447.*)

**20.** Line *t* rises to the right. True

**21.** Every line that is perpendicular to *t* has slope $\frac{3}{2}$. False

**22.** The line that contains points (−1, 0) and (3, 6) is parallel to *t*. False

**23.** Every line that is parallel to *t* has slope $\frac{2}{3}$. True

**Line *j* has the equation $2x - y = 10$.** (*See pp. 448–452.*)

**24.** Does *j* pass through the origin? No

**25.** Does *j* pass through the point (5, 1)? No

**26.** On line *j*, when $y = 4$, $x =$ __?__. 7

**Points *A*, *B*, *C*, and *D* have the coordinates shown.** (*See pp. 453–456.*)

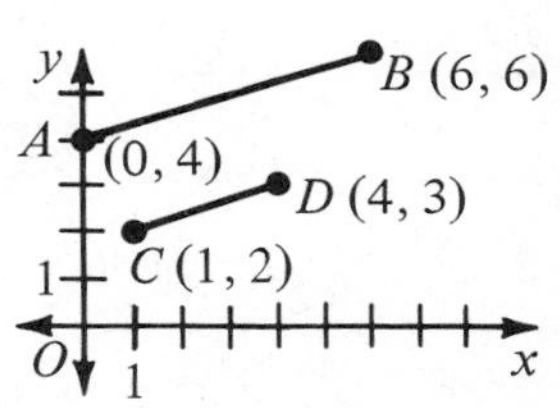


**27.** *Prove:* $\overleftrightarrow{AB} \parallel \overleftrightarrow{CD}$

**28.** *Prove:* $CD = \frac{1}{2}AB$

**Refer to the figure shown. Find each of the following.**

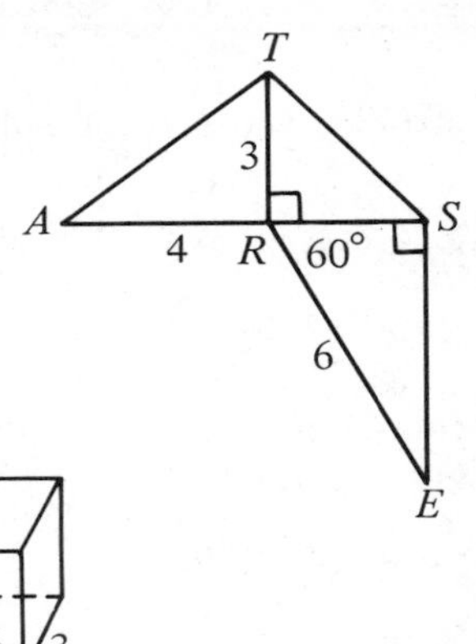


1. $SR$ 3  2. $SE$ $3\sqrt{3}$

3. $TS$ $3\sqrt{2}$  4. $TA$ 5

5. The perimeter of $\triangle TAR$ 12

6. The area of $\triangle STA$ $10\frac{1}{2}$

**Refer to the rectangular solid shown.**

7. Find the value of $x$. 5

8. Find the length $d$ of the diagonal. $\sqrt{29}$

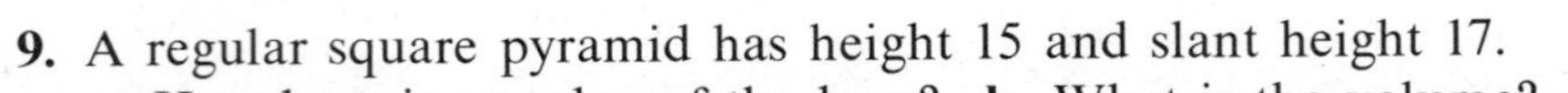

9. A regular square pyramid has height 15 and slant height 17.
 **a.** How long is an edge of the base? **b.** What is the volume? a. 16; b. 1280

10. A cone has radius 5 and height 12. Find:
 **a.** the slant height **b.** the total area **c.** the volume
 a. 13; b. $90\pi$; c. $100\pi$

**Refer to $\triangle BIG$. Express each ratio in simplest form.**

11. $\sin B$ $\frac{4}{5}$ 12. $\cos G$ $\frac{4}{5}$

13. $\tan B$ $\frac{4}{3}$ 14. $\sin G$ $\frac{3}{5}$

**Complete. Use the table on page 418.**

15. $\sin E =$ _?_ .906 16. $\tan S =$ _?_ .700

17. To the nearest tenth, $y =$ _?_. 7.0

**Complete.**

18. Point $D$ lies in quadrant _?_. III

19. The coordinates of point $A$ are (_?_, _?_). (−2, 3)

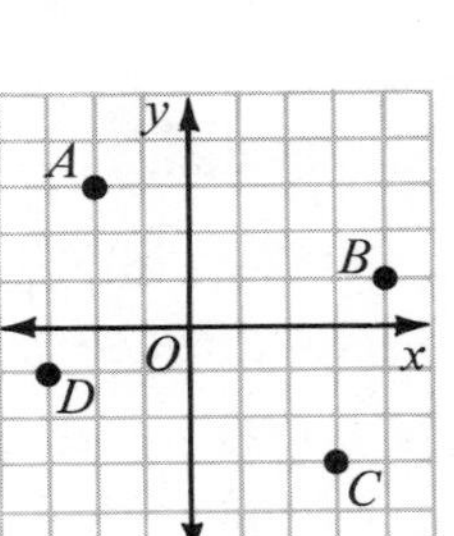


20. The length of $\overline{AD}$ is _?_. $\sqrt{17}$

21. The midpoint of $\overline{DC}$ is _?_. (0, −2)

22. The slope of $\overleftrightarrow{AD}$ is _?_. 4

23. The slope of $\overleftrightarrow{DC}$ is _?_. $-\frac{1}{3}$

24. Any line perpendicular to $\overleftrightarrow{AB}$ has slope _?_. 3

25. Prove that quadrilateral $ABCD$ is a parallelogram.

# Acknowledgments

**Creative Illustrations:** Page xii, Philip W. Garland
Chapter Openers, Steven Lindblom
Other, Walter Fournier

**Photos were provided by the following sources:**

Page 34 Ellis Herwig-STOCK, BOSTON
Page 65 Fredrik D. Bodin-STOCK, BOSTON
Page 98 Tyrone Hall
Page 125 Owen Franken-STOCK, BOSTON
Page 184 Cary Wolinsky-STOCK, BOSTON
Page 211 Editorial Photocolor Archives, Inc.
Page 224 Courtesy of John Hancock Mutual Life Insurance Co.
Page 253 Courtesy Museo Nacional De Artes E Industrias Populares, Mexico City
Page 266 Donald Dietz-STOCK, BOSTON
Page 299 Tyrone Hall
Page 306 Alinari, Scala
Page 307 Michael Holford Photographs
Page 327 Tyrone Hall
Page 368 1. NOAA 2. Walter G. Hodsdon 3. Joel E. Arem, Ph.D., F.G.A.
Page 369 Editorial Photocolor Archives, Inc.
Page 376 Ellis Herwig-STOCK, BOSTON

# Table of Squares

| Number | Square | Number | Square | Number | Square | Number | Square |
|---|---|---|---|---|---|---|---|
| $n$ | $n^2$ | $n$ | $n^2$ | $n$ | $n^2$ | $n$ | $n^2$ |
| **1** | 1 | **26** | 676 | **51** | 2601 | **76** | 5776 |
| **2** | 4 | **27** | 729 | **52** | 2704 | **77** | 5929 |
| **3** | 9 | **28** | 784 | **53** | 2809 | **78** | 6084 |
| **4** | 16 | **29** | 841 | **54** | 2916 | **79** | 6241 |
| **5** | 25 | **30** | 900 | **55** | 3025 | **80** | 6400 |
| **6** | 36 | **31** | 961 | **56** | 3136 | **81** | 6561 |
| **7** | 49 | **32** | 1024 | **57** | 3249 | **82** | 6724 |
| **8** | 64 | **33** | 1089 | **58** | 3364 | **83** | 6889 |
| **9** | 81 | **34** | 1156 | **59** | 3481 | **84** | 7056 |
| **10** | 100 | **35** | 1225 | **60** | 3600 | **85** | 7225 |
| **11** | 121 | **36** | 1296 | **61** | 3721 | **86** | 7396 |
| **12** | 144 | **37** | 1369 | **62** | 3844 | **87** | 7569 |
| **13** | 169 | **38** | 1444 | **63** | 3969 | **88** | 7744 |
| **14** | 196 | **39** | 1521 | **64** | 4096 | **89** | 7921 |
| **15** | 225 | **40** | 1600 | **65** | 4225 | **90** | 8100 |
| **16** | 256 | **41** | 1681 | **66** | 4356 | **91** | 8281 |
| **17** | 289 | **42** | 1764 | **67** | 4489 | **92** | 8464 |
| **18** | 324 | **43** | 1849 | **68** | 4624 | **93** | 8649 |
| **19** | 361 | **44** | 1936 | **69** | 4761 | **94** | 8836 |
| **20** | 400 | **45** | 2025 | **70** | 4900 | **95** | 9025 |
| **21** | 441 | **46** | 2116 | **71** | 5041 | **96** | 9216 |
| **22** | 484 | **47** | 2209 | **72** | 5184 | **97** | 9409 |
| **23** | 529 | **48** | 2304 | **73** | 5329 | **98** | 9604 |
| **24** | 576 | **49** | 2401 | **74** | 5476 | **99** | 9801 |
| **25** | 625 | **50** | 2500 | **75** | 5625 | **100** | 10,000 |

# Table of Square Roots

The square roots are given correct to three decimal places.

| Number $n$ | Positive Square Root $\sqrt{n}$ | Number $n$ | Positive Square Root $\sqrt{n}$ | Number $n$ | Positive Square Root $\sqrt{n}$ | Number $n$ | Positive Square Root $\sqrt{n}$ |
|---|---|---|---|---|---|---|---|
| **1** | 1 | **26** | 5.099 | **51** | 7.141 | **76** | 8.718 |
| **2** | 1.414 | **27** | 5.196 | **52** | 7.211 | **77** | 8.775 |
| **3** | 1.732 | **28** | 5.292 | **53** | 7.280 | **78** | 8.832 |
| **4** | 2 | **29** | 5.385 | **54** | 7.348 | **79** | 8.888 |
| **5** | 2.236 | **30** | 5.477 | **55** | 7.416 | **80** | 8.944 |
| **6** | 2.449 | **31** | 5.568 | **56** | 7.483 | **81** | 9 |
| **7** | 2.646 | **32** | 5.657 | **57** | 7.550 | **82** | 9.055 |
| **8** | 2.828 | **33** | 5.745 | **58** | 7.616 | **83** | 9.110 |
| **9** | 3 | **34** | 5.831 | **59** | 7.681 | **84** | 9.165 |
| **10** | 3.162 | **35** | 5.916 | **60** | 7.746 | **85** | 9.220 |
| **11** | 3.317 | **36** | 6 | **61** | 7.810 | **86** | 9.274 |
| **12** | 3.464 | **37** | 6.083 | **62** | 7.874 | **87** | 9.327 |
| **13** | 3.606 | **38** | 6.164 | **63** | 7.937 | **88** | 9.381 |
| **14** | 3.742 | **39** | 6.245 | **64** | 8 | **89** | 9.434 |
| **15** | 3.873 | **40** | 6.325 | **65** | 8.062 | **90** | 9.487 |
| **16** | 4 | **41** | 6.403 | **66** | 8.124 | **91** | 9.539 |
| **17** | 4.123 | **42** | 6.481 | **67** | 8.185 | **92** | 9.592 |
| **18** | 4.243 | **43** | 6.557 | **68** | 8.246 | **93** | 9.644 |
| **19** | 4.359 | **44** | 6.633 | **69** | 8.307 | **94** | 9.695 |
| **20** | 4.472 | **45** | 6.708 | **70** | 8.367 | **95** | 9.747 |
| **21** | 4.583 | **46** | 6.782 | **71** | 8.426 | **96** | 9.798 |
| **22** | 4.690 | **47** | 6.856 | **72** | 8.485 | **97** | 9.849 |
| **23** | 4.796 | **48** | 6.928 | **73** | 8.544 | **98** | 9.899 |
| **24** | 4.899 | **49** | 7 | **74** | 8.602 | **99** | 9.950 |
| **25** | 5 | **50** | 7.071 | **75** | 8.660 | **100** | 10 |

# Review Exercises

## CHAPTER 1

**In the diagram, $\overline{AD} \perp \overline{FC}$ and $\angle DOE = 30°$.**
**a. Find the measures of the following angles.**
**b. Then classify each as acute, right, or obtuse.**

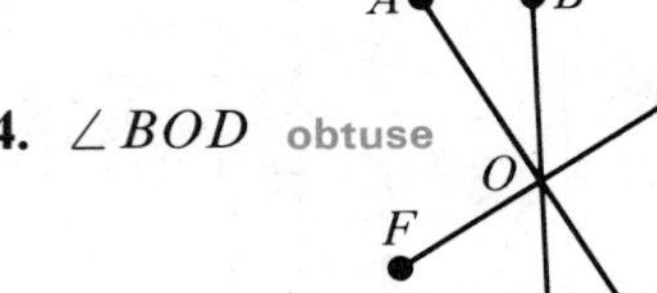


1. $\angle BOA$ acute 2. $\angle BOF$ obtuse 3. $\angle COD$ right 4. $\angle BOD$ obtuse

5. $\angle BOA$ and $\angle DOE$ are called __?__ angles. vertical

6. Name an angle equal to $\angle BOD$. $\angle EOA$

**In the diagram, $\overrightarrow{OX}$ bisects $\angle WOY$ and $\overrightarrow{OY}$ bisects $\angle XOZ$.**

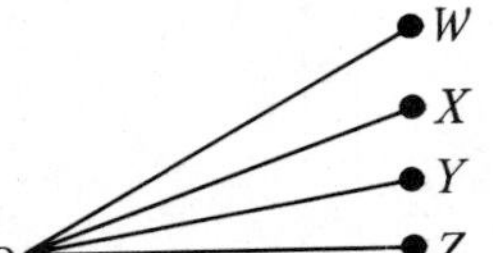


7. $\angle WOX = \angle$ __?__ XOY 8. $\angle YOZ = \angle$ __?__ XOY

9. Which postulate allows you to conclude that $\angle WOX = \angle YOZ$? Substitution

**Refer to the rectangular solid shown.**

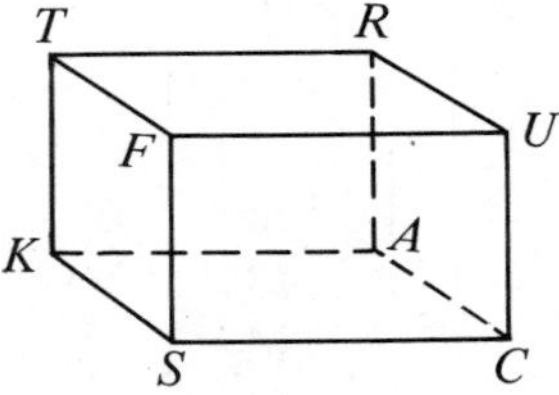


10. $K$, $S$, $F$, and __?__ are coplanar points. $T$

11. Plane $TFUR \parallel$ plane __?__ KSCA

12. Name two planes that intersect in $\overleftrightarrow{FS}$. TFSK; UFSC

13. How many planes contain points $R$, $U$, $F$, and $S$? none

14. Construct a 90° angle.

## CHAPTER 2

**Given information: $\overline{AB} \perp \overline{BC}$ and $\overline{AD} \perp \overline{DC}$.**

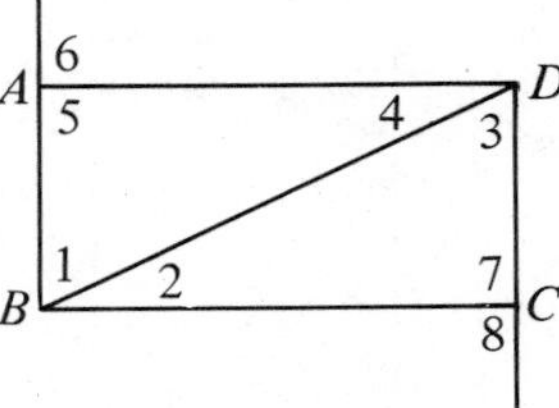


1. $\angle 1$ and $\angle$ __?__ 2 are called complementary angles.

2. $\angle 5$ and $\angle 6$ are called __?__ angles. supplementary

3. If $\angle 1 = \angle 3$, state the theorem that allows you to conclude that $\angle 2 = \angle 4$. Theorem 1, page 42

4. If $\angle 5 = \angle 7$, state the theorem that allows you to conclude that $\angle 6 = \angle 8$. Theorem 2, page 43

**Exercises 5–11 refer to the figure.**

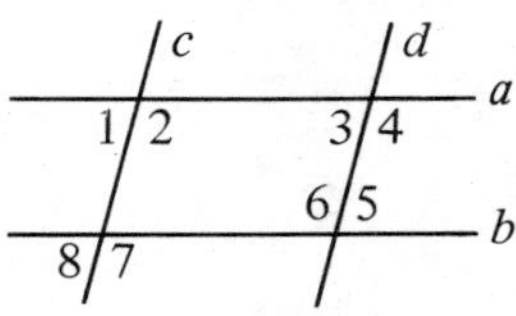

Exercises 5–11

5. $\angle 1$ and $\angle 8$ are called __?__ angles. corresponding

6. $\angle 2$ and $\angle$ __?__ 3 are called same-side interior angles.

7. $\angle 6$ and $\angle 7$ are called __?__ angles. alternate interior

**Use the given information to tell which lines must be parallel.**

**8.** $\angle 3 = \angle 5$ $a \parallel b$ **9.** $\angle 1 = \angle 3$ $c \parallel d$ **10.** $\angle 8 = \angle 5$ $c \parallel d$ **11.** $\angle 4 + \angle 5 = 180°$ $a \parallel b$

**12.** Write a complete proof in two-column form.
*Given:* $\angle 2 = \angle 3$
$\overrightarrow{QS}$ bisects $\angle PQR$.
*Prove:* $\overleftrightarrow{PQ} \parallel \overleftrightarrow{SR}$

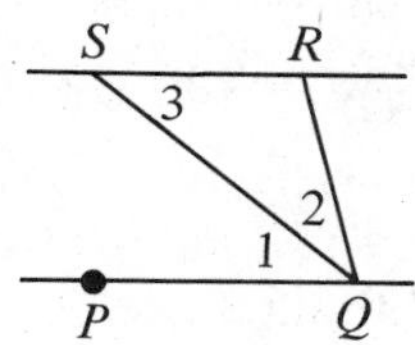


**13.** Draw an acute angle, $\angle A$. Then construct an angle equal to $\angle A$.

## CHAPTER 3

**In each exercise, find the value of *x*.**

**1.** 75

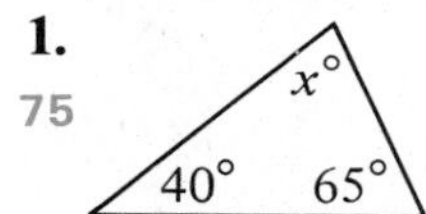


**2.** 30

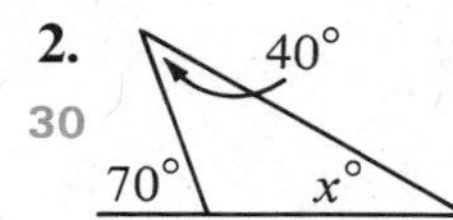


**3.** 30

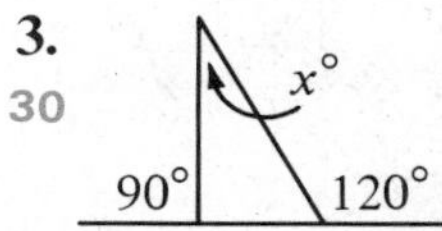


**4.** In $\triangle ABC$, $AB = AC$.
**a.** $\triangle ABC$ must be a(n) _?_ triangle. isosceles
**b.** Is it possible that $\triangle ABC$ is an equilateral triangle? Yes
**c.** Is it possible that $\triangle ABC$ is an obtuse triangle? Yes
**d.** Is it possible that $\triangle ABC$ is an acute triangle? Yes

**5.** Suppose $\triangle ANT \cong \triangle LER$.
**a.** $AT =$ _?_ LR **b.** _?_ $= ER$ NT **c.** $\angle N = \angle$ _?_ E

**Write SSS, SAS, ASA, AAS, or HL to indicate a method you could use to prove two triangles congruent.**

**6.** SAS

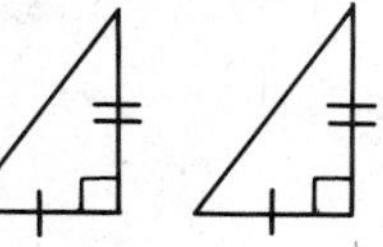

**7.** ASA

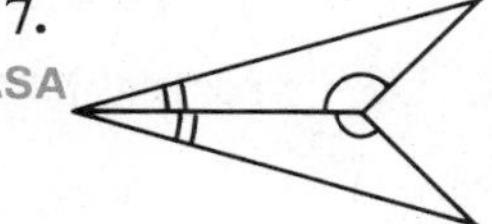

**8.** AAS

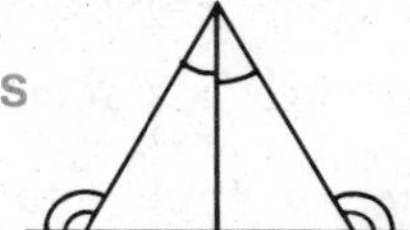

**9.** Write a complete proof in two-column form.
*Given:* $\overline{AB} \perp \overline{XY}$
$AX = AY$
*Prove:* $\triangle ABX \cong \triangle ABY$

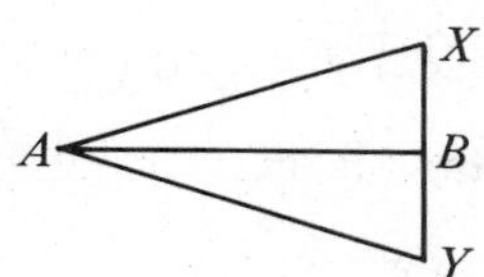

## CHAPTER 4

1. Suppose that $\triangle RUN \cong \triangle TEX$. What reason can you write to support the statements: $UN = EX$ and $\angle N = \angle X$? Corresponding parts of $\cong$ △s are $=$.

2. Draw a large $\triangle ABC$ with $\overline{AB}$ clearly longer than $\overline{AC}$. Draw the altitude $\overline{AH}$ from point $A$ and the median $\overline{AM}$ from point $A$.

3. Draw a figure like the one for Exercise 2, but much larger. Construct the perpendicular bisectors of any two sides of the triangle. Then construct a circle circumscribed about $\triangle ABC$.

**In each diagram, equal angles are marked. Find $x$.**

4. 5

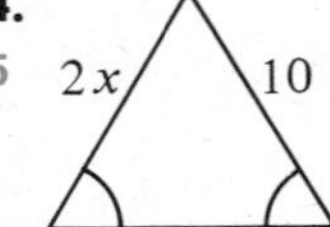


5. 6

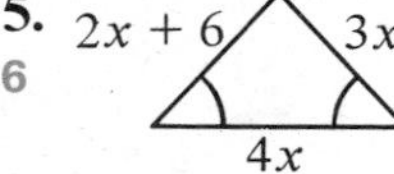


6. 4

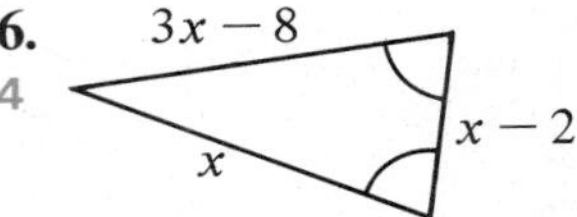


**Write complete proofs in two-column form.**

7. *Given:* $\angle A = \angle X$; $AB = XY$; $AC = XZ$
   *Prove:* $BC = YZ$

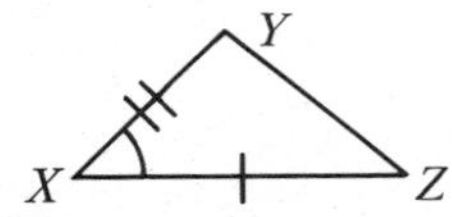


8. *Given:* $RS = TS$
   *Prove:* $\angle 3 = \angle 2$

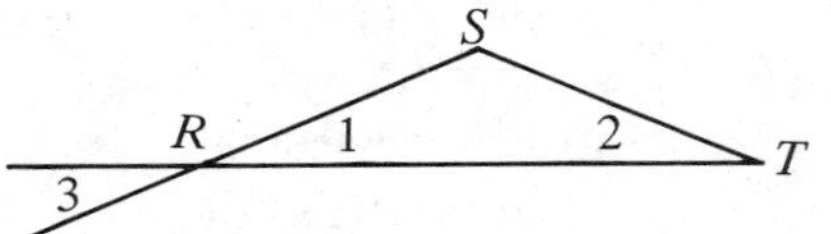


## CHAPTER 5

**Classify each statement as true or false.**

1. An octagon has ten sides. False
2. A regular polygon is equilateral. True
3. Every square is a rectangle. True
4. Every rectangle is a square. False
5. The interior angle sum of a hexagon is $720°$. True
6. In a regular pentagon, each interior angle has measure $110°$. False
7. The diagonals of a rhombus are perpendicular. True
8. The diagonals of a trapezoid bisect each other. False
9. The diagonals of a parallelogram bisect each other. True
10. The legs of a trapezoid are parallel. False

11. If the opposite angles of a quadrilateral are equal, then it must be a parallelogram. False

12. If a quadrilateral has two $80°$ angles and two $100°$ angles, then it must be a parallelogram. False

13. Base angles of an isosceles trapezoid are supplementary. False

14. The diagonals of a rectangle are equal. True

15. Write a complete proof in two-column form.
*Given:* $X$, $Y$, and $Z$ are the midpoints of the sides of $\triangle ABC$.
*Prove:* $AXYZ$ is a ▱.

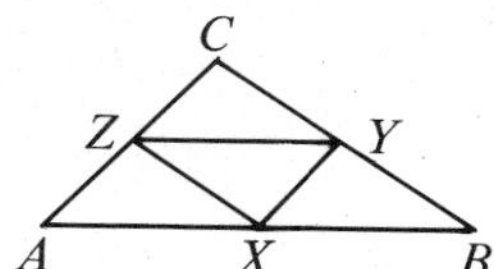


## CHAPTER 6

1. A rectangle has sides 7 m and 3 m. Find the perimeter and the area. $p = 20$ m; $A = 21$ m$^2$

2. Find the area of a square whose perimeter is 12 cm. 9 cm$^2$

**Find the area of the parallelogram, the triangle, and the trapezoid.**

3. 40 — 6, 4, 10

4. 30 — 5, 6, 12

5. 63 — 8, 6, 7, 13

**In each diagram, find the value of $x$.**

6. $\sqrt{130}$

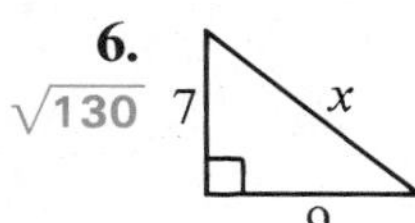


7. 15 — 9, 12, $x$

8. 10

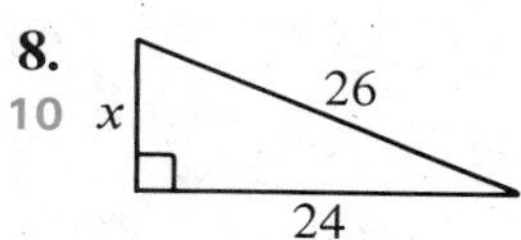


**Three sides of a triangle are given. Classify the triangle as acute, right, or obtuse.**

9. 3, 4, 5 right

10. 3, 4, 6 obtuse

11. 7, 7, 7 acute

**Find the circumference of each circle, in terms of $\pi$, given:**

12. $r = 6$ $12\pi$

13. $r = 1.5$ $3\pi$

14. $d = 8$ $8\pi$

15–17. Use 3.14 for $\pi$. Find the area of each circle described above, correct to tenths. 15. 37.7 16. 9.4 17. 25.1

## CHAPTER 7

**Express each ratio in simplest form.**

1. $\frac{15}{9}$ $\frac{5}{3}$
2. $\frac{24}{36}$ $\frac{2}{3}$
3. $\frac{15}{20}$ $\frac{3}{4}$
4. $\frac{3ac}{9ab} (a \neq 0,\ b \neq 0)$ $\frac{c}{3b}$
5. 18:20 9:10
6. 9:12:15 3:4:5
7. 2 m:40 cm 5:1
8. 3 km:500 m 6:1
9. $\frac{SA}{AL}$ $\frac{3}{2}$
10. $\frac{SR}{ST}$ $\frac{3}{5}$
11. $\frac{AR}{LT}$ $\frac{3}{5}$
12. $\frac{TR}{RS}$ $\frac{2}{3}$

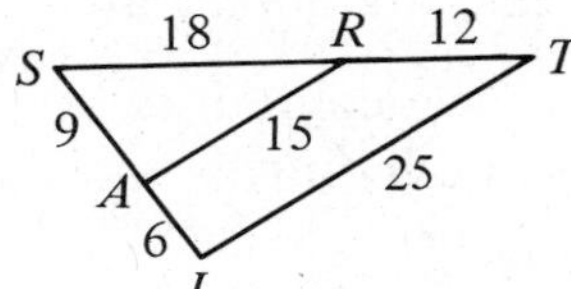


Exercises 9–12

**Find the value of $x$.**

13. $\frac{4}{x} = \frac{6}{9}$ 6
14. $\frac{18}{x} = \frac{9}{4}$ 8
15. $x:9 = 6:27$ 2
16. $\frac{x-3}{4} = \frac{x}{8}$ 6
17. Two bags of cookies cost $1.78. How much will 5 bags cost? $4.45

**Exercises 18 and 19 refer to the diagram.**

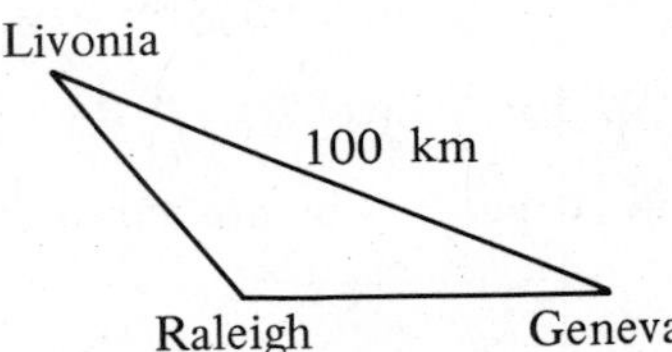


18. Measure the distance on the map between Livonia and Geneva to the nearest centimeter. Then give the scale of the map. 4 cm; 1 cm : 25 km
19. Find the actual distance between Raleigh and Geneva. 62.5 km
20. Make a scale drawing of a soccer field 100 m by 60 m.

## CHAPTER 8

**State whether the following polygons must be similar.**

1. Any two right triangles No
2. Any two regular pentagons Yes
3. Any two congruent polygons Yes
4. Any two isosceles trapezoids No

**Find the values of $x$ and $y$ in each diagram.**

5.

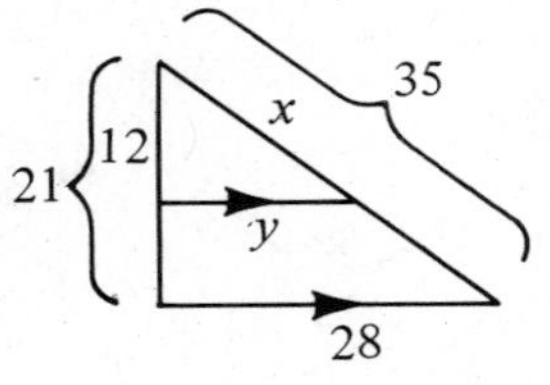


$x = 20;\ y = 16$

6.

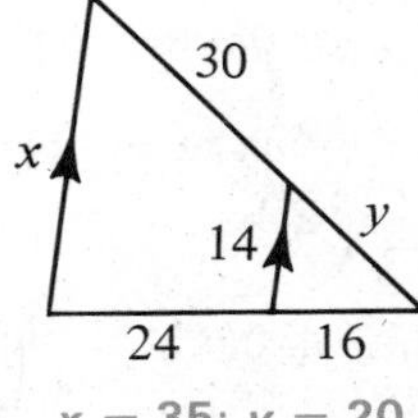


$x = 35;\ y = 20$

7.

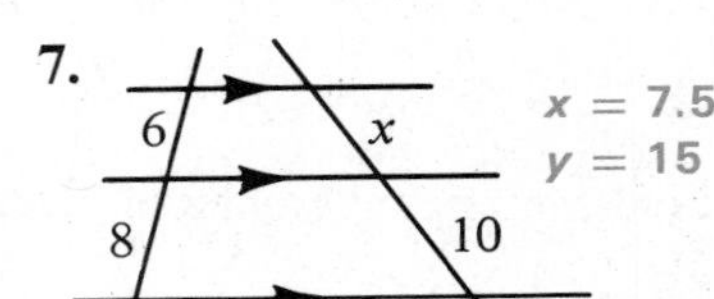


$x = 7.5$
$y = 15$

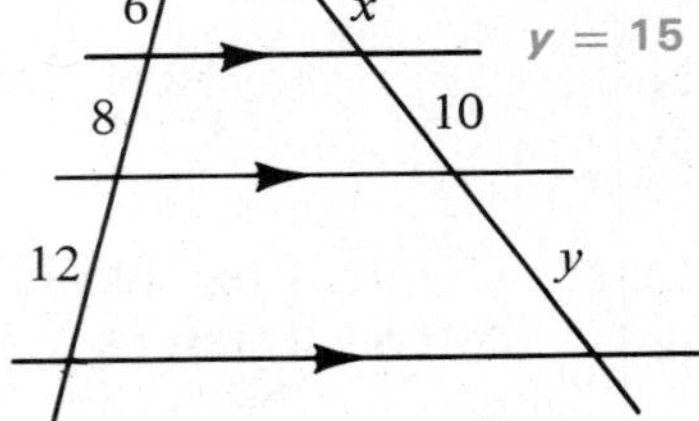

**Exercises 8–10 refer to the figure shown.**

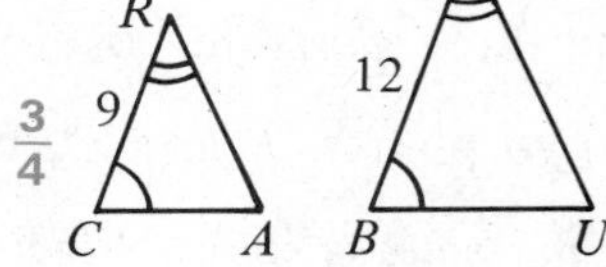


8. Which postulate supports the statement:

$$\triangle CAR \sim \triangle BUS?$$ AA Postulate

9. Find the ratio of the perimeters of the triangles. $\frac{3}{4}$

10. Find the ratio of the areas of the triangles. $\frac{9}{16}$

11. Write a proof in two-column form.
*Given:* Trapezoid $ABCD$
*Prove:* $\frac{AO}{CO} = \frac{BO}{DO}$
(*Hint:* Find two similar triangles.)

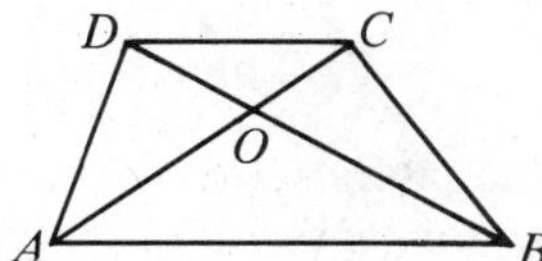


CHAPTER 9

**In the diagram, $\overleftrightarrow{UV}$ is tangent to $\odot O$. $\widehat{AB} = 70°$ and $\widehat{BC} = 80°$. Find the measure of the arc or angle.**

1. $\widehat{ABC}$ 150°
2. $\widehat{AXC}$ 210°
3. $\angle OBU$ 90°
4. $\angle AOB$ 70°
5. $\angle ACB$ 35°
6. $\angle CBV$ 40°

**$\overline{YZ}$ is a diameter of $\odot P$. $\overline{YZ} \perp \overline{RT}$.**

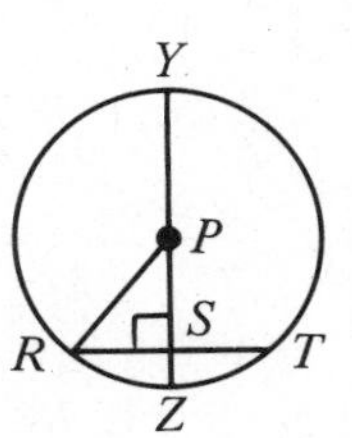


7. If $\widehat{RT} = 100°$, then $\widehat{RZ} =$ _?_° 50 and $\widehat{RY} =$ _?_°. 130
8. If $RS = 7$, then $ST =$ _?_ 7 and $RT =$ _?_. 14
9. If $PR = 10$ and $PS = 8$, then $RS =$ _?_. 6
10. If $YZ = 30$ and $RT = 18$, then $PS =$ _?_. 12

11. If $\widehat{AJ} = 60°$ and $\widehat{KB} = 40°$, then $\angle AVJ =$ _?_°. 50
12. If $\widehat{JB} = 170°$ and $\angle AVK = 155°$, then $\widehat{AK} =$ _?_°. 140

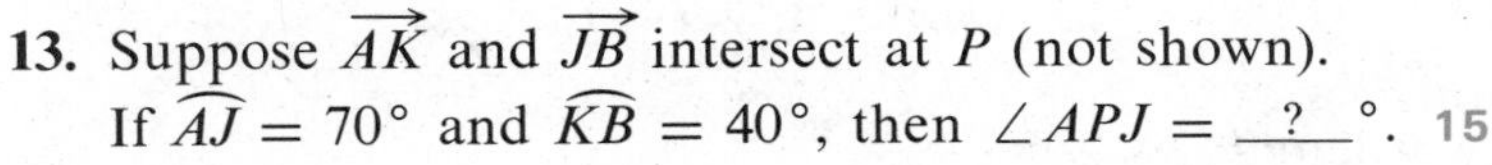

13. Suppose $\overrightarrow{AK}$ and $\overrightarrow{JB}$ intersect at $P$ (not shown).
If $\widehat{AJ} = 70°$ and $\widehat{KB} = 40°$, then $\angle APJ =$ _?_°. 15

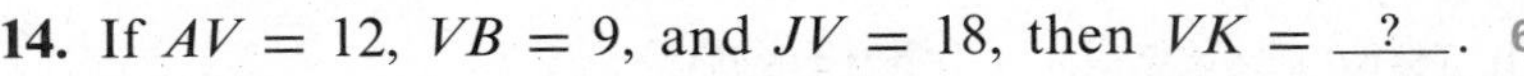

14. If $AV = 12$, $VB = 9$, and $JV = 18$, then $VK =$ _?_. 6

15. Construct a circle. Then construct a tangent to the circle.

## CHAPTER 10

intersecting, parallel, skew

1. Name three possible positions of two different lines, $j$ and $k$.

2. Name three possible positions of a line $l$ and a plane $X$. intersecting, parallel, perpendicular

3. Can two planes, $P$ and $Q$, be called *skew* planes? No

**A rectangular solid is shown. Find:**

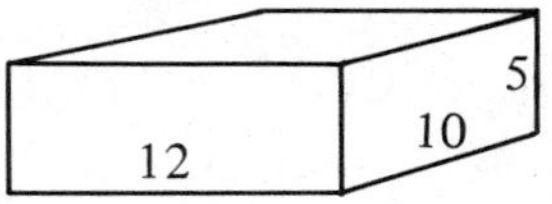


4. The area of a base 120

5. The lateral area 220

6. The total area 460

7. The volume 600

**In each exercise, find a. the lateral area b. the total area c. the volume. In Exercises 8 and 9, express your answers in terms of $\pi$.**

8.

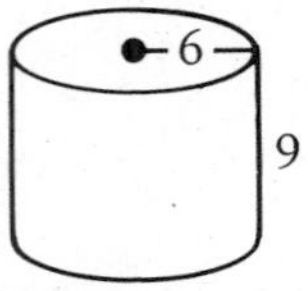


Cylinder

a. $108\pi$
b. $180\pi$
c. $324\pi$

9.

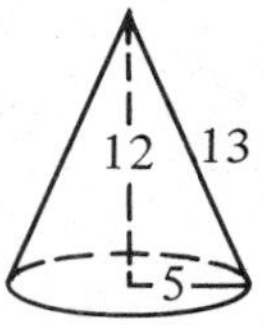


Cone

a. $65\pi$
b. $90\pi$
c. $100\pi$

10.

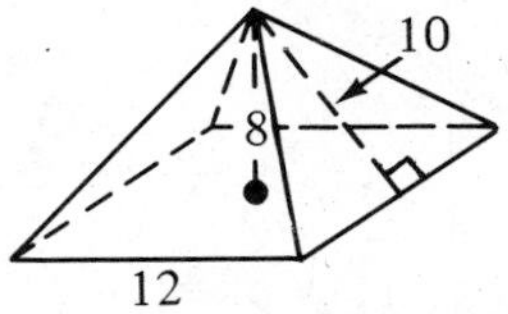


Regular square pyramid

10. a. 240
b. 384
c. 384

11. In a certain cylinder, the radius is 3 and the height is 2. Find the volume correct to tenths. (Use 3.14 for $\pi$.) 56.5

12. A sphere has radius 6. Find the area and volume in terms of $\pi$. $A = 144\pi$ $V = 288\pi$

13. The area of a sphere is $36\pi$. Find the volume in terms of $\pi$. $36\pi$

14. The slant height of a cone is 8, and the lateral area is $24\pi$. Find the diameter. 6

## CHAPTER 11

**Find the exact values of $x$ and $y$.**

1.

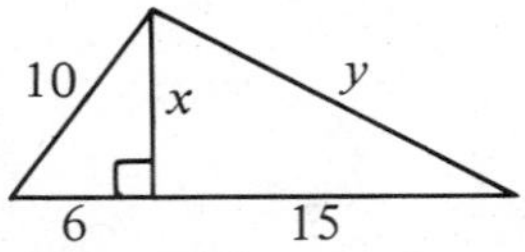


$x = 8;\ y = 17$

2.

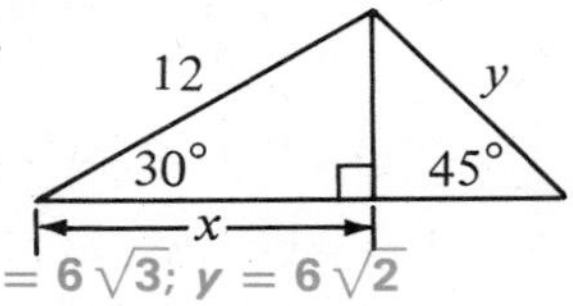


$x = 6\sqrt{3};\ y = 6\sqrt{2}$

3.

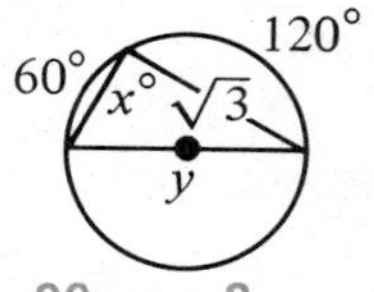


$x = 90;\ y = 2$

**Find the area of each polygon.**

4. A square with diagonals of length $8\sqrt{2}$ 64

5. A rectangle with width 5 and diagonals of length 13 60

6. A $30°$-$60°$-$90°$ triangle with hypotenuse of length 4 $2\sqrt{3}$

7. An equilateral triangle with sides 6 cm long $9\sqrt{3}\text{ cm}^2$

8. A parallelogram with sides 4 m and 8 m, and with a 60° angle $16\sqrt{3}$

9. An isosceles triangle with sides of length 13, 13, and 10 60

10. A box is 12 cm by 9 cm by 7 cm. Find the length of a diagonal. $\sqrt{274}$

11. Suppose a cone has diameter 12 and height 8. Find: **a.** the radius 6 **b.** the slant height 10 **c.** the total area $96\pi$ **d.** the volume. $96\pi$

**Find $x$, correct to tenths. Use the table on page 418.**

**12.** 8.2

10

35°

$x$

**13.** 4.3

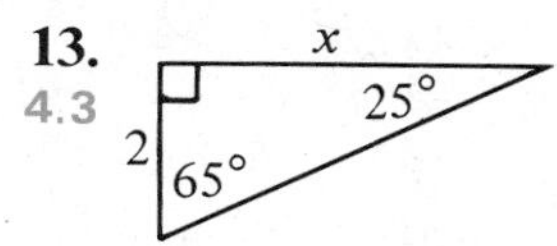


**14.** 4.1

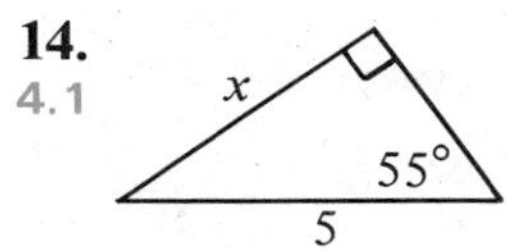


CHAPTER 12

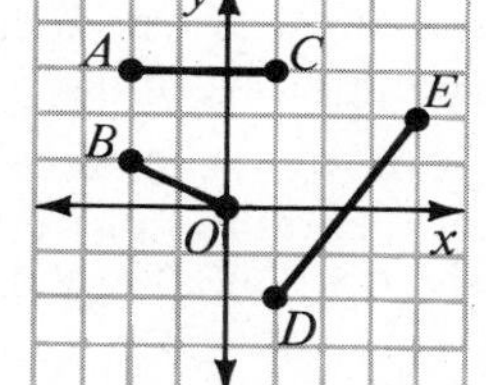


1. Point $B$ lies in quadrant _?_. II

2. The coordinates of point $C$ are (_?_, _?_). (1, 3)

3. $AC$ = _?_ 3, and $OB$ = _?_. $\sqrt{5}$

4. The midpoint of $\overline{OB}$ has coordinates (_?_, _?_). $(-1, \frac{1}{2})$

5. The slope of $\overline{AC}$ is _?_ 0, and the slope of $\overline{DE}$ is _?_ $\frac{4}{3}$.

6. Does point (3, 1) lie on the graph of the equation $5x - y = 13$? No

7. The slope of line $j$ is $\frac{3}{8}$. What is the slope of:
   **a.** any line parallel to $j$? $\frac{3}{8}$ **b.** any line perpendicular to $j$? $-\frac{8}{3}$

8. The vertices of a triangle are $K(-2, 3)$, $E(3, 5)$, and $L(7, -5)$. What angle of $\triangle KEL$ is a right angle? $\angle KEL$

9. Use the equation $2x + 3y = 12$.
   **a.** Copy and complete the table of values.
   **b.** Using a pair of coordinate axes, plot the points. Then draw the graph of $2x + 3y = 12$.

| $x$ | $y$ |
|---|---|
| 0 | ? 4 |
| 6 ? | 0 |
| 3 | ? 2 |
| −3 | ? 6 |

10. Draw the graph of the equation $x = 3$.

11. The vertices of a triangle are $A(-1, -1)$, $B(3, -3)$, and $C(3, 2)$. Prove that $\triangle ABC$ is an isosceles triangle. $AC = BC = 5$

# Answers to Self-Tests

## CHAPTER 1

Page 12 **1.** true **2.** false **3.** true **4.** true **5.** point $R$ **6.** $\angle PQS$ **7.** $\angle PQR$ **8.** $180°$

Page 20 **1.** right **2.** acute **3.** obtuse **4.** straight **5.** $\angle BED$, $\angle AEF$; $\angle BEA$, $\angle DEF$ **6.** $\angle ABF$, $\angle FBC$

Page 34 **1.**

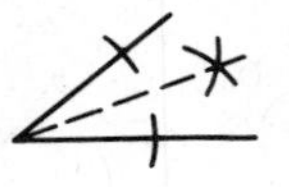

**2.** The Addition Postulate **3.** The Substitution Postulate **4.** 2; 5 **5.** $W$ **6.** $WXYZ$ **7.** $\overleftrightarrow{WX}$

## CHAPTER 2

Page 49 **1.** $70°$ **2.** $142°$ **3.** $\angle SAL$ **4.** $\angle SAK$ **5.** Hyp.: you read the newspaper every day; Concl.: you are well informed **6.** If you are well informed, then you read the newspaper every day.

Page 74 **1.** A postulate is accepted without proof; a theorem is proved. **2.** $\angle 2$, $\angle 7$; $\angle 3$, $\angle 6$ **3.** $\angle 2$, $\angle 3$; $\angle 6$, $\angle 7$ **4.** $\angle 1 = \angle 3 = \angle 8 = 130°$; $\angle 2 = \angle 4 = \angle 5 = \angle 7 = 50°$ **5.** $x = 70$; $y = 50$ **6.** Show that corresponding angles are equal, alternate interior angles are equal, same-side interior angles are supplementary, or both lines are perpendicular to a third line in the same plane. **7.** 1. $l \parallel m$ (Given) 2. $\angle 2 = \angle 3$ (If 2 $\parallel$ lines are cut by a trans., alt. int. angles are equal.) 3. $\angle 1 = \angle 2$ (Given) 4. $\angle 1 = \angle 3$ (Subst. Post.) **8.**

A

m

## CHAPTER 3

Page 92 **1.** 40 **2.** 120 **3.** 70 **4.** 74 **5.** d or c **6.** a **7.** c **8.** b

Page 104 **1.** $BOJ$ **2.** $\angle O$ **3.** $EP$ **4.** 1. Given 2. From algebra 3. Given: $D$ is the midpt. of $\overline{XY}$. 4. SSS Post.

Page 115 **1.** 1. $\angle 1 = \angle 2$ (Given: $\overrightarrow{TV}$ bisects $\angle ETO$.) 2. $TE = TO$ (Given) 3. $TV = TV$ (From algebra) 4. $\triangle TEV \cong \triangle TOV$ (SAS Post.) **2.** 1. $\angle 1 = \angle 2$; $\angle 3 = \angle 4$ (Given: $\overleftrightarrow{TV}$ bisects $\angle ETO$ and $\angle EVO$.) 2. $TV = TV$ (From algebra) 3. $\triangle TEV \cong \triangle TOV$ (ASA Post.)

Page 122 **1.** SAS, ASA, AAS **2.** 1. $\angle 1$ and $\angle 2$ are right angles. (Given: $\overline{RT} \perp \overline{SV}$) 2. $RS = TV$; $RM = TM$ (Given) 3. $\triangle RMS \cong \triangle TMV$ (HL Thm.)

## CHAPTER 4

Page 139 **1.** 1. $RM = TM$; $UM = SM$ (Given) 2. $\angle RMU = \angle TMS$ (Vertical angles are equal.) 3. $\triangle RMU \cong \triangle TMS$ (SAS Post.) 4. $RU = TS$ (Corr. parts of $\cong$ ⚠ are $=$.) **2.** 1. $\angle X = \angle Y = 90°$ (Given) 2. $AX = AY$ (Given) 3. $AB = AB$ (From algebra) 4. $\triangle AXB \cong \triangle AYB$ (HL Thm.) 5. $\angle 1 = \angle 2$ (Corr. parts of $\cong$ ⚠ are $=$.) **3.** SSS

Page 152

**1.**

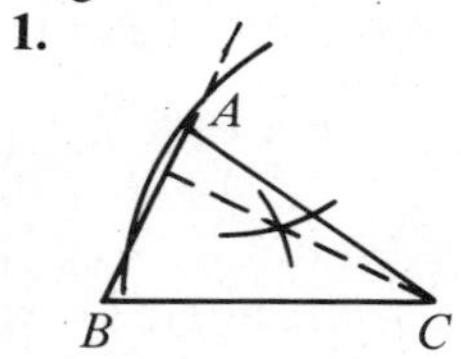


**2.**

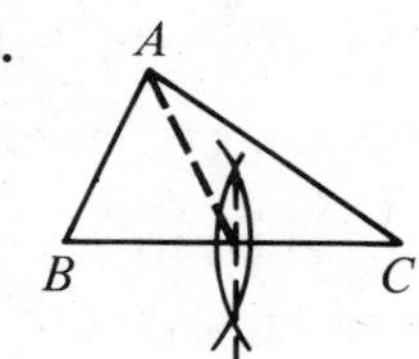


**3.**

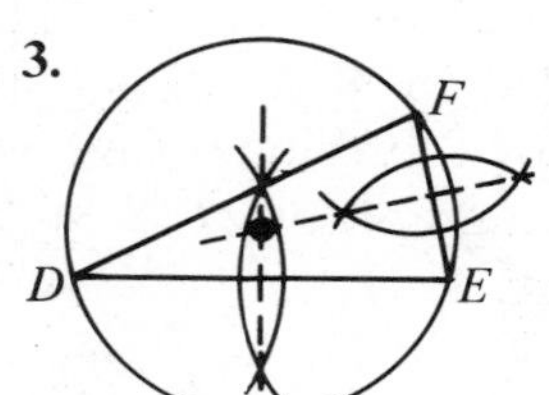


**4.**

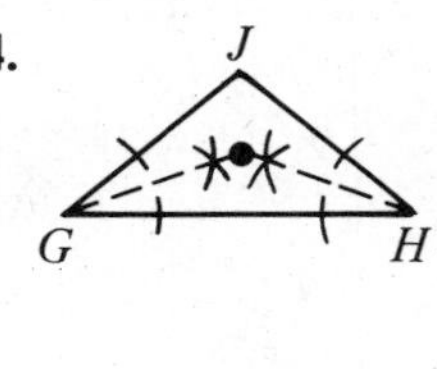


Page 163 **1.** If 2 sides of a triangle are equal, then the angles opposite those sides are equal. **2.** 5 **3.** 4 **4.** 12 **5.** 60 **6.** 40 **7.** 44

## CHAPTER 5

Page 179 **1.** For example: 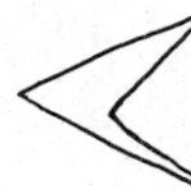

**2.** For example: 

**3.** For example: 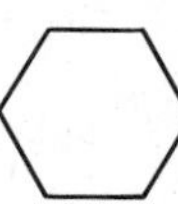

**4.** 120° **5.** 60°

Page 189 **1.** A quadrilateral with both pairs of opposite sides parallel **2.** A quadrilateral with just one pair of opposite sides parallel **3.** A parallelogram with four equal sides **4.** A parallelogram with four right angles **5.** A parallelogram with four right angles and four equal sides **6.** $\overline{CD}$ **7.** $\overline{AD}$ **8.** *BX* **9.** 5 **10.** *BCD* **11.** 3 **12.** *BCD* or *DAB*

Page 200 **1.** $BD = 12$; $BE = 6$ **2.** $\angle 1 = \angle 4 = 25°$; $\angle 2 = 90°$; $\angle 3 = 65°$ **3.** 28

**4.** 1. $WZ = XY$; $\angle 1 = \angle 2$ (Given)
2. $\overline{WZ} \parallel \overline{XY}$ (If 2 lines are cut by a trans. so that alt. int. angles are equal, the lines are $\parallel$.) 3. *WXYZ* is a ▱. (If a quad. has 1 pair of opp. sides both $\parallel$ and equal, the quad. is a ▱.)

Page 209 **1.** 9 **2.** $\angle G = \angle O = 60°$; $\angle A = 120°$ **3.** *PTKL, SPKT, PKAT* **4.** 10 **5.** 9

## CHAPTER 6

Page 224 **1. a.** 26 **b.** 30 **2. a.** 5 cm **b.** 20 cm **3.** 48 **4.** 60

Page 233 **1.** 20 **2.** 12 **3.** 84 **4.** 91 **5.** 26

Page 241 **1.** 10 **2.** 4 **3.** 10 **4.** 50 **5.** obtuse **6.** right **7.** acute **8.** right

Page 250 **1.** $\frac{C}{d}$ **2.** 3.14 **3.** $d = 10$; $C = 10\pi$; $A = 25\pi$ **4.** $r = 8$; $C = 16\pi$; $A = 64\pi$ **5.** $r = 10$; $d = 20$; $A = 100\pi$ **6.** $r = 6$; $d = 12$; $C = 12\pi$

## CHAPTER 7

Page 269 **1.** $\frac{2}{3}$ **2.** $\frac{5}{3}$ **3.** 5:8 **4.** 1:2:3 **5.** 14 **6.** 15 **7.** 9 **8.** 2 **9.** $3.20 **10.** $220

Page 275 **1.** about 5 cm; 5 cm:20 km or $\frac{1}{400{,}000}$ **2.** 16 km **3.** 8 km **4.** For example: Scale: $\frac{1}{2000}$

## CHAPTER 8

Page 292 **1.** *JOK* **2.** *OK*; *KJ* **3.** 4:8 or 1:2 **4.** *J* **5.** not similar **6.** similar **7.** not similar **8.** similar

Page 303 **1.** $x = 6$; $y = 15$ **2.** $x = 9$; $y = 2\frac{1}{4}$ **3.** 1:3; 1:9 **4.** 3:7, 9:49 **5.** 5:6; 5:6

## CHAPTER 9

Page 327 **1.** $\overline{OX}$ or $\overline{OY}$ **2.** $\overline{XY}$ **3.** $\overleftrightarrow{ST}$ **4.** $\overleftrightarrow{PQ}$ or $\overline{PQ}$ **5.** $\overline{ST}$ **6.** tangent **7.** 80° **8.** 280° **9.** 2 **10.**

Page 337 **1.** 6 **2.** 32° **3.** 12 **4.** 40° **5.** 76° **6.** 156°; 204° **7.** 30° **8.** For example: (Note that a rhombus inscribed in a circle must be a square.)

Page 346 **1.** 50° **2.** 126° **3.** 120° **4.** 10 **5.** 6 **6.** 25° **7.** 17° **8.** 110°

## CHAPTER 10

Page 368 **1.** *DSTE, ETUF* **2.** *CDSR, FETU* **3.** $\overleftrightarrow{CF}$, $\overleftrightarrow{DE}$, $\overleftrightarrow{CR}$, or $\overleftrightarrow{DS}$ **4.** 184 **5.** 160 **6.** $64\pi$ **7.** $192\pi$ **8.** $256\pi$

Page 380 **1.**

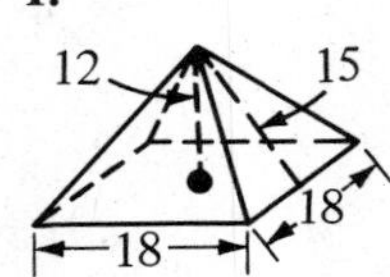


**2.** 540
**3.** 864
**4.** 1296 **5.** 5
**6.** $15\pi$ **7.** $24\pi$
**8.** $12\pi$ **9.** To the nearest integer, 201
**10.** To the nearest integer, 268

## CHAPTER 11

Page 402 **1.** $x = 12$; $y = 9$ **2.** $x = 2$; $y = 2\sqrt{2}$ **3.** $x = 5$; $y = 5\sqrt{3}$ **4.** 18 **5.** $27\sqrt{3}$ **6.** $27\sqrt{3}$

Page 409 **1.** 12 cm **2.** 4 **3.** $16\pi$ **4.** 260

Page 418 **1.** $\frac{8}{15}$ **2.** $\frac{8}{17}$ **3.** $\frac{8}{17}$ **4.** $\frac{15}{17}$

**5.** $x = 14.3$ **6.** $y = 16.4$; $z = 11.5$

## CHAPTER 12

Page 437 **1.** $(5, -4)$ **2.** $(1, 2)$ **3.** $(1, -1)$ **4.** 6 **5.** 10 **6.** 3 **7.** 13 **8.** $\left(-3, -2\frac{1}{2}\right)$

Page 447 **1.** horizontal **2.** vertical **3.** $\frac{4}{3}$ **4.** $-2$ **5.** $\frac{3}{7}$ **6.** $\frac{2}{5}$

Page 456 **1.** no **2.** $(0, 8)$; $(8, 0)$; $(3, 5)$ **3.** $(0, -4)$; $(3, 0)$; $\left(5, 2\frac{2}{3}\right)$

**4.** For example:

| $x$ | $y$ |
|---|---|
| 3 | 4 |
| 4 | 2 |
| 5 | 0 |
| 6 | $-2$ |

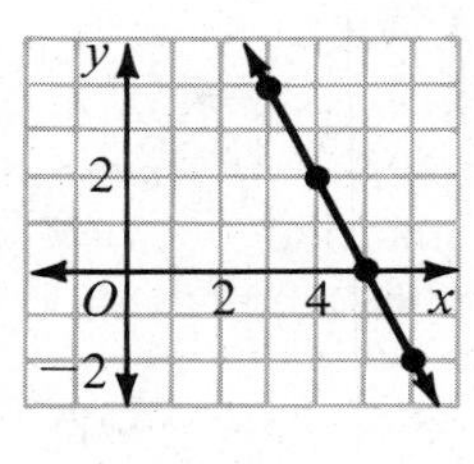


**5.** Slope of $\overline{AB} = 0 =$ slope of $\overline{DC}$. Slope of $\overline{AD} = 4 =$ slope of $\overline{BC}$. Therefore, $\overline{AB} \parallel \overline{DC}$ and $\overline{AD} \parallel \overline{BC}$. By definition, $ABCD$ is a parallelogram.

## POSTULATES

THE ADDITION POSTULATE If $a = b$ and $c = d$, then $a + c = b + d$. *page 25*

THE SUBTRACTION POSTULATE If $a = b$ and $c = d$, then $a - c = b - d$. *page 25*

THE MULTIPLICATION POSTULATE If $a = b$, then $ac = bc$. *page 25*

THE DIVISION POSTULATE If $a = b$ and $c \neq 0$, then $\frac{a}{c} = \frac{b}{c}$. *page 26*

THE SUBSTITUTION POSTULATE If $a = b$, then $a$ can be substituted for $b$ in any equation or inequality. *page 26*

POSTULATE 1 Through any two points there is exactly one line. *page 30*

POSTULATE 2 Through any three noncollinear points there is exactly one plane. *page 30*

POSTULATE 3 If two points lie in a plane, then the line joining them lies in that plane. *page 30*

POSTULATE 4 If two planes intersect, then their intersection is a line. *page 30*

POSTULATE 5 (The Ruler Postulate) Each point on a line can be paired with exactly one real number called its coordinate. The distance between two points is the positive difference of their coordinates. *page 31*

POSTULATE 6 (The Protractor Postulate) Suppose $O$ is a point of $\overleftrightarrow{XY}$. Consider all rays with endpoint $O$ which lie on one side of $\overleftrightarrow{XY}$. Each ray can be paired with exactly one real number between 0 and 180. *page 31*

POSTULATE 7 If two parallel lines are cut by a transversal, then corresponding angles are equal. *page 61*

POSTULATE 8 If two lines and a transversal form equal corresponding angles, then the lines are parallel. *page 66*

POSTULATE 9 (The SSS Postulate) If three sides of one triangle are equal to the corresponding parts of another triangle, the triangles are congruent. *page 99*

POSTULATE 10 (The SAS Postulate) If two sides and the included angle of one triangle are equal to the corresponding parts of another triangle, the triangles are congruent. *page 106*

POSTULATE 11 (The ASA Postulate) If two angles and the included side of one triangle are equal to the corresponding parts of another triangle, the triangles are congruent. *page 111*

POSTULATE 12 The area of a rectangle is given by the formula: Area = base $\times$ height *page 216*

POSTULATE 13 (The AA Postulate) If two angles of one triangle are equal to two angles of another triangle, then the triangles are similar. *page 287*

## THEOREMS

Chapter 2 Introducing Proof

THEOREM 1 If two angles are complements of equal angles (or of the same angle), then the two angles are equal. *page 42*

THEOREM 2 If two angles are supplements of equal angles (or of the same angle), then the two angles are equal. *page 43*

THEOREM 3 Vertical angles are equal. *page 43*

THEOREM 4 If two parallel lines are cut by a transversal, then alternate interior angles are equal. *page 62*

THEOREM 5 If two parallel lines are cut by a transversal, then same-side interior angles are supplementary. *page 62*

THEOREM 6 If two lines and a transversal form equal alternate interior angles, then the lines are parallel. *page 66*

THEOREM 7 If two lines and a transversal form supplementary same-side interior angles, then the lines are parallel. *page 66*

THEOREM 8 In a plane, if two lines are each perpendicular to a third line, then the two lines are parallel. *page 66*

Chapter 3 Triangles

THEOREM 1 The angle sum of a triangle is 180°. *page 84*

COROLLARY An exterior angle of a triangle is equal to the sum of the two opposite angles of the triangle. *page 85*

THEOREM 2 (AAS Theorem) If two angles and a non-included side of one triangle are equal to the corresponding parts of another triangle, the triangles are congruent. *page 116*

THEOREM 3 (HL Theorem) If the hypotenuse and a leg of one right triangle are equal to the corresponding parts of another right triangle, the triangles are congruent. *page 116*

Chapter 4 Using Congruent Triangles

THEOREM 1 Any point on the perpendicular bisector of a segment is equidistant from the endpoints of the segment. *page 141*

THEOREM 2 Any point that is equidistant from the endpoints of a segment is on the perpendicular bisector of the segment. *page 141*

THEOREM 3 If two sides of a triangle are equal, then the angles opposite those sides are equal. *page 153*

COROLLARY An equilateral triangle is also equiangular, and each angle has measure 60°. *page 153*

THEOREM 4 If two angles of a triangle are equal, then the sides opposite those angles are equal. *page 158*

COROLLARY If a triangle is equiangular, it is also equilateral. *page 158*

Chapter 5 Polygons

THEOREM 1 If a convex polygon has $n$ sides, then its angle sum is given by the formula $S = (n - 2) \times 180°$. *page 176*

THEOREM 2 The exterior angle sum of any convex polygon, one angle at each vertex, is 360°. *page 177*

THEOREM 3 Opposite sides of a parallelogram are equal. *page 186*

THEOREM 4 Opposite angles of a parallelogram are equal. *page 186*

THEOREM 5 Consecutive angles of a parallelogram are supplementary. *page 186*

THEOREM 6 Diagonals of a parallelogram bisect each other. *page 186*

THEOREM 7 The diagonals of a rectangle are equal. *page 191*

THEOREM 8 The diagonals of a rhombus are perpendicular, and they bisect the angles of the rhombus. *page 191*

THEOREM 9 The midpoint of the hypotenuse of a right triangle is equidistant from the three vertices. *page 192*

THEOREM 10 If a quadrilateral has one pair of opposite sides that are both parallel and equal, then the quadrilateral is a parallelogram. *page 195*

THEOREM 11 If a quadrilateral has both pairs of opposite sides equal, then the quadrilateral is a parallelogram. *page 196*

THEOREM 12 If a quadrilateral has diagonals that bisect each other, then the quadrilateral is a parallelogram. *page 196*

THEOREM 13 The base angles of an isosceles trapezoid are equal. *page 202*

THEOREM 14 The median of a trapezoid has two properties: **(1)** It is parallel to the bases. **(2)** Its length equals half the sum of the base lengths. *page 202*

THEOREM 15 (The Midpoints Theorem) The segment joining the midpoints of two sides of a triangle is parallel to the third side and half as long. *page 206*

Chapter 6 Areas

THEOREM 1 The area of a square is given by the formula: Area = side squared *page 217*

THEOREM 2 The area of a parallelogram is given by the formula: Area = base × height *page 222*

THEOREM 3 The area of a triangle is given by the formula: Area = $\frac{1}{2}$ × base × height *page 225*

THEOREM 4 The area of a trapezoid is given by the formula: Area = $\frac{1}{2}$ × height × sum of the bases *page 230*

THEOREM 5 (The Pythagorean Theorem) In a right triangle, the square of the hypotenuse is equal to the sum of the squares of the legs. *page 235*

THEOREM 6 If the square of one side of a triangle is equal to the sum of the squares of the other two sides, then the triangle is a right triangle. *page 238*

Chapter 8 Similar Polygons

THEOREM 1 (The Triangle Proportionality Theorem) If a line intersects a triangle and is parallel to one side, then it divides the other two sides proportionally. *page 295*

COROLLARY If three parallel lines intersect two transversals, they divide the transversals proportionally. *page 296*

THEOREM 2 If two similar polygons have a scale factor $a:b$, then **(1)** the ratio of their perimeters is $a:b$; **(2)** the ratio of their areas is $a^2:b^2$. *page 301*

Chapter 9 Circles

THEOREM 1 A radius drawn to a point of tangency is perpendicular to the tangent. *page 318*

THEOREM 2 If a line lies in the plane of a circle and is perpendicular to a radius at its outer endpoint, the line is tangent to the circle. *page 318*

THEOREM 3 In a circle, equal central angles have equal minor arcs. *page 324*

THEOREM 4 In a circle, equal minor arcs have equal central angles. *page 324*

THEOREM 5 In a circle, equal chords have equal arcs and equal arcs have equal chords. *page 329*

THEOREM 6 In a circle, equal chords are equidistant from the center. Chords that are equidistant from the center are equal. *page 329*

THEOREM 7 A diameter that is perpendicular to a chord bisects the chord and its arc. *page 329*

THEOREM 8 An inscribed angle is equal to half its intercepted arc. *page 333*

THEOREM 9 An angle formed by a chord and a tangent is equal to half its intercepted arc. *page 334*

THEOREM 10 An angle formed by two chords is equal to half the sum of the intercepted arcs. *page 338*

THEOREM 11 An angle formed by two secants is equal to half the difference of the intercepted arcs. *page 338*

THEOREM 12 If two chords intersect inside a circle, the product of the lengths of the segments of one chord equals the product of the lengths of the segments of the other. *page 342*

Chapter 10 Areas and Volumes of Solids

THEOREM 1 Suppose two similar solids have scale factor $a:b$. Then: **(1)** the ratio of corresponding segments is $a:b$; **(2)** the ratio of the areas is $a^2:b^2$; **(3)** the ratio of the volumes is $a^3:b^3$. *page 381*

Chapter 11 Right Triangles

THEOREM 1 In a 45°-45°-90° triangle, the hypotenuse is $\sqrt{2}$ times as long as a leg. *page 395*

THEOREM 2 In a 30°-60°-90° triangle, **a.** the hypotenuse is twice as long as the shorter leg; **b.** the longer leg is $\sqrt{3}$ times as long as the shorter leg. *page 396*

## CONSTRUCTIONS

CONSTRUCTION 1 *Given:* An angle *Construct:* A bisector of the angle *page 21*

CONSTRUCTION 2 *Given:* A line and a point on the line *Construct:* A perpendicular to the line through the point *page 22*

CONSTRUCTION 3 *Given:* A line and a point not on the line *Construct:* A perpendicular to the line through the point *page 22*

CONSTRUCTION 4 *Given:* An angle *Construct:* An angle equal to the given angle *page 71*

CONSTRUCTION 5 *Given:* A line and a point not on the line *Construct:* A line that passes through the point and is parallel to the given line *page 72*

CONSTRUCTION 6 *Given:* A segment *Construct:* A perpendicular bisector of the segment *page 140*

CONSTRUCTION 7 *Given:* A triangle *Construct:* A circle passing through the vertices of the triangle *page 149*

CONSTRUCTION 8 *Given:* A triangle *Construct:* An inscribed circle *page 150*

CONSTRUCTION 9 *Construct:* A 60° angle *page 159*

CONSTRUCTION 10 *Given:* Point $A$ on $\odot O$ *Construct:* A tangent to $\odot O$ at point $A$ *page 319*

# Appendix

## Cardboard Models and Pyramid Volume

The pyramid shown at the right is not a regular pyramid. But the volume of the pyramid—in fact, the volume of *every* pyramid—is given by the formula $V = \frac{1}{3}Bh$. This appendix will help you see that this is true.

In the figure, $\overline{XR} \perp$ plane $RST$.

Study the prism shown. Our original pyramid $X$-$RST$ (vertex $X$, base $RST$) is a part of the prism. Think of the rest of the prism as a pyramid whose base is rectangle $SYZT$ and whose vertex is point $X$.

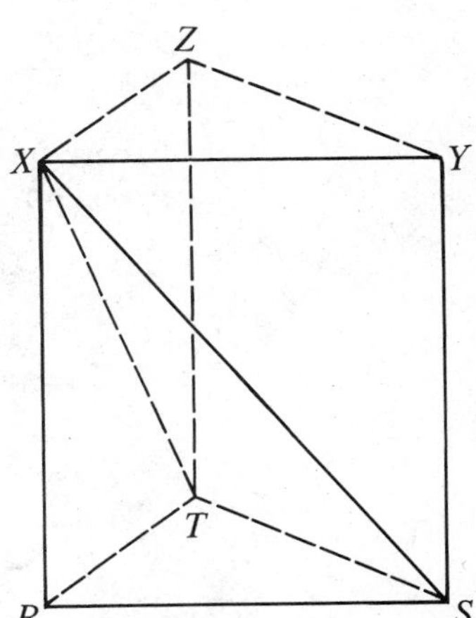


Here pyramid $X$-$SYZT$ is drawn in a position that helps you think of rectangle $SYZT$ as the base. A plane can be passed through points $X$, $Y$, and $T$, forming two triangular pyramids. Each of them has $X$ as its vertex. One base is $\triangle TSY$. The other base is $\triangle YZT$.

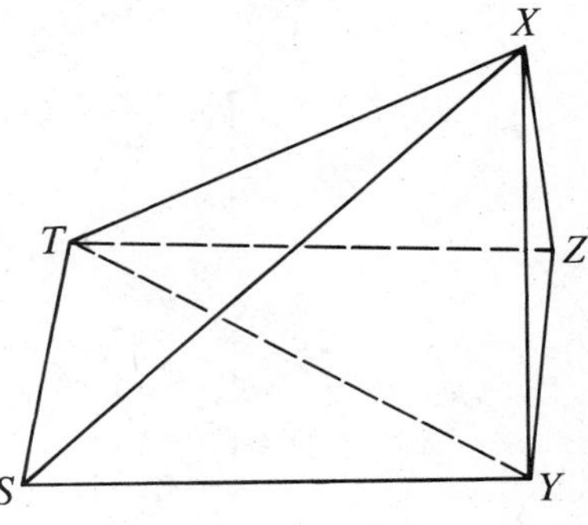

You can make cardboard models of the prism and the three pyramids by following the directions below. Use thin sheets of cardboard large enough for you to measure lengths in centimeters. Score the dotted lines (cut part way through the surface of the cardboard). Then bend along the dotted lines so that the scored side is on the outside of your model. Fold in the tabs (shaded in the diagrams) and paste or tape the models.

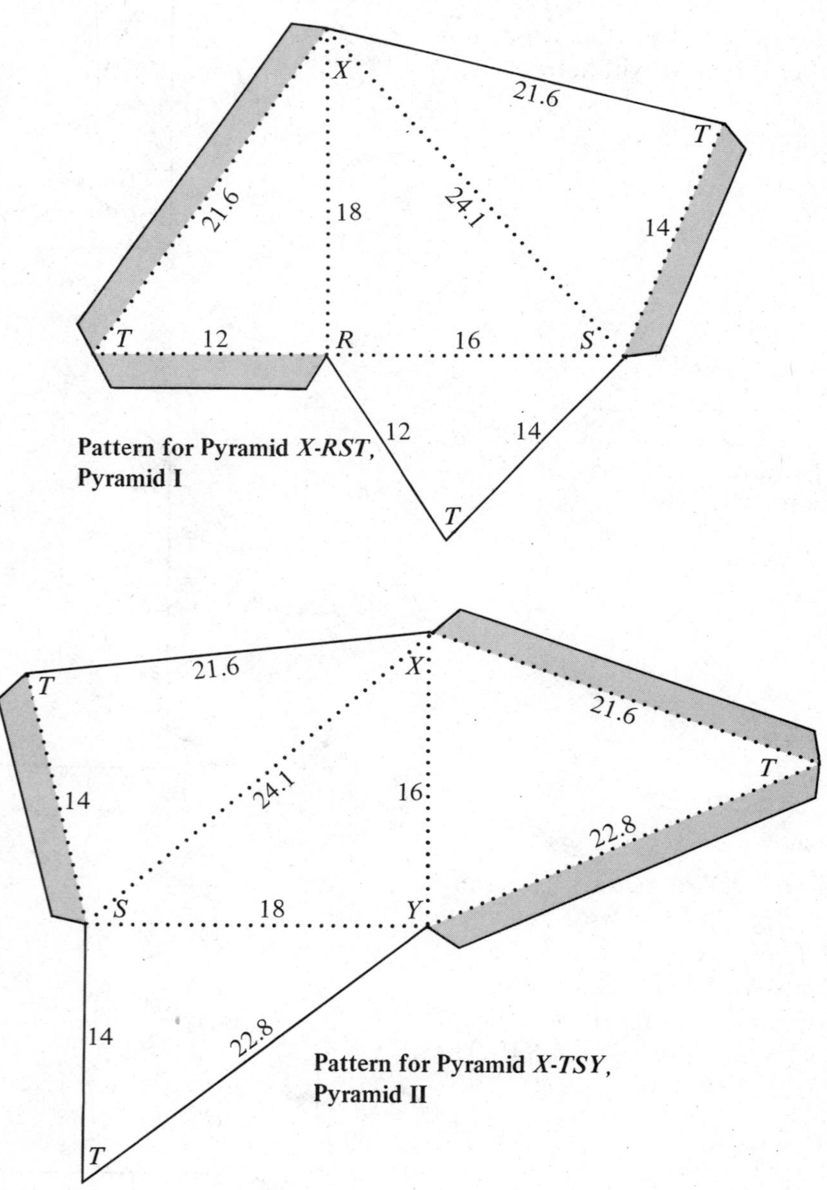


**Pattern for Pyramid *X-RST*, Pyramid I**

**Pattern for Pyramid *X-TSY*, Pyramid II**

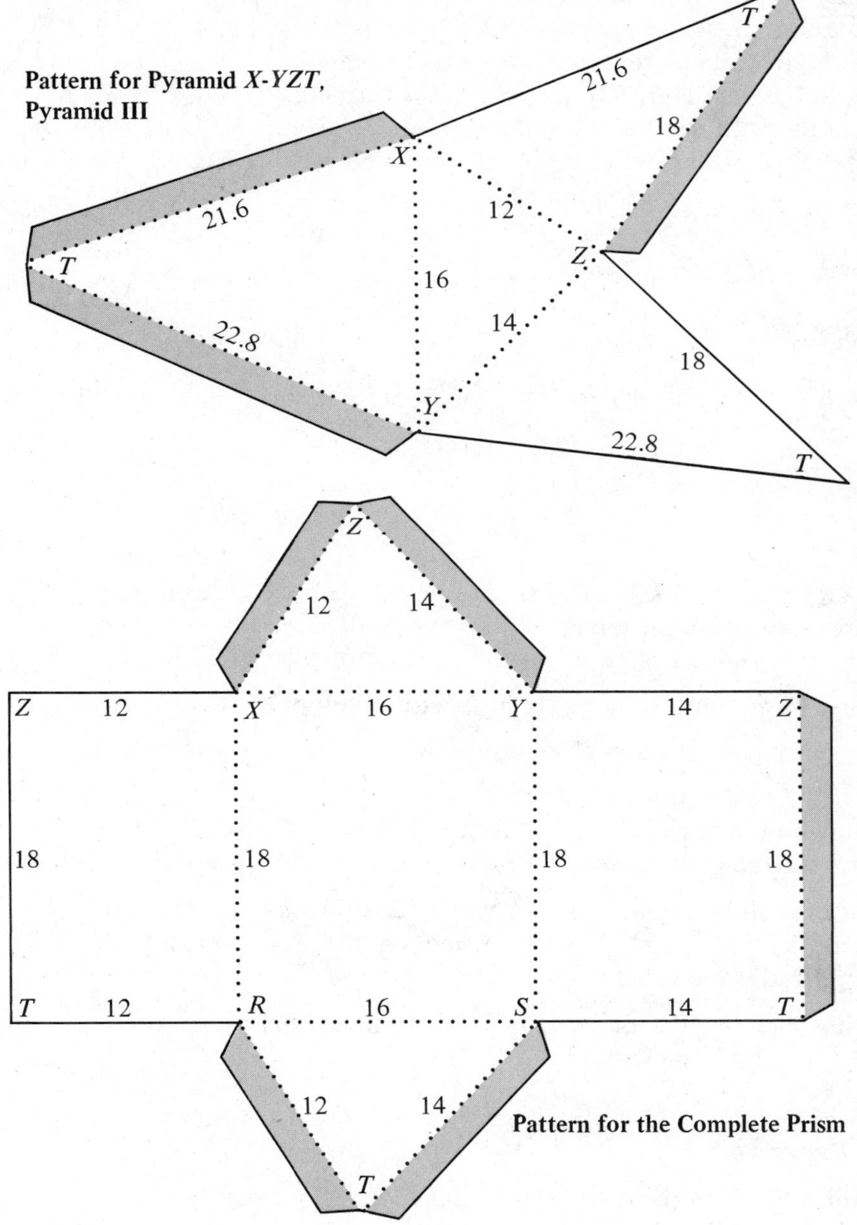


Place pyramids II and III alongside each other to form a rectangular pyramid *X-SYZT*. The bases of these pyramids have equal areas, and the pyramids have the same altitude. The volume of pyramid II is equal to the volume of pyramid III. For a comparison of pyramids I and II see Exercise 1.

The formula $V = \frac{1}{3}Bh$ can be proved for pyramids that are not triangular. To see how, study pentagonal pyramid $X$-$RSTUV$ which has been separated into three triangular pyramids with base areas $B_1$, $B_2$, and $B_3$, as shown. Since we know that the volume of a triangular pyramid is given by the formula $V = \frac{1}{3}Bh$, we can conclude:

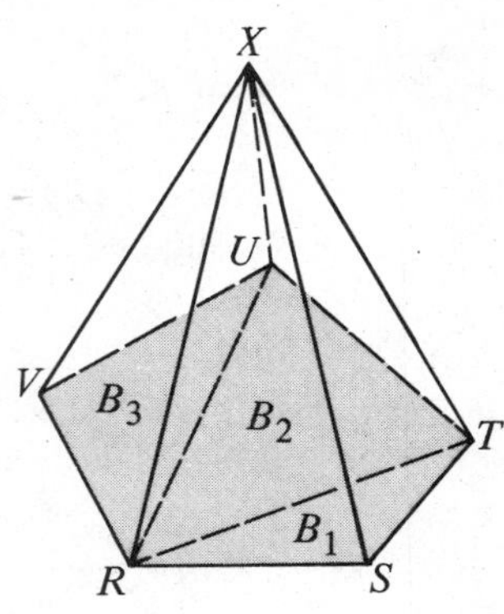


Volume of $X$-$RST = \frac{1}{3}B_1h$

Volume of $X$-$RTU = \frac{1}{3}B_2h$

Volume of $X$-$RUV = \frac{1}{3}B_3h$

Total volume $= \frac{1}{3}B_1h + \frac{1}{3}B_2h + \frac{1}{3}B_3h = \frac{1}{3}(B_1 + B_2 + B_3)h = \frac{1}{3}Bh$

## Exercises

1. Let $\triangle XRS$ and $\triangle SYX$ be the bases of pyramids I and II. Compare the base areas and altitudes of the pyramids. Explain why the volume of pyramid I is equal to the volume of pyramid II.
2. Explain why pyramids I and III have equal volumes.
3. Explain why the volume of pyramid I is given by the formula $V = \frac{1}{3}Bh$.
4. Find the volume of pyramid III. (To find the area of base $XYZ$, use the formula on page 228.) Express your answer in radical form. $\sqrt{6615} = 21\sqrt{15}$
5. The patterns show the length of $\overline{XS}$ to be 24.1. This is an approximation of the true length. Find the true length of $\overline{XS}$. Express your answer in radical form. $2\sqrt{145}$
6. Find the true lengths of $\overline{XT}$ and $\overline{YT}$. Express your answers in radical form. $XT = 6\sqrt{13}$; $YT = 2\sqrt{130}$

## Optional Exercise

The pyramid $X$-$RST$ on page 481 has lateral edge $\overline{XR}$ perpendicular to the base. However, the discussion above applies to *every* triangular pyramid. Make models of a prism and three pyramids using the following lengths.

$RS = XY = 16$ $\quad ST = YZ = 14$ $\quad RT = XZ = 12$

$XR = YS = ZT = 18$ $\quad XS = 23.1$ $\quad XT = 19.7$ $\quad YT = 18.7$

# Appendix

## Inequalities in Triangles

Much of your work with triangles has concerned the equality of certain segments or certain angles. It is interesting, however, to consider cases where unequal segments or angles are involved.

By following the steps outlined in A–D below you can arrive at the four conclusions suggested. Although each conclusion can be formally proved, you may accept them as true.

A 1. Draw any triangle $ABC$ and show the exterior $\angle 4$ at $A$.

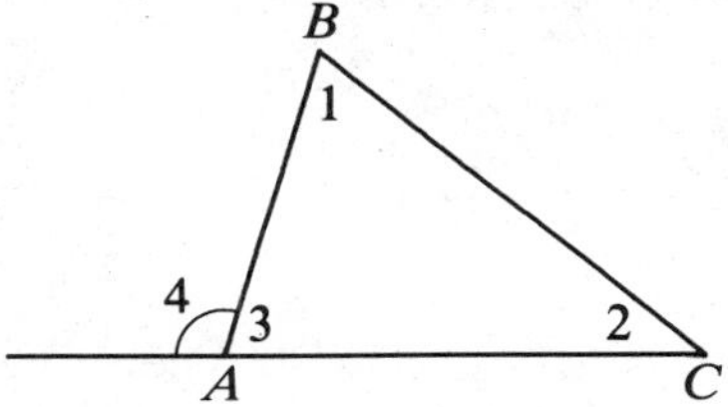


2. $\angle 4 = \angle 1 + \angle 2$ (See p. 85.)
3. Compare $\angle 4$ and $\angle 1$. It follows from Step 2 that $\angle 4$ is greater than $\angle 1$. ($\angle 4 > \angle 1$.)
4. Compare $\angle 4$ and $\angle 2$. Is $\angle 4 > \angle 2$ or $\angle 4 < \angle 2$? $>$

*Conclusion:* The exterior angle of a triangle is greater than either of the two opposite angles.

B 1. Draw $\triangle ABC$ with $AB > AC$.

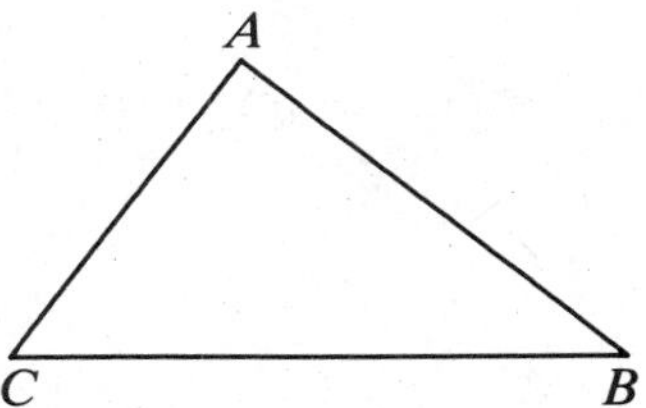


2. Use your protractor to measure $\angle B$ and $\angle C$.
3. Compare $\angle B$ and $\angle C$. Is $\angle C > \angle B$ or $\angle C < \angle B$? $>$
4. Is the larger angle opposite the longer side, $\overline{AB}$? yes

*Conclusion:* If two sides of a triangle are unequal, then the angles opposite them are unequal in the same order.

Do you see why the words "in the same order" are important in this conclusion? They mean that the largest angle is opposite the longest side and the smallest angle is opposite the shortest side.

C 1. Draw $\triangle DEF$ with $\angle D > \angle F$.

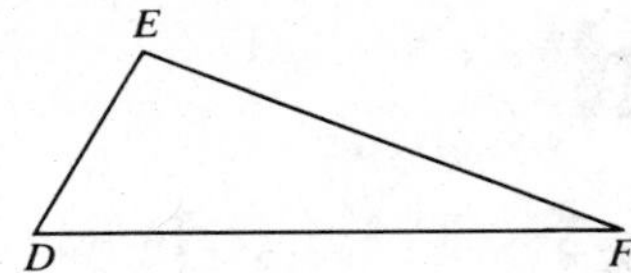


2. Measure $\overline{DE}$ and $\overline{EF}$ to the nearest centimeter.
3. Compare $DE$ and $EF$. Is $EF > DE$ or $EF < DE$? $<$
4. Is the longer side opposite the greater angle? yes

*Conclusion:* If two angles of a triangle are unequal, then the sides opposite these angles are unequal in the same order.

Again, we use the words "in the same order" in our conclusion.

D The fourth inequality has been discussed earlier, on page 165. But let us review it.

1. Draw a large triangle $ABC$.

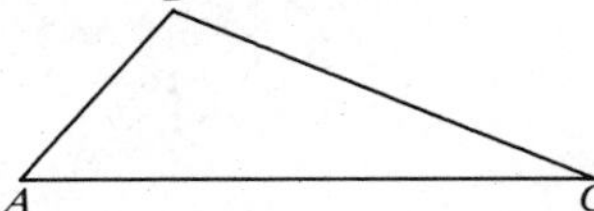


2. Measure each side and record your results to the nearest centimeter.

   $AB = \underline{?}$ 2 $\qquad AC = \underline{?}$ 4 $\qquad BC = \underline{?}$ 3

3. Substitute from Step 2 to find the following sums:

   $AB + AC = \underline{?} + \underline{?} = \underline{?}$ $\quad 2 + 4 = 6$

   $AC + BC = \underline{?} + \underline{?} = \underline{?}$ $\quad 4 + 3 = 7$

   $AB + BC = \underline{?} + \underline{?} = \underline{?}$ $\quad 2 + 3 = 5$

4. Complete, using $>$, $=$, or $<$.

   $AB + AC \underline{?} BC$ $\quad >$

   $AC + BC \underline{?} AB$ $\quad >$

   $AB + BC \underline{?} AC$ $\quad >$

*Conclusion:* In a triangle, the sum of the lengths of any two sides is greater than the length of the third side.

## Written Exercises

**Use the properties A–D in solving the following exercises.**

**Given $\triangle ABC$ with $\angle 4$ an exterior angle at $A$. Write $=$, $>$, or $<$ to make these statements correct.**

**1.** $\angle 1 + \angle 2 \underline{?} \angle 4$ $\quad =$

**2.** $\angle 4 \underline{?} \angle 2$ $\quad >$

**3.** $\angle 1 \underline{?} \angle 4$ $\quad <$

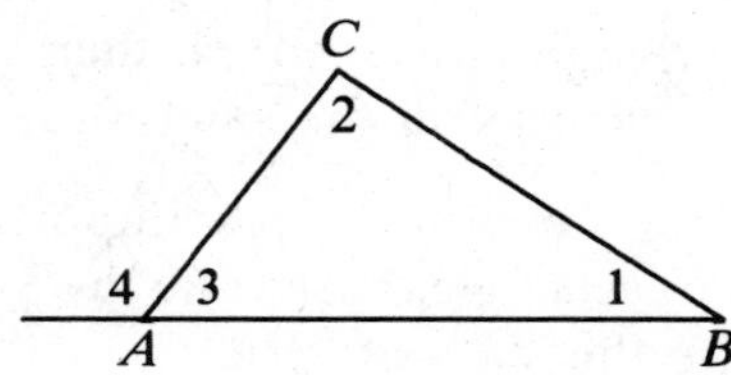

4. Using the figure below, state one of the four properties to support the statement: $\angle D > \angle E$.

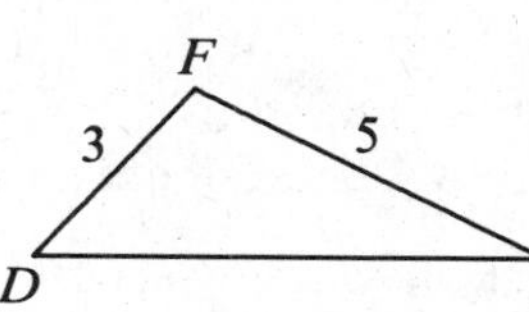


If two sides of a $\triangle$ are unequal, then the angles opposite them are unequal in the same order.

**Write $<$ or $>$ and give a reason for your choice.**

5. $\angle C \underline{\ ?\ } \angle A$ $<$; $5 < 5.2$

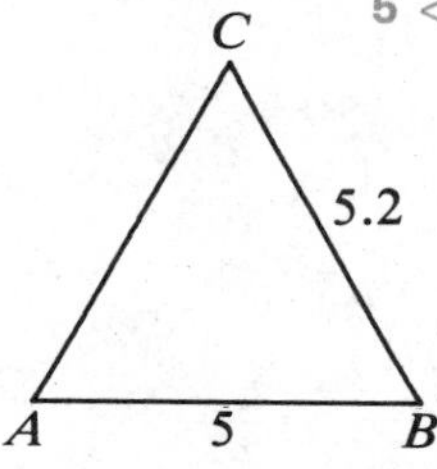


6. $\angle C \underline{\ ?\ } \angle B$ $>$; $9 > 8.9$

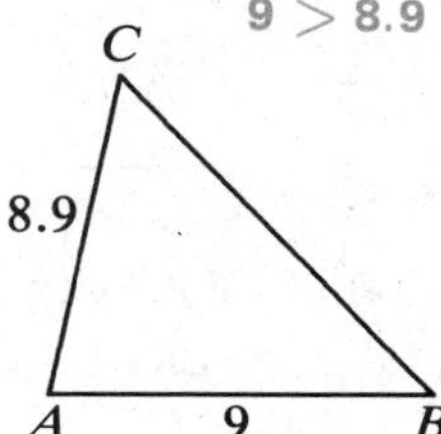


**In Exercises 7–9:**
**a. name the largest angle in the triangle;**
**b. name the smallest angle in the triangle.**

7.

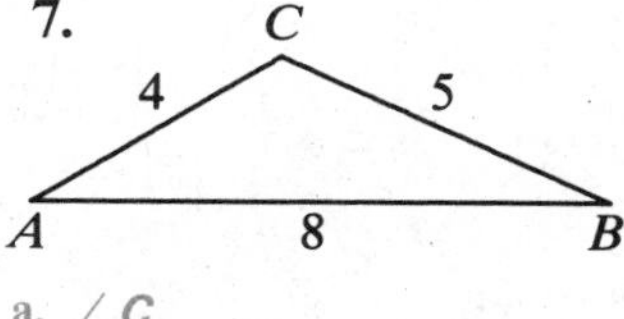


a. $\angle C$
b. $\angle B$

8.

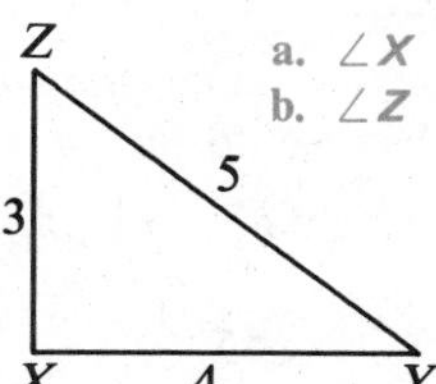


9.

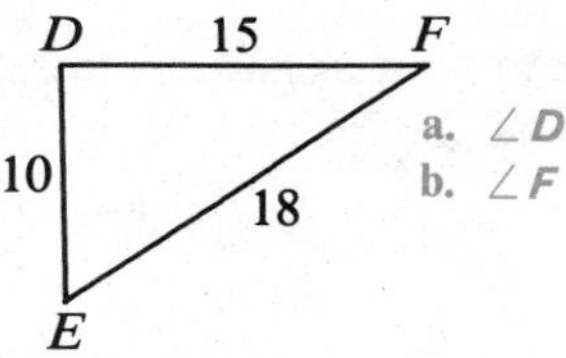


**In Exercises 10–12:**
**a. name the shortest side of the triangle;**
**b. name the longest side of the triangle.**

10.

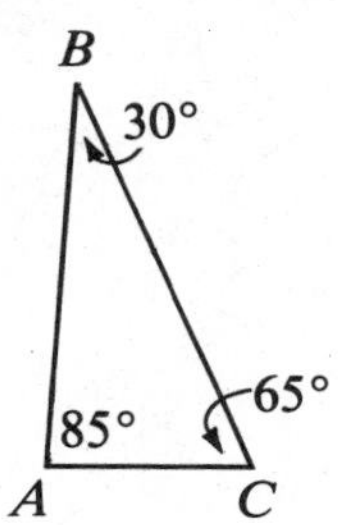


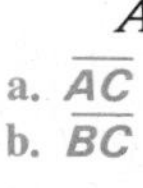


11.

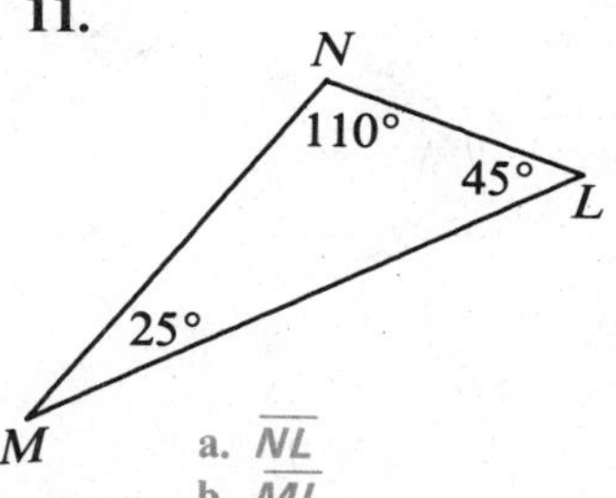


12.

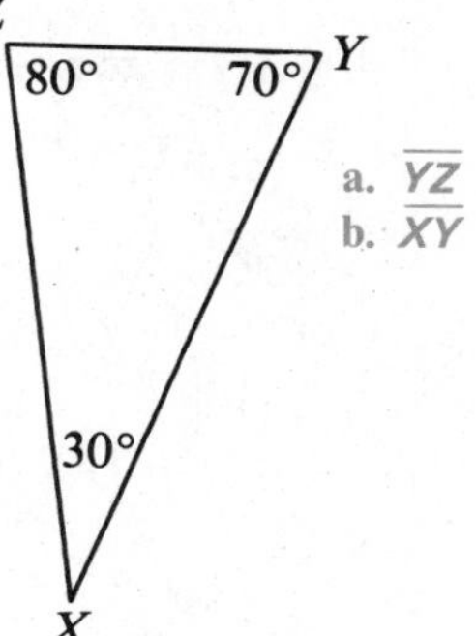

**Construct triangles having sides of the given lengths. If a construction is impossible, give the reason.** (Drawings omitted)

**13.** 6 cm, 8 cm, 10 cm

**14.** 3 cm, 4 cm, 8 cm

**15.** 2 cm, 6 cm, 9 cm

**16.** 11 cm, 4 cm, 9 cm

**17.** 4 cm, 6 cm, 2 cm

**18.** 2.5 cm, 4.1 cm, 5.0 cm

14. impossible $7 < 8$
15. impossible $8 < 9$
17. impossible $6 = 6$

**19.** Draw a right triangle *ABC*. Show that its hypotenuse, $\overline{AB}$, is its longest side.

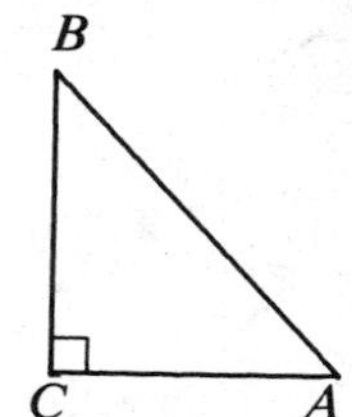


$\angle A$ and $\angle B$ are comp. Hence, $\angle C > \angle A$ and $\angle C > \angle B$, and $\overline{AB}$ is the longest side because it is opposite the largest angle.

**20.** Given $\overline{XY} \perp \overline{AB}$. Show that $\overline{XY}$ is the shortest segment from point *X* to $\overline{AB}$. (Hint: Let $\overline{XZ}$ be any other segment from *X* to $\overline{AB}$.)

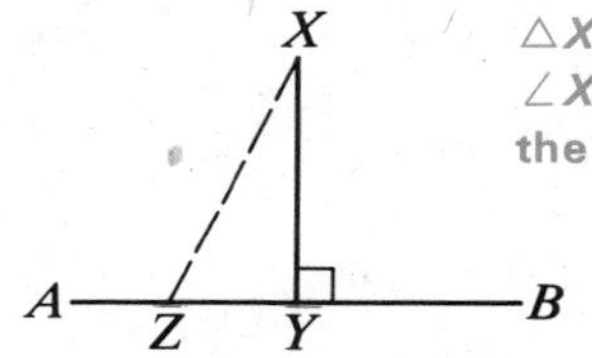


$\triangle XYZ$ is a right $\triangle$ because $\overline{XY} \perp \overline{AB}$, $\angle XYZ$ is the right $\angle$, hence $\overline{XZ}$ is the longest side, and $XY < XZ$.

**The figures are not accurately drawn. If they were, name the side in each figure that would be the longest. Name the side that would be the shortest.**

**21.**

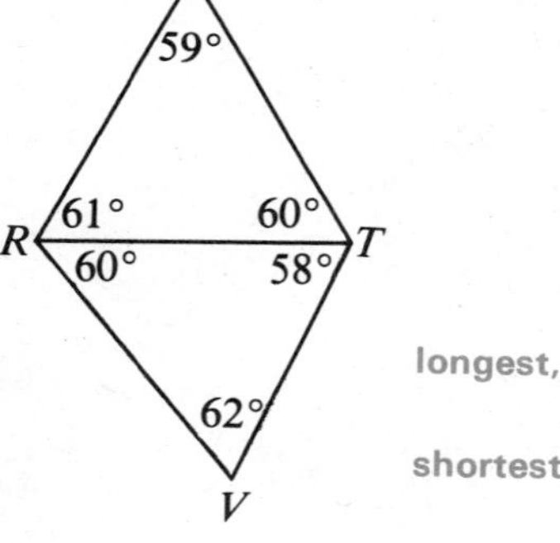


longest, $\overline{ST}$

shortest, $\overline{RV}$

**22.**

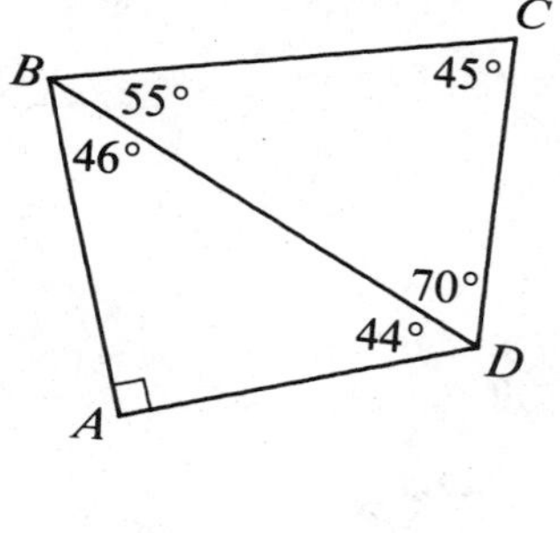


longest, $\overline{BC}$

shortest, $\overline{AB}$

# Glossary

A

**acute angle** (p. 13) An angle whose measure is between 0° and 90°.
**acute triangle** (p. 89) A triangle with three acute angles.
**altitude of a triangle** (pp. 144, 225) A segment, drawn from any vertex, perpendicular to the line that contains the opposite side. The opposite side is considered to be the *base* of the triangle.

**angle** (p. 8) A figure formed by two rays or two segments with a common endpoint. $B$ is the *vertex* of $\angle ABC$. $\overrightarrow{BA}$ and $\overrightarrow{BC}$ are the *sides* of $\angle ABC$.

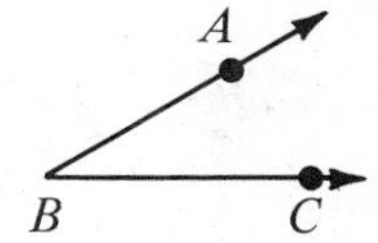


**arc** (p. 323) Part of a circle. A *semicircle,* such as $\widehat{ABC}$, is exactly half a circle. A *minor arc,* such as $\widehat{AB}$ or $\widehat{BC}$, is less than a semicircle. A *major arc,* such as $\widehat{BAC}$ or $\widehat{ACB}$, is greater than a semicircle.

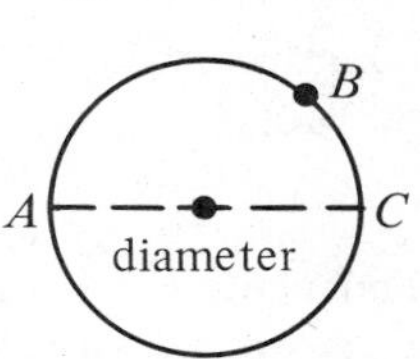


**area** (p. 216) The amount of surface in a region. Area is measured in square units.

B

**bisector of an angle** (p. 18) A ray or a line which divides an angle into two equal angles. If $\angle AOX = \angle BOX$, $\overrightarrow{OX}$ bisects $\angle AOB$.

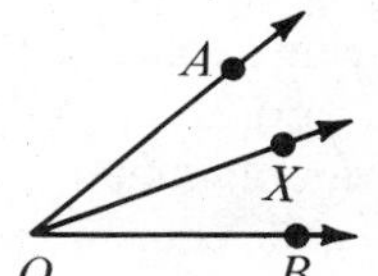


**bisector of an arc** (p. 328) A line, ray, or segment that contains the midpoint of an arc.
**bisector of a segment** (p. 140) A segment, ray, or line that contains the midpoint of a segment.

C

**central angle of a circle** (p. 323) An angle whose vertex is the center of a circle.
**chord of a circle** (p. 314) A segment that joins two points on a circle.
**circle** (p. 242) A figure, in a plane, whose points are all the same distance from a particular point in the plane. This point is the *center* of the circle.

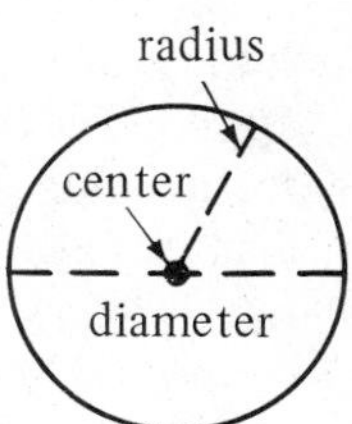


**circumference** (p. 242) The distance around a circle.
**circumscribed circle** (pp. 149, 330) A circle is circumscribed about a polygon when each vertex of the polygon lies on the circle.
**circumscribed polygon** (p. 330) A polygon is circumscribed about a circle when each side of the polygon is tangent to the circle.
**collinear points** (p. 4) Points that lie on one line.

**common tangent** (p. 319) A line that is tangent to each of two coplanar circles. A common *internal* tangent intersects the segment joining the centers of the circles. A common *external* tangent does not intersect the segment joining the centers of the circles.

**complementary angles** (p. 42) Two angles whose measures total 90°.

**conclusion** (p. 46) A result reached by reasoning. In a statement of the form "If $A$, then $B$," $B$ is the conclusion.

**cone** (p. 373) The *base* of a right circular cone is circular. Any segment that joins the vertex to a point on the circle is a *slant height* of the cone.

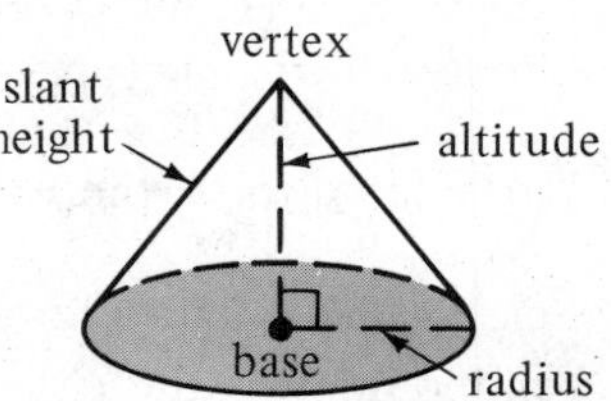


**congruent triangles** (p. 93) $\triangle ABC \cong \triangle DEF$ if the following statements are true:

$$\angle A = \angle D \qquad \angle B = \angle E \qquad \angle C = \angle F$$
$$AB = DE \qquad BC = EF \qquad AC = DF$$

**consecutive sides of a polygon** (p. 173) Two sides which intersect.

**consecutive vertices of a polygon** (p. 173) The endpoints of a side.

**constructing a geometric figure** (p. 21) Drawing a figure using only a straightedge and a compass.

**converse of a statement** (p. 46) A statement formed by exchanging the hypothesis and the conclusion of the given statement.

**convex polygon** (p. 172) Imagine fitting a rubber band along the edges of a polygon. If the rubber band fits snugly, the polygon is convex.

**coordinate(s)** (pp. 5, 426) On a number line, the number paired with a point. In the coordinate plane, the numbers which are paired with a point. Point (2, 4) has *x-coordinate* 2 and *y-coordinate* 4.

**coordinate axes** (p. 426) The horizontal and vertical number lines in the coordinate plane.

**coordinate plane** (p. 426) A plane which contains a horizontal number line (the *x-axis*) and a vertical number line (the *y-axis*). Every point in the coordinate plane can be named by a pair of numbers.

**coplanar lines** (p. 60) Lines that lie in one plane.

**coplanar points** (p. 29) Points that lie on one plane.

**corollary of a theorem** (p. 85) A statement which can be proved easily by applying a theorem.

**corresponding parts of two polygons** (p. 93) In $\triangle ABC$ and $\triangle DEF$, if point $A$ is matched with point $D$, $B$ with $E$, and $C$ with $F$, then (1) the *corresponding sides* are $\overline{AB}$ and $\overline{DE}$, $\overline{BC}$ and $\overline{EF}$, and $\overline{AC}$ and $\overline{DF}$; (2) the corresponding angles are $\angle A$ and $\angle D$, $\angle B$ and $\angle E$, and $\angle C$ and $\angle F$.

**cylinder** (p. 365) In a right circular cylinder, the *bases* are congruent circles which are parallel. Any segment that is perpendicular to the bases and has an endpoint in each base is an *altitude* of the right circular cylinder.

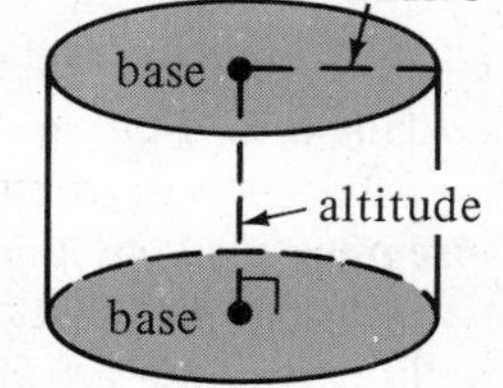

## D

**diagonal of a polygon** (p. 173) A segment which joins two nonconsecutive vertices of the polygon.

**diameter of a circle** (p. 314) A chord that passes through the center of a circle. Also, the length of such a chord.

**distance from a point to a line** (p. 328) The length of the perpendicular segment from the point to the line.

## E

**equal angles** (p. 13) Two angles whose measures are equal.

**equal arcs of a circle** (p. 323) Two arcs whose measures are equal.

**equal segments** (p. 130) Two segments whose lengths are equal.

**equal sides** (p. 89) Two sides whose lengths are equal.

**equiangular polygon** (p. 173) A polygon with all angles equal.

**equiangular triangle** (p. 89) A triangle with all angles equal.

**equidistant points** (p. 140) If $AB = AC$, then $A$ is equidistant from $B$ and $C$.

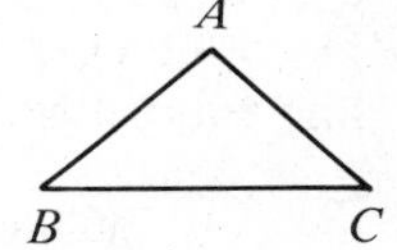


**equilateral polygon** (p. 173) A polygon with all sides equal.

**equilateral triangle** (p. 89) A triangle with all sides equal.

## G

**graph of an equation** (p. 448) The geometric figure which contains all the points whose coordinates make the equation a true statement, and no other points.

## H

**hypotenuse of a right triangle** (p. 89) The side opposite the right angle. The longest side of a right triangle.

**hypothesis** (p. 46) Information that is given. In a statement of the form "If $A$, then $B$," $A$ is the hypothesis.

## I

**if . . . then statement** (p. 46) A statement of the form "If $A$, then $B$."

**inscribed angle** (p. 333) An angle whose vertex lies on a circle and whose sides are chords of the circle.

**inscribed circle** (pp. 150, 330) A circle is inscribed in a polygon when each side of the polygon is tangent to the circle.

**inscribed polygon** (p. 330) A polygon is inscribed in a circle when each vertex of the polygon lies on the circle.

**intercepted arc(s)** (pp. 333, 334, 338) In each figure, the angle intercepts the arc or arcs shown in color.

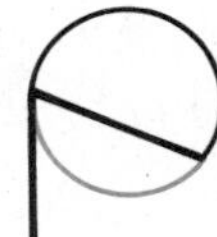

**intersecting lines** (pp. 16, 354) Two lines that meet in one point. Two intersecting lines are coplanar.

**intersecting planes** (pp. 30, 355) Two planes that meet in one line.

**isosceles trapezoid** (p. 201) A trapezoid with equal legs. There are two pairs of *base angles:* $\angle 1$ and $\angle 2$, $\angle 3$ and $\angle 4$.

base
3 4
leg leg
1 2
base

**isosceles triangle** (p. 89) A triangle with at least two equal sides. $\angle 1$ and $\angle 2$ are the *base angles.* $\angle 3$ is the *vertex angle.*

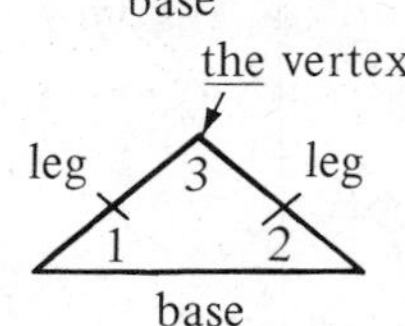


## L

**lateral area** (p. 360) In a right prism or a regular pyramid, the sum of the areas of the lateral faces. In a cylinder or a cone, the area of the lateral surface.
**legs of a right triangle** (p. 89) The two sides other than the hypotenuse.
**legs of a trapezoid** (p. 201) The nonparallel sides of a trapezoid.
**length of a segment** (p. 5) The distance between the endpoints of a segment.
**line parallel to a plane** (p. 354) A line and a plane which have no point in common.
**line perpendicular to a plane** (p. 354) A line which is perpendicular to every line in the plane that passes through the point of intersection.

## M

**measure of an angle** (p. 8) The number of degrees of an angle. The number is greater than 0 and less than or equal to 180.
**measure of a major arc** (p. 323) The difference of 360° and the measure of the minor arc.
**measure of a minor arc** (p. 323) The measure of its central angle.
**measure of a semicircle** (p. 323) The measure of a semicircle is 180°.
**median of a trapezoid** (p. 201) The segment joining the midpoints of the legs of a trapezoid.
**median of a triangle** (p. 144) A segment that joins a vertex of a triangle to the midpoint of the opposite side.
**midpoint of an arc** (p. 328) If $\widehat{CM} = \widehat{MD}$, then $M$ is the midpoint of $\widehat{CD}$.
**midpoint of a segment** (p. 5) Point $M$ is the midpoint of $\overline{AB}$ if $M$ lies on $\overline{AB}$ and $AM = MB$.

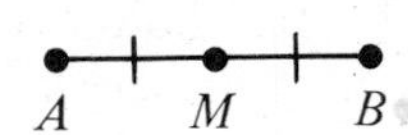


## N

**noncollinear points** (p. 29) Points that do not all lie on one line.
**number line** (p. 5) A line which matches points with the real numbers.

## O

**obtuse angle** (p. 13) An angle whose measure is between 90° and 180°.
**obtuse triangle** (p. 89) A triangle with one obtuse angle.
**origin of the coordinate plane** (p. 426) The point in which the coordinate axes intersect. Point (0, 0).

## P

**parallel line and plane** (p. 354) A line and a plane that have no point in common.

**parallel lines** (p. 60) Two coplanar lines that have no point in common.

**parallel lines cut by a transversal** (p. 60) The following angles are formed:
*alternate interior angles:* $\angle 3$ and $\angle 6$, $\angle 4$ and $\angle 5$
*corresponding angles:* $\angle 1$ and $\angle 5$, $\angle 2$ and $\angle 6$, $\angle 3$ and $\angle 7$, $\angle 4$ and $\angle 8$
*interior angles:* $\angle 3$, $\angle 4$, $\angle 5$, $\angle 6$
*same-side interior angles:* $\angle 3$ and $\angle 5$, $\angle 4$ and $\angle 6$

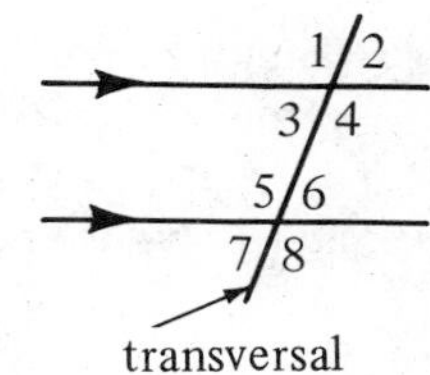


**parallel planes** (p. 30) Two planes that have no points in common.

**parallelogram** (p. 180) A quadrilateral with both pairs of opposite sides parallel. Either pair of sides may be considered the *bases.*

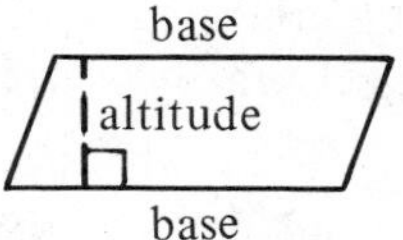


**perimeter** (p. 218) The distance around a region; the sum of the lengths of the sides of a polygon.

**perpendicular bisector of a segment** (p. 140) A segment bisector that is perpendicular to the segment.

**perpendicular lines** (p. 13) Two lines that meet to form four right angles.

**perpendicular planes** (p. 355) If a plane contains a line that is perpendicular to another plane, the two planes are perpendicular.

**pi** (p. 243) A Greek letter denoted by $\pi$. The quotient $\frac{\text{circumference}}{\text{diameter}}$ for any circle.

**plotting a point** (p. 426) Locating the point in the coordinate plane.

**polygon** (p. 172) The figure shows one example of a polygon. Parts of a polygon are named as shown. $\angle 2$ is an *exterior angle.* $\angle 1$ is an *interior angle.*

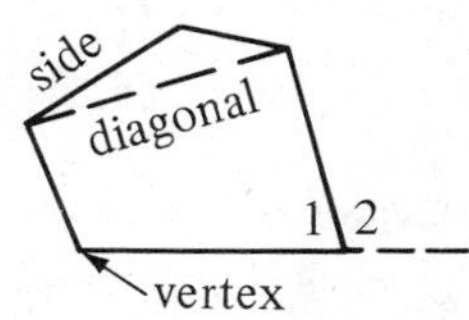


**postulate** (p. 25) A statement which is accepted without proof.

**proportion** (p. 263) An equation which states that two ratios are equal. In the proportion $\frac{4}{6} = \frac{2}{3}$, 6 and 2 are the *means,* and 4 and 3 are the *extremes.*

## Q

**quadrilateral** (p. 172) A polygon with four sides.

## R

**radius of a circle** (p. 314) A segment that joins the center and a point on the circle. Also, the length of such a segment.

**ratio** (p. 260) If $a$ and $b$ are numbers and $b \neq 0$, the ratio of $a$ to $b$ is the quotient $\frac{a}{b}$. This is sometimes denoted by $a:b$.

**ray** (p. 4) Part of a line. $\overrightarrow{AB}$ starts at *endpoint A*, goes through point *B*, and continues indefinitely.

**rectangle** (p. 180) A parallelogram with four right angles. Any side of a rectangle may be considered a *base*.

**rectangular solid** (pp. 359, 403) A right prism whose *bases* are rectangular. The segment shown in color is a *diagonal* of the rectangular solid.

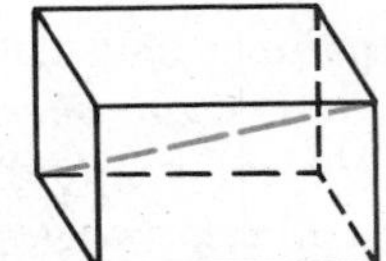

**regular polygon** (p. 173) A polygon which is both equilateral and equiangular.

**regular pyramid** (p. 369) The *base* of a regular pyramid is a regular polygon. The *lateral faces* are congruent isosceles triangles. The altitude from the vertex of a face is a *slant height*.

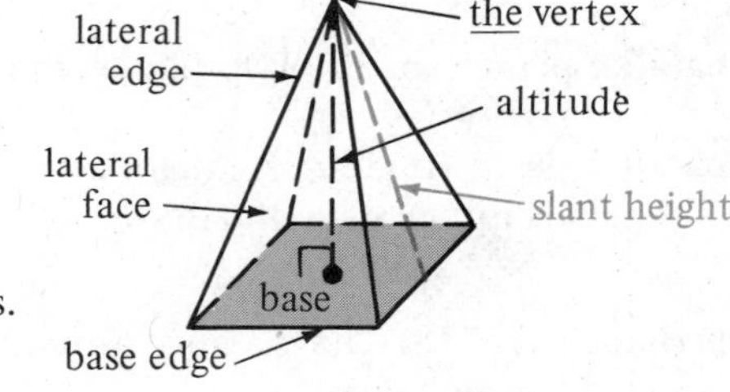


**rhombus** (p. 180) A parallelogram with four equal sides.

**right angle** (p. 13) An angle whose measure is 90°.

**right prism** (p. 359) In a right prism, the *bases* are congruent and parallel. The *lateral faces* are rectangular. The *lateral edges* are perpendicular to the bases. Any segment, such as a lateral edge, that is perpendicular to the bases and has an endpoint on each base, is an *altitude* of the right prism.

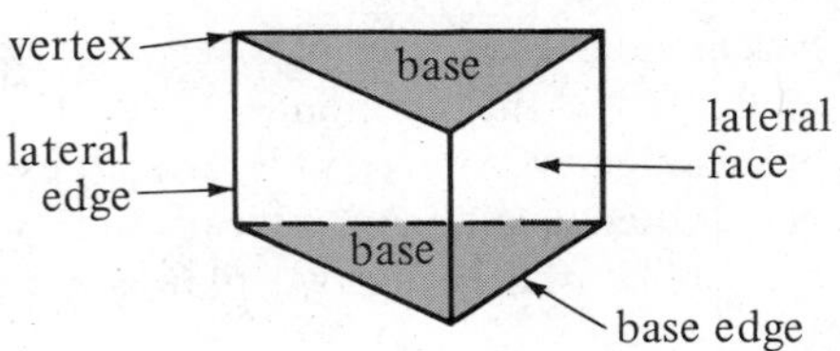


**right triangle** (p. 89) A triangle with one right angle. The hypotenuse is the longest side of a right triangle.

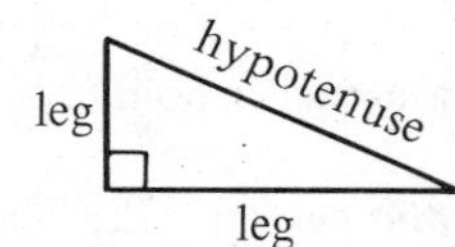


## S

**scale** (p. 270) The ratio of a distance in a drawing to the actual distance represented.

**scale factor of two similar polygons** (p. 283) The ratio of two corresponding sides.

**scalene triangle** (p. 89) A triangle with no two sides equal.

**secant of a circle** (p. 314) A line that contains a chord.

**segment** (p. 4) Part of a line. *A* and *B* are the *endpoints* of $\overline{AB}$.

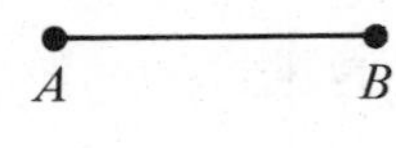


**similar polygons** (p. 282) Two polygons with the same shape. In two similar polygons:
(1) Corresponding angles are equal.
(2) Corresponding sides are in proportion.

**similar solids** (p. 381) Two solids with the same shape. In two similar solids:
(1) Corresponding angles are equal.
(2) Corresponding segments are in proportion.

**skew lines** (p. 60) Two lines that are not coplanar and do not intersect.

**slope of a line** (pp. 438, 439) $\frac{\text{rise}}{\text{run}}$. Also, if a line contains points $(x_1, y_1)$ and $(x_2, y_2)$, then the slope of the line is $\frac{y_2 - y_1}{x_2 - x_1}$, provided $x_1 \neq x_2$.

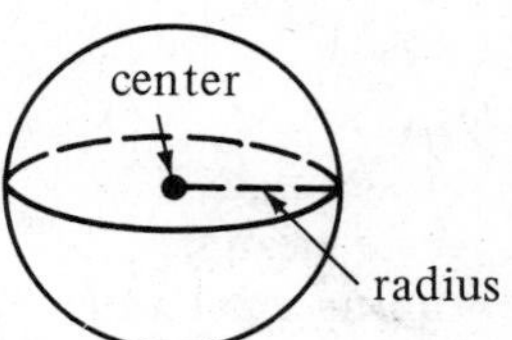


**sphere** (p. 314) A figure in space whose points are the same distance from a particular point. This point is the *center* of the sphere.

**square** (p. 180) A parallelogram with four right angles and four equal sides.
**straight angle** (p. 13) An angle whose measure is 180°.
**supplementary angles** (p. 43) Two angles whose measures total 180°.

## T

**tangent to a circle** (p. 314) A line or segment, in the plane of a circle, that intersects the circle in exactly one point. This point is the *point of tangency*.

**tangent circles** (p. 319) Two coplanar circles that are tangent to a line at one point. $\odot R$ and $\odot S$ are *externally* tangent. $\odot S$ and $\odot T$ are *internally* tangent.

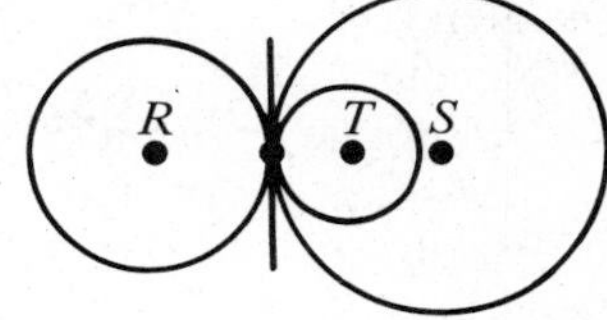


**theorem** (p. 42) A statement that can be proved.
**total area** (p. 360) The sum of the lateral area and the area of the base or bases.

**trapezoid** (p. 180) A quadrilateral with just one pair of opposite sides parallel. The segment joining the midpoints of the legs is the *median* of a trapezoid.

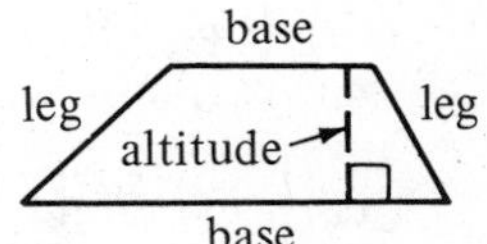


**triangle** (p. 13) A polygon with three sides. In $\triangle ABC$, each of points $A$, $B$, and $C$ is a *vertex* of the triangle. $\overline{AB}$, $\overline{BC}$, and $\overline{AC}$ are the *sides* of the triangle. $\angle 1$, $\angle 2$, and $\angle 3$ are the *angles* of the triangle. $\angle 4$ is an *exterior angle* of $\triangle ABC$. $\angle 1$ and $\angle 2$ are *opposite angles* with respect to exterior $\angle 4$.

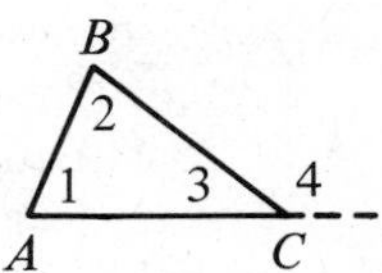


**trigonometric ratios** (pp. 410, 414)

*tangent* of $\angle A = \frac{\text{leg opposite } \angle A}{\text{leg adjacent to } \angle A}$

*sine* of $\angle A = \frac{\text{leg opposite } \angle A}{\text{hypotenuse}}$

*cosine* of $\angle A = \frac{\text{leg adjacent to } \angle A}{\text{hypotenuse}}$

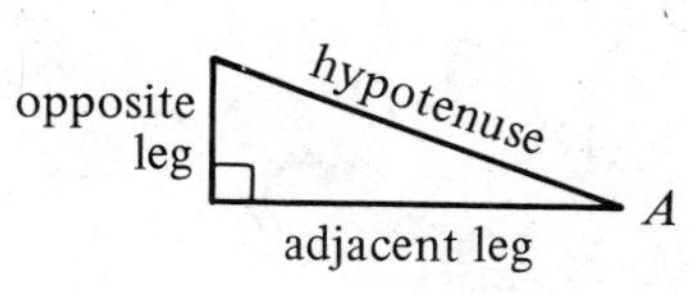


## V

**vertical angles** (p. 16) Two angles formed by intersecting lines. $\angle 1$ and $\angle 2$ are vertical angles.

**volume** (p. 360) The amount of space in a solid. Volume is measured in cubic units.

# Index

## Q



## R



## S

BCDEFGHIJ-RM-898765